CRIMINAL LAW

CASES AND MATERIALS

By

Cynthia Lee 1961-
Professor of Law
The George Washington University

and

Angela Harris 1961-
Professor of Law
Boalt Hall School of Law
University of California, Berkeley

AMERICAN CASEBOOK SERIES®

THOMSON
™
WEST

Mat #40202868

American Casebook Series and West Group are trademarks registered in the U.S. Patent and Trademark Office.

© 2005 Thomson/West
      610 Opperman Drive
      P.O. Box 64526
      St. Paul, MN 55164–0526
      1–800–328–9352

Printed in the United States of America

ISBN 0–314–15128–1

TEXT IS PRINTED ON 10% POST CONSUMER RECYCLED PAPER

This book is dedicated to

Kenichi Haramoto

Preface

Like most Criminal Law casebooks, this book is meant to introduce students to the basic doctrines and methods of American substantive criminal law, both in jurisdictions whose penal codes continue to reflect the common law and in those jurisdictions that have adopted, in whole or in part, the Model Penal Code. Three features, however, distinguish this book from others in the field.

First, this book consistently focuses on the cultural context of substantive criminal law. Chapter 15, entitled "Culture and Crime," makes this focus most explicit. In Chapter 15, we provide readings that consider the cultural meanings of crime and the cultural meanings of punishment from the point of view of offenders, the public, and criminal justice insiders. Additionally, throughout the book, we provide resources for thinking about how substantive criminal law is shaped both by "legal culture" – the systematic needs of lawyers (especially prosecutors) and judges who make the criminal system run – and by the broader culture of the society in which we live. We are particularly concerned with the ways in which American culture is internally divided along lines of race, gender, class, and sexuality.

A second feature that distinguishes this book from others in the market is its treatment of substantive criminal law as a course in public law. We provide many links between criminal law and constitutional law, from the basic elements of a crime, such as the act requirement and the mens rea requirement, to particular crimes, such as conspiracy and sodomy, to constitutional doctrines that bear directly upon criminal law, such as the equal protection clause, the due process clause, and the prohibition against cruel and unusual punishment. The book also highlights some of the systemic issues raised by the use of state power against the lives and liberties of citizens, such as the fundamental "dilemma of discretion" and the separation of powers.

Finally, we have tried to make this a flexible and user-friendly book, for the law student as well as for new teachers of the subject, by providing introductory text at the beginning of each chapter (as well as at the beginning of many sections in the chapters) and by keeping the notes and questions to a minimum. We also tried to lightly edit the cases in order to give the reader fuller factual context. Because of the importance of context, we made an effort to provide additional information about the defendant or the case not provided in the judicial opinion, whenever possible.

Most of the citations and footnotes in the excerpted cases and articles have been omitted. We inserted three asterisks to indicate textual omissions from the excerpted cases and articles. Numbered footnotes indicate footnotes in the original. Footnotes in lowercase letters indicate casebook author footnotes which we have added to enhance the material.

We hope readers will find this a fresh and accessible introduction to the substantive criminal law. We also hope that students, even if they never practice criminal law, will take away a sense of its centrality in the American cultural imagination and its implications not only for the incarcerated but for the legal system itself.

ACKNOWLEDGMENTS

We wish to thank and acknowledge the many people who helped with the production of this casebook.

Angela Harris gratefully thanks her students in Criminal Law, section 4, Fall 2004, for their patience, good humor, and enthusiastic agreement with these materials as they evolved in draft. Angela Harris also thanks Ayn Lowry, who shepherded her through the many years of logistical nightmares that accompanied the many versions of supplemental materials that preceded this book.

Cynthia Lee thanks the following students (in alphabetical order) from the George Washington University Law School who helped with the production of this casebook: Ralph Chris Berg, Dave Berman, Liza Meyers, Thomas Moir, Guillermo Billy Santiso, Lauren Voss. Cynthia Lee also thanks Kathryn Parente for her hard work, patience, and cheerful demeanor throughout the many drafts of this casebook, Lesliediana Jones for assistance with copyright matters, Herb Somers for library support, and Mary Dini for secretarial assistance during her last two weeks at the George Washington University Law School. Cynthia Lee also thanks former Dean Michael Young and Interim Dean Roger Trangsrud for supporting this project through research assistance and summer research stipends.

Finally, we both would like to thank the following colleagues for helpful comments, suggestions, and/or support for the project: Erik Luna, Ellen Podgor, David Robinson, and Daniel Solove.

Table of Cases

The principal cases are in bold types. Cases cited or discussed in the text are in roman type. References are to pages. Cases cited in principal cases and within other quoted materials are not included.

Table of Authorities

This table lists books and articles extracted or referred to in the casebook. (Newspaper articles and citations to federal documents are not included.) The sources are presented in alphabetical order. References are to pages. Authorities cited in principal cases or within quoted materials are not included.

Books

Black's Law Dictionary (7th ed.), 342

Brenner, Claudia, *Eight Bullets: One Woman's Story of Surviving Anti-Gay Violence* (1995), 398

3 Coke, Institutes (1648), 346.

Dressler, Joshua, *Cases and Materials on Criminal Law* (2d ed. 1999), 242

Dressler, Joshua, *Understanding Criminal Law* (3d ed. 2001), 167, 207, 323, 340, 719

Estrich, Susan, *Real Rape* (Harv. Univ. Press 1987), 491

Fletcher, George P., *A Crime of Self-Defense: Bernhard Goetz and the Law on Trial* (Univ. Of Chicago Press 1988), 728

Goldstein, Dershowitz, and Schwarz, *Criminal Law: Theory and Process* (1974), 425

Hall, Jerome, *Theft, Law and Society* (1952), 624

Harris, Paul, *Black Rage Confronts the Law* (NYU Press 1997), 878

Johnson, Philip E., *Criminal Law: Cases, Materials and Text* (6th ed. 2000), 820

Johnson, Philip E., *Teacher's Manual for Criminal Law: Cases, Materials and Text* (4th ed. 1990), 425

Katz, Leo, *Bad Acts and Guilty Minds: Conundrums of the Criminal Law* (Univ. Of Chicago Press 1987), 12

LaFave, Wayne R. & Austin Scott, Jr., *Criminal Law* (2d ed. 1986), 962

Lee, Cynthia, *Murder and the Reasonable Man: Passion and Fear in the Criminal Courtroom* (NYU Press 2003), 734, 736

Robinson, Paul H., *Criminal Law Case Studies* (2d ed. 2002), 290

Schulhofer, Stephen, *Unwanted Sex: The Culture of Intimidation and the Failure of the Law* (Harv. Univ. Press 1998), 518

Walker, Lenore E.A., *The Battered Woman* (1979), 744, 752

Walker, Lenore E.A., *The Battered Woman Syndrome* (2d ed. 1984), 752

Wang, Lu-in, *Hate Crimes Law* (2004 Supp.), 162

White, James Boyd, *Making Sense of*

Articles

Student-Authored Works

Copyright Acknowledgments

We are thankful to the copyright holders who gave us permission to reprint excerpts from the following works:

American Bar Association Journal, *Statutory Rape Laws: Does it Make Sense to Enforce Them in an Increasingly Permissive Society?*, 82 A.B.A. J. 86 (1996).

American Law Institute, Model Penal Code and Commentaries, copyright © 1962, 1980, and 1985 by The American Law Institute.

Ashby, Charles, *The Right to Be Apathetic: Iverson Case Raises Questions About Good Samaritan Laws*, Los Angeles Daily Journal, Sept. 2, 1998, at 1.

Associated Press, *Epileptic Convicted of Assault Cleared*, Los Angeles Daily Journal, Sept. 25, 1997, at 5.

Austin, Regina , *"The Black Community," Its Lawbreakers, and a Politics of Identification*, 65 S. Cal. L. Rev. 1769 (1992).

Bair, Jeffrey, *Killer of Thief Wins Wide Support*, The San Diego Union Tribune, Dec. 27, 1994, at A-8. Copyright permission granted by the Associated Press.

Blecker, Robert , *Haven or Hell? Inside Lorton Central Prison: Experiences of Punishment Justified*, 42 Stan. L. Rev. 1149 (1990).

Braithwaite, John, *A Future Where Punishment is Marginalized: Realistic or Utopian?*, 46 UCLA L. Rev. 1727 (1999).

Brown, Kevin, *The Social Construction of a Rape Victim: Stories of African-American Males about the Rape of Desirée Washington*, in *Black Men on Race, Gender and Sexuality: A Critical Reader* (Carbado ed. 1999).

Bucy, Pamela H., *Corporate Ethos: A Standard for Imposing Corporate Criminal Liability*, 75 Minn. L. Rev. 1095 (1991).

Butler, Paul D., *Race-Based Jury Nullification: Case-in-Chief*, 30 J. Marshall L. Rev. 911 (1997).

Butler, Paul, *Walking While Black: Encounters With the Police on My Street*, Legal Times, Nov. 10, 1997, at 23.

Coker, Donna K., *Heat of Passion and Wife Killing: Men Who Batter/Men Who Kill*, 2 S. Cal. Rev. L. & Women's Stud. 71 (1992).

Coleman, Doriane Lambelet, *Individualizing Justice Through Multiculturalism: The Liberals' Dilemma*, 96 Colum. L. Rev. 1093 (1996).

Delgado, Richard, *Ascription of Criminal States of Mind: Toward a Defense Theory for the Coercively Persuaded ("Brainwashed") Defendant*, 63 Minn. L. Rev. 1 (1978).

Delgado, Richard, *No: Selective Enforcement Targets 'Unpopular' Men*, 82 A.B.A. J. 86 (1996).

Delgado, Richard, *"Rotten Social Background": Should the Criminal Law Recognize A Defense of Severe Environmental Deprivation?*, 3 Law & Inequality J. 9 (1985).

Dressler, Joshua, *Professor Delgado's "Brainwashing" Defense: Courting a Determinist Legal System*, 63 Minn. L. Rev. 335 (1979).

Dressler, Joshua, *When "Heterosexual" Men Kill "Homosexual" Men: Reflections on Provocation Law, Sexual Advances, and the "Reasonable Man" Standard*, 85 J. Crim. L. & Criminology 726 (1995).

Dubber, Markus Dirk, *Policing Possession: The War on Crime and the End of Criminal Law*, 91 J. Crim. L. & Criminology 829 (2001).

Ehisen, Rich, *The Battle Over Medical Marijuana*, California Journal, July 1, 2003, at 36.

Gruner, Richard, *To Let the Punishment Fit the Organization: Sanctioning Corporate Offenders Through Corporate Probation*, 16 Am. J. Crim. L. 1 (1988).

Gunning, Isabelle R., *Two Forms of Justice: Iverson Case – Nevada and California Authorities Ought to Reexamine David Cash's Actions*, L.A. Times, Sept. 21, 1998, at B5

Tigar, Michael E., *The Right of Property and the Law of Theft*, 62 Tex. L. Rev. 1443 (1984).

Vidmar, Neil & Regina A. Schuller, *Juries and Expert Evidence: Social Framework Testimony*, 52 Law & Contemp. Probs. 133 (1989).

Volpp, Leti, *(Mis)identifying Culture: Asian Women and the "Cultural Defense"*, 17 Harv. Women's L.J. 57 (1994).

Volpp, Leti, *On Culture, Difference, and Domestic Violence*, 11 Am. U.J. Gender, Soc. Pol'y & Law 393 (2003).

Weisberg, Robert, *Criminal Law, Criminology, and the Small World of Legal Scholars*, 63 U. Colo. L. Rev. 521 (1992).

White, James Boyd, *Making Sense of What We Do: The Criminal Law as a System of Meaning*, in *Heracles' Bow: Essays on the Rhetoric and Poetics of the Law* (Wisc. Univ. Press 1985).

Summary of Contents

Table of Contents

Appendix

CRIMINAL LAW

CASES AND MATERIALS

Chapter 1

BASIC PRINCIPLES OF THE CRIMINAL LAW

INTRODUCTION

When law students begin their study of the criminal law, they often expect to deal with exciting search and seizure issues, illegal arrests, questionable interrogations, tainted confessions, and the like. In other words, they imagine a fun-filled course packed with the sorts of issues that occupy the episodes of T.V. shows like *Law & Order* and *NYPD Blue*. When they find out that substantive criminal law deals with none of these subjects, they may be disappointed. At most law schools, the constitutional restrictions on searches and seizures, arrests, interrogations and confessions are covered in the basic Criminal Procedure class, not Criminal Law. Criminal procedure concerns the legal limits on how people identified as possible or actual criminals may be treated by law enforcement personnel, by prosecuting attorneys, by the judiciary, and by the prison system. It is the law of criminal procedure (and to some extent the law of evidence and trial procedure) that makes for the exciting courtroom action portrayed in movies and television shows.

Substantive criminal law, however, is interesting and important in its own right. Substantive criminal law (hereafter simply *criminal law*) answers these questions: How do various jurisdictions define their criminal offenses? What are the basic elements common to every crime in the Anglo-American tradition? What does the prosecution have to prove in order for the fact-finder to find a person guilty? What are the elements of particular crimes, like murder, rape, or burglary? What distinguishes first degree from second degree murder?

Criminal law also answers the question, what level of punishment does the person who has committed a crime deserve? The rules of criminal law tell us what a person must do to be considered guilty of a crime, but not everyone who has technically violated a statute will be treated in the same way. Sometimes the issue is whether a person ought to be considered capable of committing a crime at all. For example, the insanity defense is based on the theory that people who commit crimes because they are insane lack the capacity to make moral choices which is a prerequisite for criminal punishment. Other times, assuming the person is capable of moral choice, the issue is whether and to what extent that choice reflected values and beliefs shared by many in our

1

culture, rendering the person's actions excusable or justifiable. For example, a person who kills someone else in the "heat of passion" is considered less blameworthy than a person who kills someone else in cold blood. A person who kills in self defense may not be considered blameworthy at all.

As the preceding paragraph suggests, criminal law is inextricably intertwined with issues of morality. This being the case, answers to the questions it asks may vary from person to person. Thus, criminal law in part engages one's moral intuitions, and criminal law is often taught as a branch of moral philosophy.

But people do not develop their moral intuitions in a vacuum. We grow up in a *culture*, socialized by family, friends, schools and mass media into accepting some broad beliefs and rejecting others. Like any other culture, Anglo-American culture includes widely-held ideas about responsibility, blame, and punishment, and these ideas have shaped our criminal law. In this book, we approach criminal law as a system of cultural meaning, and Anglo-American criminal law as a reflection of Anglo-American moral culture.

This is where things get really interesting, for no culture is monolithic. First, cultural meanings change over time. Second, the same culture may contain conflicting beliefs and values. Third, cultures often contain subcultures with very different traditions and perspectives, and this is certainly true of the United States. Some of these subcultures emerge because the United States is a multicultural nation, composed of immigrants (voluntary and involuntary) from many different countries. Other subcultures have emerged through the long-term effects of social inequality: men and women, for example, are sometimes said to live in different cultures. When there is no cultural consensus on moral issues, whose view gets written into the law? Should the trier of fact – whether a judge or a jury – be educated about different cultural perspectives on a person's behavior? When does a legal rule or doctrine become so lacking in support from contemporary moral culture that it should be abolished or radically altered? What are the means by which such a rule or doctrine may be changed so as to reflect a new moral consensus? What is the proper relationship between culture and morality? These are some of the questions raised by the study of substantive criminal law.

In addition to being a system of cultural meaning, criminal law is part of a legal system, and this in itself raises interesting and important issues. Criminal law reflects popular morality, but law is also partly autonomous from morality. Not everything that is a moral duty is necessarily also a legal duty. To what extent should criminal law reflect the minimum standards of behavior necessary to a functioning society, and to what extent should it push people to be better to one another than they might otherwise choose? What is the appropriate role for each of the different institutions that shape and enforce substantive criminal law – judges, juries, trial courts, appellate courts, legislatures? What discretion is or should be available to each institutional actor to apply or interpret the law the way she or he sees fit? How is that discretion limited – by constitutional rules, by rules of interpretation, by the actions of other actors within the criminal justice system?

The study of criminal law, then, is both the study of what is and what ought to be. You will learn what the rules are and also have the chance to examine critically whether those rules serve the goals of reflecting a general cultural and moral consensus, striking an appropriate balance between how we would like people to act in a perfect world and what we can reasonably expect of them, and facilitating the efficient and just operation of a necessarily imperfect legal system. This is not the flashy stuff of *Law & Order*, but it is just as pressing.

THE AIMS OF THE CRIMINAL LAW
Henry M. Hart, Jr.
23 Law & Contemp. Probs. 401 (1958)

* * * What do we mean by "crime" and "criminal"? Or, put more accurately, what should we understand to be "the method of the criminal law," the use of which is in question? This latter way of formulating the preliminary inquiry is more accurate, because it pictures the criminal law as a process, a way of doing something, which is what it is. * * *

What then are the characteristics of this method?

1. The method operates by means of a series of directions, or commands, formulated in general terms, telling people what they must or must not do. Mostly, the commands of the criminal law are "must-nots," or prohibitions, which can be satisfied by inaction. "Do not murder, rape, or rob." But some of them are "musts," or affirmative requirements, which can be satisfied only by taking a specifically, or relatively specifically, described kind of action. "Support your wife and children," and "File your income tax return."

2. The commands are taken as valid and binding upon all those who fall within their terms when the time comes for complying with them, whether or not they have been formulated in advance in a single authoritative set of words. They speak to members of the community, in other words, in the community's behalf, with all the power and prestige of the community behind them.

3. The commands are subject to one or more sanctions for disobedience which the community is prepared to enforce.

Thus far, it will be noticed, nothing has been said about the criminal law which is not true also of a large part of the noncriminal, or civil, law. The law of torts, the law of contracts, and almost every other branch of private law that can be mentioned operate, too, with general directions prohibiting or requiring described types of conduct, and the community's tribunals enforce these commands. What, then, is distinctive about the method of the criminal law?

Can crimes be distinguished from civil wrongs on the ground that they constitute injuries to society generally which society is interested in preventing? The difficulty is that society is interested also in the due fulfillment of contracts and the avoidance of traffic accidents and most of the other stuff of civil litigation. The civil law is framed and interpreted and enforced with a constant eye to these social interests. Does the distinction lie in the fact that proceedings to enforce the criminal law are instituted by public officials rather than private complainants? The difficulty is that public officers may also bring many kinds of "civil" enforcement actions – for an injunction, for the recovery of a "civil" penalty, or even for the detention of the defendant by public authority. Is the distinction, then, in the peculiar character of what is done to people who are adjudged to be criminals? The difficulty is that, with the possible exception of death, exactly the same kinds of unpleasant consequences, objectively considered, can be and are visited upon unsuccessful defendants in civil proceedings. * * *

4. What distinguishes a criminal from a civil sanction and all that distinguishes it, it is ventured, is the judgment of community condemnation which accompanies and justifies its imposition. As Professor Gardner wrote not long ago, in a distinct but cognate connection:

> The essence of punishment for moral delinquency lies in the criminal conviction itself. One may lose more money on the stock market than in a court-room; a prisoner of war camp may well provide a harsher environment than a state prison; death on the field of battle has the same physical characteristics as death by sentence of law. It is the expression of the community's hatred, fear, or contempt for the convict which alone characterizes physical hardship as punishment.

If this is what a "criminal" penalty is, then we can say readily enough what a "crime" is. It is not simply anything which a legislature chooses to call a "crime." It is not simply antisocial conduct which public officers are given a responsibility to suppress. It is not simply any conduct to which a legislature chooses to attach a "criminal" penalty. It is conduct which, if duly shown to have taken place, will incur a formal and solemn pronouncement of the moral condemnation of the community. * * *

At least under existing law, there is a vital difference between the situation of a patient who has been committed to a mental hospital and the situation of an inmate of a state penitentiary. The core of the difference is precisely that the patient has not incurred the moral condemnation of his community, whereas the convict has.

A.   SOURCES OF CRIMINAL LAW

Law students often find substantive criminal law frustrating because there is no nationwide criminal code. Each of the fifty states, the District of Columbia and the federal government has its own criminal code (also known as a penal code). The United States military, in addition, has its own criminal code. Fortunately, even though criminal provisions differ from jurisdiction to jurisdiction, there are certain basic principles of criminal law which are sufficiently common to most jurisdictions to enable generalizations about the basic elements of most crimes and the basic elements of most defenses. In addition, all the criminal laws of every jurisdiction of the United States are subject to the same constraints imposed by the United States Constitution.

Because the United States began as colonies of England, all criminal codes in the United States broadly recognize the crimes and defenses developed by English judges over many centuries and then imported here. However, the definition of these crimes and defenses, and how penal codes should be read and interpreted, depends on whether one is in a jurisdiction in which the code principally follows the common law or one in which the code has incorporated reforms taken from the Model Penal Code. For short, we can speak of these as *common law* jurisdictions and *Model Penal Code* jurisdictions.

In common law jurisdictions, judges continue to play an important role in shaping the criminal law. Courts in these jurisdictions must interpret statutes that are often very old and that may incorporate archaic language and concepts. Judges in common law jurisdictions both definitively interpret the meaning of criminal statutes and occasionally go beyond the statutes to announce new rules of their own. This book will contain many excerpts from appellate court opinions in order to articulate and examine criminal law in common law jurisdictions.

Other jurisdictions have recently sought to update and reform their criminal codes. Most of these reform efforts have been influenced by the Model Penal Code (hereafter MPC). The MPC is a product of the American Law

Institute (ALI), an organization composed of judges, lawyers, and law professors. When the ALI was organized, it saw itself as a body of experts that would try to influence state law by writing "restatements" of various subject matter areas, like Torts and Contracts. These restatements purported to simply set forth the common law of all the states in a clear, organized, and comprehensive way, but in fact they often incorporated significant reforms. The ALI hoped that the states would change their own laws to conform with the restatements, and many of these restatements have been highly influential with state legislatures.

When it came to the criminal law, the ALI concluded that the statutory and case law of the various states was such a hopelessly confusing and obsolete mishmash that "restatement" would be the wrong word. Instead, the ALI drafted its own criminal code from scratch. Drafting of the MPC began in 1952, and in 1962, after thirteen tentative drafts with accompanying explanatory Commentaries, the ALI approved and published its Proposed Official Draft of the MPC. Although no state has adopted the MPC in its entirety, between 1962 and 1984 thirty-four states enacted completely new criminal codes, all of them influenced to some extent by the MPC. In these jurisdictions, the language of the statute is more important than prior decisions of judges in figuring out "what the law is." You will find excerpts from the MPC in the Appendix to this casebook.

In common law jurisdictions, then, one primarily relies on the decisions of judges to find out what the criminal law is; in MPC jurisdictions, one primarily relies on the statutory language itself. In both kinds of jurisdictions, however, criminal law is influenced by federal law. Congress has no general constitutional authority to make criminal law, so the principal authority for enacting criminal statutes lies with the states, rather than the federal government. However, Congress does enact many criminal statutes (including, for example, drug laws) by virtue of its power over interstate commerce. Congress also has the authority to make criminal law for the District of Columbia, for the military, and for territories under its jurisdiction, such as Indian reservations. For our purposes, however, the most important source of federal law is the United States Constitution. The Constitution does not specifically set forth any crimes or defenses. However, some provisions of the Constitution set limitations on the way states can criminally punish behavior. We will examine some of these limitations in Chapter 2.

B.   JUSTIFICATIONS FOR PUNISHMENT

Two principles that are integral to the Anglo-American legal system are (1) it is unacceptable to use force against another human being without a good (legal) reason, and (2) the state should not invade individual freedoms without a good (legal) reason. The enforcement of the criminal law means that the state uses force to deprive people of their freedoms, and occasionally their lives. Criminal punishment in our society is therefore a practice in need of a justification.

The arguments traditionally used to justify criminal punishment come from moral philosophy. These moral justifications for punishment are not only discussed by theorists, but are frequently used by policymakers in public debate and by attorneys and judges in legal proceedings to evaluate the efficiency and fairness of the criminal justice system. Legislators and judges use concepts taken from moral philosophy when writing or revising criminal statutes, when sentencing convicted criminals, and when making "policy" arguments about the fairness of a law. We therefore need to briefly examine these philosophical principles in order to understand the traditional justifications for punishment.

Traditional moral reasoning is usually divided into two types: *consequentialist* and *nonconsequentialist*. The consequentialist believes that actions are morally right if, and only if, they result in desirable consequences. The primary consequentialist theory of punishment is called *utilitarianism*. Utilitarians tend to look forward at the predictable effects of punishment on the offender and/or society. The nonconsequentialist, in contrast, believes that actions are morally right or wrong in themselves, regardless of the consequences. The primary nonconsequentialist theory of punishment is called *retributivism*. Retributivists typically look backwards at the harm caused by the crime and attempt to calibrate the punishment to the crime. Debates over criminal law and policy usually involve a mixture of utilitarian and retributivist arguments.

The first excerpt in this chapter, a famous English case, provides fodder for a rich discussion regarding the basic theories of punishment. The second excerpt represents a contemporary American use of the traditional justifications for punishment in a sentencing decision. The third excerpt looks at the traditional justifications for punishment as they play out in a contemporary American prison.

REGINA v. DUDLEY AND STEPHENS
Queen's Bench Division
14 Q.B.D. 273 (1884)

* * * The two prisoners, Thomas Dudley and Edwin Stephens, were indicted for the wilful murder of Richard Parker on July 25, 1884, on the high seas, within the jurisdiction of the Admiralty of England. They were tried at the

winter assizes at Exeter on Nov. 6, 1884, before Huddleston, B., when at the suggestion of the learned judge, the jury returned a special verdict, setting out the facts, and referred the matter to the Divisional Court for its decision.

The special verdict was as follows:

The jurors, upon their oath, say and find that, on July 5, 1884, the prisoners, with one Brooks, all able-bodied English seamen, and the deceased, also an English boy, between seventeen and eighteen years of age, the crew of an English yacht, were cast away in a storm on the high seas, 1,600 miles from the Cape of Good Hope, and were compelled to put into an open boat. That in this boat they had no supply of water and no supply of food, except two 1 lb. tins of turnips, and for three days they had nothing else to subsist upon. That on the fourth day they caught a small turtle, upon which they subsisted for a few days, and this was the only food they had up to the twentieth day, when the act now in question was committed. That on the twelfth day the remains of the turtle were entirely consumed, and for the next eight days they had nothing to eat. That they had no fresh water, except such rain as they from time to time caught in their oilskin capes. That the boat was drifting on the ocean, and it was probably more than a thousand miles away from land. That on the eighteenth day, when they had been seven days without food and five without water, the prisoners spoke to Brooks as to what should be done if no succour came, and suggested that someone should be sacrificed to save the rest, but Brooks dissented, and the boy to whom they were understood to refer was not consulted. That on July 24, the day before the act now in question, the prisoner Dudley proposed to Stephens and to Brooks that lots should be cast who should be put to death to save the rest, but Brooks refused to consent, and it was not put to the boy, and in point of fact there was no drawing of lots. That on that day the prisoners spoke of their having families, and suggested that it would be better to kill the boy that their lives should be saved, and the prisoner Dudley proposed that if there was no vessel in sight by the morrow morning the boy should be killed. That next day, July 25, no vessel appearing, Dudley told Brooks that he had better go and have a sleep, and made signs to Stephens and Brooks that the boy had better be killed. The prisoner Stephens agreed to the act, but Brooks dissented from it. That the boy was then lying at the bottom of the boat quite helpless, and extremely weakened by famine and by drinking sea water, and unable to make any resistance, nor did he ever assent to his being killed. The prisoner, Captain Dudley, offered a prayer, asking forgiveness for them all if either of them should be tempted to commit a rash act, and that their souls might be saved. That the prisoner Dudley, with the assent of the prisoner Stephens, went to the boy, and telling him that his time was come, put a knife into his throat and killed him then and there. That the three men fed upon the body and blood of the boy for four days. That on the fourth day after the act had been committed, the boat was picked up by a passing vessel, and the prisoners were rescued still alive, but in the lowest state of prostration. That they were carried to the port of Falmouth, and committed for trial at Exeter. That, if the men had not fed upon the body of the boy, they would probably not have survived to be so picked up and rescued, but would within the four days have died of famine. That the boy, being in a much weaker condition, was likely to have died before them. That at the time of the act in question there was no sail in sight, nor any reasonable prospect of relief. That under the circumstances there appeared to the prisoners every probability that, unless they then fed, or very soon fed, upon the boy or one of themselves, they would die of starvation. That there was no appreciable chance of saving life except by killing someone for the others to eat. That assuming any necessity to kill anybody, there was no greater necessity for killing the boy than any of the three men.

But whether [the killing of Parker by Dudley and Stephens] be felony and murder or not the said jurors so as aforesaid chosen, tried, and sworn, are ignorant, and pray the advice of the court therupon.
Dec. 9, 1884.

The following judgment of the court was delivered by LORD COLERIDGE, C.J. -

The two prisoners, Thomas Dudley and Edwin Stephens, were indicted for the murder of Richard Parker on the high seas on July 25 in the present year. They were tried before Huddleston, B., at Exeter on Nov. 6, and, under the direction of my learned brother, the jury returned a special verdict, the legal effect of which has been argued before us, and on which we are now to pronounce judgment. From the facts, stated with the cold precision of a special verdict, it appears sufficiently that the prisoners were subject to terrible temptation and to sufferings which might break down the bodily power of the strongest man, and try the conscience of the best. Other details yet more harrowing, facts still more loathsome and appalling, were presented to the jury, and are to be found recorded in my learned brother's notes. But nevertheless this is clear, that the prisoners put to death a weak and unoffending boy upon the chance of preserving their own lives by feeding upon his flesh and blood after he was killed, and with a certainty of depriving him of any possible chance of survival. The verdict finds in terms that: "if the men had not fed upon the body of the boy, they would probably not have survived . . ." and that "the boy, being in a much weaker condition, was likely to have died before them." They might possibly have been picked up next day by a passing ship; they might possibly not have been picked up at all; in either case it is obvious that the killing of the boy would have been an unnecessary and profitless act. It is found by the verdict that the boy was incapable of resistance, and, in fact, made none; and it is not even suggested that his death was due to any violence on his part attempted against, or even so much as feared by, them who killed him. Under these circumstances the jury say they are ignorant whether those who killed him were guilty of murder, and have referred it to this court to say what [are] the legal consequences which follow from the facts which they have found.

[HIS LORDSHIP dealt with objections taken by counsel for the prisoners which do not call for report, and continued.:] There remains to be considered the real question in the case - whether killing, under the circumstances set forth in the verdict, be or be not murder. * * *

First, it is said that it follows, from various definitions of murder in books of authority - which definitions imply, if they do not state, the doctrine - that, in order to save your own life you may lawfully take away the life of another, when that other is neither attempting nor threatening yours, nor is guilty of any illegal act whatever towards you or anyone else. But, if these definitions be looked at, they will not be found to sustain the contention. * * * [I]t is clear that Bracton is speaking of necessity in the ordinary sense, the repelling by violence - violence justified so far as it was necessary for the object - any illegal violence used towards oneself.* * * Lord Hale regarded the private necessity which justified, and alone justified, the taking the life of another for the safeguard of one's own to be what is commonly called self-defence. . . . Lord Hale himself has made it clear, for, in the chapter in which he deals with the exemption created by compulsion or necessity, he thus expresses himself (1 Hale, P.C. 51):

> If a man be desperately assaulted, and in peril of death, and cannot otherwise escape, unless to satisfy his assailant's fury he will kill an innocent person then present, the fear and actual force will not acquit him of the crime and punishment of murder if he commit the act, for he ought rather to die himself than to kill an innocent; but if he cannot otherwise save his own life, the law permits him in his own defence to kill the assailant, for, by the violence of the assault and the offence committed upon him by the assailant himself, the law of nature and necessity hath made him his own protector. * * *

Is there, then, any authority for the proposition which has been presented to us? Decided cases there are none. * * *

Except for the purpose of testing how far the conservation of a man's own life is in all cases and under all circumstances an absolute, unqualified, and paramount duty, we exclude from our consideration all the incidents of war. We are dealing with a case of private homicide, not one imposed upon men in the service of their Sovereign or in the defence of their country. It is admitted that deliberate killing of this unoffending and unresisting boy was clearly murder, unless the killing can be justified by some well-recognised excuse admitted by the law. It is further admitted that there was in this case no such excuse, unless the killing was justified by what has been called necessity. But the temptation to the act which existed here was not what the law has ever called necessity. Nor is this to be regretted. Though law and morality are not the same, and though many things may be immoral which are not necessarily illegal, yet the absolute divorce of law from morality would be of fatal consequence, and such divorce would follow if the temptation to murder in this case were to be held by law an absolute defence of it. It is not so.

To preserve one's life is generally speaking, a duty, but it may be the plainest and the highest duty to sacrifice it. War is full of instances in which it is a man's duty not to live, but to die. The duty, in case of shipwreck, of a captain to his crew, of the crew to the passengers, of soldiers to women and children * * * - these duties impose on men the moral necessity, not of the preservation, but of the sacrifice, of their lives for others, from which in no country - least of all it is to be hoped in England - will men ever shirk, as indeed they have not shrunk. It is not correct, therefore, to say that there is any absolute and unqualified necessity to preserve one's life. * * *

It is not needful to point out the awful danger of admitting the principle which has been contended for. Who is to be the judge of this sort of necessity? By what measure is the comparative value of lives to be measured? Is it to be strength, or intellect, or what? It is plain that the principle leaves to him who is to profit by it to determine the necessity which will justify him in deliberately taking another's life to save his own. In this case the weakest, the youngest, the most unresisting was chosen. Was it more necessary to kill him than one of the grown men? The answer must be, No. * * *

There is no path safe for judges to tread but to ascertain the law to the best of their ability, and to declare it according to their judgment, and if in any case the law appears to be too severe on individuals, to leave it to the Sovereign to exercise that prerogative of mercy which the Constitution has entrusted to the hands fittest to dispense it. It must not be supposed that, in refusing to admit temptation to be an excuse for crime, it is forgotten how terrible the temptation was, how awful the suffering, how hard in such trials to keep the judgment straight and the conduct pure. We are often compelled to set up standards we cannot reach ourselves, and to lay down rules which we could not ourselves satisfy. But a man has no right to declare temptation to be an excuse, though he might himself have yielded to it, nor allow compassion for the criminal to change or weaken in any manner the legal definition of the crime. It is, therefore, our duty to declare that the prisoners' act in this case was wilful murder; that the facts as stated in the verdict are no legal justification of the homicide; and to say that, in our unanimous opinion, they are, upon this special verdict, guilty of murder.

The Lord Chief Justice thereupon passed sentence of death in the usual form.[a]

Judgment for the Crown.

Note

Do you think the sentence of death was an appropriate punishment? Consider five different theories of punishment: (1) general deterrence (punishment to deter others from committing the same or similar offenses), (2) specific deterrence (punishment to deter the individual defendant from committing the same crime in the future), (3) rehabilitation (reforming the defendant through vocational training, counseling, drug rehabilitation, etc.), (4) incapacitation (incarceration to keep the defendant away from other members of society), and (5) retribution (giving the defendant what he deserves).

PEOPLE V. SUITTE
New York State Supreme Court, Appellate Division
455 N.Y.S.2d 675, 90 A.D.2d 80 (App. Div. 1982)

LAZER, Justice Presiding.

The defendant has pleaded guilty to criminal possession of a weapon in the fourth degree, a class A misdemeanor. The sentence we review consists of 30 days of imprisonment and three years of probation, the jail time to be a condition of and to run concurrently with the period of probation. Execution of the sentence has been stayed pending this appeal. * * *

When arrested in January, 1981, for unauthorized use of a motor vehicle, based on what seems to have been a misunderstanding, James Suitte was found to possess a loaded Sterling .25 calibre automatic pistol. Although Mr. Suitte had registered the gun in North Carolina when he acquired it there in 1973, he carried it unlicensed in this State for the seven and one-half-year period

---

[a] Apparently, a pardon had been arranged in advance, so even though Dudley and Stephens were sentenced to death, they served only six months in prison. Leo Katz, BAD ACTS AND GUILTY MINDS: CONUNDRUMS OF THE CRIMINAL LAW 25 (1987). Haunted by memories of what happened on the dinghy, Stephens lost his mental facilities. *Id.* Dudley moved to Australia, became an opium addict, and then died of the bubonic plague. *Id.*

preceding his arrest. College educated for three years, Mr. Suitte is 46 years old, has been married for 25 years, and has two children, aged 14 and 21 years. He has never before been convicted of a crime. Although he admits he was aware of New York's gun licensing requirement, he claims that the gun was necessary for protection because the tailor shop he operates is located in a high crime area of the Bronx.

The plea of guilty was a bargained one. Originally charged with the class D felony of criminal possession of a weapon in the third degree, Mr. Suitte was permitted to plead to the misdemeanor of possession in the fourth degree. In imposing sentence under the new gun statute and its mandatory one year imprisonment provision -- publicized in the State as the "toughest gun law in the country" -- the sentencing Judge found the mandatory one year jail provision too severe. He noted, however, "the Legislature, the community and indeed this Court [are] concerned with the proliferation of guns and the possession of guns by individuals in the community, regardless of the reasons, and we have such a possession in this case." He then exercised his discretion under the statute and imposed a jail sentence of 30 days plus three years probation. The jail portion of the sentence is the focus of the appeal.

The new gun statute has substantially increased the penal sanctions for possession and sale of illegal weapons. The major change from previous law is the mandatory imposition of a prison sentence of at least one year upon conviction of possession of a loaded weapon outside the home or place of business. The legislation contains additional procedures, however, which, inter alia, permit imposition of a lesser sentence upon conviction of possession in the fourth degree if "the court having regard to the nature and circumstances of the crime and to the history and character of the defendant, is of the opinion that such sentence would be unduly harsh." This mitigation inquiry relative to possession in the fourth degree is limited to individuals who have not been convicted of either a felony or a class A misdemeanor within the preceding five years. Other provisions of the new law prohibit preindictment plea bargaining, restrict post-indictment plea bargaining and expedite the processing of licensing requests.

The statute is an obvious expression of the State's reaction to the current avalanche of gun-related crimes. In approving the law, Governor Carey proclaimed:

> We must bring an end to the proliferation of illegal handguns
> in New York and the intolerable assaults on law enforcement
> officers and law-abiding citizens. We must let it be known that
> New York has the toughest gun law in the country and that it

will be strictly enforced. We are determined to rid our streets of those who would do violence to its citizens.

The Governor viewed the amended gun law as even more stringent than that of Massachusetts, which had been considered the strictest in the country. Mayor Koch termed the legislation "a significant first step in the fight to remove illegal handguns from the streets of our city."

Early returns on the law -- later ones are not available -- indicate that applications for gun licenses have increased, fewer gun possession cases have been reduced to misdemeanors, and sentences of incarceration have been imposed in more instances than before the law. Slightly more than half of the adults convicted of gun possession received at least the mandatory one-year minimum.

Whatever its ultimate success in a nation bedeviled by handguns, there can be no doubt that the State's 1980 legislation represents a vivid manifestation of public policy intended to make illegal possession of guns a serious criminal offense accompanied by the strong prospect of punishment by penal servitude. While we note our colleague's negative view of the wisdom of the statute, it is not for the court to pass on the wisdom of the Legislature, for that body "has latitude in determining which ills of society require criminal sanctions, and in imposing, as it reasonably views them, punishments, even mandatory ones, appropriate to each." We turn, then, to the role of the judiciary in enforcing this public mandate that the crime of illegal possession of a gun be impressed upon all as a serious offense against society.

It is scarcely worth repetition to observe that a sentencing determination is a matter committed to the exercise of the sentencing court's discretion, for it is that court's primary responsibility. Sentencing involves consideration of the crimes charged, the particular circumstances of the offender, and the purposes of a penal sanction.

As has been oft-stated, the four principal objectives of punishment are deterrence, rehabilitation, retribution and isolation. While deterrence includes individual deterrence directed at preventing the specific offender from repeating the same or other criminal acts, it also includes general deterrence which aims to discourage the general public from recourse to crime. Rehabilitation is directed, of course, at reform of the individual, while retribution includes "the reaffirmation of societal norms for the purpose of maintaining respect for the norms themselves," community condemnation, and the community's emotional desire to punish the offender. Isolation serves simply to segregate the offender from society so as to prevent criminal conduct during the period of incarceration. It is clear that the principal aim of the 1980 gun legislation is general deterrence.

The most difficult problem confronting the sentencing judge is determination of the priority and relationship between the objectives of punishment, a matter of considerable and continuing debate. Inevitably, there are bound to be differences of opinion in the relative values assigned these factors in particular cases. The theories frequently are in unavoidable and constant conflict and those that prevail in the sentencer's mind obviously decide the degree of punishment. Much of the controversy and criticism swirling about the contemporary sentencing scene relates to inequitable disparities between sentences for the same or similar crimes. The disparities derive primarily from differing philosophies and attitudes of judges and a lack of consensus concerning the goals of criminal justice.

Appellate review of sentences obviously is a useful means of diminishing sentencing disparity and ensuring the imposition of fair sentences. Nevertheless, the limited nature of appellate review of sentences is a recognition that "the sentencing decision is a matter committed to the exercise of the [sentencing] court's discretion." A reviewing court lacks some of the first-hand knowledge of the case that the sentencing judge is in a position to obtain, and therefore the sentencer's decision should be afforded high respect. As a consequence, abuse of discretion is the test most frequently cited as the one to be applied. The abuse of discretion standard is especially befitted to an era in which most convictions derive from plea bargains where the bargaining leverages of the respective parties to the agreement are ofttimes more important in fixing the degree of the crime pleaded to and the other limits of the sentence to be imposed than matters of guilt, fault, character, mitigative circumstances or other factors which might otherwise seem more relevant. Nevertheless, since the Legislature has empowered us to modify sentences "as a matter of discretion in the interest of justice" and our general review powers include the right to do whatever the trial court could have done even in matters entrusted to the discretion of that court, we can substitute our own discretion for that of a trial court which has not abused its discretion in the imposition of a sentence. The power to substitute discretion helps us to meet recommended sentence review standards by making any disposition the sentencing court could have made, except an increased sentence. Without the substitution power, our ability to rectify sentencing disparities, reach extraordinary situations, and effectively set sentencing policy through the development of sentencing criteria, would be sorely handicapped.

Appellate review determines whether the sentence is excessive to the extent that there was a failure to observe the principles of sentencing. In such review, the court takes a "second look" at the sentences in light of the societal aims which such sanctions should achieve. But in reducing any sentence, the appellate body must be sensitive to the fact that its actions become guidelines for the trial court to follow in the imposition of future sentences under circumstances similar to the case reviewed.

In the current case, there has been no abuse of discretion and we perceive neither a failure to observe sentencing principles nor a need to impose a different view of discretion than that of the sentencing judge. True, the defendant does not appear to be a danger to society or in apparent need of rehabilitation. It is plain, however, that the sentencing court viewed general deterrence as the overriding principle, and we cannot say that the emphasis was erroneous or that the interests of justice call for a reduction. Deterrence is the primary and essential postulate of almost all criminal law systems. In this era of conflict between the adherents of the rehabilitation model and those who advocate determinative sentencing, it is hardly debatable that prisons do deter even if the degree of deterrence and the types of persons deterred remain in dispute. Even when imposing an "individualized" sentence, the judge may look beyond the offender to the presumed effect of the sentence on others. Indeed, the primary purpose behind mandatory sentence laws is to impose swift and certain punishment on the offender. A short definite period of confinement under the circumstances has been seen as the most effective method of deterrence. As Marvin Frankel has written, general deterrence may be satisfied through "relatively short but substantially inexorable sentences to prison." Some commentators have concluded that lesser punishment for firearm crimes, e.g., fines, probation or suspended sentences, is not significant enough to have any real deterrent effect.

In emphasizing the mandatory minimum sentence and the purpose of deterrence, the new gun legislation intended to convey to the public a "get tough" message on crime. In this regard, the advertisements heralding the new law are significant; thus: "If you get caught carrying an illegal handgun, you'll go to jail for one year. No plea bargaining. No judges feeling sorry for you. Just one year in jail."

With such a background, we cannot view the new gun law as containing a blanket exception of first offenders from the scope of its penal provisions. The statute's provisions for mitigation are not carte blanche for the commission of one offense free of the threat of a sentence of custodial detention. The sense of the new law is to deter all unlicensed handgun possessions, whether the offense is the first or a repeat. The special mitigation inquiry is not intended to provide automatic probation for those without prior criminal records. The penalty to be imposed is a matter for the trial court's broad discretion within the limits imposed by the Legislature. In balancing the public and private interests represented in the criminal justice process, the sentencing court's decision in this case was neither inconsistent with sound sentencing principles, nor inappropriate. We see nothing obscene about a 30-day jail sentence (which is subject to a 10-day reduction for good behavior) for possession of a gun, particularly when the defendant has a history of carrying the weapon for over seven years with knowledge of the law's requirements.

Reduction of the current sentence by this court would proclaim to those listening that the new gun law presents no threat of jail to first criminal offenders. Such a reduction would also declare to the trial bench that a judge who imposes a 30-day jail sentence on such a first offender has either abused his discretion or that this court disagrees with the sentencer's evaluation of the relevant sentencing factors. Finally, reduction would be this court's expression that violation of the gun law is nothing serious.

Accordingly, the sentence is affirmed.

O'CONNOR, Justice (dissenting).

In his usual scholarly and impelling style, my esteemed confrere of the majority, Justice LAZER, reviews the principles and discusses the rationale attendant upon sentencing and its appellate review. And so we go pell mell on our merry, merry way! More crimes are committed, more police make more arrests, more D.A.'s process more cases, more judges commit more people to jail, and here, the majority would affirm a jail sentence despite the presence of what, by any standard, was an abuse of sentencing discretion that warrants, nay demands, a reduction to probation. I cannot agree.

Recently released Justice Department figures for 1981 indicate that there were 369,000 adults in Federal and State prisons at the end of that year, plus nearly 157,000 in local jails. The National Council on Crime and Delinquency reports that the United States trails only the Soviet Union and South Africa (what a combination!) in its per capita rate of incarceration and, contrary to popular belief, in the severity of the punishments it inflicts! And in spite of it all, the crime rate continues to soar. * * *

It seems to me that it's about time we begin to find, in matters such as this where no violence or even threat of violence is present, alternatives to jail. I further believe that rather than joining those who bend before the incessant cry of a rightly outraged public for vengeance we, as appellate judges, should seek to put some sanity into the sentences we approve under these circumstances.

I agree with the principle, articulated in the majority opinion, that an appellate court ought not disturb a sentence in the absence of an abuse of discretion by the sentencing court or unless the interest of justice so requires.

I further agree that a workable test for applying this principle is whether the alleged excessiveness of the challenged sentence in fact demonstrates a failure by the sentencing court to observe the purposes of sentencing: individual and general deterrence, rehabilitation, retribution and isolation. I can even agree to the soundness of visiting upon one individual a punishment greater than would have been his had the sentencing court not decided to make an example of him in order to curb sharply a sudden manifestation in the general public of pernicious conduct previously endemic to certain subclasses, e.g., drug abuse, or to overcome widespread public intransigence to legislated curbs on historically unregulated conduct such as gun possession. But I disagree with the majority's statement that the sentencing judge, rather than this court, may on an ad hoc basis, subject only to personal predilections, establish the coefficients to the four variables of deterrence, rehabilitation, retribution and isolation in this sentencing formula. This court should not abdicate its responsibility for the assignment of appropriate, if somewhat inexact, weights to these factors in the discharge of its obligation to control sentencing discretion within the overarching limits fixed by the Penal Law.

Is it just or proper that we permit one sentencing judge to count general deterrence as the overriding factor in this gun possession case under the new anti-gun law, with the implication that another sentencing judge in a factually identical case may switch the emphasis in the formula to another factor, e.g., rehabilitation? Bear in mind that the difference resulting from our toleration of such ad hoc legislating by sentencing judges is incarceration, and I most vehemently reject any argument that incarceration is but a gentle escalation of sanctions to the point at which a real deterrent effect can finally be ascertained operating on the populace. After all, 30 days in the county jail will surely cripple the spirit of any otherwise law-abiding citizen who honestly believed that the cost of unlawfully possessing a gun (discounted tremendously by the infinitesimally small probability of being caught) outweighed the benefit of protecting his life while conducting his livelihood in an urban war zone. I submit that it is we, as the Appellate Division, that should assign the approximate values to the parameters of the sentencing formula (to the extent possible), and that we should restrict sentencing judges to their proper role in applying this legal formula, as so weighted, to the facts as they find them in individual cases.

I pose the questions:

(1) Is it a proper exercise of discretion to sentence to jail a first offender who poses no serious threat to the community?

(2) Does the nature of the crime here committed make it a serious threat to the community?

With these thoughts in mind, let us look at the case at bar.

On the morning of January 20, 1981, while driving through Nassau County on his way to his place of business in New York City, the defendant was stopped and arrested on a bench warrant charging him with the unauthorized use of a motor vehicle.

The validity of that warrant, or the merits of the complaint upon which it was issued, are not before the court at this time, but it should be noted that it is defendant's contention that the charge is totally without substance, arising, he alleges, out of a misunderstanding involving the return by him of a rented automobile.

Be that as it may, upon his arrest he was found in possession of a loaded Sterling .25 caliber automatic pistol. He was promptly charged with the crime of criminal possession of a weapon in the third degree, a class D felony, was convicted on his plea of guilty to possession in the fourth degree, a class A misdemeanor, and was sentenced to three years probation with the special condition that he serve a determinate sentence of 30 days in the Nassau County Correctional Center. Execution of that sentence has been stayed pending appeal.

Upon appeal to this court as excessive, that sentence has been affirmed by my confreres of the majority. I respectfully disagree and strongly suggest that under the facts and circumstances here extant, it is totally inappropriate and completely counterproductive to impose a jail sentence for however short a period of time.

An objective review of the record establishes that this defendant, a successful businessman, with three years of college education, is married and the father of two children, a daughter, aged 21, and a son, 14 years of age.

Since 1973 the defendant has owned and operated a custom tailer [sic] shop which is located in a high-crime area of the Bronx. A prior owner of the shop had been stabbed during one of several robberies that took place before defendant became the proprietor. The defendant lawfully purchased the gun in question in North Carolina and properly registered it in that State.

According to the arresting officers, the defendant was "very cooperative" when arrested, and readily admitted that he knew that it was illegal to carry an unregistered pistol in New York City and stated that although he had inquired about obtaining a gun permit, he had never completed the process. The defendant told the police that he thought he needed the gun for self-protection.

The Probation Report contains this significant appraisal:

The present offense is the defendant's only criminal conviction and his first criminal charge in 21 years. He appears to be a devoted father and husband, as well as a productive member of society. There is no evidence of criminal intent in his possession of this weapon and his desire for protection in his business neighborhood is justified.

No one can sustain this defendant, or any person, in the illegal possession of a loaded firearm. It is a clear violation of law and calls for an appropriate sanction and penalty. But under the clear and compelling circumstances here present, is it appropriate or fair or just to send this first offender off to jail for 30 days, 10 days or even one day? To me, such a sentence based upon these facts is cruel and harsh and borders on the obscene.

It is beyond cavil that violent crime is ever on the increase and that it is, in all its terrifying aspects, continuously creating conditions of unspeakable horror on the streets of our cities. Out of these jungle conditions in crescendo fashion, the cry of an aroused and frightened public is heard demanding, with good reason, swift and effective measures to contain and to curtail the monstrous abominations which are daily visited upon them. The fire is fueled by those who should and do know better but who, seizing upon a popular theme, pick up the cry and, by some total distortion of reason, imply that the fault lies with the judiciary and suggest that tougher and longer prison sentences are the solution. The Legislature responds by passing more and more mandatory sentencing laws and the press and other news media not infrequently give at least tacit approval to such measures. And all the time, judges, sitting in the eye of the storm, know that the catastrophic rise in crime bespeaks a failure not alone of society, but of the family, the church, the schools, the home and of the economic and political structure of the State itself. We know, too, that there are as many reasons for crime as there are people who commit it and we have long since learned that there is no simple solution or ready answer to the problem. I have previously expressed my disapproval of mandatory sentences because of a firmly held opinion that mandatory sentences give to a worried and frightened public the illusion of protection, that they do not deter the criminal and, worst of all, that they incapacitate a major section of the system of criminal justice in denying discretion to the courts. Are we really ready to give up on the theory that the punishment fit the crime?

To the issue before us--to tack on an additional jail sentence for the possession and/or use of the gun, loaded or unloaded, in or about the commission of a crime, makes much sense and may even be effective. However, to send an otherwise law-abiding citizen to jail on his first offense under the facts of this case makes no sense, accomplishes no good and creates nothing but untoward hardship and bitterness. I respectfully dissent and would modify the sentence by striking the 30-day period of incarceration.

HAVEN OR HELL?
INSIDE LORTON CENTRAL PRISON:
EXPERIENCES OF PUNISHMENT JUSTIFIED
Robert Blecker[a]
42 Stan. L. Rev. 1149 (1990)

I. INTRODUCTION

* * *

A. *The Problem: Justifying Punishment*

Why and how should we punish these criminals? A fearful and furious citizen may demand: "First, get them off the streets; keep them away from us. Make them suffer: They deserve it. Teach them a lesson they will not forget. And let their pain and suffering be an example to others. Maybe then, having been punished, someday, somehow, these criminals will feel remorse, change their attitudes, and productively reintegrate into society." Drawing upon sentiments and concepts implicit in the Bible and the works of Plato, Hobbes, Beccaria, Kant, Bentham, and a host of contemporary commentators, the citizen urges that punishment serve as incapacitation, retribution, general deterrence, specific deterrence, and rehabilitation.

The precise definition of each concept differs with each advocate, antagonist, or analyst. Essentially, however, *incapacitation* is rendering harmless to society a person otherwise inclined to crime. *Retribution* is the intentional infliction of pain and suffering on a criminal to the extent he deserves it because he has willingly committed a crime. *General deterrence* is the pressure that the example of one criminal's pain and suffering exerts on potential criminals to forgo their contemplated crimes. *Specific deterrence* is the pressure that unpleasant memories of incarceration exert on a released convict, which cause him to obey the law. *Rehabilitation* is the acquisition of skills or values which convert a criminal into a law-abiding citizen. * * *

---

[a]Robert Blecker, a criminal law professor at New York Law School, interviewed street criminals in Lorton prison and on the streets of Washington, D.C. from 1986 to 1999.

Those who do [prioritize] among the various justifications or purposes of punishment, almost without exception address the problem conceptually, as a matter of logic or philosophy. Without discussion, they assume that an appropriate blend of retribution, deterrence, incapacitation, and rehabilitation ultimately translates into a number, or number range, such as "10 years in prison" or "5-to-15 years in prison." A legislature or court need merely increase or decrease the length of the "sentence" to increase or decrease retribution, rehabilitation, deterrence, or incapacitation. Often this abstraction is obscured: the number *becomes* the punishment rather than a symbol of its duration which is only one dimension of a prisoner's actual pain and suffering.

Punishment, however, is not merely the quantity of time in prison. *The reality of each criminal's punishment consists in the experience of that punishment.* What actually happens to prisoners -- their daily pain and suffering inside prison -- is the only true measure of whether the traditional concepts have meaning, the traditional goals are fulfilled, the traditional definitions apply. Only through the prisoners' experience can we test the categories, clarify these concepts, and set priorities. * * * This study, then, attempts to bridge the gap between traditional penal philosophy and the actual experience of punishment.

B. Limits of the Study

* * * [T]he author and John Allen, inmate # 129375, have spent hundreds of hours together inside Lorton Central Prison, documenting the daily lives of Johnny's friends and acquaintances. We have probed deeply, exploring with the prisoners their childhood, their street hustles, their political views, their moral codes, their philosophy of life, and, of course, their experience inside the "joint" (the prison).

We did not calculate exactly how many inmates took each position, nor did we even attempt a truly representative sample of Lorton Central prisoners. Johnny, in his mid-forties, had friends who were generally older and more thoughtful than average. Moreover, Lorton Central is hardly a typical prison: In a 68-acre complex about 25 miles south of Washington, D.C., in lush Virginia farmland, strips of dormitories house approximately 1300 long-term felons who have committed serious street crimes in Washington. True to the concept of "home rule" for the nation's capital, the prison administration is mostly black; the prison population is more than 99 percent black. This is *not,* then, a statistical analysis. It is a field study -- a philosophical field study -- of one prison only. And although this study hardly qualifies as an account of an average prison experience across the United States, the national focus on Washington, D.C.'s reaction to its crime-infested streets makes it at least symbolically significant, and the interviews ensure that this composite account is revealing, because its source is real. * * *

II. INSIDE LORTON CENTRAL

Retribution, deterrence (general and specific), rehabilitation, and incapacitation represent overlapping and antithetical perspectives on why, when, and to what degree criminals should undergo pain and suffering through punishment. In order to evaluate these various definitions, justifications, and goals of punishment, therefore, we need to know whether and how prisoners do in fact suffer inside Lorton Central.

Of course everyone's "bit" -- time spent in prison -- is different. One individual feels a loss of freedom more or less than another. A forced separation from home, and the streets, and entrance into a new prison environment can be more or less painful. Losing family ties may cause a criminal to suffer differently at different stages of life. And in the course of each day, moment to moment, a prisoner's experience of prison changes. * * *

C. Haven or Hell?

* * * What is the real experience of Lorton? Obviously it depends. Some guys breeze through it; others live in agony. Even Douglas Wright who called Lorton a "playground" qualified it: "[A] playground to all those youngsters who don't know what's happening."

Almost uniformly the older inmates condemn Lorton Central as a "deathtrap." "You can get killed because you have no protection," said Danny Bethel, one of many prisoners who has been stabbed. "You can't go to a dark room; you can't take a bucket and wash your clothes without realizing it's possible you might not come out. It's no such place as that you're guaranteed to see tomorrow. You go to bed with a nightmare, and the only peace that you ever get is not waking up at all." * * *

III. THE EXPERIENCE OF LORTON CENTRAL JUSTIFIED

A. Retribution

He who kills a man shall be put to death. . . . When a man causes a disfigurement in his neighbor, as he has done it shall be done to him, fracture for fracture, eye for eye, tooth for tooth; as he has disfigured a man, he shall be disfigured. *Leviticus 24:17-20*

Retribution is perhaps the oldest measure of punishment: like for like -- pain and suffering for pain and suffering. The Bible commands: "[A]s he has done, it shall be done to him." Scorned by a shrinking majority of scholars, retribution continues to be embraced by a large majority of citizens. Retributivists have recognized that strict repayment is not always possible: If a criminal takes out the only eye of a one-eyed man, surely to take out only one of his two good eyes is not full retribution, whereas to take them both out is not exact recompense. Retribution has advanced beyond exact retaliation to become what it is today -- *proportional punishment.* Punishment should be proportional to the gravity of the crime.

Retributivists differ as to the appropriate length and intensity of punishment attaching to particular crimes. Some may see violent crime as incomparably more deserving of punishment than non-violent crime; others may feel that crimes which affect the public generally, such as illegally dumping toxic wastes, or cheating the elderly out of their life savings, or a public official's bribe-receiving deserve the greater punishment. To a degree these differences of opinion are subjective and arbitrary, but only to a degree. Since Aristotle, *malum in se,* a thing bad in itself, has been distinguished from *malum prohibitum,* a thing bad only because defined as illegal, or as inmate Alvin Hines called it, "a man-made crime." Murder, rape, robbery: These are serious crimes, bad in themselves. But is selling drugs? In 1990, a small but respectable chorus including judges and legislators calls for the legalization of narcotics. Yet, during this era of prohibition, many prisoners are serving very long and painful sentences for engaging in truly consensual transactions that perhaps should not be illegal, while others for whom killing is a business decision, who maintain deadly workplaces or poison our water are sentenced to community service or not punished at all. Is this proportional? Proportional to what? To the criminal's culpable mental state, to his conduct, to the ultimate harm caused? * * *

In theory, prison life should be tougher for serious felons, and by privileges and courtesies extended, it should be relatively more comfortable for less serious offenders. But inside Lorton Central, theory and reality do not match.

Inside Central a man's crime is virtually ignored. Officers routinely deny that they treat a prisoner with an eye to his record, to his crime, to his "evil" choice that brought him to prison. Captain Frank Townshend, a long-time, well-respected, tough-but-fair officer, insisted that he never looks at a man's record when he deals with him lest he be "prejudiced. Everyone is entitled to the same treatment here, regardless of what they did to get here. What a man is in here for is not our concern."

"Do you read their records?" Sergeant Cody was asked.

"I am not here to do that."

"You don't care what a guy has done to get in here? It makes no difference to you what he has done out there?".

"No difference. He has been to court and he has been sentenced and that is that. I am just to keep him safeguarded by the process of law."

All officers interviewed agreed: They never consult a man's record, and sometimes for good reasons. "If you know a man is a murderer, you may fear him, and he will sense that. They pick up those things," said one officer, "so I don't want to know. I make it a point not to know." One female officer offered a similar rationale. She does not check the records, for if she discovers a man is a rapist, she will feel apprehensive about disciplining him. Even when officers do know the criminals' records, they do not treat the more serious offenders more harshly. Rather, they concentrate on behavior which may cause problems in prison. "Inside, a thief is more dangerous than a murderer," observed Sergeant Shipley. "The thief will continue to steal whenever he can, and get himself or someone else stabbed or killed. So he's the one, day to day, that you have to come down hard on." * * *

Overwhelmingly then, by their actions and attitudes consistent with official D.C. Department of Corrections policy, officers and inmates reject retribution as a goal of punishment on the inside for past conduct on the outside. To them, the judge metes out punishment by setting the number of years during which all inmates will be equally deprived of liberty. The officers see no point in trying to make prison more painful for prisoners because they "deserve" it, unless they deserve it for their conduct inside prison. By consciously ignoring prisoners' criminal records, however, officers unwittingly help sever the essential retributive connection between the past crime committed and the present punishment experienced. As Captain Townshend said, "It's none of my business. What a man is like in here is what I'm concerned with, not what he did out there."

The prisoners further help cut all connection between crime on the street and punishment inside the joint. With the exception of rape which they scorn, and child molestation or crimes against the elderly for which a prisoner may be ostracized or physically attacked, whatever a person did on the outside is his own business. Each man is a hustler, trying to survive. * * *

B. General Deterrence

Deterrence lies at the very source of Western culture. Although the Old Testament is retributive in its measure of punishment -- an eye for an eye -- it is fundamentally deterrent in its justification and purpose. Over and over, the Bible calls for harsh punishment, not only because an individual deserves it on account of his past transgression, but also for the future benefit it will bring to others: "[T]hen you shall do to him as he had meant to do to his brother . . . . And the rest shall hear, and fear, and shall never again commit any such evil among you." * * *

According to the psychology expounded by Beccaria and Bentham, a rational pleasure seeker defers immediate illegal gratification because a threat of future punishment weighs decisively in his pleasure/pain, cost/benefit calculus. Convicts as well as commentators dismiss this psychology of the rational prudent calculating maximizer as fantastic -- an ideal inapplicable to the streets: General deterrence is unreal and unworkable; people do not consciously weigh costs and benefits before they engage in crime.

A litmus question to the inmates at Lorton Central -- "Before you pulled the trigger [or robbed] did you ever think about what would happen if you were caught?" -- revealed minds unconcerned with future punishment in moments immediately surrounding the criminal act:

"Nah, never thought about it," said inmate David Basnight, "until one time, and that's probably why I got caught. I just stood there, looking at the camera, thinking."

"Did you ever think about getting caught?" inmate Harry Rowe was asked.

"No."

"Never occurred to you?"

"No."

"Never thought about going to jail?"

"Well, *I'd been told,* but you know, I ain't never really thought about it . . . ."

"And the day you did it, it never passed through your mind that 'Hey, I might get caught, this might be the last day'?"

"No, I ain't think . . . that weren't on my mind. Just getting the money and getting away."

The pressing problem of the moment -- getting away -- includes not getting shot, and not getting caught, which may subconsciously include a future trial and eventually a prison term. But conscious calculation is not so much of punishment as of pulling it off and escaping.

"Did you ever think about getting caught before you did the things you did?" Johnny asked inmate Anthony Chandler Bey.

"Nah, only afterwards."

"Were you aware of the type of sentences other people were getting for robbery?"

"No."

"If you had been aware of the large sentences, would it have stopped you? Would it have made you stop and think about it?"

"Yeah, it would have made me stop and think."

"Would it have stopped you from doing the crime?"

"I don't think so. I think I would have been more aware. Wouldn't just go up and do it. Know what's happening. Look it over first. I think being aware of the sentence part, then I would have looked more deeply into it."

"Seeing another hustler fall, you say 'he did something foolish,' something you're not going to do," mused Itchy Brooks. "Sometimes a guy try to find out what he did so he won't do the same. That's the only deterrent effect that has."

When the possibility of being caught only causes a more disciplined hustler to take greater precautions or to switch to safer crimes, has deterrence succeeded?

Some criminals may be undeterrable because they do not calculate, but others are undeterrable because they do. "I had a job," said inmate Wade Briggs, "but I saw that the same amount of money it took me four weeks to work for, I could make in one day."

"They were going to put me in the army," declared Itchy, "but I figured why go six thousand miles away to kill someone, and put your life in jeopardy for a principle you might not even agree with for one hundred fifty dollars a month, when you can place your life in jeopardy for a much shorter period of time at the bank, and when you get away with it you can live well for awhile. It makes no sense.

"If I worked, there wasn't much chance of my getting more than a few thousand dollars a year and here's a chance of my getting two hundred fifty thousand dollars in a day or so. It was worth it to take the risk. Plus the federal statistics show that only a little over half of all bank robbers are caught. And eighty percent of those just ran in and grabbed the stuff. People in the banks are instructed not to create the kind of situation where somebody's going to get hurt. Because the money's insured. And really the professional is not going there to hurt nobody. He's going there to get the money. Since he knows they're instructed not to offer resistance, that's the way it's done." * * *

"The average black kid in the ghetto after that first knockdown knows that the old bootstrap trick is not really there," observed Sergeant Edmonds. "And he just takes a look around at his aunts and uncles, his parents and cousins, and he assesses how far they reached up this ladder of success. How much have they gained? And he is saying to himself 'Gee they don't got very much, old raggedy clothes, living in a run-down dump.' Then he looks right across the street. Here Joe Slick pulls up: He's got this great big shiny car, the best looking clothes on, he's got his jewelry on, he's got a fine looking woman with him. The guy says 'Now that's what I want,' because this guy's got it. He is not equating that with the whole picture, but he is looking at the for-now." * * *

Family visits at Lorton could provide a most compelling occasion for images and pain to combine and produce maximum deterrence. But they don't.

Sergeant Edmonds reminisced about his first year at the prison: "It was Christmas of '80. We had a tree down in the visiting hall and in the cell blocks. And as the kids came in, the fathers came out of their cells carrying gifts. It was a mixed emotion day for me, to look at the picture we projected to the younger kids when they came here to visit. Just to watch the expression on their faces, how they would light up when they came through the control area out front. We shook them down, brought them inside. They got on the bus, rode down to the visiting hall, their eyes just lit up. They were all aglow, watching this door, waiting for their father to come through that door into that visiting hall. And they just ran to him and flung themselves on him. It made you conscious of your younger existence. And how you felt about your father. My father was in the military, so we had that kind of 'father's home, boat's in!' He's going to be here in a few minutes and everybody is all excited about it. And everybody is rushing to him. It gave me the same kind of feeling watching them.

"But by the same token, it made the children feel that this was a good place, because all the good things that occurred to them in a family sense were occurring right here inside an institution where their father was locked away at. And being punished at. So it did not build a sense of 'this is a bad place;' it built the sense of 'this is a good place' -- the experience for a lot of them, of seeing for the first time both parents together, hugging and embracing and enjoying each other's company. And the kids running around the visiting hall or out in the field, having a good time with other kids from their neighborhoods within the city. * * *

"I talked to one of the young boys in the visiting hall one day, and he says to me, 'When I come to Lorton, you not going to beat up on me.' And I asked him, 'Well, why would you want to come to Lorton?' And he said, 'Because my father's here.' It was weird to have a child think that way. Because he really did not understand what it was about. He did not understand the meanness and ugliness of it. After that two hours is up and his father had to go back into the jungle, where he had to fight for his survival until his next visiting day, if he was lucky enough to make it and not get stabbed. Put on his best civilian clothes and come to the visiting hall. And spend another two hours with the family."

"When the kids visit, you give them your best smile," Itchy agreed. "We're relaxed; nothing jumps off at the visiting hall. But they don't see our face change as we leave the hall." * * *

C. Incapacitation

Originally prison's sole purpose was to hold prisoners until trial or punishment. Today, incarceration -- taking criminals from the streets and confining them -- remains prison's front line, and perhaps bottom line, justification. The experience inside may not be retributive, it may not rehabilitate the inmate, nor deter him or others, but at least that criminal is removed from society and to the prison, where he is disabled from committing further crimes. * * *

Even though sentences have gotten much longer and inmates believe escape is not that difficult today, very few prisoners plan or attempt it. * * * What keeps them inside? Less a fear of being shot while scaling the fence, than the punishment which follows an unsuccessful escape attempt: Transfer. Lorton, Virginia is easily accessible to Washington, D.C. As Reggie Brooks said, "They got three or four of their little buddies serving life sentences with them here, and they're in heaven." A transfer to Wala Wala [*sic*], Leavenworth or another remote prison cuts off an inmate from his family, friends, his familiar environment. Punishing escape with transfer deters; it is also ironically retributive.

An inmate who does not escape, however, is not necessarily incapacitated. Incapacitation requires more than confinement. While incarcerated, an inmate must commit no crimes against society. Prisoners inside Central rarely assault visitors, teachers, counselors, or officers, mostly because they fear transfer. But prisoners often kill prisoners. Inside Lorton Central serious stabbings and murder attempts are an everyday event. Every inmate who wants a weapon has one. "There's no way to stop them," said Captain Townshend. "They can make them out of anything. If I was an inmate, I'd have one for my own security."

Prisoners disagree over which is more dangerous, the joint or the streets. Inside Lorton Central there are very few guns, whereas the streets of Washington, D.C. have become a battlefield. On the other hand, in the closed environment inside Central, there is nowhere to run, nowhere to hide. On the street when a guy cuts in line or "rips you off," you can ignore it. You will probably never see him again. But inside Lorton Central, with everyone watching on the side-lines, you must counter such disrespect, or others will take advantage of you. "In the street when you're doing something wrong you're seldom doing it in your neighborhood," said Johnny. "Lorton *is* the neighborhood. Each time you take a pair of tennis shoes, a radio, a sweatsuit, you risk your life." * * *

Thus, from the outside, the prisoners of Lorton Central seem to be incapacitated. Rarely do they cross the perimeter or even test it. Inside the prison, however, crime -- the sale and possession of narcotics, theft, assault, and murder -- is rampant. In the words of inmate Pete Arnold, "It's a fucking zoo."

D. Specific Deterrence

In theory, then, having committed no crimes while he is incarcerated, the prisoner, once released, carries with him painful memories of his prison experience, which continue to haunt him, pressuring him to avoid criminality and live the straight life. In theory.

If, as Hobbes defined it, memory is "decaying sense," then painful prison memories have a very short half-life: "In twenty-five days you've forgotten the experience of twenty-five years," said Itchy Brooks. "All the lessons you learned." Pressed in the streets, memories of Lorton quickly fade. The immediate dangers, the uncertainty, and the insecurity can seem worse than life in Central with its "three hots and a cot."

"I know what the penitentiary is about. I've dealt with it," said Leo Simms. "Inside, I guess I know I can deal with it. If you check my records it seems I am able to deal with the institution better than I do with the street. You can institutionalize a person. I know what to expect here. I can be inside any institution for a week, and I can close my eyes and know the routine from hour to hour. It doesn't offer me any challenges. It's a lesser threat than I would have in the street. The decisions you have to make in the free world you don't have to make here. I know it's sad to say, a guy my age, but you can get in the habit of having people make decisions for you. You have many guys in this institution that cry every day about wanting to get out, but their actions dictate different, because in their heart they can't really want to go, because they don't know how to make it out there. We have a closeness that you don't have in the street . . . . When you're sick here, everyone want to know how you are. You might have twenty guys . . . . It's sad but it offers something to individuals that you don't get in the street." * * *

Dr. Reynolds, Chief [Psychologist] at Maximum, summed it up bleakly: "Before the first time, they don't think about it; after the first time they get used to it." "When I was on the street," said Robert Moffitt, "I used to say to myself 'I wish I could go to jail for about six months or a year maybe, just to get myself together.' Jail is about the only place a man can get himself cleaned up." Specific deterrence fails miserably when prison becomes a refuge.

For some inmates, Central is not so much a refuge, but an acceptable, if unpleasant, necessity. "I operate on the premise of my being a hustler and this [is] part of it, part of the game that comes with it. It's a deterrent as far as educational things," said Rodney Hunt. "I won't make the same mistakes in the future. I'll do it another way."

"How many people that's doing the time that you're doing for the crime that you did would say that 'I'm not going to do that no more'?" Johnny asked Leo Simms.

"I've talked to many guys here in Lorton, and they want to talk about a *new way* of doing it," said Leo. "But as far as not doing it, I don't think I've talked to one that has in his mind not to do that, period. Just another way." * * *

"You come here for stealing a car, you leave here knowing how to crack a safe," Itchy said. "This is a crime factory."

Prison experience, then, fails as a specific deterrent for the ex-convict on the streets who remembers it as a refuge, or accepts it as an inevitable part of hustling life. And the experience fails to specifically deter those it makes more cautious or those ex-convicts it opens up to new criminal opportunities. Most perversely, out on the street, specific deterrence fails when a convict's obvious indifference to repeating a long bit may make him an even more effective hustler. His threats are credible -- "I've done hard time; I can do it again."

He may come out more vicious than he went in. "Prison is not a healthy place to be," said Itchy. "The people in the community say, 'Well, it's not intended to be. We don't want it to be.' Fine, so when a guy come to the gate to blow your fucking head off, then that's what you apparently wanted. You should have expected it. Because that's exactly what the fuck you're doing. When you put a man in prison and you say 'life,' then make that life. Or you're asking for it."

"What do you do with a Doberman Pinscher when you want him to be mean? You make him hungry and keep him chained up, restrained from everything. When you let him loose he goes wild. It's no different with us," Itchy said. "You in such a state of deprivation when you leave here, you want *everything* and you want it *now*. You don't want to wait. You've been waiting too long. You've been waiting on too many lines. You done took shit from too many people. You ain't taking any more shit.

"So when you go on the street with that attitude you're dangerous. And that's that. This is a monster. But where did that monster come from? You were a small monster when you came but you're a giant one when you go out of here."

Why, then, doesn't every ex-prisoner return to prison? Why is any Lorton Central ex-con ever deterred? Two factors, often noted in the literature, were reflected inside the prison. "I would never come back to this place," insisted Danny Bethel. "I've overstayed my welcome. I'm too old for it and I can't take it no more. There comes a time in all of us where it's time to quit. There's no force, there's no power that can make me commit a crime. My time's over; I'm just not coming back." For many, like Bethel, Johnny, and Leo, the aging process itself makes specific deterrence work. * * *

Family is the great motivator. "It would be a lot different for me if I had a second chance," mused Earl Grier. "What it boils down to on this charge and me doing this time, is that it really wasn't worth it compared to what I have lost since I been here. I had a nice home; all my family was together. Now all my children are spread all over: Southeast, Northeast, Maryland, New York."

"Thinking about your family and their dependence on you is more of an immediate deterrent than the prison itself," explained Johnny, determined never to return. Not being with his grandmother before she died, not being able to protect and influence his children, not being able to guide his grandchildren into educated drug-free lives, eats at him. * * *

E. Rehabilitation: "An Eye Patch For An Eye"

    * * * Rehabilitation -- or reformation -- essentially consists of the acquisition of attitudes, values, habits and skills by which an "enlightened" criminal comes to value himself as a member of a society in which he can function productively and lawfully. This glossy definition is appealing, but reveals little of the rehabilitative process with its pitfalls and problems. * * *

1. Back out, back in.

    "This place is not working," observed Sergeant Edmonds, stating the obvious. "But you cannot change it inside and not change the outside. Even if a guy has good intentions, and says, 'I am going to get out and go straight, be a good father, be a good provider.' He goes back out into the system we are in. He is a convicted criminal. That's one strike against him. He's black or Hispanic, so he's got two strikes against him. When he gets back out there, who's going to hire him? The average business really does not want a convict employee. What did he do? Can he be trusted? How will other employees feel with him around? So if he gets a job, it's going to be a low-level, low-paying job. But his aspirations are as high as anybody else's out there. He wants the American dream too. A lot of them get into crime because they want the American dream. The reasons that brought him here never changed. The have-nots want to have." * * *

    Itchy described the psychological corrosion of a prisoner, released after a long bit, initially determined to stay out: "You're going in the street," said Itchy, "with the fifty dollars they give you and you have a whole new situation where you haven't been making no decisions for four or five years and now you have to make them all. You haven't had to do nothing but make ugly faces and look tough in here to get by. Now looking tough don't get you nothing. So you're out there and all your good intentions, all that shit don't amount to a hill of beans, because it's back to real life, it's back to the survival struggle. . . . You're out there and everything is falling apart; everybody's got a family except you -- yours fell apart a long time ago while you were in here.

    "And your buddies come by and say 'let's take a drink.' 'Man, no, I got some things I'm trying to do' and that lasts for awhile. Because you see yourself accomplishing something, you see yourself trying to do something. But then after a few months go by and you're still in the same situation you was, you see yourself making no progress, your prospects are the same as the day you came out. Nobody's seriously offering you anything. You got some people telling you 'well if you go down and sit outside the union somebody will come by and offer you a day's work.' What is a day's work going to do toward paying the rent? You don't got enough money to more than get you a drink, or buy you some dope and put yourself out of your misery. The next thing you know, you find that all this stuff about Lorton is fuzzy in your mind. 'Damn, I sure did rough in Lorton. But at least somebody had their foot on my neck and kept me from doing better. Now, here, nobody got their foot on my neck and I still can't do better.' Then you start backsliding. You start going around with your buddies and doing things you hadn't planned on doing."

"When you leave here," said Johnny, "You don't have no money. The people you know in the street are hustling. A guy may offer you some drugs, or somebody going to say 'Here's five or six hundred dollars. Go downtown and get yourself a couple of outfits.' And then the same guy, a couple of days later, going to say 'Hey, what you doing?' And you say 'I ain't doing nothing yet. I'm still looking around.' In the course of a few weeks you're getting back into the swing of things. And then this guy come back again in the Mercedes Benz or the BMW and that six is gone. And he say 'Hey, you ready to go to work now?' And you say, 'Of course.'" * * *

Some prisoners, however, nearing the end of their term can look forward to returning to society with a home, a family, a job. Sergeant Edmonds portrayed the pressure on them: " * * * Once he goes through the halfway house, does his six months, he is back out there. The structured life that was here, all those little supports, all those bricklets that we built up here, we have now in the process of putting him back into society removed piece by piece, until all of a sudden, he is now standing on the concrete on North Capitol Street, a free man, free to do what he wants to do with himself. Somewhere up in here, he misses those supports. Even though he hated the hell out of them, supposedly, when he was here. He still misses those supports, all the friends he had if he did that kind of time, are here in Lorton. They are not out there. They are here.

"The same people that came to visit him, the same lady, children came to visit him, now have to alter their life to fit him in. Before, they didn't have to do that. They just had Tuesdays, Thursdays, Saturdays and Sundays to visit in two hour blocks and back to whatever they were doing. Now he is there full-time. They have to integrate him into their being. Slap! 'I am back.' He wants to carry the same authoritative manner that he had when they came for those couple of hours visit. In charge. But they have lived independent of him, with the exception of the visits. Resentment builds. He is now a liability instead of an asset. Because he's not making the kind of money that is going to help motivate and lift them. What little that they now have, have to be shared with someone else. The food bill goes up. The use of the automobile is shared. All of the things that they had, now have to be shared with this guy. Even though they love him, this is a sharing thing now.

"He notices that the irritation factor is setting in, arguments ensue, words are exchanged. Now, it is crystal clear to him that something is wrong here. By now, the woman is saying 'Jesus, man, you're a drain on the family, you got to bring some money in here, we ain't going to live like this.'

"And it gets back to 'What do I know how to do? Back on the Avenue. You are talking to your friends. You have resisted them. Maybe for six or seven months. You have resisted the temptation to put the package in your hand, or do a deal to make some money. A lot of the guys who have gotten out, the guys they see on the streets, those same role models are still out there living the high life, wads of money.

"One day you are coming up out of McDonald's, dirty and greasy, going home into the shit, arguments, and all that because you are not providing. You're choking, you are stifling them to death. And he says 'Give me the package; fuck McDonald's.' He knows from that point he's on his way home. This is his home, Lorton. The rhetoric is the rhetoric. This is home." * * *

F. The Unjustified Experience at Lorton: A Summary

Traditionally, the principal definitions, justifications, and purposes of punishment -- retribution, general deterrence, specific deterrence, incapacitation, and rehabilitation -- have been singly advocated in the literature. Inside Lorton Central they have been singularly violated. * * *

Lorton Central may be unique among prisons in the United States, but in its failure to achieve the traditional goals of punishment, it suffers their common fate. The problem may lie in the categories themselves, used for centuries by legislatures, courts, philosophers, and law professors, with a most casual relationship to reality.

C.   THE PRESUMPTION OF INNOCENCE AND PROOF BEYOND A REASONABLE DOUBT

In American litigation, criminal trials begin with the prosecution's attempt to establish the defendant's guilt. The reason why the prosecution goes first in a trial is the presumption of innocence, which has been described by the Supreme Court as "that bedrock 'axiomatic and elementary' principle whose 'enforcement lies at the foundation of the administration of our criminal law.'" *In re Winship*, 397 U.S. 358 (1970). The formal way of saying that the prosecution has the responsibility for establishing the defendant's guilt – rather than the defendant having the responsibility for establishing his or her innocence – is that in a criminal case, the prosecution bears the *burden of proof.*[a]

The *standard of proof* in litigation describes the level of certainty the fact-finder must reach before ruling for the party with the burden of proof. In an American criminal trial, the prosecution's standard of proof is "beyond a reasonable doubt." This is the most difficult standard of proof to meet in American law; in civil cases, in contrast, the standard is usually "a preponderance of the evidence," meaning "more likely than not."

Why is the burden of proof in a criminal trial so onerous? In *Winship,* the Supreme Court set forth some reasons for placing such a heavy burden on the government:

> The reasonable-doubt standard plays a vital role in the American scheme of criminal procedure. It is a prime instrument for reducing the risk of convictions resting on factual error. * * * As the dissenters in the New York Court of Appeals observed, and we agree, "a person accused of a crime . . . would be at a severe disadvantage, a disadvantage amounting to a lack of fundamental fairness, if he could be adjudged guilty and imprisoned for years on the strength of the same evidence as would suffice in a civil case."

> The requirement of proof beyond a reasonable doubt has this vital role in our criminal procedure for cogent reasons. The accused during a criminal prosecution has at stake interests of immense importance, both because of the possibility that he may lose his liberty upon conviction and because of the certainty that he would be stigmatized by the conviction. Accordingly, a society that values the good name and freedom of every individual should not condemn a man for commission of a crime when there is reasonable doubt about his guilt. * * *

---

[a]There are two types of burdens of proof: the *burden of production* and the *burden of persuasion.* The burden of production is the initial responsibility to produce evidence in support of a claim. The burden of persuasion is the ultimate responsibility of proving that a given offense was committed or that the elements of an asserted defense are either present (the defendant's position) or absent (the prosecutor's position). In a criminal case, the burden of persuasion as to charged offenses always rests with the prosecution. The burden of persuasion as to a defense may rest with the prosecution or the defendant, depending on the type of defense asserted. For simplicity's sake, however, it is common to simply speak of the "burden of proof."

Moreover, use of the reasonable-doubt standard is indispensable to command the respect and confidence of the community in applications of the criminal law. It is critical that the moral force of the criminal law not be diluted by a standard of proof that leaves people in doubt whether innocent men are being condemned. It is also important in our free society that every individual going about his ordinary affairs have confidence that his government cannot adjudge him guilty of a criminal offense without convincing a proper factfinder of his guilt with utmost certainty.

The reasonable doubt standard is not just a good idea; it is the law. In *Winship*, the Court held that the Due Process Clause of the Fifth and Fourteenth Amendments of the U.S. Constitution "protects the accused against conviction except upon proof beyond a reasonable doubt of every fact necessary to constitute the crime with which he is charged." 397 U.S. at 364.

Because the prosecution always retains the burden of proof beyond a reasonable doubt in order to secure a conviction, one possible defense strategy is simply to create a reasonable doubt about some element of the crime. This kind of strategy is sometimes described as a *case-in-chief* defense, or a *prima facie* case defense. Suppose, for example, that the defendant has been charged with theft, and one element of that crime is the intentional taking of the property of another. By simply creating a reasonable doubt about whether the taking was intentional or merely accidental, the defense can win and the defendant can be acquitted. This kind of defense may not require the introduction of any evidence; it requires only that the defendant "poke holes" in the prosecution's story.[b]

---

[b]In *Mullaney v. Wilbur*, 421 U.S. 684, 95 S.Ct. 1881, 44 L.Ed.2d 508 (1975), and *Patterson v. New York*, 432 U.S. 197, 97 S.Ct. 2319, 53 L.Ed.2d 281 (1977), the Supreme Court considered the issue of whether a state could, consistent with the Due Process Clause, effectively transform the elements of a substantive crime into the elements of an affirmative defense, so as to place the burden of proof on the defendant to disprove his guilt. In *Mullaney*, the Court reversed the defendant's conviction, finding that the trial court's instruction to the jury that the defendant bore the burden of proving that he acted in the heat of passion on sudden provocation and therefore lacked the malice required for murder unconstitutionally shifted the burden of proving every essential element of the crime from the prosecution to the defense. In *Patterson*, the Court upheld a New York statutory scheme that placed the burden of proving the defense of extreme emotional disturbance (the Model Penal Code's version of the common law defense of provocation) on the defendant. The defendant argued that given *Mullaney*, this scheme was unconstitutional. The Court, over a dissent by three Justices, disagreed: "To recognize at all a mitigating circumstance does not require the

However, a second strategy is also available to the defense: admitting the basic crime, but arguing for acquittal based on extenuating circumstances. For instance, the defendant can admit that she took the victim's property, but argue that the taking was justified: she stole the victim's fire extinguisher in order to put out a fire that would have otherwise killed an entire family of innocent people. Or, the defendant can admit she stole the property, but argue that she should nevertheless be excused from criminal punishment: she believed the fire extinguisher was actually a transmission device for messages from Saturn, and that she needed to receive and translate these messages in order to save the Earth. This kind of defense – in which the defendant admits guilt as to the charged offense, but claims he nevertheless should be acquitted of that offense either because he was justified in acting the way he did or because he should be excused – is called an *affirmative defense.* In contrast to the burden of persuasion for the case in chief, which always remains on the prosecution as a matter of constitutional law, the legislature may place the burden of persuasion regarding an affirmative defense on the defendant. In such a case, the defendant has the responsibility to prove the elements of any justification or excuse defense[c] he or she asserts at trial. In situations in which the legislature has allocated the burden of persuasion to the defendant, the defendant is usually required to prove the affirmative defense by a preponderance of the evidence, the same standard used in civil trials.

What does "reasonable doubt" mean? Consider the following representative jury instructions.

DISTRICT OF COLUMBIA CRIMINAL JURY INSTRUCTIONS
Instruction 2.09
REASONABLE DOUBT
4th ed., Young Lawyers Section, Bar Association of the District of Columbia, 1993

Reasonable doubt, as the name implies, is a doubt based on reason, a doubt for which you can give a reason. It is such a doubt as would cause you, after careful and candid and impartial consideration of all the evidence, to be so

---

State to prove its nonexistence in each case in which the fact is put in issue, if in its judgment this would be too cumbersome, too expensive, and too inaccurate." 432 U.S. at 209.

[c] The distinction between justifications and excuses is discussed in Chapter 10.

undecided that you cannot say that you are firmly convinced of the defendant's guilt. It is such a doubt as would cause a reasonable person to hesitate or pause in the graver or more important transactions of life. However, it is not a fanciful doubt, nor a whimsical doubt, nor a doubt based on conjecture. It is a doubt which is based on reason. The government is not required to establish guilt beyond all doubt, or to a mathematical certainty or a scientific certainty. Its burden is to establish guilt beyond a reasonable doubt.

VIRGINIA MODEL JURY INSTRUCTIONS CRIMINAL
Instruction No. 2.100
Reasonable Doubt and Presumption of Innocence
Michie, 2002

The defendant is presumed to be innocent. You should not assume the defendant is guilty because he has been indicted and is on trial. This presumption of innocence remains with the defendant throughout the trial and is enough to require you to find the defendant not guilty unless and until the Commonwealth proves each and every element of the offense beyond a reasonable doubt. This does not require proof beyond all possible doubt, nor is the Commonwealth required to disprove every conceivable circumstance of innocence. However, suspicion or probability of guilt is not enough for a conviction.

There is no burden on the defendant to produce any evidence.

A reasonable doubt is a doubt based on your sound judgment after a full and impartial consideration of all the evidence in the case.

CALIFORNIA JURY INSTRUCTIONS – CRIMINAL
2.90. Presumption of Innocence–Reasonable Doubt–Burden of Proof
7th ed., West, 2003

A defendant in a criminal action is presumed to be innocent until the contrary is proved, and in case of a reasonable doubt whether [his] [her] guilt is satisfactorily shown, [he] [she] is entitled to a verdict of not guilty. This presumption places upon the People the burden of proving [him] [her] guilty beyond a reasonable doubt.

Reasonable doubt is defined as follows: It is not a mere possible doubt; because everything relating to human affairs is open to some possible or imaginary doubt. It is that state of the case which, after the entire comparison and consideration of all the evidence, leaves the minds of the jurors in that condition that they cannot say they feel an abiding conviction of the truth of the charge.

D.   STANDARDS OF REVIEW

Before a criminal trial has ended, at the close of the prosecution's case in chief, a defendant may move for a "directed verdict" of acquittal, in which the judge directs the jury to acquit for lack of evidence. After the trial is completed, if the defendant is convicted, he or she may appeal the conviction to a higher court for review of the sufficiency of the evidence. What standard of proof should the trial judge apply to a motion for directed verdict? What standard of proof should an appellate court apply when reviewing the evidence supporting a conviction?

It may be surprising, at first glance, to learn that in these situations the trial judge and the appellate judge or judges do not apply the reasonable-doubt standard. Instead, the *standard of review* is a more complex one. On a motion for a directed verdict, the trial judge asks herself or himself, not whether the prosecution has proved its case beyond a reasonable doubt, but whether the prosecution has introduced sufficient evidence such that a rational jury *could* decide that the prosecution has proved its case beyond a reasonable doubt. On an appeal based on the sufficiency of the evidence, the question for the appellate court is, again, not whether the prosecution has proved its case beyond a reasonable doubt, but rather whether a rational jury *could have*, on the evidence presented, found the defendant guilty beyond a reasonable doubt. These standards suggest that when the evidence is ambiguous, the appellate court reviewing a conviction will give the prosecution, not the defendant, the benefit of the doubt. The following case helps illuminate this counter-intuitive standard of review.

CURLEY v. UNITED STATES
United States Court of Appeals, District of Columbia
160 F.2d 229 (D.C. Cir. 1947)

PRETTYMAN, Associate Justice.

Appellants were indicted for violation of the mail fraud statute and for conspiracy to violate that statute. Trial was had before a jury. At the conclusion of the case for the prosecution, the defendants moved for directed verdicts of acquittal. The court denied the motions. Defendants Curley and Fuller stood on the motions and offered no evidence. Defendant Smith presented eight character witnesses and proffered certain documentary evidence. These three defendants were convicted on the conspiracy count. * * * The appeals were consolidated for argument.

[Curley and the other defendants were members of "the Group," a business organization involved in government procurement for housing and defense-related contracts.]

* * * In the negotiation of the contracts, representations were made in the name of the Group as to business controlled by it, its staff, its assets, and the existing status of various government projects. The money was received by the Group under agreements that it be held as deposits and returned if contemplated business projects did not materialize. The representations were false, and the agreements were not kept, except that three refunds were made from funds paid in by other people. The Group was represented as having within its control the designation of contractors on certain government housing projects and war work. It had none. It represented [itself] as having large amounts of cash in bank and extensive security holdings. It had no such amounts or holdings. Certain housing projects were represented as having been approved by the Federal Housing Administration. They had not been. Commitments on financing were represented as having been made by financial institutions on certain projects. No such commitments had been made. These various representations were inducements for the contracts made by the Group with its customers or clients. They were made verbally, in letters, in contract agreements, and in a brochure widely distributed. The money received as deposits was not held but was spent as received. * * *

[Curley's claim at trial was that, although he served as President of the Group, there was no proof that he was involved in any significant way in the fraudulent activities of the Group.]

The functions of the jury include the determination of the credibility of witnesses, the weighing of the evidence, and the drawing of justifiable inferences of fact from proven facts. It is the function of the judge to deny the jury any opportunity to operate beyond its province. The jury may not be permitted to conjecture merely, or to conclude upon pure speculation or from passion, prejudice or sympathy. The critical point in this boundary is the existence or non-existence of a reasonable doubt as to guilt. If the evidence is such that reasonable jurymen must necessarily have such a doubt, the judge must require acquittal, because no other result is permissible within the fixed bounds of jury consideration. But if a reasonable mind might fairly have a reasonable doubt or might fairly not have one, the case is for the jury, and the decision is for the jurors to make. The law recognizes that the scope of a reasonable mind is broad. Its conclusion is not always a point certain, but, upon given evidence, may be one of a number of conclusions. Both innocence and guilt beyond reasonable doubt may lie fairly within the limits of reasonable conclusion from given facts. The judge's function is exhausted when he determines that the evidence does or does not permit the conclusion of guilt beyond reasonable doubt within the fair operation of a reasonable mind.

The true rule, therefore, is that a trial judge, in passing upon a motion for directed verdict of acquittal, must determine whether upon the evidence, giving full play to the right of the jury to determine credibility, weigh the evidence, and draw justifiable inferences of fact, a reasonable mind might fairly conclude guilt beyond a reasonable doubt. If he concludes that upon the evidence there must be such a doubt in a reasonable mind, he must grant the motion; or, to state it another way, if there is no evidence upon which a reasonable mind might fairly conclude guilt beyond reasonable doubt, the motion must be granted. If he concludes that either of the two results, a reasonable doubt or no reasonable doubt, is fairly possible, he must let the jury decide the matter. In a given case, particularly one of circumstantial evidence, that determination may depend upon the difference between pure speculation and legitimate inference from proven facts. The task of the judge in such case is not easy, for the rule of reason is frequently difficult to apply, but we know of no way to avoid that difficulty. * * *

The crucial question at this point seems to us to be whether [Curley] knew of the wrongful acts being committed in the name of the Group. Because, if he knew, reasonable minds might fairly conclude that he must necessarily have been a participant in the scheme, i.e., a conspirator; that no other hypothesis is consistent with that knowledge and his acts. Was such knowledge on his part a legitimate inference from the proven facts? It seems to us that it was. He was president of the corporation. He was frequently in its offices. He introduced customers. He personally attempted to arrange with a bank for a 'loan' which was to be left on deposit, a sham depiction of financial substance. The misrepresentations made by the Group were total, not incidental or occasional. They were made not to occasional customers or clients but to all of them. The misrepresentations were not as to whether a group, in control of certain contracts, was also in control of others; this Group had control of no contracts whatever. The misrepresentations were not as to incidents of the staff and organization of the Group; it had no staff worthy of the name. The Group did not have funds which it might legitimately use for operating expenses and, by inadvertence or misconduct of an individual, dip into other funds which it was obligated to hold on deposit; it had no funds whatever, other than the deposits. Occasional, incidental or partial misrepresentation or misappropriation by one officer of a corporation may be unimpressive as a basis for imputing knowledge to another officer; but total misrepresentation of the corporate affairs and total diversion of funds is substantial ground for an inference of knowledge on the part of an active and experienced president. The jury might fairly and legitimately infer as a fact from the proven facts that Curley knew of the wrongs being committed. As we have said, if he knew, his proven activities with and on behalf of the Group might fairly lead, if not compel, reasonable men to conclude that he must necessarily have been a participant in the plans of the Group. It cannot be said that upon all this evidence reasonable minds must necessarily doubt that Curley was a participant in the activities of the Group. * * *

The decision in the case rests squarely upon the rule of law governing the action of the trial judge upon the motion for directed verdict of acquittal and the action of an appellate court upon a verdict of conviction. We agree, as Curley contends, that upon the evidence reasonable minds might have had a reasonable doubt. As much might be said in many, if not in most, criminal cases. The jury, within the realm of reason, might have concluded that it was possible that Curley was merely a figurehead, that he had complete faith in Fuller, that he never asked any questions, that he was never informed as to the contents of contracts with customers or the financial statements or the use of the money; in short, that it was possible that he was as much put upon as were the customers. If the jury had concluded that such was a reasonable possibility, it might have had a reasonable doubt as to guilt. But, as we have stated, that possibility is not the criterion which determines the action of the trial judge upon the motion for directed verdict and is not the basis upon which this court must test the validity of the verdict and the judgment. If the evidence reasonably permits a verdict of acquittal or a verdict of guilt, the decision is for the jury to make. In such case, an appellate court cannot disturb the judgment of the jury. If we ourselves doubted Curley's guilt, that doubt would be legally immaterial, in view of the evidence and the rule of law applicable. However, we think it proper to add, under the circumstances of the case, that to us, as to the jury, there is no doubt. * * *

Affirmed.

WILBUR K. MILLER, Associate Justice (dissenting).

It is my view that the jury should have been instructed to find the appellant, James M. Curley, not guilty. The wrongs were done by Fuller. Curley made no representations to anybody. He did not participate in negotiations with customers. He signed no letters, executed no contracts. He did not know of the brochure or the financial statement. He received no money or other thing of value. All this is admitted, even recited, in the court's opinion.

Whether Curley was guilty depended therefore, on whether he knew of the wrongful acts being committed in the name of the Group. That, the court correctly says, is the crucial question with respect to him. There was no criminal intent if he did not know. If he knew, then it would follow that he had become a conspirator with Fuller. But the evidence of knowledge must be clear, not equivocal.

It is true, of course, that whether Curley had knowledge of Fuller's wrongdoing could not be proved directly, but could only be inferred from what Curley did. Nevertheless, the presumption of innocence insists that there be no equivocation in that proof. As always, it must convince beyond a reasonable doubt. If it be not of that quality, if it be not clear but equivocal, then the jury must not be permitted to speculate that the defendant is guilty. * * *

To prove guilt beyond a reasonable doubt does not mean merely to prove certain facts which are as consistent with innocence as guilt. To me the expression means to submit evidence which produces in the minds of the jurors an abiding and conscientious conviction, to a moral certainty, that the accused is guilty. I am aware of the fact that his classic paraphrase of proof beyond a reasonable doubt by Chief Justice Shaw of Massachusetts has been criticized of late, but I do not agree with the critics. Reasonable doubt is not eliminated by evidence from which the jury may draw either of two irreconcilable inferences. * * *

E.   THE ROLE OF THE JURY

The jury plays an influential role in the criminal justice system.[a] The Sixth Amendment to the U.S. Constitution guarantees that "in all criminal prosecutions, the accused shall enjoy the right to a speedy and public trial by an impartial jury."[b] This means that unless the defendant waives his or her right to

---

[a]The importance of jury decision-making has been reaffirmed in several recent cases. In *Apprendi v. New Jersey*, 530 U.S. 466 (2000), the United States Supreme Court ruled that the constitutional right to a trial by jury includes the right to have the jury decide any fact, other than the fact of a prior conviction, that increases the penalty for the crime beyond the prescribed statutory maximum. In *Ring v. Arizona,* 536 U.S. 584 (2002), the Court extended the rule of *Apprendi* by holding that juries, not judges, must decide any and all facts leading to the imposition of the death penalty.

[b]Despite this broad language suggesting the right to a jury trial in *all* criminal cases, the Supreme Court has held that the right to a jury trial applies only to individuals charged with at least one non-petty offense (i.e., an offense for which imprisonment of more than six months is authorized). *See Blanton v. City of Las Vegas*, 489 U.S. 538 (1989). A defendant charged with multiple petty offenses is not entitled to a jury trial even if the aggregate potential penalty is greater than six months. *Lewis v. United States*, 518 U.S. 322 (1996).

a jury trial and elects to be tried by a judge, his guilt or innocence will be determined by a jury of twelve individuals.[c]

Although the judge gives jurors detailed instructions on the law they are supposed to apply to the case, the jury is not strictly obligated to follow the law. If the jury acquits the defendant even in the face of overwhelming evidence of guilt, the judge is not permitted to punish the jury nor can the judge overturn the jury's not guilty verdict. The act of returning a verdict contrary to law is called jury nullification. A longstanding debate exists over whether jurors should be informed of their power to nullify. On the one hand are individuals who, like the members of the Fully Informed Jury Association (FIJA), believe that jurors should be informed of their power to ignore the law so that justice can be done in all cases, not simply in the cases in which a member of the jury happens to know of the nullification power and tells his fellow jurors. FIJA members have shown up on the steps of courthouses, passing out leaflets informing potential jurors of their power to bring in a verdict of conscience when they find that a law is objectionable, unjust or unfair.

On the other hand are individuals who believe that jury nullification threatens the rule of law and invites chaos. According to these individuals, if jurors feel they are free to reach any verdict they choose regardless of the law, jury verdicts are likely to produce widely disparate treatment for similarly situated defendants.

In 1995, George Washington University law professor Paul Butler ignited a new debate in the nullification arena when he suggested African American jurors should engage in racially based jury nullification in cases involving African American defendants charged with non-violent crimes. An excerpt from Professor Butler's provocative essay as well as a powerful response by Andrew Liepold follow *People v. Williams*, a case in which the California Supreme Court had to decide whether a trial judge acted properly when he discharged a juror who admitted that he was uncomfortable convicting an 18-year-old male defendant of statutory rape for having what the defendant

---

[c]In the federal courts and in most state courts, the defendant is tried before a jury of 12 persons and the jury's verdict must be unanimous. If the jury cannot come to a unanimous verdict, the judge will declare a mistrial due to a hung jury and the prosecutor may either re-file charges or drop the case. Some states permit non-unanimous verdicts. Some states permit juries to be comprised of less than twelve persons. The Supreme Court has upheld the use of non-unanimous jury verdicts and juries of less than twelve persons. *See, e.g., Apodaca v. Oregon*, 406 U.S. 404 (1972), *Johnson v. Louisiana*, 406 U.S. 356 (1972). If, however, a six-person jury is used, its verdict must be unanimous. *Burch v. Louisiana*, 441 U.S. 130 (1979).

claimed was consensual sex with his 16-year-old girlfriend. If the jury has the power to acquit even in the face of overwhelming evidence of guilt, is it fair for a judge to discharge a juror who seems inclined to exercise this power?

PEOPLE v. WILLIAMS
Supreme Court of California
25 Cal.4th 441, 21 P.3d 1209, 106 Cal.Rptr.2d 295 (2001)

GEORGE, C.J.

* * * [T]he charges in this case arose from three incidents involving defendant and his former girlfriend. Only the first incident is relevant to the issue upon which we granted review.

At the time of the December 31, 1994, incident, defendant was 18 years of age and his girlfriend, Jennifer B., was 16 years of age. Both defendant and Jennifer B. testified that they engaged in sexual intercourse on that date; however, defendant testified it was consensual, and Jennifer B. testified defendant forced her to engage in intercourse by threatening her with knives.

At trial, prior to the attorneys' closing arguments, the court indicated that it would instruct the jury that it could convict defendant of unlawful sexual intercourse with a minor as a lesser offense included within the charged offense of rape. Defendant's objection was overruled.

During argument, defense counsel made the following statement: "Something else has happened in this case. * * * They have added misdemeanors to all the charges you heard. They added statutory rape suddenly without notice or preparation. Now, what is the role of a juror on the statutory misdemeanor rape? Your role as a juror is to fairly apply the law. That's why we don't want computers. We need the input of fair people, [defendant]'s peers, if you will. Law as you know is not uniformly applied. I can see five cars speeding and the highway patrol is not likely to arrest any of the five. Mores, custom[s] change. Times change. And the law must be applied fairly. So if the law is not being applied fairly, that's why you need fair jurors. Now there is a case called *Duncan versus Alaska* [Louisiana]. It's the Supreme Court of the United States. And I would like to read to you just two lines: 'The guarantee of jury trial in the federal and state Constitutions reflect a profound judgment about the way in which law should be enforced and justice administered. A right to jury trial is granted to criminal defendants in order to prevent oppression by the government.' And further on in the case at the end are the lovely words, 'A jury may, at times, afford a higher justice by refusing to enforce harsh laws.' Please understand."[2]

During the first day of deliberations, the trial court received a message from the jury foreperson indicating that Juror No. 10 "refuses to adhere to Judge's instruction to uphold the law in regard to rape and statutory rape, crime Section 261.5(b) of the Penal Code. He believes the law is wrong and, therefore, will not hear any discussions."[3] In response, the trial court questioned Juror No. 10 outside the presence of the other jurors:

THE COURT: [I]t's been reported to me that you refuse to follow my instructions on the law in regard to rape and unlawful sexual intercourse, that you believe the law to be wrong and, therefore, you will not hear any discussion on that subject. Is that correct?

[JUROR]: Pretty much, yes.

THE COURT: All right. Are you governed by what was said during argument by counsel?

[JUROR]: Yes.

THE COURT: You understand that there was an improper suggestion and that it's a violation of the Rules of Professional Conduct?

[JUROR]: No, I don't know that.

---

[2]The language quoted by defense counsel actually is from the decision in *Duncan v. Louisiana.* The "lovely words" quoted by defense counsel appear in Justice Harlan's dissenting opinion. Defense counsel did not quote the parenthetical phrase following those words, which raises concerns about the concept of juror nullification: "A jury may, at times, afford a higher justice by refusing to enforce harsh laws (although it necessarily does so haphazardly, raising the questions whether arbitrary enforcement of harsh laws is better than total enforcement, and whether the jury system is to be defended on the ground that jurors sometimes disobey their oaths)."

[3]The jury foreperson brought this matter to the court's attention on the foreperson's own initiative, without prior instruction or direction by the court. The trial in the present case occurred prior to the adoption of CALJIC No. 17.41.1, which states, in part: "[S]hould it occur that any juror refuses to deliberate or expresses an intention to disregard the law . . . it is the obligation of the other jurors to immediately advise the Court of the situation." Because this instruction was not given, we have no occasion in this case to address the appropriateness or validity of this instruction. This issue is pending before us in a number of cases.

THE COURT: All right. Well, I'm telling you that's what it was. And I would remind you too that you took an oath at the outset of the case in the following language: 'Do you and each of you understand and agree that you will well and truly try the cause now pending before this Court and a true verdict render according only to the evidence presented to you and to the instructions of the Court.' You understand that if you would not follow the instructions that have been given to you by the court that you would be violating that oath? Do you understand that?

[JUROR]: I understand that.

THE COURT: Are you willing to abide by the requirements of your oath?

[JUROR]: I simply cannot see staining a man, a young man, for the rest of his life for what I believe to be a wrong reason.

THE COURT: Well, you understand that statutory rape or unlawful sexual intercourse has been described to you as a misdemeanor? Did you follow that in the instructions?

[JUROR]: I've been told it is a misdemeanor. I still don't see--if it were a $10 fine, I just don't see convicting a man and staining his record for the rest of his life. I think that is wrong. I'm sorry, Judge.

THE COURT: What you're saying is not the law either concerning that particular aspect.

[JUROR]: I'm trying as best I can, Judge. And I'm willing to follow all the rules and regulations on the entire rest of the charges, but on that particular charge, I just feel duty-bound to object.

THE COURT: So you're not willing then to follow your oath?

[JUROR]: That is correct.

The trial court, over defendant's objection, excused Juror No. 10, replaced him with an alternate juror, and instructed the jury to begin its deliberations anew. The next day, the jury convicted defendant of the above described charges, including unlawful sexual intercourse with a minor.

III

A trial court's authority to discharge a juror is granted by Penal Code section 1089, which provides in pertinent part: "If at any time, whether before or after the final submission of the case to the jury, a juror dies or becomes ill, or upon other good cause shown to the court is found to be unable to perform his duty, or if a juror requests a discharge and good cause appears therefor, the court may order him to be discharged and draw the name of an alternate, who shall then take his place in the jury box, and be subject to the same rules and regulations as though he had been selected as one of the original jurors." "We review for abuse of discretion the trial court's determination to discharge a juror and order an alternate to serve. If there is any substantial evidence supporting the trial court's ruling, we will uphold it." * * *

A juror who refuses to follow the court's instructions is "unable to perform his duty" within the meaning of Penal Code section 1089. As soon as a jury is selected, each juror must agree to render a true verdict "'according only to the evidence presented . . . and *to the instructions of the court.*'" * * *

Defendant contends, however, that the trial court's order denied him his right to trial by jury, because Juror No. 10 properly was exercising his alleged right to engage in juror nullification by refusing to follow the law regarding unlawful sexual intercourse with a minor. But defendant has cited no case, and we are aware of none, that holds that a trial court violates the defendant's right to a jury trial by excusing a juror who refuses to follow the law. The circumstance that, as a practical matter, the jury in a criminal case may have the ability to disregard the court's instructions in the defendant's favor without recourse by the prosecution does not diminish the trial court's authority to discharge a juror who, the court learns, is unable or unwilling to follow the court's instructions.

It long has been recognized that, in some instances, a jury has the ability to disregard, or nullify, the law. A jury has the ability to acquit a criminal defendant against the weight of the evidence. A jury in a criminal case may return inconsistent verdicts. A court may not direct a jury to enter a guilty verdict "no matter how conclusive the evidence." * * *

The jury's power to nullify the law is the consequence of a number of specific procedural protections granted criminal defendants. Chief Justice Bird, quoting Judge Learned Hand's description of jury nullification as the jury's "'assumption of a power which they had no right to exercise, but to which they were disposed through lenity,'" observed: "This power is attributable to two unique features of criminal trials. First, a criminal jury has the right to return a general verdict which does not specify how it applied the law to the facts, or for that matter, what law was applied or what facts were found. * * * Second, the constitutional double jeopardy bar prevents an appellate court from disregarding the jury's verdict in favor of the defendant and ordering a new trial on the same charge." The United States Supreme Court has referred to the ability of a jury in a criminal case to nullify the law in the defendant's favor as "the unreviewable power of a jury to return a verdict of not guilty for impermissible reasons."[6]

But the circumstance that the prosecution may be powerless to challenge a jury verdict or finding that is prompted by the jury's refusal to apply a particular law does not lessen the obligation of each juror to obey the court's instructions. More than a century ago, the United States Supreme Court recognized that jurors are required to follow the trial court's instructions.* * *

This view has deep roots. In 1835, in *United States v. Battiste*, Justice Story, sitting as a circuit justice, instructed the jury in a criminal case that they were the judges of the facts, but not of the law, stating: "[T]hey have the physical power to disregard the law, as laid down to them by the court. But I deny, that, in any case, civil or criminal, they have the moral right to decide the law according to their own notions, or pleasure. On the contrary, I hold it the most sacred constitutional right of every party accused of a crime, that the jury should respond as to the facts, and the court as to the law. It is the duty of the court to instruct the jury as to the law; and it is the duty of the jury to follow the law, as it is laid down by the court. This is the right of every citizen; and it is his only protection. If the jury were at liberty to settle the law for themselves, the effect would be, not only that the law itself would be most uncertain, from the different views, which different juries might take of it; but in case of error, there would be no remedy or redress by the injured party; for the court would not have any right to review the law as it had been settled by the jury. Indeed, it would be almost impracticable to ascertain, what the law, as settled by the jury, actually was. * * * Every person accused as a criminal has a right to be tried according to the law of the land, the fixed law of the land; and not by the law as a jury may

---

[6]A jury is able to nullify the law only under certain limited circumstances. In a civil case, the jury's ability to nullify a law is sharply curtailed. The court may direct the jury in a civil case to enter a particular verdict, and a verdict that is not supported by substantial evidence or is contrary to the law may be vacated on a motion for new trial or the resulting judgment may be reversed on appeal. Even in a criminal prosecution, the jury's ability to nullify the law is limited when it acts to the defendant's detriment. If the evidence is "insufficient to sustain a conviction," the court "shall order the entry of a judgment of acquittal." A verdict convicting a defendant that is not supported by substantial evidence, or is contrary to law, may be vacated on a motion for new trial, or the resulting judgment may be reversed on appeal.

understand it, or choose, from wantonness, or ignorance, or accidental mistake, to interpret it."[7]

In *United States v. Powell,* the high court reaffirmed the rule that verdicts in a criminal prosecution need not be consistent but, at the same time, the court recognized that jurors are obligated to follow the law. * * * The court explained the rule permitting inconsistent verdicts in criminal cases "as a recognition of the jury's historic function, in criminal trials, as a check against arbitrary or oppressive exercises of power by the Executive Branch." (*Ibid.*; see also *Williams v. Florida* ["The purpose of the jury trial . . . is to prevent oppression by the Government. . . . Given this purpose, the essential feature of a jury obviously lies in the interposition between the accused and his accuser of the commonsense judgment of a group of laymen, and in the community participation and shared responsibility that results from that group's determination of guilt or innocence"].) * * *

[I]t is important not to encourage or glorify the jury's power to disregard the law. While that power has, on some occasions, achieved just results, it also has led to verdicts based upon bigotry and racism.[9] A jury that disregards the law and, instead, reaches a verdict based upon the personal views and beliefs of the jurors violates one of our nation's most basic precepts: that we are "a government of laws and not men."

---

[7]"Today the constitutions of three states--Georgia, Indiana, and Maryland-- provide that jurors shall judge questions of law as well as fact. In all three states, however, judicial decisions have essentially nullified the constitutional provisions. The unambiguous rule in other American jurisdictions is that questions of law are for the court to decide. Juries must 'take their law' as the trial judge declares it."

[9]Jury nullification includes "acquittals by all-white, southern juries of white defendants who killed, assaulted, or harassed civil rights activists or African Americans generally." As one federal circuit court has observed:

> [A]lthough the early history of our country includes the occasional *Zenger* trial or acquittals in fugitive slave cases, more recent history presents numerous and notorious examples of jurors nullifying-- cases that reveal the destructive potential of a practice Professor Randall Kennedy of the Harvard Law School has rightly termed a 'sabotage of justice.' Consider, for example, the two hung juries in the 1964 trials of Byron De La Beckwith in Mississippi for the murder of NAACP field secretary Medgar Evers, or the 1955 acquittal of J.W. Millam and Roy Bryant for the murder of fourteen-year-old Emmett Till, [citation]--shameful examples of how nullification has been used to sanction murder and lynching.

The only case cited by the parties or that we have found that has addressed the specific issue raised in the present case--i.e., whether a trial court may remove a juror who discloses, during jury deliberations, that he or she will not apply the law as instructed by the court--is *U.S. v. Thomas,* involving a prosecution for violation of federal narcotics laws. In *Thomas,* pursuant to the provisions of rule 23(b) of the Federal Rules of Criminal Procedure permitting the court to dismiss a juror for "just cause" and have a verdict returned by the remaining 11 jurors, a juror was dismissed during deliberations. The court of appeals held "that--as an obvious violation of a juror's oath and duty--a refusal to apply the law as set forth by the court constitutes grounds for dismissal under Rule 23(b)." Restating "some basic principles regarding the character of our jury system," the Court of Appeals concluded: "Nullification is, by definition, a violation of a juror's oath to apply the law as instructed by the court. . . . We categorically reject the idea that, in a society committed to the rule of law, jury nullification is desirable or that courts may permit it to occur when it is within their authority to prevent."

The court in *Thomas* added: " 'A jury has no more "*right*" to find a "guilty" defendant "not guilty" than it has to find a "not guilty" defendant "guilty," and the fact that the former cannot be corrected by a court, while the latter can be, does not create a right out of the power to misapply the law. Such verdicts are lawless, a denial of due process and constitute an exercise of erroneously seized power.'

Although the court in *Thomas* ultimately concluded that the trial court in that case had erred in dismissing the juror in question, because the record suggested that the juror's views may well have been motivated by doubts about the defendant's guilt rather than by an intent to nullify the law, the *Thomas* opinion left no doubt that when the record does establish that a deliberating juror is unwilling to apply the law as instructed by the court, "a juror's purposeful disregard of the law as set forth in the court's instruction may constitute just cause for that juror's removal under Rule 23(b)." * * *

In the present case there is ample evidence in the record to support the trial court's finding that Juror No. 10 was unable to perform his duties as a juror. The juror stated that he objected to the law concerning unlawful sexual intercourse and expressly confirmed that he was unwilling to abide by his oath to follow the court's instructions. The juror's inability to perform his duties thus appears in the record "as a demonstrable reality." The trial court acted properly in excusing Juror No. 10 on this basis.

IV

Jury nullification raises issues that go to the heart of our constitutional form of government. These issues sometimes arise when defendants, as a matter of conscience, choose to violate laws as a means of protest, or to violate laws they view as unjust. Such cases cause us to examine the meaning of the cherished right to trial by jury.

It is striking that the debate over juror nullification remains vigorous after more than a hundred years. But it is equally significant that, during this time, no published authority has restricted a trial court's authority to discharge a juror when the record demonstrates that the juror is unable or unwilling to follow the court's instructions.

"Championing a jury's refusal to apply the law as instructed is inconsistent with the very notion of the rule of law. As the young Abraham Lincoln said in a related context, 'let me not be understood as saying there are no bad laws, or that grievances may not arise for the redress of which no legal provisions have been made. I mean to say no such thing. But I do mean to say that although bad laws, if they exist, should be repealed as soon as possible, still, while they continue in force, for the sake of example, they should be religiously observed.'"

Encouraging a jury to nullify a law it finds unjust or to act as the "conscience of the community" by disregarding the court's instructions may sound lofty, but such unchecked and unreviewable power can lead to verdicts based upon bigotry and racism. Jurors who do not feel bound to follow the law can act capriciously, to the detriment of the accused. In addition to refusing to follow laws they view as unjust, such jurors could choose to disregard instructions mandated by the Legislature not to read media accounts of the trial, not to discuss the case with others, or not to conduct their own investigation by visiting the crime scene. The jury might feel free to ignore the presumption of innocence or find the defendant guilty even though some jurors harbor a reasonable doubt. A jury might disregard an instruction not to draw an inference from the exercise of a privilege and assume the defendant must be guilty if he or she chooses not to testify. In a capital case, a juror could vote to impose the death penalty without considering mitigating evidence. Some jurors might decide not to view a defendant's confession with caution or not require corroboration of the testimony of an accomplice. A jury even might determine that deliberations are too difficult and decide the defendant's guilt by the flip of a coin.

These are just a few of the many instructions required by the Legislature that a juror might choose to ignore if encouraged to nullify the law.

Jury nullification is contrary to our ideal of equal justice for all and permits both the prosecution's case and the defendant's fate to depend upon the whims of a particular jury, rather than upon the equal application of settled rules of law. As one commentator has noted: "When jurors enter a verdict in contravention of what the law authorizes and requires, they subvert the rule of law and subject citizens--defendants, witnesses, victims, and everyone affected by criminal justice administration--to power based on the subjective predilections of twelve individuals. They affect the rule of men, not law." A nullifying jury is essentially a lawless jury.

We reaffirm, therefore, the basic rule that jurors are required to determine the facts and render a verdict in accordance with the court's instructions on the law. A juror who is unable or unwilling to do so is "unable to perform his [or her] duty" as a juror and may be discharged.

V

The judgment of the Court of Appeal is affirmed.

RACE-BASED JURY NULLIFICATION: CASE-IN-CHIEF
Paul D. Butler
30 J. Marshall L. Rev. 911 (1997)
* * *

I was a Special Assistant United States Attorney in the District of Columbia. I represented the United States of America and used that power to put African-American people in prison. Like a lot of prosecutors, that pretty much was my job description. While at the U.S. Attorney's Office, I saw and did things that profoundly changed the way that I viewed my work as a prosecutor and my responsibilities as an African-American man.

* * * The reality is this: as we speak, one-third of African-American young men are under criminal justice supervision. The reality is that, as we speak, over half of the women in state prison are African-American and over half of the men in federal and state prisons are African-American.

My journey took me to the academy. I teach criminal law. My students learned that prison is for people who are the most dangerous and the most immoral in our society. Is there anyone here who really believes that over half of the most immoral and dangerous people in the United States are African-American when they constitute only 12 percent of the population?

When I look at those statistics, I think that punishment, prison, and criminal law have become the way that we treat the problems of the poor, especially poor African-American people. I think that is immoral. I am confident that one day we, as a society, will understand that, but African-American people cannot afford to wait that long. If the present rate of incarceration of African-Americans continues, by the year 2010 the majority of African-American men between the ages of 18 and 40 will be in prison, the majority.

Now, to prevent that kind of "just us" justice, I advocate a program of black self-help outside and inside the courtroom. Outside the courtroom self-help includes the kind of community-building efforts that many of us are already engaged in: mentoring, tutoring, after-school programs, providing legal and medical care to the poor, working with inmates, and taking better care of our families. Our ancestors taught the world that it takes a village to raise a child, and we need to increase those efforts one hundred-fold. Inside the courtroom self-help includes the responsible use of prosecutorial discretion, especially by black prosecutors. It also includes selective jury nullification for victimless crimes. I am going to spend the balance of my time talking about selective jury nullification because it is part of my solution to the unfairness in the criminal justice system.

* * *According to the Department of Justice, for virtually every crime African-Americans are disproportionately arrested, prosecuted, convicted and imprisoned.

That is true of murder, manslaughter, rape, drug possession, drug distribution, theft and gambling. Why is that? Why do African-Americans commit so many crimes, or do they really? Maybe it is just discrimination that accounts for this apparent disproportionate black criminality. To give you a sense of the justice of selective nullification, I am going to describe quickly two racial critiques of American criminal justice: a liberal critique, and one that I call radical, although the radical critique is made by a lot of people who do not think of themselves as radical.

First, I will discuss the liberal racial critique of American justice. According to the critique, American criminal justice is racist because it is controlled primarily by white people who are unable to escape the culture's dominant message of white supremacy. Therefore, white people are inevitably, even if unintentionally, prejudiced. These white actors include legislatures, police, prosecutors, judges and jurors. These white actors exercise their discretion to make and enforce the criminal law in a discriminatory fashion.

Sometimes this discrimination is overt, as in the case of people like Mark Fuhrman or the police officers who beat up Rodney King. Sometimes it is unintentional, such as a white juror who invariably credits the testimony of a white witness over a black witness. I think that the most persuasive case for the liberal critique is with drug cases. According to the Department of Justice, black people do not commit any more drug offenses than whites. They are about 12 percent of drug offenders, which is exactly proportionate to their share of the population. Now, I know this does not surprise all of you who have been on college campuses, and if you think about it, it is probably consistent with our knowledge of the real world, too. * * *

The Department of Justice agrees, and the conclusion is borne out by statistics. But get this: of people who are incarcerated for drug use, African-Americans are more than 70 percent. African-Americans are 12 percent of the offenders, but 74 percent of the people locked up for the offense. That sounds like discrimination, and when I talk to my police and prosecutor friends, they agree that it is a kind of discrimination. However, many make the argument that it is discrimination that is good for the black community: it is more law enforcement, which is a good thing. When I talk about my proposal for nullification, we will come back to that idea. For now, understand that I think that drug offenses are the best argument for the liberal critique on American criminal justice.

However, I mentioned another critique, one that I called radical. What is this critique? What is the radical critique of why there are so many more blacks in prison than whites and other minorities? The radical critique does not discount the role of discrimination in accounting for this racial disparity, but it also does not say that most or all of the blame is due to discrimination. It offers a more structural fundamental explanation for black crime. * * *

* * * The answer to why there is so much black crime is rooted more in sociology than in either psychology or biology. Prominent American criminologist Norval Morris says that "an adverse social and subcultural background is statistically more is criminogenic than psychosis." How about that? So, unsurprisingly then, virtually all of the sociological theories predict high levels of African-American criminal behavior. A short quote, if you will indulge me, from Michael Tonry:

> Crime by young disadvantaged black men [does not] result primarily from their individual moral failures but from their misfortune of being born in places and times and under circumstances that make crime, drug use and gang membership

look like reasonable choices, choices from a narrow range of not very attractive options.[10]

* * * One interesting thing is what the liberal and the radical critiques do not say. They do not say that prison is a bad place for every African-American criminal. Rather, liberal critics tend to say that law enforcement in the white community should be leveled up to law enforcement in the black community. For example, white communities should have the same kind of police presence. Alternatively, these critics might say that law enforcement should be leveled down in black communities. For example, the government should not prosecute black drug users and sellers any more than it prosecutes white or Asian-American or Latino drug users and sellers.

Our radical critics, on the other hand, might encourage incarceration of African-Americans when it has some proven social benefit, some utilitarian benefit, usually like rehabilitation or incapacitation or sentencing with a proven deterrent effect. This is an important point because one almost never hears any racial critic saying that black murderers or rapists or child abusers should not be punished. That includes African-American jurors who engage in jury nullification. In fact, in my experience, black jurors are happy to send violent black criminals to prison, because these jurors, like most jurors, have good sense. It is almost always in the interests of the community to isolate dangerous people, even if the reason those people are dangerous might be due to circumstances beyond their control.

What are the costs to the black community of so much law enforcement? What are the costs of having one out of three of our young men under criminal justice supervision? Racial critics identify many costs: economic and social costs, including the lack of a black male presence particularly in the African-American community; the lack of male role models and male income; the perceived dearth or the lack of marriage-eligible African-American men, among others. So when we start talking about specific cases in which nullification would occur, I will mention drug cases as one great example. You might say, "Well, that's not a victimless crime." I ask you to keep in mind that law enforcement is also not victimless. Law enforcement also has opportunity costs.

* * * Nullification is a partial cure that I come to reluctantly and for moral reasons. To me it is not enough to say that there is a power to nullify;

---

[10] *See* Michael Tonry, MALIGN NEGLECT: RACE, CRIME AND PUNISHMENT IN AMERICA 29-30 (1995)

there also has to be some moral basis for this power. In the article I make several moral claims as to the power. I am going to quickly tell you about two.

One is this phenomenon of democratic domination. It is a critical race concept. The reason why I believe that African-American jurors have a moral claim to selective nullification is based on this idea that they do not effectively have a say; they do not have the say that they should in the making of the law. They are the victims of the tyranny of the majority. * * * Let me tell you how it works in the context of the criminal justice system. With every crime bill, the Black Political Caucus--the national one or the one in the state--will make the argument, "Hey, guys, instead of spending all this money building prisons, let's spend some money on rehabilitation, on job training, on education. Those are the root causes of crime." In the Black Political Caucus' belief, the white majority will just say no. It will be legislated away, as we saw happen in the two most recent crime bills. That is always the case. We know that there are better ways to stop crime than prison building, including, for example, financial incentives for kids to stay in school. Rand Corporation released a report that said you prevent more crime per dollar spent by giving kids money to stay in school than you do by building prisons.

The second most powerful way to stop crime is parental training, teaching some of these kids who are having babies how to be good parents. Studies show that such training prevents more crime than the deterrent effect of prison. Now, that does not shock a lot of you. It does not shock a lot of legislators either, but, unfortunately, the majority seems to prefer the punishment regime. We have certainly seen that with powder cocaine versus crack cocaine today. You all know the disparity: you get the same punishment for one gram of crack that you get for 100 grams of powder.[a] A lot of African-Americans and other people thought that that was unfair. The political majority's response to the African-American community was, "Well, if you don't like racially biased disparity, don't acquit crack dealers; what you ought to do is change the law." The way you change the federal sentencing law is to lobby the U.S. Sentencing Commission. At least that is the way you always did it before this proposal for jury nullification.

The Sentencing Commission was lobbied by civil rights groups, and they agreed that that disparity was unfair. They recommended to the U.S. Congress and to the President that the crack-versus-powder disparity be

----

[a] Butler refers to a federal punishment differential between possession of powder cocaine and possession of crack cocaine. *See, e.g.,* U.S. Sentencing Comm'n, Federal Sentencing Guidelines Manual § 2D1.1(c) (1994). For a discussion of a similar punishment regime in the state of Minnesota, *see State v. Russell* in Chapter 2.

changed. However, for some reason the U.S. Congress and the President, Bill Clinton, just said no. They preferred the punishment regime. Again, this is typical when it comes to the way lawmakers deal with the criminal justice system as it applies to African-Americans. "Democratic domination" is Derrick Bell's name for it, and for me it is a moral reason as to why nullification is appropriate.

The third moral claim African-Americans have to the power of jury nullification is what I call the symbolic role of black jurors. If you look at Supreme Court cases, they often have the occasion to discuss black jurors. They do so because of our country's sad history of excluding black people from juries. The Court said that is a bad thing because black jurors serve this symbolic function. Essentially they symbolize the fairness and the impartiality of the law. The Court says that excluding black jurors undermines public confidence in the criminal justice system. The Court has also found that black jurors are especially important in race-related cases.

* * * What about an African-American juror who endorses racial critiques of the American criminal justice system? She does not hold any confidence in the integrity of the system. So if she is aware of the implicit message that the Supreme Court says her presence sends, maybe she does not want to be the vehicle for that message.

Again, that brings us to selective nullification. For violent crimes, for crimes with victims, there should be no nullification. If the juror is convinced beyond a reasonable doubt in such cases, then she should convict and be happy to do so. In my experience prosecuting cases for violent crimes, Washington, D.C. jurors are happy to put those people in prison. It is in everybody's interests to get those people off the streets, and certainly these jurors are acting in their self interests. In Chicago, for example, jurors know that nullified, violent African-American criminals are not going to move to the largely white communities of Bridgeport or Cicero; they are going to move to the predominantly black South Shore, they are going to move to the primarily African-American West Side. Thus, these jurors have no interest in emancipating violent African-American criminals. The problem is that separating violent criminals from their communities is not the main use of prisons. Most people are in prison for nonviolent conduct.

A lot of people are imprisoned for drug offenses, and I think that jurors in those cases should consider nullification. For possession cases, I encourage nullification. For distribution cases I do not encourage it, but I think it is an option that jurors should consider. Jurors should weigh factors that judges weigh now in the sentencing determination. For example, I would never encourage nullification for anyone who sells drugs to children. I might well suggest it for a nonviolent distributor of marijuana. There are two purposes of this selective nullification: black self-help, and, less importantly, political protest. The black self-help prevents people from being punished when there are better alternatives, as I discussed earlier.

The political protest part is to encourage an end to this madness of locking up African-Americans when white people do not get locked up for the identical crimes. Again, this is borne out by those drug statistics. According to the Justice Department, black people do not use drugs any more than whites -- it is just that African-Americans get locked up more for drug charges. People ask what the black community would look like if drug offenders were not incarcerated. We know the answer to that: it would look like the white community. Again, the white community does not resort to the punishment regime for dealing with drug problems. I agree with that. I think punishment is not a smart way to deal with substance abuse. I think that when it comes to law enforcement, what is good enough for white people is good enough for African-Americans.

I hope that nullification would encourage rehabilitation for non-criminal means of dealing with the problem. I do not like drugs. I wish people would not use them. I have seen them ruin people's lives. I might also add that I have seen alcohol ruin people's lives, but I also do not support locking up alcohol users and distributors. So I hope that nullification will spark the return of rehabilitation and crime prevention.

*   *   *

"Is American criminal justice just?" To me the answer is obviously not. There are too many African-Americans in prison who do not belong there. Do you really think that 50 percent of the most dangerous and immoral people in the United States are black? That is what our justice system tells us about black people. If you do not agree with that, if you do not believe that, then you must agree that we need fundamental change.

The second question is, "If not jury nullification, then what?" I do not want to hear that African-Americans should write to Congress. We tried that. It did not work. The house that African-Americans live in is on fire, and when your house is on fire, you do not write to Congress. You do not ask the people who set the fire to put it out; you leave the building. That is what my proposal for selective jury nullification encourages.

RACE-BASED JURY NULLIFICATION: REBUTTAL
(PART A)
Andrew D. Leipold
30 J. Marshall L. Rev. 923 (1997)

* * *[D]o I think that the criminal justice system is perfect the way it is? Of course not. Do I think there are severe problems involving race and justice? Of course I do. Do I think the answer is selective jury nullification? Not even remotely.

Professor Butler says he does not want to hear us suggest that the answer is to write to Congress. That answer fails, he says, because right now the house is on fire, suggesting that more dramatic and more immediate action is needed. But even if the house is on fire, I do not think we should embrace a solution that involves fanning the flames and making the fire worse. This is what I fear selective race-based jury nullification will do.

Let me briefly outline a few of my concerns about Professor Butler's plan. The first two are technical, lawyer-type arguments. The last two address philosophical concerns I have about his proposal.

The first technical point involves the impact of Professor Butler's proposal on the makeup of juries. I agree with Paul entirely about the importance of African-Americans serving on juries, and the Supreme Court opinions he cites came out exactly right. It is critically important to have juries that are reflective of community sentiments and community norms. Given this, we should ask ourselves what juries will look like if large numbers of African-American potential jurors were to embrace the Butler plan. I think the answer, without a doubt, is that there would be fewer African-Americans seated on juries than there are today. * * *

If potential African-American jurors were to embrace the Butler plan, and if they were honest during voir dire, their belief in jury nullification would at least give prosecutors a race-neutral explanation for removing these jurors with their peremptory strikes. In addition, if the jurors were candid in admitting that they came to the jury box with a very strong presumption of acquitting a defendant regardless of what the facts show, such jurors could almost certainly be removed for cause. Since there are no limits on the number of challenges for cause, every African-American juror who believed in race-based nullification might be excused in certain cases. The result would inevitably be juries that are less diverse; this surely can not be part of the solution that Professor Butler seeks.

My second technical argument is that juries are incapable of making reasoned nullification decisions, because at trial they will not be given the information they need. At the heart of Professor Butler's plan is the notion that juries should engage in a cost-benefit analysis when deciding whether to convict. Jurors are supposed to look at the defendant and ask, "Even if this defendant committed the crime charged, what are the rewards of keeping this person out of jail, and what are the risks to the community of letting this person stay free?" The problem is that juries will never hear the evidence that would help them answer this question.

Consider the problem in the context of a simple drug possession case. If we were sitting on a jury, what would we like to know about the defendant before we decided whether to nullify his conviction? We would probably want to know whether the defendant is contrite. We would want to know whether he had a criminal record, and if so, how serious were his prior crimes. We might want to know whether there was anyone else involved in the crime who is more blameworthy. We might wonder how the prosecution enforces this crime against others: are African-Americans disproportionately targeted or arrested for this type of crime? We might also want to know about the potential sentences the defendant would face if convicted; under our cost-benefit analysis, we might be more willing to nullify if the defendant faced a stiff, mandatory sentence.

The problem is that almost none of this information is admissible at trial. Defendants cannot be forced to testify, so the jurors will often be unable to evaluate the defendant's contrition. Evidence of prior crimes is usually inadmissible, as is information on possible sentences or the prosecution's enforcement scheme. In short, through no fault of their own, jurors just will not be able to engage in a meaningful cost-benefit analysis. The best they would be able to do is speculate, based on what they think might be going on, rather than on what is actually going on in the case at hand. * * *

There are undoubtedly other groups that will feel that they, too, do not get a fair shake from the criminal justice system and they, too, should come to the jury box with an eye toward nullifying the convictions of members of their groups. "What's so bad about that," you ask? "Maybe that's the way all juries should decide cases." The problem with nullification is that once we tell a jury, directly or indirectly, that it is okay to engage in an uninformed cost-benefit analysis, we have no moral basis for complaining about any decision that a jury makes.

Assume that a jury nullifies in the case of a young African-American defendant who has been charged with simple possession. Maybe this is a good result: maybe in that specific case, society is better off keeping another African-American kid out of jail, away from a very harsh sentence. But now assume that the next jury comes back and says, "Yes, we think this defendant battered his wife, but you know, she decided to stay in the marriage rather than get a divorce, it looks like she provoked him by spending too much time at her job, she was nagging him, et cetera, and we are not going to send this guy to jail." When a jury recently acquitted a defendant who had raped a woman at knife point because the woman was "asking for it" by dressing in a provocative manner, this also sounded like a cost-benefit analysis. We might be repelled by this reasoning, but we do not have any standing to complain about the process by which the outcome was reached. Those juries also engaged in a cost-benefit analysis, the same process approved of by the Butler plan. * * *

The final concern I have is at the broadest philosophical level. It is a comment that makes me very sad to have to raise at all: whether you go to jail or get set free should not depend on the color of your skin. Using race as the reason for acquitting or convicting is a bad idea, and no matter how strategic the reasoning and no matter how good our intentions, it is still wrong. It is wrong because it encourages the kind of stereotyping that had led to problems in the first place. It is wrong because we are telling people that they will never get equal justice in the courts and so you should take whatever you can get, however you can get it, and be satisfied with that. In short, the plan raises the flag of surrender in the fight for equal justice under the law.

Note

The constitutions of Indiana, Maryland, and Georgia contain provisions which empower the jury to determine both law and fact, but courts have limited the application of these provisions. The Indiana Constitution provides that "[i]n all criminal cases whatever, the jury shall have the right to determine the law and the facts[,]" but it has been held that "that right is not without limitation[ ] ... [and the jury] may not arbitrarily reject the instructions of the court." *Fuquay v. Indiana*, 583 N.E.2d 154, 156 (Ind. Ct. App. 1991). Maryland's constitution states that "[i]n the trial of all criminal cases, the Jury shall be the Judges of Law, as well as of fact," but the Fourth Circuit Court of Appeals has indicated that juries in criminal cases are not given unrestricted powers in applying the law, and in fact, "[t]he powers of the jury are hedged in a number of ways." *Wyley v. Warden, Maryland Penitentiary*, 372 F.2d 742, 743-44 (4th Cir. 1967). The Georgia Constitution provides that "[i]n criminal cases . . .the jury shall be the judges of the law and the facts." Yet, "it has long been settled that this language ... means that jurors are 'made absolutely and exclusively judges of the facts in the case [and] they are, in this sense only, judges of the law.'" *Hall v. State*, 201 Ga. App. 133, 410 S.E.2d 448, 451 (Ct. App. 1991) (quoting *Harris v. State*, 190 Ga. 258, 9 S.E.2d 183 (1940)) (citation omitted).

There have been occasional proposals made to systematically inform juries of their power to nullify. For example, in 1990 Oregon voters rejected an initiative measure that would have required judges in criminal trials to instruct juries with the following language:

> If you decide that the prosecution has proven beyond reasonable doubt every element of the criminal charge but * * * you cannot in good conscience support a guilty verdict, you are not required to do so. To reach a verdict which you believe is just, each of you has the right to consider to what extent the defendant's actions have actually caused harm or otherwise violated your sense of right and wrong. If you believe justice requires it, you may also judge both the merits of the law under which the defendant has been charged and the wisdom of applying that law to the defendant. * * * The court cautions that with the exercise of this right comes the full moral responsibility for the verdict you bring in.

See Fauvre v. Roberts, 309 Or. 691, 791 P.2d 128 (1990). Would you have voted for this law?

F.   STATUTORY INTERPRETATION

As we have seen, the primary source of criminal law in the United States is statutory law. No statute, however, is self-interpreting, and judges play an important role in deciding what a particular statute means and how it should apply to particular cases. Whether the jurisdiction is one whose penal code is based on the common law of England or one whose penal code has incorporated the Model Penal Code in whole or in part, judges must develop ways to interpret statutes in ways that serve a number of goals. These goals include respecting the "plain language" of the statutory text; discerning and effectuating the intent of the legislature or, in the case of an initiative, the voters; and making sure that the interpretation of a particular statute in one case does not contradict its interpretation in another case.

Judges in England and the United States have developed a body of informal rules over time to help them interpret statutes. Some of these rules address what values a judge should prioritize when reading a statute: for example, the rule that the interpreter should always begin with the text of the statute itself. Other rules concern efficiency in the administration of justice: for example, the rule that statutes should be interpreted in such a way as to avoid constitutional problems. Still other rules address grammar and syntax issues that frequently arise in textual interpretation. Two of these -- *noscitur a sociis* and *ejusdem generis* -- are described in the case that follows. Finally, some rules of statutory interpretation, such as the "rule of lenity" also discussed in the following case, reflect basic principles of fairness: under the rule of lenity, all doubts when reading a criminal statute should be resolved in favor of the defendant, in recognition of the important liberty interests at stake and the presumption of innocence. Collectively, these various sorts of interpretive rules are referred to as "canons of statutory construction."

This alternative term for statutory interpretation – "statutory construction" – reminds us that the process of interpretation is as much an art as a science. Although judges are supposed to apply the law and not make it, when statutory language is broad, ambiguous, or outdated, the line between applying and making can become exceedingly fine. Indeed, as students of literary interpretation know, in a sense to read a text is always in some sense to "construct" its meaning. In Chapter 2, we will explore some of the constitutional implications of the fuzzy boundary between discovering and making meaning.

UNITED STATES v. DAURAY
215 F.3d 257 (2d Cir. 2000)

JACOBS, Circuit Judge:

Defendant-appellant Charles Dauray was arrested in possession of pictures (or photocopies of pictures) cut from one or more magazines. He was convicted following a jury trial in the United States District Court for the District of Connecticut of violating 18 U.S.C. § 2252(a)(4)(B), which punishes the possession of (inter alia) "matter," three or more in number, "which contain any visual depiction" of minors engaging in sexually explicit conduct. On appeal from the judgment of conviction, Dauray argues that the wording of § 2252(a)(4)(B) – which has since been amended – is ambiguous as applied to possession of three or more pictures, and that the rule of lenity should therefore apply to resolve this ambiguity in his favor. We agree, reverse the conviction, and direct that the indictment be dismissed.

BACKGROUND

On May 13, 1994, an officer of the Connecticut Department of Environmental Protection approached Dauray's car in a state park and found Dauray in possession of thirteen unbound pictures of minors. The pictures were pieces of magazine pages and photocopies of those pages. On November 18, 1998, a federal grand jury returned a one-count indictment, charging Dauray with possessing child pornography in violation of 18 U.S.C. § 2252(a)(4)(B).

The version of the statute then in force punished the possession of "3 or more books, magazines, periodicals, films, video tapes, or other matter" that have passed in interstate or foreign commerce and "which contain any visual depiction" showing (or produced by using) a minor engaged in sexually explicit conduct. 18 U.S.C. § 2252(a)(4)(B) (1994) (amended 1998). The statute defined "sexually explicit conduct" in part as "actual or simulated -- lascivious exhibition of the genitals or pubic area of any person."

Dauray and the government stipulated at trial to the facts that bear upon this appeal. One stipulation provided that "[i] on or about May 13, 1994, Charles Dauray possessed the visual depictions which have been introduced into evidence; and [ii] Charles Dauray was aware of the contents of these visual depictions and thus he knew that genitalia of minors appear in each of them." A second stipulation was that the visual depictions were transported in interstate commerce. The jury therefore had only to decide whether the visual depictions showed "minor[s] engaging in sexually explicit conduct," i.e., whether they depicted the "lascivious exhibition of the genitals or pubic area." The jury found Dauray guilty, and by special interrogatory specified the four of the thirteen pieces of evidence that met the statutory definition.

The district court then considered Dauray's pretrial motion, on which the court had earlier reserved decision, to dismiss the indictment for failure to charge an offense. Dauray argued that each of the four pictures specified by the jury was in itself a "visual depiction" and therefore could not be "other matter which contain any visual depiction." Therefore, he reasoned, the indictment failed to charge an offense. The district court concluded that the pictures Dauray possessed were "other matter" within the plain meaning of § 2252(a)(4)(B), and for the same reason denied Dauray's request to apply the rule of lenity.

Dauray was sentenced on April 30, 1999 to 36 months of imprisonment, followed by three years of supervised release, and a $50 special assessment.

DISCUSSION

The statute under which Dauray was convicted has since been amended. At the time, the statute provided in pertinent part:

(a) Any person who--
(4) ...
(B) knowingly possesses 3 or more books, magazines, periodicals, films, video tapes, or other matter which contain any visual depiction that has been mailed, or has been shipped or transported in interstate or foreign commerce, or which was produced using materials which have been

mailed or so shipped or transported, by any means including by computer, if--

(i) the producing of such visual depiction involves the use of a minor engaging in sexually explicit conduct; and

(ii) such visual depiction is of such conduct;

shall be punished as provided in subsection (b) of this section.

18 U.S.C. § 2252(a)(4)(B) (1994) (emphasis added).

The question presented on appeal is whether individual pictures are "other matter which contain any visual depiction" within the meaning of § 2252(a)(4)(B). This question of first impression is one of law, which we review de novo.

Notwithstanding diligent efforts to construe § 2252(a)(4)(B), we conclude that it can be read either to support or to defeat this indictment. We therefore apply the rule of lenity to resolve the ambiguity in Dauray's favor.

I.

A.   Plain Meaning.

Our starting point in statutory interpretation is the statute's plain meaning, if it has one. Congress provided no definition of the terms "other matter" or "contain." We therefore consider the ordinary, common-sense meaning of the words.

Among the several dictionary definitions of the verb "to contain," Dauray presses one, and the government emphasizes another. (i) "To contain" means "to have within: hold." Webster's Third New International Dictionary 491 (unabridged ed.1981). Dauray argues that a picture is not a thing that contains itself. Thus in the natural meaning of the word, a pictorial magazine "contains" pictures, but it is at best redundant to say that a picture "contains" a picture. (ii) "To contain" also means "to consist of wholly or in part: comprise; include," *id.*, and the government argues that each underlying piece of paper is "matter" (as opposed perhaps to anti-matter) that contains the picture printed on it. It is also possible, applying this latter meaning, to say that each picture, composed of paper and ink, is matter that contains its imagery.

The district court assumed that Congress meant to employ both meanings. The district court thus recognized that one critical word of the statute lends itself to (at least) two meanings, only one of which can sustain the conviction, but then assumed, without resort to tools of construction, that the statutory language was drafted to support every meaning that would impose punishment. Resort to tools of construction is necessary in this case, however, to decide whether the language used gave adequate notice that this defendant's conduct was forbidden by this statute.

The plain meaning of another critical term – "other matter" – is also elusive. The dictionary defines "matter" as "the substance of which a physical object is composed." Webster's Third New International Dictionary 1394. Everything is more or less organized matter (as Napoleon observed). But Congress employed "matter" in a specific context, as the final, general term at the end of a list. We must "consider not only the bare meaning of the word but also its placement and purpose in the statutory scheme. '[T]he meaning of statutory language, plain or not, depends on context.'" Other courts have construed "other matter" in § 2252(a)(4)(B) as "simply something which, at a minimum, must be capable of containing a visual depiction." These definitions are unhelpful for our purposes.

There is no doubt that a pictorial magazine is "matter" that "contains" visual images. But no court that has construed § 2252(a)(4)(B) has considered whether a loose photograph clipped from such a magazine is itself "matter" that "contains" a visual image. The First Circuit recently held that a single negative film strip containing three images constituted only one piece of "matter" under § 2252(a)(4)(B). The court noted that "[h]ad Congress meant for the number of images to be the relevant criterion, it would have likely stated as much." The case concerned the character of singular "matter" containing multiple images, not whether each image--if loosed from the container--could itself constitute prohibited "matter."

Every other case that construes the term "other matter" has involved whether an individual computer graphics file is a "matter." These cases consider whether a computer file has the capacity to "contain a visual depiction," whether the general term "other matter" extends the statute's prohibition to a medium that is unenumerated in the list (and unlikely to have been thought of when the statute was drafted), and whether the proper analog to a graphics file is a page in a book or a book in a library. These cases have no evident bearing on whether a single magazine (which it was no crime to possess at the time of Dauray's arrest, no matter how many pages and pictures it contained) can become prohibited material simply by detaching the staples that bind the pages. * * *

B.   Canons of Construction.

Because the government and Dauray each rely on a reasonable meaning of § 2252(a)(4)(B), we resort to the canons of statutory interpretation to help resolve the ambiguity.

1. Lists and Other Associated Terms. Two related canons inform our analysis of the meaning of "other matter." First, the meaning of doubtful terms or phrases may be determined by reference to their relationship with other associated words or phrases (*noscitur a sociis*). Second, "where general words follow a specific enumeration of persons or things, the general words should be limited to persons or things similar to those specifically enumerated" (*ejusdem generis*). In this case, "other matter" should be construed to complete the class of items or things in the list preceding it, namely "books, magazines, periodicals, films, [or] video tapes."

Dauray argues that the listed items form a category of picture containers that can enclose within them multiple visual depictions. Because a picture taken from a magazine is not itself a picture container, like books or magazines, but is rather a thing abstracted from its container, Dauray contends that a picture in itself cannot be considered "other matter" within the meaning of the statute, and that possession of three of them is not prohibited.

But these canons equally support the government's argument. The list – at a sufficient level of generality, and completed by the catch-all "other matter" -- can be read to include any physical medium or method capable of presenting visual depictions. A picture cut from a magazine, considered as paper and ink employed to exhibit images, can be said to contain an image or as many images as can be perceived in a picture or photograph, which depends on how one looks at it.

2. Statutory Structure. "[A] statute is to be considered in all its parts when construing any one of them." The Protection of Children Against Sexual Exploitation Act contains four substantive subsections (of which § 2252(a)(4) is one): § 2252(a)(1) prohibits the interstate transportation of child pornography; § 2252(a)(2) prohibits the receipt or distribution of it; and § 2252(a)(3) prohibits its sale or possession with intent to sell. Only § 2252(a)(4) specifies that the conduct forbidden involves "books, magazines, periodicals, films, video tapes or other matter which contain" the pornography. The others more simply forbid "any visual depiction" of child pornography, period. Dauray and the government both find support in this statutory structure.

According to Dauray, the different drafting demonstrates that Congress knew how to prohibit the possession of individual pictures if it wanted to do so. The plain language of the other sections--each of which targets "any visual depiction"--is such that if Dauray had transported, distributed or sold the pictures he merely possessed, he would have violated the law unambiguously.

But the government could argue: that the transport, distribution and sale of child pornography are most harmful to children, and were therefore prohibited regardless of the medium or number of visual depictions; that Congress did not want to cast so fine a net in the context of mere possession in order to assure that the accidental possessor of one piece of pornography avoids liability while the collector does not; and that Congress implemented the distinction by punishing only persons who possess a threshold number (three) of anything that contains pornographic images, i.e., "books, magazines, periodicals, films, video tapes or other matter." If the statute simply read "3 or more visual depictions," then the accidental possession of one pictorial magazine could violate the statute. The difference between the language in § 2252(a)(4) and the other subsections is therefore (according to this view) fully consistent with a congressional intent to punish the possession of three or more individual pictures, postcards, posters, still frames, or even fragments of magazine pages.

3. Statutory Amendment. A statute should be construed to be consistent with subsequent statutory amendments. In 1998, Congress amended the statute by replacing "3 or more" with "1 or more" of the same list of "books, magazines, periodicals, films, video tapes or other matter." At the same time, Congress established an affirmative defense for a defendant who could show that he possessed "less than three matters containing" child pornography and "promptly and in good faith ... took reasonable steps to destroy" the pornography or report it to law enforcement officials without disseminating it to others. According to the government, the list, with its catch-all of "other matter," is designed to reach even an individual photograph. That could have been accomplished without the list, however, by an amendment that simply prohibits possession of "1 or more visual depictions." Dauray argues with some force that the list is superfluous post-amendment unless it serves to distinguish a "container" such as a magazine, from its contents, such as individual pictures cut from the magazine's pages. The government on this appeal makes no response to this argument, which is not to say that no response can be made.

4. Avoiding Absurdity. A statute should be interpreted in a way that avoids absurd results. Whichever interpretation one accepts, the statute tends to produce absurd results. Dauray's reading would prohibit the possession of three books, each of which contains one image, but allow the possession of stacks of unbound photographs. Equally absurd, the government's reading would prohibit the possession of three individual photographs (unless they were mounted in a single album), but allow the possession of two thick illustrated tomes.

C.   Legislative History.

When the plain language and canons of statutory interpretation fail to resolve statutory ambiguity, we will resort to legislative history. Unfortunately, "[e]xamination of [§ 2252's] legislative history . . . reveals no insight as to what Congress intended the precise scope of 'other matter' to be."

II.

Due process requires that a criminal statute "give fair warning of the conduct that it makes a crime." "[B]efore a man can be punished as a criminal under the Federal law his case must be 'plainly and unmistakably' within the provisions of some statute." The rule of lenity springs from this fair warning requirement. "In criminal prosecutions the rule of lenity requires that ambiguities in the statute be resolved in the defendant's favor." This expedient "ensures fair warning by so resolving ambiguity in a criminal statute as to apply it only to conduct clearly covered."

But "[b]ecause the meaning of language is inherently contextual," the Supreme Court has "declined to deem a statute 'ambiguous' for purposes of lenity merely because it was possible to articulate a construction more narrow than that urged by the Government." "Instead, [the Court has] always reserved lenity for those situations in which a reasonable doubt persists about a statute's intended scope even after resort to 'the language and structure, legislative history, and motivating policies' of the statute." It is a "doctrine of last resort."

Here, we have done what we can. We have read the plain language of § 2252(a)(4)(B), considered the traditional canons of statutory construction, looked for legislative history, and canvassed potentially relevant case law. And we are left with no more than a guess as to the proper meaning of the ambiguous language here.

While it is true that "our role as a court is to apply the provision as written, not as we would write it," the statute's ambiguity makes it impossible for us to apply the provision in this case without simply guessing about congressional intent. Indeed, the government conceded at oral argument that Dauray would not have violated the statute had his pictures been found in a photo album rather than in an unbound stack.

The government did not show that the pictures at issue were taken from more than a single magazine. At the time of Dauray's arrest, the statute did not forbid possession of such a magazine. Nor did the statute give Dauray notice that removing several pictures from the magazine, and keeping them, would subject him to criminal penalties. This result is unconstitutionally surprising. Under these circumstances, we must apply the rule of lenity and resolve the ambiguity in Dauray's favor.

CONCLUSION

For the foregoing reasons, the judgment is hereby reversed.

KATZMANN, Circuit Judge, dissenting.

I respectfully dissent from the majority's well-argued opinion. I would not apply the rule of lenity in this case. In *Muscarello v. U.S.*, the Supreme Court stated that the "simple existence of some statutory ambiguity ... is not sufficient to warrant application of that rule, for most statutes are ambiguous to some degree." The Court continued: "To invoke the rule, we must conclude that there is a grievous ambiguity or uncertainty in the statute." I do not think that there is such a "grievous ambiguity or uncertainty" in the statute before us, or that we can make "no more than a guess as to what Congress intended." The statute requires that the visual depiction be contained within books, magazines, periodicals, films, video tapes, or other matter. The word "contain" in the statute, consistent with its purposes, could mean both "comprise" and "hold" and still, in my view, not lead to "grievous ambiguity or uncertainty." Nothing in the statute itself or in the legislative record suggests that Congress did not intend to use both ordinary meanings of the word "contain." It makes sense, given the statute's purposes, that a photograph could be understood – quite naturally – to "contain" a visual depiction.

I fully agree with the majority that the statute could result in some incongruous interpretations. But in the end, I conclude that we must "apply the provision as written, not as we would write it."

Chapter 2

CONSTITUTIONAL LIMITATIONS
ON THE POWER TO PUNISH

INTRODUCTION

Although legislatures have primary authority for making criminal laws, all United States law, whether criminal or civil, is subject to the requirements of the United States Constitution. In addition, each state has its own constitution, which is binding upon the law of that state. Although constitutional opinions are scattered throughout this book, this chapter focuses on four federal constitutional limitations that are particularly fundamental to understanding criminal law. These limitations are the "void for vagueness" doctrine applied to state and federal governments through the Due Process Clause of the Fifth and Fourteenth Amendments; the "Cruel and Unusual" Punishment Clause of the Eighth Amendment; the Equal Protection Clause of the Fourteenth Amendment; and the Supremacy Clause, Art. VI, clause 2.

In addition to introducing the reader to some substantive restrictions on legislative power to create and punish crimes, this chapter introduces the reader to some of the tensions that emerge from the system of separation of powers and the federal system in the United States. Under the system of separation of powers, the legislature is the body primarily charged with passing laws that reflect the will of the general public at any given time; the judiciary's task is to protect non-majority interests and enforce the long-term, fundamental interests of the people as a whole by enforcing constitutional guarantees. The courts, then, often find themselves caught between the desire to carry out the will of the majority and the desire to restrain the majority in the name of fundamental principles.

The federal system also produces characteristic dilemmas for judges interpreting the federal Constitution. For example, in theory, individual states should have the latitude to pursue different paths, and pass laws that reflect the will of their own voters. This suggests that criminal law will look very different in different states. The fact that the Constitution has nationwide application, however, creates a pressure toward uniformity. As we will see, the tensions emerging both from the system of separation of powers and from the system of federalism often emerge in subtle (and sometimes not-so-subtle) battles between courts, between courts and legislatures, and sometimes within courts.

Finally, a common theme of this chapter and Chapter One is the theme of discretion. Although one of the aims of the criminal law, as we will see in *Papachristou v. Jacksonville,* is to subject all citizens equally to "the rule of law," in fact discretion in the system cannot be eliminated, only exposed and subjected to scrutiny. We have already seen this to be true in the case of jury nullification: the structure of the American system gives juries unreviewable discretion to free people being tried for a crime. In this chapter, we will see how judges have made an effort to control or challenge the discretion of police and prosecutors, how legislatures have attempted to control the discretion of judges, and how judges attempt to control the discretion of legislatures. The majority in *McCleskey v. Kemp* concedes that some level of discretion in the criminal justice system is inevitable, but suggests that this discretion is both good and bad. Is it possible to control the "bad" exercise of discretion and maintain the "good"?

A.   FOURTEENTH AMENDMENT DUE PROCESS: VOID FOR VAGUENESS DOCTRINE

The Due Process Clause of the Fifth and Fourteenth Amendments ("nor shall any person . . . be deprived of life, liberty, or property, without due process of law") has been interpreted to impose upon legislatures the duty to draft statutes that are clearly understandable. This requirement serves two purposes: providing fair notice to citizens of what conduct is prohibited, and, perhaps more importantly, limiting police discretion to arrest and jury discretion to imprison people they don't like. *Papachristou v. Jacksonville, Kolender v. Lawson,* and *Chicago v. Morales* illustrate how this "void for vagueness" doctrine works.

PAPACHRISTOU v. CITY OF JACKSONVILLE
Supreme Court of the United States
405 U.S. 156, 92 S.Ct. 839, 31 L.Ed.2d 110 (1972)

Mr. Justice DOUGLAS delivered the opinion of the Court.

This case involves eight defendants who were convicted in a Florida municipal court of violating a Jacksonville, Florida, vagrancy ordinance.[1] Their

---

[1] Jacksonville Ordinance Code § 26--57 provided at the time of these arrests and convictions as follows:

> Rogues and vagabonds, or dissolute persons who go about begging, common gamblers, persons who use juggling or unlawful games or plays, common drunkards, common night walkers, thieves, pilferers or pickpockets, traders in stolen property, lewd, wanton and lascivious persons, keepers of gambling places, common railers and brawlers, persons wandering or strolling around from place to place

convictions, entailing fines and jail sentences (some of which were suspended), were affirmed by the Florida Circuit Court in a consolidated appeal. * * * The case is here on a petition for certiorari, which we granted. For reasons which will appear, we reverse.

At issue are five consolidated cases. Margaret Papachristou, Betty Calloway, Eugene Eddie Melton, and Leonard Johnson were all arrested early on a Sunday morning, and charged with vagrancy -- 'prowling by auto.'

Jimmy Lee Smith and Milton Henry were charged with vagrancy--'vagabonds.'

Henry Edward Heath and a codefendant were arrested for vagrancy--'loitering' and 'common thief.'

Thomas Owen Campbell was charged with vagrancy--'common thief.'

Hugh Brown was charged with vagrancy--'disorderly loitering on street' and 'disorderly conduct--resisting arrest with violence.'

The facts are stipulated. Papachristou and Calloway are white females. Melton and Johnson are black males. Papachristou was enrolled in a job-training program sponsored by the State Employment Service at Florida Junior College in Jacksonville. Calloway was a typing and shorthand teacher at a state mental institution located near Jacksonville. She was the owner of the automobile in which the four defendants were arrested. Melton was a Vietnam war veteran who had been released from the Navy after nine months in a veterans' hospital. On the date of his arrest he was a part-time computer helper while attending

---

without any lawful purpose or object, habitual loafers, disorderly persons, persons neglecting all lawful business and habitually spending their time by frequenting houses of ill fame, gaming houses, or places where alcoholic beverages are sold or served, persons able to work but habitually living upon the earnings of their wives or minor children shall be deemed vagrants and, upon conviction in the Municipal Court shall be punished as provided for Class D offenses.

Class D offenses at the time of these arrests and convictions were punishable by 90 days' imprisonment, $500 fine, or both. Jacksonville Ordinance Code § 1--8 (1965). The maximum punishment has since been reduced to 75 days or $450. § 304.101 (1971).

We are advised that at present the Jacksonville vagrancy ordinance is § 330.107 and identical with the earlier one except that 'juggling' has been eliminated.

college as a full-time student in Jacksonville. Johnson was a tow-motor operator in a grocery chain warehouse and was a lifelong resident of Jacksonville.

At the time of their arrest the four of them were riding in Calloway's car on the main thoroughfare in Jacksonville. They had left a restaurant owned by Johnson's uncle where they had eaten and were on their way to a nightclub. The arresting officers denied that the racial mixture in the car played any part in the decision to make the arrest. The arrest, they said, was made because the defendants had stopped near a used-car lot which had been broken into several times. There was, however, no evidence of any breaking and entering on the night in question.

Of these four charged with 'prowling by auto' none had been previously arrested except Papachristou who had once been convicted of a municipal offense.

Jimmy Lee Smith and Milton Henry (who is not a petitioner) were arrested between 9 and 10 a.m. on a weekday in downtown Jacksonville, while waiting for a friend who was to lend them a car so they could apply for a job at a produce company. Smith was a part-time produce worker and part-time organizer for a Negro political group. He had a common-law wife and three children supported by him and his wife. He had been arrested several times but convicted only once. Smith's companion, Henry, was an 18-year-old high school student with no previous record of arrest.

This morning it was cold, and Smith had no jacket, so they went briefly into a dry cleaning shop to wait, but left when requested to do so. They thereafter walked back and forth two or three times over a two-block stretch looking for their friend. The store owners, who apparently were wary of Smith and his companion, summoned two police officers who searched the men and found neither had a weapon. But they were arrested because the officers said they had no identification and because the officers did not believe their story.

Heath and a codefendant were arrested for "loitering" and for "common thief." Both were residents of Jacksonville, Heath having lived there all his life and being employed at an automobile body shop. Heath had previously been arrested but his codefendant had no arrest record. Heath and his companion were arrested when they drove up to a residence shared by Heath's girl friend and some other girls. Some police officers were already there in the process of arresting another man. When Heath and his companion started backing out of the driveway, the officers signaled to them to stop and asked them to get out of the car, which they did. Thereupon they and the automobile were searched. Although no contraband or incriminating evidence was found, they were both arrested, Heath being charged with being a 'common thief' because he was reputed to be a thief. The codefendant was charged with 'loitering' because he was standing in the driveway, an act which the officers admitted was done only at their command.

[The facts describing the arrests of Campbell and Brown have been omitted.]

This ordinance is void for vagueness, both in the sense that it 'fails to give a person of ordinary intelligence fair notice that his contemplated conduct is forbidden by the statute,' and because it encourages arbitrary and erratic arrests and convictions. * * *

Living under a rule of law entails various suppositions, one of which is that '(all persons) are entitled to be informed as to what the State commands or forbids.' * * *

The poor among us, the minorities, the average householder are not in business and not alerted to the regulatory schemes of vagrancy laws; and we assume they would have no understanding of their meaning and impact if they read them. Nor are they protected from being caught in the vagrancy net by the necessity of having a specific intent to commit an unlawful act.

The Jacksonville ordinance makes criminal activities which by modern standards are normally innocent. 'Nightwalking' is one. Florida construes the ordinance not to make criminal one night's wandering, only the 'habitual' wanderer or, as the ordinance describes it, 'common night walkers.' We know, however, from experience that sleepless people often walk at night, perhaps hopeful that sleep-inducing relaxation will result.

Luis Munoz-Marin, former Governor of Puerto Rico, commented once that 'loafing' was a national virtue in his Commonwealth and that it should be encouraged. It is, however, a crime in Jacksonville.

'(P)ersons able to work but habitually living upon the earnings of their wives or minor children' -- like habitually living 'without visible means of support' -- might implicate unemployed pillars of the community who have married rich wives.

'(P)ersons able to work but habitually living upon the earnings of their wives or minor children' may also embrace unemployed people out of the labor market, by reason of a recession or disemployed by reason of technological or so-called structural displacements.

Persons 'wandering or strolling' from place to place have been extolled by Walt Whitman and Vachel Lindsay. The qualification 'without any lawful purpose or object' may be a trap for innocent acts. Persons 'neglecting all lawful business and habitually spending their time by frequenting . . . places where alcoholic beverages are sold or served' would literally embrace many members of golf clubs and city clubs. * * *

The difficulty is that these activities are historically part of the amenities of life as we have known them. They are not mentioned in the Constitution or in the Bill of Rights. These unwritten amenities have been in part responsible for giving our people the feeling of independence and self-confidence, the feeling of creativity. These amenities have dignified the right of dissent and have honored the right to be nonconformists and the right to defy submissiveness. They have encouraged lives of high spirits rather than hushed, suffocating silence. * * *

This aspect of the vagrancy ordinance before us is suggested by what this Court said in 1876 about a broad criminal statute enacted by Congress: 'It would certainly be dangerous if the legislature could set a net large enough to catch all possible offenders, and leave it to the courts to step inside and say who could be rightfully detained, and who should be set at large.'

While that was a federal case, the due process implications are equally applicable to the States and to this vagrancy ordinance. Here the net cast is large, not to give the courts the power to pick and choose but to increase the arsenal of the police. * * *

Another aspect of the ordinance's vagueness appears when we focus, not on the lack of notice given a potential offender, but on the effect of the unfettered discretion it places in the hands of the Jacksonville police. Caleb Foote, an early student of this subject, has called the vagrancy-type law as offering 'punishment by analogy.' Such crimes, though long common in Russia, are not compatible with our constitutional system. We allow our police to make arrests only on 'probable cause,' a Fourth and Fourteenth Amendment standard applicable to the States as well as to the Federal Government. Arresting a person on suspicion, like arresting a person for investigation, is foreign to our system, even when the arrest is for past criminality. Future criminality, however, is the common justification for the presence of vagrancy statutes. * * *

Those generally implicated by the imprecise terms of the ordinance -- poor people, nonconformists, dissenters, idlers--may be required to comport themselves according to the life style deemed appropriate by the Jacksonville police and the courts. Where, as here, there are no standards governing the exercise of the discretion granted by the ordinance, the scheme permits and encourages an arbitrary and discriminatory enforcement of the law. It furnishes a convenient tool for 'harsh and discriminatory enforcement by local prosecuting officials, against particular groups deemed to merit their displeasure.' It results in a regime in which the poor and the unpopular are permitted to 'stand on a public sidewalk . . . only at the whim of any police officer.' * * *

A presumption that people who might walk or loaf or loiter or stroll or frequent houses where liquor is sold, or who are supported by their wives or who look suspicious to the police are to become future criminals is too precarious for a rule of law. The implicit presumption in these generalized vagrancy standards -- that crime is being nipped in the bud -- is too extravagant to deserve extended treatment. Of course, vagrancy statutes are useful to the police. Of course, they are nets making easy the roundup of so-called undesirables. But the rule of law implies equality and justice in its application. Vagrancy laws of the Jacksonville type teach that the scales of justice are so tipped that even-handed administration of the law is not possible. The rule of law, evenly applied to minorities as well as majorities, to the poor as well as the rich, is the great mucilage that holds society together.

The Jacksonville ordinance cannot be squared with our constitutional standards and is plainly unconstitutional.

Reversed.

CAN A PERSON BE FREE TO WANDER WITHOUT WORRY OF ARREST?
Leon Lindsay
The Christian Science Monitor, Midwestern Edition, May 12, 1982, at 3[a]

Edward C. Lawson is not a lawyer, but one day next fall he plans to stand before the US Supreme Court and argue his case – a right of any citizen, though few have taken advantage of it. When Mr. Lawson appears before the high court bench, the justices may hear an impressive plea based on what he calls "the most important part of the Bill of Rights" – the Fourth Amendment, which guarantees "The right of the people to be secure in their persons . . . against unreasonable searches and seizures. . . ."

They also will see – unless court protocol requires that he cut his hair and wear a business suit – what might have prompted San Diego police to detain or arrest him more than 15 times between March 1975 and January 1977. They will at least see what Lawson believes is the chief reason for these incidents: He is black.

Prosecuted twice for violating Section 647(e) of the California Penal Code, an anti-vagrancy law, Lawson was convicted once. That began a five-year process of appeals that will culminate in the Supreme Court. Lawson is a bachelor in his mid-30s who heads his own San Francisco-based consulting and entrepreneurial firm. A vegetarian who says he does not smoke, drink, or "do dope," he also is a firm advocate of physical and mental fitness. To help maintain both, Lawson says, he walks everywhere he can. Distances of 10 or 12 miles do not faze him, nor is he concerned about the time consumed.

What did San Diego policemen, patrolling residential or business streets in their cruisers, see that prompted them to stop him? They saw a tall, slender black man striding along the sidewalk or roadside, most likely wearing a plain T-shirt and white trousers. The most outstanding feature is his hair; braided in the style of the Rastafarian religious sect (of which he is not a member), it is just below shoulder length. On his feet are sneakers or basketball shoes. And, if it is late at night and perhaps a little chilly, Lawson might wear a loose-fitting white jacket much like those worn by hospital workers.

Apparently because police saw Lawson walking at certain times and in certain areas in which his presence seemed unusual, they stopped him and demanded identification. He says that the first few times it happened he presented the identification he always carries and explained his presence. After a while, however, he began to feel that this was wrong, and he would ask the police why they wanted him to account for himself. Thus the 15 documented occasions, one of which led to his conviction.

Appeals in the case labeled *Lawson v. Kolender* (San Diego Police Chief William Kolender) led through state courts to the US District Court, where the judge overruled the conviction and the statute, noting that "a person who is stopped on less than probable cause cannot be punished for failing to identify himself." But the court also ruled that because the arresting officers had acted in "good faith" under the law, Lawson could not seek to recover damages from them.

The case then went to the federal Court of Appeals (Ninth Circuit), which on Oct. 15, 1981, upheld the district court's decision holding 647(e) unconstitutional and also ruled that a jury trial must be held to determine whether the policemen had acted in good faith and whether Lawson could collect the $150,000 in damages he seeks. The court of appeals held that the California law "intrudes upon the Fourth Amendment's proscription against unreasonable searches and seizures . . . (and) violates the due process clause because it encourages arbitrary and discriminatory enforcement." The court also said that the law "contains a vague enforcement standard which is susceptible to arbitrary enforcement; or . . . fails to give fair and adequate notice of the type of conduct prohibited."

Lawyers for the state attorney general's office and the City of San Diego, who appealed that decision to the Supreme Court, hold that the law is needed by police to help prevent crimes such as robbery, burglary, and rape. They hold that there has been sufficient experience with this and similar laws across the United States to establish safe guidelines for its enforcement. * * *

Although Lawson attended college only sporadically and puts little value on formal education, the New York City native is articulate and well-informed. He has no record other than the one conviction in San Diego. He makes clear that he does not believe it was his hair or the way he dressed that caused police to stop him. Laws like 647(e), he asserts, are directed "against the prevailing minority" in many US cities. "In certain places that means blacks. In other places it means Hispanics. Hippies in the 1960s would routinely and consistently find themselves describing to someone (in law enforcement) where they were going or what they were doing. "The law becomes a form of instantaneous punishment, to discourage certain kinds of people from being in certain areas," says Lawson. "There is nothing unique about what happened to me. . . . What they were doing was that they were stopping a black who was in an area or (out at) a time that they deemed he should not be." * * *

KOLENDER v. LAWSON
Supreme Court of the United States
461 U.S. 352, 103 S.Ct. 1855, 75 L.Ed.2d 903 (1983)

JUSTICE O'CONNOR delivered the opinion of the Court.

This appeal presents a facial challenge[a] to a criminal statute that requires persons who loiter or wander on the streets to provide a "credible and reliable" identification and to account for their presence when requested by a peace officer under circumstances that would justify a stop under the standards of Terry v. Ohio.[b] We conclude that the statute as it has been construed is unconstitutionally vague within the meaning of the Due Process Clause of the Fourteenth

---

[a]A distinction is made in constitutional law between a "facial" challenge to a statute or other government action, and a challenge "as applied." A "facial" challenge means that the plaintiff is claiming that the law is unconstitutional in all its applications. A challenge "as applied" means that the law is generally sound, but is unconstitutional with respect to the plaintiff (and other people who might be similarly situated).

[b]Terry v. Ohio, 392 U.S. 1 (1968), held that the police have the power to stop and question any person upon "reasonable suspicion" of criminal activity, and the further power to frisk that person upon reasonable suspicion that the suspect is armed and dangerous. This kind of stop is called a Terry detention or Terry stop.

Amendment by failing to clarify what is contemplated by the requirement that a suspect provide a "credible and reliable" identification. Accordingly, we affirm the judgment of the court below.

I

Appellee Edward Lawson was detained or arrested on approximately 15 occasions between March 1975 and January 1977 pursuant to Cal. Penal Code Ann. § 647(e).[3] Lawson was prosecuted only twice, and was convicted once. The second charge was dismissed.

Lawson then brought a civil action in the District Court for the Southern District of California seeking a declaratory judgment that § 647(e) is unconstitutional, a mandatory injunction to restrain enforcement of the statute, and compensatory and punitive damages against the various officers who detained him. The District Court found that § 647(e) was overbroad because "a person who is stopped on less than probable cause cannot be punished for failing to identify himself." The District Court enjoined enforcement of the statute, but held that Lawson could not recover damages because the officers involved acted in the good-faith belief that each detention or arrest was lawful. * * *

The Court of Appeals affirmed the District Court determination as to the unconstitutionality of § 647(e). * * *

The officers appealed to this Court from that portion of the judgment of the Court of Appeals which declared §647(e) unconstitutional and which enjoined its enforcement. We noted probable jurisdiction pursuant to 28 U.S.C. § 1254(2).

---

[3]The District Court failed to find facts concerning the particular occasions on which Lawson was detained or arrested under § 647(e). However, the trial transcript contains numerous descriptions of the stops given both by Lawson and by the police officers who detained him. For example, one police officer testified that he stopped Lawson while walking on an otherwise vacant street because it was late at night, the area was isolated, and the area was located close to a high crime area. Another officer testified that he detained Lawson, who was walking at a late hour in a business area where some businesses were still open, and asked for identification because burglaries had been committed by unknown persons in the general area. The appellee states that he has never been stopped by police for any reason apart from his detentions under § 647(e).

II

In the courts below, Lawson mounted an attack on the facial validity of §647(e).[c] "In evaluating a facial challenge to a state law, a federal court must, of course, consider any limiting construction that a state court or enforcement agency has proffered." As construed by the California Court of Appeal, §647(e) requires that an individual provide "credible and reliable" identification when requested by a police officer who has reasonable suspicion of criminal activity sufficient to justify a *Terry* detention. "Credible and reliable" identification is defined by the State Court of Appeal as identification "carrying reasonable assurance that the identification is authentic and providing means for later getting in touch with the person who has identified himself." In addition, a suspect may be required to "*account for his presence* . . . to the extent that it assists in producing credible and reliable identification . . . ." Under the terms of the statute, failure of the individual to provide "credible and reliable" identification permits the arrest.

III

Our Constitution is designed to maximize individual freedoms within a framework of ordered liberty. Statutory limitations on those freedoms are examined for substantive authority and content as well as for definiteness or certainty of expression.

As generally stated, the void-for-vagueness doctrine requires that a penal statute define the criminal offense with sufficient definiteness that ordinary people can understand what conduct is prohibited and in a manner that does not encourage arbitrary and discriminatory enforcement. Although the doctrine focuses both on actual notice to citizens and arbitrary enforcement, we have recognized recently that the more important aspect of the vagueness doctrine "is not actual notice, but the other principal element of the doctrine – the requirement that a legislature establish minimal guidelines to govern law enforcement." Where the legislature fails to provide such minimal guidelines, a criminal statute may permit "a standardless sweep [that] allows policemen, prosecutors, and juries to pursue their personal predilections."

---

[c] California Penal Code Ann. § 647(e) (West 1970) provides:

Every person who commits any of the following acts is guilty of disorderly conduct, a misdemeanor:...(e) Who loiters or wanders upon the streets or from place to place without apparent reason or business and who refuses to identify himself and to account for his presence when requested by any peace officer so to do, if the surrounding circumstances are such as to indicate to a reasonable man that the public safety demands such identification.

Section 647(e), as presently drafted and as construed by the state courts, contains no standard for determining what a suspect has to do in order to satisfy the requirement to provide a "credible and reliable" identification. As such, the statute vests virtually complete discretion in the hands of the police to determine whether the suspect has satisfied the statute and must be permitted to go on his way in the absence of probable cause to arrest. An individual, whom police may think is suspicious but do not have probable cause to believe has committed a crime, is entitled to continue to walk the public streets "only at the whim of any police officer" who happens to stop that individual under §647(e). Our concern here is based upon the "potential for arbitrarily suppressing First Amendment liberties. . . ." In addition, §647(e) implicates consideration of the constitutional right to freedom of movement. * * *

At oral argument, the appellants confirmed that a suspect violates §647(e) unless "the officer [is] satisfied that the identification is reliable." In giving examples of how suspects would satisfy the requirement, appellants explained that a jogger, who was not carrying identification, could, depending on the particular officer, be required to answer a series of questions concerning the route that he followed to arrive at the place where the officers detained him, or could satisfy the identification requirement simply by reciting his name and address.

It is clear that the full discretion accorded to the police to determine whether the suspect has provided a "credible and reliable" identification necessarily "[entrusts] lawmaking 'to the moment-to-moment judgment of the policeman on his beat.'" Section 647(e) "furnishes a convenient tool for 'harsh and discriminatory enforcement by local prosecuting officials, against particular groups deemed to merit their displeasure,'" and "confers on police a virtually unrestrained power to arrest and charge persons with a violation." In providing that a detention under §647(e) may occur only where there is the level of suspicion sufficient to justify a *Terry* stop, the State ensures the existence of "neutral limitations on the conduct of individual officers." Although the initial detention is justified, the State fails to establish standards by which the officers may determine whether the suspect has complied with the subsequent identification requirement.

Appellants stress the need for strengthened law enforcement tools to combat the epidemic of crime that plagues our Nation. The concern of our citizens with curbing criminal activity is certainly a matter requiring the attention of all branches of government. As weighty as this concern is, however, it cannot justify legislation that would otherwise fail to meet constitutional standards for definiteness and clarity. Section 647(e), as presently construed, requires that "suspicious" persons satisfy some undefined identification requirement, or face criminal punishment. Although due process does not require "impossible standards" of clarity, this is not a case where further precision in the statutory language is either impossible or impractical.

IV

We conclude §647(e) is unconstitutionally vague on its face because it encourages arbitrary enforcement by failing to describe with sufficient particularity what a suspect must do in order to satisfy the statute. Accordingly, the judgment of the Court of Appeals is affirmed, and the case is remanded for further proceedings consistent with this opinion.

It is so ordered.

[JUSTICE BRENNAN's concurring opinion and JUSTICE WHITE's dissenting opinion have been omitted.]

Note

Interestingly, the California legislature never revised the loitering statute which was struck down in *Kolender v. Lawson* in a way that specifically addressed the U.S. Supreme Court's concerns. The legislature merely made some minor revisions to the statute in an attempt to make the statute gender-neutral. Section 647(e) of the California Penal Code currently reads:

§ 647. Disorderly conduct

Every person who commits any of the following acts is guilty of disorderly conduct, a misdemeanor:

(e) Who loiters or wanders upon the streets or from place to place without apparent reason or business and who refuses to identify himself or herself and to account for his or her presence when requested by any peace officer so to do, if the surrounding circumstances would indicate to a reasonable person that the public safety demands this identification.

WALKING WHILE BLACK: ENCOUNTERS WITH THE POLICE ON MY STREET

Paul Butler[a]

Legal Times, Nov. 10, 1997, at 23[b]

Sometimes being a scholar of criminal procedure and a black man seems redundant.

I am walking in the most beautiful neighborhood in the District of Columbia. Though I'm coming home from work, I feel as though I'm on a nature walk: I spy deer and raccoons and hear ridiculously noisy birds. And even more unusual in Washington: black and white people. Living next door to each other. It's more like Disney World than the stereotypical image of Washington, D.C.

It is the neighborhood where I am fortunate enough to reside, and I am ashamed that the walk is unfamiliar; it is occasioned by my broken car. The time is about 9 p.m., and the streets are mostly deserted. When I'm about three blocks from home, a Metropolitan Police car, passing by, slows down. I keep walking, and the car makes a right turn, circles the block, and meets me. There are three officers inside. Their greeting is, "Do you live around here?"

I have been in this place before. I know that answering the question will be the beginning, not the end, of an unpleasant conversation--"Where do you live?" "It's kind of cold to be walking, isn't it?" "Can I see some I.D.?"-- that I don't feel like having.

So I ask a question instead: "Why do you want to know?" The three officers exchange a glance--the "we got a smartass on our hands" glance. I get it a lot.

"Is it against the law to walk on the sidewalk if I don't live around here?" When no response is immediately forthcoming, I say, "Have a nice evening, officers," and head toward home.

---

[a]Paul Butler is a Professor of Law at The George Washington University Law School in Washington, D.C.

The police now use an investigative technique that probably has a name other than cat-and-mouse, but that is the most accurate description. They park their car on the side of the road, turn off their lights, and watch me walk. When I pass out of their range of vision, they zip the car up to where they can see me.

In this fashion we arrive on the block where I live. I have a question, and so I stop and wait. For once, I have the power to summon the police immediately, quicker even than the president, who lives about seven miles away. Sure enough, as soon as I pause, the car does too. The police and I have a conversation, consisting mostly of questions.

"Why are you following me?"

"Why won't you tell us where you live?"

"What made you stop me?"

"We don't see a lot of people walking in this neighborhood."

"Are you following me because I'm black?"

"No, we're black too."

This answer is true, but it is not responsive. I ask the officers if they have ever been followed around a store by a security guard. They all say yes. The senior officer--a sergeant--says that it doesn't bother her because she knows she's not a thief.

I ask if that's how the kid in the Eddie Bauer case should have felt. A Prince George's County police officer, moonlighting as a security guard, made an African-American teen-ager take off the shirt he was wearing and go home to get a receipt in order to prove that he had not stolen the shirt from the store. Testifying about how that made him feel, the black man-child cried. The case had been in the news the previous week because a jury awarded the boy $850,000. Nonetheless, the sergeant says she isn't aware of it.

The officers tell me that they're suspicious because this is not a neighborhood where they usually see people walking. Furthermore, they know everybody who lives in the neighborhood and they don't know me. I ask if they know who lives there, pointing down the road to the house where I have lived for 14 months. Yes, they answer, yes, they do.

And so I walk. I walk up my stairs. I sit on my porch. I wait. I wait because I am a professor of criminal procedure. I wait because I remember the last time, with different officers, in a different place, when I "cooperated." Which meant that I let them search my car. Or rather, I let one search while the other watched me. With his hand resting near his gun. On 16th Street. Cars whizzed by. I pretended that I was invisible.

Now the officers park their car and position its spotlight on my face. All three of them join me on my porch.

"Do you live here?"

"Yes, I do."

"Can we see some identification?"

"No, you may not."

During the antebellum period of our nation's history, blacks were required to carry proof of their status, slave or free, at all times. Any black unsupervised by a white was suspect. In North Carolina, to make it easier for law enforcement, nonslave blacks had to wear shoulder patches with the word "free."

The District of Columbia, through its three agents standing on my porch, tells me: "If you live here, go inside. It's too cold to be out."

I am content where I am. So, the police announce, are they. They will not leave me until I produce some I.D. or enter the house.

I have arrived home late because I worked late, writing about a book for the Harvard Law Review. The book, which I'm carrying in my knapsack, is Race, Crime and the Law, by Randall Kennedy. Since apparently none of us has anything better to do, I take the book out of my sack and show the officers Chapter 4, "Race, Law, and Suspicion: Using Color as a Proxy for Dangerousness." The chapter contains several stories just like this one. It quotes Harvard Professor Henry Louis Gates Jr. * * * "There's a moving violation that many African-Americans know as D.W.B.: Driving While Black."

But this, I announce, is the first time I've ever heard of "walking while black." I point to the big window of my beautiful house. I tell the police that I have seen people, mostly white, walking down the street at all times of the day and night, and I have never heard them questioned about their right to be there. That is why I will not show them my identification. This is not apartheid South Africa, and I don't need a pass card.

The officers are not interested. In fact, they announce, they're getting angry. There have been burglaries in this neighborhood and car vandalism. The police are just doing their job, and I--I am wasting the taxpayers' money. One officer theorizes that I'm homeless. Another believes that I'm on drugs. The one thing of which they are certain is that I don't live here in the house on whose porch I sit. And when they find out who I "really" am, I will be guilty of unlawful entry, a misdemeanor. * * *

The sergeant tells me that since I'm being "evasive," she will interview my neighbors. The two officers who remain radio for backup. They give the dispatcher the wrong address, and I correct them. Soon a second patrol car, with two more officers, arrives. I am cold but stubborn.

Finally, my neighbor comes outside and identifies me. I'm free now-- free to be left alone. Free to walk on a public street. Free to sit on my porch, even if it is cold.

But first, we--the five law enforcement officers and I--look to my neighbor for vindication, a moral to justify the last hour of our lives. My neighbor is black like us. He says that he is always happy to see police patrolling the neighborhood. But, he adds, many white people walk late at night, and they are not questioned about their right to be there. My neighbor tells the officers that they are always welcome to stop by his house for coffee. And he goes home. The sergeant invites me to a crime prevention meeting at the police station in a few weeks. Then the five officers get into their two cars and drive away.

As for me, I'm still searching for a moral. My neighborhood does not seem so beautiful anymore. I got my car repaired right away: I had enjoyed the walk, but I dreaded the next set of officers. Sometimes I prefer to leave criminal procedure at the office. Sometimes I like a walk to be simply a walk.

But sometimes I am willing for my walk to serve as a hypothetical, for the police, and for you, reader, about the Fourth Amendment and its protection against unreasonable government intrusion. If I had a television show, I would say, "Kids, don't try this at home." It is unfortunate, but other uppity Negroes have gotten themselves shot for less than what I did. The officers I encountered were professional, even if the male officers were not especially polite. They never led me to believe that they would physically harm me or even falsely arrest me. It is sad that I should feel grateful for that, but I do.

One reason that I felt safer with the officers was because they were African-American. They might stop me because I'm black, but I didn't think they would be as quick on the draw as nonblack officers, who are more susceptible to the hype. The black officer's construct of me--a black man walking in a neighborhood where people don't often walk at night--was burglary suspect, or homeless person, or drug addict. The white officer's construct--even during a traffic stop--is violent black man. At least that is what is communicated by the approach with the hand on the gun, the order to exit the car, and the patdown search. Not every time, but often enough.

Because the officers were black, I was especially angry. They should've known better.

What is reasonable law enforcement? There are neighborhoods in this city that covet police officers as concerned about crime prevention as these officers seemed to be. Like my neighbor, I had been pleased to see police patrols--at least until the police patrolled me. Still, I could excuse the intrusion as the price of life in the big city if everybody had to pay the price. But everybody does not. Ultimately, my protest is less about privacy and more about discrimination.

Most courts say that police may consider race in assessing suspicion. It is probably true that there are more black than white burglars and car thieves in the District. In *United States v. Weaver*, the U.S. Court of Appeals for the 8th Circuit said of racial profiles:

> [F]acts are not to be ignored simply because they may be unpleasant. . . . Race, when coupled with other factors is a lawful factor in the decision to approach and ultimately detain a suspect. We wish it were otherwise, but we take the facts as they are presented to us, not as we would like them to be.

But the fact is also that most of the black people who walk in my neighborhood are, like me, law-abiding. And the fact is that some white people are not law-abiding. Race is so imprecise a proxy for criminality that it is, in the end, useless.

The police officers made me an offer before they left. If I wanted to know when they stopped white people who walked in my neighborhood, they would tell me. They would ring my doorbell any time, day or night, to let me know. Ironically, considering the officers' lack of interest in Professor Kennedy's book, their offer is also his suggestion. Kennedy believes in colorblindness, including in assessments of suspicion. He writes:

> [I]nstead of placing a racial tax on minorities, government should, if necessary, increase taxes across the board. . . . It should be forced to inconvenience everyone . . . by subjecting all . . . to questioning. The reform I support, in other words,

does not entail lessened policing. It only insists that the costs of policing be allocated on a nonracial basis.

I turned down the offer, thinking that the police might begin to question every walker in my neighborhood just to make a point. That would not make me feel any safer, and it would inconvenience the neighbors.

In retrospect, I made the wrong decision. I hadn't wanted to draw the enmity of my neighbors by causing them to be treated like criminal suspects. Or like black men. Sometimes the law gets me confused about the difference. Kennedy is correct: It is a confusion everyone should share.

CITY OF CHICAGO v. MORALES
Supreme Court of the United States
527 U.S. 41, 119 S.Ct. 1849, 144 L.Ed.2d 67 (1999)

JUSTICE STEVENS announced the judgment of the Court and delivered the opinion of the Court with respect to Parts I, II, and V, and an opinion with respect to Parts III, IV, and VI, in which JUSTICE SOUTER and JUSTICE GINSBURG join.

In 1992, the Chicago City Council enacted the Gang Congregation Ordinance, which prohibits "criminal street gang members" from "loitering" with one another or with other persons in any public place. The question presented is whether the Supreme Court of Illinois correctly held that the ordinance violates the Due Process Clause of the Fourteenth Amendment to the Federal Constitution.

I

Before the ordinance was adopted, the city council's Committee on Police and Fire conducted hearings to explore the problems created by the city's street gangs, and more particularly, the consequences of public loitering by gang members. Witnesses included residents of the neighborhoods where gang members are most active, as well as some of the aldermen who represent those areas. * * *

The council found that a continuing increase in criminal street gang activity was largely responsible for the city's rising murder rate, as well as an escalation of violent and drug related crimes. It noted that in many neighborhoods throughout the city, "the burgeoning presence of street gang members in public places has intimidated many law abiding citizens." Furthermore, the council stated that gang members "establish control over identifiable areas . . . by loitering in those areas and intimidating others from entering those areas; and . . . members of criminal street gangs avoid arrest by committing no offense punishable under existing laws when they know the police are present . . . ." It further found that "loitering in public places by criminal street gang members creates a justifiable fear for the safety of persons and property in the area" and that "aggressive action is necessary to preserve the city's streets and other public places so that the public may use such places without fear." Moreover, the council concluded that the city "has an interest in discouraging all persons from loitering in public places with criminal gang members."

The ordinance creates a criminal offense punishable by a fine of up to $500, imprisonment for not more than six months, and a requirement to perform up to 120 hours of community service. Commission of the offense involves four predicates. First, the police officer must reasonably believe that at least one of the two or more persons present in a "public place" is a "criminal street gang member." Second, the persons must be "loitering," which the ordinance defines as "remaining in any one place with no apparent purpose." Third, the officer must then order "all" of the persons to disperse and remove themselves "from the area." Fourth, a person must disobey the officer's order. If any person, whether a gang member or not, disobeys the officer's order, that person is guilty of violating the ordinance.

Two months after the ordinance was adopted, the Chicago Police Department promulgated General Order 92-4 to provide guidelines to govern its enforcement. That order purported to establish limitations on the enforcement discretion of police officers "to ensure that the anti-gang loitering ordinance is not enforced in an arbitrary or discriminatory way." The limitations confine the authority to arrest gang members who violate the ordinance to sworn "members of the Gang Crime Section" and certain other designated officers, and establish detailed criteria for defining street gangs and membership in such gangs. In addition, the order directs district commanders to "designate areas in which the presence of gang members has a demonstrable effect on the activities of law abiding persons in the surrounding community," and provides that the ordinance "will be enforced only within the designated areas." The city, however, does not release the locations of these "designated areas" to the public.

II

During the three years of its enforcement, the police issued over 89,000 dispersal orders and arrested over 42,000 people for violating the ordinance. * * *

We granted certiorari, and now affirm. Like the Illinois Supreme Court, we conclude that the ordinance enacted by the city of Chicago is unconstitutionally vague.

III

The basic factual predicate for the city's ordinance is not in dispute. As the city argues in its brief, "the very presence of a large collection of obviously brazen, insistent, and lawless gang members and hangers-on on the public ways intimidates residents, who become afraid even to leave their homes and go about their business. That, in turn, imperils community residents' sense of safety and security, detracts from property values, and can ultimately destabilize entire neighborhoods." The findings in the ordinance explain that it was motivated by these concerns. We have no doubt that a law that directly prohibited such intimidating conduct would be constitutional, but this ordinance broadly covers a significant amount of additional activity. Uncertainty about the scope of that additional coverage provides the basis for respondents' claim that the ordinance is too vague. * * *

[A]s the United States recognizes, the freedom to loiter for innocent purposes is part of the "liberty" protected by the Due Process Clause of the Fourteenth Amendment. We have expressly identified this "right to remove from one place to another according to inclination" as "an attribute of personal liberty" protected by the Constitution. Indeed, it is apparent that an individual's decision to remain in a public place of his choice is as much a part of his liberty as the freedom of movement inside frontiers that is "a part of our heritage" or the right to move "to whatsoever place one's own inclination may direct" identified in Blackstone's Commentaries. * * *

Vagueness may invalidate a criminal law for either of two independent reasons. First, it may fail to provide the kind of notice that will enable ordinary people to understand what conduct it prohibits; second, it may authorize and even encourage arbitrary and discriminatory enforcement. Accordingly, we first consider whether the ordinance provides fair notice to the citizen and then discuss its potential for arbitrary enforcement.

IV

"It is established that a law fails to meet the requirements of the Due Process Clause if it is so vague and standardless that it leaves the public uncertain as to the conduct it prohibits . . . ." The Illinois Supreme Court recognized that the term "loiter" may have a common and accepted meaning, but the definition of that term in this ordinance – "to remain in any one place with no apparent purpose" – does not. It is difficult to imagine how any citizen of the city of Chicago standing in a public place with a group of people would know if he or she had an "apparent purpose." If she were talking to another person, would she have an apparent purpose? If she were frequently checking her watch and looking expectantly down the street, would she have an apparent purpose?

Since the city cannot conceivably have meant to criminalize each instance a citizen stands in public with a gang member, the vagueness that dooms this ordinance is not the product of uncertainty about the normal meaning of "loitering," but rather about what loitering is covered by the ordinance and what is not. The Illinois Supreme Court emphasized the law's failure to distinguish between innocent conduct and conduct threatening harm.[24] * * *

The city's principal response to this concern about adequate notice is that loiterers are not subject to sanction until after they have failed to comply with an officer's order to disperse. "Whatever problem is created by a law that criminalizes conduct people normally believe to be innocent is solved when persons receive actual notice from a police order of what they are expected to do." We find this response unpersuasive for at least two reasons.

First, the purpose of the fair notice requirement is to enable the ordinary citizen to conform his or her conduct to the law. "No one may be required at peril of life, liberty or property to speculate as to the meaning of penal statutes." Although it is true that a loiterer is not subject to criminal sanctions unless he or she disobeys a dispersal order, the loitering is the conduct that the ordinance is designed to prohibit. If the loitering is in fact harmless and innocent, the dispersal order itself is an unjustified impairment of liberty. If the police are able to decide arbitrarily which members of the public they will order to disperse, then the Chicago ordinance becomes indistinguishable from the law we held invalid in *Shuttlesworth v. Birmingham.* Because an officer may issue an order only after prohibited conduct has already occurred, it cannot provide the kind of advance notice that will protect the putative loiterer from being ordered to disperse. Such an order cannot retroactively give adequate warning of the boundary between the permissible and the impermissible applications of the law. * * *

V

The broad sweep of the ordinance also violates "'the requirement that a legislature establish minimal guidelines to govern law enforcement.'" There are no such guidelines in the ordinance. In any public place in the city of Chicago, persons who stand or sit in the company of a gang member may be ordered to

---

[24]One of the trial courts that invalidated the ordinance gave the following illustration: "Suppose a group of gang members were playing basketball in the park, while waiting for a drug delivery. Their apparent purpose is that they are in the park to play ball. The actual purpose is that they are waiting for drugs. Under this definition of loitering, a group of people innocently sitting in a park discussing their futures would be arrested, while the 'basketball players' awaiting a drug delivery would be left alone."

disperse unless their purpose is apparent. The mandatory language in the enactment directs the police to issue an order without first making any inquiry about their possible purposes. It matters not whether the reason that a gang member and his father, for example, might loiter near Wrigley Field is to rob an unsuspecting fan or just to get a glimpse of Sammy Sosa leaving the ballpark; in either event, if their purpose is not apparent to a nearby police officer, she may – indeed, she "shall" – order them to disperse. * * *

VI

* * * We recognize the serious and difficult problems testified to by the citizens of Chicago that led to the enactment of this ordinance. "We are mindful that the preservation of liberty depends in part on the maintenance of social order." However, in this instance the city has enacted an ordinance that affords too much discretion to the police and too little notice to citizens who wish to use the public streets.

Accordingly, the judgment of the Supreme Court of Illinois is Affirmed.

JUSTICE SCALIA, dissenting.

The citizens of Chicago were once free to drive about the city at whatever speed they wished. At some point Chicagoans (or perhaps Illinoisans) decided this would not do, and imposed prophylactic speed limits designed to assure safe operation by the average (or perhaps even subaverage) driver with the average (or perhaps even subaverage) vehicle. This infringed upon the "freedom" of all citizens, but was not unconstitutional.

Similarly, the citizens of Chicago were once free to stand around and gawk at the scene of an accident. At some point Chicagoans discovered that this obstructed traffic and caused more accidents. They did not make the practice unlawful, but they did authorize police officers to order the crowd to disperse, and imposed penalties for refusal to obey such an order. Again, this prophylactic measure infringed upon the "freedom" of all citizens, but was not unconstitutional.

Until the ordinance that is before us today was adopted, the citizens of Chicago were free to stand about in public places with no apparent purpose – to engage, that is, in conduct that appeared to be loitering. In recent years, however, the city has been afflicted with criminal street gangs. As reflected in the record before us, these gangs congregated in public places to deal in drugs, and to terrorize the neighborhoods by demonstrating control over their "turf." Many residents of the inner city felt that they were prisoners in their own homes. Once again, Chicagoans decided that to eliminate the problem it was worth restricting some of the freedom that they once enjoyed. The means they took was similar to the second, and more mild, example given above rather than the first: Loitering was not made unlawful, but when a group of people occupied a public place without an apparent purpose and in the company of a known gang member, police officers were authorized to order them to disperse, and the failure to obey such an order was made unlawful. The minor limitation upon the free state of nature that this prophylactic arrangement imposed upon all Chicagoans seemed to them (and it seems to me) a small price to pay for liberation of their streets. * * *

JUSTICE THOMAS, with whom THE CHIEF JUSTICE and JUSTICE SCALIA join, dissenting.

The duly elected members of the Chicago City Council enacted the ordinance at issue as part of a larger effort to prevent gangs from establishing dominion over the public streets. By invalidating Chicago's ordinance, I fear that the Court has unnecessarily sentenced law-abiding citizens to lives of terror and misery. The ordinance is not vague. "Any fool would know that a particular category of conduct would be within [its] reach." Nor does it violate the Due Process Clause. The asserted "freedom to loiter for innocent purposes," is in no way "'deeply rooted in this Nation's history and tradition.'" I dissent.

I

The human costs exacted by criminal street gangs are inestimable. In many of our Nation's cities, gangs have "virtually overtaken certain neighborhoods, contributing to the economic and social decline of these areas and causing fear and lifestyle changes among law-abiding residents." Gangs fill the daily lives of many of our poorest and most vulnerable citizens with a terror that the Court does not give sufficient consideration, often relegating them to the status of prisoners in their own homes.

The city of Chicago has suffered the devastation wrought by this national tragedy. Last year, in an effort to curb plummeting attendance, the Chicago Public Schools hired dozens of adults to escort children to school. The youngsters had become too terrified of gang violence to leave their homes alone. The children's fears were not unfounded. In 1996, the Chicago Police Department estimated that there were 132 criminal street gangs in the city. Between 1987 and 1994, these gangs were involved in 63,141 criminal incidents, including 21,689 nonlethal violent crimes and 894 homicides. Many of these criminal incidents and homicides result from gang "turf battles," which take place on the public streets and place innocent residents in grave danger.

Before enacting its ordinance, the Chicago City Council held extensive hearings on the problems of gang loitering. Concerned citizens appeared to testify poignantly as to how gangs disrupt their daily lives. Ordinary citizens like Ms. D'Ivory Gordon explained that she struggled just to walk to work:

> When I walk out my door, these guys are out there . . . . They watch you . . . . They know where you live. They know what time you leave, what time you come home. I am afraid of them. I have even come to the point now that I carry a meat cleaver to work with me . . . . I don't want to hurt anyone, and I don't want to be hurt. We need to clean these corners up. Clean these communities up and take it back from them.

Eighty-eight-year-old Susan Mary Jackson echoed her sentiments, testifying, "We used to have a nice neighborhood. We don't have it anymore . . . . I am scared to go out in the daytime . . . . you can't pass because they are standing. I am afraid to go to the store. I don't go to the store because I am afraid. At my age if they look at me real hard, I be ready to holler." Another long-time resident testified:

> I have never had the terror that I feel everyday when I walk down the streets of Chicago . . . . I have had my windows broken out. I have had guns pulled on me. I have been threatened. I get intimidated on a daily basis, and it's come to the point where I say, well, do I go out today. Do I put my ax in my briefcase. Do I walk around dressed like a bum so I am not looking rich or got any money or anything like that.

Following these hearings, the council found that "criminal street gangs establish control over identifiable areas . . . by loitering in those areas and intimidating others from entering those areas." It further found that the mere presence of gang members "intimidates many law abiding citizens" and "creates a justifiable fear for the safety of persons and property in the area." It is the product of this democratic process – the council's attempt to address these social ills – that we are asked to pass judgment upon today.

II

As part of its ongoing effort to curb the deleterious effects of criminal street gangs, the citizens of Chicago sensibly decided to return to basics. The ordinance does nothing more than confirm the well-established principle that the police have the duty and the power to maintain the public peace, and, when necessary, to disperse groups of individuals who threaten it. * * *

Today, the Court focuses extensively on the "rights" of gang members and their companions. It can safely do so – the people who will have to live with the consequences of today's opinion do not live in our neighborhoods. Rather, the people who will suffer from our lofty pronouncements are people like Ms. Susan Mary Jackson; people who have seen their neighborhoods literally destroyed by gangs and violence and drugs. They are good, decent people who must struggle to overcome their desperate situation, against all odds, in order to raise their families, earn a living, and remain good citizens. As one resident described, "There is only about maybe one or two percent of the people in the city causing these problems maybe, but it's keeping 98 percent of us in our houses and off the streets and afraid to shop." By focusing exclusively on the imagined "rights" of the two percent, the Court today has denied our most vulnerable citizens the very thing that JUSTICE STEVENS elevates above all else – the "freedom of movement." And that is a shame. I respectfully dissent.

[The concurring opinions of JUSTICE O'CONNOR and JUSTICE KENNEDY have been omitted.]

Note

Tracey Meares and Dan Kahan explain why the anti-gang loitering ordinance passed by the Chicago City Council in the summer of 1992 was favored by residents of the mostly poor, minority, inner-city neighborhoods where the ordinance would likely be enforced:

> In fact, it may be precisely because they care so deeply about [the youths likely to be affected by the anti-gang loitering ordinance] that residents of the inner-city prefer relatively mild gang loitering and curfew laws over draconian penalty enhancements for gang crimes, severe mandatory minimum prison sentences for drug distribution, and similarly punitive measures. Inner-city residents may believe these harsher penalties visit an intolerably destructive toll on the whole community. The pervasive sense of linked fate between the majority of inner city residents and the youths affected by curfews and gang loitering ordinances again furnishes a compelling reason not to second guess the community's determination that such measures enhance rather than detract from liberty.

Tracey L. Meares and Dan M. Kahan, *The Wages of Antiquated Procedural Thinking: A Critique of Chicago v. Morales*, 1998 U. Chi. Legal F. 197, at 210.

In February of 2000, the Chicago City Council passed a new ordinance, aimed at inconveniencing drug traffickers and gang members by allowing the police to disperse groups of people hanging out in the street. The new ordinance defines "gang loitering" as "remaining in any one place under circumstances that would warrant a reasonable person to believe the purpose or effect of that behavior is to enable a criminal street gang to establish control over identifiable areas, to intimidate others from entering those areas or to conceal illegal activities." Chi. Mun. Code § 8-4-015 (2003). Officers must tell people being targeted as loiterers that they are violating the ordinance, that they must disperse, and that they may not return for at least three hours under penalty of arrest; they also must give the putative loiterers reasonable time to disperse before being arrested. Finally, the ordinance may be enforced only in neighborhoods the police superintendent designates as "hot zones." Margaret Graham Tebo, *Second City Tries Again: Chicago Hopes New Loitering Law Avoids Constitutional Defects*, 86 A.B.A. J. 28 (2000).

B.   THE EIGHTH AMENDMENT: CRUEL AND UNUSUAL PUNISHMENT AND THE PRINCIPLE OF PROPORTIONALITY

The Eighth Amendment states, "Excessive bail shall not be required, nor excessive fines imposed, nor cruel and unusual punishments inflicted." Although the Supreme Court has been internally divided on this issue, a majority of Justices have maintained that punishments that are out of proportion to the crime violate the cruel and unusual punishment clause. *Coker v. Georgia* remains one of the leading Supreme Court cases concerning the application of the cruel and unusual punishment clause in the death penalty context. In *Ewing v. California,* the Supreme Court attempts to reconcile prior decisions pointing in different directions on the application of the proportionality principle to non-death cases. In *Ramirez v. Castro*, the Ninth Circuit Court of Appeals struggles with how to apply *Ewing.*

COKER v. GEORGIA
Supreme Court of the United States
433 U.S. 584, 97 S.Ct. 2861, 53 L.Ed.2d 982 (1977)

MR. JUSTICE WHITE announced the judgment of the Court and filed an opinion in which MR. JUSTICE STEWART, MR. JUSTICE BLACKMUN, and MR. JUSTICE STEVENS, joined.

Georgia Code Ann. § 26-2001 (1972) provides that "[a] person convicted of rape shall be punished by death or by imprisonment for life, or by imprisonment for not less than one nor more than 20 years." Punishment is determined by a jury in a separate sentencing proceeding in which at least one of the statutory aggravating circumstances must be found before the death penalty may be imposed. Petitioner Coker was convicted of rape and sentenced to death. Both the conviction and the sentence were affirmed by the Georgia Supreme Court. Coker was granted a writ of certiorari, limited to the single claim, rejected by the Georgia court, that the punishment of death for rape violates the Eighth Amendment, which proscribes "cruel and unusual punishments" and which must be observed by the States as well as the Federal Government.

I

While serving various sentences for murder, rape kidnaping, and aggravated assault, petitioner escaped from the Ware Correctional Institution near Waycross, Ga., on September 2, 1974. At approximately 11 o'clock that night, petitioner entered the house of Allen and Elnita Carver through an unlocked kitchen door. Threatening the couple with a "board," he tied up Mr. Carver in the bathroom, obtained a knife from the kitchen, and took Mr. Carver's money and the keys to the family car. Brandishing the knife and saying "you know what's going to happen to you if you try anything, don't you," Coker then raped Mrs. Carver. Soon thereafter, petitioner drove away in the Carver car, taking Mrs. Carver with him. Mr. Carver, freeing himself, notified the police; and not long thereafter petitioner was apprehended. Mrs. Carver was unharmed.

Petitioner was charged with escape, armed robbery, motor vehicle theft, kidnaping, and rape. Counsel was appointed to represent him. Having been found competent to stand trial, he was tried. The jury returned a verdict of guilty, rejecting his general plea of insanity. A sentencing hearing was then conducted in accordance with the procedures dealt with at length in *Gregg v. Georgia.* The jury was instructed that it could consider as aggravating circumstances whether the rape had been committed by a person with a prior record of conviction for a capital felony and whether the rape had been committed in the course of committing another capital felony, namely, the armed robbery of Allen Carver. The court also instructed, pursuant to statute, that even if aggravating circumstances were present, the death penalty need not be imposed if the jury found they were outweighed by mitigating circumstances, that is, circumstances not constituting justification or excuse for the offense in question, "but which, in fairness and mercy, may be considered as extenuating or reducing the degree" of moral culpability or punishment. The jury's verdict on the rape count was death by electrocution. Both aggravating circumstances on which the court instructed were found to be present by the jury.

II

* * * It is now settled that the death penalty is not invariably cruel and unusual punishment within the meaning of the Eighth Amendment; it is not inherently barbaric or an unacceptable mode of punishment for crime; neither is it always disproportionate to the crime for which it is imposed. It is also established that imposing capital punishment, at least for murder, in accordance

with the procedures provided under the Georgia statutes saves the sentence from the infirmities which led the Court to invalidate the prior Georgia capital punishment statute in *Furman v. Georgia*.[a]

In sustaining the imposition of the death penalty in *Gregg,* however, the Court firmly embraced the holdings and dicta from prior cases to the effect that the Eighth Amendment bars not only those punishments that are "barbaric" but also those that are "excessive" in relation to the crime committed. Under *Gregg,* a punishment is "excessive" and unconstitutional if it (1) makes no measurable contribution to acceptable goals of punishment and hence is nothing more than the purposeless and needless imposition of pain and suffering; or (2) is grossly out of proportion to the severity of the crime. A punishment might fail the test on either ground. Furthermore, these Eighth Amendment judgments should not be, or appear to be, merely the subjective views of individual Justices; judgment should be informed by objective factors to the maximum possible extent. To this end, attention must be given to the public attitudes concerning a particular sentence - history and precedent, legislative attitudes, and the response of juries reflected in their sentencing decisions are to be consulted. In *Gregg,* after giving due regard to such sources, the Court's judgment was that the death penalty for deliberate murder was neither the purposeless imposition of severe punishment nor a punishment grossly disproportionate to the crime. But the Court reserved the question of the constitutionality of the death penalty when imposed for other crimes.

III

That question, with respect to rape of an adult woman, is now before us. We have concluded that a sentence of death is grossly disproportionate and excessive punishment for the crime of rape and is therefore forbidden by the Eighth Amendment as cruel and unusual punishment.

A

---

[a] In *Furman v. Georgia*, 408 U.S. 238, 92 S.Ct. 2726, 33 L.Ed.2d 346 (1972), the Supreme Court, in a 5-4 decision, effectively invalidated capital punishment as it was currently being practiced in the United States. Three Justices – Douglas, Stewart, and White – held that because juries in Georgia exercised essentially unfettered discretion in deciding which murderers should receive the death penalty and which should not, there was an unconstitutionally substantial risk that the death penalty was being imposed in an arbitrary and capricious, as well as a racially discriminatory, manner. Two other Justices, writing separately – Brennan and Marshall – came to the conclusion that the death penalty was unconstitutional in all circumstances. Chief Justice Burger and Justices Blackmun, Powell, and Rehnquist would have upheld the Georgia scheme against constitutional attack.

As advised by recent cases, we seek guidance in history and from the objective evidence of the country's present judgment concerning the acceptability of death as a penalty for rape of an adult woman. At no time in the last 50 years have a majority of the States authorized death as a punishment for rape. In 1925, 18 States, the District of Columbia, and the Federal Government authorized capital punishment for the rape of an adult female. By 1971 just prior to the decision in *Furman* v. *Georgia,* that number had declined, but not substantially, to 16 States plus the Federal Government. *Furman* then invalidated most of the capital punishment statutes in this country, including the rape statutes, because, among other reasons, of the manner in which the death penalty was imposed and utilized under those laws.

With their death penalty statutes for the most part invalidated, the States were faced with the choice of enacting modified capital punishment laws in an attempt to satisfy the requirements of Furman or of being satisfied with life imprisonment as the ultimate punishment for *any* offense. Thirty-five States immediately reinstituted the death penalty for at least limited kinds of crime. * * *

In reviving death penalty laws to satisfy *Furman*'s mandate, none of the States that had not previously authorized death for rape chose to include rape among capital felonies. Of the 16 States in which rape had been a capital offense, only three provided the death penalty for rape of an adult woman in their revised statutes - Georgia, North Carolina, and Louisiana. * * *

The current judgment with respect to the death penalty for rape is not wholly unanimous among state legislatures, but it obviously weighs very heavily on the side of rejecting capital punishment as a suitable penalty for raping an adult woman.

B

It was also observed in *Gregg* that "[t]he jury... is a significant and reliable objective index of contemporary values because it is so directly involved" and that it is thus important to look to the sentencing decisions that juries have made in the course of assessing whether capital punishment is an appropriate penalty for the crime being tried. * * *

According to the factual submissions in this Court, out of all rape convictions in Georgia since 1973... 63 cases had been reviewed by the Georgia Supreme Court as of the time of oral argument; and of these, 6 involved a death sentence, 1 of which was set aside, leaving 5 convicted rapists now under sentence of death in the State of Georgia. Georgia juries have thus sentenced rapists to death six times since 1973. This obviously is not a negligible number; and the State argues that as a practical matter juries simply reserve the extreme sanction for extreme cases of rape and that recent experience surely does not prove that jurors consider the death penalty to be a disproportionate punishment for every conceivable instance of rape, no matter how aggravated. Nevertheless, it is true that in the vast majority of cases, at least 9 out of 10, juries have not imposed the death sentence.

IV

These recent events evidencing the attitude of state legislatures and sentencing juries do not wholly determine this controversy, for the Constitution contemplates that in the end our own judgment will be brought to bear on the question of the acceptability of the death penalty under the Eighth Amendment. Nevertheless, the legislative rejection of capital punishment for rape strongly confirms our own judgment, which is that death is indeed a disproportionate penalty for the crime of raping an adult woman. * * *

Rape is without doubt deserving of serious punishment; but in terms of moral depravity and of the injury to the person and to the public, it does not compare with murder, which does involve the unjustified taking of human life. Although it may be accompanied by another crime, rape by definition does not include the death of or even the serious injury to another person. The murderer kills; the rapist, if no more than that, does not. Life is over for the victim of the murderer; for the rape victim, life may not be nearly so happy as it was, but it is not over and normally is not beyond repair. We have the abiding conviction that the death penalty, which "is unique in its severity and irrevocability," is an excessive penalty for the rapist who, as such, does not take human life. * * *

The judgment of the Georgia Supreme Court upholding the death sentence is reversed, and the case is remanded to that court for further proceedings not inconsistent with this opinion.

So ordered.

MR. CHIEF JUSTICE BURGER, with whom MR. JUSTICE REHNQUIST joins, dissenting.

*   *   *
(1)

On December 5, 1971, the petitioner, Ehrlich Anthony Coker, raped and then stabbed to death a young woman. Less than eight months later Coker kidnaped a second young woman. After twice raping this 16-year-old victim, he stripped her, severely beat her with a club, and dragged her into a wooded area where he left her for dead. He was apprehended and pleaded guilty to offenses stemming from these incidents. He was sentenced by three separate courts to three life terms, two 20-year terms, and one 8-year term of imprisonment. Each judgment specified that the sentences it imposed were to run consecutively rather than concurrently. Approximately 1 1/2 years later, on September 2, 1974, petitioner escaped from the state prison where he was serving these sentences. He promptly raped another 16-year-old woman in the presence of her husband, abducted her from her home, and threatened her with death and serious bodily harm. It is this crime for which the sentence now under review was imposed.

The Court today holds that the State of Georgia may not impose the death penalty on Coker. In so doing, it prevents the State from imposing any effective punishment upon Coker for his latest rape. The Court's holding, moreover, bars Georgia from guaranteeing its citizens that they will suffer no further attacks by this habitual rapist. In fact, given the lengthy sentences Coker must serve for the crimes he has already committed, the Court's holding assures that petitioner - as well as others in his position - will henceforth feel no compunction whatsoever about committing further rapes as frequently as he may be able to escape from confinement and indeed even within the walls of the prison itself. To what extent we have left States "elbow-room" to protect innocent persons from depraved human beings like Coker remains in doubt. * * *

Unlike the plurality, I would narrow the inquiry in this case to the question actually presented: Does the Eighth Amendment's ban against cruel and unusual punishment prohibit the State of Georgia from executing a person who has, within the space of three years, raped three separate women, killing one and attempting to kill another, who is serving prison terms exceeding his probable lifetime and who has not hesitated to escape confinement at the first available opportunity? Whatever one's view may be as to the State's constitutional power to impose the death penalty upon a rapist who stands before a court convicted for the first time, this case reveals a chronic rapist whose continuing danger to the community is abundantly clear. * * *

[O]nce the Court has held that "the punishment of death does not invariably violate the Constitution," *Gregg v. Georgia,* it seriously impinges upon the State's legislative judgment to hold that it may not impose such sentence upon an individual who has shown total and repeated disregard for the welfare, safety, personal integrity, and human worth of others, and who seemingly cannot be deterred from continuing such conduct. I therefore would hold that the death sentence here imposed is within the power reserved to the State and leave for another day the question of whether such sanction would be proper under other circumstances. * * *

[The concurring opinions of JUSTICE BRENNAN and JUSTICE MARSHALL have been omitted.]

Note

Since *Coker v. Georgia*, two states, Louisiana and Georgia, have passed legislation making it a capital offense to rape a child under the age of 12. Michael Higgins, *Is Capital Punishment for Killers Only? State Seeks Death Penalty Against Child Rapists, Raising Constitutional Questions*, 83 A.B.A. J. 30 (1997). The U.S. Supreme Court has not yet decided whether imposing the death penalty for child rape violates the Eighth Amendment's prohibition against cruel and unusual punishment. Is the rape of a child more heinous than the rape of an adult woman, thus justifying the death penalty? Should death ever be allowed as punishment for a crime that does not involve the killing of a human being?

In response to the Douglas-Stewart-White position in *Furman* that juries' standardless exercise of discretion in the decision to impose capital punishment is a violation of the cruel and unusual punishment clause, some states eliminated jury discretion altogether. For instance, North Carolina amended its homicide law to impose the death penalty for all those convicted of first degree murder. This scheme was struck down by the Supreme Court in *Woodson v. North Carolina*, 428 U.S. 280, 96 S.Ct. 2978, 49 L.Ed.2d 944 (1976). According to the Court, this scheme did not successfully avoid the unfettered discretion problem, because the choice to convict a defendant of first-degree versus second-degree murder was still essentially standardless. In addition, according to the Court, the North Carolina approach failed to "allow the particularized consideration of relevant aspects of the character and record of each convicted defendant before the imposition upon him of a sentence of death;" and this, too, was a constitutional violation.

The states that sought to reinstate the death penalty eventually settled on the procedures set forth in the Model Penal Code as a way to balance the interest in constraints on discretion with the interest in individualized treatment. Under the Model Penal Code system, capital trials are bifurcated into a guilt phase and a punishment phase. *See* Model Penal Code § 210.6(2). In the punishment phase, the jury decides whether death should be imposed by reference to statutorily prescribed "mitigating" and "aggravating" factors. *See* Model Penal Code § 210.6(3) and § 210.6(4). This scheme was approved by the Court in *Gregg v. Georgia*, handed down the same day as *Woodson*. 428 U.S. 153, 96 S.Ct. 2909, 49 L.Ed.2d 859 (1976).

At least one Justice subsequently lost faith in the Model Penal Code system as a way to balance the constitutional requirements of individualized treatment and guided discretion. In *Callins v. Collins*, 510 U.S. 1141, 114 S.Ct. 1127, 127 L.Ed.2d 435 (1994), a case in which the Court denied a petition for writ of certiorari by a death row inmate, Justice Blackmun wrote:

Twenty years have passed since this Court declared that the death penalty must be imposed fairly, and with reasonable consistency, or not at all, and, despite the effort of the States and courts to devise legal formulas and procedural rules to meet this daunting challenge, the death penalty remains fraught with arbitrariness, discrimination, caprice, and mistake. This is not to say that the problems with the death penalty today are identical to those that were present 20 years ago. Rather, the problems that were pursued down one hole with procedural rules and verbal formulas have come to the surface somewhere else, just as virulent and pernicious as they were in their original form. Experience has taught us that the constitutional goal of eliminating arbitrariness and discrimination from the administration of death, can never be achieved without compromising an equally essential component of fundamental fairness – individualized sentencing. * * *

From this day forward, I no longer shall tinker with the machinery of death.

Justice Blackmun retired from the Court several months later.

EWING v. CALIFORNIA
Supreme Court of the United States
538 U.S. 11, 123 S.Ct. 1179, 155 L.Ed.2d 108 (2003)

JUSTICE O'CONNOR announced the judgment of the Court and delivered an opinion in which THE CHIEF JUSTICE and JUSTICE KENNEDY join.

In this case, we decide whether the Eighth Amendment prohibits the State of California from sentencing a repeat felon to a prison term of 25 years to life under the State's "Three Strikes and You're Out" law.

I

A

California's three strikes law reflects a shift in the State's sentencing policies toward incapacitating and deterring repeat offenders who threaten the public safety. The law was designed "to ensure longer prison sentences and greater punishment for those who commit a felony and have been previously convicted of serious and/or violent felony offenses." * * *

B

California's current three strikes law consists of two virtually identical statutory schemes "designed to increase the prison terms of repeat felons." When a defendant is convicted of a felony, and he has previously been convicted of one or more prior felonies defined as "serious" or "violent" in Cal. Penal Code Ann. §§ 667.5 and 1192.7, sentencing is conducted pursuant to the three strikes law. Prior convictions must be alleged in the charging document, and the defendant has a right to a jury determination that the prosecution has proved the prior convictions beyond a reasonable doubt.

If the defendant has one prior "serious" or "violent" felony conviction, he must be sentenced to "twice the term otherwise provided as punishment for the current felony conviction." If the defendant has two or more prior "serious" or "violent" felony convictions, he must receive "an indeterminate term of life imprisonment." Defendants sentenced to life under the three strikes law become eligible for parole on a date calculated by reference to a "minimum term," which is the greater of (a) three times the term otherwise provided for the current conviction, (b) 25 years, or (c) the term determined by the court pursuant to § 1170 for the underlying conviction, including any enhancements.

Under California law, certain offenses may be classified as either felonies or misdemeanors. These crimes are known as "wobblers." Some crimes that would otherwise be misdemeanors become "wobblers" because of the defendant's prior record. For example, petty theft, a misdemeanor, becomes a "wobbler" when the defendant has previously served a prison term for committing specified theft-related crimes. Other crimes, such as grand theft, are "wobblers" regardless of the defendant's prior record. Both types of "wobblers" are triggering offenses under the three strikes law only when they are treated as felonies. Under California law, a "wobbler" is presumptively a felony and "remains a felony except when the discretion is actually exercised" to make the crime a misdemeanor.

In California, prosecutors may exercise their discretion to charge a "wobbler" as either a felony or a misdemeanor. Likewise, California trial courts have discretion to reduce a "wobbler" charged as a felony to a misdemeanor either before preliminary examination or at sentencing to avoid imposing a three strikes sentence. In exercising this discretion, the court may consider "those factors that direct similar sentencing decisions," such as "the nature and circumstances of the offense, the defendant's appreciation of and attitude toward the offense, . . . [and] the general objectives of sentencing."

California trial courts can also vacate allegations of prior "serious" or "violent" felony convictions, either on motion by the prosecution or *sua sponte*. In ruling whether to vacate allegations of prior felony convictions, courts consider whether, "in light of the nature and circumstances of [the defendant's] present felonies and prior serious and/or violent felony convictions, and the particulars of his background, character, and prospects, the defendant may be deemed outside the [three strikes] scheme's spirit, in whole or in part." Thus, trial courts may avoid imposing a three strikes sentence in two ways: first, by reducing "wobblers" to misdemeanors (which do not qualify as triggering offenses), and second, by vacating allegations of prior "serious" or "violent" felony convictions.

C

On parole from a 9-year prison term, petitioner Gary Ewing walked into the pro shop of the El Segundo Golf Course in Los Angeles County on March 12, 2000. He walked out with three golf clubs, priced at $399 apiece, concealed in his pants leg. A shop employee, whose suspicions were aroused when he observed Ewing limp out of the pro shop, telephoned the police. The police apprehended Ewing in the parking lot.

Ewing is no stranger to the criminal justice system. In 1984, at the age of 22, he pleaded guilty to theft. The court sentenced him to six months in jail (suspended), three years' probation, and a $300 fine. In 1988, he was convicted of felony grand theft auto and sentenced to one year in jail and three years' probation. After Ewing completed probation, however, the sentencing court reduced the crime to a misdemeanor, permitted Ewing to withdraw his guilty plea, and dismissed the case. In 1990, he was convicted of petty theft with a prior and sentenced to 60 days in the county jail and three years' probation. In 1992, Ewing was convicted of battery and sentenced to 30 days in the county jail and two years' summary probation. One month later, he was convicted of theft and sentenced to 10 days in the county jail and 12 months' probation. In January 1993, Ewing was convicted of burglary and sentenced to 60 days in the county jail and one year's summary probation. In February 1993, he was convicted of possessing drug paraphernalia and sentenced to six months in the county jail and three years' probation. In July 1993, he was convicted of appropriating lost property and sentenced to 10 days in the county jail and two years' summary probation. In September 1993, he was convicted of unlawfully possessing a firearm and trespassing and sentenced to 30 days in the county jail and one year's probation.

In October and November 1993, Ewing committed three burglaries and one robbery at a Long Beach, California, apartment complex over a 5-week period. He awakened one of his victims, asleep on her living room sofa, as he tried to disconnect her video cassette recorder from the television in that room. When she screamed, Ewing ran out the front door. On another occasion, Ewing accosted a victim in the mailroom of the apartment complex. Ewing claimed to have a gun and ordered the victim to hand over his wallet. When the victim resisted, Ewing produced a knife and forced the victim back to the apartment itself. While Ewing rifled through the bedroom, the victim fled the apartment screaming for help. Ewing absconded with the victim's money and credit cards.

On December 9, 1993, Ewing was arrested on the premises of the apartment complex for trespassing and lying to a police officer. The knife used in the robbery and a glass cocaine pipe were later found in the back seat of the patrol car used to transport Ewing to the police station. A jury convicted Ewing of first-degree robbery and three counts of residential burglary. Sentenced to nine years and eight months in prison, Ewing was paroled in 1999.

Only 10 months later, Ewing stole the golf clubs at issue in this case. He was charged with, and ultimately convicted of, one count of felony grand theft of personal property in excess of $ 400. As required by the three strikes law, the prosecutor formally alleged, and the trial court later found, that Ewing had been convicted previously of four serious or violent felonies for the three burglaries and the robbery in the Long Beach apartment complex.

At the sentencing hearing, Ewing asked the court to reduce the conviction for grand theft, a "wobbler" under California law, to a misdemeanor so as to avoid a three strikes sentence. Ewing also asked the trial court to exercise its discretion to dismiss the allegations of some or all of his prior serious or violent felony convictions, again for purposes of avoiding a three strikes sentence. Before sentencing Ewing, the trial court took note of his entire criminal history, including the fact that he was on parole when he committed his latest offense. The court also heard arguments from defense counsel and a plea from Ewing himself.

In the end, the trial judge determined that the grand theft should remain a felony. The court also ruled that the four prior strikes for the three burglaries and the robbery in Long Beach should stand. As a newly convicted felon with two or more "serious" or "violent" felony convictions in his past, Ewing was sentenced under the three strikes law to 25 years to life.

The California Court of Appeal affirmed in an unpublished opinion. Relying on our decision in *Rummel v. Estelle,* the court rejected Ewing's claim that his sentence was grossly disproportionate under the Eighth Amendment. Enhanced sentences under recidivist statutes like the three strikes law, the court reasoned, serve the "legitimate goal" of deterring and incapacitating repeat offenders. The Supreme Court of California denied Ewing's petition for review, and we granted certiorari. We now affirm.

II

A

The Eighth Amendment, which forbids cruel and unusual punishments, contains a "narrow proportionality principle" that "applies to noncapital sentences." We have most recently addressed the proportionality principle as applied to terms of years in a series of cases beginning with *Rummel v. Estelle.*

In *Rummel*, we held that it did not violate the Eighth Amendment for a State to sentence a three-time offender to life in prison with the possibility of parole. Like Ewing, Rummel was sentenced to a lengthy prison term under a recidivism statute. Rummel's two prior offenses were a 1964 felony for "fraudulent use of a credit card to obtain $ 80 worth of goods or services," and a 1969 felony conviction for "passing a forged check in the amount of $ 28.36." His triggering offense was a conviction for felony theft – "obtaining $ 120.75 by false pretenses."

This Court ruled that "having twice imprisoned him for felonies, Texas was entitled to place upon Rummel the onus of one who is simply unable to bring his conduct within the social norms prescribed by the criminal law of the State." The recidivism statute "is nothing more than a societal decision that when such a person commits yet another felony, he should be subjected to the admittedly serious penalty of incarceration for life, subject only to the State's judgment as to whether to grant him parole." We noted that this Court "has on occasion stated that the Eighth Amendment prohibits imposition of a sentence that is grossly disproportionate to the severity of the crime." But "outside the context of capital punishment, successful challenges to the proportionality of particular sentences have been exceedingly rare."

Although we stated that the proportionality principle "would . . . come into play in the extreme example . . . if a legislature made overtime parking a felony punishable by life imprisonment," we held that "the mandatory life sentence imposed upon this petitioner does not constitute cruel and unusual punishment under the Eighth and Fourteenth Amendments." * * *

Three years after *Rummel*, in *Solem v. Helm,* 463 U.S. 277 (1983), we held that the Eighth Amendment prohibited "a life sentence without possibility of parole for a seventh nonviolent felony." The triggering offense in *Solem* was "uttering a 'no account' check for $100." We specifically stated that the Eighth Amendment's ban on cruel and unusual punishments "prohibits . . . sentences that are disproportionate to the crime committed," and that the "constitutional principle of proportionality has been recognized explicitly in this Court for almost a century." The *Solem* Court then explained that three factors may be relevant to a determination of whether a sentence is so disproportionate that it violates the Eighth Amendment: "(i) the gravity of the offense and the harshness of the penalty; (ii) the sentences imposed on other criminals in the same jurisdiction; and (iii) the sentences imposed for commission of the same crime in other jurisdictions."

Applying these factors in *Solem*, we struck down the defendant's sentence of life without parole. We specifically noted the contrast between that sentence and the sentence in *Rummel*, pursuant to which the defendant was eligible for parole. Indeed, we explicitly declined to overrule *Rummel*: "Our conclusion today is not inconsistent with *Rummel* v. *Estelle*."

Eight years after *Solem*, we grappled with the proportionality issue again in *Harmelin v. Michigan*. *Harmelin* was not a recidivism case, but rather involved a first-time offender convicted of possessing 672 grams of cocaine. He was sentenced to life in prison without possibility of parole. A majority of the Court rejected Harmelin's claim that his sentence was so grossly disproportionate that it violated the Eighth Amendment. The Court, however, could not agree on why his proportionality argument failed. JUSTICE SCALIA, joined by THE CHIEF JUSTICE, wrote that the proportionality principle was "an aspect of our death penalty jurisprudence, rather than a generalizable aspect of Eighth Amendment law." He would thus have declined to apply gross disproportionality principles except in reviewing capital sentences.

JUSTICE KENNEDY, joined by two other Members of the Court, concurred in part and concurred in the judgment. JUSTICE KENNEDY specifically recognized that "the Eighth Amendment proportionality principle also applies to noncapital sentences." He then identified four principles of proportionality review – "the primacy of the legislature, the variety of legitimate penological schemes, the nature of our federal system, and the requirement that proportionality review be guided by objective factors" – that "inform the final one: The Eighth Amendment does not require strict proportionality between crime and sentence. Rather, it forbids only extreme sentences that are 'grossly disproportionate' to the crime." JUSTICE KENNEDY'S concurrence also stated that *Solem* "did not mandate" comparative analysis "within and between jurisdictions."

The proportionality principles in our cases distilled in JUSTICE KENNEDY'S concurrence guide our application of the Eighth Amendment in the new context that we are called upon to consider.

B

For many years, most States have had laws providing for enhanced sentencing of repeat offenders. Yet between 1993 and 1995, three strikes laws effected a sea change in criminal sentencing throughout the Nation. These laws responded to widespread public concerns about crime by targeting the class of offenders who pose the greatest threat to public safety: career criminals. As one of the chief architects of California's three strikes law has explained: "Three Strikes was intended to go beyond simply making sentences tougher. It was intended to be a focused effort to create a sentencing policy that would use the judicial system to reduce serious and violent crime."

Throughout the States, legislatures enacting three strikes laws made a deliberate policy choice that individuals who have repeatedly engaged in serious or violent criminal behavior, and whose conduct has not been deterred by more conventional approaches to punishment, must be isolated from society in order to protect the public safety. Though three strikes laws may be relatively new, our tradition of deferring to state legislatures in making and implementing such important policy decisions is longstanding.

Our traditional deference to legislative policy choices finds a corollary in the principle that the Constitution "does not mandate adoption of any one penological theory." A sentence can have a variety of justifications, such as incapacitation, deterrence, retribution, or rehabilitation. Some or all of these justifications may play a role in a State's sentencing scheme. Selecting the sentencing rationales is generally a policy choice to be made by state legislatures, not federal courts.

When the California Legislature enacted the three strikes law, it made a judgment that protecting the public safety requires incapacitating criminals who have already been convicted of at least one serious or violent crime. Nothing in the Eighth Amendment prohibits California from making that choice. To the contrary, our cases establish that "States have a valid interest in deterring and segregating habitual criminals." Recidivism has long been recognized as a legitimate basis for increased punishment.

California's justification is no pretext. Recidivism is a serious public safety concern in California and throughout the Nation. According to a recent report, approximately 67 percent of former inmates released from state prisons were charged with at least one "serious" new crime within three years of their release. In particular, released property offenders like Ewing had higher recidivism rates than those released after committing violent, drug, or public-order offenses. * * *

The State's interest in deterring crime also lends some support to the three strikes law. We have long viewed both incapacitation and deterrence as rationales for recidivism statutes: "[A] recidivist statute['s] . . . primary goals are to deter repeat offenders and, at some point in the life of one who repeatedly commits criminal offenses serious enough to be punished as felonies, to segregate that person from the rest of society for an extended period of time." Four years after the passage of California's three strikes law, the recidivism rate of parolees returned to prison for the commission of a new crime dropped by nearly 25 percent. Even more dramatically:

> [A]n unintended but positive consequence of 'Three Strikes' has been the impact on parolees leaving the state. More California parolees are now leaving the state than parolees from other jurisdictions entering California. This striking turnaround started in 1994. It was the first time more parolees left the state than entered since 1976. This trend has continued and in 1997 more than 1,000 net parolees left California.

To be sure, California's three strikes law has sparked controversy. Critics have doubted the law's wisdom, cost-efficiency, and effectiveness in reaching its goals. This criticism is appropriately directed at the legislature, which has primary responsibility for making the difficult policy choices that underlie any criminal sentencing scheme. We do not sit as a "superlegislature" to second-guess these policy choices. It is enough that the State of California has a reasonable basis for believing that dramatically enhanced sentences for habitual felons "advances the goals of [its] criminal justice system in any substantial way."

III

Against this backdrop, we consider Ewing's claim that his three strikes sentence of 25 years to life is unconstitutionally disproportionate to his offense of "shoplifting three golf clubs." We first address the gravity of the offense compared to the harshness of the penalty.[a] At the threshold, we note that Ewing incorrectly frames the issue. The gravity of his offense was not merely "shoplifting three golf clubs." Rather, Ewing was convicted of felony grand theft for stealing nearly $1,200 worth of merchandise after previously having been convicted of at least two "violent" or "serious" felonies. Even standing alone, Ewing's theft should not be taken lightly. His crime was certainly not "one of the most passive felonies a person could commit." To the contrary, the Supreme Court of California has noted the "seriousness" of grand theft in the context of proportionality review. Theft of $1,200 in property is a felony under federal law and in the vast majority of States.

---

[a]Justice O'Connor's opinion addresses only one of the three factors outlined in *Solem v. Helm*, the gravity of the offense and the harshness of the penalty. O'Connor does not go on to compare Ewing's sentence to sentences imposed on other criminals in California, nor does she compare Ewing's sentence to sentences imposed for commission of the same crime in other jurisdictions. Justice Kennedy, concurring in *Harmelin v. Michigan*, expressed the view that such comparative analysis is not mandatory.

That grand theft is a "wobbler" under California law is of no moment. Though California courts have discretion to reduce a felony grand theft charge to a misdemeanor, it remains a felony for all purposes "unless and until the trial court imposes a misdemeanor sentence." * * * In Ewing's case, however, the trial judge justifiably exercised her discretion not to extend such lenient treatment given Ewing's long criminal history.

In weighing the gravity of Ewing's offense, we must place on the scales not only his current felony, but also his long history of felony recidivism. Any other approach would fail to accord proper deference to the policy judgments that find expression in the legislature's choice of sanctions. In imposing a three strikes sentence, the State's interest is not merely punishing the offense of conviction, or the "triggering" offense: "It is in addition the interest . . . in dealing in a harsher manner with those who by repeated criminal acts have shown that they are simply incapable of conforming to the norms of society as established by its criminal law." To give full effect to the State's choice of this legitimate penological goal, our proportionality review of Ewing's sentence must take that goal into account.

Ewing's sentence is justified by the State's public-safety interest in incapacitating and deterring recidivist felons, and amply supported by his own long, serious criminal record. Ewing has been convicted of numerous misdemeanor and felony offenses, served nine separate terms of incarceration, and committed most of his crimes while on probation or parole. His prior "strikes" were serious felonies including robbery and three residential burglaries. To be sure, Ewing's sentence is a long one. But it reflects a rational legislative judgment, entitled to deference, that offenders who have committed serious or violent felonies and who continue to commit felonies must be incapacitated. The State of California "was entitled to place upon [Ewing] the onus of one who is simply unable to bring his conduct within the social norms prescribed by the criminal law of the State."

We hold that Ewing's sentence of 25 years to life in prison, imposed for the offense of felony grand theft under the three strikes law, is not grossly disproportionate and therefore does not violate the Eighth Amendment's prohibition on cruel and unusual punishments. The judgment of the California Court of Appeal is affirmed.

It is so ordered.

Justice SCALIA, concurring.

In my opinion in *Harmelin v. Michigan* [501 U.S. 957, 984, 985, 111 S.Ct. 2680, 115 L.Ed.2d 836 (1991)], I concluded that the Eighth Amendment's prohibition of "cruel and unusual punishments" was aimed at excluding only certain modes of punishment, and was not a "guarantee against disproportionate sentences." Out of respect for the principle of stare decisis, I might nonetheless accept the contrary holding of *Solem v. Helm* --that the Eighth Amendment contains a narrow proportionality principle -- if I felt I could intelligently apply it. This case demonstrates why I cannot.

Proportionality -- the notion that the punishment should fit the crime -- is inherently a concept tied to the penological goal of retribution. "[I]t becomes difficult even to speak intelligently of 'proportionality,' once deterrence and rehabilitation are given significant weight," -- not to mention giving weight to the purpose of California's three strikes law: incapacitation. In the present case, the game is up once the plurality has acknowledged that "the Constitution does not mandate adoption of any one penological theory," and that a "sentence can have a variety of justifications, such as incapacitation, deterrence, retribution, or rehabilitation." That acknowledgment having been made, it no longer suffices merely to assess "the gravity of the offense compared to the harshness of the penalty;" that classic description of the proportionality principle (alone and in itself quite resistant to policy-free, legal analysis) now becomes merely the "first" step of the inquiry. Having completed that step (by a discussion which, in all fairness, does not convincingly establish that 25-years-to-life is a "proportionate" punishment for stealing three golf clubs), the plurality must then add an analysis to show that "Ewing's sentence is justified by the State's public-safety interest in incapacitating and deterring recidivist felons."

Which indeed it is -- though why that has anything to do with the principle of proportionality is a mystery. Perhaps the plurality should revise its terminology, so that what it reads into the Eighth Amendment is not the unstated proposition that all punishment should be reasonably proportionate to the gravity of the offense, but rather the unstated proposition that all punishment should reasonably pursue the multiple purposes of the criminal law. That formulation would make it clearer than ever, of course, that the plurality is not applying law but evaluating policy.

Because I agree that petitioner's sentence does not violate the Eighth Amendment's prohibition against cruel and unusual punishments, I concur in the judgment.

[The concurring opinion of JUSTICE THOMAS and the dissents of JUSTICES STEVENS and BREYER, joined by JUSTICES SOUTER and GINSBURG, have been omitted.]

RAMIREZ v. CASTRO

United States Court of Appeals for the Ninth Circuit

365 F.3d 755 (9th Cir. 2004)

WARDLAW, Circuit Judge:

The State of California through its Attorney General, Bill Lockyer, appeals from the district court's judgment granting a writ of habeas corpus to petitioner Isaac Ramirez on the grounds that (1) his 25-years-to-life sentence under California's "Three Strikes" law violated his Eighth Amendment right to be free from cruel and unusual punishment, and (2) the California Court of Appeal's decision to the contrary was objectively unreasonable under 28 U.S.C. § 2254(d)(1). We have jurisdiction under 28 U.S.C. §§ 1291 and 2253, and we affirm the district court.

In May 1996, Ramirez was caught walking out of a Sears department store in broad daylight carrying a $199 VCR for which he had not paid. He immediately surrendered to authorities and returned the VCR; the encounter was without violence. For this crime, prosecutors could have charged Ramirez with a petty theft misdemeanor, punishable by up to six months in county jail. Instead, prosecutors chose to use two nonviolent shoplifting offenses to which Ramirez pleaded guilty in 1991, for both of which he served one sentence of just over six months in county jail, to charge him with one count of petty theft with a prior theft-related conviction, a "wobbler" offense in California punishable as a felony.

That exercise of prosecutorial discretion had grave consequences for Ramirez. After he was convicted of this "wobbler" felony, the jury found that Ramirez's 1991 "robbery" convictions were "strikes" for purposes of California's Three Strikes law enacted in 1994. The trial court thereafter denied Ramirez's motion to strike one or both of his two prior shoplifts, even though it had indicated before trial that it was inclined to do so, and sentenced Ramirez to 25 years to life in prison, with no eligibility for parole until he had served 25 years. The California Court of Appeal affirmed the sentence.

The sentence imposed upon Ramirez for his three shoplifting offenses is more severe than the sentence he would have faced had any one of his three crimes been murder, manslaughter, or rape. Considering the objective factors of this case and performing the fact-specific analysis of Ramirez's criminal history as we are required to do under Supreme Court precedent, we hold that this is an "exceedingly rare" case in which the sentence imposed is grossly disproportionate to the crimes committed, in violation of the Eighth Amendment.
* * *

I

* * * On October 9, 1991, a criminal complaint was filed in Orange County, California charging Ramirez with two counts of second-degree robbery, i.e., willfully and unlawfully taking personal property "by means of force and fear" in violation of Penal Code §§ 211, 212.5(c), and 213(a)(2), a "serious felony" under § 1192.7(c)(19). Each count was punishable by a prison term of two, three, or five years. The first count was for a January 1991 shoplift of merchandise from a Lucky's grocery store, for which Ramirez's older sister was also charged with second-degree commercial burglary. The only "force" related to the offense was that the getaway car, driven by a third person, ran over a security guard's foot causing a "minor injury." The second count was for a September 1991 shoplift at a K-Mart department store. The only "force" related to that offense was that Ramirez pushed a security guard away with his open hand as he was running out of the store. Neither incident involved weapons or violence in furtherance of the crime.

Prosecutors offered Ramirez a plea bargain, pursuant to which he would be sentenced to one year in county jail and three years of probation in exchange for his guilty plea to the two felony counts. They allegedly told Ramirez that if he did not take the plea his sister would be sentenced to five years in prison. On October 22, 1991, Ramirez took the plea. By doing so, he could not have agreed to put two "strikes" on his record, as California did not enact its Three Strikes law until more than two and one-half years later. Ramirez was released after serving six months and 20 days in county jail; he completed his probationary period without incident.

B

After years without any contact with law enforcement, on May 5, 1996, Ramirez shoplifted a $199 VCR from a Sears department store in Montclair, California by placing the VCR in a box, sealing the box with store security tape previously obtained from a friend, and walking out of the store. There was no report of any force or violence associated with the offense. Indeed, when the authorities approached him in the Montclair Plaza parking lot, Ramirez surrendered without resistance, admitted his crime, and returned the VCR. When asked why he had tried to steal the VCR, Ramirez replied, "I don't know. I did something stupid."

For this shoplift of merchandise valued under $400, Ramirez could have been charged with petty theft, a misdemeanor offense punishable by a maximum sentence of six months in jail. Instead, San Bernardino County prosecutors charged Ramirez with one count of petty theft with a prior theft-related conviction under § 666. In light of his two prior "serious felony" convictions under § 1192.7,[2] a conviction for this "wobbler" felony offense would bring Ramirez within the scope of California's Three Strikes law, exposing him to a possible sentence of 25 years to life in prison.[3] The "wobbler" offense would be treated as a felony unless and until either the prosecution decided to charge it as a misdemeanor, or the trial court reduced it to a misdemeanor at the preliminary hearing or at sentencing to avoid application of the Three Strikes law.

Ramirez's trial began on January 27, 1997, and the jury convicted him on January 28, 1997. On January 29, 1997, in a bifurcated proceeding, a jury found true the allegations that Ramirez suffered two prior serious felony "strikes." The trial court then held a sentencing hearing and considered Ramirez's renewed motion to strike one or both of his priors. Were the court to strike one of his priors, his maximum sentence for the instant offense would have been "twice the term otherwise provided as punishment for the current felony conviction," or six years in prison.

At the hearing, Ramirez admitted committing the petty theft of the VCR, but stated that a sentence of 25 years to life in prison was too severe. He told the sentencing judge that he had worked hard since his 1991 offenses to turn his life around, purchasing two businesses, attending school, receiving certificates in parenting and substance abuse, and establishing child support and visitation. Despite his efforts, his wife lost her job, he lost both businesses and his home, and he was forced to file for bankruptcy. His attorney described Ramirez's nonviolent petty theft of the VCR as "a simple situation of backslide." With respect to the 1991 K-Mart offense, Ramirez admitted that he "may have pushed the gentleman away to run" but stated he did not commit "any violent act" and was not "a violent person." He told the judge that "you're sentencing my children as well because they [will] feel the pain," and that he had already paid the price for the 1991 offenses by serving almost a year in jail for those crimes. Ramirez said even a six-year prison sentence for the instant offense would be "too much."

The judge denied Ramirez's motion to strike, reasoning:

---

[2] In 1996, Ramirez's prior second-degree robbery convictions were not "violent" felonies for purposes of a Three Strikes sentence, as only first-degree robbery was then so defined. In 2000, well after Ramirez was convicted and sentenced, the Three Strikes law was amended such that "any robbery" is now a "violent felony" for purposes of a Three Strikes sentence.

[3] For purposes of a Three Strikes sentence, "[t]he fact that [the defendant's] prior convictions were adjudicated in a single proceeding does not mean that they constitute one prior conviction; two strikes can arise from one case."

I think possibly one of the problems is that we've treated theft offenses so lightly over the years, and there's just a whole lot of reasons for that, but it's come to the point where, I think, that many people have just decided it's no big deal, and Mr. Ramirez has indicated he thinks that even five or six years for this crime would be too much.

And in looking at your history, it seems that there has been a constant pattern, and the Court is just not confident that it won't continue to be a pattern. Yes, there was a five-year gap, but I also understand that part of that time Mr. Ramirez was out of the state, and I'm not going to assume that there's anything that happened that we didn't know about, but it seems that he came right back to it and committed this theft offense again, and the pattern, the priors were thefts from stores, they were shoplifts.

It just seems to be a constant pattern, and Mr. Ramirez indicates that he's straightened his life out, but it didn't seem to stop him from doing this crime. If this had just been a sudden impulse kind of thing, it would be different, but this was clearly planned, and there was a sophistication involved in bringing the [security] tape in and the way he planned out the picking up the box and walking out and looking around and the fact that he planned ahead. He was going to -- he had a buyer for the object already. I mean, what's happened is that Mr. Ramirez has become a professional thief, and it's just real clear from all the evidence.

I did indicate earlier that I had an intention to strike one of the priors prior to trial, but that was before I heard all the facts and realized the planning and sophistication that did go into this crime, and at this point I am not inclined to strike either or both of the priors.

Mr. Ramirez stated that I'm sentencing his children, but I'm not the one that's doing that. I'm afraid you're the one who did that when you committed this offense.

I know you didn't realize when you pled to those prior robberies that this would ultimately be the consequence, but there certainly was plenty of publicity about this law since it was passed, and you should have known better, but I think you just had the attitude that, like you said, interpreting what you said, that it was really no big deal, and I've really already paid enough for that theft, in other words, it was just some minor thing. Well, the People of the state has [sic] decided that it's not going to be a minor thing anymore if somebody continues to commit these crimes, and they've decided that the penalty should be 25 to life, and I think the circumstances in this case fit that, and I don't feel compelled to strike those priors.

The judge then sentenced Ramirez to 25 years to life in prison under the Three Strikes law, which required Ramirez to serve 25 years before he would become eligible for parole. He was incarcerated at Ironwood State Prison, a Security Level III facility for inmates with "several prior prison terms or significant behavioral problems." The court denied his subsequent motion for resentencing.

On direct appeal, Ramirez claimed, inter alia, that his sentence violated the Eighth Amendment's prohibition of cruel and unusual punishment. On September 8, 1998, the California Court of Appeal affirmed Ramirez's conviction and sentence in an unpublished, reasoned opinion. * * *

C

On May 24, 2000, Ramirez filed this habeas petition. On March 22, 2002, the magistrate judge filed its report and recommendation. Analyzing Ramirez's Eighth Amendment claim under *Harmelin v. Michigan*; *Solem v. Helm*; and *Rummel v. Estelle*, * * * the magistrate judge found that Ramirez's sentence: (1) raised an inference of gross disproportionality to the gravity of Ramirez's nonviolent offense, for which he would have received a sentence of one year in jail or three years in prison but for California's Three Strikes law; (2) was more severe than the sentences for most violent crimes in California, including second-degree murder, voluntary manslaughter, rape, and sexual assault on a minor, and, further, if Ramirez's prior convictions had been for these violent offenses instead of a theft-related offense, he would have received only six months in jail; and (3) was more severe than the sentence he would have received in any other state with the possible exception of Louisiana. * * *

On June 14, 2002, the district court adopted the magistrate's report and recommendation in its entirety. On June 17, 2002, the district court entered its judgment granting Ramirez a writ of habeas corpus and ordering his release from custody forthwith. On June 27, 2002, after serving nearly five and one-half years of his sentence, Ramirez was released from prison. He has lived in California under parole supervision for nearly two years without incident.

The State appealed. The parties completed their briefing on February 24, 2003, with Ramirez filing his answering brief in pro se. The matter was calendared for oral argument on July 18, 2003 in Pasadena, California. * * *

Ramirez told the Court that he had been a model inmate during his nearly six years in prison, receiving no write-ups and serving as an inmate representative. He said that he had benefitted from this time in prison, which he described as a "healing period," using it to free himself of addiction, to develop a deep and lasting spirituality, and to set his life on the right course. The State's counsel argued that Ramirez was a dangerous recidivist for whom the State had a strong interest in returning to prison for the remainder of his Three Strikes sentence. * * *

II

We review de novo a district court's decision to grant a petition for habeas corpus under 28 U.S.C. § 2254. We may affirm the decision to grant a petition "on any ground supported by the record, even if it differs from the rationale of the district court." * * *

III

[The court discusses *Rummel, Solem, Harmelin,* and *Ewing.*]

In *Andrade II,* the Supreme Court reversed a decision by a three-judge panel of our Court granting Andrade's petition for a writ of habeas corpus on the ground that his Three Strikes sentence violated the Eighth Amendment's gross disproportionality principle. Applying the AEDPA standard, the Supreme Court held the California Court of Appeal's decision affirming Andrade's sentence was neither contrary to, nor an unreasonable application of, clearly established federal law.

For stealing a total of $153 worth of videotapes from two different K-Mart department stores on separate occasions in November 1995, Andrade was sentenced, in light of his prior theft-related offenses, to two consecutive Three Strikes sentences of 25 years to life, with no eligibility for parole until he served 50 years in prison. Like the plurality in *Ewing,* the Court looked beyond Andrade's two most recent convictions to detail his extensive criminal history, during which he had been "in and out of state and federal prison since 1982."

In January 1982, [Andrade] was convicted of a misdemeanor theft offense and was sentenced to 6 days in jail with 12 months' probation. Andrade was arrested again in November 1982 for multiple counts of first-degree residential burglary. He pleaded guilty to at least three of those counts, and in April of the following year he was sentenced to 120 months in prison. In 1988, Andrade was convicted in federal court of transportation of marijuana and was sentenced to eight years in federal prison. In 1990, he was convicted in state court for a misdemeanor petty theft offense and was ordered to serve 180 days in jail. In September 1990, Andrade was convicted again in federal court for the same felony of transportation of marijuana and was sentenced to 2,191 days in federal prison. And in 1991, Andrade was arrested for a state parole violation -- escape from federal prison. He was paroled from the state penitentiary system in 1993.

As a threshold matter, the Court held that the "only relevant clearly established law" for purposes of its AEDPA review of the California Court of Appeal's decision rejecting Andrade's Eighth Amendment challenge was the "gross disproportionality principle" developed in *Rummel* and *Solem* and distilled in Justice Kennedy's concurrence in *Harmelin*, the "precise contours" of which "are unclear." The Court then held that the state court's decision was not contrary to these precedents because it had appropriately relied upon *Rummel* in affirming Andrade's sentence, and his case was not materially indistinguishable from either *Rummel* or *Solem*. Finally, the Supreme Court held the state court's decision was not an unreasonable application of these precedents because the proportionality principle affords legislatures broad discretion in determining appropriate sentences for recidivists, and it was not objectively unreasonable for the state court to decide in light of Andrade's criminal history that his sentence was not outside the "contours" of the proportionality principle and thus not the "extraordinary case" resulting in a sentence that violated the Eighth Amendment.

With all of these Supreme Court decisions in mind, we now turn to Ramirez's case.

IV

A

Unlike the Three Strikes sentences analyzed in *Ewing* and *Andrade II*, Ramirez's extreme sentence raises an inference of gross disproportionality when compared to the gravity of his most recent offense and criminal history.

That Ramirez's sentence is harsh is beyond any dispute. Indeed, it appears there are only two more severe sentences available to anyone convicted of a crime in California: life without the possibility of parole and death. Because the 25-year minimum of his indeterminate life sentence may not be reduced by credit for good behavior or working while in prison, Ramirez's "real time term" of 25 years in prison is more than twice the length of the real time term at issue in *Rummel*, where parole was available after 12 years. * * *

The question therefore is whether Ramirez's extreme sentence is justified by the gravity of his most recent offense and criminal history. We hold that it is not.

The core conduct of Ramirez's most recent offense, his nonviolent shoplift of a $199 VCR, is misdemeanor petty theft punishable by up to six months in county jail. Ramirez's offense was chargeable as a "wobbler" felony only by virtue of his prior theft-related conviction. While perhaps not "one of the most passive felonies a person could commit," Ramirez's nonviolent petty theft is nevertheless akin to the triggering felony in *Solem* (uttering a "no account" check for $100), and is easily distinguished from the offense triggering a life sentence in *Harmelin* (possession of over one and one-half pounds of cocaine). Because Ramirez's nonviolent shoplift did not "threaten[ ] to cause grave harm to society," it clearly would not by itself justify the sentence he received. But because Ramirez was sentenced as a recidivist under the Three Strikes law, "in weighing the gravity" of his offense in our proportionality analysis, "we must place on the scales not only his current felony," but also his criminal history.

Ramirez's prior criminal history is comprised solely of two 1991 convictions for second-degree robbery obtained through a single guilty plea, for which his total sentence was one year in county jail and three years probation. These second-degree robberies were "serious" felonies within the meaning of § 1192.7 (and thus for purposes of a Three Strikes sentence), but these crimes were nonviolent in nature. No weapons were involved in the offenses. The "force" reported in these shoplifting crimes -- the basis by which prosecutors could charge them as second-degree robberies -- was a "minor injury" caused when somebody else drove over the foot of a grocery store security guard, and that Ramirez pushed a K-Mart security guard out of his way as he fled the store. As the sentencing court initially and correctly found, these offenses are more accurately described as "confrontation petty theft and not really robbery, notwithstanding the convictions."

The true nature of these crimes is further reflected in the one-year jail sentence offered by prosecutors in exchange for Ramirez's guilty plea to the two felonies. Each count of second-degree robbery exposed Ramirez to a possible prison sentence of two, three, or five years. In California, only felonies are punishable by incarceration in state prison, while a misdemeanor is punishable by six months in county jail. Thus, the one-year jail sentence prosecutors offered, which is also the maximum Ramirez could have received were he instead charged and convicted of two counts of misdemeanor petty theft is not consistent with a desire to punish Ramirez's crimes as "serious felonies."

Moreover, this single, one-year jail sentence was the only period of incarceration ever imposed upon Ramirez prior to his Three Strikes sentence. Before receiving a sentence of 25 years to life in state prison, Ramirez had spent one period of six months and 20 days in county jail; he had never been sentenced to or served time in state prison.

The gravity of Ramirez's criminal history thus pales in comparison to the lengthy recidivist histories discussed above in *Solem, Ewing*, and *Andrade.* * * * Ramirez's criminal history is also minimal in comparison to the statewide averages for Three Strikes offenders recognized by the Supreme Court in Ewing. *See* 538 U.S. at 27-28, 123 S.Ct. 1179 (summarizing a 1996 Sacramento Bee study that found California's Three Strikes offenders averaged five prior felony convictions apiece with the vast majority -- about 84 percent -- having been convicted of at least one violent crime such as homicide, attempted murder, and sexual assault). * * *

We recognize that California's legislature has primacy and great latitude in determining appropriate punishment, and that California's Three Strikes law may serve the State's legitimate goals of incapacitating serious and violent recidivist criminals and deterring recidivist crime in California. But we find these state interests less compelling in this particular case, in which the "seriousness" of Ramirez's felony convictions is belied both by the nonviolent nature of those offenses and by the fact that the State offered Ramirez jail time instead of seeking to punish him with a sentence in state prison. Indeed, it is doubtful that California's Three Strikes law, passed largely in response to the infamous 1993 kidnaping and murder of 12-year-old Polly Klaas, was ever intended to apply to a nonviolent, three-time shoplifter such as Ramirez.

In any event, neither the "harm caused or threatened to the victim or society," nor the "absolute magnitude" of Ramirez's three shoplifts justifies the Three Strikes sentence in this case. These "objective factors" and those discussed above demonstrate that Ramirez's sentence is grossly disproportionate to the crimes he committed in violation of the Eighth Amendment. In other words, while a sentence of 25 years to life for felons with recidivist histories such as those in Ewing and Andrade does not violate the gross disproportionality principle, that sentence weighed against the gravity of Ramirez's offense raises an inference of gross disproportionality in light of the nature and paucity of his criminal history.

Because this is the extremely rare case that gives rise to an inference of gross disproportionality, we turn to a comparative analysis of Ramirez's sentence.

B

Under an intrajurisdictional analysis, we "compare the sentences imposed on other criminals in the same jurisdiction. If more serious crimes are subject to the same penalty, or to less serious penalties, that is some indication that the punishment at issue may be excessive." * * *

* * * California punishes far more serious and violent crimes much less severely than the Three Strikes sentence imposed upon Ramirez for his three shoplifting crimes. *See, e.g.,* § 190 (second-degree murder punishable by 15 years to life in prison); § 193 (voluntary manslaughter punishable by up to 11 years); § 264 (rape punishable by up to 8 years); § 288 (sexual assault on a minor punishable by up to 8 years). The availability of parole for prisoners convicted of these and other serious and violent offenses results in even less severe sentences. For example, the Board of Prison Terms regulations recommend that parole be made available after 19-21 years to a prisoner convicted of second-degree murder involving the most aggravated circumstances, e.g., "severe trauma inflicted with deadly intensity" such as "beating, clubbing, stabbing, strangulation" or "multiple wounds inflicted with a weapon" upon a victim that had "little or no personal relationship" with the prisoner or whose death occurred during a "robbery, rape, or other felony." * * *

The State argues that we should compare Ramirez's sentence to recidivist offenders sentenced under the Three Strikes law rather than first-time violent crime offenders, and that "when a proper comparison is made, it is apparent that [recidivist] defendants with more serious or violent triggering offenses are punished more harshly than Ramirez." Although we agree that comparison to other recidivist sentences is relevant, the State misses the point when it argues, for example, that a hypothetical defendant with two strikes would receive an even harsher Three Strikes sentence if that defendant used a firearm in his triggering offense. This hypothetical case is not relevant to our intrajurisdictional comparative analysis of Ramirez's sentence. What would be relevant is a case in which another defendant received a 25 years to life sentence after committing just three shoplifting crimes, or having spent only one brief period of incarceration in county jail for his "strikes," or having some similar minor criminal history. The State has not cited such a case and we have not found any.

Moreover, an internal policy memorandum dated December 19, 2000 from Los Angeles County District Attorney Steve Cooley to all Deputy District Attorneys in the County, which was attached as an exhibit to Attorney General Lockyer's declaration in this case, makes clear that Ramirez probably would not have faced a Three Strikes sentence at all if he had committed his petty VCR theft just a couple of years later, and on the other side of the San Bernardino/Los Angeles county line:

> The Three Strikes law, Penal Code §§ 1170.12(a)-(d), provides a powerful tool for obtaining life sentences in cases involving habitual criminal offenders. However, unless used judiciously, it also has the potential for injustice and abuse in the form of disproportionately harsh sentences for relatively minor crimes.

The Three Strikes statutory scheme appropriately authorizes the use of prosecutorial discretion in its implementation. As prosecutors, it is our legal and ethical obligation to exercise this discretion in a manner that assures proportionality, evenhanded application, predictability and consistency. Moreover, the potential for coercive plea-bargaining must be avoided. Penal Code Section 1170.12(d)(2) authorizes prosecutors to move to dismiss or strike a qualifying prior felony conviction in the furtherance of justice pursuant to Penal Code Section 1385. In this context, "in furtherance of justice" requires consideration of the constitutional rights of the defendant and the interests of society. [citations] Proper exercise of prosecutorial discretion protects society and preserves confidence in and respect for the criminal justice system.

Cf. Greg Krikorian, *Three-Strikes Law Has Little Effect, Study Says*, L.A. TIMES, Mar. 5, 2004, at B1. (recognizing that District Attorney Cooley declines to prosecute "most nonviolent offenses and lesser drug charges as third strikes," even though Los Angeles County generates approximately 40% of the Three Strikes cases in California).

Thus, our intrajurisdictional comparative analysis of Ramirez's sentence indicates that it is excessive for the crimes he has committed, which supports our conclusion that his sentence violates the gross disproportionality principle of the Eighth Amendment.

C

Under an interjurisdictional analysis, we "compare the sentences imposed for commission of the same crime in other jurisdictions." * * *

[The court discusses sentences in Rhode Island, Texas, West Virginia, and Louisiana for crimes similar to Ramirez's, and finds that "none of these states would have imposed a sentence upon Ramirez anywhere near as harsh as 25 years to life." The court further finds that "the maximum sentence Ramirez could have received under the United States Sentencing Guidelines, which also take into account the criminal history of a defendant, is seven months in prison -- a term that pales in comparison with his Three Strikes sentence."]

For all of the foregoing reasons, we believe the California Court of Appeal's determination that Ramirez's sentence did not violate the Eighth Amendment is incorrect. * * *

V

* * *

Ramirez's sentence of 25 years to life in prison is grossly disproportionate to the offenses he committed. The California Court of Appeal's decision to the contrary is an objectively unreasonable application of clearly established federal law because it erroneously characterizes and otherwise fails to consider the unique, objective factual circumstances of Ramirez's case. Because this is indeed the "exceedingly rare" case, Ramirez is entitled to habeas relief under 28 U.S.C. § 2254(d)(1).

AFFIRMED.

Note

Under ancient English common law, the writ of habeas corpus allowed any court to bring a person being held in jail or prison before it, in order to ensure that the detention or imprisonment was not illegal. In the United States, the writ of habeas corpus was incorporated into the federal criminal code at 28 U.S.C. §§ 2254 and 2255; it is most often employed in criminal cases post-conviction, in order to raise constitutional claims in the federal system after direct appeals through the state system have failed.

The Effective Death Penalty Act (AEDPA), signed into law by President Clinton in 1996 in the wake of the Oklahoma City bombing, dramatically heightened the standard for granting review under section 2254. Under AEDPA, in order to grant a review of post-conviction constitutional claims, a federal court must find "that the adjudication of the claim: (1) resulted in a decision that was contrary to, or involved unreasonable application of, clearly established Federal law, as determined by the Supreme Court of the United States; or (2) resulted in a decision that was based on an unreasonable determination of the facts in light of the evidence presented in the State court proceeding." 28 U.S.C. § 2254(d) (2002).

C.   EQUAL PROTECTION

The Equal Protection Clause of the Fourteenth Amendment (understood by the courts to apply to the federal government through the Fifth Amendment Due Process Clause) prohibits each state government from denying to "any person within its jurisdiction the equal protection of the laws." This clause has been interpreted by the courts to prohibit governments from treating people differently based on their race unless such treatment serves a "compelling state interest" and is "narrowly tailored" to serve that interest. (Discrimination based on gender is subjected to a slightly more generous standard.) This standard is commonly referred to as "strict scrutiny," because very few government actions can satisfy this stringent test.

Over the last few decades, however, the Supreme Court has applied this so-called "strict scrutiny" only to racial discrimination that is "intentional." Non-intentional conduct that results in people being treated differently on the basis of their race is subjected to a much lower level of scrutiny: In such cases, the court only asks if the state action has a "rational basis." *McCleskey v. Kemp* illustrates the Supreme Court's approach to the intent requirement in the context of criminal law. *State v. Russell* involves an equal protection challenge brought under Minnesota's state constitution, and reflects a different approach to rational basis review.

McCLESKEY v. KEMP
Supreme Court of the United States
481 U.S. 279, 107 S.Ct. 1756, 95 L.Ed.2d 262 (1987)

JUSTICE POWELL delivered the opinion of the Court.

* * *

I

McCleskey, a black man, was convicted of two counts of armed robbery and one count of murder in the Superior Court of Fulton County, Georgia, on October 12, 1978. McCleskey's convictions arose out of the robbery of a furniture store and the killing of a white police officer during the course of the robbery. The evidence at trial indicated that McCleskey and three accomplices planned and carried out the robbery. All four were armed. McCleskey entered the front of the store while the other three entered the rear. McCleskey secured the front of the store by rounding up the customers and forcing them to lie face down on the floor. The other three rounded up the employees in the rear and tied them up with tape. The manager was forced at gunpoint to turn over the store receipts, his watch, and $6. During the course of the robbery, a police officer, answering a silent alarm, entered the store through the front door. As he was walking down the center aisle of the store, two shots were fired. Both struck the officer. One hit him in the face and killed him.

Several weeks later, McCleskey was arrested in connection with an unrelated offense. He confessed that he had participated in the furniture store robbery, but denied that he had shot the police officer. At trial, the State introduced evidence that at least one of the bullets that struck the officer was fired from a .38 caliber Rossi revolver. This description matched the description of the gun that McCleskey had carried during the robbery. The State also introduced the testimony of two witnesses who had heard McCleskey admit to the shooting.

The jury convicted McCleskey of murder. At the penalty hearing, the jury heard arguments as to the appropriate sentence. Under Georgia law, the jury could not consider imposing the death penalty unless it found beyond a reasonable doubt that the murder was accompanied by one of the statutory aggravating circumstances. The jury in this case found two aggravating circumstances to exist beyond a reasonable doubt: the murder was committed during the course of an armed robbery; and the murder was committed upon a peace officer engaged in the performance of his duties. In making its decision whether to impose the death sentence, the jury considered the mitigating and aggravating circumstances of McCleskey's conduct. McCleskey offered no mitigating evidence. The jury recommended that he be sentenced to death on the murder charge and to consecutive life sentences on the armed robbery charges. The court followed the jury's recommendation and sentenced McCleskey to death.

On appeal, the Supreme Court of Georgia affirmed the convictions and the sentences. This Court denied a petition for a writ of certiorari. The Superior Court of Fulton County denied McCleskey's extraordinary motion for a new trial. McCleskey then filed a petition for a writ of habeas corpus in the Superior Court of Butts County. After holding an evidentiary hearing, the Superior Court denied relief. The Supreme Court of Georgia denied McCleskey's application for a certificate of probable cause to appeal the Superior Court's denial of his petition and this Court again denied certiorari.

McCleskey next filed a petition for a writ of habeas corpus in the Federal District Court for the Northern District of Georgia. His petition raised 18 claims, one of which was that the Georgia capital sentencing process is administered in a racially discriminatory manner in violation of the Eighth and Fourteenth Amendments to the United States Constitution. In support of his claim, McCleskey proffered a statistical study performed by Professors David C. Baldus, Charles Pulaski, and George Woodworth (the Baldus study) that purports to show a disparity in the imposition of the death sentence in Georgia based on the race of the murder victim and, to a lesser extent, the race of the defendant. The Baldus study is actually two sophisticated statistical studies that examine over 2,000 murder cases that occurred in Georgia during the 1970's. The raw numbers collected by Professor Baldus indicate that defendants charged with killing white persons received the death penalty in 11% of the cases, but defendants charged with killing blacks received the death penalty in only 1% of the cases. The raw numbers also indicate a reverse racial disparity according to the race of the defendant: 4% of the black defendants received the death penalty, as opposed to 7% of the white defendants.

Baldus also divided the cases according to the combination of the race of the defendant and the race of the victim. He found that the death penalty was assessed in 22% of the cases involving black defendants and white victims; 8% of the cases involving white defendants and white victims; 1% of the cases involving black defendants and black victims; and 3% of the cases involving white defendants and black victims. Similarly, Baldus found that prosecutors sought the death penalty in 70% of the cases involving black defendants and white victims; 32% of the cases involving white defendants and white victims; 15% of the cases involving black defendants and black victims; and 19% of the cases involving white defendants and black victims.

Baldus subjected his data to an extensive analysis, taking account of 230 variables that could have explained the disparities on nonracial grounds. One of his models concludes that, even after taking account of 39 nonracial variables, defendants charged with killing white victims were 4.3 times as likely to receive a death sentence as defendants charged with killing blacks. According to this model, black defendants were 1.1 times as likely to receive a death sentence as other defendants. Thus, the Baldus study indicates that black defendants, such as McCleskey, who kill white victims have the greatest likelihood of receiving the death penalty. * * *

II

McCleskey's first claim is that the Georgia capital punishment statute violates the Equal Protection Clause of the Fourteenth Amendment.[7] He argues that race has infected the administration of Georgia's statute in two ways: persons who murder whites are more likely to be sentenced to death than persons who murder blacks, and black murderers are more likely to be sentenced to death than white murderers. As a black defendant who killed a white victim, McCleskey claims that the Baldus study demonstrates that he was discriminated against because of his race and because of the race of his victim. In its broadest form, McCleskey's claim of discrimination extends to every actor in the Georgia capital sentencing process, from the prosecutor who sought the death penalty and the jury that imposed the sentence, to the State itself that enacted the capital

---

[7]Although the District Court rejected the findings of the Baldus study as flawed, the Court of Appeals assumed that the study is valid and reached the constitutional issues. Accordingly, those issues are before us. As did the Court of Appeals, we assume the study is valid statistically without reviewing the factual findings of the District Court. Our assumption that the Baldus study is statistically valid does not include the assumption that the study shows that racial considerations actually enter into any sentencing decisions in Georgia. Even a sophisticated multiple-regression analysis such as the Baldus study can only demonstrate a *risk* that the factor of race entered into some capital sentencing decisions and a necessarily lesser risk that race entered into any particular sentencing decision.

punishment statute and allows it to remain in effect despite its allegedly discriminatory application. We agree with the Court of Appeals, and every other court that has considered such a challenge, that this claim must fail.

A

Our analysis begins with the basic principle that a defendant who alleges an equal protection violation has the burden of proving "the existence of purposeful discrimination." A corollary to this principle is that a criminal defendant must prove that the purposeful discrimination "had a discriminatory effect" on him. Thus, to prevail under the Equal Protection Clause, McCleskey must prove that the decisionmakers in *his* case acted with discriminatory purpose. He offers no evidence specific to his own case that would support an inference that racial considerations played a part in his sentence. Instead, he relies solely on the Baldus study. McCleskey argues that the Baldus study compels an inference that his sentence rests on purposeful discrimination. McCleskey's claim that these statistics are sufficient proof of discrimination, without regard to the facts of a particular case, would extend to all capital cases in Georgia, at least where the victim was white and the defendant is black.

The Court has accepted statistics as proof of intent to discriminate in certain limited contexts. First, this Court has accepted statistical disparities as proof of an equal protection violation in the selection of the jury venire in a particular district. Although statistical proof normally must present a "stark" pattern to be accepted as the sole proof of discriminatory intent under the Constitution, "because of the nature of the jury-selection task, . . . we have permitted a finding of constitutional violation even when the statistical pattern does not approach [such] extremes." Second, this Court has accepted statistics in the form of multiple-regression analysis to prove statutory violations under Title VII of the Civil Rights Act of 1964.[a]

But the nature of the capital sentencing decision, and the relationship of the statistics to that decision, are fundamentally different from the corresponding elements in the venire-selection or Title VII cases. Most importantly, each particular decision to impose the death penalty is made by a petit jury selected from a properly constituted venire. Each jury is unique in its composition, and the Constitution requires that its decision rest on consideration of innumerable factors that vary according to the characteristics of the individual defendant and the facts of the particular capital offense. Thus, the application of an inference drawn from the general statistics to a specific decision in a trial and sentencing

---

[a]Title VII of the Civil Rights Act of 1964 forbids employers from discriminating in their employment practices on the basis of race, color, religion, sex, or national origin.

simply is not comparable to the application of an inference drawn from general statistics to a specific venire-selection or Title VII case. In those cases, the statistics relate to fewer entities, and fewer variables are relevant to the challenged decisions.

Another important difference between the cases in which we have accepted statistics as proof of discriminatory intent and this case is that, in the venire-selection and Title VII contexts, the decisionmaker has an opportunity to explain the statistical disparity. Here, the State has no practical opportunity to rebut the Baldus study. "Controlling considerations of . . . public policy" dictate that jurors "cannot be called . . . to testify to the motives and influences that led to their verdict." Similarly, the policy considerations behind a prosecutor's traditionally "wide discretion" suggest the impropriety of our requiring prosecutors to defend their decisions to seek death penalties, "often years after they were made." Moreover, absent far stronger proof, it is unnecessary to seek such a rebuttal, because a legitimate and unchallenged explanation for the decision is apparent from the record: McCleskey committed an act for which the United States Constitution and Georgia laws permit imposition of the death penalty.

Finally, McCleskey's statistical proffer must be viewed in the context of his challenge. McCleskey challenges decisions at the heart of the State's criminal justice system. "One of society's most basic tasks is that of protecting the lives of its citizens and one of the most basic ways in which it achieves the task is through criminal laws against murder." Implementation of these laws necessarily requires discretionary judgments. Because discretion is essential to the criminal justice process, we would demand exceptionally clear proof before we would infer that the discretion has been abused. The unique nature of the decisions at issue in this case also counsels against adopting such an inference from the disparities indicated by the Baldus study. Accordingly, we hold that the Baldus study is clearly insufficient to support an inference that any of the decisionmakers in McCleskey's case acted with discriminatory purpose.

B

McCleskey also suggests that the Baldus study proves that the State as a whole has acted with a discriminatory purpose. He appears to argue that the State has violated the Equal Protection Clause by adopting the capital punishment statute and allowing it to remain in force despite its allegedly discriminatory application. But "'discriminatory purpose' . . . implies more than intent as volition or intent as awareness of consequences. It implies that the decisionmaker, in this case a state legislature, selected or reaffirmed a particular course of action at least in part 'because of,' not merely 'in spite of,' its adverse effects upon an identifiable group." For this claim to prevail, McCleskey would have to prove that the Georgia Legislature enacted or maintained the death penalty statute *because of* an anticipated racially discriminatory effect. In *Gregg v. Georgia* this Court found that the Georgia capital sentencing system could operate in a fair and neutral manner. There was no evidence then, and there is none now, that the Georgia Legislature enacted the capital punishment statute to further a racially discriminatory purpose.

Nor has McCleskey demonstrated that the legislature maintains the capital punishment statute because of the racially disproportionate impact suggested by the Baldus study. * * * Accordingly, we reject McCleskey's equal protection claims. * * *

III

McCleskey also argues that the Baldus study demonstrates that the Georgia capital sentencing system violates the Eighth Amendment. We begin our analysis of this claim by reviewing the restrictions on death sentences established by our prior decisions under that Amendment.

A

The Eighth Amendment prohibits infliction of "cruel and unusual punishments." This Court's early Eighth Amendment cases examined only the "particular methods of execution to determine whether they were too cruel to pass constitutional muster." Subsequently, the Court recognized that the constitutional prohibition against cruel and unusual punishments "is not fastened to the obsolete but may acquire meaning as public opinion becomes enlightened by a humane justice." In *Weems*, the Court identified a second principle inherent in the Eighth Amendment, "that punishment for crime should be graduated and proportioned to offense." * * *

IV

A

In light of our precedents under the Eighth Amendment, McCleskey cannot argue successfully that his sentence is "disproportionate to the crime in the traditional sense." He does not deny that he committed a murder in the course of a planned robbery, a crime for which this Court has determined that the death penalty constitutionally may be imposed. His disproportionality claim "is of a different sort." McCleskey argues that the sentence in his case is disproportionate to the sentences in other murder cases.

Because McCleskey's sentence was imposed under Georgia sentencing procedures that focus discretion "on the particularized nature of the crime and the particularized characteristics of the individual defendant," we lawfully may presume that McCleskey's death sentence was not "wantonly and freakishly" imposed and thus that the sentence is not disproportionate within any recognized meaning under the Eighth Amendment.

B

Although our decision in *Gregg* as to the facial validity of the Georgia capital punishment statute appears to foreclose McCleskey's disproportionality argument, he further contends that the Georgia capital punishment system is arbitrary and capricious in *application*, and therefore his sentence is excessive, because racial considerations may influence capital sentencing decisions in Georgia. We now address this claim.

To evaluate McCleskey's challenge, we must examine exactly what the Baldus study may show. Even Professor Baldus does not contend that his statistics *prove* that race enters into any capital sentencing decisions or that race was a factor in McCleskey's particular case. Statistics at most may show only a likelihood that a particular factor entered into some decisions. There is, of course, some risk of racial prejudice influencing a jury's decision in a criminal case. There are similar risks that other kinds of prejudice will influence other criminal trials. The question "is at what point that risk becomes constitutionally unacceptable," McCleskey asks us to accept the likelihood allegedly shown by the Baldus study as the constitutional measure of an unacceptable risk of racial prejudice influencing capital sentencing decisions. This we decline to do. * * *

McCleskey's argument that the Constitution condemns the discretion allowed decisionmakers in the Georgia capital sentencing system is antithetical to the fundamental role of discretion in our criminal justice system. Discretion in the criminal justice system offers substantial benefits to the criminal defendant. Not only can a jury decline to impose the death sentence, it can decline to convict or choose to convict of a lesser offense. Whereas decisions against a defendant's interest may be reversed by the trial judge or on appeal, these discretionary exercises of leniency are final and unreviewable. Similarly, the capacity of prosecutorial discretion to provide individualized justice is "firmly entrenched in American law." As we have noted, a prosecutor can decline to charge, offer a plea bargain, or decline to seek a death sentence in any particular case. Of course, "the power to be lenient [also] is the power to discriminate," but a capital punishment system that did not allow for discretionary acts of leniency "would be totally alien to our notions of criminal justice."

C

At most, the Baldus study indicates a discrepancy that appears to correlate with race. Apparent disparities in sentencing are an inevitable part of our criminal justice system. The discrepancy indicated by the Baldus study is "a far cry from the major systemic defects identified in *Furman*." As this Court has recognized, any mode for determining guilt or punishment "has its weaknesses and the potential for misuse." Specifically, "there can be 'no perfect procedure for deciding in which cases governmental authority should be used to impose death.'" Despite these imperfections, our consistent rule has been that constitutional guarantees are met when "the mode [for determining guilt or punishment] itself has been surrounded with safeguards to make it as fair as possible." Where the discretion that is fundamental to our criminal process is involved, we decline to assume that what is unexplained is invidious. In light of the safeguards designed to minimize racial bias in the process, the fundamental value of jury trial in our criminal justice system, and the benefits that discretion provides to criminal defendants, we hold that the Baldus study does not demonstrate a constitutionally significant risk of racial bias affecting the Georgia capital sentencing process.

We have held that discretion in a capital punishment system is necessary to satisfy the Constitution. Yet, the dissent now claims that the "discretion afforded such prosecutors and jurors in the Georgia capital sentencing system" violates the Constitution by creating "opportunities for racial considerations to influence criminal proceedings." The dissent contends that in Georgia "no guidelines govern prosecutorial decisions...and [that] Georgia provides juries with no list of aggravating and mitigating factors, nor any standard for balancing them against one another." Prosecutorial decisions necessarily involve both judgmental and factual decisions that vary from case to case. Thus, it is difficult to imagine guidelines that would produce the predictability sought by the dissent without sacrificing the discretion essential to a humane and fair system of criminal justice. Indeed, the dissent suggests no such guidelines for prosecutorial discretion.

Two additional concerns inform our decision in this case. First, McCleskey's claim, taken to its logical conclusion, throws into serious question the principles that underlie our entire criminal justice system. The Eighth Amendment is not limited in application to capital punishment, but applies to all penalties. Thus, if we accepted McCleskey's claim that racial bias has impermissibly tainted the capital sentencing decision, we could soon be faced with similar claims as to other types of penalty. Moreover, the claim that his sentence rests on the irrelevant factor of race easily could be extended to apply to claims based on unexplained discrepancies that correlate to membership in other minority groups, and even to gender. Similarly, since McCleskey's claim relates to the race of his victim, other claims could apply with equally logical force to statistical disparities that correlate with the race or sex of other actors in the criminal justice system, such as defense attorneys or judges. Also, there is no logical reason that such a claim need be limited to racial or sexual bias. If arbitrary and capricious punishment is the touchstone under the Eighth

Amendment, such a claim could – at least in theory – be based upon any arbitrary variable, such as the defendant's facial characteristics, or the physical attractiveness of the defendant or the victim, that some statistical study indicates may be influential in jury decisionmaking. As these examples illustrate, there is no limiting principle to the type of challenge brought by McCleskey. The Constitution does not require that a State eliminate any demonstrable disparity that correlates with a potentially irrelevant factor in order to operate a criminal justice system that includes capital punishment. As we have stated specifically in the context of capital punishment, the Constitution does not "plac[e] totally unrealistic conditions on its use."

Second, McCleskey's arguments are best presented to the legislative bodies. It is not the responsibility – or indeed even the right – of this Court to determine the appropriate punishment for particular crimes. It is the legislatures, the elected representatives of the people, that are "constituted to respond to the will and consequently the moral values of the people." Legislatures also are better qualified to weigh and "evaluate the results of statistical studies in terms of their own local conditions and with a flexibility of approach that is not available to the courts." Capital punishment is now the law in more than two-thirds of our States. It is the ultimate duty of courts to determine on a case-by-case basis whether these laws are applied consistently with the Constitution. Despite McCleskey's wide-ranging arguments that basically challenge the validity of capital punishment in our multiracial society, the only question before us is whether in his case the law of Georgia was properly applied. We agree with the District Court and the Court of Appeals for the Eleventh Circuit that this was carefully and correctly done in this case.

VI

Accordingly, we affirm the judgment of the Court of Appeals for the Eleventh Circuit.

It is so ordered.

JUSTICE BRENNAN, with whom JUSTICE MARSHALL joins, and with whom JUSTICE BLACKMUN and JUSTICE STEVENS join in all but Part I, dissenting.

I

Adhering to my view that the death penalty is in all circumstances cruel and unusual punishment forbidden by the Eighth and Fourteenth Amendments, I would vacate the decision below insofar as it left undisturbed the death sentence imposed in this case. This Court observes that "the *Gregg*-type statute imposes unprecedented safeguards in the special context of capital punishment," which "ensure a degree of care in the imposition of the death penalty that can be described only as unique." Notwithstanding these efforts, murder defendants in Georgia with white victims are more than four times as likely to receive the death sentence as are defendants with black victims. Nothing could convey more powerfully the intractable reality of the death penalty: "that the effort to eliminate arbitrariness in the infliction of that ultimate sanction is so plainly doomed to failure that it – and the death penalty – must be abandoned altogether."

Even if I did not hold this position, however, I would reverse the Court of Appeals, for petitioner McCleskey has clearly demonstrated that his death sentence was imposed in violation of the Eighth and Fourteenth Amendments. * * *

II

At some point in this case, Warren McCleskey doubtless asked his lawyer whether a jury was likely to sentence him to die. A candid reply to this question would have been disturbing. First, counsel would have to tell McCleskey that few of the details of the crime or of McCleskey's past criminal conduct were more important than the fact that his victim was white. Furthermore, counsel would feel bound to tell McCleskey that defendants charged with killing white victims in Georgia are 4.3 times as likely to be sentenced to death as defendants charged with killing blacks. In addition, frankness would compel the disclosure that it was more likely than not that the race of McCleskey's victim would determine whether he received a death sentence: 6 of every 11 defendants convicted of killing a white person would not have received the death penalty if their victims had been black, while, among defendants with aggravating and mitigating factors comparable to McCleskey's, 20 of every 34 would not have been sentenced to die if their victims had been black. Finally, the assessment would not be complete without the information that cases involving black defendants and white victims are more likely to result in a death sentence than cases featuring any other racial combination of defendant and victim. The story could be told in a variety of ways, but McCleskey could not fail to grasp its essential narrative line: there was a significant chance that race would play a prominent role in determining if he lived or died. * * *

IV

The Court cites four reasons for shrinking from the implications of McCleskey's evidence: the desirability of discretion for actors in the criminal justice system, the existence of statutory safeguards against abuse of that discretion, the potential consequences for broader challenges to criminal sentencing, and an understanding of the contours of the judicial role. While these concerns underscore the need for sober deliberation, they do not justify rejecting evidence as convincing as McCleskey has presented.

The Court maintains that petitioner's claim "is antithetical to the fundamental role of discretion in our criminal justice system." It states that "where the discretion that is fundamental to our criminal process is involved, we decline to assume that what is unexplained is invidious."

Reliance on race in imposing capital punishment, however, is antithetical to the very rationale for granting sentencing discretion. Discretion is a means, not an end. It is bestowed in order to permit the sentencer to "trea[t] each defendant in a capital case with that degree of respect due the uniqueness of the individual." The decision to impose the punishment of death must be based on a "particularized consideration of relevant aspects of the character and record of each convicted defendant." Failure to conduct such an individualized moral inquiry "treats all persons convicted of a designated offense not as unique individual human beings, but as members of a faceless, undifferentiated mass to be subjected to the blind infliction of the penalty of death."

Considering the race of a defendant or victim in deciding if the death penalty should be imposed is completely at odds with this concern that an individual be evaluated as a unique human being. Decisions influenced by race rest in part on a categorical assessment of the worth of human beings according to color, insensitive to whatever qualities the individuals in question may possess. Enhanced willingness to impose the death sentence on black defendants, or diminished willingness to render such a sentence when blacks are victims, reflects a devaluation of the lives of black persons. When confronted with evidence that race more likely than not plays such a role in a capital sentencing system, it is plainly insufficient to say that the importance of discretion demands that the risk be higher before we will act – for in such a case the very end that discretion is designed to serve is being undermined. * * *

The Court next states that its unwillingness to regard petitioner's evidence as sufficient is based in part on the fear that recognition of McCleskey's claim would open the door to widespread challenges to all aspects of criminal sentencing. Taken on its face, such a statement seems to suggest a fear of too much justice. Yet surely the majority would acknowledge that if striking evidence indicated that other minority groups, or women, or even persons with blond hair, were disproportionately sentenced to death, such a state of affairs would be repugnant to deeply rooted conceptions of fairness. The prospect that there may be more widespread abuse than McCleskey documents may be dismaying, but it does not justify complete abdication of our judicial role. The Constitution was framed fundamentally as a bulwark against governmental power, and preventing the arbitrary administration of punishment is a basic ideal of any society that purports to be governed by the rule of law.

In fairness, the Court's fear that McCleskey's claim is an invitation to descend a slippery slope also rests on the realization that any humanly imposed system of penalties will exhibit some imperfection. Yet to reject McCleskey's powerful evidence on this basis is to ignore both the qualitatively different character of the death penalty and the particular repugnance of racial discrimination, considerations which may properly be taken into account in determining whether various punishments are "cruel and unusual." Furthermore, it fails to take account of the unprecedented refinement and strength of the Baldus study.

It hardly needs reiteration that this Court has consistently acknowledged the uniqueness of the punishment of death. "Death, in its finality, differs more from life imprisonment than a 100-year prison term differs from one of only a year or two. Because of that qualitative difference, there is a corresponding difference in the need for reliability in the determination that death is the appropriate punishment." Furthermore, the relative interests of the state and the defendant differ dramatically in the death penalty context. The marginal benefits accruing to the state from obtaining the death penalty rather than life imprisonment are considerably less than the marginal difference to the defendant between death and life in prison. Such a disparity is an additional reason for tolerating scant arbitrariness in capital sentencing. * * *

The Court also maintains that accepting McCleskey's claim would pose a threat to all sentencing because of the prospect that a correlation might be demonstrated between sentencing outcomes and other personal characteristics. Again, such a view is indifferent to the considerations that enter into a determination whether punishment is "cruel and unusual." Race is a consideration whose influence is expressly constitutionally proscribed. We have expressed a moral commitment, as embodied in our fundamental law, that this specific characteristic should not be the basis for allotting burdens and benefits. Three constitutional amendments, and numerous statutes, have been prompted specifically by the desire to address the effects of racism. "Over the years, this Court has consistently repudiated 'distinctions between citizens solely because of their ancestry' as being 'odious to a free people whose institutions are founded upon the doctrine of equality.'" Furthermore, we have explicitly acknowledged the illegitimacy of race as a consideration in capital sentencing. That a decision to impose the death penalty could be influenced by *race* is thus a particularly repugnant prospect, and evidence that race may play even a modest role in levying a death sentence should be enough to characterize that sentence as "cruel and unusual." * * *

Furthermore, the Court's fear of the expansive ramifications of a holding for McCleskey in this case is unfounded because it fails to recognize the uniquely sophisticated nature of the Baldus study. McCleskey presents evidence that is far and away the most refined data ever assembled on any system of punishment, data not readily replicated through casual effort. Moreover, that evidence depicts not merely arguable tendencies, but striking correlations, all the more powerful because nonracial explanations have been eliminated. Acceptance of petitioner's evidence would therefore establish a remarkably stringent standard of statistical evidence unlikely to be satisfied with any frequency. * * *

V

* * * Warren McCleskey's evidence confronts us with the subtle and persistent influence of the past. His message is a disturbing one to a society that has formally repudiated racism, and a frustrating one to a Nation accustomed to regarding its destiny as the product of its own will. Nonetheless, we ignore him at our peril, for we remain imprisoned by the past as long as we deny its influence in the present.

It is tempting to pretend that minorities on death row share a fate in no way connected to our own, that our treatment of them sounds no echoes beyond the chambers in which they die. Such an illusion is ultimately corrosive, for the reverberations of injustice are not so easily confined. "The destinies of the two races in this country are indissolubly linked together," and the way in which we choose those who will die reveals the depth of moral commitment among the living. * * *

[JUSTICE BLACKMUN's dissenting opinion has been omitted.]

JUSTICE ISN'T BLIND
Richard Morin[a]
Washington Post, September 3, 2000, at B5

A black man is run over and killed by a drunken driver. A typical sentence: two years in prison. A white man is run over and killed by a drunken driver. A typical sentence: four years in prison. A white woman is run over and killed by a drunken driver. A typical sentence: seven years in prison.

Three similar crimes. Three equally blameless victims. Three different punishments – a pattern that is entirely common, assert two economists who have studied the influence of victims' sex and race on sentencing in homicide cases.

Edward Glaeser of Harvard University and Bruce Sacerdote of Dartmouth College found that people convicted of vehicular homicide, for

---

[a]Robert Morin is a staff writer and columnist for The Washington Post.

example, received sentences that were 56 percent longer if they killed a woman than if the victim had been a man. But a driver who killed a black person got a sentence that was 53 percent shorter than he would have received if the victim had been white, if all other key factors about the crime, the killer and the victim held constant. * * *

Glaeser and Sacerdote based their conclusions on a random sampling of 2,800 homicide cases drawn from prosecutors' files in 33 urban counties by the Bureau of Justice Statistics. The data set included the characteristics of the offenders, the victims and the outcomes of the trials. That allowed the researchers to control for the effects of factors such as the killers' and victims' prior criminal histories, the type of offense and details of the crime – in addition to personal characteristics such as age, gender, race and income. They confirmed some key findings with data from Alabama, a state with similarly complete records and a relatively large number of vehicular homicides.

The sentencing pattern for the crime of vehicular homicide is particularly noteworthy, they say, because its victims are "essentially random." Unlike other types of homicides, victims of vehicular homicide typically are people who happened by chance to be in the wrong place at the wrong time – the perfect natural experiment to test the impact of the victim's race, gender and other characteristics on sentencing.

They also found these effects were large in other types of homicides. Overall, "murderers who kill black victims receive 26.8 percent shorter sentences" than they would have received if the victims had been white, they wrote. "Murderers who kill male victims receive 40.6 percent shorter sentences [than murderers who kill female victims]," other key factors being equal.

They also found that the race of the victims had far more to do with sentence length than the race of the killers, after controlling for various factors including the defendants' prior criminal records.

What explains the apparent tendency of judges and juries to go lighter on killers whose victims are black but throw the book at killers whose victims are women? One troubling possibility suggested by Glaeser and Sacerdote: "vengeance." That's a factor that some social scientists argue is important, though rarely acknowledged, in sentencing decisions. In the case of female victims, they argue that vengeance may take the form of outrage over the death of an "innocent" woman to produce a disproportionately long sentence. But in the case of black victims, they speculate that this "taste for vengeance" may take a different form – overt or, more likely, unconscious racism that significantly devalues the life of a black victim by going lighter on the convicted killer. "The racial effects may be despicable," they concluded – but apparently they are all too real.

STATE v. RUSSELL
Supreme Court of Minnesota
477 N.W.2d 886 (Minn. 1991)

WAHL, J.

We are asked, in this pretrial appeal, to consider the following certified question:

> Does Minnesota Statute 152.023, Subd. 2(1) (1989), as it is applied, violate the equal protection clauses of the Fourteenth Amendment of the United States Constitution and the Minnesota Constitution, Article 1, Section 2?

Under Minn. Stat. §152.023, subd. 2, a person is guilty of a third degree offense if he or she possesses three or more grams of cocaine base [hereinafter "crack cocaine"]. Under the same statute, a person must possess ten or more grams of cocaine powder to be guilty of the same offense. A person who possesses less than 10 grams of cocaine powder is guilty of a fifth degree offense.

Pursuant to these statutes, possession of three grams of crack cocaine carries a penalty of up to 20 years in prison while possession of an equal amount of cocaine powder carries a penalty of up to five years in prison. Under the sentencing guidelines, the presumptive sentence for possession of three grams of crack cocaine is an executed 48 months imprisonment. The presumptive sentence for possession of an equal amount of cocaine powder is a stayed 12 months of imprisonment and probation.

Defendants, five African-American men who were charged with violating Minn. Stat. §152.023, subd. 2, jointly moved the trial court to dismiss the charges on the ground that the statute has a discriminatory impact on black persons and violates the equal protection guarantees of the federal and state constitutions.

The trial court found that crack cocaine is used predominantly by blacks and that cocaine powder is used predominantly by whites.[1] As a result, a far greater percentage of blacks than whites are sentenced for possession of three or more grams of crack cocaine under Minn. Stat. §152.023 with more severe

---

[1]Among the many statistics provided to the trial court were those showing that of all persons charged with possession of cocaine base in 1988, 96.6% were black. Of all persons charged with possession of powder cocaine, 79.6% were white.

consequences than their white counterparts who possess three or more grams of cocaine powder. The trial court concluded that the law has a discriminatory impact on black persons.

The trial court then determined that no rational basis supported the distinction between crack-cocaine and cocaine powder and that the law therefore violated constitutional guarantees of equal protection. The trial court granted the defendants' joint motion to dismiss and certified the question of the statute's constitutionality to the court of appeals. * * * We granted a joint petition for accelerated review filed by both the state and the defendants. * * * We affirm.

Review of an equal protection challenge under the federal rational basis test requires (1) a legitimate purpose for the challenged legislation, and (2) that it was reasonable for the lawmakers to believe that use of the challenged classification would promote that purpose.[2]

The state argues that the challenged statute passes muster under that test. It contends that the legislature has a permissible and legitimate interest in regulating the possession and sale of crack cocaine and cocaine powder and that it was reasonable for lawmakers to believe that the three grams of crack – ten grams of powder classification would regulate the possession of those drugs by the "street level" dealers at whom the statute was primarily aimed.

Even if we were to agree with the state's argument as to the analysis under the federal test, we strike the statute as unconstitutional under the rational basis test as articulated under Minnesota law. Since the early eighties, this court has, in equal protection cases, articulated a rational basis test that differs from the federal standard, requiring:

> (1) The distinctions which separate those included within the classification from those excluded must not be manifestly arbitrary or fanciful but must be genuine and substantial, thereby providing a natural and reasonable basis to justify legislation adapted to peculiar conditions and needs; (2) the classification must be genuine or relevant to the purpose of the

---

[2] To invoke strict scrutiny of a statute that has a racially discriminatory impact, under current federal equal protection analysis, requires a showing that the legislature enacted the particular statute "'because of' not merely 'in spite of'" an anticipated racially discriminatory effect. *McCleskey v. Kemp,* 481 U.S. 279, 298, 95 L.Ed.2d 262 , 107 S.Ct. 1756 (1987). This standard not only places a virtually insurmountable burden on the challenger, who has the least access to the information necessary to establish a possible invidious purpose, but it also defies the fundamental tenets of equal protection. * * *

law; that is there must be an evident connection between the distinctive needs peculiar to the class and the prescribed remedy; and (3) the purpose of the statute must be one that the state can legitimately attempt to achieve.

*   *   *

We therefore hold that under our state constitutional standard of rational basis review the challenged statute cannot stand. First, the statute fails for lack of a genuine and substantial distinction between those inside and outside the class. In order to meet this standard, the state must provide more than anecdotal support for classifying users of crack cocaine differently from users of cocaine powder. The primary justification advanced by the state in support of the crack/cocaine classification is that it serves to facilitate prosecution of "street level" drug dealers. The three grams of crack - ten grams of powder formula was adopted because it was thought those amounts indicated a level at which dealing, not merely using, took place.

The primary testimony before the legislature on the distinction between crack cocaine and cocaine powder in terms of the respective amounts of the drugs that indicate street-level dealing came from Mr. James Kamin of the Hennepin County Attorney's Office. He stated at legislative hearings that his knowledge of the quantities possessed by drug dealers did not come from study but "simply from talking with people like Sergeant Strauss and informants, people who have been convicted or are being prosecuted for drug offenses. My knowledge of these numbers come from the streets."

This purely anecdotal testimony does not establish a substantial and genuine distinction. A statutory distinction that provides the basis for prescribing widely disparate criminal penalties is not sufficiently justified when based on the anecdotal observations of one expert witness. This is especially true in light of evidence presented that undermines the conclusion reached by the legislature. For instance, respondents point to a recent report by the Minnesota Department of Public Safety Office of Drug Policy that states that police and prosecutors contacted by researchers are not persuaded by the "street dealer" distinction because they believe that most cocaine powder users are dealers as well. Without more factual support, the three grams of crack – ten grams of powder distinction appears to be based upon an arbitrary rather than a genuine and substantial distinction.

The second proffered basis for the disparate treatment of crack versus cocaine powder users is that crack is more addictive and dangerous than cocaine powder. The evidence on this point similarly fails to establish a genuine and substantial distinction between those inside and outside the class. The primary legislative testimony on this point was presented by Michael Strauss, an officer from the Minneapolis Narcotics Division, who testified from his experience and training in the Narcotics Division but who did not profess to be a trained scientist.

Further evidence on the chemical properties and physiological effects of crack and cocaine powder was presented to the trial court through the testimony of Dawn Speier, a chemist for the City of Minneapolis. She testified that there is a difference between crack and cocaine powder in the severity of the attack on the central nervous system and respiratory function, and, based on what she had read or heard, that a smaller amount of crack will produce the same effect as cocaine powder. She also testified, however, that the mood altering ingredient in both powder and base was the same – cocaine. Further, she testified that the difference in effect between the two was based on the way the drug was ingested (cocaine powder being generally sniffed through the nostrils, crack cocaine being smoked). In fact, Speier confirmed that if cocaine powder is dissolved in water and injected intravenously, the effect on the body is similar to the effect of smoking crack cocaine. Thus, as respondents argue, evidence as to the degree of dangerousness between crack and cocaine powder is based on testimony as to effects resulting from different methods of ingestion, rather than on an inherent difference between the forms of the drug. Disparate treatment of crack and powder cocaine users is not justified on the basis of crack's greater dangerousness when there is evidence that powder cocaine could readily produce the effects purported to justify a harsher penalty for possession of crack.

There is also evidence in the legislative record that there is more violence associated with the use of crack than with the use of cocaine powder. This evidence is not only anecdotal, but pales in light of official observation that if there is more violence associated with crack use, "that difference could be caused more by factors such as gang warfare and certain group behaviors than by the pharmacological effects of crack." Although under the more deferential rational basis test, we may not second guess the scientific accuracy of legislative determinations of fact absent overwhelming contrary evidence, the rational basis test under the Minnesota Constitution requires more factual support than is present here to establish a genuine and substantial distinction between the two substances.

The crack-cocaine distinction also fails because the classification is not relevant to the statutory purpose. Without more evidence to support the asserted dealership levels of drug possession, the three grams of crack - ten grams of cocaine distinction does not further its statutory purpose of penalizing street level drug dealers. Without more evidence, it is as easily assumed that individuals jailed for possession of three grams of crack are mere personal users who were arbitrarily penalized as dealers. Furthermore, a statute which permits a person possessing less than ten grams of powder cocaine, which can be easily converted into more than three grams of crack, to be punished only for 5th degree possession of cocaine, is not only irrelevant to its purpose of penalizing drug dealers, it is also arbitrary and unreasonable.

Lastly, the crack-cocaine classification, while perhaps aimed at the legitimate purpose of eradicating street level drug dealers, employs an illegitimate means to achieve that purpose. The legislature determined that three grams of crack and ten grams of powder indicate a level at which dealing, not merely using, takes place. Once possession of the indicated amounts is proved, intent to sell is presumed, justifying a harsher penalty than that for mere possession. In effect, the statute punishes a person for possession with intent to sell without requiring the prosecution to prove, as an element of the crime, that an actual sale was intended, thus creating an irrebuttable presumption of fact. This court has recognized that statutes creating conclusive presumptions of law or fact have been almost uniformly declared unconstitutional as denying due process of law. Because the statute creates an irrebuttable presumption of intent to sell without affording the defendant an affirmative defense of lack of intent to sell, and on the basis of that presumption automatically metes out a harsher punishment, the means chosen to affect its purposes are constitutionally suspect.

We answer the certified question in the affirmative and affirm the decision of the trial court.

Affirmed.

COYNE, J., dissenting

I respectfully dissent: First, because the majority has abandoned the recognized rule for reviewing a facially neutral crime control statute in favor of an activist form of judicial review which allows the court to substitute its view of the basis for and efficacy of the statute for that of the legislature; and second, because, based on its assumption that crack cocaine and cocaine powder are identical substances – a matter on which experts disagree – the majority proceeds on the false premise that the legislature may not found a legislative distinction on differences in the form and marketing of the two substances.

I begin my analysis by emphasizing the limitations on this court's role vis a vis the legislature in matters relating to crime control and the punishment of crimes. As we have stated in other contexts, the judicial branch of government in Minnesota has no inherent authority to set the terms or conditions of punishment for a criminal act. Instead, the power to define appropriate punishment for criminal conduct rests with the legislature as a corollary to its broader power to define what acts constitute criminal conduct. Justice Powell stated it this way in *McCleskey v. Kemp*:

> It is not the responsibility – or indeed even the right – of this Court to determine the appropriate punishment for particular crimes. It is the legislatures, the elected representatives of the people, that are 'constituted to respond to the will and consequently the moral values of the people.'

Everyone agrees that under the equal protection clause the legislature is not free to make punishment turn on "an unjustifiable standard such as race, religion, or other arbitrary classification." However, in reviewing the constitutionality of legislation under the equal protection clause we should remember the words of Justice Holmes, which are as true today as they were nearly 90 years ago:

> Great constitutional provisions must be administered with caution. Some play must be allowed for the joints of the machine, and it must be remembered that legislatures are ultimate guardians of the liberties and welfare of the people in quite as great a degree as the courts.

We should not lightly or casually presume discriminatory purpose by the legislature.

Certainly, courts must subject any law that makes a classification based on race – any law that is not neutral on its face – to the "most rigid scrutiny" and must strike down the legislation as violative of equal protection unless the state can justify the law by demonstrating that the weightiest of considerations necessitated its enactment. But a law like the statute at issue, which is facially neutral and serves ends properly within the power of government to pursue, is not invalid under the equal protection clause unless the party attacking it can prove discriminatory intent or purpose.

Proof of discriminatory intent or purpose requires more, however, than showing that the legislature relied on anecdotal evidence, that the legislature's action is of doubtful wisdom, or that the legislature was aware that the law might "affect a greater proportion of one race than of another." The evidence must affirmatively demonstrate an invidious motive or purpose – that is, that the legislature acted as it did, at least in part, "because of an anticipated discriminatory effect" and not simply "'in spite of,' its adverse effects upon an identifiable group." Only when it has been established that a discriminatory purpose was "a motivating factor" in the legislature's decision, is judicial deference no longer justified.

As background to a consideration of the validity of the Minnesota law which was enacted in 1989, it should be noted that the Minnesota legislation was preceded by the federal Anti-Drug Abuse Act of 1986. That act amended 21

U.S.C. §841(b)(1)(B) to equate 100 grams of cocaine powder and 1 gram of cocaine base or crack cocaine – the so-called "100 to 1 ratio" – for the purpose of determining punishment. Under the federal act an offense involving mixtures weighing 5 grams or more containing cocaine base was subject to the same harsh punishment as an offense involving mixtures weighing 500 grams or more containing cocaine powder. Our own Eighth Circuit, in rejecting a Fifth Amendment due process challenge to the act, pointed to the fact that Congress considered cocaine base or crack cocaine to be more dangerous than cocaine powder because of crack's potency, its more highly addictive nature, and its greater accessibility because of its relatively low cost. I further note that the act has withstood claims that it violates Fifth Amendment equal protection. As stated in *United States v. Cyrus:*

> A legislative body need not explicitly state its reasons for passing legislation so long as a court can devine [sic] some rational purpose. Here, such purposes are readily apparent. Crack is far more addictive than cocaine. It is far more accessible due to its relatively low cost. And it has experienced an explosion of popularity. Any one of these factors would furnish a rational basis for the [100 to 1] distinction.

While considering ways of addressing the crisis created by crack cocaine, the 1989 Minnesota legislature heard testimony similar to that which in 1986 prompted Congress to adopt the "100 to 1 ratio." For example, the legislature was presented with evidence that crack cocaine and cocaine powder are not, as defendants contend and as the majority unjustifiably assumes, the same substance but different substances justifying dissimilar legislative treatment. The record demonstrates that although crack cocaine is derived from cocaine powder, the two substances have both a slightly different chemical composition and a different pharmacological effect. The unique characteristics of crack cocaine were discussed not only in the legislative hearings but also in the affidavit of defendants' own expert in this litigation, M. Dawn Speier, Public Health Chemist for the City of Minneapolis. According to her, smoking crack cocaine "delivers a highly concentrated dose – at least 3 times that delivered by snorting an equivalent dose of cocaine powder – to the brain" and "abusers lose control faster with crack smoking than with snorting [powder]." Similarly, other experts have opined that "although it can take months or years for a nasal cocaine [powder] user to progress from recreational use, this can happen within days to weeks with crack." The combination of the low cost per unit of crack cocaine and the highly addictive nature of the substance has created an epidemic of crack trafficking and use, has fueled gang behavior, has destroyed individuals (including innocent babies, who, as a result of their mothers' addiction, are born addicted), has destroyed families, and has ruined entire neighborhoods, prompting one of the authors of the 1989 legislation to conclude that crack cocaine is "by far the single most dangerous drug ever encountered." * * *

In conclusion, the power to define what act constitutes a crime and to fix the punishment for that crime rests with the legislature. This court has neither the obligation nor the right to interfere with legislation dealing with the control of crime without a very good reason. Absent some evidence of discriminatory intent or purpose, the fact that more black persons than white persons violate Minn. Stat. §152.023, subd. 2(1) (1989) is not a basis for declaring the statute unconstitutional although it may well be indicative of deep-seated societal failings. Social problems, however, are seldom susceptible of facile definition or scientific proof or easy resolution. In my view, the cumulative evidence the legislature considered and the thoughtful remarks of the bill's authors and of other legislators exhibit only a commendable, concerted, and reasoned good faith effort to address a serious social problem.

Because I believe that Minn. Stat. §152.023, subd. 2(1) (1989) meets the equal protection requirements of both the United States Constitution and the Minnesota Constitution, I would answer the certified question "no" and reverse the trial court.

D.   FEDERALISM AND THE SUPREMACY CLAUSE

The Constitution establishes a federalist system in which authority is divided between the federal government and the states. The Constitution's enumeration of powers belonging to the federal government, *see* Art. I, § 8, serves to limit the reach of the federal government, preserving the authority of the states over issues of public health, safety, and welfare.

The Supremacy Clause of the U.S. Constitution, Art. VI, clause 2, provides: "This Constitution, and the Laws of the United States which shall be made in Pursuance thereof; * * * shall be the supreme Law of the Land; and the Judges in every State shall be bound thereby, any Thing in the Constitution or Laws of any State to the Contrary notwithstanding." This language sets forth the principle that any constitutionally sound federal law trumps a conflicting state law. The Supremacy Clause thus plays a vital role as arbiter when state and federal laws conflict. The boundary between state and federal power, however, is a murky one, as the two levels of government jockey for position against one another. *Oregon v. Ashcroft* and the article that follows illustrate some current tensions between the federal government and the states over issues such as the right to physician-assisted suicide and the right to use marijuana for medical purposes.

OREGON v. ASHCROFT

United States Court of Appeals for the Ninth Circuit
368 F.3d 1118 (9th Cir. 2004)

TALLMAN, Circuit Judge:

A doctor, a pharmacist, several terminally ill patients, and the State of Oregon challenge an interpretive rule issued by Attorney General John Ashcroft which declares that physician assisted suicide violates the Controlled Substances Act of 1970 ("CSA"). This so-called "Ashcroft Directive" criminalizes conduct specifically authorized by Oregon's Death With Dignity Act. We hold that the Ashcroft Directive is unlawful and unenforceable because it violates the plain language of the CSA, contravenes Congress' express legislative intent, and oversteps the bounds of the Attorney General's statutory authority. * * *

The Ashcroft Directive purports to interpret and implement the CSA, which Congress enacted as Title II of the Comprehensive Drug Abuse Prevention and Control Act of 1970. The stated purpose of the CSA is "to provide increased research into, and prevention of, drug abuse and drug dependence . . . and to strengthen existing law enforcement authority in the field of drug abuse."

Under the CSA, it is unlawful to prescribe or dispense controlled substances without a federal registration. The CSA originally provided automatic federal registration for state-licensed health-care practitioners. The Attorney General could revoke a practitioner's federal registration only if the practitioner falsified his or her registration application, was convicted of a felony related to a controlled substance, or had his or her state license suspended or revoked.

In 1971, pursuant to his authority to issue rules regulating controlled substances under the CSA, then-Attorney General John Mitchell promulgated the following regulation:

> A prescription for a controlled substance to be effective must be issued for a legitimate medical purpose by an individual practitioner acting in the usual course of his professional practice . . . . An order purporting to be a prescription issued not in the usual course of professional treatment . . . is not a prescription within the meaning and intent of . . . the Act and the person knowingly filling such a purported prescription, as well as the person issuing it, shall be subject to the penalties provided for violations of the provisions of law relating to controlled substances.

This regulation exposed properly licensed and registered physicians to federal prosecution for distributing prescription drugs outside "the usual course of professional practice."

In 1984, Congress amended the CSA to give broader authority to the Attorney General. The Attorney General is now authorized to revoke a physician's prescription privileges upon his determination that the physician has "committed such acts as would render his registration . . . inconsistent with the public interest[.]" When determining which acts are inconsistent with the public interest, the Attorney General must consider the following factors:

> (1) The recommendation of the appropriate State licensing board or professional disciplinary authority;

> (2) The applicant's expertise in dispensing . . . controlled substances;

> (3) The applicant's conviction record under Federal or State laws relating to the manufacture, distribution, or dispensing of controlled substances;

> (4) Compliance with applicable State, Federal, or local laws relating to controlled substances;

> (5) Such other conduct which may threaten the public health and safety.

Although this provision gives the Attorney General new discretion over the registration of health care practitioners, Congress explained that "the amendment would continue to give deference to the opinions of State licencing authorities, since their recommendations are the first of the factors to be considered[.]"

Against this backdrop of federal regulation, in 1994, the State of Oregon enacted by ballot measure the country's first law authorizing physician assisted suicide. Oregon's Death With Dignity Act authorizes physicians to prescribe lethal doses of controlled substances to terminally ill Oregon residents according to procedures designed to protect vulnerable patients and ensure that their decisions are reasoned and voluntary.[3] Oregon voters reaffirmed their support

---

[3]Under Oregon's Death With Dignity Act, only adult Oregon residents suffering from an incurable disease likely to result in death within six months are eligible for a lethal prescription. A patient's diagnosis must be confirmed by two independent physicians. Patients must sign a written request for the prescription in the presence of two witnesses attesting that the patient is competent and acting voluntarily.

for the Death With Dignity Act on November 4, 1997, by defeating a ballot measure that sought to repeal the law.

Soon thereafter, several members of Congress, including then-Senator John Ashcroft, urged then-Attorney General Janet Reno to declare that physician assisted suicide violated the CSA. She declined to do so. In a letter dated January 5, 1998, Attorney General Reno explained that the CSA was not "intended to displace the states as the primary regulators of the medical profession, or to override a state's determination as to what constitutes legitimate medical practice." She concluded that "the CSA does not authorize [the Drug Enforcement Administration ("DEA")] to prosecute, or to revoke DEA registration of, a physician who has assisted in a suicide in compliance with Oregon law."

With a change of administrations came a change of perspectives. On November 9, 2001, newly appointed Attorney General John Ashcroft reversed the position of his predecessor and issued the Directive at issue here. The Ashcroft Directive proclaims that physician assisted suicide serves no "legitimate medical purpose" under 21 C.F.R. § 1306.04 and that specific conduct authorized by Oregon's Death With Dignity Act "may 'render [a practitioner's] registration . . . inconsistent with the public interest' and therefore subject to possible suspension or revocation." The Directive specifically targets health care practitioners in Oregon and instructs the DEA to enforce this determination "regardless of whether state law authorizes or permits such conduct by practitioners."

To be perfectly clear, we take no position on the merits or morality of physician assisted suicide. We express no opinion on whether the practice is inconsistent with the public interest or constitutes illegitimate medical care. This case is simply about who gets to decide. All parties agree that the question before us is whether Congress authorized the Attorney General to determine that physician assisted suicide violates the CSA. We hold that the Attorney General lacked Congress' requisite authorization. The Ashcroft Directive violates the "clear statement" rule, contradicts the plain language of the CSA, and contravenes the express intent of Congress.

We begin with instructions from the Supreme Court that the "earnest and profound debate about the morality, legality, and practicality of physician-assisted suicide" belongs among state lawmakers. *Washington v. Glucksberg*, 521 U.S. 702, 735 (1997). In *Glucksberg*, Justice O'Connor emphasized that "states are presently undertaking extensive and serious evaluation of physician-assisted suicide. . . . In such circumstances, the . . . challenging task of crafting appropriate procedures for safeguarding . . . liberty interests is entrusted to the 'laboratory' of the States . . . in the first instance." Here, Oregon voters have twice declared their support for the legalization of physician assisted suicide in their state. We disagree with the dissent's suggestion that this court, rather than the Attorney General, is interfering with the democratic process.

The principle that state governments bear the primary responsibility for evaluating physician assisted suicide follows from our concept of federalism, which requires that state lawmakers, not the federal government, are "the primary regulators of professional [medical] conduct." The Supreme Court has made the constitutional principle clear: "Obviously, direct control of medical practice in the states is beyond the power of the federal government."[6]

By criminalizing medical practices specifically authorized under Oregon law, the Ashcroft Directive interferes with Oregon's authority to regulate medical care within its borders and therefore "alters the 'usual constitutional balance between the States and the Federal Government.'" Under these circumstances, "it is incumbent on the federal courts to be certain of Congress' intent" before finding that federal authority supercedes state law.

Unless Congress' authorization is "unmistakably clear," the Attorney General may not exercise control over an area of law traditionally reserved for state authority, such as regulation of medical care. * * *

The Ashcroft Directive is invalid because Congress has provided no indication -- much less an "unmistakably clear" indication -- that it intended to authorize the Attorney General to regulate the practice of physician assisted suicide. By attempting to regulate physician assisted suicide, the Ashcroft Directive invokes the outer limits of Congress' power by encroaching on state authority to regulate medical practice. Because Congress has not clearly authorized such an intrusion, the Ashcroft Directive violates the clear statement rule. We need not, and therefore do not, decide whether the Ashcroft Directive actually exceeds Commerce Clause boundaries, but only that it "invokes the outer limits of Congress' power" without explicit authority from Congress.

The Ashcroft Directive not only lacks clear congressional authority, it also violates the plain language of the CSA. We hold that the Directive exceeds the scope of federal authority under the CSA, misconstrues the Attorney

---

[6]As noted in *Younger v. Harris*:

The concept [of federalism] does not mean blind deference to "States' Rights" any more than it means centralization of control over every important issue in our National Government and its courts. The Framers rejected both these courses. What the concept does represent is a system in which there is sensitivity to the legitimate interests of both State and National Governments, and in which the National Government, anxious though it may be to vindicate and protect federal rights and federal interests, always endeavors to do so in ways that will not unduly interfere with the legitimate activities of the States.

General's role under the statute, and fails to follow explicit instructions for revoking physician prescription privileges.

The CSA expressly limits federal authority under the Act to the "field of drug abuse." Contrary to the Attorney General's characterization, physician assisted suicide is not a form of drug "abuse" that Congress intended the CSA to cover. Physician assisted suicide is an unrelated, general medical practice to be regulated by state lawmakers in the first instance.

In sum, the CSA was enacted to combat drug abuse. To the extent that it authorizes the federal government to make decisions regarding the practice of medicine, those decisions are delegated to the Secretary of Heath and Human Services, not to the Attorney General. The Attorney General's unilateral attempt to regulate general medical practices historically entrusted to state lawmakers interferes with the democratic debate about physician assisted suicide and far exceeds the scope of his authority under federal law. We therefore hold that the Ashcroft Directive is invalid and may not be enforced.

The petitions for review are GRANTED. The injunction previously entered by the district court is ORDERED continued in full force and effect as the injunction of this court.

[J. CLIFFORD WALLACE's dissenting opinion has been omitted.]

THE BATTLE OVER MEDICAL MARIJUANA
Rich Ehisen
California Journal, July 1, 2003, at 36[a]

Ever since the United States declared independence from England, Uncle Sam and his 50 wards - otherwise known as the federal government and the states - have been squabbling over how to divide the exercise of authority. The boundary between the two shifts constantly depending on the inclination of the president and his administration, the philosophical bent of the U.S. Supreme Court and the various demands and needs of the states.

In the past, the confrontations have covered some of the most profound issues in American history, including slavery, segregation and creation of a national currency. But now that boundary is being tested by something of an odd subject - an illegal substance known as marijuana. A few states - the most notable, California - say marijuana use ought to be legal if prescribed by a doctor for critically ill patients, and they have sanctioned growing the plant for medicinal purposes. Uncle Sam, on the other hand, says

---

[a]Printed with permission of California Journal, Sacramento, California.

marijuana is illegal, period, and has used the federal police power to shut down marijuana operations considered legal by states.

The trend that put the states on a collision course with the federal government has been gaining steam in recent years, prompted in large measure by the passage of various initiatives. California authorized it in November 1996 with passage of Proposition 215, which gave people with serious medical conditions the legal ability to use marijuana as a means of alleviating the physical pain of their illness. The federal ground shifted in 2001, however, when a more conservative Bush administration replaced the Clinton administration and began to cast a gimlet eye on medicinal marijuana.

Proposition 215 notwithstanding, the U.S. Drug Enforcement Administration (DEA) has arrested and prosecuted people it says violated federal laws prohibiting marijuana cultivation, sale and use. So, which laws take precedence - state laws that authorized the activity or federal laws that ban it?

Two recent high-profile arrests in California have focused attention on the issue and spawned both local and national reactions that could have a dramatic effect on whether the DEA will continue to have that same power in the future.

The first case revolves around the arrest and conviction of Ed Rosenthal of Oakland, who federal prosecutors say was warehousing pot for sale. During the January 2003 trial, U.S. District Judge Charles Breyer refused to allow jurors to hear that the 58-year-old Rosenthal, a self-proclaimed "pot guru" who once wrote an advice column for High Times magazine, was stockpiling the plant for medical use and was doing so legally according to California law.

Rosenthal's conviction sparked an angry reaction from one juror, who wrote in a San Jose Mercury News editorial that she felt she had "helped send a man to prison who doesn't belong there." It also inspired more than two dozen members of Congress in April to introduce HR 1717, dubbed the "Truth in Trials Act," which would allow individuals accused of violating federal marijuana laws to introduce evidence in federal court that shows they were following state medicinal-use laws.

"This is an issue of states' rights, plain and simple," said California Representative Sam Farr (D-Carmel), lead sponsor of the bill. "The voters of California have passed a medical marijuana initiative, but the federal government has exhibited little respect for our state's laws. U.S. Attorney General John Ashcroft has insisted that his authority is of greater consequence than California's Proposition 215, a 1996 initiative passed by five million voters that would allow doctors to recommend medical marijuana to patients in pain."

Barely two weeks after the introduction of HR 1717, the city and county of Santa Cruz filed suit in federal court against Ashcroft and the DEA in response to an administration raid at a nearby farm. The farm is the home of Valerie Corral, who co-founded WAMM, the Wo/Men's Alliance for Medical Marijuana and who also served on the state advisory board that drafted Proposition 215. The suit claims seven defendants have had their medication "illegally reduced" since the raid, causing "insurmountable" pain and even death among some WAMM members. * * *

The raid also prompted state Attorney General Bill Lockyer to get into the act. In September 2002, Lockyer, who lost his mother and younger sister to cancer, fired off an angry letter to Ashcroft. Lockyer acknowledged the need to bring state and federal law together, but he also complained that "surely an administration with a proper sense of balance, proportion and respect for states' rights could and should reconsider the DEA's policy and redirect its resources." Lockyer also insinuated that the hard line taken by the Bush administration was to blame, noting that the raids began in earnest only in 2001, five years after voters approved Proposition 215.

Lockyer's letter also questioned the fiscal prudence of the DEA targeting small marijuana cooperatives. "A medicinal marijuana provider such as the Santa Cruz collective represents little danger to the public," Lockyer wrote, "and it is certainly not a concern which would warrant diverting scarce federal resources away from the fight against domestic methamphetamine production, heroine distribution or international terrorism, to cite just a few far more worthy priorities."

Outgoing DEA Director Asa Hutchinson fired back, telling Lockyer that the benefits of medicinal marijuana were not scientifically proven and that pot was still a federally banned drug. He also noted that Proposition 215 did not change federal law, saying that the government had never in the past "approved medicine by popular referendum" and that it "would be ill-advised to start now."

Hence, the dilemma. * * *

[S]ince 1996, voters in eight states - Alaska, Arizona, California, Colorado, Maine, Nevada, Oregon and Washington - have taken the law into their own hands by approving ballot propositions that allow for medicinal marijuana use. In 2000, the Hawaii Legislature approved such use on its own, which then-Governor Ben Cayetano signed into law. This made Hawaii the first state where medicinal marijuana use laws originated with elected officials rather than a voter referendum.

More recently, lawmakers in New York, Connecticut and Maryland introduced similar legislation. Connecticut's died on a narrow vote in the full House, while New York's recently cleared its first committee. Despite heavy lobbying from the Bush administration, Maryland's Republican Governor Bob Ehrlich signed legislation in May 2003 making his state the 10th to allow medicinal use of marijuana.

To bolster their case that federal law ought to apply in this instance, federal officials express skepticism that marijuana has medicinal value. During visits to Maryland to urge Ehrlich to veto that state's marijuana legislation, White House drug czar John Walters called medical marijuana legislation "cruel" and a "hoax." Advocates, on the other hand, point to a 1999 report issued by the National Academy of Sciences, Institute of Medicine, which stated that "scientific data indicate the potential therapeutic value of cannabinoid drugs, primarily THC, for pain relief, control of nausea and vomiting, and appetite stimulation" as proof of pot's medicinal value. The study also noted that "smoked marijuana is a crude THC delivery system that also delivers harmful substances into the system." * * *

Despite opposition from the DEA and others, polls in several states show that public opinion strongly favors the medical use of marijuana. A March 2002 poll by the Lucas organization showed 73 percent of Connecticut voters approve of the issue while a Time magazine poll from November 2002 showed support from 80 percent of the respondents in a national survey. A Pew Research Center poll from March 2001 showed 73 percent of U.S. respondents support allowing doctors "to prescribe marijuana."

What is less clear is how states are going to convince the Bush administration that they should make their own rules. And the federal government has financial muscle to flex in this bout. In June, for instance, two Republican congressmen, Mark Souder of Indiana and Tom Davis of Virginia, introduced legislation to give the drug czar the authority to shift up to 5 percent of the $230 million White House Office of Drug Policy budget away from states that allow medical marijuana use. That money would instead go to federal authorities.

Stanford law professor Robert Weisberg summed up the debate during a recent television appearance on the PBS news show "California Connected" by saying that he doubted the federal government was really concerned with medical marijuana. "But what they are bothered by," he said, "is the 'in your face' attitude of California saying, 'We defy federal law.'"

Chapter 3

THE ACT REQUIREMENT

INTRODUCTION

Most crimes in the United States consist of four basic elements: (1) a prohibited act that results in some kind of social harm (in legalese, an "actus reus"); (2) a prohibited mental state (in legalese, a "mens rea," or guilty mind); (3) a chain of causation that links the defendant's actions with the social harm; and (4) concurrence between the mens rea and the actus reus. This chapter examines the requirement of an act.

The act requirement is better thought of as an umbrella term that ties together at least five loosely related doctrines or concepts. First, there is the notion that in the United States, a person should not be convicted solely on the basis of her thoughts, but also must have done something that caused some sort of social harm. Second, there is the notion that this act must not have been compelled or committed by the government itself. Third is the requirement that the defendant's act must have been voluntary. Fourth is the general rule that there can be no criminal liability for an omission unless the person who failed to act had a legal duty to act. Finally, there is the notion that "status crimes" are unconstitutional: people should only be criminally punished for their conduct, not simply for being a certain kind of person.

Although the Supreme Court has located the source of this last doctrine in the Constitution, most of the other doctrines associated with the act requirement are considered to be based on fundamental principles of common law rather than on a particular statutory, constitutional, or precedential rule. This is also true, as we will see, of the mens rea requirement: though it is considered fundamental, it is not rooted in the Constitution.

Another commonality between the act requirement and the mens rea requirement is that the real subject of both elements of criminal law is culpability. We have just defined mens rea in a narrow sense as the prohibited mental state necessary to the commission of a crime. In legal theory, however, mens rea is also understood more broadly to refer to the idea that people should not be criminally punished unless they are somehow morally blameworthy. Mens rea in this broad sense is thus an outgrowth of the theory of retribution; and both the requirement of an act and the requirement of some kind of

158

prohibited mental state have to do with making sure that the people we punish criminally are people we as a culture consider morally blameworthy.

A.   ACTING VERSUS THINKING: THE PROSCRIPTION AGAINST THOUGHT CRIMES

One of the basic principles of criminal law is that the state cannot punish a person merely because he has bad thoughts. The criminal law generally requires an act in addition to a culpable mind-set before an individual can be held criminally liable.

The next two excerpts explore the limits of this principle. Can or should an individual be punished for writing about evil deeds in his private journal? Can or should one be punished more severely if he commits a violent crime against an individual because of his race, religion, national origin, gender, or sexual orientation? Is there a principled reason for drawing a distinction between these two types of cases?

JAILED "ON THE PRECIPICE" OF CRIME
Sandy Theis
Newhouse News Service, August 8, 2003[a]

Instead of acting on his fantasies, Brian Dalton confronted his demons by writing a journal filled with fictional tales of child molestation and torture.

For this thought crime, Dalton became the first person in America imprisoned for fictitious writings. His case is being watched closely by constitutional scholars who argue that personal diaries are protected by the First Amendment, and by anti-pornography crusaders who counter that Dalton is a threat to society.

There is little dispute that Dalton is a troubled man. His writings were so graphic that grand jurors asked police to stop reading them after just two pages, and a psychologist hired by the prosecution said they were among the most disturbing things he'd encountered in his 21-year practice. Dalton's stories center on three children, ages 10 and 11, who are caged in a basement, molested and sexually tortured. Yet court records show no evidence that he acted on these dark fantasies.

---

[a]Reprinted courtesy of Newhouse News Service.

Still, Dalton pleaded guilty in July 2001 to pandering obscenity involving a minor,[b] a crime that falls under Ohio's broadly written pornography law.

"I remember testifying against the language when I was the ACLU director," said Benson Wolman, one of Dalton's lawyers and a former director of the American Civil Liberties Union of Ohio. 'It says no person shall 'create, reproduce or publish' these materials, and I remember giving testimony to the effect of: 'Wait a minute. This means that if somebody writes something down in a diary they can be prosecuted for it.' And I was assured that 'no, no our prosecutors wouldn't do anything like that.'"

Not only did Franklin County (Columbus) prosecutors go after Dalton, but his initial lawyer, Isabella Dixon-Thomas (now a candidate for Columbus city attorney) never raised the obvious First Amendment or privacy issues posed by the case. She later asked to withdraw Dalton's guilty plea so she could raise them, but the trial judge refused her request.

Dalton is serving a seven-year prison sentence.

The ACLU eventually intervened. On July 17, an appeals court dismissed the guilty plea, said Dalton was denied his constitutional right to an effective lawyer, and sent the case back for a new trial.[c]

Franklin County Prosecutor Ron O'Brien said he would ask the Ohio Supreme Court to hear the case.

The case is noteworthy for the issues it raises, as well as the players involved.

Along with top-tier ACLU lawyers from the left, Dalton's legal team includes Jeff Sutton, President George W. Bush's newest appointee to the 6th U.S. Circuit Court of Appeals and a lawyer the left has loved to hate. According

---

[b]The Ohio statute criminalizing "pandering obscenity involving a minor" defines the crime as creating, reproducing, publishing, advertising, selling, delivering, displaying, buying, procuring, possessing, etc. any obscene material that has a minor as one of its participants or portrayed observers.

[c]In March 2004, Franklin County Common Pleas Judge David Cain dismissed the child pornography charge against Dalton, ruling that the statute under which he was charged only applies to acts involving real children and noting that it was clear that Dalton's stories were never intended to be distributed. *See Porn Charge Tossed in Journal Case*, Chicago Tribune, March 5, 2004, at 20.

to Wolman, "Sutton called up and volunteered; he was astounded by what happened in the trial court."

The appeals court appeared to share his astonishment.

The scholarly but blunt opinion details mistakes made by the trial judge and by Dixon-Thomas, saying she erroneously concluded that some of Dalton's writings were based on the molestation of his cousin rather than a fictional character. This misunderstanding was significant, the appeals court said, because it affected her legal advice to Dalton. As the appeals court noted, "The private possession of obscene material is constitutionally protected. . . . However, the private possession of child pornography may be constitutionally prohibited."

Prosecutors are trying to keep Dalton locked up, arguing his wicked writings are part of a pattern that proves he is a threat to society. They contend that he had "admitted to prior sex offenses," although he was never charged, and say some of this writings show that he "is on the precipice of offending against another real child."

Prosecutors also note what is perhaps the case's greatest irony: Dalton's past psychological treatment required him "to keep a 'deviant sexual fantasy' journal." The writings helped to monitor his fantasies and teach Dalton how to avoid "triggers" that would spark his deviant behavior.

In other words, Dalton's writings were therapeutic not pornographic.

Note

The idea that "thought crimes" are prohibited under American law suggests that the defendant must have committed some kind of action in addition to having thoughts in order to be prosecuted. Drawing a bright line between thought and action, however, is not easy. Reality looks more like a continuum of intertwined thought and action from the first fleeting idea related to a criminal act to the completed crime. At what point along that continuum is it appropriate for the police to step in?

The criminal law tries to answer this question through its treatment of the so-called "inchoate" crimes endeavor to criminalize conduct leading up to the completed social harm, so that the police may apprehend a person before the social harm occurs.[a] Similarly, anti-stalking and anti-harassment statutes allow

---

[a]The inchoate crimes are discussed in Chapters 11 and 13.

the police to step in before the social harm has been completed. Such statutes punish "threats" as actions in and of themselves.

The next case, *Wisconsin v. Mitchell*, examines the controversial subject of hate crimes law. In response to crimes of violence with racist or bigoted overtones, legislatures at both the state and federal levels have passed a variety of penal laws specifically addressing such "hate crimes." *See* Lu-in Wang, HATE CRIMES LAW § 1:2 (2004 Supp.). Critics of hate crimes laws have argued that increasing the penalty for a crime because the defendant was motivated by racial or other bias amounts to criminalizing bad thoughts in violation of the First Amendment. Professor Lu-in Wang describes the difference between laws punishing hate crimes and laws punishing hate speech:

> Generally, prosecution under a hate crime statute requires that the individual committed some predicate offense set out in the statute with the animus specified in a hate crime statute, with the statute operating to enhance the punishment imposed for the predicate offense. Those statutes that do not depend on the commission of a predicate offense, and simply punish the utterance of racist or bigoted speech, or the commission of bigoted acts that are substantially equivalent to speech, are hate speech laws. * * *

Id.

WISCONSIN v. MITCHELL
Supreme Court of the United States
508 U.S. 476, 113 S. Ct 2194, 124 L.Ed.2d 436 (1993)

REHNQUIST, CHIEF JUSTICE

Respondent Todd Mitchell's sentence for aggravated battery was enhanced because he intentionally selected his victim on account of the victim's race. The question presented in this case is whether this penalty enhancement is prohibited by the First and Fourteenth Amendments. We hold that it is not.

On the evening of October 7, 1989, a group of young black men and boys, including Mitchell, gathered at an apartment complex in Kenosha, Wisconsin. Several members of the group discussed a scene from the motion picture "Mississippi Burning," in which a white man beat a young black boy who was praying. The group moved outside and Mitchell asked them: " 'Do you all feel hyped up to move on some white people?' " Shortly thereafter, a young white boy approached the group on the opposite side of the street where they were standing. As the boy walked by, Mitchell said: "'You all want to fuck somebody up? There goes a white boy; go get him.'" Mitchell counted to three and pointed in the boy's direction. The group ran toward the boy, beat him severely, and stole his tennis shoes. The boy was rendered unconscious and remained in a coma for four days.

After a jury trial in the Circuit Court for Kenosha County, Mitchell was convicted of aggravated battery. That offense ordinarily carries a maximum sentence of two years' imprisonment. But because the jury found that Mitchell had intentionally selected his victim because of the boy's race, the maximum sentence for Mitchell's offense was increased to seven years under § 939.645. That provision enhances the maximum penalty for an offense whenever the defendant "[i]ntentionally selects the person against whom the crime ... is committed ... because of the race, religion, color, disability, sexual orientation, national origin or ancestry of that person...." The Circuit Court sentenced Mitchell to four years' imprisonment for the aggravated battery.

Mitchell unsuccessfully sought postconviction relief in the Circuit Court. Then he appealed his conviction and sentence, challenging the constitutionality of Wisconsin's penalty-enhancement provision on First Amendment grounds. The Wisconsin Court of Appeals rejected Mitchell's challenge, but the Wisconsin Supreme Court reversed. The Supreme Court held that the statute "violates the First Amendment directly by punishing what the legislature has deemed to be offensive thought." It rejected the State's contention "that the statute punishes only the 'conduct' of intentional selection of a victim." According to the court, "[t]he statute punishes the 'because of' aspect of the defendant's selection, the *reason* the defendant selected the victim, the *motive* behind the selection." And under *R.A.V. v. St. Paul*, "the Wisconsin legislature cannot criminalize bigoted thought with which it disagrees."

We granted certiorari because of the importance of the question presented and the existence of a conflict of authority among state high courts on the constitutionality of statutes similar to Wisconsin's penalty-enhancement provision. We reverse. * * *

The State argues that the statute does not punish bigoted thought, as the Supreme Court of Wisconsin said, but instead punishes only conduct. While this argument is literally correct, it does not dispose of Mitchell's First Amendment challenge. To be sure, our cases reject the "view that an apparently limitless variety of conduct can be labeled 'speech' whenever the person engaging in the conduct intends thereby to express an idea." Thus, a physical assault is not by any stretch of the imagination expressive conduct protected by the First Amendment.

But the fact remains that under the Wisconsin statute the same criminal conduct may be more heavily punished if the victim is selected because of his race or other protected status than if no such motive obtained. Thus, although the statute punishes criminal conduct, it enhances the maximum penalty for conduct motivated by a discriminatory point of view more severely than the same conduct engaged in for some other reason or for no reason at all. Because the only reason for the enhancement is the defendant's discriminatory motive for selecting his victim, Mitchell argues (and the Wisconsin Supreme Court held) that the statute violates the First Amendment by punishing offenders' bigoted beliefs.

Traditionally, sentencing judges have considered a wide variety of factors in addition to evidence bearing on guilt in determining what sentence to impose on a convicted defendant. The defendant's motive for committing the offense is one important factor. Thus, in many States the commission of a murder, or other capital offense, for pecuniary gain is a separate aggravating circumstance under the capital sentencing statute.

But it is equally true that a defendant's abstract beliefs, however obnoxious to most people, may not be taken into consideration by a sentencing judge. In *Dawson*, the State introduced evidence at a capital sentencing hearing that the defendant was a member of a white supremacist prison gang. Because "the evidence proved nothing more than [the defendant's] abstract beliefs," we held that its admission violated the defendant's First Amendment rights. In so holding, however, we emphasized that "the Constitution does not erect a *per se* barrier to the admission of evidence concerning one's beliefs and associations at sentencing simply because those beliefs and associations are protected by the First Amendment." Thus, in *Barclay v. Florida*, we allowed the sentencing judge to take into account the defendant's racial animus towards his victim. The evidence in that case showed that the defendant's membership in the Black Liberation Army and desire to provoke a "race war" were related to the murder of a white man for which he was convicted. Because "the elements of racial hatred in [the] murder" were relevant to several aggravating factors, we held that the trial judge permissibly took this evidence into account in sentencing the defendant to death.

Mitchell suggests that *Dawson* and *Barclay* are inapposite because they did not involve application of a penalty-enhancement provision. But in *Barclay* we held that it was permissible for the sentencing court to consider the defendant's racial animus in determining whether he should be sentenced to death, surely the most severe "enhancement" of all. And the fact that the Wisconsin Legislature has decided, as a general matter, that bias-motivated offenses warrant greater maximum penalties across the board does not alter the result here. For the primary responsibility for fixing criminal penalties lies with the legislature.* * *

Moreover, the Wisconsin statute singles out for enhancement bias-inspired conduct because this conduct is thought to inflict greater individual and societal harm. For example, according to the State and its *amici,* bias-motivated crimes are more likely to provoke retaliatory crimes, inflict distinct emotional harms on their victims, and incite community unrest. The State's desire to redress these perceived harms provides an adequate explanation for its penalty-enhancement provision over and above mere disagreement with offenders' beliefs or biases * * *

For the foregoing reasons, we hold that Mitchell's First Amendment rights were not violated by the application of the Wisconsin penalty-enhancement provision in sentencing him. The judgment of the Supreme Court of Wisconsin is therefore reversed, and the case is remanded for further proceedings not inconsistent with this opinion.

It is so ordered.

B.   ACTING ON ONE'S OWN VERSUS ACTING UNDER STATE COMPULSION: "SITUATIONAL OFFENSES"

MARTIN v. STATE
Alabama Court of Appeals
31 Ala. App. 334, 17 So.2d 427 (Ct. App. 1944)

SIMPSON, JUDGE.

Appellant was convicted of being drunk on a public highway, and appeals. Officers of the law arrested him at his home and took him onto the highway, where he allegedly committed the proscribed acts, viz., manifested a drunken condition by using loud and profane language.

The pertinent provisions of our statute are: "Any person who, while intoxicated or drunk, appears in any public place where one or more persons are present, * * * and manifests a drunken condition by boisterous or indecent conduct, or loud and profane discourse, shall, on conviction, be fined," etc.

Under the plain terms of this statute, a voluntary appearance is presupposed. The rule has been declared, and we think it sound, that an accusation of drunkenness in a designated public place cannot be established by proof that the accused, while in an intoxicated condition, was involuntarily and forcibly carried to that place by the arresting officer.

Conviction of appellant was contrary to this announced principle and, in our view, erroneous. * * *

Reversed and rendered.

Note

Although the number of true "situational offenses" is very small, these cases bear a family resemblance to three other more common kinds of cases. First are "entrapment" cases. If law enforcement officials go too far in encouraging a citizen to commit a crime, and then arrest her for it, she will have a valid affirmative defense. Second, in some circumstances it is a valid defense to a crime that one reasonably relied on the advice of a person with the official responsibility to enforce the law that was broken. This defense is analyzed as a "mistake of law" and will be discussed in Chapter 5. Finally, if a person uses physical force or the threat of force to cause the defendant to commit a crime, the defendant may be able to raise the affirmative defense of "duress" to escape culpability. This defense will be discussed in Chapter 10.

C. ACTING VOLUNTARILY VERSUS ACTING INVOLUNTARILY: THE UNCONSCIOUSNESS DEFENSE

In general, a person cannot be convicted of a crime unless he or she commits a voluntary (i.e. volitional) act that causes social harm. A volitional act is a movement of the body willed by the actor. Professor Joshua Dressler explains the difference between volitional and non-volitional acts:

> [Consider] the difference in meaning of the following two sentences: (1) "I raised my arm;" and (2) "My arm came up." Both statements suggest that a bodily movement has occurred. Yet, the difference in language expresses our understanding of the difference between a voluntary act (as described in the first sentence) and an involuntary one (the second sentence). In both cases, the arm movement was the result of impulses from the actor's brain. But, in the first sentence, the implication is that the act was the result of something more than mere physiological brain activity. That extra "something" was the more sophisticated thought process that goes into the "decision" to raise one's arm. . . . With a voluntary act, a human being –

a person – and not simply an organ of a human being, causes the bodily action.

Thus, when *D*'s arm strikes V as the result of an epileptic seizure, we sense that *D*'s *body*, but not *D* the person, has caused the impact. The movement of *D*'s arm is similar to a tree branch bending in the wind and striking *V*. When *D* "wills" her arm to move, however, we feel that *D*, and not simply her body, is responsible for *V*'s injury. Her "acting self" is implicated. A personal, human agency is involved in causing the bodily contact.[a]

Habitual acts are generally considered volitional even if "the actor is unaware of what she is doing as she is doing it." Dressler explains:

> One should be careful not to assume that an act is involuntary simply because the actor is unaware of what she is doing as she is doing it. For example, people act habitually: a chain-smoker may light up a cigarette "without thinking"; a driver coming home from work may change lanes on the freeway at precisely the same place each day, without even noticing that she is doing this. Although, at our best, we are aware of both our external and internal (mental) surroundings, sometimes we "don't notice that [we] notice . . . [We are] aware of everything except [ourselves]." In this sense, consciousness is a matter of degree, and the law treats habitual acts as falling on the voluntary side of the continuum.[b]

The next case, *State v. Decina*, involves the actions of a man who suffered an epileptic seizure at the wheel of his car with fatal consequences. The Court of Appeals of New York appears to deviate from the general rule that one cannot be held criminally liable for non-volitional acts, focusing most of its opinion on the recklessness of Mr. Decina's conduct which is really a question of mens rea. Are you persuaded by the court's reasoning?

---

[a] Joshua Dressler, UNDERSTANDING CRIMINAL LAW 86 (3d ed. 2001).

[b] *Id.*

STATE v. DECINA

Court of Appeals of New York

2 N.Y.2d 133, 138 N.E.2d 799, 157 N.Y.S.2d 558 (1956)

FROESSEL, JUDGE

At about 3:30 p.m. on March 14, 1955, a bright, sunny day, defendant was driving, alone in his car, in a northerly direction on Delaware Avenue in the city of Buffalo. The portion of Delaware Avenue here involved is 60 feet wide. At a point south of an overhead viaduct of the Erie Railroad, defendant's car swerved to the left, across the center line in the street, so that it was completely in the south lane, traveling 35 to 40 miles per hour.

It then veered sharply to the right, crossing Delaware Avenue and mounting the easterly curb at a point beneath the viaduct and continued thereafter at a speed estimated to have been about 50 or 60 miles per hour or more. During this latter swerve, a pedestrian testified that he saw defendant's hand above his head; another witness said he saw defendant's left arm bent over the wheel, and his right hand extended towards the right door.

A group of six schoolgirls were walking north on the easterly sidewalk of Delaware Avenue, two in front and four slightly in the rear, when defendant's car struck them from behind. One of the girls escaped injury by jumping against the wall of the viaduct. The bodies of the children struck were propelled northward onto the street and the lawn in front of a coal company, located to the north of the Erie viaduct on Delaware Avenue. Three of the children, 6 to 12 years old, were found dead on arrival by the medical examiner, and a fourth child, 7 years old, died in a hospital two days later as a result of injuries sustained in the accident.

After striking the children, defendant's car continued on the easterly sidewalk, and then swerved back onto Delaware Avenue once more. It continued in a northerly direction, passing under a second viaduct before it again veered to the right and remounted the easterly curb, striking and breaking a metal lamppost. With its horn blowing steadily – apparently because defendant was "stooped over" the steering wheel – the car proceeded on the sidewalk until it finally crashed through a 7 1/4-inch brick wall of a grocery store, injuring at least one customer and causing considerable property damage.

When the car came to a halt in the store, with its horn still blowing, several fires had been ignited. Defendant was stooped over in the car and was "bobbing a little." To one witness he appeared dazed, to another unconscious, lying back with his hands off the wheel. Various people present shouted to defendant to turn off the ignition of his car, and "within a matter of seconds the horn stopped blowing and the car did shut off."

Defendant was pulled out of the car by a number of bystanders and laid down on the sidewalk. To a policeman who came on the scene shortly he appeared "injured, dazed"; another witness said that "he looked as though he was knocked out, and his arm seemed to be bleeding." An injured customer in the store, after receiving first aid, pressed defendant for an explanation of the accident and he told her: "I blacked out from the bridge."

When the police arrived, defendant attempted to rise, staggered and appeared dazed and unsteady. When informed that he was under arrest, and would have to accompany the police to the station house, he resisted and, when he tried to get away, was handcuffed. The foregoing evidence was adduced by the People, and is virtually undisputed – defendant did not take the stand nor did he produce any witnesses.

From the police station defendant was taken to the E. J. Meyer Memorial Hospital, a county institution, arriving at 5:30 p.m. * * *

On the evening of that day, after an interne [sic] had visited and treated defendant and given orders for therapy, Dr. Wechter, a resident physician in the hospital and a member of its staff, came to his room. * * *

He asked defendant how he felt and what had happened. Defendant, who still felt a little dizzy or blurry, said that as he was driving he noticed a jerking of his right hand, which warned him that he might develop a convulsion, and that as he tried to steer the car over to the curb he felt himself becoming unconscious, and he thought he had a convulsion. He was aware that children were in front of his car, but did not know whether he had struck them.

Defendant then proceeded to relate to Dr. Wechter his past medical history, namely, that at the age of 7 he was struck by an auto and suffered a marked loss of hearing. In 1946 he was treated in this same hospital for an illness during which he had some convulsions. Several burr holes were made in his skull and a brain abscess was drained. Following this operation defendant had no convulsions from 1946 through 1950. In 1950 he had four convulsions, caused by scar tissue on the brain. From 1950 to 1954 he experienced about 10 or 20 seizures a year, in which his right hand would jump although he remained fully conscious. In 1954, he had 4 or 5 generalized seizures with loss of consciousness, the last being in September, 1954, a few months before the accident. Thereafter he had more hospitalization, a spinal tap, consultation with a neurologist, and took medication daily to help prevent seizures.

On the basis of this medical history, Dr. Wechter made a diagnosis of Jacksonian epilepsy, and was of the opinion that defendant had a seizure at the time of the accident. Other members of the hospital staff performed blood tests and took an electroencephalogram during defendant's three-day stay there. The testimony of Dr. Wechter is the only testimony before the trial court showing that defendant had epilepsy, suffered an attack at the time of the accident, and had knowledge of his susceptibility to such attacks.

Defendant was indicted and charged with violating section 1053-a of the Penal Law. Following his conviction, after a demurrer[a] to the indictment was overruled, the Appellate Division, while holding that the demurrer was properly overruled, reversed on the law, the facts having been "examined" and found "sufficient." * * *

We turn first to the subject of defendant's cross appeal, namely, that his demurrer should have been sustained, since the *indictment* here does not charge a crime. The indictment states essentially that defendant, *knowing* "that he was subject to epileptic attacks or other disorder rendering him likely to lose consciousness for a considerable period of time," was culpably negligent "in that he *consciously* undertook to and *did operate* his Buick sedan on a public highway" (emphasis supplied) and "while so doing" suffered such an attack which caused said automobile "to travel at a fast and reckless rate of speed, jumping the curb and driving over the sidewalk" causing the death of 4 persons. In our opinion, this clearly states a violation of section 1053-a of the Penal Law.[b] The statute does not require that a defendant must deliberately intend to kill a human being, for that would be murder. Nor does the statute require that he knowingly and consciously follow the precise path that leads to death and destruction. It is sufficient, we have said, when his conduct manifests a "disregard of the consequences which may ensue from the act, and indifference to the rights of others. No clearer definition, applicable to the hundreds of varying circumstances that may arise, can be given. Under a given state of facts, whether negligence is culpable is a question of judgment."

---

[a]A demurrer is a pleading filed by the defendant, which admits the matters of fact alleged in the complaint, but alleges that they are insufficient as a matter of law to state a cause of action.

[b]Section 1053-a, Criminal negligence in operation of vehicle resulting in death, provided that "A person who operates or drives any vehicle of any kind in a reckless or culpably negligent manner, whereby a human being is killed, is guilty of criminal negligence in the operation of a vehicle resulting in death." New York courts had previously held that the terms "criminal negligence" and "culpably negligent" represented a state of mind closer to recklessness than ordinary negligence.

Assuming the truth of the indictment, as we must on a demurrer, this defendant knew he was subject to epileptic attacks and seizures that might strike at any time. He also knew that a moving motor vehicle uncontrolled on a public highway is a highly dangerous instrumentality capable of unrestrained destruction. With this *knowledge*, and without anyone accompanying him, he deliberately took a chance by making a conscious choice of a course of action, in disregard of the consequences which he knew might follow from his conscious act, and which in this case did ensue. How can we say as a matter of law that this did not amount to culpable negligence within the meaning of section 1053-a?

To hold otherwise would be to say that a man may freely indulge himself in liquor in the same hope that it will not affect his driving, and if it later develops that ensuing intoxication causes dangerous and reckless driving resulting in death, his unconsciousness or involuntariness at that time would relieve him from prosecution under the statute. His awareness of a condition which he knows may produce such consequences as here, and his disregard of the consequences, renders him liable for culpable negligence, as the courts below have properly held. To have a sudden sleeping spell, an unexpected heart or other disabling attack, without any prior knowledge or warning thereof, is an altogether different situation, and there is simply no basis for comparing such cases with the flagrant disregard manifested here. * * *

Accordingly, the Appellate Division properly sustained the lower court's order overruling the demurrer, as well as its denial of the motion in arrest of judgment on the same ground.

JUDGE DESMOND, concurring in part and dissenting in part.

I agree that the judgment of conviction cannot stand but I think the indictment should be dismissed because it alleges no crime. Defendant's demurrer should have been sustained.

The indictment charges that defendant knowing that "he was subject to epileptic attacks or other disorder rendering him likely to lose consciousness" suffered "an attack and loss of consciousness which caused the said automobile operated by the said defendant to travel at a fast and reckless rate of speed" and to jump a curb and run onto the sidewalk "thereby striking and causing the death" of 4 children. Horrible as this occurrence was and whatever necessity it may show for new licensing and driving laws, nevertheless this indictment charges no crime known to the New York statutes. Our duty is to dismiss it.

Section 1053-a of the Penal Law describes the crime of "criminal negligence in the operation of a vehicle resulting in death." Declared to be guilty of that crime is "A person who operates or drives any vehicle of any kind in a reckless or culpably negligent manner, whereby a human being is killed." The essentials of the crime are, therefore, first, vehicle operation in a culpably negligent *manner*, and, second, the resulting death of a person. This indictment asserts that defendant violated section 1053-a, but it then proceeds in the language quoted in the next-above paragraph of this opinion to describe the way in which defendant is supposed to have offended against that statute. That descriptive matter shows that defendant did *not* violate section 1053-a. No *operation* of an automobile in a reckless manner is charged against defendant. The excessive speed of the car and its jumping the curb were "caused," says the indictment itself, by defendant's prior "attack and loss of consciousness." Therefore, what defendant is accused of is *not* reckless or culpably negligent driving, which necessarily connotes and involves consciousness and volition. The fatal assault by this car was after and because of defendant's failure of consciousness. To say that one drove a car in a reckless manner in that his unconscious condition caused the car to travel recklessly is to make two mutually contradictory assertions. One cannot be "reckless" while unconscious. One cannot while unconscious "operate" a car in a culpably negligent manner or in any other "manner." The statute makes criminal a particular kind of knowing, voluntary, immediate operation. It does not touch at all the involuntary presence of an unconscious person at the wheel of an uncontrolled vehicle. To negative the possibility of applying section 1053-a to these alleged facts we do not even have to resort to the rule that all criminal statutes are closely and strictly construed in favor of the citizen and that no act or omission is criminal unless specifically and in terms so labeled by a clearly worded statute. * * *

Numerous are the diseases and other conditions of a human being which make it possible or even likely that the afflicted person will lose control of his automobile. Epilepsy, coronary involvements, circulatory diseases, nephritis, uremic poisoning, diabetes, Meniere's syndrome, a tendency to fits of sneezing, locking of the knee, muscular contractions – any of these common conditions may cause loss of control of a vehicle for a period long enough to cause a fatal accident. An automobile traveling at only 30 miles an hour goes 44 feet in a second. Just what is the court holding here? No less than this: that a driver whose brief blackout lets his car run amuck and kill another has killed that other by reckless driving. But any such "recklessness" consists necessarily not of the erratic behavior of the automobile while its driver is unconscious, but of his driving at all when he knew he was subject to such attacks. Thus, it must be that such a blackout-prone driver is guilty of reckless driving whenever and as soon as he steps into the driver's seat of a vehicle. Every time he drives, accident or no accident, he is subject to criminal prosecution for reckless driving or to revocation of his operator's license. * * *

When section 1053-a was new it was assailed as unconstitutional on the ground that the language "operates or drives any vehicle of any kind in a reckless or culpably negligent manner" was too indefinite since a driver could only guess as to what acts or omissions were meant. * * * [G]iving section 1053-1 the new meaning assigned to it permits punishment of one who did not drive in any forbidden manner but should not have driven at all, according to the present theory. No motorist suffering from any serious malady or infirmity can with impunity drive any automobile at any time or place, since no one can know what physical conditions make it "reckless" or "culpably negligent" to drive an automobile. Such a construction of a criminal statute offends against due process and against justice and fairness. * * *

A whole new approach may be necessary to the problem of issuing or refusing drivers' licenses to epileptics and persons similarly afflicted. But the absence of adequate licensing controls cannot in law or in justice be supplied by criminal prosecutions of drivers who have violated neither the language nor the intendment of any criminal law.

Entirely without pertinence here is any consideration of driving while intoxicated or while sleepy, since those are conditions presently known to the driver, not mere future possibilities or probabilities.

The demurrer should be sustained and the indictment dismissed.

INTERPRETIVE CONSTRUCTION IN THE SUBSTANTIVE CRIMINAL LAW
Mark Kelman
33 Stan. L. Rev. 591 (1981)

* * * By interpretive construction, I refer to processes by which concrete situations are reduced to substantive legal controversies: It refers both to the way we construe a factual situation and to the way we frame the possible rules to handle the situation. What then follows logically, if not chronologically, is rational rhetoricism – the process of presenting the legal conclusions that result when interpretive constructs are applied to the "facts." * * *

Legal argument can be made only *after* a fact pattern is characterized by interpretive constructs. Once these constructs operate, a single legal result seems inevitable, a result seemingly deduced on general principle. These constructs appear both in conscious and unconscious forms in standard legal discourse. * * *

*   *   *

The voluntary act requirement. Unconscious shifting between broad and narrow time frames * * * arises in applying the criminal law's voluntary act requirement. In *Martin v. State*, police officers arrested the defendant at his home and took him onto a public highway, where the defendant used loud and profane language. He was convicted under a statute prohibiting public exhibition of a drunken condition. The appellate court reversed, holding that the defendant was involuntarily and forcibly carried to the public place by the arresting officers. The court concluded, uncontroversially, that an involuntary act cannot give rise to liability. But in *People v. Decina*, the court sustained the defendant's conviction for negligent homicide, though at the time his car struck the victims, he was unconscious as a result of an epileptic fit, not voluntarily operating the vehicle. The court held that the defendant was culpable because he had made a conscious decision to drive, knowing that an epileptic attack was possible.

The hidden interpretive time-framing construct becomes visible when one tries to square *Martin* with *Decina*. In *Decina*, the court opened up the time frame, declaring that if the defendant commits a voluntary act at time one which poses a risk of causing an involuntary harm later–drives the car knowing he is a blackout-prone epileptic–then the second act–crashing while unconscious–will be deemed voluntary. But the defendant in *Martin*, as well, may have done *something* voluntarily (before the police came) that posed a risk that he would get arrested and carried into public in his drunken state. While it is plausible that Martin was arrested on an old warrant and could not foresee that he would wind up in public on this occasion, it is quite possible that the defendant was arrested for activity he was engaging in at home: for instance, beating his wife. Why did the court not consider saying that the voluntary act at time one (wife beating) both posed a risk of and caused a harmful involuntary act at time two (public drunkenness) and assessing the voluntariness of the alleged criminal act with reference to the wider time-framed scenario? It cannot be that the involuntary, harmful act at time two was unforeseeable. The probability of an epileptic blackout is almost certainly far lower than the probability of ending up in public after engaging in behavior likely to draw police attention. * * *

EPILEPTIC CONVICTED OF ASSAULT CLEARED
Associated Press[a]
Los Angeles Daily Journal, Sept. 25, 1997, at 5[b]

ARLINGTON, Va. – A man with epilepsy who was convicted of assault for grabbing a woman's arm during a seizure has been cleared after convincing a judge that he wasn't in control of himself. Scott D. Vining was found guilty in July after he grabbed the woman on a commuter train in the Washington suburbs and refused to let go. A third passenger intervened. On Tuesday, when he had been scheduled to be sentenced, Arlington County Judge Griffin T. Garnett Jr. dismissed the verdict after seeing videotapes of Vining having seizures, including some in which he lunged at people. The tapes were shot over six days at George Washington University Hospital. Vining voluntarily stopped taking his medication to prove that his epilepsy could cause the behavior he exhibited on May 19. The prosecutor who had obtained Vining's conviction joined the defense in seeking the dismissal.

In finding Vining guilty, Garnett had discounted a letter from the man's doctor and testimony about his previous seizures. Vining, 35, had faced up to a year in jail and a $2,500 fine.

The woman Vining grabbed on the train, Lavita Haugabrook, was not in court Tuesday, but her mother and stepfather were and were distressed by the judge's decision. "I don't believe this," said Diane Johnson, shaking her head. "He hasn't said one time, 'I'm sorry.'" Outside the courtroom, however, Vining did just that. "I am deeply, deeply sorry about what your daughter experienced," he told Ms. Johnson. "I had no knowledge . . . If I had, I would have done everything humanly possible to explain what happened."

Alexandra K. Finucane, vice president of the Epilepsy Foundation of America, said the case "demonstrates the crying need for educating not only the general public about epilepsy but also the police, prosecutors and even the judiciary."

---

[a]Reprinted with permission of The Associated Press.

[b]Copyright 2003 Daily Journal Corp. Reprinted with permission. The Daily Journal's definition of reprint and posting permission does not include the copying by third parties.

D. ACTING VERSUS FAILING TO ACT: LIABILITY FOR OMISSIONS

Despite the general rule that a voluntary act that causes the social harm is necessary to satisfy the actus reus requirement, criminal liability can be based upon an omission if the defendant had a legal duty to act and was physically capable of acting. The omission which replaces the voluntary act must also cause the social harm, and the defendant must act with the requisite mens rea in order to be convicted of the offense.

The courts have recognized five situations in which individuals have a legal duty to act:

(1) when there is a *special relationship* between the defendant and the victim, such as the relationship between husbands and wives, parents and children, and masters and servants;

(2) when the defendant enters into a *contract* which requires him either explicitly or implicitly to act in a particular way (e.g., a contractual duty to provide care to an elderly individual);

(3) when there is a *statutory duty* to act (such as the duty to pay federal taxes found in the Internal Revenue Code);

(4) when the defendant *creates the risk* of harm to the victim; and

(5) when the defendant, who otherwise would not have a duty to act, *voluntarily assumes care* of a person in need of help.

In order to be held criminally liable for an omission, the defendant must have been physically capable of acting. For example, if the defendant is a mother whose child falls into a swimming pool, the mother ordinarily would have a duty to rescue her child (or at least attempt such a rescue) because of the special relationship recognized by courts between parents and their children. If the mother just stands there and watches her child drown, not jumping into the swimming pool to attempt a rescue, she could be charged with negligent homicide as long as she had the requisite mental state required for commission of that crime. Given the "physically capable of acting" requirement, however, if the mother did not know how to swim or could not swim because of some physical limitation, then she could not be held criminally liable for her failure to jump into the pool. She might, however, be held criminally liable for failing to throw her child a life preserver if a life preserver was available and she was physically capable of throwing it to her child.

Additionally, the defendant must have known of the facts giving rise to the need for action. For example, if a mother is swimming in a lake and does not know that her daughter is drowning five feet away from her, the mother cannot be held liable for her failure to rescue her daughter.

The first two cases in this section discuss some of the ways a person can be held criminally liable for a failure to act. The remaining materials examine the general American rule that there is no legal duty to rescue a total stranger. In particular, these materials explore the question whether it is wise to adopt Good Samaritan statutes that attempt to reverse the general American rule by imposing a statutory duty to rescue or at least call for help when one knows that another individual is in need of assistance.

1.   **Establishing the Duty to Act**

PEOPLE v. BEARDSLEY
Supreme Court of Michigan
150 Mich. 206, 113 N.W. 1128 (1907)

MCALVAY, J.C..

Respondent was convicted of manslaughter before the circuit court for Oakland county, and was sentenced to the State prison at Jackson for a minimum term of one year and a maximum term not to exceed five years. He was a married man living at Pontiac, and at the time the facts herein narrated occurred, he was working as a bartender and clerk at the Columbia Hotel. He lived with his wife in Pontiac, occupying two rooms on the ground floor of a house. Other rooms were rented to tenants, as was also one living room in the basement. His wife being temporarily absent from the city, respondent arranged with a woman named Blanche Burns, who at the time was working at another hotel, to go to his apartments with him. He had been acquainted with her for some time. They knew each other's habits and character. They had drunk liquor together, and had on two occasions been in Detroit and spent the night together in houses of assignation. On the evening of Saturday, March 18, 1905, he met her at the place where she worked, and they went together to his place of residence. They at once began to drink and continued to drink steadily, and remained together, day and night, from that time until the afternoon of the Monday following, except when respondent went to his work on Sunday afternoon. There was liquor at these rooms, and when it was all used they were served with bottles of whiskey and beer by a young man who worked at the Columbia Hotel, and who also attended respondent's fires at the house. He was the only person who saw them in the house during the time they were there together. Respondent gave orders for liquor by telephone. On Monday afternoon, about one o'clock, the young man went to the house to see if anything was wanted. At this time he heard respondent say they must fix up the rooms, and the woman must not be found there by his wife, who was likely to return at any time. During this visit to the house the woman sent the young man to a drug store to purchase, with money she gave him, camphor and morphine tablets. He procured both articles. There were six grains of morphine in quarter-grain tablets. She concealed the morphine from respondent's notice, and was discovered putting something into her mouth by him and the young man as they were returning from the other room after taking a drink of beer. She in fact was taking morphine. Respondent struck the box from her hand. Some of the tablets fell on the floor, and of these, respondent crushed several with his foot. She picked up and swallowed two of them, and the young man put two of them in the spittoon. Altogether it is probable she took from three to four grains of morphine. The young man went away soon after this. Respondent called him by telephone about an hour later, and after he came to the house requested him to take the woman into the room in the basement which was occupied by a Mr. Skoba. She was in a stupor and did not rouse when spoken to. Respondent was too intoxicated to be of any assistance and the young man proceeded to take her downstairs. While doing this Skoba arrived, and together they put her in his room on the bed. Respondent requested Skoba to look after her, and let her out the back way when she waked up. Between nine and ten o'clock in the evening Skoba became alarmed at her condition. He at once called the city marshal and a doctor. An examination by them disclosed that she was dead.

　　　　Many errors are assigned by respondent, who asks to have his conviction set aside. The principal assignments of error are based upon the charge of the court, and refusal to give certain requests to charge, and are upon the theory that under the undisputed evidence in the case, as claimed by the people and detailed by the people's witnesses, the respondent should have been acquitted and discharged. In the brief of the prosecutor his position is stated as follows:

> It is the theory of the prosecution that the facts and circumstances attending the death of Blanche Burns in the house of respondent were such as to lay upon him a duty to care for her, and the duty to take steps for her protection, the failure to take which, was sufficient to constitute such an omission as would render him legally responsible for her death. * * * There is no claim on the part of the people that the respondent was in any way an active agent in bringing about the death of Blanche Burns, but simply that he owed her a duty which he failed to perform, and that in consequence of such failure on his part she came to her death.

Upon this theory a conviction was asked and secured.

The law recognizes that under some circumstances the omission of a duty owed by one individual to another, where such omission results in the death of the one to whom the duty is owing, will make the other chargeable with manslaughter. This rule of law is always based upon the proposition that the duty neglected must be a legal duty, and not a mere moral obligation. It must be a duty imposed by law or by contract, and the omission to perform the duty must be the immediate and direct cause of death.

Although the literature upon the subject is quite meagre and the cases few, nevertheless, the authorities are in harmony as to the relationship which must exist between the parties to create the duty, the omission of which establishes legal responsibility. One authority has briefly and correctly stated the rule, which the prosecution claims should be applied to the case at bar, as follows:

> If a person who sustains to another the legal relation of protector, as husband to wife, parent to child, master to seaman, etc., knowing such person to be in peril of life, willfully or negligently fails to make such reasonable and proper efforts to rescue him as he might have done without jeopardizing his own life or the lives of others, he is guilty of manslaughter at least, if by reason of his omission of duty the dependent person dies.

> So one who from domestic relationship, public duty, voluntary choice, or otherwise, has the custody and care of a human being, helpless either from imprisonment, infancy, sickness, age, imbecility, or other incapacity of mind or body, is bound to execute the charge with proper diligence and will be held guilty of manslaughter, if by culpable negligence he lets the helpless creature die.

The following brief digest of cases gives the result of our examination of American and English authorities, where the doctrine of criminal liability was involved when death resulted from an omission to perform a claimed duty. We discuss no cases where statutory provisions are involved. In *Territory v. Manton,* a husband was convicted of manslaughter for leaving his intoxicated wife one winter's night lying in the snow, from which exposure she died. The conviction was sustained on the ground that a legal duty rested upon him to care for and protect his wife, and that his neglect to perform that duty, resulting in her death, he was properly convicted.

State v. Smith is a similar case. A husband neglected to provide clothing and shelter for his insane wife. He left her in a bare room without fire during severe winter weather. Her death resulted. The charge in the indictment is predicated upon a known legal duty of the husband to furnish his wife with suitable protection.

In *State v. Behm,* the conviction of a mother of manslaughter for exposing her infant child without protection, was affirmed upon the same ground.

State v. Noakes was a prosecution and conviction of a husband and wife for manslaughter. A child of a maid servant was born under their roof. They were charged with neglecting to furnish it with proper care. In addition to announcing the principle in support of which the case is already cited, the court said:

> To create a criminal liability for neglect by nonfeasance, the neglect must also be of a personal, legal duty, the natural and ordinary consequences of neglecting which would be dangerous to life.

In reversing the case for error in the charge – not necessary to here set forth – the court expressly stated that it did not concede that respondents were under a legal duty to care for this child because it was permitted to be born under their roof, and declined to pass upon that question. * * *

The case of *Regina v. Nicholls,* was a prosecution of a penniless old woman, a grandmother, for neglecting to supply an infant grandchild left in her charge with sufficient food and proper care. The case was tried at assizes in Stafford before Brett, J., who said to the jury:

> If a grown up person chooses to undertake the charge of a human creature, helpless either from infancy, simplicity, lunacy, or other infirmity, he is bound to execute that charge without (at all events) wicked negligence, and if a person who has chosen to take charge of a helpless creature lets it die by wicked negligence, that person is guilty of manslaughter.

* * * The charge of this nisi prius judge recognizes the principle that a person may voluntarily assume the care of a helpless human being, and having assumed it, will be held to be under an implied legal duty to care for and protect such person. The duty assumed being that of caretaker and protector to the exclusion of all others.

Another English case decided in the appellate court, Lord Coleridge, C.J., delivering the opinion, is *Regina v. Instan.* An unmarried woman without means lived with and was maintained by her aged aunt. The aunt suddenly became very sick, and for ten days before her death was unable to attend to herself, to move about, or to do anything to procure assistance. Before her death no one but the prisoner had any knowledge of her condition. The prisoner continued to live in the house at the cost of the deceased and took in the food supplied by the tradespeople. The prisoner did not give food to the deceased, or give or procure any medical or nursing attendance for her; nor did she give notice to any neighbor of her condition or wants, although she had abundant opportunity and occasion to do so. In the opinion, Lord Coleridge, speaking for the court, said:

> It is not correct to say that every moral obligation is a legal duty; but every legal duty is founded upon a moral obligation. In this case, as in most cases, the legal duty can be nothing else than taking upon one's self the performance of the moral obligation. There is no question whatever that it was this woman's clear duty to impart to the deceased so much of that food, which was taken into the house for both and paid for by the deceased, as was necessary to sustain her life. The deceased could not get it for herself. She could only get it through the prisoner. It was the prisoner's clear duty at common law to supply it to the deceased, and that duty she did not perform. Nor is there any question that the prisoner's failure to discharge her legal duty, if it did not directly cause, at any rate accelerated, the death of the deceased. There is no case directly on the point; but it would be a slur and a stigma upon our law if there could be any doubt as to the law to be derived from the principle of decided cases, if cases were necessary. There was a clear moral obligation, and a legal duty founded upon it; a duty willfully disregarded and the death was at least accelerated, if not caused, by the nonperformance of the legal duty.

*   *   *

Seeking for a proper determination of the case at bar by the application of the legal principles involved, we must eliminate from the case all consideration of mere moral obligation, and discover whether respondent was under a legal duty towards Blanche Burns at the time of her death, knowing her to be in peril of her life, which required him to make all reasonable and proper effort to save her; the omission to perform which duty would make him responsible for her death. This is the important and determining question in this case. If we hold that such legal duty rested upon respondent it must arise by implication from the facts and circumstances already recited. The record in this case discloses that the deceased was a woman past 30 years of age. She had been twice married. She was accustomed to visiting saloons and to the use of intoxicants. She previously had made assignations with this man in Detroit at least twice. There is no evidence or claim from this record that any duress, fraud, or deceit had been practiced upon her. On the contrary it appears that she went upon this carouse with respondent voluntarily and so continued to remain with him. Her entire conduct indicates that she had ample experience in such affairs.

It is urged by the prosecutor that the respondent "stood towards this woman for the time being in the place of her natural guardian and protector, and as such owed her a clear legal duty which he completely failed to perform." The cases cited and digested establish that no such legal duty is created based upon a mere moral obligation. The fact that this woman was in his house created no such legal duty as exists in law and is due from a husband towards his wife, as seems to be intimated by the prosecutor's brief. Such an inference would be very repugnant to our moral sense. Respondent had assumed either in fact or by implication no care or control over his companion. Had this been a case where two men under like circumstances had voluntarily gone on a debauch together and one had attempted suicide, no one would claim that this doctrine of legal duty could be invoked to hold the other criminally responsible for omitting to make effort to rescue his companion. How can the fact that in this case one of the parties was a woman, change the principle of law applicable to it? Deriving and applying the law in this case from the principle of decided cases, we do not find that such legal duty as is contended for existed in fact or by implication on the part of respondent towards the deceased, the omission of which involved criminal liability. We find no more apt words to apply to this case than those used by Mr. Justice Field in *United States v. Knowles*:

> In the absence of such obligations, it is undoubtedly the moral duty of every person to extend to others assistance when in danger; * * * and if such efforts should be omitted by any one when they could be made without imperiling his own life, he would, by his conduct, draw upon himself the just censure and reproach of good men; but this is the only punishment to which he would be subjected by society.

Other questions discussed in the briefs need not be considered. The conviction is set aside, and respondent is ordered discharged.

COMMONWEALTH V. HOWARD
Superior Court of Pennsylvania
265 Pa. Super. 535, 402 A.2d 674 (Super Ct. 1979)

HOFFMAN, Judge:

Appellant contends that the Commonwealth failed to prove her guilty of involuntary manslaughter beyond a reasonable doubt because the evidence was insufficient to prove that her actions were reckless or directly caused the death of her five year old daughter. We conclude that the evidence was sufficient to prove all the essential elements of the crime, and therefore, we affirm.

Appellant resided with her daughter and a boyfriend, Edward Watts. For a period of several weeks before the child's death, Watts regularly beat the child and subjected her to various forms of sadistic abuse. Appellant also struck the child on occasion, sometimes with a belt or strap. On the evening of March 5, 1977, during the course of a beating by Watts, the child fell and hit her head on a piece of furniture. When appellant could not awaken her child the next morning, Watts called the police and fabricated a story to explain the child's injuries, which included a bloodied nose and bruised forehead. The child was pronounced dead on arrival at a local hospital. The stated cause of death was multiple injuries to the head and trunk.[1]

Under Section 2504 of our Crimes Code, 18 Pa.C.S.A. § 2504, "A person is guilty of involuntary manslaughter when as a direct result of the doing of an unlawful act in a reckless or grossly negligent manner, or the doing of a lawful act in a reckless or grossly negligent manner, he causes the death of another person." Although there was evidence in the record that appellant struck her child on occasion, the lower court in this waiver trial premised appellant's culpability on her failure to protect her child from the more regular and severe

---

[1] A post-mortem examination of the child revealed 43 major categories of external wounds. Of these, some were recent, some were several days old, and others were more remote. The medical examiner also described numerous internal injuries to the child, including extensive contusions of the scalp, a bilateral subdural hemorrhage, internal bleeding and swelling in the brain, laceration of the lung tissues, and a remote fracture of the right sixth rib (since healed), which indicated the injury was at least several weeks old and probably older. The examiner stated that the internal injuries were the result of the same multiple blunt impacts on the child's body which caused the various external injuries. Some of the child's injuries also revealed various types of sadistic torture practiced upon her, which we will not detail here.

beatings inflicted upon her by Watts. We affirm because we conclude that the evidence was sufficient to prove that appellant's failure to protect the child was a direct cause of her death, and that such failure was reckless or grossly negligent under the circumstances.

Preliminarily we note that an omission to act may create criminal culpability under our Crimes Code even though the law defining the offense, as here, requires an "act," where "a duty to perform the omitted act is otherwise imposed by law." 18 Pa.C.S.A. § 301(b)(2). Here, appellant and the victim stood in the relation of parent and child. A parent has the legal duty to protect her child, and the discharge of this duty requires affirmative performance.

Next we must examine whether the child's death was "a direct result of" appellant's failure to protect her child from Watts' beatings and abuse. While the immediate cause of the child's death was multiple injuries to the head and trunk, inflicted on the child by Watts over a period of several weeks, appellant may still be held culpable for her continuing failure to protect the child during all that time. * * * [W]e hold that appellant's failure to protect her child from Watts' savagery was a direct cause of death sufficient to impose criminal culpability.

Lastly, we must consider whether appellant's failure to protect her child was, under these circumstances, reckless or grossly negligent. Section 302(b)(3) of the Crimes Code, 18 Pa.C.S.A. § 302(b)(3) states:

> A person acts recklessly with respect to a material element of an offense when he consciously disregards a substantial and unjustifiable risk that the material element exists or will result from his conduct. The risk must be of such a nature and degree that, considering the nature and intent of the actor's conduct and the circumstances known to him, its disregard involves a gross deviation from the standard of conduct that a reasonable person would observe in the actor's situation.

*   *   *

Here appellant witnessed and had full knowledge of a continuing pattern of severe beatings, abuse, and sadistic torture inflicted on her child by Watts over a period of at least several weeks. However, appellant did nothing to protect her child. She never evicted or even discouraged Watts. She never reported anything to the public authorities. Taken together with the evidence of different ages and severity of the child's injuries this is sufficient to show that appellant consciously disregarded a manifestly apparent risk to the health and safety of her young child and that this neglect was a gross deviation from the standard of conduct the reasonable parent would observe under the circumstances. It is this long period of knowing yet apathetic acquiescence in her child's undoubted agony which satisfies the culpability requirements of the involuntary manslaughter statute.

Judgment of sentence affirmed.

MOTHERHOOD AND CRIME
Dorothy E. Roberts
79 Iowa L. Rev. 95 (1993)

* * * I usually push my criminal law students to determine the extent of the obligation mothers owe their children when we discuss *Commonwealth v. Howard* [402 A.2d 674 (Pa. Super. Ct. 1979)]. In Howard, a mother was convicted of manslaughter for failing to protect her young child from her boyfriend's deadly abuse. "Must a mother forego all self-interest, take on any risk, in order to avoid criminal liability?" I ask. "Must she even risk injury to herself in order to ensure her children's safety?" At least one student will invariably respond: "A mother must be willing to give up her own life in order to protect her children from harm." * * *

The law compels and legitimates prevailing relationships of power. Criminal law not only defines and mandates socially acceptable behavior, it also shapes the way we perceive ourselves and our relationships to others. Legal rules reward conduct that fulfills a woman's maternal role and punish conduct that conflicts with mothering. Society's construction of mother, its image of what constitutes a good mother and what constitutes a bad mother, facilitates its continuing control of women. Society considers women who fail to meet the ideal of motherhood deviant or criminal. It stigmatizes unwed mothers, unfit mothers, and women who do not become mothers for violating the dominant norm. Considering our society's general neglect of children, it is probable that laws which punish mothers' conduct do so just as much to enforce gender roles as to protect children. * * *

The starkest example of criminal law's suppression of a mother's personal identity is the prosecution of women for failing to protect their children from another's abuse. In 1991, a Tennessee jury convicted Denise Maupin of aiding and abetting the first degree murder of her two-year-old son, Michael. The day her son died, Ms. Maupin left her two children at home in the care of her boyfriend, Thomas Hale, while she went to her first day of work at a local fast food restaurant. When she returned home she found that Hale had beaten Michael until he was barely conscious for wetting his pants. Michael died that night in the hospital. The court sentenced Denise Maupin to life imprisonment.

In 1992, the prosecutor in Kings County, New York, charged Mrs. G. with sexual abuse of her children, and, in the alternative, neglect for failing to protect them from their father's sexual abuse. The case came to the attention of the authorities when Mrs. G. went to the 68th police precinct for help after her husband violently assaulted her. After referral to the Victim Services Agency, she told a caseworker that her husband had been molesting the children, as well as beating her. At trial, Mrs. G. testified that her husband would threaten her, punch and kick her, and bang her head against the wall for trying to intervene when he abused the children. In 1987, Mrs. G. fled from her husband and moved in with her sister in Florida. Not long afterwards, Mr. G. located his wife through a private detective. He harassed his wife and her sister until she returned to him in New York. Two experts testified at the trial that Mrs. G. suffered from battered woman's syndrome, which deprived her of the ability to protect herself and her children. Nevertheless, the judge entered a finding of neglect, imposing strict liability.

Courts hold mothers responsible for violence in the family. Society considers child abuse a failure of a mother's natural capacity to nurture and protect. Even though men are at least as likely as women to abuse children, psychological theory and social service practice generally attribute child abuse to maternal deficiency. With respect to the failure of child abuse researchers to study the father's role, Judith Martin observes, "[T]he mother is not only expected to be most deeply and intimately concerned with child-rearing; she is also at fault should any mischance occur in that process. No matter who actually harms the child, mother has failed in her duty to create a safe environment for her young." The criminal law reflects this dominant social science view of a mother's responsibility for child abuse. * * *

COMMONWEALTH v. PESTINIKAS

Superior Court of Pennsylvania
421 Pa. Super. 371 617 A.2d 1339 (Super Ct. 1992)

WIEAND, J.

The principal issue in this appeal is whether a person can be prosecuted criminally for murder when his or her failure to perform a contract to provide food and medical care for another has caused the death of such other person. The trial court answered this question in the affirmative and instructed the jury accordingly. The jury thereafter found Walter and Helen Pestinikas guilty of murder of the third degree in connection with the starvation and dehydration death of ninety-two (92) year old Joseph Kly. On direct appeal from the judgment of sentence, the defendants contend that the trial court misapplied the law and gave the jury incorrect instructions. They argue, therefore, that they are entitled to an arrest of judgment because of the insufficiency of the evidence against them or at least a new trial because of the trial court's erroneous instructions to the jury.* * *

Joseph Kly met Walter and Helen Pestinikas in the latter part of 1981 when Kly consulted them about prearranging his funeral. In March, 1982, Kly, who had been living with a stepson, was hospitalized and diagnosed as suffering from Zenker's diverticulum, a weakness in the walls of the esophagus, which caused him to have trouble swallowing food. In the hospital, Kly was given food which he was able to swallow and, as a result, regained some of the weight which he had lost. When he was about to be discharged, he expressed a desire not to return to his stepson's home and sent word to appellants that he wanted to speak with them. As a consequence, arrangements were made for appellants to care for Kly in their home on Main Street in Scranton, Lackawanna County.

Kly was discharged from the hospital on April 12, 1982. When appellants came for him on that day they were instructed by medical personnel regarding the care which was required for Kly and were given a prescription to have filled for him. Arrangements were also made for a visiting nurse to come to appellants' home to administer vitamin B-12 supplements to Kly. Appellants agreed orally to follow the medical instructions and to supply Kly with food, shelter, care and the medicine which he required.

According to the evidence, the prescription was never filled, and the visiting nurse was told by appellants that Kly did not want the vitamin supplement shots and that her services, therefore, were not required. Instead of giving Kly a room in their home, appellants removed him to a rural part of Lackawanna County, where they placed him in the enclosed porch of a building, which they owned, known as the Stage Coach Inn. This porch was approximately nine feet by thirty feet, with no insulation, no refrigeration, no bathroom, no sink and no telephone. The walls contained cracks which exposed the room to outside weather conditions. Kly's predicament was compounded by appellants' affirmative efforts to conceal his whereabouts. Thus, they gave misleading information in response to inquiries, telling members of Kly's family that they did not know where he had gone and others that he was living in their home.

After Kly was discharged from the hospital, appellants took Kly to the bank and had their names added to his savings account. Later, Kly's money was transferred into an account in the names of Kly or Helen Pestinikas, pursuant to which moneys could be withdrawn without Kly's signature. Bank records reveal that from May, 1982, to July, 1983, appellants withdrew amounts roughly consistent with the three hundred ($300) dollars per month which Kly had agreed to pay for his care. Beginning in August, 1983 and continuing until Kly's death in November, 1984, however, appellants withdrew much larger sums so that when Kly died, a balance of only fifty-five ($55) dollars remained. In the interim, appellants had withdrawn in excess of thirty thousand ($30,000) dollars.

On the afternoon of November 15, 1984, when police and an ambulance crew arrived in response to a call by appellants, Kly's dead body appeared emaciated, with his ribs and sternum greatly pronounced. Mrs. Pestinikas told police that she and her husband had taken care of Kly for three hundred ($300) dollars per month and that she had given him cookies and orange juice at 11:30 a.m. on the morning of his death. A subsequent autopsy, however, revealed that Kly had been dead at that time and may have been dead for as many as thirty-nine (39) hours before his body was found. The cause of death was determined to be starvation and dehydration. Expert testimony opined that Kly would have experienced pain and suffering over a long period of time before he died.

At trial, the Commonwealth contended that after contracting orally to provide food, shelter, care and necessary medicine for Kly, appellants engaged in a course of conduct calculated to deprive Kly of those things necessary to maintain life and thereby cause his death. The trial court instructed the jury that appellants could not be found guilty of a malicious killing for failing to provide food, shelter and necessary medicines to Kly unless a duty to do so had been imposed upon them by contract. The court instructed the jury, inter alia, as follows:

> In order for you to convict the defendants on any of the homicide charges or the criminal conspiracy or recklessly endangering charges, you must first find beyond a reasonable doubt that the defendants had a legal duty of care to Joseph Kly.

> There are but two situations in which Pennsylvania law imposes criminal liability for the failure to perform an act. One of these is where the express language of the law defining the offense provides for criminal [liability] based upon such a failure. The other is where the law otherwise imposes a duty to act.

> Unless you find beyond a reasonable doubt that an oral contract imposed a duty to act upon Walter and Helen Pestinikas, you must acquit the defendants.

Appellants contend that this was error.

The applicable law appears at 18 Pa.C.S. § 301(a) and (b) as follows:

(a) General rule.– A person is not guilty of an offense unless his liability is based on conduct which includes a voluntary act or the omission to perform an act of which he is physically capable.

(b) Omission as basis of liability.– Liability for the commission of an offense may not be based on an omission unaccompanied by action unless:

> (1) the omission is expressly made sufficient by the law defining the offense; or

> (2) a duty to perform the omitted act is otherwise imposed by law.

With respect to subsection (b), Toll, in his invaluable work on the Pennsylvania Crimes Code, has commented

> . . . [Subsection (b)] states the conventional position with respect to omissions unaccompanied by action as a basis of liability. Unless the omission is expressly made sufficient by the law defining the offense, a duty to perform the omitted act must have been otherwise imposed by law for the omission to have the same standing as a voluntary act for purposes of liability. It should, of course, suffice, as the courts now hold, that the duty arises under some branch of the civil law. If it does, this minimal requirement is satisfied, though whether the omission constitutes an offense depends as well on many other factors. * * *

In *Jones v. United States* the court stated:

There are at least four situations in which the failure to act may constitute breach of a legal duty. One can be held criminally liable: first, where a statute imposes a duty to care for another; second, where one stands in a certain status relationship to another; third, where one has assumed a contractual duty to care for another; and fourth, where one has voluntarily assumed the care of another and so secluded the helpless person as to prevent others from rendering aid.

[T]he duty must be one which the party is bound to perform by law or by contract, and not one the performance of which depends simply upon his humanity, or his sense of justice or propriety. It has been said that a legal duty to assist another does not arise out of a mere moral duty. * * *

Consistently with this legal thinking we hold that when, in 18 Pa.C.S. § 301(b)(2), the statute provides that an omission to do an act can be the basis for criminal liability if a duty to perform the omitted act has been imposed by law, the legislature intended to distinguish between a legal duty to act and merely a moral duty to act. A duty to act imposed by contract is legally enforceable and, therefore, creates a legal duty. It follows that a failure to perform a duty imposed by contract may be the basis for a charge of criminal homicide if such failure causes the death of another person and all other elements of the offense are present. Because there was evidence in the instant case that Kly's death had been caused by appellants' failure to provide the food and medical care which they had agreed by oral contract to provide for him, their omission to act was sufficient to support a conviction for criminal homicide, and the trial court was correct when it instructed the jury accordingly.

Our holding is not that every breach of contract can become the basis for a finding of homicide resulting from an omission to act. A criminal act involves both a physical and mental aspect. An omission to act can satisfy the physical aspect of criminal conduct only if there is a duty to act imposed by law. A failure to provide food and medicine, in this case, could not have been made the basis for prosecuting a stranger who learned of Kly's condition and failed to act. Even where there is a duty imposed by contract, moreover, the omission to act will not support a prosecution for homicide in the absence of the necessary mens rea. For murder, there must be malice. Without a malicious intent, an omission to perform duties having their foundation in contract cannot support a conviction for murder. In the instant case, therefore, the jury was required to find that appellants, by virtue of contract, had undertaken responsibility for providing necessary care for Kly to the exclusion of the members of Kly's family. This would impose upon them a legal duty to act to preserve Kly's life. If they maliciously set upon a course of withholding food and medicine and thereby caused Kly's death, appellants could be found guilty of murder. * * *

Having found no valid reason for disturbing the jury's verdicts, we conclude that the judgments of sentence must be, as they are,

AFFIRMED.

[The dissenting opinion by J. DEL SOLE has been omitted.]

2.   **The "No Duty to Rescue" Rule and the Debate Over "Good Samaritan" Statutes**

THE RIGHT TO BE APATHETIC: IVERSON CASE RAISES QUESTIONS ABOUT GOOD SAMARITAN LAWS

Charles Ashby
Los Angeles Daily Journal, Sept. 2, 1998, at 1[a]

LAS VEGAS – Ignore thy neighbor. That is every American's right. That may seem morally reprehensible, but long-established legal precedent in the United States releases Americans from any duty to help one another. Unless the situation involves withholding evidence of a crime or helping to cover one up, it is not illegal, in most states, to witness a crime or accident and then fail to step in to prevent it or fail to report it to authorities.

Which is why charges will not be filed against 20-year-old David Cash, the Los Angeles man who seemingly could have stopped the brutal sexual assault and strangulation of a 7-year-old girl in a Nevada casino last year, a Clark County, Nev[ada], prosecutor said. Despite the growing outcry for charges against Cash, Ben Graham, chief deputy district attorney for the Clark County district attorney's office, said he will not be prosecuted. "Clark County has come under a lot of intense pressure because of this," Graham said. "But he really didn't violate any crime." There is not enough evidence to charge Cash with any crime, he said, whether it is obstruction of justice or accessory after the fact, since he neither gained anything from the crime nor actively tried to cover it up. To be guilty as an accessory, Graham explained, a person has to aid, abet or encourage someone to commit a crime.

Common-Law Line of Authority

"What you have is a long, long common-law line of authority that unless you're in a special class or in a special relationship, you really have no duty to act," Graham said. "Historically, mere presence, being there when a crime is committed, is not chargeable. Our laws are basically laws of 'do not.' We seldom require anyone to go do anything." He sees the moral question, on the other hand, as a simple one: Anyone should have done whatever he could to stop the murder of Sherrice Iverson, he said.

Iverson was killed during the wee hours of May 25, 1997, as she played in a casino in Primm, Nevada. As her father gambled, two Long Beach buddies, Cash and Jeremy Strohmeyer, 19, struck up a game of tag with the child. When she dashed into the women's bathroom, Strohmeyer followed her, then Cash. In the restroom – as he peered over the stall – Cash reportedly watched as Strohmeyer began to sexually assault the girl. He then left the restroom, telling no one what he saw, according to an interview in the Los Angeles Times.

While Cash expressed sympathy for Strohmeyer, he displayed a notable absence of feeling for the child – and no regret for not reporting the crime. "I'm not going to get upset over someone else's life," Cash reportedly said. "I just worry about myself first. I'm not going to lose sleep over somebody else's problems."

Strohmeyer has been charged with murder in the sexual assault and strangulation of the girl. If convicted at the trial, which began Monday, Strohmeyer could face a death sentence.[a] He is being represented by Los Angeles criminal defense attorney Leslie Abramson.

Clark County defense lawyer Tom Pitaro * * * sees a defense if Cash were to be charged with a crime. * * * "If you were defending him, you would say he didn't have a duty to do anything; therefore, he didn't cause any harm. He just didn't prevent any – and there's no [law] against that."

Whether there should be is a subject of mounting national interest. In recent years, the idea of requiring intervention gained ground in several states and with respect to certain types of people, for instance children. Teachers gained new legal responsibilities in recent years, requiring them to report suspected child-abuse cases, Pitaro said. Failure to do so can result in civil and, in some states, criminal penalties.

Nevada Assemblyman Richard Perkins, D-Clark County, has requested that a [G]ood Samaritan bill be drafted to make silence such as Cash's illegal. Currently only Minnesota, Wisconsin, Vermont, Rhode Island and Massachusetts have duty-to-rescue laws that apply to the general public. Other states have considered the idea, chiefly since Princess Diana's death in Paris last year, when paparazzi following the car were said to be taking pictures of the accident rather than helping those inside. France long has had a [Good]

---

[a] After this article was published, Strohmeyer pled guilty to murder in exchange for an agreement by prosecutors not to seek the death penalty. He was sentenced to life without the possibility of parole.

Samaritan law that requires people who witness accidents to assist in some way.
* * *

Those states that make it criminal not to offer aid also safeguard the person offering the aid through general liability protections. And a person is not expected to render aid that would endanger oneself or cause a person to neglect a duty to others. Pitaro says any good defense lawyer would see those "protections" as loopholes in the law that would allow an easy acquittal.

The oldest "general duty to rescue" law in the United States is Wisconsin's, approved in 1983. As a result, there is little case law interpreting it. Wisconsin's law carries a misdemeanor punishment for failing to follow it. It was upheld by the Wisconsin Court of Appeals in 1994 in *State v. LaPlante*, 521 N.W.2d 448. In that case, the court said to gain a conviction, the prosecution must prove that the accused believed a crime was being committed and that a victim was exposed to bodily harm, said Gary Watchke, legislative analyst for the Wisconsin Legislative Reference Bureau.

[Good] Samaritan laws that govern professionals, such as a doctor, firefighter or police officer, are different, Watchke said. Such professionals accept responsibility to people they do not personally know because of the nature of their jobs. Good Samaritan laws are needed to protect them from liability, encouraging them to help when they are needed, he said.

TWO FORMS OF JUSTICE: IVERSON CASE - NEVADA AND CALIFORNIA AUTHORITIES OUGHT TO REEXAMINE DAVID CASH'S ACTIONS
Isabelle R. Gunning
L.A. Times, Sept. 21, 1998, at B5

One year and four months ago, Jeremy Strohmeyer followed little 7-year-old Sherrice Iverson into a casino ladies' room. His friend, David Cash, followed after them. There, Strohmeyer kidnapped, sexually assaulted and strangled Sherrice to death while Cash, according to his own testimony, watched the assault begin and then left without notifying authorities. Strohmeyer pleaded guilty to all the crimes, facing a lifetime in prison, and Cash remains at UC Berkeley. The disparate legal treatment of two young men who both appear so morally culpable has raised a lot of passions, causing even a noted criminal defense attorney, Strohmeyer's own Leslie Abramson, to call angrily for some retribution against Cash.

So why hasn't Cash been charged? Many in the African American community believe that the whole case is about race. South-Central activists were highly critical of the Nevada district attorney's willingness to accept a plea offer from Strohmeyer, wondering if the prosecution wouldn't have been more eager to seek the death penalty through a trial if the victim were white and wealthy. Maybe. As a former public defender, it seems to me that the deal was typical when a defendant faces a real possibility of the death penalty. Moreover, as an opponent of the death penalty, I agree with Sherrice's father when he said, "Killing that boy won't bring my baby back."

But when it comes to Cash, I wonder. This is not Mississippi in 1963. There is no great racist plot. Indeed, the public unease and outrage against Cash is a multiracial affair with blacks and browns, whites and reds, yellows and "mixeds" all horrified by his actions and indifference. But is there a subtle, perhaps unconscious combination of racial and class privilege causing the authorities to balk at charging a young middle-class white man with a bright future at an elite public university? Would they be so hesitant if he were darker hued, had no high school degree and had the uncertain economic future that too many young, poor black and brown men face?

It is said that neither Nevada nor California can charge Cash because neither state has a "Good Samaritan" law – and they should. I disagree with the pundits who oppose such laws with concerns that range from the infrequency with which Vermont uses its law to the suggestion that these laws turn "us into informants on each other." It doesn't matter if the new law is rarely used. Ideally, we hope that all criminal laws will rarely need to be used. What matters is that we believe that the moral obligation to help under certain circumstances is important. If so, then we should have a law for whenever it is needed. And these laws have less to do with us becoming informants on each other and everything to do with what we should already be doing for each other: helping each other out in times of need, regardless of our differences, because we are all part of a community. * * *

3.   Sample Good Samaritan Statutes

HAWAII'S GOOD SAMARITAN STATUTE
Haw. Rev. Stat. Ann. § 663-1.6. (Michie 1995)

[§ 663-1.6]. Duty to assist.

(a)   Any person at the scene of a crime who knows that a victim of the crime is suffering from serious physical harm shall obtain or attempt to obtain aid from law enforcement or medical personnel if the person can do so without danger or peril to any person. Any person who violates this subsection is guilty of a petty misdemeanor.

(b)   Any person who provides reasonable assistance in compliance with subsection (a) shall not be liable in civil damages unless the person's acts constitute gross negligence or wanton acts or omissions, or unless the person receives or expects to receive remuneration. Nothing contained in this subsection shall alter existing law with respect to tort liability of a physician licensed to practice under the laws of this State committed in the ordinary course of the physician's practice.

(c)   Any person who fails to provide reasonable assistance in compliance with subsection (a) shall not be liable for any civil damages.

VERMONT'S GOOD SAMARITAN STATUTE
Vt. Stat. Ann. tit. 12 , § 519 (2002)

§ 519 Emergency medical care

(a)   A person who knows that another is exposed to grave physical harm shall, to the extent that the same can be rendered without danger or peril to himself or without interference with important duties owed to others, give reasonable assistance to the exposed person unless that assistance or care is being provided by others.

(b)   A person who provides reasonable assistance in compliance with subsection (a) of this section shall not be liable in civil damages unless his acts constitute gross negligence or unless he will receive or expects to receive remuneration. Nothing contained in this subsection shall alter existing law with respect to tort liability of a practitioner of the healing arts for acts committed in the ordinary course of his practice.

(c)   A person who willfully violates subsection (a) of this section shall be fined not more than $100.00.

E.   ACTING VERSUS HAVING A STATUS: "STATUS CRIMES"

One aspect of the act requirement has been constitutionalized: the idea that people should be punished only for their conduct and not being a certain kind of person. In *Robinson v. California*, the first case in this section, the United States Supreme Court addressed the question whether the state of California could punish a person for being a narcotics addict. In *Powell v. Texas*, the Court had to decide whether the state of Texas could punish a chronic alcoholic for being drunk in public. Both defendants argued that because of their addictions, their conduct was not entirely voluntary. As you read these cases, think about whether you are persuaded by the Court's explanation for treating the two cases differently.

ROBINSON v. CALIFORNIA
Supreme Court of the United States
370 U.S. 660, 82 S.Ct. 1417, 8 L.Ed.2d 758 (1962)

STEWART, JUSTICE

A California statute makes it a criminal offense for a person to "be addicted to the use of narcotics." This appeal draws into question the constitutionality of that provision of the state law, as construed by the California courts in the present case.

The appellant was convicted after a jury trial in the Municipal Court of Los Angeles. The evidence against him was given by two Los Angeles police officers. Officer Brown testified that he had had occasion to examine the appellant's arms one evening on a street in Los Angeles some four months before the trial. The officer testified that at that time he had observed "scar tissue and discoloration on the inside" of the appellant's right arm, and "what appeared to be numerous needle marks and a scab which was approximately three inches below the crook of the elbow" on the appellant's left arm. The officer also testified that the appellant under questioning had admitted to the occasional use of narcotics. * * *

The appellant testified in his own behalf, denying the alleged conversations with the police officers and denying that he had ever used narcotics or been addicted to their use. He explained the marks on his arms as resulting from an allergic condition contracted during his military service. His testimony was corroborated by two witnesses.

The trial judge instructed the jury that the statute made it a misdemeanor for a person "either to use narcotics, or to be addicted to the use of narcotics . . . . That portion of the statute referring to the 'use' of narcotics is based upon the 'act' of using. That portion of the statute referring to 'addicted to the use' of narcotics is based upon a condition or status. They are not identical. . . . To be addicted to the use of narcotics is said to be a status or condition and not an act. It is a continuing offense and differs from most other offenses in the fact that [it] is chronic rather than acute; that it continues after it is complete and subjects the offender to arrest at any time before he reforms. The existence of such a chronic condition may be ascertained from a single examination, if the characteristic reactions of that condition be found present."

The judge further instructed the jury that the appellant could be convicted under a general verdict if the jury agreed *either* that he was of the "status" *or* had committed the "act" denounced by the statute. "All that the People must show is either that the defendant did use a narcotic in Los Angeles County, or that while in the City of Los Angeles he was addicted to the use of narcotics . . . ."

Under these instructions the jury returned a verdict finding the appellant "guilty of the offense charged." * * * We noted probable jurisdiction of this appeal because it squarely presents the issue whether the statute as construed by the California courts in this case is repugnant to the Fourteenth Amendment of the Constitution. * * *

It would be possible to construe the statute under which the appellant was convicted as one which is operative only upon proof of the actual use of narcotics within the State's jurisdiction. But the California courts have not so construed this law. * * *

This statute, therefore, is not one which punishes a person for the use of narcotics, for their purchase, sale or possession, or for antisocial or disorderly behavior resulting from their administration. It is not a law which even purports to provide or require medical treatment. Rather, we deal with a statute which makes the "status" of narcotic addiction a criminal offense, for which the offender may be prosecuted "at any time before he reforms." California has said that a person can be continuously guilty of this offense, whether or not he has ever used or possessed any narcotics within the State, and whether or not he has been guilty of any antisocial behavior there.

It is unlikely that any State at this moment in history would attempt to make it a criminal offense for a person to be mentally ill, or a leper, or to be afflicted with a venereal disease. A State might determine that the general health and welfare require that the victims of these and other human afflictions be dealt with by compulsory treatment, involving quarantine, confinement, or sequestration. But, in the light of contemporary human knowledge, a law which made a criminal offense of such a disease would doubtless be universally thought to be an infliction of cruel and unusual punishment in violation of the Eighth and Fourteenth Amendments.

We cannot but consider the statute before us as of the same category. In this Court counsel for the State recognized that narcotic addiction is an illness. Indeed, it is apparently an illness which may be contracted innocently or involuntarily. We hold that a state law which imprisons a person thus afflicted as a criminal, even though he has never touched any narcotic drug within the State or been guilty of any irregular behaviour there, inflicts a cruel and unusual punishment in violation of the Fourteenth Amendment. To be sure, imprisonment for ninety days is not, in the abstract, a punishment which is either cruel or unusual. But the question cannot be considered in the abstract. Even one day in prison would be a cruel and unusual punishment for the "crime" of having a common cold.

We are not unmindful that the vicious evils of the narcotics traffic have occasioned the grave concern of government. There are, as we have said, countless fronts on which those evils may be legitimately attacked. We deal in this case only with an individual provision of a particularized local law as it has so far been interpreted by the California courts.

Reversed.

JUSTICE CLARK, dissenting.

The Court finds § 11721 of California's Health and Safety Code, making it an offense to "be addicted to the use of narcotics," violative of due process as "a cruel and unusual punishment." I cannot agree. * * *

Apart from prohibiting specific acts such as the purchase, possession and sale of narcotics, California has taken certain legislative steps in regard to the status of being a narcotic addict – a condition commonly recognized as a threat to the State and to the individual. The Code deals with this problem in realistic stages. At its incipiency narcotic addiction is handled under § 11721 of the Health and Safety Code which is at issue here. It provides that a person found to be addicted to the use of narcotics shall serve a term in the county jail of not less than 90 days nor more than one year, with the minimum 90-day confinement applying in all cases without exception. Provision is made for parole with periodic tests to detect readdiction. * * *

Where narcotic addiction has progressed beyond the incipient, volitional stage, California provides for commitment of three months to two years in a state hospital. * * * This proceeding is clearly civil in nature with a purpose of rehabilitation and cure.* * * Thus, the "criminal" provision applies to the incipient narcotic addict who retains self-control, requiring confinement of three months to one year and parole with frequent tests to detect renewed use of drugs. Its overriding purpose is to cure the less seriously addicted person by preventing further use. On the other hand, the "civil" commitment provision deals with addicts who have lost the power of self-control, requiring hospitalization of up to two years. Each deals with a different type of addict but with a common purpose. * * *

In the instant case the proceedings against the petitioner were brought under the volitional-addict section. There was testimony that he had been using drugs only four months with three to four relatively mild doses a week. At arrest and trial he appeared normal. His testimony was clear and concise, being simply that he had never used drugs. The scabs and pocks on his arms and body were caused, he said, by "overseas shots" administered during army service preparatory to foreign assignment. He was very articulate in his testimony but the jury did not believe him, apparently because he had told the clinical expert while being examined after arrest that he had been using drugs, as I have stated above. The officer who arrested him also testified to like statements and to scabs – some 10 or 15 days old – showing narcotic injections. There was no evidence in the record of withdrawal symptoms. Obviously he could not have been committed under § 5355 as one who had completely "lost the power of self-control." The jury was instructed that narcotic "addiction" as used in § 11721 meant strongly disposed to a taste or practice or habit of its use, indicated by the use of narcotics often or daily. A general verdict was returned against petitioner, and he was ordered confined for 90 days to be followed by a two-year parole during which he was required to take periodic Nalline tests. * * *

The majority acknowledges, as it must, that a State can punish persons who purchase, possess or use narcotics. Although none of these acts are harmful to society in themselves, the State constitutionally may attempt to deter and prevent them through punishment because of the grave threat of future harmful conduct which they pose. Narcotics addiction – including the incipient, volitional addiction to which this provision speaks – is no different. California courts have taken judicial notice that "the inordinate use of a narcotic drug tends to create an irresistible craving and forms a habit for its continued use until one becomes an addict, and he respects no convention or obligation and will lie, steal, or use any other base means to gratify his passion for the drug, being lost to all considerations of duty or social position." Can this Court deny the legislative and judicial judgment of California that incipient, volitional narcotic addiction poses a threat of serious crime similar to the threat inherent in the purchase or possession of narcotics? And if such a threat is inherent in addiction, can this Court say that California is powerless to deter it by punishment?

It is no answer to suggest that we are dealing with an involuntary status and thus penal sanctions will be ineffective and unfair. The section at issue applies only to persons who use narcotics often or even daily but not to the point of losing self-control. When dealing with involuntary addicts California moves only through § 5355 of its Welfare Institutions Code which clearly is not penal. Even if it could be argued that § 11721 may not be limited to volitional addicts, the petitioner in the instant case undeniably retained the power of self-control and thus to him the statute would be constitutional. Moreover, "status" offenses have long been known and recognized in the criminal law. A ready example is drunkenness, which plainly is as involuntary after addiction to alcohol as is the taking of drugs. * * *

I would affirm the judgment.

[JUSTICE DOUGLAS' and JUSTICE HARLAN'S concurring opinions and JUSTICE WHITE'S dissenting opinion have been omitted.]

POWELL v. TEXAS
Supreme Court of the United States
392 U.S. 514, 88 S.Ct. 2145, 20 L.Ed.2d 1254 (1968)

MR. JUSTICE MARSHALL announced the judgment of the Court and delivered an opinion in which THE CHIEF JUSTICE, MR. JUSTICE BLACK, and MR. JUSTICE HARLAN join.

In late December 1966, appellant was arrested and charged with being found in a state of intoxication in a public place, in violation of Texas Penal Code, Art. 477 (1952), which reads as follows:

"Whoever shall get drunk or be found in a state of intoxication in any public place, or at any private house except his own, shall be fined not exceeding one hundred dollars."

Appellant was tried in the Corporation Court of Austin, Texas, found guilty, and fined $20. He appealed to the County Court at Law No. 1 of Travis County, Texas, where a trial *de novo* was held. His counsel urged that appellant was "afflicted with the disease of chronic alcoholism," that "his appearance in public [while drunk was] . . . not of his own volition," and therefore that to punish him criminally for that conduct would be cruel and unusual, in violation of the Eighth and Fourteenth Amendments to the United States Constitution.

The trial judge in the county court, sitting without a jury, made certain findings of fact but ruled as a matter of law that chronic alcoholism was not a defense to the charge. He found appellant guilty, and fined him $50. There being no further right to appeal within the Texas judicial system, appellant appealed to this Court; we noted probable jurisdiction.

I.

The principal testimony was that of Dr. David Wade, a Fellow of the American Medical Association, duly certificated in psychiatry. His testimony consumed a total of 17 pages in the trial transcript. Five of those pages were taken up with a recitation of Dr. Wade's qualifications. In the next 12 pages Dr. Wade was examined by appellant's counsel, cross-examined by the State, and re-examined by the defense, and those 12 pages contain virtually all the material developed at trial which is relevant to the constitutional issue we face here. Dr. Wade sketched the outlines of the "disease" concept of alcoholism; noted that there is no generally accepted definition of "alcoholism"; alluded to the ongoing debate within the medical profession over whether alcohol is actually physically "addicting" or merely psychologically "habituating"; and concluded that in either case a "chronic alcoholic" is an "involuntary drinker," who is "powerless not to drink," and who "loses his self-control over his drinking." He testified that he had examined appellant, and that appellant is a "chronic alcoholic," who "by the time he has reached [the state of intoxication] . . . is not able to control his behavior, and [who] . . . has reached this point because he has an uncontrollable compulsion to drink." Dr. Wade also responded in the negative to the question whether appellant has "the willpower to resist the constant excessive consumption of alcohol." He added that in his opinion jailing appellant without medical attention would operate neither to rehabilitate him nor to lessen his desire for alcohol.

On cross-examination, Dr. Wade admitted that when appellant was sober he knew the difference between right and wrong, and he responded affirmatively to the question whether appellant's act of taking the first drink in any given instance when he was sober was a "voluntary exercise of his will." Qualifying his answer, Dr. Wade stated that "these individuals have a compulsion, and this compulsion, while not completely overpowering, is a very strong influence, an exceedingly strong influence, and this compulsion coupled with the firm belief in their mind that they are going to be able to handle it from now on causes their judgment to be somewhat clouded."

Appellant testified concerning the history of his drinking problem. He reviewed his many arrests for drunkenness; testified that he was unable to stop drinking; stated that when he was intoxicated he had no control over his actions and could not remember them later, but that he did not become violent; and admitted that he did not remember his arrest on the occasion for which he was being tried. On cross-examination, appellant admitted that he had had one drink on the morning of the trial and had been able to discontinue drinking. In relevant part, the cross-examination went as follows:

"Q. You took that one at eight o'clock because you wanted to drink?

"A. Yes, sir.

"Q. And you knew that if you drank it, you could keep on drinking and get drunk?

"A. Well, I was supposed to be here on trial, and I didn't take but that one drink.

"Q. You knew you had to be here this afternoon, but this morning you took one drink and then you knew that you couldn't afford to drink any more and come to court; is that right?

"A. Yes, sir, that's right.

"Q. So you exercised your will power and kept from drinking anything today except that one drink?

"A. Yes, sir, that's right.

*   *   *

On redirect examination, appellant's lawyer elicited the following:
"Q. Leroy, isn't the real reason why you just had one drink today because you just had enough money to buy one drink?

"A. Well, that was just give [sic] to me.

"Q. In other words, you didn't have any money with which you could buy any drinks yourself?

"A. No, sir, that was give [sic] to me.

"Q. And that's really what controlled the amount you drank this morning, isn't it?

"A. Yes, sir.

"Q. Leroy, when you start drinking, do you have any control over how many drinks you can take?

"A. No, sir."

Evidence in the case then closed. The State made no effort to obtain expert psychiatric testimony of its own, or even to explore with appellant's witness the question of appellant's power to control the frequency, timing, and location of his drinking bouts, or the substantial disagreement within the medical profession concerning the nature of the disease, the efficacy of treatment and the prerequisites for effective treatment. It did nothing to examine or illuminate what Dr. Wade might have meant by his reference to a "compulsion" which was "not completely overpowering," but which was "an exceedingly strong influence," or to inquire into the question of the proper role of such a "compulsion" in constitutional adjudication. Instead, the State contented itself with a brief argument that appellant had no defense to the charge because he "is legally sane and knows the difference between right and wrong." * * *

III.

Appellant claims that his conviction on the facts of this case would violate the Cruel and Unusual Punishment Clause of the Eighth Amendment as applied to the States through the Fourteenth Amendment. The primary purpose of that clause has always been considered, and properly so, to be directed at the method or kind of punishment imposed for the violation of criminal statutes; the nature of the conduct made criminal is ordinarily relevant only to the fitness of the punishment imposed.

Appellant, however, seeks to come within the application of the Cruel and Unusual Punishment Clause announced in *Robinson v. California,* 370 U.S. 660 (1962), which involved a state statute making it a crime to "be addicted to the use of narcotics." This Court held there that "a state law which imprisons a person thus afflicted [with narcotic addiction] as a criminal, even though he has never touched any narcotic drug within the State or been guilty of any irregular behavior there, inflicts a cruel and unusual punishment. . . ."

On its face the present case does not fall within that holding, since appellant was convicted, not for being a chronic alcoholic, but for being in public while drunk on a particular occasion. The State of Texas thus has not sought to punish a mere status, as California did in *Robinson;* nor has it attempted to regulate appellant's behavior in the privacy of his own home. Rather, it has imposed upon appellant a criminal sanction for public behavior which may create substantial health and safety hazards, both for appellant and for members of the general public, and which offends the moral and esthetic sensibilities of a large segment of the community. This seems a far cry from convicting one for being an addict, being a chronic alcoholic, being "mentally ill, or a leper. . . ." * * *

It is suggested in dissent that *Robinson* stands for the "simple" but "subtle" principle that "[criminal] penalties may not be inflicted upon a person for being in a condition he is powerless to change." In that view, appellant's "condition" of public intoxication was "occasioned by a compulsion symptomatic of the disease" of chronic alcoholism, and thus, apparently, his behavior lacked the critical element of *mens rea.* Whatever may be the merits of such a doctrine of criminal responsibility, it surely cannot be said to follow from *Robinson.* The entire thrust of *Robinson*'s interpretation of the Cruel and

Unusual Punishment Clause is that criminal penalties may be inflicted only if the accused has committed some act, has engaged in some behavior, which society has an interest in preventing, or perhaps in historical common law terms, has committed some *actus reus.* * * *

Ultimately, then, the most troubling aspects of this case, were *Robinson* to be extended to meet it, would be the scope and content of what could only be a constitutional doctrine of criminal responsibility. In dissent it is urged that the decision could be limited to conduct which is "a characteristic and involuntary part of the pattern of the disease as it afflicts" the particular individual, and that "[it] is not foreseeable" that it would be applied "in the case of offenses such as driving a car while intoxicated, assault, theft, or robbery." That is limitation by fiat. In the first place, nothing in the logic of the dissent would limit its application to chronic alcoholics. If Leroy Powell cannot be convicted of public intoxication, it is difficult to see how a State can convict an individual for murder, if that individual, while exhibiting normal behavior in all other respects, suffers from a "compulsion" to kill, which is an "exceedingly strong influence," but "not completely overpowering." Even if we limit our consideration to chronic alcoholics, it would seem impossible to confine the principle within the arbitrary bounds which the dissent seems to envision. * * *

Traditional common-law concepts of personal accountability and essential considerations of federalism lead us to disagree with appellant. We are unable to conclude, on the state of this record or on the current state of medical knowledge, that chronic alcoholics in general, and Leroy Powell in particular, suffer from such an irresistible compulsion to drink and to get drunk in public that they are utterly unable to control their performance of either or both of these acts and thus cannot be deterred at all from public intoxication. * * *

Affirmed.

MR. JUSTICE FORTAS, with whom MR. JUSTICE DOUGLAS, MR. JUSTICE BRENNAN, and MR. JUSTICE STEWART join, dissenting.

* * * The sole question presented is whether a criminal penalty may be imposed upon a person suffering the disease of "chronic alcoholism" for a condition – being "in a state of intoxication" in public – which is a characteristic part of the pattern of his disease and which, the trial court found, was not the consequence of appellant's volition but of "a compulsion symptomatic of the disease of chronic alcoholism." We must consider whether the Eighth Amendment, made applicable to the States through the Fourteenth Amendment, prohibits the imposition of this penalty in these rather special circumstances as "cruel and unusual punishment." This case does not raise any question as to the right of the police to stop and detain those who are intoxicated

in public, whether as a result of the disease or otherwise; or as to the State's power to commit chronic alcoholics for treatment. Nor does it concern the responsibility of an alcoholic for criminal *acts*. We deal here with the mere *condition* of being intoxicated in public. * * *

* * * *Robinson* stands upon a principle which, despite its subtlety, must be simply stated and respectfully applied because it is the foundation of individual liberty and the cornerstone of the relations between a civilized state and its citizens: Criminal penalties may not be inflicted upon a person for being in a condition he is powerless to change. In all probability, Robinson at some time before his conviction elected to take narcotics. But the crime as defined did not punish this conduct. The statute imposed a penalty for the offense of "addiction" – a condition which Robinson could not control. Once Robinson had become an addict, he was utterly powerless to avoid criminal guilt. He was powerless to choose not to violate the law.

In the present case, appellant is charged with a crime composed of two elements – being intoxicated and being found in a public place while in that condition. The crime, so defined, differs from that in *Robinson*. The statute covers more than a mere status. But the essential constitutional defect here is the same as in *Robinson,* for in both cases the particular defendant was accused of being in a condition which he had no capacity to change or avoid. The trial judge sitting as trier of fact found, upon the medical and other relevant testimony, that Powell is a "chronic alcoholic." He defined appellant's "chronic alcoholism" as "a disease which destroys the afflicted person's will power to resist the constant, excessive consumption of alcohol." He also found that "a chronic alcoholic does not appear in public by his own volition but under a compulsion symptomatic of the disease of chronic alcoholism." I read these findings to mean that appellant was powerless to avoid drinking; that having taken his first drink, he had "an uncontrollable compulsion to drink" to the point of intoxication; and that, once intoxicated, he could not prevent himself from appearing in public places. * * *

The findings in this case, read against the background of the medical and sociological data to which I have referred, compel the conclusion that the infliction upon appellant of a criminal penalty for being intoxicated in a public place would be "cruel and inhuman punishment" within the prohibition of the Eighth Amendment. This conclusion follows because appellant is a "chronic alcoholic" who, according to the trier of fact, cannot resist the "constant excessive consumption of alcohol" and does not appear in public by his own volition but under a "compulsion" which is part of his condition.

I would reverse the judgment below.

[MR. JUSTICE BLACK'S concurring opinion, with whom MR. JUSTICE HARLAN joins, and MR. JUSTICE WHITE'S concurring opinion have been omitted. MR. JUSTICE FRANKFURTER took no part in the consideration of this decision.]

Chapter 4

THE MENS REA REQUIREMENT

INTRODUCTION

The term mens rea has at least two different meanings. Mens rea is sometimes used in a broad sense to refer to culpability generally. In this sense, mens rea means the kind of moral blameworthiness that ought to make a person criminally responsible for his or her actions. When we use this broader meaning, we are often seeking to determine whether we, within the constraints of Western moral culture, feel comfortable blaming the defendant for what happened. This is a question of retribution: who deserves blame and punishment?

As a technical matter, however, mens rea refers to "the particular mental state provided for in the definition of the offense."[a] The narrower definition of mens rea is sometimes referred to as the scienter or intent requirement. The subject of this chapter is mens rea in the narrow sense.

The study of mens rea reveals some dramatic differences between jurisdictions that primarily incorporate the English common law and jurisdictions that have incorporated the Model Penal Code (MPC). The English common law produced a wide variety of terms used to describe a person's mental state, including terms like "wilfully," "maliciously," "corruptly," "intentionally," "knowingly," "recklessly," and "negligently." Within the common law system, these terms have no necessary relationship to one another, and they do not even always mean the same thing from statute to statute. Judges working within the common law tradition also developed a distinction between "specific intent" and "general intent" statutes which is best analyzed historically rather than logically, yet which is important to understand because of its doctrinal implications.

Thus, when interpreting a penal code that continues to rely on the common law tradition for its mens rea language, be prepared to use the tools of statutory interpretation introduced in earlier chapters. As we will see in *United States v. Holloway*, excerpted below, understanding what mental states are

---

[a]Joshua Dressler, UNDERSTANDING CRIMINAL LAW § 10.02[C] (3d ed. 2001).

comprehended by the statute often requires a long, torturous trip into legislative history and precedent.

The drafters of the MPC attempted to avoid these problems by rationalizing their mens rea terms. As you can see by examining § 2.02 of the MPC, there are only four mens rea terms under the MPC. These terms – purpose, knowledge, recklessness, and negligence – are precisely defined, they have a logical relationship to one another, and they always mean the same thing wherever they appear.

A.   THE HISTORICAL DEVELOPMENT OF MENS REA

REGINA V. CUNNINGHAM
Court of Criminal Appeal, 1957
41 Crim.App. 155, 2 Q.B. 396, 2 All. Eng. Rep. 412

BYRNE, J. read the judgment of the court: * * *

The appellant was convicted * * * upon an indictment framed under section 23 of the Offences Against the Person Act, 1861, which charged that he unlawfully and maliciously caused to be taken by Sarah Wade a certain noxious thing, namely coal gas, so as thereby to endanger the life of the said Sarah Wade. The facts were that the appellant was engaged to be married, and Mrs. Wade, his prospective mother-in-law was the tenant of a house, No. 7a, Bakes Street, Bradford, which was unoccupied but which was to be occupied by the appellant after his marriage. Mrs. Wade and her husband, an elderly couple, lived in the house next door. At one time the two houses had been one, but when the building was converted into two houses a wall had been erected to divide the cellars of the two houses, and that wall was composed of rubble loosely cemented.

On the evening of Jan. 17 last, the appellant went to the cellar of No. 7a, Bakes Street, wrenched the gas meter from the gas pipes and stole it, together with its contents. * * * The facts were not really in dispute, and in a statement to a police officer the appellant said: "All right I will tell you, I was short of money, I had been off work for three days, I got 8 shillings from the gas meter. I tore it off the wall and threw it away." Although there was a stop tap within two feet of the meter, the appellant did not turn off the gas, with the result that a very considerable volume of gas escaped, some of which seeped through the wall of the cellar and partially asphyxiated Mrs. Wade, who was asleep in her bedroom next door, with the result that her life was endangered. * * *

The act of the appellant was clearly unlawful and, therefore, the real question for the jury was whether it was also malicious within the meaning of section 23 of the Offences Against the Person Act, 1861.

* * * Section 23 provides as follows:

"Whosoever shall unlawfully and maliciously administer to or cause to be administered to or taken by any other person any poison or other destructive or noxious thing, so as thereby to endanger the life of such person, or so as thereby to inflict upon such person any grievous bodily harm, shall be guilty of felony . . ."

Counsel argued * * * that the learned judge misdirected the jury as to the meaning of the word "maliciously." * * *

* * * [T]he following principle * * * was propounded by the late Professor C.S. Kenny in the first edition of his Outlines of Criminal Law published in 1902 * * *: "* * * in any statutory definition of a crime, 'malice' must be taken not in the old vague sense of 'wickedness' in general, but as requiring either (i) an actual intention to do the particular kind of harm that in fact was done, or (ii) recklessness as to whether such harm should occur or not (i.e. the accused has foreseen that the particular kind of harm might be done, and yet has gone on to take the risk of it). It is neither limited to, nor does it indeed require, any ill-will towards the person injured." * * *

In his summing-up, the learned judge directed the jury as follows: * * *

'Unlawful' does not need any definition. It is something forbidden by law. What about 'malicious'? 'Malicious' for this purpose means wicked – something which he has no business to do and perfectly well knows it. 'Wicked' is as good a definition as any other which you would get. * * *

With the utmost respect to the learned judge, we think it is incorrect to say that the word "malicious" in a statutory offence merely means wicked. We think the learned judge was, in effect, telling the jury that if they were satisfied that the appellant acted wickedly – and he had clearly acted wickedly in stealing the gas meter and its contents – they ought to find that he had acted maliciously in causing the gas to be taken by Mrs. Wade so as thereby to endanger her life. In our view, it should have been left to the jury to decide whether, even if the appellant did not intend the injury to Mrs. Wade, he foresaw that the removal of the gas meter might cause injury to someone but nevertheless removed it. We are unable to say that a reasonable jury, properly directed as to the meaning of the word "maliciously" in the context of section 23, would, without doubt, have convicted.

In these circumstances, this court has no alternative but to allow the appeal and quash the conviction.

B.   PROBLEMS OF STATUTORY INTERPRETATION

Sometimes a statute expressly includes a mental state, but it is not clear which element or elements that mental state modifies. In such cases, the court must utilize canons of statutory construction to figure out the legislature's intent. The Supreme Court illustrates this process in *United States v. Yermian*. As you read the case, think about how the court would rule if operating under the Model Penal Code.

UNITED STATES v. YERMIAN
Supreme Court of the United States
468 U.S. 63, 104 S.Ct. 2936, 82 L.Ed.2d 53 (1984)

JUSTICE POWELL delivered the opinion of the Court.

It is a federal crime under 18 U.S.C. § 1001 to make any false or fraudulent statement in any matter within the jurisdiction of a federal agency. To establish a violation of § 1001, the Government must prove beyond a reasonable doubt that the statement was made with knowledge of its falsity. This case presents the question whether the Government also must prove that the false statement was made with actual knowledge of federal agency jurisdiction.

I

Respondent Esmail Yermian was convicted in the District Court of Central California on three counts of making false statements in a matter within the jurisdiction of a federal agency, in violation of § 1001. The convictions were based on false statements respondent supplied his employer in connection with a Department of Defense security questionnaire. Respondent was hired in 1979 by Gulton Industries, a defense contractor. Because respondent was to have access to classified material in the course of his employment, he was required to obtain a Department of Defense Security Clearance. To this end, Gulton's security officer asked respondent to fill out a "Worksheet For Preparation of Personnel Security Questionnaire."

In response to a question on the worksheet asking whether he had ever been charged with any violation of law, respondent failed to disclose that in 1978 he had been convicted of mail fraud. * * * In describing his employment history, respondent falsely stated that he had been employed by two companies that had in fact never employed him. The Gulton security officer typed these false representations onto a form entitled "Department of Defense Personnel Security Questionnaire." Respondent reviewed the typed document for errors and signed a certification stating that his answers were "true, complete, and correct to the best of [his] knowledge" and that he understood "that any misrepresentation or false statement . . . may subject [him] to prosecution under section 1001 of the United States Criminal Code." * * *

Government investigators subsequently discovered that respondent had submitted false statements on the security questionnaire. Confronted with this discovery, respondent acknowledged that he had responded falsely to questions regarding his criminal record and employment history. On the basis of these false statements, respondent was charged with three counts in violation of § 1001.

At trial, respondent admitted to having actual knowledge of the falsity of the statements he had submitted in response to the Department of Defense Security Questionnaire. He explained that he had made the false statements so that information on the security questionnaire would be consistent with similar fabrications he had submitted to Gulton in his employment application. Respondent's sole defense at trial was that he had no actual knowledge that his false statements would be transmitted to a federal agency.[2]

Consistent with this defense, respondent requested a jury instruction requiring the Government to prove not only that he had actual knowledge that his statements were false at the time they were made, but also that he had actual knowledge that those statements were made in a matter within the

---

[2]Respondent maintained this defense despite the fact that both the worksheet and the questionnaire made reference to the Department of Defense, and the security questionnaire signed by respondent was captioned "Defense Department." The latter document also contained a reference to the "Defense Industrial Security Clearance Office," stated that respondent's work would require access to "secret" material, and informed respondent that his signature would grant "permission to the Department of Defense to obtain and review copies of [his] medical and institutional records." Nevertheless, respondent testified that he had not read the form carefully before signing it and thus had not noticed either the words "Department of Defense" on the first page or the certification printed above the signature block.

jurisdiction of a federal agency. The District Court rejected that request and instead instructed the jury that the Government must prove that respondent "knew or should have known that the information was to be submitted to a government agency." Respondent's objection to this instruction was overruled, and the jury returned convictions on all three counts charged in the indictment.

The Court of Appeals for the Ninth Circuit reversed, holding that the District Court had erred in failing to give respondent's requested instruction. The Court of Appeals read the statutory terms "knowingly and willfully" to modify both the conduct of making false statements and the circumstance that they be made "in any matter within the jurisdiction of [a federal agency]." The court therefore concluded that "as an essential element of a section 1001 violation, the government must prove beyond a reasonable doubt that the defendant knew at the time he made the false statement that it was made in a matter within the jurisdiction of a federal agency." The Court of Appeals rejected the Government's argument that the "reasonably foreseeable" standard provided by the District Court's jury instructions satisfied any element of intent possibly associated with the requirement that false statements be made within federal agency jurisdiction.

The decision of the Court of Appeals for the Ninth Circuit conflicts with decisions by the three other Courts of Appeals that have considered the issue. We granted certiorari to resolve the conflict, and now reverse.

II

The only issue presented in this case is whether Congress intended the terms "knowingly and willfully" in § 1001 to modify the statute's jurisdictional language, thereby requiring the Government to prove that false statements were made with actual knowledge of federal agency jurisdiction. The issue thus presented is one of statutory interpretation. Accordingly, we turn first to the language of the statute.

A

The relevant language of § 1001 provides:

> Whoever, in any matter within the jurisdiction of any department or agency of the United States knowingly and willfully . . . makes any false, fictitious or fraudulent statements or representations, . . . shall be fined. . . .

The statutory language requiring that knowingly false statements be made "in any matter within the jurisdiction of any department or agency of the United States" is a jurisdictional requirement. Its primary purpose is to identify the factor that makes the false statement an appropriate subject for federal concern. Jurisdictional language need not contain the same culpability requirement as other elements of the offense. Indeed, we have held that "the existence of the fact that confers federal jurisdiction need not be one in the mind of the actor at the time he perpetrates the act made criminal by the federal statute." Certainly in this case, the statutory language makes clear that Congress did not intend the terms "knowingly and willfully" to establish the standard of culpability for the jurisdictional element of § 1001. The jurisdictional language appears in a phrase separate from the prohibited conduct modified by the terms "knowingly and willfully." Any natural reading of § 1001, therefore, establishes that the terms "knowingly and willfully" modify only the making of "false, fictitious or fraudulent statements," and not the predicate circumstance that those statements be made in a matter within the jurisdiction of a federal agency. Once this is clear, there is no basis for requiring proof that the defendant had actual knowledge of federal agency jurisdiction. The statute contains no language suggesting any additional element of intent, such as a requirement that false statements be "knowingly made in a matter within federal agency jurisdiction," or "with the intent to deceive the Federal Government." On its face, therefore, § 1001 requires that the Government prove that false statements were made knowingly and willfully, and it unambiguously dispenses with any requirement that the Government also prove that those statements were made with actual knowledge of federal agency jurisdiction.[7] Respondent's argument that the legislative history of the statute supports a contrary interpretation is unpersuasive. * * *

III

Respondent argues that absent proof of actual knowledge of federal agency jurisdiction, § 1001 becomes a "trap for the unwary," imposing criminal sanctions on "wholly innocent conduct." Whether or not respondent fairly may characterize the intentional and deliberate lies prohibited by the statute (and manifest in this case) as "wholly innocent conduct," this argument is not sufficient to overcome the express statutory language of § 1001. Respondent does not argue that Congress lacks the power to impose criminal sanctions for deliberately false statements submitted to a federal agency, regardless of

---

[7]Because the statutory language unambiguously dispenses with an actual knowledge requirement, we have no occasion to apply the principle of lenity urged by the dissent.

whether the person who made such statements actually knew that they were being submitted to the Federal Government. That is precisely what Congress has done here. In the unlikely event that § 1001 could be the basis for imposing an unduly harsh result on those who intentionally make false statements to the Federal Government, it is for Congress and not this Court to amend the criminal statute.

IV

Both the plain language and the legislative history establish that proof of actual knowledge of federal agency jurisdiction is not required under § 1001. Accordingly, we reverse the decision of the Court of Appeals to the contrary.

It is so ordered.

JUSTICE REHNQUIST, with whom JUSTICE BRENNAN, JUSTICE STEVENS, and JUSTICE O'CONNOR join, dissenting.

It is common ground that in a prosecution for the making of false statements the Government must prove that the defendant actually knew that the statements were false at the time he made them. The question presented here is whether the Government must also prove that the defendant actually knew that his statements were made in a matter within "the jurisdiction of any department or agency of the United States." The Court concludes that the plain language and the legislative history of 18 U.S.C. § 1001 conclusively establish that the statute is intended to reach false statements made without actual knowledge of federal involvement in the subject matter of the false statements. I cannot agree.
* * *

I

I think that in this case, "[a]fter 'seiz[ing] everything from which aid can be derived,' we are left with an ambiguous statute." Notwithstanding the majority's repeated, but sparsely supported, assertions that the evidence of Congress' intent not to require actual knowledge is "convincing," and "unambiguou[s]," I believe that the language and legislative history of § 1001 can provide "no more than a guess as to what Congress intended." I therefore think that the canon of statutory construction which requires that "ambiguity concerning the ambit of criminal statutes . . . be resolved in favor of lenity," is applicable here. Accordingly, I would affirm the Court of Appeals' conclusion that actual knowledge of federal involvement is a necessary element for conviction under § 1001.

The federal false-statements statute, 18 U.S.C. § 1001, provides that [whoever], *in any matter within the jurisdiction of any department or agency of the United States* knowingly and willfully . . . makes any false, fictitious or fraudulent statements or representations, . . . shall be fined not more than $10,000 or imprisoned not more than five years, or both.

The majority correctly begins its analysis with the language of the statute, but in my view, it incorrectly concludes that the statutory language is unambiguous.

In drawing that conclusion, the Court does no more than point out that the "in any matter" language is placed at the beginning of the sentence in a phrase separate from the later phrase specifying the prohibited conduct. The Court then concludes that under any "natural reading" of the statute, it is clear that "knowingly and willfully" modify only the phrase specifying the prohibited conduct. Although "there is no errorless test for identifying or recognizing 'plain' or 'unambiguous' language" in a statute, the Court's reasoning here amounts to little more than simply pointing to the ambiguous phrases and proclaiming them clear. In my view, it is quite impossible to tell which phrases the terms "knowingly and willfully" modify, and the magic wand of *ipse dixit* does nothing to resolve that ambiguity. * * *

[T]he fact that the Court's "natural reading" has not seemed so natural to the judges of the Ninth and Fifth Circuits, nor for that matter to me, indicates that the Court's reading, though certainly a plausible one, is not at all compelled by the statutory language. * * *

I respectfully dissent.

HOLLOWAY v. UNITED STATES
Supreme Court of the United States
526 U.S. 1, 119 S.Ct. 966, 143 L.Ed.2d 1 (1999)

JUSTICE STEVENS delivered the opinion of the Court.

Carjacking "with the intent to cause death or serious bodily harm" is a federal crime.[1] The question presented in this case is whether that phrase

---

[1] As amended by the Violent Crime Control and Law Enforcement Act of 1994, § 60003(a) (14), 108 Stat. 1970, and by the Carjacking Correction Act of 1996, § 2, 110 Stat. 3020, the statute provides:

Whoever, *with the intent to cause death or serious bodily harm* requires the Government to prove that the defendant had an unconditional intent to kill or harm in all events, or whether it merely requires proof of an intent to kill or harm if necessary to effect a carjacking. Most of the judges who have considered the question have concluded, as do we, that Congress intended to criminalize the more typical carjacking carried out by means of a deliberate threat of violence, rather than just the rare case in which the defendant has an unconditional intent to use violence regardless of how the driver responds to his threat.

I

A jury found petitioner guilty on three counts of carjacking, as well as several other offenses related to stealing cars. In each of the carjackings, petitioner and an armed accomplice identified a car that they wanted and followed it until it was parked. The accomplice then approached the driver, produced a gun, and threatened to shoot unless the driver handed over the car keys. The accomplice testified that the plan was to steal the cars without harming the victims, but that he would have used his gun if any of the drivers had given him a "hard time." When one victim hesitated, petitioner punched him in the face but there was no other actual violence.

The District Judge instructed the jury that the Government was required to prove beyond a reasonable doubt that the taking of a motor vehicle was committed with the intent "to cause death or serious bodily harm to the person from whom the car was taken." After explaining that merely using a gun to frighten a victim was not sufficient to prove such intent, he added the following statement over the defendant's objection:

---

takes a motor vehicle that has been transported, shipped, or received in interstate or foreign commerce from the person or presence of another by force and violence or by intimidation, or attempts to do so, shall --

(1) be fined under this title or imprisoned not more than 15 years, or both,

(2) if serious bodily injury (as defined in section 1365 of this title, including any conduct that, if the conduct occurred in the special maritime and territorial jurisdiction of the United States, would violate section 2241 or 2242 of this title) results, be fined under this title or imprisoned not more than 25 years, or both, and

(3) if death results, be fined under this title or imprisoned for any number of years up to life, or both, or sentenced to death.

In some cases, intent is conditional. That is, a defendant may intend to engage in certain conduct only if a certain event occurs.

In this case, the government contends that the defendant intended to cause death or serious bodily harm if the alleged victims had refused to turn over their cars. If you find beyond a reasonable doubt that the defendant had such an intent, the government has satisfied this element of the offense . . . .

In his postverdict motion for a new trial, petitioner contended that this instruction was inconsistent with the text of the statute. The District Judge denied the motion, stating that there "is no question that the conduct at issue in this case is precisely what Congress and the general public would describe as carjacking, and that Congress intended to prohibit it in § 2119." He noted that the statute as originally enacted in 1992 contained no intent element but covered all carjackings committed by a person "possessing a firearm." A 1994 amendment had omitted the firearm limitation, thus broadening the coverage of the statute to encompass the use of other weapons, and also had inserted the intent requirement at issue in this case. The judge thought that an "odd result" would flow from a construction of the amendment that "would no longer prohibit the very crime it was enacted to address except in those unusual circumstances when carjackers also intended to commit another crime -- murder or a serious assault." Moreover, the judge determined that even though the issue of conditional intent has not been discussed very often, at least in the federal courts, it was a concept that scholars and state courts had long recognized.

Over a dissent that accused the majority of "a clear judicial usurpation of congressional authority," the Court of Appeals affirmed. * * *

II

Writing for the Court in *United States v. Turkette,* Justice White reminded us that the language of the statutes that Congress enacts provides "the most reliable evidence of its intent." For that reason, we typically begin the task of statutory construction by focusing on the words that the drafters have chosen. In interpreting the statute at issue, "we consider not only the bare meaning" of the critical word or phrase "but also its placement and purpose in the statutory scheme."

The specific issue in this case is what sort of evil motive Congress intended to describe when it used the words "with the intent to cause death or serious bodily harm" in the 1994 amendment to the carjacking statute. More precisely, the question is whether a person who points a gun at a driver, having decided to pull the trigger if the driver does not comply with a demand for the car keys, possesses the intent, at that moment, to seriously harm the driver. In our view, the answer to that question does not depend on whether the driver immediately hands over the keys or what the offender decides to do after he gains control over the car. At the relevant moment, the offender plainly does have the forbidden intent.

The opinions that have addressed this issue accurately point out that a carjacker's intent to harm his victim may be either "conditional" or "unconditional." The statutory phrase at issue theoretically might describe (1) the former, (2) the latter, or (3) both species of intent. Petitioner argues that the "plain text" of the statute "unequivocally" describes only the latter: that the defendant must possess a specific and unconditional intent to kill or harm in order to complete the proscribed offense. To that end, he insists that Congress would have had to insert the words "if necessary" into the disputed text in order to include the conditional species of intent within the scope of the statute. Because Congress did not include those words, petitioner contends that we must assume that Congress meant to provide a federal penalty for only those carjackings in which the offender actually attempted to harm or kill the driver (or at least intended to do so whether or not the driver resisted).

We believe, however, that a commonsense reading of the carjacking statute counsels that Congress intended to criminalize a broader scope of conduct than attempts to assault or kill in the course of automobile robberies. As we have repeatedly stated, "'the meaning of statutory language, plain or not, depends on context.'" When petitioner's argument is considered in the context of the statute, it becomes apparent that his proffered construction of the intent element overlooks the significance of the placement of that element in the statute. The carjacking statute essentially is aimed at providing a federal penalty for a particular type of robbery. The statute's *mens rea* component thus modifies the act of "taking" the motor vehicle. It directs the factfinder's attention to the defendant's state of mind at the precise moment he demanded or took control over the car "by force and violence or by intimidation." If the defendant has the proscribed state of mind at that moment, the statute's scienter element is satisfied. * * *

Two considerations strongly support the conclusion that a natural reading of the text is fully consistent with a congressional decision to cover both species of intent. First, the statute as a whole reflects an intent to authorize federal prosecutions as a significant deterrent to a type of criminal activity that was a matter of national concern. Because that purpose is better served by construing the statute to cover both the conditional and the unconditional species of wrongful intent, the entire statute is consistent with a normal interpretation of the specific language that Congress chose. Indeed, petitioner's interpretation would exclude from the coverage of the statute most of the conduct that Congress obviously intended to prohibit.

Second, it is reasonable to presume that Congress was familiar with the cases and the scholarly writing that have recognized that the "specific intent" to commit a wrongful act may be conditional. The facts of the leading case on the point are strikingly similar to the facts of this case. In *People v. Connors*, the Illinois Supreme Court affirmed the conviction of a union organizer who had pointed a gun at a worker and threatened to kill him forthwith if he did not take off his overalls and quit work. The Court held that the jury had been properly instructed that the "specific intent to kill" could be found even though that intent was "coupled with a condition" that the defendant would not fire if the victim complied with his demand. That holding has been repeatedly cited with approval by other courts and by scholars. Moreover, it reflects the views endorsed by the authors of the Model [Penal] Code. The core principle that emerges from these sources is that a defendant may not negate a proscribed intent by requiring the victim to comply with a condition the defendant has no right to impose; "an intent to kill, in the alternative, is nevertheless an intent to kill." * * *

In short, we disagree with petitioner's reading of the text of the Act and think it unreasonable to assume that Congress intended to enact such a truncated version of an important criminal statute.[14] The intent requirement of § 2119 is satisfied when the Government proves that at the moment the defendant demanded or took control over the driver's automobile the defendant possessed the intent to seriously harm or kill the driver if necessary to steal the car (or, alternatively, if unnecessary to steal the car). Accordingly, we affirm the judgment of the Court of Appeals.

It is so ordered.

JUSTICE SCALIA, dissenting.

The issue in this case is the meaning of the phrase, in 18 U.S.C. § 2119, "with the intent to cause death or serious bodily harm." (For convenience' sake, I shall refer to it in this opinion as simply intent to kill.) As recounted by the Court, petitioner's accomplice, Vernon Lennon, "testified that the plan was to steal the cars without harming the victims, but that he would have used his gun

---

[14]We also reject petitioner's argument that the rule of lenity should apply in this case. We have repeatedly stated that "'the rule of lenity applies only if, after seizing everything from which aid can be derived, . . . we can make no more than a guess as to what Congress intended.'"

if any of the drivers had given him a 'hard time.'" The District Court instructed the jury that the intent element would be satisfied if petitioner possessed this "conditional" intent. Today's judgment holds that instruction to have been correct.

I dissent from that holding because I disagree with the following, utterly central, passage of the opinion:

> [A] carjacker's intent to harm his victim may be either 'conditional' or 'unconditional.' The statutory phrase at issue theoretically might describe (1) the former, (2) the latter, or (3) both species of intent.

I think, to the contrary, that in customary English usage the unqualified word "intent" does not usually connote a purpose that is subject to any conditions precedent except those so remote in the speaker's estimation as to be effectively nonexistent – and it *never* connotes a purpose that is subject to a condition which the speaker hopes will not occur. (It is this last sort of "conditional intent" that is at issue in this case, and that I refer to in my subsequent use of the term.) "Intent" is "[a] state of mind in which a person seeks to accomplish a given result through a course of action." Black's Law Dictionary 810 (6th ed. 1990). One can hardly "seek to accomplish" a result he hopes will not ensue.

The Court's division of intent into two categories, conditional and unconditional, makes the unreasonable seem logical. But Aristotelian classification says nothing about linguistic usage. Instead of identifying *two* categories, the Court might just as readily have identified three: unconditional intent, conditional intent, and feigned intent. But the second category, like the third, is simply not conveyed by the word "intent" alone. There is intent, conditional intent, and feigned intent, just as there is agreement, conditional agreement, and feigned agreement – but to say that in either case the noun alone, without qualification, "theoretically might describe" all three phenomena is simply false. Conditional intent is no more embraced by the unmodified word "intent" than a sea lion is embraced by the unmodified word "lion."

If I have made a categorical determination to go to Louisiana for the Christmas holidays, it is accurate for me to say that I "intend" to go to Louisiana. And that is so even though I realize that there are some remote and unlikely contingencies – "acts of God," for example – that might prevent me. (The fact that these remote contingencies are always implicit in the expression of intent accounts for the humorousness of spelling them out in such expressions as "if I should live so long," or "the Good Lord willing and the creek don't rise.") It is less precise, though tolerable usage, to say that I "intend" to go if my purpose is conditional upon an event which, though not virtually certain to happen (such as my continuing to live), is reasonably likely to happen, and which I hope will happen. I might, for example, say that I "intend" to go even if my plans depend upon receipt of my usual and hoped-for end-of-year bonus.

But it is *not* common usage – indeed, it is an unheard-of usage – to speak of my having an "intent" to do something, when my plans are contingent upon an event that is not virtually certain, and that I hope will not occur. When a friend is seriously ill, for example, I would not say that "I intend to go to his funeral next week." I would have to make it clear that the intent is a conditional one: "I intend to go to his funeral next week if he dies." The carjacker who intends to kill if he is met with resistance is in the same position: he has an "intent to kill if resisted"; he does not have an "intent to kill." No amount of rationalization can change the reality of this normal (and as far as I know exclusive) English usage. The word in the statute simply will not bear the meaning that the Court assigns. * * *

Notwithstanding the clear ordinary meaning of the word "intent," it would be possible, though of course quite unusual, for the word to have acquired a different meaning in the criminal law. The Court does not claim – and falls far short of establishing – such "term-of-art" status. It cites five state cases (representing the majority view among the minority of jurisdictions that have addressed the question) saying that conditional intent satisfies an intent requirement; but it acknowledges that there are cases in other jurisdictions to the contrary. As I understand the Court's position, it is not that the former cases are right and the latter wrong, so that "intent" in criminal statutes, a term of art in that context, includes conditional intent; but rather that "intent" in criminal statutes *may* include conditional intent, depending upon the statute in question. That seems to me not an available option. It is so utterly clear in normal usage that "intent" does *not* include conditional intent, that only an accepted convention in the criminal law could give the word a different meaning. And an accepted convention is not established by the fact that some courts have thought so some times. One must decide, I think, which line of cases is correct, and in my judgment it is that which rejects the conditional-intent rule.

There are of course innumerable federal criminal statutes containing an intent requirement, ranging from intent to steal, to intent to defeat the provisions of the Bankruptcy Code, to intent that a vessel be used in hostilities against a friendly nation, to intent to obstruct the lawful exercise of parental rights. Consider, for example, 21 U.S.C. § 841, which makes it a crime to possess certain drugs with intent to distribute them. Possession alone is also a crime, but a lesser one. Suppose that a person acquires and possesses a small quantity of cocaine for his own use, and that he in fact consumes it entirely himself. But assume further that, at the time he acquired the drug, he told his wife not to worry about the expense because, if they had an emergency need for money, he could always resell it. If conditional intent suffices, this person, who has never sold drugs and has never "intended" to sell drugs in any normal sense, has been guilty of possession with intent to distribute. Or consider 18 U.S.C. § 2390, which makes it a crime to enlist within the United States "with intent to serve in armed hostility against the United States." Suppose a Canadian enlists in the Canadian army in the United States, intending, of course, to fight all of Canada's wars, including (though he neither expects nor hopes for it) a war against the United States. He would be criminally liable. These examples make it clear, I think, that the doctrine of conditional intent cannot reasonably be applied across-the-board to the criminal code. I am unaware that any equivalent absurdities result from reading "intent" to mean what it says – a conclusion strongly supported by the fact that the Government has cited only a single case involving another federal statute, from over two centuries of federal criminal jurisprudence, applying the conditional-intent doctrine (and that in circumstances where it would not at all have been absurd to require real intent). The course selected by the Court, of course – "intent" is sometimes conditional and sometimes not – would require us to sift through these many statutes one-by-one, making our decision on the basis of such ephemeral indications of "congressional purpose" as the Court has used in this case, to which I now turn. * * *

The Court confidently asserts that "petitioner's interpretation would exclude from the coverage of the statute most of the conduct that Congress obviously intended to prohibit." It seems to me that one can best judge what Congress "obviously intended" not by intuition, but by the words that Congress enacted, which in this case require intent (not conditional intent) to kill. Is it implausible that Congress intended to define such a narrow federal crime? Not at all. The era when this statute was passed contained well publicized instances of not only carjackings, and not only carjackings involving violence or the threat of violence (as of course most of them do); but also of carjackings in which the perpetrators senselessly harmed the car owners when that was entirely unnecessary to the crime. I have a friend whose father was killed, and whose mother was nearly killed, in just such an incident – after the car had already been handed over. It is not at all implausible that Congress should direct its attention to this particularly savage sort of carjacking – where killing the driver is part of the intended crime.

Indeed, it seems to me much more implausible that Congress would have focused upon the ineffable "conditional intent" that the Court reads into the statute, sending courts and juries off to wander through "would-a, could-a, should-a" land. It is difficult enough to determine a defendant's actual intent; it is infinitely more difficult to determine what the defendant planned to do upon the happening of an event that the defendant hoped would not happen, and that he himself may not have come to focus upon. There will not often be the accomplice's convenient confirmation of conditional intent that exists in the present case. Presumably it will be up to each jury whether to take the carjacker ("Your car or your life") at his word. Such a system of justice seems to me so arbitrary that it is difficult to believe Congress intended it. Had Congress meant to cast its carjacking net so broadly, it could have achieved that result – and eliminated the arbitrariness – by defining the crime as "carjacking under threat of death or serious bodily injury." Given the language here, I find it much more plausible that Congress meant to reach – as it said – the carjacker who intended to kill.

In sum, I find the statute entirely unambiguous as to whether the carjacker who hopes to obtain the car without inflicting harm is covered. Even if ambiguity existed, however, the rule of lenity would require it to be resolved in the defendant's favor. The Government's statement that the rule of lenity "has its *primary* application in cases in which there is some doubt whether the legislature intended to criminalize conduct that might otherwise appear to be innocent," is carefully crafted to conceal the fact that we have repeatedly applied the rule to situations just like this. For example, in *Ladner v. United States,* the statute at issue made it a crime to assault a federal officer with a deadly weapon. The defendant, who fired one shotgun blast that wounded two federal officers, contended that under this statute he was guilty of only one, and not two, assaults. The Court said, in an opinion joined by all eight Justices who reached the merits of the case:

> This policy of lenity means that the Court will not interpret a federal criminal statute so as to increase the penalty that it places on an individual when such an interpretation can be based on no more than a guess as to what Congress intended. If Congress desires to create multiple offenses from a single act affecting more than one federal officer, Congress can make that meaning clear. We thus hold that the single discharge of a shotgun alleged by the petitioner in this case would constitute only a single violation of § 254.

In *Bell v. United States,* the issue was similar: whether transporting two women, for the purpose of prostitution, in the same vehicle and on the same trip, constituted one or two violations of the Mann Act. In an opinion authored by Justice Frankfurter, the Court said:

When Congress leaves to the Judiciary the task of imputing to Congress an undeclared will, the ambiguity should be resolved in favor of lenity. And this is not out of any sentimental consideration, or for want of sympathy with the purpose of

Congress in proscribing evil or antisocial conduct. It may fairly be said to be a presupposition of our law to resolve doubts in the enforcement of a penal code against the imposition of a harsher punishment.

If that is no longer the presupposition of our law, the Court should say so, and reduce the rule of lenity to an historical curiosity. But if it remains the presupposition, the rule has undeniable application in the present case. If the statute is not, as I think, clear in the defendant's favor, it is at the very least ambiguous and the defendant must be given the benefit of the doubt. * * *

[JUSTICE THOMAS' dissenting opinion has been omitted.]

C.   INTENT

Under the modern common law, intent is defined in two ways. First, one acts with the requisite intent if it is his or her conscious object or purpose to cause a certain result or to engage in certain prohibited conduct. Alternatively one "intends" a particular social harm if one knows to a virtual certainty that one's actions will cause that social harm. In other words, intent at common law is equated with either "conscious object" or "knowledge to a virtual certainty."

The Model Penal Code uses the term "purposely" to reflect a mental state akin to the first common law definition of intent. Note, however, that "intent" under the common law also encompasses what the Model Penal Code calls "knowledge." *See* Model Penal Code § 2.02(2)(a).

1.   Inferring Intent from Circumstantial Evidence

Because of difficulties inherent in proving intent, courts have adopted legal shortcuts which allow the fact finder in a murder case to infer an intent to kill when absolute proof of such intent is lacking. One such shortcut is the "natural and probable consequences" doctrine explained in *State v. Fugate*. In other cases, courts have been reluctant to permit shortcuts to proving intent. *Virginia v. Black* is an example of such reluctance.

STATE v. FUGATE

Court of Appeals of Ohio, Second District

36 Ohio App. 2d 131, 303 N.E.2d 313 (Ohio App. 2d Dist. 1973)

KERNS, J.

The defendant, Herbert Lee Fugate, appellant herein, was tried by a jury and convicted of armed robbery and first degree murder. From the judgment and sentence thereupon entered by the Court of Common Pleas of Montgomery County, Fugate has perfected an appeal to this court.

On April 15, 1971, the appellant entered the Point Garage located at the intersection of Hamilton and McLain Streets with a loaded sixteen-gauge shotgun. In the process of robbing the owner of the garage, Sylvester Leingang, Fugate struck him on two different occasions with the barrel of the shotgun, causing severe head wounds. He then ordered his victim, Mr. Leingang, into the basement of the garage where he shot and killed him.

At the time of the robbery and killing, Fugate was 19 years of age, weighed approximately 175, and was over 6 feet tall. The decedent was 66 years of age. The fatal wound extended laterally from the left rear toward the right front of the body of Leingang.

The first assignment of error is based upon the proposition that the killing was not done "purposely" as required by R.C. 2901.01, and in support of this alleged error the appellant has alluded to a number of cases which show that an intent to kill is essential to a conviction for first degree murder. The cited cases have little more than academic interest in this case unless the jury was required to accept the testimony of Fugate that the shooting was accidental to the exclusion of all other evidence presented at the trial.

But the jury was not so limited in its consideration of the evidence. The element of intent may be, and usually is, determined from attendant circumstances, and the composite picture developed by the evidence in this case is particularly suited to a reasonable finding that the killing was done purposely. As stated in *State v. Salter:* "intent is a mental phenomenon, and in order to determine whether an intent to do a certain act existed, the circumstances surrounding the act must be examined and the intent determined therefrom." Or as set forth in paragraph four of the syllabus in *State v. Huffman:* "The intent of an accused person dwells in his mind. Not being ascertainable by the exercise of any or all of the senses, it can never be proved by the direct testimony of a third person and it need not be." * * *

"It is the law of Ohio that an intent to kill may be presumed where the natural and probable consequence of a wrongful act is to produce death, and such intent may be deduced from all the surrounding circumstances, including the instrument used to produce death, and the manner of inflicting a fatal wound."

In the present case, the evidence, and the inferences reasonably deducible therefrom, amply support the jury findings as to every essential element of the crime. The first assignment of error is overruled. * * *

We find no prejudicial error in the record, and the judgment of the Court of Common Pleas will be affirmed.

Judgment affirmed.

VIRGINIA v. BLACK
Supreme Court of the United States
538 U.S. 343, 123 S.Ct. 1536, 155 L.Ed.2d 535 (2003)

JUSTICE O'CONNOR announced the judgment of the Court and delivered the opinion of the Court with respect to Parts I, II, and III, and an opinion with respect to Parts IV and V, in which THE CHIEF JUSTICE, JUSTICE STEVENS, and JUSTICE BREYER join.

In this case we consider whether the Commonwealth of Virginia's statute banning cross burning with "an intent to intimidate a person or group of persons" violates the First Amendment. We conclude that while a State, consistent with the First Amendment, may ban cross burning carried out with the intent to intimidate, the provision in the Virginia statute treating any cross burning as prima facie evidence of intent to intimidate renders the statute unconstitutional in its current form.

I

Respondents Barry Black, Richard Elliott, and Jonathan O'Mara were convicted separately of violating Virginia's cross-burning statute, § 18.2-423. That statute provides:

> It shall be unlawful for any person or persons, with the intent of intimidating any person or group of persons, to burn, or cause to be burned, a cross on the property of another, a highway or other public place. Any person who shall violate any provision of this section shall be guilty of a Class 6 felony.

Any such burning of a cross shall be prima facie evidence of an intent to intimidate a person or group of persons.

On August 22, 1998, Barry Black led a Ku Klux Klan rally in Carroll County, Virginia. Twenty-five to thirty people attended this gathering, which occurred on private property with the permission of the owner, who was in attendance. The property was located on an open field just off Brushy Fork Road (State Highway 690) in Cana, Virginia.

When the sheriff of Carroll County learned that a Klan rally was occurring in his county, he went to observe it from the side of the road. During the approximately one hour that the sheriff was present, about 40 to 50 cars passed the site, a "few" of which stopped to ask the sheriff what was happening on the property. Eight to ten houses were located in the vicinity of the rally. Rebecca Sechrist, who was related to the owner of the property where the rally took place, "sat and watched to see wha[t][was] going on" from the lawn of her in-laws' house. She looked on as the Klan prepared for the gathering and subsequently conducted the rally itself.

During the rally, Sechrist heard Klan members speak about "what they were" and "what they believed in." The speakers "talked real bad about the blacks and the Mexicans." One speaker told the assembled gathering that "he would love to take a .30/.30 and just random[ly] shoot the blacks." The speakers also talked about "President Clinton and Hillary Clinton," and about how their tax money "goes to ... the black people." Sechrist testified that this language made her "very ... scared."

At the conclusion of the rally, the crowd circled around a 25- to 30-foot cross. The cross was between 300 and 350 yards away from the road. According to the sheriff, the cross "then all of a sudden ... went up in a flame." As the cross burned, the Klan played Amazing Grace over the loudspeakers. Sechrist stated that the cross burning made her feel "awful" and "terrible."

When the sheriff observed the cross burning, he informed his deputy that they needed to "find out who's responsible and explain to them that they cannot do this in the State of Virginia." The sheriff then went down the driveway, entered the rally, and asked "who was responsible for burning the cross." Black responded, "I guess I am because I'm the head of the rally." The sheriff then told Black, "[T]here's a law in the State of Virginia that you cannot burn a cross and I'll have to place you under arrest for this."

Black was charged with burning a cross with the intent of intimidating a person or group of persons, in violation of § 18.2-423. At his trial, the jury was instructed that "intent to intimidate means the motivation to intentionally put a person or a group of persons in fear of bodily harm. Such fear must arise from the willful conduct of the accused rather than from some mere temperamental timidity of the victim." The trial court also instructed the jury that "the burning of a cross by itself is sufficient evidence from which you may infer the required intent." When Black objected to this last instruction on First Amendment grounds, the prosecutor responded that the instruction was "taken straight out of the [Virginia] Model Instructions." The jury found Black guilty, and fined him $2,500. The Court of Appeals of Virginia affirmed Black's conviction.

On May 2, 1998, respondents Richard Elliott and Jonathan O'Mara, as well as a third individual, attempted to burn a cross on the yard of James Jubilee. Jubilee, an African-American, was Elliott's next-door neighbor in Virginia Beach, Virginia. Four months prior to the incident, Jubilee and his family had moved from California to Virginia Beach. Before the cross burning, Jubilee spoke to Elliott's mother to inquire about shots being fired from behind the Elliott home. Elliott's mother explained to Jubilee that her son shot firearms as a hobby, and that he used the backyard as a firing range.

On the night of May 2, respondents drove a truck onto Jubilee's property, planted a cross, and set it on fire. Their apparent motive was to "get back" at Jubilee for complaining about the shooting in the backyard. Respondents were not affiliated with the Klan. The next morning, as Jubilee was pulling his car out of the driveway, he noticed the partially burned cross approximately 20 feet from his house. After seeing the cross, Jubilee was "very nervous" because he "didn't know what would be the next phase," and because "a cross burned in your yard ... tells you that it's just the first round."

Elliott and O'Mara were charged with attempted cross burning and conspiracy to commit cross burning. O'Mara pleaded guilty to both counts, reserving the right to challenge the constitutionality of the cross-burning statute. The judge sentenced O'Mara to 90 days in jail and fined him $2,500. The judge also suspended 45 days of the sentence and $1,000 of the fine.

At Elliott's trial, the judge originally ruled that the jury would be instructed "that the burning of a cross by itself is sufficient evidence from which you may infer the required intent." At trial, however, the court instructed the jury that the Commonwealth must prove that "the defendant intended to commit cross burning," that "the defendant did a direct act toward the commission of the cross burning," and that "the defendant had the intent of intimidating any person or group of persons." The court did not instruct the jury on the meaning of the word "intimidate," nor on the prima facie evidence provision of § 18.2-423. The jury found Elliott guilty of attempted cross burning and acquitted him of conspiracy to commit cross burning. It sentenced Elliott to 90 days in jail and a $2,500 fine. The Court of Appeals of Virginia affirmed the convictions of both Elliott and O'Mara.

Each respondent appealed to the Supreme Court of Virginia, arguing that § 18.2-423 is facially unconstitutional. The Supreme Court of Virginia consolidated all three cases, and held that the statute is unconstitutional on its face. It held that the Virginia cross-burning statute "is analytically indistinguishable from the ordinance found unconstitutional in *R.A.V. v. St. Paul.* The Virginia statute, the court held, discriminates on the basis of content since it "selectively chooses only cross burning because of its distinctive message." The court also held that the prima facie evidence provision renders the statute overbroad because "[t]he enhanced probability of prosecution under the statute chills the expression of protected speech." * * *

We granted certiorari.

II

Cross burning originated in the 14th century as a means for Scottish tribes to signal each other * * * Cross burning in this country, however, long ago became unmoored from its Scottish ancestry. Burning a cross in the United States is inextricably intertwined with the history of the Ku Klux Klan.

The first Ku Klux Klan began in Pulaski, Tennessee, in the spring of 1866. Although the Ku Klux Klan started as a social club, it soon changed into something far different. The Klan fought Reconstruction and the corresponding drive to allow freed blacks to participate in the political process. Soon the Klan imposed "a veritable reign of terror" throughout the South. The Klan employed tactics such as whipping, threatening to burn people at the stake, and murder. The Klan's victims included blacks, southern whites who disagreed with the Klan, and "carpetbagger" northern whites.

The activities of the Ku Klux Klan prompted legislative action at the national level. In 1871, "President Grant sent a message to Congress indicating that the Klan's reign of terror in the Southern States had rendered life and property insecure." In response, Congress passed what is now known as the Ku Klux Klan Act. President Grant used these new powers to suppress the Klan in South Carolina, the effect of which severely curtailed the Klan in other States as well. By the end of Reconstruction in 1877, the first Klan no longer existed.

The genesis of the second Klan began in 1905, with the publication of Thomas Dixon's *The Clansmen: An Historical Romance of the Ku Klux Klan.* Dixon's book was a sympathetic portrait of the first Klan, depicting the Klan as a group of heroes "saving" the South from blacks and the "horrors" of

Reconstruction. Although the first Klan never actually practiced cross burning, Dixon's book depicted the Klan burning crosses to celebrate the execution of former slaves. Cross burning thereby became associated with the first Ku Klux Klan. When D.W. Griffith turned Dixon's book into the movie *The Birth of a Nation* in 1915, the association between cross burning and the Klan became indelible. In addition to the cross burnings in the movie, a poster advertising the film displayed a hooded Klansman riding a hooded horse, with his left hand holding the reins of the horse and his right hand holding a burning cross above his head. Soon thereafter, in November 1915, the second Klan began.

From the inception of the second Klan, cross burnings have been used to communicate both threats of violence and messages of shared ideology. The first initiation ceremony occurred on Stone Mountain near Atlanta, Georgia. While a 40-foot cross burned on the mountain, the Klan members took their oaths of loyalty. This cross burning was the second recorded instance in the United States. The first known cross burning in the country had occurred a little over one month before the Klan initiation, when a Georgia mob celebrated the lynching of Leo Frank by burning a "gigantic cross" on Stone Mountain that was "visible throughout" Atlanta.

The new Klan's ideology did not differ much from that of the first Klan. As one Klan publication emphasized, "We avow the distinction between [the] races, ... and we shall ever be true to the faithful maintenance of White Supremacy and will strenuously oppose any compromise thereof in any and all things." Violence was also an elemental part of this new Klan. By September 1921, the New York World newspaper documented 152 acts of Klan violence, including 4 murders, 41 floggings, and 27 tar-and-featherings.

Often, the Klan used cross burnings as a tool of intimidation and a threat of impending violence. For example, in 1939 and 1940, the Klan burned crosses in front of synagogues and churches. After one cross burning at a synagogue, a Klan member noted that if the cross burning did not "shut the Jews up, we'll cut a few throats and see what happens." In Miami in 1941, the Klan burned four crosses in front of a proposed housing project, declaring, "We are here to keep niggers out of your town .... When the law fails you, call on us." And in Alabama in 1942, in "a whirlwind climax to weeks of flogging and terror," the Klan burned crosses in front of a union hall and in front of a union leader's home on the eve of a labor election. These cross burnings embodied threats to people whom the Klan deemed antithetical to its goals. And these threats had special force given the long history of Klan violence.

The Klan continued to use cross burnings to intimidate after World War II. In one incident, an African-American "school teacher who recently moved his family into a block formerly occupied only by whites asked the protection of city police * * * after the burning of a cross in his front yard." And after a cross burning in Suffolk, Virginia during the late 1940's, the Virginia Governor stated that he would "not allow any of our people of any race to be subjected to terrorism or intimidation in any form by the Klan or any other organization." These incidents of cross burning, among others, helped prompt Virginia to enact its first version of the cross-burning statute in 1950. * * *

To this day, regardless of whether the message is a political one or whether the message is also meant to intimidate, the burning of a cross is a "symbol of hate." And while cross burning sometimes carries no intimidating message, at other times the intimidating message is the *only* message conveyed. For example, when a cross burning is directed at a particular person not affiliated with the Klan, the burning cross often serves as a message of intimidation, designed to inspire in the victim a fear of bodily harm. Moreover, the history of violence associated with the Klan shows that the possibility of injury or death is not just hypothetical. The person who burns a cross directed at a particular person often is making a serious threat, meant to coerce the victim to comply with the Klan's wishes unless the victim is willing to risk the wrath of the Klan. Indeed, as the cases of respondents Elliott and O'Mara indicate, individuals without Klan affiliation who wish to threaten or menace another person sometimes use cross burning because of this association between a burning cross and violence.

In sum, while a burning cross does not inevitably convey a message of intimidation, often the cross burner intends that the recipients of the message fear for their lives. And when a cross burning is used to intimidate, few if any messages are more powerful.

III

A

The First Amendment, applicable to the States through the Fourteenth Amendment, provides that "Congress shall make no law ... abridging the freedom of speech." The hallmark of the protection of free speech is to allow "free trade in ideas"--even ideas that the overwhelming majority of people might find distasteful or discomforting. Thus, the First Amendment "ordinarily" denies a State "the power to prohibit dissemination of social, economic and political doctrine which a vast majority of its citizens believes to be false and fraught with evil consequence." The First Amendment affords protection to symbolic or expressive conduct as well as to actual speech.

The protections afforded by the First Amendment, however, are not absolute, and we have long recognized that the government may regulate certain categories of expression consistent with the Constitution. The First Amendment permits "restrictions upon the content of speech in a few limited areas, which are 'of such slight social value as a step to truth that any benefit that may be derived from them is clearly outweighed by the social interest in order and morality.'"

Thus, for example, a State may punish those words "which by their very utterance inflict injury or tend to incite an immediate breach of the peace." We have consequently held that fighting words -- "those personally abusive epithets which, when addressed to the ordinary citizen, are, as a matter of common knowledge, inherently likely to provoke violent reaction"--are generally proscribable under the First Amendment * * * And the First Amendment also permits a State to ban a "true threat."

"True threats" encompass those statements where the speaker means to communicate a serious expression of an intent to commit an act of unlawful violence to a particular individual or group of individuals. The speaker need not actually intend to carry out the threat. Rather, a prohibition on true threats "protect[s] individuals from the fear of violence" and "from the disruption that fear engenders," in addition to protecting people "from the possibility that the threatened violence will occur." Intimidation in the constitutionally proscribable sense of the word is a type of true threat, where a speaker directs a threat to a person or group of persons with the intent of placing the victim in fear of bodily harm or death. Respondents do not contest that some cross burnings fit within this meaning of intimidating speech, and rightly so.

B

The Supreme Court of Virginia ruled that in light of *R.A.V. v. City of St. Paul*, even if it is constitutional to ban cross burning in a content-neutral manner, the Virginia cross-burning statute is unconstitutional because it discriminates on the basis of content and viewpoint. It is true, as the Supreme Court of Virginia held, that the burning of a cross is symbolic expression. The reason why the Klan burns a cross at its rallies, or individuals place a burning cross on someone else's lawn, is that the burning cross represents the message that the speaker wishes to communicate. Individuals burn crosses as opposed to other means of communication because cross burning carries a message in an effective and dramatic manner.

The fact that cross burning is symbolic expression, however, does not resolve the constitutional question. The Supreme Court of Virginia relied upon *R.A.V. v. City of St. Paul*, to conclude that once a statute discriminates on the basis of this type of content, the law is unconstitutional. We disagree.

In *R.A.V.,* we held that a local ordinance that banned certain symbolic conduct, including cross burning, when done with the knowledge that such conduct would "'arouse anger, alarm or resentment in others on the basis of race, color, creed, religion or gender'" was unconstitutional. We held that the ordinance did not pass constitutional muster because it discriminated on the basis of content by targeting only those individuals who "provoke violence" on a basis specified in the law. The ordinance did not cover "[t]hose who wish to use 'fighting words' in connection with other ideas--to express hostility, for example, on the basis of political affiliation, union membership, or homosexuality." This content-based discrimination was unconstitutional because it allowed the city "to impose special prohibitions on those speakers who express views on disfavored subjects." * * *

* * * Virginia's statute does not run afoul of the First Amendment insofar as it bans cross burning with intent to intimidate. Unlike the statute at issue in *R.A.V.,* the Virginia statute does not single out for opprobrium only that speech directed toward "one of the specified disfavored topics." It does not matter whether an individual burns a cross with intent to intimidate because of the victim's race, gender, or religion, or because of the victim's "political affiliation, union membership, or homosexuality." Moreover, as a factual matter it is not true that cross burners direct their intimidating conduct solely to racial or religious minorities. * * * The First Amendment permits Virginia to outlaw cross burnings done with the intent to intimidate because burning a cross is a particularly virulent form of intimidation. Instead of prohibiting all intimidating messages, Virginia may choose to regulate this subset of intimidating messages in light of cross burning's long and pernicious history as a signal of impending violence. Thus, just as a State may regulate only that obscenity which is the most obscene due to its prurient content, so too may a State choose to prohibit only those forms of intimidation that are most likely to inspire fear of bodily harm. A ban on cross burning carried out with the intent to intimidate is fully consistent with our holding in *R.A.V.* and is proscribable under the First Amendment.

IV

The Supreme Court of Virginia ruled in the alternative that Virginia's cross-burning statute was unconstitutionally overbroad due to its provision stating that "[a]ny such burning of a cross shall be prima facie evidence of an intent to intimidate a person or group of persons." The Commonwealth added the prima facie provision to the statute in 1968. The court below did not reach whether this provision is severable from the rest of the cross-burning statute under Virginia law. * * *

The prima facie evidence provision, as interpreted by the jury instruction, renders the statute unconstitutional. * * * The prima facie evidence provision permits a jury to convict in every cross-burning case in which defendants exercise their constitutional right not to put on a defense. And even where a defendant like Black presents a defense, the prima facie evidence provision makes it more likely that the jury will find an intent to intimidate regardless of the particular facts of the case. The provision permits the Commonwealth to arrest, prosecute, and convict a person based solely on the fact of cross burning itself. * * *

As the history of cross burning indicates, a burning cross is not always intended to intimidate. Rather, sometimes the cross burning is a statement of ideology, a symbol of group solidarity. It is a ritual used at Klan gatherings, and it is used to represent the Klan itself. Thus, "[b]urning a cross at a political rally would almost certainly be protected expression." Indeed, occasionally a person who burns a cross does not intend to express either a statement of ideology or intimidation. Cross burnings have appeared in movies such as *Mississippi Burning*, and in plays such as the stage adaptation of Sir Walter Scott's *The Lady of the Lake*.

The prima facie provision makes no effort to distinguish among these different types of cross burnings. It does not distinguish between a cross burning done with the purpose of creating anger or resentment and a cross burning done with the purpose of threatening or intimidating a victim. It does not distinguish between a cross burning at a public rally or a cross burning on a neighbor's lawn. It does not treat the cross burning directed at an individual differently from the cross burning directed at a group of like-minded believers. It allows a jury to treat a cross burning on the property of another with the owner's acquiescence in the same manner as a cross burning on the property of another without the owner's permission. * * *

For these reasons, the prima facie evidence provision, as interpreted through the jury instruction and as applied in Barry Black's case, is unconstitutional on its face. * * *

V

With respect to Barry Black, we agree with the Supreme Court of Virginia that his conviction cannot stand, and we affirm the judgment of the Supreme Court of Virginia. With respect to Elliott and O'Mara, we vacate the judgment of the Supreme Court of Virginia, and remand the case for further proceedings.

It is so ordered.

[The opinion of Mr. JUSTICE STEVENS, concurring in the judgment, has been omitted.]

JUSTICE THOMAS, dissenting.

In every culture, certain things acquire meaning well beyond what outsiders can comprehend. That goes for both the sacred, and the profane. I believe that cross burning is the paradigmatic example of the latter.

I

Although I agree with the majority's conclusion that it is constitutionally permissible to "ban * * * cross burning carried out with intent to intimidate," I believe that the majority errs in imputing an expressive component to the activity in question. In my view, whatever expressive value cross burning has, the legislature simply wrote it out by banning only intimidating conduct undertaken by particular means. A conclusion that the statute prohibiting cross burning with intent to intimidate sweeps beyond a prohibition on certain conduct into the zone of expression overlooks not only the words of the statute but also reality.

A

"In holding [the ban on cross burning with intent to intimidate] unconstitutional, the Court ignores Justice Holmes' familiar aphorism that 'a page of history is worth a volume of logic.'"

To me, the majority's brief history of the Ku Klux Klan only reinforces [the] common understanding of the Klan as a terrorist organization, which, in its endeavor to intimidate, or even eliminate those its dislikes, uses the most brutal of methods.

Such methods typically include cross burning – a "tool for the intimidation and harassment of racial minorities, Catholics, Jews, Communists, and any other groups hated by the Klan." * * *

* * * [T]he perception that a burning cross is a threat and a precursor of worse things to come is not limited to blacks. Because the modern Klan expanded the list of its enemies beyond blacks and "radicals," to include Catholics, Jews, most immigrants, and labor unions, a burning cross is now widely viewed as a signal of impending terror and lawlessness. * * *

Accordingly, this statute prohibits only conduct, not expression. And, just as one cannot burn down someone's house to make a political point and then seek refuge in the First Amendment, those who hate cannot terrorize and intimidate to make their point. In light of my conclusion that the statute here addresses only conduct, there is no need to analyze it under any of our First Amendment tests.

Because I would uphold the validity of this statute, I respectfully dissent.

[The opinions of Mr. JUSTICE SCALIA, with whom JUSTICE THOMAS joins as to Parts I and II, concurring in part, concurring in the judgment in part, and dissenting in part, and the opinion of Mr. JUSTICE SOUTER, with whom JUSTICE KENNEDY and JUSTICE GINSBURG join, concurring in the judgment in part and dissenting in part, have been omitted.]

2.   The Doctrine of "Transferred Intent"

One of the basic principles of criminal law is the idea that an intent to do one thing, such as intending to steal rum, cannot be used as a substitute for an intent to do another thing, such as intending to burn down a ship. *Regina v. Faulkner*, 13 Cox C.C. 550 (1877). If the statute requires an intent to burn down a ship, then the government must prove that the defendant's conscious object or purpose was to burn down the ship, or that the defendant knew to a virtual certainty that his actions would cause the ship to burn down. An intent to steal rum is not the same as an intent to burn down a ship. An intent to light a match in order to steal that rum is a far cry from purposefully burning down a ship or knowing that one's actions will burn down the ship.

What if an individual attempts to shoot and kill one person X, misses, and instead kills another person Y? Can that individual be held criminally liable for intentionally murdering Y?

If an intent to do one thing cannot be used as proof of an intent to do another completely different thing, then one might surmise that an individual who intends to shoot and kill one person, but instead by mistake shoots and kills another person, cannot be held criminally liable for intentionally killing that other person (although he might be liable for recklessly killing that individual). Under both the common law and the Model Penal Code, *see* Model Penal Code § 2.03(2), however, the shooter can be held criminally liable for intentionally killing the other person even if that other person was in fact an unintended victim. The court in *People v. Scott* explains why.

PEOPLE v. SCOTT

Supreme Court of California
14 Cal.4th 544, 927 P.2d 288, 59 Cal.Rptr.2d 178 (1996)

BROWN, J.

A jury convicted defendants Damien Scott and Derrick Brown of various crimes for their part in a drive-by shooting which resulted in the death of one person and injury to several others. We must decide in this case whether the doctrine of transferred intent may be used to assign criminal liability to a defendant who kills an unintended victim when the defendant is also prosecuted for the attempted murder of an intended victim.

Under the classic formulation of California's common law doctrine of transferred intent, a defendant who shoots with the intent to kill a certain person and hits a bystander instead is subject to the same criminal liability that would have been imposed had "'the fatal blow reached the person for whom intended.'" In such a factual setting, the defendant is deemed as culpable as if he had accomplished what he set out to do.

Here, it was established at trial that defendants fired an automatic weapon into a public park in an attempt to kill a certain individual, and fatally shot a bystander instead. The case presents the type of factual setting in which courts have uniformly approved reliance on the transferred intent doctrine as the basis of determining a defendant's criminal liability for the death of an unintended victim. Consistent with a line of decisions beginning with *Suesser* nearly a century ago, we conclude that the jury in this case was properly instructed on a transferred intent theory of liability for first degree murder. * * *

I.   BACKGROUND

In May 1991, Calvin Hughes became the target of a family vendetta. While Hughes and Elaine Scott were romantically involved, Hughes and his sister, Eugenia Griffin, shared Scott's apartment. After the bloom faded from the romance, relations between Hughes and Scott became increasingly acrimonious and one night Hughes and Scott got into a physical altercation. Defendant Damien Scott and codefendant Derrick Brown, Scott's adult sons, came to her aid and forced Hughes and Griffin out of the apartment.

A few days later, Hughes borrowed Griffin's car and, accompanied by his friend Gary Tripp, returned to Scott's place to retrieve his personal belongings. When Scott attempted to bar his entry, Hughes forced his way into the apartment and gathered his things. On his way out, he heard Scott threaten to page her sons.

Hughes and Tripp drove to Jesse Owens Park in South Los Angeles to meet Griffin. Nathan Kelley and his teenage son, Jack Gibson, had parked nearby. As Hughes stood beside Kelley's car, talking to him through the open window, three cars entered the park. Gunfire erupted. Defendant Scott and codefendant Brown, riding in the first car, sprayed the area with bullets. Hughes took cover behind the front bumper of Kelley's car. When there was a lull in the shooting, Hughes sprinted toward the park gym. A renewed hail of gunfire followed him. A bullet hit the heel of his shoe. The shooting stopped when Hughes took cover behind the gym. The gunmen left the park.

In the aftermath, the victims discovered both Kelley's and Griffin's vehicles had been riddled with bullets; Gary Tripp had been shot in the leg and buttocks; and Jack Gibson had been killed when a bullet struck him in the head.

In an amended multicount information, defendant Scott and codefendant Brown were jointly charged with the murder of Jack Gibson; attempted murder of Calvin Hughes and Gary Tripp; and assault with a firearm on Calvin Hughes, Nathan Kelley, Gary Tripp, and Eugenia Griffin. * * *

At a second trial following mistrial due to a deadlocked jury, the prosecutor sought to establish that Jack Gibson was the unintended victim of defendants' premeditated and deliberate intent to kill Calvin Hughes. At the prosecution's request, the trial court instructed the jury on transferred intent using a modified version of CALJIC No. 8.65. The court stated as follows: "As it relates to the charge of murder, where one attempts to kill a certain person, but by mistake or inadvertence kills a different person, the crime, if any, so committed is the same as though the person originally intended to be killed, had been killed." The jury was also instructed on second degree express malice and implied malice murder.

The jury convicted both defendants of second degree murder, two counts of attempted murder, and two counts of assault with a firearm. * * *

Defendants appealed their convictions and, in a published decision, the Court of Appeal modified and affirmed the judgments of conviction. In relevant part, the Court of Appeal rejected defendants' argument that a transferred intent instruction only applies when the prosecution elects to charge the defendant with first degree murder of the unintended victim, and not also with attempted murder of the intended victim.

We granted defendant Scott's petition for review.

The jury convicted defendants of second degree murder for fatally shooting the unintended victim. It cannot be determined from the verdicts, however, whether the jury relied on the transferred intent instruction to convict defendants of second degree murder on an express malice theory, or whether it reached that verdict through a finding of implied malice. Consequently, it is necessary to decide whether a transferred intent instruction was properly given in this case.

II.   DISCUSSION

The common law doctrine of transferred intent was applied in England as early as the 16th century. The doctrine became part of the common law in many American jurisdictions, including that of California, and is typically invoked in the criminal law context when assigning criminal liability to a defendant who attempts to kill one person but accidentally kills another instead. Under such circumstances, the accused is deemed as culpable, and society is harmed as much, as if the defendant had accomplished what he had initially intended, and justice is achieved by punishing the defendant for a crime of the same seriousness as the one he tried to commit against his intended victim. Under the classic formulation of the common law doctrine of transferred intent, the defendant's guilt is thus "exactly what it would have been had the blow fallen upon the intended victim instead of the bystander."

In California, the transferred intent doctrine was first addressed in *Suesser*. The defendant in that case was convicted of first degree murder and sentenced to death for fatally shooting an individual under the erroneous belief he was firing at a different person named Allen, whom the defendant deliberately and with premeditation intended to kill. On appeal, the defendant argued the trial court erred in refusing his request to instruct the jury that malice must exist towards the person actually killed, and that if the defendant shot the deceased erroneously believing him to be Allen, he was guilty of only second degree murder. The trial court instructed instead in accordance with the common law doctrine of transferred intent, explaining to the jury that the defendant was guilty of the same degree of murder as if he had killed Allen instead of the deceased.

Persuaded by the reasoning of commentators and the weight of authority from other jurisdictions, *Suesser* held that the common law doctrine of transferred intent survived the enactment of California's murder statute. The opinion in *Suesser* does not expressly state the rationale behind the rule of transferred intent. One of the out-of-state decisions cited by the *Suesser* court did so succinctly, however. In *State v. Murray,* the defendant was convicted of first degree murder for killing a bystander in an attempt on the life of another person. The Oregon Supreme Court affirmed the judgment because the defendant "exhibited the same malignity and recklessness in the one event he would have displayed in the other, and the consequences to society are just as fearful."

Suesser and a number of other California decisions present the classic "bad aim" cases in which a defendant who attempts to kill one individual and inadvertently kills a bystander instead is convicted of murder on the theory of transferred intent. Courts in these cases have uniformly rejected the defendants' argument that their convictions were based on insufficient evidence of intent to kill. * * *

Nor is application of the transferred intent doctrine under these circumstances foreclosed by the prosecutor having charged defendants with attempted murder of the intended victim. Contrary to what its name implies, the transferred intent doctrine does not refer to any actual intent that is capable of being "used up" once it is employed to convict a defendant of a specific intent crime against the intended victim.

Courts and commentators have long recognized that the notion of creating a whole crime by "transferring" a defendant's intent from the object of his assault to the victim of his criminal act is, as Dean Prosser aptly describes it, a "bare-faced" legal fiction. The legal fiction of transferring a defendant's intent helps illustrate why, as a theoretical matter, a defendant can be convicted of murder when she did not intend to kill the person *actually killed*. The transferred intent doctrine does not, however, denote an actual "transfer" of "intent" from the intended victim to the unintended victim. Rather, as applied here, it connotes a *policy* – that a defendant who shoots at an intended victim with intent to kill but misses and hits a bystander instead should be subject to the same criminal liability that would have been imposed had he hit his intended mark. It is the policy underlying the doctrine, rather than its literal meaning, that compels the conclusion that a transferred intent instruction was properly given in this case.

Conversely, reliance on a transferred intent theory of liability for the first degree murder of the unintended victim did not prevent the prosecutor from also charging defendants with attempted murder of the intended victim. As previously recounted, defendants shot at an intended victim, missed him, and killed another individual instead. In their attempt to kill the intended victim, defendants committed crimes against two persons. They may be held accountable for the death of the unintended victim on a theory of transferred intent. Their criminal liability for attempting to kill the intended victim is that which the law assigns, here, in accordance with the attempted murder statute.

Defendant Scott argues that when an accused is charged with attempted murder of the intended victim, and transferred intent is used to assign a defendant's liability for the killing of an unintended victim, the defendant is being prosecuted as if he intended to kill two people rather than one. Defendant asserts that, under these circumstances, transferred intent should not be applied. He finds support for this proposition in *People v. Birreuta*, where the court stated that a murderer who premeditates and deliberates two killings is more culpable, and should be punished more severely, than the murderer who intends to kill only one victim and inadvertently kills another.

In *Birreuta,* the defendant was convicted of two counts of first degree murder for fatally shooting both an intended and an unintended victim. The court reversed the conviction that was based on the theory of transferred intent, holding that when the intended victim is killed, it is unnecessary to rely on the fiction of transferred intent. According to the court, the defendant's premeditation and deliberation can be directly and fully employed in prosecuting the first degree murder of the intended victim.

The *Birreuta* court viewed killers who premeditatedly and deliberately kill two people as more culpable than those who only intend to kill one person and mistakenly kill another in the attempt. The court noted that when the transferred intent doctrine is applied to hold the latter accountable for the accidental killing as a first degree murder, this distinction in culpability disappears.

We observe that although application of the transferred intent doctrine in the classic bad aim cases has been consistent, in cases involving crimes relating to both intended and unintended victims, reliance on the doctrine to assign criminal liability has led to mixed results. Some courts simply apply the rule of *Suesser* without addressing the question whether the death of, or injury to, the intended as well as the unintended victim requires a different analysis. Other courts acknowledge the potential for analytical distinctions but reach conflicting resolutions. The court in *People v. Carlson* stated, in dictum, that transferred intent "applies even though the original object of the assault is killed as well as the person whose death was the accidental or the unintended result of the intent to kill the former." The court in *Birreuta* expressed a contrary view, holding the transferred intent doctrine did not apply when both intended and unintended victims are killed.

Because the facts of the case presented here do not involve the fatal shooting of both an intended and unintended victim, we have no occasion to determine whether *Birreuta*'s reasoning or its conclusion is correct, and we decline to express a view on that decision. As previously discussed, the evidence at trial in this case was that defendants' attempt to kill one person resulted in the killing of an innocent bystander. Under these circumstances, *Suesser* and its progeny have uniformly applied the common law doctrine of transferred intent to assign a defendant's criminal liability for the killing of the unintended victim. Consistent with the line of decisions beginning with *Suesser* nearly a century ago, because defendants shot at one person with an intent to kill, missed him, and killed a bystander instead, they may be held accountable for a crime of the same seriousness as the one they would have committed had they hit their intended target. * * *

III.   DISPOSITION

The judgment of the Court of Appeal affirming the judgments of conviction is affirmed.

Note

Joshua Dressler argues that even in the classic "bad aim" case, the fiction of transferred intent is unnecessary:

> For example, assume that *D*, intending to kill *X*, accidentally kills *Y* instead. According to the transferred intent doctrine *D*'s intent to kill *X* is transferred to *Y*. But why? The *actus reus* of common law murder is "the killing of *a* human being by another human being." Assume that the *mens rea* of the offense is "intent to kill." In this context, the latter phrase means that the defendant must intend to kill "*a* human being." The identity of the intended victim, however, is immaterial. Therefore, if the prosecutor proves that a human being – any human being – has been killed by *D*, the crime of murder has been proven; the *actus reus* of the offense (the killing of a human being, *Y*) has occurred; and *D* possessed the required *mens rea* (*D* intended to kill a human being, *X*). There is no need to transfer the intent to kill from *X* to *Y*.

Joshua Dressler, CASES AND MATERIALS ON CRIMINAL LAW 139 (2d ed.1999).

3.   The Specific Intent/ General Intent Distinction

The common law draws a distinction between specific intent and general intent crimes. Although the distinction is better understood as the product of history than of logic, it is important for students and practitioners to be familiar with it because different legal rules apply depending on whether the defendant is charged with a specific intent or a general intent crime. *People v. Atkins* explains how to determine whether an offense is a specific intent or a general intent crime and why it matters to the defendant who wishes to present evidence of voluntary intoxication in his defense.

PEOPLE v. ATKINS
Supreme Court of California
25 Cal.4th 76, 18 P.3d 660, 104 Cal.Rptr.2d 738 (2001)

CHIN, J.

Is evidence of voluntary intoxication admissible, under Penal Code section 22, on the issue of whether defendant formed the required mental state for arson? We conclude that such evidence is not admissible because arson is a general intent crime. Accordingly, we reverse the judgment of the Court of Appeal.

FACTS AND PROCEDURAL HISTORY

On September 26, 1997, defendant told his friends that he hated Orville Figgs and was going to burn down Figgs's house.

On the afternoon of September 27, defendant and his brother David drove by Figgs's home on the Ponderosa Sky Ranch. Defendant "flipped the bird" at Figgs as they passed by.

Later that day, around 5:00 p.m., a neighbor saw David drive a white pickup truck into the Ponderosa Sky Ranch canyon, but could not tell if he had a passenger. Around 9:00 p.m., the same neighbor saw the pickup truck drive out of the canyon at a high rate of speed. A half-hour later, a fire was reported. Shortly after 10:00 p.m., Figgs was awakened by a neighbor. Because the fire was rapidly approaching his house, Figgs set up a fire line. The fire came within 150 feet of his house.

At 9:00 or 9:30 p.m., one of defendant's friends saw defendant at David's apartment. He was angrily throwing things around. When asked if defendant was heavily intoxicated, the friend replied, "Yes. Agitated, very agitated."

The county fire marshall, Alan Carlson, responded to the fire around 1:30 a.m. and saw a large fire rapidly spreading in the canyon below the ranch. He described fire conditions on that night as "extreme." Both the weather and the vegetation were particularly dry. The wind was blowing from 12 to 27 miles per hour, with gusts up to 50 miles per hour. The canyon had heavy brush, trees, grass, and steep sloping grades. The fire could not be controlled for three days and burned an area from 2.5 to 2.8 miles long.

The fire marshall traced the origin of the fire to an approximately 10-foot square area that was completely burned and smelled of "chainsaw mix," a combination of oil and gasoline. A soil sample taken from that area tested positive for gasoline. About 40 feet away, the marshall found defendant's wallet, which was near a recently opened beer can, and tire tracks. He also found a disposable lighter nearby and two more beer cans in other parts of the canyon. All the cans had the same expiration date.

Several days later, defendant spoke with the fire marshall. After waiving his *Miranda* rights, defendant told the marshall that he and his brother had spent much of the day drinking. They then drove in David's white pickup to the Ponderosa Sky Ranch canyon, where they drank some more and stayed between three and one-half to five hours. Defendant saw that the area was in poor condition and decided to burn some of the weeds. His family had once lived there. He pulled out the weeds, placed them in a small pile in a cleared area, retrieved a plastic gasoline jug from David's truck, and from the jug poured "chainsaw mix" on the pile of weeds. Defendant put the jug down a few feet away and lit the pile of weeds with a disposable lighter. The fire quickly spread to the jug and got out of hand. He and David tried to put the fire out, unsuccessfully. They panicked and fled while the jug was still burning. Defendant told the marshall that he meant no harm, claimed the fire was an accident, but admitted that he and his family had hard feelings with the Figgs family.

The marshall testified that the fire had not been started in a cleared area. The area was covered with vegetation, and there was no evidence that the fire started accidentally during a debris burn or that someone had tried to put it out. The marshall opined that the fire was intentionally set.

An information charged defendant with arson of forest land. The trial court instructed on arson[2] and on the lesser offenses of arson to property unlawfully causing a fire of forest land and misdemeanor unlawfully causing a fire of property. It described arson and all lesser offenses as general intent crimes and further instructed that voluntary intoxication is not a defense to arson

---

[2]   The trial court defined arson, in the language of CALJIC No. 14.80, as follows: "Any person who willfully and maliciously sets fire to or burns or causes to be burned any forest land is guilty of arson in violation of [section 451, subdivision (c)]. * * * The word 'willfully' means intentionally.* * *"

and the lesser crimes and does not relieve defendant of responsibility for the crime. The jury found defendant guilty as charged.

Defendant appealed, arguing that evidence of voluntary intoxication was admissible to show that he lacked the requisite mental state for arson. The Court of Appeal agreed. It reasoned that, as defined in its prior decisions of *In re Stonewall F.*, the mens rea for arson is the intent to set fire to or burn or cause to be burned forest land, a specific mental state, as to which voluntary intoxication evidence is admissible under section 22, subdivision (b). The court reversed because the instruction that voluntary intoxication was not a defense to arson "denied defendant the opportunity to prove he lacked the required mental state."

We granted the People's petition for review on the issue of whether evidence of voluntary intoxication is admissible, under section 22, to negate the required mental state for arson.

DISCUSSION

Section 22 provides, as relevant:

(a) No act committed by a person while in a state of voluntary intoxication is less criminal by reason of his or her having been in that condition. * * *

(b) Evidence of voluntary intoxication is admissible solely on the issue of whether or not the defendant actually formed a required specific intent, or, when charged with murder, whether the defendant premeditated, deliberated, or harbored express malice aforethought.

Evidence of voluntary intoxication is inadmissible to negate the existence of general criminal intent. In *People v. Hood*, * * * we held that intoxication was relevant to negate the existence of a specific intent, but not a general intent, and that assault is a general intent crime for this purpose. We stated:

The distinction between specific and general intent crimes evolved as a judicial response to the problem of the intoxicated offender. That problem is to reconcile two competing theories of what is just in the treatment of those who commit crimes while intoxicated. On the one hand, the moral culpability of a drunken criminal is frequently less than that of a sober person effecting a like injury. On the other hand, it is commonly felt that a person who voluntarily gets drunk and while in that state commits a crime should not escape the consequences.

Before the nineteenth century, the common law refused to give any effect to the fact that an accused committed a crime while intoxicated. The judges were apparently troubled by this rigid traditional rule, however, for there were a number of attempts during the early part of the nineteenth century to arrive at a more humane, yet workable, doctrine. The theory that these judges explored was that evidence of intoxication could be considered to negate intent, whenever intent was an element of the crime charged. As Professor Hall notes, however, such an exculpatory doctrine could eventually have undermined the traditional rule entirely, since some form of *mens rea* is a requisite of all but strict liability offenses. To limit the operation of the doctrine and achieve a compromise between the conflicting feelings of sympathy and reprobation for the intoxicated offender, later courts both in England and this country drew a distinction between so-called specific intent and general intent crimes.

Although we noted in *Hood* that specific and general intent have been notoriously difficult terms to define and apply, we set forth a general definition distinguishing the two intents: "When the definition of a crime consists of only the description of a particular act, without reference to intent to do a further act or achieve a future consequence, we ask whether the defendant intended to do the proscribed act. This intention is deemed to be a general criminal intent. When the definition refers to defendant's intent to do some further act or achieve some additional consequence, the crime is deemed to be one of specific intent." The basic framework that *Hood* established in designating a criminal intent as either specific or general for purposes of determining the admissibility of evidence of voluntary intoxication has survived.

Defendant argues that arson requires the specific intent to burn the relevant structure or forest land, a mental state that may be negated by evidence of voluntary intoxication. The People argue that arson is a general intent crime with a mental state that cannot be negated by such evidence. The Courts of Appeal have disagreed on the intent requirement for arson. * * *

We agree with the People that arson requires only a general criminal intent and that the specific intent to set fire to or burn or cause to be burned the relevant structure or forest land is not an element of arson. * * *

As relevant here, the proscribed acts within the statutory definition of arson are to (1) set fire to; (2) burn; or (3) cause to be burned, any structure, forest land, or property. Language that typically denotes specific intent crimes, such as "with the intent" to achieve or "for the purpose of" achieving some further act, is absent from section 451. "A crime is characterized as a 'general intent' crime when the required mental state entails only an intent to do the act that causes the harm; a crime is characterized as a 'specific intent' crime when the required mental state entails an intent to cause the resulting harm." The statute does not require an additional specific intent to burn a "structure, forest land, or property," but rather requires only an intent to do the act that causes the harm. * * * Thus, the intent requirement for arson fits within the *Hood* definition of general intent, i.e., the description of the proscribed act fails to refer to an intent to do a further act or achieve a future consequence. * * *

Finally, we reject defendant's argument that the withholding of voluntary intoxication evidence to negate the mental state of arson violates his due process rights by denying him the opportunity to prove he did not possess the required mental state. (*Montana v. Egelhoff*, 518 U.S. 37 (1996)).[a]

CONCLUSION

We reverse the judgment of the Court of Appeal and remand the case to the Court of Appeal for further proceedings consistent with this opinion.

Note

As *Atkins* suggests, the specific intent/general intent distinction evolved as a pragmatic strategy to deal with the problem of the intoxicated offender. Over time, however, courts began to rely upon the distinction in other areas of criminal law jurisprudence. We will encounter it again, for example, when we study the law of mistake.

The Model Penal Code does not employ the specific intent/general intent distinction.

D.　KNOWLEDGE

Another mens rea term used in both common law and Model Penal Code jurisdictions is the mental state of "knowledge." Under the common law, a person knows of a fact if he either is aware of that fact or correctly believes the fact exists. Many jurisdictions recognize a third way of proving knowledge,

---

[a] We will study *Montana v. Egelhoff* in Chapter 10.

equating positive or actual knowledge with wilful blindness or deliberate ignorance. The Ninth Circuit Court of Appeals discusses wilful blindness in *United States v. Jewell.*

UNITED STATES v. JEWELL
United States Court of Appeals for the Ninth Circuit
532 F.2d 697 (9th Cir. 1976)

BROWNING, CIRCUIT JUDGE

* * *

Appellant defines "knowingly" in 21 U.S.C. §§ 841 and 960 to require that positive knowledge that a controlled substance is involved be established as an element of each offense.[a] On the basis of this interpretation, appellant argues that it was reversible error to instruct the jury that the defendant could be convicted upon proof beyond a reasonable doubt that if he did not have positive knowledge that a controlled substance was concealed in the automobile he drove over the border, it was solely and entirely because of the conscious purpose on his part to avoid learning the truth. The majority concludes that this contention is wrong in principle, and has no support in authority or in the language or legislative history of the statute.

It is undisputed that appellant entered the United States driving an automobile in which 110 pounds of marihuana worth $6,250 had been concealed in a secret compartment between the trunk and rear seat. Appellant testified that he did not know the marihuana was present. There was circumstantial evidence from which the jury could infer that appellant had positive knowledge of the presence of the marihuana, and that his contrary testimony was false.[2] On the

---

[a] 21 U.S.C. § 841 provides in part: "[I]t shall be unlawful for any person knowingly or intentionally – (1) to manufacture, distribute, or dispense, or possess with intent to manufacture, distribute, or dispense, a controlled substance * * *."

21 U.S.C. § 960 provides in part: "Any person who * * * knowingly or intentionally imports or exports a controlled substance, * * * shall be punished * * *."

[2] Appellant testified that a week before the incident in question he sold his car for $100 to obtain funds "to have a good time." He then rented a car for about $100, and he and a friend drove the rented car to Mexico. Appellant and his friend were unable to adequately explain their whereabouts during the period of about 11 hours between the time they left Los Angeles and the time they admitted arriving in Mexico.

Their testimony regarding acquisition of the load car follows a pattern common in these cases: they were approached in a Tijuana bar by a stranger who other hand there was evidence from which the jury could conclude that appellant spoke the truth that although appellant knew of the presence of the secret compartment and had knowledge of facts indicating that it contained marihuana, he deliberately avoided positive knowledge of the presence of the contraband to avoid responsibility in the event of discovery.[3] If the jury concluded the latter was indeed the situation, and if positive knowledge is required to convict, the jury would have no choice consistent with its oath but to find appellant not guilty even though he deliberately contrived his lack of positive knowledge. * * *

---

identified himself only by his first name "Ray." He asked them if they wanted to buy marihuana, and offered to pay them $100 for driving a car north across the border. Appellant accepted the offer and drove the load car back, alone. Appellant's friend drove appellant's rented car back to Los Angeles.

Appellant testified that the stranger instructed him to leave the load car at the address on the car registration slip with the keys in the ashtray. The person living at that address testified that he had sold the car a year earlier and had not seen it since. When the Customs agent asked appellant about the secret compartment in the car, appellant did not deny knowledge of its existence, but stated that it was in the car when he got it.

There were many discrepancies and inconsistencies in the evidence reflecting upon appellant's credibility. Taking the record as a whole, the jury could have concluded that the evidence established an abortive scheme, concocted and carried out by appellant from the beginning, to acquire a load of marihuana in Mexico and return it to Los Angeles for distribution for profit.

[3]Both appellant and his companion testified that the stranger identified as "Ray" offered to sell them marihuana and, when they declined, asked if they wanted to drive a car back to Los Angeles for $100. Appellant's companion "wanted no part of driving the vehicle." He testified, "It didn't sound right to me." Appellant accepted the offer. The Drug Enforcement Administration agent testified that appellant stated "he thought there was probably something wrong and something illegal in the vehicle, but that he checked it over. He looked in the glove box and under the front seat and in the trunk, prior to driving it. *He didn't find anything, and, therefore, he assumed that the people at the border wouldn't find anything either.*" (emphasis added). Appellant was asked at trial whether he had seen the special compartment when he opened the trunk. He responded, "Well, you know, I saw a void there, but I didn't know what it was." He testified that he did not investigate further. The Customs agent testified that when he opened the trunk and saw the partition he asked appellant "when he had that put in." Appellant told the agent "that it was in the car when he got it."

The jury would have been justified in accepting all of the testimony as true and concluding that although appellant was aware of facts making it virtually certain that the secret compartment concealed marihuana, he deliberately refrained from acquiring positive knowledge of the fact.

Appellant tendered an instruction that to return a guilty verdict the jury must find that the defendant knew he was in possession of marihuana. The trial judge rejected the instruction because it suggested that "absolutely, positively, he has to know that it's there." The court said, "I think, in this case, it's not too sound an instruction because we have evidence that if the jury believes it, they'd be justified in finding he actually didn't know what it was – he didn't because he didn't want to find it."

The court instructed the jury . . . that the government must prove beyond a reasonable doubt that the defendant "knowingly" brought the marihuana into the United States and that he "knowingly" possessed the marihuana. The court continued:

> The Government can complete their burden of proof by proving, beyond a reasonable doubt, that if the defendant was not actually aware that there was marijuana in the vehicle he was driving when he entered the United States his ignorance in that regard was solely and entirely a result of his having made a conscious purpose to disregard the nature of that which was in the vehicle, with a conscious purpose to avoid learning the truth.

The legal premise of these instructions is firmly supported by leading commentators here and in England. Professor Rollin M. Perkins writes, "One with a deliberate antisocial purpose in mind . . . may deliberately 'shut his eyes' to avoid knowing what would otherwise be obvious to view. In such cases, so far as criminal law is concerned, the person acts at his peril in this regard, and is treated as having 'knowledge' of the facts as they are ultimately discovered to be." J. Edwards, writing in 1954, introduced a survey of English cases with the statement, "For well-nigh a hundred years, it has been clear from the authorities that a person who deliberately shuts his eyes to an obvious means of knowledge has sufficient mens rea for an offence based on such words as . . . 'knowingly.'" Professor Glanville Williams states, on the basis of both English and American authorities, "To the requirement of actual knowledge there is one strictly limited exception. . . . (T)he rule is that if a party has his suspicion aroused but then deliberately omits to make further enquiries, because he wishes to remain in ignorance, he is deemed to have knowledge." Professor Williams concludes, "The rule that wilful blindness is equivalent to knowledge is essential, and is found throughout the criminal law."[7]

The substantive justification for the rule is that deliberate ignorance and positive knowledge are equally culpable. The textual justification is that in common understanding one "knows" facts of which he is less than absolutely certain. To act "knowingly," therefore, is not necessarily to act only with positive knowledge, but also to act with an awareness of the high probability of the existence of the fact in question. When such awareness is present, "positive" knowledge is not required.

This is the analysis adopted in the Model Penal Code. Section 2.02(7) states: "When knowledge of the existence of a particular fact is an element of an offense, such knowledge is established if a person is aware of a high probability of its existence, unless he actually believes that it does not exist." As the Comment to this provision explains, "Paragraph (7) deals with the situation British commentators have denominated 'wilful blindness' or 'connivance,' the case of the actor who is aware of the probable existence of a material fact but does not satisfy himself that it does not in fact exist." * * *

There is no reason to reach a different result under the statute involved in this case. Doing so would put this court in direct conflict with Courts of Appeals in two other circuits that have approved "deliberate ignorance" instructions in prosecutions under 21 U.S.C. § 841(a), or its predecessor, 21 U.S.C. § 174. * * *

Appellant's narrow interpretation of "knowingly" is inconsistent with the Drug Control Act's general purpose to deal more effectively "with the growing menace of drug abuse in the United States." Holding that this term

---

[7]Mr. Williams' concluding paragraph reads in its entirety:

The rule that wilful blindness is equivalent to knowledge is essential, and is found throughout the criminal law. It is, at the same time, an unstable rule, because judges are apt to forget its very limited scope. A court can properly find wilful blindness only where it can almost be said that the defendant actually knew. He suspected the fact; he realised its probability; but he refrained from obtaining the final confirmation because he wanted in the event to be able to deny knowledge. This, and this alone, is wilful blindness. It requires in effect a finding that the defendant intended to cheat the administration of justice. Any wider definition would make the doctrine of wilful blindness indistinguishable from the civil doctrine of negligence in not obtaining knowledge.

introduces a requirement of positive knowledge would make deliberate ignorance a defense. It cannot be doubted that those who traffic in drugs would make the most of it. This is evident from the number of appellate decisions reflecting conscious avoidance of positive knowledge of the presence of contraband – in the car driven by the defendant or in which he is a passenger, in the suitcase or package he carries, in the parcel concealed in his clothing.

It is no answer to say that in such cases the fact finder may infer positive knowledge. It is probable that many who performed the transportation function, essential to the drug traffic, can truthfully testify that they have no positive knowledge of the load they carry. Under appellant's interpretation of the statute, such persons will be convicted only if the fact finder errs in evaluating the credibility of the witness or deliberately disregards the law.

It begs the question to assert that a "deliberate ignorance" instruction permits the jury to convict without finding that the accused possessed the knowledge required by the statute. Such an assertion assumes that the statute requires positive knowledge. But the question is the meaning of the term "knowingly" in the statute. If it means positive knowledge, then, of course, nothing less will do. But if "knowingly" includes a mental state in which the defendant is aware that the fact in question is highly probable but consciously avoids enlightenment, the statute is satisfied by such proof.

It is worth emphasizing that the required state of mind differs from positive knowledge only so far as necessary to encompass a calculated effort to avoid the sanctions of the statute while violating its substance. "A court can properly find wilful blindness only where it can almost be said that the defendant actually knew." In the language of the instruction in this case, the government must prove, "beyond a reasonable doubt, that if the defendant was not actually aware . . . his ignorance in that regard was solely and entirely a result of . . . a conscious purpose to avoid learning the truth."

No legitimate interest of an accused is prejudiced by such a standard, and society's interest in a system of criminal law that is enforceable and that imposes sanctions upon all who are equally culpable requires it.

The conviction is affirmed.

[The opinion of JUDGE KENNEDY, with whom JUDGES ELY, HUFSTEDLER and WALLACE join dissenting, is omitted.]

E.   STRICT LIABILITY CRIMES

Some statutes do not include a mental state element. In such cases, the court must determine whether the legislature purposely left out a mental state element because it wanted to treat the crime as one of strict liability (one for which the government need not prove any mental state) or whether the omission was inadvertent. In *Morissette v. United States*, the Supreme Court explains that when a statute is silent as to mens rea, the ordinary presumption is that a mental state is required for criminal liability.

MORISSETTE v. UNITED STATES
Supreme Court of the United States
342 U.S. 246, 72 S.Ct. 240, 96 L.Ed. 288 (1951)

MR. JUSTICE JACKSON delivered the opinion of the Court.

This would have remained a profoundly insignificant case to all except its immediate parties had it not been so tried and submitted to the jury as to raise questions both fundamental and far-reaching in federal criminal law, for which reason we granted certiorari.

On a large tract of uninhabited and untilled land in a wooded and sparsely populated area of Michigan, the Government established a practice bombing range over which the Air Force dropped simulated bombs at ground targets. These bombs consisted of a metal cylinder about forty inches long and eight inches across, filled with sand and enough black powder to cause a smoke puff by which the strike could be located. At various places about the range signs read "Danger – Keep Out – Bombing Range." Nevertheless, the range was known as good deer country and was extensively hunted.

Spent bomb casings were cleared from the targets and thrown into piles "so that they will be out of the way." They were not stacked or piled in any order but were dumped in heaps, some of which had been accumulating for four years or upwards, were exposed to the weather and rusting away.

Morissette, in December of 1948, went hunting in this area but did not get a deer. He thought to meet expenses of the trip by salvaging some of these casings. He loaded three tons of them on his truck and took them to a nearby farm, where they were flattened by driving a tractor over them. After expending this labor and trucking them to market in Flint, he realized $84.

Morissette, by occupation, is a fruit stand operator in summer and a trucker and scrap iron collector in winter. An honorably discharged veteran of World War II, he enjoys a good name among his neighbors and has had no blemish on his record more disreputable than a conviction for reckless driving.

The loading, crushing and transporting of these casings were all in broad daylight, in full view of passers-by, without the slightest effort at concealment. When an investigation was started, Morissette voluntarily, promptly and candidly told the whole story to the authorities, saying that he had no intention of stealing but thought the property was abandoned, unwanted and considered of no value to the Government. He was indicted, however, on the charge that he "did unlawfully, wilfully and knowingly steal and convert" property of the United States of the value of $84, in violation of 18 U.S.C. § 641, which provides that "whoever embezzles, steals, purloins, or knowingly converts" government property is punishable by fine and imprisonment. Morissette was convicted and sentenced to imprisonment for two months or to pay a fine of $200. The Court of Appeals affirmed, one judge dissenting.

On his trial, Morissette, as he had at all times told investigating officers, testified that from appearances he believed the casings were cast-off and abandoned, that he did not intend to steal the property, and took it with no wrongful or criminal intent. The trial court, however, was unimpressed, and ruled: "He took it because he thought it was abandoned and he knew he was on government property. . . . That is no defense. . . . I don't think anybody can have the defense they thought the property was abandoned on another man's piece of property." The court stated: "I will not permit you to show this man thought it was abandoned. . . . I hold in this case that there is no question of abandoned property." The court refused to submit or to allow counsel to argue to the jury whether Morissette acted with innocent intention. It charged: "And I instruct you that if you believe the testimony of the government in this case, he intended to take it. . . . He had no right to take this property. . . . And it is no defense to claim that it was abandoned, because it was on private property. . . . And I instruct you to this effect: That if this young man took this property (and he says he did), without any permission (he says he did), that was on the property of the United States Government (he says it was), that it was of the value of one cent or more (and evidently it was), that he is guilty of the offense charged here. If you believe the government, he is guilty. . . . The question on intent is whether or not he intended to take the property. He says he did. Therefore, if you believe either side, he is guilty." Petitioner's counsel contended, "But the taking must have been with a felonious intent." The court ruled, however: "That is presumed by his own act."

The Court of Appeals suggested that "greater restraint in expression should have been exercised," but affirmed the conviction because, "As we have interpreted the statute, appellant was guilty of its violation beyond a shadow of doubt, as evidenced even by his own admissions." Its construction of the statute is that it creates several separate and distinct offenses, one being knowing conversion of government property. The court ruled that this particular offense requires no element of criminal intent. This conclusion was thought to be required by the failure of Congress to express such a requisite and this Court's decisions in *United States v. Behrman* and *United States v. Balint*.[a]

I.

In those cases this Court did construe mere omission from a criminal enactment of any mention of criminal intent as dispensing with it. If they be deemed precedents for principles of construction generally applicable to federal penal statutes, they authorize this conviction. Indeed, such adoption of the literal reasoning announced in those cases would do this and more – it would sweep out of all federal crimes, except when expressly preserved, the ancient requirement of a culpable state of mind. We think a resume of their historical background is convincing that an effect has been ascribed to them more comprehensive than was contemplated and one inconsistent with our philosophy of criminal law.

The contention that an injury can amount to a crime only when inflicted by intention is no provincial or transient notion. It is as universal and persistent in mature systems of law as belief in freedom of the human will and a consequent ability and duty of the normal individual to choose between good and evil. A relation between some mental element and punishment for a harmful act is almost as instinctive as the child's familiar exculpatory "But I didn't mean to," and has afforded the rational basis for a tardy and unfinished substitution of deterrence and reformation in place of retaliation and vengeance as the motivation for public prosecution. Unqualified acceptance of this doctrine by English common law in the Eighteenth Century was indicated by Blackstone's sweeping statement that to constitute any crime there must first be a "vicious will." Common-law commentators of the Nineteenth Century early pronounced the same principle, although a few exceptions not relevant to our present problem came to be recognized.

---

[a] In *United States v. Behrman,* the Court held that the Anti-Narcotic Act of 1914 which made it a crime to sell, barter, exchange or give away certain drugs could be applied to a physician who prescribed large amounts of heroin and cocaine to a known addict regardless of the doctor's intent or knowledge. In *United States v. Balint,* the Court held that a New York anti-narcotic statute did not make knowledge an element of the offense, and therefore the indictment did not have to charge that the defendants sold the prescribed drugs knowing them to be prohibited.

Crime, as a compound concept, generally constituted only from concurrence of an evil-meaning mind with an evil-doing hand, was congenial to an intense individualism and took deep and early root in American soil.[9] As the states codified the common law of crimes, even if their enactments were silent on the subject, their courts assumed that the omission did not signify disapproval of the principle but merely recognized that intent was so inherent in the idea of the offense that it required no statutory affirmation. Courts, with little hesitation or division, found an implication of the requirement as to offenses that were taken over from the common law. The unanimity with which they have adhered to the central thought that wrongdoing must be conscious to be criminal is emphasized by the variety, disparity and confusion of their definitions of the requisite but elusive mental element. However, courts of various jurisdictions, and for the purposes of different offenses, have devised working formulae, if not scientific ones, for the instruction of juries around such terms as "felonious intent," "criminal intent," "malice aforethought," "guilty knowledge," "fraudulent intent," "wilfulness," "*scienter*," to denote guilty knowledge, or "*mens rea*," to signify an evil purpose or mental culpability. By use or combination of these various tokens, they have sought to protect those who were not blameworthy in mind from conviction of infamous common-law crimes.

However, the *Balint* and *Behrman* offenses belong to a category of another character, with very different antecedents and origins. The crimes there involved depend on no mental element but consist only of forbidden acts or omissions. This, while not expressed by the Court, is made clear from examination of a century-old but accelerating tendency, discernible both here and in England, to call into existence new duties and crimes which disregard any ingredient of intent. The industrial revolution multiplied the number of workmen exposed to injury from increasingly powerful and complex mechanisms, driven by freshly discovered sources of energy, requiring higher precautions by employers. Traffic of velocities, volumes and varieties unheard of came to subject the wayfarer to intolerable casualty risks if owners and drivers were not to observe new cares and uniformities of conduct. Congestion of cities and crowding of quarters called for health and welfare regulations undreamed of in simpler times. Wide distribution of goods became an instrument of wide distribution of harm when those who dispersed food, drink, drugs, and even securities, did not comply with reasonable standards of quality, integrity, disclosure and care. Such dangers have engendered increasingly numerous and detailed regulations which heighten the duties of those in control

---

[9] Holmes, The Common Law, considers intent in the chapter on The Criminal Law, and earlier makes the pithy observation: "Even a dog distinguishes between being stumbled over and being kicked."

of particular industries, trades, properties or activities that affect public health, safety or welfare.

While many of these duties are sanctioned by a more strict civil liability, lawmakers, whether wisely or not, have sought to make such regulations more effective by invoking criminal sanctions to be applied by the familiar technique of criminal prosecutions and convictions. This has confronted the courts with a multitude of prosecutions, based on statutes or administrative regulations, for what have been aptly called "public welfare offenses." These cases do not fit neatly into any of such accepted classifications of common-law offenses, such as those against the state, the person, property, or public morals. Many of these offenses are not in the nature of positive aggressions or invasions, with which the common law so often dealt, but are in the nature of neglect where the law requires care, or inaction where it imposes a duty. Many violations of such regulations result in no direct or immediate injury to person or property but merely create the danger or probability of it which the law seeks to minimize. While such offenses do not threaten the security of the state in the manner of treason, they may be regarded as offenses against its authority, for their occurrence impairs the efficiency of controls deemed essential to the social order as presently constituted. In this respect, whatever the intent of the violator, the injury is the same, and the consequences are injurious or not according to fortuity. Hence, legislation applicable to such offenses, as a matter of policy, does not specify intent as a necessary element. The accused, if he does not will the violation, usually is in a position to prevent it with no more care than society might reasonably expect and no more exertion than it might reasonably exact from one who assumed his responsibilities. Also, penalties commonly are relatively small, and conviction does no grave damage to an offender's reputation. Under such considerations, courts have turned to construing statutes and regulations which make no mention of intent as dispensing with it and holding that the guilty act alone makes out the crime. This has not, however, been without expressions of misgiving.

The pilot of the movement in this country appears to be a holding that a tavernkeeper could be convicted for selling liquor to an habitual drunkard even if he did not know the buyer to be such. Later came Massachusetts holdings that convictions for selling adulterated milk in violation of statutes forbidding such sales require no allegation or proof that defendant knew of the adulteration. Departures from the common-law tradition, mainly of these general classes, were reviewed and their rationale appraised by Chief Justice Cooley, as follows:

> I agree that as a rule there can be no crime without a criminal intent; but this is not by any means a universal rule. . . . Many statutes which are in the nature of police regulations, as this is, impose criminal penalties irrespective of any intent to violate

them; the purpose being to require a degree of diligence for the protection of the public which shall render violation impossible.

* * * It was not until recently that the Court took occasion more explicitly to relate abandonment of the ingredient of intent, not merely with considerations of expediency in obtaining convictions, nor with the *malum prohibitum* classification of the crime, but with the peculiar nature and quality of the offense. We referred to ". . . a now familiar type of legislation whereby penalties serve as effective means of regulation," and continued, "such legislation dispenses with the conventional requirement for criminal conduct – awareness of some wrongdoing. In the interest of the larger good it puts the burden of acting at hazard upon a person otherwise innocent but standing in responsible relation to a public danger." But we warned: "Hardship there doubtless may be under a statute which thus penalizes the transaction though consciousness of wrongdoing be totally wanting."

Neither this Court nor, so far as we are aware, any other has undertaken to delineate a precise line or set forth comprehensive criteria for distinguishing between crimes that require a mental element and crimes that do not. We attempt no closed definition, for the law on the subject is neither settled nor static. * * *

Stealing, larceny, and its variants and equivalents, were among the earliest offenses known to the law that existed before legislation; they are invasions of rights of property which stir a sense of insecurity in the whole community and arouse public demand for retribution, the penalty is high and, when a sufficient amount is involved, the infamy is that of a felony, which, says Maitland, is ". . . as bad a word as you can give to man or thing." State courts of last resort, on whom fall the heaviest burden of interpreting criminal law in this country, have consistently retained the requirement of intent in larceny-type offenses. If any state has deviated, the exception has neither been called to our attention nor disclosed by our research.

Congress, therefore, omitted any express prescription of criminal intent from the enactment before us in the light of an unbroken course of judicial decision in all constituent states of the Union holding intent inherent in this class of offense, even when not expressed in a statute. Congressional silence as to mental elements in an Act merely adopting into federal statutory law a concept of crime already so well defined in common law and statutory interpretation by the states may warrant quite contrary inferences than the same silence in creating an offense new to general law, for whose definition the courts have no guidance except the Act. * * *

We hold that mere omission from § 641 of any mention of intent will not be construed as eliminating that element from the crimes denounced.

Reversed.

COMMONWEALTH v. BARONE
276 Pa. Super. 282, 419 A.2d 457 (Pa. Super. Ct. 1980)

CERCONE, President Judge:

The Commonwealth brings the instant appeal from the trial court's order granting of appellee's demurrer to the charge of homicide by vehicle, Motor Vehicle Code, 75 Pa.C.S. § 3732 (1977). Ms. Barone filed a cross-appeal challenging an earlier order of court dismissing various of her earlier petitions and motions attacking the constitutionality of this statute. Albeit for different reasons, the majority of this Court agree that the order of the trial court discharging appellant should be affirmed.

(1) Section 3732 of the Motor Vehicle Code provides:

> Any person who unintentionally causes the death of another person while engaged in the violation of any law of this Commonwealth or municipal ordinance applying to the operation or use of a vehicle or to the regulation of traffic is guilty of homicide by vehicle, a misdemeanor of the first degree, when the violation is the cause of death.

The Commonwealth argues and the Dissent agrees that the words of this provision are precise and unambiguous. From this the Commonwealth further reasons that this statute unequivocally evidences a legislative intent to impose the severe penal sanctions of up to five years imprisonment and a possible fine, on drivers who, no matter how unintentionally, cause a death while operating a vehicle in violation of any statewide or municipal rule regulating operation or use of an auto. In our opinion, the above language is not susceptible to such a "plain meaning" approach. After having examined the legislative history of this enactment, we would hold that the legislature intended to select culpable negligence as defined in the Crimes Code * * * as its touchstone for punishment. * * *

Section 305 provides in pertinent part:

"(a) The requirements of culpability prescribed by . . . Section 302 of this title . . . do not apply to:

(2) offenses defined by statutes other than this title, insofar as a legislative purpose to impose absolute liability for such offenses or with respect to any material element thereof plainly appears.

This section of the Crimes Code is essentially identical to the parallel provision of the Model Penal Code, § 205(1)(b) (1962). The Comments to this proviso expressly observe "(t)hat this section makes a frontal attack on absolute or strict liability in penal law, whenever the offense carries a possibility of sentence of imprisonment." Implementation of this strong common law tradition against strict penal responsibility is found in the Code's commandment that legislation should not be found to impose strict liability unless a legislative intent to do so "plainly appears." With this in mind, our Court should not liberally apply this "plainly appears" test, but rather should carefully scrutinize the legislature's use of any settled terms which have heretofore been commonly associated with "fault."

The above approach, however, is not novel to Pennsylvania appellate courts. Our courts, as the Dissent correctly points out, have customarily adhered to the following principles of statutory construction 1) When the legislature employs language which is plain and unambiguous, there is no longer justification to resort to the rules of statutory construction; 2) In deciding whether a word or phrase is plain and unambiguous within the meaning of the above principle, an appellate court is to construe the word or phrase in accordance with its common and approved usage and; 3) If our legislature has utilized a word or phrase which is centuries old in our common law jurisprudence, we must interpret it consistently with its heritage in our legal traditions.

I begin with the words that are used to delineate the offense in this case. The critical word in the title is "homicide." In this Commonwealth, our court has uniformly interpreted enactments which carry this solemn title as requiring that the voluntary act which caused the death be done with some degree of fault, that is, intentionally, knowingly, recklessly, or more recently negligently. The legislature has further provided that the "homicide" which is punishable is that which is caused "unintentionally" while operating a motor vehicle. Taken in context, "unintentional" plainly means only that the conduct causing the death was not done purposely or with design. It neither plainly negatives the above understanding of the term "homicide" nor does it modify the phrase "while engaged in the violation of any law of this Commonwealth or municipal ordinance applying to the operation or use of a vehicle or to the regulation of traffic" in such an unambiguous manner as to preclude a judgment that the violation must still be "negligent." Viewed from this perspective, the above words and phrases could be read as either evidencing a legislative purpose to impose strict criminal responsibility or to fix accountability only for negligent violations. In our opinion, the plain meaning analysis of both the Dissent and Judge Spaeth's Concurring Opinion have obscured a simple fact. In civil law, the dual purpose for employing criminal statutory violations as standards is both to compensate the innocent victim and to deter the actor from repeating the harm causing act or omission. The criminal statute which serves as the index, however, does not share this compensation function, but rather is customarily drafted to protect the public at large from the conduct it prohibits. Underlying the criminal statute is the notion that punishment is necessary in order to reform or teach the accused not to repeat the offense and to deter others from imitating him. With regard to this particular statute, if the ultimate goal is to protect the public from imprudent driver conduct, then what purpose is to be served by punishing an operator who may have acted reasonably and prudently under the circumstances. To demonstrate, failing to adhere to the left-right-left rule when merging into traffic involves more risk to others; however, in a civil action a jury of the defendant's peers may find that it was not unreasonable to omit to observe this rule when the defendant is rushing an injured person to a hospital. To hold, as the Dissent does, that this same defendant may be criminally punished without reference to his state of mind simply does not make sense. If, with reference to the accused's evaluation of and perception of the operative factors, his conduct conforms to what is socially acceptable under the same or similar circumstances, how does this mark him as one who needs to suffer punishment? Does this statute envision punishing such an operator or separating him from his family and the remainder of society for five years? Does it seek to reduce traffic fatalities by deterring operators from exercising such care in the future? We surmise that it does not. Accordingly, we must reject the Dissent's plain meaning analysis and move to the Statutory Construction Act, for further guidance in answering the question sub judice.

a.

Where, as here, we determine that the words or phrases of an act are equivocal or ambiguous, legislative intention may be ascertained by examining the circumstances which surrounded enactment, the harm sought to be regulated and prevented, the object sought to be obtained, the consequences of any particular construction, and the germane legislative history

Circumstances Surrounding Enactment

In 1966 Congress passed the Highway Safety Act of 1966. This act authorized the United States Secretary of Transportation to adopt standards for all state highway safety programs. Pursuant to this mandate, the Secretary promulgated a standard on "Codes and Laws." This standard required all states to conduct comparative traffic law studies which would eventually be used to yield state legislation providing for uniform rules of the road within each state and the nation. Variations in state law were to be detected by comparing the states' current laws with the specimen provisions contained in the then effective version of the Uniform Vehicle Code. The states' progress in embracing this standard was to be monitored by the United States Department of Transportation.

The initial report was published in January of 1973. The report revealed that Pennsylvania's traffic laws were among the most outdated and non-uniform in the United States. Employing the provisions of the U.V.C. as the norm, the study ranked Pennsylvania 49 out of 51 jurisdictions. Alarmed by the consequences of failing to comply with the standard,[20] the Pennsylvania Department of Justice secured a Federal Highway-Safety Grant to finance research on a proposed revision of the Motor Vehicle Code. In retrospect, therefore, the subject legislation was not an isolated amendment to the Motor Vehicle Code motivated solely by the carnage on our roadways and the "inadequacy" of our involuntary manslaughter statute. Rather, the vehicular homicide proviso was but one aspect of a massive overhauling of all Pennsylvania rules of the road.

Harm to be remedied and object sought to be obtained.

As alluded to above, the primary legislative intent in revising the rules of the road chapter of the Motor Vehicle Code was to eliminate highway accidents and delays which were due in large degree to both Pennsylvania and non-resident operators proceeding on the highways on the basis of different and obsolete rules of driver conduct. Regarding the legislation sub judice, the prime object sought to be obtained was no different than that which provoked the modernization of all the rules of the road, i.e., uniformity. Not surprisingly, therefore, the legislature turned to the U.V.C. as a model for its homicide by vehicle provision. Of course, as the Dissent observes, there were additional possible reasons why the legislature chose to enact a distinct offense governing vehicular homicides. Foremost among these other reasons might have been a desire to reduce the fatalities on our roadways, and a corresponding recognition of the limited utility of our involuntary manslaughter statute in coping with the problem. However, both of these weighty concerns are not jeopardized by reading the subject statute as not dispensing with the requirement that the harm causing violation must nevertheless be culpable. More directly, to credit the legislature with an intent to deter life endangering conduct on our roadways is

---

[20] Failure to meet any standard under the Act could have resulted in a ten percent reduction in federally allocated highway building funds and a loss of all funds available under the Highway Safety Act.

to acknowledge that in order for punishment to be efficacious and just under this provision, it must be predicated upon the accused's awareness of the factors which made his conduct criminal. Thus, conviction, punishment, and sentence may well provide inadvertent violators with an additional incentive to take more care in both evaluating the risks they consciously create and those which they unreasonably fail to perceive. In either case, however, the assumption which underlies the punishment is that the actor ignored the operative factors in creating a risk of harm to others. Confronted with imprisonment, the violator may indeed think twice prior to speeding through a densely populated neighborhood. On the other hand, to suggest as the Dissent does that our legislature intentionally chose to disregard the social utility of the driver's conduct is to impute to the legislature a harshness and shortsightedness which we cannot. While there is always some risk associated with driving an auto, we do not think that the legislature in its collective wisdom intended to abrogate the possibility of a finding that the risk taken was reasonable under the particular circumstances.

Other Statutes

Nor do the supposed shortcomings of our involuntary manslaughter statute alone justify a determination that the vehicular homicide proviso was intended to create strict criminal responsibility. This Court has recently ruled that the convenience of investigation and prosecution is not the polestar in ascertaining what the essential elements of an offense are or what degree of culpability must accompany them. We concede that the history of this proviso confirms a legislative judgment that a distinct offense was needed due to the reluctance of juries to convict for involuntary manslaughter in fatal traffic accident cases; however, we dispute that this history supports the further proposition that as a result of this difficulty the legislature threw in the proverbial towel and deemed it essential to punish every violator no matter how reasonable his conduct. Faced with this difficulty, we reason that the legislature intended to adopt an intermediate response.

It is true that under the present involuntary manslaughter statute a negligent operator completely escapes any criminal punishment unless the violation which precipitated death was perpetrated "in a reckless or grossly negligent manner." We suggest that the legislature intended to fill this void not by punishing every death causing violation, but rather only intended to reach those violations in which there has been a "gross deviation" from the required standard of care. To hold otherwise is to completely confuse and obscure the distinctions between legality, justification, excuse, and culpability in the law of vehicular homicide. In passing this statute, we do not discern that the legislature abandoned its heretofore sensitive approach to the law of homicide generally. We read the subject provision as merely supplementing the already existing law as relates to deaths caused by Motor Vehicle Code violations. Thus, this provision being within this general conceptual framework, it continues to recognize that Motor Vehicle Code violations may involve differing species of culpability. For example, it is more aggravating to cause a death through an intentional violation rather than reckless, and worse to bring it about through reckless violation than negligent violation.[26] In the past, Pennsylvania law punished the former two, it did not punish the latter. The latter until now has been an innocent homicide. Accordingly, as the Dissent concedes there was a need for a new offense governing deaths resulting from negligent violations of the rules of the road. This is that measure and we would so hold.

IV.

The only remaining question is whether the trial court properly sustained Ms. Barone's demurrer to the charge. In reviewing the propriety of this action, "the test to be applied . . . is whether the evidence of record and the inferences reasonably drawn therefrom would support a guilty verdict, and in making our determination we must read the evidence in the light most favorable to the Commonwealth." Instantly, the focus of our inquiry is whether the Commonwealth's evidence was sufficient to prove beyond a reasonable doubt that Ms. Barone's conduct amounted to "a gross deviation from the standard of care that a reasonable person would observe in (her) situation."

Thus viewed, the Commonwealth adduced the following. On September 14, 1977, Ms. Barone was on route to her place of employment in a two-door, brown Toyota. At approximately 8:00 a.m. she arrived at the intersection of Bethel Grant Road and Morris Road in Upper Gwynedd Township, Montgomery County. The weather was clear and the roadways dry. As she approached the intersection, she observed a stop sign and initially obeyed its command to come to a complete stop. As is often the case at a major thoroughfare during this time of day, traffic was heavy. She observed this traffic for approximately two to three minutes waiting for an opportunity to safely cross the intersection. Subsequently, Ms. Barone apparently either failed to look to her right or misjudged the distance and rate of speed of the oncoming traffic and proceeded into the intersection. While in the intersection her auto was struck by a motorcycle resulting in the motorcycle operator's death. Commonwealth witnesses also testified that prior to impact Ms. Barone neither sounded her horn

---

[26] We are not unmindful of the difficulty of the jury's discriminating between recklessness and negligence when both of the above statutory offenses are submitted for its consideration. We are, however, confident that our lower courts are capable of devising formulations which clarify the distinctions between the two mental states. See Model Penal Code, § 2.02, Comment at 124-28.

nor did she apply her brakes in an effort to avoid the collision. We are persuaded that based upon the above the jury could not have properly found that Ms. Barone's actions amounted to "a gross deviation from the standard of care that a reasonable person would observe in (her) situation." We are convinced that no jury of reasonable men and women could have found a gross deviation from the applicable standard of care in light of the undisputed fact that Ms. Barone waited patiently at the stop sign for several minutes before proceeding into the intersection. Under these circumstances, such conduct could not have established a violation of section 3732.

Accordingly, we would affirm the lower court's determination that the above evidence was not sufficient to go to the jury.

Order affirmed and defendant discharged.

SPAETH, Judge, concurring:

* * * The dissent has concluded that section 3732 should be construed to create strict criminal liability, and I agree (although I regard the issue as exceedingly close, and respect the President Judge's contrary conclusion).[2] The dissent has also concluded, however, that as so construed, section 3732 is constitutional, and as to this, I disagree; in my opinion, section 3732 represents a violation of due process, perhaps not under the federal constitution, but certainly under our state constitution.

I

Statutes creating, or arguably creating, strict criminal liability have required the courts to engage in a distinctive analysis, not usual in the criminal law. Before examining the statute involved in the present case, therefore, it is important to review the cases, so that one may understand how this analysis has developed and what its distinctive features are. In conducting this review, it will

---

[2] An argument may be made that section 3732 does not, by the Commonwealth's construction, impose strict liability but liability for negligence, the theory being that it is negligent for someone to violate a traffic law. However, a mere violation of a traffic law may not constitute even civil negligence, and definitely will not constitute criminal negligence as defined under section 302(b)(4) of the Crimes Code. See 18 Pa.C.S. s 302(b)(4) (criminal negligence is conduct that "involves a gross deviation from the standard of care that a reasonable person would use in the actor's situation"). Accordingly, if the Commonwealth's construction of section 3732 is correct, the section must be labelled a strict criminal liability section.

be convenient to look first at the federal cases, and then at the cases decided by our Supreme Court and by this court.

A
The Federal Cases

"The existence of mens rea is the rule of, rather than the exception to, the principles of Anglo-American criminal jurisprudence." "The contention that an injury can amount to a crime only when inflicted by intention is no provincial or transient notion. It is as universal and persistent in mature systems of law as belief in freedom of the human will and a consequent ability and duty of the normal individual to choose between good and evil." The concept of strict criminal liability is apparently of relatively recent origin in our system of law, and has been the subject of Supreme Court scrutiny on only a very few occasions. In only one case, *Morissette*, has the Court undertaken a full discussion of the problems presented by a statute creating, or arguably creating, a strict liability crime.

[The concurrence discusses a line of Supreme Court cases concerning public welfare offenses, including *Morissette*.]

Two important principles may be derived from *Morissette*; it is these principles that render distinctive the analysis to be employed when examining a statute creating, or arguably creating, strict criminal liability. The first principle is that in determining whether the imposition of strict criminal liability is consistent with due process, several factors, including the policy and intent of the legislature, the origins of the offense, the reasonableness of the standards imposed, and the punishment and stigma attached to a conviction, must be considered. The second principle is that in considering these several factors, a court must shuttle back and forth, between the question whether the statute can be construed as not requiring proof of criminal intent, and the question whether, if so construed, the statute will violate due process; the answer to one of these questions will color, or affect, the answer to the other. Thus in *Morissette* the Court was persuaded to construe the statute as not creating strict criminal liability but instead as requiring proof of intent. * * *

* * * [I]f the penalty is not relatively small, and the conviction does gravely besmirch -- then the elimination of the element of criminal intent may be violative of the due process clause. * * *

Sometimes it has been held that a requirement of intent may not be read into the statute, but that even when so construed, the relevant factors are such that the statute does not violate due process. Thus, in *United States v. Ayo-Gonzalez*, the Fifth Circuit applies the *Morissette-Holdridge* analysis to determine whether the Bartlett Act prohibited unintentional fishing incursions by foreign vessels in United States waters. After an extensive examination of the policy of the Act and its legislative history, the court concluded that no proof of intent was required to sustain a conviction. The court also concluded that this creation of strict criminal liability did not violate due process because the conviction did not invite moral stigma and the maximum sentence of one year imprisonment was not too severe. * * *

Other times it has been held that a requirement of intent may be read into the statute, if the result will be that then the statute will not violate due process. Thus, in *United States v. Heller*, the Sixth Circuit concluded that to sustain a conviction under a federal statute making it a crime to transmit any demand or request for a ransom the prosecutor was required to prove that the defendant had an intent to extort. The court reached this conclusion after making the analysis prescribed in *Morissette* and *Holdridge*. Especially pertinent to the decision were the legislative history of the statute and the severity of the punishment.

Finally, other times it has been held that a requirement of intent may not be read into a statute, even though the result is that the statute will then violate due process. *See Lambert v. California.*[a] * * *

[The concurrence then discusses the Pennsylvania caselaw.]

II

It is now in order to apply the * * * analysis to the present case. The first step will be to determine whether, in enacting section 3732, the legislature intended to make homicide by vehicle a strict liability crime. If it appears that the legislature did so intend, the second step will be to determine whether the section violates due process. If it appears that it does, the third, and last, step will be to re-examine the section, to determine whether it may be saved, or whether it must be declared unconstitutional.

[After analyzing the legislative history, the concurrence concludes that the legislature intended to make this crime one of strict liability.]

* * * [I]f the legislature had intended to limit criminal violations under section 3732 to reckless or negligent defendants, it need not have enacted the section at all, for those defendants were already subject to prosecution for involuntary manslaughter under section 2504 of the Crimes Code. Indeed, a consideration

---

[a] *Lambert v. California* is excerpted in Chapter 5.

of the crime of involuntary manslaughter provides what seems to me a probably correct explanation of why the legislature intended to create strict criminal liability under section 3732. The cases demonstrate that the Commonwealth has had difficulty in obtaining convictions for involuntary manslaughter, for proof of a traffic violation may not be proof of recklessness or gross negligence. It seems probable that in enacting section 3732, the legislature intended to overcome this difficulty by broadening the scope of liability to include those persons who merely violated traffic ordinances. * * *

B
When construed to create strict criminal liability, does section 3732 violate due process?

In testing the constitutionality of a statute creating strict criminal liability, the two most important considerations are the severity of the possible punishment and the moral stigma that may be attached to a conviction. As the Sixth Circuit stated in *United States v. Heller*, "Certainly if Congress attempted to define a (strict liability) offense that placed an onerous stigma on an offender's reputation and that carried a severe penalty, the Constitution would be offended."

1

Appellee's conviction under section 3732 of homicide by vehicle places a most onerous stigma on her reputation.

The Commentary, Homicide by Vehicle, states that the use of the term "homicide by vehicle," as compared with the term "manslaughter," "lessen(s) the stigma attached to convictions." If this be so, the stigma attached nevertheless remains most onerous. As Henry Hart has observed, one cannot truthfully say to any defendant that there is nothing wrong with being labeled a criminal. Especially is this so when the crime is "homicide by vehicle." Labels may not be ignored. To be labeled a rapist or murderer places a far more onerous stigma on a person than to be labeled as someone convicted of misbranding a drug. While the word "homicide," by itself, means only the killing of a human being, included within this definition are the terms "murder" and "manslaughter." Indeed, the Crimes Code defines the term "criminal homicide" so as to include "murder" and "manslaughter." Adding the phrase "by vehicle" does little to lessen the stigma attached to the word "homicide," except perhaps among lawyers. In popular parlance, "homicide" is usually equated with "murder." * * *

While there apparently has been no case holding what type of a conviction does such grave damage to reputation as to violate the federal due process clause, it must be noted that the stigma attached to "homicide by vehicle" is different from, and far more serious than, the stigma attached to such crimes as the fishing violation considered in *United States v. Ayo-Gonzalez* * * *. This court has been extremely concerned with the unfair effects that a criminal record may have upon a defendant's future. Indeed, it is not an overstatement to say that to saddle appellee in this case with a homicide record might result in more damage to her future than even the imprisonment she may receive for her conviction. * * *

I acknowledge that despite the foregoing scholarly commentary, the federal courts have held that a sentence of imprisonment may be imposed for conviction of a strict liability crime. *United States v. Balint* (five years); *United States v. Freed* (ten years); *United States v. Mowat* (six months imprisonment); *United States v. Ayo-Gonzalez* (one year imprisonment). *But see United States v. Heller* (possible twenty year term is too severe for a strict liability crime). It is because of these cases that I said at the beginning of this opinion that "perhaps" section 3732 did not violate federal due process. It very well may violate federal due process, for in addition to carrying a sentence of imprisonment, conviction "gravely besmirch(es)" the defendant's reputation. However, I know of no federal case resting a finding of violation of due process on damage to reputation alone.

How the federal courts would decide such a case need not concern us, for under the decisions of our Supreme Court and of this court, it is settled that imposition of imprisonment upon conviction of a strict liability crime does constitute a violation of due process under our State constitution.

In *Commonwealth v. Koczwara*, the defendant was convicted of violating the Pennsylvania Liquor Code by serving alcohol to minors. The evidence established that an employee of the defendant served the minors when the defendant was not present and without the defendant's knowledge. Nevertheless the defendant was convicted, fined, and sentenced to three months imprisonment. On appeal the Supreme Court noted that the crime was a violation of a mere "regulatory provision," "generally enforceable by light penalties, and although violations are labelled crimes, the considerations applicable to them are totally different from those applicable to true crimes, which involve moral delinquency and which are punishable by imprisonment or another serious penalty." Although concluding that the legislature could create such strict criminal liability, the Court held that to imprison the defendant violated due process under the Pennsylvania Constitution.

While *Koczwara* involved vicarious liability, it is nevertheless controlling on the issue presented in this case because of the distinction made by the Court between, on the one hand, true crimes, and on the other hand, strict liability (including vicarious liability) crimes. The Court made it clear that to imprison someone for anything other than a true crime was unconstitutional; and it defined a true crime as one that involves both "moral delinquency" and "personal causation." From this distinction the conclusion followed that since strict liability (including vicarious liability) crimes are not true crimes, they may not constitutionally be punished by imprisonment. Thus in *Koczwara* our Supreme Court went beyond *Balint*, and the federal cases following it, and gave judicial recognition to the views of Sayre and the other commentators, that since strict liability crimes are not true crimes they should not be punished like true crimes.

C
Is it possible to save section 3732?

Since, when construed to create strict criminal liability, section 3732 violates due process, both because conviction too gravely besmirches the defendant's reputation and because the punishment is too severe, it is necessary to proceed to the third, and final, step of the * * * analysis, and re-examine the section to determine whether after all it may be construed so that it will not violate due process. Two possible constructions suggest themselves.

1

The first possible construction would be to construe section 3732 as not imposing strict criminal liability. * * * Nevertheless, the difficulty, which I find insuperable, would be that then we should have to answer the question if section 3732 does not create strict criminal liability, what sort of conduct does it make culpable? By its own terms section 3732 does not refer to intentional conduct. The only remaining forms of culpable conduct would seem to be either recklessness or negligence. However, if section 3732 is construed to require proof of either of these, it becomes a duplicate of section 2504 of the Crimes Code, which defines involuntary manslaughter as a crime:

> (a) General rule. A person is guilty of involuntary manslaughter when as a direct result of the doing of an unlawful act in a reckless or grossly negligent manner, or the doing of a lawful act in a reckless or grossly negligent manner, he causes the death of another person.

It would be to some extent absurd to have two different criminal statutes apply to the same conduct. * * *

2

The second possible construction would be to construe section 3732 as creating strict criminal liability, but to save it by removing that part or parts that result in a violation of due process. That is what the Supreme Court did in *Commonwealth v. Koczwara*, where instead of striking down the section of the Liquor Code involved, the Court merely removed from the section the sanction of imprisonment. To save section 3732, however, one would have to remove from it not only the sanction of imprisonment but also the label "homicide by vehicle"; for as discussed above, what renders the section a violation of due process is the combination of a too severe penalty and a too onerous stigma. Removing both the sanction of imprisonment and creating a new name for the crime would amount to re-writing the section and would be an encroachment upon the legislative function.

3

I am thus left with the conclusion that rather than attempt to save section 3732, it should be declared unconstitutional. The legislature would then be free to produce a constitutional version of the section, if it should so desire.

I should affirm the decision of the lower court.

WIEAND, Judge, dissenting:

I respectfully dissent.

      * * *

The language of the section defining homicide by vehicle is precise and unambiguous. As it pertains to the facts of the instant case, the only culpability required is a violation of a law "applying to the operation or use of a vehicle or to the regulation of traffic." Highway safety and the means for achieving it are legitimately, even uniquely, within the legislature's area of concern. Because automobiles are potentially hazardous instrumentalities, the legislature, in the public interest, may adopt traffic regulations and rules of the road reasonably calculated to promote care on the part of those who use its highways. Apparently alarmed by the deplorable carnage on our highways, the legislature determined that potential prosecution for involuntary manslaughter was an inadequate response. Motorists are generally reputable citizens. When one of them is involved in an automobile accident resulting in death to another person, the cause frequently is a negligent violation of a rule of the road or speed limit. A reckless disregard for the safety of others is frequently absent, and when it is present, it is often difficult to prove beyond a reasonable doubt. Therefore, the legislature determined to make criminal responsibility dependent upon violation of a traffic law and not necessarily on culpable or criminal negligence. * * *

Homicide by vehicle, as I have observed, is the legislature's response to a high fatality rate on the public highways. The standard adopted to define the offense, i.e., a violation of a traffic law that causes a death, is not unreasonable. Motorists cannot justly complain that they will be held criminally accountable for the consequences if they violate the Vehicle Code. These factors, I believe, are controlling. Contrary to appellee's argument, the classification of the offense as a misdemeanor of the first degree and the fixing of a maximum sentence equivalent to that prescribed for involuntary manslaughter are not determinative. These considerations must yield to the paramount interest of the legislature in establishing laws which regulate the operation of vehicles on the highways of the Commonwealth. In previous due process challenges to motor vehicle regulations, Pennsylvania courts have invariably upheld statutes that evidenced a reasonable relation to the legislative purpose and were not arbitrary or capricious. I conclude that the offense of homicide by vehicle is not an unreasonable method to effectuate a legitimate state safety policy.

I express no opinion, of course, concerning the wisdom of the legislature's decision to provide criminal responsibility without recklessness or gross negligence. Neither do I express an opinion concerning the legislature's decision to classify homicide by vehicle as a criminal offense equal in seriousness to involuntary manslaughter. * * *

Chapter 5

MISTAKE AND IGNORANCE

INTRODUCTION

We have already seen how the criminal law deals with one kind of mistake when we studied the doctrine of transferred intent in Chapter 4. In "transferred intent" cases, the defendant mistakenly hurts a different victim than the one intended. Suppose, in contrast, the defendant commits the prohibited act with some kind of belief that turns out to have been wrong? How should the criminal law respond? These questions are the subject of this chapter.

The law of mistake and ignorance can be very confusing, but you will not go wrong if you remember one simple point: mistake is the flip side of mens rea. That is, the question of whether the defendant's ignorance or mistaken belief is a defense can only be answered by understanding what mental state the statute requires. It is important to know whether you are interpreting a penal code that relies primarily on the common law or one that relies on the Model Penal Code when considering questions of mistake. The common law approach to mistake and ignorance relies on the distinction we examined in Chapter 4 between specific intent and general intent crimes. The common law approach also incorporates a second distinction: between mistakes of fact and mistakes of law. The Model Penal Code does not observe the specific intent/general intent distinction; nor does it distinguish between mistakes of fact and mistakes of law. *See* Model Penal Code § 2.04.

We have observed that the main thing to keep in mind when considering whether mistake or ignorance is a defense is what mental state the statute requires. This is another way of saying that mistake and ignorance are usually case-in-chief defenses (see Chapter 1). However, there are some situations, both in common law-based and MPC-based penal codes, where reliance on an official interpretation of the law is a defense. In this situation, the defendant's mistake of law is an affirmative defense.

A. MISTAKES OF FACT

The common law rules regarding mistakes of fact are fairly simple, turning on the distinction between specific intent and general intent crimes. If one is charged with a specific intent crime, an honest mistake that negates the specific intent required for commission of the offense is a complete defense. The mistake need not be reasonable as long as it is in good faith.[a]

If one is charged with a general intent crime, a mistake of fact that negates an element of the crime must be both honest and reasonable to exculpate. A minority of common law jurisdictions subject the general intent defendant's mistake-of-fact claim to even further scrutiny, employing either a moral wrong or legal wrong test. These doctrines are explained in *Bell v. State*.

The next two cases both involve claims of mistake-of-fact. *People v. Navarro* provides a clear explanation of the common law rules for mistakes of fact. *Bell v. State* examines whether a state legislature can, consistent with due process, preclude a mistake of age defense to a charge of promoting prostitution in the first degree.

PEOPLE v. NAVARRO

Appellate Department, Superior Court of California, Los Angeles
99 Cal. App. 3d Supp. 1, 160 Cal.Rptr. 692 (Cal. Super. App. 1979)

DOWDS, J.

Defendant, charged with a violation of Penal Code section 487, subdivision 1, grand theft, appeals his conviction after a jury trial of petty theft, a lesser but necessarily included offense. His contention on appeal is that the jury was improperly instructed. The only facts set forth in the record on appeal are that defendant was charged with stealing four wooden beams from a construction site and that the state of the evidence was such that the jury could have found that the defendant believed either (1) that the beams had been abandoned as worthless and the owner had no objection to his taking them or (2) that they had substantial value, had not been abandoned and he had no right to take them.

---

[a]For example, let's say Sally is charged with larceny, a specific intent crime which is defined as the taking and carrying away of another's personal property with intent to permanently deprive the possessor of such property, after mistakenly taking Robert's black umbrella believing it was her own. Sally can argue mistake of fact as a defense and will likely be acquitted if the jury believes that Sally honestly thought Robert's black umbrella was her own. Even if Sally's mistake was unreasonable – Sally's umbrella was blue, so she should have known that Robert's black umbrella was not her umbrella – Sally will be exonerated because she lacked the specific intent to permanently deprive Robert of his umbrella.

The court refused two jury instructions proposed by defendant reading as follows:

Defendant's A

If one takes personal property with the good faith belief that the property has been abandoned or discarded by the true owner, he is not guilty of theft. This is the case even if such good faith belief is unreasonable. The prosecutor must prove beyond a reasonable doubt that the defendant did not so believe for you to convict a defendant of theft.

Defendant's B

If one takes personal property with the good faith belief that he has permission to take the property, he is not guilty of theft. This is the case even if such good faith belief is unreasonable. The prosecutor must prove beyond a reasonable doubt that the defendant did not so believe for you to convict a defendant of theft.

Instead, the court instructed the jury in the words of the following modified instructions:

Modified-Defendant's A

If one takes personal property in the reasonable and good faith belief that the property has been abandoned or discarded by the true owner, he is not guilty of theft.

Modified-Defendant's B

If one takes personal property in the reasonable and good faith belief that he has the consent or permission of the owner to take the property, he is not guilty of theft.
If you have a reasonable doubt that the defendant had the required criminal intent as specified in these instructions, the defendant is entitled to an acquittal.

Accordingly, the question for determination on appeal is whether the defendant should be acquitted if there is a reasonable doubt that he had a good faith belief that the property had been abandoned or that he had the permission of the owner to take the property or whether that belief must be a reasonable one as well as being held in good faith. * * *

Evidence was presented * * * from which the jury could have concluded that defendant believed that the wooden beams had been abandoned and that the owner had no objection to his taking them, i.e., that he lacked the specific criminal intent required to commit the crime of theft (intent permanently to deprive an owner of his property).

* * *

The proper rule, it seems to us, is set forth in Perkins on Criminal Law: "If no specific intent or other special mental element is required for guilt of the offense charged, a mistake of fact will not be recognized as an excuse unless it was based upon reasonable grounds . . . . [On the other hand, because] of the requirement of a specific intent to steal there is no such thing as larceny by negligence. One does not commit this offense by carrying away the chattel of another in the mistaken belief that it is his own, no matter how great may have been the fault leading to this belief, if the belief itself is genuine."

La Fave and Scott, Handbook on Criminal Law sets forth at page 357 what the authors call the ". . . rather simple rule that an honest mistake of fact or law is a defense when it negates a required mental element of the crime . . ." As an example they refer to the crime of receiving stolen property, stating ". . . if the defendant by a mistake of either fact or law did not know the goods were stolen, even though the circumstances would have led a prudent man to believe they were stolen, he does not have the required mental state and thus may not be convicted of the crime."

In the instant case the trial court in effect instructed the jury that even though defendant in good faith believed he had the right to take the beams, and thus lacked the specific intent required for the crime of theft, he should be convicted unless such belief was reasonable. In doing so it erred. It is true that if the jury thought the defendant's belief to be unreasonable, it might infer that he did not in good faith hold such belief. If, however, it concluded that defendant in good faith believed that he had the right to take the beams, even though such belief was unreasonable as measured by the objective standard of a hypothetical reasonable man, defendant was entitled to an acquittal since the specific intent required to be proved as an element of the offense had not been established.

* * *

The judgment is reversed.

BELL v. STATE

Court of Appeals of Alaska
668 P.2d 829 (1983)

BRYNER, Chief Judge.

Willie B. Bell appeals his convictions for promoting prostitution in the first degree in violation of AS 11.66.110(a)(2) and managing a prostitution enterprise in violation of AS 11.66.120(a)(1). He also appeals the sentence imposed. We affirm.

Bell was a twenty-nine-year-old army sergeant when he procured two sixteen-year-old girls, C.R. and M.J., and one fourteen-year-old girl, D.W., for prostitution. C.R. began living with Bell and engaging in prostitution after Bell promised to marry her and to buy her a new car and new clothing. At Bell's direction, D.W. and M.J. worked as prostitutes in May, 1980. On May 22, 1980, Bell assaulted M.J., claiming that she had been drinking instead of "working." Fearing that Bell would harm them, C.R. and M.J. left him and contacted police, who obtained a search warrant to record conversations between M.J., C.R. and Bell. A telephone conversation between Bell and C.R. and a conversation involving Bell, M.J. and C.R. were recorded pursuant to the warrant and used as evidence against Bell.

The indictment returned against Bell charged two counts of promoting prostitution in the first degree, alleging that he induced D.W. to engage in prostitution when she was under the age of sixteen (Count I), and that he induced C.R. to engage in prostitution by means of force (Count II). Count III of the indictment, as it went to the jury, alleged that Bell was guilty of attempted promotion of prostitution in the first degree, regarding M.J. The indictment also alleged that Bell managed, supervised, controlled or owned a prostitution enterprise other than a house of prostitution (Count IV). Bell was convicted of Counts I and IV. On Count II, Bell was acquitted of the charge but convicted of the lesser-included offense of promoting prostitution in the third degree. On Count III, Bell was found not guilty of the charge but guilty of the lesser-included offense of attempted promotion of prostitution in the third degree. Bell was not sentenced on Counts II and III. Superior Court Judge Milton M. Souter sentenced Bell to a five-year term with two years suspended on Count I, and a four-year term with three years suspended on Count IV. The sentences for these offenses were to run concurrently. Subsequently, Judge Souter refused to reduce the sentence.

On appeal, Bell argues that: (1) he should have been allowed to present a reasonable mistake of age defense to the charge contained in Count I * * * .

I. MISTAKE OF AGE

Bell asserts that the trial court erred in refusing to give a proposed jury instruction providing for a reasonable mistake of age defense to the charge of inducing a person under the age of sixteen to engage in prostitution in violation of AS 11.66.110(a)(2).[2] Bell argues that AS 11.66.110(b) violates his due process rights under the United States and Alaska constitutions by expressly precluding mistake of age as a defense to the charge of violating AS 11.66.110(a)(2). We find this argument unpersuasive and conclude that the

---

[2] AS 11.66.110 provides:

PROMOTING PROSTITUTION IN THE FIRST DEGREE.
(a) A person commits the crime of promoting prostitution in the first degree if he
> (1) induces or causes a person to engage in prostitution through the use of force;
> (2) as other than a patron of a prostitute, induces or causes a person under 16 years of age to engage in prostitution; or
> (3) induces or causes a person in his legal custody to engage in prostitution.

(b) In a prosecution under (a)(2) of this section, it is not a defense that the defendant reasonably believed that the person he induced or caused to engage in prostitution was 16 years of age or older.
(c) Promoting prostitution in the first degree is a class B felony.

The jury was instructed on the elements of this offense. The court then instructed that:

> It is not a defense to the crime charged in Count I of the Indictment that the defendant reasonably believed that the person he induced or caused to engage in prostitution was 16 years of age or older.

The instruction proposed by Bell stated:

> It is a defense to Count I of the indictment, Inducing a Person Under 16 Years of Age to Engage in Prostitution, that the defendant reasonably and in good faith believed that the female person was of the age of sixteen years or older, even though, in fact, she was under the age of sixteen years. If from all the evidence you have a reasonable doubt as to the question whether defendant reasonably and in good faith believed that she was sixteen years of age or older, you must give the defendant the benefit of that doubt and find him not guilty.

legislature may, consistent with the requirements of constitutional due process, preclude mistake of age from constituting a defense to the crime of promoting prostitution in the first degree.

It is apparent that the legislature considered procurement of a person under sixteen to be an aggravated form of promoting prostitution. The commentary to the Revised Criminal Code, 2 Senate Journal, Supplement No. 47, at 109 (1978), states that by denying a defendant the defense of reasonable mistake as to age, creation of strict liability was intended as to the element of the offense involving age of the victim. * * *

Bell correctly states the well-recognized rule in this jurisdiction that criminal intent is a necessary ingredient of criminal liability and that one charged with criminal conduct must have an awareness or consciousness of wrongdoing. *Speidel v. State,* 460 P.2d 77, 78 (Alaska 1969). In *Speidel,* the awareness of wrongdoing was in the context of a larceny-type crime, for which courts have historically required a specific intent to wrongfully deprive. In *Alex v. State,* 484 P.2d 677 (Alaska 1971), the supreme court discussed the intent required for non-larceny crimes:

> However, as applied to crimes generally, what is imperative, is that an accused's act be other than simply inadvertent or neglectful. What is essential is not an awareness that a given conduct is a "wrongdoing" in the sense that it is proscribed by law, but rather, an awareness that one is committing the specific acts which are defined by law as a "wrongdoing." It is, however, no defense that one was not aware that his acts were wrong in the sense that they were proscribed by law. So long as one acts intentionally, with cognizance of his behavior, he acts with the requisite awareness of wrongdoing.

We believe this language is applicable to Bell's actions, since he was consciously committing the acts proscribed by law. As an element of this offense, Bell was required to be aware that he was procuring women to engage in acts of prostitution. Indeed, the jurors in this case were instructed that they must be convinced beyond a reasonable doubt that the defendant engaged in conduct which caused or induced [D.W.] to engage in prostitution; [and] that the defendant engaged in said conduct with the specific intent to cause or induce [D.W.] to engage in prostitution.

Thus, while Bell was not required to know the age of those whom he procured, this is not to say that the offense did not require *mens rea* or a culpable mental state.

We also note that AS 11.66.110(b) is in accord with the common law view that there should be no exculpation for mistake where, if the facts had been as the actor believed them to be, his conduct would still be illegal or immoral.[4] As Bell recognizes on appeal, his conduct would still have been illegal even if D.W. had been sixteen or over. AS 11.66.130(a)(2).[5] * * *

In continuing to press his claim that AS 11.66.110(b) imposes an unconstitutional standard, Bell relies upon *State v. Guest,* 583 P.2d 836 (Alaska 1978), in which the supreme court upheld a trial court's decision to instruct the jury on a defense of reasonable mistake of age in a statutory rape case. Following the reasoning of *Speidel* and *Alex,* the court stated that an intent requirement must be read into former AS 11.15.120 to save it from unconstitutionality. To refuse a defense of mistake of age in a statutory rape case, according to the *Guest* court, would be to impose significant criminal liability without any criminal mental element.

Bell relies most heavily upon the following language in *Guest:*

It has been urged in other jurisdictions that where an offender is aware he is committing an act of fornication he therefore has sufficient criminal intent to justify a conviction for statutory rape because what was done would have been unlawful under the facts as he thought them to be. We reject this view. While it is true that under such circumstances a mistake of fact does not serve as a complete defense, we believe that it should serve

---

[4] In the landmark case of *Regina v. Prince,* L.4., 2 Cr.Cas.Res. 154 (1875), the defendant was convicted of taking a girl under sixteen years of age from under the care of her father, even though the defendant reasonably believed she was older. The defense of mistake of age was disallowed on the ground that removal of an unmarried girl from the lawful custody of her parents would have been a crime even had she been as old as he believed. Hence, the defendant acted at his peril.

[5] AS 11.66.130 provides, in relevant part:

(a) A person commits the crime of promoting prostitution in the third degree if, with intent to promote prostitution, he ...
      (2) as other than a patron of a prostitute, induces or causes a person 16 years of age or older to engage in prostitution ....
(b) Promoting prostitution in the third degree is a class A misdemeanor.

to reduce the offense to that which the offender would have been guilty of had he not been mistaken. Thus, if an accused had a reasonable belief that the person with whom he had sexual intercourse was sixteen years of age or older, he may not be convicted of statutory rape. If, however, he did not have a reasonable belief that the victim was eighteen years of age or older, he may still be criminally liable for contribution to the delinquency of a minor.

The court cited in support of its position section 2.04(2) of the Model Penal Code (Proposed Official Draft 1962), which provides:

> Although ignorance or mistake would otherwise afford a defense to the offense charged, the defense is not available if the defendant would be guilty of another offense had the situation been as he supposed. In such case, however, the ignorance or mistake of the defendant shall reduce the grade and degree of the offense of which he may be convicted to those of the offense of which he would be guilty had the situation been as he supposed.

We believe the problem addressed in *Guest* is distinguishable from the issue at hand. As we have stated, Bell did not lack criminal intent; he intended to promote prostitution. The court in *Guest* was careful to point out that fornication was not itself a crime, so that it could not have been considered as a lesser-included offense of statutory rape. Also, although the court went on to observe that Guest *might* still have been guilty of contributing to the delinquency of a minor under former AS 11.40.130 if he did not have a reasonable belief that his partner was under eighteen, it is clear that Bell was *necessarily* guilty of promoting prostitution in the third degree if the facts were as he supposed them to be.

*　　*　　*

We hold that AS 11.66.110(b), which expressly dispenses with mistake of age as a defense to promoting prostitution in the first degree, does not violate due process of law. We therefore conclude that the trial court did not err in rejecting Bell's challenge to the instruction on mistake of age. * * *

The conviction and sentence are AFFIRMED.

Note

Regina v. Prince, mentioned in *Bell,* is usually cited for the principle that if the defendant's conduct is morally wrong, there is no violation of the culpability principle if the conduct is criminally punished without regard to mens rea. In addition to this "moral wrong" doctrine, courts in jurisdictions that incorporate the common law sometimes articulate a "legal wrong" doctrine: even if the defendant can assert a reasonable mistake of fact, he or she will not be exculpated if, had the facts been as the defendant believed them to be, she or he would still be guilty of some other crime.

The Model Penal Code does not distinguish between specific intent and general intent crimes. Under the MPC, a mistake of fact is a defense if it negates the mental state required for commission of the offense. *See* Model Penal Code § 2.04(1). The MPC, however, also applies a rule that is similar to the common law's legal wrong doctrine. Under the MPC, even if the defendant's mistake negates the mental state required for commission of the offense, if the defendant would be guilty of another defense if the facts were as he believed them to be, then he will be found guilty of the charged offense. *See* Model Penal Code § 2.04(2). The MPC, however, in contrast to the common law legal wrong doctrine, allows the defendant to be punished only at the penalty set for the other, lesser crime, not the charged offense.

B. MISTAKES OF LAW

Under both the common law and the Model Penal Code, the general rule regarding mistakes of law is that ignorance of the law is no excuse. Except in certain limited circumstances described below, a person cannot defend against a crime by claiming that he did not know what he was doing was unlawful.

There are three qualifications to the general rule that ignorance of the law is no excuse. First, a person who reasonably relies on an official interpretation of the law that turns out to be erroneous (also known as "entrapment by estoppel") can be exonerated. Second, ignorance of the law can be a defense to a crime if knowledge that the prohibited conduct is unlawful is an element of the crime. In such a case, the defendant's lack of knowledge will negate the mens rea required for commission of the offense. Third, the U.S. Supreme Court has held that under certain limited circumstances, the prosecution of a person who lacks fair notice of a legal duty imposed by law can violate due process. We will study each of these three exceptions in the cases below.

Finally, should it be a defense to a crime that the defendant was a recent immigrant to the United States, not familiar with United States laws or mores, and that the behavior that constituted the crime was appropriate behavior in light of the immigrant's own culture? The "cultural defense" will be examined in Chapter 10.

1.   Official Interpretation of the Law (a.k.a. "Entrapment by Estoppel")

Although the law in this area is very confused and uncertain, jurisdictions whose penal codes primarily incorporate the common law have sometimes acknowledged an affirmative defense to defendants who commit crimes upon reliance on official statements of the law, whether set forth in judicial rulings or in oral or written statements by officials. This "reliance" or "estoppel" defense is sometimes referred to as "entrapment by estoppel," because it shares with the doctrine of entrapment the policy that citizens should not be coerced into criminal behavior by government officials and then punished for it. Section 2.04(3) of the Model Penal Code codifies this affirmative defense.

PEOPLE v. MARRERO
Court of Appeals of New York
69 N.Y.2d 382, 507 N.E.2d 1068, 515 N.Y.S.2d 212 (1987)

BELLACOSA, J.

The defense of mistake of law is not available to a Federal corrections officer arrested in a Manhattan social club for possession of a loaded .38 caliber automatic pistol who claimed he mistakenly believed he was entitled, pursuant to the interplay of CPL 2.10, 1.20 and Penal Law §265.20, to carry a handgun without a permit as a peace officer. * * *

On the trial of the case, the court rejected the defendant's argument that his personal misunderstanding of the statutory definition of a peace officer is enough to excuse him from criminal liability under New York's mistake of law statute (Penal Law §15.20). The court refused to charge the jury on this issue and defendant was convicted of criminal possession of a weapon in the third degree. We affirm the Appellate Division order upholding the conviction.

Defendant was a Federal corrections officer in Danbury, Connecticut, and asserted that status at the time of his arrest in 1977. He claimed at trial that there were various interpretations of fellow officers and teachers, as well as the peace officer statute itself, upon which he relied for his mistaken belief that he could carry a weapon with legal impunity.

The starting point for our analysis is the New York mistake statute as an outgrowth of the dogmatic common-law maxim that ignorance of the law is no excuse. The central issue is whether defendant's personal misreading or misunderstanding of a statute may excuse criminal conduct in the circumstances of this case. * * *

The [common law rule], which was to encourage the societal benefit of individuals' knowledge of and respect for the law, is underscored by Justice Holmes' statement: "It is no doubt true that there are many cases in which the criminal could not have known that he was breaking the law, but to admit the excuse at all would be to encourage ignorance where the law-maker has determined to make men know and obey, and justice to the individual is rightly outweighed by the larger interests on the other side of the scales." (Holmes, The Common Law, at 48 [1881]).

The revisors of New York's Penal Law intended no fundamental departure from this common-law rule in Penal Law §15.20, which provides in pertinent part:

§15.20. *Effect of ignorance or mistake upon liability.*

*   *   *

2. A person is not relieved of criminal liability for conduct because he engages in such conduct under a mistaken belief that it does not, as a matter of law, constitute an offense, unless such mistaken belief is founded upon an official statement of the law contained in (a) a statute or other enactment * * * (d) an interpretation of the statute or law relating to the offense, officially made or issued by a public servant, agency, or body legally charged or empowered with the responsibility or privilege of administering, enforcing or interpreting such statute or law.

This section was added to the Penal Law as part of the wholesale revision of the Penal Law in 1965. When this provision was first proposed, commentators viewed the new language as codifying "the established common law maxim on mistake of law, while at the same time recognizing a defense when the erroneous belief is founded upon an 'official statement of the law.'"

The defendant claims as a first prong of his defense that he is entitled to raise the defense of mistake of law under section 15.20 (2) (a) because his mistaken belief that his conduct was legal was founded upon an official statement of the law contained in the statute itself.[1] Defendant argues that his mistaken interpretation of the statute was reasonable in view of the alleged ambiguous wording of the peace officer exemption statute, and that his "reasonable" interpretation of an "official statement" is enough to satisfy the requirements of subdivision (2) (a).   However, the whole thrust of this exceptional exculpatory concept, in derogation of the traditional and common-law principle, was intended to be a very narrow escape valve. Application in this case would invert that thrust and make mistake of law a generally applied or available defense instead of an unusual exception which the very opening words of the mistake statute make so clear, i.e., "A person is not relieved of criminal liability for conduct * * * unless" (Penal Law §15.20). * * *

The prosecution further counters defendant's argument by asserting that one cannot claim the protection of mistake of law under section 15.20 (2) (a) simply by misconstruing the meaning of a statute but must instead establish that the statute relied on actually permitted the conduct in question and was only later found to be erroneous. To buttress that argument, the People analogize New York's official statement defense to the approach taken by the Model Penal Code (MPC). Section 2.04 of the MPC provides:

> Section 2.04. *Ignorance or Mistake.*
>
> *   *   *
>
> (3) A belief that conduct does not legally constitute an offense is a defense to a prosecution for that offense based upon such conduct when * * * (b) he acts in reasonable reliance upon an official statement of the law, *afterward determined to be invalid or erroneous*, contained in (i) a statute or other enactment.

---

[1] Under New York Penal Law § 265.02, a person is guilty of criminal possession of a weapon in the third degree when "[s]uch person possesses any loaded firearm." N.Y. PENAL LAW § 265.02 (McKinney 2004). New York Penal Law § 265.20 (exemptions) states that section 265.02 shall not apply to possession of any weapons by "peace officers as defined in subdivision thirty-three of section 1.20 of the criminal procedure law." N.Y. PENAL LAW § 265.20. New York's Criminal Procedure Law § 1.20(33) defines "peace officer" as including "[a]n attendant, or an official, or guard of any state prison *or of any penal correctional institution*." N.Y. CRIM. PROC. LAW § 1.20 (emphasis added).

Although the drafters of the New York statute did not adopt the precise language of the Model Penal Code provision with the emphasized clause, it is evident and has long been believed that the Legislature intended the New York statute to be similarly construed. In fact, the legislative history of section 15.20 is replete with references to the influence of the Model Penal Code provision. * * *

The "official statement" component in the mistake of law defense in both paragraphs (a) and (d) adds yet another element of support for our interpretation and holding. Defendant tried to establish a defense under Penal Law §15.20 (2) (d) as a second prong. But the interpretation of the statute relied upon must be "officially made or issued by a public servant, agency or body legally charged or empowered with the responsibility or privilege of administering, enforcing or interpreting such statute or law." We agree with the People that the trial court also properly rejected the defense under Penal Law §15.20 (2) (d) since none of the interpretations which defendant proffered meets the requirements of the statute.* * *

Strong public policy reasons underlie the legislative mandate and intent which we perceive in rejecting defendant's construction of New York's mistake of law defense statute. If defendant's argument were accepted, the exception would swallow the rule. Mistakes about the law would be encouraged, rather than respect for and adherence to law. There would be an infinite number of mistake of law defenses which could be devised from a good-faith, perhaps reasonable but mistaken, interpretation of criminal statutes, many of which are concededly complex. Even more troublesome are the opportunities for wrongminded individuals to contrive in bad faith solely to get an exculpatory notion before the jury.* * *

Accordingly, the order of the Appellate Division should be affirmed.

HANCOCK, JR., J. [dissenting.]

The rule adopted by the majority prohibiting the defense of mistake of law under Penal Law §15.20 (2) (a) in the circumstances here is directly contrary to the plain dictates of the statute and a rejection of the jurisprudential reforms and legislative policies underlying its enactment. For these reasons, as more fully explained herein, we cannot agree with this decision.* * *

II

Penal Law §15.20 (effect of ignorance or mistake upon liability), in pertinent part, provides: "2. A person is not relieved of criminal liability for conduct because he engages in such conduct under a mistaken belief that it does not, as a matter of law, constitute an offense, unless such mistaken belief is founded upon an official statement of the law contained in (a) a statute or other enactment."

It is fundamental that in interpreting a statute, a court should look first to the particular words of the statute in question, being guided by the accepted rule that statutory language is generally given its natural and most obvious meaning. Here, there is but one natural and obvious meaning of the statute: that if a defendant can establish that his mistaken belief was "founded upon" his interpretation of "an official statement of the law contained in * * * [a] statute," he should have a defense. No other natural and obvious meaning has been suggested.

It is difficult to imagine a case more squarely within the wording of Penal Law §15.20 (2) (a) or one more fitted to what appears clearly to be the intended purpose of the statute than the one before us. For this reason it is helpful to discuss the statute and its apparent intended effect in the light of what defendant contends was his mistaken belief founded on an official statement of the law contained in a statute. * * *

Defendant's mistaken belief that, as a Federal corrections officer, he could legally carry a loaded weapon without a license was based on the express exemption from criminal liability under Penal Law §265.02 accorded in Penal Law §265.20 (a) (1) (a) to "peace officers" as defined in the Criminal Procedure Law and on his reading of the statutory definition for "peace officer" in CPL 2.10 (25) as meaning a correction officer "of *any* penal correctional institution," including an institution not operated by New York State. Thus, he concluded erroneously that, as a corrections officer in a Federal prison, he was a "peace officer" and, as such, exempt by the express terms of Penal Law §265.20 (a) (1) (a). This mistaken belief, based in good faith on the statute defining "peace officer" is, defendant contends, the precise sort of "mistaken belief * * * founded upon an official statement of the law contained in * * * a statute or other enactment" which gives rise to a mistake of law defense under Penal Law §15.20 (2) (a). He points out, of course, that when he acted in reliance on his belief he had no way of foreseeing that a court would eventually resolve the question of the statute's meaning against him and rule that his belief had been mistaken, as three of the five-member panel at the Appellate Division ultimately did in the first appeal.

The majority, however, has accepted the People's argument that to have a defense under Penal Law §15.20 (2) (a) "a defendant must show that the statute *permitted his conduct*, not merely that he believed it did." Here, of course, defendant cannot show that the statute permitted his conduct. To the contrary, the question has now been decided by the Appellate Division and it is settled that defendant. was not exempt under Penal Law §265.20 (a) (1) (a). Therefore, the argument goes, defendant can have no mistake of law defense. * * *

Nothing in the statutory language suggests the interpretation urged by the People and adopted by the majority: that Penal Law §15.20 (2) (a) is available to a defendant *not* when he has mistakenly read a statute *but only* when he has correctly read and relied on a statute which is later invalidated. Such a construction contravenes the general rule that penal statutes should be construed against the State and in favor of the accused and the Legislature's specific directive that the revised Penal Law should not be strictly construed but "must be construed according to the fair import of [its] terms to promote justice and effect the objects of the law."

More importantly, the construction leads to an anomaly: only a defendant who is *not mistaken* about the law when he acts has a mistake of law defense. In other words, a defendant can assert a defense under Penal Law §15.20 (2) (a) only when his reading of the statute is *correct – not mistaken*. Such construction is obviously illogical; it strips the statute of the very effect intended by the Legislature in adopting the mistake of law defense. * * * An interpretation of a statute which produces an unreasonable or incongruous result and one which defeats the obvious purpose of the legislation and renders it ineffective should be rejected.

Finally, the majority's disregard of the natural and obvious meaning of Penal Law §15.20 (2) (a) so that a defendant mistaken about the law is deprived of a defense under the statute amounts, we submit, to a rejection of the obvious legislative purposes and policies favoring jurisprudential reform underlying the statute's enactment. It is self-evident that in enacting Penal Law §15.20 (2) as part of the revision and modernization of the Penal Law the Legislature intended to effect a needed reform by abolishing what had long been considered the unjust archaic common-law rule totally prohibiting mistake of law as a defense. Had it not so intended it would simply have left the common-law rule intact. In place of the abandoned *"ignorantia legis"* common-law maxim the Legislature enacted a rule which permits *no defense for ignorance of law* but *allows a mistake of law defense* in specific instances, including the one presented here: when the defendant's erroneous belief is founded on an "official statement of the law." * * *

Although expressing its evident conviction that the statute should be treated as an "exceptional exculpatory concept * * * intended to be a very narrow escape valve," the majority cites no language in the statute or in the legislative history supporting its views or the construction of Penal Law §15.20 (2) (a) which seems so contrary to the statute's plain language and evident purpose. Despite the assertion that such construction reflects "appropriate precedential awareness" the majority cites no precedential authority.

Instead, the majority bases its decision on an analogous provision in the Model Penal Code and concludes that despite its totally different wording and meaning Penal Law §15.20 (2) (a) should be read as if it were Model Penal Code §2.04 (3) (b) (i). But New York in revising the Penal Law did not adopt the Model Penal Code. As in New Jersey, which generally adopted the Model Penal Code but added one section which is substantially more liberal, New York followed parts of the Model Penal Code provisions and rejected others. In *People v Goetz,* we said that the Legislature's rejection of the verbatim provisions of the Model Penal Code was crucial in determining its intent in drafting the statute. The significance of the alterations here can be no different.

While Penal Law §15.20 (2) and Model Penal Code §2.04 are alike in their rejection of the strict common-law rule, they are not alike in wording and differ significantly in substance. * * * In respect to the defense based upon an actor's reliance on an official statement of law contained in a statute the Model Penal Code and the New York statute are totally dissimilar. The Model Penal Code *does not* permit a defense for someone who acts in good faith upon a *mistaken belief* that a specific statute authorizes his conduct. The defense is limited to an act in reliance on an official statement of law in a statute "afterward determined to be *invalid or erroneous.*" The New York statute, in contrast, specifically *permits* the defense when the actor proceeds under "a *mistaken belief*" that his conduct does not "constitute an offense" when that "*mistaken belief* is founded upon an official statement of the law contained in * * * a statute."

Thus, the precise phrase in the Model Penal Code limiting the defense under section 2.04 (3) (b) (i) to reliance on a statute "afterward determined to be invalid or erroneous" which, if present, would support the majority's narrow construction of the New York statute, is omitted from Penal Law §15.20 (2) (a). How the Legislature can be assumed to have enacted the very language which it has specifically rejected is not explained. * * *

III

Any fair reading of the majority opinion, we submit, demonstrates that the decision to reject a mistake of law defense is based on considerations of public policy and on the conviction that such a defense would be bad, rather than on an analysis of CPL 15.20 (2) (a) under the usual principles of statutory construction. The majority warns, for example, that if the defense were permitted "the exception would swallow the rule"; that "[mistakes] about the law would be encouraged"; that an "infinite number of mistake of law defenses * * * could be devised"; and that "wrongminded individuals [could] contrive in bad faith solely to get an exculpatory notion before the jury." * * *

It is no answer to protest that the defense may become a "false and diversionary stratagem[]" or that "wrongminded individuals [could] contrive" an "infinite number of mistake of law defenses"; for it is the very business of the courts to separate the true claims from the false. * * * Justice Holmes wrote in commenting on John Austin's argument that permitting the mistake of law defense would present courts with problems they were not prepared to solve: "If justice requires the fact to be ascertained, the difficulty of doing so is no ground for refusing to try."

IV

* * *There should be a reversal and defendant should have a new trial in which he is permitted to assert a defense of mistake of law under Penal Law §15.20 (2) (a).

Note

Apparently, Marrero purchased his .38 caliber pistol from a gun dealer in New York who told him that he didn't need a permit for the gun because federal corrections officers are considered "peace officers" under New York law. Paul H. Robinson, CRIMINAL LAW CASE STUDIES 33 (2d ed. 2002); Dan M. Kahan, *Ignorance of the Law Is an Excuse – But Only for the Virtuous*, 96 Mich. L. Rev. 127, 131 (1997) (suggesting that local gun dealers "routinely sold weapons to federal prison guards without demanding proof that the guards were licensed to carry such weapons."). Marrero also spoke to the instructor of a local criminal justice course, who supported this interpretation of the law. *Id.*

The trial judge in Marrero's case initially agreed with Marrero's reading of the law and granted his motion to dismiss the indictment. *Id.* at 131-32. The state appealed, and the appellate court voted 3-2 to reverse the trial court's ruling and reinstate the indictment. *Id.* at 132. Are any of these facts relevant to Marrero's mistake of law claim? Should they be?

UNITED STATES V. CLEGG
United States Court of Appeals for the Ninth Circuit
846 F.2d 1221 (9th Cir. 1988)

PER CURIAM

Eugene Ray Clegg is charged with exporting firearms in violation of 18 U.S.C. § 922(a)(1) (1982) and 22 U.S.C. § 2778(b)(2), (c) (1982). * * *

Facts

Prior to his arrest in September 1982, Clegg taught at an American school in Islamabad, Pakistan. According to Clegg, United States officials, affiliated with various agencies of our government, solicited, encouraged and assisted his efforts to supply weapons to Afghan rebels resisting Soviet occupation of their country. Believing that this solicitation, encouragement, and assistance constituted official permission to transport arms, Clegg smuggled arms through Pakistan to the Afghan rebels. He was arrested in Pakistan, where he was imprisoned. Upon his release, United States marshals escorted him back to this country. He returned home facing charges of exporting firearms in violation of federal law. In defending against these charges, Clegg seeks to prove that he acted in reasonable good-faith reliance on statements of United States officials that led him to believe he was lawfully transporting guns.

The acts on which Clegg claims to have relied include the following alleged events, occurrence of which Clegg proposes to prove at trial: (1) that Lieutenant Colonel Durham of the United States Army, second in command in Pakistan, informed Clegg that the United States supplied arms to Afghan rebels, and that the United States wanted Clegg to smuggle arms to the rebels; (2) that Durham offered to put Clegg in contact with the rebels, that he later became aware of Clegg's smuggling, that he helped Clegg to plan a large secret arms shipment which never took place, and that he supplied Clegg with arms for resale to Afghan rebels on one occasion; (3) that Colonel Maugher of the United States Army, who was director of military intelligence for the United States in Pakistan, knew of Clegg's activities, and that Maugher once sold ammunition to Clegg with the understanding that it was destined for resale to the rebels; and (4) that several other individual government officials, whose positions led Clegg to believe that they had power to authorize arms shipments to the rebels, knew of Clegg's shipments and on at least one occasion assisted Clegg in shipping arms. * * *

Discussion

A. This case is controlled by our recent decision in *United States v. Tallmadge*. In *Tallmadge*, we reviewed a conviction for violation of 18 U.S.C. § 922(h)(1) (1982), which prohibits convicted felons from receiving firearms. Tallmadge defended on the ground that his state felony conviction had been reduced to a misdemeanor. While that fact alone did not bring him outside the sweep of section 922, we exonerated Tallmadge because he had disclosed these facts to a licensed firearm dealer and the dealer had sold him the weapon anyway.

In reaching this conclusion, we reasoned as follows:

> In the matter before us, the uncontradicted evidence established that Tallmadge received and possessed firearms in reliance upon the representation of a federally licensed gun dealer that a person convicted of a felony in a state court could purchase firearms if the offense had subsequently been reduced to a misdemeanor. We have no doubt that under the doctrine of entrapment by estoppel a person could not be prosecuted under 18 U.S.C. §§ 922(h)(1) and 1202(a)(1) if an ATF official had represented that a person convicted of a felony can purchase firearms after the charge has been reduced to a misdemeanor. Here, the misleading statement regarding the lawfulness of Tallmadge's proposed conduct was made by a licensee of the federal government. * * *

> The Department of the Treasury requires a licensed firearms dealer and a prospective buyer to fill out a form entitled Firearms Transaction Record to permit the licensee to determine if he may lawfully sell a firearm to such person. The form also requires the firearms dealer "to alert the transferee [buyer] of certain restrictions on the receipt and possession of arms." The form further provides that "[t]he transferor [seller] of the firearm is responsible for determining the lawfulness of the transaction...." To fulfill this duty the form provides that the firearms dealer "should be familiar with the Gun Control Act of 1968 and Title VII, Unlawful Possession or Receipt of Firearms, and 27 CFR Part 178 (Commerce in Firearms and Ammunition)." Thus, Congress has not only granted certain persons the exclusive right to engage in the business of selling firearms, it has also given them the [a]ffirmative duty of inquiring of a prospective buyer whether he has a criminal record that would make it unlawful for him to purchase a

firearm. In addition, the Treasury Department requires licensees to inform buyers concerning the restrictions imposed by Congress on the purchase of firearms. Clearly, the United States Government has made licensed firearms dealers federal agents in connection with the gathering and dispensing of information on the purchase of firearms. Under these circumstances, we believe that a buyer has the right to rely on the representations of a licensed firearms dealer, who has been made aware of all the relevant historical facts, that a person may receive and possess a weapon if his felony conviction has been reduced to a misdemeanor.

We view this as an a fortiori case. Tallmadge was dealing with a licensed firearm dealer, a private party. Clegg alleges that he dealt not merely with government officials, but with officials of the highest rank. Moreover, Clegg, unlike Tallmadge, was operating far from the territory of the United States, in a place not obviously covered by American law. If Tallmadge was entitled to rely upon the representations of the gun dealer as a complete defense, we can hardly deny the same defense to Clegg. Whatever our disagreements may be with the court's ruling in *Tallmadge*, it is the law of the circuit and we are bound to follow it. * * *

The judgment of the district court is AFFIRMED.

SKOPIL, Circuit Judge, dissenting.

I dissent from the majority's holding that Clegg is entitled to assert a mistake of law defense to the charges of exporting firearms without a license. Generally, ignorance of the law or a mistake as to the law's requirements cannot be a defense in a criminal prosecution. An exception has been created to provide for the legitimate reliance on an official interpretation of law. * * *

Nothing in my search of the record in this case discloses the requisite reliance on an official interpretation of the law. Even assuming that Clegg dealt with officials possessing the requisite authority[1] to suspend the law, Clegg never

---

[1] The majority does not specifically address the issue of what authority the official must possess. In *United States v. Barker*, 546 F.2d 940, 946-49 (D.C.Cir.1976), Judge Wilkey approved the use of a mistake of law defense for someone who relied on the "apparent authority" of a government official. Other circuits have adopted a stricter standard by requiring that the government official have actual authority. *See United States v. Duggan*, 743 F.2d 59, 84 (2d Cir.1984). In *Tallmadge*, we seemed to conclude that a licensed firearms dealer is an agent of the

alleges these officials authorized the unlawful conduct or told him that his activities were lawful. In fact, Clegg admits that he was involved in gun running [activities] before he ever became acquainted with these officials. As the majority notes in its summary of Clegg's allegations, various officials of the United States may have become aware of Clegg's activities. Moreover, several officials may have actually helped Clegg in his quest to supply arms to Afghan rebels. Liberally construed, the officials' conduct may amount to what the majority terms "solicitation, encouragement, and assistance" to Clegg. Nevertheless, in my opinion, there is still lacking any allegation of an official representation that Clegg's conduct was lawful. Hence, Clegg may well have had the aid of various United States officials. This does not make his conduct lawful. I would reverse the district court's ruling that Clegg is entitled to assert the defense.

STATE V. FRIDLEY
Supreme Court of North Dakota
335 N.W.2d 785 (N.D. 1983)

PAULSON, Justice.

Gaylord Duane Fridley [Fridley] appeals from a judgment of conviction entered in the Stark County Court of Increased Jurisdiction on September 23, 1982, upon a jury's verdict finding him guilty of driving while his license was revoked. We affirm.

On the evening of April 1, 1982, Fridley was stopped for speeding in Dickinson by two auxiliary police officers of the Dickinson Police Department. A routine driver's license check revealed that Fridley's driver's license had been revoked. Fridley was subsequently arrested and cited for driving while his license was revoked, in violation of § 39-06-42 of the North Dakota Century Code.

Fridley demanded a jury trial. [The state made a motion in limine to prevent Fridley from introducing evidence in support of his mistake argument on the ground that it was irrelevant and would only confuse the jury.] Fridley resisted the State's motion in limine on the grounds that his defense to the charge would rest upon the statutorily defined defense of excuse based upon mistake of law, pursuant to §§ 12.1-05-08 and 12.1-05-09, N.D.C.C.,

---

United States empowered by statute to interpret the law. *See Tallmadge*, 829 F.2d at 774. Here, the majority simply notes that Clegg dealt with "officials of the highest rank" but does not decide whether such officials are empowered either to provide Clegg with a license to export arms or to suspend the license requirement.

respectively. Fridley said his defense would be based on his mistaken assumption that he was legally authorized to drive at the time he was arrested.

The State's motion in limine was heard by the court on the same day as the trial. Fridley contended during his offer of proof that after he received notice of his license revocation, he contacted by telephone, in March of 1982, a person named "Debbie" of the Drivers License Division in regard to the procedures necessary for obtaining a work permit to drive. According to Fridley, "Debbie" told him that he must take a driver's test, that he must forward $10.00 along with his "SR-22 Form," and that he should send his driver's license with his application for a work permit to the Drivers License Division. Fridley stated that he was told he would then be without a driver's license for seven days. Fridley testified that he interpreted the substance of his conversation with "Debbie" to mean that his driver's license would be revoked for a period of seven days commencing only when these requested materials "hit the Bismarck office." * * *

In response to the State's motion in limine, Fridley also requested the following jury instruction based upon §§ 12.1-05-08 and 12.1-05-09, N.D.C.C.:

> Gaylord Fridley's conduct may be excused if he believe [sic] the facts were such that his conduct was necessary because of an official interpretation by the Drivers License Division. If you find that this belief is negligently or recklessly held, you may find that Gaylord Fridley was not justified in relying upon the interpretation by the personnel at the Drivers License Division. However, if you find that Gaylord Fridley, in good faith, relied upon the interpretation of the personnel at the Drivers License Division, and it is proved to your satisfaction by a preponderance of the evidence, then you should find Gaylord Fridley not guilty.

The court refused Fridley's requested jury instruction and granted the State's motion in limine prohibiting the defendant "from making any reference to contacts made through the Drivers License Division after the official written decision by the hearing officer" revoking his license. The court determined that any reference to statements made by "Debbie" at the Drivers License Division would constitute hearsay. * * * The trial court also determined that, under § 12.1-05-09, N.D.C.C., the statements purportedly made by "Debbie" concerning the procedures for obtaining a work permit did not qualify as an "official interpretation" of the law defining driving while one's license is revoked. The court also concluded that there was no basis for granting the defendant's requested jury instruction because, as a matter of law, there had been no showing of "reasonable reliance" on an official statement or interpretation of the law. * * *

The jury found Fridley guilty of driving while his license was revoked on September 13, 1982. The court fined Fridley $400.00 and sentenced him to serve 30 days in jail, with 15 days suspended on the condition that he have no moving traffic violations for a period of one year. Fridley appeals.

In his appeal Fridley contends that the trial court erred in granting the State's motion in limine, thus precluding him from presenting evidence to establish his defense of excuse based upon mistake of law. We hold that the trial court properly granted the State's motion in limine -- not on the basis of the reasons given by the trial court for its decision -- but on the basis that, as a matter of law, the defense of excuse, based upon mistake of law, is not applicable to prosecutions under § 39-06-42, N.D.C.C., a strict liability offense for which proof of culpability is not required. * * *

Section 39-06-42(1), N.D.C.C., under which Fridley was convicted, provides in pertinent part as follows:

> 39-06-42. Penalty for driving while license suspended or revoked -- Impoundment of vehicle number plates -- Authority of cities.
>
> 1. Except as provided in chapters 39-16 and 39-16.1, and in section 39-06.1-11, any person who drives a motor vehicle on any public highway of this state at a time when his license or privilege so to do is suspended or revoked shall be guilty of a class B misdemeanor....

It is evident that § 39-06-42(1), N.D.C.C., does not contain a mental culpability requirement. Although § 12.1-02-02(2), N.D.C.C., provides that if a statute defining a crime does not specify any culpability requirement and does not provide explicitly that a person may be guilty without culpability, the culpability that is required is "willfully," past decisions of our court have restricted the application of § 12.1-02-02(2), N.D.C.C., to offenses defined in Title 12.1, N.D.C.C., alone. In addition, we have previously pointed out that § 39-06-42, N.D.C.C., is one of several strict liability offenses found throughout our Century Code. * * *

Section 12.1-05-09, N.D.C.C., provides:

> 12.1-05-09. Mistake of law .-- Except as otherwise expressly provided, a person's good faith belief that conduct does not

constitute a crime is an affirmative defense if he acted in reasonable reliance upon a statement of the law contained in:

1. A statute or other enactment.
2. A judicial decision, opinion, order, or judgment.
3. An administrative order or grant of permission.
4. An official interpretation of the public servant or body charged by law with responsibility for the interpretation, administration, or enforcement of the law defining the crime.

Chapter 12.1-05 of the North Dakota Century Code "is an almost complete adoption of Chapter 6 of the Proposed [Federal Criminal] Code dealing with defenses involving justification and excuse." The language of § 12.1-05-09, N.D.C.C., is identical to § 609 of the Proposed Federal Criminal Code. It is therefore helpful, as an aid to interpreting the North Dakota mistake of law statute, to examine the Comments of the draftsmen of the Proposed Federal Criminal Code.

The Final Report, supra at page 53, contains, in relevant part, the following Comment regarding § 609:

> This section sets forth those circumstances under which a person is excused from criminal liability for his conduct because he mistakenly believed his conduct did not constitute a crime. *The defense is not available for infractions where proof of culpability is generally not required.* [Emphasis added.]

Although the above-quoted Comment indicates that the defense of mistake of law is not applicable to "infractions" where proof of culpability is not required, we believe the same holds true in regard to § 39-06-42, N.D.C.C., a class B misdemeanor for which proof of culpability is not required. * * *

In the instant case, allowing the assertion of the mistake of law defense, which rests upon a defendant's "good faith belief" that his conduct does not constitute a crime, is difficult to reconcile with the concept of a strict liability offense for which proof of a culpable state of mind is not required. * * *

For the reasons stated in this opinion, the judgment of conviction is affirmed.

2.   Ignorance or Mistake That Negates the Mens Rea

As mentioned above, if one is charged with an offense which makes knowledge that the prohibited conduct is unlawful an element of the crime, then one can argue that one's lack of knowledge as to the unlawfulness of one's conduct negates an essential element of the crime. This type of mistake is a complete defense. In *Cheek v. United States* and *Bryan v. United States*, the U.S. Supreme Court discusses and explains the meaning of this type of mistake defense.

CHEEK v. UNITED STATES
Supreme Court of the United States
498 U.S. 192, 111 S.Ct. 604, 112 L.Ed.2d 617 (1991)

JUSTICE WHITE delivered the opinion of the Court.

Title 26, §7201 of the United States Code provides that any person "who willfully attempts in any manner to evade or defeat any tax imposed by this title or the payment thereof" shall be guilty of a felony. Under 26 U.S.C. § 7203, "any person required under this title . . . or by regulations made under authority thereof to make a return . . . who willfully fails to . . . make such return" shall be guilty of a misdemeanor. This case turns on the meaning of the word "willfully" as used in §§ 7201 and 7203.

I

Petitioner John L. Cheek has been a pilot for American Airlines since 1973. He filed federal income tax returns through 1979 but thereafter ceased to file returns. He also claimed an increasing number of withholding allowances – eventually claiming 60 allowances by mid-1980 – and for the years 1981 to 1984 indicated on his W-4 forms that he was exempt from federal income taxes. In 1983, petitioner unsuccessfully sought a refund of all tax withheld by his employer in 1982. Petitioner's income during this period at all times far exceeded the minimum necessary to trigger the statutory filing requirement.

As a result of his activities, petitioner was indicted for 10 violations of federal law. He was charged with six counts of willfully failing to file a federal income tax return for the years 1980, 1981, and 1983 through 1986, in violation of 26 U.S.C. §7203. He was further charged with three counts of willfully attempting to evade his income taxes for the years 1980, 1981, and 1983 in violation of §7201. In those years, American Airlines withheld substantially less than the amount of tax petitioner owed because of the numerous allowances and exempt status he claimed on his W-4 forms. The tax offenses with which petitioner was charged are specific intent crimes that require the defendant to have acted willfully.

At trial, the evidence established that between 1982 and 1986, petitioner was involved in at least four civil cases that challenged various aspects of the federal income tax system. In all four of those cases, the plaintiffs were informed by the courts that many of their arguments, including that they were not taxpayers within the meaning of the tax laws, that wages are not income, that the Sixteenth Amendment does not authorize the imposition of an income tax on individuals, and that the Sixteenth Amendment is unenforceable, were frivolous or had been repeatedly rejected by the courts. During this time period, petitioner also attended at least two criminal trials of persons charged with tax offenses. In addition, there was evidence that in 1980 or 1981 an attorney had advised Cheek that the courts had rejected as frivolous the claim that wages are not income.[4]

Cheek represented himself at trial and testified in his defense. He admitted that he had not filed personal income tax returns during the years in question. He testified that as early as 1978, he had begun attending seminars sponsored by, and following the advice of, a group that believes, among other things, that the federal tax system is unconstitutional. Some of the speakers at these meetings were lawyers who purported to give professional opinions about the invalidity of the federal income tax laws. Cheek produced a letter from an attorney stating that the Sixteenth Amendment did not authorize a tax on wages and salaries but only on gain or profit. Petitioner's defense was that, based on the indoctrination he received from this group and from his own study, he sincerely believed that the tax laws were being unconstitutionally enforced and that his actions during the 1980-1986 period were lawful. He therefore argued that he had acted without the willfulness required for conviction of the various offenses with which he was charged.

In the course of its instructions, the trial court advised the jury that to prove "willfulness" the Government must prove the voluntary and intentional violation of a known legal duty, a burden that could not be proved by showing mistake, ignorance, or negligence. The court further advised the jury that an objectively reasonable good-faith misunderstanding of the law would negate willfulness, but mere disagreement with the law would not. The court described Cheek's beliefs about the income tax system and instructed the jury that if it

---

[4]The attorney also advised that despite the Fifth Amendment, the filing of a tax return was required and that a person could challenge the constitutionality of the system by suing for a refund after the taxes had been withheld, or by putting himself "at risk of criminal prosecution."

found that Cheek "honestly and reasonably believed that he was not required to pay income taxes or to file tax returns," a not guilty verdict should be returned.

After several hours of deliberation, the jury sent a note to the judge that stated in part:

> We have a basic disagreement between some of us as to if Mr. Cheek honestly & reasonably believed that he was not required to pay income taxes . . . . Page 32 [the relevant jury instruction] discusses good faith misunderstanding & disagreement. Is there any additional clarification you can give us on this point?

The District Judge responded with a supplemental instruction containing the following statements:

> [A] person's opinion that the tax laws violate his constitutional rights does not constitute a good faith misunderstanding of the law. Furthermore, a person's disagreement with the government's tax collection systems and policies does not constitute a good faith misunderstanding of the law.

At the end of the first day of deliberation, the jury sent out another note saying that it still could not reach a verdict because "we are divided on the issue as to if Mr. Cheek honestly & reasonably believed that he was not required to pay income tax." When the jury resumed its deliberations, the District Judge gave the jury an additional instruction. This instruction stated in part that "an honest but unreasonable belief is not a defense and does not negate willfulness," and that "advice or research resulting in the conclusion that wages of a privately employed person are not income or that the tax laws are unconstitutional is not objectively reasonable and cannot serve as the basis for a good faith misunderstanding of the law defense." The court also instructed the jury that "persistent refusal to acknowledge the law does not constitute a good faith misunderstanding of the law." Approximately two hours later, the jury returned a verdict finding petitioner guilty on all counts.[6]

---

[6]A note signed by all 12 jurors also informed the judge that although the jury found petitioner guilty, several jurors wanted to express their personal opinions of the case and that notes from these individual jurors to the court were "a complaint against the narrow & hard expression under the constraints of the law." At least two notes from individual jurors expressed the opinion that petitioner sincerely believed in his cause even though his beliefs might have been unreasonable.

Petitioner appealed his convictions, arguing that the District Court erred by instructing the jury that only an objectively reasonable misunderstanding of the law negates the statutory willfulness requirement. The United States Court of Appeals for the Seventh Circuit rejected that contention and affirmed the convictions. * * * Because the Seventh Circuit's interpretation of "willfully" as used in these statutes conflicts with the decisions of several other Courts of Appeals, we granted certiorari.

II

The general rule that ignorance of the law or a mistake of law is no defense to criminal prosecution is deeply rooted in the American legal system. Based on the notion that the law is definite and knowable, the common law presumed that every person knew the law. This common-law rule has been applied by the Court in numerous cases construing criminal statutes.

The proliferation of statutes and regulations has sometimes made it difficult for the average citizen to know and comprehend the extent of the duties and obligations imposed by the tax laws. Congress has accordingly softened the impact of the common-law presumption by making specific intent to violate the law an element of certain federal criminal tax offenses. Thus, the Court almost 60 years ago interpreted the statutory term "willfully" as used in the federal criminal tax statutes as carving out an exception to the traditional rule. This special treatment of criminal tax offenses is largely due to the complexity of the tax laws. In *United States v. Murdock,* the Court recognized that:

> Congress did not intend that a person, by reason of a bona fide misunderstanding as to his liability for the tax, as to his duty to make a return, or as to the adequacy of the records he maintained, should become a criminal by his mere failure to measure up to the prescribed standard of conduct.

The Court held that the defendant was entitled to an instruction with respect to whether he acted in good faith based on his actual belief. * * *

Subsequent decisions have refined this proposition. In *United States v. Bishop,* we described the term "willfully" as connoting "a voluntary, intentional violation of a known legal duty," and did so with specific reference to the "bad faith or evil intent" language employed in *Murdock.* Still later, *United States v. Pomponio* addressed a situation in which several defendants had been charged with willfully filing false tax returns. * * * Taken together, *Bishop* and *Pomponio* conclusively establish that the standard for the statutory willfulness requirement is the "voluntary, intentional violation of a known legal duty."

III

Cheek accepts the *Pomponio* definition of willfulness, but asserts that the District Court's instructions and the Court of Appeals' opinion departed from that definition. In particular, he challenges the ruling that a good-faith misunderstanding of the law or a good-faith belief that one is not violating the law, if it is to negate willfulness, must be objectively reasonable. We agree that the Court of Appeals and the District Court erred in this respect.

A

Willfulness, as construed by our prior decisions in criminal tax cases, requires the Government to prove that the law imposed a duty on the defendant, that the defendant knew of this duty, and that he voluntarily and intentionally violated that duty. We deal first with the case where the issue is whether the defendant knew of the duty purportedly imposed by the provision of the statute or regulation he is accused of violating, a case in which there is no claim that the provision at issue is invalid. In such a case, if the Government proves actual knowledge of the pertinent legal duty, the prosecution, without more, has satisfied the knowledge component of the willfulness requirement. But carrying this burden requires negating a defendant's claim of ignorance of the law or a claim that because of a misunderstanding of the law, he had a good-faith belief that he was not violating any of the provisions of the tax laws. This is so because one cannot be aware that the law imposes a duty upon him and yet be ignorant of it, misunderstand the law, or believe that the duty does not exist. In the end, the issue is whether, based on all the evidence, the Government has proved that the defendant was aware of the duty at issue, which cannot be true if the jury credits a good-faith misunderstanding and belief submission, whether or not the claimed belief or misunderstanding is objectively reasonable.

In this case, if Cheek asserted that he truly believed that the Internal Revenue Code did not purport to treat wages as income, and the jury believed him, the Government would not have carried its burden to prove willfulness, however unreasonable a court might deem such a belief. Of course, in deciding whether to credit Cheek's good-faith belief claim, the jury would be free to consider any admissible evidence from any source showing that Cheek was aware of his duty to file a return and to treat wages as income, including evidence showing his awareness of the relevant provisions of the Code or regulations, of court decisions rejecting his interpretation of the tax law, of authoritative rulings of the Internal Revenue Service, or of any contents of the personal income tax return forms and accompanying instructions that made it plain that wages should be returned as income.[7]

We thus disagree with the Court of Appeals' requirement that a claimed good-faith belief must be objectively reasonable if it is to be considered as possibly negating the Government's evidence purporting to show a defendant's awareness of the legal duty at issue. Knowledge and belief are characteristically questions for the factfinder, in this case the jury. Characterizing a particular belief as not objectively reasonable transforms the inquiry into a legal one and would prevent the jury from considering it. * * *

It was therefore error to instruct the jury to disregard evidence of Cheek's understanding that, within the meaning of the tax laws, he was not a person required to file a return or to pay income taxes and that wages are not taxable income, as incredible as such misunderstandings of and beliefs about the law might be. Of course, the more unreasonable the asserted beliefs or misunderstandings are, the more likely the jury will consider them to be nothing more than simple disagreement with known legal duties imposed by the tax laws and will find that the Government has carried its burden of proving knowledge.

B

Cheek asserted in the trial court that he should be acquitted because he believed in good faith that the income tax law is unconstitutional as applied to him and thus could not legally impose any duty upon him of which he should have been aware. Such a submission is unsound. * * *

Claims that some of the provisions of the tax code are unconstitutional are submissions of a different order. They do not arise from innocent mistakes caused by the complexity of the Internal Revenue Code. Rather, they reveal full knowledge of the provisions at issue and a studied conclusion, however wrong, that those provisions are invalid and unenforceable. Thus in this case, Cheek paid his taxes for years, but after attending various seminars and based on his own study, he concluded that the income tax laws could not constitutionally require him to pay a tax.

---

[7]Cheek recognizes that a "defendant who knows what the law is and who disagrees with it . . . does not have a bona fide misunderstanding defense," but asserts that "a defendant who has a bona fide misunderstanding of [the law] does not 'know' his legal duty and lacks willfulness." The Reply Brief for Petitioner, at 13, states: "We are in no way suggesting that Cheek or anyone else is immune from criminal prosecution if he knows what the law is, but believes it should be otherwise, and therefore violates it."

We do not believe that Congress contemplated that such a taxpayer, without risking criminal prosecution, could ignore the duties imposed upon him by the Internal Revenue Code and refuse to utilize the mechanisms provided by Congress to present his claims of invalidity to the courts and to abide by their decisions. There is no doubt that Cheek, from year to year, was free to pay the tax that the law purported to require, file for a refund and, if denied, present his claims of invalidity, constitutional or otherwise, to the courts. Also, without paying the tax, he could have challenged claims of tax deficiencies in the Tax Court, § 6213, with the right to appeal to a higher court if unsuccessful. Cheek took neither course in some years, and when he did was unwilling to accept the outcome. As we see it, he is in no position to claim that his good-faith belief about the validity of the Internal Revenue Code negates willfulness or provides a defense to criminal prosecution under §§ 7201 and 7203. Of course, Cheek was free in this very case to present his claims of invalidity and have them adjudicated, but like defendants in criminal cases in other contexts, who "willfully" refuse to comply with the duties placed upon them by the law, he must take the risk of being wrong.

We thus hold that in a case like this, a defendant's views about the validity of the tax statutes are irrelevant to the issue of willfulness and need not be heard by the jury, and, if they are, an instruction to disregard them would be proper. For this purpose, it makes no difference whether the claims of invalidity are frivolous or have substance. It was therefore not error in this case for the District Judge to instruct the jury not to consider Cheek's claims that the tax laws were unconstitutional. However, it was error for the court to instruct the jury that petitioner's asserted beliefs that wages are not income and that he was not a taxpayer within the meaning of the Internal Revenue Code should not be considered by the jury in determining whether Cheek had acted willfully.

IV

For the reasons set forth in the opinion above, the judgment of the Court of Appeals is vacated, and the case is remanded for further proceedings consistent with this opinion.

It is so ordered.

JUSTICE SOUTER took no part in the consideration or decision of this case.

JUSTICE SCALIA, concurring in the judgment.

I concur in the judgment of the Court because our cases have consistently held that the failure to pay a tax in the good-faith belief that it is not legally owing is not "willful." I do not join the Court's opinion because I do not agree with the test for willfulness that it directs the Court of Appeals to apply on remand.

As the Court acknowledges, our opinions from the 1930's to the 1970's have interpreted the word "willfully" in the criminal tax statutes as requiring the "bad purpose" or "evil motive" of "intentionally violating a known legal duty." It seems to me that today's opinion squarely reverses that long-established statutory construction when it says that a good-faith erroneous belief in the unconstitutionality of a tax law is no defense. It is quite impossible to say that a statute which one believes unconstitutional represents a "known legal duty."
* * *

I find it impossible to understand how one can derive from the lonesome word "willfully" the proposition that belief in the nonexistence of a textual prohibition excuses liability, but belief in the invalidity (*i.e.*, the legal nonexistence) of a textual prohibition does not. One may say, as the law does in many contexts, that "willfully" refers to consciousness of the act but not to consciousness that the act is unlawful. Or alternatively, one may say, as we have said until today with respect to the tax statutes, that "willfully" refers to consciousness of both the act *and* its illegality. But it seems to me impossible to say that the word refers to consciousness that some legal text exists, without consciousness that that legal text is binding, *i.e.*, with the good-faith belief that it is not a valid law. Perhaps such a test for criminal liability would make sense (though in a field as complicated as federal tax law, I doubt it), but some text other than the mere word "willfully" would have to be employed to describe it – and that text is not ours to write.

Because today's opinion abandons clear and longstanding precedent to impose criminal liability where taxpayers have had no reason to expect it, because the new contours of criminal liability have no basis in the statutory text, and because I strongly suspect that those new contours make no sense even as a policy matter, I concur only in the judgment of the Court.

[JUSTICE BLACKMUN's dissenting opinion has been omitted.]

BRYAN v. UNITED STATES
Supreme Court of the United States
524 U.S. 184, 118 S.Ct. 1939, 141 L.Ed.2d 197 (1998)

JUSTICE STEVENS delivered the opinion of the Court.

Petitioner was convicted of "willfully" dealing in firearms without a federal license. The question presented is whether the term "willfully" in 18

U.S.C. § 924(a)(1)(D) requires proof that the defendant knew that his conduct was unlawful, or whether it also requires proof that he knew of the federal licensing requirement.

I

In 1968 Congress enacted the Omnibus Crime Control and Safe Streets Act. 82 Stat. 197-239. In Title IV of that Act Congress made findings concerning the impact of the traffic in firearms on the prevalence of lawlessness and violent crime in the United States and amended the Criminal Code to include detailed provisions regulating the use and sale of firearms. As amended, 18 U.S.C. § 922 defined a number of "unlawful acts"; subsection (a)(1) made it unlawful for any person except a licensed dealer to engage in the business of dealing in firearms.[2] Section 923 established the federal licensing program and repeated the prohibition against dealing in firearms without a license, and § 924 specified the penalties for violating "any provision of this chapter." Read literally, § 924 authorized the imposition of a fine of up to $5,000 or a prison sentence of not more than five years, "or both," on any person who dealt in firearms without a license even if that person believed that he or she was acting lawfully.[3] As enacted in 1968, § 922(a)(1) and § 924 omitted an express scienter requirement and therefore arguably imposed strict criminal liability on every unlicensed dealer in firearms. The 1968 Act also omitted any definition of the term "engaged in the business" even though that conduct was an element of the unlawful act prohibited by § 922(a)(1).

In 1986 Congress enacted the Firearms Owners' Protection Act (FOPA), in part, to cure these omissions. The findings in that statute explained that additional legislation was necessary to protect law-abiding citizens with

---

[2] 82 Stat. 228. The current version of this provision, which is substantially the same as the 1968 version, is codified at 18 U.S.C. § 922(a)(1)(A). It states:

(a) It shall be unlawful –
(1) for any person –
(A) except a licensed importer, licensed manufacturer, or licensed dealer, to engage in the business of importing, manufacturing, or dealing in firearms, or in the course of such business to ship, transport, or receive any firearm in interstate or foreign commerce.

[3] § 924. Penalties

(a) Whoever violates any provision of this chapter . . . shall be fined not more than $5,000 or imprisoned not more than five years, or both.

respect to the acquisition, possession, or use of firearms for lawful purposes.[4] FOPA therefore amended § 921 to include a definition of the term "engaged in the business,"[5] and amended § 924 to add a scienter requirement as a condition to the imposition of penalties for most of the unlawful acts defined in § 922. For three categories of offenses the intent required is that the defendant acted "knowingly"; for the fourth category, which includes "any other provision of this chapter," the required intent is that the defendant acted "willfully."[6] The §

---

[4]The Congress finds that − . . . .

(b)(2) additional legislation is required to reaffirm the intent of the Congress, as expressed in section 101 of the Gun Control Act of 1968, that 'it is not the purpose of this title to place any undue or unnecessary Federal restrictions or burdens on law-abiding citizens with respect to the acquisition, possession, or use of firearms appropriate to the purpose of hunting, trapshooting, target shooting, personal protection, or any other lawful activity, and that this title is not intended to discourage or eliminate the private ownership or use of firearms by law-abiding citizens for lawful purposes.

[5]Section 921 of title 18, United States Code, is amended − . . . .

(21) The term 'engaged in the business' means − . . . .

(C) as applied to a dealer in firearms, as defined in section 921(a)(11)(A), a person who devotes time, attention, and labor to dealing in firearms as a regular course of trade or business with the principal objective of livelihood and profit through the repetitive purchase and resale of firearms, but such term shall not include a person who makes occasional sales, exchanges, or purchases of firearms for the enhancement of a personal collection or for a hobby, or who sells all or part of his personal collection of firearms . . . .

[6] Title 18 U.S.C. § 924(a)(1) currently provides:

Except as otherwise provided in this subsection, subsection (b), (c), or (f) of this section, or in section 929, whoever−
(A) knowingly makes any false statement or representation with respect to the information required by this chapter to be kept in the records of a person licensed under this chapter or in applying for any license or exemption or relief from disability under the provisions of this chapter;
(B) knowingly violates subsection (a)(4), (f), (k), (r), (v), or (w) of section 922;

922(a)(1)(A) offense at issue in this case is an "other provision" in the "willfully" category.

II

The jury having found petitioner guilty, we accept the Government's version of the evidence. That evidence proved that petitioner did not have a federal license to deal in firearms; that he used so-called "straw purchasers" in Ohio to acquire pistols that he could not have purchased himself; that the straw purchasers made false statements when purchasing the guns; that petitioner assured the straw purchasers that he would file the serial numbers off the guns; and that he resold the guns on Brooklyn street corners known for drug dealing. The evidence was unquestionably adequate to prove that petitioner was dealing in firearms, and that he knew that his conduct was unlawful.[8] There was, however, no evidence that he was aware of the federal law that prohibits dealing in firearms without a federal license.

Petitioner was charged with a conspiracy to violate 18 U.S.C. § 922(a)(1)(A), by willfully engaging in the business of dealing in firearms, and with a substantive violation of that provision. After the close of evidence, petitioner requested that the trial judge instruct the jury that petitioner could be convicted only if he knew of the federal licensing requirement,[10] but the judge

---

> (C) knowingly imports or brings into the United States or any possession thereof any firearm or ammunition in violation of section 922(*l*); or
> (D) willfully violates any other provision of this chapter, shall be fined under this title, imprisoned not more than five years, or both.

[8] Why else would he make use of straw purchasers and assure them that he would shave the serial numbers off the guns? Moreover, the street corner sales are not consistent with a good-faith belief in the legality of the enterprise.

[10] KNOWLEDGE OF THE LAW

> The Federal Firearms Statute which the Defendant is charged with, conspiracy to violate and with allegedly violated *[sic]*, is a specific intent statute. You must accordingly find, beyond a reasonable doubt, that Defendant at all relevant times charged, acted with the knowledge that it was unlawful to engage in the business of firearms distribution lawfully purchased by a legally permissible transferee or gun purchaser . . . . You must be persuaded that with the actual knowledge of the federal firearms licensing laws Defendant acted in

rejected this request. Instead, the trial judge gave this explanation of the term "willfully":

> A person acts willfully if he acts intentionally and purposely and with the intent to do something the law forbids, that is, with the bad purpose to disobey or to disregard the law. Now, the person need not be aware of the specific law or rule that his conduct may be violating. But he must act with the intent to do something that the law forbids.

Petitioner was found guilty on both counts. On appeal he argued that the evidence was insufficient because there was no proof that he had knowledge of the federal licensing requirement, and that the trial judge had erred by failing to instruct the jury that such knowledge was an essential element of the offense. The Court of Appeals affirmed. It concluded that the instructions were proper and that the Government had elicited "ample proof" that petitioner had acted willfully.

Because the Eleventh Circuit has held that it is necessary for the Government to prove that the defendant acted with knowledge of the licensing requirement, we granted certiorari to resolve the conflict.

III

The word "willfully" is sometimes said to be "a word of many meanings" whose construction is often dependent on the context in which it appears. Most obviously it differentiates between deliberate and unwitting conduct, but in the criminal law it also typically refers to a culpable state of mind. As we explained in *United States v. Murdock*, a variety of phrases have been used to describe that concept.[12] As a general matter, when used in the criminal context, a "willful" act is one undertaken with a "bad purpose." In other words, in order to establish a "willful" violation of a statute, "the Government must prove that the defendant acted with knowledge that his conduct was unlawful."

---

knowing and intentional violation of them.

[12] The word often denotes an act which is intentional, or knowing, or voluntary, as distinguished from accidental. But when used in a criminal statute it generally means an act done with a bad purpose. The word is also employed to characterize a thing done without ground for believing it is lawful or conduct marked by careless disregard whether or not one has the right so to act.

Petitioner argues that a more particularized showing is required in this case for two principal reasons. First, he argues that the fact that Congress used the adverb "knowingly" to authorize punishment of three categories of acts made unlawful by § 922 and the word "willfully" when it referred to unlicensed dealing in firearms demonstrates that the Government must shoulder a special burden in cases like this. This argument is not persuasive because the term "knowingly" does not necessarily have any reference to a culpable state of mind or to knowledge of the law. As Justice Jackson correctly observed, "the knowledge requisite to knowing violation of a statute is factual knowledge as distinguished from knowledge of the law." Thus, in *United States v. Bailey*, we held that the prosecution fulfills its burden of proving a knowing violation of the escape statute "if it demonstrates that an escapee knew his actions would result in his leaving physical confinement without permission." And in *Staples v. United States*, we held that a charge that the defendant's possession of an unregistered machine gun was unlawful required proof "that he knew the weapon he possessed had the characteristics that brought it within the statutory definition of a machine gun." It was not, however, necessary to prove that the defendant knew that his possession was unlawful. Thus, unless the text of the statute dictates a different result, the term "knowingly" merely requires proof of knowledge of the facts that constitute the offense.

With respect to the three categories of conduct that are made punishable by § 924 if performed "knowingly," the background presumption that every citizen knows the law makes it unnecessary to adduce specific evidence to prove that "an evil-meaning mind" directed the "evil-doing hand." More is required, however, with respect to the conduct in the fourth category that is only criminal when done "willfully." The jury must find that the defendant acted with an evil-meaning mind, that is to say, that he acted with knowledge that his conduct was unlawful.

Petitioner next argues that we must read § 924(a)(1)(D) to require knowledge of the law because of our interpretation of "willfully" in two other contexts. In certain cases involving willful violations of the tax laws, we have concluded that the jury must find that the defendant was aware of the specific provision of the tax code that he was charged with violating. Similarly, in order to satisfy a willful violation in *Ratzlaf*, we concluded that the jury had to find that the defendant knew that his structuring of cash transactions to avoid a reporting requirement was unlawful. Those cases, however, are readily distinguishable. Both the tax cases and *Ratzlaf* involved highly technical statutes that presented the danger of ensnaring individuals engaged in apparently innocent conduct. As a result, we held that these statutes "carve out an exception to the traditional rule" that ignorance of the law is no excuse and require that the defendant have knowledge of the law. The danger of convicting individuals engaged in apparently innocent activity that motivated our decisions in the tax cases and *Ratzlaf* is not present here because the jury found that this petitioner knew that his conduct was unlawful.

Thus, the willfulness requirement of § 924(a)(1)(D) does not carve out an exception to the traditional rule that ignorance of the law is no excuse; knowledge that the conduct is unlawful is all that is required. * * *

Accordingly, the judgment of the Court of Appeals is affirmed.

It is so ordered.

JUSTICE SCALIA, with whom THE CHIEF JUSTICE and JUSTICE GINSBURG join, dissenting.

Petitioner Sillasse Bryan was convicted of "willfully" violating the federal licensing requirement for firearms dealers. The jury apparently found, and the evidence clearly shows, that Bryan was aware in a general way that some aspect of his conduct was unlawful. The issue is whether that general knowledge of illegality is enough to sustain the conviction, or whether a "willful" violation of the licensing provision requires proof that the defendant knew that his conduct was unlawful specifically because he lacked the necessary license. On that point the statute is, in my view, genuinely ambiguous. Most of the Court's opinion is devoted to confirming half of that ambiguity by refuting Bryan's various arguments that the statute clearly requires specific knowledge of the licensing requirement. The Court offers no real justification for its implicit conclusion that either (1) the statute unambiguously requires only general knowledge of illegality, or (2) ambiguously requiring only general knowledge is enough. Instead, the Court curiously falls back on "the traditional rule that ignorance of the law is no excuse" to conclude that "knowledge that the conduct is unlawful is all that is required." In my view, this case calls for the application of a different canon – "the familiar rule that, 'where there is ambiguity in a criminal statute, doubts are resolved in favor of the defendant.'"

Title 18 § 922(a)(1)(A) makes it unlawful for any person to engage in the business of dealing in firearms without a federal license. That provision is enforced criminally through § 924(a)(1)(D), which imposes criminal penalties on whoever "willfully violates any other provision of this chapter." The word "willfully" has a wide range of meanings, and "'its construction [is] often . . . influenced by its context.'" In some contexts it connotes nothing more than "an act which is intentional, or knowing, or voluntary, as distinguished from accidental." In the present context, however, inasmuch as the preceding three subparagraphs of § 924 specify a *mens rea* of "knowingly" for *other* firearms offenses, see §§ 924(a)(1)(A)-(C), a "willful" violation under § 924(a)(1)(D) must require some mental state more culpable than mere intent to perform the forbidden act. The United States concedes (and the Court apparently agrees) that the violation is not "willful" unless the defendant knows in a general way that his conduct is unlawful.

That concession takes this case beyond any useful application of the maxim that ignorance of the law is no excuse. Everyone agrees that § 924(a)(1)(D) requires some knowledge of the law; the only real question is *which* law? The Court's answer is that knowledge of *any* law is enough – or, put another way, that the defendant must be ignorant of *every* law violated by his course of conduct to be innocent of willfully violating the licensing requirement. The Court points to no textual basis for that conclusion other than the notoriously malleable word "willfully" itself. Instead, it seems to fall back on a presumption (apparently derived from the rule that ignorance of the law is no excuse) that even where ignorance of the law *is* an excuse, that excuse should be construed as narrowly as the statutory language permits.

I do not believe that the Court's approach makes sense of the statute that Congress enacted. I have no quarrel with the Court's assertion that "willfully" in § 924(a)(1)(D) requires only "general" knowledge of illegality – in the sense that the defendant need not be able to recite chapter and verse from Title 18 of the United States Code. It is enough, in my view, if the defendant is generally aware that the *actus reus* punished by the statute – dealing in firearms without a license – is illegal. But the Court is willing to accept a *mens rea* so "general" that it is entirely divorced from the *actus reus* this statute was enacted to punish. That approach turns § 924(a)(1)(D) into a strange and unlikely creature. Bryan would be guilty of "willfully" dealing in firearms without a federal license even if, for example, he had never heard of the licensing requirement but was aware that he had violated the law by using straw purchasers or filing the serial numbers off the pistols. The Court does not even limit (for there is no rational basis to limit) the universe of relevant laws to federal *firearms* statutes. Bryan would also be "acting with an evil-meaning mind," and hence presumably be guilty of "willfully" dealing in firearms without a license, if he knew that his street-corner transactions violated New York City's business licensing or sales tax ordinances. (For that matter, it ought to suffice if Bryan knew that the car out of which he sold the guns was illegally double-parked, or if, in order to meet the appointed time for the sale, he intentionally violated Pennsylvania's speed limit on the drive back from the gun purchase in Ohio.) Once we stop focusing on the conduct the defendant is actually charged with (*i.e.,* selling guns without a license), I see no principled way to determine *what* law the defendant must be conscious of violating.

Congress is free, of course, to make criminal liability under one statute turn on knowledge of another, to use its firearms dealer statutes to encourage compliance with New York City's tax collection efforts, and to put judges and juries through the kind of mental gymnastics described above. But these are strange results, and I would not lightly assume that Congress intended to make liability under a federal criminal statute depend so heavily upon the vagaries of local law – particularly local law dealing with completely unrelated subjects. If we must have a presumption in cases like this one, I think it would be more reasonable to presume that, when Congress makes ignorance of the law a defense to a criminal prohibition, it ordinarily means ignorance of the unlawfulness of the specific conduct punished *by that criminal prohibition*.

That is the meaning we have given the word "willfully" in other contexts where we have concluded it requires knowledge of the law. *See, e.g., Ratzlaf*, 510 U.S. at 149 ("To convict Ratzlaf of the crime with which he was charged, . . . the jury had to find he knew the structuring in which he engaged was unlawful"); *Cheek v. United States*, 498 U.S. 192, 201 ("The standard for the statutory willfulness requirement is the 'voluntary, intentional violation of a known legal duty.' . . . The issue is whether the defendant knew of the duty purportedly imposed by the provision of the statute or regulation he is accused of violating"). The Court explains these cases on the ground that they involved "highly technical statutes that presented the danger of ensnaring individuals engaged in apparently innocent conduct." That is no explanation at all. The complexity of the tax and currency laws may explain why the Court interpreted "willful" to require some awareness of illegality, as opposed to merely "an act which is intentional, or knowing, or voluntary, as distinguished from accidental." But it *in no way* justifies the distinction the Court seeks to draw today between knowledge of the law the defendant is actually charged with violating and knowledge of *any* law the defendant could conceivably be charged with violating. * * *

* * * It is common ground that the statutory context here requires some awareness of the law for a § 924(a)(1)(D) conviction, but the statute is simply ambiguous, or silent, as to the precise contours of that *mens rea* requirement. In the face of that ambiguity, I would invoke the rule that "'ambiguity concerning the ambit of criminal statutes should be resolved in favor of lenity.'"

> The rule that penal laws are to be construed strictly, is, perhaps, not much less old than construction itself. It is founded on the tenderness of the law for the rights of individuals; and on the plain principle that the power of punishment is vested in the legislative, not in the judicial department.

In our era of multiplying new federal crimes, there is more reason than ever to give this ancient canon of construction consistent application: by fostering uniformity in the interpretation of criminal statutes, it will reduce the occasions on which this Court will have to produce judicial havoc by resolving in defendants' favor a circuit conflict regarding the substantive elements of a federal crime.

I respectfully dissent.

3.   Fair Notice and Due Process (the *Lambert* Exception)

LAMBERT v. CALIFORNIA
Supreme Court of the United States
355 U.S. 225, 78 S.Ct. 240, 2 L.Ed.2d 228 (1957)

MR. JUSTICE DOUGLAS delivered the opinion of the Court.

Section 52.38 (a) of the Los Angeles Municipal Code defines "convicted person" as follows:

> Any person who, subsequent to January 1, 1921, has been or hereafter is convicted of an offense punishable as a felony in the State of California, or who has been or who is hereafter convicted of any offense in any place other than the State of California, which offense, if committed in the State of California, would have been punishable as a felony.

Section 52.39 provides that it shall be unlawful for "any convicted person" to be or remain in Los Angeles for a period of more than five days without registering; it requires any person having a place of abode outside the city to register if he comes into the city on five occasions or more during a 30-day period; and it prescribes the information to be furnished the Chief of Police on registering. Section 52.43 (b) makes the failure to register a continuing offense, each day's failure constituting a separate offense.

Appellant, arrested on suspicion of another offense, was charged with a violation of this registration law. The evidence showed that she had been at the time of her arrest a resident of Los Angeles for over seven years. Within that period she had been convicted in Los Angeles of the crime of forgery, an offense which California punishes as a felony. Though convicted of a crime punishable as a felony, she had not at the time of her arrest registered under the Municipal Code. At the trial, appellant asserted that §52.39 of the Code denies her due process of law and other rights under the Federal Constitution, unnecessary to enumerate. The trial court denied this objection. The case was tried to a jury which found appellant guilty. The court fined her $250 and placed her on probation for three years. * * * The case is here on appeal.* * * [W]e now hold that the registration provisions of the Code as sought to be applied here violate the Due Process requirement of the Fourteenth Amendment.

The registration provision, carrying criminal penalties, applies if a person has been convicted "of an offense punishable as a felony in the State of California" or, in case he has been convicted in another State, if the offense "would have been punishable as a felony" had it been committed in California. No element of willfulness is by terms included in the ordinance nor read into it by the California court as a condition necessary for a conviction.

We must assume that appellant had no actual knowledge of the requirement that she register under this ordinance, as she offered proof of this defense which was refused. The question is whether a registration act of this character violates due process where it is applied to a person who has no actual knowledge of his duty to register, and where no showing is made of the probability of such knowledge.

We do not go with Blackstone in saying that "a vicious will" is necessary to constitute a crime, for conduct alone without regard to the intent of the doer is often sufficient. There is wide latitude in the lawmakers to declare an offense and to exclude elements of knowledge and diligence from its definition. But we deal here with conduct that is wholly passive – mere failure to register. It is unlike the commission of acts, or the failure to act under circumstances that should alert the doer to the consequences of his deed. The rule that "ignorance of the law will not excuse" is deep in our law, as is the principle that of all the powers of local government, the police power is "one of the least limitable." On the other hand, due process places some limits on its exercise. Engrained in our concept of due process is the requirement of notice. Notice is sometimes essential so that the citizen has the chance to defend charges. Notice is required before property interests are disturbed, before assessments are made, before penalties are assessed. Notice is required in a myriad of situations where a penalty or forfeiture might be suffered for mere failure to act. * * *

Registration laws are common and their range is wide. Many such laws are akin to licensing statutes in that they pertain to the regulation of business activities. But the present ordinance is entirely different. Violation of its provisions is unaccompanied by any activity whatever, mere presence in the city being the test. Moreover, circumstances which might move one to inquire as to the necessity of registration are completely lacking. At most the ordinance is but a law enforcement technique designed for the convenience of law enforcement agencies through which a list of the names and addresses of felons then residing in a given community is compiled. The disclosure is merely a compilation of former convictions already publicly recorded in the jurisdiction where obtained.

Nevertheless, this appellant on first becoming aware of her duty to register was given no opportunity to comply with the law and avoid its penalty, even though her default was entirely innocent. She could but suffer the consequences of the ordinance, namely, conviction with the imposition of heavy criminal penalties thereunder. We believe that actual knowledge of the duty to register or proof of the probability of such knowledge and subsequent failure to comply are necessary before a conviction under the ordinance can stand. As Holmes wrote in The Common Law, "A law which punished conduct which would not be blameworthy in the average member of the community would be too severe for that community to bear." Its severity lies in the absence of an opportunity either to avoid the consequences of the law or to defend any prosecution brought under it. Where a person did not know of the duty to register and where there was no proof of the probability of such knowledge, he may not be convicted consistently with due process. Were it otherwise, the evil would be as great as it is when the law is written in print too fine to read or in a language foreign to the community.

Reversed.

MR. JUSTICE FRANKFURTER, whom MR. JUSTICE HARLAN and MR. JUSTICE WHITTAKER join, dissenting.

The present laws of the United States and of the forty-eight States are thick with provisions that command that some things not be done and others be done, although persons convicted under such provisions may have had no awareness of what the law required or that what they did was wrongdoing. The body of decisions sustaining such legislation, including innumerable registration laws, is almost as voluminous as the legislation itself. The matter is summarized in *United States v. Balint*: "Many instances of this are to be found in regulatory measures in the exercise of what is called the police power where the emphasis of the statute is evidently upon achievement of some social betterment rather than the punishment of the crimes as in cases of *mala in se*."

Surely there can hardly be a difference as a matter of fairness, of hardship, or of justice, if one may invoke it, between the case of a person wholly innocent of wrongdoing, in the sense that he was not remotely conscious of violating any law, who is imprisoned for five years for conduct relating to narcotics, and the case of another person who is placed on probation for three years on condition that she pay $250, for failure, as a local resident, convicted under local law of a felony, to register under a law passed as an exercise of the State's "police power." * * *

STATE V. BRYANT

Court of Appeals of North Carolina
594 S.E.2d 202 (N.C. Ct. App. 2004)

GEER, Judge.

Defendant Roy Eugene Bryant, formerly a resident of South Carolina, appeals from his conviction for failure to register in North Carolina as a sex offender when he moved to this State from South Carolina. He also appeals from his conviction as a habitual felon. We hold that North Carolina's sex offender registration statute is unconstitutional as applied to an out-of-state offender who lacked notice of his duty to register upon moving to North Carolina. We therefore reverse defendant's convictions.

Facts

On 19 November 1991, in Pickens County, South Carolina, defendant pled guilty to third degree criminal sexual conduct and was sentenced to a term of ten years imprisonment. Prior to his 9 April 2000 release from the custody of the South Carolina Department of Corrections, defendant signed a "Notice of Sex Offender Registry" form. On the form, he indicated that he would be living with his mother in Greenville, South Carolina. On 17 August 2000, defendant completed a registration form notifying authorities that he had moved to Pickens County, South Carolina.

In the fall of 2000, defendant was working with a traveling fair. While the fair was in Winston-Salem, North Carolina, defendant suffered a broken jaw. After being treated at a hospital, defendant chose to remain in Winston-Salem rather than moving on with the fair. In November 2000, defendant moved in with a woman he had met at the fair and lived with her at 4373 Grove Avenue in Winston-Salem.

On 30 March 2001, Kelly Wilkinson, a detective with the Winston-Salem Police Department, had occasion to perform a check of defendant's criminal record. She discovered that defendant was registered as a sex offender in South Carolina, but was not registered in North Carolina. During an interview at the police department, defendant told the detective that his address was currently 4373 Grove Avenue in Winston-Salem.

On 2 April 2001, Wilkinson contacted Sharon Reid, the deputy sheriff with the Forsyth County Sheriff's Department responsible for maintaining the county's sex offender registry, and notified her that defendant was a convicted sex offender who was not registered in North Carolina. After verifying this information, Reid determined that the offense for which defendant was convicted in South Carolina had a statutory equivalent in North Carolina that would trigger the duty to register. Defendant was then arrested and indicted for failure to register as a sex offender. He was subsequently also indicted for having attained the status of habitual felon.

Prior to trial, defendant filed a motion seeking a declaration that the North Carolina sex offender registration statute's failure to provide out-of-state persons with notice of the duty to register in North Carolina violated defendant's equal protection and due process rights under the Fourteenth Amendment of the United States Constitution. Following the trial court's denial of the motion, a jury found defendant guilty as to both the failure to register and habitual felon charges. The trial court sentenced defendant to 133 to 169 months imprisonment.

Discussion

Defendant assigns as error the trial court's denial of his motion to declare N.C. Gen.Stat. Chapter 14, Article 27A unconstitutional as applied to residents of other states who move to North Carolina. Defendant's central argument is that the statutory scheme, which imposes a duty to register with county authorities on certain sex offenders, violates the right to due process of out-of-state residents who move to North Carolina by allowing them to be convicted of the offense without notice of the duty to register.

N.C. Gen.Stat. § 14-208.7 establishes a duty to register for certain sex offenders who reside within North Carolina, as well as those who move into North Carolina from other states:

> A person who is a State resident and who has a reportable conviction shall be required to maintain registration with the sheriff of the county where the person resides. If the person moves to North Carolina from outside this State, the person shall register within 10 days of establishing residence in this State, or whenever the person has been present in the State for 15 days, whichever comes first.

A person required to register must notify the sheriff of the county with whom the person last registered of any change of address within ten days. Failure to comply with the registration and change-of-address provisions is a felony:

> (a) A person required by this Article to register who does any of the following is guilty of a Class F felony:

(1) Fails to register.

(2) Fails to notify the last registering sheriff of a change of address.

With respect to in-state sex offenders, the statute provides that a prison official shall notify the offender of the duty to register at least ten days, but not more than 30 days, before the offender is due to be released from a penal institution. The statute contains no provision for notification of sex offenders moving to North Carolina from another state of North Carolina's registration requirements.

This Court has previously held that the registration statute "has no requirement of knowledge or intent, so as to require that the State prove either [a] defendant knew he was in violation of or intended to violate the statute when he failed to register his change of address." Nevertheless, as this Court observed in *Young*, "although ignorance of the law is no excuse, and the statute at issue does not require the State to prove intent, due process requires that [a] defendant have knowledge, actual or constructive, of the statutory requirements before he can be charged with its violation."

The *Young* Court based its holding on *Lambert v. California.* * * *

This Court observed in *Young* that "in line with due process notice requirements, our Legislature has written the [sex offender registration] statute such that it mandates a convicted sex offender be notified of the registration requirements. Under ordinary circumstances such a provision would work to remove the statute from due process notice attacks." The Court further held, however: "N.C. Gen.Stat. § 14-208.11 does not provide adequate notice for an incompetent sex offender to comply with the statute's requirements. Due process requires not just the mechanical act of notifying a defendant or the automatic assumption that the notice is good, but in fact, we believe due process requires that notice be synonymous with the ability to comply."

This Court reasoned that although Young, who had been adjudicated incompetent, was provided with sufficient notice of the registration requirement to satisfy due process for any reasonable and prudent man, Young was not a reasonable and prudent man. Therefore, what constituted "actual notice" to a reasonable and prudent man was not sufficient notice to Young.

Under *Young*, the question presented by this appeal is whether Article 27A of the General Statutes, although sufficient to supply notice to reasonable and prudent residents of North Carolina "[u]nder ordinary circumstances," provides adequate notice for due process purposes to offenders moving into

North Carolina from other states. To comply with *Lambert* and *Young*, due process requires either a showing of actual or constructive notice.

We first observe that defendant was not given actual notice of his duty to register by North Carolina authorities. The North Carolina sex offender registration statute lacks any provision for providing notice of the registration duty to new residents; its notice provisions are limited to defendants who are convicted in North Carolina courts and released from North Carolina prisons. In contrast, other states employ various procedures designed to notify new residents who are sex offenders of their duty to register. * * *

Young and *Lambert*, however, both recognize that even in the absence of statutorily required notification, a defendant may have received sufficient notice through other means to comply with due process. The State contends that defendant received notice in South Carolina of his obligation to register in any new state to which he moved. We do not believe that South Carolina's notification procedures, as they existed during the pertinent time period, were sufficient to give defendant notice that he was required to register in North Carolina.

The State's witness Michael Stobbe, an employee with the Inmates Records Section of the South Carolina Department of Corrections ("SCDOC"), testified that a "Notice of Sex Offender Registry" form is routinely used to notify inmates being released from SCDOC custody of their duty to register. The inmate signs and dates the form, and an employee witnesses the form. In this case, the form was duly signed by defendant on 20 March 2000. The form stated, in pertinent part:

> Pursuant to Section 23-3-430 of [the] Code of Laws of South Carolina, any person who has been convicted, pled guilty or nolo contendere of offenses deemed sexual in nature must register with the Sheriff's Office in their county of residence....

> Inmates being released from the South Carolina Department of Corrections at the completion of their sentence to any early release program, to community supervision, or upon parole must register with the Sheriff's Office in their county of residence within 24 hours of release.

> If an inmate who is required to register moves out of the State of South Carolina, s/he is required to provide written notice to the county sheriff where s/he was last registered in South Carolina within 10 days of the change of address to a new state.

A person must send written notice of change of address to the county Sheriff's Office in the new county and the county where s/he previously resided within 10 days of moving to a new residence. Any person required to register under this program shall be required to register annually for life.

The form specified that defendant had been informed orally and in writing that he was required to "abide by the registry conditions set forth in Title 23, Chapter 3, Article 7 [of the South Carolina Code]." There was no reference to the laws of any other state.

With respect to offenders moving out of South Carolina to another state, SCDOC's "Notice of Sex Offender Registry" form gives clear notice only of a duty to report the move to the Sheriff's Office in the former county of residence. Although in addition to requiring that notice, the form contains a separate paragraph referring to a duty to inform the Sheriff's Office in "the new county," the form is ambiguous as to whether "the new county" means only a county within South Carolina or also applies to counties within a new state.

This form should be construed with reference to the statute on which it is modeled, which provides:

> If any person required to register under this article changes his address into another county in South Carolina, the person must register with the county sheriff in the new county within ten days of establishing the new residence. The person must also provide written notice within ten days of the change of address in the previous county to the county sheriff with whom the person last registered.

S.C.Code Ann. § 23-3-460. The statute contains no like provision for moves outside South Carolina. The statute thus suggests that the "the new county" referred to in the form means a new county within South Carolina. In order to find notice, we would have to conclude that an offender in South Carolina would construe a form in a manner inconsistent with the statute on which it was based. We are unwilling to do so.

Although *Young* and *White* hold that notice may also be received orally, the record contains no indication that defendant had been told by anyone of his need to register in any state to which he moved. Stobbe admitted that he did not know whether anyone read the form to defendant. The form, in any event, states only that defendant was orally advised of the requirement that he comply with South Carolina law. Detective Wilkinson, who interviewed defendant in March 2001, testified only that when she asked defendant, "Why have you not bothered to register in the State of North Carolina?" he "had no real answer for that" -- a response arguably consistent with a lack of knowledge. Detective Wilkinson acknowledged that defendant never gave any indication that he knew he had to register in North Carolina.

The State alternatively contends that defendant had constructive notice of his duty to register. The State argues, citing a New York trial court decision, *People v. Patterson*, that sex offender registration laws are so pervasive that defendant must have known that he was required to register in other states. The court observed in *Patterson* that "[a]s time goes on and these State laws lose their novelty, it will be increasingly difficult to say that sex offenders do not have fair warning that sex offender registration laws exist, even in the absence of mandatory individual notice requirements like those set out in [the New York statute]." We do not, however, believe that mere knowledge that most states have registration requirements is sufficient today to establish knowledge that an offender must register in states other than the one in which he was originally convicted. * * *

We note that had South Carolina officials complied with the mandate of 42 U.S.C. § 14071(b)(1)(A)(iii), or had the North Carolina legislature enacted a provision requiring state officials to inform new residents with reportable convictions of their duty to register, this defendant's due process argument would likely have failed. As written, our current sex offender registration statute does not adequately address the reality of our mobile society, in which people frequently move across state lines. Our General Assembly should revisit this statute to provide a procedure enabling the State to ensure that convicted sex offenders who move to North Carolina from another state comply with North Carolina's registration requirements.

We hold that N.C. Gen.Stat. § 14-208.11 is unconstitutional as applied to a person convicted in another state who has moved to North Carolina and lacks notice of his duty to register in North Carolina. Defendant's conviction under N.C. Gen.Stat. § 14-208.11 must, therefore, be reversed. As defendant's habitual felon conviction was dependent on that conviction, it too must be reversed. Because of our disposition of this matter, we need not address defendant's remaining assignments of error.

Reversed.

Chapter 6

CAUSATION AND CONCURRENCE

A.   CAUSATION

The third basic element of a crime is the causation requirement.[a] Causation is actually part of the actus reus requirement. Recall that the actus reus consists of (1) a voluntary act (or omission when the defendant has a legal duty to act) that (2) *causes* (3) the social harm. Because causation analysis can become quite complicated, courts tend to treat causation as a separate element of the crime.

It is important not to confuse causation as it is defined and dealt with in tort law with causation as it is defined and dealt with in criminal law. "Because of the higher stakes in the criminal law, and its especially strong commitment to personal, rather than vicarious, responsibility, some courts expressly provide that a tort conception of causation is insufficient to impose criminal responsibility. Instead, a stricter test, requiring a closer connection between the defendant's conduct and the resulting harm, may be applied."[b]

Two types of causation must be proven to establish criminal liability. First, the defendant's conduct must be an actual or but-for cause of the social harm. Second, the defendant's conduct must be the proximate or legal cause of the social harm.

---

[a]As mentioned in an earlier chapter, not all crimes require a causal link between the actus reus and the social harm. Causation is namely required for result crimes (crimes which are defined in terms of a prohibited result), but not for conduct crimes (crimes which are defined in terms of prohibited conduct). Joshua Dressler, UNDERSTANDING CRIMINAL LAW §9.10[D] (3d ed. 2001). For example, proof that the defendant's act or omission caused the social harm is required for the crime of murder which is defined in terms of a prohibited result (the death of a human being). Causation, however, is not an element of the crime of speeding, which is defined in terms of prohibited conduct (driving over the speed limit).

[b] Joshua Dressler, UNDERSTANDING CRIMINAL LAW § 14.01[C] (3d ed. 2001).

1.   Actual (or "But For") Causation

The first inquiry a court makes is whether the defendant is an actual cause (a.k.a. cause-in-fact or "but for" cause) of the social harm. Many different factors may have caused the social harm. The actual cause inquiry merely determines whether the defendant's conduct (or omission) is one of those causal factors. It narrows down the field of actors who might be held criminally liable for the social harm.

In order to determine whether the defendant is an actual cause of the social harm, courts apply the "but for" test. Under this test, the court asks, "But for D's voluntary act (or omission where D had a duty to act), would the social harm have occurred *when it did*?" If the answer to this question is "no" (without D's conduct, the social harm would not have occurred when it did), then D is an actual cause.

2.   Proximate Causation

The second inquiry a court makes is whether the defendant was the proximate cause of the social harm. The defendant must be both an actual cause and the proximate cause (and perform a voluntary act with the requisite mens rea) in order to be found criminally liable.

At base, the proximate cause inquiry is an examination into the question whether it is fair and just to hold the defendant criminally liable. There are no hard and fast rules governing this inquiry. Generally speaking, when the defendant's conduct is the direct cause of the social harm (when there are no intervening causes), courts tend to find that it is fair and just to hold the defendant criminally liable for the resulting harm. When intervening causes (acts or events that come after the defendant's act but before the social harm and also contribute causally to the social harm) are present, many courts apply intervening cause analysis to decide whether to hold the defendant criminally liable.

Intervening cause analysis differs depending on whether the intervening cause is characterized as a dependent (or responsive) intervening cause or an independent (or coincidental) intervening cause. A dependent intervening cause is one that is dependent upon or responsive to the defendant's voluntary act. An independent intervening cause is one that is independent of or coincidental to the defendant's voluntary act. If the intervening cause is dependent, the general rule is that the defendant is the proximate cause unless the intervening cause is extremely unusual or bizarre. If the intervening cause is independent, the defendant is generally relieved of criminal liability (i.e., not the proximate cause) unless the intervening cause is foreseeable. Sometimes courts simply focus on the foreseeability of the social harm, as opposed to the foreseeability of the intervening cause.

When courts are uncomfortable with the result obtained through intervening cause analysis they may rely on other factors when deciding whether to hold the defendant criminally liable as the proximate cause. As you read the cases in this chapter, think about what other factors seem to influence courts deciding causation cases.

COMMONWEALTH v. REMENTER
Superior Court of Pennsylvania
410 Pa. Super. 9, 598 A.2d 1300 (Super. Ct. 1991)

BECK, J.

On April 19, 1989, the decedent Mary Berry was crushed to death beneath the wheels of a passer-by's automobile while attempting to escape from an ongoing assault by her boyfriend, appellant Charles Rementer. Appellant was charged with having caused the death of Mary Berry and was convicted of murder in the third degree[a] at a non-jury trial. He appeals from the judgment of sentence which was imposed after the denial of post-verdict motions. He raises two primary challenges to his conviction. Appellant first argues that the evidence at trial was insufficient to prove that his conduct caused the death of the victim. He also alleges that the Commonwealth failed to prove malice, an essential element of third degree murder. We affirm.

Appellant's conviction for third degree murder arose from events which occurred during the early evening hours of April 19, 1989 in Philadelphia. On that evening, at about 6:30 p.m., the decedent Berry and appellant entered a bar together at 7th and Oregon. The bartender serving them, who had known Berry for many years, noted that Berry and appellant were arguing, although the bartender could not discern the substance of the argument. During the argument Berry became "very upset" and was "crying hysterical[ly]."

---

[a]Under Pennsylvania law, murder in the first degree is an intentional killing, punishable by death or life imprisonment. Murder in the second degree is one committed while the defendant is engaged in the perpetration of a felony (i.e., the felony murder rule) and is punishable by life imprisonment. Murder in the third degree encompasses all other kinds of murder, and is punishable by up to 40 years in prison. *See* 18 Pa. Cons. Stat. §§ 1102, 2502.

Shortly thereafter, Berry left the bar and got into her cab, which was parked outside and which she drove for a living. A moment later, appellant followed her, got into the driver's side where Berry was sitting, shoved her into the passenger's seat and drove away.

An out-of-town trucker, Brent Murphy, was taking a break from loading his truck a few blocks from the bar when he saw Berry's cab. Berry was hanging out of the passenger window, screaming "Help me, he's trying to kill me." The driver of the cab, identified as appellant, was holding on to Berry, beating her and pulling her hair. Berry, by "fighting and kicking", had managed to get one leg out of the passenger window, but all the while appellant was "trying to pull her back in by her hair."

While Murphy watched, Berry struggled away from appellant and fell out of the passenger window. Appellant also left the car and continued the assault on Berry, beating her "with his fists in the face" while she was lying on the ground. Murphy ran into a nearby supermarket and told somebody to call the police. When he emerged from the store, appellant was holding Berry against the cab while he continued to beat her. Murphy heard Berry say, "Don't hurt me, Charlie." Appellant pulled Berry into the cab, held her down, shut the door and drove away. About ten minutes later, a short distance away, Murphy saw the police. Berry was dead and the police had been summoned. Murphy explained to the police what he had witnessed moments earlier.

Meanwhile, three young men were standing at a nearby intersection. One of them, David Brotnitsky, saw appellant and Berry standing and arguing under the bridge of the I-95 on-ramp. Berry's cab was parked nearby on Water Street. Appellant punched Berry in the face and Berry ran away from him. Appellant pursued her, grabbed her and dragged her back to the cab. At first, appellant threw Berry in the back seat but she again managed to escape. Appellant then "got out after her and threw her in the front seat." Thinking that the fight was over, Brotnitsky stopped paying attention. The next thing he noticed was that the police had arrived on Water Street to investigate Berry's death.

Another witness, John Smith, was driving towards Water Street when he saw Berry's cab moving slow[ly] along the curb with the passenger door open. Smith yelled and asked the occupants what was going on. Just then, Berry ran from the cab towards Smith's car shouting unintelligible pleas for help. Another occupant of Smith's car suggested finding a police officer. As he pulled away Smith saw Berry in the rear view mirror. She was lying on the street and a station wagon was driving away "from her body."

Joseph Campbell was also in the vicinity when he saw "Charlie," whom he recognized from the neighborhood, and Berry fighting and arguing. Berry was shouting for help and running from appellant. Campbell saw appellant punch Berry in the head. Berry then ran towards oncoming cars, finally stopping at a station wagon. From where he was standing a short distance away, Campbell saw Berry grab on to the window of the station wagon and then fall. No more than two minutes passed from the time Campbell saw appellant strike Berry in the face to the time she fell beneath the wheels of the station wagon to her death.

The station wagon referred to by Smith and Campbell was driven by Vito Michielli. Michielli and his wife and two small children were on Water Street that evening driving home from a shopping trip. Berry and appellant approached his car forcing him to stop. Berry was screaming "help me" and "let me in" and attempted to open the back door of the station wagon. Michielli and his wife were frightened and the children began to cry. The Michiellis' reaction was to lock all the doors and attempt to close the windows of the car. Mr. Michielli reached out of his window, pushed Berry away and sped off. Not until several days later, when a local newspaper reported the incident and Berry's tragic death, did Michielli realize that in leaving the scene his car had run over Berry.

Michielli's wife also testified. She said that she first saw Berry running up the middle of the street toward their car. Mrs. Michielli stated that appellant was chasing her and that when they reached the Michiellis' car, he was "right behind her." Berry went over to the driver's side of the station wagon and appellant went to the passenger side. Mrs. Michielli saw Berry reach in to open the rear door of the car and heard her scream, "Help me, Help me, please let me in." Mr. Michielli pushed Berry away from the car and immediately drove off. Mrs. Michielli was also unaware at the time that the incident had ended with Berry's death.

The medical examiner's report revealed that Berry had suffered "blunt head trauma consistent with direct blows to the face, recent contusions to the chin, right and left cheeks near the nose and contused lacerations to the upper and lower lips, on the inside of the mouth." The medical examiner also found that Berry sustained a crush injury of the chest," consistent with a motor vehicle passing over the body." There were also fractures of the skull and of the ribs. The coroner's report, as stipulated to by the parties at trial, concluded that the crush injury was the cause of death. Finally, the Mobile Crime Unit discovered a large clump of Berry's hair inside the cab, which had been forcibly pulled from Berry's head.

At trial, appellant testified on his own behalf. He stated that both he and Berry had injected cocaine earlier on the day of her death. He testified that they were arguing and that they had also been drinking. Appellant stated that he drove Berry's cab out of concern for her welfare because she was "acting schizy from the cocaine." According to appellant, Berry's pleas for help were entirely unprovoked by him. He said that he pulled her back into the cab to prevent her from hurting herself and from "making a scene." Appellant admitted striking Berry but claimed that he did so out of anger because his attempts to calm her down by talking rationally had failed. He also claimed that he hit her only once, did not mean to hurt her and did not intend to kill her.

The trial court found appellant guilty of murder in the third degree. Following the denial of post-trial motions, appellant was sentenced to a term of imprisonment of four to twelve years. On appeal he argues that the Commonwealth failed to present sufficient evidence to establish two essential elements of third degree murder, i.e., causation and malice. We will address each challenge separately. * * *

[I]t is undisputed that causation constitutes an essential element of the offense of murder which the Commonwealth must prove beyond a reasonable doubt. * * * The issue regarding causation plainly arises in the instant case because the immediate cause of Berry's death was the crushing blow received under the wheels of Michielli's station wagon. Appellant argues that by the time Berry ran over to Michielli's car the "unfortunate domestic dispute" had ended and that therefore Berry's death had an accidental and intervening cause. Thus, according to appellant, the chain of causation between his assault on Berry and her resulting death had been broken. As such, he argues, his actions did not constitute a sufficiently direct cause of Berry's death. Moreover, appellant argues that Berry's death was not foreseeable and stemmed not from his assault but from independent actions by Berry for which he, appellant, cannot be held culpable. We reject these claims.

Certain fundamental principles guide our inquiry. First, it is well established that the tort theory of causation will not suffice to impose criminal responsibility. This principle was first explicitly adopted by the supreme court in *Commonwealth v. Root* which held that ". . . the accused is not guilty unless his conduct was a cause of death sufficiently direct as to meet the requirements of the *criminal*, and not the *tort*, law." The *Root* court explained: "Legal theory which makes guilt or innocence of criminal homicide depend upon such accidental and fortuitous circumstances as are now embraced by modern tort law's encompassing concept of proximate cause is too harsh to be just." Thus, a "more direct causal connection is required for conviction."

It is difficult to draw a bright line between causation in the criminal law and in the tort law. Certain principles can, however, be ascertained. In order to impose criminal liability, causation must be direct and substantial. Defendants should not be exposed to a loss of liberty based on the tort standard which only provides that the event giving rise to the injury is a substantial factor. Although typically the tort context refers only to substantial and not to direct and substantial as in the criminal context, the additional language in the criminal law does not provide much guidance. Therefore, criminal causation has come to involve a case-by-case social determination; i.e., is it just or fair under the facts of the case to expose the defendant to criminal sanctions. In other words, was the defendant's conduct so directly and substantially linked to the actual result as to give rise to the imposition of criminal liability or was the actual result so remote and attenuated that it would be unfair to hold the defendant responsible for it?

Many cases have grappled with the concept of what constitutes a legally sufficient causal connection where, as here, the immediate cause of death was not the blow dealt by the defendant's hand. We have concluded, from a careful reading of these cases and from analysis provided by criminal law commentators, that the resolution of the causation issue here and in analogous cases involves a two part inquiry. The first part of the inquiry requires us to decide whether the defendant's conduct was an operative cause of the victim's death. With respect to establishing a causal relationship between conduct and result, our crimes code poses a threshold factual requirement and that is, the conduct must be "an antecedent but for which the result in question would not have occurred." Thus, if the victim's death is attributable *entirely* to other factors and not at all brought about by the defendant's conduct, no causal connection exists and no criminal liability for the result can attach. The second part of the test raises the question of whether the result of defendant's actions were so extraordinarily remote or attenuated that it would be unfair to hold the defendant criminally responsible.

In discussing the first part of the test we point out that the defendant's conduct need not be the sole cause of the victim's death in order to establish causal connection. In *Commonwealth v. Skufca,* a parent left two small children trapped inside a locked apartment while she went out for the evening. A fire started which suffocated the children who were impossible to rescue due to their mother's action in locking them inside an unattended apartment. Suffocation through smoke inhalation was the immediate medical cause of death. In upholding the involuntary manslaughter conviction of the parent, the supreme court emphasized:

> [I]t has never been the law of this Commonwealth that criminal responsibility must be confined to a sole or immediate cause of death . . . . Criminal responsibility is properly assessed against one whose conduct was a direct and substantial factor in

producing the death even though other factors combined with that conduct to achieve the result.

* * * In *Commonwealth v. Cheeks,* the victim was stabbed in the abdomen by the defendant during a robbery. The stabbing necessitated an operation which resulted in complications including abdominal distention. As a result of the victim's post-operative condition, tubes were inserted through the victim's nostrils and into his stomach. The victim was disoriented, uncooperative and confused and pulled out the tubes on several occasions. Finally, he pulled out a tube, gagged and asphyxiated. The defendant in *Cheeks* argued that the stab wound was not the cause of death and that the victim's own actions had intervened as an independent act of causation. The supreme court disagreed. The court found that "the fact that the stabbing was not the immediate cause of death is not controlling." The stabbing was an operative link in a chain of events which resulted in the victim's death. The court saw defendant's conduct as the cause which necessarily triggered the series of events which ended in the victim's death.

However, causation-in-fact, the "but for" element of assessing the causal connection, alone will not necessarily determine criminal culpability.[4] If it did, little would distinguish tort liability from criminal liability. Our cases emphasize that a criminal conviction requires "a more direct causal connection" than tort concepts. Thus not only do we demand that the defendant's conduct actually cause the victim's death in that "it is an antecedent but for which the result in question would not have occurred," we also question, in cases such as the instant one, whether the fatal result was so extraordinary, remote or attenuated that it would be unfair to hold the defendant criminally responsible for it.

In our view, it is this second prong of the causation inquiry which is in fact at issue when our cases impose a "stricter" or "more direct" test for criminal causation than is needed for tort liability. Thus, the defendant's conduct must bear a direct and substantial relationship to the fatal result in order to impose criminal culpability. Put another way, if the fatal result was an unnatural or

---

[4]In explaining the inadequacy of the but-for inquiry in assessing ultimate criminal liability, the comments to the Model Penal Code use the following illustration to demonstrate a causal connection which might satisfy the but-for test but which, due to remoteness of result, would not constitute legally sufficient causation:
For example, if the defendant attempted to shoot his wife, with the result that she retired to her parents' country home and died there from falling off a horse, no one would think that he should be held guilty for murder, though he did intend her death and his attempt to kill her was a but-for cause of her encounter with the horse. ***

obscure consequence of the defendant's actions, our sense of justice would prevent us from allowing the result to impact on the defendant's guilt.

This concept is often addressed in terms of foreseeability. For instance, in *Commonwealth v. Skufca*, in which a parent was held to have legally caused the death of her children who died of smoke inhalation after being trapped in a room by their mother, the court noted: "Although suffocation due to the fire was the immediate cause of the children's death, appellant's unlawful conduct in leaving them locked in the room, without supervision, for several hours, susceptible to numerous foreseeable dangers, was the legal cause of their death." * * *

In *Commonwealth v. Lang*, this court found that a police officer's death during a high speed pursuit of a fleeing defendant on a motorcycle was a "foreseeable" and direct consequence of the defendant's conduct and "not a fortuitous or coincidental event." In *Lang*, we found that "[the defendant] knew or should have known that his actions, speeding and attempting to elude arrest, were likely to result in injury to someone: either to himself, to some innocent third party, or to the pursuing police officer."

In contrast to the above-cited and similar cases, is *Commonwealth v. Colvin* wherein the actual result was so remote and fortuitous that it must be said to have no bearing on the defendant's culpability. In *Colvin*, this court reversed an involuntary manslaughter conviction due to insufficiency of evidence on causation. In that case, the defendant threw a stone at a house, breaking a window. The noise the mischief made was heard by only one member of the household. That person immediately informed his mother, who had not heard the stone hit the house, about what had just happened and the mother collapsed and died. Implicit in the court's finding that the causal connection was not "direct" enough, is an appreciation that the fatal result was so remote and attenuated from the risks hazarded by the defendant's unlawful conduct in throwing the stone, that it had no "bearing on the liability of the actor or on the gravity of his offense."

In light of the foregoing principles, we examine appellant's claim that the evidence at trial was insufficient to establish the necessary causal connection between his conduct and Berry's resulting death. Appellant first contends that the argument he was having with Berry was over by the time she approached Michielli's car for aid and that, therefore, her actions in seeking refuge in the station wagon cannot be attributed to him. Berry's actions were not provoked by his assault but were spontaneous and unrelated to the "earlier dispute," appellant argues, and therefore, his conduct cannot be said to have caused her death.

This argument that there was no dispute occurring at the time Berry ran to Michielli's car is belied by considerable evidence which, when viewed in the

light most favorable to the Commonwealth, establishes quite the contrary. As described above, several witnesses testified to the ferocity and tenacity of appellant's assault on Berry and all the observations attested to occurred within minutes of Berry's death. Campbell testified that he saw Berry shouting and running for help. He said appellant punched Berry in the head no more than two minutes before she fell to her death beneath the wheels of the car. Smith, Campbell and the Michiellis all testified that Berry's actions right up until the instant of her death were accompanied by cries for help, a fact which completely refutes appellant's claim that her actions were not taken in response to his conduct. Finally, Mrs. Michielli stated that when Berry approached their car, appellant was chasing her and was right behind her. Appellant's contention that the "dispute" had ended is wholly without support in the record.

Appellant further argues that Berry's death occurred through such an unforeseeable chain of events that his conduct cannot be said to have caused the fatal result. We disagree. The evidence at trial plainly established that appellant subjected Berry to a brutal and persistent assault from which she continually attempted to escape. In the first place, it is completely natural and foreseeable that any victim of an assault would respond to the danger by trying to escape it. In fact, it is difficult to imagine behavior which is more responsive or more predictable than fleeing from a deadly assault. Moreover, Berry's actions were particularly likely in the context of the instant case. Berry was clearly intent upon escaping her assailant at any cost and attempted to do so repeatedly. She tried climbing out of the car window, only to be beaten and pulled back into the car. She ran away from appellant twice after that and each time was violently forced back into the car by appellant. Just before Berry escaped for the last, and fatal, time, the cab was seen moving along the street with the passenger door open. The risk that Berry might suffer serious injury or death either during the assault or in her attempt to avoid it, was inherent in the situation appellant's attack created. In our view, the fatal result of appellant's assault is not rendered unforeseeable merely because the precise agency of death, i.e. the Michielli's station wagon, could not have been foretold. Appellant perpetrated a deadly assault on the decedent in and around an automobile on a public street with other moving vehicles in close proximity. It is absurd to argue that the fatal result was so extraordinary or accidental that appellant should not be held criminally liable for the consequences of his conduct. We find that more than sufficient evidence was adduced at trial from which the factfinder could conclude that appellant's conduct was the legal cause of Berry's death. * * *

Judgment of sentence affirmed.

STATE v. GOVAN

Court of Appeals of Arizona, Division One, Department B
154 Ariz. 611, 744 P.2d 712 (Ct. App. 1987)

GREER, J.

On May 13, 1985, appellant was indicted on one count of second degree murder. Following a jury trial, he was convicted on October 18, 1985, of the lesser-included offense of manslaughter. He was sentenced to a mitigated term of imprisonment of six years.

The incident which gave rise to the criminal charges in this case occurred on April 5, 1980. The appellant and Ms. Sharon Keeble, with whom he had been living for three years, argued over the appellant's alleged molestation of the victim's teenage daughter. The victim eventually fired a shot at the appellant. The appellant then left the scene, but later that day returned and was observed again arguing with the victim. The victim borrowed a neighbor's telephone and attempted to call the police. While the victim was attempting to dial the phone, the appellant pulled a gun out of his pocket and shot at the victim, striking her in the neck. As a result she was paralyzed from the neck down. The appellant told police that he had not intended to shoot the victim, but had drawn his gun and fired behind him without taking aim.

On May 1, 1980, the state charged appellant with aggravated assault for shooting Ms. Keeble. During Ms. Keeble's hospitalization, appellant visited her and they were subsequently married. The aggravated assault charge was dismissed without prejudice on March 11, 1981. Due to her quadriplegia Ms. Keeble suffered from several ailments and needed constant care. In January, 1985, the victim contracted pneumonia and died. Appellant was subsequently charged with second degree murder and convicted of manslaughter. * * *

The appellant argues that he cannot be convicted of anything because there was no evidence to show that the shot he fired caused the quadriplegia of the victim. Defense counsel argued that the state needed to bring in a doctor from every institution that treated Ms. Keeble to show that the quadriplegia was the direct result of the gunshot wound. He then concluded that, "as to the rest of it, I would just say there is insufficient evidence." In denying the motion, the trial court properly noted that there was uncontroverted evidence that the victim had been taken immediately to a hospital in the Phoenix area and remained a quadriplegic until her death. In addition, both of the doctors who testified at trial said, without objection, that the cause of death was pneumonia stemming from the quadriplegia, which was caused by a gunshot wound to the neck.

In this case, there was substantial, if not overwhelming, evidence that the gunshot to the victim's neck resulted in her immediate paralysis and quadriplegia. It was not error to deny the motion for judgment of acquittal.

The appellant also argues, based on *State v. Hall,* that the death was not the natural result of his having shot the victim. In *Hall,* the court first distinguished between cases where an intervening event was a coincidence and those where it was a response to the defendant's prior actions. It then stated that

> A defendant's actions may still be a proximate cause of death regardless of the type of intervening act that occurred, but as 'common sense would suggest, the perimeters of legal cause are more closely drawn when the intervening cause was a matter of coincidence rather than response.'

Thus, an intervening cause that was a coincidence will be a superseding cause when it was unforeseeable. Alternatively, an intervening cause that was a response will be a superseding cause only where it was abnormal and unforeseeable. Appellant's action would not be a proximate cause of Ms. Keeble's death if the chain of natural effects and causes was either non-existent because of or broken by intervening events which were unforeseeable and hence were superseding events. Here there were no intervening events which could be characterized as superseding. In this case, it is clear that the gunshot wound resulted in the quadriplegia. Furthermore, medical testimony proved that the quadriplegia, including the complications caused by the tracheostomy, eventually resulted in a "response" to that condition, which resulted in the victim's death. Thus, the appellant's conduct was a proximate cause of the victim's death and he is criminally liable for it.

The appellant refines his argument on appeal to contend that the victim simply gave up her will to live, and this broke the chain of causation between the shooting and her death. He points out that the victim did not seek medical attention for at least two weeks after she knew that she was ill.

This argument was never presented to the trial court. Ordinarily we would not review a matter not argued below, but to allow a conviction to stand that is not supported by the evidence would be fundamental error. However, we do not find appellant's argument persuasive. Although a victim may break the chain of causation by voluntarily doing harm to himself, this should not be so when an individual causes the victim to commit suicide or lose the will to live because of extreme pain from wounds inflicted by the appellant, or when the wound has rendered the victim irresponsible. The impact of quadriplegia on a person's physical and mental well-being may be equated with the effects of extreme pain. Thus, the rationale in *Hall* applies also to the relationship between the gunshot wound and the alleged loss of will to live. The appellant's conduct could be regarded as a proximate cause of the victim's death, and he would still be criminally liable for it.

Judgment and sentence affirmed.

HENDERSON v. KIBBE

Supreme Court of the United States

431 U.S. 145, 97 S.Ct. 1730, 52 L.Ed.2d 203 (1977)

STEVENS, J.

Respondent is in petitioner's custody pursuant to a conviction for second-degree murder. The question presented to us is whether the New York State trial judge's failure to instruct the jury on the issue of causation was constitutional error requiring a Federal District Court to grant habeas corpus relief. Disagreeing with a divided panel of the Court of Appeals for the Second Circuit, we hold that it was not.

On the evening of December 30, 1970, respondent and his codefendant encountered a thoroughly intoxicated man named Stafford in a bar in Rochester, N. Y. After observing Stafford display at least two $100 bills, they decided to rob him and agreed to drive him to a nearby town. While in the car, respondent slapped Stafford several times, took his money, and, in a search for concealed funds, forced Stafford to lower his trousers and remove his boots. They then abandoned him on an unlighted, rural road, still in a state of partial undress, and without his coat or his glasses. The temperature was near zero, visibility was obscured by blowing snow, and snow banks flanked the roadway. The time was between 9:30 and 9:40 p.m.

At about 10 p.m., while helplessly seated in a traffic lane about a quarter mile from the nearest lighted building, Stafford was struck by a speeding pickup truck. The driver testified that while he was traveling 50 miles per hour in a 40-mile zone, the first of two approaching cars flashed its lights - presumably as a warning which he did not understand. Immediately after the cars passed, the driver saw Stafford sitting in the road with his hands in the air. The driver neither swerved nor braked his vehicle before it hit Stafford. Stafford was pronounced dead upon arrival at the local hospital.

Respondent and his accomplice were convicted of grand larceny, robbery, and second-degree murder. Only the conviction of murder, as defined in N. Y. Penal Law §125.25 (2), is now challenged. That statute provides that "[a] person is guilty of murder in the second degree" when "[under] circumstances evincing a depraved indifference to human life, he recklessly engages in conduct which creates a grave risk of death to another person, *and thereby causes the death of another person.*" (Emphasis added.)

Defense counsel argued that it was the negligence of the truckdriver, rather than the defendants' action, that had caused Stafford's death, and that the defendants could not have anticipated the fatal accident.[4] On the other hand, the prosecution argued that the death was foreseeable and would not have occurred but for the conduct of the defendants who therefore were the cause of death.[5] Neither party requested the trial judge to instruct the jury on the meaning of the statutory requirement that the defendants' conduct "thereby cause[d] the death of another person," and no such instruction was given. * * *

The Appellate Division of the New York Supreme Court affirmed respondent's conviction. Although respondent did not challenge the sufficiency of the instructions to the jury in that court, Judge Cardamone dissented on the ground that the trial court's charge did not explain the issue of causation or

---

[4] "... [Y]ou are going to have to honestly come to the conclusion that here is three people, all three drinking, and that these two, or at least my client were in a position to perceive this grave risk, be aware of it and disregard it. Perceive that Mr. Stafford would sit in the middle of the northbound lane, that a motorist would come by who was distracted by flashing lights in the opposite lane, who then froze at the wheel, who then didn't swerve, didn't brake, and who was violating the law by speeding, and to make matters worse, he had at that particular time, because of what the situation was, he had low beams on, that is a lot of anticipation. That is a lot of looking forward. Are you supposed to anticipate that somebody is going to break the law when you move or do something? I think that is a reasonable doubt."

[5] "As I mentioned not only does the first count contain reference to and require proof of a depraved indifference to a human life, it proves that the defendant recklessly engaged in conduct which created a risk of death in that they caused the death of George Stafford. Now, I very well know, members of the jury, you know, that quite obviously the acts of both of these defendants were not the only the direct or the most preceding cause of his death. If I walked with one of you downtown, you know, and we went across one of the bridges and you couldn't swim and I pushed you over and you drowned because you can't swim, I suppose you can say, well, you drowned because you couldn't swim. But of course, the fact is that I pushed you over. The same thing here. Sure, the death, the most immediate, the most preceding, the most direct cause of Mr. Stafford's death was the motor vehicle.... But how did he get there? Or to put it differently, would this man be dead had it not been for the acts of these two defendants? And I submit to you, members of the jury, that the acts of these two defendants did indeed cause the death of Mr. Stafford. He didn't walk out there on East River Road. He was driven out there. His glasses were taken and his identification was taken and his pants were around his ankles."

include an adequate discussion of the necessary mental state. That judge expressed the opinion that "the jury, upon proper instruction, could have concluded that the victim's death by an automobile was a remote and intervening cause."

The New York Court of Appeals also affirmed. It identified the causation issue as the only serious question raised by the appeal, and then rejected the contention that the conduct of the driver of the pickup truck constituted an intervening cause which relieved the defendants of criminal responsibility for Stafford's death. The court held that it was "not necessary that the ultimate harm be intended by the actor. It will suffice if it can be said beyond a reasonable doubt, as indeed it can be here said, that the ultimate harm is something which should have been foreseen as being reasonably related to the acts of the accused."[7] The court refused to consider the adequacy of the charge to the jury because that question had not been raised in the trial court.

Respondent then filed a petition for a writ of habeas corpus in the United States District Court for the Northern District of New York. The District Court held that the respondent's attack on the sufficiency of the charge failed to raise a question of constitutional dimension and that, without more, "the charge is not reviewable in a federal habeas corpus proceeding."

The Court of Appeals for the Second Circuit reversed * * * On the merits, the court held that since the Constitution requires proof beyond a reasonable doubt of every fact necessary to constitute the crime, the failure to

---

[7]The New York court added:

"We subscribe to the requirement that the defendants' actions must be a *sufficiently direct cause* of the ensuing death before there can be any imposition of criminal liability, and recognize, of course, that this standard is greater than that required to serve as a basis for tort liability. Applying these criteria to the defendants' actions, we conclude that their activities on the evening of December 30, 1970 were a sufficiently direct cause of the death of George Stafford so as to warrant the imposition of criminal sanctions. In engaging in what may properly be described as a despicable course of action, Kibbe and Krall left a helplessly intoxicated man without his eyeglasses in a position from which, because of these attending circumstances, he could not extricate himself and whose condition was such that he could not even protect himself from the elements. The defendants do not dispute the fact that their conduct evinced a depraved indifference to human life which created a grave risk of death, but rather they argue that it was just as likely that Stafford would be miraculously rescued by a good [S]amaritan. We cannot accept such an argument. There can be little doubt but that Stafford would have frozen to death in his state of undress had he remained on the shoulder of the road. The only alternative left to him was the highway, which in his condition, for one reason or another, clearly foreboded the probability of his resulting death."

instruct the jury on an essential element as complex as the causation issue in this case created an impermissible risk that the jury had not made a finding that the Constitution requires.

Because the Court of Appeals decision appeared to conflict with this Court's holding in *Cupp v. Naughten*, we granted certiorari. * * *

I

The Court has held "that the Due Process Clause protects the accused against conviction except upon proof beyond a reasonable doubt of every fact necessary to constitute the crime with which he is charged." One of the facts which the New York statute required the prosecution to prove is that the defendants' conduct caused the death of Stafford. As the New York Court of Appeals held, the evidence was plainly sufficient to prove that fact beyond a reasonable doubt. It is equally clear that the record requires us to conclude that the jury made such a finding.

There can be no question about the fact that the jurors were informed that the case included a causation issue that they had to decide. The element of causation was stressed in the arguments of both counsel. The statutory language, which the trial judge read to the jury, expressly refers to the requirement that defendants' conduct "cause[d] the death of another person." The indictment tracks the statutory language; it was read to the jurors and they were given a copy for use during their deliberations. The judge instructed the jury that all elements of the crime must be proved beyond a reasonable doubt. Whether or not the arguments of counsel correctly characterized the law applicable to the causation issue, they surely made it clear to the jury that such an issue had to be decided. It follows that the objection predicated on this Court's holding in *Winship* is without merit.

II

* * * The New York Court of Appeals concluded that the evidence of causation was sufficient because it can be said beyond a reasonable doubt that the "ultimate harm" was "something which should have been foreseen as being reasonably related to the acts of the accused." It is not entirely clear whether the court's reference to "ultimate harm" merely required that Stafford's death was foreseeable, or, more narrowly, that his death by a speeding vehicle was

foreseeable.[14] In either event, the court was satisfied that the "ultimate harm" was one which "should have been foreseen." Thus, an adequate instruction would have told the jury that if the ultimate harm should have been foreseen as being reasonably related to defendants' conduct, that conduct should be regarded as having caused the death of Stafford.

The significance of the omission of such an instruction may be evaluated by comparison with the instructions that were given. One of the elements of respondent's offense is that he acted "recklessly." By returning a guilty verdict, the jury necessarily found, in accordance with its instruction on recklessness, that respondent was "aware of and consciously disregard[ed] a substantial and unjustifiable risk" that death would occur. A person who is "aware of and consciously disregards" a substantial risk must also foresee the ultimate harm that the risk entails. Thus, the jury's determination that the respondent acted recklessly necessarily included a determination that the ultimate harm was foreseeable to him.

In a strict sense, an additional instruction on foreseeability would not have been cumulative because it would have related to an element of the offense not specifically covered in the instructions given. But since it is logical to assume that the jurors would have responded to an instruction on causation consistently with their determination of the issues that were comprehensively explained, it is equally logical to conclude that such an instruction would not have affected their verdict.[16] Accordingly, we reject the suggestion that the omission of more complete instructions on the causation issue "so infected the entire trial that the resulting conviction violated due process." Even if we were to make the unlikely assumption that the jury might have reached a different

---

[14]The passage of the opinion quoted in n. 7, *supra,* emphasizes the obvious risk of death by freezing, suggesting that defendants need not have foreseen the precise manner in which the death did occur.

[16]In fact, it is not unlikely that a complete instruction on the causation issue would actually have been favorable to the prosecution. For example, an instruction might have been patterned after the following example given in W. LaFave & A. Scott, CRIMINAL LAW 260 (1972):

> *A,* with intent to kill *B,* only wounds *B,* leaving him lying
> unconscious in the unlighted road on a dark night, and then *C,*
> driving along the road, runs over and kills *B.* Here *C's* act is a
> matter of coincidence rather than a response to what *A* has done, and
> thus the question is whether the subsequent events were foreseeable,
> as they undoubtedly were in the above illustration.

Such an instruction would probably have been more favorable to the prosecution than the instruction on recklessness which the court actually gave.

verdict pursuant to an additional instruction, that possibility is too speculative to justify the conclusion that constitutional error was committed.

The judgment is reversed.

It is so ordered.

B.   CONCURRENCE

The final basic element of a crime is the concurrence requirement which mandates a connection between the *actus reus* and the *mens rea*. Two types of concurrence must be present. First, "the defendant must possess the requisite *mens rea* at the same moment that her voluntary conduct (or omission) causes the social harm (the *actus reus*)." Joshua Dressler, UNDERSTANDING CRIMINAL LAW § 15.01 (3d ed. 2001). This is called temporal concurrence because the focus is on whether the required *mens rea* was present at the same time that the defendant performed the *actus reus*. Second, the mens rea must be the motivating force behind the *actus reus*. This is called motivational concurrence. As you read the following cases, decide for yourself whether the concurrence requirement was satisfied.

THABO MELI v. REGINAM
Privy Council
[1954] 1 All E.R. 373

Jan. 13. LORD REID: The four appellants in this case were convicted of murder after a trial before Sir Walter Harragin, judge of the High Court of Basutoland, in March, 1953. The appeal which has been heard by this Board dealt with two matters: first, whether the conclusions of the learned judge on questions of fact were warranted: and secondly, whether, on a point of law, the accused are entitled to have the verdict quashed.

On the first matter, there really is no ground for criticizing the learned judge's treatment of the facts. It is established by evidence, which was believed and which is apparently credible, that there was a preconceived plot on the part of the four accused to bring the deceased man to a hut and there to kill him, and then to fake an accident, so that the accused should escape the penalty for their act. The deceased man was brought to the hut. He was there treated to beer and was at least partially intoxicated; and he was then struck over the head in accordance with the plan of the accused. Witnesses say that while the deceased was seated and bending forward he was struck a heavy blow on the back of the head with a piece of iron like the instrument produced at the trial. But a post-mortem examination showed that his skull had not been fractured and medical evidence was to the effect that a blow such as the witness described would have produced more severe injuries than those found at the post-mortem examination. There is at least doubt whether the weapon which was produced as being like the weapon which was used could have produced the injuries that were found, but it may be that this weapon is not exactly similar to the one which was used, or it may be that the blow was a glancing blow and produced less severe injuries than those which one might expect. In any event, the man was unconscious after receiving the blow, but he was not then dead. There is no evidence that the accused then believed that he was dead, but their Lordships are prepared to assume from their subsequent conduct that they did so believe; and it is only on that assumption that any statable case can be made for this appeal. The accused took out the body, rolled it over a low krantz or cliff, and dressed up the scene to make it look like an accident. Obviously, they believed at that time that the man was dead, but it appears from the medical evidence that the injuries which he received in the hut were not sufficient to cause the death and that the final cause of his death was exposure when he was left unconscious at the foot of the krantz.

The point of law which was raised in this case can be simply stated. It is said that two acts were done:–first, the attack in the hut; and, secondly, the placing of the body outside afterwards–and that they were separate acts. It is said that, while the first act was accompanied by mens rea, it was not the cause of death; but that the second act, while it was the cause of death, was not accompanied by mens rea; and on that ground, it is said that the accused are not guilty of murder, though they may have been guilty of culpable homicide. It is said that the mens rea necessary to establish murder is an intention to kill, and that there could be no intention to kill when the accused thought that the man was already dead, so their original intention to kill had ceased before they did the act which caused the man's death. It appears to their Lordships impossible to divide up what was really one series of acts in this way. There is no doubt that the accused set out to do all these acts in order to achieve their plan, and as parts of their plan; and it is much too refined a ground of judgment to say that, because they were under a misapprehension at one stage and thought that their guilty purpose had been achieved before, in fact, it was achieved, therefore they are to escape the penalties of the law. Their Lordships do not think that this is a matter which is susceptible of elaboration. There appears to be no case, either in South Africa or England, or for that matter elsewhere, which resembles the present. Their Lordships can find no difference relevant to the present case between the law of South Africa and the law of England; and they are of the opinion that by both laws there can be no separation such as that for which the accused contend. Their crime is not reduced from murder to a lesser crime merely because the accused were under some misapprehension for a time during the completion of their criminal plot.

Their Lordships must, therefore, humbly advise Her Majesty that this appeal should be dismissed.

Appeal dismissed.

STATE v. ROSE
Supreme Court of Rhode Island
112 R.I. 402, 311 A.2d 281 (1973)

ROBERTS, J.

These are two indictments, one (No. 70-573) charging the defendant, Henry Rose, with leaving the scene of an accident, death resulting, in violation of G. L. 1956 (1968 Reenactment) §31-26-1[1] and the other (No. 70-572) charging the defendant with manslaughter. The defendant was tried on both indictments to a jury in the Superior Court, and a verdict of guilty was returned in each case. Thereafter the defendant's motions for a new trial were denied, and he is now prosecuting a bill of exceptions[a] in each case in this court.

These indictments followed the death of David J. McEnery, who was struck by defendant's motor vehicle at the intersection of Broad and Summer Streets in Providence at about 6:30 p.m. on April 1, 1970. According to the testimony of a bus driver, he had been operating his vehicle north on Broad Street and had stopped at a traffic light at the intersection of Summer Street. While the bus was standing there, he observed a pedestrian starting to cross Broad Street, and as the pedestrian reached the middle of the southbound lane he was struck by a "dirty, white station wagon" that was proceeding southerly on Broad Street. The pedestrian's body was thrown up on the hood of the car. The bus driver further testified that the station wagon stopped momentarily, the body of the pedestrian rolled off the hood, and the car immediately drove off

---

[1]General Laws 1956 (1968 Reenactment) § 31-26-1 reads, in part, as follows: "Duty to stop in accidents resulting in personal injury. – (a) The driver of any vehicle knowingly involved in an accident resulting in injury to or death of any person shall immediately stop such vehicle at the scene of such accident or as close thereto as possible but shall then forthwith return to and in every event shall remain at the scene of the accident until he has fulfilled the requirements of § 31-26-3. Every such stop shall be made without obstructing traffic more than is necessary. * * *"

[a]Black's Law Dictionary (7th ed.) defines a bill of exceptions as a formal written statement signed by the trial judge and presented to the appellate court of a party's objections or exceptions taken during trial and the grounds upon which they are founded.

along Broad Street in a southerly direction. The bus operator testified that he had alighted from his bus, intending to attempt to assist the victim, but was unable to locate the body.

Subsequently, it appears from the testimony of a police officer, about 6:40 p.m. the police located a white station wagon on Haskins Street, a distance of some 610 feet from the scene of the accident. The police further testified that a body later identified as that of David J. McEnery was wedged beneath the vehicle when it was found and that the vehicle had been registered to defendant.

Testifying on behalf of the state was a Robert Buckley, who stated that he had worked with defendant and that about 5 p.m. on the day of the accident he had gone to a place located in Central Falls that he identified as The Palms where he met defendant about 5:15 p.m. Buckley further testified that about 7 p.m. that evening defendant phoned him, told him that he had been involved in an accident, and asked Buckley to help him look for his car. According to Buckley, he picked up defendant's girl friend, identified as Pat, and went to the vicinity of the accident and drove around for some time but was unable to locate the car.

Buckley testified that later he picked up defendant, who asked him to take him to a cafe in Central Falls known as The Well, where he would attempt to establish an alibi. After arriving at The Well, defendant asked Buckley to take him to the Central Falls police station, where defendant reported that his car had been stolen from in front of The Well sometime between 5:30 p.m. and 9 p.m. on that day. Buckley later drove defendant to Pat's home, and while there defendant answered a telephone call. After the telephone call had been completed, defendant told Buckley that "a guy had been killed." According to Buckley, defendant "was denying it on the phone" during the conversation. * * *

The defendant here argues that in neither case did the evidence exclude any reasonable hypothesis or theory of the innocence of defendant. In so arguing in case No. 70-572, charging defendant with manslaughter, defendant directs our attention to the fact that the court charged the jury that there was no evidence in the case of culpable negligence on the part of defendant up to and including the time at which Mr. McEnery was struck by the station wagon. * * *

The defendant is contending that if the evidence is susceptible of a finding that McEnery was killed upon impact, he was not alive at the time he was being dragged under defendant's vehicle and defendant could not be found guilty of manslaughter. An examination of the testimony of the only medical witness makes it clear that, in his opinion, death could have resulted immediately upon impact by reason of a massive fracture of the skull. The medical witness also testified that death could have resulted a few minutes after the impact but conceded that he was not sure when it did occur.

We are inclined to agree with defendant's contention in this respect. Obviously, the evidence is such that death could have occurred after defendant had driven away with McEnery's body lodged under his car and, therefore, be consistent with guilt. On the other hand, the medical testimony is equally consistent with a finding that McEnery could have died instantly upon impact and, therefore, be consistent with a reasonable conclusion other than the guilt of defendant. It is clear, then, that, the testimony of the medical examiner lacking any reasonable medical certainty as to the time of the death of McEnery, we are unable to conclude that on such evidence defendant was guilty of manslaughter beyond a reasonable doubt. Therefore, we conclude, with respect to Indictment No. 70-572, that it was error to deny defendant's motion for a directed verdict of acquittal.

We are unable, however, to reach the same conclusion concerning the denial of the motion for a directed verdict of acquittal with respect to Indictment No. 70-573, in which defendant was charged with leaving the scene of an accident. The testimony adduced through the bus driver clearly establishes that at the time McEnery was struck his body was thrown up on the hood of the car and that while the car was standing still the body rolled off the hood and thereupon defendant drove off in a southerly direction. Later, the police found defendant's station wagon on a side street some 610 feet from the point of impact with McEnery's body wedged under the front of the car. The circumstances here are clearly consistent with a hypothesis of guilt, but it is clear that they are not consistent with any other reasonable hypothesis. We conclude, therefore, with respect to Indictment No. 70-573, that the trial court did not err in denying the motion for a directed verdict.

Because we conclude that the trial court erred in denying defendant's motion for a directed verdict of acquittal in the case charging him with manslaughter, it is unnecessary for us to consider his contentions of error concerning his motion for a new trial in that case. * * *

Chapter 7

CRIMINAL HOMICIDE

INTRODUCTION

The term "criminal homicide" encompasses a host of different crimes, all involving the unlawful killing of a human being by another human being. Criminal homicide can be divided into two main categories: murder and manslaughter. Under both the common law and contemporary penal codes, murder is broadly defined as the unlawful killing of a human being by another human being with malice aforethought. Manslaughter is the unlawful killing of a human being by another human being without malice aforethought.

The law of homicide has changed very slowly in the last few centuries. Even the Model Penal Code drafters, who sought to update the criminal law in many ways, altered the common law of homicide very little. So in this area the content of the law is fairly clear and well-settled. The interesting issues with respect to homicide involve policy -- the "goodness of fit" between the criminal law and the society to which it applies. Two issues in this regard are whether the law of homicide should change more than it has, and whether the law we have is applied fairly.

Should the law of homicide change? Homicide is generally considered reprehensible but, as we will see, some kinds of homicides have traditionally been considered more heinous than other kinds. As times change, cultural assessments of the relative seriousness of various homicide crimes may change as well. As you read the materials in this chapter, consider whether the assessments of relative evil made by the common law structure still fit contemporary American life and, if not, how the law ought to change.

A second issue in the law of homicide, one particularly relevant for practitioners of criminal law, is how to ensure that prosecutors, defense counsel, judges, and fact-finders fairly apply settled law. Even if the law generally reflects a cultural consensus in terms of categorizing homicides, jury members, judges, and attorneys may consciously or unconsciously bring conflicting assumptions and even prejudices to the table. As you read the materials in this chapter, consider whether and how this kind of "bad discretion" to apply the law unequally can be curbed.

A third policy problem that arises in the law of homicide is one we first examined when we studied the doctrine of transferred intent: the tension between a "culpability" approach and a "social harm" approach to criminal punishment. When a person has died, does it make more sense to inquire into the badness of the perpetrator or to focus on punishing the bad result? Is there a way that the criminal law can do both?

A. DEFINITIONAL ISSUES

Homicide law makes unlawful the unexcused, unjustified killing of a human. But what constitutes "killing" and what constitutes "a human?" Two definitional issues – one that pertains to the beginning of the human life cycle and one to the end of the human life cycle – should be mentioned before we proceed.

With respect to the beginning of the human life cycle, under English common law the prohibition on homicide applied as soon as a person was "born alive." Thus, the seventeenth-century English jurist Edward Coke wrote: "If a woman be quick with child [a fetus has "quickened" when the mother can feel its movements], and by a potion or otherwise killeth it in her wombe, or if a man beat her, whereby the childe dyeth in her body, and she is delivered of a dead childe, this is a great misprision [misdemeanor], and no murder; but if the childe be born alive and dyeth of the potion, battery, or other cause, this is murder; for in law it is accounted a reasonable creature, *in rerum natura*, when it is born alive." 3 Coke, Institutes 58 (1648). Some contemporary American penal codes that incorporate the common law have been interpreted to incorporate this "born alive" rule. *See, e.g., Keeler v. Superior Court*, 2 Cal.3d 619 (1970).

At the same time, United States constitutional law protects a woman's right to choose an abortion by balancing the woman's interest in bodily autonomy with the state's interest in protecting human life. In *Roe v. Wade*, 410 U.S. 113 (1973), and again in *Planned Parenthood of Southeastern Pennsylvania v. Casey*, 505 U.S. 833 (1992), the Court identified "viability" -- the ability of a fetus to live outside the womb -- as the fulcrum of this balance. In these cases, the Court set out three principles:

> First is a recognition of the right of the woman to choose to have an abortion before viability and to obtain it without undue interference from the State. * * * Second is a confirmation of the State's power to restrict abortions after fetal viability, if the law contains exceptions for pregnancies which endanger the woman's life or health. And third is the principle that the State has legitimate interests from the outset of the pregnancy in

protecting the health of the woman and the life of the fetus that
may become a child.

Casey, 505 U.S. at 846. Based on these principles, a state may criminalize the
killing of a fetus as long as the law contains exceptions that protect the mother's
constitutional rights.

The states have incorporated the common law tradition, constitutional
requirements, and moral values in different ways in their penal codes. For
instance, § 210.0(1) of the Model Penal Code, along with several states,
incorporates the common law, defining "human being" for the purposes of
homicide law as "a person who has been born and is alive." Some states
specifically criminalize the death or injury of a viable fetus. *See, e.g.*, Ind. Code
Ann. § 35-42-1-1 (defining the killing of a viable fetus as murder); *State v. Ard*,
505 S.E.2d 328 (S.C. 1998) (permitting the death penalty to be imposed for the
killing of a fetus). Other states criminally punish the death or injury of a "quick"
fetus, even if it is not viable. *See* Ark. Code Ann. § 5-1-102(13)(B) (Supp. 1999)
(including a fetus twelve weeks or older in the definition of a "person"); *People
v. Davis*, 872 P.2d 591 (Cal. 1994) (holding that a murder prosecution is
permissible when a fetus is seven to eight weeks old); 720 Ill. Comp. Stat. 5/9-
1.2, -2.1, -3.2, 5/12-3.1, -4.4 (permitting homicide prosecutions for the killing
of a fetus at any stage of development). Finally, a few states punish the injury
or death of a fetus by amplifying the penalties against killing or harming a
pregnant woman. *See, e.g.*, Kan. Stat. Ann. §§ 21-3440, -3441 (1995) (creating
heightened penalties for felonies and misdemeanors resulting in a miscarriage).

At the other end of the human life cycle, advances in medicine have
made it possible for people to be kept alive much longer after a severe injury
than was possible at English common law. Contemporary American criminal
codes have adapted to this new reality in several ways. First, all fifty states and
the District of Columbia now interpret "death" to include "brain death," in
which respiration and heartbeat continue but the person has no brain function
left. A majority of these jurisdictions have adopted the Uniform Determination
of Death Act (UDDA) promulgated by the National Conference of
Commissioners on Uniform State Laws. According to the UDDA, "An
individual who has sustained either (1) irreversible cessation of circulatory or
respiratory functions, or (2) irreversible cessation of all functions, including the
brain stem, is dead. A determination of death must be made in accordance with
accepted medical standards." Uniform Determination of Death Act §1. The
UDDA seeks both to shield physicians who follow accepted medical practice
from liability, and to facilitate organ transplant. Thus, recognizing "brain death"
means that the actions of physicians in turning off life support or engaging in
transplant surgery do not break the chain of causation, and the person who
originally caused the fatal injury can be criminally prosecuted. *See, e.g., People*

v. Eulo, 472 N.E.2d 286 (N.Y. 1984); *Commonwealth v. Golston*, 366 N.E.2d 744 (Mass. 1977).

B.   CATEGORIZING HOMICIDES

Although the common law and Model Penal Code approaches to homicide share the central distinction between murder and manslaughter, these terms are differently defined under the two systems. Thus, an overview will be useful.

As a point of departure, it may be useful to know that under both the common law approach and the Model Penal Code, "malice" and "malice aforethought" have lost their everyday meaning. Thus, "malice" no longer means meanness or evil, and "aforethought" no longer refers to premeditation. "Malice aforethought" should rather be understood as a legal term of art or technical label for the mens rea of murder.

In penal codes that primarily rely on the common law, an unlawful killing of a human being is committed with "malice aforethought" when any one of four conditions are present:

1.   An intent to kill;

2.   An intent to commit serious bodily injury;[a]

3.   An "abandoned and malignant heart" or "depraved heart" (a.k.a. depraved heart murder); or

4.   The felony murder rule applies.

If the defendant intends to kill, he acts with "express" malice. If malice aforethought is shown in any other way, it is considered "implied" malice.

When proof of murder depends on proof of malice aforethought, what kind of evidence will be sufficient? As we have seen, intent to kill may be inferred from circumstantial evidence. Another evidentiary rule typically observed in jurisdictions that have incorporated the common law is the

---

[a] Not all jurisdictions recognize intent to commit serious bodily injury as a means of proving malice aforethought. Where it is recognized, the rule reflects a desire to prevent defendants charged with murder from simply arguing, "But I didn't mean to kill," and in that way creating a reasonable doubt.

"deadly weapon rule," which permits (but does not require) the jury to infer intent to kill when the defendant has used a deadly weapon[b] aimed at a vital part of the human body. When attempting to infer intent to kill or to seriously injure, the jury is also permitted to rely on the "natural and probable consequences" doctrine introduced in Chapter 4.

Manslaughter is defined under the common law approach as the unlawful killing of a human being by another human being without malice aforethought. Most common law-based jurisdictions recognize two types of manslaughter: voluntary manslaughter and involuntary manslaughter.

Voluntary manslaughter, the more serious type of manslaughter, is an intentional killing that would normally qualify as second degree murder, but which is reduced to the lesser crime of voluntary manslaughter through the application of a partial defense, such as provocation (also known as heat of passion), imperfect self defense, or diminished capacity. We will study the doctrine of provocation later in this chapter. Imperfect self-defense and diminished capacity are discussed in Chapter 10. A typical sentence for voluntary manslaughter might run from three to eleven years in prison.

Involuntary manslaughter is the least serious form of criminal homicide in many jurisdictions, carrying penalties from two to five years in prison. Generally speaking, a defendant may be charged with involuntary manslaughter if he or she brought about the death of another human being through "criminal negligence," a legal term of art that is defined sometimes as gross negligence and sometimes as recklessness. As you will see in this chapter, states are not consistent regarding the mental state required for involuntary manslaughter.

Some states that follow the common law recognize an additional homicide crime: vehicular manslaughter. Where vehicular manslaughter is recognized, it often carries penalties even lower than those for involuntary manslaughter. In California, for example, a conviction for involuntary manslaughter may be punished with imprisonment for two, three, or four years, whereas a conviction for vehicular manslaughter may result in less than a year in jail. *See* Cal. Penal Code § 193.

---

[b] States are not in agreement about what constitutes a "deadly weapon." In some states, a "deadly weapon" is an instrument designed for the purpose of causing death or serious bodily injury. Other jurisdictions define "deadly weapon" as any substance capable of causing death or serious bodily injury. *See* Model Penal Code §210.0(4).

Section 210.1 of the Model Penal Code defines criminal homicide as the purposeful, knowing, reckless, or negligent death of another human being, thus calling into play the four mens rea elements defined in § 2.02. Criminal homicide is murder when it is committed purposely or knowingly, or when it is committed recklessly "under circumstances manifesting extreme indifference to the value of human life." *See* § 210.2. This recklessness and indifference is presumed if the actor is engaged or is an accomplice to the commission of, attempt to commit, or flight after committing or attempting to commit, certain other crimes. This formulation represents the MPC drafters' response to the common law doctrines of "depraved heart" murder and felony murder. The Model Penal Code does not recognize degrees of murder.

Section 210.3 defines manslaughter as criminal homicide (1) when it is committed recklessly (but without circumstances manifesting extreme indifference to the value of human life) and (2) when a homicide that would otherwise be murder "is committed under the influence of extreme mental or emotional disturbance for which there is reasonable explanation or excuse." This latter formulation represents the MPC drafters' response to the common law doctrine of heat of passion.

C. DEGREES OF MURDER (FIRST DEGREE VS. SECOND DEGREE MURDER)

Many jurisdictions divide common law murder into two degrees, an approach initiated by Pennsylvania over two centuries ago and widely copied by other states. In these jurisdictions, a murder charge will be raised to first degree murder upon proof that (1) the murder involved "premeditation and deliberation," (2) the murder was committed using a means specified in the first degree murder statute, such as lying in wait, poison, or torture, or (3) the murder occurred during the commission or attempted commission of an enumerated felony (namely rape, robbery, burglary, or arson).

Although the words "premeditation" and "deliberation" are often treated as synonyms, they are not one and the same. Premeditation generally means that the killer must have reflected upon and thought about the killing in advance. No particular length of time is required for premeditation. Indeed, some jurisdictions observe the "wink of an eye" doctrine, under which premeditation can occur in an instant. Deliberation refers to the *quality* of the accused's thought processes. In general, a killing that is deliberate is one that is undertaken with a cool head.

A recurring question in the courts is how fact-finders ought to interpret circumstantial evidence of premeditation and deliberation. How, for example, should evidence of multiple blows be interpreted -- as evidence of deliberation, or as evidence of an unthinking frenzy? How should fact-finders interpret situations in which the victim took a long time to die? In each of the following cases, the court had to decide whether there was sufficient evidence of premeditation and deliberation to sustain a first degree murder conviction. Do the opinions set out logical and usable guidelines for finding premeditation and deliberation? Does the requirement of premeditation and deliberation itself make sense as a way of isolating the very worst homicides, or should other factors be equally or more important?

STATE v. BROWN

Supreme Court of Tennessee
836 S.W.2d 530 (Tenn. 1992)

Daughtrey, Justice.

This capital case arose from the death of four-year-old Eddie Eugene Brown and the subsequent conviction of his father for first-degree murder, as well as for child neglect.[1] After careful review, we have reached the conclusion that the evidence introduced at trial is not sufficient to support a conviction for first-degree murder. We therefore hold that the defendant's conviction must be reduced to second-degree murder.

1. Factual Background

The victim in this case, Eddie Eugene Brown, was born in early February 1982, the son of defendant Mack Edward Brown and his co-defendant, Evajean Bell Brown, who were not living together at the time of Eddie's birth and were later divorced. * * *

Mack had been living with his wife and his son for less than a year when Eddie died. The Brown's next-door neighbor testified that, at around 3:40 a.m. on April 10, 1986, she heard yelling and screaming in their apartment. She distinctly heard a man's voice say, "Shut up. Get your ass over here. Sit down. Shut up. I know what I'm doing." She also heard a woman's voice say, "Stop, don't do that. Leave me alone. Stop don't do that." She testified that the fight went on for 30 minutes and that she heard a sound which she described as a "thump, like something heavy hit the wall." The only other evidence introduced concerning the events of that morning was the tape of Evajean's call for an ambulance. At 8:59 a.m. she telephoned for help for her son, stating that he "fell down some steps and he's not breathing."

---

[1] Eddie's mother was charged as well, but her trial ended in a mistrial and because of double jeopardy considerations, she cannot be retried.

The paramedics who answered the call tried to revive Eddie but were unsuccessful. His heartbeat was reestablished at the hospital, but as it turned out, he was already clinically brain-dead. One of the treating nurses later testified that at that point, Eddie was being kept alive only for purposes of potential organ donation.

Various examinations indicated that the child had suffered two, and possibly three, skull fractures. * * * The CT scan showed a cerebral edema, or swelling of the brain, which was more pronounced on the right side of the brain than the left, and which had shifted the midline of Eddie's brain toward the left. The pathologist who performed the autopsy noted the presence of vomit in Eddie's lungs and explained that swelling in the brain can cause vomiting. He theorized that repeated blows to Eddie's head caused cerebral hemorrhages and swelling. According to the expert, this pressure in the skull resulted in Eddie's aspiration of his own vomit and his ultimate death. He testified further that the swelling process could have taken as long as four or five hours to a day, or as little as 15 minutes.[3]

A neurological surgeon testified that Eddie's brain injuries were, at least in part, consistent with contrecoup[4] injuries, which occur when the head is violently shaken back and forth. The surgeon explained that there is a limited amount of fluid between the brain and the skull. That fluid generally serves as a shock absorber, but when the skull and brain are moving at a sufficient velocity and the skull suddenly stops, the fluid is not an adequate buffer between the delicate brain tissue and the hard skull surface. As he described this phenomenon at trial, "when the skull stops the brain slaps up against it," resulting in severe bruising and swelling of the brain.

In addition to his cranial and cerebral injuries, Eddie had several internal injuries. When Eddie's internal organs were removed for donation, the county medical examiner observed hemorrhaging in the duodenum section of his intestine. He testified that such localized hemorrhaging was consistent with a blow by a fist to the upper portion of the abdomen. Additionally, blood was found in the child's stool and urine, and his liver enzymes were elevated. There was testimony to the effect that these conditions may have resulted from cardiac

---

[3] The significance of this testimony is that the child could have sustained these injuries at 4 a.m. (when a neighbor heard the fight between his parents) and not have begun the process of vomiting and dying until just before the ambulance was called at 9 a.m.

[4] The neurological surgeon testified that "contrecoup" is French for "back and forth."

arrest, but that they are also consistent with blows to the abdomen, liver, and kidneys.

Finally, Eddie had bruises of varying ages on his face, scalp, ears, neck, chest, hips, legs, arms, buttocks, and scrotum. He had a large abrasion on his shoulder, scratches on his neck and face, and a round, partially healed wound on his big toe which, according to one of his treating nurses, was consistent with a cigarette burn.[5] He had lacerations on both his ears at the scalp. He had linear bruises consistent with being struck with a straight object. The autopsy revealed an old lesion at the base of his brain which was evidence of a head injury at least two weeks before his death. X-rays revealed a broken arm which had not been treated and which had occurred three to five weeks before his death. The injury to his arm was confirmed by a witness who had noticed his arm hanging limply and then later noticed it in a homemade sling. * * *

Brown's statement indicates that around two or three o'clock on the morning of April 10, 1986, he and his wife both spanked Eddie because Eddie had urinated and defecated on the floor. The defendant admitted to another spanking, after he had sent Eddie to bed, and after he and his wife had a fight over money. As the defendant described it, it was during this spanking that his "mood began to kind of snap and let go." He said that he remembered going to Eddie's bedroom and remembered ordering Evajean out of the room. Although he denied remembering anything other than spanking Eddie's bottom with the open part of his hand, he stated that he was afraid he had beaten Eddie during the time that everything "went blank." The only thing he clearly recalled before that point was Eddie "staring at [him] mean" and saying, "I hate you! I hate you!" He stated that his next memory was of going downstairs and hearing Eddie behind him, falling onto the landing and into the door.

When the police questioned the defendant, his right hand was badly swollen. He explained that several days prior to April 10, he had injured his hand while working on his car and had sought medical treatment at Fort Sanders Hospital. They put a splint on his hand and gave him pain medication. He denied having struck Eddie with his right hand, stating that "[i]t hurts so bad there ain't no way." The hospital's records indicate that on April 3, the defendant's hand was x-rayed and splinted. The records do not indicate that there was any break in the skin on the hand.

With the consent of the defendant, the police searched the apartment and recovered numerous items stained with blood consistent with Eddie's blood

---

[5] There was testimony that Mack Brown smoked cigarettes but Evajean did not. * * *

type, including an adult pajama top, a brown paper bag from the living room floor, and several towels and wash cloths. Police also found a bandage under the kitchen sink which was stained with blood consistent with Eddie's blood type. The blood on this bandage material was on the outside near the adhesive tape, not on the inner surface, which would have been next to the skin of the person wearing the bandage. The pants the defendant was wearing at the time of his arrest also had blood stains on them that were consistent with Eddie's blood type. A number of other items collected from the apartment tested positive for human blood, but the type of blood could not be determined because there was too little blood or they had been washed. These items included the couch cover, a pillow case and sheets taken from Eddie's bed, paint chips from the wall in Eddie's room, a child's undershirt and socks, and a three-by-five inch section of the living room rug. * * *

2. Sufficiency of the Evidence

We are asked first to decide whether the evidence was sufficient to support the verdict of first-degree murder. The defendant argues principally that premeditation was not shown. * * *

* * * The statute in effect at the time of the homicide in this case defined first-degree murder as follows:

> Every murder perpetrated by means of poison, lying in wait, or by other kind of willful, deliberate, malicious, and premeditated killing, or committed in the perpetration of, or attempt to perpetrate, any murder in the first degree, arson, rape, robbery, burglary, larceny, kidnapping, aircraft piracy, or the unlawful throwing, placing or discharging of a destructive device or bomb, is murder in the first degree.

T.C.A. § 39-2-202(a) (1982).

Based upon our review of the record, we conclude that the evidence in this case is insufficient to establish deliberation and premeditation. Hence, the defendant's conviction for first-degree murder cannot stand. However, we do find the evidence sufficient to sustain a conviction of second-degree murder.

At common law, there were no degrees of murder, but the tendency to establish a subdivision by statute took root relatively early in the development of American law. The pattern was set by a 1794 Pennsylvania statute that identified the more heinous kinds of murder as murder in the first degree, with all other murders deemed to be murder in the second degree. Some states have subdivided the offense into three or even four degrees of murder, but since the enactment of the first such statute in 1829, Tennessee has maintained the distinction at two. It is one which this Court has found to be "not only founded in mercy and humanity, but . . . well fortified by reason."[8]

* * * Because conviction of second-degree murder also requires proof of intent and malice, the two distinctive elements of first-degree murder are deliberation and premeditation.

* * * [P]erhaps the two most oft-repeated propositions with regard to the law of first-degree murder, that the essential ingredient of first-degree murder is premeditation and that premeditation may be formed in an instant, are only partially accurate, because they are rarely quoted in context. In order to establish first-degree murder, the premeditated killing must also have been done deliberately, that is, with coolness and reflection. As noted in *Rader v. State*:

> When the murder is not committed in the perpetration of, or attempt to perpetrate any of the felonies named in the [statute], then, in order to constitute murder in the first degree, it must be perpetrated by poison or lying in wait, or some other kind of willful, deliberate, malicious, and premeditated killing; that is to say, the deliberation and premeditation must be akin to the deliberation and premeditation manifested where the murder is by poison or lying in wait. * * *

The obvious point to be drawn from this discussion is that even if intent (or "purpose to kill") and premeditation ("design") may be formed in an instant, deliberation requires some period of reflection, during which the mind is "free from the influence of excitement, or passion."

Despite admonitions in the opinions of the Tennessee Supreme Court during the nineteenth century and early part of the twentieth century regarding the necessity of maintaining a clear line of demarcation between first- and second-degree murder, that line has been substantially blurred in later cases. The culprit appears to be the shortcutting of analysis, commonly along three or four different tracks.

One of those has been the same error decried by Justice Turney in 1872, i.e., the use of the terms "premeditation" and "deliberation" interchangeably, or sometimes collectively, to refer to the same concept. * * *

---

[8] At common law and in Tennessee prior to 1829, the only penalty provided for murder was death; the creation of second-degree murder introduced the possibility of a life sentence upon conviction.

Another weakness in our more recent opinions is the tendency to overemphasize the speed with which premeditation may be formed. The cases convert the proposition that no specific amount of time between the formation of the design to kill and its execution is required to prove first-degree murder, into one that requires virtually no time lapse at all, overlooking the fact that while intent (and perhaps even premeditation) may indeed arise instantaneously, the very nature of deliberation requires time to reflect, a lack of impulse, and, as the older cases had held at least since 1837, a "cool purpose." * * *

A more recent version of Wharton's Criminal Law, however, returns the discussion of premeditation and deliberation to its roots:

> Although an intent to kill, without more, may support a prosecution for common law murder, such a murder ordinarily constitutes murder in the first degree only if the intent to kill is accompanied by premeditation and deliberation. 'Premeditation' is the process simply of thinking about a proposed killing before engaging in the homicidal conduct; and 'deliberation' is the process of carefully weighing such matters as the wisdom of going ahead with the proposed killing, the manner in which the killing will be accomplished, and the consequences which may be visited upon the killer if and when apprehended. 'Deliberation' is present if the thinking, i.e., the 'premeditation,' is being done in such a cool mental state, under such circumstances, and for such a period of time as to permit a 'careful weighing' of the proposed decision.

C. Torcia, Wharton's Criminal Law § 140 (14th ed. 1979). * * *

Logically, of course, the fact that repeated blows (or shots) were inflicted on the victim is not sufficient, by itself, to establish first-degree murder. Repeated blows can be delivered in the heat of passion, with no design or reflection. Only if such blows are inflicted as the result of premeditation and deliberation can they be said to prove first-degree murder. * * *

This discussion leads us inevitably to the conclusion that Mack Brown's conviction for first-degree murder in this case cannot be sustained. The law in Tennessee has long recognized that once the homicide has been established, it is presumed to be murder in the second degree. The state bears the burden of proof on the issue of premeditation and deliberation sufficient to elevate the offense to first-degree murder.

Here, there simply is no evidence in the record that in causing his son's death, Mack Brown acted with the premeditation and deliberation required to establish first-degree murder. There is proof, circumstantial in nature, that the defendant acted maliciously toward the child, in the heat of passion or anger, and without adequate provocation -- all of which would make him guilty of second-degree murder. The only possible legal basis upon which the state might argue that a first-degree conviction can be upheld in this case is the proof in the record that the victim had sustained "repeated blows." It was on this basis, and virtually no other, that we upheld a similar first-degree murder conviction for the death of a victim of prolonged child abuse in *State v. LaChance*. In view of our foregoing discussion concerning the shortcomings of such an analysis, we find it necessary to depart from much of the rationale underlying that decision.

In abandoning *LaChance*, we are following the lead of a sister state. In *Midgett v. State*, the Arkansas Supreme Court was asked to affirm the first-degree murder conviction of a father who had killed his eight-year-old son by repeated blows of his fist. As was the case here, there was a shocking history of physical abuse to the child, established both by eyewitness testimony and by proof of old bruises and healed fractures.

　　* * * [T]he *Midgett* court noted:

> The appellant argues, and we must agree, that in a case of child abuse of long duration the jury could well infer that the perpetrator comes not to expect death of the child from his action, but rather that the child will live so that the abuse may be administered again and again. Had the appellant planned his son's death, he could have accomplished it in a previous beating. . . . The evidence in this case supports only the conclusion that the appellant intended not to kill his son but to further abuse him or that his intent, if it was to kill the child, was developed in a drunken, heated, rage while disciplining the child. Neither of those supports a finding of premeditation or deliberation.

The Arkansas court, in strengthening the requirements for proof of premeditation and deliberation in a first-degree murder case involving a victim of child abuse, found it necessary to overrule prior case law to the extent that it was inconsistent with the opinion in *Midgett*. We do the same here. Like the *Midgett* court, we do not condone the homicide in this case, or the sustained abuse of the defenseless victim, Eddie Brown. We simply hold that in order to sustain the defendant's conviction, the proof must conform to the statute. Because the state has failed to establish sufficient evidence of first-degree murder, we reduce the defendant's conviction to second-degree murder and remand the case for resentencing. * * *

STATE v. BINGHAM

Supreme Court of Washington

105 Wash. 2d 820, 719 P.2d 109 (1986)

GOODLOE, J.

In this case, we review the sufficiency of the evidence of the premeditation element in an aggravated first degree murder conviction. The Court of Appeals found the evidence insufficient and reversed and remanded for resentencing for second degree murder. We affirm the Court of Appeals decision.

On February 18, 1982, the raped and strangled body of Leslie Cook, a retarded adult, was found in a pasture in Sequim. Cook was last seen alive on February 15, 1982, with respondent Charles Dean Bingham. The Clallam County Prosecutor, by amended information, charged Bingham with aggravated first degree (premeditated) murder, rape being the aggravating circumstance. The prosecutor also notified Bingham that the State would seek the death penalty.

The evidence presented at trial showed that on February 15, Cook and Bingham got off a bus together in Sequim about 6 p.m. There was no evidence that they knew each other before this time. They visited a grocery store and two residences. Cook was last seen at the residence of Wayne Humphrey and Enid Pratt where Bingham asked for a ride back to Port Angeles. When he was told no, Bingham said they would hitchhike. They left together heading toward the infrequently traveled Old Olympic Highway. None of the witnesses who saw the two heard any argument or observed any physical contact between them. Three days later, Cook's body was found in a field about a quarter mile from the Humphrey-Pratt residence.

At trial, King County Medical Examiner Reay described the results of the autopsy he performed on Cook's body. The cause of death was "asphyxiation through manual strangulation," accomplished by applying continuous pressure to the windpipe for approximately 3 to 5 minutes. Cook had a bruise on her upper lip, more likely caused by a hand being pressed over her mouth than by a violent blow. Tears were found in Cook's vaginal wall and anal ring. Spermatozoa were present. These injuries were inflicted antemortem. Also, there was a bite mark on each of Cook's breasts. Reay testified that these occurred perimortem or postmortem.

Two forensic odontologists testified that the bite mark on one breast matched Bingham's teeth. No conclusive determination could be made with respect to the other bite mark.

The prosecutor's theory, as revealed in both his opening statement and closing argument, was that Bingham wanted to have sex with Cook and that he had to kill her in order to do so. The prosecutor hypothesized that Bingham had started the act while Cook was alive, and that he put his hand over her mouth and then strangled her in order to complete the act. The prosecutor also told the jury that the murder would be premeditated if Bingham had formed the intent to kill when he began to strangle Cook, and thought about that intent for the 3 to 5 minutes it took her to die.

The court instructed the jury on aggravated first degree murder and on the lesser included offenses of first and second degree murder and first degree manslaughter. The court also gave Bingham's proposed instruction on voluntary intoxication.

The jury found Bingham guilty of aggravated first degree murder. The jury also found, in the penalty phase, that the State had failed to prove that there were insufficient mitigating circumstances to warrant leniency. The trial court therefore sentenced Bingham to life imprisonment without the possibility of release or parole. * * *

We must determine whether evidence of premeditation was sufficiently demonstrated in order for the issue to go to the jury and in order to sustain a finding of premeditated killing. * * *

Bingham was charged with first degree murder pursuant to RCW 9A.32.030(1)(a), which requires for conviction "a premeditated intent to cause the death of another." The element of premeditation distinguishes first and second degree murder. Section (1)(a) of the second degree murder statute, RCW 9A.32.050, requires for conviction "intent to cause the death of another person but without premeditation."

The only statutory elaboration on the meaning of premeditation is found in RCW 9A.32.020(1), which states that premeditation "must involve more than a moment in point of time." Washington case law further defines premeditation as "the mental process of thinking beforehand, deliberation, reflection, weighing or reasoning for a period of time, however short." We recently approved an instruction which defined premeditation as "the deliberate formation of and reflection upon the intent to take a human life."

Premeditation may be shown by direct or circumstantial evidence. Circumstantial evidence can be used where the inferences drawn by the jury are reasonable and the evidence supporting the jury's verdict is substantial. In this case, the State presented no direct evidence. The issue thus becomes whether sufficient circumstantial evidence of premeditation was presented. Bingham was not charged with felony murder.[a]

To show premeditation, the State relied on the pathologist's testimony that manual strangulation takes 3 to 5 minutes. The State argues this time is an appreciable amount of time in which Bingham could have deliberated. Bingham argues that time alone is not enough and that other indicators of premeditation must be shown. * * *

We agree with the Court of Appeals majority that to allow a finding of premeditation only because the act takes an appreciable amount of time obliterates the distinction between first and second degree murder. Having the opportunity to deliberate is not evidence the defendant did deliberate, which is necessary for a finding of premeditation. Otherwise, any form of killing which took more than a moment could result in a finding of premeditation, without some additional evidence showing reflection. Holding a hand over someone's mouth or windpipe does not necessarily reflect a decision to kill the person, but possibly only to quiet her or him. Furthermore, here a question of the ability to deliberate or reflect while engaged in sexual activity exists. * * *

The facts of a savage murder generate a powerful drive, almost a juggernaut for jurors, and indeed for judges, to crush the crime with the utmost condemnation available, to seize whatever words or terms reflect maximum denunciation, to cry out murder "in the first degree." But it is the task and conscience of a judge to transcend emotional momentum with reflective analysis. The judge is aware that many murders most brutish and bestial are committed in a consuming frenzy or heat of passion, and that these are in law only murder in the second degree. * * *

---

[a]Apparently, the prosecutor did not charge Bingham with felony murder because he thought felony murder was a lesser included offense of aggravated first degree murder, and that the jury would be instructed on felony murder before deliberations. The trial court, however, rejected the prosecutor's proposed instruction on felony murder. The Court of Appeals of Washington upheld the trial court's decision on this issue, stating: "We believe the evidence also would have supported a finding of felony murder . . . However, the State did not charge Bingham with felony murder. The trial judge correctly refused to instruct the jury that felony murder was a lesser included offense of the crime as charged." *State v. Bingham*, 40 Wash. App. 553, 699 P.2d 262 (Ct. App. 1985).

Exercising our responsibility, we find manual strangulation alone is insufficient evidence to support a finding of premeditation. We affirm the Court of Appeals decision.

CALLOW, J. (dissenting)

I would reinstate the aggravated first degree murder conviction of defendant. Sufficient evidence was presented on premeditation for that issue to be submitted to the jury. The decision on that issue is the function of the jury; not to be taken away. * * *

The rule announced by the majority seems to be that premeditation must take place *before the commencement* of the act that results in death. Take the farmer's son who begins to fill the bin with wheat as a joke on his brother sleeping at its bottom. Then, realizing that he will inherit the whole farm if he persists, he does so and causes his brother's death. He had time to premeditate and did so in the middle of the act. He has committed aggravated first degree murder. That a murderer originally commenced an act without intending death does not grant him a carte blanche to persist when he realizes that to do so will kill his victim. * * *

The testimony of Dr. Donald Reay, Chief Medical Examiner for King County, who performed the autopsy on Leslie Cook, is illuminating as to what is necessary to effect death by manual strangulation. * * *

Q Doctor, when you say manual strangulation, you mean the hands?

A Yes, correct.

Q Okay, now how long does it take someone to die by manual strangulation, doctor?

A Ordinarily the process will take three to five minutes.

Q And what sort of force or what sort of action is required during that three to five minutes period?

A The requirement is to stop the blood flow to the brain and at the same time prevent a person from breathing. The result is that they become oxygen deficient and the heart is sensitive over a period of time and leads to lack of oxygen that develops an abnormal rhythm which proceeds to death.

Q Doctor, does unconsciousness come before death in a case of manual strangulation?

A Oh, yes. Yes.

Q And how long does it take before someone is unconscious, do you know?

A If a well placed hold about the neck, it can take a matter of seconds. We have done some tests where a person becomes unconscious in a matter of six to seven seconds, if the vessels are pinched in a very quick fashion.

Q And death ensues within three to five minutes?

A Yes, that may be unconsciousness, but if the pressure is released the person will wake up. It's a hold that sometimes is used by law enforcement, but if the pressure is sustained then the brain goes without oxygen and in addition the airways collapse over the lungs and heart go without oxygen and there are deficits building up which affect the heart and it starts to develop abnormal beats or rhythms and eventually leads to death.

Q Doctor, does this sort of asphyxiation by manual strangulation in this instance, does it take a steady pressure for that three to five minute period?

A Yes, the pressure can vary, certainly, but the important thing is to include the airway and the arterial supply. One or the other will effectively do it.

* * *

If one sits quietly and watches the clock for 3 to 5 minutes, an appreciation of the fullness of that length of time pervades one's thoughts. The jury was entitled to put itself in the shoes of the victim and the murderer. The victim would have gone from apprehension to fear, terror, and then lapsed into unconsciousness. During this time the victim, in all likelihood, would have struggled and the defendant would have watched all of this in the eyes of his victim. As to the defendant, the continued, deliberate exertion of strength required for that length of time was substantial. By the fact of death, we know that not once during all that it took to effect death did he desist from accomplishing his purpose. * * *

The State presented substantial circumstantial evidence on the issue of premeditation. The trial court properly left that issue to the jury. The jury found that the defendant did premeditate. I would reinstate the first degree murder conviction of the defendant.

Note

Judge Goodloe, writing for the majority in *State v. Bingham*, questions whether a man can "deliberate or reflect while engaged in sexual activity." Do you find this reason in support of the majority's finding that there was insufficient evidence of premeditation persuasive?

GILBERT v. STATE

Court of Appeals of Florida, Fourth District
487 So. 2d 1185, 11 Fla. L. Weekly 1007 (Fla. Dist. Ct. App. 1986)

WALDEN, J.

Upon trial by jury, Roswell Gilbert was found guilty of the premeditated murder of his wife, Emily, in contravention of section 782.04(1)(a)1, Florida Statutes (1981). He, at age 75, was sentenced to life imprisonment. Under section 775.082, Florida Statutes (1981), there is a mandatory minimum sentence of 25 years. Thus, Mr. Gilbert would be incarcerated until he reached the age of 100 years before he would be eligible for release.

Mr. and Mrs. Gilbert lived together in a Fort Lauderdale condominium. They had been married for 51 years. Emily suffered from osteoporosis and Alzheimer's Disease. Her physician, Dr. Hidalgo, had prescribed Percodan to help alleviate the pain of the arthritis. The dosage was for moderate pain. There is no doubt that she was in pain because of the osteoporosis and sometimes confused because of the Alzheimer's.

At trial, appellant's attorney called a couple of Emily's friends, in addition to Dr. Hidalgo, to testify as to her physical and emotional condition before her death.

On direct examination Lillian Irvin testified that Emily was in a lot of pain because of the arthritis. One day, while Lillian was in her condominium office, Emily came in looking for appellant. She was upset and crying. He was in a condominium meeting, so Lillian called him out of the meeting to come and attend to his wife. When he arrived Emily said, "I'm so sick, I want to die, I'm so sick . . . Ros I want to die, I want to die."

On cross-examination Lillian testified that Emily would come down from her tenth floor apartment every day to either look for appellant or walk around the condominium pool. The couple also went out to lunch every day.

Jacqueline Rhodes also testified for the defense. She stated that Emily had deteriorated during the last two years of their acquaintance. She was forgetful at times and in pain because of her back. In Jacqueline's opinion appellant had always been very kind and attentive to his wife.

On one particular occasion, Jacqueline went to the Gilberts' apartment and saw Emily lying on the sofa crying and looking very sick. This struck Jacqueline as particularly indicative of Emily's condition.

Appellant testified in his own defense. He recounted their lives together from the first incident of osteoporosis, which was approximately eight years before her death. As time progressed the arthritis worsened and then Emily began to lose her memory. This was diagnosed as Alzheimer's Disease. The manifestation of Emily's illness which appeared to bother appellant the most was her increased dependence on him.

Appellant then described the events which led up to Emily's death. On March 2, Emily had another bout with osteoporosis. The next day he took her to the hospital. Emily did not want to stay there and became uncooperative and insisted on going home. Finally, appellant decided it was best to take her home. This made Emily feel better.

On March 4, the day of the killing, appellant took Emily out to lunch as usual. When they got back he gave her four Percodan tablets, put her on the sofa and went to a condominium meeting. A few minutes later Emily followed him down to the meeting. Appellant left the meeting and took Emily back to their apartment. As she lay on the sofa, she said, "Please, somebody help me. Please, somebody help me." In his own words this is how appellant killed Emily:

> Who's that somebody but me, you know, and there she was in pain and all this confusion and I guess if I got cold as icewater that's what had happened. I thought to myself, I've got to do it, it's got to be mine, I've got to end her suffering, this can't go on.

> I went in. The gun was up on the top shelf with a clip in it. I loaded it with one shell, pulled the clip out. I don't like to leave loaded guns laying around.

Well, then I shot her in the head. I felt her pulse, I could still feel it. I thought, Oh, my God, I loused it up.

I went back to the shop. This time I was shaking. I wasn't cold as ice at all. Back to the shop, put another round in the gun, came back, put another bullet in her head.

The only comforting thing, the first shot there was no convulsive reaction, just her right hand shook like that fast and her head went over the impacted bullet and it slowly came down, didn't make any noise except her mouth just opened slowly like that and then, you know, I thought it hit so fast she didn't know what happened. Then I felt her pulse. It turned out I was wrong. The pulse keeps going after this episode for a few minutes anyway. I didn't know that. I just thought I had, you know -- and the second time I fired I felt the pulse seemed to be gone. So I somehow got to the telephone and called the security guard downstairs and I said, "I just killed my wife," and --

His attorney continued the questioning:

[Mr. Varon:] Ros, why did you use a gun?

[Appellant:] I think poison is a horrible way to die. There's no such thing as instantaneous death with poison. I know nothing about poisons but I know that and I know nothing about poisons, I didn't have any. If I did have any, I wouldn't know how to use it. I'd probably louse it up, just get her terribly sick and that's not going to do any --

Q Ros --

A Firing a shot in the head will cause cessation of all consciousness in one millisecond, one thousandth of a second. I'm sure she didn't even hear the gun go off and I've been asked that question.

. . . .

Q Why did you think that or did you feel that you're the only one that could have ended her suffering?

A Natural conclusion. I can't go to the medical people. They have no cure for Alzheimer's. The osteoporosis was getting worse slowly in time. Everything looked like it was converging to a climax.

Q Ros --

A I couldn't see any other end than her dying. If I put her in a nursing home, well, after that hospital thing I don't think a nursing home would take her. The hospital certainly wouldn't take her.

So I put her in a nursing home and they won't let me stay there and she's separated from me. It would be a horrible death for her. She would die.

Then I can't confide in my friends without getting them involved, you know, in this sort of thing that I did. I couldn't go to the doctor. He is a professional. He is duly bound to report it to the authorities and they would pull me out of the picture.

The whole thing was a mess and the only solution to me was to terminate her suffering. That's all.

Q Now, Ros --

A If I could continue?

Q Yes, please.

A I didn't consider what would happen to me at all. The only important thing was to terminate her suffering. I could take care of whatever happens to me and it's happening right now and that was of no consequence to me.

Sure, I know I was breaking the law but there seems to be things more important than the law, at least to me in my private tragedy. So it's murder. So what?

On cross-examination appellant testified that he had never talked with Emily about killing her and had decided to shoot her from behind so she would not see the gun.

The record reveals that up until the time of her death, Emily was always neat and well-dressed, wearing makeup, jewelry, and coordinated outfits. She also went to the hairdresser every two weeks up until the last week of her life.

Her doctor testified that Emily could have lived for another five to ten years. She was never bedridden or completely incapacitated. * * *

In the case at hand there was no evidence that Emily left a mercy will. It is ridiculous and dangerous to suggest, as appellant does, that a constructive mercy will was left when Emily (or anyone else who is sick) said/says, "I'm so sick I want to die." Such a holding would judicially sanction open season on people who, although sick, are also chronic complainers. Because there was no mercy will, appellant's good faith intentions do not come into play. "Good faith" is not a legal defense to first degree murder. * * *

Finally, this court notices that this aged defendant has been a peaceful, law-abiding and respected citizen up until this time. No one has suggested that he will again kill someone or enter upon a criminal career. However, the absolute rigidity of the statutory mandatory minimum sentences do not permit consideration of these factors or, for that matter, they, different from the sentencing guidelines, do not take into account any mitigating circumstances. Whether such sentences should somehow be moderated so as to allow a modicum of discretion and whether they should allow distinctions to be made in sentencing between different kinds of wrongdoers, for instance, between a hired gangster killer and one, however misguided, who kills for love or mercy, are all questions which, under our system, must be decided by the legislature and not by the judicial branch. We leave it there.

Having completely considered the written and oral appellate presentation, the judgment of conviction is

AFFIRMED.

GLICKSTEIN, J., concurring specially.

I agree in general with the reasoning of the majority, and entirely concur in the result. * * *

I have some concern, [however], about the hint in the main opinion that trial courts should be enabled to vary minimum mandatory sentences according to the "kind" of wrongdoer; e.g., hired killer versus misguided mercy killer. I do not favor opening the door to such distinctions.

My thoughts lie with the victim, who was silenced forever by appellant's criminal act. She would be no more dead if a hired gangland killer had pulled the trigger.

Can it be that we feel more comfortable about imposing severe punishment on persons we perceive to belong to a separate tribe, whom we label criminals, than on those we see as members of our own tribe? In fact, we are all members of a common humanity.

The Decalogue states categorically, "Thou shalt not murder." It draws no distinction between murder by members of the middle class and murder by members of an underclass. It draws no distinction between murder by a family member and murder by a stranger. It draws no distinction between murder out of a misguided notion of compassion and murder for hire.

The victims in all such cases are equally dead. If the act was deliberate, the minimum penalty should not vary with the actor's purported motivation.

The concept of permissive mitigation of the minimum penalty based upon a claim the motive for the killing was compassion is even more difficult to accept when the offender is sophisticated, educated and mature, and has enjoyed opportunities in life to make choices.

Note

Under both the common law tradition and the Model Penal Code, suicide (killing oneself) and euthanasia (killing another out of mercy rather than ill-will) are illegal.[a] Several states have passed statutes explicitly criminalizing physician-assisted suicide. However, one jurisdiction in the United States – Oregon – has gone against this trend, legalizing physician-assisted suicide through passage of the Oregon Death with Dignity Act, adopted by voters in 1994. As one commentator describes its provisions:

---

[a] Euthanasia is commonly divided into two types, active and passive. "Active euthanasia involves prescribing medication or treatments aimed at shortening a person's life and alleviating his or her suffering. * * * Passive euthanasia may take two forms: one is abstention from performing acts that prolong the patient's life. An example may be refraining from connecting a patient to a respirator or to a resuscitation machine. The other form involves discontinuation of actions designed to sustain life. This means withdrawing machines to which the patient has already been connected." Raphael Cohen-Almagor, *Euthanasia and Physician-Assisted Suicide in the Democratic World: A Legal Overview*, 16 N.Y. Int'l L. Rev. 1, 2-3 (2003).

The Death with Dignity Act specifically permits competent, terminally ill adult Oregon residents to obtain prescriptions from their doctors for the purpose of lethal self-administration. * * * The attending physician is assigned specific responsibilities under the Act, including to determine whether the patient has a terminal disease, whether the patient is competent, whether the patient is a resident of Oregon, and, perhaps most importantly, to ensure that the patient has made an informed decision. Before a patient may qualify to end his or her life under the Act, a consulting physician must also confirm the attending physician's diagnosis that the patient has a terminal disease and independently determine that the patient is competent and has made a voluntary and informed decision. The attending or consulting physician must also refer the patient to a psychological counselor if either doctor believes that the patient "may be suffering from a psychiatric or psychological disorder or depression causing impaired judgment." In such a case, the Act specifically prohibits the prescription of medication for the purpose of ending the patient's life until the counselor determines that the patient is not suffering from depression or any other psychological disorder. The patient is also encouraged to notify family members of his decision, and the Act requires a waiting period between the patient's request and physician's prescription of the medication.

Comment, *The Oregon Death with Dignity Act: A Successful Model or a Legal Anomaly Vulnerable To Attack?*, 40 Hous. L. Rev. 1387, 1391-92 (2004).

How often has the Act been utilized? The Comment continues:

During the five-year period from 1998 through 2002, 198 prescriptions of lethal doses were written in accordance with the Death with Dignity Act. Of these 198 prescription recipients, 129 died after ingesting the medication; the remaining patients either died from their underlying disease or were still alive at the time the fifth-year data was compiled. Moreover, the 129 PAS [physician-assisted suicide] deaths in Oregon during the five-year study comprise less than one-eighth of one percent of Oregon resident deaths.

Id. at 1392.

Although Oregon is the only United States jurisdiction that formally allows assisted suicide, even in jurisdictions where euthanasia is a crime juries sometimes refuse to apply the law. Raphael Cohen-Almagor reports on the strange career of Dr. Jack Kevorkian, nicknamed "Dr. Death," who reportedly helped more than 130 terminal patients to die, some with the aid of a machine he invented to help people commit suicide by automatically injecting first a narcotic and then a lethal dose of potassium chloride.

> In Michigan, a special statute was passed in 1993 to stop Dr. Jack Kevorkian from assisting patients to die. However, Dr. Kevorkian stood trial several times and in all instances the juries refused to convict him of violating that statute, although Kevorkian admitted he had assisted people to commit suicide. Kevorkian was acquitted on the grounds that his main intent was to relieve pain, not to cause death. In November 1998, he actively performed euthanasia on Thomas Youk, stood trial and was convicted of second-degree murder and of delivering a controlled substance for the purpose of injecting Youk with lethal drugs. Kevorkian was given a jail sentence of 10 to 25 years on the second-degree murder conviction, and 3 to 7 years on the "controlled substance" conviction.

Raphael Cohen-Almagor, *Euthanasia and Physician-Assisted Suicide in the Democratic World: A Legal Overview*, 16 N.Y. Int'l L. Rev. 1, 19-20 (2003).

Should the law recognize a constitutionally-protected liberty interest in an individual's right to take her own life, and if so, should that right encompass the right to involve others, such as physicians, in implementing the patient's decision? In *Washington v. Glucksberg*, 521 U.S. 702 (1997), the Supreme Court held that the right to commit suicide was *not* a liberty interest protected by the Due Process Clause of the Fourteenth and Fifth Amendments. Moreover, the Court held that governments have a legitimate government interest in prohibiting suicide and euthanasia, including the preservation of human life; the protection of the integrity and ethics of the medical profession; the protection of vulnerable groups from abuse, neglect, and mistake; and the protection of disabled and terminally ill people from prejudice, negative and inaccurate stereotypes, and societal indifference. *Glucksberg*, 521 U.S. at 703. Therefore, the state of Washington was free to enforce a statute banning physician-assisted suicide.

On the same day that the Court handed down *Glucksberg*, it also decided *Vacco v. Quill*, 521 U.S. 793 (1997). In that case, physicians had asked for a judgment that New York's laws prohibiting physician-assisted suicide were unconstitutional under the Equal Protection Clause, given that New York permitted competent patients to refuse life-saving medical treatment. The physicians argued that such a refusal is practically equivalent to a physician-assisted suicide, so the law should not allow the former while criminalizing the latter. The Court rejected the equal protection challenge, asserting that "[t]he distinction between letting a patient die and making that patient die is important, logical, rational, and well established: It comports with fundamental legal principles of causation . . ." *Vacco v. Quill*, 521 U.S. at 793-94. Do you agree with the Court?

D.   THE DOCTRINE OF PROVOCATION (VOLUNTARY MANSLAUGHTER)

One of the ways an intentional killing can be mitigated from murder to voluntary manslaughter is through the doctrine of provocation, also known as the heat of passion defense. Under this doctrine, one who kills in response to legally adequate provocation is treated as having acted without malice aforethought, the mens rea required for murder. In reality, however, the defendant who claims provocation often acts with an intent to kill or an intent to grievously injure, two means of proving malice aforethought. The better way to think about provocation is that the defendant's culpability is mitigated, not because of the absence of malice aforethought, but because of culturally-sanctioned sympathy with his or her loss of self control. Thus, the provocation defense is often described as a concession to human weakness.

Over the years, American jurisdictions have embraced three different approaches to determining whether a defendant charged with murder is entitled to a voluntary manslaughter instruction: (1) the early common law (categorical) test; (2) the modern "reasonable man" (later "reasonable person") test; and (3) the Model Penal Code's extreme mental or emotional disturbance defense. These different approaches are discussed in greater detail below.

Historically, the provocation defense developed through the desire of common law judges to align the dictates of the criminal law with Anglo-American cultural mores. One note-writer observes that the cultural notion of "honor" had much to do with the emergence of provocation doctrine:

> In English society, a man was bound by a code of honor that strictly defined the parameters of appropriate behavior during particular forms of social intercourse. Since the protection of a man's "natural honor" was contingent on his conformity to this behavior, the honor code was much more pervasive and influential than the loose rules of etiquette that structure modern society. "Men of honour" -- men who took their natural

honor seriously -- were expected to retaliate swiftly and forcefully in the face of an affront. The act of retaliation, regardless of the consequences, would negate the threat to honor. "What is more," explains [Jeremy Horder], "[the man of honor] was not expected to retaliate reluctantly . . . . He was expected to resent the affront, and to retaliate in anger." [Jeremy Horder, PROVOCATION AND RESPONSIBILITY 25-30 (1992).]

Anger, rage, and retaliatory measures, then, were culturally programmed reactions, "implanted" in the psyches of sixteenth-century English males as not only justifiable, but also obligatory courses of action. To the extent that men of honor believed retaliatory actions were the direct functions of courage, retaliatory "boxes on the ear," fist fights, and even duels were encouraged in English society. Moreover, the code of honor did not simply dictate that men were obliged to engage in some form of ambiguous "angered retaliation"; the form of retaliation was strictly regulated by culturally defined principles of proportionality. These rules of proportionality, as well as the principle of natural honor they reflected, were explicitly embodied in early-modern manslaughter laws.

Note, James J. Sing, *Culture as Sameness: Toward a Synthetic View of Provocation and Culture in the Criminal Law*, 108 Yale L.J. 1845, 1867 (1999).

Sing argues further that understood from this perspective, the doctrine of heat of passion as originally developed was not a concession to human frailty (and thus a type of excuse), but rather a recognition that anger and passion are in some circumstances justified by the prevailing culture (and thus a type of justification). As you read the cases below, consider whether in the context of contemporary Anglo-American culture heat of passion is conceptualized as a justification, an excuse, or a little of both.[a]

1. The Early Common Law's Categorical Approach to Provocation

The first approach to provocation, which emerged in the 1700s, was called the early common law or categorical test. Under this approach, one could

---

[a] For further discussion regarding the distinction between justifications and excuses, *see* the Introduction to Chapter 10.

claim the provocation mitigation if and only if one killed in response to: (1) an aggravated assault or battery, (2) the observation of a serious crime against a close relative, (3) an illegal arrest, (4) mutual combat, or (5) catching one's wife in the act of adultery. Only these categories of provocative acts were recognized at early common law as adequate provocation, and judges themselves created and applied these categories. Provocation was considered a question of "law," rather than "fact."

One categorical rule which has survived throughout the years even in modern jurisdictions is the "mere words" rule. Under this rule, mere words are never enough to constitute legally adequate provocation. The mere words rule made sense under the early common law categorical approach, when judges strictly controlled the kinds of situations subject to the provocation doctrine, but makes less sense under the modern trend which allows the jury to decide on a case by case basis whether there was adequate provocation.

Even though the mere words rule has been observed as a general matter, courts have made exceptions in certain situations. The next case, *People v. Ambro*, illustrates one long-standing exception to the mere words rule.

PEOPLE v. AMBRO
Appellate Court of Illinois, Second District
153 Ill. App. 3d 1, 505 N.E.2d 381 (App. Ct. 1987)

NASH, J.

After a jury trial, defendant, George Ambro, was convicted of murdering his wife, Ruth Ambro, and sentenced to a term of 20 years' imprisonment. On appeal, defendant contends . . . the trial court erred in refusing to instruct the jury on the offense of voluntary manslaughter based on provocation. * * *

Defendant and Ruth Ambro were married on May 25, 1974, and, at the time of the killing on March 28, 1985, the couple had two children, Jocelyn and Bethany, ages six and two years old. In 1978, the couple began experiencing marital difficulties and Ruth attempted suicide. In June 1984, the couple separated until Ruth returned to their Elgin residence two weeks later. During late 1984 and early 1985, the couple's marital problems worsened. Defendant testified that the couple did not have marital relations until after December 1984, and Ruth would stay out at night until 4:30 a.m. without explanation. He stated he became suspicious of her activities when he observed that Ruth was wearing different types of underwear and discovered she had purchased birth control pills.

In January 1985, the couple joined a marital counselling [sic] group, and on March 20, 1985, Ruth informed the group that she no longer loved defendant and was going to divorce him. Defendant stated that he attempted suicide shortly thereafter. On March 26, 1985, Ruth met with an attorney and scheduled a meeting for March 29, 1985, to sign a petition for dissolution of the marriage.

Defendant testified that he returned home from work on the evening of March 28, 1985, at approximately 5:30 p.m. and Ruth immediately began bickering. * * * [T]he couple had dinner and argued about Ruth's treatment of the children. Defendant accused Ruth of mistreating Bethany by hitting her and not feeding her properly and asked Ruth if she was taking her frustration toward defendant out on the child. Defendant stated that when Ruth picked up Bethany's high chair and threw it back about three feet, he became very upset and confused. * * *

After Bethany was put to bed, the couple continued their argument. Defendant stated he was cleaning the kitchen counter and was holding two knives in his hand when his wife, who was on the living room sofa, told him that he had no right to complain about her handling of the children because he "had no right to the children." She then called defendant an alcoholic and told him that he did not love the children and that she was going to take them away from him. Defendant testified he could not describe his feelings at that point and had never had such feelings before. He went to the living room, kneeled beside Ruth and asked her what he could do to restore their relationship. Ruth said, "I have another man and when we make love I feel like it was." She then said, "I know you want to kill me. Pull that knife and make it easy for me." Defendant then stabbed Ruth with a knife, testifying that he had no conscious knowledge of doing so or an intent to stab her. He immediately called the police, but Ruth never regained consciousness and died soon after being brought to the hospital. At trial, medical testimony established that the wife died from a single stab wound through the heart. * * *

Defendant tendered a jury instruction defining the offense of manslaughter based on provocation, but the trial court sustained an objection by the State and refused to submit it to the jury, which was instructed only on the charge of murder. After deliberations, the jury convicted defendant of murder and he was sentenced to a term of 20 years' imprisonment.

We consider first defendant's contention that the trial court erred in refusing to instruct the jury on the offense of voluntary manslaughter based on provocation. Defendant argues that it was error to refuse his tendered instruction based on section 9 -- 2(a) of the Criminal Code of 1961 (Code) (Ill. Rev. Stat. 1985, ch. 38, par. 9 -- 2(a)), which defines voluntary manslaughter. That section states:

A person who kills an individual without lawful justification commits voluntary manslaughter if at the time of the killing he is acting under a sudden and intense passion resulting from serious provocation by:

(1) The individual killed * * *.

* * * Serious provocation is conduct sufficient to excite an intense passion in a reasonable person.

Defendant asserts that the evidence warranted submission of the manslaughter instruction to the jury. In resolving this issue, we must first determine whether the evidence relating to the conduct of Ruth Ambro prior to the killing is, if believed by the jury, the type of provocation contemplated under section 9 -- 2(a) of the Code. In *People v. Matthews*, the court characterized this requirement by stating:

> Passion on the part of the slayer, no matter how violent will not relieve him from liability for murder unless it is engendered by a provocation which the law recognizes as being reasonable and adequate. If the provocation is not sufficient the crime is murder.

The general rule in Illinois is that the only categories of provocation which are considered sufficiently serious to reduce the crime of murder to voluntary manslaughter are substantial physical injury or assault, mutual quarrel or combat, illegal arrest, and adultery with the offender's spouse.[a] Mere words, however aggravated, abusive, opprobrious, or indecent, are not sufficient provocation. Moreover, adultery by a spouse has generally been limited to those instances where the parties were discovered in the act of adultery or immediately before or after its commission.

An apparent exception to these general rules, based on verbal revelations of infidelity and other conduct, has been recognized in two Illinois cases in which convictions for voluntary manslaughter were affirmed. In *People v. Ahlberg,* the defendant's killing of his wife was the culmination of a series of events. In that case, defendant's wife moved out of the house with the children

---

[a]Under the early common law's categorical approach to provocation, this last category of legally adequate provocation was limited to husbands who caught their wives in the act of adultery. Wives who caught their husbands in the act were not considered adequately provoked to merit a reduction in the charge from murder to manslaughter.

without informing her husband, and he looked for her for several days. When the victim finally contacted him, she informed the defendant that she was getting a divorce because she was tired of "being the nice school teacher's wife," that he had never satisfied her sexually, and that she had found an older man who could love her and her two children more than he could. Under these circumstances, the reviewing court considered that it would be a "direct refutation of logic and a miscarriage of justice" to follow the rule that mere words are insufficient to cause provocation serious enough to support a conviction for manslaughter.

In *People v. Carr*, defendant and his wife had engaged in frequent arguments in the six months preceding the shooting, most of them over the husband's suspicions of infidelity by her. Defendant's wife then moved out of their home, and defendant informed a cousin of the victim that he would kill his wife if she tried to remove any furniture from their home. The wife returned two weeks later to remove some furniture. The couple began arguing, and, when the wife told him, "At least now I have a real man," defendant shot her. The appellate court cited *Ahlberg* with approval and concluded that the evidence was sufficient to support defendant's conviction for voluntary manslaughter.

In *People v. Harris*, the court reviewed the two cases and noted that both *Ahlberg* and *Carr* involved situations where the revelation of adultery was one of a series of provoking statements or circumstances. The court then determined that "these cases do not support the proposition that Illinois has adopted the more liberal approach concerning verbal communication of the fact of adultery as provocation." We agree with that conclusion, since neither *Ahlberg* nor *Carr* were based on mere verbal conduct. In both cases, there was a history of ongoing marital discord, a wife who evidenced an intent to permanently leave her husband, insulting remarks concerning the husband's masculinity, and an announcement of adultery by the wife.

In the present case, defendant and his wife had been experiencing marital difficulties for seven years and, as in *Carr*, defendant began to suspect her of infidelity shortly before he killed her. One week before her death, Ruth told the couple's marital-counselling group and defendant that she no longer loved her husband and was going to seek a divorce. She then contacted an attorney to draft a petition for dissolution of the marriage and informed defendant of her actions. On the evening of the killing, defendant became upset over his wife's treatment of Bethany and her threats of seeking a divorce, and the couple engaged in repeated arguments during which the wife implied that defendant was not the father of her children, called him an alcoholic, and told him she was going to take the children when she left him. When defendant knelt beside his wife and asked how he could restore their relationship, she informed him of her adultery and then goaded him to kill her.

These facts closely parallel the series of events found to constitute serious provocation in *Ahlberg* and *Carr* and, in our view, go beyond the provocation elements in those cases, since the victim here goaded defendant to kill her. On these facts, we conclude the present case falls within the exception recognized in *Ahlberg* and *Carr* and find that the wife's conduct was the type of provocation which Illinois law recognizes as sufficiently serious, if believed by the jury, to reduce the crime of murder to voluntary manslaughter. * * *

Accordingly, the judgment of the trial court is reversed and the cause remanded for a new trial.

Reversed and remanded.[b]

Note

Courts have made exceptions to the mere words rule in a few other situations. For example, in *State v. Tackett*, 8 N.C. 210 (1820), the Supreme Court of North Carolina ordered a new trial for a white man who was convicted of murdering a slave, suggesting that a white man who kills another man's slave in response to words of reproach uttered by that slave is entitled to claim provocation. In explaining why a new trial was in order, the court noted that the trial court's instruction to the jury (that the case was to be determined by the same rules and principles of law as if the deceased, a slave, had been a white man) was in error. According to the court, it was appropriate to grant more leniency to a white man who kills a slave than to a white man who kills another white man because:

> It exists in the nature of things, that where slavery prevails, the relation between a white man and a slave differs from that, which subsists between free persons; and every individual in the community feels and understands, that the homicide of a slave may be extenuated by acts which would not produce a legal provocation if done by a white person. * * *

> It is a rule of law, that neither words of reproach, insulting gestures, nor a trespass against goods or land, are provocations sufficient to free the party killing from the guilt of murder, where he made use of a deadly weapon. But it cannot be laid

---

[b] In 1989, the Supreme Court of Illinois overruled *People v. Ambro*, *People v. Ahlberg*, and *People v. Carr*, holding that a wife's confession of adultery, no matter how insulting, does not constitute legally adequate provocation. *People v. Chevalier*, 544 N.E.2d 942 (Ill. 1989).

down as a rule, that some of these provocations, if offered by a slave, well known to be turbulent and disorderly, would not extenuate the killing, if it were instantly done under the heat of passion, and without circumstances of cruelty.

Should courts recognize an exception to the mere words rule for persons of color who kill in response to a racist epithet? Professor Camille Nelson argues that the doctrine of provocation should be expanded to include an appreciation of serial or cumulative provocation. Under her proposal, a black man who has suffered countless acts of racism would be able to claim provocation from being called the "N word." She explains:

> Such recognition of "serial provocation" would better appreciate the reality of racist abuses. Unlike the case of the battered woman who might be in a longstanding relationship with her abuser, victims of racism are bombarded by various abuses from many different persons and sources. If the accused is a black person who has been the victim of routine racist microaggressions, the racist act or racist insult should be situated in the context of such racism. Psychiatrists who have studied black populations view such microaggressions as "incessant and cumulative" assaults on black self-esteem. Racism affects mental well-being, in addition to causing stress, by compromising the self-concept of the person subjected to racial abuses.

Camille A. Nelson, *(En)raged or (En)gaged: The Implications of Racial Context to the Canadian Provocation Defence*, 35 U. Rich. L. Rev. 1007, 1051 (2002).

2. The Modern "Reasonable Person" Test

In the late 1800s, many American jurisdictions began to abandon the categorical approach to provocation in favor of an approach that utilized a reasonableness requirement to determine which types of behavior could be considered legally adequate provocation. Under the modern test for provocation in jurisdictions that have incorporated the common law, the jury must find: (1) the defendant actually acted in a heat of passion; (2) the heat of passion was provoked by an act or event that would have also provoked a reasonable person in the defendant's shoes to lose self control; (3) the defendant did not have sufficient time to "cool off" between the provocative act or event and the killing; and (4) a reasonable person in the defendant's shoes would not have had sufficient time to cool. Additionally, there must be a causal connection between the provocation, the passion, and the killing, meaning both that the provocation is what actually provoked the killing and that the person killed is either the provoker or someone acting in concert with the provoker.

Although the modern test for provocation gives more decision-making power to the jury than the early common law approach, jurisdictions following the common law continue to differ with respect to how much of provocation doctrine should be implemented by the judge and how much should be left to the jury. In some jurisdictions, judges continue to impose rules on what situations may legally constitute adequate provocation. In other jurisdictions, the jury is given virtually free rein to hear the facts and decide whether the alleged provocation was adequate. *People v. Berry*, which follows, is an example of the latter approach.

PEOPLE v. BERRY
Supreme Court of California
18 Cal.3d 509, 556 P.2d 777, 134 Cal.Rptr. 415 (1976)

SULLIVAN, J.

Defendant Albert Joseph Berry was charged by indictment with one count of murder and one count of assault by means of force likely to produce great bodily injury. The assault was allegedly committed on July 23, 1974, and the murder on July 26, 1974. In each count, the alleged victim was defendant's wife, Rachel Pessah Berry. A jury found defendant guilty as charged and determined that the murder was of the first degree. Defendant was sentenced to state prison for the term prescribed by law. He appeals from the judgment of conviction.

Defendant contends that there is sufficient evidence in the record to show that he committed the homicide while in a state of uncontrollable rage caused by provocation and flowing from a condition of diminished capacity and therefore that it was error for the trial court to fail to instruct the jury on voluntary manslaughter as indeed he had requested. He claims: (1) that he was entitled to an instruction on voluntary manslaughter as defined by statute since the killing was done upon a sudden quarrel or heat of passion; and (2) that he was also entitled to an instruction on voluntary manslaughter in the context of a diminished capacity defense since malice was negatived by mental defect or disease. We agree with defendant as to the first instruction, but not as to the second.

Defendant, a cook, 46 years old, and Rachel Pessah, a 20-year-old girl from Israel, were married on May 27, 1974. Three days later Rachel went to Israel by herself, returning on July 13, 1974. On July 23, 1974, defendant choked Rachel into unconsciousness. She was treated at a hospital where she reported her strangulation by defendant to an officer of the San Francisco Police Department. On July 25, Inspector Sammon, who had been assigned to the case, met with Rachel and as a result of the interview a warrant was issued for defendant's arrest.

While Rachel was at the hospital, defendant removed his clothes from their apartment and stored them in a Greyhound Bus Depot locker. He stayed overnight at the home of a friend, Mrs. Jean Berk, admitting to her that he had choked his wife. On July 26, he telephoned Mrs. Berk and informed her that he had killed Rachel with a telephone cord on that morning at their apartment. The next day Mrs. Berk and two others telephoned the police to report a possible homicide and met Officer Kelleher at defendant's apartment. They gained entry and found Rachel on the bathroom floor. A pathologist from the coroner's office concluded that the cause of Rachel's death was strangulation. Defendant was arrested on August 1, 1974, and confessed to the killing.

At trial defendant did not deny strangling his wife, but claimed through his own testimony and the testimony of a phychiatrist, Dr. Martin Blinder, that he was provoked into killing her because of a sudden and uncontrollable rage so as to reduce the offense to one of voluntary manslaughter. He testified that upon her return from Israel, Rachel announced to him that while there she had fallen in love with another man, one Yako, and had enjoyed his sexual favors, that he was coming to this country to claim her and that she wished a divorce. Thus commenced a tormenting two weeks in which Rachel alternately taunted defendant with her involvement with Yako and at the same time sexually excited defendant, indicating her desire to remain with him. Defendant's detailed testimony, summarized below, chronicles this strange course of events.

After their marriage, Rachel lived with defendant for only three days and then left for Israel. Immediately upon her return to San Francisco she told defendant about her relationship with and love for Yako. This brought about further argument and a brawl that evening in which defendant choked Rachel and she responded by scratching him deeply many times. Nonetheless they continued to live together. Rachel kept taunting defendant with Yako and demanding a divorce. She claimed she thought she might be pregnant by Yako. She showed defendant pictures of herself with Yako. Nevertheless, during a return trip from Santa Rosa, Rachel demanded immediate sexual intercourse with defendant in the car, which was achieved; however upon reaching their apartment, she again stated that she loved Yako and that she would not have intercourse with defendant in the future.

On the evening of July 22nd defendant and Rachel went to a movie where they engaged in heavy petting. When they returned home and got into bed, Rachel announced that she had intended to make love with defendant, 'But I am saving myself for this man Yako, so I don't think I will.' Defendant got out of bed and prepared to leave the apartment whereupon Rachel screamed and yelled at him. Defendant choked her into unconsciousness.

Two hours later defendant called a taxi for his wife to take her to the hospital. He put his clothes in the Greyhound bus station and went to the home of his friend Mrs. Berk for the night. The next day he went to Reno and returned the day after. Rachel informed him by telephone that there was a warrant for his arrest as a result of her report to the police about the choking incident. On July 25th defendant returned to the apartment to talk to Rachel, but she was out. He slept there overnight. Rachel returned around 11 a.m. the next day. Upon seeing defendant there, she said, 'I suppose you have come here to kill me.' Defendant responded, 'yes,' changed his response to 'no,' and then again to 'yes,' and finally stated 'I have really come to talk to you.' Rachel began screaming. Defendant grabbed her by the shoulder and tried to stop her screaming. She continued. They struggled and finally defendant strangled her with a telephone cord.

Dr. Martin Blinder, a physician and psychiatrist, called by the defense, testified that Rachel was a depressed, suicidally inclined girl and that this suicidal impulse led her to involve herself ever more deeply in a dangerous situation with defendant. She did this by sexually arousing him and taunting him into jealous rages in an unconscious desire to provoke him into killing her and thus consummating her desire for suicide. Throughout the period commencing with her return from Israel until her death, that is from July 13 to July 26, Rachel continually provoked defendant with sexual taunts and incitements, alternating acceptance and rejection of him. This conduct was accompanied by repeated references to her involvement with another man; it led defendant to choke her on two occasions, until finally she achieved her unconscious desire and was strangled. Dr. Blinder testified that as a result of this cumulative series of provocations, defendant at the time he fatally strangled Rachel, was in a state of uncontrollable rage, completely under the sway of passion.

We first take up defendant's claim that on the basis of the foregoing evidence he was entitled to an instruction on voluntary manslaughter as defined by statute which is 'the unlawful killing of a human being, without malice . . . upon a sudden quarrel or heat of passion.' In *People v. Valentine*, this court, in an extensive review of the law of manslaughter, specifically approved the following quotation from *People v. Logan* as a correct statement of the law: 'In the present condition of our law it is left to the jurors to say whether or not the facts and circumstances in evidence are sufficient to lead them to believe that the defendant did, or to create a reasonable doubt in their minds as to whether or not he did, commit his offense under a heat of passion. The jury is further to be admonished and advised by the court that this heat of passion must be such a passion as would naturally be aroused in the mind of an ordinarily reasonable person under the given facts and circumstances, and that, consequently, no defendant may set up his own standard of conduct and justify or excuse himself because in fact his passions were aroused, unless further the jury believe that the facts and circumstances were sufficient to arouse the passions of the ordinarily reasonable man.... For the fundamental of the inquiry is whether or not the defendant's reason was, at the time of his act, so disturbed or obscured by some passion--not necessarily fear and never, of course, the passion for revenge--to such an extent as would render ordinary men of average disposition liable to act rashly or without due deliberation and reflection, and from this passion rather than from judgment.'

We further held in *Valentine* that there is no specific type of provocation required by section 192 and that verbal provocation may be sufficient. In *People v. Borchers,* in the course of explaining the phrase "heat of passion" used in the statute defining manslaughter we pointed out that "passion" need not mean "rage" or "anger" but may be any "(v)iolent, intense, high-wrought or enthusiastic emotion" and concluded there "that defendant was aroused to a heat of 'passion' by a series of events over a considerable period of time . . ." Accordingly we there declared that evidence of admissions of infidelity by the defendant's paramour, taunts directed to him and other conduct, "supports a finding that defendant killed in wild desperation induced by (the woman's) long continued provocatory conduct." We find this reasoning persuasive in the case now before us. Defendant's testimony chronicles a two-week period of provocatory conduct by his wife Rachel that could arouse a passion of jealousy, pain and sexual rage in an ordinary man of average disposition such as to cause him to act rashly from this passion. It is significant that both defendant and Dr. Blinder testified that the former was in the heat of passion under an uncontrollable rage when he killed Rachel.

The Attorney General contends that the killing could not have been done in the heat of passion because there was a cooling period, defendant having waited in the apartment for 20 hours. However, the long course of provocatory conduct, which had resulted in intermittent outbreaks of rage under specific provocation in the past, reached its final culmination in the apartment when Rachel began screaming. Both defendant and Dr. Blinder testified that defendant killed in a state of uncontrollable rage, of passion, and there is ample evidence in the record to support the conclusion that this passion was the result of the long course of provocatory conduct by Rachel, just as the killing emerged from such conduct in Borchers. * * *

[A]s we have already explained, the court did commit error in refusing to instruct on voluntary manslaughter based on sudden quarrel or heat of passion.

HEAT OF PASSION AND WIFE KILLING: MEN WHO BATTER/MEN WHO KILL
Donna K. Coker
2 S. Cal. Rev. L. & Women's Stud. 71 (1992)[a]

* * * [H]omicide law divides sane individuals who intentionally kill into two major categories: those who premeditate murder and those who act in the heat of passion. Social stereotypes of wife-killing that characterize the killer as a previously non-violent man who "snapped" under pressure, roughly parallel the understandings which underlie heat-of-passion doctrine. However, this social stereotype is grossly inaccurate when applied to men who are identified as "batterers" and when applied to the general category of husband-wife killings. Violence perpetrated by abusive men is purposeful, not spontaneous; the majority of men who kill their wives have a documented history of violent assaults. Furthermore, one would expect to find empirical evidence of wife-killers who fit the stereotype of the heat-of-passion killer in those reports of forensic psychiatrists whose job it is to aid defense counsel, yet these reports seem to confirm that men who kill and men who batter have remarkably similar personality traits and similar motivations. While further research is needed before we can determine whether or not the "impassioned" wife-killer exists, if he does exist, he is apparently part of a very small group of wife-killers.

* * * The case of *People v. Berry* appears in many criminal law textbooks as well as legal treatises, generally for the proposition that the question of "cooling off" is a jury question. * * *

At his trial, Berry offered only two defense witnesses: himself and a psychiatrist, Dr. Martin Blinder. Dr. Blinder testified that

> [Rachel] was a depressed, suicidally inclined girl [sic] and . . . this suicidal impulse led her to involve herself even more deeply in a dangerous situation with defendant. She did this by sexually arousing him and taunting him into jealous rages in an unconscious desire to provoke him into killing her and thus consummating her desire for suicide.

---

[a]Reprinted with the permission of the *California Review of Law and Women's Studies*.

The defense needed Blinder's testimony for two different, but equally critical, reasons. First, the fact that Berry had a prior conviction for stabbing and injuring his second wife had already been ruled admissible. Blinder's testimony was required to neutralize this damaging fact, but, in fact, Blinder went one step better by explaining that Berry's past violence resulted from his repeated emotional victimization at the hands of women. Second, Blinder's testimony was needed most obviously in order to cast the killing as a heat of passion killing and, in particular, to explain the 20-hour wait in Rachel's apartment as a result of *cumulative* passion and not premeditation and lying-in-wait. The result was psychiatric testimony that brilliantly–if tautologically–turned facts about Berry that suggested the antithesis to a "heat of passion killer"–i.e., a proclivity for violence, a history of serious prior assaults on the victim identical in kind to the fatal assault, Berry's stabbing of his ex-wife under remarkably similar circumstances, and a psychological profile fitting that of an abuser–into evidence of Berry's increasing provocation as the result of Rachel's relentless "taunting." * * *

In essence, Berry's defense was that he *was* the sort of man who abused women – but the twist was [Dr. Martin] Blinder's psychiatric explanation that Berry's violence was a result of his choosing women who enraged him and provoked him to violence. The fact that Berry had a prior conviction for assaulting his ex-wife with a butcher knife, that in past relationships with other women he had destroyed their property, forcing former girlfriends to "put him out of the house, locking the door," indicated to Blinder the personality of the *women* with whom Berry involved himself, more than it demonstrated Berry's dangerous and abusive nature. Blinder testified that these women "offer[ed] him the promise of comfort but ultimately deliver[ed] . . . emotional pain." Yet Blinder's testimony provides a classic portrait of an abuser. Berry was *most* dangerous when women threatened to leave him. Berry was "emotionally dependent" on wives and girlfriends; he threatened physical violence in order to control women; he destroyed women's property; and he had a history of violent relationships with wives and lovers. The Supreme Court's opinion read Dr. Blinder's testimony to focus narrowly on the effect of *Rachel's* "provocative" behavior on Berry's mental state. Dr. Blinder's testimony, however, refers to a cumulative rage resulting from the provocation of *all* the women in Berry's entire life.

> Q: . . . How would you characterize [Berry's] state of mind . . . [at the time of the homicide]?

> A: . . . I would say that he was in a state of uncontrollable rage which was a product of having to contend with what seems to me an incredibly provacative [sic] situation, an incredibly provacative [sic] young woman, and *that this immediate*

situation was superimposed upon Mr. Berry having encountered the situation time and time again. So that we have a cumulative effect dating back to the way his mother dealt with him.

. . .

Q: . . . [Y]ou say that the situation involving Rachel Berry and Albert Berry . . . was the product of . . . cumulative . . . provocations. Now, specifically, what would you base your opinion as to provocations on?

. . .

A: . . . We have two factors here. . . . The past history, that is, the history of this man well in advance of his meeting the deceased. And then the history of his relationship with her. And I think the two go together. . . . After 15 years [of marriage to his second wife] and five children, his wife leaves him for . . . another man. . . . They continued to live together, during which time his wife taunted him about her boyfriend. . . .

One night while they were having sex, his wife [calls him by the name of her boyfriend.] Despondent and enraged at the same time, he went into the kitchen, obtained a knife, and stabbed his wife in the abdomen. And she was not serious. He only got to spend a year in jail for that. . . .

So we have this pattern of enormous dependency on these women and then rupture of the relationship with tremendous rage, almost uncontrollable. I think in one instance he put his foot through the stereo . . . he had purchased for one of these girls [sic] . . . .

So we see a succession of women, beginning with his mother, who offer the promise of comfort but ultimately deliver indifference and emotional pain.

The irony of this defense testimony is found in its confirmation that Berry had a *propensity* to assault wives and lovers under circumstances in which he claimed the woman's infidelity provoked him. Rachel, then, became the recipient of Berry's cumulative rage against *all* the past women in his life. In a tautological way, Berry's past abuse of other women was used to strengthen his claim of *Rachel's* provocative nature: Berry had a pattern of involvement with emotionally abusive women; his violence was in response to their "abuse"–never the other way around. Rachel was involved with Berry; therefore, it is more than likely that Rachel emotionally abused Berry and that his violence was the result of provocation occasioned by her abuse. Dr. Blinder makes this leap of logic quite explicit in response to the District Attorney's attempt to probe his knowledge of Rachel's (supposed) subconscious suicidal motivation:

> Q: . . . [A]ssuming that [Rachel's suicidal] statement was made after the time of . . . her first husband's tragic accidental death. Would that have any effect [on your assessment] as to her [suicidal] state of mind?
>
> A: . . . Not much, Mr. Winkler. *Any woman who engaged in a relationship with [Berry] clearly has serious depressive and suicidal impulses.*

Again, the District Attorney attempted to highlight Blinder's complete reliance on Berry for his clinical assessment of Rachel and Berry's former lovers:

> Q: . . . Really, everything that you have [about Rachel] basically is what Mr. Berry tells you about her?
>
> A: . . . Well, let's put it this way, Mr. Winkler. . . . We're looking at a man who's had a series of relationships which have been in the same pattern time after time and which have all ended in much the same way, not perhaps the violent outcome but at least psychologically the same kind of outcome. It would be very surprising if Mr. Berry did any better in this relationship than he did with all the others.
>
> Q: . . . You are basing your opinion that [Berry] had these types of relationships primarily on what Mr. Berry tells you, is that correct . . . ?
>
> A: . . . Well, in part. I think I am basing it primarily on my ability to detect, identify familiar clinical patterns and some of the data that Mr. Berry gives me fits into this clinical pattern. . . . When you get a total longitudinal history of this man, *one can almost draw up the nature of his relationships with women* without his telling you a great deal about them.

* * *

Indicia of premeditation of the obsessive, brooding kind characteristic of batterers is clear in *Berry*. Berry himself said in his police statement, "I deliberately waited to kill her. No pretense, no bullshi[t], no nothing." Berry's long wait for Rachel to return home provides further evidence. His two prior assaults on Rachel also suggest premeditation, but the court's failure to understand the escalating, obsessive nature of wife battering prevents its recognition. The opinion relies on Blinder's explanation that the two prior assaults were evidence of Berry's increasingly provoked state. In fact, prior assaults just as easily support a "rehearsal" model or provide evidence of Berry's resort to increasingly dangerous tactics in order to control Rachel. Berry's ambivalence–his uncertainty about whether or not he intended to kill Rachel–and the fact that his two prior assaults of Rachel were similar in kind though not in severity, strongly point to the kind of "locked-in"–"it all depends on what *she* does"–sense of causality that mark the most dangerous of abusive men. Berry's confession evidences this kind of ambivalence. He requests to go back on the record to say, "I knew damn well when I was waiting for her, I'd probably kill her" but at trial testified that when Rachel asked if he'd come to kill her, he first said "yes" then "no" then "yes" again. While Berry admits that he knew he would *probably* kill her," he also states that his intent was to make her stop screaming: "She come in the door. She started screaming. I told her to shut up. All I wanted to do was talk. She kept screaming at me. I grabbed her and we wrestled . . . and I tried to shut her up. She wouldn't stop screaming. I wrapped the phone cord around her [neck]." * * *

    * * * The California Supreme Court opinion repeatedly echoes the tenor of Blinder's words – using terms such as "the result" or "culmination" – terms that diffuse responsibility and make Berry's violence seem inevitable and uncontrollable. For example, the opinion notes that Rachel's provocative behavior "resulted" in Berry's attacks; her confession of her love affair with Yacob "brought about further argument and a brawl that evening [after she returned from Israel] in which defendant choked Rachel and she responded by scratching him deeply many times." Rachel's "taunts and incitements" "led defendant to choke her on two occasions, until finally [Rachel] achieved her unconscious desire [for suicide] and was strangled." And the court further notes that "[Rachel's] long course of provocatory conduct . . . had resulted in intermittent outbreaks of rage . . . [which] reached its final culmination in the apartment when Rachel began screaming."

    Time and again the court identifies Rachel as the actor and Berry as the one who is acted upon. The violence "results," a brawl is "brought about" by Rachel's behavior, and Berry is therefore "led" to choke her. * * *

    * * * Berry portrayed himself, and likely believed himself to be, the real victim. When asked by the police why he didn't just leave Rachel – "[w]hat made you want to take her life first?" he responded:

I had so much planned in the future, everything. We were going to open up a restaurant when she came back [from Israel]. Had it all planned we were going to move, we were going to get out of that apartment because of bad memories . . . . I never denied her anything. She could have anything – as a matter of fact, when she was in Israel I sent her my last God damn hundred dollars.

This testimony portrays a man who is feeling great disappointment and loss. It also portrays a man wholly captured by his own perspective of reality – unable to imagine what was motivating Rachel. Berry's pain, no doubt, was genuine, but it was not his pain that killed Rachel. * * *

Though Blinder's testimony focused on Rachel's "provocative" sexual behavior, the truth is that Berry didn't kill Rachel until it appeared that she might make good on her threat to leave him. * * * Of course, a defense witness tells it from the perspective of the accused, but in this circumstance, the defendant's perspective is largely that of the Court and that of the Law, as well. That perspective, * * * suggests that a woman's "abandonment" of a husband is provocative – and that a woman's preference of another lover is provocation of the worst sort.

PROVOKED REASON IN MEN AND WOMEN: HEAT-OF-PASSION MANSLAUGHTER AND IMPERFECT SELF-DEFENSE

Laurie J. Taylor
33 UCLA L. Rev. 1679 (1986)

* * * Women are almost always killed by men, often by those with whom they have had an intimate relationship. Therefore, it is not surprising that in heat-of-passion killings of women, the passion often is connected to the victim's sexuality. Many defendants in the early English cases that define voluntary manslaughter were men who had killed their wives or their wives' lovers upon discovering them in the act of adultery. The earliest case specifying that provocation, not revenge, must be the cause of a killing for it to be considered manslaughter involved the prosecution of a defendant for killing his wife's lover. The court ordered that the defendant be burned in the hand and "'directed the executioner to burn him gently, because there could not be greater provocation than this.'" The case that first enumerated the categories of adequate provocation involved a man who killed another man in a quarrel, but the court was especially solicitous of one category: "Jealousy is the rage of a man, and adultery is the highest invasion of property. . . . a man cannot receive a higher provocation." The court lamented that killing the lover was merely partially excused and not justifiable. One writer maintains that "'the pre-

statutory English law of provocation amounted to little more than a re-statement of the established rule which admitted the defence where one spouse [sic] discovered the other in the act of adultery.'"

This writer's use of the term "spouse" is misleading: for almost three centuries only husbands could invoke the defense of provocation when they killed after witnessing adultery. While the law sympathized with the jealous rage of men, it assumed that wives did not experience similar rage. In 1946, 275 years after a court first announced the defense of provocation, an English court finally stated that wives who killed their husbands or their husbands' lovers could also avail themselves of the defense.

Adultery evoked a similar response from United States courts. The case some consider the first American use of the reasonable man standard for provocation focused on whether assault with intent to murder after learning of adultery justified a finding of heat of passion. The "honor defense" or "unwritten law" that allowed a court to acquit a defendant entirely when he killed to protect his honor (i.e., his exclusive right to possess the sexuality of his wife and his female relatives) had supporters in the legal community as recently as fifty years ago. Until the 1960s and 1970s, statutes in four states made it justifiable for the husband to kill his wife's lover.[87] * * *

Historically, when a defendant claimed adultery as provocation, courts lessened traditional requirements for adequate provocation. From 1871 to 1946, a line of English cases held that words alone could sufficiently provoke if those words confessed adultery. American courts have held that discovery of a letter revealing completed adultery could sufficiently provoke a defendant, and that learning in other ways of a wife's infidelity sufficed as well. Some courts have even held that killing to prevent adultery justifies acquittal, and that a man coming upon his wife and her lover in the act of adultery can claim self-defense if he kills the lover.

Partially excusing homicide because the discovery of adultery provides adequate provocation effectively sends a message to a defendant that although

---

[87] * * * These states were Georgia, New Mexico, Texas, and Utah. In *Reed v. State*, 123 Tex. Crim. 348, 59 S.W.2d 122 (1933), the court held that a wife who killed a woman committing adultery with her husband was not justified by the Texas statute [even though that statute provided that a husband who killed his wife's lover would be completely justified if he caught them in the act of adultery]. *See also* * * * *Scroggs v. State*, 94 Ga. App. 28, 93 S.E.2d 583 (1956) (wife killing to prevent adultery is justified, but were she to kill in the heat of passion upon discovering commission of husband's adultery, she would be guilty of manslaughter).

his act was wrong, he is not entirely blameworthy. Acquitting a defendant who kills to prevent or in reaction to adultery, * * * implies societal approval of the act itself and tells the defendant that there has been no social harm. The quality of the relationship between the defendant and the victim is irrelevant, except that the law recognizes the defense only when the relationship is legal marriage. The law of provocation endorses men's ownership of women's sexuality by expressly sanctioning violent reactions by husbands to their wives' infidelity.

Although the defense of provocation upon the discovery of adultery now applies to women as well as to men, it is a shallow concession to equality that bears little legitimacy or meaning. Cases and social studies show that women rarely react to their husband's infidelity with deadly violence. In contrast, men who kill their wives or lovers frequently act after accusing them of infidelity.

Note

Laurie Taylor argues that "[f]emale homicide is so different from male homicide that women and men may be said to live in two different cultures, each with its own 'subculture of violence.'" Laurie J. Taylor, *Provoked Reason in Men and Women: Heat-of-Passion Manslaughter and Imperfect Self-Defense*, 33 UCLA L.Rev. 1679, 1681 (1986). Statistics compiled by the United States Bureau of Justice Statistics between 1976 and 2002 support Taylor's claim that homicide is highly gendered. First, men commit far more homicides than women in general. For example, in the year 2002 men were almost 10 times more likely to commit homicide than women.[1] Second, women are significantly more likely to be the victims of intimate homicide than men. In the time period 1976-2002, about one-third of female victims of homicide were killed by an "intimate" (defined as spouses, ex-spouses, boyfriends, and girlfriends), whereas only about 3-4 percent of male homicide victims were killed by an intimate.[2] Finally, although statistics on this point are difficult to find, the data appear to indicate that women are disproportionately the killers of infants and children. *See, e.g.*, Lynne Marie Kohm and Thomas Scott Liverman, *Prom Mom Killers: The Impact of Blame Shift and Distorted Statistics on Punishment for Neonaticide*, 9 Wm. & Mary J. Women & L. 43, 53-54 (2002) (according to a study by the Centers for Disease Control, 89 percent of infants killed on the day

---

[1] Bureau of Justice Statistics, "Homicide Trends in the U.S.: Trends by Gender," available at http://www.ojp.usdoj.gov/bjs/homicide/gender.htm (visited January 24, 2005).

[2] U.S. Bureau of Justice Statistics, "Homicide Trends in the U.S.: Intimate Homicide," available at http://www.ojp.usdoj.gov/bjs/homicide/intimates.htm (visited January 24, 2005).

of their birth were killed by their mothers; according to a report by the Department of Human Health and Services, mothers perpetrate 78 percent of fatal child abuse); *see generally* Michelle Oberman, *Mothers Who Kill: Coming to Terms with Modern American Infanticide*, 34 Am. Crim. L. Rev. 1 (1996). If Taylor's assertion that there are gendered "subcultures of violence" is correct, what should be the law's response? For example, if men tend to kill their wives, ex-wives, and girlfriends and women tend to kill their babies and children, what might sex equality require?

Taylor argues that "cumulative rage," as exemplified in *Berry*, should not be recognized as an emotion adequate for mitigation to voluntary manslaughter, but that "cumulative terror" should be, recognizing that many women kill their male partners in response to physical and/or psychological abuse. Is this a fair result? As we will see when we study the doctrine of self-defense, battered women who kill their abusers are not always able to meet the requirements for a valid claim of self-defense. For such women, provocation may be the only defense available to avoid a murder conviction.

3.   Who Is "The Reasonable Person"?

In jurisdictions that follow the common law, a determination that the defendant's homicide should be treated as voluntary manslaughter rather than murder requires a determination that a *"reasonable person"* in the defendant's situation would have been provoked to act in the heat of passion. Even the Model Penal Code, which instructs jurors to consider the situation from the point of view of the actor (i.e. defendant), requires jurors to find that the defendant's explanation for his mental or emotional disturbance is a *reasonable* one. Thus reasonableness is a key component of the provocation defense in both common law and Model Penal Code jurisdictions.

The reasonable person test raises several questions. Does a reasonable person ever kill in the heat of passion? Isn't this a contradiction in terms? If so, why are we using the reasonable person as a standard for judging unreasonable behavior? Moreover, who is the reasonable person? Is the reasonable person the average person or the ideal person? Does the reasonable person look like the defendant, and if so to what extent? Does the reasonable person carry all the beliefs and assumptions of her culture, including its prejudices?

One of the classic discussions of the reasonable person rule took place in a 1978 English case, *Director of Public Prosecutions v. Camplin*. The defendant was a 15 year old boy who killed an older man by splitting his skull with a chapati pan after they had sex, allegedly against the boy's will, subsequent to which the defendant laughed at him. At trial, the defense suggested to the jury that they should take his age into account and judge his actions by the standard of a reasonable 15 year old boy. The trial judge rejected this idea and instructed the jury to judge Camplin by the standard of a reasonable adult. Camplin was found guilty of murder.

The question certified for appeal to the House of Lords was whether the standard should have been that of the reasonable adult or a reasonable boy. The Lords wrote several opinions. Lord Diplock suggested that "the public policy that underlay the adoption of the 'reasonable man' test in the common law doctrine of provocation was to reduce the incidence of fatal violence by preventing a person relying on his own exceptional pugnacity or excitability as an excuse for loss of self control." Lord Simon added that "it would be unjust that the drunk man or one exceptionally pugnacious or bad-tempered or over-sensitive should be able to claim that these matters rendered him peculiarly susceptible to the provocation offered, where the sober and even-tempered man would hang for his homicide." The Lords appeared to agree, in light of these considerations, that the reasonable person is "An ordinary person of either sex, not exceptionally excitable or pugnacious, but possessed of such powers of self-control as everyone is entitled to expect that his fellow citizens will exercise in society as it is today." Furthermore, the Lords held that the trial judge erred in instructing the jury to hold the 15 year old defendant to the standard of an adult man; rather, "the reasonable man referred to in the [standard] is a person having the power of self-control to be expected of an ordinary person of the . . . age of the [defendant]. . . ."

The common law thus seems to draw a line between physical or demographic characteristics that might be pertinent to the gravity of the provocation and the defendant's reaction to it, and characteristics pertaining purely to the defendant's powers of judgment or self-control, such as drunkenness or ill-temper. In its application, however, the operation of the reasonable person standard has been less than clear. This is particularly true with respects to situations that inflame some people but not others in the same society. Consider the following materials on the reasonable person in a homophobic culture.

HOMOPHOBIA IN MANSLAUGHTER: THE HOMOSEXUAL ADVANCE AS INSUFFICIENT PROVOCATION

Robert B. Mison
80 Cal. L. Rev. 133 (1992)[a]

INTRODUCTION

The question is simple: Should a nonviolent sexual advance in and of itself constitute sufficient provocation to incite a reasonable man to lose his self-control and kill in the heat of passion? If so, the defendant will be guilty of voluntary manslaughter, not murder. This sexual-advance defense could be used by a male or a female who claims that he or she killed in reaction to the victim's sexual advance. As the law now stands, however, only a homosexual advance can mitigate murder to manslaughter.

Consider the following story[5] in which the defendant successfully raised the homosexual-advance defense to mitigate his crime. A young man is out drinking heavily with his friends. His car breaks down and he hitches a ride from another man, the victim. Together they drive around looking for women for sex. After a while, the young man asks, "Where can I get a blow job?" The victim-to-be responds, "I can handle that." They continue to drive around, stopping at a convenience store for some cigarettes before going to a baseball field at a local school. They wander into the shadows where the victim pulls down his pants and underwear and attempts to embrace the young man. But the young man kicks him, stomps on him, takes his money, and leaves the victim to die on the isolated field. Before leaving the scene, the young man returns to the victim's car and carefully wipes it clean of his fingerprints.

At his trial, the young man claims that the victim's homosexual overture provoked him to lose his self-control and kill. He took the money and wiped his fingerprints from the car only as an afterthought. Defense counsel argues that a reasonable jury could find the victim's homosexual advance sufficient provocation for the defendant's acts and requests the judge to instruct the jury on the lesser included offense of voluntary manslaughter. The prosecution does not object. The judge, satisfied that a reasonable jury could find the victim's

---

[a] © 1992 by the *California Law Review*. Reprinted from *California Law Review* by permission of the University of California, Berkeley.

[5] This story is a retelling of *Schick v. State,* 570 N.E.2d 918, 921-22 (Ind. Ct. App. 1991).

sexual advance adequate provocation, permits defense counsel to argue provocation and agrees to instruct the jury on voluntary manslaughter. The jury finds the young man guilty -- of voluntary manslaughter.

So unfolds a homosexual-advance case. Regardless of the ultimate verdict, allowing the defense to argue provocation and instructing the jury on the reduced charge of voluntary manslaughter in cases such as the foregoing is both immoral and inconsistent with the goals of modern criminal jurisprudence. Although the sufficiency of provocation is normally a question for the fact finder, judges may decide as a matter of law that no rational jury could find an alleged homosexual advance sufficient provocation to kill. With few exceptions, however, trial courts have permitted juries to make that decision as a matter of fact. The continued use and acceptance of this defense sends a message to juries and the public that if someone makes a homosexual overture, such an advance may be sufficient provocation to kill that person. This reinforces both the notions that gay men are to be afforded less respect than heterosexual men, and that revulsion and hostility are natural reactions to homosexual behavior. * * *

WHEN "HETEROSEXUAL" MEN KILL "HOMOSEXUAL" MEN: REFLECTIONS ON PROVOCATION LAW, SEXUAL ADVANCES, AND THE "REASONABLE MAN" STANDARD
Joshua Dressler
85 J. Crim. L. & Criminology 726 (1995)[a]

* * * In a recent article, Robert Mison asked the following "simple" question: "Should a nonviolent homosexual advance in and of itself constitute sufficient provocation to incite a reasonable man to lose his self-control and kill in the heat of passion" and, as a consequence, be convicted of manslaughter, rather than murder? Mison's answer was that it should not. Although trial courts almost always instruct juries on the provocation defense in homosexual-advance cases, Mison concluded that "judges should hold, as a matter of law, that a homosexual advance alone is not sufficient provocation to incite a 'reasonable man' to kill." * * *

As Mison claims, discrimination against gay men and lesbians is a serious legal problem, in part due to public (and judicial) ignorance regarding homosexuals and homosexuality. Nonetheless, Mison fails to make the case for a blanket rejection of the provocation defense in NHA [non-violent homosexual

[a]Reprinted by special permission of Northwestern University School of Law, *Journal of Criminal Law and Criminology.*

advance] prosecutions. One reason he fails is that he oversimplifies the motivations underlying the violence perpetrated in such cases. The primary reason he fails, however, is that he misapprehends the rationale of the provocation defense and the character of the Reasonable Man in provocation law. * * *

Mison. . . errs in his description of the Reasonable Man who should serve as the objective standard in heat-of-passion cases. Mison writes:

> The reasonable man is an ideal, reflecting the standard to which society wants its citizens and system of justice to aspire. It is an "entity whose life is said to be the public embodiment of rational behavior." If the reasonable man is the embodiment of both rational behavior and the idealized citizen, a killing based simply on a homosexual advance reflects neither rational nor exemplary behavior. The argument is not that the ordinary person would not be provoked by a homosexual advance, but rather that a reasonable person should not be provoked to kill by such an advance.

* * *

In the provocation area, the law does not deal with an idealized human being, because an ideal Reasonable Man, by definition, would never become angry enough that he would lose his self-control and kill solely on the basis of passion, rather than reason. Instead, the provocation defense is based on the principle that the defendant is, unfortunately, just like other ordinary human beings. That is why the defense represents a "concession to human weakness."

The Reasonable Man in the context of provocation law, therefore, is more appropriately described as the Ordinary Man (i.e., a person who possesses ordinary human weaknesses). There is more to be said on this subject, but it is sufficient for immediate purposes to emphasize that the Ordinary Man is someone far less praiseworthy than the Reasonable Man that Mison has in mind. * * *

Mison would probably argue that the law is wrong to justify or even to excuse homophobic-based anger; therefore, the actor's out-of-control reaction is wholly unjustifiable and inexcusable. But this argument goes too far. It is not necessarily the case that a person who kills after a NHA does so as the result of intolerance, bigotry, or homophobia.

It is true, of course, that a person who responds to a homosexual advance acts with knowledge of the provoker's sexual orientation, but the victim's status as a homosexual is not necessarily a motivation for the killing. Consider, again, the NHA cases that have found their way to the appellate courts. Most men - including non-homophobic heterosexuals and gay men - would justifiably become indignant if a stranger nonconsensually touched their genitals, fondled their buttocks, or committed a sexual act upon them while they slept. Certainly a woman would become outraged if a man touched her breasts, patted her on the buttocks, or had sexual relations with her while she was asleep. In such circumstances, no one would characterize her indignant response as heterophobic or anti-male in nature. And although a woman in such circumstances would probably not become angry enough to kill in response to the male's conduct (whereas a man might kill in a similar case of a homosexual advance), this difference in response is not necessarily the result of the man's homophobia and the woman's non-heterophobia. Instead, the difference may be that he is a he and she is a she.

The point is that an unwanted sexual advance is a basis for justifiable indignation. The reason it is far more likely that a man would kill under such circumstances than a woman, is that women rarely kill when provoked, but men frequently do. As noted, the provocation defense partially excuses what is primarily male behavior. However, heterosexual and homosexual advance cases are alike in certain key regards: (1) indignation in response to a violation of one's sexual privacy or autonomy is justifiable; (2) anger, one possible manifestation of such indignation, is justifiable or excusable; (3) any resulting killing is wholly unjustifiable; but (4) if the invasion of privacy is significant, ordinary, fallible human beings might become so upset that their out-of-control reaction deserves mitigated punishment. Thus, in short, there is a valid, non-homophobic basis for recognizing a partial excuse in many sexual-advance cases.

This is not meant to suggest that a heterosexual man on the receiving end of a homosexual advance is responding to the violation of his sexual privacy in a sexual-orientation-neutral way. While a sexual advance may be unwanted because the recipient does not have a sexual interest in the particular individual who is acting aggressively, if the sexual advance is homosexual in nature, and the recipient of the advance is exclusively heterosexual, the fact that the advance is homosexual in character will be a reason for the recipient's angry reaction.

Nor is this meant to suggest that the displeasure with which the heterosexual recipient reacts - enough anger that he might ultimately lose self-control - is not often aggravated by the fact that, for some men, the thought of participating in a homosexual act is physically (as distinguished from morally) repulsive. Human sexual desires are profoundly complicated and inherently personal. Consequentially, a person's distaste for a particular type of sexual act is, in a significant sense, a natural reaction of that person. Unless one assumes that people freely choose their sexual orientation and freely decide which sexual acts will give them pleasure, it is impossible to fairly condemn those heterosexual or homosexual males or females who find some sexual acts - including some sexual activities with persons of their own orientation - extremely distasteful and, therefore, emotionally upsetting.

A heterosexual person's repulsion at the thought of participating in a homosexual act is not always evidence of homophobia. A person may find homosexual conduct distasteful, but not hate homosexuals or want harm to befall them in their personal lives. Indeed, few human actions, especially those related to sexual feelings, are the result of a single motive or emotional strain. When a woman is angered because a man touches her against her will, her emotions may have multiple explanations: anger at the invasion of her sexual privacy; hatred of such "piggish" behavior; fear of another, perhaps greater, invasion of her autonomy. All that the law realistically can do in NHA cases is measure the actor's response - which might, but need not, have homophobic qualities to it - against the standard of the Ordinary Man in the actor's situation. * * *

COMMONWEALTH v. CARR
Superior Court of Pennsylvania
398 Pa. Super. 306, 580 A.2d 1362 (Super. Ct. 1990)

WIEAND, J.

In this appeal from a sentence of life imprisonment imposed for murder of the first degree, the principal issue is whether the trial court erred when it disallowed evidence of the defendant's psychosexual history to show the likelihood of a killing in the heat of passion aroused by defendant's observation of two women engaged in homosexual lovemaking.

On May 13, 1988, Claudia Brenner and Rebecca Wight were hiking along the Appalachian Trail in Adams County, when they found an appropriate campsite and stopped for the night. There, they were resting and engaging in lesbian lovemaking when Claudia Brenner was shot in the right arm. After a short pause, additional shots were fired, as a result of which Brenner was struck four additional times in and about her face, neck and head. Rebecca Wight ran for cover behind a tree and was shot in the head and back. Brenner attempted to help Wight, who was unable to walk, but was unable to rouse her. Brenner thereupon went for help, but by the time help arrived, Wight was dead. Suspicion subsequently focused on Stephen Roy Carr. He was arrested and taken into custody on a fugitive warrant from the State of Florida and made statements which incriminated himself in the shooting. He was subsequently tried non-jury before the Honorable Oscar Spicer and found guilty of murder in the first degree.

Carr defended at trial on grounds, inter alia, that he had shot Brenner and Wight in the heat of passion caused by the serious provocation of their nude homosexual love-making. In support of this defense and to show the existence of passion, Carr offered to show a history of constant rejection by women, including his mother who may have been involved in a lesbian relationship, sexual abuse while in prison in Florida, inability to hold a job, and retreat to the mountains to avoid further rejection. This was relevant, he contended, to show that he was impassioned when provoked by the "show" put on by the women, including their nakedness,[a] their hugging and kissing and their oral sex. The trial court refused to allow evidence of Carr's psychosexual history, finding it irrelevant.

The crime of voluntary manslaughter is defined by the Pennsylvania Crimes Code as follows:

> A person who kills an individual without lawful justification commits voluntary manslaughter if at the time of the killing he is acting under a sudden and intense passion resulting from serious provocation. . . .

In *Commonwealth v. Copeland,* the Court said:

> The passion which will reduce an unlawful killing to voluntary manslaughter must be caused by legally adequate provocation. The test for determining the existence of legally adequate provocation is an objective test.

In making the objective determination as to what constitutes sufficient provocation reliance may be placed upon the cumulative impact of a series of related events. The ultimate test for adequate provocation remains whether a reasonable man, confronted with this series of events, [would have become] impassioned to the extent that his mind was "incapable of cool reflection." * * *

If sufficient provocation exists, the fact finder must also determine whether the defendant actually acted in the heat of passion when he committed

---

[a]In *Eight Bullets: One Woman's Story of Surviving Anti-Gay Violence,* Claudia Brenner explains that she was partially dressed and Rebecca was fully dressed when the shooting happened.

the homicide and thus whether the provocation led directly to the killing or whether there was sufficient "cooling" period so that a reasonable man would have regained his capacity to reflect.

The sight of naked women engaged in lesbian lovemaking is not adequate provocation to reduce an unlawful killing from murder to voluntary manslaughter. It is not an event which is sufficient to cause a reasonable person to become so impassioned as to be incapable of cool reflection. A reasonable person would simply have discontinued his observation and left the scene; he would not kill the lovers. Whatever a person's views about homosexuality, the law does not condone or excuse the killing of homosexuals any more than it condones the killing of heterosexuals. Similarly, it does not recognize homosexual activity between two persons as legal provocation sufficient to reduce an unlawful killing of one or both of the actors by a third person from murder to voluntary manslaughter.

A trial court must make an initial determination whether sufficient evidence has been presented of serious provocation. In the instant case, the judge was both court and jury. Appellant was permitted to show the nature of the activities in which his victims were engaged when he came upon them in the woods. "In a provocation defense, the actions of the victim establishing provocation are relevant. Those are the victim's actions on the [day] in question because the provocation must lead *directly* to the killing." After it had been determined that these activities were inadequate to provoke a heat of passion response, however, appellant's rejection by women and his mother's sexual preference were irrelevant. Appellant's history of misfortunes are not events which are in any way related to the events which he claims provoked him on May 13, 1988. An accused cannot, by recalling some past injury or insult, establish a foundation for a manslaughter verdict. The trial court did not err when it excluded evidence of appellant's psychosexual history. * * *

The judgment of sentence is affirmed.

4.   The Model Penal Code's Extreme Emotional Disturbance Test

The Model Penal Code's provocation doctrine is found in § 210.3(b), which permits a homicide that would otherwise be murder to be considered manslaughter when it is committed "under the influence of extreme mental or emotional disturbance for which there is reasonable explanation and excuse." This provision further provides that "The reasonableness of such explanation or excuse shall be determined from the viewpoint of a person in the actor's situation under the circumstances as he believes them to be." The MPC approach, therefore, appears much more "subjective" than the common law approach.

When you read *State v. Dumlao*, think about how the Model Penal Code's approach to provocation differs from both the early common law approach and the modern test for provocation. Is the Model Penal Code approach an improvement on these other approaches? How would *Berry* and *Ambro* be decided under the MPC?

STATE v. DUMLAO
Intermediate Court of Appeals of Hawaii
6 Haw. App. 173, 715 P.2d 822 (Ct. App. 1986)

HEEN, J.

Defendant Vidado B. Dumlao (Dumlao) appeals from his conviction of murder. He argues on appeal that the trial court erred in refusing to give his requested manslaughter instruction. Relying on *State v. O'Daniel,* he contends there was sufficient evidence that he shot his mother-in-law, Pacita M. Reyes (Pacita), while "under the influence of extreme mental or emotional disturbance for which there [was] a reasonable explanation" to support an instruction under HRS §707-702(2) (1976).[2] We agree and reverse. * * *

---

[2]HRS §707-702(2) reads as follows:
Manslaughter. * * *
(2) In a prosecution for murder it is a defense, which reduces the offense to manslaughter, that the defendant was, at the time he caused the death of the other person, under the influence of extreme mental or emotional disturbance for which there is a reasonable explanation. The reasonableness of the explanation shall be determined from the view-point of a person in the defendant's situation under the circumstances as he believed them to be. * * *

Since HRS §707-702(2) is derived from MPC §210.3,[9] we may look to the commentaries and cases from other jurisdictions explaining and construing that section for insight into the meaning of the language of our statute. We will examine the first element of §707-702 first.

A.

"Extreme mental or emotional disturbance" sometimes is, but should not be, confused with the "insanity" defense. The point of the extreme emotional disturbance defense is to provide a basis for mitigation that differs from a finding of mental defect or disease precluding criminal responsibility. The disturbance was meant to be understood in relative terms as referring to a loss of self-control due to intense feelings. * * *

An explanation of the term "extreme emotional disturbance" which reflects the situational or relative character of the concept was given in *People v. Shelton,* as follows:

> [T]hat extreme emotional disturbance is the emotional state of an individual, who: (a) has no mental disease or defect that rises to the level established by Section 30.05 of the Penal Law; and (b) is exposed to an extremely unusual and overwhelming stress; and (c) has an extreme emotional reaction to it, as a result of which there is a loss of self-control and reason is overborne by intense feelings, such as passion, anger, distress, grief, excessive agitation or other similar emotions.[12]

---

[9]Section 210.3 states in pertinent part as follows:

Manslaughter

(1) Criminal homicide constitutes manslaughter when:
* * *
(b) a homicide which would otherwise be murder is committed under the influence of extreme mental or emotional disturbance for which there is reasonable explanation or excuse. The reasonableness of such explanation or excuse shall be determined from the viewpoint of a person in the actor's situation under the circumstances as he believes them to be.

[12]The extreme emotional disturbance defense is also broader than the heat of passion doctrine which it replaced, in that a cooling off period intervening between the fatal act and the disturbance does not negate the defense. "A spontaneous explosion is not required." Rather, "a significant mental trauma" could have "affected a defendant's mind for a substantial period of time, simmering in the unknown subconscious and then inexplicably coming to the fore."

It is clear that in adopting the "extreme mental or emotional disturbance" concept, the MPC intended to define the provocation element of manslaughter in broader terms than had previously been done. It is equally clear that our legislature also intended the same result when it adopted the language of the MPC.

We turn then to the second prong of our analysis, the test to determine the reasonableness of the explanation for the mental or emotional disturbance. It is here that the most significant change has been made in the law of manslaughter.

B.

The anomaly of the reasonable person test was corrected by the drafters of the MPC through the development of an objective/subjective test of reasonableness. Dressler explains that,

> [I]t makes the test more, although not entirely, subjective, by requiring the jury to test the reasonableness of the actor's conduct, "from the viewpoint of a person in the actor's situation." Thus, the actor's sex, sexual preference, pregnancy, physical deformities, and similar characteristics are apt to be taken into consideration in evaluating the reasonableness of the defendant's behavior.

The drafters of the Model Penal Code (MPC) found it "shocking" that the common law disregarded the fact that the passage of time sometimes served only to increase rather than diminish outrage. MPC §201.3 at 48, Comments (Tent. Draft No. 9, 1959). They said:

> Though it is difficult to state a middle ground between a standard which ignores all individual peculiarities and one which makes emotional distress decisive regardless of the nature of its cause, we think that such a statement is essential. For surely if the actor had just suffered a traumatic injury, if he were blind or were distraught with grief, if he were experiencing an unanticipated reaction to a therapeutic drug, it would be deemed atrocious to appraise his crime for purposes of sentence without reference to any of these matters. They are material because they bear upon the inference as to the actor's character that it is fair to draw upon the basis of his act. So too . . . where lapse of time increased rather than diminished the extent of the outrage perpetrated on the actor, . . . it was shocking in our view to hold this vital fact to be irrelevant.

This more subjective version of the provocation defense goes substantially beyond the common law by abandoning preconceptions of what constitutes adequate provocation, and giving the jury wider scope.

Under the prior law of provocation, personal characteristics of the defendant were not to be considered. Under the MPC a change from the old provocation law and the reasonable person standard has been effected by requiring the factfinder to focus on a person in the defendant's situation. Thus, the MPC, while requiring that the explanation for the disturbance must be reasonable, provides that the reasonableness is determined from the defendant's viewpoint. The phrase "actor's situation," as used in §210.3(b) of the MPC, is designedly ambiguous and is plainly flexible enough to allow the law to grow in the direction of taking account of mental abnormalities that have been recognized in the developing law of diminished responsibility.

Moreover, the MPC does not require the provocation to emanate from the victim as was argued by the State here.

In light of the foregoing discussion and the necessity of articulating the defense in comprehensible terms, we adopt the test enunciated by the New York Court of Appeals in *People v. Casassa:*

> [W]e conclude that the determination whether there was reasonable explanation or excuse for a particular emotional disturbance should be made by viewing the subjective, internal situation in which the defendant found himself and the external circumstances as he perceived them at the time, however inaccurate that perception may have been, and assessing from that standpoint whether the explanation . . . for his emotional disturbance was reasonable, so as to entitle him to a reduction of the crime charged from murder . . . to manslaughter . . . .

The language of HRS §707-702(2) indicates that the legislature intended to effect the same change in the test for manslaughter in Hawaii's law as was made by the MPC. Therefore, we hold that under HRS §707-702(2) the broader sweep of the emotional disturbance defense applies when considering whether an offense should be reduced from murder to manslaughter. To hold that the pre-penal code law of provocation continues to hold sway would be to render the language of §707-702(2) meaningless.

Thus, we hold in the instant case that the trial court was required to instruct the jury as requested by Dumlao, if there was any evidence to support a finding that at the time of the offense he suffered an "extreme mental or emotional disturbance" for which there was a "reasonable explanation" when the totality of circumstances was judged from his personal viewpoint.

We turn now to the question of whether there was evidence to support the proffered instruction.

II.

In the instant case, there was evidence of the following:

Arthur Golden, M.D., Dumlao's expert witness, stated at trial that his diagnosis of Dumlao was one of "paranoid personality disorder," which is a "long range, almost lifetime or certainly over many, many years, emotional or mental disorder. It is almost a way of functioning."

Dr. Golden diagnosed Dumlao as having unwarranted suspiciousness, one of the basic indicators of the "paranoid personality disorder." That unwarranted suspiciousness included pathological jealousy, which Dumlao suffered throughout his ten-year marriage. Dumlao harbored the belief that other males, including his wife's relatives, were somehow sexually involved with her. He could never figure out exactly who or where or how, yet this extreme suspiciousness persisted.

Dr. Golden described the second major sign of Dumlao's paranoid personality disorder as hypersensitivity, characterized by being easily slighted or quick to take offense, and a readiness to counterattack when a threat was perceived. For example, when somebody glanced or gazed at his wife, he would consider it a personal affront and could well believe that a sexual overture had been made to her. Dr. Golden believed that at the time of the offense Dumlao felt the need to counterattack because Dumlao perceived a very substantial threat. Dr. Golden stated that "[p]erhaps an ordinary individual in his situation would not have. He did."

Dr. Golden gave other examples from Dumlao's history, illustrating his extreme and irrational reactions to outwardly normal events.

Dr. Golden's observations were supported by the testimony of the State's witnesses Eduardo, Agapito and Pedrito Reyes, his brothers-in-law, as well as Florentina, his wife, and Gaudencio Dumlao, his father. For example, according to Florentina, during their entire marriage Dumlao's extreme jealousy had caused him to beat and kick her, throw a knife at her, [and] threaten her with his gun. He threatened on numerous occasions to beat or kill her. Dumlao accused her of having sexual relations with her brothers. Moreover, he would get angry for no more reason than that she might be behind some man in the checkout line at the store, and Dumlao would conclude that she was "talking to him or whatever, like that" and become jealous.

Dumlao's extreme and irrational jealousy concerning his wife was known to all the family members. According to Agapito, they couldn't even talk to their sister in Dumlao's presence. "If we have to talk to her, we have to talk from a distance because he suspects us." Furthermore, Dumlao "never allowed us to talk in a group."

Dumlao's testimony, describing his own perceptions of the night in question, further confirms the nature of his extreme jealousy. Dumlao described how he became suspicious and jealous of his wife that night because of the way that Agapito looked at him:

> A. I had this feeling that something going to happen when I leave because the action that I seen -- Agapito.

> Q. What action? * * *

> A. He look at me on, the kine. He make sure -- he make sure that -- I don't know, making sure if I stay -- if I leave the house or I don't know so I got the bad feeling so I never leave. * * *

> Q. Why did you have this feeling that he would go into your wife's bedroom?

> A. Jealousy arose. * * *

> Q. What did you do? Did you do anything after you went back to your bedroom?

> A. I wake up my wife, questioned her. * * *

> A. If he -- if she had something to do with my brother-in-law, Agapito.

> Q. What do you mean, had something to do with your brother-in-law, Agapito? * * *

> A. Sexual relation. * * *

> Q. What happened after you insisted on her answering you?

A. She got up so I lay down -- I laid down on the bedroom so I -- I kick or push her on the side over there.

Dumlao went on to describe how, after his father had counseled him and he went back in the room, he could hear the voices of the others talking in the living room. He thought that they were talking about him. He then came out to "investigate" with his gun in his waistband. He saw "Pedrito with his eyes at me, burning eye, angry eye, angry," and he saw Eduardo and Agapito alongside Pedrito. Dumlao testified that Pedrito rushed at him holding a knife in his hand, saying, "My sister suffer ten years. You going to pay. Now you going to pay." He testified that when he pulled his gun to "try and scare [Pedrito]," the gun went off, firing the bullet that struck and killed Pacita.

CONCLUSION

Reviewing the evidence within the context of the meaning of HRS §707-702(2), we conclude that it was sufficient to require the trial court to give Dumlao's requested instruction on manslaughter. There was evidence, "no matter how weak, inconclusive or unsatisfactory," that Dumlao killed Pacita while under the influence of "extreme emotional disturbance." Whether a jury will agree that there was such a disturbance or that the explanation for it was reasonable we cannot say. However, Dumlao was entitled to have the jury make that decision using the objective/subjective test.

The fact that the other witnesses contradicted his testimony concerning an attack by Pedrito, and that his testimony that he was only trying to scare Pedrito does not comport with the manslaughter defense, does not detract from Dumlao's right to the instruction based on the above evidence. Dumlao was entitled to an instruction on every theory of defense shown by the evidence. It was the jury's province to determine the weight and credibility of that evidence.

Reversed and remanded for new trial.

Note

Victoria Nourse undertook a study of intimate murder cases involving claims of provocation to see what kinds of claims were being deemed legally adequate by judges. Nourse found that in Model Penal Code jurisdictions, a frequent factual scenario in the intimate murder cases in which a male defendant was allowed to argue provocation to the jury involved departure, attempted separation, or rejection by the female partner. In many of these cases, the fatal violence that resulted in the female partner's death was preceded by her act of filing for divorce, attempting to end a casual dating relationship, breaking off an engagement, or trying to enforce a protective stay away order. Nourse reports:

> Departure is not an official category in the law of murder, but it is a frequent factual scenario in intimate murder cases in reform jurisdictions. In my study, over one-quarter of the MPC claims (twenty-six percent) that reached juries involved what I classify as a departure. By contrast, in common law jurisdictions, no departure claim in this category reached a jury. In none of these departure claims did the court report that the defendant acted because the victim was having an affair. In each, there was evidence that the "provoking" party sought to leave the relationship and that the parties' relationship was over, ending, or about to end. In all but one case, the provoking party was a woman. * * *
>
> The MPC asks juries to consider the defendant's "situation," and sometimes those situations include not only the defendant's perception of the situation but also his perception of the equities of the situation. For example, the defendant in [a case summarized earlier] came from his girlfriend's home to kill his wife, who wanted a divorce. If the law asks us to adopt the defendant's perspective, we must put on the shoes of one who is himself unfaithful to a relationship. Or consider the defendant in the *Perry* case. In that case, the defendant became enraged when a sheriff sought to execute a court order requiring him to leave his house. If we must adopt the defendant's perspective, we must put on the shoes of one claiming that a lawful court order (obtained upon representations that the defendant had refused to leave the home and was feared by his wife) entitled him to our compassion. In both of these cases, * * * juries were permitted by law to conclude that manslaughter was the appropriate verdict based on an EED theory. That the triers of fact in these cases returned murder verdicts does not diminish the fact that the law permitted these cases to come out quite differently, allowing defendants with essentially "unclean hands" to claim the law's leniency.

Victoria Nourse, *Passion's Progress: Modern Law Reform and the Provocation Defense*, 106 Yale L.J. 1331, 1354-55 (1997). Do these findings suggest that the MPC was a step backward rather than a step forward for women?

Some states, such as Maryland, have attempted a compromise reform. Rather than completely abolishing the doctrine of provocation, Maryland bars the use of the provocation defense when a person kills in response to discovering his or her spouse in the act of adultery. Do you think categorical exclusions (like the Maryland statute reprinted below) are a good idea?

MARYLAND CRIMINAL LAW CODE §2-207
Md. Code Ann., Crim. Law §2-207

§ 2-207. Manslaughter

(b) Spousal adultery not a mitigating factor. -- The discovery of one's spouse engaged in sexual intercourse with another does not constitute legally adequate provocation for the purpose of mitigating a killing from the crime of murder to voluntary manslaughter even though the killing was provoked by that discovery.

E.   DEPRAVED HEART MURDER

Section 188 of the California Penal Code reads: "* * * [M]alice may be express or implied. It is express when there is manifested a deliberate intention unlawfully to take away the life of a fellow creature. It is implied, when no considerable provocation appears, or when the circumstances attending the killing show an abandoned and malignant heart."

This provision is fairly representative of the law in jurisdictions that follow the common law. When an individual intentionally kills another human being, that individual is said to have acted with "express malice." In other situations, when there is a killing but no proof of an intent to kill, the law may nevertheless "imply" malice. One of these situations, as the California Penal Code suggests, is when the individual who kills acts with "an abandoned and malignant heart." This type of murder is called depraved heart murder and is usually treated as murder in the second degree.

How does the prosecutor go about proving an abandoned and malignant heart? Although different jurisdictions have different names for this concept – "depraved heart," "abandoned and malignant heart," "wantonness," "extreme indifference to human life" – the common law approach has been fairly well settled. Malice will be implied in a homicide case if it can be shown that the defendant acted with gross recklessness and an extreme indifference to human life, meaning that the defendant realized that his actions created a substantial and unjustified risk of death and yet went ahead and committed the actions anyway. It is important to distinguish this kind of non-intentional homicide from a death that follows from the defendant's grossly negligent or even reckless behavior. Homicides that involve a "depraved heart" can be punished as second-degree murder; homicides that involve only gross negligence or simple recklessness can only be punished as involuntary manslaughter. The following cases explore the difference between the state of mind required for a depraved heart murder conviction and the state of mind required for an involuntary manslaughter conviction.

COMMONWEALTH V. MALONE
Supreme Court of Pennsylvania
354 Pa. 180, 47 A.2d 445 (1946)

MAXEY, CHIEF JUSTICE

This is an appeal from the judgment and sentence under a conviction of murder in the second degree. William H. Long, age 13 years, was killed by a shot from a 32-caliber revolver held against his right side by the defendant, then aged 17 years. These youths were on friendly terms at the time of the homicide. The defendant and his mother, while his father and brother were in the U. S. Armed Forces, were residing in Lancaster, Pa., with the family of William H. Long, whose son was the victim of the shooting.

On the evening of February 26th, 1945, when the defendant went to a moving picture theater, he carried in the pocket of his raincoat a revolver which he had obtained at the home of his uncle on the preceding day. In the afternoon preceding the shooting, the decedent procured a cartridge from his father's room and he and the defendant placed it in the revolver.

After leaving the theater, the defendant went to a dairy store and there met the decedent. Both youths sat in the rear of the store ten minutes, during which period the defendant took the gun out of his pocket and loaded the chamber to the right of the firing pin and then closed the gun. A few minutes later, both youths sat on stools in front of the lunch counter and ate some food. The defendant suggested to the decedent that they play 'Russian Poker.'[1] Long replied; 'I don't care; go ahead.' The defendant then placed the revolver against the right side of Long and pulled the trigger three times. The third pull resulted in a fatal wound to Long. The latter jumped off the stool and cried: 'Oh! Oh! Oh!' and Malone said: 'Did I hit you, Billy? Gee, Kid, I'm sorry.' Long died from the wounds two days later.

---

[1] It has been explained that 'Russian Poker' is a game in which the participants, in turn, place a single cartridge in one of the five chambers of a revolver cylinder, give the latter a quick twirl, place the muzzle of the gun against the temple and pull the trigger, leaving it to chance whether or not death results to the trigger puller.

The defendant testified that the gun chamber he loaded was the first one to the right of the firing chamber and that when he pulled the trigger he did not 'expect to have the gun go off.' He declared he had no intention of harming Long, who was his friend and companion. The defendant was indicted for murder, tried and found guilty of murder in the second degree and sentenced to a term in the penitentiary for a period not less than five years and not exceeding ten years. A new trial was refused and after sentence was imposed, an appeal was taken.

Appellant alleges certain errors in the charge of the court and also contends that the facts did not justify a conviction for any form of homicide except involuntary manslaughter. This contention we over-rule.... At common law, the 'grand criterion' which 'distinguished murder from other killing' was malice on the part of the killer and this malice was not necessarily 'malevolent to the deceased particularly' but 'any evil design in general; the dictate of a wicked, depraved and malignant heart.' Among the examples that Blackstone cites of murder is 'coolly discharging a gun among a multitude of people,' causing the death of someone of the multitude. * * *

When an individual commits an act of gross recklessness for which he must reasonably anticipate that death to another is likely to result, he exhibits that "wickedness of disposition, hardness of heart, cruelty, recklessness of consequences, and a mind regardless of social duty" which proved that there was at that time in him "the state or frame of mind termed malice." This court has declared that if a driver "wantonly, recklessly, and in disregard of consequences" hurls "his car against another, or into a crowd" and death results from that act "he ought * * * to face the same consequences that would be meted out to him if he had accomplished death by wantonly and wickedly firing a gun."

In *Com. v. Hillman*, the charge of the court below was approved by this court. In that charge appears this statement: 'Malice in law means a depraved and wicked heart that is reckless and disregards the rights of others. Reckless conduct that results in the death of another is malice. To illustrate that: If a man fires a gun into a crowd and kills another it is murder, because the fact of the reckless shooting of a gun into a crowd is malice in law. That wicked and depraved disposition and that recklessness and disregard of human life is malice.'

In *Com. v. Knox*, the following instructions by the trial judge in a murder case was held by this court not to be error: 'When a man uses a gun loaded with powder and shot and aimed at a vital part of the body of another and discharges it, he must be presumed to know that death is likely to follow.' * * *

The killing of William H. Long by this defendant resulted from an act intentionally done by the latter, in reckless and wanton disregard of the consequences which were at least sixty per cent certain from his thrice attempted discharge of a gun known to contain one bullet and aimed at a vital part of Long's body. This killing was, therefore, murder, for malice in the sense of a wicked disposition is evidenced by the intentional doing of an uncalled-for act in callous disregard of its likely harmful effects on others. The fact that there was no motive for this homicide does not exculpate the accused. In a trial for murder proof of motive is always relevant but never necessary.

All the assignments of error are overruled and the judgment is affirmed. The record is remitted to the court below so that the sentence imposed may be carried out.

STATE v. DAVIDSON
Supreme Court of Kansas
267 Kan. 667, 987 P.2d 335 (1999)

ALLEGRUCCI, J.

Defendant Sabine Davidson was convicted of reckless second-degree murder and endangering a child. She appeals her conviction of reckless second-degree murder in the death of 11-year-old Christopher Wilson, who was killed by defendant's Rottweiler dogs. * * *

On appeal, defendant argues that her conduct did not constitute reckless second-degree murder in law or in fact. The question we must resolve is whether Davidson's conduct constituted reckless second-degree murder as defined in K.S.A. 1998 Supp. 21-3402(b), and, if so, whether the State presented evidence sufficient to sustain a conviction of reckless second-degree murder.

Davidson's challenge to the law and the evidence rests on the same premise: that the State proved only that she failed to confine her dogs. K.S.A. 1998 Supp. 21-3402(b) requires the State to prove that her conduct "manifested extreme indifference to the value of human life." At best, she argues that her conduct constituted a negligent omission to confine the dogs and she should have been charged with involuntary manslaughter. Simply stated, she argues that the crime of second-degree murder does not fit her conduct.

We are struck by Davidson's lack of candor concerning her conduct relevant to Chris' death. The State's evidence established Davidson's conduct consisted of much more than a failure "to confine the family's dogs." She conveniently ignores significant aspects of her conduct that contributed to the tragic death of Chris.

The State's evidence established numerous earlier incidents involving defendant's dogs. A woman who babysat for defendant in the summer of 1995 testified about two incidents involving defendant's dogs. On one occasion the witness, who had been told it would be all right to do so, let a German shepherd out of its cage, and the shepherd attacked a puppy. When the sitter intervened, the shepherd "snipped" at her. On another occasion, a Rottweiler puppy belonging to the Davidsons nipped at their 3-year-old daughter's calves, leaving teeth marks and making her cry. When told about it, defendant laughed.

Fifteen-year-old Margaret Smith, who lived near the Davidsons, testified that sometime during the 1995-96 school year, two dogs chased her and Jeffrey Wilson away from the school bus stop as they waited there in the morning. She believed that the dogs belonged to the Davidsons. Jeffrey remembered only one dog involved in that incident. It was a Rottweiler, and he was certain it belonged to the Davidsons. He also testified that he rode fast when bicycling past the Davidson house because the dogs inside the fence were big and they jumped and barked "like they wanted to attack us."

Deputy Shumate had been to the Davidson house in January 1996 when one of the neighbors complained about their dogs running loose. The complainant said that his wife was afraid of the dogs, a German shepherd and a Rottweiler. * * *

Learie Thompson, who lives near the Davidsons, complained to the sheriff's office in January 1996 because the Davidsons' dogs were in his yard. He recalled three to five times earlier when the dogs were loose and came into his yard. For the most part, the dogs Thompson saw in his yard were German shepherds. Thompson testified that he was afraid of the Davidsons' dogs because they were big and aggressive toward people. When the dogs were in their fenced enclosure, they would rage and growl and try to get out of the fence. For some time after he complained to the sheriff, Thompson did not see the dogs outside their fenced enclosure. Then early on the morning that Chris was killed, as Thompson opened his garage door to leave for work, the Davidsons' three Rottweiler dogs rushed into the garage. Thompson jumped up onto his truck. The dogs stood on their hind legs and growled and bared their teeth at him for several minutes. Responding to Thompson's cries, his wife activated the garage door mechanism. It made a noise as it was engaging, and the dogs ran away.

Eleven-year-old Daniel Stevens recalled an incident in the spring of 1996 when he and Chris were riding their bicycles and were chased by two barking Rottweilers. In January 1997, he was chased by one Rottweiler when he was riding his bicycle. Both times the dogs ran as far as the turn in the road and then went back to the Davidsons' house.

One incident occurred at the intersection where Chris was killed. On June 14, 1996, Tony Van Buren, who lives directly across the street from the Davidson house, was out in his front yard in the evening when he heard dogs barking. He saw three Rottweilers forming a semicircle around two young children, who were approximately 3 to 5 years old. As the children moved, the dogs moved, too, and maintained a consistent distance. He ran into his house, told his wife to call the sheriff, and got a pistol and a ball bat. Yelling as he went, Van Buren ran toward the dogs and children. When he got about halfway there, the dogs turned and went up to the Davidson house. The gate to the fenced enclosure was open approximately 4 to 6 inches. Van Buren opened it more and the two smaller dogs went in. Van Buren tried to coax the third dog through the gate, but it barked and growled at him and then disappeared around the house. When the sheriff's deputy arrived, Van Buren talked with her for a little bit. The third dog returned to the fenced area, and Van Buren was able to open the gate and get the dog to go in. Van Buren went to the Davidsons' door and rang the bell. No one answered. He also tried to telephone them, but their line had been disconnected. * * *

Schutzhund is a dog sport developed in Germany that involves tracking, obedience, retrieving, and protection work. In protection work, the dog attacks an "agitator." The agitator wears a protective suit and padded sleeve. The dog is taught to bite the sleeve and hold on, even when being hit by the agitator's stick, until the handler gives the command "out." Bridget Bernardi, who used to train Schutzhund dogs in Germany, testified that her experiences with Schutzhund clubs in this country had not been positive because participants lacked knowledge about the sport and that their dogs' biting conduct seemed more aggressive and less like a game. * * *

Defendant took various German shepherds and Rottweilers that belonged to her to meetings of Schutzhund clubs in Kansas and Oklahoma. Debbie Lutz, president and training director of the Tornado Alley Schutzhund Club in Topeka, testified that defendant attended one session. Defendant brought a dog that was not crated as it should have been. Robert Armstead, president and training director of an Oklahoma City Schutzhund club, testified that defendant attended several sessions of the club in 1996. She brought two German shepherds and one Rottweiler. Her handling of her dogs "was very, very poor." She focused exclusively on the protection work aspect of Schutzhund and completely ignored obedience and tracking. * * *

In addition to keeping and breeding German shepherds, defendant in 1995 began purchasing Rottweilers. Bernardi testified that defendant bought three from her, five from other kennels, and one from a breeder in Germany. * * *

On the day Chris was killed, April 24, 1997, * * * Violet Wilson dropped her two younger sons, Chris, 11, and Tramell, 9, off at the school bus stop shortly after 7:15 a.m. The bus stop was located near the residences of Tony Van Buren and defendant. While waiting for the bus, Tramell noticed that defendant's dogs were digging at the fence like they "really wanted to get out." When the dogs got out of the fence, they ran toward the boys, who climbed up into a tree in Van Buren's yard. The three dogs surrounded the tree and barked at the boys for several minutes before the biggest dog left and the other two followed it.

Chris wanted to get down out of the tree and see where the dogs had gone and what they were doing. Tramell urged him to stay in the tree, but Chris got down and looked around for the dogs.

When the school bus arrived at 7:30, no children were at the stop, but the driver noticed two book bags and a musical instrument had been left there. The driver saw Tramell up in a tree on Van Buren's lot. Tramell got out of the tree, ran to the bus stop, gathered up the bags and instruments, and got on the bus. As he got on, Tramell said something about Chris, which the driver thought sounded like Chris had run the dog home. The driver waited several minutes before repositioning the bus to let Chris know that he needed to hurry up. After moving the bus, the driver could see in the side mirror that there were three large black dogs down in the ravine. The dogs appeared to be fighting over something; they were jumping back and forth and thrashing their heads from side to side. One of the children on the bus said, "It looks like they have a rag doll." Then the driver realized that the dogs had Chris. The only movement of Chris' body was that caused by the thrashing motion of the dogs.

The driver began honking the bus horn in an effort to distract the dogs, and she radioed the dispatcher. There were approximately 20 children on the bus, and the driver then made an effort to divert their attention away from the ravine and to calm them.

When David Morrison, a sheriff's deputy, arrived, the bus driver told him that the boy and the dogs were in the ravine. As Morrison walked toward them, the dogs noticed him and moved quickly and steadily in his direction. Morrison could see that Chris was not moving. Morrison's shouts and gestures did not divert the dogs, which continued to move straight toward him with a large male in the lead. Morrison could see blood on the lead dog's face and forelegs. When the lead dog was approximately 15 feet away from him, Morrison shot and killed him. One of the children on the bus testified that the lead dog had been the one at Chris' neck.

The other two dogs began to run away. Another officer, Sergeant Mataruso, who had just arrived, fired shots at the fleeing dogs. Morrison ran down into the ravine and found Chris. The boy had no pulse. The grass around his body was torn up, and there was a lot of blood spread around the area. Items of clothing, some ripped up, and shoes were scattered about.

When Deputy Shumate arrived, he saw a dead dog in the road. Mataruso told him that he had shot at, and probably wounded, another dog that had been seen running toward a house. Shumate went to the Davidson house, where he found the wounded dog and killed it. Shumate told Mr. and Mrs. Davidson that a child had been attacked by their dogs; he then arrested them. They asked no questions about the identity or condition of the child. Inside the house, there was a dog confined in a large plastic pet carrier. Shumate testified that "the dog was growling, sort of barking, and moving the pet carrier all over the floor like it was trying to get out of the carrier to get at me." The third dog was shot and killed by a highway patrolman later in the day.

An autopsy revealed that Chris had died as a result of trauma from animal bites. There were many injuries, but those affecting the head and neck were immediately responsible for his death. The boy's esophagus and carotid artery were torn. His neck had been broken, and the bones splintered and crushed. * * *

The dogs that killed Chris were Rottweilers. The one killed by Morrison was an 80-pound male. The other two were females of 70 pounds and 54 pounds, respectively.

The Rottweiler that was confined in a crate inside the Davidsons' house when police went there after Chris' death was placed in the Junction City police kennel. When a kennel worker approached its cage, the dog "went nuts," forcefully lunging at the gate and showing her full set of teeth. When defendant was told of the incident, she laughed. Later, while the dog was housed at the humane society, a friend of the Davidsons took his young daughter with him to check on the dog. The dog's behavior was unlike what he had observed when it was at the Davidsons' house. It charged at the fence, and they "could see her back molars." The man was so scared that his knees felt rubbery and his heart pounded. Tom Brenneman tested the dog and found that it had had very little obedience training, but that it had some Schutzhund protection training and bit the bite sleeve hard.

In addition to finding the Rottweiler inside the house, police found books, magazines, catalogues, and videotapes on the subject of Schutzhund. There was a catalogue of Schutzhund protective gear. A puppy-breeding setup occupied the basement of the house. * * *

Defendant told police that she let the dogs out about 6:30 a.m. on April 24, 1997. Then she took a sleeping pill and went to sleep on the living room couch. Later, when she was told that her dogs had attacked a boy, she said, "The dead one should be one of the Wilson boys." She said that the Wilson boys teased her dogs whenever they came around her property so that the dogs barked and got aggressive when the boys were in the area. She also said that the boy had been at the bus stop, and that is how she knew who was attacked.

Defendant told police that she and her husband had discussed putting a chain on the gate to the fenced enclosure because the dogs got out of that gate "all the time." There was no chain on the gate, however. At trial, defendant testified that after Bernardi watched one of the Rottweilers open the gate by lifting the latch, she put a padlock through the hole in the latch so that it could not be lifted. Defendant testified that after padlocking the latch, she had no more reports of the dogs getting out.

A videotape made by Deputies Snyder and Popovich shows that the Davidsons' back and side yards are enclosed by a 6-foot-tall chain link fence. The gate fastening device is a typical horseshoe-shaped hinged latch. In a horizontal position the arms of the latch are on either side of an adjacent upright fence post on which the next section of fence is attached. A locked padlock through the hole in the latch on the Davidsons' gate kept the latch in a horizontal position. The fence post along with the latch should have kept the gate closed, but the post was easily moved far enough from the vertical for the latch to slip past. On the videotape, Snyder opened and closed the "padlocked" gate without much effort. The manager of the fence company that installed the fence and gate testified that the posts were set in concrete. After watching the videotape, he testified that it looked like the post had been loosened because dirt had been dug out around the concrete footing of it. With regard to the latch, he said, "It would appear that over the course of time it had widened from probably . . . considerable pressure being put on the gate while the latch was in the closed position." The fence was installed in 1993.

Reckless second-degree murder, also known as depraved heart murder, was defined by the legislature as "the killing of a human being committed . . . unintentionally but recklessly under circumstances manifesting extreme indifference to the value of human life." * * *

The State cites other jurisdictions in which dog owners have been convicted of manslaughter for killings committed by their dogs. No case has been cited, nor are we aware of a case, where a dog owner has been convicted of second-degree murder.[a] * * *

Here, defendant argues that 21-3402(b) is not applicable to her conduct. In her view, the State's evidence establishes only that she failed to secure the dogs. She then argues that her conduct, as a matter of law, is not reckless second-degree murder. * * *

Defendant's argument in law and in fact is based on the State's failure to establish a "depraved heart scienter." It is difficult at times to follow her arguments, but she seems to imply that the State has failed to prove foreseeability, i.e., that she had knowledge the dogs would attack someone, let alone harm or kill someone. Thus, she argues the State failed to prove that her conduct was inherently dangerous to human life and that she was indifferent to that danger. In her view, her conduct did not rise to that level of reckless conduct manifesting an extreme indifference to the value of human life. * * *

Here, defendant argues that all she did was let the dogs into the fenced area, take a pill, and go to sleep. This argument conveniently ignores significant aspects of her conduct that contributed to the tragic death of Chris. The State presented evidence that she selected powerful dogs with a potential for aggressive behavior and that she owned a number of these dogs in which she fostered aggressive behavior by failing to properly train the dogs. She ignored the advice from experts on how to properly train her dogs and their warnings of the dire results which could occur from improper training. She was told to socialize her dogs and chose not to do so. She ignores the evidence of the dogs getting out on numerous occasions and her failure to properly secure the gate. She ignored the aggressive behavior her dogs displayed toward her neighbors and their children. The State presented evidence that she created a profound risk and ignored foreseeable consequences that her dogs could attack or injure someone. The State is not required to prove that defendant knew her dogs would

---

[a] In March 2002, Marjorie Knoller was convicted of second-degree murder and involuntary manslaughter in the death of her apartment neighbor Diane Whipple. Jaxon Van Derbeken, *Why Jury Called It Murder*, S.F. Chronicle, March 22, 2002. In January 2001, Whipple was beginning to enter her apartment just as Knoller was leaving to take Bane, a 120 pound Presa Canario, and another dog for an evening walk. Bane pounced on Whipple and mauled her to death. San Francisco Superior Court Judge James Warren later threw out the murder conviction on the ground that the evidence did not show that Knoller "subjectively knew on January 26 that her conduct was such that a human being was likely to die." Rene Sanchez, *Murder Conviction Overturned in California Dog-Mauling Case*, Wash. Post, June 18, 2002, at A10. The judge did not dismiss Knoller's conviction for involuntary manslaughter.

attack and kill someone. It was sufficient to prove that her dogs killed Chris and that she could have reasonably foreseen that the dogs could attack or injure someone as a result of what she did or failed to do.

Davidson was charged with reckless second-degree murder. The jury was instructed that in order to establish the charge, it would have to be proved that defendant killed Christopher Wilson "unintentionally but recklessly under circumstances showing extreme indifference to the value of human life." "Recklessly" was defined as "conduct done under circumstances that show a realization of the imminence of danger to the person of another and a conscious and unjustifiable disregard of that danger." The jury also was instructed that it could consider the lesser included offense of involuntary manslaughter, either an unintentional killing done recklessly or an unintentional killing done in the commission of the offense of permitting a dangerous animal to be at large. The jury found that defendant's conduct involved an extreme degree of recklessness.

In *Robinson*, the court stated that "recklessness that can be assimilated to purpose or knowledge is treated as depraved heart second-degree murder, and less extreme recklessness is punished as manslaughter." Here, the evidence, viewed in a light most favorable to the State, showed that defendant created an unreasonable risk and then consciously disregarded it in a manner and to the extent that it reasonably could be inferred that she was extremely indifferent to the value of human life. The evidence was sufficient to enable a rational factfinder to find Davidson guilty of reckless second-degree murder. Thus, the district court properly submitted the charge of reckless second-degree murder to the jury, and the evidence was sufficient to support the jury's verdict.

The judgment of the district court is affirmed.

Note

Judge Allegrucci, writing for the majority in *State v. Davidson*, stated, "The State is not required to prove that defendant *knew* her dogs would attack and kill someone. It is sufficient to prove ... that she could have *reasonably foreseen* that the dogs could attack or injure someone as a result of what she did or failed to do." To convict Ms. Davidson of reckless second-degree murder, however, the jury had to find that she acted "recklessly" which is defined as "conduct done under circumstances that show a *realization* of the imminence of danger to the person of another and a *conscious* and unjustified disregard of that danger." If recklessness was the mental state required for a second-degree murder conviction, was Judge Allegrucci's statement correct as a matter of law?

Did the State provide sufficient evidence that Ms. Davidson realized (i.e., was aware of) the risk of death posed by her dogs and consciously disregarded this risk? Would your answer to this question change if you learned that Davidson was a German national, and therefore English was not likely her first language? Suppose the evidence suggested she had been thrown out of three Schutzhund clubs?

May drunk driving provide the basis for a second-degree murder prosecution? In *People v. Watson,* 30 Cal.3d 290 (1981), the Supreme Court of California held that a man who had gone to a bar, consumed large quantities of beer, and then, while driving home, struck another car, killing the passengers, could be charged with murder. Said the court, quoting a previous opinion, "One who wilfully consumes alcoholic beverages to the point of intoxication, knowing that he thereafter must operate a motor vehicle, thereby combining sharply impaired physical and mental faculties with a vehicle capable of great force and speed, reasonably may be held to exhibit a conscious disregard of the safety of others." One justice dissented sharply, however:

> The fact that respondent was under the influence of alcohol made his driving more dangerous. A high percentage of accidents is caused by such drivers. No one holds a brief for this type of activity. However, a rule should not be promulgated by this court that driving while under the influence of alcohol is sufficient to establish an act "likely to kill." Death or injury is not the probable result of driving while under the influence of alcohol. "Thousands, perhaps hundreds of thousands, of Californians each week reach home without accident despite their driving intoxicated." * * *

> How does respondent's state of mind at the time he drove to the bar and began drinking justify an inference that he had a reckless state of mind at the time of the accident? This meager evidence does not justify the inference that by drinking alcohol he harbored a conscious disregard for life when he later drove his car! I submit that the majority's reasoning that such an inference may be drawn to support a finding of implied malice will be used to establish second degree murder in every case in which a person drives a car to a bar, a friend's home, or a party, drinks alcohol so that he is under its influence, drives away and is involved in a fatal accident.

Id. at 305.

F.   INVOLUNTARY MANSLAUGHTER

Generally speaking, there are two ways a prosecutor can secure an involuntary manslaughter conviction. First, the prosecutor can prove that the defendant had the requisite mens rea for involuntary manslaughter. Many jurisdictions use the term "criminal negligence" to describe the mental state necessary for an involuntary manslaughter conviction. "Criminal negligence," like the term "malice aforethought," is a legal term of art which has been defined in different ways. In most jurisdictions, something more than ordinary civil negligence is required; this state of mind is sometimes described as "gross negligence" and sometimes even "recklessness." However, a minority of courts, like the Court of Appeals of Washington in *State v. Williams*, have held that simple negligence is all that is required for an involuntary manslaughter conviction.

Since the difference between a reckless state of mind and a negligent state of mind (whether ordinary or gross) turns on whether the defendant was aware of a substantial and unjustifiable risk and chose to disregard it (recklessness requiring awareness of the risk and negligence not requiring such awareness), the mental state required and how it is defined can make a significant difference in the odds of conviction. In the following cases, the courts take different views on the mental state required for an involuntary manslaughter conviction. Pay careful attention to the terminology used to describe the required mental state and the definitions of these terms that the courts provide. Some of these definitions conflict with the usual meanings of the terms defined.

A second way one can be convicted of involuntary manslaughter is through application of the misdemeanor manslaughter rule. Because this doctrine can be understood as a kind of mini-felony murder rule, we will examine it in more detail after we have studied felony murder.

COMMONWEALTH v. WELANSKY
Supreme Judicial Court of Massachusetts
316 Mass. 383, 55 N.E.2d 902 (1944)

LUMMUS, J.

On November 28, 1942, and for about nine years before that day, a corporation named New Cocoanut Grove, Inc., maintained and operated a "night club" in Boston, having an entrance at 17 Piedmont Street, for the furnishing to the public for compensation of food, drink, and entertainment consisting of orchestra and band music, singing and dancing. It employed about eighty persons. The corporation, its officers and employees, and its business, were completely dominated by the defendant Barnett Welansky. * * * He owned, and held in his own name or in the names of others, all the capital stock. He leased some of the land on which the corporate business was carried on, and owned the rest, although title was held for him by his sister. He was entitled to, and took, all the profits. Internally, the corporation was operated without regard to corporate forms, as though the business were that of the defendant as an individual. It was not shown that responsibility for the number or condition of safety exits had been delegated by the defendant to any employee or other person.

The defendant was accustomed to spend[ing] his evenings at the night club, inspecting the premises and superintending the business. On November 16, 1942, he became suddenly ill, and was carried to a hospital, where he was in bed for three weeks and remained until discharged on December 11, 1942. During his stay at the hospital, although employees visited him there, he did not concern himself with the night club, because, as he testified, he "knew it would be all right" and that "the same system . . . [he] had would continue" during his absence. There is no evidence of any act, omission or condition at the night club on November 28, 1942, (apart from the lighting of a match hereinafter described), that was not within the usual and regular practice during the time before the defendant was taken ill when he was at the night club nearly every evening. * * *

* * * A little after ten o'clock on the evening of Saturday, November 28, 1942, the night club was well filled with a crowd of patrons. It was during the busiest season of the year. An important football game in the afternoon had attracted many visitors to Boston. Witnesses were rightly permitted to testify that the dance floor had from eighty to one hundred persons on it, and that it was "very crowded." Witnesses were rightly permitted to give their estimates, derived from their observations, of the number of patrons in various parts of the night club. Upon the evidence it could have been found that at that time there were from two hundred fifty to four hundred persons in the Melody Lounge, from four hundred to five hundred in the main dining room and the Caricature Bar, and two hundred fifty in the Cocktail Lounge. * * *

A bartender in the Melody Lounge noticed that an electric light bulb which was in or near the cocoanut husks of an artificial palm tree in the corner had been turned off and that the corner was dark. He directed a sixteen year old bar boy who was waiting on customers at the tables to cause the bulb to be lighted. A soldier sitting with other persons near the light told the bar boy to leave it unlighted. But the bar boy got a stool, lighted a match in order to see the bulb, turned the bulb in its socket, and thus lighted it. The bar boy blew the match out, and started to walk away. Apparently the flame of the match had ignited the palm tree and that had speedily ignited the low cloth ceiling near it, for both flamed up almost instantly. The fire spread with great rapidity across the upper part of the room, causing much heat. The crowd in the Melody Lounge rushed up the stairs, but the fire preceded them. People got on fire while on the stairway. The fire spread with great speed across the foyer and into the Caricature Bar and the main dining room, and thence into the Cocktail Lounge. Soon after the fire started the lights in the night club went out. The smoke had a peculiar odor. The crowd were panic stricken, and rushed and pushed in every direction through the night club, screaming, and overturning tables and chairs in their attempts to escape.

The door at the head of the Melody Lounge stairway was not opened until firemen broke it down from outside with an axe and found it locked by a key lock, so that the panic bar could not operate. Two dead bodies were found close to it, and a pile of bodies about seven feet from it. The door in the vestibule of the office did not become open, and was barred by the clothing rack. The revolving door soon jammed, but was burst out by the pressure of the crowd. The head waiter and another waiter tried to get open the panic doors from the main dining room to Shawmut Street, and succeeded after some difficulty. The other two doors to Shawmut Street were locked, and were opened by force from outside by firemen and others. Some patrons escaped through them, but many dead bodies were piled up inside them. A considerable number of patrons escaped through the Broadway door, but many died just inside that door. Some employees, and a great number of patrons, died in the fire. Others were taken out of the building with fatal burns and injuries from smoke, and died within a few days.

I. *The pleadings, verdicts, and judgments.*

The defendant, his brother James Welansky, and Jacob Goldfine, were indicted for manslaughter in sixteen counts of an indictment numbered 413, each count for causing the death of a person described as "Jane Doe," "John Doe," or the like. The first six counts were quashed, leaving the last ten counts. Later a motion by the Commonwealth was allowed, substituting in each of the last ten counts the real name of a victim. Voluntarily the Commonwealth filed specifications as to those counts, by which it specified among other things that the alleged misconduct of the defendant consisted in causing or permitting or failing reasonably to prevent defective wiring, the installation of inflammable decorations, the absence of fire doors, the absence of "proper means of egress properly maintained" and "sufficient proper" exits, and overcrowding. Some other specifications -- such as failure to prevent the unlawful employment of minors -- plainly had little or no relation to any wanton or reckless conduct that might result in manslaughter. * * * Another indictment numbered 414 in sixteen counts was returned against the same three persons. * * *

The defendant was found guilty upon counts 7 to 16 inclusive of indictment 413 and upon counts 7 to 15 inclusive of indictment 414. He was sentenced to imprisonment in the State prison upon each count for a term of not less than twelve years and not more than fifteen years, the first day of said term to be in solitary confinement and the residue at hard labor, the sentences to run concurrently. * * *

II. *The principles governing liability.*

The Commonwealth disclaimed any contention that the defendant intentionally killed or injured the persons named in the indictments as victims. It based its case on involuntary manslaughter through wanton or reckless conduct. The judge instructed the jury correctly with respect to the nature of such conduct.

Usually wanton or reckless conduct consists of an affirmative act, like driving an automobile or discharging a firearm, in disregard of probable harmful consequences to another. But where, as in the present case, there is a duty of care for the safety of business visitors invited to premises which the defendant controls, wanton or reckless conduct may consist of intentional failure to take such care in disregard of the probable harmful consequences to them or of their right to care.

To define wanton or reckless conduct so as to distinguish it clearly from negligence and gross negligence is not easy. * * * The words "wanton" and "reckless" are practically synonymous in this connection, although the word "wanton" may contain a suggestion of arrogance or insolence or heartlessness that is lacking in the word "reckless." * * *

The standard of wanton or reckless conduct is at once subjective and objective, as has been recognized ever since *Commonwealth v. Pierce*. Knowing facts that would cause a reasonable man to know the danger is equivalent to knowing the danger. The judge charged the jury correctly when he said, "To constitute wanton or reckless conduct, as distinguished from mere negligence, grave danger to others must have been apparent, and the defendant must have chosen to run the risk rather than alter his conduct so as to avoid the act or omission which caused the harm. If the grave danger was in fact realized by the defendant, his subsequent voluntary act or omission which caused the harm amounts to wanton or reckless conduct, no matter whether the ordinary man would have realized the gravity of the danger or not. But even if a particular defendant is so stupid [or] so heedless . . . that in fact he did not realize the grave danger, he cannot escape the imputation of wanton or reckless conduct in his dangerous act or omission, if an ordinary normal man under the same circumstances would have realized the gravity of the danger. A man may be reckless within the meaning of the law although he himself thought he was careful." * * *

The words "wanton" and "reckless" are thus not merely rhetorical or vituperative expressions used instead of negligent or grossly negligent. They express a difference in the degree of risk and in the voluntary taking of risk so marked, as compared with negligence, as to amount substantially and in the eyes of the law to a difference in kind. For many years this court has been careful to preserve the distinction between negligence and gross negligence, on the one hand, and wanton or reckless conduct on the other. In pleadings as well as in statutes the rule is that "negligence and wilful and wanton conduct are so different in kind that words properly descriptive of the one commonly exclude the other."

Notwithstanding language used commonly in earlier cases, and occasionally in later ones, it is now clear in this Commonwealth that at common law conduct does not become criminal until it passes the borders of negligence and gross negligence and enters into the domain of wanton or reckless conduct. There is in Massachusetts at common law no such thing as "criminal negligence." * * *

To convict the defendant of manslaughter, the Commonwealth was not required to prove that he caused the fire by some wanton or reckless conduct. Fire in a place of public resort is an ever present danger. It was enough to prove that death resulted from his wanton or reckless disregard of the safety of patrons in the event of fire from any cause. * * *

Judgment affirmed.

Note

The fire at the New Cocoanut Grove stirred up a torrent of angry emotions which may have encouraged the prosecution of Mr. Welansky who was ill in the hospital at the time of the fire. Professor Phillip Johnson comments on the *Welansky* case:

> It appears that the public of Boston and the newspapers felt an enormous psychological need to find a scapegoat for the Coconut Grove fire, in which hundreds of people died horribly.

Initially, there was a call for prosecution of the 16-year-old busboy who apparently started the fire. He seems to have been a model youth from an impoverished background, however, and public opinion soon turned towards more suitable scapegoats. There were attacks in the newspapers upon a variety of public officials who were responsible in varying degrees for failing to require that the unsafe conditions be rectified. A fire inspector had reported on conditions at the nightclub just eight days before the fire, and had found them to be fairly acceptable. Eventually, the newspaper attacks came to center on the owners of the club, and Welansky was indicted.

In fact, the cause of the fire was never satisfactorily explained and the degree to which any negligence on the part of Welansky contributed to it remained highly speculative. In 1970, the Boston Fire Department concluded a renewed investigation of the case and found that the cause of the fire could not be determined. At that time, the busboy who had supposedly started the fire, now 44 years old, was still receiving abusive telephone calls blaming him for the fire.

Philip Johnson, TEACHER'S MANUAL for CRIMINAL LAW: CASES, MATERIALS AND TEXT (4th ed. 1990), *citing* Goldstein, Dershowitz, and Schwarz, CRIMINAL LAW: THEORY AND PROCESS (1974).

In 1993, the city's fire department reopened its investigation into the fire and found new evidence that the club's air conditioning system was filled with methyl chloride on the night of the fire. Methyl chloride is a flammable alternative to the usual coolants. *New Theory Offered on Deadly 1942 Blaze*, Las Vegas Review Journal, Sept. 25, 1993, at 8A.

STATE v. WILLIAMS
Court of Appeals of Washington
4 Wash. App. 908, 484 P.2d 1167 (Ct. App. 1971)

HOROWITZ, C.J.

Defendants, husband and wife, were charged by information filed October 3, 1968, with the crime of manslaughter for negligently failing to supply their 17-month child with necessary medical attention, as a result of which he died on September 12, 1968. Upon entry of findings, conclusions and judgment of guilty, sentences were imposed on April 22, 1969. Defendants appeal.

The defendant husband, Walter Williams, is a 24-year-old full-blooded Sheshont Indian with a sixth-grade education. His sole occupation is that of laborer. The defendant wife, Bernice Williams, is a 20-year-old part Indian with an 11th grade education. At the time of the marriage, the wife had two children, the younger of whom was a 14-month son. Both parents worked and the children were cared for by the 85-year-old mother of the defendant husband. The defendant husband assumed parental responsibility with the defendant wife to provide clothing, care and medical attention for the child. Both defendants possessed a great deal of love and affection for the defendant wife's young son.

The court expressly found:

> That both defendants were aware that William Joseph Tabafunda was ill during the period September 1, 1968 to September 12, 1968. The defendants were ignorant. They did not realize how sick the baby was. They thought that the baby had a toothache and no layman regards a toothache as dangerous to life. They loved the baby and gave it aspirin in hopes of improving its condition. They did not take the baby to a doctor because of fear that the Welfare Department would take the baby away from them. They knew that medical help was available because of previous experience. They had no excuse that the law will recognize for not taking the baby to a doctor.

> The defendants Walter L. Williams and Bernice J. Williams were negligent in not seeking medical attention for William Joseph Tabafunda.

> That as a proximate result of this negligence, William Joseph Tabafunda died.

From these and other findings, the court concluded that the defendants were each guilty of the crime of manslaughter as charged.

Defendants take no exception to [these] findings but contend that the findings do not support the conclusions that the defendants are guilty of manslaughter as charged. The contentions raise two basic issues, (1) the existence of the duty to furnish medical aid charged by the information to be violated and the seriousness of the breach required; and (2) the issue of proximate cause, *i.e.,* whether defendants were put on notice, in time to save the child's life, that medical care was required. Because the nature of the duty and the quality or seriousness of the breach are closely interrelated, our discussion of the first issue involved will embrace both matters.

Parental duty to provide medical care for a dependent minor child was recognized at common law and characterized as a natural duty. In Washington, the existence of the duty is commonly assumed and is stated at times without reference to any particular statute. * * * On the question of the quality or seriousness of breach of the duty, at common law, in the case of involuntary manslaughter, the breach had to amount to more than mere ordinary or simple negligence -- gross negligence was essential. In Washington, however, RCW 9.48.060 (since amended by Laws of 1970, ch. 49, § 2) and RCW 9.48.150 supersede both voluntary and involuntary manslaughter as those crimes were defined at common law. Under these statutes the crime is deemed committed even though the death of the victim is the proximate result of only simple or ordinary negligence.

The concept of simple or ordinary negligence describes a failure to exercise the "ordinary caution" necessary to make out the defense of excusable homicide. Ordinary caution is the kind of caution that a man of reasonable prudence would exercise under the same or similar conditions. If, therefore, the conduct of a defendant, regardless of his ignorance, good intentions and good faith, fails to measure up to the conduct required of a man of reasonable prudence, he is guilty of ordinary negligence because of his failure to use "ordinary caution." If such negligence proximately causes the death of the victim, the defendant, as pointed out above, is guilty of statutory manslaughter. * * *

The remaining issue of proximate cause requires consideration of the question of when the duty to furnish medical care became activated. If the duty to furnish such care was not activated until after it was too late to save the life of the child, failure to furnish medical care could not be said to have proximately caused the child's death. Timeliness in the furnishing of medical care also must be considered in terms of "ordinary caution." The law does not mandatorily require that a doctor be called for a child at the first sign of any indisposition or illness. The indisposition or illness may appear to be of a minor or very temporary kind, such as a toothache or cold. If one in the exercise of ordinary caution fails to recognize that his child's symptoms require medical attention, it cannot be said that the failure to obtain such medical attention is a breach of the duty owed. In our opinion, the duty as formulated in *People v. Pierson*, properly defines the duty contemplated by our manslaughter statutes. The court there said:

> We quite agree that the Code does not contemplate the necessity of calling a physician for every trifling complaint with which the child may be afflicted which in most instances may be overcome by the ordinary household nursing by members of the family; that a reasonable amount of discretion is vested in

parents, charged with the duty of maintaining and bringing up infant children; and that the standard is at what time would an ordinarily prudent person, solicitous for the welfare of his child and anxious to promote its recovery, deem it necessary to call in the services of a physician.

It remains to apply the law discussed to the facts of the instant case. * * *

Dr. Gale Wilson, the autopsy surgeon and chief pathologist for the King County Coroner, testified that the child died because an abscessed tooth had been allowed to develop into an infection of the mouth and cheeks, eventually becoming gangrenous. This condition, accompanied by the child's inability to eat, brought about malnutrition, lowering the child's resistance and eventually producing pneumonia, causing the death. Dr. Wilson testified that in his opinion the infection had lasted for approximately 2 weeks, and that the odor generally associated with gangrene would have been present for approximately 10 days before death. He also expressed the opinion that had medical care been first obtained in the last week before the baby's death, such care would have been obtained too late to have saved the baby's life. Accordingly, the baby's apparent condition between September 1 and September 5, 1968 became the critical period for the purpose of determining whether in the exercise of ordinary caution defendants should have provided medical care for the minor child.

The testimony concerning the child's apparent condition during the critical period is not crystal clear, but is sufficient to warrant the following statement of the matter. The defendant husband testified that he noticed the baby was sick about 2 weeks before the baby died. The defendant wife testified that she noticed the baby was ill about a week and a half or 2 weeks before the baby died. The evidence showed that in the critical period the baby was fussy; that he could not keep his food down; and that a cheek started swelling up. The swelling went up and down, but did not disappear. In that same period, the cheek turned "a bluish color like." The defendants, not realizing that the baby was as ill as it was or that the baby was in danger of dying, attempted to provide some relief to the baby by giving the baby aspirin during the critical period and continued to do so until the night before the baby died. The defendants thought the swelling would go down and were waiting for it to do so; and defendant husband testified, that from what he had heard, neither doctors nor dentists pull out a tooth "when it's all swollen up like that." There was an additional explanation for not calling a doctor given by each defendant. Defendant husband testified that "the way the cheek looked, . . . and that stuff on his hair, they would think we were neglecting him and take him away from us and not give him back." Defendant wife testified that the defendants were "waiting for the swelling to go down," and also that they were afraid to take the child to a doctor for fear that the doctor would report them to the welfare department, who, in turn, would take the child away. "It's just that I was so scared of losing him." They testified that they had heard that the defendant husband's cousin lost a child that way. The evidence showed that the defendants did not understand the significance or seriousness of the baby's symptoms. However, there is no evidence that the defendants were physically or financially unable to obtain a doctor, or that they did not know an available doctor, or that the symptoms did not continue to be a matter of concern during the critical period. Indeed, the evidence shows that in April 1968 defendant husband had taken the child to a doctor for medical attention.

In our opinion, there is sufficient evidence from which the court could find, as it necessarily did, that applying the standard of ordinary caution, *i.e.,* the caution exercisable by a man of reasonable prudence under the same or similar conditions, defendants were sufficiently put on notice concerning the symptoms of the baby's illness and lack of improvement in the baby's apparent condition in the period from September 1 to September 5, 1968 to have required them to have obtained medical care for the child. The failure so to do in this case is ordinary or simple negligence, and such negligence is sufficient to support a conviction of statutory manslaughter.

The judgment is affirmed.

Note

The Court of Appeals of Washington was unmoved by the defendants' claim that the reason they did not take the baby to the doctor was because they were afraid the doctor would report them to the welfare department which would then take the baby away. Whether the defendants acted negligently turns on the reasonableness or unreasonableness of their actions. The question of reasonableness depends in turn on the fact finder's construction of the reasonable person. Who is the "reasonable person" against whom these American Indian parents should be compared? Should the fact finder consider class, age, gender, level of education, or ethnicity? Consider the following.

INDIAN CHILD WELFARE ACT OF 1978
P.L. 95-608
HOUSE REPORT NO. 95-1386
July 24, 1978

* * * The wholesale separation of Indian children from their families is perhaps the most tragic and destructive aspect of American Indian life today.

Surveys of states with large Indian populations conducted by the Association of American Indian Affairs (AAIA) in 1969 and again in 1974 indicate that approximately 25-35 percent of all Indian children are separated from their families and placed in foster homes, adoptive homes, or institutions. In some states the problem is getting worse: in Minnesota, one in every eight Indian children under 18 years of age is living in an adoptive home; and, in 1971-72, nearly one in every four Indian children under 1 year of age was adopted.

The disparity in placement rates for Indians and non-Indians is shocking. In Minnesota, Indian children are placed in foster care or in adoptive homes at a per capita rate five times greater than non-Indian children. In Montana, the ratio of Indian foster-care placement is at least 13 times greater. In South Dakota, 40 percent of all adoptions made by the State's Department of Public Welfare since 1967-68 are of Indian children, yet Indians make up only 7 percent of the juvenile population. The number of South Dakota Indian children living in foster homes is per capita, nearly 16 times greater than the non-Indian rate. In the state of Washington, the Indian adoption rate is 19 times greater and the foster care rate 10 times greater. In Wisconsin, the risk run by Indian children of being separated from their parents is nearly 1,600 percent greater than it is for non-Indian children. Just as Indian children are exposed to these great hazards, their parents are too. * * *

The Indian child welfare crisis will continue until the standards for defining mistreatment are revised. Very few Indian children are removed from their families on the grounds of physical abuse. One study of a North Dakota reservation showed that these grounds were advanced in only 1 percent of the cases. Another study of a tribe in the Northwest showed the same incidence. The remaining 99 percent of the cases were argued on such vague grounds as "neglect" or "social deprivation" and on allegations of the emotional damage the children were subjected to by living with their parents. Indian communities are often shocked to learn that parents they regard as excellent caregivers have been judged unfit by non-Indian social workers.

In judging the fitness of a particular family, many social workers, ignorant of Indian cultural values and social norms, make decisions that are wholly inappropriate in the context of Indian family life and so they frequently discover neglect or abandonment where none exists.

For example, the dynamics of Indian extended families are largely misunderstood. An Indian child may have scores of, perhaps more than a hundred, relatives who are counted as close, responsible members of the family. Many social workers, untutored in the ways of Indian family life or assuming them to be socially irresponsible, consider leaving the child with persons outside the nuclear family as neglect and thus as grounds for terminating parental rights. * * *

One of the grounds most frequently advanced for taking Indian children from their parents is the abuse of alcohol. However, this standard is applied unequally. In areas where rates of problem drinking among Indians and non-Indians are the same, it is rarely applied against non-Indian parents. Once again cultural biases frequently affect decision making. * * *

G.   THE FELONY MURDER RULE

Under the common law felony murder rule (also known as the second degree felony murder rule), a person who kills during the commission or attempted commission of a felony has committed second degree murder. (The felon's accomplices may also be convicted of second degree murder. We will explore the question of what makes a person an accomplice in Chapter 12.)

In addition to the common law doctrine of felony murder, many jurisdictions that follow the common law also elevate, by statute, certain homicides to first-degree murder status if the killing occurred during the perpetration or attempted perpetration of an enumerated felony (i.e., a felony specified in the first degree murder statute). The felonies that are typically enumerated are rape, robbery, arson, burglary, and kidnaping.

In *People v. Aaron*, excerpted below, the Supreme Court of Michigan described the history of the felony murder rule:

> Felony murder has never been a static, well-defined rule at common law, but throughout its history has been characterized by judicial reinterpretation to limit the harshness of the application of the rule. Historians and commentators have concluded that the rule is of questionable origin and that the reasons for the rule no longer exist, making it an anachronistic remnant, "a historic survivor for which there is no logical or practical basis for existence in modern law." * * *

> At early common law, the felony-murder rule went unchallenged because at that time practically all felonies were punishable by death. It was, therefore, "of no particular moment whether the condemned was hanged for the initial felony or for the death accidentally resulting from the felony." Thus... no injustice was caused directly by application of the rule at that time. * * *

Case law of Nineteenth-Century England reflects the efforts of the English courts to limit the application of the felony-murder doctrine. In [a] case involving a death resulting from arson, Judge Stephen instructed the jury as follows:

> [Instead] of saying that any act done with intent to commit a felony and which causes death amounts to murder, it should be reasonable to say that any act known to be dangerous to life and likely in itself to cause death, done for the purpose of committing a felony which causes death, should be murder.

In this century, the felony-murder doctrine was comparatively rarely invoked in England and in 1957 England abolished the felony-murder rule. * * *

Is felony murder a strict liability crime? The answer might plausibly be "no," because the prosecution has to prove some kind of mens rea in order to get a conviction: the state of mind required for commission of the underlying felony. On the other hand, the answer might be "yes, in some cases." This is because under the felony murder rule, a person may be convicted of murder even if she had no intent to kill and was not reckless or negligent with respect to the risk of death. That is to say, accidental deaths that occur in the commission of or attempt to commit a felony are covered by the felony murder rule. Because of its relative indifference to mens rea, the felony murder rule is in tension with the rest of homicide law, which focuses, as we have seen, on the actor's culpability as the primary way of meting out punishment.

PEOPLE v. STAMP

Court of Appeal of California, Second Appellate District, Division Three
2 Cal. App. 3d 203, 82 Cal.Rptr. 598 (Ct. App. 1969)

COBEY, ACTING P.J.

These are appeals by Jonathan Earl Stamp, Michael John Koory and Billy Dean Lehman, following jury verdicts of guilty of robbery and murder, both in the first degree. Each man was given a life sentence on the murder charge together with the time prescribed by law on the robbery count.

Defendants appeal their conviction of the murder of Carl Honeyman who, suffering from a heart disease, died between 15 and 20 minutes after Koory and Stamp held up his business, the General Amusement Company, on October 26, 1965, at 10:45 a.m. * * *

On this appeal appellants primarily rely upon their position that the felony-murder doctrine should not have been applied in this case due to the unforeseeability of Honeyman's death. * * *

Defendants Koory and Stamp, armed with a gun and a blackjack, entered the rear of the building housing the offices of General Amusement Company, ordered the employees they found there to go to the front of the premises, where the two secretaries were working. Stamp, the one with the gun, then went into the office of Carl Honeyman, the owner and manager. Thereupon Honeyman, looking very frightened and pale, emerged from the office in a "kind of hurry." He was apparently propelled by Stamp who had hold of him by an elbow.

The robbery victims were required to lie down on the floor while the robbers took the money and fled out the back door. As the robbers, who had been on the premises 10 to 15 minutes, were leaving, they told the victims to remain on the floor for five minutes so that no one would "get hurt."

Honeyman, who had been lying next to the counter, had to use it to steady himself in getting up off the floor. Still pale, he was short of breath, sucking air, and pounding and rubbing his chest. As he walked down the hall, in an unsteady manner, still breathing hard and rubbing his chest, he said he was having trouble "keeping the pounding down inside" and that his heart was "pumping too fast for him." A few minutes later, although still looking very upset, shaking, wiping his forehead and rubbing his chest, he was able to walk in a steady manner into an employee's office. When the police arrived, almost immediately thereafter, he told them he was not feeling very well and that he had a pain in his chest. About two minutes later, which was 15 or 20 minutes after the robbery had occurred, he collapsed on the floor. At 11:25 he was pronounced dead on arrival at the hospital. The coroner's report listed the immediate cause of death as heart attack.

The employees noted that during the hours before the robbery Honeyman had appeared to be in normal health and good spirits. The victim was an obese, 60-year-old man, with a history of heart disease, who was under a great deal of pressure due to the intensely competitive nature of his business. Additionally, he did not take good care of his heart.

Three doctors, including the autopsy surgeon, Honeyman's physician, and a professor of cardiology from U.C.L.A., testified that although Honeyman had an advanced case of atherosclerosis, a progressive and ultimately fatal disease, there must have been some immediate upset to his system which precipitated the attack. It was their conclusion in response to a hypothetical question that but for the robbery there would have been no fatal seizure at that time. The fright induced by the robbery was too much of a shock to Honeyman's system. There was opposing expert testimony to the effect that it could not be said with reasonable medical certainty that fright could ever be fatal. * * *

Appellant's contention that the evidence was insufficient to prove that the robbery factually caused Honeyman's death is without merit. The test on review is whether there is substantial evidence to uphold the judgment of the trial court, and in so deciding this court must assume in the case of a jury trial the existence of every fact in favor of the verdict which the jury could reasonably have deduced from the evidence. A review of the facts as outlined above shows that there was substantial evidence of the robbery itself, that appellants were the robbers, and that but for the robbery the victim would not have experienced the fright which brought on the fatal heart attack. * * *

Appellant's contention that the felony-murder rule is inapplicable to the facts of this case is also without merit. Under the felony-murder rule of section 189 of the Penal Code, a killing committed in either the perpetration of or an attempt to perpetrate robbery is murder of the first degree. This is true whether the killing is wilfull, deliberate and premeditated, or merely accidental or unintentional, and whether or not the killing is planned as a part of the commission of the robbery.

The doctrine presumes malice aforethought on the basis of the commission of a felony inherently dangerous to human life. This rule is a rule of substantive law in California and not merely an evidentiary shortcut to finding malice as it withdraws from the jury the requirement that they find either express malice or the implied malice which is manifested in an intent to kill. Under this rule no intentional act is necessary other than the attempt to or the actual commission of the robbery itself. When a robber enters a place with a deadly weapon with the intent to commit robbery, malice is shown by the nature of the crime. * * *

The doctrine is not limited to those deaths which are foreseeable. Rather a felon is held strictly liable for *all* killings committed by him or his accomplices in the course of the felony. As long as the homicide is the direct causal result of the robbery the felony-murder rule applies whether or not the death was a natural or probable consequence of the robbery. So long as a victim's predisposing physical condition, regardless of its cause, is not the *only* substantial factor bringing about his death, that condition, and the robber's ignorance of it, in no way destroys the robber's criminal responsibility for the death. So long as life is shortened as a result of the felonious act, it does not matter that the victim might have died soon anyway. In this respect, the robber takes his victim as he finds him. * * *

The judgment is affirmed.

Note

Another example of the reach of the felony murder rule comes from a newspaper report involving the death of an 87-year-old man who was accidentally shoved during an altercation between a security guard and a shoplifter:

> * * * JC Penney security guard Harry Delatorre, 20, and [Jesse] Rhodes were wrestling over a pair of women's acidwash Levi Jeans [which Delatorre thought Rhodes was attempting to steal] when they accidentally shoved [Stanley Dollin], who was slowly strolling down the crowded avenue in the afternoon, Berkeley Homicide Inspector Bob Maloney said. [Dollin sustained head injuries and died three days later. Rhodes was charged with first degree murder.]
>
> If convicted, Rhodes will be sentenced to 25 years in state prison.
>
> "Maybe there is some humanity in the system for this poor, humble and physically weak woman," McWilliams said. "This doesn't make sense to her, she's not a killer. She has a long history of petty theft, but she is not a killer."

Patricia Jacobus, *Rash of Unrelated August Killings Plagues Berkeley*, The Daily Californian, August 16, 1989, p. 1.

Courts troubled by the spectacle of accidental deaths being treated as murders have attempted to limit the operation of the felony murder rule with additional rules. Four such limiting rules are found in many jurisdictions that recognize felony murder. These are (1) the inherently dangerous felony limitation; (2) the "res gestae" requirement, (3) the merger doctrine; and (4) the agency rule. The cases in this section outline these limitations on the felony murder rule.

The tension between the social-harm approach of the felony murder rule and the culpability approach of the rest of murder doctrine, and the byzantine complexity caused by judges' attempts to limit the scope of felony murder by creating limiting rules, has led some to call for the abolition of the felony murder rule. As a policy matter, can felony murder be justified? On what grounds – retribution, deterrence, incapacitation? The last case in this section, *People v. Aaron*, considers some of these questions.

1. The Inherently Dangerous Felony Limitation

PEOPLE v. PATTERSON
Supreme Court of California
49 Cal.3d 615, 778 P.2d 549, 262 Cal.Rptr. 195 (1989)

* * * According to the testimony at the preliminary hearing, victim Jennie Licerio and her friend Carmen Lopez had been using cocaine on a daily basis in the months preceding Licerio's death. On the night of November 25, 1985, the two women were with defendant in his motel room. There, all three drank "wine coolers," inhaled "lines" of cocaine, and smoked "coco puffs" (hand-rolled cigarettes containing a mixture of tobacco and cocaine). Defendant furnished the cocaine. When Licerio became ill, Lopez called an ambulance. Defendant stayed with the two women until the paramedics and the police arrived. The paramedics were unable to revive Licerio, who died of acute cocaine intoxication.

The People filed an information charging defendant with one count each of murder (Pen. Code, § 187), possession of cocaine (Health & Saf. Code, § 11350), and possession of cocaine for sale (Health & Saf. Code, § 11351). Defendant was also charged with three counts of violating Health and Safety Code section 11352, in that he "did willfully, unlawfully and feloniously transport, import into the State of California, sell, furnish, administer, and give away, and attempt to import into the State of California and transport a controlled substance, to wit: cocaine."

Defendant moved under Penal Code section 995 to set aside that portion of the information charging him with murder, contending the evidence presented at the preliminary hearing did not establish probable cause to believe he had committed murder. In opposing the motion, the People * * * relied solely on the second degree felony-murder doctrine. They argued that by furnishing cocaine defendant committed an inherently dangerous felony, thus justifying application of the rule. The trial court denied the motion. However, when the case was reassigned for trial, the court dismissed the murder charge under Penal Code section 1385. In compliance with Penal Code section 1385's requirement that "[the] reasons for the dismissal must be set forth in an order entered upon the minutes," the court gave this explanation in its minute order: "Court finds that violation of 11351 H & S and 11352 H & S are not inherently dangerous to human life and on the Courts [*sic*] own motion orders count 1 of the information dismissed in the interest of justice under section 1385 P.C." * * *

The Court of Appeal affirmed the dismissal of the murder count. Based on its review of the applicable decisions of this court, the Court of Appeal felt compelled to analyze Health and Safety Code section 11352 in its entirety (as opposed to only that portion of the statute actually violated in the present case) to determine whether defendant had committed an inherently dangerous felony. The court observed that section 11352 could be violated in various nonhazardous ways, such as transporting or offering to transport controlled substances. As the court said, "The latter acts are obviously not inherently dangerous to human life." While recognizing that the murder charge against defendant rested on his *furnishing* cocaine to the victim, the court concluded that, viewing the statute "in the abstract," a violation of section 11352 could not be characterized as an inherently dangerous felony.

The Court of Appeal reached this conclusion reluctantly. The court noted that consideration of the entire statute, which included offenses unrelated to defendant's conduct, had brought the second degree felony-murder rule "to the brink of logical absurdity." The court suggested that "[if] the rule is not abolished, it should be codified by the legislature with meaningful guidelines to effectuate its use." * * *

Discussion

1.   *Second degree felony-murder doctrine*

There is no precise statutory definition for the second degree felony-murder rule. In *People v. Ford*, we defined the doctrine as follows: "A homicide that is a direct causal result of the commission of a felony inherently dangerous to human life (other than the six felonies enumerated in Pen. Code § 189) constitutes at least second degree murder. In determining whether the felony is inherently dangerous, "we look to the elements of the felony in the abstract, not the particular 'facts' of the case."

The Court of Appeal's opinion in this case criticized the second degree felony-murder rule in its present form, suggesting the doctrine should either be completely eliminated or considerably "reformed." In response, defendant and amici curiae on his behalf have urged us to abolish the rule. The People and their amici curiae, on the other hand, have asked that we "reform" the doctrine by looking solely to the actual conduct of a defendant, thereby dispensing with the requirement that the elements of the offense be viewed in the abstract. We decline both invitations for the reasons discussed below.

The second degree felony-murder doctrine has been a part of California's criminal law for many decades.   In recent years, we have characterized the rule as "anachronistic" and "disfavored", based on the view of many legal scholars that the doctrine incorporates an artificial concept of strict criminal liability that "erodes the relationship between criminal liability and moral culpability." The Legislature, however, has taken no action to alter this judicially created rule, and has declined our more recent suggestion in *People v. Dillon*, that it reconsider the rules on first and second degree felony murder and misdemeanor manslaughter. In this case, our limited purpose in granting the People's petition for review was to determine the applicability of the second degree felony-murder doctrine to the crime of furnishing cocaine. We decline defendant's invitation that we determine the continued vitality of the rule.

We also turn down the People's invitation that we expand the second degree felony-murder doctrine by eliminating the requirement of *People v. Williams*, that the elements of the offense be viewed "in the abstract," and by adopting a new standard focusing instead on the actual conduct of a defendant in determining whether the felony is inherently dangerous. * * *

Sound reasons support the *Williams* rule. As we observed in *People v. Burroughs*: "This form of [viewed-in-the-abstract] analysis is compelled because there is a killing in every case where the rule might potentially be applied. If in such circumstances a court were to examine the particular facts of the case prior to establishing whether the underlying felony is inherently dangerous, the court might well be led to conclude the rule applicable despite any unfairness which might redound to the defendant by so broad an application: the existence of the dead victim might appear to lead inexorably to the conclusion that the underlying felony is exceptionally hazardous." * * *

3.   *Meaning of the term "inherently dangerous to human life"*

For the guidance of the trial court on remand, we shall elaborate on the meaning of the term "inherently dangerous to life" for purposes of the second degree felony-murder doctrine.

The felony-murder rule generally acts as a substitute for the *mental state* ordinarily required for the offense of murder. We observed in *People v. Satchell*: "Under well-settled principles of criminal liability a person who kills -- whether or not he is engaged in an independent felony at the time -- is guilty of murder *if he acts with malice aforethought.* The felony-murder doctrine, whose ostensible purpose is to deter those engaged in felonies from killing negligently or accidentally, operates to posit the existence of that crucial mental state -- and thereby to render irrelevant evidence of actual malice or the lack thereof -- when the killer is engaged in a felony whose inherent danger to human life renders logical an imputation of malice on the part of all who commit it." * * *

The second degree felony-murder rule eliminates the need for the prosecution to establish the *mental* component. The justification therefor is that, when society has declared certain inherently dangerous conduct to be felonious, a defendant should not be allowed to excuse himself by saying he was unaware of the danger to life because, by declaring the conduct to be felonious, society has warned him of the risk involved. * * *

We therefore conclude -- by analogy to the established definition of the term "dangerous to life" in the context of the implied malice element of second degree murder -- that, for purposes of the second degree felony-murder doctrine, an "inherently dangerous felony" is an offense carrying "a high probability" that death will result. A less stringent standard would inappropriately expand the scope of the second degree felony-murder rule reducing the seriousness of the act which a defendant must commit in order to be charged with murder.

We share the concern Chief Justice Lucas has expressed in his dissent regarding the tragic effects that the abuse of illegal drugs, particularly "crack" cocaine, has on our society. However, it is the Legislature, rather than this court, that should determine whether expansion of the second degree felony-murder rule is an appropriate method by which to address this problem. In the absence of specific legislative action, we must determine the scope of the rule by applying the established definition of inherent dangerousness.

We reverse the decision of the Court of Appeal, and direct that court to remand the matter to the trial court for further proceedings consistent with this opinion.

Lucas, C.J., concurring and dissenting:

I concur in the judgment. As several prior cases have indicated, the second degree felony-murder doctrine performs a valuable function in deterring the commission of crimes which, though involving no express or implied malice, are nonetheless so inherently dangerous as to justify a murder charge when a death occurs during their commission. Accordingly, the majority quite properly refuses to accept defendant's invitations (1) to abrogate the doctrine entirely, or (2) to permit consideration of other felonies not involved in the case in determining the inherent dangerousness of the defendant's own offense.

I dissent, however, to the majority's unrealistic, unwise and unprecedented definition of inherent dangerousness as involving "a high probability of death." With that one broad, gratuitous stroke, the majority has precluded application of the second degree felony-murder doctrine to most, if not all, drug furnishing offenses (as well as many nondrug offenses), thereby overruling or disapproving, sub silentio, several prior cases of this court and the Court of Appeal. * * *

Each of the foregoing cases held that a second degree murder charge could be founded upon the furnishing of illegal, dangerous drugs. No mention whatever was made of any need to show a "high probability" of death in those cases. The courts therein simply concluded that *an inherent danger to life* was sufficient to warrant a felony murder charge. * * *

Because the drug furnishing statutes must be viewed *in the abstract* for purposes of applying the second degree felony-murder doctrine, as a practical matter the majority's new "high probability" requirement will be impossible to satisfy in any case arising under those statutes, for to my knowledge none of them involves drugs so dangerous that death is a *highly probable* result. At a time when our society faces a serious "crack" cocaine crisis of epidemic proportions, the majority's holding is particularly unwelcome. I note that neither defendant nor the People urged adoption of the "high probability" standard -- the issue remained unbriefed throughout the appeal process.

We recently set forth in *People* v. *Burroughs*, another second degree felony-murder case, the correct and proper test for determining the inherent dangerousness of an offense. There, we referred to a felony "inherently so dangerous that by its very nature, it cannot be committed without creating *a substantial risk* that someone will be killed . . . ." This formulation was not the creation of the *Burroughs* court. As one commentator has observed, citing English cases from 1887 and 1898, at common law the second degree felony-murder rule was "limited by the requirement that the commission of a felony involve *substantial human risk* . . . ."

Applying the foregoing test in the context of a drug furnishing offense, the relevant question would be whether furnishing a particular drug such as cocaine or heroin created a substantial risk of death. Although that test may be difficult for the prosecution to meet, the majority's alternative test will entirely foreclose the possibility of a murder charge in all of these cases.

As I have indicated, the purpose of the felony-murder rule is to *deter* the commission of inherently dangerous felonies. Certainly that purpose is furthered by deterring offenses bearing a substantial risk of death, as well as those offenses involving a greater likelihood of death. As the court in a similar case (involving heroin furnishing) explained, "knowledge that the death of a person to whom heroin is furnished *may* result in a conviction for murder should have some effect on the defendant's readiness to do the furnishing." * * *

The anomalous and inconsistent nature of the majority's holding is confirmed by the fact that a defendant can be charged with *first* degree felony murder by committing such offenses as burglary, robbery, rape or child molestation, none of which offenses, viewed in the abstract, involves a high probability of death, although each of which may present substantial risks of death. If a first degree murder charge can be based on an offense not involving a high probability of death, surely the lesser charge of second degree murder can be based on similar offenses, so long as the requisite substantial risk of death can be demonstrated.

For all the foregoing reasons, I dissent to the majority's improper new formulation of the standard for determining inherent dangerousness.

[JUSTICE MOSK's and JUSTICE PANELLI's concurring and dissenting opinions have been omitted.]

HINES v. STATE
Supreme Court of Georgia
276 Ga. 491, 578 S.E.2d 868 (2003)

FLETCHER, C.J.

While hunting, Robert Lee Hines mistook his friend Steven Wood for a turkey and shot him dead. A jury convicted Hines of felony murder based on the underlying crime of possession of a firearm by a convicted felon, but acquitted him of felony murder based on the underlying felony of misuse of a firearm while hunting. * * *

Taken in the light most favorable to the jury's verdict of guilty, the evidence at trial showed that, late in the afternoon of April 8, 2001, Hines and some of his friends and relatives went turkey hunting. They split into two groups, with Hines and his friend Randy Stoker hunting together in one area, and the victim, the victim's wife, and Hines's son hunting in a different area, approximately one-fourth mile away. As the sky was growing dark, Hines heard a turkey gobble, "saw it fan out and shot." Hines's shot went through heavy foliage and hit the victim approximately eighty feet away. Immediately thereafter, the victim's wife screamed, "You shot Wood." Hines and his son went for help, but the victim died before help could arrive.

On his return, Hines tried to convince his son and Stoker to take responsibility for the shooting. They both refused. The entire group, however, agreed to say that they did not know who had shot Wood. Hines removed his camouflage clothing and hid his shotgun and hunting gear before the police arrived.

Two days later, Hines admitted he had shot Wood and showed the police where he had hidden his shotgun. Hines's son showed the police where he had hidden Hines's hunting clothing and gear, which included unopened cans of beer. An open beer can and foam insulation wrap that belonged to Hines were found near where Hines had fired the fatal shot.

We conclude that the evidence at trial was sufficient for a reasonable trier of fact to have found Hines guilty beyond a reasonable doubt of the crimes for which he was convicted. * * *

Hines contends that a convicted felon's possession of a firearm while turkey hunting cannot be one of the inherently dangerous felonies required to support a conviction for felony murder. "The only limitation on the type of felony that may serve as an underlying felony for a felony murder conviction is that the felony must be inherently dangerous to human life." A felony is "inherently dangerous" when it is "'dangerous per se'" or "'by its circumstances creates a foreseeable risk of death.'" Depending on the facts, possession of a firearm by a convicted felon can be an inherently dangerous felony.

In *Ford v. State*, the defendant was a convicted felon who was unloading a handgun when it accidentally discharged, went through the floor, and killed an occupant of the apartment below. A jury convicted Ford for felony murder based on his felonious possession of a firearm. This Court reversed, finding that, because no evidence showed the defendant knew there was an apartment below him or that the victim was present, his possession of a firearm could not support a conviction for felony murder.

In contrast to *Ford*, Hines intentionally fired his shotgun intending to hit his target. He had been drinking before he went hunting, and there was evidence that he had been drinking while hunting. He knew that other hunters were in the area and was unaware of their exact location. He also knew that other people visited the area in which he was hunting. He took an unsafe shot at dusk, through heavy foliage, at a target eighty feet away that he had not positively identified as a turkey. Under these circumstances, we conclude that Hines's illegal possession of a firearm created a foreseeable risk of death. Accordingly, Hines's violation of the prohibition against convicted felons possessing firearms was an inherently dangerous felony that could support a felony murder conviction. * * *

Judgment affirmed. All the Justices concur, except Sears, P. J., who dissents.

SEARS, PRESIDING JUSTICE, dissenting.

Because I conclude that circumstances surrounding Hines's commission of the status felony of possessing a firearm were not inherently dangerous within the meaning of our decision in *Ford v. State*, I dissent to the majority's affirmance of Hines's conviction of felony murder.

In *Ford*, this Court held that for a felony to serve as the basis for a felony murder conviction, it had to be inherently dangerous by its very nature or had to be committed under circumstances creating a foreseeable risk of death. We also held that the imputation of malice that justifies the felony murder rule is dependent on the "perpetrator's life-threatening state of mind accompanying [the] commission [of the underlying felony]." In *Ford*, however, we did not specify how to determine whether a particular felony, either by its nature or as it was committed, was inherently dangerous to human life. Because of the severe punishments that accompany a conviction of murder and because it is illogical to impute malice for purposes of felony murder " ' "from the intent to commit a felony not [foreseeably] dangerous to human life," ' " I conclude that for purposes of our felony-murder doctrine, a felony is inherently dangerous per se or as committed if it carries "'a high probability' that [a human] death will result." This standard will ensure that our felony murder rule is not inappropriately expanded by "reducing the seriousness of the act which a defendant must commit in order to be charged with murder."

In the present case, I conclude that the possession of a firearm by Hines was not committed in a fashion that was inherently dangerous and that carried a high probability that death would result. The fact that Hines was hunting, a dangerous sport; the fact that he had been drinking before he went hunting; the fact that he was hunting at dusk; and the fact that he fired a shot when he knew other hunters were in the general area in which he was hunting may establish that Hines was negligent, but do not establish that his acts created a high probability that death to a human being would result, or that he had a "life-threatening state of mind." Moreover, as for the fatal shot, Hines testified that he heard a turkey gobble, that he "saw it fan out," and that he then fired at the object. Even though Hines may not, as stated by the majority, have positively identified his target as a turkey, he had to make a split-second decision regarding his target and concluded, based on hearing a gobble and seeing something "fan out," that the object was a turkey. I cannot conclude that, under these circumstances, the failure of the hunter to identify his target beyond doubt carried a high probability that a human being would be killed or that he acted with a "life-threatening state of mind." The death in this case is clearly a tragic incident, and Hines's conduct before and after the shooting was reprehensible. But the sanction of life in prison for murder should be reserved for cases in which the defendant's moral failings warrant such punishment. Here, the application of the felony murder statute to Hines's actions punishes him more severely than his culpability merits. In this regard, Hines will be serving the same punishment – life in prison – as an arsonist convicted of felony murder who firebombed an apartment that he knew was occupied, causing the death of two young children, and the same punishment as an armed robber convicted of felony murder who entered a store with a firearm and shot and killed a store employee. This result is unwarranted and unnecessary, as Hines could be prosecuted and convicted of an appropriate lesser crime, such as involuntary manslaughter or the misuse of a firearm while hunting.[13]

One final note. Hunting is a time-honored recreational activity encouraged by the State of Georgia and enjoyed by many of our State's citizens. No doubt a number of hunters have probably engaged in negligent hunting practices similar to those in this case. Although I do not condone such careless practices, neither can I agree with subjecting so many hunters to the possibility of spending life in prison when they do not fastidiously follow proper hunting procedures and accidentally shoot a fellow hunter.

For the foregoing reasons, I dissent to the majority opinion.

2.   The Res Gestae Requirement

A second consideration in the application of the felony murder rule is the res gestae requirement. The res gestae requirement has two parts. First, the felony and the homicide must be close in time and distance. In other words, there must be both temporal and geographical proximity between the homicide and the felony. Recall that in order for the felony murder rule to apply, the killing must occur "during the commission or attempted commission" of a felony. Clearly, the felony murder rule does not apply if the killing occurs *before* the felony. One might also presume that the felony murder rule does not apply if the killing occurs *after* the commission of the felony. Courts, however, have expanded the time period during which the felony is said to be occurring by holding that felony murder liability continues until the felon reaches a place of temporary safety. The first case in this section, *People v. Bodely*, discusses this "place of temporary safety" rule. Second, the res gestae requirement demands a causal connection between the felony and the homicide. Courts, however, are not in agreement regarding how much of a causal connection is required. Some courts merely require a but-for causal connection. *See, e.g., People v. Stamp, supra*. Others, like the court in *King v. Commonwealth* below, require a greater causal connection between the felonious conduct and the death.

---

[13]Hines was in fact convicted of this crime in the present case.

PEOPLE v. BODELY

Court of Appeal of California, Sixth Appellate District
32 Cal. App. 4th 311, 38 Cal.Rptr.2d 72 (Ct. App. 1995)

MIHARA, J.

The question presented by this case is whether a killing which occurs during the perpetrator's flight from a burglary[a] occurs "in the perpetration" of the burglary and therefore is felony murder. We conclude that such a killing is felony murder and affirm the judgment.

FACTS

Defendant entered a supermarket, grabbed $75 out of a cash register and ran. Several supermarket employees pursued him. He ran out of the supermarket into the parking lot and got into his car. Joseph Andre, who was in the parking lot at the time, joined in the chase. Andre ran in front of defendant's car and put his hands on the hood as if to stop the car. Andre then went to the driver's side window of defendant's car, put his arm inside the car and told defendant to stop. Defendant drove away, jerking the car sharply to the left. Defendant's car hit Andre, knocking Andre onto the hood of the car. Andre then fell off of the hood and struck the back of his head on the pavement. This impact resulted in Andre's death. Defendant sped up and drove away. Defendant was convicted of first degree murder, burglary and an unrelated robbery and committed to state prison. On appeal, he challenges only the murder conviction.

ANALYSIS

"All murder . . . which is committed in the perpetration of, or attempt to perpetrate . . . burglary . . . is murder of the first degree." Defendant claims that Andre's death did not occur "in the perpetration of . . . burglary" because defendant had already left the burglarized structure when he caused Andre's death. Defendant concedes that felony-murder liability continues throughout the

---

[a] Under California Penal Code § 459, the offense of burglary requires entrance into "any structure which has walls on all sides and is covered by a roof" (*People v. Stickman,* 34 Cal. 242 (1867)) with "intent to commit grand or petit larceny or any felony."

flight of a perpetrator from the scene of a *robbery*[b] until the perpetrator reaches a place of temporary safety. However, he claims that the perpetration of burglary "is over" when the burglar leaves the structure, because burglary, unlike robbery, does not require the perpetrator to asport any loot.[c] Hence, in defendant's view, the flight of the perpetrator from a burglary is not part of the perpetration of the offense. The only authority on point is *People v. Fuller*, which resolved this precise issue against defendant. Defendant asks us not to follow *Fuller*.[d]

The Attorney General asks us to follow *Fuller* and hold that the perpetration of a felony does not end for purposes of felony-murder liability until the perpetrator has "reached a place of temporary safety." Numerous California Supreme Court decisions hold that the perpetration of a *robbery* continues, for felony-murder liability purposes, so long as the robbers are in flight from the scene of the crime and have not reached a place of temporary safety. While this so-called "escape rule" was originally justified by an analysis based on when the crime of robbery was "complete," the California Supreme Court has more recently explained that the duration of felony-murder liability is not determined by considering whether the felony itself has been completed. Instead, "the homicide is committed in the perpetration of the felony if the killing and the felony are *parts of one continuous transaction*."

If we apply this "one continuous transaction" analysis, no rationale supports limiting the escape rule exclusively to robbery. The perpetrator's immediate escape from the scene of a crime is no less a part of the same continuous transaction which includes the crime when the crime is burglary than when the crime is robbery. Burglary and robbery, like many other crimes, are generally technically "complete" for purposes of criminal liability prior to the escape of the perpetrator. However, "the escape rule serves the legitimate public policy considerations of deterrence and culpability" by extending felony-murder liability beyond the technical completion of the crime. While the California

---

[b] California Penal Code § 211 defines robbery as "the felonious taking of personal property in the possession of another, from his person or immediate presence, and against his will, accomplished by means of force or fear."

[c] "Asportation" is the technical term for "taking and carrying away" in the law of theft.

[d] In *People v. Fuller*, the Court of Appeal for the Fifth District of California held that flight following a burglary is considered part of the same transaction as long as the felon has not yet reached a place of temporary safety. The court also held that the felony murder rule applies to both escaping robbers and escaping burglars. 86 Cal. App. 3d 618 (1978).

Supreme Court has never actually decided the precise issue raised here, its various statements on this subject reflect that the escape rule is not limited to the crime of robbery. In *People v. Bigelow,* the California Supreme Court explained that "the test used in felony-murder cases to determine when a killing is so closely related to an underlying felony as to justify an enhanced punishment for the killing" is that ". . . the crime continues until the criminal has reached a place of temporary safety." In *People v. Cooper,* the California Supreme Court mentioned that ". . . the potential of felony-murder liability of *burglars* continues through the escape until the perpetrators reach a place of temporary safety" and cited *Fuller* for this proposition.* * *

Since the application of the escape rule to burglary is consistent with the "one continuous transaction" test, we conclude that felony-murder liability continues during the escape of a burglar from the scene of the burglary until the burglar reaches a place of temporary safety.

CONCLUSION

The judgment is affirmed.

COTTLE, P.J., and WUNDERLICH, J., concurred.

KING v. COMMONWEALTH
Court of Appeals of Virginia
6 Va. App. 351, 368 S.E.2d 704 (Ct. App. 1988)

COLEMAN, J.

* * * Nelson James King appeals his conviction of second degree murder under the statute. He argues that he could not be convicted of second degree murder for the accidental death of a cofelon occurring during the commission of a felony. He also argues that the trial court erred in instructing the jury on the elements of the offense. We hold that because the death was not caused by an act of the felons in furtherance of the felony, appellant is not criminally liable for the death.

On October 17, 1984, King and his copilot, Mark Lee Bailey, were flying a Beechcraft Bonanza airplane carrying over five hundred pounds of marijuana to the New River Valley airport in Dublin, Virginia. They were flying for Wallace Thrasher, who owned the airplane and ran the drug smuggling operation. King was a licensed pilot; Bailey was not. The two encountered heavy cloud cover and fog near Mt. Airy, North Carolina and apparently became lost. In an effort to navigate through the cloud cover and fog, they flew the plane to a lower altitude in order to follow U.S. Route 52. Bailey was piloting the plane at this time. As Bailey flew, King was examining navigation maps in an attempt to determine the plane's whereabouts. The airplane crashed into Fancy Gap Mountain killing Bailey almost instantly. King was thrown from the plane and survived. King was charged with felony homicide under Code §18.2-33 for Bailey's death. A jury convicted King of second degree murder under the statute and recommended a six-year penitentiary sentence.

Code §18.2-33 defines second degree felony homicide: "The killing of one accidentally, contrary to the intention of the parties, while in the prosecution of some felonious act other than those specified in §§ 18.2-31 and 18.2-32, is murder of the second degree and is punishable as a Class 3 felony." This statute and its companion, §18.2-32, defining first degree felony-murder, codify the common law doctrine of felony-murder. The doctrine was developed to elevate to murder a homicide committed during the course of a felony by imputing malice to the killing. The justification for imputing malice was the theory that the increased risk of death or serious harm occasioned by the commission of a felony demonstrated the felon's lack of concern for human life. The doctrine was originally limited, therefore, to felonies that were inherently or foreseeably dangerous. The purpose of the doctrine was to deter inherently dangerous felonies by holding the felons responsible for the consequences of the felony, whether intended or not. While the range of felonies which may be a predicate for the felony-murder conviction has changed, the function of the doctrine is still to elevate to murder a homicide resulting from a felony by imputing malice. * * *

The second degree felony-murder statute in Virginia contemplates a killing with malice. Indeed, "the commission of *any* felonious act . . . supplies the malice which raises the incidental homicide to the level of second-degree murder." It does not follow, however, that any death of any person which occurs during the period in which a felony is being committed will subject the felon to criminal liability under the felony-murder rule. To construe our statute to encompass every accidental death occurring during the commission of a felony, regardless of whether it causally relates to or results from the commission of the felony, is to make felons absolutely liable for the accidental death of another even though such death is fortuitous and the product of causes wholly unrelated to the commission of the felony. Recognizing the potentially harsh and far reaching effects of such a construction of the felony-murder doctrine, the Virginia courts, as well as others, have limited its application. In order for the incidental accidental killing to be murder, the homicide must be criminal in nature and must contain the elements or attributes of criminal homicide cognizable at common law.

One of the most significant factors in defining the scope of the felony-murder doctrine involves the causation required between the felony and the death. Previous decisions of the Virginia Supreme Court have found it unnecessary to decide whether "a mere nexus" between the death and predicate felony is sufficient to satisfy the statute or whether a more direct causal relationship is required. We must address that issue at this time.

In Virginia, it is clear when the homicide is within the *res gestae* of the initial felony and emanates therefrom, it is committed in the perpetration of that felony. The Court explained that "the felony-murder statute applies where the killing is so closely related to the felony in time, place, and causal connection as to make it a part of the same criminal enterprise." * * *

In a leading case involving the felony-murder doctrine, which the Virginia Supreme Court has cited with approval, the Pennsylvania Supreme Court addressed the causation problem at length. Rejecting their previous standard of proximate cause, the court stated:

> In adjudging a felony-murder, it is to be remembered at all times that the thing which is imputed to a felon for a killing incidental to his felony is *malice* and *not the act of killing*. The mere coincidence of homicide and felony is not enough to satisfy the requirements of the felony-murder doctrine . . . . " Death must be a consequence of the felony . . . and not merely coincidence."

The court noted further: "[T]he 'causation' requirement for responsibility in a felony-murder is that the homicide stem from the commission of the felony." The *Redline* court noted that the malice of the underlying felony attaches to whatever else the criminal may do in connection with the felony. Therefore, "the killing must have been done by the defendant or by an accomplice or confederate or by one acting in furtherance of the felonious undertaking."

The implications of this reasoning are threefold. First, only acts causing death which are committed by those involved in the felony can be the basis for a conviction. Second, the act causing death must result from some effort to further the felony before malice can be imputed to that act. Third, there must be some act attributable to the felons which causes death. It is not sufficient that death be only temporally related to commission of the felony. Death must be directly related in time, place, and causal connection to the commission of the felony; the felony or acts in furtherance thereof must contribute to cause the death to constitute a "killing" within the felony-murder statute. * * *

In the present case, King and Bailey were in the airplane to further the felony of possession of marijuana with the intent to distribute. They were flying over the mountains while committing the felony. The time and the place of the death were closely connected with the felony. However, no causal connection exists between the felony of drug distribution and the killing by a plane crash. Thus, no basis exists to find that the accidental death was part or a result of the criminal enterprise. In the felony-murder cases cited above, death, to be considered an "accidental killing" within the statute, has resulted from a particular act which was an integral part of the felony or an act in direct furtherance of the felony -- shooting a gun, striking a match, distributing cocaine. In this case, there is no such act which caused the death. Thus, there has been no homicide, or unlawful killing by another, for which a cofelon can be held accountable. Bailey, who was flying the plane at the time of the crash, was not killed by King or by any act of King which was in furtherance of the felony. We see no "act of killing" which we can attribute to King or to the felony. The felony-murder rule does not exist to enable courts to impute "the act of killing" where an accidental death results from fortuitous circumstances and the only connection with the felony is temporal. The cause of Bailey's death was Bailey's piloting and adverse weather conditions. The accident stemmed not from the possession or distribution of drugs, but from fog, low cloud cover, pilot error, and inexperience. Had Bailey and King been transporting drugs in an automobile when they encountered heavy fog and Bailey, not seeing a curve, had driven off the mountain, the legal consequences would be the same. The commission of the felony merely accounted for their presence at the location of the accident, and nothing directly related to the commission of the felony caused the accident. Thus, flying into the mountain was not a direct consequence of the felony. Had the plane been flying low or recklessly to avoid detection, for example, the crash would be a consequence or action which was directly intended to further the felony and a different result might obtain. * * *

The Commonwealth argues that the jury could infer that King's conduct in the commission of the underlying felony was inherently dangerous to human life and that his action of putting the plane in a dangerous position and allowing an unlicensed pilot to fly caused the crash. Accepting without comment the Commonwealth's argument that the evidence established involuntary manslaughter based on King's antecedent negligence, the evidence still establishes no causal relationship between the felony of possession of marijuana and the death by plane crash. If King and Bailey had been transporting legal cargo that day, the crash would still have occurred. It is true, of course, that but for the felony, King and Bailey probably would not have been in the plane. However, criminal liability for felony-murder requires more than a finding that "but for" the felony the parties would not have been present at the time and location of the accidental death. The act or acts causing death must have been directly calculated to further the felony or necessitated by the commission of the felony. Such a causal connection is absent in this case.

Because we reverse the conviction on the grounds stated above, we do not address the issue of the trial judge's jury instructions.

Reversed and dismissed.

3. The Merger Doctrine

PEOPLE v. SMITH

Supreme Court of California

35 Cal.3d 798, 678 P.2d 886, 201 Cal.Rptr. 311 (1984)

Mosk, J.

Defendant appeals from a judgment convicting her of second degree murder, felony child abuse, and child beating. The court sentenced her to imprisonment for 15 years to life on the murder count and stayed service of sentence on the 2 remaining counts to avoid double punishment. The principal issue on appeal is whether felony child abuse may serve as the underlying felony to support a conviction of second degree murder on a felony-murder theory. We conclude that because the acts constituting such child abuse in the present case were an integral part of the homicide, the offense merged into the homicide; it was therefore error to give a felony-murder instruction, and the judgment must be reversed insofar as it convicts defendant of second degree murder.

Defendant and her two daughters, three-and-a-half-year-old Bethany (Beth) and two-year-old Amy, lived with David Foster. On the day Amy died, she refused to sit on the couch instead of the floor to eat a snack. Defendant became angry, took Amy into the children's bedroom, spanked her and slapped her in the face. Amy then went towards the corner of the bedroom which was often used for discipline; defendant hit her repeatedly, knocking her to the floor. Foster then apparently joined defendant to "assist" in Amy's discipline. Beth testified that both Foster and defendant were striking Amy, who at that point had been at least partially undressed by defendant. Defendant and Foster used both their hands and a paddle on the child, and were also biting her. In addition, Beth testified that Foster put a wastebasket on Amy's head and hit her on the head with his fist.[3] Eventually, defendant knocked the child backwards and she fell, hitting her head on the closet door.

Amy stiffened and went into respiratory arrest. Defendant and Foster took her to the hospital, where defendant admitted that she "beat her too hard." She also stated that Foster had not come home until after the incident. Amy died that evening. Her injuries were consistent with compressive force caused by numerous blows by hands, fists, and a paddle. The severe head injury that was the direct cause of death occurred within an hour before the child was brought to the hospital.

Defendant testified that although she had spanked Amy on the day in question, she then left Amy in the children's room. Foster, believing additional discipline was warranted, went into the room, closed the door and began shouting at Amy. Although defendant heard thumping noises, she was not overly concerned because Foster had behaved similarly in the past and Amy had not been injured. After a half hour, defendant became somewhat worried and entered the room. She observed that Amy had a puffy lip, and bite marks and bruises all over her lower body. Foster left the room at defendant's request after defendant said she would continue the discipline. Defendant then shouted at Amy for 15 to 20 minutes to allow Foster time to "cool off." To avoid the possibility that Foster might also attack Beth, she took Beth into another bedroom and closed the door. Foster returned to the children's room and began slapping Amy because she would not look at him. Defendant testified she was afraid that if she interfered she would become the object of Foster's attack. She stated that although she realized that Amy was being abused, she did not believe the child's life was in danger. Defendant eventually did intervene, at which point Amy stiffened and fainted. Defendant expressed a desire to take the child to hospital, but Foster objected because of his concern about the possible effect on his probation status. Defendant therefore agreed to take all responsibility for Amy's injuries and initially did so in her statement at the hospital. As noted above, however, defendant later denied any active involvement in the beating that led to Amy's death.

I

The court gave the jury the standard instructions defining murder, malice aforethought, second degree murder, second degree felony murder, and manslaughter. The second degree felony-murder instruction informed the jury

---

[3] Apparently Beth was in another room during the incident but claimed she could see "a little bit" despite her testimony that both the door to the room she was in and the door to Amy's room were closed.

that an unlawful killing, whether intentional, unintentional, or accidental, is second degree murder if it occurs during the commission of a felony inherently dangerous to human life, and that felony child abuse is such a crime. Defendant contends that on the facts of this case the crime of felony child abuse was an integral part of and included in fact within the homicide, and hence that it merged into the latter under the rule of *People v. Ireland.* We agree.

Our opinions have repeatedly emphasized that felony murder, although the law of this state, is a disfavored doctrine: "We have recognized that the rule is much censured 'because it anachronistically resurrects from a bygone age a 'barbaric' concept that has been discarded in the place of its origin" and because 'in almost all cases in which it is applied it is unnecessary' and 'it erodes the relation between criminal liability and moral culpability.' Accordingly, we have reiterated that this "highly artificial concept" "should not be extended beyond any rational function that it is designed to serve." "Applying this principle to various concrete factual circumstances, we have sought to insure that the [doctrine] . . . be given the narrowest possible application consistent with its ostensible purpose -- which is to deter those engaged in felonies from killing negligently or accidentally."

In accord with this policy, we restricted the scope of the felony-murder rule in *Ireland* by holding it inapplicable to felonies that are an integral part of and included in fact within the homicide. In that case the defendant and his wife were experiencing serious marital difficulties which eventually culminated in defendant's drawing a gun and killing his wife. The jury was instructed that it could find the defendant guilty of second degree felony murder if it determined that the homicide occurred during the commission of the underlying felony of assault with a deadly weapon. Like all felony-murder instructions, this instruction had the "effect of '[relieving] the jury of the necessity of finding one of the elements of the crime of murder' to wit, malice aforethought." We reasoned that "the utilization of the felony-murder rule in circumstances such as those before us extends the operation of that rule 'beyond any rational function that it is designed to serve.' To allow such use of the felony-murder rule would effectively preclude the jury from considering the issue of malice aforethought in all cases wherein homicide has been committed as a result of a felonious assault − a category which includes the great majority of all homicides. This kind of bootstrapping finds support neither in logic nor in law. We therefore hold that *a second degree felony-murder instruction may not properly be given when it is based upon a felony which is an integral part of the homicide and which the evidence produced by the prosecution shows to be an offense included in fact within the offense charged."* (Italics added.)

Very soon after *Ireland* we again had occasion to consider the question of merger in *People v. Wilson.* There the defendant forcibly entered his estranged wife's apartment carrying a shotgun. Once inside the apartment, he fatally shot a man in the living room and proceeded to break into the bathroom where he killed his wife. The jury was instructed on second degree felony murder based on the underlying felony of assault with a deadly weapon, and convicted the defendant of second degree murder of the man. We determined that the predicate felony was a "necessary ingredient of the homicide" and reversed under *Ireland*, which explicitly prohibited use of the felony-murder rule in such circumstances.

The defendant was also convicted of the first degree murder of his wife, and we reversed that conviction on similar grounds. The jury was instructed on first degree felony murder on the theory that the homicide was committed in the course of a burglary because the defendant had entered the premises with intent to commit a felony, i.e., assault with a deadly weapon. We held that the felony-murder rule cannot apply to burglary-murder cases in which "the entry would be nonfelonious but for the intent to commit the assault, and the assault is an integral part of the homicide and is included in fact in the offense charged . . . ." Because under *Ireland* the "elements of the assault were necessary elements of the homicide," the felony of burglary based on an intent to commit assault was included in fact in the homicide. We reasoned that "Where a person enters a building with an intent to assault his victim with a deadly weapon, he is not deterred by the felony-murder rule. That doctrine can serve its purpose only when applied to a felony independent of the homicide." We concluded that an instruction telling the jury that "the intent to assault makes the entry burglary and that the burglary raises the homicide resulting from the assault to first degree murder without proof of malice aforethought and premeditation" used the same bootstrap reasoning we condemned in *Ireland*.

In *People v. Sears,* we followed *Wilson* in a slightly different factual situation. There the defendant entered a cottage with the intent to assault his estranged wife. In the course of the assault, her daughter intervened and was killed by the defendant. The People argued that this situation was distinguishable on the ground that the felony of burglary with intent to assault the wife was "independent of the homicide" of the daughter and therefore the felony-murder rule could apply. We rejected the theory, holding that "It would be anomalous to place the person who intends to attack one person and in the course of the assault kills another inadvertently or in the heat of battle in a worse position than the person who from the outset intended to attack both persons and killed one or both. Where a defendant assaults one or more persons killing one, his criminal responsibility for the homicide should not depend upon which of the victims died but should be the greatest crime committed viewing each victim of the attack individually and without regard to which in fact died. This result is reached in application of existing principles of transferred intent, and it is unnecessary to resort to the felony-murder rule." *Sears* thus reiterated our view that the felony-murder rule should be applied narrowly rather than expansively.

In addition to the offenses of assault with a deadly weapon and burglary with intent to assault, the felony of discharging a firearm at an inhabited dwelling has also been held to merge into a resulting homicide; thus, application of the felony-murder rule in this situation is similarly prohibited. The *Wesley* court reasoned that because "The discharge of the firearms by the defendants was the means by which the homicide was committed and was *in fact* an 'integral part' and a 'necessary element' of the homicide," the felony was not independent of the homicide.

Cases in which the second degree felony-murder doctrine has withstood an *Ireland* attack include those in which the underlying felony was furnishing narcotics; driving under the influence of narcotics; poisoning food, drink or medicine; armed robbery; kidnaping; and finally, felony child abuse by malnutrition and dehydration; and felony child endangering by beating. With the exception of *Northrop* (felony child endangering by beating), however, none of these decisions involved an underlying felony that has as its principal purpose an assault on the person of the victim.

In *People v. Burton, supra,* we refined the *Ireland* rule by adding the caveat that the felony-murder doctrine may nevertheless apply if the underlying offense was committed with an "independent felonious purpose." Even if the felony was included within the facts of the homicide and was integral thereto, a further inquiry is required to determine if the homicide resulted "from conduct for an independent felonious purpose" as opposed to a "single course of conduct with a single purpose." In cases like *Ireland*, the "purpose of the conduct was the very assault which resulted in death"; on the other hand, "in the case of armed robbery, as well as the other felonies enumerated in section 189 of the Penal Code, there is an independent felonious purpose, namely in the case of robbery to acquire money or property belonging to another."

Our task is to apply the foregoing rules to the offense at issue here -- felony child abuse defined by section 273a, subdivision (1).[4] We recognize that

---

[4]Section 273a, subdivision (1), provided: "Any person who, under circumstances or conditions likely to produce great bodily harm or death, willfully causes or permits any child to suffer, or inflicts thereon unjustifiable physical pain or mental suffering, or having the care or custody of any child, willfully causes or permits the person or health of such child to be injured, or willfully causes or permits such child to be placed in such situation that its person or health is endangered, is punishable by imprisonment in the county jail not exceeding 1 year, or in the state

a violation of its terms can occur in a wide variety of situations: the definition broadly includes both active and passive conduct, i.e., child abuse by direct assault and child endangering by extreme neglect. Two threshold considerations, however, govern all types of conduct prohibited by this law: first, the conduct must be willful; second, it must be committed "under circumstances or conditions likely to produce great bodily harm or death." Absent either of these elements, there can be no violation of the statute.

The language of *Ireland, Wilson* and *Burton* bars the application of the felony-murder rule "where the purpose of the conduct was the very assault which resulted in death." In cases in which the violation of section 273a, subdivision (1), is a direct assault on a child that results in death (i.e., causing or permitting a child to suffer or inflicting thereon unjustifiable physical pain), it is plain that the purpose of the child abuse was the "very assault which resulted in death." It would be wholly illogical to allow this kind of assaultive child abuse to be bootstrapped into felony murder merely because the victim was a child rather than an adult, as in *Ireland.*

In the present case the homicide was the result of child abuse of the assaultive variety. Thus, the underlying felony was unquestionably an "integral part of" and "included in fact" in the homicide within the meaning of *Ireland.*[5] Furthermore, we can conceive of no independent purpose for the conduct, and the People suggest none; just as in *Ireland*, the purpose here was the very assault that resulted in death. To apply the felony-murder rule in this situation would extend it "beyond any rational function that it is designed to serve." We reiterate that the ostensible purpose of the felony-murder rule is not to deter the underlying felony, but instead to deter negligent or accidental killings that may occur in the course of committing that felony. When a person *willfully* inflicts unjustifiable physical pain on a child under these circumstances, it is difficult to see how the assailant would be further deterred from killing negligently or accidentally in the course of that felony by application of the felony-murder rule.

In *Ireland*, we reasoned that one who violates section 245 is not deterred by the felony-murder rule. The elements of section 245 and the offense here are

---

prison for not less than 1 year nor more than 10."

[5] This conclusion is further supported by the finding of the trial court that to punish defendant for felony child abuse (and child beating) in addition to murder would constitute double punishment for the same act in violation of section 654.

strikingly similar;[6] the principal difference is that the assault prohibited by section 273a is committed on a child. Accordingly, despite our deep abhorrence of the crime of child abuse, we see no escape from our duty to apply the merger doctrine we carefully enunciated in *Ireland* and its progeny. * * *

The People argue that the present case is controlled by *People v. Shockley*,[a] but that decision is distinguishable on its facts. In *Shockley*, the death followed from malnutrition and dehydration; by contrast, the cause of death here was unquestionably a severe beating. The *Shockley* court envisaged this very distinction when it stated that "Where the underlying felony is based on an independent felony *not related to the assault causing the murder*, a different result follows." Here the death of the child was directly caused by an assault that in turn was the basis of the charge of felony child abuse; on these facts, *Ireland* compels application of the merger rule.[7]

It was therefore error to give a felony-murder instruction in this case. The People cannot show that no juror relied on the erroneous instruction as the sole basis for finding defendant guilty of murder. In these circumstances it is settled that the error must be deemed prejudicial. Because we reverse on this ground, we need not reach defendant's alternate claim that felony child abuse is not a felony inherently dangerous to human life within the meaning of the second degree felony-murder rule, or other asserted errors in instructions bearing on the murder count. * * *

The judgment is reversed insofar as it convicts defendant of second degree murder; in all other respects the judgment is affirmed.

---

[6] Section 245, subdivision (a)(1), prohibits assault with a deadly weapon or "by any means of force likely to produce great bodily injury."

[a] In *Shockley*, the court held that "the act of leaving [a] child in a position that endangers its person or health is clearly collateral and independent of any design to cause death" and is therefore not subject to the merger doctrine. *People v. Shockley*, 79 Cal. App. 3d 669, 677 (1978).

[7] Because of this factual distinction we need not address the question whether the merger doctrine applies when the defendant is guilty of felony child abuse of the nonassaultive variety, e.g., by extreme neglect -- as in *Shockley* -- or by failure to intervene when a child in his care or custody is placed in a life-endangering situation.

4. **Third Party Killings: The Agency Rule**

STATE v. CANOLA

Supreme Court of New Jersey
73 N.J. 206, 374 A.2d 20 (1977)

CONFORD, J.

Defendant, along with three confederates, was in the process of robbing a store when a victim of the robbery, attempting to resist the perpetration of the crime, fatally shot one of the cofelons. The sole issue for our resolution is whether, under N.J.S.A. 2A:113-1, defendant may be held liable for felony murder. A divided part of the Appellate Division determined the question in the affirmative. Because of the dissent, the appeal is here as of right.

The facts of this case * * * may be summarized as follows. The owner of a jewelry store and his employee, in an attempt to resist an armed robbery, engaged in a physical skirmish with one of the four robbers. A second conspirator, called upon for assistance, began shooting, and the store owner returned the gunfire. Both the owner and the felon, one Lloredo, were fatally shot in the exchange, the latter by the firearm of the owner.

Defendant and two others were indicted on two counts of murder, one count of robbery and one count of having been armed during the robbery. The murder counts were based on the deaths, respectively, of the robbery victim and the co-felon. After trial on the murder counts defendant was found guilty on both and was sentenced to concurrent terms of life imprisonment. The Appellate Division unanimously affirmed the conviction for the murder of the robbery victim, and this court denied a petition for certification addressed thereto. However, when the Appellate Division majority upheld the trial court's denial of a motion to dismiss the count addressed to the homicide of the co-felon, Judge Handler dissented.

Conventional formulations of the felony murder rule would not seem to encompass liability in this case. * * * A recent study of the early formulations of the felony murder rule by such authorities as Lord Coke, Foster and Blackstone and of later ones by Judge Stephen and Justice Holmes concluded that they were concerned solely with situations where the felon or a confederate did the actual killing. Contrary to the division of view in the modern American cases on the point, it has been observed that the English courts never applied the felony murder rule to hold a felon guilty of the death of his co-felon at the hands of the intended victim.

The precise issue in the present case is whether a broader concept than the foregoing – specifically, liability of a felon for the death of a co-felon effected by one resisting the felony – is required by the language of our statute applicable to the general area of felony murder. N.J.S.A. 2A:113-1. This reads:

> If any person, in committing or attempting to commit arson, burglary, kidnapping, rape, robbery, sodomy or any unlawful act against the peace of this State, of which the probable consequences may be bloodshed, kills another, *or if the death of anyone ensues from the committing or attempting to commit any such crime or act... then such person so killing is guilty of murder.* (emphasis added).

* * * The Appellate Division majority was of the view that the above-emphasized portion of the statute, referred to by it as the "ensues clause," compelled the result it arrived at. It said:

> * * * In our view the statute indicates an intention on the part of the Legislature to extend criminal responsibility beyond that imposed upon a felon at common law and to hold liable all participants in an armed robbery for deaths which occur during the commission of the crime.

Judge (now Justice) Handler, in dissenting, cited the decisions representing the majority view in those other jurisdictions which had considered the general question, and said they hold that "a felon cannot be found guilty for the death of an accomplice occurring during the commission of the felony." * * * * For reasons to be more fully explicated, we are in accord with the conclusion arrived at in the dissent. * * *

It is clearly the majority view throughout the country that, at least in theory, the doctrine of felony murder does not extend to a killing, although growing out of the commission of the felony, if directly attributable to the act of one other than the defendant or those associated with him in the unlawful enterprise. This rule is sometimes rationalized on the "agency" theory of felony murder.[2]

---

[2] The classic statement of the theory is found in an early case applying it in a context pertinent to the case at bar, *Commonwealth v. Campbell,* as follows:

> No person can be held guilty of homicide unless the act is either actually or constructively his, and it cannot be his act in either sense unless committed by his own hand or by some one acting in concert

A contrary view, which would attach liability under the felony murder rule for *any* death proximately resulting from the unlawful activity – even the death of a co-felon – notwithstanding the killing was by one resisting the crime, does not seem to have the present allegiance of any court.

At one time the proximate cause theory was espoused by the Pennsylvania Supreme Court. The reasoning of the *Almeida* decision, involving the killing of a policeman shot by other police attempting to apprehend robbers, was distinctly circumvented when the question later arose whether it should be applied to an effort to inculpate a defendant for the killing of his co-felon at the hands of the victim of the crime. *Commonwealth v. Redline*. The court there held against liability. Examining the common-law authorities relied upon by the *Almeida* majority, the *Redline* court concluded:

> As already indicated, *Almeida* was, itself, an extension of the
> felony-murder doctrine by judicial decision and is not to be
> extended in its application beyond facts such as those to which
> it was applied.

The court then held that "in order to convict for felony murder, *the killing must have been done by the defendant or by an accomplice or confederate or by one acting in furtherance of the felonious undertaking*." The court refused, however, actually to overrule the *Almeida* decision, thereby creating a distinction (although the opinion indicates it was a half-hearted one) between the situation in which the victim was an innocent party and the killing therefore merely "excusable" and that in which the deceased was a felon and the killing thus "justifiable." Twelve years later the Pennsylvania court did overrule *Almeida* in a case involving Almeida's companion, Smith. The court noted, *inter alia*, the harsh criticism leveled against the common-law felony rule, its doubtful deterrent effect, the failure of the cases cited in *Almeida* to support the conclusions reached therein, the inappropriateness of tort proximate-cause principles to homicide prosecution, and the "will-of-the-wisp" distinction drawn by the *Almeida* court between justifiable and excusable homicides. * * *

The California cases have taken a wholly unique course in this area of the criminal law. The Court of Appeal, influenced by the early Pennsylvania cases, first adopted the proximate cause theory. In *People v. Harrison,* the court held the defendants guilty of first degree murder when the owner of a store being robbed exchanged gunfire with the robbers and killed an employee. But in *People v. Washington,* the Supreme Court refused to hold a surviving felon

---

with him or in furtherance of a common object or purpose.

liable for the death of a co-felon, instead reverting to the common law view of *Campbell, supra,* and overruling *People v. Harrison.* It said:

> Accordingly, for a defendant to be guilty of murder under the felony-murder rule the act of killing must be committed by the defendant or by his accomplice acting in furtherance of their common design.

In *dicta*, however, the court stated that it was not necessary to invoke the felony murder rule in order to imply the malice requisite for murder and that such malice is evident when the defendant does an act (*apart* from the felony) "that involves a high degree of probability that it will result in death." Accordingly, in *People v. Gilbert,* while adhering to the notion that for the strict liability of the felony murder rule to apply the felon or his accomplice must do the killing, the court recognized the implication of *Washington* that "entirely apart from the felony murder rule, malice may be established when a defendant initiates a gun battle, and that under such circumstances he may be convicted of murder for a killing committed by another." * * *

To be distinguished from the situation before us here, and from the generality of the cases discussed above, are the so-called "shield" cases. The first of these were the companion cases of *Taylor v. State,* and *Keaton v. State.* In attempting to escape after robbing a train, defendants thrust the brakeman in front of them as a shield, as a result of which he was fatally shot by law officers. The court had no difficulty in finding defendants guilty of murder. The court in *Taylor* noted the correctness of the *Campbell* case doctrine that a person could not be held liable for homicide unless the act is either actually or constructively committed by him, but indicated it was inapplicable to a case where defendants forced deceased to occupy a place of danger in order that they might carry out the crime. In *Keaton*, the court said defendant would be responsible for the "reasonable, natural and probable result of his act" of placing deceased in danger of his life. The conduct of the defendants in cases such as these is said to reflect "express malice," justifying a murder conviction. * * *

Reverting to our immediate task here, it is to determine whether our own statute necessarily mandates the proximate cause concept of felony murder, as thought by the Appellate Division majority. It is fair to assume, initially, that the Legislature had no special reason in 1796 to ordain a rule of felony murder beyond that generally accepted in Anglo-American jurisprudence at the end of the eighteenth century. As above noted, there was then no precedent, either English or American, for holding the felon for killings at the hands of others than the felon himself or those confederated with him -- that is to say, the so called agency rule held sway. But as seen above, the view of the Appellate Division was that the "ensues clause" of N.J.S.A. 2A:113-1 must be deemed to have expanded the culpability of the felon to killings by others not confederated with him, if proximately related to the felonious enterprise, else the clause would be meaningless surplusage in the act. However, other plausible motivations for the ensues clause can be postulated consistent with a legislative intent to adhere to the traditional limitations of the felony murder doctrine. * * *

[I]t is inescapable that the ensues clause is connected with the conclusion of the section, "then such person so killing is guilty of murder." This fortifies the view that even as to a death which "ensues" from the commission or attempt to commit the felony, liability for murder is intended to be restricted to the person "so killing," *i.e.*, the felon or his agents, not third persons, conformably with the limitation of the Pennsylvania *Redline* doctrine. * * *

With such background, and assuming the statute is facially susceptible of the interpretation here advocated by the State, it is appropriate to consider the public policy implications of the proposed doctrine as an extension of prior assumptions in this State as to the proper limitations of the felony murder rule.

Most modern progressive thought in criminal jurisprudence favors restriction rather than expansion of the felony murder rule. A leading text states: "The felony murder rule is somewhat in disfavor at the present time. The courts apply it when the law requires, but they do so grudgingly and tend to restrict its application where the circumstances permit." It has frequently been observed that although the rule was logical at its inception, when all felonies were punishable by death, its survival to modern times when other felonies are not though to be as blameworthy as premeditated killings is discordant with rational and enlightened views of criminal culpability and liability. * * *

The final report of the New Jersey Criminal Law Revision Commission was, however, unwilling totally to reject the felony murder rule, concluding instead:

> It is true that we have no way of knowing how many of the homicides resulting in felony murder convictions were committed purposefully, knowingly or recklessly and how many were negligent or accidental. But it is our belief that this rule of law does lead some to refuse to assume a homicidal risk in committing other crimes.

The proposed New Jersey Penal Code does nevertheless offer limited defenses not hitherto available under the felony murder rule, and it confines the rule to deaths caused by the felon or his co-felons "in the course of and in furtherance of [the felony]." This is standard "agency theory" formulation and would seem intended to exclude liability for acts of persons other than felons or co-felons though generally arising out of the criminal episode.

In view of all of the foregoing, it appears to us regressive to extend the application of the felony murder rule beyond its classic common-law limitation to acts by the felon and his accomplices, to lethal acts of third persons not in furtherance of the felonious scheme. The language of the statute does not compel it, and, as indicated above, is entirely compatible with the traditional limitations of the rule. Tort concepts of foreseeability and proximate cause have shallow relevance to culpability for murder in the first degree. Gradations of criminal liability should accord with degree of moral culpability for the actor's conduct. * * *

It is our judgment that if the course of the law as understood and applied in this State for almost 200 years is to be altered so drastically, it should be by express legislative enactment.

The judgment of the Appellate Division is modified so as to strike the conviction and sentencing of defendant for murder of the co-felon Lloredo.

SULLIVAN, J. (concurring in result only).

The practical result of the majority holding is that even though some innocent person or a police officer be killed during the commission of an armed robbery, the felon would bear no criminal responsibility of any kind for that killing as long as it was not at the hand of the felon or a confederate. The legislative intent, as I see it, is otherwise.

The thrust of our felony murder statute, N.J.S.A. 2A:113-1, is to hold the criminal liable for any killing which ensues during the commission of a felony, even though the felon, or a confederate, did not commit the actual killing. The only exception I would recognize would be the death of a co-felon, which could be classified as a justifiable homicide and not within the purview of the statute.

The Legislature should act promptly to clarify the situation resulting from the majority opinion. If it does not extend the felony murder statute to encompass a killing during the commission of a felony not at the hand of the felon or confederate, it should, at least, provide that the felon be chargeable with manslaughter for such killing (in addition to liability for the felony).

I therefore concur in the result but only for the reason stated above.

[C.J. HUGHES' dissent has been omitted.]

Note

Following the decision in *State v. Canola*, the New Jersey legislature seemed to take Justice Sullivan's advice, amending its Penal Code to provide that "criminal homicide constitutes murder when: * * * the actor * * * is engaged in the commission of, or an attempt to commit, or flight after committing or attempting to commit [a designated felony], and * * * any person causes the death of a person other than one of the participants." N.J. Stat. Ann. § 2C:11-3(a)(1)(3) (2004).

In California, a new theory of second-degree murder has emerged: "provocative act murder." Under this theory, when a defendant or his accomplice commits a "provocative act" and his victim or a police officer kills in reasonable response to that act, the defendant can be found guilty of murder.

Does this doctrine violate the agency rule? The California courts have said no: provocative act murder is based on an expansion of the so-called "gun battle rule," under which an actor who initiates a gun battle with law enforcement can be held guilty of second-degree murder on a depraved heart murder theory. Provocative act murder, therefore, is not a species of felony murder.

5.   Should the Common Law Felony Murder Rule Be Abolished?

In March 2004, a mother in Northwest Washington, D. C. was charged with first-degree felony murder for giving her 10-month old daughter a fatal dose of methadone. Apparently, the mother, who took methadone during her pregnancy, began using a medicine dropper to add methadone to her baby's formula two or three times a week to quiet the baby, who was born addicted to the drug, after seeing the baby's godmother do so shortly after the baby came home from the hospital. It is not clear that the mother was even aware that her actions were putting her child at risk of death. Is application of the felony murder rule appropriate in a situation like this?

In the next case, the Supreme Court of Michigan takes a harsh look at the common law felony murder rule and decides that it should be abolished. The court, however, retains Michigan's first degree felony murder rule. As you read *People v. Aaron,* think about the distinction between the common law felony murder rule and the first degree felony murder rule, and whether you agree with the Michigan Supreme Court's decision.

PEOPLE v. AARON

Supreme Court of Michigan
409 Mich. 672, 299 N.W.2d 304 (1980)

FITZGERALD, J.

The existence and scope of the felony-murder doctrine have perplexed generations of law students, commentators and jurists in the United States and England, and have split our own Court of Appeals. In these cases, we must decide whether Michigan has a felony-murder rule which allows the element of malice required for murder to be satisfied by the intent to commit the underlying felony or whether malice must be otherwise found by the trier of fact. We must also determine what is the *mens rea* required to support a conviction under Michigan's first-degree murder statute. * * *

Facts

Defendant Aaron was convicted of first-degree felony murder as a result of a homicide committed during the perpetration of an armed robbery. The jury was instructed that they could convict defendant of first-degree murder if they found that defendant killed the victim during the commission or attempted commission of an armed robbery. The trial court refused defendant's request to instruct on lesser included offenses. The Court of Appeals affirmed and we remanded the case to the trial court for entry of a judgment of conviction of the lesser included offense of second-degree murder and for resentencing. Defendant subsequently filed an application for reconsideration with this Court. * * *

[A]n examination of the felony-murder rule indicates that the doctrine is of doubtful origin. Derived from the misinterpretation of case law, it went unchallenged because of circumstances which no longer exist. The doctrine was continuously modified and restricted in England, the country of its birth, until its ultimate rejection by Parliament in 1957.

III. Limitation [on] the Felony-Murder Doctrine in the United States

While only a few states have followed the lead of Great Britain in abolishing felony murder, various legislative and judicial limitations on the doctrine have effectively narrowed the scope of the rule in the United States. Perkins states that the rule is "somewhat in disfavor at the present time" and that "courts apply it where the law requires, but they do so grudgingly and tend to restrict its application where circumstances permit."

The draftsmen of the Model Penal Code have summarized the limitations imposed by American courts as follows:

(1) "The felonious act must be dangerous to life."

(2) and (3) "The homicide must be a natural and probable consequence of the felonious act." "Death must be 'proximately' caused." Courts have also required that the killing be the result of an act done in the furtherance of the felonious purpose and not merely coincidental to the perpetration of a felony. These cases often make distinctions based on the identity of the victim (*i.e.,* whether the decedent was the victim of the felony or whether he was someone else, *e.g.,* a policeman or one of the felons) and the identity of the person causing the death.

(4) "The felony must be *malum in se.*"

(5) "The act must be a common-law felony."

(6) "The period during which the felony is in the process of commission must be narrowly construed."

(7) "The underlying felony must be 'independent' of the homicide." *
* *

Kentucky and Hawaii have specifically abolished the felony-murder doctrine. The commentary to Hawaii's murder statute is instructive as to that state's reasoning in abolishing the doctrine:

> Even in its limited formulation the felony-murder rule is still objectionable. It is not sound principle to convert an accidental, negligent, or reckless homicide into a murder simply because, without more, the killing was in furtherance of a criminal objective of some defined class. Engaging in certain penally-prohibited behavior may, of course, evidence a recklessness sufficient to establish manslaughter, or a practical certainty or intent, with respect to causing death, sufficient to establish murder, but such a finding is an independent determination which must rest on the facts of each case. * * *

The numerous modifications and restrictions placed upon the common-law felony-murder doctrine by courts and legislatures reflect dissatisfaction with the harshness and injustice of the rule. Even though the felony-murder doctrine survives in this country, it bears increasingly less resemblance to the traditional felony-murder concept. To the extent that these modifications reduce the scope and significance of the common-law doctrine, they also call into question the continued existence of the doctrine itself.

IV. The Requirement of Individual Culpability for Criminal Responsibility

"If one had to choose the most basic principle of the criminal law in general * * * it would be that criminal liability for causing a particular result is not justified in the absence of some culpable mental state in respect to that result * * *." The most fundamental characteristic of the felony-murder rule violates this basic principle in that it punishes all homicides, committed in the perpetration or attempted perpetration of proscribed felonies whether intentional, unintentional or accidental, without the necessity of proving the relation between the homicide and the perpetrator's state of mind. This is most evident when a killing is done by one of a group of co-felons. The felony-murder rule completely ignores the concept of determination of guilt on the basis of individual misconduct. The felony-murder rule thus "erodes the relation between criminal liability and moral culpability."

The felony-murder rule's most egregious violation of basic rules of culpability occurs where felony murder is categorized as first-degree murder. All other murders carrying equal punishment require a showing of premeditation, deliberation and willfulness while felony murder only requires a showing of intent to do the underlying felony. Although the purpose of our degree statutes is to punish more severely the more culpable forms of murder, an accidental killing occurring during the perpetration of a felony would be punished more severely than a second-degree murder requiring intent to kill, intent to cause great bodily harm, or wantonness and willfulness. Furthermore, a defendant charged with felony murder is permitted to raise defenses only to the mental element of the felony, thus precluding certain defenses available to a defendant charged with premeditated murder who may raise defenses to the mental element of murder *(e.g.,* self-defense, accident). Certainly, felony murder is no more reprehensible than premeditated murder.

LaFave & Scott explain the felony-murder doctrine's failure to account for a defendant's moral culpability as follows:

> The rationale of the doctrine is that one who commits a felony is a bad person with a bad state of mind, and he has caused a bad result, so that we should not worry too much about the fact that the fatal result he accomplished was quite different and a good deal worse than the bad result he intended. Yet it is a general principle of criminal law that one is not ordinarily criminally liable for bad results which differ greatly from intended results.

Termed as a "somewhat primitive rationale" it is deserving of the observation made by one commentator that "the felony-murder doctrine gives rise to what can only be described as an emotional reaction, not one based on logical and abstract principles."

Another writer states:

It is an excuse based on the rough moral notion that a man who intentionally commits a felony must have a wicked heart, and therefore 'ought to be punished' for the harm which he has done accidentally. It is to guard against this kind of reasoning that our modern rules of evidence exclude in most cases any communication to the jury of a prisoner's previous misdeeds. * * *

The United States Supreme Court has reaffirmed on several occasions the importance of the relationship between culpability and criminal liability. * * *

The contention that an injury can amount to a crime only when inflicted by intention is no provincial or transient notion. It is as universal and persistent in mature systems of law as belief in freedom of the human will and a consequent ability and duty of the normal individual to choose between good and evil. A relation between some mental element and punishment for a harmful act is almost as instinctive as the child's familiar exculpatory 'But I didn't mean to,' and has afforded the rational basis for a tardy and unfinished substitution of deterrence and reformation in place of retaliation and vengeance as the motivation for public prosecution.

Morissette v. United States, 342 U.S. 246, 250-251; 72 S.Ct. 240; 96 L.Ed. 288 (1952).

Whether a death results in the course of a felony (thus giving rise to felony-murder liability) turns on fortuitous events that do not distinguish the intention or moral culpability of the defendants.

Lockett v. Ohio, 438 U.S. 586, 620, 98 S.Ct. 2954; 57 L.Ed.2d 973 (1978) (Mr. Justice Marshall's concurring opinion).

* * *

V. The Felony-Murder Doctrine in Michigan

A. Murder and Malice Defined

In order to understand the operation of any state's felony-murder doctrine, initially it is essential to understand how that state defines murder and malice.

In Michigan, murder is not statutorily defined. This Court early defined the term as follows:

> Murder is where a person of sound memory and discretion unlawfully kills any reasonable creature in being, in the peace of the state, with malice prepense or aforethought, either express or implied.

Thus, malice aforethought is the "grand criterion" which elevates a homicide, which may be innocent or criminal, to murder. However, "[the] nature of malice aforethought is the source of much of the confusion that attends the law of homicide." Overbroad and ill-considered instructions on malice have plagued appellate courts for decades.

We agree with the following analysis of murder and malice aforethought presented by LaFave & Scott:

> Though murder is frequently defined as the unlawful killing of another 'living human being' with 'malice aforethought', in modern times the latter phrase does not even approximate its literal meaning. Hence it is preferable not to rely upon that misleading expression for an understanding of murder but rather to consider the various types of murder (typed according to the mental element) which the common law came to recognize and which exist today in most jurisdictions:
>
> (1) intent-to-kill murder;
>
> (2) intent-to-do-serious-bodily-injury murder;
>
> (3) depraved-heart murder [wanton and willful disregard that the natural tendency of the defendant's behavior is to cause death or great bodily harm]; and
>
> (4) felony murder.

Under the common law, which we refer to in defining murder in this state, each of the four types of murder noted above has its own mental element which independently satisfies the requirement of malice aforethought. It is, therefore, not necessary for the law to imply or for the jury to infer the intention to kill once the finder of fact determines the existence of any of the other three mental states because each one, by itself, constitutes the element of malice aforethought.

Our focus in this opinion is upon the last category of murder, *i.e.*, felony murder. We do not believe the felony-murder doctrine, as some courts and commentators would suggest, abolishes the requirement of malice, nor do we believe that it equates the *mens rea* of the felony with the *mens rea* required for a non-felony murder. We construe the felony-murder doctrine as providing a separate definition of malice, thereby establishing a fourth category of murder. The effect of the doctrine is to recognize the intent to commit the underlying felony, in itself, as a sufficient *mens rea* for murder. This analysis of the felony-murder doctrine is consistent with the historical development of the doctrine.

The question we address today is whether Michigan recognizes the felony-murder doctrine and, accordingly, the category of malice arising from the underlying felony. The relevant inquiry is first whether Michigan has a statutory felony-murder doctrine. If it does not, it must then be determined whether Michigan has or should have a common-law felony-murder doctrine.

B. Statutory Felony Murder

Michigan does not have a statutory felony-murder doctrine which designates as murder any *death* occurring in the course of a felony without regard to whether it was the result of accident, negligence, recklessness or willfulness. Rather, Michigan has a statute which makes a *murder* occurring in the course of one of the enumerated felonies a first-degree murder:

> Murder which is perpetrated by means of poison, lying in wait, or other wilful, deliberate, and premeditated killing, or which is committed in the perpetration, or attempt to perpetrate arson, criminal sexual conduct in the first or third degree, robbery, breaking and entering of a dwelling, larceny of any kind, extortion, or kidnapping, is murder of the first degree, and shall be punished by imprisonment for life. * * *

Michigan case law also makes it clear that the purpose of our first-degree murder statute is to graduate punishment and that the statute only serves to raise an already established *murder* to the first-degree level, not to transform a death, without more, into a murder. * * *

Thus, we conclude that Michigan has not codified the common-law felony-murder rule. The use of the term "murder" in the first-degree statute requires that a murder must first be established before the statute is applied to elevate the degree.

C. Common-Law Felony Murder in Michigan

The prosecution argues that even if Michigan does not have a statutory codification of the felony-murder rule, the common-law definition of murder included a homicide in the course of a felony. Thus, the argument continues, once a homicide in the course of a felony is proven, under the common-law felony-murder rule a murder has been established and the first-degree murder statute then becomes applicable. This Court has ruled that the term murder as used in the first-degree murder statute includes all types of murder at common law. Hence, we must determine whether Michigan in fact has a common-law felony-murder rule.

Our research has uncovered no Michigan cases, nor do the parties refer us to any, which have expressly considered whether Michigan has or should continue to have a common-law felony-murder doctrine. * * *

However, our finding that Michigan has never specifically adopted the doctrine which defines malice to include the intent to commit the underlying felony is not the end of our inquiry. In Michigan, the general rule is that the common law prevails except as abrogated by the Constitution, the Legislature or this Court.

This Court has not been faced previously with a decision as to whether it should abolish the felony-murder doctrine. Thus, the common-law doctrine remains the law in Michigan. Moreover, the assumption by appellate decisions that the doctrine exists, combined with the fact that Michigan trial courts have applied the doctrine in numerous cases resulting in convictions of first-degree felony murder, requires us to address the common-law felony-murder issue. The cases before us today squarely present us with the opportunity to review the doctrine and to consider its continued existence in Michigan. Although there are no Michigan cases which specifically abrogate the felony-murder rule, there exists a number of decisions of this Court which have significantly restricted the doctrine in Michigan and which lead us to conclude that the rule should be abolished. * * *

Our review of Michigan case law persuades us that we should abolish the rule which defines malice as the intent to commit the underlying felony. Abrogation of the felony-murder rule is not a drastic move in light of the significant restrictions this Court has already imposed. Further, it is a logical extension of our decisions as discussed above.

We believe that it is no longer acceptable to equate the intent to commit a felony with the intent to kill, intent to do great bodily harm, or wanton and willful disregard of the likelihood that the natural tendency of a person's behavior is to cause death or great bodily harm. In *People v Hansen*, this Court said that "[malice] requires an intent to cause the very harm that results or some harm of the same general nature, or an act done in wanton or wilful disregard of the plain and strong likelihood that such harm will result." In a charge of felony murder, it is the murder which is the harm which is being punished. A defendant who only intends to commit the felony does not intend to commit the harm that results and may or may not be guilty of perpetrating an act done in wanton or willful disregard of the plain and strong likelihood that such harm will result. Although the circumstances surrounding the commission of the felony may evidence a greater intent beyond the intent to commit the felony, or a wanton and willful act in disregard of the possible consequence of death or serious injury, the intent to commit the felony, of itself, does not connote a "man-endangering-state-of-mind." Hence, we do not believe that it constitutes a sufficient *mens rea* to establish the crime of murder.

Accordingly, we hold today that malice is the intention to kill, the intention to do great bodily harm, or the wanton and willful disregard of the likelihood that the natural tendency of defendant's behavior is to cause death or great bodily harm. We further hold that malice is an essential element of any murder, as that term is judicially defined, whether the murder occurs in the course of a felony or otherwise. The facts and circumstances involved in the perpetration of a felony may evidence an intent to kill, an intent to cause great bodily harm, or a wanton and willful disregard of the likelihood that the natural tendency of defendant's behavior is to cause death or great bodily harm; however, the conclusion must be left to the jury to infer from all the evidence.
* * *

VI. Practical Effect of Abrogation of the Common-Law Felony-Murder Doctrine

From a practical standpoint, the abolition of the category of malice arising from the intent to commit the underlying felony should have little effect on the result of the majority of cases. In many cases where felony murder has been applied, the use of the doctrine was unnecessary because the other types of malice could have been inferred from the evidence.

Abrogation of this rule does not make irrelevant the fact that a death occurred in the course of a felony. A jury can properly *infer* malice from evidence that a defendant intentionally set in motion a force likely to cause death or great bodily harm. Thus, whenever a killing occurs in the perpetration or attempted perpetration of an inherently dangerous felony, in order to establish malice the jury may consider the "nature of the underlying felony and the circumstances surrounding its commission." If the jury concludes that malice existed, they can find murder and, if they determine that the murder occurred in the perpetration or attempted perpetration of one of the enumerated felonies, by statute the murder would become first-degree murder.

The difference is that the jury may not find malice from the intent to commit the underlying felony alone. The defendant will be permitted to assert any of the applicable defenses relating to *mens rea* which he would be allowed to assert if charged with premeditated murder. The latter result is reasonable in light of the fact that felony murder is certainly no more heinous than premeditated murder. The prosecution will still be able to prove first-degree murder without proof of premeditation when a homicide is committed with malice, as we have defined it, and the perpetration or attempted perpetration of an enumerated felony is established. Hence, our first-degree murder statute continues to elevate to first-degree murder a *murder* which is committed in the perpetration or attempted perpetration of one of the enumerated felonies.

As previously noted, in many circumstances the commission of a felony, particularly one involving violence or the use of force, will indicate an intention to kill, an intention to cause great bodily harm, or wanton or willful disregard of the likelihood that the natural tendency of defendant's behavior is to cause death or great bodily harm. Thus, the felony-murder rule is not necessary to establish *mens rea* in these cases.

In the past, the felony-murder rule has been employed where unforeseen or accidental deaths occur and where the state seeks to prove vicarious liability of co-felons. In situations involving the vicarious liability of co-felons, the individual liability of each felon must be shown. It is fundamentally unfair and in violation of basic principles of individual criminal culpability to hold one felon liable for the unforeseen and unagreed-to results of another felon. In cases where the felons are acting intentionally or recklessly in pursuit of a common plan, the felony-murder rule is unnecessary because liability may be established on agency principles.

Finally, in cases where the death was purely accidental, application of the felony-murder doctrine is unjust and should be precluded. The underlying felony, of course, will still be subject to punishment. * * *

Thus, in the three situations in which the felony-murder doctrine typically has applied, the rule is either unnecessary or contrary to fundamental principles of our criminal law.

It is submitted that this is one of the most persuasive arguments in favor of abolition of the doctrine: it is not necessary to the establishment of criminal liability in the majority of cases in which it has been applied, and its application to those cases in which death occurred wholly by accident -- *i.e.*, without intent or likelihood of harm -- is contrary to the modern trend toward establishment of culpability as the basis of criminal liability.

[It] is unsatisfactory and inelegant to have a rule of law which, whenever it is applied, is either unnecessary (as in the case where dangerous violence is knowingly used) or unjust (as in the case where the risk of death is not foreseen). * * *

VII. Conclusion

Whatever reasons can be gleaned from the dubious origin of the felony-murder rule to explain its existence, those reasons no longer exist today. Indeed, most states, including our own, have recognized the harshness and inequity of the rule as is evidenced by the numerous restrictions placed on it. The felony-murder doctrine is unnecessary and in many cases unjust in that it violates the basic premise of individual moral culpability upon which our criminal law is based.

We conclude that Michigan has no statutory felony-murder rule which allows the mental element of murder to be satisfied by proof of the intention to commit the underlying felony. Today we exercise our role in the development of the common law by abrogating the common-law felony-murder rule. We hold that in order to convict a defendant of murder, as that term is defined by Michigan case law, it must be shown that he acted with intent to kill or to inflict great bodily harm or with a wanton and willful disregard of the likelihood that the natural tendency of his behavior is to cause death or great bodily harm. We further hold that the issue of malice must always be submitted to the jury.

The first-degree murder statute will continue to operate in that all *murder* committed in the perpetration or attempted perpetration of the enumerated felonies will be elevated to first-degree murder.

This decision shall apply to all trials in progress and those occurring after the date of this opinion.

In *Aaron*, the judgment of conviction of second-degree murder is reversed and this case is remanded to the trial court for a new trial. * * *

H. THE MISDEMEANOR MANSLAUGHTER DOCTRINE

Under the misdemeanor-manslaughter doctrine, a homicide that occurs during the commission of a misdemeanor (an unlawful act not amounting to a felony) constitutes involuntary manslaughter. Courts have placed various limitations on the application of the misdemeanor manslaughter doctrine, just as they have on felony murder. For instance, in some jurisdictions the doctrine only applies to deaths that occur during the commission of a misdemeanor that is *malum in se* (evil in and of itself). In these jurisdictions, a *malum prohibitum* offense (an act or omission that does not carry any particular moral opprobrium) cannot serve as the trigger for a misdemeanor manslaughter conviction. Some states do not apply the merger rule, but do apply an "inherently dangerous" restriction, holding that the underlying misdemeanor must be inherently dangerous to life or safety. Some states will not apply the doctrine if the underlying crime is a strict liability crime (one which requires no mens rea at all). Other states place no limitations on the type of act that can serve as the underlying misdemeanor or unlawful act. Some states require that the misdemeanor be the actual and proximate cause of the death. Other states do not require any causal relationship between the commission of the misdemeanor and the death. In *Todd v. State*, the Court of Appeal of Florida discusses the requirements for an involuntary manslaughter conviction under the misdemeanor manslaughter doctrine as it is applied in Florida.

TODD v. STATE
Court of Appeal of Florida, Fifth District
594 So. 2d 802, 17 Fla. L. Weekly D 369 (Ct. App. 1992)

GRIFFIN, J.

On March 18, 1990, appellant entered the Lighthouse Church and stole $110 from the collection plate. The theft was witnessed by several members of the congregation, one of whom, Richard Voegltin, took off in his car in pursuit of appellant. During the pursuit, Mr. Voegltin, who had a preexisting heart condition, began to experience cardiac dysrhythmia. He lost control of his vehicle, collided with a tree at low speed and died of cardiac arrest.

The state charged appellant with manslaughter, alleging that he caused the death of Mr. Voegltin by committing the misdemeanor offense of petty theft which caused Voegltin to pursue him in order to recover the stolen property. Appellant filed a motion to dismiss, asserting that, because it cannot be said with any reasonable degree of medical certainty that Mr. Voegltin died as a result of chasing appellant, because Mr. Voegltin was at high risk of having a heart attack due to his preexisting medical condition, and because the appellant had no knowledge of this preexisting medical condition, the manslaughter charge should be dismissed. The trial court denied the motion to dismiss. We reverse.

The issue, as presented to us, is whether Florida recognizes the misdemeanor manslaughter rule. Reduced to basics, the misdemeanor manslaughter rule is that an unintended homicide which occurs during the commission of an unlawful act not amounting to a felony constitutes the crime of involuntary manslaughter. It is sometimes referred to more broadly as "unlawful act manslaughter." * * *

The misdemeanor manslaughter rule has been the subject of surprisingly little analysis, although in their Handbook on Criminal Law, LaFave and Scott have included a detailed discussion and critique of this theory of criminal responsibility. They suggest that "the trend today, barely underway, is to abolish altogether this type of involuntary manslaughter . . . ." The authors posit that to punish as homicide the result of an unlawful act that is unintended and produced without any consciousness of the risk of producing it is "too harsh" and "illogical."

One of the few secondary sources cited by LaFave and Scott on this topic is a 1939 law review article by I. Wilner entitled *Unintentional Homicide In the Commission of an Unlawful Act.* In this article the author argues that the principal historic purpose of this rule was not, in fact, punishment of the homicide but vigorous punishment of the underlying "unlawful act," which in most cases was a violation of some property right.

Because of the facial simplicity of the misdemeanor manslaughter rule, its application by courts has led to some rather extraordinary findings of criminal liability for homicide. For example, in 1926 a Texas court found liability for manslaughter on the following facts: The victim discovered the defendant committing adultery with the victim's wife. Adultery was a misdemeanor in Texas. The victim made a murderous attack on the defendant. In defending himself against the murderous attack, the defendant killed the victim. The court decided that since the victim's murderous attack was a foreseeable reaction to the defendant's criminal misconduct, the defendant was guilty of manslaughter. In *Commonwealth v. Mink,* the defendant was attempting to commit suicide, but her fiancee [sic] intervened to try to stop her and was accidentally killed by the defendant. Because suicide was an unlawful act *malum in se,* the court found defendant guilty of manslaughter.

Over time, this theory of criminal responsibility has developed many complexities. Courts differ about whether the unlawful act must amount to a criminal offense and whether different standards should apply for *malum in se* or *malum prohibitum* offenses. In this case, neither of these issues is of concern.

The offense in this case is a *malum in se* misdemeanor offense under the criminal law of Florida. However, the other principal point of divergence in the development of the misdemeanor manslaughter rule - the issue of causation - is critical to this case.

The views on the requirement of causation in unlawful act manslaughter differ widely among the various jurisdictions. In some instances, no causal relationship at all has been required. At the other extreme is the requirement that there be not only a direct causal relationship between the unlawful act and the death, but that the death must be a natural and probable consequence of the offense. An example cited by Wilner is the case of *Votre v. State,* where, contrary to statute, the defendant gave whiskey to the victim, who was a minor. Consumption of the alcohol caused the victim to suffer a heart attack of which he died. The Indiana court held that the defendant was not guilty of manslaughter because the homicide must follow both as a part of the perpetration of the unlawful act and as a natural and probable consequence of it. * * *

Florida courts, by simply interpreting the statutory definition of manslaughter ("the killing of a human being by the act, procurement, or culpable negligence of another, without lawful justification. . ."), appear always to have understood the importance of causation as an element of this type of homicide. Our courts also have appreciated the foreseeability element of causation. * * *

In this case, even if it were assumed that the stress of pursuit brought on the heart attack, it cannot be said that the petty theft was the legal cause of Mr. Voegltin's death. The crime itself was a minor property offense. There is no suggestion of any touching or any threat to anyone's person. This is not even a case, like a purse snatching, where violence was necessary to produce the theft. Nor is it asserted that Mr. Voegltin died from fright or horror at witnessing the crime. The state's traverse specifically asserts that it was the pursuit that caused the fatal heart attack. Although the petty theft did trigger a series of events that concluded in the death of Mr. Voegltin and was, in that sense, a "cause" of the death, the petty theft did not encompass the kind of direct, foreseeable risk of physical harm that would support a conviction of manslaughter. The relationship between the unlawful act committed (petty theft) and the result effected (death by heart attack during pursuit in an automobile) does not meet the test of causation historically or currently required in Florida for conviction of manslaughter.

REVERSED.

Chapter 8

SEXUAL OFFENSES

INTRODUCTION

In 1961, when the Model Penal Code was promulgated, American law closely reflected the Anglo-American common law, which recognized three basic sexual offenses: forcible rape, statutory rape, and sodomy. Forcible rape was typically defined as "the carnal knowledge of a woman, not the perpetrator's wife, forcibly and against her will." Statutory rape was typically defined as sexual intercourse with a female under the age of consent, where the age of consent varied from age 18 to age 10.

Statutory and forcible rape shared some common features. First, neither crime contained an explicit mens rea as an essential element of the crime. Statutory rape is often called a strict liability crime, since knowledge of the girl's age has traditionally not been required. Forcible rape has been treated as a general intent crime. Second, both kinds of rape, forcible and statutory, assumed that the victim would be a woman and the perpetrator would be a man. Third, both kinds of rape, forcible and statutory, focused on heterosexual, vaginal intercourse as the actus reus element of the crime. Under this definition, an assault in which an object other than a penis is put in the victim's vagina would not fall under the traditional definition of forcible rape. Similarly, the forcible rape of a male child by a male adult would not constitute forcible rape. Nor would oral or anal intercourse, whether by force or with a child. Finally, the penalties for forcible rape and statutory rape were similar: for both crimes the range of possible punishments was extremely broad, from as low as three years in prison, to as high as the death penalty. This wide range of penalties gave enormous discretion to the sentencing judge.

In addition to statutory and forcible rape, the American criminal law of a generation ago punished sodomy, also ominously referred to in many statutes as "the crime against nature." *See Wainwright v. Stone*, 414 U.S. 21 (1973) (upholding, against a void-for-vagueness charge, a Florida statute that punished "the abominable and detestable crime against nature, either with mankind or beast"). Under English common law as originally adopted by the United States, sodomy always included anal intercourse between men. It also sometimes included any sexual contact with an animal, and sometimes both same-sex and cross-sex oral sex. Notice, therefore, that although same-sex relations between men were uniformly criminalized within the common law tradition, same-sex relations between women were more ambiguously treated: lesbian relations might or might not be a crime, depending on the jurisdiction. At English common law, sodomy was a capital offense. Even after sodomy stopped being a capital offense, the penalties were quite high, with 10 or 20 year maximums being common.

As with statutory rape, at common law neither non-consent nor force were elements of the crime of sodomy. The absence of a force element meant that the defense could not win an acquittal by questioning whether the victim really resisted or whether his or her resistance was adequate, a question that traditionally lay at the center of many forcible rape prosecutions. The absence of a non-consent element in sodomy law meant that married men could be convicted of sodomy against their wives, even in states where marital rape was not a crime. More importantly, the absence of a non-consent element of sodomy meant that prosecutors could convict consenting adults, such as gay and lesbian couples.

In contrast to rape and sodomy, prostitution was not a crime at common law. In the United States, prostitution was not widely criminalized until the Progressive Era (roughly 1880 to 1920), when a moral panic about the social evils of prostitution and the "white slave trade" it engendered took hold of the public. By 1961, the vast majority of United States jurisdictions punished prostitution and related crimes such as owning a brothel.

The Model Penal Code represents the cutting edge of modernization in the law of sexual offenses circa 1961. Since that time, however, state and federal legislatures, and federal courts interpreting the Constitution, have changed some aspects of the law of sexual offenses even further. The law of forcible rape has changed the most dramatically: the law seems to be moving to reconceptualize forcible rape not as a crime against a woman's honor, but as a crime against a person's sexual autonomy. The law of sodomy has similarly been drastically altered by judicial recognition of the liberty interests of consenting, adult same-sex partners. In contrast, the law of statutory rape and the law of prostitution have remained relatively stable since 1961.

A.   FORCIBLE RAPE

In contrast to homicide law in the United States, which has changed very little since the founding of the nation, the law of forcible rape has changed in fundamental ways since the founding of the nation. First, the states have gone in different directions in reforming their laws. Some states, like Michigan, have followed the MPC in trying to create a unified body of sexual assault law with many different gradations. Other states have been more haphazard. For example, California has simply created more sex crimes whenever there is a public outcry, without trying to integrate them into a coherent whole. The California Penal Code has separate provisions criminalizing forcible rape, sodomy, oral copulation, penetration with an object, lewd and lascivious acts with a child under 14, spousal rape, sexual assault of an animal, and many other crimes. Therefore, although the law of homicide is easy to categorize into a generic "common law approach" and "MPC approach," forcible rape law is much more varied, and must be described in terms of trends.

Second, and more importantly, the basic purposes of forcible rape law are being rethought in contemporary times as Western culture regarding sexuality and gender undergoes rapid changes. Some of the changes in forcible rape doctrine are a direct result of feminist activism. Other changes have occurred as norms concerning sexuality have changed drastically in the last couple of generations.

As you read the materials on forcible rape, keep in the back of your mind some policy questions upon which we as a society have yet to reach consensus. First, what is the harm caused by rape? Are there analogies to other crimes that are useful in answering this question? Is rape a type of violence like assault and battery? Is it a forcible taking of sex? (Some commentators have suggested, for example, that rape should be analogized to armed robbery.) Or, are the harms of rape sui generis?

The second policy question to keep in mind is a corollary of the first. What interests does rape law protect, and what interests should it protect? Does it (and should it) protect male access to female bodies? Does it (and should it) protect people's sexual autonomy? Does it (and should it) protect people against bad sex?

Third, is all rape equal, or are there good reasons to treat different kinds of rape differently? If we do want to separate out certain rapes as deserving of more punishment than others, how do we identify those rapes? Several possible criteria are suggested by existing doctrine: (1) mens rea (Are intentional rapes worse than reckless or negligent ones?); (2) the presence or absence of a relationship between the perpetrator and the victim (Is stranger rape worse than acquaintance rape, or the other way around?); (3) the presence or absence of violence (Is a rape at gunpoint worse than a rape by threats and intimidation?); and (4) the presence or absence of meaningful consent (Is a rape of a mentally retarded victim or a victim who is comatose more or less heinous than the rape of someone clearly able to say "no"?). Consider whether and how these various sorting criteria might be reflected in the law.

Fourth, what kinds of doctrinal rules will both further the goals of preventing and redressing rape and protecting the rights of defendants? As you will see in the materials that follow, the cultural context of rape law enforcement is pervaded with class and race bias.

Finally, do we need to look beyond the criminal justice system to solve the problem of rape? Should we look to mediation and the tort system? To social education?

1.   The Element of Force or Threat of Force

In many forcible rape cases, the critical question is whether the defendant used force or threat of force to accomplish the sexual intercourse. At one time, states required proof of physical resistance by the victim. A woman claiming she was raped had to resist her attacker "to her utmost" in order to prove the sexual intercourse was by force or threat of force and without her consent. Most (though not all) jurisdictions have eliminated the resistance requirement for the reasons offered in Justice Wilner's dissenting opinion in *Rusk v. State*. Even without an explicit resistance requirement, however, evidence of resistance plays an important role in establishing the elements of force and non-consent. Moreover, judges and jurors often look for evidence of resistance by the victim and may be skeptical of the victim's claim of rape if the victim did not physically resist. The next several cases focus on whether there was sufficient evidence of force or threat of force to support a rape conviction, but the question of resistance remains just below the surface.

RUSK v. STATE
Court of Special Appeals of Maryland
43 Md. App. 476, 406 A.2d 624 (Ct. Spec. App. 1979)

THOMPSON, J.

* * * Edward Salvatore Rusk, the appellant, was convicted in the Criminal Court of Baltimore of rape in the second degree and of assault. He was sentenced to concurrent terms of ten years for the rape and five years for the assault. The appellant does not challenge the conviction for assault but only for the rape. We will, therefore, affirm the assault conviction.

The prosecutrix was a twenty-one year old mother of a two-year old son. She was separated from her husband but not yet divorced. Leaving her son with her mother, she attended a high school reunion after which she and a female friend, Terry, went bar hopping in the Fells Point area of Baltimore. They drove in separate cars. At the third bar the prosecutrix met appellant. * * *

They had a five or ten minute conversation in the bar; at the end of which the prosecutrix said she was ready to leave. Appellant requested a ride home and she agreed. When they arrived at appellant's home, the prosecutrix parked at the curb on the side of the street opposite his rooming house but did not turn off the ignition. She put the car in park and appellant asked her to come up to his apartment. She refused. He continued to ask her to come up, and she testified she then became afraid. While trying to convince him that she didn't want to go to his apartment she mentioned that she was separated and if she did, it might cause her marital problems particularly if she were being followed by a detective. The appellant then took the keys out of the car and walked over to her side of the car, opened the door and said, "Now will you come up?" The prosecutrix then told him she would. She stated:

> At that point, because I was scared, because he had my car keys. I didn't know what to do. I was someplace I didn't even know where I was. It was in the city. I didn't know whether to run. I really didn't think, at that point, what to do. Now, I know that I should have blown the horn. I should have run. There were a million things I could have done. I was scared, at that point, and I didn't do any of them.

The prosecutrix followed appellant into the rowhouse, up the stairs, and into the apartment. When they got into appellant's room, he said that he had to go to the bathroom and left the room for a few minutes. The prosecutrix made no attempt to leave. When appellant came back, he sat on the bed while she sat on the chair next to the bed. He turned the light off and asked her to get on the bed with him. He started to pull her onto the bed and also began to remove her blouse. She stated she took off her slacks and removed his clothing because "he asked [her] to do it." After they both undressed, prosecutrix stated:

> I was still begging him to please let, you know, let me leave. I said, 'you can get a lot of other girls down there, for what you want,' and he just kept saying, 'no,' and then I was really scared, because I can't describe, you know, what was said. It was more the look in his eyes; and I said, at that point – I didn't know what to say; and I said, 'If I do what you want, will you let me go without killing me?' Because I didn't know, at that point, what he was going to do; and I started to cry; and when I did, he put his hands on my throat, and started lightly to choke me; and I said, 'If I do what you want, will you let me go?' And he said, yes, and at that time, I proceeded to do what he wanted me to.

She stated that she performed oral sex and they then had sexual intercourse.[1]

* * *

The Court of Appeals of Maryland last spoke on the amount of force required to support a rape conviction in *Hazel v. State,* when the Court said:

"Force is an essential element of the crime and to justify a conviction, the evidence must warrant a conclusion either that the victim resisted and her resistance was overcome by force or that she was prevented from resisting by threats to her safety."[2]

---

[1] If we could say at this point that there is enough evidence for a reasonable fact finder to say such threat of force is solely that which overcame her will to resist, the conduct of both following intercourse would belie that conclusion:

"A. All right. Now, after the sexual intercourse came to a conclusion, what is the very next thing that took place?

A. I asked him if I could leave now, and he said, 'Yes;' and I got up and got dressed; and he got up and got dressed; and he walked me to my car, and asked if he could see me again; and I said, 'Yes;' and he asked me for my telephone number; and I said, 'No, I'll see you down [at] Fell's Point sometime,' just so I could leave.

Q. What is the reason that you said that you would meet him the next day?

A. I didn't say the next day, and I just said I would see him down there only so I could leave. I didn't know what else to say. I had no intention of meeting him again."

After arriving home she said:

"I sat in the car, thinking about it a while, and I thought I wondered what would happen if I hadn't of done what he wanted me to do. So I thought the right thing to do was to go report it, and I went from there to Hillendale to find a police car."

If, in quiet contemplation after the act, she had to wonder what would have happened, her submission on the side of prudence seems hardly justified. Indeed, if she had to wonder afterward, how can a fact finder reasonably conclude that she was justifiably in fear sufficient to overcome her will to resist, at the time.

[2] Since *Hazel*, the Maryland Legislature has codified extensively the law pertaining to sexual offenses providing in Md. Code, Art. 27, § 463 as follows: "(a) What constitutes. – A person is guilty of rape in the second degree if the person engages in vaginal intercourse with another person: (1) By force or threat of force against the will and without the consent of the other person...." The statute has made

In all of the victim's testimony we have been unable to see any resistance on her part to the sex acts and certainly can we see no fear as would overcome her attempt to resist or escape as required by *Hazel*. Possession of the keys by the accused may have deterred her vehicular escape but hardly a departure seeking help in the rooming house or in the street. We must say that "the way he looked" fails utterly to support the fear required by *Hazel*. * * *

As we said in *Winegan v. State*:

> [Where] the victim's story could not be corroborated by wounds, bruises or disordered clothing, the lack of consent could be shown by fear based upon reasonable apprehension. * * *

The State argues * * * that the evidence that the accused "started lightly to choke me" as well as the circumstances of being in a somewhat strange part of town late at night were sufficient to overcome the will of a normal twenty-one year old married woman. We are not impressed with the argument. * * *

[W]e find the evidence legally insufficient to warrant a conclusion that appellant's words or actions created in the mind of the victim a reasonable fear that if she resisted, he would have harmed her, or that faced with such resistance, he would have used force to overcome it. The prosecutrix stated that she was afraid, and submitted because of "the look in his eyes." After both were undressed and in the bed, and she pleaded to him that she wanted to leave, he started to lightly choke her. At oral argument it was brought out that the "lightly choking" could have been a heavy caress. We do not believe that "lightly choking" along with all the facts and circumstances in the case, were sufficient to cause a reasonable fear which overcame her ability to resist. In the absence of any other evidence showing force used by appellant, we find that the evidence was insufficient to convict appellant of rape.

Judgment on the rape conviction reversed. * * *

WILNER, J. [dissenting]

With the deepest respect for the generally superior wisdom of may colleagues who authored or endorsed the majority Opinion, but with the equally profound conviction that, in this case, they have made a serious mistake, I record this dissent.

---

no change in the force as required by *Hazel*.

The majority's error, in my judgment, is not in their exposition of the underlying principles of law that must govern this case, but rather in the manner that they have applied those principles. The majority have trampled upon the first principle of appellate restraint. Under the guise of judging the sufficiency of the evidence presented against appellant, they have tacitly – perhaps unwittingly, but nonetheless effectively – substituted their own view of the evidence (and the inferences that may fairly be drawn from it) for that of the judge and jury. In so doing, they have not only improperly invaded the province allotted to those tribunals, but, at the same time, have perpetuated and given new life to myths about the crime of rape that have no place in our law today. * * *

Md. Annot. Code art. 27, § 463(a) considers three types of conduct as constituting second degree rape. We are concerned only with the first: a person is guilty of rape in the second degree if he (1) engages in vaginal intercourse with another person, (2) by force or threat of force, (3) against the will, and (4) without the consent of the other person. There is no real question here as to the first, third, or fourth elements of the crime. The evidence was certainly sufficient to show that appellant had vaginal intercourse with the victim, and that such act was against her will and without her consent. The point at issue is whether it was accomplished by force or threat of force; and I think that in viewing the evidence, that point should remain ever clear. Consent is not the issue here, only whether there was sufficient evidence of force or the threat of force.

Unfortunately, courts, including in the present case a majority of this one, often tend to confuse these two elements – force and lack of consent – and to think of them as one. They are not. They mean, and require, different things. What seems to cause the confusion – what, indeed, has become a common denominator of both elements – is the notion that the victim must actively resist the attack upon her. If she fails to offer sufficient resistance (sufficient to the satisfaction of the judge), a court is entitled, or at least presumes the entitlement, to find that there was no force or threat of force, or that the act was not against her will, or that she actually consented to it, or some unarticulated combination or synthesis of these elements that leads to the ultimate conclusion that the victim was not raped. Thus it is that the focus is almost entirely on the extent of resistance – the victim's acts, rather than those of her assailant. Attention is directed not to the wrongful stimulus, but to the victim's reactions to it. Right or wrong, that seems to be the current state of the Maryland law; and, notwithstanding its uniqueness in the criminal law, and its illogic, until changed by statute or the Court of Appeals, I accept it as binding.

But what is required of a woman being attacked or in danger of attack? How much resistance must she offer? Where is that line to be drawn between requiring that she either risk serious physical harm, perhaps death, on the one hand, or be termed a willing partner on the other? Some answers were given in *Hazel v. State,* although, as in so many cases, they were stated in the context of both the requirement of force and the lack of consent. * * *

From these pronouncements in *Hazel,* this Court has articulated what the majority refers to as a "rule of reason" – i.e., that "where the victim's story could not be corroborate by wounds, bruises or disordered clothing, the lack of consent could be shown by fear based upon reasonable apprehension." As so phrased, I do not consider this to be a rule of reason at all; it is highly unreasonable, and again mixes the element of consent with that of force. But what I do accept is what the Court of Appeals said in Hazel: (1) if the acts and threats of the defendant were reasonably calculated to create in the mind of the victim -- having regard to the circumstances in which she was placed – a real apprehension, due to fear, of imminent bodily harm, serious enough to impair or overcome her will to resist, then such acts and threats are the equivalent of force; (2) submission is not the equivalent of consent; and (3) the real test is whether the assault was committed without the consent and against the will of the prosecuting witness.

Upon this basis, the evidence against appellant must be considered. Judge Thompson recounts most, but not quite all, of the victim's story. The victim – I'll call her Pat – attended a high school reunion. She had arranged to meet her girlfriend Terry there. The reunion was over at 9:00, and Terry asked Pat to accompany her to Fell's Point. Pat had gone to Fell's Point with Terry on a few prior occasions, explaining in court: "I've never met anybody [there] I've gone out with. I met people in general, talking in conversation, most of the time people that Terry knew, not that I have gone down there, and met people as dates." She agreed to go, but first called her mother, who was babysitting with Pat's two-year old son, to tell her that she was going with Terry to Fell's Point, and that she would not be home late. It was just after 9:00 when Pat and Terry, in their separate cars, left for Fell's Point, alone.

They went to a place called Helen's and had one drink. They stayed an hour or so and then walked down to another place (where they had another drink), stayed about a half hour there, and went to a third place. Up to this point, Pat conversed only with Terry, and did not strike up any other acquaintanceships. Pat and Terry were standing against a wall when appellant came over and said hello to Terry, who was conversing with someone else at the time. Appellant then began to talk with Pat. They were both separated, they both had young children; and they spoke about those things. Pat said that she had been ready to leave when appellant came on the scene, and that she only talked with him for five or ten minutes. It was then about midnight. Pat had to get up with her baby in the morning and did not want to stay out late.

Terry wasn't ready to leave. As Pat was preparing to go, appellant asked if she would drop him off on her way home. She agreed because she thought he was a friend of Terry's. She told him, however, as there walked to her car, "I'm just giving a ride home, you know, as a friend, not anything to be, you now, thought of other than a ride." He agreed to that condition.

Pat was completely unfamiliar with appellant's neighborhood. She had no idea where she was. When she pulled up to where appellant said he lived, she put the car in park, but left the engine running. She said to appellant "Well, here, you know, you are home." Appellant then asked Pat to come up with him and she refused. He persisted in his request, as did she in her refusal. She told him that even if she wanted to come up, she dared not do so. She was separated and it might cause marital problems for her. Finally, he reached over, turned off the ignition, took her keys, got out of the car, came around to her side, opened the door, and said to her, "Now, will you come up?"

It was at this point that Pat followed appellant to his apartment, and it is at this point that the majority of this Court begins to substitute its judgment for that of the trial court and jury. We know nothing about Pat and appellant. We don't know how big they are, what they look like, what their life experiences have been. We don't know if appellant is larger or smaller than she, stronger or weaker. We don't know what the inflection was in his voice as he dangled her car keys in front of her. We can't tell whether this was in a jocular vein or a truly threatening one. We have no idea what his mannerisms were. The trial judge and the jury could discern some of these things, of course, because they could observe the two people in court and could listen to what they said and how they said it. But all we know is that, between midnight and 1:00 a.m., in a neighborhood that was strange to Pat, appellant took her car keys, demanded that she accompany him, and most assuredly implied that unless she did so, at the very least, she might be stranded.

Now, let us interrupt the tale for a minute and consider the situation. Pat did not honk the horn; she did not scream; she did not try to run away. Why, she was asked. "I was scared. I didn't think at the time what to do." Later, on cross-examination: "At that point, because I was scared, because he had my car keys. I didn't know what to do. I was someplace I didn't even know where I was. It was in the city. I didn't know whether to run. I really didn't think, at that point, what to do. Now, I know that I should have blown the [h]orn. I should have run. There were a million things I could have done. I was scared, at that point, and I didn't do any of them." What, counsel asked, was she afraid of? "Him," she replied. What was she scared that he was going to do? "Rape me, but I didn't say that. It was the way he looked at me, and said, 'Come on up, come on up;' and when he took the keys, I knew that was wrong. I just didn't say, are you going to rape me." * * *

How does the majority opinion view these events? It starts by noting that Pat was a 21-year old mother who was separated from her husband but not yet divorced, as though that had some significance. To me, it has none, except perhaps (when coupled with the further characterization that Pat and Terry had gone "bar hopping") to indicate an underlying suspicion, for which there is absolutely no support in the record, that Pat was somehow "on the make." Even more alarming, and unwarranted, however, is the majority's analysis of Pat's initial reflections on whether to report what had happened. Ignoring completely her statement that she "didn't want to go through what I'm going through now," the majority, in footnote 1, cavalierly and without any foundation whatever, says:

> If, in quiet contemplation after the act, she had to wonder what would have happened, her submission on the side of prudence seems hardly justified. Indeed, if she had to wonder afterward, how can a fact finder reasonably conclude that she was justifiably in fear sufficient to overcome her will to resist, at the time.

It is this type of reasoning – if indeed "reasoning" is the right word for it – that is particularly distressing. The concern expressed by Pat, made even more real by the majority opinion of this court, is one that is common among rape victims, and largely accounts for the fact that most incidents of forcible rape go unreported by the victim. If appellant had desired, and Pat had given, her wallet instead of her body, there would be no question about appellant's guilt of robbery. Taking the car keys under those circumstances would certainly have supplied the requisite threat of force or violence and negated the element of consent. No one would seriously contend that because she failed to raise a hue and cry she had consented to the theft of her money. Why then is such life-threatening action necessary when it is her personal dignity that is being stolen?

Rape has always been considered a most serious crime, one that traditionally carried the heaviest penalty. But until recently, it remained shrouded in the taboos and myths of a Victorian age, and little real attention was given to how rapes occur, how they may be prevented, and how a victim can best protect herself from injury when an attack appears inevitable. The courts are as responsible for this ignorance and the misunderstandings emanating from it as any other institution in society, and it is high time that they recognize reality.

Rape is on the increase in the United States. The Uniform Crime Reports compiled by the F.B.I show more than a doubling in both the absolute number of forcible rapes and in the rate per 100,000 population between 1965 and 1974. Between 1973 and 1977, forcible rape has increased 19%. As the result of the Battelle Study, we now know some things about this crime that we could only guess at before. Nearly half of the rapes occur when this one did, between 8:00 p.m. and 2:00 a.m., and, as in this case, approximately one-third of rape victims had come into contact with their assailants voluntarily, under circumstances other than hitchhiking. Physical force is absent in over half of reported cases and, in a third of the cases, no weapon is involved. * * *

Of particular significance is what was learned about resistance. The most common type of resistance offered by victims is verbal. Note: verbal resistance is resistance! In cases arising in the large cities, only 12.7% of the victims attempted flight, and only 12% offered physical resistance. The reason for this is apparent from the next thing learned: that "[rape] victims who resisted were more likely to be injured than ones who did not." The statistics showed, for rapes in large cities, that, where physical resistance was offered, over 71% of the victims were physically injured in some way, 40% requiring medical treatment or hospitalization.

Said the Report: "These results indicate one possible danger of the popular notion (and some statutory requirements) that a victim of an attack should resist to her utmost."

In a second volume of the Report, intended for prosecutors, some of the social attitudes about rape were discussed. With respect to resistance, it was noted:

> Perhaps because most women's experience and expertise with violence tends to be minimal, they are unlikely to engage in physical combat or succeed when they do. Many women employ what is referred to as 'passive resistance.' This can include crying, being slow to respond, feigning an inability to understand instructions or telling the rapist they are pregnant, diseased or injured. While these techniques may not always be successful, their use does suggest that the victim is surely not a willing partner.

In contrast to some of the inferences sought to be drawn by the majority from Pat's reactions, the Report further points out:

> Rather than expressing their emotions, some victims respond to a rape with a calm, composed demeanor or 'controlled reaction.' These victims do not wish to exhibit emotions, especially in front of a stranger or authority figure like the prosecutor. Psychologically it is important for these victims to demonstrate that they can handle stress in a mature and adult manner. The appearance of casualness hides and may avoid

true and often intense emotions. This 'control' may result in victim responses which are considered inappropriate such as giggling, smiling or even laughing. Unfortunately this type of response can cause others to doubt the victim's account of the rape.

Finally, perhaps in response to the oft-quoted comment of Matthew Hale that still pervades societal thinking about rape ("[Rape] is an accusation easily to be made and hard to be proved, and harder to be defended by the party accused, tho never so innocent"), the Report observes:

> On a national average, 15 percent of all forcible rapes reported to the police were 'determined by investigation' to be unfounded. Given the inherent skepticism of many criminal justice personnel to rape victims and the harassment and invasion of privacy that a reporting victim is likely to confront, it is doubtful that many false accusations proceed past the initial report. Curtis (1974) asserts that 'contrary to widespread opinion, there is in fact little hard empirical evidence that victims in rape lie more than, say victims in robbery.' Undoubtedly, there are false reports. However, the danger posed by the myth that women 'cry rape' is that police officers and prosecutors will believe it and then place the burden on the victims to prove the contrary. * * *

Where does this leave us but where we started? A judge and a jury, observing the witnesses and hearing their testimony, concluded without dissent that there was sufficient evidence to find beyond a reasonable doubt that appellant had sexual intercourse with Pat by force or threat of force against her will and without her consent; in other words, that the extent of her resistance and the reasons for her failure to resist further were reasonable. No claim is made here that the jury was misinstructed on the law of rape. Yet a majority of this Court, without the ability to see and hear the witnesses, has simply concluded that, in their judgment, Pat's fear was not a reasonable one, or that there was no fear at all (a point that appellant conceded at oral argument before the Court en banc). In so doing, they have ignored the fact of a young woman alone in a strange neighborhood at 1:00 in the morning with a man who had taken her keys and was standing at her open car door demanding that she come with him; they have ignored that she offered the very type of verbal resistance that is prudent, common, and recommended by law enforcement agencies; they have ignored that the reasonableness of Pat's apprehension is inherently a question of fact for the jury to determine. Brushing all of this aside, they have countermanded the judgment of the trial court and jury and declared Pat to have been, in effect, an adulteress. * * *

Note

The government appealed the decision you just read, and in 1981, the Court of Appeals of Maryland (Maryland's highest court) reversed the intermediate court of appeals, holding that the reversal of Rusk's rape conviction was in error because the reasonableness of Pat's fear was a question of fact for the jury, not the appellate court, to decide. *State v. Rusk*, 424 A.2d 720 (Md. 1981). Three judges vigorously dissented, however, on the ground that "there is no evidence to support the majority's conclusion that the prosecutrix was forced to submit to sexual intercourse, certainly not fellatio." Continued the dissent:

> While courts no longer require a female to resist to the utmost or to resist where resistance would be foolhardy, they do require her acquiescence in the act of intercourse to stem from fear generated by something of substance. She may not simply say, "I was really scared," and thereby transform consent or mere unwillingness into submission by force. These words do not transform a seducer into a rapist. She must follow the natural instinct of every proud female to resist, by more than mere words, the violation of her person by a stranger or an unwelcomed friend. She must make it plain that she regards such sexual acts as abhorrent and repugnant to her natural sense of pride. She must resist unless the defendant has objectively manifested his intent to use physical force to accomplish his purpose. The law regards rape as a crime of violence. The majority today attenuates this proposition. It declares the innocence of an at best distraught young woman. It does not demonstrate the defendant's guilt of the crime of rape.

424 A.2d 733.

Professor Susan Estrich notes that "*State v. Rusk* is one of the most vigorously debated rape cases in recent volumes of the case reporters." Susan Estrich, REAL RAPE 63 (1987). "All told, twenty-one judges, including the trial judge, reviewed the sufficiency of evidence. Ten concluded that Rusk was a rapist; eleven that he was not." *Id.*

STATE v. ALSTON

Supreme Court of North Carolina
310 N.C. 399, 312 S.E.2d 470 (1984)

MITCHELL, JR. A.J.

The defendant raises on appeal the question whether the evidence of his guilt of kidnapping and second degree rape was sufficient to support his convictions of those crimes. For reasons discussed herein, we conclude the evidence was insufficient to support his conviction of either crime.

The State's evidence tended to show that at the time the incident occurred the defendant and the prosecuting witness in this case, Cottie Brown, had been involved for approximately six months in a consensual sexual relationship. During the six months the two had conflicts at times and Brown would leave the apartment she shared with the defendant to stay with her mother. She testified that she would return to the defendant and the apartment they shared when he called to tell her to return. Brown testified that she and the defendant had sexual relations throughout their relationship. Although she sometimes enjoyed their sexual relations, she often had sex with the defendant just to accommodate him. On those occasions, she would stand still and remain entirely passive while the defendant undressed her and had intercourse with her.

Brown testified that at times their consensual sexual relations involved some violence. The defendant had struck her several times throughout the relationship when she refused to give him money or refused to do what he wanted. Around May 15, 1981, the defendant struck her after asking for money that she refused to give him. Brown left the apartment she shared with the defendant and moved in with her mother. She did not have intercourse with the defendant after May 15 until the alleged rape on June 15. After Brown left the defendant, he called her several times and visited her at Durham Technical Institute where she was enrolled in classes. When he visited her they talked about their relationship. Brown testified that she did not tell him she wanted to break off their relationship because she was afraid he would be angry.

On June 15, 1981, Brown arrived at Durham Technical Institute by taxicab to find the defendant standing close to the school door. The defendant blocked her path as she walked toward the door and asked her where she had moved. Brown refused to tell him, and the defendant grabbed her arm, saying that she was going with him. Brown testified that it would have taken some effort to pull away. The two walked toward the parking lot and Brown told the defendant she would walk with him if he let her go. The defendant then released her. She testified that she did not run away from him because she was afraid of him. She stated that other students were nearby.

Brown stated that she and the defendant then began a casually paced walk in the neighborhood around the school. They walked, sometimes side by side, sometimes with Brown slightly behind the defendant. As they walked they talked about their relationship. Brown said the defendant did not hold her or help her along in any way as they walked. The defendant talked about Brown's "dogging" him and making him seem a fool and about Brown's mother's interference in the relationship. When the defendant and Brown left the parking lot, the defendant threatened to "fix" her face so that her mother could see he was not playing. While they were walking out of the parking lot, Brown told the defendant she wanted to go to class. He replied that she was going to miss class that day.

The two continued to walk away from the school. Brown testified that the defendant continually talked about their relationship as they walked, but that she paid little attention to what he said because she was preoccupied with her own thoughts. They passed several people. They walked along several streets and went down a path close to a wooded area where they stopped to talk. The defendant asked again where Brown had moved. She asked him whether he would let her go if she told him her address. The defendant then asked whether the relationship was over and Brown told him it was. He then said that since everyone could see her but him he had a right to make love to her again. Brown said nothing.

The two turned around at that point and began walking towards a street they had walked down previously. Changing directions, they walked in the same fashion they had walked before -- side by side with Brown sometimes slightly behind. The defendant did not hold or touch Brown as they walked. Brown testified that the defendant did not say where they were going but that, when he said he wanted to make love, she knew he was going to the house of a friend. She said they had gone to the house on prior occasions to have sex. The defendant and Brown passed the same group of men they had passed previously. Brown did not ask for assistance because some of the men were friends of the defendant, and she assumed they would not help. The defendant and Brown continued to walk to the house of one of the defendant's friends, Lawrence Taylor.

When they entered the house, Taylor was inside. Brown sat in the living room while the defendant and Taylor went to the back of the house and talked. When asked why she did not try to leave when the defendant and Taylor were in the back of the house, Brown replied, "[There] was nowhere to go. I don't know. I just didn't." The defendant returned to the living room area and turned on the television. He attempted to fix a broken fan. Brown asked Taylor for a cigarette, and he gave her one.

The defendant began talking to Brown about another man she had been seeing. By that time Taylor had gone out of the room and perhaps the house. The defendant asked if Brown was "ready." The evidence tended to show that she told him "no, that I wasn't going to bed with him." She testified that she did not want to have sex with the defendant and did not consent to do so at any time on June 15.

After Brown finished her cigarette, the defendant began kissing her neck. He pulled her up from the chair in which she had been sitting and started undressing her. He noticed that she was having her menstrual period, and she sat down pulling her pants back up. The defendant again took off her pants and blouse. He told her to lay down on a bed which was in the living room. She complied and the defendant pushed apart her legs and had sexual intercourse with her. Brown testified that she did not try to push him away. She cried during the intercourse. Afterwards they talked. The defendant told her he wanted to make sure she was not lying about where she lived and that he would not let her up unless she told him.

After they dressed they talked again about the man Brown had been seeing. They left the house and went to the defendant's mother's house. After talking with the defendant's mother, Brown took a bus home. She talked with her mother about taking out a complaint against the defendant but did not tell her mother she and the defendant had had sex. Brown made a complaint to the police the same day.

The defendant continued to call Brown after June 15, but she refused to see him. One evening he called from a telephone booth and told her he had to talk. When he got to her apartment he threatened to kick her door down and Brown let him inside. Once inside he said he had intended merely to talk to her but that he wanted to make love again after seeing her. Brown said she sat and looked at him, and that he began kissing her. She pulled away and he picked her up and carried her to the bedroom. He performed oral sex on her and she testified that she did not try to fight him off because she found she enjoyed it. The two stayed together until morning and had sexual intercourse several times that night. Brown did not disclose the incident to the police immediately because she said she was embarrassed.

The defendant put on no evidence and moved at the close of the State's evidence for dismissal of both charges based on insufficiency of evidence. The trial court denied the motions and the majority in the Court of Appeals affirmed the trial court.

Upon the defendant's motion to dismiss, the question for the court is whether substantial evidence was introduced of each element of the offense charged and that the defendant was the perpetrator. Substantial evidence is "such relevant evidence as a reasonable mind might accept as adequate to support a conclusion." The issue of substantiality is a question of law for the court. If the evidence is sufficient only to raise a suspicion or conjecture as to either the commission of the offense or the identity of the perpetrator, the motion to dismiss should be allowed. This is true even though the suspicion is strong.

The court is to consider the evidence in the light most favorable to the State in ruling on a motion to dismiss. The State is entitled to every reasonable intendment and inference to be drawn from the evidence; contradictions and discrepancies do not warrant dismissal – they are for the jury to resolve. * * *

In his second assignment of error the defendant contends there was no substantial evidence that the sexual intercourse between Brown and him was by force and against her will. He argues that the evidence was insufficient to allow the trial court to submit the issue of his guilt of second degree rape to the jury. After a review of the evidence, we find this argument to have merit.

Second degree rape involves vaginal intercourse with the victim both by force and against the victim's will. Consent by the victim is a complete defense, but consent which is induced by fear of violence is void and is no legal consent.

A defendant can be guilty of raping even his mistress or a "common strumpet." This is so because consent to sexual intercourse freely given can be withdrawn at any time prior to penetration. If the particular act of intercourse for which the defendant is charged was both by force and against the victim's will, the offense is rape without regard to the victim's consent given to the defendant for prior acts of intercourse.

Where as here the victim has engaged in a prior continuing consensual sexual relationship with the defendant, however, determining the victim's state of mind at the time of the alleged rape obviously is made more difficult. Although inquiry in such cases still must be made into the victim's state of mind at the time of the alleged rape, the State ordinarily will be able to show the victim's lack of consent to the specific act charged only by evidence of statements or actions by the victim which were clearly communicated to the defendant and which expressly and unequivocally indicated the victim's withdrawal of any prior consent and lack of consent to the particular act of intercourse.

In the present case the State introduced such evidence. It is true, of course, that Brown gave no physical resistance to the defendant. Evidence of physical resistance is not necessary to prove lack of consent in a rape case in this jurisdiction. Brown testified unequivocally that she did not consent to sexual intercourse with the defendant on June 15. She was equally unequivocal in testifying that she submitted to sexual intercourse with the defendant only because she was afraid of him. During their walk, she told the defendant that their relationship was at an end. When the defendant asked her if she was "ready" immediately prior to having sexual intercourse with her, she told him "no, that I wasn't going to bed with him." Even in the absence of physical resistance by Brown, such testimony by her provided substantial evidence that the act of sexual intercourse was against her will.

The State did not offer substantial evidence, however, of the element of force. As we have stated, actual physical force need not be shown in order to establish force sufficient to constitute an element of the crime of rape. Threats of serious bodily harm which reasonably induce fear thereof are sufficient. In the present case there was no substantial evidence of either actual or constructive force.

The evidence in the present case tended to show that, shortly after the defendant met Brown at the school, they walked out of the parking lot with the defendant in front. He stopped and told Brown he was going to "fix" her face so that her mother could see he was not "playing." This threat by the defendant and his act of grabbing Brown by the arm at the school, although they may have induced fear, appeared to have been unrelated to the act of sexual intercourse between Brown and the defendant. More important, the record is devoid of evidence that Brown was in any way intimidated into having sexual intercourse with the defendant by that threat or any other act of the defendant on June 15. Brown said she did not pay a lot of attention to what the defendant said because she was thinking about other things. She specifically stated that her fear of the defendant was based on an experience with him prior to June 15 and that on June 15 he did not hold her down or threaten her with what would happen if she refused to submit to him. The State failed to offer substantial evidence of force used or threatened by the defendant on June 15 which related to his desire to have sexual intercourse on that date and was sufficient to overcome the will of the victim.

We note that the absence of an explicit threat is not determinative in considering whether there was sufficient force in whatever form to overcome the will of the victim. It is enough if the totality of the circumstances gives rise to a reasonable inference that the unspoken purpose of the threat was to force the victim to submit to unwanted sexual intercourse. The evidence introduced in the present case, however, gave rise to no such inference. Under the peculiar facts of this case, there was no substantial evidence that threats or force by the defendant on June 15 were sufficiently related to sexual conduct to cause Brown to believe that she had to submit to sexual intercourse with him or suffer harm. Although Brown's general fear of the defendant may have been justified by his conduct on prior occasions, absent evidence that the defendant used force or threats to overcome the will of the victim *to resist the sexual intercourse alleged to have been rape*, such general fear was not sufficient to show that the defendant used the force required to support a conviction of rape.

In summary, we think that the State's evidence was sufficient to show that the act of sexual intercourse in question was against Brown's will. It was not sufficient, however, to show that the act was accomplished by actual force or by a threat to use force unless she submitted to sexual intercourse. Since the State did not introduce substantial evidence of the element of force required to sustain a conviction of rape, the trial court erred in denying the defendant's motion to dismiss the case against the defendant for second degree rape.

For the foregoing reasons, we reverse the opinion of the Court of Appeals holding that there was no error in the defendant's trial for kidnapping and second degree rape and remand this action to the Court of Appeals for its further remand to the Superior Court, Durham County, for the entry of directed verdicts in favor of the defendant.

COMMONWEALTH v. BERKOWITZ
Superior Court of Pennsylvania
415 Pa. Super. 505, 609 A.2d 1338 (Super. Ct. 1992)

PER CURIAM

Appellant appeals from judgment of sentence imposed following convictions of rape and indecent assault. We are called upon to determine the degree of physical force necessary to complete the act of rape in Pennsylvania. We find that under the totality of the circumstances, evidence of sufficient force was not adduced herein. * * * Accordingly, we discharge appellant on the rape conviction. * * *

I. FACTS AND PROCEDURAL HISTORY

In the spring of 1988, appellant and the victim were both college sophomores at East Stroudsburg State University, ages twenty and nineteen years old, respectively. They had mutual friends and acquaintances. On April nineteenth of that year, the victim went to appellant's dormitory room. What transpired in that dorm room between appellant and the victim thereafter is the subject of the instant appeal.

During a one day jury trial held on September 14, 1988, the victim gave the following account during direct examination by the Commonwealth. At roughly 2:00 on the afternoon of April 19, 1988, after attending two morning classes, the victim returned to her dormitory room. There, she drank a martini to "loosen up a little bit" before going to meet her boyfriend, with whom she had argued the night before. Roughly ten minutes later she walked to her boyfriend's dormitory lounge to meet him. He had not yet arrived.

Having nothing else to do while she waited for her boyfriend, the victim walked up to appellant's room to look for Earl Hassel, appellant's roommate. She knocked on the door several times but received no answer. She therefore wrote a note to Mr. Hassel, which read, "Hi Earl, I'm drunk. That's not why I came to see you. I haven't seen you in a while. I'll talk to you later, [victim's name]." She did so, although she had not felt any intoxicating effects from the martini, "for a laugh."

After the victim had knocked again, she tried the knob on the appellant's door. Finding it open, she walked in. She saw someone lying on the bed with a pillow over his head, whom she thought to be Earl Hassel. After lifting the pillow from his head, she realized it was appellant. She asked appellant which dresser was his roommate's. He told her, and the victim left the note.

Before the victim could leave appellant's room, however, appellant asked her to stay and "hang out for a while." She complied because she "had time to kill" and because she didn't really know appellant and wanted to give him "a fair chance." Appellant asked her to give him a back rub but she declined, explaining that she did not "trust" him. Appellant then asked her to have a seat on his bed. Instead, she found a seat on the floor, and conversed for a while about a mutual friend. No physical contact between the two had, to this point, taken place.

Thereafter, however, appellant moved off the bed and down on the floor, and "kind of pushed [the victim] back with his body. It wasn't a shove, it was just kind of a leaning-type of thing." Next appellant "straddled" and started kissing the victim. The victim responded by saying, "Look, I gotta go. I'm going to meet [my boyfriend]." Then appellant lifted up her shirt and bra and began fondling her. The victim then said "no."

After roughly thirty seconds of kissing and fondling, appellant "undid his pants and he kind of moved his body up a little bit." The victim was still saying "no" but "really couldn't move because [appellant] was shifting at [her] body so he was over [her]." Appellant then tried to put his penis in her mouth. The victim did not physically resist, but rather continued to verbally protest, saying "No, I gotta go, let me go," in a "scolding" manner.

Ten or fifteen more seconds passed before the two rose to their feet. Appellant disregarded the victim's continual complaints that she "had to go," and instead walked two feet away to the door and locked it so that no one from the outside could enter.

Then, in the victim's words, "[appellant] put me down on the bed. It was kind of like – he didn't throw me on the bed. It's hard to explain. It was kind of like a push but no. . . ." She did not bounce off the bed. "It wasn't slow like a romantic kind of thing, but it wasn't a fast shove either. It was kind of in the middle."

Once the victim was on the bed, appellant began "straddling" her again while he undid the knot in her sweatpants. He then removed her sweatpants and underwear from one of her legs. The victim did not physically resist in any way while on the bed because appellant was on top of her, and she "couldn't like go anywhere." She did not scream out at anytime because, "[i]t was like a dream was happening or something."

Appellant then used one of his hands to "guide" his penis into her vagina. At that point, after appellant was inside her, the victim began saying "no, no to him softly in a moaning kind of way . . . because it was just so scary." After about thirty seconds, appellant pulled out his penis and ejaculated onto the victim's stomach.

Immediately thereafter, appellant got off the victim and said, "Wow, I guess we just got carried away." To this the victim retorted, "No, we didn't get carried away, you got carried away." The victim then quickly dressed, grabbed her school books and raced downstairs to her boyfriend who was by then waiting for her in the lounge.

Once there, the victim began crying. Her boyfriend and she went up to his dorm room where, after watching the victim clean off appellant's semen from her stomach, he called the police.

Defense counsel's cross-examination elicited more details regarding the contact between appellant and the victim before the incident in question. The victim testified that roughly two weeks prior to the incident, she had attended a school seminar entitled, "Does 'no' sometimes means 'yes'?" Among other things, the lecturer at this seminar had discussed the average length and circumference of human penises. After the seminar, the victim and several of her friends had discussed the subject matter of the seminar over a speaker-telephone with appellant and his roommate Earl Hassel. The victim testified that during that telephone conversation, she had asked appellant the size of his penis.

According to the victim, appellant responded by suggesting that the victim "come over and find out." She declined.

When questioned further regarding her communications with appellant prior to the April 19, 1988 incident, the victim testified that on two other occasions, she had stopped by appellant's room while intoxicated. During one of those times, she had laid down on his bed. When asked whether she had asked appellant again at that time what his penis size was, the victim testified that she did not remember.

Appellant took the stand in his own defense and offered an account of the incident and the events leading up to it which differed only as to the consent involved. According to appellant, the victim had begun communication with him after the school seminar by asking him of the size of his penis and of whether he would show it to her. Appellant had suspected that the victim wanted to pursue a sexual relationship with him because she had stopped by his room twice after the phone call while intoxicated, laying down on his bed with her legs spread and again asking to see his penis. He believed that his suspicions were confirmed when she initiated the April 19, 1988 encounter by stopping by his room (again after drinking), and waking him up.

Appellant testified that, on the day in question, he did initiate the first physical contact, but added that the victim warmly responded to his advances by passionately returning his kisses. He conceded that she was continually "whispering . . . no's," but claimed that she did so while "amorously . . . passionately" moaning. In effect, he took such protests to be thinly veiled acts of encouragement. When asked why he locked the door, he explained that "that's not something you want somebody to just walk in on you [doing.]"

According to appellant, the two then laid down on the bed, the victim helped him take her clothing off, and he entered her. He agreed that the victim continued to say "no" while on the bed, but carefully qualified his agreement, explaining that the statements were "moaned passionately." According to appellant, when he saw a "blank look on her face," he immediately withdrew and asked "is anything wrong, is something the matter, is anything wrong." He ejaculated on her stomach thereafter because he could no longer "control" himself. Appellant testified that after this, the victim "saw that it was over and then she made her move. She gets right off the bed . . . she just swings her legs over and then she puts her clothes back on." Then, in wholly corroborating an aspect of the victim's account, he testified that he remarked, "Well, I guess we got carried away," to which she rebuked, "No, we didn't get carried, you got carried away.'"

After hearing both accounts, the jury convicted appellant of rape and indecent assault.... Appellant was then sentenced to serve a term of imprisonment of one to four years for rape and a concurrent term of six to twelve months for indecent assault. Post-trial bail was granted pending this timely appeal. * * *

II. SUFFICIENCY OF THE EVIDENCE

Appellant's argument in this regard was well summarized by appellant's counsel in his brief.

> * * * Mr. Berkowitz prays that this Court overturns his rape conviction. He asks that this Court define the parameters between what may have been unacceptable social conduct and the criminal conduct necessary to support the charge for forcible rape.
>
> We contend that upon review, the facts show no more than what legal scholars refer to as "reluctant submission." The complainant herself admits that she was neither hurt nor threatened at any time during the encounter. She admits she never screamed or attempted to summon help. The incident occurred in a college dormitory in the middle of the afternoon.
>
> There has never been an affirmed conviction for forcible rape under similar circumstances. Not one factor which this Court has considered significant in prior cases, exists here. The uncontroverted evidence fails to establish forcible compulsion.

The Commonwealth counters:

> Viewing the evidence and its inferences in the light most favorable to the Commonwealth, the jury's conclusion that the Defendant's forcible conduct overcame [the victim's] will is reasonable. The assault was rapid and the victim was physically overcome. Because she was acquainted with the Defendant, [the victim] had no reason to be fearful or suspicious of him and her resorting to verbal resistance only is understandable. More importantly, perhaps, it is only her lack of consent that is truly relevant. It is entirely reasonable to believe that the Defendant sat on her, pushed her on the bed and penetrated her before she had time to fully realize her plight and raise a hue and cry. If the law required active resistance, rather [than] the simple absence of consent, speedy penetration would

immunize the most violent attacks and the goal-oriented rapist would reap an absurd reward. Certainly a victim must communicate her objections. But, contrary to the Defendant's arguments, Pennsylvania law says she can "just say no." [The victim] said "no." She said it repeatedly, clearly and sternly. She was rapidly, forcibly raped and deserves the protection of the law.

With the Commonwealth's position, the trial court agreed. We cannot.

In viewing the evidence, we remain mindful that credibility determinations were a matter solely for the fact finder below. On appeal, we must examine the evidence in the light most favorable to the Commonwealth drawing all reasonable inferences therefrom. If a jury could have reasonably determined from the evidence adduced that all of the necessary elements of the crime were established, then the evidence will be deemed sufficient to support the verdict.

In Pennsylvania, the crime of rape is defined by statute as follows:

A person commits a felony of the first degree when he engages in sexual intercourse with another person not his spouse:

(1) by forcible compulsion;
(2) by threat of forcible compulsion that would prevent resistance by a person of reasonable resolution;
(3) who is unconscious; or
(4) who is so mentally deranged or deficient that such person is incapable of consent.

18 Pa.C.S.A. § 3121. A statutory caveat to this rule may be found in section 3107 of title 18.

Resistance Not Required

The alleged victim need not resist the actor in prosecution under this chapter: Provided, however, that nothing in this section shall be construed to prohibit a defendant from introducing evidence that the alleged victim consented to the conduct in question.

The contours of Pennsylvania's rape statute, however, are not immediately apparent. As our Supreme Court explained in the landmark case, *Commonwealth v. Rhodes*:

"[F]orcible compulsion" as used in section 3121(1) includes not only physical force or violence but also moral, psychological or intellectual force used to compel a person to engage in sexual intercourse against that person's will.

Closely related to section 3121(1) is section 3121(2) which applies to the situation where "forcible compulsion" is not actually used but is threatened. That section uses the phrase "by threat of forcible compulsion that would prevent resistance by a person of reasonable resolution." The Model Penal Code used the terminology "compels her to submit by any threat that would prevent resistance by a woman of ordinary resolution" and graded that offense as gross sexual imposition, a felony of the third degree. The Pennsylvania legislature rejected the concept that sexual intercourse compelled by "gross imposition" should be graded as a less serious offense and, therefore, enacted section 3121(2). By use of the phrase "person of reasonable resolution," the legislature introduced an objective standard regarding the use of *threats* of forcible compulsion to prevent resistance (as opposed to actual application of "forcible compulsion.").

The determination of whether there is sufficient evidence to demonstrate beyond a reasonable doubt that an accused engaged in sexual intercourse by forcible compulsion (which we have defined to include "not only physical force or violence, but also moral, psychological or intellectual force used to compel a person to engage in sexual intercourse against that person's will"), or by the threat of such forcible compulsion that would prevent resistance by a person of reasonable resolution *is, of course, a determination that will be made in each case based upon the totality of the circumstances that have been presented to the fact finder.* Significant factors to be weighed in that determination would include the respective ages of the victim and the accused, the respective mental and physical conditions of the victim and the accused, the atmosphere and physical setting in which the incident was alleged to have taken place, the extent to which the accused may have been in a position of authority, domination or custodial control over the victim, and whether the victim was under duress. This list of possible factors is by no means exclusive.

Before us is not a case of mental coercion. There existed no significant disparity between the ages of appellant and the victim. They were both college sophomores at the time of the incident. Appellant was age twenty; the victim was nineteen. The record is devoid of any evidence suggesting that the physical or mental condition of one party differed from the other in any material way. Moreover, the atmosphere and physical setting in which the incident took place was in no way coercive. The victim walked freely into appellant's dorm room in the middle of the afternoon on a school day and stayed to talk of her own volition. There was no evidence to suggest that appellant was in any position of authority, domination or custodial control over the victim. Finally, no record evidence indicates that the victim was under duress. Indeed, nothing in the record manifests any intent of appellant to impose "moral, psychological or intellectual" coercion upon the victim.

Nor is this a case of a threat of forcible compulsion. When asked by defense counsel at trial whether appellant had at any point threatened her in any manner, the victim responded, "No, he didn't." Moreover, careful review of the record fails to reveal any express or even implied threat that could be viewed as one which, by the objective standard applicable herein, "would prevent resistance by a person of reasonable resolution."

Rather, the Commonwealth contends that the instant rape conviction is supported by the evidence of actual physical force used to complete the act of intercourse. Essentially, the Commonwealth maintains that, viewed in the light most favorable to it, the record establishes that the victim did not consent to engage in the intercourse, and thus, any force used to complete the act of intercourse thereafter constituted "forcible compulsion."

In response, appellant urges that the victim's testimony itself precludes a finding of "forcible compulsion." Appellant essentially argues that the indisputable lack of physical injuries and physical resistance proves that the evidence was insufficient to establish rape.

In beginning our review of these arguments, it is clear that any reliance on the victim's absence of physical injuries or physical resistance is misplaced. Although it is true that the instant victim testified that she was not "physically hurt in any fashion," and that it was "possible that [she] took no physical action to discourage [appellant]," such facts are insignificant in a sufficiency determination. As our Supreme Court has made clear, "'rape . . . is defined, not in terms of the physical injury to the victim, but in terms of the effect it has on the victim's volition.'" Similarly, our legislature has expressly commanded that the "victim *need not resist* the actor in prosecutions under" Chapter 31. As the *Rhodes* Court observed, this legislative mandate was intended to make it clear that "lack of consent is not synonymous with lack of resistance." Thus, while the *presence* of actual injury or physical resistance might well indicate "forcible compulsion," we are compelled to conclude that the absence of either or both is not fatal to the Commonwealth's case.

What is comparatively uncertain, however, in the absence of either an injury or resistance requirement, is the precise degree of actual physical force necessary to prove "forcible compulsion." As the *Rhodes* Court has made clear, no precise definition of the term "forcible compulsion" may be found.

The "force necessary to support convictions for rape and involuntary deviate sexual intercourse *need only be such as to establish lack of consent and to induce the woman to submit without additional resistance* . . . The degree of force required to constitute rape [or involuntary deviate sexual intercourse] is *relative* and *depends upon the facts and particular circumstances of the case.*"

The *Rhodes* Court specifically refused to "delineate all of the possible circumstances that might tend to demonstrate that sexual intercourse was engaged in by forcible compulsion or by threat of forcible compulsion within the meaning of [title 18] section 3121(1) and (2)." Rather, the Court left that delineation to evolve "in the best tradition of the common law – by development of a body of case law. . . . [W]hether there is sufficient evidence to demonstrate . . . that an accused engaged in sexual intercourse by forcible compulsion . . . is, of course, a determination that will be made in each case based on the *totality of the circumstances*. . . ." Thus, the ultimate task for the fact finder remains the question of whether, under the totality of circumstances, "the victim . . . was forced to . . . engage in sexual intercourse . . . *against his or her will.*"

Here, the victim testified that the physical aspects of the encounter began when appellant "kind of pushed me back with his body. It wasn't a shove, it was just kind of a leaning-type thing." She did not testify that appellant "pinned" her to the floor with his hands thereafter; she testified that he "started kissing me . . . [and] lift[ing] my shirt [and] bra . . . straddling me kind of . . . shifting at my body so that he was over me." When he attempted to have oral sex with her, appellant "knelt up straight . . . [and] tried to put his penis in my mouth . . . and after he obviously couldn't . . . he, we got up." Although appellant then locked the door, his act cannot be seen as an attempt to imprison the victim since she knew and testified that the type of lock on the door of appellant's dorm room simply prevented those on the outside from entering but could be opened from the inside without hindrance. Appellant did not push, shove or throw the victim to his bed; he "put" her on the bed, not in a "romantic" way, but not with a "fast shove either." Once on the bed, appellant did not try to restrain the victim with his hands in any fashion. Rather, while she was "just kind of laying there," he "straddled" her, "quick[ly] undid" the knot in her sweatpants, "took off" her sweatpants and underwear, placed the "weight of his body" on top of her and "guided" his penis inside her vagina.

Even in the light most favorable to the Commonwealth, the victim's testimony as to the physical aspects of the encounter cannot serve as a basis to prove "forcible compulsion." The cold record is utterly devoid of any evidence regarding the respective sizes of either appellant or the victim. As such, we are left only to speculate as to the coercive effect of such acts as "leaning" against the victim or placing the "weight of his body" on top of her. This we may not do. Moreover, even if the record indicated some disparity in the respective weights or strength of the parties, such acts are not themselves inconsistent with consensual relations. Except for the fact that appellant was on top of the victim before and during intercourse, there is no evidence that the victim, if she had wanted to do so, could not have removed herself from appellant's bed and walked out of the room without any risk of harm or danger to herself whatsoever. These circumstances simply cannot be bootstrapped into sexual intercourse by forcible compulsion.

Similarly inconclusive is the fact that the victim testified that the act occurred in a relatively brief period of time. The short time frame might, without more, indicate that the victim desired the sexual encounter as easily as it might that she didn't, given the fact that no threats or mental coercion were alleged. At most, therefore, the physical aspects of the encounter establishes that appellant's sexual advances may have been unusually rapid, persistent and virtually uninterrupted. However inappropriate, undesirable or unacceptable such conduct may be seen to be, it does not, standing alone, prove that the victim was "forced to engage in sexual intercourse against her will."

The only evidence which remains to be considered is the fact that both the victim and appellant testified that throughout the encounter, the victim repeatedly and continually said "no." Unfortunately for the Commonwealth, under the existing statutes, this evidence alone cannot suffice to support a finding of "forcible compulsion."

Evidence of verbal resistance is unquestionably relevant in a determination of "forcible compulsion." At least twice previously this Court has given weight to the failure to heed the victim's oral admonitions. In each such case, however, evidence of verbal resistance was only found sufficient where coupled with a sufficient threat of forcible compulsion, mental coercion, or actual physical force of a type inherently inconsistent with consensual sexual intercourse. Thus, although evidence of verbal protestations may be relevant to prove that the intercourse was against the victim's will, it is not dispositive or sufficient evidence of "forcible compulsion."

If the legislature had intended to define rape, a felony of the first degree, as non-consensual intercourse, it could have done so. It did not do this. It defined rape as sexual intercourse by "forcible compulsion." If the legislature means what it said, then where as here no evidence was adduced by the Commonwealth which established either that mental coercion, or a threat, or force inherently inconsistent with consensual intercourse was used to complete the act of intercourse, the evidence is insufficient to support a rape conviction. Accordingly, we hold that the trial court erred in determining that the evidence adduced by the Commonwealth was sufficient to convict appellant of rape. * * *

IV. CONCLUSION

For the foregoing reasons, we conclude that the evidence adduced by the Commonwealth was insufficient to convict appellant of rape. * * * The remaining issues appellant raises need not be addressed in view of this disposition. Accordingly, we *discharge* appellant as to the rape conviction. * * *

[There were no dissenting opinions.]

Note

Professor Lynne Henderson argues that "a primary impediment to recognition that rape is a real and frequent crime is a widely accepted cultural 'story' of heterosexuality that results in an unspoken 'rule' of male innocence and female guilt in law." Lynne Henderson, *Rape and Responsibility*, 11 Law & Phil. 127 (1992). Henderson explains:

> * * * We as a society still see women as responsible for "controlling" heterosexuality, and blame them when they do not, despite a concomitant belief that emphasizes male initiation and persistence in sexual matters. In bourgeois culture, in a bizarre distortion of causality, girls are raised to believe that their dress, makeup, hairstyle, walk, and talk determine male reactions. As Susan Estrich noted in 1985, Ann Landers, the popular advice columnist wrote, "'the woman who 'repairs to some private place for a few drinks and a little shared affection' has, by her acceptance of such a cozy invitation, given the man reason to believe she is a candidate to whatever he might have in mind.'" Landers doesn't seem to have changed her mind in the intervening years, despite feminist efforts to combat the ideology of female responsibility for rape. Landers published the following letter in 1991:

> > Dear Ann Landers: I hope I can put into words my personal theory on date rape...There is no hiding a man's arousal. Usually, the female enjoys bringing it on every bit as much as the man enjoys the experience. It is all part of human nature.

> > The problem is that for many men, there is only one way to end arousal and that is

ejaculation. At the height of ecstasy, does the female partner think the man is going to excuse himself, go...and take a cold shower? No way. *He wants the final act.*

...If the female partner has made up her mid that there is NOT going to be penetration, she should put a stop to the proceedings at the very first sign of male arousal. A female who doesn't want the total [sic] sexual experience should have healthy respect for flashing red warning light. If she goes beyond this point she could be in trouble.

Here, women control sex, but men lose control, and it is "only natural." Males are incapable of being aroused and then going without intercourse. Heterosexual contact or play inevitably requires intercourse. Men are entitled if women lead them on. Landers seemingly approves this vision, responding "I see a great deal of logic in what you have said" and ending her commentary with the statement that "The female who agrees to hours of petting but does not want to complete the sex act is asking for trouble and she will probably get it." Thus, because women are expected to control sexual activity, perversely they become responsible for rape.

Id. at 138-39. Do you agree with Professor Henderson or Ann Landers?

After *Berkowitz* was decided, the Pennsylvania Senate unanimously approved legislation that would have eliminated the force or the threat of force requirement for a rape conviction. In other words, sexual intercourse without the victim's consent and against the victim's will would have been sufficient for rape under the proposed legislation. *"No" Enough in State's Rape Bill*, S.D. Union Trib., June 15, 1994, at A-6. The Senate's action, however, did not carry the day. The Pennsylvania rape statute today still requires "forcible compulsion" or a "threat of forcible compulsion that would prevent resistance by a person of reasonable resolution." 18 Pa. Crim. Stat. Ann. § 3121 (2003).

Should the crime of rape be redefined to eliminate the force or threat of force element? In *State of New Jersey in the Interest of M.T.S.*, the Supreme Court of New Jersey doesn't formally eliminate the force requirement, but accomplishes almost the same result by suggesting that the requirement is satisfied simply by the act of sexual penetration without the permission of the victim.

STATE OF NEW JERSEY
IN THE INTEREST OF M.T.S.
Supreme Court of New Jersey
129 N.J. 422, 609 A.2d 1266 (1992)

HANDLER, J.

Under New Jersey law a person who commits an act of sexual penetration using physical force or coercion is guilty of second-degree sexual assault. The sexual assault statute does not define the words "physical force." The question posed by this appeal is whether the element of "physical force" is met simply by an act of non-consensual penetration involving no more force than necessary to accomplish that result.

That issue is presented in the context of what is often referred to as "acquaintance rape." The record in the case discloses that the juvenile, a seventeen-year-old boy, engaged in consensual kissing and heavy petting with a fifteen-year-old girl and thereafter engaged in actual sexual penetration of the girl to which she had not consented. There was no evidence or suggestion that the juvenile used any unusual or extra force or threats to accomplish the act of penetration.

The trial court determined that the juvenile was delinquent for committing a sexual assault. The Appellate Division reversed the disposition of delinquency, concluding that non-consensual penetration does not constitute sexual assault unless it is accompanied by some level of force more than that necessary to accomplish the penetration.

We granted the State's petition for certification.

I

The issues in this case are perplexing and controversial. We must explain the role of force in the contemporary crime of sexual assault and then define its essential features. We then must consider what evidence is probative to establish the commission of a sexual assault. The factual circumstances of this case expose the complexity and sensitivity of those issues and underscore the analytic difficulty of those seemingly-straightforward legal questions.

On Monday, May 21, 1990, fifteen-year-old C.G. was living with her mother, her three siblings, and several other people, including M.T.S. and his girlfriend. A total of ten people resided in the three-bedroom town-home at the time of the incident. M.T.S., then age seventeen, was temporarily residing at the home with the permission of the C.G.'s mother; he slept downstairs on a couch. C.G. had her own room on the second floor. At approximately 11:30 p.m. on May 21, C.G. went upstairs to sleep after having watched television with her mother, M.T.S., and his girlfriend. When C.G. went to bed, she was wearing underpants, a bra, shorts, and a shirt. At trial, C.G. and M.T.S. offered very different accounts concerning the nature of their relationship and the events that occurred after C.G. had gone upstairs. The trial court did not credit fully either teenager's testimony.

C.G. stated that earlier in the day, M.T.S. had told her three or four times that he "was going to make a surprise visit up in [her] bedroom." She said that she had not taken M.T.S. seriously and considered his comments a joke because he frequently teased her. She testified that M.T.S. had attempted to kiss her on numerous other occasions and at least once had attempted to put his hands inside of her pants, but that she had rejected all of his previous advances.

C.G. testified that on May 22, at approximately 1:30 a.m., she awoke to use the bathroom. As she was getting out of bed, she said, she saw M.T.S., fully clothed, standing in her doorway. According to C.G., M.T.S. then said that "he was going to tease [her] a little bit." C.G. testified that she "didn't think anything of it"; she walked past him, used the bathroom, and then returned to bed, falling into a "heavy" sleep within fifteen minutes. The next event C.G. claimed to recall of that morning was waking up with M.T.S. on top of her, her underpants and shorts removed. She said "his penis was into [her] vagina." As soon as C.G. realized what had happened, she said, she immediately slapped M.T.S. once in the face, then "told him to get off [her], and get out." She did not scream or cry out. She testified that M.T.S. complied in less than one minute after being struck; according to C.G., "he jumped right off of [her]." She said she did not know how long M.T.S. had been inside of her before she awoke.

C.G. said that after M.T.S. left the room, she "fell asleep crying" because "[she] couldn't believe that he did what he did to [her]." She explained that she did not immediately tell her mother or anyone else in the house of the events of that morning because she was "scared and in shock." According to C.G., M.T.S. engaged in intercourse with her "without [her] wanting it or telling him to come up [to her bedroom]." By her own account, C.G. was not otherwise harmed by M.T.S.

At about 7:00 a.m., C.G. went downstairs and told her mother about her encounter with M.T.S. earlier in the morning and said that they would have to "get [him] out of the house." While M.T.S. was out on an errand, C.G.'s mother gathered his clothes and put them outside in his car; when he returned, he was told that "[he] better not even get near the house." C.G. and her mother then filed a complaint with the police.

According to M.T.S., he and C.G. had been good friends for a long time, and their relationship "kept leading on to more and more." He had been living at C.G.'s home for about five days before the incident occurred; he testified that during the three days preceding the incident they had been "kissing and necking" and had discussed having sexual intercourse. The first time M.T.S. kissed C.G., he said, she "didn't want him to, but she did after that." He said C.G. repeatedly had encouraged him to "make a surprise visit up in her room."

M.T.S. testified that at exactly 1:15 a.m. on May 22, he entered C.G.'s bedroom as she was walking to the bathroom. He said C.G. soon returned from the bathroom, and the two began "kissing and all," eventually moving to the bed. Once they were in bed, he said, they undressed each other and continued to kiss and touch for about five minutes. M.T.S. and C.G. proceeded to engage in sexual intercourse. According to M.T.S., who was on top of C.G., he "stuck it in" and "did it [thrust] three times, and then the fourth time [he] stuck it in, that's when [she] pulled [him] off of her." M.T.S. said that as C.G. pushed him off, she said "stop, get off," and he "hopped off right away."

According to M.T.S., after about one minute, he asked C.G. what was wrong; she replied with a back-hand to his face. He recalled asking C.G. what was wrong a second time, and her replying, "how can you take advantage of me or something like that." M.T.S. said that he proceeded to get dressed and told C.G. to calm down, but that she then told him to get away from her and began to cry. Before leaving the room, he told C.G., "I'm leaving ... I'm going with my real girlfriend, don't talk to me ... I don't want nothing to do with you or anything, stay out of my life ... don't tell anybody about this ... it would just screw everything up." He then walked downstairs and went to sleep.

On May 23, 1990, M.T.S. was charged with conduct that if engaged in by an adult would constitute second-degree sexual assault of the victim, contrary to *N.J.S.A.* 2C:14-2c(1). * * * Following a two-day trial on the sexual assault charge, M.T.S. was adjudicated delinquent. After reviewing the testimony, the court concluded that the victim had consented to a session of kissing and heavy petting with M.T.S. The trial court did not find that C.G. had been sleeping at the time of penetration, but nevertheless found that she had not consented to the actual sexual act. Accordingly, the court concluded that the State had proven second-degree sexual assault beyond a reasonable doubt. On appeal, following the imposition of suspended sentences on the sexual assault and the other remaining charges, the Appellate Division determined that the absence of force beyond that involved in the act of sexual penetration precluded a finding of second-degree sexual assault. It therefore reversed the juvenile's adjudication of delinquency for that offense.

II

The New Jersey Code of Criminal Justice, *N.J.S.A.* 2C:14-2c(1), defines "sexual assault" as the commission "of sexual penetration" "with another person" with the use of "physical force or coercion."[3] An unconstrained reading of the statutory language indicates that both the act of "sexual penetration" and the use of "physical force or coercion" are separate and distinct elements of the offense. Neither the definitions section of *N.J.S.A.* 2C:14-1 to -8, nor the remainder of the Code of Criminal Justice provides assistance in interpreting the words "physical force." The initial inquiry is, therefore, whether the statutory words are unambiguous on their face and can be understood and applied in accordance with their plain meaning. The answer to that inquiry is revealed by the conflicting decisions of the lower courts and the arguments of the opposing parties. T he trial court held that "physical force" had been established by the sexual penetration of the victim without her consent. The Appellate Division believed that the statute requires some amount of force more than that necessary

---

[3] The sexual assault statute, *N.J.S.A.:* 2C:14-2c(1), reads as follows:

c. An actor is guilty of sexual assault if he commits an act of sexual penetration with another person under any one of the following circumstances:
(1) The actor *uses physical force or coercion,* but the victim does not sustain severe personal injury;
(2) The victim is one whom the actor knew or should have known was physically helpless, mentally defective or mentally incapacitated;
(3) The victim is on probation or parole, or is detained in a hospital, prison or other institution and the actor has supervisory or disciplinary power over the victim by virtue of the actor's legal, professional or occupational status;
(4) The victim is at least 16 but less than 18 years old and:
(a) The actor is related to the victim by blood or affinity to the third degree; or
(b) The actor has supervisory or disciplinary power over the victim; or
(c) The actor is a foster parent, a guardian, or stands in loco parentis within the household;
(5) The victim is at least 13 but less than 16 years old and the actor is at least 4 years older than the victim.

Sexual assault is a crime of the second degree.

to accomplish penetration.

The parties offer two alternative understandings of the concept of "physical force" as it is used in the statute. The State would read "physical force" to entail any amount of sexual touching brought about involuntarily. A showing of sexual penetration coupled with a lack of consent would satisfy the elements of the statute. The Public Defender urges an interpretation of "physical force" to mean force "used to overcome lack of consent." That definition equates force with violence and leads to the conclusion that sexual assault requires the application of some amount of force in addition to the act of penetration.

Current judicial practice suggests an understanding of "physical force" to mean "any degree of physical power or strength used against the victim, even though it entails no injury and leaves no mark." Resort to common experience or understanding does not yield a conclusive meaning. The dictionary provides several definitions of "force," among which are the following: (1) "power, violence, compulsion, or constraint exerted upon or against a person or thing," (2) "a general term for exercise of strength or power, esp. physical, to overcome resistance," or (3) "strength or power of any degree that is exercised without justification or contrary to law upon a person or thing." *Webster's Third New International Dictionary* 887 (1961). Thus, as evidenced by the disagreements among the lower courts and the parties, and the variety of possible usages, the statutory words "physical force" do not evoke a single meaning that is obvious and plain. Hence, we must pursue avenues of construction in order to ascertain the meaning of that statutory language. Those avenues are well charted. When a statute is open to conflicting interpretations, the court seeks the underlying intent of the legislature, relying on legislative history and the contemporary context of the statute. * * *

The provisions proscribing sexual offenses found in the Code of Criminal Justice, *N.J.S.A.* 2C:14-2c(1), became effective in 1979, and were written against almost two hundred years of rape law in New Jersey. The origin of the rape statute that the current statutory offense of sexual assault replaced can be traced to the English common law. Under the common law, rape was defined as "carnal knowledge of a woman against her will." American jurisdictions generally adopted the English view, but over time states added the requirement that the carnal knowledge have been forcible, apparently in order to prove that the act was against the victim's will. As of 1796, New Jersey statutory law defined rape as "carnal knowledge of a woman, forcibly and against her will." Those three elements of rape – carnal knowledge, forcibly, and against her will -- remained the essential elements of the crime until 1979.

Under traditional rape law, in order to prove that a rape had occurred, the state had to show both that force had been used and that the penetration had been against the woman's will. Force was identified and determined not as an independent factor but in relation to the response of the victim, which in turn implicated the victim's own state of mind. Thus, the perpetrator's use of force became criminal only if the victim's state of mind met the statutory requirement. The perpetrator could use all the force imaginable and no crime would be committed if the state could not prove additionally that the victim did not consent. Although the terms "non-consent" and "against her will" were often treated as equivalent, under the traditional definition of rape, both formulations squarely placed on the victim the burden of proof and of action. * * *

The presence or absence of consent often turned on credibility. To demonstrate that the victim had not consented to the intercourse, and also that sufficient force had been used to accomplish the rape, the state had to prove that the victim had resisted. According to the oft-quoted Lord Hale, to be deemed a credible witness, a woman had to be of good fame, disclose the injury immediately, suffer signs of injury, and cry out for help. Courts and commentators historically distrusted the testimony of victims, "assuming that women lie about their lack of consent for various reasons: to blackmail men, to explain the discovery of a consensual affair, or because of psychological illness." Evidence of resistance was viewed as a solution to the credibility problem; it was the "outward manifestation of nonconsent, [a] device for determining whether a woman actually gave consent." * * *

In many jurisdictions the requirement was that the woman have resisted to the utmost. "Rape is not committed unless the woman oppose the man to the utmost limit of her power." * * *

Critics of rape law agreed that the focus of the crime should be shifted from the victim's behavior to the defendant's conduct, and particularly to its forceful and assaultive, rather than sexual, character. Reformers also shared the goals of facilitating rape prosecutions and of sparing victims much of the degradation involved in bringing and trying a charge of rape. There were, however, differences over the best way to redefine the crime. Some reformers advocated a standard that defined rape as unconsented-to sexual intercourse; others urged the elimination of any reference to consent from the definition of rape. Nonetheless, all proponents of reform shared a central premise: that the burden of showing non-consent should not fall on the victim of the crime. In dealing with the problem of consent the reform goal was not so much to purge the entire concept of consent from the law as to eliminate the burden that had been placed on victims to prove they had not consented.

Similarly, with regard to force, rape law reform sought to give independent significance to the forceful or assaultive conduct of the defendant and to avoid a definition of force that depended on the reaction of the victim. Traditional interpretations of force were strongly criticized for failing to acknowledge that force may be understood simply as the invasion of "bodily integrity." In urging that the "resistance" requirement be abandoned, reformers sought to break the connection between force and resistance. * * *

III

* * * The reform statute defines sexual assault as penetration accomplished by the use of "physical force" or "coercion," but it does not define either "physical force" or "coercion" or enumerate examples of evidence that would establish those elements. Some reformers had argued that defining "physical force" too specifically in the sexual offense statute might have the effect of limiting force to the enumerated examples. The task of defining "physical force" therefore was left to the courts. * * *

[T]he New Jersey Code of Criminal Justice does not refer to force in relation to "overcoming the will" of the victim, or to the "physical overpowering" of the victim, or the "submission" of the victim. It does not require the demonstrated non-consent of the victim. As we have noted, in reforming the rape laws, the Legislature placed primary emphasis on the assaultive nature of the crime, altering its constituent elements so that they focus exclusively on the forceful or assaultive conduct of the defendant. * * *

The intent of the Legislature to redefine rape consistent with the law of assault and battery is further evidenced by the legislative treatment of other sexual crimes less serious than and derivative of traditional rape. The Code redefined the offense of criminal sexual contact to emphasize the involuntary and personally-offensive nature of the touching. Sexual contact is criminal under the same circumstances that render an act of sexual penetration a sexual assault, namely, when "physical force" or "coercion" demonstrates that it is unauthorized and offensive. Thus, just as any unauthorized touching is a crime under traditional laws of assault and battery, so is any unauthorized sexual contact a crime under the reformed law of criminal sexual contact, and so is any unauthorized sexual penetration a crime under the reformed law of sexual assault.

The understanding of sexual assault as a criminal battery, albeit one with especially serious consequences, follows necessarily from the Legislature's decision to eliminate non-consent and resistance from the substantive definition of the offense. Under the new law, the victim no longer is required to resist and therefore need not have said or done anything in order for the sexual penetration to be unlawful. The alleged victim is not put on trial, and his or her responsive or defensive behavior is rendered immaterial. We are thus satisfied that an interpretation of the statutory crime of sexual assault to require physical force in addition to that entailed in an act of involuntary or unwanted sexual penetration would be fundamentally inconsistent with the legislative purpose to eliminate any consideration of whether the victim resisted or expressed non-consent. * * *

Because the statute eschews any reference to the victim's will or resistance, the standard defining the role of force in sexual penetration must prevent the possibility that the establishment of the crime will turn on the alleged victim's state of mind or responsive behavior. We conclude, therefore, that any act of sexual penetration engaged in by the defendant without the affirmative and freely-given permission of the victim to the specific act of penetration constitutes the offense of sexual assault. Therefore, physical force in excess of that inherent in the act of sexual penetration is not required for such penetration to be unlawful. The definition of "physical force" is satisfied under *N.J.S.A.* 2C:14-2c(1) if the defendant applies any amount of force against another person in the absence of what a reasonable person would believe to be affirmative and freely-given permission to the act of sexual penetration. * * *

Today the law of sexual assault is indispensable to the system of legal rules that assures each of us the right to decide who may touch our bodies, when, and under what circumstances. The decision to engage in sexual relations with another person is one of the most private and intimate decisions a person can make. Each person has the right not only to decide whether to engage in sexual contact with another, but also to control the circumstances and character of that contact. No one, neither a spouse, nor a friend, nor an acquaintance, nor a stranger, has the right or the privilege to force sexual contact.

We emphasize as well that what is now referred to as "acquaintance rape" is not a new phenomenon. Nor was it a "futuristic" concept in 1978 when the sexual assault law was enacted. Current concern over the prevalence of forced sexual intercourse between persons who know one another reflects both greater awareness of the extent of such behavior and a growing appreciation of its gravity. Notwithstanding the stereotype of rape as a violent attack by a stranger, the vast majority of sexual assaults are perpetrated by someone known to the victim. One respected study indicates that more than half of all rapes are committed by male relatives, current or former husbands, boyfriends or lovers. Similarly, contrary to common myths, perpetrators generally do not use guns or knives and victims generally do not suffer external bruises or cuts. Although this more realistic and accurate view of rape only recently has achieved widespread public circulation, it was a central concern of the proponents of reform in the 1970s.

The insight into rape as an assaultive crime is consistent with our evolving understanding of the wrong inherent in forced sexual intimacy. It is one that was appreciated by the Legislature when it reformed the rape laws, reflecting an emerging awareness that the definition of rape should correspond fully with the experiences and perspectives of rape victims. Although reformers focused primarily on the problems associated with convicting defendants accused of violent rape, the recognition that forced sexual intercourse often takes place between persons who know each other and often involves little or no violence comports with the understanding of the sexual assault law that was embraced by the Legislature. Any other interpretation of the law, particularly one that defined force in relation to the resistance or protest of the victim, would directly undermine the goals sought to be achieved by its reform. * * *

Accordingly, we reverse the judgment of the Appellate Division and reinstate the disposition of juvenile delinquency for the commission of second-degree sexual assault.

2.   What Counts (or should count) as Consent?

Forcible rape generally requires proof that the sexual intercourse was without the consent of the victim. What if a woman initially consents to sexual intercourse, but then changes her mind? Should a man who persists in having sexual intercourse under such circumstances be found guilty of rape? The California Supreme Court provides its answers to these questions in *In re John Z.* What would Ann Landers say?

What if the victim said "no," but the defendant honestly believed she meant "yes"? Should a man who honestly but mistakenly believed his female partner was consenting, even though she said no, be absolved of liability for rape? The question of whether a mistaken belief in consent should be a defense raises the issue: What is the mens rea of rape?

Under the common law, rape was and continues to be described as general intent crime, suggesting that the intent to have sexual intercourse (intent to do the actus reus of rape) is the only mental state required for commission of the crime. One famous English case held, however, that a defendant could defend against a rape charge by claiming that he honestly believed the victim was consenting. *See Regina v. Morgan*, 1976 A.C. 182, 214. According to the *Morgan* court, a rape defendant may be acquitted even if his belief is completely unreasonable. *Morgan* suggests that forcible rape should be considered a specific intent crime because the defendant must intend more than just intercourse; in order to be convicted of rape, he must intend to have intercourse with a partner who does not consent.

In the United States, most jurisdictions recognize a mistake defense, but require that the defendant's mistake as to the victim's consent must be honest *and reasonable* in order to constitute a complete defense. Note that assertion of this affirmative defense (honest and reasonable belief in consent) is different from a claim that the victim was actually consenting.

What constitutes a reasonable belief in consent? If a substantial percentage of women say no when they really mean yes, is it "reasonable" for a man to think that a woman who says no really means yes? Several studies indicate that many women say "no" when they actually want to engage in sexual intercourse. Stephen Schulhofer, author of UNWANTED SEX: THE CULTURE OF INTIMIDATION AND THE FAILURE OF LAW (1998), reports:

> A 1988 survey of undergraduates at Texas A & M University presents an especially detailed look at this problem. Over 600 women were asked whether they had ever engaged in acts of token resistance when they really wanted to have sex. Thirty-nine percent of the women reported that they sometimes said "no" even though they "had every intention to and were willing to engage in sexual intercourse." Of the sexually experienced women in the survey, 61 percent said that they had done so. Though these women were willing to engage in intercourse – eventually – they didn't necessarily want the men to disregard their "no" and force them to submit right away. Instead, many of the women wanted their dates to wait or "talk me into it." But when a woman's "no" is equivocal, it means that her date, if he reads her intention correctly, should continue to press her for sex, perhaps in a physically assertive way. In fact, some of the women said that they told their date "no" because they "want[ed] him to be more physically aggressive."

> An obvious concern in this 1988 study is that the Texas A & M women may not be typical. The authors cautioned that students there showed an unusually strong tendency to view male-female relationships as adversarial and to endorse the kinds of assumptions about gender roles that were prevalent in the 1950s. But subsequent studies elsewhere report strikingly similar findings, with no regional differences. A 1994 study of students at universities in Hawaii, Texas, and the Midwest found that 38 percent of the women sometimes said "no" when they meant yes. In a 1995 study at Penn State, 37 percent of the women reported having said "no" when they meant yes. For most women, most of the time, "no" does mean no. But

sometimes it means maybe or "try harder to talk me into it." Sometimes, for some women, it means "get physical." * * *

Should the law require an affirmative yes as evidence of consent? In 1996, Antioch College implemented a new Sexual Offense Prevention Policy (reprinted below) requiring men and women engaging in sexual activity to acquire willing and verbal consent for each individual sex act. The policy met a firestorm of controversy.

In re JOHN Z.

Supreme Court of California

29 Cal.4th 756, 60 P.3d 183, 128 Cal.Rptr.2d 783 (2003)

CHIN, J.

We granted this case to settle a conflict in Court of Appeal decisions as to whether the crime of forcible rape (Pen. Code, § 261, subd. (a)(2)) is committed if the female victim consents to an initial penetration by her male companion, and then withdraws her consent during an act of intercourse, but the male continues against her will. (*Compare People v. Vela* (1985) 172 Cal. App. 3d 237, 218 Cal.Rptr. 161 (*Vela*) [no rape committed] *with People v. Roundtree* (2000) 77 Cal.App.4th 846, 91 Cal.Rptr.2d 921 (*Roundtree*) [rape committed].) We agree with *Roundtree* and the Court of Appeal in the present case that a withdrawal of consent effectively nullifies any earlier consent and subjects the male to forcible rape charges if he persists in what has become nonconsensual intercourse.

The juvenile court * * * found that [the defendant] committed forcible rape. * * * He was committed to Crystal Creek Boys Ranch. On appeal, defendant contends the evidence is insufficient to sustain the finding that he committed forcible rape. We disagree.

FACTS

The following facts are largely taken from the Court of Appeal opinion in this case. During the afternoon of March 23, 2000, 17-year-old Laura T. was working at Safeway when she received a call from Juan G., whom she had met about two weeks earlier. Juan wanted Laura to take him to a party at defendant's home and then return about 8:30 p.m. to pick him up. Laura agreed to take Juan to the party, but since she planned to attend a church group meeting that evening she told him she would be unable to pick him up.

Sometime after 6:00 p.m., Laura drove Juan to defendant's residence. Defendant and Justin L. were present. After arranging to have Justin L.'s stepbrother, P. W., buy them alcohol, Laura picked up P. W. and drove him to the store where he bought beer. Laura told Juan she would stay until 8:00 or 8:30 p.m. Although defendant and Juan drank the beer, Laura did not.

During the evening, Laura and Juan went into defendant's parents' bedroom. Juan indicated he wanted to have sex but Laura told him she was not ready for that kind of activity. Juan became upset and went into the bathroom. Laura left the bedroom and both defendant and Justin asked her why she "wouldn't do stuff." Laura told them that she was not ready.

About 8:10 p.m., Laura was ready to leave when defendant asked her to come into his bedroom to talk. She complied. Defendant told her that Juan had said he (Juan) did not care for her; defendant then suggested that Laura become his girlfriend. Juan entered the bedroom and defendant left to take a phone call.

When defendant returned to the bedroom, he and Juan asked Laura if it was her fantasy to have two guys, and Laura said it was not. Juan and defendant began kissing Laura and removing her clothes, although she kept telling them not to. At some point, the boys removed Laura's pants and underwear and began "fingering" her, "playing with [her] boobs" and continued to kiss her. Laura enjoyed this activity in the beginning, but objected when Juan removed his pants and told defendant to keep fingering her while he put on a condom. Once the condom was in place, defendant left the room and Juan got on top of Laura. She tried to resist and told him she did not want to have intercourse, but he was too strong and forced his penis into her vagina. The rape terminated when, due to Laura's struggling, the condom fell off. Laura told Juan that "maybe it's a sign we shouldn't be doing this," and he said "fine" and left the room. (Although Juan G. was originally a codefendant, at the close of the victim's testimony he admitted amended charges of sexual battery and unlawful sexual intercourse, a misdemeanor.)

Laura rolled over on the bed and began trying to find her clothes; however, because the room was dark she was unable to do so. Defendant, who had removed his clothing, then entered the bedroom and walked to where Laura was sitting on the bed and "he like rolled over [her] so [she] was pushed back down to the bed." Laura did not say anything and defendant began kissing her and telling her that she had "a really beautiful body." Defendant got on top of Laura, put his penis into her vagina "and rolled [her] over so [she] was sitting on top of him." Laura testified she "kept . . . pulling up, trying to sit up to get it out . . . and he grabbed my hips and pushed me back down and then he rolled me back over so I was on my back . . . and . . . kept saying, will you be my girlfriend." Laura "kept like trying to pull away" and told him that "if he really did care about me, he wouldn't be doing this to me and if he did want a relationship, he should wait and respect that I don't want to do this." After about 10 minutes, defendant got off Laura, and helped her dress and find her keys. She then drove home.

On cross-examination, Laura testified that when defendant entered the room unclothed, he lay down on the bed behind her and touched her shoulder with just enough pressure to make her move, a nudge. He asked her to lie down and she did. He began kissing her and she kissed him back. He rolled on top of her, inserted his penis in her and, although she resisted, he rolled her back over, pulling her on top of him. She was on top of him for four or five minutes, during which time she tried to get off, but he grabbed her waist and pulled her back down. He rolled her over and continued the sexual intercourse. Laura told him that she needed to go home, but he would not stop. He said, "just give me a minute," and she said, "no, I need to get home." He replied, "give me some time" and she repeated, "no, I have to go home." Defendant did not stop, "he just stayed inside of me and kept like basically forcing it on me." After about a "minute, minute and [a] half," defendant got off Laura.

Defendant testified, admitting that he and Juan were kissing and fondling Laura in the bedroom, but claimed it was with her consent. He also admitted having sexual intercourse with Laura, again claiming it was consensual. He claimed he discontinued the act as soon as Laura told him that she had to go home.

DISCUSSION

Although the evidence of Laura's initial consent to intercourse with John Z. was hardly conclusive, we will assume for purposes of argument that Laura impliedly consented to the act, or at least tacitly refrained from objecting to it, until defendant had achieved penetration. (But see § 261.6 [defining the type of consent at issue under section 261 as "positive cooperation in act or attitude pursuant to an exercise of free will"].) As will appear, we conclude that the offense of forcible rape occurs when, during apparently consensual intercourse, the victim expresses an objection and attempts to stop the act and the defendant forcibly continues despite the objection.

Vela held that where the victim consents to intercourse at the time of penetration but thereafter withdraws her consent, any use of force by her assailant past that point is not rape. The court in *Vela* found "scant authority" on point, relying on two out-of-state cases which had held that if consent is given prior to penetration, no rape occurs despite the withdrawal of consent during intercourse itself. According to *Vela*, these cases held that "the presence or absence of consent at the moment of initial penetration appears to be the crucial point in the crime of rape."

Vela agreed with these cases, reasoning that "the essence of the crime of rape is the outrage to the person and feelings of the female resulting from the nonconsensual violation of her womanhood. When a female willingly consents to an act of sexual intercourse, the penetration by the male cannot constitute a violation of her womanhood nor cause outrage to her person and feelings. If she withdraws consent during the act of sexual intercourse and the male forcibly continues the act without interruption, the female may certainly feel outrage because of the force applied or because the male ignores her wishes, but the sense of outrage to her person and feelings could hardly be of the same magnitude as that resulting from an initial nonconsensual violation of her womanhood. It would seem, therefore, that the essential guilt of rape as stated in . . . section 263 is lacking in the withdrawn consent scenario."

With due respect to *Vela* and the two sister state cases on which it relied, we find their reasoning unsound. First, contrary to *Vela*'s assumption, we have no way of accurately measuring the level of outrage the victim suffers from being subjected to continued forcible intercourse following withdrawal of her consent. We must assume the sense of outrage is substantial. More importantly, section 261, subdivision (a)(2), defines rape as "an act of sexual intercourse accomplished with a person not the spouse of the perpetrator . . . . where it is accomplished against a person's will by means of force, violence, duress, menace, or fear of immediate and unlawful bodily injury on the person or another." Nothing in section 261 conditions the act of rape on the degree of outrage of the victim. Section 263 states that "the essential guilt of rape consists in the outrage to the person and feelings of the victim of the rape. Any sexual penetration, however slight, is sufficient to complete the crime." But no California case has held that the victim's outrage is an element of the crime of rape. * * *

As the Court of Appeal in this case stated, "while outrage of the victim may be the cause for criminalizing and severely punishing forcible rape, outrage by the victim is not an element of forcible rape. Pursuant to section 261, subdivision (a)(2), forcible rape occurs when the act of sexual intercourse is accomplished against the will of the victim by force or threat of bodily injury and it is immaterial at what point the victim withdraws her consent, so long as that withdrawal is communicated to the male and he thereafter ignores it."

In the present case, assuming arguendo that Laura initially consented to, or appeared to consent to, intercourse with defendant, substantial evidence shows that she withdrew her consent and, through her actions and words, communicated that fact to defendant. Despite the dissent's doubt in the matter, no reasonable person in defendant's position would have believed that Laura continued to consent to the act. As the Court of Appeal below observed, "Given [Laura's testimony], credited by the court, there was nothing equivocal about her withdrawal of any initially assumed consent."

Vela appears to assume that, to constitute rape, the victim's objections must be raised, or a defendant's use of force must be applied, *before* intercourse commences, but that argument is clearly flawed. One can readily imagine situations in which the defendant is able to obtain penetration before the victim can express an objection or attempt to resist. Surely, if the defendant thereafter ignores the victim's objections and forcibly continues the act, he has committed "an act of sexual intercourse accomplished . . . . against a person's will by means of force . . . ."

Defendant, candidly acknowledging *Vela*'s flawed reasoning, contends that, in cases involving an initial consent to intercourse, the male should be permitted a "reasonable amount of time" in which to withdraw, once the female raises an objection to further intercourse. As defendant argues, "By essence of the act of sexual intercourse, a male's primal urge to reproduce is aroused. It is therefore unreasonable for a female and the law to expect a male to cease having sexual intercourse immediately upon her withdrawal of consent. It is only natural, fair and just that a male be given a reasonable amount of time in which to quell his primal urge . . . ."

We disagree with defendant's argument. Aside from the apparent lack of supporting authority for defendant's "primal urge" theory, the principal problem with his argument is that it is contrary to the language of section 261, subdivision (a)(2): Nothing in the language of section 261 or the case law suggests that the defendant is entitled to persist in intercourse once his victim withdraws her consent.

In any event, even were we to accept defendant's "reasonable time" argument, in the present case he clearly was given ample time to withdraw but refused to do so despite Laura's resistance and objections. Although defendant testified he withdrew as soon as Laura objected, for purposes of appeal we need not accept this testimony as true in light of Laura's contrary testimony. As noted above, Laura testified that she struggled to get away when she was on top of defendant, but that he grabbed her waist and pushed her down onto him. At this point, Laura told defendant that if he really cared about her, he would respect her wishes and stop. Thereafter, she told defendant *three* times that she needed to go home and that she did not accept his protestations he just needed a "minute." Defendant continued the sex act for at least four or five minutes after Laura *first* told him she had to go home. According to Laura, after the *third* time she asked to leave, defendant continued to insist that he needed more time and "just stayed inside of me and kept like basically forcing it on me," for about a "minute, minute and [a] half." Contrary to the dissent's concerns, the force defendant exerted in resisting Laura's attempts to stop the act was clearly ample to satisfy section 261, subdivision (a)(2). * * *

We disapprove *Vela*, to the extent that decision is inconsistent with our opinion. The judgment of the Court of Appeal is affirmed.

BROWN, J. (dissenting):

A woman has an absolute right to say "no" to an act of sexual intercourse. After intercourse has commenced, she has the absolute right to call a halt and say "no more," and if she is compelled to continue, a forcible rape is committed. Although California's rape statutes are gender neutral, the criminalization of more subtle forms of sexual violence reflects a new view of women as "responsible, autonomous beings who possess the right to personal, sexual, and bodily self-determination." Thus, both courts and legislatures have expanded the concept of rape to include spousal rape, lesser degrees of rape, and what has been characterized as postpenetration rape.

To the extent the majority holds the clear withdrawal of consent nullifies any earlier consent and forcible persistence in what then becomes nonconsensual intercourse is rape, not assault and battery as the Court of Appeal held in *People v. Vela*, I concur in that portion of its reasoning. However, because the majority ignores critical questions about the nature and sufficiency of proof in a postpenetration rape case, I cannot concur in the rest of the majority opinion. The majority opinion is deficient in several respects. First, the opinion fails to consider whether the victim's statements in this case clearly communicated her withdrawal of consent. Second, there is no attempt to define what constitutes force in this context. Finally, questions about wrongful intent are given short shrift.

The People must prove the elements of a crime beyond a reasonable doubt. As relevant to this case, "Rape is an act of sexual intercourse ... with a person not the spouse of the perpetrator" "accomplished against a person's will by means of force, violence, duress, menace, or fear of immediate and unlawful bodily injury on the person or another." Presumably, in a postpenetration rape case, the prosecution still has the burden of showing, beyond a reasonable doubt, that the victim clearly communicated withdrawal of consent and the defendant exercised some degree of force to continue. Moreover, a defendant's reasonable and good faith mistake of fact regarding a person's consent to sexual intercourse is a defense to rape. To be acquitted, a defendant need only raise a reasonable doubt as to his reasonable and honest belief in consent. Thus, to convict in such a case, the People must prove the absence of such a belief *beyond a reasonable doubt*.

Ordinarily, these cases involve a credibility contest in which the victim tells one story, the defendant another. The trial judge in this juvenile matter relied primarily on Laura's testimony and rejected John Z.'s testimony in its entirety. Even so, "assuming arguendo that Laura initially consented to, or appeared to consent to, intercourse with defendant," the facts in this case, as described solely by the prosecution witness, create doubt both about the withdrawal of consent and the use of force.

This is a sordid, distressing, sad little case. From any perspective, its facts are appalling. Laura T., a 17-year-old girl, finds herself alone in a house with four young men, ranging in age from 16 to 21. One of them, Juan, is "sort of" her boyfriend. Laura and Juan met at a bus stop near her workplace and had known each other for about two weeks when they arrived at the "party" at John Z.'s house on March 23, 2000. Laura drove to the party in her own vehicle. She planned to drop Juan off and leave. The other partygoers were unknown to Laura. John Z. was introduced to her after they arrived. Instead of leaving, Laura remained at John Z.'s house for several hours. During the evening she was openly affectionate with Juan, and sporadically engaged in some mutual kissing with John Z.-in the kitchen and later in the master bedroom when Juan was sulking in the bathroom.

This is how she described subsequent events:

Around 8:00 p.m., Laura decided she was ready to leave. Before she walked out the door, John asked if he could talk to her. She walked back into the house and went into his bedroom, which was completely dark. She did not ask to turn on the light. She entered the room willingly and was not restrained from leaving. They sat in the dark, talking. John told her Juan never cared about her, was only "using [her] and anyone else could use [her] too." John said he really liked her; she should dump Juan and become John's girlfriend. When Juan came into the bedroom, Laura confronted him with what John had said. He denied it. The boys asked if she had ever fantasized about having "two guys." Laura said she had not, but she continued to sit on the bed in John's darkened bedroom with both Juan and John while one or both of them removed various items of her clothing. At first, she tried to replace her clothing, but after pulling her bra back into place a couple of times, she made no further efforts to retrieve her clothes. Asked why she did not leave, she responded: "There is no reason. I just didn't. I didn't think about it. I had already tried to leave once, and they asked me to go in the bedroom and talk."

Feeling there was "no point in fighting" because there was nothing she could do about it anyway, she laid back on the bed, with Juan on one side of her and John on the other. She did not say anything and she was not fighting or resisting while the rest of her clothing was removed. The boys were "fingering" her and playing with her "boobs" and kissing her and "like just trying to like keep me satisfied type of thing." She acknowledged that she enjoyed these activities, enjoyed it "because it was like a threesome"; she was laughing and liked being the center of attention.

After that prelude and after she had intercourse with Juan, which ended when the condom kept falling off and she told him perhaps that was a sign they "shouldn't be doing this," we come to the facts which form the basis of John Z.'s adjudication. According to Laura, she was sitting on the bed naked when John Z. came into the room, naked or partially unclothed. She had been unable to find her clothes in the dark. John sat on the bed behind her and touched her with one hand on her shoulder. He did not pull or push her backward. He nudged her with one hand. His left hand was in a cast. She laid back down on the bed. John began kissing her. She kissed him back. He climbed on top of her and achieved penetration. She did not say anything. She did not push him away, slap him or strike him. He made no threats and he did not hurt her. John asked her repeatedly "will you be my girlfriend?"

He rolled over so she was on top. She remained in that position for four to five minutes. Although he held her only with one hand on her waist-not hard enough for her to feel the pressure or to create a bruise-she was unable to extricate herself or break the connection. There was no conversation when intercourse began and she said nothing while she was on top of him. When she found herself on the bottom again, she said: "If he really did care about me, he wouldn't be doing this to me and if he really did want a relationship, he should wait and respect that I don't want to do this." John responded: "I really do care about you." She never "officially" told him she did not want to have sexual intercourse.

Sometime later she said: "I should be going now." "I need to go home." John said: "Just give me a minute." Several minutes later, she said again: "I need to get home." He said: "[G]ive me some time." She said: "No. I have to go home." The third time she told him she had to go home she was a little more urgent. She never "officially" cried, but she was starting to. When asked if at anytime while having intercourse with John Z., she had told him "no," Laura answers: "No," and repeats her contingent statement. Calling a halt, her answers suggest, was entirely John Z.'s responsibility. He said he cared about her, "but he still just let it happen."

The majority finds Laura's "actions and words" clearly communicated withdrawal of consent in a fashion "no reasonable person in defendant's position" could have mistaken. But, Laura's silent and ineffectual movements could easily be misinterpreted. And, none of her statements are unequivocal. While Laura may have felt these words clearly conveyed her unwillingness, they could reasonably be understood as requests for reassurance or demands for speed. And, Laura's own testimony demonstrates that is precisely how John Z. interpreted what she said. Indeed, Laura demonstrates a similar ambivalence. When asked if she had made it clear to John that she didn't want to have sex, Laura says "I thought I had," but she acknowledges she "never officially told him" she did not want to have sexual intercourse. When asked by the prosecutor on redirect why she told John "I got to go home," Laura answers: "Because I had to get home so my mom wouldn't suspect anything."

Furthermore, even if we assume that Laura's statements evidenced a clear intent to withdraw consent, sexual intercourse is not transformed into rape merely because a woman changes her mind. As the majority acknowledges, by reason of Penal Code sections 261 and 263, " '[t]he crime of rape therefore is necessarily committed when a victim withdraws her consent during an act of sexual intercourse but is *forced* to complete the act. The statutory requirements of the offense are met as the act of sexual intercourse is *forcibly* accomplished against the victim's will.' " In other words, an act of sexual intercourse becomes rape under these circumstances if all the elements of rape are present. Under the facts of this case, however, it is not clear that Laura was forcibly compelled to continue. All we know is that John Z. did not instantly respond to her statement that she needed to go home. He requested additional time. He did not demand it. Nor did he threaten any consequences if Laura did not comply.

The majority relies heavily on John Z.'s failure to desist immediately. But, it does not tell us how soon would have been soon enough. Ten seconds? Thirty? A minute? Is persistence the same thing as force? And even if we conclude persistence should be criminalized in this situation, should the penalty be the same as for forcible rape? Such questions seem inextricably tied to the question of whether a reasonable person would know that the statement "I need to go home" should be interpreted as a demand to stop. Under these circumstances, can the withdrawal of consent serve as a proxy for both compulsion and wrongful intent?

The majority finds these deficiencies insignificant because this is a juvenile adjudication. But, if John Z. is convicted of a felony as an adult, the same juvenile adjudication will qualify as a strike.[a] * * *

I respectfully dissent.

THE ANTIOCH COLLEGE SEXUAL OFFENSE PREVENTION POLICY
Approved by the Board of Trustees on June 8, 1996

* * *

CONSENT

1.   For the purpose of this policy, "consent" shall be defined as follows: the act of willingly and verbally agreeing to engage in specific sexual behavior. See (4) below when sexual behavior is mutually and simultaneously initiated.

Because of the importance of communication and the potential dangers when misunderstanding exists in a sexual situation, those involved in any sexual interaction need to share enough of a common understanding to be able to adequately communicate: 1) requests for consent; and, 2) when consent is given, denied or withdrawn.

Note: Recognized American and international sign languages are considered a form of verbal language for the purpose of this policy.

2.   When sexual behavior is not mutually and simultaneously initiated, then the person who initiates sexual behavior is responsible for verbally asking for the consent of the other individual(s) involved.

3.   The person with whom sexual contact/conduct is initiated shall verbally express his/her willingness or must verbally express consent, and/or express his/her lack of willingness by words, actions, gestures, or any other previously agreed upon communication. Silence and/or non-communication must never be interpreted as consent.

---

[a]Justice Brown is referring to California's Three Strikes law which mandates 25 years for an individual with two strikes, i.e. two prior serious or violent felonies, who is convicted of a third felony which does not have to be serious or violent.

4.   When sexual behavior is mutually and simultaneously initiated, then the persons involved share responsibility for getting/giving or refusing/denying consent by words, actions, gestures or by any other previously agreed upon communication.

5.   Obtaining consent is an on-going process in any sexual interaction. Verbal consent should be obtained with each new level of physical and/or sexual behavior in any given interaction, regardless of who initiates it. Asking "Do you want to have sex with me?" is not enough. The request for consent must be specific to each act.

6.   If someone has initially consented but then stops consenting during a sexual interaction, she/he should communicate withdrawal of consent verbally (example: saying "no" or "stop") and/or through physical resistance (example: pushing away). The other individual(s) must stop immediately.

7.   In order for consent to be meaningful and valid under this policy:

      a)   the person not initiating must have judgment and control unimpaired by any drug or intoxicant administered to prevent her/his resistance, and/or which has been administered surreptitiously, by force or threat of force, or by deception;

      b)   the person not initiating must have judgment and control unimpaired by mental dysfunction which is known to the person initiating;

      c)   the person not initiating must not be asleep or unconscious;

      d)   the person initiating must not have forced, threatened, coerced, or intimidated the other individual(s) into engaging in sexual behavior.

8.   To knowingly take advantage of someone who is under the influence of alcohol, drugs, prescribed or over-the-counter medication is not acceptable behavior in the Antioch community.

3.   **Toward a Right of Sexual Autonomy?**

THE FEMINIST CHALLENGE IN CRIMINAL LAW
Stephen J. Schulhofer[a]
143 U. Pa. L. Rev. 2151 (1995)

* * * Several examples will illustrate the far-reaching implications of the conception of autonomy that is already broadly accepted within our culture. First, when is consent lacking? "No" means no, obviously. But an intrusion on the person requires more than just the absence of a clear "no." A physical intrusion on the person requires actual permission.

Would anyone think that a medical patient's ambivalence, or an ambiguous "maybe," was a consent to medical treatment or surgery? Obviously, anything less than clear affirmative permission would never count as consent. Imagine Atlas, an Olympic weightlifter, consulting a doctor about whether to have surgery on his elbow. The doctor really wants to perform the operation. He thinks Atlas will be very happy with the experience. But the weightlifter is uncertain. He thinks things may not work out the way the doctor has promised. And there is a risk of picking up a serious infection. So Atlas hesitates, says he just is not sure. Can the doctor just go ahead and start cutting? Would we ever treat the weightlifter's silence or indecision as equivalent to consent? No, obviously, but why not? No one compelled him to submit. If he really objected, all he had to do was say so! Yet we would never consider silence or ambivalence as equivalent to consent for surgery. To say that is not to patronize Atlas; it is simply to recognize an obvious violation of the physical autonomy of his person.

Why should the physical autonomy of a woman's body not be entitled to the same respect in a sexual encounter? Clear proof of an unequivocal "no" should not be required. Consent for an intimate physical intrusion into the body should mean in sexual interactions what it means in every other context -- affirmative permission clearly signaled by words or conduct. There are many ways to make permission clear without verbalizing the word "yes," and permission certainly need not be in writing. But permission must be an affirmative indication of actual willingness. Silence and ambivalence are not permission.

---

[a] Reprinted by permission.

Next, what if a woman does agree? What kinds of constraints violate her autonomy? Autonomy cannot mean freedom from all constraints upon choice, but it does entail freedom from those constraints that our culture identifies as illegitimate. The scope of that freedom is marked by the rights to bodily integrity and personal independence that existing legal principles already protect. This modest conception of personal autonomy offers boundaries that are specific and, yet, far reaching.

One example is sexual harassment in the workplace. This looks like an area that is hardly ripe for criminal sanctions. But if a supervisor tries to get sexual favors by offering a promotion (or by threatening to veto one), he is confronting the employee with alternatives (no matter whether we call them offers or threats) that his position gives him no right to impose. If the supervisor used his position to get an economic payoff from the employee, he would be guilty of extortion. If a professor threatened to withhold a good grade or a good recommendation until he got some cash from a student, again he would be guilty of extortion.

The worker or student should have the same right to control her sexuality that she has to control her wages or her bank account. What makes the woman's consent invalid is not that the supervisor's act involves too much pressure. What makes the consent invalid is that rules already settled in our culture deny the supervisor the right to require an employee to choose between her promotion and her legally protected interests. One of those interests should be -- and is -- her sexual independence. For the same reason, the high school principal who allegedly obtained sex from a student by threatening to block her graduation should certainly be guilty of a crime.

Two variations will make the implications clearer. Suppose that a highly paid fashion model wants to land a film role to enhance her career. The company's casting director says that unless she sleeps with him, she will not get the part. If you are looking for excessive pressure, this case will seem a lot harder than that of the student or employee. You may not feel sympathy for the model at all. But whether you feel sympathy or not, the violation of her autonomy is the same as in the previous cases. The man's action is extortionate, just as if he had insisted on a side-payment in cash. There is an improper constraint on the woman's freedom of choice under background rights that are already settled in our culture.

The converse of the model's situation, the "hard case" for this analysis, is that of a needy mother of four who finds a partner willing to support her. Suppose that the relationship deteriorates, and the man threatens to kick her out of the apartment unless she continues to meet his sexual demands. Obviously, the needy mother has far less freedom of choice than the successful fashion model does. But the relevant question has to be whether the man's threatened actions are illicit. In the model's situation, the pressure may be slight, but it is clearly impermissible. In the mother's case, the pressure, though severe, might not be illicit. A sexual quid pro quo is not a legitimate condition of ordinary employment, but sexual fulfillment is, for both men and women, an appropriate and valued goal of ongoing, intimate personal relationships. Thus, although the man's action in imposing a sexual condition on his willingness to continue his relationship with the needy mother could be criticized as insensitive in many contexts, it nonetheless involves an exercise of his autonomy that society ordinarily considers legitimate and worthy of social protection. It makes sense to ask whether the nature of the relationship is sufficient to give her a right to remain in the apartment or to receive financial support, and if she does have such a right, the man's threats should render any consent to sex invalid. But if existing norms do not protect her from this sort of economic pressure, then her decision to remain in the relationship, although highly constrained, is not improperly tainted, and her consent to sex would therefore be valid.

With these principles in mind, we can return to the cases mentioned earlier -- the man who takes the woman's car keys and the man whose intimidated girlfriend no longer tries to fight back. In the first case, there is a kind of consent, ultimately the woman says "OK," but the consent is tainted by a clear violation of her right to leave. In the second case, there is never any affirmative permission at all. These cases make clear that one thing missing in the law of rape is some way to punish sexual misconduct that is not physically violent. It is as if we had a law against armed robbery but no law against theft. The way to fill that gap is not to try expanding what we mean by force but to have statutes punishing, as an offense distinct from forcible rape, any sexual imposition without valid consent. Thus, the men in these two cases should, at a minimum, be convicted of sexual misconduct.

We get these results without having to sort out degrees of force and without having to treat women as dominated or disempowered. The key is in the background structure of rights and privileges that determine what uses of personal power and institutional position are permissible, against either the weak or the strong, against either men or women in our society.

This approach identifies a baseline of existing rights, and it leaves room for evolution in the standards for valid consent. Respect for a woman's autonomy should mean that her interest in controlling her sexual choices receives just as much protection as any person's interest in controlling her property, her labor, or her freedom of action in other areas of life.

Note

Professor Schulhofer argues that the law of sexual offenses should protect a broad right of sexual autonomy.

> [T]he law of sexual abuse should be reorganized around two . . . distinct groups of offenses, with one or two degrees of each. "Rape" should reach intercourse by force, in the sense of actual or threatened physical violence. A new offense, "sexual abuse" or "sexual misconduct" would reach nonviolent interference with freedom of choice. To restrain the impact of cultural inertia on interpretation of the latter offense, it might even be named "nonviolent sexual abuse" or "sexual misconduct without force."

Stephen J. Schulhofer, *Taking Sexual Autonomy Seriously*, 11 Law & Phil. 35, 74 (1992).

Today, many states punish more than just forcible rape. Sexual intercourse with a person who is unconscious or mentally or developmentally challenged and sexual intercourse procured by some types of fraud are examples of sexual offenses that do not involve the element of force or threat of force, yet are defined as rape in some jurisdictions. Do such crimes reflect Schulhofer's concept of a right of sexual autonomy?

In *State v. Scherzer*, the court examines a case involving apparently consensual and nonforcible intercourse with a mentally retarded girl. The next case, *Boro v. Superior Court*, discusses the common law distinction between fraud-in-the-factum and fraud-in-the-inducement. At common law, if sexual intercourse was procured by deceit or fraud about the nature of the act (i.e., fraud-in-the-factum), then the victim's consent was considered null and void. If, however, the victim was induced to engage in the sexual intercourse by a false promise or some other deceit, but knew she was consenting to sexual intercourse, then her consent was considered valid for purposes of rape law and a charge of rape could not be sustained.[a] Does this distinction in *Boro* make sense? Is it trying to do the work that a right to sexual autonomy might accomplish more straightforwardly?

---

[a] Although sexual intercourse achieved by fraud-in-the-inducement was not considered rape at common law, in some jurisdictions, it was deemed the lesser crime of seduction by statute.

STATE v. SCHERZER

Superior Court of New Jersey
301 N.J. Super. 363, 694 A.2d 196 (1997)

SHEBELL, P.J

In May 1990, defendants, Kevin Scherzer and Kyle Scherzer, twin brothers, were indicted, along with three co-defendants, Peter Quigley, Richard Corcoran, Jr., and John Maher, on various sexual assault charges allegedly committed against a mentally defective victim, M.G. In September 1990, the prosecutor's application to have three juveniles, Christopher Archer, his brother Paul Archer, and Bryant Grober, tried as adults was granted. Therefore, in September 1991, a superseding indictment was obtained charging all eight defendants with second degree conspiracy to commit aggravated sexual assault (Count One); two counts of first degree aggravated sexual assault (sexual penetration of mentally defective person) (Counts Two and Four); two counts of first degree aggravated sexual assault (sexual penetration using physical force or coercion) (Counts Three and Five); and four counts of third degree aggravated criminal sexual contact (Counts Six, Seven, Eight, and Nine). * * *

* * * The three appellants, Kevin Scherzer, Kyle Scherzer and Christopher Archer, were convicted of second degree conspiracy to commit aggravated sexual assault (Count One), and first degree aggravated sexual assault by force or coercion (Count Three). They were acquitted of Counts Four through Nine. In addition, Christopher Archer and Kevin Scherzer were convicted of first degree aggravated sexual assault upon a mentally defective person (Count Two), and Kyle Scherzer was convicted of the lesser included offense of second degree attempted aggravated sexual assault. * * *

Kyle and Kevin Scherzer and Christopher Archer, appeal. * * *

FACTS

M.G. lived in Glen Ridge most of her life, where she attended special education classes at the elementary and middle schools. In 1989, when seventeen years of age, she attended classes for the "educably mentally retarded" at West Orange High School. She participated in athletics programs, such as softball and basketball, at Glen Ridge High School. Defendants were also Glen Ridge residents and M.G. had known them since grade school.

At trial M.G. testified that on the afternoon of March 1, 1989, she went to Carteret Park in Glen Ridge, to play basketball. There she saw the Archer brothers, Corcoran, and another boy. While she was shooting baskets, Christopher Archer, Grober, Quigley, and two other boys greeted her. In her direct testimony, M.G. said that Grober told her that if she went to the Scherzers' basement with them she would get to go out with Paul. However, on cross-examination she said that she went up to Grober, placed her hand on his crotch, and said something to the effect of "Nice package you have there. Would you like a blow job?" On redirect, she stated the latter testimony was a lie, as she did not want to hurt people.

She said she walked to the Scherzers' house with Christopher Archer, who put his arm around her shoulders. She viewed this as "romantic." When they arrived, there were already "a lot of people" on the stairs and in the basement. Others started setting up chairs near the couch, while she and Grober sat on the couch. M.G. said that when some of the boys asked her to, she took off her sweat pants and T-shirt. Thereafter, at the urging of the boys, sexual activity occurred beginning with M.G. inserting her fingers in her vagina, her masturbating and performing fellatio on five of the young men, permitting Kevin to insert a broomstick and Christopher to insert the handle of a baseball bat into her vagina. She said she permitted Corcoran to put a small stick in her vagina. Four of the boys also sucked on her breasts. Before she left, some of the boys told her "not to tell anybody" or they would tell her mother and she would "get in trouble."

Paul Archer, called on behalf of the defense, testified to a different account of the events. He said he and Quigley went to the park because he had heard some baseball players would be throwing the ball around. When they arrived, they went over to talk to the Scherzer brothers and some other friends who were on the basketball court. Soon afterward, Grober and Christopher arrived. Then M.G. arrived carrying a basketball and went directly to Grober. Paul overheard M.G. say, "Bryant, you're really hot. You're sexy. I like your bod[y]. You have a nice package." Grober appeared startled. Paul said that in all the years he had known Grober, he had never before seen him engage in conversation with M.G. After M.G. made these comments to Grober, Paul saw her reach for Grober's crotch, and Grober lunged back. M.G. then asked if Grober wanted a "blow job." At first Grober did not take her seriously, but after they talked, he asked if she meant it.

Paul and Quigley walked to the Scherzers' house, where there were "a couple of guys" playing Nintendo in the basement. Soon, Grober and M.G. appeared. Paul observed Grober drop his pants, and M.G. kneel down and perform fellatio. After a while, he saw Grober rest his hand on M.G.'s shoulder, but did not observe him exert pressure. Grober then moved his hand to the top of M.G.'s head, but once again no pressure was exerted. He did not hear M.G. say any words of resistance. According to Paul, the entire act took about thirty seconds. Grober then sat down and did not participate in any other sexual activity with M.G.

According to Paul, M.G., who was "totally in control" of the events, then said that "that blow job just got me so horny, I want to have sex with someone." When no one responded, she stood up, pulled down her pants, and then laid down on the couch. He said she then placed her fingers followed by the other objects into her vagina voluntarily. Kevin and Christopher helped her move the broomstick in and out. On cross-examination, Paul admitted that he had testified, when the judge was taking his guilty plea, that his brother and Kevin had inserted the broomstick into M.G., but said that testimony was a mistake.

He said that as people started to leave, M.G. walked to him, pulled up her shirt and bra, and said, "Paul, don't you like my breasts?" She asked him to touch them, but he refused. He said no one else touched her breasts, nor did he observe M.G. masturbating any of the boys or anyone doing anything with a stick. When M.G. asked if the boys wanted to "come back another day and do it again," no one responded. Some of the boys said, "[Y]ou're not going to say anything about this?" and she said no. He said that the entire incident, from the time M.G. first walked up to Grober at the park until she left the basement, lasted about twenty minutes.

Three boys who said they left the basement soon after the sexual activity began testified for the State. They agreed that M.G.'s activities with Grober, which is all they witnessed, appeared to be voluntary, as they did not see Grober use any force.

The first adult to whom M.G. related the incident was her swimming instructor, who testified that on March 3, 1989, after the swim class, M.G. came to talk to her, but seemed hesitant. M.G. said she had gone to a party during the week, that there were boys there, and that "something had happened." When asked what happened, M.G. said she did not want to talk about it now. The next day the instructor talked to M.G. in the locker room. M.G. told her she had gone to someone's basement and the boys asked her to "suck their dicks" and "stuck something up [her] butt." The instructor told M.G.'s classroom teacher at West Orange High School about the incident. The teacher informed M.G.'s parents about a week after the incident occurred. When M.G. learned that the instructor had told others about the incident, she was angry and said that it was her own fault that the "boys got in trouble" and that "she was going to lie."

M.G.'s mother took her to a gynecologist on March 14, 1989, however, a pelvic examination showed nothing abnormal. Her mother first met with the Glen Ridge police on March 22, 1989, and on March 27, 1989, M.G. and her mother met with Detective Sheila Byron. They brought a stick M.G. had brought home after the incident. Detective Byron became the principal investigator on the case.

M.G. gave the prosecution four statements – on April 7, May 5, May 18, and August 3, 1989. In the third statement the word "forced" in the phrase "additional acts were forced upon me" was crossed out and changed to "done." The investigator who took the statement from M.G. testified that he made the change because he did not think she knew "what the concept of the word force was." However, under cross-examination, M.G. testified that she requested the change because the acts were not forced on her. * * *

The State presented numerous witnesses who testified concerning M.G.'s personality, mental acuity, and the way she was perceived by others. A teacher who taught M.G. and other educable mentally retarded students at West Orange High School, said that M.G. functioned verbally on a second-grade level, had poor self-esteem, and was "very easily led" by people whom she hoped would like her. An instructor, who in 1982 taught tennis to a group of children that included M.G. and the Archers, all about eleven or twelve at the time, testified that the other children, including the Archers, would call M.G. "stupid" and "a retard." He said that when he offered M.G. the opportunity to be in a different group, she said those boys were her friends and she wanted to be with them.

Dawn Lipinski, the sister of M.G.'s friend Jennifer Lipinski, testified that "everyone knows that [M.G.] is different." She also said that M.G. would "do anything that she's asked to do" and that she had never heard her say no to any request. M.G.'s sister also said that everybody knew that M.G. was different. She testified that M.G. talks as if she is five or six years old, cannot follow simple instructions, and does not understand money. As an example of how easily led M.G. was, her sister said that when M.G. was five years old, a group of children, including Kyle and Kevin, persuaded her to eat dog feces.

M.G.'s mother testified about the social problems that emerged when M.G. was attending Columbia High School in Maplewood in 1987. She said M.G. would act the part of the class clown, setting herself up for ridicule. M.G.'s teachers at Columbia were concerned she might be raped. This led her mother to have her gynecologist prescribe birth control pills for her. M.G.'s mother also testified that, prior to the incident, M.G. had received sexual phone calls from Christopher Archer.

A guidance counselor at Columbia High School, testified about the sexual incidents in which M.G. was involved while at Columbia. M.G. told someone that "she wanted to be fucked," she would regularly exchange sexual comments with a group of football players in the cafeteria, and someone once touched her breast in health class. After these incidents, the guidance counselor claimed to have told M.G. that she had a right to refuse to allow someone to touch her body, but she could not understand this concept, especially when the person touching her was a friend.

The young men who testified at trial about the incident, three for the State and one for the defense, Paul Archer, all acknowledged it was common knowledge that M.G. was different. She was described as hard to communicate with, and as "slower, simple," something one could recognize after a few minutes of conversation. She associated mainly with younger children, was subjected to teasing, was the butt of jokes, was in special education classes, and was called "a retard."

The State presented three expert witnesses: Dr. Susan Esquilin, a psychologist specializing in the area of sexual abuse; Dr. Gerald Meyerhoff, a psychiatrist specializing in the field of child and adolescent psychiatry and mental retardation in children and adolescents; and Dr. Ann Burgess, a registered nurse with a doctorate in psychiatric mental health nursing and a specialist in the field of rape trauma.

Dr. Esquilin administered an I.Q. test on which M.G. scored 64, the mildly-mentally retarded range. On the adaptive behavior test, which measures daily living skills, M.G. scored in the top half, when compared to other retarded people. According to Esquilin, M.G. had a high risk of victimization because "she so focused on what somebody else wants and needs and not what she feels she wants and needs. . . . She's likely to do what anybody asks her to do." Esquilin expressed the opinion that M.G. is mentally defective, as she is incapable of exercising the right to refuse to engage in sexual conduct, and understands coercion only as the use of physical force. To M.G., her sexuality was a way of pleasing others. Esquilin's review of the Ferraez tapes strengthened her opinion that M.G. was susceptible to coercion and social pressure and that she had an immature concept of friendship.

Dr. Meyerhoff diagnosed M.G. as mildly-mentally retarded and suffering from attention-deficit hyperactivity disorder, residual state. * * * In his opinion, M.G. was "mentally defective" because although she understood that she was engaging in conduct of a sexual nature, she did not understand that she had the right to refuse to participate in the sexual activity. * * * Under cross-examination he acknowledged M.G. was at times sexually aggressive because sexual activity fulfilled her need for friendship, which "was an important part of her life." He also acknowledged that she was capable of lying and being deceptive.

Dr. Burgess, who had co-authored a pioneering study on rape trauma syndrome ("RTS") in 1974, testified about the kinds of reactions she had observed in rape victims and how her observations served to dispel such common myths as that victims immediately report a rape or that all victims display an emotional demeanor after an attack. She said that adolescent rape victims often do not disclose information about rape immediately, especially when the assailant is known to them, because they have divided loyalties about the assailant and fear retaliation. Recantation may be a way of protecting the assailant from getting into trouble or for the victim to deny that the rape occurred. * * *

Additionally, Burgess testified that M.G. suffered from RTS, as M.G. reported the incident only to people with whom she felt safe, and because of the type of friendship she desired with defendants. * * *

I

We first consider whether the judge erred in denying defendants' judgments of acquittal and whether the jury's verdicts were against the weight of evidence. * * *

[The court holds that there was sufficient evidence to support the defendants' conviction for conspiracy to commit aggravated sexual assault.]

The judge also denied defendants' motions for judgments of acquittal on the counts charging aggravated sexual assault under N.J.S.A. 2C:14-2a(5)(a) and (b). The offenses are defined by the Code as follows:

> a. An actor is guilty of aggravated sexual assault if he commits an act of sexual penetration with another person under any one of the following circumstances:
>
> . . . .
>
> (5) The actor is aided or abetted by one or more other persons and either of the following circumstances exists:
> (a) The actor uses *physical force or coercion,* or
> (b) The victim is one whom the actor knew or should have known was physically helpless, *mentally defective* or mentally incapacitated; . . . .

[Emphasis added.]

Under N.J.S.A. 2C:14-1c, "sexual penetration" can mean vaginal intercourse, fellatio, or insertion of fingers or objects into the vagina either by the actor or by the victim upon the actor's instruction, with depth of insertion irrelevant to whether the crime was committed. In *State in the Interest of M.T.S.,* the Supreme Court held that the definition of "physical force" in *N.J.S.A.* 2C:14-2a(5)(a) is satisfied "if the defendant applies any amount of force against another person in the absence of what a reasonable person would believe to be affirmative and freely-given permission to the act of sexual penetration." There need be no more physical force than that "inherent in the act of sexual penetration." * * *

Therefore, on the third count, the State had to prove that defendants engaged in an act of sexual penetration while aided or abetted by at least one other person and that defendants used force or coercion. Viewing the State's evidence as to defendants' use of force or coercion in a light most favorable to it * * *, we are convinced that the State failed to present enough evidence to prove to a reasonable jury that force or coercion were used against M.G. Her testimony and conduct clearly reflect that her engaging in the sexual activity in question was voluntary for purposes of N.J.S.A. 2C:14-2a(5)(a), and did not involve force or coercion.

M.G. never testified that the sexual activity was done without her consent. There was no evidence that physical force without permission, as defined by *M.T.S,* was used by defendants. Nor did we find it reasonable on the evidence presented to infer that force or coercion was engaged in by or on behalf of defendants. Persuasion is not coercion under N.J.S.A. 2C:14-2a(5)(a) merely because the victim is mentally defective, as such conduct is specifically covered under subsection (b). Nor is there any indication that M.G. was in any way intimidated by the size or number of the boys present.

In any event, even if a judgment of acquittal were denied, Count Three, charging penetration using physical force or coercion, must ultimately fail as a manifest denial of justice. Paul Archer and two other boys present testified to the absence of force and the voluntariness of M.G.'s actions in the Scherzer basement. M.G.'s own testimony fails to support a finding of force or coercion. She said on direct that she went to the basement because Grober said she would be able to go out with Paul Archer if she did. Even if defendants did lure her to the basement with promises of a date with Paul, the trial judge correctly instructed the jury that being promised a date with Paul was not enough to constitute criminal coercion. Moreover, on cross-examination she said that she went up to Grober at the park, placed her hand on his crotch, and asked him if he wanted her to give him a blow job. Although on redirect, she said that the latter testimony was a lie, Paul testified to substantially that account of the incident. M.G. also said that she did not try to leave the basement because she wanted to stay, and that she could have left if she wanted to. M.G. said she had the prosecutor change the word "forced" to "done" in her August 3, 1989 statement because the acts were not forced on her. * * * The jury also heard Dr.

Meyerhoff describe M.G. as sexually aggressive. Under no proper theory of force or coercion could a reasonable jury find those elements of the offense beyond a reasonable doubt on the admissible facts and applicable law.

However, a different conclusion results as to Count Two. N.J.S.A. 2C:14-1(h) defines "mentally defective" as a condition that renders one "temporarily or permanently incapable of understanding the nature of [one's] conduct, including, but not limited to, being incapable of providing consent." The Supreme Court clarified this definition [in a case called *Olivio*] by specifying that the mentally defective person must be "unable to comprehend the distinctively sexual nature of the conduct, or incapable of understanding or exercising the right to refuse to engage in such conduct with another." Thus, as to this count, the inquiry is whether the State presented sufficient evidence for a reasonable jury to conclude that defendants, knowing that M.G. was mentally defective, purposely engaged in sexual penetration while aided or abetted by at least one other person.

The State presented two experts, Doctors Esquilin and Meyerhoff, who expressed their opinion that M.G. was mentally defective under the *Olivio* standard because, although M.G. understood that she was engaging in conduct of a sexual nature, she did not understand that she had the right to refuse. Defendants had known her since grade school, and thus it was reasonable to infer they were aware of this defect. M.G.'s tennis teacher testified that in 1982 the Archers were among those who called M.G. "stupid" and "a retard." M.G.'s sister and Dawn Lipinski both testified that everyone knew that M.G. was "different."

M.G.'s friends, family, and teachers testified to her inability to say no to any request because she wanted to please people and to her use of sexuality to make friends. Lipinski said she had never heard M.G. say no to any request. M.G.'s sister related an incident that occurred when M.G. was five years old – a group of children, including Kyle and Kevin, persuaded her to eat dog feces – as an example of how easily led she was. M.G.'s mother testified about phone calls of a sexual nature that M.G. received from Christopher Archer. M.G.'s high school guidance counselor testified that after she learned M.G. was engaging in sexual conversations with a group of football players in the cafeteria and had allowed someone to touch her breast in health class, she told M.G. that she had a right not to allow someone to touch her body, but that she did not appear to understand the concept, especially when the person touching her was someone she considered to be a friend.

The State presented ample evidence that all three defendants were aware of M.G.'s acquiescent nature in sexual and other matters and that they had taken advantage of that aspect of her personality in the past. Even if they could not be expected to have labeled her as "mentally defective," they, as reasonable young persons were shown under the circumstances presented to have known that M.G. did not understand that she could say no to a request. This we hold to be sufficient under N.J.S.A. 2C:14-2a(5)(b).

There was no dispute that vaginal penetration of M.G. occurred, and according to M.G.'s testimony, all three defendants were involved in either preparing, inserting, or trying to insert, either the broom handle or the bat into M.G. while she lay on the couch. That the bat may not have actually entered M.G. is irrelevant since it touched her vaginal area. * * *

* * * We conclude that as to the convictions on all counts other than Count Three, it does not appear "that there was a miscarriage of justice under the law."

Quite the contrary, the evidence weighed heavily in favor of the jury's verdicts. Only on the force or coercion count, was there insufficient evidence of the use of force or coercion. On the basis of the permissible evidence presented to the jury, we conclude that the jury could rationally have found that all the elements required to prove the remaining counts on which defendants were convicted were proved beyond a reasonable doubt and that the jury's verdicts were not against the weight of evidence. * * *

We vacate defendants' convictions only on Count Three. * * *

The judge on resentencing must note that defendants were not proved to have committed sexual assault by force or coercion and that consequently all have one less conviction. * * *

Affirmed in part and reversed in part.   Remanded for resentencing.

BORO v. SUPERIOR COURT

Court of Appeal of California, First Appellate District, Division One
163 Cal. App. 3d 1224, 210 Cal.Rptr. 122 (Ct. App. 1985)

NEWSOM, J.

By timely petition filed with this court, petitioner Daniel Boro seeks a writ of prohibition to restrain further prosecution of count II of the information on file against him in San Mateo County Superior Court No. C-13489 charging him with a violation of Penal Code section 261, subdivision (4), rape: "an act of sexual intercourse accomplished with a person not the spouse of the perpetrator, under any of the following circumstances: . . . (4) Where a person is at the time unconscious of the nature of the act, and this is known to the accused."[1]

Petitioner contends that his motion to dismiss should have been granted with regard to count II because the evidence at the preliminary hearing proved that the prosecutrix, Ms. R., was aware of the "nature of the act" within the meaning of section 261, subdivision (4). The Attorney General contends the opposite, arguing that the victim's agreement to intercourse was predicated on a belief – fraudulently induced by petitioner – that the sex act was necessary to save her life, and that she was hence unconscious of the *nature* of the act within the meaning of the statute.

In relevant part the factual background may be summarized as follows. Ms. R., the rape victim, was employed as a clerk at the Holiday Inn in South San Francisco when, on March 30, 1984, at about 8:45 a.m., she received a telephone call from a person who identified himself as "Dr. Stevens" and said that he worked at Peninsula Hospital.

"Dr. Stevens" told Ms. R. that he had the results of her blood test and that she had contracted a dangerous, highly infectious and perhaps fatal disease; that she could be sued as a result; that the disease came from using public toilets; and that she would have to tell him the identity of all her friends who would then have to be contacted in the interest of controlling the spread of the disease.

"Dr. Stevens" further explained that there were only two ways to treat the disease. The first was a painful surgical procedure – graphically described – costing $9,000, and requiring her uninsured hospitalization for six weeks. A second alternative, "Dr. Stevens" explained, was to have sexual intercourse with an anonymous donor who had been injected with a serum which would cure the disease. The latter, nonsurgical procedure would only cost $4,500. When the victim replied that she lacked sufficient funds the "doctor" suggested that $1,000 would suffice as a down payment. The victim thereupon agreed to the nonsurgical alternative and consented to intercourse with the mysterious donor, believing "it was the only choice I had."

After discussing her intentions with her work supervisor, the victim proceeded to the Hyatt Hotel in Burlingame as instructed, and contacted "Dr. Stevens" by telephone. The latter became furious when he learned Ms. R. had informed her employer of the plan, and threatened to terminate his treatment, finally instructing her to inform her employer she had decided not to go through

---

[1] The District Attorney agreed to dismiss Count I which charged Boro with forcible rape.

with the treatment. Ms. R. did so, then went to her bank, withdrew $1,000 and, as instructed, checked into another hotel and called "Dr. Stevens" to give him her room number.

About a half hour later the defendant "donor" arrived at her room. When Ms. R. had undressed, the "donor," petitioner, after urging her to relax, had sexual intercourse with her.

At the time of penetration, it was Ms. R.'s belief that she would die unless she consented to sexual intercourse with the defendant: as she testified, "My life felt threatened, and for that reason and that reason alone did I do it."

Petitioner was apprehended when the police arrived at the hotel room, having been called by Ms. R.'s supervisor. Petitioner was identified as "Dr. Stevens" at a police voice lineup by another potential victim of the same scheme.

Upon the basis of the evidence just recounted, petitioner was charged [under] section 261, subdivision (4) – rape "[where] a person is at the time unconscious of the nature of the act, and this is known to the accused." * * *

The People's position is stated concisely: "We contend, quite simply, that at the time of the intercourse Ms. R., the victim, was 'unconscious of the nature of the act': because of [petitioner's] misrepresentation she believed it was in the nature of a medical treatment and not a simple, ordinary act of sexual intercourse." Petitioner, on the other hand, stresses that the victim was plainly aware of the *nature* of the act in which she voluntarily engaged, so that her motivation in doing so (since it did not fall within the proscription of section 261, subdivision (2)) is irrelevant.

Our research discloses sparse California authority on the subject. A victim need not be totally and physically unconscious in order that section 261, subdivision (4) apply. In *People v. Minkowski*, the defendant was a physician who "treated" several victims for menstrual cramps. Each victim testified that she was treated in a position with her back to the doctor, bent over a table, with feet apart, in a dressing gown. And in each case the "treatment" consisted of the defendant first inserting a metal instrument, then substituting an instrument which "felt different" – the victims not realizing that the second instrument was in fact the doctor's penis. The precise issue before us was never tendered in *People* v. *Minkowski* because the petitioner there *conceded* the sufficiency of evidence to support the element of consciousness.

The decision is useful to this analysis, however, because it exactly illustrates certain traditional rules in the area of our inquiry. Thus, as a leading authority has written, "if deception causes a misunderstanding as to the fact itself (fraud in the *factum*) there is no legally-recognized consent because what happened is not that for which consent was given; whereas consent induced by fraud is as effective as any other consent, so far as direct and immediate legal consequences are concerned, if the deception relates not to the thing done but merely to some collateral matter (fraud in the inducement)."

The victims in *Minkowski* consented, not to sexual intercourse, but to an act of an altogether different nature, penetration by medical instrument. The consent was to a pathological, and not a carnal, act, and the mistake was, therefore, in the *factum* and not merely in the inducement.

Another relatively common situation in the literature on this subject – discussed in detail by Perkins is the fraudulent obtaining of intercourse by impersonating a spouse. As Professor Perkins observes, the courts are not in accord as to whether the crime of rape is thereby committed. "[The] disagreement is not in regard to the underlying principle but only as to its application. Some courts have taken the position that such a misdeed is fraud in the inducement on the theory that the woman consents to exactly what is done (sexual intercourse) and hence there is no rape; other courts, with better reason it would seem, hold such a misdeed to be rape on the theory that it involves fraud in the *factum* since the woman's consent is to an innocent act of marital intercourse while what is actually perpetrated upon her is an act of adultery. Her innocence seems never to have been questioned in such a case and the reason she is not guilty of adultery is because she did not consent to adulterous intercourse. Statutory changes in the law of rape have received attention earlier and need not be repeated here."

In California, of course, we have by statute adopted the majority view that such fraud is in the *factum*, not the inducement, and have thus held it to vitiate consent. It is otherwise, however, with respect to the conceptually much murkier statutory offense with which we here deal, and the language of which has remained essentially unchanged since its enactment.

The language itself could not be plainer. It defines rape to be "an act of sexual intercourse" with a nonspouse, accomplished where the victim is "at the time unconscious of the nature of the act . . ." Nor, as we have just seen, can we entertain the slightest doubt that the Legislature well understood how to draft a statute to encompass fraud in the *factum* and how to specify certain fraud in the inducement as vitiating consent. Moreover, courts of this state have previously confronted the general rule that fraud in the inducement does not vitiate consent. * * *[5]

[T]he Attorney General cites *People v. Howard.* There, the court dealt with section 288a, subdivision (f) and section 286, subdivision (f) making criminal oral copulation or sodomy between adults where one person is "unconscious of the nature of the act." But in *Howard, supra* the victim was a 19-year-old with the mental capacity of a 6-to-8-year-old, who "simply [did] not understand the nature of the act in which he [participated]." Whether or not we agree with the *Howard* court's analysis, we note that here, in contrast, there is not a shred of evidence on the record before us to suggest that as the result of mental retardation Ms. R. lacked the capacity to appreciate the nature of the sex act in which she engaged. On the contrary, her testimony was clear that she precisely understood the "nature of the act," but, motivated by a fear of disease, and death, succumbed to petitioner's fraudulent blandishments.

To so conclude is not to vitiate the heartless cruelty of petitioner's scheme, but to say that it comprised crimes of a different order than a violation of section 261, subdivision (4).

Let a peremptory writ of prohibition issue restraining respondent from taking further action upon count II (a violation of Pen. Code, § 261, subd. (4)) in *People v. Daniel Kayton Boro*... other than dismissal. The stay of trial heretofore imposed shall remain in effect until the finality of this opinion.

Note

After getting his rape with an unconscious victim charge dismissed, Boro, believe it or not, did the same thing to another woman and was prosecuted again. *See* Patricia Falk, *Rape By Fraud and Rape By Coercion*, 64 Brooklyn L. Rev. 39, 57 (1998). This time, he was less fortunate because in response to *Boro v. Superior Court*, the California legislature amended the Penal Code in 1985 to punish cases involving fraud-in-the-inducement. *See* Cal. Penal Code § 266c.

---

[5] It is not difficult to conceive of reasons why the Legislature may have consciously wished to leave the matter where it lies. Thus, as a matter of degree, where consent to intercourse is obtained by promises of travel, fame, celebrity and the like -- ought the liar and seducer to be chargeable as a rapist? Where is the line to be drawn?

4. Rape and Race

THE SOCIAL CONSTRUCTION OF A RAPE VICTIM
Stories of African-American Males
about the Rape of Desirée Washington
Kevin Brown
in BLACK MEN ON RACE, GENDER, AND SEXUALITY: A CRITICAL READER
(Carbado ed. 1999)

THE "VICTIMIZATION" OF MIKE TYSON: STORIES FROM THE HOME FRONT

As one might expect, from the time Tyson was accused of raping Desirée Washington until he was finally sentenced, the "accusation" was a hot topic of conversation. I had a number of discussions about the accusation with other African-American males living in Indianapolis. When the accusation was first made, I asked a lot of my friends what they thought. None of us seriously entertained the possibility that Mike Tyson might actually be convicted of rape; any doubt was resolved in favor of Mike Tyson. I do not remember a single male speaking up for Desirée Washington.

A typical discussion occurred at the barbershop in which I get my hair cut. Anyone familiar with the African-American male community knows that to really take the pulse of the community about a particular issue, you must discuss it at a barbershop. The barbershop is more than a place to get your haircut – it is also a cultural institution. The barbershop is a place where we (males) hang out and receive part of our initiation into the finer points of being a male.

I put the issue of Mike Tyson on the floor by asking a question for general discussion to anyone who was willing to take it up: "What do you think about the claim by Desirée Washington that she was raped by Mike Tyson?" Desirée had no supporters here. Among the comments that were fairly typical were: "Well, she got in his limousine, didn't she?" "His limousine showed up at her hotel room at 2:00 in the morning?" "What do you expect, if you go out with a man at 2:00 in the morning." "No doubt the reason that she is doing this is because, like he said, she was probably mad because he didn't walk her to the limousine." From these comments, an initial image of Desirée took shape. I thought to myself, it's obvious, she must have consented. Not only that, I thought this woman must be crazy. Imagine doing all this because someone would not walk her to the limousine. As for Mike, he was being victimized by a vindictive and unstable woman.

Another discussion that I had prior to the trial was with a friend of mine who was closely involved in organizing the boxing matches that took place during the Summer Celebration. Here was an opportunity for me to get an inside scoop on what had occurred. I asked my friend if he thought Mike had raped Desirée Washington. He responded, "[yeah] he did it, but we have got some things on her, too, she wasn't completely innocent." The confident tone in his voice and what he said implied that Desirée might have brought this on herself.

This kind of inside information was precisely what I had hoped to find when I called him – the real inside story that would give me the complete picture so that I could understand precisely what had happened. So I asked, "Oh, really? Well, what did she do?"

I assumed that he was about to divulge the damning piece of evidence. You know, the piece of evidence that Perry Mason always hit the murderer with when they were on the stand in the final ten minutes of an otherwise dull episode. As he gave his response, his voice suggested quiet confidence that this piece of information would be the deciding piece of evidence. "She violated curfew."

Hmmm, I thought, that is serious business. She broke a pageant rule that was there for her protection. No doubt these rules were, in part, to protect the contestants from this kind of situation. If only she had followed the rules, this would not have happened.

Prior to the trial, it was clear that all those I had discussed the rape with were resolving all doubt in favor of Mike Tyson. At least that view is consistent with the law; a person (man?) (white man?) accused of rape, especially date rape, is presumed innocent until proven guilty beyond a reasonable doubt.

No one I talked to believed that Tyson would or should be convicted. Therefore, the verdict by the Indianapolis jury had a profound effect on our image of the "victim" in the rape. After Mike was convicted, he did not appear to lose any support. Shortly after the verdict, I went back to the same barbershop and once again raised the issue. This time I sought to find out what people thought the appropriate punishment should be. I asked my barber, an older man whose judgment I have come to respect through our many conversations over the past ten years, for his opinion.

"Do you think Mike Tyson should go to jail?"

"If he did it, and I'm not saying he did," my barber responded, "but if he did, I think that, well, maybe you ought to be lenient here. Perhaps he needs counseling, if he did it. And in fact, you know, there was a White guy this past summer who was also convicted of rape, and he received a suspended sentence."

This was the beginning of the redefinition of Mike as the victim. Before the conviction, Mike was being victimized by an unbalanced and jealous woman. Now he was also being victimized by the "White" criminal justice system.

If he did it! Even though Mike Tyson had been convicted by a jury that had heard all of the legally admissible evidence and therefore was certainly more knowledgeable about the case than my barber, he (and now I) was not willing to accept that verdict as a pronouncement of what had actually occurred. Those unfamiliar with African-American culture may ask how my barber could now say, "If he did it." According to the Indianapolis poll, 67 percent of African-Americans polled believed that Tyson was unfairly convicted and another 11 percent believed that, although he was guilty, his sentence was unfair. Only 7 percent of the African-Americans polled believed that Tyson got what he deserved. The remaining 15 percent expressed no opinion on the issue. In contrast, 40 percent of the Whites polled believed that Tyson got what he deserved. Only 28 percent believed he was unfairly convicted, while an additional 10 percent believed that, though he was guilty, his sentence was unfair. The remaining 22 percent expressed no opinion.

My barber's response tapped into two dominant beliefs in African-American culture. First, Blacks, and particularly Black males, cannot expect fair treatment by America's White criminal justice system. The same poll also indicated that 37 percent of the Whites and 70 percent of the Blacks believed that the judicial system treats Blacks and Whites differently. In Tyson's prosecution, ten of the twelve jurors who voted for conviction were White, and both the judge and prosecutor were White. When African-Americans talk about racism in the criminal justice system, this is part of what we mean – prosecution, judgment, and convictions of African-Americans by Whites. Comparing the sentencing of Mike Tyson to that of some White person convicted of the same crime was also based upon this same notion. It becomes even easier to view Tyson's prosecution in a racial context when it is juxtaposed against the acquittal of William Kennedy for date rape.

Viewing Tyson as a victim of the White criminal justice system completely changes the interpretation and understanding of his prosecution, conviction, and punishment. Mike Tyson's conviction is not just his individual conviction. Rather, it is a symbolic of the American judicial system's harsh treatment of African-Americans, particularly males. To support Tyson, then, is to fight against racial domination of African-Americans.

The second belief that my barber tapped into was that the fight against racial subordination will usually trump the fight against the sexual subordination of African-American women in the Black community. Although it is true that a Sister had been raped by a Brother, Tyson was now a victim of racism in the criminal justice system. Despite the fact that Brothers certainly want to support Sisters, concerns about the Sisters must wait until after we have dealt with Man (resolved the racial issue). Let us not forget, we have been trying to resolve the racial issue for over 370 years.

After my barber responded, another Brother in the barbershop joined in and brought up the fact that Desirée had appeared on television the night before and told her side of the story. During this program, she made it clear she had not received any compensation for her appearance. One of the other barbers in the shop pointed out that, although it may be true that Desirée did not get any money before the program aired, she very well could have received payment right after the program was shown. Another patron, seizing on this possibility, responded, "You know that show was on at 7:00 or 8:00, that doesn't tell you what she got paid at 9:00 or 10:00." Another Brother said, "Even if she didn't get paid for this particular appearance, she is going to get money from the tabloids. She is going to sue, she is going to get plenty of money. This women is going to be set for the rest of her life. God damn! Some people are lucky."

Now the motives for Desirée's not toeing the traditional line – racism trumps sexism – were out in the open. Desirée was out for herself. This wily eighteen-year-old college freshman from Coventry, Rhode Island, was too sophisticated and worldly for Mike Tyson. She was doing all this for the money. Desirée had just hit the lottery and was going to cash in big. And the terrible thing about it was that this Sister, in conjunction with the White criminal justice system, had brought down another Brother in order to advance her own greedy self-interest. * * *

The next day, I happened to be flipping channels on the television and turned to a station delivering the Indianapolis news. I tuned in just in time to see a number of African-American ministers and community leaders pleading for leniency and mercy for Mike Tyson. One of the ministers pointed out that the Bible said, "'blessed are the merciful' and we are simply asking for mercy for Mike Tyson." Just like that, the sentencing of Mike Tyson had become a religious issue. I thought, well, if God is on Mike's side, then he must be innocent.

One of the Black reporters at the news conference responded to this statement by asking the minister, "Doesn't the Bible also command that thou shalt not engage in fornication?" A split of religious authority had occurred, but this split was quickly resolved. The minister who had quoted the Bible retorted to this imprudent question by reminding the reporter that it was the Black community leaders who had gotten African-Americans hired at the local television stations: "It was from us pressuring the stations you work at that got you your job." So now the issue of leniency for Mike Tyson had become an issue of loyalty to the African-American community.

As I prepared my remarks for this Conference, I started to think about the mental images that were in my mind. I sensed my outrage about how Mike Tyson had been victimized. He had been victimized by a criminal justice system. He had been victimized by a woman who had consented to have sex with him. He was then victimized by her again when she decided to take him down to advance her own greedy self-interest. He was victimized by a lawyer who failed to provide him with an adequate defense. He had been victimized by a jury that had been pressured into returning a guilty verdict against him. He was victimized, victimized, victimized.

THE "DE-VICTIMIZATION" OF MIKE TYSON

In a few moments of quiet reflection about the Tyson-Washington incident, a number of things began to occur to me that were obvious in so many ways. Only two people actually know that happened that night in that hotel room. With the passage of time and the need to envision the incident in the way that supported their articulated versions, even Mike and Desirée may now have difficulty recalling exactly what happened. The others and I were collectively constructing a story of what happened, from bits and pieces of information and preexisting thought patterns. Like authors of books, makers of films, or writers of poetry, we were putting meaning into an otherwise meaningless situation. And once this was done, we acted as if our story was what actually happened.

Why was the view of Tyson as the victim so easy to formulate and to accept? The answer stared me in the face. Most of my construction of Tyson as the victim proceeded from one of the most fundamental beliefs in the African-American community. Justice is White. The postconviction redefinition of Tyson as a victim occurred because of the fundamental belief that a Black man could not expect justice within the American criminal justice system. Never mind the fact that Tyson could afford the best lawyer money can buy. Never mind the fact that there were (only) two African-Americans on the jury.

If Tyson had been convicted by an all-Black jury, with an African-American prosecutor and judge, my perception of the incident would have been significantly different. The ability to construct an image of Tyson as a victim of racism in the criminal justice system (defined in the African-American culture as the prosecution, judgment, and conviction of Blacks by Whites) would have almost completely disappeared. With racism substantially eliminated as a concern, I could have quickly focused on other aspects of this situation. My concern about racism and oppression, however, had controlled my interpretation of the rape of Desirée Washington.

I began to think more and more about how my desire to struggle against perceived racism was keeping me from understanding other aspects of this situation. For starters, I had not been able to see Desirée Washington as the victim, and yet this is precisely what the jury saw when it convicted Tyson. As I began to think about the possibility of Desirée Washington as the victim, a number of issues about her came quickly to mind. Before, I was willing to believe that an eighteen-year-old college freshman could be so sophisticated that she could hatch a plan to take down the former heavyweight champion of the world. This required me to believe that she could easily outsmart a man who was not only seven years her senior and had been heavyweight champion of the world but who also had experienced a rough divorce.

Desirée often talked about how terrified she was that night. "Terrified" cannot possibly describe what she must have felt. I tried to imagine being an eighteen-year-old, 108 pound woman in a hotel room with a person who could arguably be considered the best fighter of all time. I had seen Mike Tyson fight heavyweights such as Michael Spinks, Trevor Berbick, and Razor Ruddick. "Terrified" is the word I would use to describe how they appeared entering the ring to face Mike Tyson. Those men were heavyweight boxers, some even heavyweight champions at the time. They also had the safety and comfort of knowing that if things got out of hand, they could lay down on the canvas and take the ten count. At least for them, there was a referee who could stop the fight.

Then there were all of those who suggested that something was wrong because Desirée Washington might profit from being raped by Mike Tyson. I thought of how many times I have heard people express sympathy for the men Tyson beat in the ring – men who were receiving millions of dollars for about two minutes worth of work. Fights that people personally paid thirty dollars or more to see. Unlike Desirée, however, these boxers had volunteered to give up their bodies to be abused by Mike Tyson.

Victimization, however, was not confined to Desirée. The implications for African-American women were victimizing as well: "Don't talk about date rape, because we won't believe you; you must have consented." "Don't cooperate with the Man in taking down a Brother, even if you think he is wrong, especially one who is a celebrity." "Your concern about your bodies and how males inflict pain on you has to be subordinated until the racial problem is resolved." Of course, I realized that African-Americans will never resolve the racial problem.

Then, finally, I realized that there was one last group of victims who were being obscured by the notion of Tyson as the victim: African-American males, including those who had to rallied to support, explain, and justify Mike Tyson's actions. In an effort to exonerate himself, Tyson used an explanation and defense of his conduct that drew on every negative stereotype about African-American males that exists. His defense portrayed black men as oversexed, prone to violent and aggressive behavior, and dumb as a brick wall. Tyson literally had been responsible for producing millions of dollars of negative publicity, reinforcing the very social construction of African-American men in dominant culture of which I had so often complained. As I was envisioning myself as fighting racism by supporting Tyson, I was also embracing and approving of the image of Black males against which I struggle so hard.

PATRIARCHAL STORIES I:
CULTURAL RAPE NARRATIVES IN THE
COURTROOM
Andrew E. Taslitz
5 S. Cal. Rev. L. & Women's Stud. 387 (1996)[a]

B. Mike Tyson: Embracing the Beast

1. Desiree's Tale

Mike Tyson embraced the image of the beast. He played directly into white tales of dangerous carnal black desires. His defense: he was so famous and such an animal that any woman who came up to his room, including Desire Washington, the woman he was charged with raping, had to know precisely why she was there.

Washington's tale was of an innocent betrayed. She was a star high school student, stereotypically beautiful, attending the Miss Black America contest as a participant. Her dad had long been a huge Tyson fan. Consequently, when Tyson visited the contestants and asked Washington out, saying he liked her because she was a "nice, Christian girl," she jumped at it and said "yes." When he neither called nor showed, however, she got ready for bed. To her surprise, he finally called at about 1:30 a.m. She said it was too late, but he said that he would be gone in the morning, so she agreed to meet him at his limousine to go out.

---

[a]Reprinted with the permission of the *California Review of Law and Women's Studies.*

When she got to the limo, however, he said he had to get something from his room, and encouraged her to accompany him for the brief stop. Once in the room, they chatted, and he was friendly. But he abruptly changed his tone, saying, "Oh, you're turning me on." She said that she did not do one night stands, and he said she was "just a baby." She was uncomfortable but did not sense danger.

She excused herself to use the bathroom. When she returned, he had stripped to his underpants. She went for her purse, saying it was time to go. But Tyson was much faster. He quickly stripped off her outer jacket, bustier, shorts, and underpants and told her not to fight. She told him to leave her alone, expressing fear she might get pregnant and saying again she did not do one night stands. She complained that he was not wearing a condom, but he said he did not need one; they would just make a baby.

He then tried putting his penis in her vagina, but it hurt, and she started crying. He then twisted her like a pretzel and licked her vagina for lubrication. She hit him, saying that Tyson had said he respected her and thought she was a good Christian girl. He ignored her, calling her "Oh, Mommy," and hurt her further. He asked whether she wanted to get on top, but when he moved to let her do so, she tried to flee. He resumed his original efforts, pulled out, and ejaculated outside of her.

When she got back to her room, she told her roommate that Tyson had "tried" to rape her, unable to admit to herself that she had been raped, and then cried. Within twenty-three hours, she had reported the rape to police and her parents. Shortly thereafter, she went to Methodist Hospital.

2. Tyson's Tart

There were several factors working in Tyson's favor. Most importantly, Washington was a black woman, invoking the theme of over-powering female lust. While Tyson, as a black male, might be viewed as a beast too, in the white stories such beasts only attack white women. What the beasts do to black women those women like anyway.

The theme of animal sexuality was reinforced by Washington's being young and attractive. Moreover, she went to a man's room at two o'clock in the morning, clearly invoking themes of breached silence. She had a motive to lie too: Tyson was wealthy, and crying rape might be a quick way to make some serious money. Moreover, Tyson had claimed Washington seemed fine until he brushed her off after the act. Angry at being treated like a one night stand, she cried rape. Indeed, had she really been raped, would she have had the strength to complete the pageant? Yet that is what she did. Furthermore, Tyson offered witnesses who testified that Washington had been friendly with Tyson before the rape. Moreover, Washington admitted she had taken the time to change her panty shield when she went to the bathroom in Tyson's hotel, hardly the behavior of a woman fearing rape. The picture seemed a clear one of the Lying Woman.

There were, however, two problems for Tyson: first, he warmly embraced, even magnified, his image as a lustful beast; and second, Washington's behavior, conduct, character, and background were radically disconnected from the image of a hypersexual whore.

3. The Beast Awakes

Even Tyson's defenders early on fed media images of Tyson as a quintessential black stud. One of the officers in charge of investigating Washington's charges put it this way:

> I've got an eighteen-year-old black victim who leading black spokesmen are trashing. I saw some professor from some small southern school on television explaining that what Mike Tyson did to Desiree was part of some black dating ritual. It's normal, he said, for black men to treat black women this way.

Tyson, rather than seek to overcome white cultural images of black men, sought, instead, to magnify them. His lawyer stressed repeatedly that Tyson was an octopus, publicly feeling female breasts and behinds everywhere he went, including at the Miss Black America contest. Every woman knew what he was about, and Washington was no exception.

Tyson's behavior before and at the trial matched this image. At a press conference, Tyson was heard saying to a friend, "I should have killed the bitch." On the stand, his usual soft-spoken manner snapped at least once, revealing an angry face on a large, powerful man. He was, testified one witness, routinely disrespectful of black women and black leaders. His testimony at trial, moreover, seemed scripted like an actor playing a role. This impression was reinforced when he became obviously rattled and uncomfortable once the prosecutor departed from the expected routine. Moreover, he admitted at trial that he had lied to the grand jury twice. At trial, he said he flatly asked Washington, "Want to screw?" as his way of asking for a date, something he had denied to the grand jury. He also told the grand jury that his bodyguard, Dale Edwards, had been in the adjacent room of Tyson's suite at the time of the rape and heard what really happened. At trial, however, he admitted this was not so and claimed he had just "assumed" Edwards had been there.

The physical evidence, moreover, seemed to confirm Tyson's bullying, something rare in a "date" rape. Washington had two small vaginal abrasions, one 1/8 of an inch wide and the other 3/8 of an inch long, making her wince with pain when the doctor inserted a speculum. Such injuries, testified a prosecution expert, are virtually unknown in consensual sex cases but occur in 10-20% of all rapes. Even the defense's own expert, called to say that such injuries can come from consensual sex, admitted he had seen such injuries only two to three times in 20,000 examinations. Her panties were also torn at the waistband, consistent with her testimony that Tyson ripped her clothes off. Additionally, blood on her panties matched the site of the injuries she described.

Tyson was, therefore, an admitted liar and beast. He reinforced, rather than re-thought, precisely those themes likely to lead to his conviction.

4. Captivated by Innocence

There was much about Desiree Washington that contradicted standard cultural tales. "Jurors were captivated by her beauty, innocence and integrity." She was small and slight next to the 260-pound Tyson. She bore the scars and blood of the bully. She was a good student and churchgoer, with a father who revered Mike Tyson. When she testified, she made clear that the thought of publicly attacking a black man in court troubled her deeply. Her image, then, was of a good, somewhat innocent kid misled. Except for her arguable lapse of judgment that night, she presented little apparent threat to the patriarchal order.

Moreover, her demeanor and relatively prompt reporting of the incident matched what was expected of a victim. She returned from Tyson's room to his limo. The limo driver had done a practicum at a mental health counseling center, where she attended women who had been raped and beaten. She thought Washington fit the profile, her eyes "frantic, dazed, and disoriented," her clothes and hair mussed, looking scared. And she kept repeating: "I don't believe him. I don't believe him. Who does he think he is?" She reported the rape quickly to her roommate (saying that he tried to rape her), 911, the hospital, and her family. Her 911 call, which was played for the jury, was powerful and fully consistent with her tale in court. It included her fears that no one would believe her or that they would think that she was just after money. Consistency, as we have seen, is something jurors expect if they are to convict in a rape case. Movingly for the jury, she explained how, like a little girl, she had to sleep with her mom many nights after the pageant to shield her from nightmares.

Greed rang hollow as a motivator as well. When Tyson had first called Washington, she had asked her roommate to come along, but the roommate had refused. It would be hard to set up a rape blackmail scheme if there had been an eyewitness. Moreover, Tyson had offered her a substantial sum of money to drop the charges, which she had refused. At trial, little more than speculation supported greed as a motivator, speculation that contradicted Washington's deeds and demeanor. However, some have argued that there were a host of procedural errors at trial that prevented Tyson from countering this image.

Once Tyson made the decision to embrace the image of the black beast, to go beyond that image and admit to, and even celebrate, abusive behavior toward black women, Washington's race began to matter less. At that point, her actions and injuries fit well the bullying theme to which Tyson was tethered, pushing the incident over the thin line from seduction to rape. Washington followed many, though not all, of the rules on silence too. By day's end, the jury decided there was a beast who needed caging, rare, very rare, where a black woman has cried pain.

B.   STATUTORY RAPE

GARNETT v. STATE
Court of Appeals of Maryland
332 Md. 571, 632 A.2d 797 (1993)

MURPHY, J.

Maryland's "statutory rape" law prohibiting sexual intercourse with an underage person is codified in Maryland Code (1957, 1992 Repl.Vol.) Art. 27, § 463, which reads in full:

Second degree rape.

(a) *What constitutes.* – A person is guilty of rape in the second degree if the person engages in vaginal intercourse with another person:

(1) By force or threat of force against the will and without the consent of the other person; or

(2) Who is mentally defective, mentally incapacitated, or physically helpless, and the person performing the act knows or should reasonably know the other person is mentally defective, mentally incapacitated, or physically helpless; or

(3) Who is under 14 years of age and the person performing the act is at least four years older than the victim.

(b) *Penalty.* — Any person violating the provisions of this section is guilty of a felony and upon conviction is subject to imprisonment for a period of not more than 20 years.

Subsection (a)(3) represents the current version of a statutory provision dating back to the first comprehensive codification of the criminal law by the Legislature in 1809. Now we consider whether under the present statute, the State must prove that a defendant knew the complaining witness was younger than 14 and, in a related question, whether it was error at trial to exclude evidence that he had been told, and believed, that she was 16 years old.

I

Raymond Lennard Garnett is a young retarded man.[a] At the time of the incident in question he was 20 years old. He has an I.Q. of 52. His guidance counselor from the Montgomery County public school system, Cynthia Parker, described him as a mildly retarded person who read on the third-grade level, did arithmetic on the 5th-grade level, and interacted with others socially at school at the level of someone 11 or 12 years of age. Ms. Parker added that Raymond attended special education classes and for at least one period of time was educated at home when he was afraid to return to school due to his classmates' taunting. Because he could not understand the duties of the jobs given him, he failed to complete vocational assignments; he sometimes lost his way to work. As Raymond was unable to pass any of the State's functional tests required for graduation, he received only a certificate of attendance rather than a high-school diploma.

---

[a]In *Atkins v. Virginia*, 536 U.S. 304 (2002), the Supreme Court held that the execution of a mentally retarded individual constitutes cruel and unusual punishment in violation of the Eighth Amendment. In reaching this conclusion, Justice Stevens, writing for the court, surveyed clinical definitions of mental retardation and found that most "require not only subaverage intellectual function, but also significant limitations in adaptive skills such as communication, self-care, and self-direction that become manifest before age 18. Mentally retarded persons frequently know the difference between right and wrong and are competent to stand trial. Because of their impairments, however, by definition they have diminished capacities to understand and process information, to communicate, to abstract from mistakes and learn from experience, to engage in logical reasoning, to control impulses, and to understand the reactions of others. There is no evidence that they are more likely to engage in criminal conduct than others, but there is abundant evidence that they often act on impulse rather than pursuant to a premeditated plan, and that in group settings they are followers rather than leaders. Their deficiencies do not warrant an exemption from criminal sanctions, but they do diminish their personal culpability." 536 U.S. at 318.

In November or December 1990, a friend introduced Raymond to Erica Frazier, then aged 13; the two subsequently talked occasionally by telephone. On February 28, 1991, Raymond, apparently wishing to call for a ride home, approached the girl's house at about nine o'clock in the evening. Erica opened her bedroom window, through which Raymond entered; he testified that "she just told me to get a ladder and climb up her window." The two talked, and later engaged in sexual intercourse. Raymond left at about 4:30 a.m. the following morning. On November 19, 1991, Erica gave birth to a baby, of which Raymond is the biological father.

Raymond was tried before the Circuit Court for Montgomery County (Miller, J.) on one count of second degree rape under §463(a)(3) proscribing sexual intercourse between a person under 14 and another at least four years older than the complainant. At trial, the defense twice proffered evidence to the effect that Erica herself and her friends had previously told Raymond that she was 16 years old, and that he had acted with that belief. The trial court excluded such evidence as immaterial, explaining:

> Under 463, the only two requirements as relate to this case are that there was vaginal intercourse, [and] that . . . Ms. Frazier was under 14 years of age and that . . . Mr. Garnett was at least four years older than she.

> In the Court's opinion, consent is no defense to this charge. The victim's representation as to her age and the defendant's belief, if it existed, that she was not under age, what amounts to what otherwise might be termed a good faith defense, is in fact no defense to what amount[s] to statutory rape.

> It is in the Court's opinion a strict liability offense.

The court found Raymond guilty. It sentenced him to a term of five years in prison, suspended the sentence and imposed five years of probation, and ordered that he pay restitution to Erica and the Frazier family. Raymond noted an appeal; we granted certiorari prior to intermediate appellate review by the Court of Special Appeals to consider the important issue presented in the case.

II

* * * Section 463(a)(3) does not expressly set forth a requirement that the accused have acted with a criminal state of mind, or mens rea. The State insists that the statute, by design, defines a strict liability offense, and that its essential elements were met in the instant case when Raymond, age 20, engaged in vaginal intercourse with Erica, a girl under 14 and more than 4 years his junior. Raymond replies that the criminal law exists to assess and punish morally culpable behavior. He says such culpability was absent here. He asks us either to engraft onto subsection (a)(3) an implicit mens rea requirement, or to recognize an affirmative defense of reasonable mistake as to the complainant's age. Raymond argues that it is unjust, under the circumstances of this case which led him to think his conduct lawful, to brand him a felon and rapist.

III

Raymond asserts that the events of this case were inconsistent with the criminal sexual exploitation of a minor by an adult. As earlier observed, Raymond entered Erica's bedroom at the girl's invitation; she directed him to use a ladder to reach her window. They engaged voluntarily in sexual intercourse. They remained together in the room for more than seven hours before Raymond departed at dawn. With an I.Q. of 52, Raymond functioned at approximately the same level as the 13-year-old Erica; he was mentally an adolescent in an adult's body. Arguably, had Raymond's chronological age, 20, matched his socio-intellectual age, about 12, he and Erica would have fallen well within the four-year age difference obviating a violation of the statute, and Raymond would not have been charged with any crime at all.

The precise legal issue here rests on Raymond's unsuccessful efforts to introduce into evidence testimony that Erica and her friends had told him she was 16 years old, the age of consent to sexual relations, and that he believed them. Thus the trial court did not permit him to raise a defense of reasonable mistake of Erica's age, by which defense Raymond would have asserted that he acted innocently without a criminal design. At common law, a crime occurred only upon the concurrence of an individual's act and his guilty state of mind. In this regard, it is well understood that generally there are two components of every crime, the *actus reus* or guilty act and the *mens rea* or the guilty mind or mental state accompanying a forbidden act. The requirement that an accused have acted with a culpable mental state is an axiom of criminal jurisprudence. Writing for the United States Supreme Court, Justice Robert Jackson observed:

> The contention that an injury can amount to a crime only when inflicted by intention is no provincial or transient notion. It is as universal and persistent in mature systems of law as belief in freedom of the human will and a consequent ability and duty of the normal individual to choose between good and evil.

* * *

To be sure, legislative bodies since the mid-19th century have created strict liability criminal offenses requiring no mens rea. Almost all such statutes responded to the demands of public health and welfare arising from the complexities of society after the Industrial Revolution. Typically misdemeanors involving only fines or other light penalties, these strict liability laws regulated food, milk, liquor, medicines and drugs, securities, motor vehicles and traffic, the labeling of goods for sale, and the like. Statutory rape, carrying the stigma of felony as well as a potential sentence of 20 years in prison, contrasts markedly with the other strict liability regulatory offenses and their light penalties.

Modern scholars generally reject the concept of strict criminal liability. Professors LaFave and Scott summarize the consensus that punishing conduct without reference to the actor's state of mind fails to reach the desired end and is unjust:

> It is inefficacious because conduct unaccompanied by an awareness of the factors making it criminal does not mark the actor as one who needs to be subjected to punishment in order to deter him or others from behaving similarly in the future, nor does it single him out as a socially dangerous individual who needs to be incapacitated or reformed. It is unjust because the actor is subjected to the stigma of a criminal conviction without being morally blameworthy. Consequently, on either a preventive or retributive theory of criminal punishment, the criminal sanction is inappropriate in the absence of *mens rea.* * *

IV

The legislatures of 17 states have enacted laws permitting a mistake of age defense in some form in cases of sexual offenses with underage persons. * * * In some states, the defense is available in instances where the complainant's age rises above a statutorily prescribed level, but is not available when the complainant falls below the defining age. In other states, the availability of the defense depends on the severity of the sex offense charged to the accused.

In addition, the highest appellate courts of four states have determined that statutory rape laws by implication required an element of mens rea as to the complainant's age. In the landmark case of *People v. Hernandez,* the California Supreme Court held that, absent a legislative directive to the contrary, a charge of statutory rape was defensible wherein a criminal intent was lacking; it reversed the trial court's refusal to permit the defendant to present evidence of his good faith, reasonable belief that the complaining witness had reached the age of consent. In so doing, the court first questioned the assumption that age alone confers a sophistication sufficient to create legitimate consent to sexual relations: "the sexually experienced 15-year-old may be far more acutely aware of the implications of sexual intercourse than her sheltered cousin who is beyond the age of consent." The court then rejected the traditional view that those who engage in sex with young persons do so at their peril, assuming the risk that their partners are underage:

> [I]f [the perpetrator] participates in a mutual act of sexual intercourse, believing his partner to be beyond the age of consent, with reasonable grounds for such belief, where is his criminal intent? In such circumstances he has not consciously taken any risk. Instead he has subjectively eliminated the risk by satisfying himself on reasonable evidence that the crime cannot be committed. If it occurs that he has been mislead, we cannot realistically conclude for such reason alone the intent with which he undertook the act suddenly becomes more heinous . . . . [T]he courts have uniformly failed to satisfactorily explain the nature of the criminal intent present in the mind of one who in good faith believes he has obtained a lawful consent before engaging in the prohibited act.

* * * Two-fifths of the states, therefore, now recognize the defense in cases of statutory sexual offenses.

V

We think it sufficiently clear, however, that Maryland's second degree rape statute defines a strict liability offense that does not require the State to prove mens rea; it makes no allowance for a mistake-of-age defense. The plain language of § 463, viewed in its entirety, and the legislative history of its creation lead to this conclusion. * * *

Section 463(a)(3) prohibiting sexual intercourse with underage persons makes no reference to the actor's knowledge, belief, or other state of mind. As we see it, this silence as to mens rea results from legislative design. First, subsection (a)(3) stands in stark contrast to the provision immediately before it, subsection (a)(2) prohibiting vaginal intercourse with incapacitated or helpless persons. In subsection (a)(2), the Legislature expressly provided as an element of the offense that "the person performing the act *knows or should reasonably know* the other person is mentally defective, mentally incapacitated, or physically helpless." In drafting this subsection, the Legislature showed itself perfectly capable of recognizing and allowing for a defense that obviates criminal intent; if the defendant objectively did not understand that the sex partner was impaired, there is no crime. That it chose not to include similar language in subsection (a)(3) indicates that the Legislature aimed to make statutory rape with underage persons a more severe prohibition based on strict criminal liability.

Second, an examination of the drafting history of § 463 during the 1976 revision of Maryland's sexual offense laws reveals that the statute was viewed as one of strict liability from its inception and throughout the amendment process. As originally proposed, Senate Bill 358 defined as a sexual offense in the first degree a sex act committed with a person less than 14 years old by an actor four or more years older. The Senate Judicial Proceedings Committee then offered a series of amendments to the bill. Among them, Amendment # 13 reduced the stipulated age of the victim from less than 14 to 12 or less. Amendment # 16 then added a provision defining a sexual offense in the second degree as a sex act with another "under 14 years of age, which age the person performing the sexual act knows or should know." These initial amendments suggest that, at the very earliest stages of the bill's life, the Legislature distinguished between some form of strict criminal liability, applicable to offenses where the victim was age 12 or under, and a lesser offense with a *mens rea* requirement when the victim was between the ages of 12 and 14.

Senate Bill 358 in its amended form was passed by the Senate on March 11, 1976. The House of Delegates' Judiciary Committee, however, then proposed changes of its own. It rejected the Senate amendments, and defined an offense of rape, without a *mens rea* requirement, for sexual acts performed with someone under the age of 14. The Senate concurred in the House amendments and S.B. 358 became law. Thus the Legislature explicitly raised, considered, and then explicitly jettisoned any notion of a *mens rea* element with respect to the complainant's age in enacting the law that formed the basis of current §463(a)(3). In the light of such legislative action, we must inevitably conclude that the current law imposes strict liability on its violators.

This interpretation is consistent with the traditional view of statutory rape as a strict liability crime designed to protect young persons from the dangers of sexual exploitation by adults, loss of chastity, physical injury, and, in the case of girls, pregnancy. The majority of states retain statutes which impose strict liability for sexual acts with underage complainants. We observe again, as earlier, that even among those states providing for a mistake-of-age defense in some instances, the defense often is not available where the sex partner is 14 years old or less; the complaining witness in the instant case was only 13. The majority of appellate courts, including the Court of Special Appeals, have held statutory rape to be a strict liability crime.

VI

Maryland's second degree rape statute is by nature a creature of legislation. Any new provision introducing an element of *mens rea*, or permitting a defense of reasonable mistake of age, with respect to the offense of sexual intercourse with a person less than 14, should properly result from an act of the Legislature itself, rather than judicial fiat. Until then, defendants in extraordinary cases, like Raymond, will rely upon the tempering discretion of the trial court at sentencing.

JUDGMENT AFFIRMED, WITH COSTS.

STATE v. YANEZ
Supreme Court of Rhode Island
716 A.2d 759 (1998)

GOLDBERG, JUSTICE.

The principal issue presented by this case is whether a reasonable mistake of fact concerning a complainant's age may be asserted as a defense to a charge of statutory-rape. For the reasons articulated in this opinion, we hold that with respect to the age requirement, first-degree child-molestation sexual assault is a strict-liability offense. Consequently a defendant charged with this offense may not introduce evidence that he or she was mistaken regarding the child's age, nor is a defendant entitled to a jury instruction regarding the same. * * *

Facts

The defendant, Alejandro Yanez (Yanez), was eighteen-years-old when he engaged in consensual sexual intercourse with Allison (a fictitious name), the victim in this case, who was thirteen-years-old at the time. The two were first introduced to each other, albeit ever so briefly, in August 1992, nearly a year before this incident. Allison testified that she was attending a Portuguese festival with a girlfriend when she saw her aunt's boyfriend, Victor Yanez (Victor), defendant's brother. According to Allison, who at that time was only twelve-years-old, Victor introduced her to Yanez. For the next eleven months Allison and Yanez had virtually no contact with each other except for the obligatory "Hello" in passing. Then one day in mid-July 1993, while Allison was walking to the local park to meet friends, she saw Yanez cruise by in his white Trans Am convertible with the top down. She testified that she waved to Yanez, who proceeded to turn the Trans Am around and offer her a ride. Since the park was only across the street, Allison declined Yanez's invitation, but when he persisted, Allison acceded. The two briefly talked during the quarter-mile trip. Yanez gave Allison his name and telephone number, and the two conversed again briefly that night on the telephone.

The next day Allison received a telephone message from either her mother or her sister that Yanez had called her and asked that she call him back. Allison returned Yanez's telephone call, and the two made arrangements to meet in the parking lot behind St. Joseph's Church in West Warwick. From the church the two left in Yanez's car and went for a ride. According to Allison, they proceeded to the home of a friend of Yanez's where they engaged in consensual sexual intercourse on the floor in a back bedroom.

Following the conclusion of their first "date" Allison returned home quite late. After entering the house, Allison proceeded directly to the bathroom to shower whereupon she was subsequently confronted by her mother. While in the bathroom, Allison's mother noticed her underwear on the floor and asked if she had engaged in sexual intercourse. Allison initially denied having had sexual intercourse that evening but later admitted the truth. Subsequently Allison's mother contacted the police, whereupon Allison admitted that she had engaged in sexual intercourse but named as her partner a person called Derek. Allison later explained that she had lied about Yanez's identity because she did not want her mother to know that she had engaged in sexual intercourse with Yanez. A subsequent police investigation revealed that Yanez admitted having had sexual intercourse with Allison but insisted that Allison had told him that she was sixteen-years-old. Allison denied having told Yanez that she was sixteen years of age and, in fact, testified that on the two or three occasions when Yanez had inquired about her age, she had responded that she was only thirteen.

Yanez was indicted on one count of first-degree child-molestation sexual assault in violation of G.L.1956 §§ 11-37-8.1 and 11-37-8.2, although the trial testimony would later reveal that this was not an isolated incident and that there were two more equally sordid, uncharged encounters.[1] At trial defense counsel made numerous attempts to introduce evidence not only demonstrating Yanez's mistaken belief concerning Allison's age but also evidence concerning Allison's apparent maturity in light of her appearance, physical development,

---

[1] Far from the dissent's contention that the uncharged sexual encounters occurred before this charged incident and that Allison and Yanez were actually dating each other, the record simply does not contain this inference.

and demeanor. The trial justice rejected this evidence and determined that in cases in which conduct is made criminal because the victim is a minor, the defense of ignorance or mistaken belief with respect to the victim's age is not available. The trial justice further indicated that he intended to charge the jury with respect to the unavailability of this defense and consequently declined to charge in accordance with Yanez's requested mistake of fact instructions. * * *

Following deliberations a Superior Court jury convicted Yanez of first-degree child-molestation sexual assault. The trial justice sentenced Yanez to the minimum twenty year sentence but suspended eighteen years of the sentence with probation. The trial justice also ordered that Yanez have no contact with Allison for twenty years and, as required by law, that Yanez register with the local police authorities as a convicted sex offender. Yanez was released on bail pending the outcome of this appeal. * * *

I

Mistake of Fact Defense

The crime of statutory-rape was legislatively created in England during the thirteenth century in order to afford special protection to those society had deemed too young to appreciate the consequences of their actions. Thus English courts, which had generally recognized the mistake of fact defense in criminal prosecutions since 1638, did not begin to discuss this defense in the context of statutory-rape cases until the later half of the nineteenth century. At that time, the mistake of fact defense was rejected by courts both in England and in the United States.

Characterizing statutory-rape as a strict-liability offense remained the law in every American jurisdiction until 1964. * * * [T]he majority of courts that have considered this issue continue to reject the reasonable mistake of a victim's age as a defense to statutory-rape and maintain their allegiance to the common law. We note that our research involving statutory-rape cases has revealed that the highest appellate courts of only four states have judicially recognized the mistake of fact defense. All four of these cases, however, are distinguishable from the case at bar.

The courts in [California and Utah] both expressly relied upon the text of their respective criminal codes, which required the concurrence of an act and a mental state in order to constitute a crime, as well as language in their codes that unless otherwise provided, ignorance or mistake of fact negates a culpable mental state. * * * Our General Laws are entirely devoid of any [similar] provisions * * *; therefore, these cases are of no aid to Yanez.

The other two cases in which the mistake of fact defense was judicially recognized are *State v. Guest,* 583 P.2d 836 (Alaska 1978), and *Perez v. State,* 111 N.M. 160, 803 P.2d 249 (1990). In both of these cases, however, the age of the victims (fifteen) closely approached the age of consent (sixteen). In addition the court in *Perez* observed that even though the mistake of fact defense is available if the victim is between the ages of thirteen and sixteen, a defendant is precluded from raising this defense when the victim is under the age of thirteen. Unlike the circumstances in *Guest* and *Perez* in which the victims were fifteen, however, Allison was only thirteen years of age. * * *

A. Statutory Interpretation

* * *

Section 11-37-8.1 provides that:

"[a] person is guilty of first degree child molestation sexual assault if he or she engages in sexual penetration with a person fourteen (14) years of age or under."

The term "sexual penetration" is defined in § 11-37-1(8) as follows:

" 'Sexual penetration' – sexual intercourse, cunnilingus, fellatio, and anal intercourse, or any other intrusion, however slight, by any part of a person's body or by any object into the genital or anal openings of another person's body, but emission of semen is not required."

Clearly the plain words and meaning of § 11-37-8.1 prohibit the sexual penetration of an underaged person and make no reference to the actor's state of mind, knowledge, or belief. In our opinion this lack of a *mens rea* results not from negligent omission but from legislative design.

Yanez correctly asserts that this Court has previously declared the existence of an implied *mens rea* element with respect to the term "sexual contact" in cases of second-degree sexual assault, and to some but not all acts of "sexual penetration" in cases of first-degree child-molestation sexual assault. These opinions represent our determination that conduct that the Legislature has included within the definitions of "sexual contact" or "sexual penetration," other than sexual intercourse, anal intercourse, cunnilingus, or fellatio, may in the absence of a *mens rea* element embrace conduct that is intended for an innocent purpose and not for purposes of sexual arousal or gratification. * * *

The Rhode Island General Assembly has divided sexual offenses into two main categories – sexual assault and child-molestation sexual assault. An examination of the pertinent provisions reveals that the Legislature has carefully distinguished between the two, explicitly requiring a *mens rea* for sexual assaults that were either unknown at common law or for those acts of sexual abuse that did not involve sexual intercourse, anal intercourse, cunnilingus, or fellatio while electing to maintain the common law's strict-liability for child-molestation sexual assault. * * *

It can be inferred from this statutory classification that the child-molestation sexual assault statutes' silence with regard to a *mens rea* "is designed to subserve the state interest of protecting female children from the severe physical and psychological consequences of engaging in coitus before attaining the age of consent in the statute." Had the Legislature intended not only to punish the act of child-molestation sexual assault but also to require a mental state, the Legislature could easily have provided for such an element. But its decision to include a *mens rea* requirement in the sexual assault statutes while declining to provide a *mens rea* requirement in the child-molestation sexual assault statutes, demonstrates that the Legislature's omission was intentional. This is a sensible and pragmatic objective with which we shall not interfere by engrafting a *mens rea* requirement where one was not intended.

B. Due-Process Argument

Despite the Legislature's design Yanez nonetheless continues to argue that § 11-37-8.1 contains an implicit element that the accused must have knowledge that the victim is fourteen years of age or younger. Yanez suggests that § 11-37-8.1 violates his due-process rights because he had neither the opportunity to learn Allison's true age nor the opportunity to present a meaningful defense concerning his reasonable mistake. In support of this argument Yanez relies on *Morissette v. United States*, in which the Supreme Court observed "that intent was so inherent in the idea of the offense that it required no statutory affirmation," and on *Griffith* in which we relied on *Morissette* and declared that § 11-37-8.1 contains an implicit *mens rea* requirement that a defendant "act with the intent of sexual arousal or gratification" and that this statute "is not a strict liability offense." * * *

[I]n order for Yanez to prove that the Legislature's exercise of its power runs afoul of the protections guaranteed by the due-process clause, Yanez must demonstrate that this practice "offends some principle of justice so rooted in the traditions and conscience of our people as to be ranked as fundamental." Yanez cannot satisfy this test. * * *

We note that at the sentencing hearing the trial justice was fully cognizant of Yanez's favorable presentence report, his work history, his expressed remorse, and his supportive family. However, there is no escaping the fact that on their very first "date" following a brief encounter lasting only two or three minutes the previous day, this eighteen-year-old defendant engaged in sexual intercourse on the bedroom floor of his friend's house with this thirteen-year-old girl. The trial justice appropriately observed that there was some measure of planning involved in Yanez's encounters with Allison, which were aimed at avoiding detection by her mother. The trial justice further noted that the fact that Allison may have been "experienced" for someone her age or that her unfortunate past might have been somewhat unstable or troubled is not a defense. Indeed, the trial justice appropriately concluded that Allison is exactly the type of victim whose vulnerability the Legislature had intended to protect and that an offense perpetrated upon one in her circumstances "is more harmful than one committed upon someone who has a stable environment." Thus, although observing that "it is the public policy of this state * * * that those who engage in sexual intercourse with a person under 14, should be treated harshly," the trial justice nonetheless fashioned a compassionate sentence designed to promote not only rehabilitation but also deterrence. In the words of the trial justice, this sentence is "[n]ot only to deter this young man from committing similar crimes, but to discourage or deter others in the community; to let them know that if they're going to succumb to passion with someone under 14 years of age, there's a very high price to pay." We agree with the trial justice and find no error in his decision. * * *

Conclusion

For the reasons articulated, we deny the defendant's appeal and affirm the judgment of conviction. The papers in this case are hereby remanded to the Superior Court.

FLANDERS, JUSTICE, dissenting.

I respectfully dissent. I cannot believe that the Legislature intended that G.L.1956 § 11-37-8.1 (Rhode Island's statutory-rape law) – carrying a mandatory-minimum sentence of twenty years in jail – should be construed by the Judiciary to bar an accused teenager's reasonable mistake-of-age defense to charges based upon his engaging in consensual sexual acts with his teenaged girlfriend. The unavoidable result of such a draconian interpretation of this law is the imposition on this defendant, Alejandro Yanez (Alex) – a young man who was barely eighteen years old at the time of this incident – of an uncommonly brutal, harsh, and undeserved punishment that is so out of whack with reality that it is virtually without parallel in any jurisdiction of the United States.[10]

---

[10] Although Alex received the minimum twenty-year sentence after the trial justice refused to consider his mistake-of-age defense, the trial justice ordered him to serve the first two years of his sentence in prison and suspended the remaining

If any legislative intent is apparent in the language used in § 11-37-8.1 to criminalize sex with children, it is the intent manifest in its title to outlaw sexual abuse of children by adults and to punish severely those who commit such "child molestation." But there is a world of difference between a crime involving intentional child molestation and a situation like this one in which two teenage lovers engage in a fully consensual act (or acts) of sexual intercourse in the mistaken belief on the part of one of them that they are both of a legal age to do so. Although their exuberant sexual behavior may be sniffed at by a tongue-clucking majority as "sordid," it is certainly not "child molestation" within the meaning of Rhode Island's statutory-rape law.[11] Any criminal statute that carries a mandatory twenty-year jail sentence and imposes a lifelong stigma as a sexual predator on any violator should be rationally interpreted to draw a distinction between these two very different scenarios – especially when, as here, the sexual conduct in question would have been unquestionably legal if Alex's sexual partner had been sixteen years old, as she allegedly said she was.

In this case, two versions of what happened vie for acceptance. According to the defense, Alex, an eighteen-year-old (who was only six months too old for participation in our juvenile court system), had been dating a mature-looking young woman whom he had met several times previously and who phoned him and asked him to go out on that fateful evening. Alex claims that the young woman told him she was sixteen when (unbeknownst to him) she was really a month and a half shy of her fourteenth birthday. Her deceit was made more credible Alex contends, by her mature and developed physical

---

eighteen years while placing Alex on probation for this period. Thus, even after Alex finishes serving his prison sentence, he will be subject to re-imprisonment for up to eighteen years if he fails to keep the peace or engages in any other conduct that causes a hearing justice to be reasonably satisfied that he has violated the terms of his probation. Moreover, he will be required to register as a convicted sex offender and will be forever stigmatized as a convicted felon and child molester. Accordingly, in the circumstances of this case I disagree with the majority's conclusion that this outcome represents "a compassionate sentence."

[11] The uncharged sexual conduct alluded to by the majority relates to testimony by Allison that she and Alex had engaged in sexual activity on other occasions, apparently *before* the charged incident occurred at the house of Alex's friend. Thus, far from painting a picture of a "sordid" one-time tryst on the floor of a dingy back room, the evidence indicated that Allison and Alex had been dating each other and that the sexual activity that grew out of their relationship was no more sordid than any other case of premarital, teenage sex. Indeed, the trial justice himself noted at the sentencing hearing that the consensual sexual encounter for which Alex was charged was not a one-time affair: "[O]n the second date they're having sexual intercourse. Apparently times have changed."

appearance, her poise, her association with older teenagers, and her evident sexual experience.[13] The defense was prepared to produce witnesses to corroborate the reasonableness of Alex's being taken in by these misrepresentations but the trial justice barred him from doing so. In any event, there is no dispute that Alex and his date engaged in fully consensual sexual relations with each other. The prosecution, on the other hand, paints Alex as a fully accountable eighteen-year-old adult who, after having been warned that the young woman was not old enough to be seeing him, nonetheless proceeded to take advantage of her, knowing full well that the allure of his relative sophistication – together with his ownership of a car and access to a friend's apartment – would work its magic on an impressionable thirteen-year-old. But because the trial justice prevented Alex from introducing any evidence concerning the reasonableness of his mistaken belief that his teenage girlfriend was of legal age to engage in consensual sex, the jury never got to hear any of this testimony.

I would hold that in this type of situation the General Assembly intended that a jury – not judges or prosecutors – is the appropriate body to sort out true cases of child molestation from those involving consensual premarital sex between teenagers based upon a mistaken but reasonably held belief that both were old enough to do so legally. To this end, a criminal defendant indicted under § 11-37-8.1 should be afforded the opportunity to defend against such charges by showing a reasonable and good-faith mistake concerning the age of his or her consenting sexual partner.

I am both surprised and disappointed that a majority of this Court believes otherwise and thinks that Rhode Island's statutory-rape law must be interpreted as a strict-liability crime when it comes to the age of the accused's sexual partner. * * *

It is true that over the last century and a half, many American jurisdictions have adopted so-called statutory-rape laws. And many of these statutes, like Rhode Island's, set out only two express elements – sexual penetration and age -- and say nothing about a required mental state. This omission is not dispositive, however. Because "intent [is] so inherent in the idea of the [criminal] offense that it require[s] no statutory affirmation," *Morissette*, 342 U.S. at 252, most criminal statutes do not specify the mental state required for the forbidden acts to constitute a crime. Rather the common-law tradition

---

[13] Indeed, by the time of Alex's trial Allison had become pregnant by a different boyfriend, a condition which she initially and falsely blamed on Alex in order to conceal her sexual activity from her family.

mandates that the forbidden acts must be the result of intentional wrongdoing.
* * *

[The judge discusses the law of rape in colonial Rhode Island, the contemporary sex assault statutes, and then discusses the public welfare rationale for strict liability.]

Unlike regulatory prohibitions directed at *mala prohibita* offenses such as the sale of adulterated milk, child molestation does not naturally fall under the heading of statutorily prohibited public-welfare offenses. Child molestation is an inherently contemptible crime against an identifiable victim. To lump such a crime with petty gambling or commercial mislabeling belittles the gravity of intentional sexual-abuse crimes. Conversely, the degree of punishment and societal opprobrium befitting true sexual-abuse crimes cannot be so cavalierly imposed without regard to the culpable intention of the actor as can the light fines and slap-on-the-wrist penalties attached to typical public-welfare offenses.
* * *

III
The Emerging Rule

The last of the triad of points I would make is that a growing number of American jurisdictions have now adopted a new and still emerging American rule that antiquates judicially imposed strict-liability schemes for statutory rape. The Model Penal Code of 1962 (MPC) expressly rejects strict liability in the rape or sexual-assault context. Section 213.3(1)(a) of that code, the rough equivalent of our § 11-37-8.1, would prohibit sexual intercourse with a female under the age of sixteen when the actor is at least four years older than the victim. But the MPC expressly allows a reasonable-mistake-of-fact defense when, as here, the alleged victim is at least ten years old, *see* 2 MPC § 213.6 cmt. 2, although the MPC does adopt an irrebuttable presumption that a child victim actually under the age of ten cannot be reasonably taken for a sixteen-year-old. The MPC approach thus has the effect of attaching a "*mens rea* of [at least] recklessness to the age element in statutory rape." 2 MPC, § 213.6 cmt.2 at 415.

Today some fifteen American states have adopted the MPC in some form. Some set a critical age higher than the MPC's common-law designation of ten (occasionally as high as fourteen or sixteen) for the no-credible-error presumption, but all these states establish penalties far more flexible than our rigid twenty-year minimum sentence – even for the most egregious type of forcible child molestation. Six additional states expressly provide for a mistake-of-fact defense without age limitation, and two states, California and New Mexico, have judicially recognized a mistake-of-age defense by construction of generic statutory provisions similar to ours. And Alaska, as noted, has held the defense to be constitutionally mandated.

In *Hernandez* the Supreme Court of California departed from its own prior decisional law that had rejected the mistake-of-fact defense in the statutory-rape context. California's statute, which punished underage intercourse as a mere misdemeanor, contained general language similar to that employed in our statute – that is language devoid of any explicit reference to an intent requirement or to strict liability. The *Hernandez* court decided that such a statute left no room for strict liability. In explaining its holding on this score, the California high court noted, "The severe penalty imposed for [statutory rape], the serious loss of reputation conviction entails, * * * and the fact that it has been regarded for centuries as a crime involving moral turpitude, make it extremely unlikely that the Legislature meant to include the morally innocent to make sure the guilty did not escape." * * *

With *Hernandez* and the MPC taking the lead, twenty-three American jurisdictions, nearly half, now explicitly recognize some form of the mistake-of-age defense.

Of those states that arguably remain in the strict-liability camp, seven states expressly disallow the defense by statute. The remaining nineteen jurisdictions either have judicial decisions construing silent rape statutes like ours or are blithely assumed to impose strict liability without a definite statute or judicial opinion directly on point. Notably, of these states that putatively impose strict liability, almost all impose no mandatory minimum sentence or provide for a relatively low minimum; and many of these statutes incorporate flexibility measures such as imposing a lighter sentence or no criminal liability when the actor and the alleged victim are relatively close in age. * * *

For the above-stated reasons I am unwilling to attribute to the General Assembly an unexpressed intention to place Rhode Island on the outermost fringes of current legal thinking and actual practice regarding the mistake-of-age defense, especially when virtually no other state in the whole country imposes such an inflexibly harsh penalty without regard to the defendant's true culpability. In my judgment the majority's conversion of § 11-37- 8.1 into a strict-liability crime in mistake-of-age cases, coupled with the statute's mandatory minimum twenty-year prison sentence and convicted sex-offender status, creates an unparalleled and unjustified "double-whammy" that rains down its crushing blows indiscriminately upon innocently intentioned teenage lovers and heinous child molesters alike. Certainly the Legislature may enact strict measures to discourage sexual intercourse with minors or to avoid teenage pregnancy. But a mandatory twenty-years-to-life sentencing range is utterly out of proportion to this goal if mistake of age is not available as a defense.

Furthermore, the General Assembly's manifest aim to punish and to deter intentional sexual molestation of children does not require the judicial creation of strict liability in this situation. Allowing a criminal defendant accused of sexual assault upon a teenaged minor to claim mistake of age as a defense will neither burden prosecutors unduly nor insulate true child molesters from societal retribution. A jury can sort out a legitimate mistake-of-age defense in this context from fabricated excuses.

In sum, absent plain language in a statute that indicates otherwise, a teenaged boy's improvident participation in premarital sex with a teenaged girl that he reasonably believed was old enough to consent should not result in that teenager beginning his adult life in prison as a convicted child molester with a mandatory minimum term of twenty years in jail hanging over his head for the foreseeable future.

For these reasons I would reverse the trial court's conviction and remand this case for a new trial that would allow Alex to raise a reasonable-mistake-of-age defense to the charges.

STATUTORY RAPE LAWS: DOES IT MAKE SENSE TO ENFORCE THEM IN AN INCREASINGLY PERMISSIVE SOCIETY?
82 A.B.A. J. 86 (1996)[a]

Statutory rape laws were enacted in the Middle Ages to protect the chastity of young women. Now they are emerging as the latest solution to the teen pregnancy problem, after a 1995 study by the Alan Guttmacher Institute found about two-thirds of teen mothers were impregnated by adult males.

In California, Gov. Pete Wilson announced in his 1996 state-of-the-state address that statutory rape is a crime that is going to be treated as such. The state allocated more than 82 million to 16 jurisdictions to step up enforcement. The highest priority for prosecution were cases resulting in pregnancies and those in which there was an age discrepancy of more than five years. Soon after, California passed a law stiffening penalties to include a $25,000 fine and nine-year prison sentence for second-time offenders.

Some call these laws a relic of an oppressive past, while others think they promote family values. The positions of law professors Michelle Oberman, DePaul University - Chicago, and Richard Delgado, University of Colorado - Boulder, are more nuanced. Oberman thinks the laws must be recast as a weapon against coerced sex, while Delgado believes they will always be subject to selective enforcement.

YES: THE RISK OF PSYCHOLOGICAL HARM TO GIRLS IS TOO GREAT
Michelle Oberman

In an era in which more than 50 percent of teens under age 18 are sexually active, it is inconceivable that we could incarcerate every person who has sex with a minor. Nonetheless, important reasons remain for enforcing, and even expanding, statutory rape laws.

These laws reflect a consensus that minors are not mature enough to make major decisions because they are vulnerable to coercion and exploitation. This concern permeates the law – minors may disaffirm their contracts, generally may not consent to their own health care, may not drink alcohol and cannot vote. Therefore, the real question facing those who see statutory rape laws as antiquated is whether minors are somehow better able to protect themselves in sexual encounters than they are in other adult endeavors. The answer from numerous sources is no.

Studies by the American Association for University Women demonstrate that, for girls in particular, adolescence is a time of acute crisis in which self-esteem, body image, academic confidence and the willingness to speak out decline precipitously. Psychologists studying girls' sexuality report that these combined sources of insecurity, coupled with the perceived importance of being attractive to males, lead many girls to look to males for validation. In short, they try to fulfill their emotional needs through sex.

What this means is that many girls consent to sexual relationships that we, as a society, can and should recognize as exploitative. Traditional rape laws, focusing on lack of consent, do nothing to combat the problem of the 14-year-old girl who says yes to a 33-year-old neighbor because sleeping with an adult makes her feel important, or who says yes to a classmate who threatens to spread rumors about her unless she sleeps with him, or who says yes to several boys because they took her out.

Such encounters often result in permanent harm to girls through depression, disease and pregnancy. The very real harms girls suffer by "consenting" to sexual exploitation provide ample justification for laws that penalize those who would prey upon them.

Most modern statutory rape laws are gender-neutral and impose criminal liability only if the "victim" is under the age of consent and the partner is older by anywhere from two to five years or more. Bright-line rules are a sensible, if imperfect, mechanism for protecting minors, since there are valid reasons to suspect coercion when a girl 15 or younger has a partner 18 or older.

However, despite their usefulness, these statutes ignore the many exploitative sexual encounters between minors of similar ages. Moreover, the failure to mention coercion, coupled with the fact that age - disparate sexual unions are commonplace, yields little guidance for enforcement. Absent an explicit focus on coercion, these laws invite selective, discriminatory enforcement.

Instead of abolishing statutory rape laws, we ought to consider how to refine them. In doing so, we must remain cognizant of the harm we seek to prevent. The "wrong" committed by coercing a minor exists independently of teen pregnancy. Although no legal solution will eliminate the risks inherent in sexual activity and allow girls to come of age safely, the law has a critical role to play in setting predatory sexual behavior off-limits.

NO: SELECTIVE ENFORCEMENT TARGETS 'UNPOPULAR' MEN

Richard Delgado

Except in the case of the very young, who of course should be protected from sexual predators, statutory rape laws are a bad idea. Most such laws provide that anyone who has sex with someone younger than a certain age--frequently 16--is guilty of the crime of rape, since an underage partner is unable to give valid consent. These laws can only be applied unevenly--and they are.

Consider: Recent surveys show the median age of first intercourse for women in the United States is 17 years and a few months; for boys, it is a little lower. This means that a high percentage of young women are victims of statutory rape, and a very large percentage of young men belong in jail. Laws that sweeping are out of touch with social norms and cannot be enforced, except selectively--and, indeed, statutory rape laws are.

Unable to prosecute the whole country, law enforcement officials apply the law principally against two groups: men, frequently older, who have sex with girls from "good homes"; and minority men, who are punished if they commit the crime of having sex with white women or impregnate a woman of color under circumstances that add to the welfare rolls.

Amending the laws, as some legislators want to do, so that they would apply with special force to men who have sex with women five or more years younger would help, but only a little: Prosecutors cannot possibly charge in every case of a 16-year-old girl who has sex with her 21-year-old boyfriend.

The laws would continue to be used as weapons to punish men who are politically unpopular, socially unacceptable, of the wrong color, or who make the mistake of having intercourse with a woman from a socially upstanding (and well-connected) family. These laws, then, uphold old notions of chastity and virginity, while providing a weapon against men from social groups we do not like.

They also deprive women in their mid- and late teens of choice under the guise of protecting that choice. In this respect, they are the modern descendants of Victorian and late medieval laws punishing the crime of seduction, which were used to protect noble families against the loss of a property right in their daughters' marriageability.

Punishments for pressured sex and sex with the very young – and even hardcore pornography, which glorifies and encourages brutal sex and rape – are socially imperative, and the same is true for sexual harassment in the workplace and elsewhere. But overbroad statutory rape laws are one of the worst ideas that the family-values crowd has produced in years.

Women rarely are charged for sex with younger men. This is perhaps as it should be--men and women stand on very different footings with respect to physical and social power. But this relative scarcity of reverse-enforcement cases should cause us to ask deeper questions: What is rape? What is consent? When is intercourse pressured, and when is it an expression of love between two autonomous individuals?

These are all important questions. But mechanistic laws, which contain overtones of Puritanism, can only impede us in addressing these matters. They are both paternalistic and patriarchal, and should be firmly resisted.

C.   SODOMY

BOWERS v. HARDWICK

Supreme Court of the United States

478 U.S. 186, 106 S.Ct. 2841, 92 L.Ed.2d 140 (1986)

WHITE, JUSTICE, delivered the opinion of the Court, in which BURGER, C.J., and POWELL, REHNQUIST, and O'CONNOR, JJ. joined.

In August 1982, respondent Hardwick (hereafter respondent) was charged with violating the Georgia statute criminalizing sodomy by committing that act with another adult male in the bedroom of respondent's home. After a preliminary hearing, the District Attorney decided not to present the matter to the grand jury unless further evidence developed.

Respondent then brought suit in the Federal District Court, challenging the constitutionality of the statute insofar as it criminalized consensual sodomy.[2] He asserted that he was a practicing homosexual, that the Georgia sodomy statute, as administered by the defendants, placed him in imminent danger of arrest, and that the statute for several reasons violates the Federal Constitution. The District Court granted the defendants' motion to dismiss for failure to state a claim.

A divided panel of the Court of Appeals for the Eleventh Circuit reversed. Relying on our decisions in *Griswold v. Connecticut, Eisenstadt v. Baird, Stanley v. Georgia,* and *Roe v. Wade,*[a] the court went on to hold that the Georgia statute violated respondent's fundamental rights because his homosexual activity is a private and intimate association that is beyond the reach

---

[2] * * * The only claim properly before the Court, therefore, is Hardwick's challenge to the Georgia statute as applied to consensual homosexual sodomy. We express no opinion on the constitutionality of the Georgia statute as applied to other acts of sodomy.

[a] In *Griswold v. Connecticut*, 381 U.S. 479 (1965), the Court struck down a Connecticut statute forbidding the use of contraceptives, holding that the statute violated the right of marital privacy. In *Eisenstadt v. Baird*, 405 U.S. 438 (1972), the Court held that it was a violation of equal protection for the State to prohibit the distribution of contraceptives to unmarried persons while allowing such distribution to married couples. In *Stanley v. Georgia*, 394 U.S. 557 (1969), the Court invalidated a law that prohibited the knowing possession of obscene materials. In *Roe v. Wade*, 410 U.S. 113 (1973), the Court held that a woman has the right to choose whether to terminate her pregnancy at least during the first trimester of pregnancy.

of state regulation by reason of the Ninth Amendment and the Due Process Clause of the Fourteenth Amendment.

Because other Courts of Appeals have arrived at judgments contrary to that of the Eleventh Circuit in this case, we granted the Attorney General's petition for certiorari questioning the holding that the sodomy statute violates the fundamental rights of homosexuals. We agree with petitioner that the Court of Appeals erred, and hence reverse its judgment.

This case does not require a judgment on whether laws against sodomy between consenting adults in general, or between homosexuals in particular, are wise or desirable. It raises no question about the right or propriety of state legislative decisions to repeal their laws that criminalize homosexual sodomy, or of state-court decisions invalidating those laws on state constitutional grounds. The issue presented is whether the Federal Constitution confers a fundamental right upon homosexuals to engage in sodomy and hence invalidates the laws of the many States that still make such conduct illegal and have done so for a very long time. The case also calls for some judgment about the limits of the Court's role in carrying out its constitutional mandate.

We first register our disagreement with the Court of Appeals and with respondent that the Court's prior cases have construed the Constitution to confer a right of privacy that extends to homosexual sodomy and for all intents and purposes have decided this case. * * *

Accepting the decisions in these cases [dealing with child rearing and education, family relationships, procreation, marriage, contraception, and abortion], we think it evident that none of the rights announced in those cases bears any resemblance to the claimed constitutional right of homosexuals to engage in acts of sodomy that is asserted in this case. No connection between family, marriage, or procreation on the one hand and homosexual activity on the other has been demonstrated, either by the Court of Appeals or by respondent. * * *

Precedent aside, however, respondent would have us announce, as the Court of Appeals did, a fundamental right to engage in homosexual sodomy. This we are quite unwilling to do. It is true that despite the language of the Due Process Clauses of the Fifth and Fourteenth Amendments, which appears to focus only on the processes by which life, liberty, or property is taken, the cases are legion in which those Clauses have been interpreted to have substantive content, subsuming rights that to a great extent are immune from federal or state regulation or proscription. Among such cases are those recognizing rights that have little or no textual support in the constitutional language.

Striving to assure itself and the public that announcing rights not readily identifiable in the Constitution's text involves much more than the imposition of the Justices' own choice of values on the States and the Federal Government, the Court has sought to identify the nature of the rights qualifying for heightened judicial protection. In *Palko v. Connecticut*, it was said that this category includes those fundamental liberties that are "implicit in the concept of ordered liberty," such that "neither liberty nor justice would exist if [they] were sacrificed."

It is obvious to us that neither of these formulations would extend a fundamental right to homosexuals to engage in acts of consensual sodomy. Proscriptions against that conduct have ancient roots. Sodomy was a criminal offense at common law and was forbidden by the laws of the original thirteen States when they ratified the Bill of Rights. In 1868, when the Fourteenth Amendment was ratified, all but 5 of the 37 States in the Union had criminal sodomy laws. In fact, until 1961, all 50 States outlawed sodomy, and today, 24 States and the District of Columbia continue to provide criminal penalties for sodomy performed in private and between consenting adults. Against this background, to claim that a right to engage in such conduct is "deeply rooted in this Nation's history and tradition" or "implicit in the concept of ordered liberty" is, at best, facetious.

Nor are we inclined to take a more expansive view of our authority to discover new fundamental rights imbedded in the Due Process Clause. The Court is most vulnerable and comes nearest to illegitimacy when it deals with judge-made constitutional law having little or no cognizable roots in the language or design of the Constitution...

Respondent, however, asserts that the result should be different where the homosexual conduct occurs in the privacy of the home. He relies on *Stanley v. Georgia*, where the Court held that the First Amendment prevents conviction for possessing and reading obscene material in the privacy of one's home: "If the First Amendment means anything, it means that a State has no business telling a man, sitting alone in his house, what books he may read or what films he may watch."

Stanley did protect conduct that would not have been protected outside the home, and it partially prevented the enforcement of state obscenity laws; but the decision was firmly grounded in the First Amendment. The right pressed upon us here has no similar support in the text of the Constitution, and it does not qualify for recognition under the prevailing principles for construing the Fourteenth Amendment. Its limits are also difficult to discern. Plainly enough, otherwise illegal conduct is not always immunized whenever it occurs in the home. Victimless crimes, such as the possession and use of illegal drugs, do not escape the law where they are committed at home. *Stanley* itself recognized that its holding offered no protection for the possession in the home of drugs, firearms, or stolen goods. And if respondent's submission is limited to the voluntary sexual conduct between consenting adults, it would be difficult, except by fiat, to limit the claimed right to homosexual conduct while leaving exposed to prosecution adultery, incest, and other sexual crimes even though they are committed in the home. We are unwilling to start down that road.

Even if the conduct at issue here is not a fundamental right, respondent asserts that there must be a rational basis for the law and that there is none in this case other than the presumed belief of a majority of the electorate in Georgia that homosexual sodomy is immoral and unacceptable. This is said to be an inadequate rationale to support the law. The law, however, is constantly based on notions of morality, and if all laws representing essentially moral choices are to be invalidated under the Due Process Clause, the courts will be very busy indeed. Even respondent makes no such claim, but insists that majority sentiments about the morality of homosexuality should be declared inadequate. We do not agree, and are unpersuaded that the sodomy laws of some 25 States should be invalidated on this basis.[8]

Accordingly, the judgment of the Court of Appeals is

Reversed.

[The opinion of Mr. JUSTICE BURGER, concurring in the judgment is omitted.]

JUSTICE POWELL, concurring.

I join the opinion of the Court. I agree with the Court that there is no fundamental right--*i.e.,* no substantive right under the Due Process Clause-- such as that claimed by respondent Hardwick, and found to exist by the Court of Appeals. This is not to suggest, however, that respondent may not be protected by the Eighth Amendment of the Constitution. The Georgia statute at issue in this case, Ga. Code Ann. § 16-6-2 (1984), authorizes a court to imprison a person for up to 20 years for a single private, consensual act of sodomy. In my view, a prison sentence for such conduct--certainly a sentence of long duration--would create a serious Eighth Amendment issue. Under the Georgia statute a single act of sodomy, even in the private setting of a home, is a felony

---

[8] Respondent does not defend the judgment below based on the Ninth Amendment, the Equal Protection Clause, or the Eighth Amendment.

comparable in terms of the possible sentence imposed to serious felonies such as aggravated battery, first-degree arson, and robbery.

In this case, however, respondent has not been tried, much less convicted and sentenced. Moreover, respondent has not raised the Eighth Amendment issue below. For these reasons this constitutional argument is not before us.

JUSTICE BLACKMUN, with whom JUSTICE BRENNAN, JUSTICE MARSHALL, and JUSTICE STEVENS join, dissenting.

This case is no more about "a fundamental right to engage in homosexual sodomy," as the Court purports to declare, than *Stanley v. Georgia* was about a fundamental right to watch obscene movies, or *Katz v. United States* was about a fundamental right to place interstate bets from a telephone booth. Rather, this case is about "the most comprehensive of rights and the right most valued by civilized men," namely, "the right to be let alone."

The statute at issue, Ga. Code Ann. § 16-6-2 (1984), denies individuals the right to decide for themselves whether to engage in particular forms of private, consensual sexual activity. The Court concludes that § 16-6-2 is valid essentially because "the laws of ... many States ... still make such conduct illegal and have done so for a very long time." But the fact that the moral judgments expressed by statutes like § 16-6-2 may be "'natural and familiar ... ought not to conclude our judgment upon the question whether statutes embodying them conflict with the Constitution of the United States.'" Like Justice Holmes, I believe that "[i]t is revolting to have no better reason for a rule of law than that so it was laid down in the time of Henry IV. It is still more revolting if the grounds upon which it was laid down have vanished long since, and the rule simply persists from blind imitation of the past." I believe we must analyze Hardwick's claim in the light of the values that underlie the constitutional right to privacy. If that right means anything, it means that, before Georgia can prosecute its citizens for making choices about the most intimate aspects of their lives, it must do more than assert that the choice they have made is an "'abominable crime not fit to be named among Christians.'"

I

In its haste to reverse the Court of Appeals and hold that the Constitution does not "confe[r] a fundamental right upon homosexuals to engage in sodomy," the Court relegates the actual statute being challenged to a footnote and ignores the procedural posture of the case before it. A fair reading of the statute and of the complaint clearly reveals that the majority has distorted the question this case presents.

First, the Court's almost obsessive focus on homosexual activity is particularly hard to justify in light of the broad language Georgia has used. Unlike the Court, the Georgia Legislature has not proceeded on the assumption that homosexuals are so different from other citizens that their lives may be controlled in a way that would not be tolerated if it limited the choices of those other citizens. Rather, Georgia has provided that "[a] person commits the offense of sodomy when he performs or submits to any sexual act involving the sex organs of one person and the mouth or anus of another." The sex or status of the persons who engage in the act is irrelevant as a matter of state law. In fact, to the extent I can discern a legislative purpose for Georgia's 1968 enactment of § 16-6-2, that purpose seems to have been to broaden the coverage of the law to reach heterosexual as well as homosexual activity. I therefore see no basis for the Court's decision to treat this case as an "as applied" challenge to § 16-6-2, or for Georgia's attempt, both in its brief and at oral argument, to defend § 16-6-2 solely on the grounds that it prohibits homosexual activity. Michael Hardwick's standing may rest in significant part on Georgia's apparent willingness to enforce against homosexuals a law it seems not to have any desire to enforce against heterosexuals. But his claim that § 16-6-2 involves an unconstitutional intrusion into his privacy and his right of intimate association does not depend in any way on his sexual orientation. * * *

II

"Our cases long have recognized that the Constitution embodies a promise that a certain private sphere of individual liberty will be kept largely beyond the reach of government." In construing the right to privacy, the Court has proceeded along two somewhat distinct, albeit complementary, lines. First, it has recognized a privacy interest with reference to certain *decisions* that are properly for the individual to make. Second, it has recognized a privacy interest with reference to certain *places* without regard for the particular activities in which the individuals who occupy them are engaged. The case before us implicates both the decisional and the spatial aspects of the right to privacy.

A

The Court concludes today that none of our prior cases dealing with various decisions that individuals are entitled to make free of governmental interference "bears any resemblance to the claimed constitutional right of homosexuals to engage in acts of sodomy that is asserted in this case." While it is true that these cases may be characterized by their connection to protection of the family, the Court's conclusion that they extend no further than this boundary ignores the warning in *Moore v. East Cleveland* against "clos[ing] our eyes to the basic reasons why certain rights associated with the family have been accorded shelter under the Fourteenth Amendment's Due Process Clause." We protect those rights not because they contribute, in some direct and material way, to the general public welfare, but because they form so central a part of an individual's life. "[T]he concept of privacy embodies the 'moral fact that a person belongs to himself and not others nor to society as a whole.'" And so we protect the decision whether to marry precisely because marriage "is an association that promotes a way of life, not causes; a harmony in living, not political faiths; a bilateral loyalty, not commercial or social projects." We protect the decision whether to have a child because parenthood alters so dramatically an individual's self-definition, not because of demographic considerations or the Bible's command to be fruitful and multiply. And we protect the family because it contributes so powerfully to the happiness of individuals, not because of a preference for stereotypical households. The Court recognized in *Roberts* that the "ability independently to define one's identity that is central to any concept of liberty" cannot truly be exercised in a vacuum; we all depend on the "emotional enrichment from close ties with others."

Only the most willful blindness could obscure the fact that sexual intimacy is "a sensitive, key relationship of human existence, central to family life, community welfare, and the development of human personality." The fact that individuals define themselves in a significant way through their intimate sexual relationships with others suggests, in a Nation as diverse as ours, that there may be many "right" ways of conducting those relationships, and that much of the richness of a relationship will come from the freedom an individual has to *choose* the form and nature of these intensely personal bonds.

In a variety of circumstances we have recognized that a necessary corollary of giving individuals freedom to choose how to conduct their lives is acceptance of the fact that different individuals will make different choices. For example, in holding that the clearly important state interest in public education should give way to a competing claim by the Amish to the effect that extended formal schooling threatened their way of life, the Court declared: "There can be no assumption that today's majority is 'right' and the Amish and others like them are 'wrong.' A way of life that is odd or even erratic but interferes with no rights or interests of others is not to be condemned because it is different." The Court claims that its decision today merely refuses to recognize a fundamental right to engage in homosexual sodomy; what the Court really has refused to recognize is the fundamental interest all individuals have in controlling the nature of their intimate associations with others.

B

The behavior for which Hardwick faces prosecution occurred in his own home, a place to which the Fourth Amendment attaches special significance. The Court's treatment of this aspect of the case is symptomatic of its overall refusal to consider the broad principles that have informed our treatment of privacy in specific cases. Just as the right to privacy is more than the mere aggregation of a number of entitlements to engage in specific behavior, so too, protecting the physical integrity of the home is more than merely a means of protecting specific activities that often take place there. Even when our understanding of the contours of the right to privacy depends on "reference to a 'place,' the essence of a Fourth Amendment violation is 'not the breaking of [a person's] doors, and the rummaging of his drawers,' but rather is 'the invasion of his indefeasible right of personal security, personal liberty and private property.'" * * *

III

The Court's failure to comprehend the magnitude of the liberty interests at stake in this case leads it to slight the question whether petitioner, on behalf of the State, has justified Georgia's infringement on these interests. I believe that neither of the two general justifications for § 16-6-2 that petitioner has advanced warrants dismissing respondent's challenge for failure to state a claim.

First, petitioner asserts that the acts made criminal by the statute may have serious adverse consequences for "the general public health and welfare," such as spreading communicable diseases or fostering other criminal activity. * * * [I]t is not surprising that the record before us is barren of any evidence to support petitioner's claim. In light of the state of the record, I see no justification for the Court's attempt to equate the private, consensual sexual activity at issue here with the "possession in the home of drugs, firearms, or stolen goods," to which *Stanley* refused to extend its protection. None of the behavior so mentioned in *Stanley* can properly be viewed as "[v]ictimless,": drugs and weapons are inherently dangerous, and for property to be "stolen," someone must have been wrongfully deprived of it. Nothing in the record before the Court provides any justification for finding the activity forbidden by § 16-6-2 to be physically dangerous, either to the persons engaged in it or to others.

The core of petitioner's defense of § 16-6-2, however, is that respondent and others who engage in the conduct prohibited by § 16-6-2 interfere with Georgia's exercise of the "'right of the Nation and of the States to maintain a decent society.'" Essentially, petitioner argues, and the Court agrees, that the fact that the acts described in § 16-6-2 "for hundreds of years, if not thousands, have been uniformly condemned as immoral" is a sufficient reason to permit a State to ban them today.

I cannot agree that either the length of time a majority has held its convictions or the passions with which it defends them can withdraw legislation from this Court's scrutiny. As Justice Jackson wrote so eloquently for the Court in *West Virginia Board of Education v. Barnette,* "we apply the limitations of the Constitution with no fear that freedom to be intellectually and spiritually diverse or even contrary will disintegrate the social organization.... [F]reedom

to differ is not limited to things that do not matter much. That would be a mere shadow of freedom. The test of its substance is the right to differ as to things that touch the heart of the existing order." It is precisely because the issue raised by this case touches the heart of what makes individuals what they are that we should be especially sensitive to the rights of those whose choices upset the majority.

The assertion that "traditional Judeo-Christian values proscribe" the conduct involved cannot provide an adequate justification for § 16-6-2. That certain, but by no means all, religious groups condemn the behavior at issue gives the State no license to impose their judgments on the entire citizenry. The legitimacy of secular legislation depends instead on whether the State can advance some justification for its law beyond its conformity to religious doctrine. A State can no more punish private behavior because of religious intolerance than it can punish such behavior because of racial animus... No matter how uncomfortable a certain group may make the majority of this Court, we have held that "[m]ere public intolerance or animosity cannot constitutionally justify the deprivation of a person's physical liberty." * * *

IV

* * * [D]epriving individuals of the right to choose for themselves how to conduct their intimate relationships poses a far greater threat to the values most deeply rooted in our Nation's history than tolerance of nonconformity could ever do. Because I think the Court today betrays those values, I dissent.

[The opinion of Mr. JUSTICE STEVENS, with whom JUSTICE BRENNAN and JUSTICE MARSHALL join dissenting, is omitted.]

Note

The decision in *Bowers v. Hardwick* was closely divided. Justice Lewis Powell provided the swing vote in favor of the Court's ruling that the State of Georgia did not violate Michael Hardwick's right of due process when it arrested him for committing sodomy with another adult male in the privacy of his own home. Apparently, Justice Powell had second thoughts about his decision. After his retirement, he told a group of students at NYU School of Law, "I think I probably made a mistake in that one," referring to his opinion in *Bowers*. Anand Agneshwar, *Ex-Justice Says He May Have Been Wrong*, National Law Journal, Nov. 5, 1990, at 3.

The next excerpt provides some interesting factual background not found in the Supreme Court's opinion.

BEYOND THE PRIVACY PRINCIPLE
Kendall Thomas
92 Colum. L. Rev. 1431 (1992)

A. *Trail of Blood: The Untold Story of* Bowers v. Hardwick

* * * Michael Hardwick's first encounter with the police power of the state of Georgia took place one morning a block away from the gay bar in Atlanta where he worked.[12] An Atlanta police officer named K.R. Torick stopped Hardwick after seeing him throw a beer bottle into a trashcan outside the bar. As Hardwick recounts the story, the officer "made me get in the car and asked me what I was doing. I told him that I worked there, which immediately identified me as a homosexual, because he knew it was a homosexual bar." Torick then issued Hardwick a ticket for drinking in public. Because of a discrepancy on the ticket between the day and the date he was to appear in court, Hardwick failed to appear. Within two hours of Hardwick's scheduled appearance, Torick went to Hardwick's house with a warrant for his arrest, only to find that he was not at home. When Hardwick returned to his apartment, his roommate told him of the police officer's visit. Hardwick then went to the Fulton County courthouse, where he paid a $50 fine. In Hardwick's words:

---

[12] This information is taken from Michael Hardwick's account of the case, which appears in Peter Irons, THE COURAGE OF THEIR CONVICTIONS, 392-403 (1988), and from Laurence Tribe's discussion of *Hardwick* in Laurence H. Tribe, AMERICAN CONSTITUTIONAL LAW, 1424-25 (2d ed. 1988). Professor Tribe argued the case on Hardwick's behalf before the Supreme Court.

> I told the county clerk the cop had already been at my house
> with a warrant and he said that was impossible. He said it takes
> forty-eight hours to process a warrant. He wrote me a receipt
> just in case I had any problems with it further down the road.
> That was that, and I thought I had taken care of it and
> everything was finished, and I didn't give it much thought.

Three weeks later, Hardwick arrived home from work to find three men whom he did not know outside his house. In his account of the incident, Hardwick admits that he has no proof that these men were police officers, "but they were very straight, middle thirties, civilian clothes."

> I got out of the car, turned around, and they said 'Michael' and
> I said yes, and they proceeded to beat the hell out of me. Tore
> all the cartilage out of my nose, kicked me in the face, cracked
> about six of my ribs. I passed out. I don't know how long I
> was unconscious.... I managed to crawl up the stairs into the
> house, into the back bedroom. What I didn't realize was that
> I'd left a trail of blood all the way back.

A few days after this incident, and nearly a month after his first visit, Officer Torick again appeared at Hardwick's home. Torick found Hardwick in his bedroom having sex with another man.

> He said, My name is Officer Torick. Michael Hardwick, you
> are under arrest. I said, For what? What are you doing in my
> bedroom? He said, I have a warrant for your arrest. I told him
> the warrant isn't any good. He said, It doesn't matter, because
> I was acting under good faith.

Torick handcuffed Hardwick and his partner and took them to jail, where they were booked, fingerprinted, and photographed. As the two men were taken to a holding tank, Hardwick recalls that the arresting officer "made sure everyone in the holding cells and guards and people who were processing us knew I was in there for 'cocksucking' and that I should be able to get what I was looking for. The guards were having a real good time with that." Some hours later, Hardwick and his partner were transferred to another part of the building in which he was being held, in the course of which the jail officers made it clear to the other inmates that the men were gay, remarking "Wait until we put [him] into the bullpen. Well, fags shouldn't mind--after all, that's why they are here." Hardwick and his partner remained in jail for the greater part of the day, when friends were permitted to post bail for their release.

Shortly after his release, Hardwick accepted an offer from the Georgia affiliate of the American Civil Liberties Union to undertake his defense in the state courts. Hardwick and his attorneys planned to challenge the constitutionality of the state sodomy law's criminalization of the sexual conduct for which he had been arrested. Before the case came to trial, however, the Fulton County District Attorney declined to seek a grand jury indictment against Hardwick on the sodomy charges. In legal terms, this did not mean that the matter was at an end; the governing statute of limitations rendered Hardwick subject to indictment on the sodomy charges at any time within the next four years. In political terms, it meant that Hardwick (and gays and lesbians throughout the state) continued to be vulnerable to harassment and violence that would likely go unchecked and unchallenged so long as the sodomy statute remained in the Georgia criminal code. Faced with this prospect, Hardwick agreed to take his constitutional claim to the federal courts. * * *

LAWRENCE v. TEXAS

Supreme Court of the United States

539 U.S. 558, 123 S.Ct. 2472, 156 L.Ed.2d 508 (2003)

KENNEDY, J.

Liberty protects the person from unwarranted government intrusions into a dwelling or other private places. In our tradition the State is not omnipresent in the home. And there are other spheres of our lives and existence, outside the home, where the State should not be a dominant presence. Freedom extends beyond spatial bounds. Liberty presumes an autonomy of self that includes freedom of thought, belief, expression, and certain intimate conduct. The instant case involves liberty of the person both in its spatial and more transcendent dimensions.

I

The question before the Court is the validity of a Texas statute making it a crime for two persons of the same sex to engage in certain intimate sexual conduct.

In Houston, Texas, officers of the Harris County Police Department were dispatched to a private residence in response to a reported weapons disturbance. They entered an apartment where one of the petitioners, John Geddes Lawrence, resided. The right of the police to enter does not seem to have been questioned. The officers observed Lawrence and another man, Tyron Garner, engaging in a sexual act. The two petitioners were arrested, held in custody over night, and charged and convicted before a Justice of the Peace.

The complaints described their crime as "deviate sexual intercourse, namely anal sex, with a member of the same sex (man)." The applicable state law is Tex. Penal Code Ann. § 21.06(a) (2003). It provides: "A person commits an offense if he engages in deviate sexual intercourse with another individual of the same sex." The statute defines "deviate sexual intercourse" as follows:

> (A) any contact between any part of the genitals of one person and the mouth or anus of another person; or
> (B) the penetration of the genitals or the anus of another person with an object.

The petitioners exercised their right to a trial *de novo* in Harris County Criminal Court. They challenged the statute as a violation of the Equal Protection Clause of the Fourteenth Amendment and of a like provision of the Texas Constitution. Those contentions were rejected. The petitioners, having entered a plea of *nolo contendere*, were each fined $200 and assessed court costs of $141.25.

The Court of Appeals for the Texas Fourteenth District considered the petitioners' federal constitutional arguments under both the Equal Protection and Due Process Clauses of the Fourteenth Amendment. After hearing the case en banc the court, in a divided opinion, rejected the constitutional arguments and affirmed the convictions. The majority opinion indicates that the Court of Appeals considered our decision in *Bowers v. Hardwick,* to be controlling on the federal due process aspect of the case. *Bowers* then being authoritative, this was proper.

We granted certiorari to consider three questions:

> 1. Whether Petitioners' criminal convictions under the Texas "Homosexual Conduct" law -- which criminalizes sexual intimacy by same-sex couples, but not identical behavior by different-sex couples -- violate the Fourteenth Amendment guarantee of equal protection of laws?

> 2. Whether Petitioners' criminal convictions for adult consensual sexual intimacy in the home violate their vital interests in liberty and privacy protected by the Due Process Clause of the Fourteenth Amendment?

> 3. Whether *Bowers v. Hardwick* should be overruled?

The petitioners were adults at the time of the alleged offense. Their conduct was in private and consensual.

II

We conclude the case should be resolved by determining whether the petitioners were free as adults to engage in the private conduct in the exercise of their liberty under the Due Process Clause of the Fourteenth Amendment to the Constitution. For this inquiry we deem it necessary to reconsider the Court's holding in *Bowers*.

There are broad statements of the substantive reach of liberty under the Due Process Clause in earlier cases, including *Pierce v. Society of Sisters* and *Meyer v. Nebraska*; but the most pertinent beginning point is our decision in *Griswold v. Connecticut*.

In *Griswold* the Court invalidated a state law prohibiting the use of drugs or devices of contraception and counseling or aiding and abetting the use of contraceptives. The Court described the protected interest as a right to privacy and placed emphasis on the marriage relation and the protected space of the marital bedroom.

After *Griswold* it was established that the right to make certain decisions regarding sexual conduct extends beyond the marital relationship. In *Eisenstadt v. Baird*, the Court invalidated a law prohibiting the distribution of contraceptives to unmarried persons. The case was decided under the Equal Protection Clause; but with respect to unmarried persons, the Court went on to state the fundamental proposition that the law impaired the exercise of their personal rights. It quoted from the statement of the Court of Appeals finding the law to be in conflict with fundamental human rights, and it followed with this statement of its own:

> It is true that in *Griswold* the right of privacy in question inhered in the marital relationship . . . . If the right of privacy means anything, it is the right of the *individual*, married or single, to be free from unwarranted governmental intrusion into matters so fundamentally affecting a person as the decision whether to bear or beget a child.

The opinions in *Griswold* and *Eisenstadt* were part of the background for the decision in *Roe v. Wade*. As is well known, the case involved a challenge to the Texas law prohibiting abortions, but the laws of other States were affected as well. Although the Court held the woman's rights were not absolute, her right to elect an abortion did have real and substantial protection as an exercise of her liberty under the Due Process Clause. The Court cited cases that protect spatial freedom and cases that go well beyond it. *Roe* recognized the right of a woman to make certain fundamental decisions affecting her destiny and confirmed once more that the protection of liberty under the Due Process Clause has a substantive dimension of fundamental significance in defining the rights of the person.

In *Carey v. Population Services Int'l*, the Court confronted a New York law forbidding sale or distribution of contraceptive devices to persons under 16 years of age. Although there was no single opinion for the Court, the law was invalidated. Both *Eisenstadt* and *Carey*, as well as the holding and rationale in *Roe*, confirmed that the reasoning of *Griswold* could not be confined to the protection of rights of married adults. This was the state of the law with respect to some of the most relevant cases when the Court considered *Bowers* v. *Hardwick*.

The facts in *Bowers* had some similarities to the instant case. A police officer, whose right to enter seems not to have been in question, observed Hardwick, in his own bedroom, engaging in intimate sexual conduct with another adult male. The conduct was in violation of a Georgia statute making it a criminal offense to engage in sodomy. One difference between the two cases is that the Georgia statute prohibited the conduct whether or not the participants were of the same sex, while the Texas statute, as we have seen, applies only to participants of the same sex. Hardwick was not prosecuted, but he brought an action in federal court to declare the state statute invalid. He alleged he was a practicing homosexual and that the criminal prohibition violated rights guaranteed to him by the Constitution. The Court, in an opinion by Justice White, sustained the Georgia law. Chief Justice Burger and Justice Powell joined the opinion of the Court and filed separate, concurring opinions. Four Justices dissented.

The Court began its substantive discussion in *Bowers* as follows: "The issue presented is whether the Federal Constitution confers a fundamental right upon homosexuals to engage in sodomy and hence invalidates the laws of the many States that still make such conduct illegal and have done so for a very long time." That statement, we now conclude, discloses the Court's own failure to appreciate the extent of the liberty at stake. To say that the issue in *Bowers* was simply the right to engage in certain sexual conduct demeans the claim the individual put forward, just as it would demean a married couple were it to be said marriage is simply about the right to have sexual intercourse. The laws involved in *Bowers* and here are, to be sure, statutes that purport to do no more than prohibit a particular sexual act. Their penalties and purposes, though, have more far-reaching consequences, touching upon the most private human conduct, sexual behavior, and in the most private of places, the home. The statutes do seek to control a personal relationship that, whether or not entitled to formal recognition in the law, is within the liberty of persons to choose without being punished as criminals.

This, as a general rule, should counsel against attempts by the State, or a court, to define the meaning of the relationship or to set its boundaries absent injury to a person or abuse of an institution the law protects. It suffices for us to acknowledge that adults may choose to enter upon this relationship in the confines of their homes and their own private lives and still retain their dignity as free persons. When sexuality finds overt expression in intimate conduct with another person, the conduct can be but one element in a personal bond that is more enduring. The liberty protected by the Constitution allows homosexual persons the right to make this choice. * * *

At the outset it should be noted that there is no longstanding history in this country of laws directed at homosexual conduct as a distinct matter. Beginning in colonial times there were prohibitions of sodomy derived from the English criminal laws passed in the first instance by the Reformation Parliament of 1533. The English prohibition was understood to include relations between men and women as well as relations between men and men. Nineteenth-century commentators similarly read American sodomy, buggery, and crime-against-nature statutes as criminalizing certain relations between men and women and between men and men. The absence of legal prohibitions focusing on homosexual conduct may be explained in part by noting that according to some scholars the concept of the homosexual as a distinct category of person did not emerge until the late 19th century. Thus early American sodomy laws were not directed at homosexuals as such but instead sought to prohibit nonprocreative sexual activity more generally. * * *

It was not until the 1970's that any State singled out same-sex relations for criminal prosecution, and only nine States have done so. . . . Over the course of the last decades, States with same-sex prohibitions have moved toward abolishing them.

In summary, the historical grounds relied upon in *Bowers* are more complex than the majority opinion and the concurring opinion by Chief Justice Burger indicate. Their historical premises are not without doubt and, at the very least, are overstated.

It must be acknowledged, of course, that the Court in *Bowers* was making the broader point that for centuries there have been powerful voices to condemn homosexual conduct as immoral. The condemnation has been shaped by religious beliefs, conceptions of right and acceptable behavior, and respect for the traditional family. For many persons these are not trivial concerns but profound and deep convictions accepted as ethical and moral principles to which they aspire and which thus determine the course of their lives. These considerations do not answer the question before us, however. The issue is whether the majority may use the power of the State to enforce these views on the whole society through operation of the criminal law. "Our obligation is to define the liberty of all, not to mandate our own moral code." * * *

As an alternative argument in this case, counsel for the petitioners and some *amici* contend that *Romer* provides the basis for declaring the Texas statute invalid under the Equal Protection Clause. That is a tenable argument, but we conclude the instant case requires us to address whether *Bowers* itself has continuing validity. Were we to hold the statute invalid under the Equal Protection Clause some might question whether a prohibition would be valid if drawn differently, say, to prohibit the conduct both between same-sex and different-sex participants.

Equality of treatment and the due process right to demand respect for conduct protected by the substantive guarantee of liberty are linked in important respects, and a decision on the latter point advances both interests. If protected conduct is made criminal and the law which does so remains unexamined for its substantive validity, its stigma might remain even if it were not enforceable as drawn for equal protection reasons. When homosexual conduct is made criminal by the law of the State, that declaration in and of itself is an invitation to subject homosexual persons to discrimination both in the public and in the private spheres. The central holding of *Bowers* has been brought in question by this case, and it should be addressed. Its continuance as precedent demeans the lives of homosexual persons.

The stigma this criminal statute imposes, moreover, is not trivial. The offense, to be sure, is but a class C misdemeanor, a minor offense in the Texas legal system. Still, it remains a criminal offense with all that imports for the dignity of the persons charged. The petitioners will bear on their record the history of their criminal convictions. Just this Term we rejected various challenges to state laws requiring the registration of sex offenders. We are advised that if Texas convicted an adult for private, consensual homosexual conduct under the statute here in question the convicted person would come within the registration laws of a least four States were he or she to be subject to their jurisdiction. This underscores the consequential nature of the punishment and the state-sponsored condemnation attendant to the criminal prohibition. Furthermore, the Texas criminal conviction carries with it the other collateral consequences always following a conviction, such as notations on job application forms, to mention but one example. * * *

The doctrine of *stare decisis* is essential to the respect accorded to the judgments of the Court and to the stability of the law. It is not, however, an inexorable command. In *Casey* we noted that when a Court is asked to overrule a precedent recognizing a constitutional liberty interest, individual or societal reliance on the existence of that liberty cautions with particular strength against reversing course. . . . [T]here has been no individual or societal reliance on *Bowers* of the sort that could counsel against overturning its holding once there are compelling reasons to do so. *Bowers* itself causes uncertainty, for the precedents before and after its issuance contradict its central holding.

The rationale of *Bowers* does not withstand careful analysis. In his dissenting opinion in *Bowers* Justice Stevens came to these conclusions:

> Our prior cases make two propositions abundantly clear. First, the fact that the governing majority in a State has traditionally viewed a particular practice as immoral is not a sufficient reason for upholding a law prohibiting the practice; neither history nor tradition could save a law prohibiting miscegenation from constitutional attack. Second, individual decisions by married persons, concerning the intimacies of their physical relationship, even when not intended to produce offspring, are a form of "liberty" protected by the Due Process Clause of the Fourteenth Amendment. Moreover, this protection extends to intimate choices by unmarried as well as married persons.

Justice Stevens' analysis, in our view, should have been controlling in *Bowers* and should control here.

Bowers was not correct when it was decided, and it is not correct today. It ought not to remain binding precedent. *Bowers v. Hardwick* should be and now is overruled.

The present case does not involve minors. It does not involve persons who might be injured or coerced or who are situated in relationships where consent might not easily be refused. It does not involve public conduct or prostitution. It does not involve whether the government must give formal recognition to any relationship that homosexual persons seek to enter. The case does involve two adults who, with full and mutual consent from each other, engaged in sexual practices common to a homosexual lifestyle. The petitioners are entitled to respect for their private lives. The State cannot demean their existence or control their destiny by making their private sexual conduct a crime. Their right to liberty under the Due Process Clause gives them the full right to engage in their conduct without intervention of the government. "It is a promise of the Constitution that there is a realm of personal liberty which the government may not enter." The Texas statute furthers no legitimate state interest which can justify its intrusion into the personal and private life of the individual.

Had those who drew and ratified the Due Process Clauses of the Fifth Amendment or the Fourteenth Amendment known the components of liberty in its manifold possibilities, they might have been more specific. They did not presume to have this insight. They knew times can blind us to certain truths and later generations can see that laws once thought necessary and proper in fact serve only to oppress. As the Constitution endures, persons in every generation can invoke its principles in their own search for greater freedom.

The judgment of the Court of Appeals for the Texas Fourteenth District is reversed, and the case is remanded for further proceedings not inconsistent with this opinion.

It is so ordered.

O'CONNOR, J. (concurring)

The Court today overrules *Bowers v. Hardwick*. I joined *Bowers*, and do not join the Court in overruling it. Nevertheless, I agree with the Court that Texas' statute banning same-sex sodomy is unconstitutional. Rather than relying on the substantive component of the Fourteenth Amendment's Due Process Clause, as the Court does, I base my conclusion on the Fourteenth Amendment's Equal Protection Clause.

The Equal Protection Clause of the Fourteenth Amendment "is essentially a direction that all persons similarly situated should be treated alike." Under our rational basis standard of review, "legislation is presumed to be valid and will be sustained if the classification drawn by the statute is rationally related to a legitimate state interest."

Laws such as economic or tax legislation that are scrutinized under rational basis review normally pass constitutional muster, since "the Constitution presumes that even improvident decisions will eventually be rectified by the democratic processes." We have consistently held, however, that some objectives, such as "a bare . . . desire to harm a politically unpopular group," are not legitimate state interests. When a law exhibits such a desire to harm a politically unpopular group, we have applied a more searching form of rational basis review to strike down such laws under the Equal Protection Clause. * * *

The statute at issue here makes sodomy a crime only if a person "engages in deviate sexual intercourse with another individual of the same sex." Sodomy between opposite-sex partners, however, is not a crime in Texas. That is, Texas treats the same conduct differently based solely on the participants.

Those harmed by this law are people who have a same-sex sexual orientation and thus are more likely to engage in behavior prohibited by §21.06.

The Texas statute makes homosexuals unequal in the eyes of the law by making particular conduct -- and only that conduct -- subject to criminal sanction. It appears that prosecutions under Texas' sodomy law are rare. This case shows, however, that prosecutions under §21.06 *do* occur. And while the penalty imposed on petitioners in this case was relatively minor, the consequences of conviction are not. As the Court notes, petitioners' convictions, if upheld, would disqualify them from or restrict their ability to engage in a variety of professions, including medicine, athletic training, and interior design. Indeed, were petitioners to move to one of four States, their convictions would require them to register as sex offenders to local law enforcement.

And the effect of Texas' sodomy law is not just limited to the threat of prosecution or consequence of conviction. Texas' sodomy law brands all homosexuals as criminals, thereby making it more difficult for homosexuals to be treated in the same manner as everyone else. Indeed, Texas itself has previously acknowledged the collateral effects of the law, stipulating in a prior challenge to this action that the law "legally sanctions discrimination against [homosexuals] in a variety of ways unrelated to the criminal law," including in the areas of "employment, family issues, and housing."

Texas attempts to justify its law, and the effects of the law, by arguing that the statute satisfies rational basis review because it furthers the legitimate governmental interest of the promotion of morality. In *Bowers*, we held that a state law criminalizing sodomy as applied to homosexual couples did not violate substantive due process. We rejected the argument that no rational basis existed to justify the law, pointing to the government's interest in promoting morality. The only question in front of the Court in *Bowers* was whether the substantive component of the Due Process Clause protected a right to engage in homosexual sodomy. *Bowers* did not hold that moral disapproval of a group is a rational basis under the Equal Protection Clause to criminalize homosexual sodomy when heterosexual sodomy is not punished.

This case raises a different issue than *Bowers:* whether, under the Equal Protection Clause, moral disapproval is a legitimate state interest to justify by itself a statute that bans homosexual sodomy, but not heterosexual sodomy. It is not. Moral disapproval of this group, like a bare desire to harm the group, is an interest that is insufficient to satisfy rational basis review under the Equal Protection Clause. Indeed, we have never held that moral disapproval, without any other asserted state interest, is a sufficient rationale under the Equal

Protection Clause to justify a law that discriminates among groups of persons. * * *

Texas argues, however, that the sodomy law does not discriminate against homosexual persons. Instead, the State maintains that the law discriminates only against homosexual conduct. While it is true that the law applies only to conduct, the conduct targeted by this law is conduct that is closely correlated with being homosexual. Under such circumstances, Texas' sodomy law is targeted at more than conduct. It is instead directed toward gay persons as a class. "After all, there can hardly be more palpable discrimination against a class than making the conduct that defines the class criminal." When a State makes homosexual conduct criminal, and not "deviate sexual intercourse" committed by persons of different sexes, "that declaration in and of itself is an invitation to subject homosexual persons to discrimination both in the public and in the private spheres." * * *

That this law as applied to private, consensual conduct is unconstitutional under the Equal Protection Clause does not mean that other laws distinguishing between heterosexuals and homosexuals would similarly fail under rational basis review. Texas cannot assert any legitimate state interest here, such as national security or preserving the traditional institution of marriage. Unlike the moral disapproval of same-sex relations -- the asserted state interest in this case -- other reasons exist to promote the institution of marriage beyond mere moral disapproval of an excluded group.

A law branding one class of persons as criminal solely based on the State's moral disapproval of that class and the conduct associated with that class runs contrary to the values of the Constitution and the Equal Protection Clause, under any standard of review. I therefore concur in the Court's judgment that Texas' sodomy law banning "deviate sexual intercourse" between consenting adults of the same sex, but not between consenting adults of different sexes, is unconstitutional.

JUSTICE SCALIA, with whom THE CHIEF JUSTICE and JUSTICE THOMAS join, dissenting.

"Liberty finds no refuge in a jurisprudence of doubt." That was the Court's sententious response, barely more than a decade ago, to those seeking to overrule *Roe v. Wade*. The Court's response today, to those who have engaged in a 17-year crusade to overrule *Bowers v. Hardwick*, is very different. The need for stability and certainty presents no barrier.

Most of the rest of today's opinion has no relevance to its actual holding -- that the Texas statute "furthers no legitimate state interest which can justify" its application to petitioners under rational-basis review. Though there is discussion of "fundamental propositions," and "fundamental decisions," nowhere does the Court's opinion declare that homosexual sodomy is a "fundamental right" under the Due Process Clause; nor does it subject the Texas law to the standard of review that would be appropriate (strict scrutiny) if homosexual sodomy *were* a "fundamental right." Thus, while overruling the *outcome* of *Bowers*, the Court leaves strangely untouched its central legal conclusion: "Respondent would have us announce . . . a fundamental right to engage in homosexual sodomy. This we are quite unwilling to do." Instead the Court simply describes petitioners' conduct as "an exercise of their liberty" -- which it undoubtedly is -- and proceeds to apply an unheard-of form of rational-basis review that will have far-reaching implications beyond this case.

I

    I begin with the Court's surprising readiness to reconsider a decision rendered a mere 17 years ago in *Bowers* v. *Hardwick.* I do not myself believe in rigid adherence to *stare decisis* in constitutional cases; but I do believe that we should be consistent rather than manipulative in invoking the doctrine. Today's opinions in support of reversal do not bother to distinguish -- or indeed, even bother to mention -- the paean to *stare decisis* coauthored by three Members of today's majority in *Planned Parenthood v. Casey.* There, when *stare decisis* meant preservation of judicially invented abortion rights, the widespread criticism of *Roe* was strong reason to *reaffirm* it:

> Where, in the performance of its judicial duties, the Court decides a case in such a way as to resolve the sort of intensely divisive controversy reflected in *Roe*[,] . . . its decision has a dimension that the resolution of the normal case does not carry . . . . To overrule under fire in the absence of the most compelling reason . . . would subvert the Court's legitimacy beyond any serious question.

    Today, however, the widespread opposition to *Bowers*, a decision resolving an issue as "intensely divisive" as the issue in *Roe*, is offered as a reason in favor of *overruling* it. * * *

    Today's opinion is the product of a Court, which is the product of a law-profession culture, that has largely signed on to the so-called homosexual agenda, by which I mean the agenda promoted by some homosexual activists directed at eliminating the moral opprobrium that has traditionally attached to homosexual conduct. I noted in an earlier opinion the fact that the American Association of Law Schools (to which any reputable law school *must* seek to belong) excludes from membership any school that refuses to ban from its job-interview facilities a law firm (no matter how small) that does not wish to hire as a prospective partner a person who openly engages in homosexual conduct.

One of the most revealing statements in today's opinion is the Court's grim warning that the criminalization of homosexual conduct is "an invitation to subject homosexual persons to discrimination both in the public and in the private spheres." It is clear from this that the Court has taken sides in the culture war, departing from its role of assuring, as neutral observer, that the democratic rules of engagement are observed. Many Americans do not want persons who openly engage in homosexual conduct as partners in their business, as scoutmasters for their children, as teachers in their children's schools, or as boarders in their home. They view this as protecting themselves and their families from a lifestyle that they believe to be immoral and destructive. The Court views it as "discrimination" which it is the function of our judgments to deter. So imbued is the Court with the law profession's anti-anti-homosexual culture, that it is seemingly unaware that the attitudes of that culture are not obviously "mainstream"; that in most States what the Court calls "discrimination" against those who engage in homosexual acts is perfectly legal; that proposals to ban such "discrimination" under Title VII have repeatedly been rejected by Congress; that in some cases such "discrimination" is *mandated* by federal statute; and that in some cases such "discrimination" is a constitutional right. *See Boy Scouts of America v. Dale,* 530 U.S. 640 (2000).

Let me be clear that I have nothing against homosexuals, or any other group, promoting their agenda through normal democratic means. Social perceptions of sexual and other morality change over time, and every group has the right to persuade its fellow citizens that its view of such matters is the best. That homosexuals have achieved some success in that enterprise is attested to by the fact that Texas is one of the few remaining States that criminalize private, consensual homosexual acts. But persuading one's fellow citizens is one thing, and imposing one's views in [the] absence of democratic majority will is something else. I would no more *require* a State to criminalize homosexual acts -- or, for that matter, display *any* moral disapprobation of them -- than I would *forbid* it to do so. What Texas has chosen to do is well within the range of traditional democratic action, and its hand should not be stayed through the invention of a brand-new "constitutional right" by a Court that is impatient of democratic change. It is indeed true that "later generations can see that laws once thought necessary and proper in fact serve only to oppress;" and when that happens, later generations can repeal those laws. But it is the premise of our system that those judgments are to be made by the people, and not imposed by a governing caste that knows best.

One of the benefits of leaving regulation of this matter to the people rather than to the courts is that the people, unlike judges, need not carry things to their logical conclusion. The people may feel that their disapprobation of homosexual conduct is strong enough to disallow homosexual marriage, but not strong enough to criminalize private homosexual acts -- and may legislate accordingly. The Court today pretends that it possesses a similar freedom of action, so that we need not fear judicial imposition of homosexual marriage, as has recently occurred in Canada (in a decision that the Canadian Government has chosen not to appeal). At the end of its opinion -- after having laid waste the foundations of our rational-basis jurisprudence -- the Court says that the present case "does not involve whether the government must give formal recognition to any relationship that homosexual persons seek to enter." Do not believe it. More illuminating than this bald, unreasoned disclaimer is the progression of thought displayed by an earlier passage in the Court's opinion, which notes the constitutional protections afforded to "personal decisions relating to *marriage*, procreation, contraception, family relationships, child rearing, and education," and then declares that "persons in a homosexual relationship may seek autonomy for these purposes, just as heterosexual persons do." Today's opinion dismantles the structure of constitutional law that has permitted a distinction to be made between heterosexual and homosexual unions, insofar as formal recognition in marriage is concerned. If moral disapprobation of homosexual conduct is "no legitimate state interest" for purposes of proscribing that conduct, and if, as the Court coos (casting aside all pretense of neutrality), "when sexuality finds overt expression in intimate conduct with another person, the conduct can be but one element in a personal bond that is more enduring," what justification could there possibly be for denying the benefits of marriage to homosexual couples exercising "the liberty protected by the Constitution?" Surely not the encouragement of procreation, since the sterile and the elderly are allowed to marry. This case "does not involve" the issue of homosexual marriage only if one entertains the belief that principle and logic have nothing to do with the decisions of this Court. Many will hope that, as the Court comfortingly assures us, this is so.

The matters appropriate for this Court's resolution are only three: Texas's prohibition of sodomy neither infringes a "fundamental right" (which the Court does not dispute), nor is unsupported by a rational relation to what the Constitution considers a legitimate state interest, nor denies the equal protection of the laws. I dissent.

PEOPLE v. SAMUELS

Court of Appeals of California, First Appellate District, Division Two
250 Cal. App. 2d 501, 58 Cal.Rptr. 439 (Ct. App. 1967)

SHOEMAKER, P.J.

Defendant Marvin Samuels was charged by indictment with two counts of conspiracy to violate Penal Code, section 311.2 (preparing and distributing obscene matter); two counts of assault by means of force likely to cause great bodily injury; and a final count of sodomy. Defendant pleaded not guilty to all charges.

The jury acquitted defendant of sodomy but found him guilty on both charges of conspiracy, one charge of aggravated assault and the offense of simple assault included in the other charge of aggravated assault. The simple assault conviction was subsequently dismissed. The court suspended the imposition of sentence, fined defendant $3,000 and placed him on probation for a period of 10 years.

Defendant appeals from the order granting probation and from an order denying his motion for new trial as to the conspiracy and aggravated assault charges. The latter order is nonappealable.

Defendant Samuels, an opthalmologist, testified that he recognized the symptoms of sadomasochism in himself, and his primary concern became to control and release his sadomasochistic urges in ways which were harmless. Through his hobby of photography, he participated in the production of several films on the [E]ast [C]oast. Three of these films depicted bound individuals being whipped. Defendant wielded the whip in two of the films and acted as the cameraman, producer and director for the third film. He testified that the apparent force of the whippings was "faked" and that cosmetics were used to supply the marks of the apparent beating. Defendant produced one of these films at the trial.

In early September 1964, defendant met Kenneth Anger in San Francisco. Anger was a self-employed film director who had made such films as "Fireworks" and "Scorpio Rising." He had also been a close friend of Dr. Kinsey from the institute by that name, had been a buyer for the institute for a period of seven years, and had an authorization to send material through the mails.

On the night of their initial meeting, Anger introduced himself to defendant and inquired whether defendant had seen "Scorpio Rising."

Defendant replied that he had not. Defendant had seen "Fireworks," however, and considered it the most sadomasochistic film he had ever seen. He told Anger that he himself had made two or three rolls of film dealing with sadomasochistic activity and was interested in having them developed. Anger volunteered to have the films developed and also told defendant that he believed that the Kinsey Institute would be very interested in examining the footage and might want the films for their collection, since they were then studying the subject of sadomasochism. Defendant agreed to mail the films to Anger's Hollywood address. There was no discussion of having the films developed at an ordinary camera store.

In the middle of September, defendant mailed the three rolls of film to Anger in Hollywood. Anger sent the rolls to a local film service laboratory, and picked up the developed film several days later. One of the rolls was badly underexposed and nearly black. The other two rolls were visible, although slightly underexposed. Anger mailed the latter two films to Dr. Gebhardt of the Kinsey Institute, having previously written him and informed him that he was on the trail of footage which he thought would interest the institute. Anger mailed the underexposed roll to defendant.

Dr. Gebhardt returned the films to Anger, who mailed them to defendant.

Anger's next contact with defendant occurred in early November. The two men dined at a San Francisco restaurant and defendant stated during the course of the dinner that he had edited the films which Anger had developed for him, and he also stated that he intended to make more films of a sadomasochistic nature. Anger again volunteered to have them developed, and told defendant to mail them to Anger's San Francisco address. Defendant indicated that an individual who would play the role of the masochist in a future film was coming from out of state. When Anger again stated that the Kinsey Institute would be interested in the films, defendant expressed a willingness to donate to the institute both the films he had already made and those he intended to make. There was never any discussion of making the films available to the general public or to anyone other than the Kinsey Institute.

After dinner, defendant and Anger went to defendant's home, where the two rolls of film which he had edited were projected. Anger saw that the two rolls had been spliced together and that a shot of a solitary figure wielding a whip had been taken from the end of one roll, where it had previously appeared, and had been cut into several pieces and reinserted at various places in the two combined rolls. This film constitutes the basis for the second conspiracy count and will hereafter be referred to as the "horizontal" film.

At the trial Anger identified defendant as the man wielding the whip.

Anger's next contact with defendant occurred in mid-November, when he received two rolls of film from him. Anger deposited the films at Schaefer's Camera Store in San Francisco, using the fictitious name of "Jackson" and giving a false address. He subsequently returned to the camera shop and was told that only one of the films had thus far been developed and returned to the shop. He paid the developing fee and picked up the film.

The other roll of film had been sent by the camera shop to the Eastman Kodak Company in Palo Alto for processing. The company contacted the Palo Alto Police Department and projected the film for certain police officers and prosecuting attorneys, who confiscated the film.

A dummy roll of film was left at Schaefer's Camera Store. On November 20, Anger picked up this film and was apprehended by the police of San Francisco. Anger was taken to the Hall of Justice where he was questioned concerning the defendant and the films.

Later that day, the Santa Clara County district attorney's office obtained a warrant authorizing a search of defendant's home for whips and other instruments of torture.

Anger and several police officers of San Francisco then drove to the Santa Clara County district attorney's office, arriving there about 7:30 p.m. They viewed the film which Inspector Nieto of San Francisco had obtained from Eastman.

This film, which will henceforth be referred to as the "vertical" film, constituted the basis for the first conspiracy count and the aggravated assault charge. It shows a gagged and naked man strung up in an unfinished room, receiving a beating with whips and lashes administered by a man whom Anger identified as defendant. There are marks on the victim's buttocks, the small of his back and further up on his body. The film contained no splices.

After viewing the film, all of the officers proceeded to defendant's Sunnyvale residence, arriving there at approximately 9 p.m. When defendant opened the door, he was informed of the search warrant, it was read to him and then handed to him. The officers then entered the house and observed that the living room was in semi-darkness and that a movie screen was set up in the living room, and a projector was on the dining room table. Two canisters of film were on the table by the projector. One canister contained the "horizontal" film, and the other contained a travelogue entitled "Fire Island," which defendant had made on the [E]ast [C]oast.

Nieto accompanied defendant into the bedroom and was subsequently joined by Logan of the district attorney's office, who advised defendant of his rights to counsel and to remain silent. Logan then asked defendant the name of the individual who was strung from the beam in the "vertical" film. Defendant replied that he did not know his name and that he had met him in a San Francisco bar. In response to further questioning, defendant said that the film had been made in an unfinished room in the Sunnyvale house. He further stated that no third party was present when the film was made, and automatic camera settings were used. He then refused to say anything further until he had consulted an attorney.

Defendant was subsequently questioned by Nieto. The man in the "vertical" film was an individual whom he had met either at a "gay" bar or at Foster's. Defendant thought his name was "George," but did not know his present whereabouts. The man approached him and stated that he was an "M" looking for an "S." The man thereafter came to defendant's home and voluntarily submitted to the beating. Defendant admitted that he was a well-known sadist and stated that he was one of the best in the business. When asked about the white substance on the face of the victim in the film, defendant stated that it was adhesive tape. He subsequently accompanied Nieto into the unfinished room in his house and identified the studs to which the victim's feet had been anchored during the filming.

Lowell Bradford, Director of the Santa Clara County Laboratory of Criminalistics and a qualified expert, testified that he had extracted certain sections from the "vertical" film by way of color slides which were then made into prints. This film, as above noted, contained no splices. His examination of the prints taken from a "representative area" of the film led him to the conclusion that the camera could not have been stopped so as to allow for the application of cosmetics and that the marks and welts which appeared on the victim during this portion of the film occurred progressively from frame to frame in slow development and were not the result of any retouching. Bradford had made a similar examination of a representative area of the "horizontal" film and had concluded that the welts on the victim had progressively developed during uninterrupted sections of the film without any indication of camera stops during which cosmetics could have been applied. There was no evidence that either the "vertical" or "horizontal" films had been retouched and Bradford was of the opinion that both films truly and correctly represented what was before the camera at the time. Edward Chong, senior county photographer, and Rudolph Stohr of the Eastman Kodak Company, were of the same opinion as to the absence of retouching and the accurate depiction of the scene before the camera.

On cross-examination, Bradford admitted that he had never examined defendant's camera, a Bolex, and was generally unfamiliar with that type of camera. With the exception of one stop early in the film, his notes indicated no other distinct stops in the "vertical" film. He saw no interruption in the continuity of action and did not know whether the clear frames were actual stops or were attributable to a shutter fault. Since he had not examined the camera, he did not know whether it had any such defect.

Bradford had also performed a laboratory examination of the riding crop, belt, cane and lash used to strike the victims in the two films and had been unable to detect any traces of blood or cosmetics.

Defendant testified on his own behalf and admitted making both films in his home. The man who had been strung up in the "vertical" film had telephoned defendant after he had let it be known in the San Francisco "underground" that he wanted volunteers for sadomasochistic films to be sent to the Kinsey Institute. Defendant arranged to meet him at the San Jose bus depot and drove him to his Sunnyvale home. After the filming had been completed, defendant drove him back to the bus depot in the "same condition he came in." During the course of the filming, which took some four hours, defendant strung the man up with hospital restraints and struck him lightly with a riding crop, pulling his punches just before striking the man's body. He stopped the camera periodically and applied cosmetics. Defendant had coached the man to move violently so as to make the film seem realistic. * * *

Dr. Robert Malone, a surgeon and physician whose practice included serving as team physician for a high school football team for a period of 10 years, was of the opinion that the marks on the victims in the "vertical" and "horizontal" films could have been caused only in part by the blows inflicted during the course of said films; that as to the "vertical" film, the dark coloration which appeared after the initial redness would not show up until at least 12 hours after the blow or trauma and certainly not within a period of a few minutes, as depicted in the film. The doctor testified at length as to the effect of the body being struck a violent blow in support of his opinion. If he were to assume that the marks did accurately depict the victim's reaction to the blows depicted in the film, his medical opinion would be that there would of necessity have been a breaking of the skin and some bleeding, which would be detectable on the instruments used to inflict the beating. He could conceive of no physiological or medical explanation for this change and believed that cosmetics must have been applied to the surface of the skin.

Defendant challenges the validity of his conviction of conspiracy and assault on numerous and diverse grounds. * * *

Defendant also contends that the consent of the victim is an absolute defense to the charge of aggravated assault and that the trial court erred in instructing the jury to the contrary. This argument cannot be sustained.

Although both parties concede that they were unable to find any California case directly in point, consent of the victim is not generally a defense to assault or battery, except in a situation involving ordinary physical contact or blows incident to sports such as football, boxing or wrestling. It is also the rule that the apparent consent of a person without legal capacity to give consent, such as a child or insane person, is ineffective.

It is a matter of common knowledge that a normal person in full possession of his mental faculties does not freely consent to the use, upon himself, of force likely to produce great bodily injury. Even if it be assumed that the victim in the "vertical" film did in fact suffer from some form of mental aberration which compelled him to submit to a beating which was so severe as to constitute an aggravated assault, defendant's conduct in inflicting that beating was no less violative of a penal statute obviously designed to prohibit one human being from severely or mortally injuring another. It follows that the trial court was correct in instructing the jury that consent was not a defense to the aggravated assault charge. * * *

The attempted appeal from the order denying a new trial is dismissed. The conviction as to aggravated assault is affirmed. The trial court is directed to vacate and set aside the convictions of conspiracy and the order of probation is vacated with directions to the trial court to reconsider the same in the light of our determination.

D.   PROSTITUTION

Prostitution was not a crime at English common law, and until the late nineteenth century prostitutes were usually punished criminally, if at all, under vagrancy, indecent exposure, and nuisance laws. In the late nineteenth and early twentieth century, however, an anti-prostitution movement emerged in the United States. This "abolitionist" movement was made up of feminists concerned with the economic, political and social subjugation of women; moral purists concerned about innocent women being dragooned into so-called "white slavery" and the sordid public spectacle of "red-light districts;" and physicians and other "social hygienists" concerned with the spread of venereal disease and other public health effects of prostitution. These reformers succeeded into whipping the public into a panic about prostitution, and at both the state and federal level both prostitution and its many manifestations were criminalized.

Although Progressive-Era reformists focused their disapproval on the procurers, pimps, and other male exploiters of prostitutes, the burden of the new criminalization largely fell on women. A Massachusetts study of the "white slave trade" published in 1914, for example, noted: "The police court records show that relatively few male patrons of prostitutes are arrested for their share in the offense involved. Just here there seems to be a lack of evenhanded justice. When men are found in a raided house they are not arrested unless taken in the act of fornication. The usual penalty for the offense for the man is a fine of $10. . . . Very rarely is even a short jail sentence imposed." Commission for the Investigation of the White Slave Traffic, So Called, Report of the Commission for the Investigation of the White Slave Traffic, H. Rep. N. 2281, at 60 (Mass. 1914).

Why the criminal law's relative lack of interest in johns as opposed to prostitutes? A commentator offers the following reasons:

> [T]he Victorian myth that men could not control their sex drives, while female sexuality was nonexistent, continued and persists today, affecting the way the justice system differentiates prostitutes and johns. Prostitutes were considered by some as a necessary evil, keeping male urges in check and preventing men from bothering other "respectable" women like their wives. In fact, many believed that
>
> > [v]ice is one of the weaknesses of men; it cannot be extirpated; if repressed unduly at one point, it will break out more violently and bafflingly elsewhere; a segregated district is really a protection to the morality of the womanhood of the city, for without it rape would be common and clandestine immorality would increase.
>
> Therefore, men were not faulted for acting upon their irrepressible desires. This may help explain the justice system's hesitancy to punish them. In contrast, women were acting against their nature by acting sexually and society sought to separate them from respectable women. Thus, legislatures enacted laws "to control female sexuality and promiscuity, even though prostitution is considered a 'necessary evil' which must exist, albeit clandestinely, to serve the sexual freedom of men."

> Another reason for the vilification of prostitutes was the threat they posed to the existing patriarchal familial structure which guarded male dominance. Prostitutes asserted independence by not relying on married life as their sole source of support and by making more money than could be had in legitimate occupations. Thus, the nineteenth-century campaign to criminalize prostitution was part of a sometimes desperate attempt to enforce norms of marriage, chastity, and propriety on women -- to keep women in the private sphere of home and family, to prevent them from supporting themselves independently of men, to encourage them to marry.

Julie Lefler, *Shining the Spotlight on Johns: Moving Toward Equal Treatment of Male Customers and Female Prostitutes*, 10 Hastings Women's L.J. 11, 14-15 (1999).

Today, should prostitution be a crime at all? What are the harms prostitution causes, and how can they be alleviated? Does the decision in *Lawrence* change the way we should think about prostitution? Consider these questions as you read the following case.

In re P.
Family Court, New York County, New York
92 Misc.2d 62, 400 N.Y.S.2d 455 (1977)

MARGARET TAYLOR, Judge.

Respondent P. is a 14 year old female. She is before this court on the complaint of D.

The petition alleges, inter alia, that "Respondent did offer to perform a deviate sexual act for U.S. currency", an act which, if committed by an adult, would constitute the crime of prostitution, Penal Law Section 230.00, a class B misdemeanor.

Paragraph Ten of the Bill of Particulars of the Corporation Counsel describes the incident as follows:

"On March 6, 1977, at about 8:30 P.M., respondent accosted complaining witness on the street and offered to engage in sexual acts with him for a fee of $10; he agreed and respondent took him to the Evans Hotel, 273 West 38 Street, New York City. Complaining witness paid $4 for the use of a room and went there with respondent."

It should be noted that the complaining witness was not charged with the violation of patronizing a prostitute, P.L. § 230.05.[2] Nor was he charged with any other crime applicable to these facts.[3]

Section 230.00 of the Penal Law reads:

> A person is guilty of prostitution when such person engages or agrees or offers to engage in sexual conduct with another person in return for a fee.

A deviate sexual act is defined by Section 130.00(2) of the Penal Law as:

> "Deviate sexual intercourse" means sexual conduct between persons not married to each other consisting of contact between the penis and the anus, the mouth and the penis, or the mouth and the vulva.

Deviate sexual intercourse, also a Class B misdemeanor, is made a crime under Section 130.38 of the Penal Law:

> Consensual Sodomy: A person is guilty of consensual sodomy when he engages in deviate sexual intercourse with another person.

Under the Family Court Act, the court can find that a respondent is a juvenile delinquent only if (a) the court finds beyond a reasonable doubt that "the respondent did any act which, if done by an adult, would constitute a crime" and (b) "the respondent requires supervision, treatment, or confinement". Both of these findings are jurisdictional and, therefore, a failure to find both elements requires dismissal of a juvenile delinquent petition.

The threshold question in all juvenile delinquency proceedings is, therefore, not whether a respondent committed a particular act but whether such an act would be a crime if committed by an adult. If not, then the court can go no further and must dismiss the petition. Accordingly, if acts committed by an adult would not constitute a crime because the criminal statute or statutes

---

[2] Patronizing a prostitute is a violation.

[3] The complaining witness could have been charged with attempted statutory rape (P.L. ss 110; 135.25(2)) or endangering the welfare of a minor (P.L. s 260.10), in addition to patronizing a prostitute.

making such alleged acts a crime were unconstitutional, such acts could not be the basis for a charge of juvenile delinquency. A youth under the age of 16 may be found to be a juvenile delinquent only if an adult who engaged in the same conduct as the youth could be found to have committed a crime. If a statute is unconstitutional as applied to adults, a statute is unconstitutional as applied to juveniles.

Inasmuch as the petition alleges that the respondent offered to perform an act of consensual sodomy for a fee, the charges brought against respondent necessarily invoke the prostitution statute and the consensual sodomy law. Respondent is specifically charged with offering to perform a "deviate" sexual act for a fee. If she had been charged with offering to perform a "normal" sexual act (i. e. fornication) for a fee, it would have been necessary for the court to deal with the question of whether a crime can be committed by offering to perform a sexual act, which in and of itself is not illegal, for money. Here, however, respondent is charged with offering to perform an act which in and of itself is proscribed by a criminal statute, the consensual sodomy law. It is necessary, therefore, for the court to examine those sections of the Penal Law and make a determination as to their constitutionality.

Respondent, by her attorney, has moved to dismiss the prostitution charge on constitutional and other grounds. For the reasons stated below, the court holds that sections 230.00, 130.38 and 130.00(2) of the Penal Law are unconstitutional under the New York State Constitution in that these statutes constitute a denial of equal protection and invade respondent's constitutionally protected right of privacy.

Article I, Section 11 of the New York State Constitution guarantees that:

No person shall be denied the equal protection of the laws of this State or any subdivision thereof.

This provision provides at least as broad protection as its federal counterpart.

The equal protection clause is offended when the state discriminates between classes of citizens similarly situated on arbitrary and unreasonable grounds not related to the objective of the legislation.

The selective enforcement of a law against a particular class of individuals on the basis of sex is no less offensive to the equal protection clause of the New York State Constitution than classification by sex on the face of the statute.

Sex is a suspect classification in New York State. Thus, sections 230.00 and 230.05 as applied are subject to strict scrutiny.

However, as the Court of Appeals notes,

> The inflexibility of the traditional equal protection approaches is readily apparent for each is polarized and outcome determinative. Modern day theorists . . . have detected a departure from traditional approaches in recent precedent and argue, convincingly, we think, that a middle level of review presently exists.

[This] middle level of review * * * requires that a court examine such factors as the classification involved, the constitutional and societal importance of the interests adversely affected and the relative invidiousness of the basis upon which the classification is drawn. This court has no interest in adopting an outcome determinative test when it is faced with these controversial challenges to the prostitution and consensual sodomy laws. Thus, all the forementioned facts will be considered when examining the constitutional challenges raised.

Until 1964, a prostitute was defined as a "female person". The legislature amended the penal law to make the prostitution statute sex neutral in its wording and it enacted a statute proscribing the act of patronizing a prostitute. Although the prostitution laws were made facially sex neutral, their historical sex bias has endured.

Prostitution is a Class B misdemeanor, carrying a penalty of up to ninety days imprisonment. A person may be found guilty of prostitution for simply "agreeing" to perform a sexual act, even if the patron is the solicitor. In contrast, patronizing a prostitute is merely a violation carrying a penalty of up to fifteen days imprisonment or up to $250 fine. The conduct engaged in by the prostitute and the patron is nearly identical and the wording of the respective statutes is quite similar.

The instant case presents clear evidence of intentional selective enforcement of the prostitution statutes against females.[6] The overwhelming majority of arrests made under section 230.00 of the Penal Law are of female prostitutes. During the first six months of 1977, 3219 arrests were made in New York County under this statute. Of those arrested, 2,944 were females and only 275 were males. Of equal importance is the fact that although 3219 arrests were

---

[6] This pattern of sex-discriminatory enforcement of prostitution laws is found nationwide.

made for prostitution, only 62 persons were charged with patronizing a prostitute. Of the 2,944 female prostitutes arrested, only 60 of their male patrons were charged with a violation. This data supports the conclusion that those assigned the task of enforcing the law harbor the attitude that women who supply sex are immoral whereas the men who demand their services are considered blameless.

The methods of enforcement used by the police contribute to the selective enforcement of the prostitution laws against females. Arrests for prostitution are rarely made on the complaint of a private citizen. A police officer must be directly solicited to make an arrest. Male undercover police officers are assigned to pose as patrons to entrap streetwalkers. However, female plainclothes officers are not presently assigned to pose as prostitutes to entrap male patrons. Thus, the method of enforcement of the prostitution laws is sex biased, aimed only at punishing the female prostitute.[9]

Thus, the court concludes that even were sex not a "suspect classification", the prostitution statutes nonetheless violate the equal protection clause. There is no, nor has the Corporation Counsel suggested any, reasonable justification for penalizing the conduct of female prostitutes more severely than the conduct of their male patrons.[10] The prostitution laws have undeniably been selectively enforced against females because of their sex. Discrimination by the

---

[9] In experimental programs in New York City and the District of Columbia, female undercover police officers were assigned to pose as prostitutes to entrap patrons. White, married, middle class and middle aged men were arrested. The public uproar of "respectable" citizens that ensued in response to these arrests caused the end of these experiments. This commonplace selective enforcement tactic designed to punish the female streetwalker and leave unscathed her white, middle aged, middle class married male client is a very costly law enforcement practice. It violates the streetwalker's right to equal protection of the law. Moreover, community support for law enforcement is eroded when the streetwalker is repeatedly arrested while patrons, pimps, hotel owners and landlords go free. The court acknowledges the community concern over the street activity connected with prostitution. But inasmuch as it is the patron who is most sensitive to arrest and who is most likely to be deterred from engaging in allegedly disruptive public conduct, non-discriminatory enforcement of the prostitution laws against all participants patrons, landlords, pimps, hotel owners and prostitutes alike could resolve the constitutional infirmity and have a significant impact upon the street problems associated with prostitution.

[10] Unofficial sources report that the vast number of prostitutes arrested under Penal Law section 230.00 (and related statutes) are non-white streetwalkers. Their customers are predominately white males. Thus, it appears that Penal Law section 230.00 works an invidious racial discrimination.

state between different classes of citizens, "'must be reasonable, not arbitrary, and must rest upon some ground of difference having a fair and substantial relationship to the objective of the legislation, so that all persons similarly circumstanced shall be treated alike.'"

This court can find no real difference between the conduct of the prostitute and the patron. The patron pays and the prostitute receives compensation for her services. Yet, under the wording of the statute and frequently in practice, the patron may be the solicitor.[11]

As a court of this state observed over fifty years ago:

> The men create the market; and the women who supply the demand pay the penalty. It is time that this unfair discrimination and injustice should cease. . . . The practical application of the law as heretofore enforced is an unjust discrimination against women in the matter of an offense, which in its very nature, if completed, requires the participation of men.

To the extent prostitution may cause a public nuisance by reason of offensive conduct on the streets or congested traffic,[12] such nuisance is caused

---

[11] To borrow a succinctly worded observation from the Court of Appeals:

"(T)he conclusion seems inescapable that lurking behind the discrimination is the imputation that females who engage in misconduct, sexual or otherwise, ought to be more censured, and their conduct subject to greater control and regulation, than males. Somewhat similar moral presumptions have been squarely rejected as a basis or excuse for sexually discriminatory legislation."

Numerous commentators share the Court of Appeals' perspective that underlying the extremely harsh treatment meted out to females engaging in sexual "mis"-conduct or commercial sex are archaic notions that a woman's place is in the narrowly circumscribed, non-public world. When females wander out of this protective sphere into the public, they "get what they deserve". Or to state the same idea more pointedly, that females are chattel, the property of one male, and therefore, have no right to be promiscuous, to self-determine to whom and when they shall bestow their "sexual favors".

[12] See Introductory memorandum of Albert H. Blumenthal, accompanying the submission of Penal Law section 240.37 to the State Assembly:

"Law abiding citizens in our cities have been increasingly subjected to by prostitute and patron alike. The Corporation Counsel does not dispute and the facts of the instant case amply demonstrate that the prostitution laws are selectively enforced against the female participant. The male patron and female prostitute are equal partners in commercial sex. This court can find no legitimate distinction between their conduct. Such intentional and selective enforcement of these laws almost exclusively against females because of their sex violates the equal protection clause of the New York State Constitution.

The respondent is charged with offering to perform a "deviate" sexual act for a fee. As indicated above, it is necessary, therefore, for the court to examine sections 130.38 and 130.00(2) of the Penal Law and make a determination as to their constitutionality.

The Penal Law only makes unlawful acts of "deviate" sexual intercourse performed by unmarried persons, whether of the opposite or same sex. Thus, the consensual sodomy statute creates a distinction between the private consensual sexual conduct of married and unmarried persons.[14]

As will appear more fully below, the private consensual sexual relations of married and unmarried persons involve a fundamental right of privacy protected by the New York State Constitution. The right of privacy does not attach to the marital relationship but to the individuals involved.

Since a fundamental interest involving life or liberty is involved in this challenge to the constitutionality of the consensual sodomy statute, this court will carefully examine the state interests claimed to be protected by the criminalization of consensual sodomy between unmarried adults. The court will not accept mere claims that "deviate" sexual intercourse is harmful and, therefore, is properly proscribed by a state statute. On the contrary, it must be demonstrated that consensual sodomy in fact harms the public health, safety or welfare.

It cannot be said that acts of deviate sexual intercourse are, in and of themselves, intrinsically harmful or unnatural, causing in the participants any

---

harassment, interference and embarrassment by persons engaged in and promoting prostitute activities. Moreover, vehicular traffic in our congested cities is often disrupted by persons engaged in this illicit activity. The public demands and should have protection from invasion of its privacy."

[14] The New York State Human Rights Law forbids discrimination on the basis of marital status. Thus, the State has clearly expressed its displeasure at distinctions based on marital status.

deviation from fundamental human nature.[15] Since 1968, when the consensual sodomy law was amended, married persons in this state have been permitted to engage in "deviate" sexual intercourse without criminal sanction. In these past nine years, no empirical evidence that consensual sodomy is intrinsically harmful has been produced. Such conduct may be freely engaged in by married persons without sanction and is a widely accepted form of sexual expression. In this state, affectional or sexual preference have not been found to be a controlling factor in matters of licensing,[17] citizenship, or admission to the bar.

Since it cannot be demonstrated that there is anything intrinsically harmful in acts of consensual sodomy between unmarried adults, can Penal Law section 130.38 be legitimated as a mode of protecting the stability of marriage and the family? There is no empirical evidence that so-called "deviate" sex, an activity that has been engaged in for centuries, has been a factor of any significance affecting the stability of marriage and the family. On the contrary, in the 17 states where consensual sodomy has been decriminalized, and the 100 nations that permit consensual sodomy, cooperative social institutions like the family remain stable.

---

[15] In late 1973, the Board of Trustees of the American Psychiatric Association (A.P.A.) decided to remove homosexuality from the list of mental diseases. This action met with the approval of the A.P.A. membership in 1974. Studies indicate that most unmarried persons engage in the sexual conduct characterized as deviate sexual intercourse. Of unmarried heterosexual persons between the ages of 18 and 24 years old, 72% of those studied performed fellatio, 69% performed cunnilingus. One-sixth of all persons under 25 years of age who have ever had coitus have engaged in anal intercourse. Studies also reveal that 20 to 25% of all males over the age of 15 have engaged in oral or anal sex with another male and 10-20% of all females over 19 years of age have engaged in oral sex with another female.

[17] Policy Statement of New York Secretary of State Mario Cuomo (June 25, 1976):

> "(T)he Department of State does not believe that affectional or sexual preference is a relevant factor in determining the grant, maintenance or renewal of licenses.

> Nor does the Department believe that convictions arising from the actions of consenting adults engaged in or seeking nonpecuniary sexual activity should be considered in determining the good character of our licensees. The Department, however, will consider such convictions when they result from sexual activity with a mentally defective, mentally incapacitated or physically helpless person."

The court has searched for, but cannot find, a proper governmental objective served by the legislature in distinguishing between the marital status of persons engaging in so-called "deviate" sexual intercourse. Completely lacking is any evidence that the conduct proscribed is more harmful to unmarried participants or that such conduct between unmarried persons is more harmful to the public.

If the consensual sodomy law was designed to prevent sexual relations between unmarried people, then "normal" sexual relations between the unmarried would also be sanctioned by the Criminal Law. Fornication, however, is not a crime in this state. If the purpose of the law is to promote conventional sex it also fails in its objective since married persons are permitted to engage in unconventional or "deviate" sexual conduct. Thus, if morality vis a vis sexual norms or the promotion of marriage are the objectives of the legislation, there is no rational let alone substantial relationship between the law itself and these legislative ends. There is no logical or factual basis on which the marital status of the participants should be decisive as to whether a mode of sexual conduct is legal or criminal. Since the classification created by section 130.38 of the Penal Law and section 130.00(2) as incorporated therein has no rational basis, the criminalization of "deviate" sexual intercourse between persons who are not married to each other is an unconstitutional denial of equal protection of the laws.

As the framers of the Federal and New York State Constitutions realized, a tension exists between the rights and powers of the government as opposed to those rights reserved to the People. As the Supreme Court observed nearly a century ago:

> No right is held more sacred, or is more carefully guarded by the Common Law, than the right of every individual to the possession and control of his own person, free from all restraint or interference from others, unless by clear and unquestionable authority of law.

It is the Bill of Rights that stands between the will of the majority and the individual. It declares that except in the direct pursuit of protecting the public health, safety or morals, the State may not interfere with the individual's right of self expression. As numerous commentators have noted, the right of privacy found in the Bill of Rights has, as its underpinnings, the concept that affording the maximum amount of opportunity for individual choice maximizes the ability of each person for self development.

Running counter to the majoritarian tide of laws is the Bill of Rights' protection of diversity and guarantee of opportunity for the disadvantaged, who are unable to gain redress through the political process, to gain expression of and protection for their views in the courts.

The Supreme Court only recently recognized in the Bill of Rights a right of privacy. But the parameters of this right are quickly being revealed. The right of privacy encompasses not just sexual conduct in the marital relationship but is broad in scope, including in its protection each individual's decision as to whether, when and in what manner he or she will engage in private intimate relations. [The judge cites *Eisenstadt v. Baird, Stanley v. Georgia, Roe v. Wade*, and *Carey v. Population Services International.*] The mantle of constitutional protection surrounding personal intimacy is not, therefore, limited to married persons. It attaches to the individual not the relationship, and protects the individual's right to engage in non-procreative, recreational sex.

Just as there is no express right to privacy included in the Federal Constitution, the New York State Constitution's protection of the right of privacy is not found on the face of that document but emanates from such protections as liberty of speech, the right to be free from unreasonable searches and seizures, and the guarantee of due process of law. * * *

With the foregoing explication of the existence of the right of privacy under the New York State Constitution and the philosophical underpinnings of this right, this court states at the outset the premise that private, intimate, consensual sexual conduct not harmful to others, even if it violates the personal moral code of many, does not violate public morality and is protected by the right of privacy. In determining whether the state has a legitimate interest in proscribing private consensual sexual conduct, "deviate" or " normal", the following questions must be dealt with:

1. What harm does such conduct pose to the public health, safety or morals?

2. Is there harm in fact? Can harm actually or empirically be shown?

3. Is the harm caused in fact by the proscribed conduct?

4. Is the legislation reasonably related to the state's legitimate objective or is the relationship between the protectible public interest and the proscribed conduct too attenuated?

This court will not accept at face value bald claims of harm to the public health, safety and morals, but will closely examine the reasonableness of the state objectives proffered by the Corporation Counsel.

In discussing above the equal protection challenge to the consensual sodomy statutes, this court discussed the harms to the public health, safety or welfare allegedly caused by "deviate" sexual intercourse. Assertions that "deviate" sexual intercourse is intrinsically harmful to the participants or that it has a deleterious effect on the moral fibre of the community by undermining the stability of marriage and the family were each shown to be unsubstantiated. Although other courts argue that the Bible prohibits "deviate" sexual conduct and, therefore, such conduct is immoral, it is this court's view that absent empirical evidence demonstrating that private, consensual "deviate" sexual acts cause harm in fact to the public health, safety or welfare the state may not legitimately proscribe such conduct. Since there is no proof that public harm is caused by consensual sodomy, the government may not intrude in private, personal decisions regarding sexual preference.

Since it has been demonstrated that there is no legitimate basis for governmental interference in private, consensual sodomy, the balance of this opinion will deal with the remaining question of whether the state may legitimately proscribe commercial, recreational sex.

It is claimed that prostitution is indeed harmful in that it spreads disease, leads to ancillary criminal conduct, encourages criminal organization and generally may be characterized as anti-social behavior both offensive and injurious to the community.

It is urged that prostitution spreads venereal disease. Without question, venereal disease is a serious threat to public health and it has apparently now reached epidemic proportions. However, all empirical data supports the conclusion of Dr. Charles Winnick of the City University, President of the American Social Health Association, that "(T)he amount of venereal disease attributable to prostitution is remaining fairly constant at a little under 5%, which is a negligible proportion compared to the amount of venereal disease we now have." Thus, a negligible amount of venereal disease is caused in fact by prostitution. The state may have a legitimate interest in seeking to eradicate even this small incidence of disease, but the attenuated relationship between prostitution and venereal disease emphasizes that it would be unreasonable to prohibit all prostitution for the sake of eradicating 5% of the "VD" health hazard.[23]

---

[23] The cost to New York taxpayers of arresting and obtaining court disposition of a prostitute has been estimated at $1705.00. Additionally, it costs the public $1250 to incarcerate a prostitute for 30 days. Over 3200 persons have been arrested and arraigned under Penal Law Section 230.00 (only one of several prostitution related offenses) during the months of January through June, 1977 in New

It is also claimed that prostitution leads to other crimes. Indeed, in this case respondent is also charged with acts which could constitute robbery and assault in the second degree if committed by an adult. Nonetheless, the Corporation Counsel has not come forward with any empirical evidence substantiating that prostitution is the cause-in-fact of ancillary crime. Indeed, it has been concluded by numerous social scientists that crimes ancillary to prostitution are a by-product of the environment to which society consigns prostitution.

> The effects of the enforcement procedures on the prostitute clearly are negative. Jail is not a deterrent. It often encourages criminal conduct. Incarceration contributes little to rehabilitation while teaching the prostitute about genuine criminal activity. She learns that other more serious crimes may pay better; she begins to view herself as a criminal. Attaching the lable "criminal" to prostitution and imposing heavy sentences blur the distinction between offering service and committing a theft.

James, Real and Ideal: The Use of Legal Sanctions as Moral Agents (1973). Because prostitution and patronizing a prostitute are criminally sanctioned, prostitutes and their patrons alike fear reporting ancillary crimes for fear of prosecution. Moreover, 70% of the women in prison for felonies were first arrested for prostitution. Thus, there is a clear inference that it is the criminalization of prostitution and not prostitution itself that leads to ancillary crime.

This court knows of no study that has substantiated the allegation that sex for money in fact causes ancillary crime. Nor has the Corporation Counsel shed any light on this subject. Due process requires that a law be reasonably related and applied to some actual or manifest evil: it must have as its objective the eradication of harm in fact caused by the proscribed conduct. The constitution limits the extent to which the state can proscribe prostitution with the purpose of eradicating an entirely distinct, severable kind of conduct. The state must proceed against ancillary crimes directly by enforcing the specific sanctions against such conduct and may not rely on the blunderbuss approach of incarcerating all prostitutes.

York County alone. As pointed out in Footnote 22 above, 70% of the persons patronizing prostitutes are 30-60 years old yet it is the 15-30 year old age group that has the highest incidence (84%) of V.D. Thus, there is no rational relationship between the objective of protecting public health and the criminalization of prostitution as a method of obtaining that objective.

The Corporation Counsel claims that prostitution encourages the spread of organized crime. There is no factual basis for this allegation. Prostitution plays "a small and declining role in organized crime's operation". Although organized crime clearly presents a threat to the general security of the public, there is no proof that prostitution is the cause in fact of organized crime. Therefore, it is improper and unreasonable for the state to proscribe prostitution as a method of curbing organized crime.

Another type of harm attributed to prostitution is that it injures the community. Underlying this claim are the allegations that commercial sex undermines the stability of the family and is simply immoral.

The law may seek to legislate morality, but it must do so without offending the constitutional protections of the due process clause and the right of privacy.

The Penal Law should act to deprive an individual of liberty only when a real and demonstrable harm to the public can result from the proscribed conduct. The state cannot rely upon the bare assertion of immorality to justify a criminal prohibition. Attempts by the state to regulate lifestyle choices on the bare assertion that the regulation serves morality is impermissible. Conduct that does not interfere with the rights and interests of others may not be regulated by the state.

Preventing harm to what is believed by many to be the central institution for social cooperation, the family, may well be a legitimate objective of the state. Most male patrons of prostitutes are married. And it is the patron who creates the demand for the services of prostitutes. Thus, if the marital contract is breached by promiscuity or the family undermined by extra-marital sexual relations, the burden of responsibility lies with the patron, not the prostitute. Yet, the penal law punishes the prostitute most severely. If the state's objective is to promote the stability of the family and commercial sex has a direct impact upon the family, then the law should focus on the conduct of the patron. However, it has never been demonstrated that commercial sex has had any affect on the stability of marriage or the family. Indeed, although prostitution has been practiced for centuries, disruption of the family has never been causally related to prostitution. Several states and numerous foreign nations have decriminalized prostitution without any indication of a concomitant decline in the vitality of the marital or family institution. *See* Vorenburg, Elizabeth and James, "The Biggest Pimp of All: Prostitution and Some Facts of Life", The Atlantic Monthly, Jan.

1977, Vol. 239 No. 1, p. 31.[25] The decriminalization of fornication in this state has not led to any reported damage to the family. This court can find no reason why commercial fornication should have a less innocuous effect on these social institutions. Thus, there is no empirical connection between prostitution, whether involving ordinary or deviate sexual intercourse, and the stability of the family. Therefore, the state cannot reasonably assert protection of marriage and the family as legitimate objectives for its regulation of prostitution.

Sex for a fee is recreational, not procreational sex. Typically, it is the female participant who receives the fee. The arguments that prostitution harms the public health, safety or welfare do not withstand constitutional scrutiny. It may be that it is the fact that a woman is accepting a fee for recreational, sexual services that triggers the governmental intrusion upon this private consensual sexual conduct. If it is paternalism that prompts the legislature to protect women by proscribing prostitution,[26] that motive is ill served by the prostitution laws since women are not protected, but rather are penally punished. Society may find something offensive about having women perform sex for money. However offensive it may be, recreational commercial sex threatens no harm to the public health, safety or welfare and, therefore, may not be proscribed.

Finally, prostitution is said to offend public sensibilities. Individual members of the public may indeed be offended by the public conduct associated with prostitution: they may be solicited on the street by prostitutes, embarrassed by the advances of streetwalkers, or find their path on the sidewalks or thoroughfares blocked. Such conduct may, indeed, be a harm legitimately of interest to the state should it constitute public disorder. This court will not decide the question of who has a right to be on the public streets. However, the court will point out that this public conduct is not caused in fact by the act of engaging in sexual relations for a fee. This harm, if any, is caused by the solicitation aspect of prostitution. The public aspect of prostitution, solicitation,

---

[25] In Amsterdam, the "red light" district is situated very near the governmental centers and wealthy residential neighborhoods. Psychologists who studied children who grew up in and frequented the district found no ill effects of the exposure of the children to prostitutes or commercial sex. In Amsterdam, it should be noted that the prostitutes are not permitted to roam the street, soliciting customers.

[26] Paternalism certainly could not be the motive in the instant case. Respondent is a 14 year old female. If the motive of this proceeding were to protect her, she would not be threatened with the loss of her liberty. Paternalism might dictate an Article Ten proceeding on her behalf. It clearly would dictate some charge against the patron, such as endangering the welfare of a minor, attempted statutory rape or criminal solicitation. None of these protective measures were taken in this case.

must be distinguished from its private aspect, the performance of consensual sexual relations for a fee in private. Street solicitation is a method of advertising the business of commercial sex. It is separable from the underlying activity. In Nevada and Great Britain, for example, prostitution has been legalized, but street solicitation is proscribed by public order, breach of the peace type statutes. Advertising is unoffensively and effectively accomplished through the use of discrete [sic] newspaper advertisements.

The prohibition of the offensive public conduct associated with the solicitation of prostitution may be a legitimate state objective. Since it has been demonstrated that only this public element of prostitution may make that conduct harmful, and that public conduct may be dealt with separately from the sexual conduct itself, it would be unreasonable for the state to completely proscribe private, sexual conduct in order to reach distinct public solicitation. Members of the public may have a protectable privacy interest: not to be repeatedly accosted on the streets by a prostitute any more than a religious zealot, peddler, alcoholic or panhandler, and not to have a group of street musicians, noisy teenagers, solicitors for charities, or streetwalkers converging at his or her doorstep. These public interests can be protected, but by less intrusive means than those now employed by the state. Private, consensual sexual conduct between adults, whether or not performed for a fee, is protected by the right of privacy. If the state has a legitimate interest in curbing public disorder, it can and must accomplish this objective without depriving the individual of his or her right to engage in private, consensual, sexual relations. The constitutionally protected right of privacy makes it incumbent upon the state to implement its policy by more reasonable, less intrusive means.

For the reasons stated, the sexual conduct charge against respondent is dismissed.

Note

The decision in *In re P.* was reversed. *In re Dora P.*, 68 A.D.2d 719, 418 N.Y.S.2d 597 (N.Y.A.D. 1 Dept. 1979). In light of *Lawrence*, was the reversal correct?

Chapter 9

THEFT OFFENSES

INTRODUCTION

Like homicide law and rape law, the law of theft shows clearly the imprints of history and culture on law. Unlike those other crimes, however, the law of theft is deeply intertwined with economics and technology. The evolution of the law of theft in the English common law reflected the emergence of capitalism: from being a crime against the person, theft became a crime against property, and evolved as the concept of property itself evolved. As one commentator concludes, "There is no better way to understand the relation between the development of capitalist legal institutions and the changing contours of the right of property than by studying the cases of those charged with stealing." Michael E. Tigar, *The Right of Property and the Law of Theft*, 62 Tex. L. Rev. 1443 (1984); *see also* Jerome Hall, THEFT, LAW AND SOCIETY (1952). Theft law has evolved, as well, in response to new technological capacities. For instance, the advent of the computer and the World Wide Web expanded the capacities of thieves, in turn prompting a new wave of criminal law reforms.

Despite the dramatic changes in political economy and technological capacity from thirteenth-century England to the present-day United States, however, some basic questions have remained the same. What is the harm caused by theft? What sorts of things constitute "property" so that they can be stolen? Can rules developed in previous centuries be altered to address current problems, and if so, at what cost? If not, what might an entirely new structure of theft look like?

Section A of this chapter examines the law of theft from a historical perspective and introduces you to the basic theft crimes -- larceny, embezzlement, and false pretenses -- and the arguably related crime of extortion. You will see that the ghosts of English common law continue to haunt contemporary American law. This section illustrates, as well, the point that to fully understand the doctrine it is necessary to understand the cultural environment in which it emerged. Section B of the chapter addresses two "aggravated" forms of theft, burglary and robbery. Section C, "Beyond Theft," addresses an issue central to present-day American political economy: the tendency to conceptualize intangible rights as property rights, including the right to honest government and the right to possess, use, and restrict information. The law of mail fraud and the emerging law of computer crimes are used as examples. Finally, section D, "Crimes of Propertylessness," examines how criminal law is used to control those who do not fit into the capitalist social order.

A.   THEFT

The Anglo-American common law of theft began with the basic crime of larceny. Later, English judges created the related crime of larceny by trick through the common law process, and Parliament created two additional statutory theft crimes, embezzlement and false pretenses. When the United States was founded, American lawmakers incorporated into their penal codes the three basic theft crimes – larceny, embezzlement, and false pretenses. Eventually, however, reformers in many states incorporated all three into a single consolidated crime of theft, hoping to escape the procedural nightmares caused by doctrinal complexity. The consolidation approach is reflected, as well, in the Model Penal Code. *See* Model Penal Code § 223.1(1).

Even where the law of theft has been consolidated, however, the ghosts of the original common law crimes continue to haunt contemporary statutes. In order to understand the contemporary law of theft, then, it is necessary to understand the growth and development of the English common law of theft.

1.   Larceny

The most ancient of the basic theft crimes is larceny, which consists of (1) the trespassory "taking" and "carrying away" of property (2) from the possession of another (3) with the intent to permanently deprive the owner of it. The "taking" must be "trespassory" -- that is, the actor must have no right to use the property. In order for a taking to be trespassory, the taking and the specific intent to permanently deprive must occur at the same time. Therefore, for example, if you lend me your laptop and after I have borrowed it for a few days I decide to take it from you permanently, I have not committed larceny. Because my intent to permanently deprive you of the property did not occur at the same time as my initial taking, the taking would not be considered trespassory.

The "carrying away" element of larceny has a technical name: asportation. The courts have held that asportation means the assertion of control over and some movement of the item contrary to the possession of the owner, no matter how slight. Thus, if I come across your laptop in the law library and, intending to steal it, I pick it up but then put it back because I realize I'm being watched, I have technically committed larceny. In contemporary law, there is some debate over how the asportation requirement applies in the retail context, where people commonly pick up merchandise and move it around within the store. *See, e.g., Craig v. State*, 410 So.2d 449, 453 (Ala. Crim. App. 1981) ("it is clear that if a shopper moves merchandise from one place to another within a store with the intention to steal it, there has been asportation and the shopper may be found guilty of larceny"); *State v. Robertson*, 2003 WL 21965059 (Wash. App. Div. 2) (unpublished opinion) (defendant, stopped by a greeter at Wal-Mart while wheeling a computer and cell phone in a cart toward the exit with the intent to steal them, was properly convicted of theft; "By falsely asserting that she had a sales receipt for the items, Robertson claimed to be the rightful owner of them and thus acted in a way that was not authorized by the true rightful owner, Wal-Mart."). *But see People v. Parrett*, 90 Misc.2d 541, 394 N.Y.S.2d 809 (N.Y. Dist. Ct. 1977) (reversing theft conviction when defendant concealed clothing in her purse, paid for other items, and was apprehended upon arriving to the second floor by escalator, on the ground that no asportation from the store had occurred).

Larceny as it existed in thirteenth-century England, however, was not a crime against property but a crime against "the king's peace." That is, the harm to be avoided was the violence -- disturbance of the peace -- that might erupt when one person openly and deliberately committed an act contrary to the lawful right of possession of another. "Property" as we know it today simply did not exist. As one commentator explains:

> Neither early Roman law nor English feudal and manorial law placed emphasis upon property as we understand that term. Neither society based its social relations upon commerce, and neither displayed a highly developed sense of the institution of property as the exclusive right to use and dispose of a thing. One's lawful possession of a beast, a plow, or a store of feed was not regarded as proprietary in the sense bourgeois law makes us familiar with; in feudal England, for example, possessing these things was an incident of a complex set of social relations based upon the reciprocal duties and obligations inherent in the concepts of fealty and vassalage. The rules against stealing were designed to interdict and punish conduct that risked disturbing public order by interfering with a right more appreciated than the right to "own" something -- the right to possess and "use" it.

Michael E. Tigar, *The Right of Property and the Law of Theft*, 62 Tex. L. Rev. 1443, 1448 (1984).

As England evolved into a commercial society, however, common law judges began to expand the scope of larceny, in the process slowly transforming the harm punished by theft from the disturbance of the royal peace to the interference with an individual's right to control a movable object. One famous way-station in this process was the decision in *The Carrier's Case*, Y.B.Pasch. 13 Edw. IV, f. 9, pl. 5 (Star Ch. and Exch. Ch.1473), reprinted in 64 Selden Society 30 (1945). A foreign merchant entrusted some bales of "woad" -- a blue dye used in the woolen industry -- to a carrier who was to bring them to Southampton. Somewhere along the way, the carrier broke the packages open and misappropriated the contents, finally abandoning the goods in London. Both the merchant and the Sheriff of London claimed the right to the bales, the sheriff on the theory (established by precedent) that goods taken feloniously and later abandoned belonged to the government.

The case was an important one politically: wool was a key industry in fifteenth-century England (even the king was a wool merchant), and the security of foreign merchants and their property was in question as well. Under existing law the situation did not constitute larceny, because the carrier's initial possession of the bales had been lawful. However, the judges of the Exchequer Chamber who took the case reported nevertheless that the carrier had committed larceny. Although the judges did not reach a consensus on the reason why, Lord Chokke's opinion came to be taken as the rule of the case. Chokke reasoned that the carrier was given the bales, not the contents. When the carrier broke the bales open, an unlawful taking of the contents occurred, constituting larceny.

This "breaking bulk" doctrine became incorporated into the law of larceny, and still survives in contemporary American law. For example, in *United States v. Mafnas*, 701 F.2d 83 (9th Cir. 1983), the defendant, the employee of an armored car service, opened bags of money in his care and removed the cash. The court held that Mafnas's crime was larceny rather than embezzlement, relying on the "breaking bulk" reasoning first publicly articulated in 1473.

2. Larceny By Trick

Another judicial expansion of the law of theft that helped transform larceny from a crime of disturbing the peace to a crime of interference with property rights occurred several centuries later, in the 1779 case of *Rex v. Pear*, 1 Leach 253 (3d London ed. 1800) (Case CV), 168 Eng. Rep. 208 (Cr. Cas. Res. 1779). Pear hired a horse, telling the owner that he was going to Surrey with it. In fact, he rode to Smithfield and sold the horse. Although the written reports of the case are in disarray, the jury apparently found that Pear had had the intent to sell even when he hired the horse, and that he had committed larceny.

The rationale for this holding was that Pear's taking of the horse had been wrongful, and therefore void, from the very beginning because it had been achieved by deceit. In order to make this idea fit the existing doctrinal structure of larceny, however, the judges needed to invent a number of legal fictions. *Rex v. Pear* came to stand for the general principle that an employer or principal retains "constructive possession" of property when she entrusts it to an employee or agent; the employee or agent receives only "custody." Therefore, when an employee or agent obtains custody of a thing through deceit, and takes custody with the specific intent to permanently deprive the owner of it, she violates the owner's (constructive) possession, commits a trespassory taking, and has committed larceny.

Although cumbersome, these legal fictions, including the quasi-metaphysical thing known as "possession," have lingered in contemporary American law. For example, in *Overstreet v. Commonwealth*, 17 Va. App. 234, 435 S.E.2d 906 (Ct. App. 1993), the court held that a defendant who had been given permission to drive a car committed larceny of the vehicle when he kept it beyond the time consented to by the owner. The court explained: "[W]here the owner gives consent to a temporary possession or a possession for a limited purpose, the expiration of that qualification creates constructive revestment of possession in the true owner." *Id.* at 908.

Under contemporary law, "constructive possession" and its corollary, "custody," are said to occur in three situations: (1) when a principal or employer delivers property to an agent or employee to use, keep, make a delivery for the principal; (2) when the owner of property loses it or mislays it and someone else finds it; and (3) a property owner delivers the property to another person as part of a transaction to be completed in the owner's presence. In any of these situations, if a person takes and carries away the property with the intent to permanently deprive the owner, the crime is larceny.

3. Embezzlement

The common law courts were not willing to extend the law of larceny infinitely, however, and the remaining key expansions of the law of theft were accomplished by statute. The crime of embezzlement is an example. Suppose I am the owner of a small business and I hire you to keep my books and pay my creditors. Instead of paying my creditors all the money they are owed, however, you surreptitiously keep a portion of it for yourself. Under the existing law of larceny, no crime has been committed. You have not committed larceny against me because I am not the owner of the missing money; the creditors are. (The most I probably have is "custody" of the money.) You have not committed larceny against my creditors because they never possessed the money; they are still waiting around to receive it.

Of course, the common law courts could have decided that constructive possession occurs whenever a person is owed a debt, holding, for example, that the instant I sold goods to the creditors they received constructive possession of the accounts payable. However, they were unwilling to stretch the concept of constructive possession quite that far. The gap thus left when the law of larceny met commercial society led to the creation of a new statutory crime called embezzlement. As Michael Tigar tells the story:

> In 1799, a bank clerk named Bazeley pocketed a hundred pound note given him by a bank customer for deposit to the customer's account. Bazeley made the credit entry, so the victim was the bank and not the customer. He was found not guilty. The bank never had "possession" of the note, the evidence being undisputed that Bazeley put it in his pocket without first putting it in the cash drawer; thus, he could not have taken from the bank's possession. He could not even be convicted on the theory of those cases dealing with misappropriation by servants, who were said to have custody of their masters' goods, although possession remained in the master. [*King v. Bazeley*, 2 Leach 835, 168 Eng.Rep. 517 (Cr.Cas.Res.1799).]

> *Bazeley* led to passage of England's first general embezzlement statute in 1799. Statutes passed earlier in the eighteenth century had dealt with embezzlement by employees of certain public or quasi-public entities, and an early seventeenth century law punished workers who embezzled wool delivered for spinning and weaving. With these exceptions, until 1799 taking by an agent or servant who had lawful possession was a breach of trust that could be remedied only by filing a civil suit.

> The embezzlement legislation and the extension of the concept of taking from constructive possession were designed to protect class interests. England was moving from mercantile to industrial capitalism. Units of trade and commerce were growing larger; the image of the solitary merchant or artisan gave way to corporate and partnership forms employing wage labor. A misappropriation between partners or joint venturers might be the stuff of which civil law suits could be made, but the hired clerk's defalcation was a matter for criminal prosecution, a hanging matter.

Tigar, *The Right of Property and the Law of Theft, supra* at 1454-55.[a]

Under contemporary law, embezzlement generally is defined as (1) the intentional conversion of (2) the property of another (3) by someone who is already in lawful possession of it (or by someone to whom it has been "entrusted"). "Conversion" means some act that seriously interferes with the owner's ability to use the property. Thus, the simple movement of an object in space -- which would be enough to constitute "asportation" for the purpose of larceny -- is not enough to constitute a conversion. Using something up, selling it, using it as collateral for a loan, giving it away, inflicting serious damage to it, or delivering it to someone not entitled to it, are all acts that would constitute conversion.

The distinction between larceny by trick and embezzlement is that, under the doctrine of larceny by trick, the defendant's initial taking is achieved by deceit and is thus considered never to constitute possession, whereas in embezzlement the defendant receives lawful possession of the property. This distinction survived transplant into contemporary American law. Many factual situations, however, create questions as to which crime properly applies. The distinction between the two crimes can mean the difference between conviction and acquittal. For example, in Virginia the theft crimes have never been consolidated, and prosecutors must therefore draft the indictment for the right offense or risk seeing the defendant acquitted. Problems frequently ensue:

> In *Gwaltney v. Commonwealth* [19 Va. App. 468, 475, 452 S.E.2d 687, 691 (1995)], for example, a bank teller stole not from her own cash drawer, but from the momentarily unattended drawer of another teller. Gwaltney argued that her crime was larceny, not embezzlement, because she had never been entrusted with the particular currency that she stole. The court ruled otherwise, finding that "Gwaltney's position of trust extended beyond the confines of her station to the entire teller line." *Gwaltney* is one of several Virginia cases that demonstrate the troublesome dilemma a prosecutor may face in choosing the appropriate charge for an indictment alleging theft by an employee. Employment relationships involve an endless variety of rules and practices that may, or may not, result in the entrustment of particular property to a particular employee. Determining how far an employee's "position of trust" extends

---

[a] Tigar's reference to the punishment for larceny points to another reason why the common law courts may have permitted larceny to grow so complex and filled with holes. Under English law, larceny was a capital crime.

may require analysis and investigation that, as a practical matter, few police officers and prosecutors are able to undertake before indictment. Conflicting rules or differences of opinion among managers within an employing company may make it impossible to prove entrustment -- or lack thereof -- beyond a reasonable doubt. Yet, that is what Virginia law currently requires.

John G. Douglass, *Rethinking Theft Crimes in Virginia*, 38 U. Rich. L. Rev. 13, 19-20 (2003).

4.   False Pretenses

The crime of false pretenses, like the crime of embezzlement, was created by statute to fill the gaps left by the expanded law of larceny. Under the doctrine of larceny by trick, as we have seen, a person who gained possession of property through deception could be found guilty of theft. But a person who gained both possession and title of property through deception was not guilty of any crime. Parliament responded to the problem with a 1757 statute making it a crime to obtain property by "false pretense."

In a commercial society where people commonly make representations intended to produce a transaction, the kind of deceit that constitutes false pretenses had to be distinguished from mere "puffing," or representations that everyone ought to recognize as exaggerated or possibly false. The defendant's intentions were made the key. As one commentator explains:

> To commit false pretenses, the perpetrator must have an "intent to defraud." Generally, such a fraud was easily formed in the typical swindle, but this was not always the case. An intent to defraud was absent where an untrue representation was made with an intent to deceive but without the intent to obtain the property that was obtained thereby, and without realization of the influence of the deceit. An omission, or silence, however, could be considered a "deceitful means or artful practice." "One who knew he was obtaining money or a chattel by his misrepresentation of fact and who received it with intent to take a fraudulent advantage of the other, has obtained it by fraud whether his original statement was made for this purpose or not." The silence, in light of full knowledge of the situation, was the equivalent of a repetition of the false statement at the moment of acquisition. An intent to defraud was also found where the person made an untrue statement innocently, but

thereafter learned of the mistake before the property was received and fraudulently failed to disclose the information upon acquisition.

False pretenses further required that the victim was deceived. Property is "not obtained by the untrue representation of fact if the real facts are known to the other. Hence it is essential to show that the owner was misled by the misrepresentation." It was also "not an indictable offense, under the statute, for one to obtain by false statements payment of a debt already due, or personal property to the possession of which he was entitled, because no injury was done."

Courtney Chetty Genco, *What Happened to* Durland*?: Mail Fraud, RICO, and Justifiable Reliance*, 68 Notre Dame L. Rev. 333, 350 (1992).

Finally, under the traditional law of false pretenses, the misrepresentation must pertain to some existing fact in the past or present, and not a "mere promise as to the future," such as the false promise to fulfill a contract. *See Durland v. United States*, 161 U.S. 306 (1896).

The modern crime of false pretenses requires: (1) a false statement of fact that (2) causes the victim (3) to pass title to the defendant. The defendant must: (4) know the statement is false; and (5) thereby intend to defraud the victim. The law of Virginia again provides an example of the pitfalls that await the unwary prosecutor.

The main challenge in distinguishing larceny by trick from the crime of false pretenses is determining whether title passed to the thief. In *Baker v. Commonwealth* [225 Va. 192, 300 S.E.2d 788 (1983)], for example, the defendant took a Jeep from a car dealer for a "test drive," leaving behind as security a truck he had fraudulently obtained elsewhere. After he failed to return the Jeep, Baker was prosecuted for false pretenses. The Supreme Court of Virginia reversed the conviction because title to the Jeep never passed to Baker. Baker's crime was larceny, not false pretenses. Identifying the crime in Baker is relatively easy, because vehicles come with paper titles issued by the state. In many cases, however, passage of title raises more intricate problems. Where a thief fraudulently obtains consumer goods in a retail transaction, his crime typically will satisfy the elements of false pretenses because Virginia's commercial code deems title to pass upon delivery of the goods. But his crime may be larceny if the small print of a consumer financing contract leaves title with the retailer. In one Virginia case, the line between false pretenses and larceny turned upon a phrase in a rental contract that required return of keys at the end of the rental period. Even in cases involving cash, the line-drawing problem may not be easy. Typically, title to currency passes with possession; but it may be otherwise where the victim places conditions on the use of the cash or uses cash as security in a more complex transaction. In such cases, the line between false pretenses and larceny may depend upon what the victim said, or thought, at the time of the crime. In sum, to be confident that false pretenses is the right charge in some close cases, a prosecutor must be a commercial law expert and a mind reader rolled into one.

John G. Douglass, *Rethinking Theft Crimes in Virginia*, 38 U. Rich. L. Rev. 13, 21-22 (2003).

5.   Consolidated Theft Statutes

Most American jurisdictions now have passed "consolidated theft statutes" which roll the three traditional theft crimes -- larceny/larceny by trick, embezzlement, and false pretenses – into a single crime of theft. The existence of a consolidated theft statute means that prosecutors do not risk having their indictment dismissed if they charge the wrong crime. American legislatures have also created new theft crimes over the years to address specific threats. However, consolidated theft statutes and even many new theft crimes continue to rely on the old common law distinctions, and therefore those distinctions continue to haunt contemporary law. The case that follows provides an example.

COMMONWEALTH v. MILLS
Supreme Judicial Court of Massachusetts
436 Mass. 387, 764 N.E.2d 854 (2002)

SPINA, J.

Following a jury trial, the defendant was found guilty of three counts of larceny from the city of Boston, in violation of G.L. c. 266, § 30; two counts of larceny by false pretenses from the Committee for Public Counsel Services (CPCS), in violation of G.L. c. 266, § 30; three counts of perjury, in violation of G.L. c. 268, § 1A; three counts of pension fraud, in violation of G.L. c. 32, § 18; two counts of procurement fraud, in violation of G.L. c. 266, § 67A; two counts of making false claims, in violation of G.L. c. 266, § 67B; and four counts of failure to make tax returns, in violation of G.L. c. 62C, § 73(c). Based on the five larceny convictions, the judge adjudicated the defendant a "common and notorious thief" pursuant to G.L. c. 266, § 40,[2] and sentenced him to serve not less than eighteen and not more than twenty years in prison with various lesser concurrent sentences on the remaining charges. The defendant filed a timely notice of appeal. The Appeals Court (1) reversed the judgment as to the indictment alleging three counts of larceny from the retirement board of the city of Boston (board), set aside those verdicts, and entered judgment for the defendant on those counts; (2) reversed the adjudication of the defendant as a common and notorious thief and vacated the sentence under G.L. c. 266, § 40; and (3) remanded the case to the Superior Court for resentencing by a different judge on the remaining indictments. We granted the Commonwealth's application for further appellate review. The issues now before us are whether the judge (1) erred in denying the defendant's motion for a required finding of not guilty with respect to the three counts of larceny from the board; (2) erred by adjudicating the defendant a common and notorious thief; and (3) considered improper factors, including the defendant's exercise of his right to remain silent, when sentencing the defendant. We reverse the judgments as to the three counts of larceny from the board, and remand those matters for a new trial; we vacate the adjudication of the defendant as a common and notorious thief, which was dependent on the three counts of larceny from the board; and we remand the remaining convictions to the Superior Court for resentencing by a different judge.

1. Background. The defendant retired in 1978 from the Boston police department after he was diagnosed with hypertensive heart disease. He applied for and received from the board a nontaxable accidental disability pension of approximately $15,500 per year. The defendant then began to run a private investigation business, Mills Investigations, Inc. (Mills Investigations), out of his home in New Hampshire.

During 1993, 1994, and 1995, the defendant spent every business day at the Middlesex Superior Court, either in the court room assigned to

---

[2] General Laws c. 266, § 40, provides: "Whoever, having been convicted, upon indictment, of larceny or of being accessory to larceny before the fact, afterward commits a larceny or is accessory thereto before the fact, and is convicted thereof upon indictment, and whoever is convicted at the same sitting of the court, as principal or accessory before the fact, of three distinct larcenies, shall be adjudged a common and notorious thief, and shall be punished by imprisonment in the state prison for not more than twenty years or in jail for not more than two and one half years."

clerk-magistrate Joseph Marshall or in Marshall's office. Beginning in April, 1994, Marshall handled most of the appointments of counsel for indigent defendants and motions for investigation funds. When the designated bar advocate was not in the courtroom, Marshall would deviate from the master list and appoint one attorney from among a group of four who were typically in the courtroom. Those four attorneys moved for investigation funds in every one of their cases and always retained the services of Mills Investigations. Marshall "rubber-stamped" his allowance of these motions off the record and in his back office where the defendant usually spent three hours a day socializing with Marshall.

For fiscal year 1993, the defendant billed CPCS for approximately $107,000 for investigative services. For fiscal year 1994, the defendant billed CPCS for approximately $197,000, representing 5,483 hours of investigative services. On forty-four occasions, the defendant submitted bills with more than twenty-four hours of work attributed to a single day. For fiscal year 1995, the defendant billed CPCS for approximately $359,000, representing 10,057 hours of investigative services. The defendant submitted 211 bills in which he claimed to have worked well over twenty-four hours in a single day (with some days as long as seventy-two hours).

Between 1992 and 1994, the defendant received approximately $45,000 in nontaxable accidental disability benefits from the board. Once approved for a disability pension, the only limitation to keeping the full amount received each year is the amount of income the recipient earns, if any, during that same time period. Following receipt of pension benefits, every disability pensioner is required by statute to file with the board a yearly earnings report, signed under the pains and penalties of perjury. The board calculates an earned income limitation for each disability pensioner, and the pensioner must refund a dollar's worth of pension for each dollar of income over the established limit. To collect money owed as a refund, the board sends bills to pensioners requesting remittance of a check in the appropriate amount. If the pensioner does not respond, the board withholds the amount due from the current pension distribution as security until payment is properly received.

The board estimated that the defendant could earn up to $30,228 in 1992, $30,820 in 1993, and $32,484 in 1994 before being liable for any refunds. For 1992, the defendant withdrew $89,637 from the corporate account of Mills Investigations for his own personal use; he reported to the board that he had earned a total of $25,000. For 1993, the defendant withdrew $65,640 from the corporate account of Mills Investigations for his own personal use; he reported to the board that he had earned a total of $17,500. For 1994, the defendant withdrew $104,494 from the corporate account of Mills Investigations for his own personal use; he reported to the board that he had earned a total of $30,000. As a result of the defendant under-reporting his earnings, the board never sought a refund of any pension money.

2. Motion for required finding of not guilty. At the close of the Commonwealth's case, the defendant presented a general motion for required findings of not guilty. The motion was denied. The defense rested without presenting any evidence, the defendant renewed his motion, and it was again denied.

The defendant now asserts that the Superior Court judge erred in denying his motion for a required finding of not guilty with respect to the larceny indictment charging him with three counts of stealing the property of the city of Boston when he submitted false earnings reports to the board. He contends that while making such fraudulent statements would violate criminal statutes for perjury, and pension fraud, such conduct did not constitute larceny. The defendant argues that he obtained his accidental disability pension payments lawfully. What he did was make it unlikely that the board would demand a refund and hold his future pension payments as security therefor. The defendant also asserts that because the judge erred in denying his motion for required findings of not guilty, his adjudication as a common and notorious thief should be vacated because only two larceny convictions (from CPCS) would remain.

In his general motion for a required finding of not guilty, the defendant stated that the evidence produced by the Commonwealth was insufficient to prove beyond a reasonable doubt that he had committed the offenses as charged in the indictments. * * * The pertinent indictment herein, for three counts of larceny under G.L. c. 266, § 30,[3] charged the defendant with stealing the property of the city of Boston, namely "money or a release of a claim to money, the value of which exceeded $250." "[T]he word 'steal' has become 'a term of art and includes the criminal taking or conversion' by way either of larceny, embezzlement or obtaining by false pretenses." These three formerly separate crimes have been merged into the one crime of larceny as defined in G.L. c. 266,

---

[3] General Laws c. 266, § 30(1), states, in pertinent part, as follows: "Whoever steals, or with intent to defraud obtains by a false pretense, or whoever unlawfully, and with intent to steal or embezzle, converts, or secretes with intent to convert, the property of another as defined in this section, whether such property is or is not in his possession at the time of such conversion or secreting, shall be guilty of larceny...."

§ 30. Larceny can be established by evidence that would have warranted a conviction upon any one of the three formerly separate charges. The purpose of the merger of these three common-law crimes of "stealing" into one statutory crime was to eliminate the possibility that a defendant indicted for one of the crimes would escape punishment if the proof at trial established another of the crimes.

General Laws c. 277, § 41, provides: "In an indictment for criminal dealing with personal property with intent to steal, an allegation that the defendant stole said property shall be sufficient; and such indictment may be supported by proof that the defendant committed larceny of the property, or embezzled it, or obtained it by false pretenses." Thus, "[t]he statute explicitly permits convictions to be supported by evidence that the defendant's theft was committed in any manner condemned by the law."

The Commonwealth was not ordered to elect its theory of the manner in which the alleged larcenies were committed. To require the Commonwealth to elect a particular theory of larceny would be to continue to afford an opportunity to frustrate the ends of justice in derogation of the specific legislative intent to eliminate the merely technical differences between three cognate and similar offenses. Here, there was no restriction in the indictment as to what legal theory of the statutory crime of larceny would be established by the evidence. As such, the proof offered by the Commonwealth with respect to the three counts of "stealing" from the board could be used to support any of the theories of larceny.

Our well-established standard of review of the denial of a motion for a required finding of not guilty is "whether, after viewing the evidence in the light most favorable to the prosecution, any rational trier of fact could have found the essential elements of the crime beyond a reasonable doubt." Where, as here, a defendant submits a generally expressed motion for a required finding of not guilty, the motion applies to any offense properly charged in the indictment and is correctly denied when the evidence supports any such properly charged offense. Therefore, we examine whether the Commonwealth presented sufficient evidence to establish the essential elements of at least one form of "stealing," namely larceny, embezzlement, or larceny by false pretenses, beyond a reasonable doubt. If so, then the Superior Court judge did not err in denying the defendant's motion for a required finding of not guilty.

"To support a conviction of larceny under G.L. c. 266, § 30, the Commonwealth is required to prove the 'unlawful taking and carrying away of the personal property of another with the specific intent to deprive the person of the property permanently.' " We agree with the well-reasoned analysis of the

Appeals Court that filing false earnings reports with the board does not constitute a trespassory taking of money, and the "release of a claim to money" is not property within the meaning of G.L. c. 266, § 30(2), or the common law.

With respect to embezzlement, the evidence should establish that the defendant "fraudulently converted" to his personal use property that was under his control by virtue of a position of "trust or confidence" and did so with the intent to deprive the owner of the property permanently. Contrary to the Commonwealth's argument that the Appeals Court added a new element to the crime of embezzlement, the existence of a confidential or fiduciary relationship between the embezzler and the victim has always been at the heart of this crime. The fraudulent conversion of property by parties who merely have a debtor-creditor relationship does not constitute embezzlement.

The defendant's filing of false earnings reports with the board, conduct intended to eliminate the possibility that the board would demand a refund of a portion of his annual accidental disability pension because of his earned income, does not establish the essential elements of embezzlement. Pursuant to G.L. c. 32, § 13(1)(b), "[p]ayments under any annuity, pension or retirement allowance ... shall be due and payable for the month on the last day of each month during the continuance of such annuity, pension or retirement allowance, as the case may be." General Laws c. 32, § 91A, provides that "[e]very person pensioned or retired under any general or special law for disability, including accidental disability, shall in each year on or before April fifteenth subscribe, under the penalties of perjury, and file with the [public employee retirement administration] commission a statement ... certifying the full amount of his earnings from earned income during the preceding year." If such earnings exceed a predetermined amount, said person "shall refund the portion of his retirement allowance for such preceding year equal to such excess and until such refund is made, his pension or retirement allowance shall be held as security therefor." This procedure establishes a debtor-creditor relationship between the recipient of a disability retirement allowance and the board. The recipient is lawfully entitled to a specified amount on a monthly basis. If, after submitting an earned income statement, it is determined that the recipient should have received a smaller disability retirement allowance because of other earned income, the recipient then must refund a portion of it to the board and future distributions will be withheld until that debt has been satisfied.

At the time the defendant filed his annual earnings reports with the board on or about April 15, 1993, April 4, 1994, and April 28, 1995, he was not "fraudulently converting" money that was under his control by virtue of a position of "trust or confidence." The money he received was merely the distribution of a government benefit to which he was lawfully entitled each month for his own personal use and to which, at the time of receipt, he obtained complete title and possession. By filing false earnings reports, the defendant was ensuring that he would not have to pay a reimbursement to the board and would not be subjected to any subsequent withholdings. While such conduct certainly constitutes perjury, and pension fraud, it is not embezzlement.

The Commonwealth contends that the nature of the relationship between an alleged embezzler and a victim is one of fact that falls within the province of the jury to decide. This would ordinarily be true where, to establish the essential elements of embezzlement, the Commonwealth must show that the defendant acquired control of property through a position of "trust or confidence." In this case, the relationship between the defendant and the board is established, as a matter of law, pursuant to G.L. c. 32, § 91A, to be that of debtor and creditor.

The final "stealing" offense that falls under the larceny statute, G.L. c. 266, § 30, is larceny by false pretenses. A prosecution for larceny by false pretenses requires proof that (1) a false statement of fact was made; (2) the defendant knew or believed that the statement was false when he made it; (3) the defendant intended that the person to whom he made the false statement would rely on it; and (4) the person to whom the false statement was made did rely on it and, consequently, parted with property.

Following his diagnosis of hypertensive heart disease, the defendant applied for, and the board made a determination that he was entitled to, an accidental disability retirement allowance. The Commonwealth has not contested the defendant's lawful entitlement to this benefit. However, when the defendant filed annual earnings reports with the board in 1993, 1994, and 1995, he stated that he had earned far less income than he had actually withdrawn from the corporate account of Mills Investigations for his own personal use. The evidence warrants a finding that the defendant knowingly made such false statements with the intent that the board would rely on them, would determine that he had not exceeded his annual earned income limitations, and, consequently, would continue to pay him the full amount of his accidental disability retirement allowance every year. This is exactly what happened; the defendant's expectations were fulfilled. The defendant's actions resulted in his receiving a greater allowance from the board than that to which he was lawfully entitled and constituted larceny by false pretenses.

We conclude that the judge did not err in denying the defendant's motion for required findings of not guilty with respect to the three counts of larceny from the board. After viewing the evidence in the light most favorable to the Commonwealth, a rational trier of fact could have found the essential elements of larceny by false pretenses beyond a reasonable doubt.

3. Jury instructions. The defendant's convictions of "stealing" from the board were based on a theory of traditional larceny because that was the only instruction given to the jury.[5] The jury were not instructed on larceny by false pretenses with respect to this indictment. The Commonwealth did not request further instructions on any other theory of larceny, and the defendant, understandably, did not object to the instructions as given.* * *

Precise instructions to the jury on the Commonwealth's theory of how the defendant "stole" from the board were critical because traditional larceny, embezzlement, and larceny by false pretenses have different required elements. The jury herein did not have the benefit of the applicable law, namely the elements of larceny by false pretenses, so as to be able to render a proper verdict. Because the jury were only given instructions as to traditional larceny, pursuant to which they found the defendant guilty, and because we have already concluded that the filing of false earnings reports with the board does not constitute traditional larceny (only larceny by false pretenses), the defendant's larceny convictions cannot stand. A new trial is required with respect to the indictment charging the defendant with three counts of larceny from the board.[7] In light of this conclusion, the defendant may not be adjudicated a common and notorious thief pursuant to G.L. c. 266, § 40.

5. Conclusion. The judgments are reversed as to the indictment alleging three counts of larceny from the board, the verdicts set aside, and the cases remanded for a new trial. The adjudication of the defendant as a common and notorious thief is vacated. The remaining convictions are remanded to the Superior Court for resentencing by a different judge.

---

[5] The judge charged the jury on the elements of larceny as follows: "In order to prove the defendant guilty of larceny, the Commonwealth must prove three things beyond a reasonable doubt. One, that the defendant took or carried away the property or money; second, that the property or money was owned or possessed by someone other than the defendant; and three, the defendant did so with the intent to deprive that person of the property permanently."

[7] The Appeals Court has pointed out that double jeopardy principles would bar retrial on a theory of larceny by false pretenses. This issue is not presently before us and is a defense that properly can be raised by motion prior to the commencement of a new trial.

B.   AGGRAVATED THEFT

1.   Burglary

UNITED STATES v. EICHMAN

United States District Court for the Southern District of New York
756 F.Supp. 143 (S.D.N.Y. 1991)

SAND, District Judge.

This criminal case involves charges arising from acts allegedly committed by the defendants at the United States Armed Forces Recruiting Station at Times Square in New York City. Count three of the indictment, brought pursuant to the Assimilative Crimes Act, 18 U.S.C. § 13 (1988), charges the defendants with burglary in the third degree in violation of N.Y.Penal Law § 140.20 (McKinney 1988). Presently before this Court are the defendants' motions to dismiss count three of the indictment, or, in the alternative, to permit an inspection of the grand jury minutes.

The issue raised by defendants' motions is what constitutes "enter[ing] . . . in a building with intent to commit a crime therein" under the burglary provisions of the New York Penal Law. The government opposes defendants' motions but asks this Court to issue a ruling on how the jury will be charged on the burglary count. For the reasons given below, this Court denies the motion to dismiss and the motion to inspect. However, we grant the government's request and set forth our determination as to how the jury will be charged with respect to the elements of the burglary count.

I. BACKGROUND

The government and the defendants are in substantial agreement as to the facts of this case. On September 11, 1990, defendants Shawn Eichman and Joseph Urgo went to the Armed Forces Recruiting Station at Times Square and climbed onto the roof of the one story structure using a ladder. Once on the roof the defendants poured motor oil over the surface of the roof and onto the exterior signs of the building. The defendants then lowered the American flag flying over the building, doused it with lighter fluid and set it on fire. Defendants claim that their activities were acts of political protest symbolizing their objection to American policy in the Persian Gulf.

Shortly after they ignited the flag, defendants were arrested on the roof by New York City police officers. The next day they were arraigned on a complaint charging attempted arson of the recruiting station. The government subsequently decided not to pursue the arson charge. Instead, the indictmentreturned by the grand jury charged defendants with three other crimes: (1) injuring and committing depredations against property of the United States, in violation of 18 U.S.C. §§ 1361, 1362 (1988); (2) reckless endangerment, in violation of 18 U.S.C. §§ 7, 13 (1988) and N.Y.Penal Law § 120.20 (McKinney 1988); and (3) burglary in the third degree, in violation of 18 U.S.C. §§ 7, 13 and N.Y.Penal Law § 140.20. * * *

On December 17, 1990, defendants moved to dismiss the burglary count of the indictment on the ground that absent an allegation that defendants entered within the four walls of the recruiting station, the government would be unable to prove the "entry" element of the burglary count at trial. * * * The government argues that the defendants' motions should be denied because the indictment pleads all the necessary elements of burglary under New York law. However, the government nonetheless asks this Court to reach the merits of defendants' argument regarding the entry element. * * *

II. DISCUSSION

* * * Defendants also argue for dismissal on the ground that the government indicted them on the burglary charge, which is the only felony count in the indictment, in order to punish them for expressing their political views. In response, the government maintains that it could have sought indictment on the charge of attempted arson, which carries a higher penalty than burglary, but did not do so because it thought that the burglary charge better fit the defendants' conduct. The decision whether to prosecute an individual, and for what crime, are matters resting in the sound discretion of the prosecuting authorities. This Court finds no reason to question the government's exercise of its prosecutorial discretion in this case. * * *

C. Government's Request for Ruling on Charge to Jury

In its Memorandum of Law in opposition to defendants' motions and again at oral argument, the government argued that while the motions should be denied, this Court nonetheless should reach the substantive issue raised therein. The government asks that we rule on how the jury would be charged with regard to the burglary count, on the ground that resolution of that question at this time is likely to advance the resolution of this case. We treat the government's request as being in the nature of a motion in limine and grant the request.

The underlying issue raised by defendants' motions is whether the defendants can be convicted of burglary under New York law if the government does not attempt to prove that they ever entered within the four walls or beneath the roof of the recruiting station. This court is convinced that they cannot.

Under New York law, a person must "enter or remain unlawfully in a building" in order to be guilty of burglary in the third degree. N.Y.Penal Law § 140.20.[1] In defining unlawful entry the Penal Law focuses on the requirement of unlawfulness, defining it in terms of lack of license or privilege to be in a building. However, the Penal Law does not define the breadth of the concept of entering in a building.

In the absence of statutory guidance, the parties place their reliance on a recent Court of Appeals decision, *People v. King*, 61 N.Y.2d 550, 463 N.E.2d 601, 475 N.Y.S.2d 260 (1984). In *King*, the defendant appealed his conviction for attempted burglary of a jewelry store. The store was on the ground floor and had a metal security gate covering the display windows and the vestibule area which led past the display windows and into the interior of the store. The defendant was apprehended after he cut a small hole in the part of the security gate directly in front of the vestibule area.

The defendant's first contention in *King* was that he should not have been convicted because it would have been impossible for him to enter the store in that the hole was not big enough for his body to pass through. The Court rejected this contention, holding that because the Penal Law does not define "enter" the term retains its common law meaning, which is that entry is accomplished when a person "intrudes within a building, no matter how slightly." Because the defendant could have put a part of his body through the hole, the entry requirement was satisfied.

The defendant's second contention was that the vestibule area was not part of the "building" within the meaning of the statute, such that his attempt to enter it was not attempted burglary. The Court also rejected this contention, holding that the "existence of the security gate, which can be pulled down to completely enclose the vestibule area from public access, albeit with a temporary fourth wall, makes the vestibule functionally indistinguishable from the space inside the display cases or the rest of the store."

In this case, both parties focus on the part of the *King* opinion which discusses the vestibule area. The government reads that part as standing for the

---

[1] The phrase "remain unlawfully" is included in the statute to cover situations where an individual has permission to enter a building, but remains after that permission has expired or been revoked. *See* N.Y.Penal Law § 140.00(5) (McKinney 1988). As such, that phrase has no application in this case.

proposition that the element of entering is satisfied so long as the defendant goes into "an area of or related to a building to which the public has been or can be denied access." The defendants interpret *King* to mean that in order to be guilty of burglary, the defendant must intrude into some enclosed space in or connected to a building.

In deciding which view of *King* is correct, the appropriate starting point is the common law of burglary since, according to the *King* Court, the element of entry still retains its common law meaning in New York. At common law, burglary was the breaking and entering of a dwelling house at night with the intent to commit a felony therein. The predominate impetus of common law burglary was "to protect the security of the home, and the person within his home." The offense was directed at preserving the internal security of the dwelling; consequently, an entry into the structure itself was an essential element of the crime. The intrusion of any part of the defendant's body, or of an object held in his hand, was sufficient to establish the element of entry. Yet there had to be some movement by the defendant across the external boundaries of the structure, some breaking of the planes created by the threshold and the four walls. Activity conducted outside the external boundaries of a dwelling, no matter how felonious, was not burglary at common law.[2]

The scope of common law burglary was expanded somewhat through the concept of curtilage. Curtilage was defined as the area within close proximity to the dwelling house. Outbuildings within the curtilage were deemed to be part of the dwelling house, such that an unlawful entry into the outbuilding was burglary. In essence, then, the effect of the concept of curtilage was to expand the definition of dwelling house; however, it did not alter the entry requirement. Thus a defendant might be convicted of burglary for stealing from a homeowner's barn, but only if he actually entered within the four walls of the barn.

Because the common law required that a defendant penetrate the exterior walls of a structure in order to be guilty of burglary, such penetration is required for the commission of statutory burglary in New York. Thus in this case, the defendants may be convicted of burglary only if the government can prove that they actually entered within the four walls or beneath the roof of the recruiting station.

This conclusion comports with the Court of Appeal's decision in King and the case law of New York's lower courts. In *King*, the vestibule of the

---

[2] Thus Lord Hale maintained that firing a gun into a house was not burglary unless some part of the weapon crossed the threshold.

jewelry store was within the planes created by the four exterior walls of the building. Thus the defendant was guilty of attempted burglary because he tried to gain entrance to the vestibule. In *People v. Bright*, the defendant's conviction for burglary was upheld where he was apprehended inside the vestibule area of a store, which was within the area encompassed by the four walls of the building. In *People v. Pringle*, the defendant's conviction for burglary was upheld where he entered a separately secured nurse's station within a prison and committed an assault. The common thread in these cases is that in all three instances, the defendants actually entered into the interiors of enclosed and separately secured structures.

In addition to its consonance with the caselaw of New York, the view of the entry requirement adopted by this Court comports with the restraints imposed by the rule of lenity. * * * Courts should decline to interpret a criminal statute to encompass situations which a reasonable layperson could not foresee as being within the ambit of the statute. In this case, there is little doubt but that the defendants knew that their actions on the rooftop of the recruiting station violated the law. Trespass, destruction of government property, reckless endangerment and perhaps even attempted arson were foreseeable charges stemming from their conduct. That the defendants could reasonably have foreseen the charge of burglary is, however, a much more doubtful proposition.

In sum, this Court is of the view that the New York Penal Law requires that a defendant actually enter within the four walls or beneath the roof of a building in order to be guilty of burglary in the third degree. At trial, the jury will be instructed that they may not convict the defendants of the burglary charge unless they find that such an entry occurred. Of course, if the government presents no evidence of such entry then the count will be dismissed.

STATE v. THIBEAULT

Supreme Judicial Court of Maine
402 A.2d 445 (Me. 1979)

DELAHANTY, Justice.

A Superior Court jury, Penobscot County, found Dale Thibeault guilty of Class B burglary. 17-A M.R.S.A. § 401(B). On April 24, 1978, Thibeault was sentenced to a term of six years at the Maine State Prison. On appeal, the defendant attacks the legality of his conviction on numerous grounds. * * *

The prosecution introduced ample evidence tending to show that on the evening of December 9, 1977, the defendant entered an apartment leased by David and Debbie Gardner with the intent, later consummated, to abscond with certain valuables.   On his case-in-chief, the defendant called one of the cotenants, David Gardner, to the stand.   Gardner testified that he had been friendly with the defendant for several years and that prior to the December 9 incident he had given the defendant blanket permission to enter his apartment at any time.   On cross-examination, Gardner allowed that he had not given the defendant permission to remove any property from the apartment.

On appeal, as at his trial, the defendant directs his attack at that segment of the jury instructions in which the presiding Justice discussed the evidence pertinent to the "license or privilege" language found in Section 401.[1]   The challenged passage reads as follows:

> Now as to the license and privilege.   There's not much of a dispute that Mr. Gardner, one of the co-tenants, gave permission but it becomes your duty under the law and considering all the facts whether or not the State has sustained its burden which I have given you beyond a reasonable doubt that the Defendant, Mr. Thibeault, knew that he was not licensed and privileged or privileged to do so with the intent to commit this crime of theft which I have defined to you. Was that a license? Was it a privilege? Was it a qualified license or privilege?   It's for you to say what was in the mutual contemplation of the parties when permission to enter was given by Mr. Gardner.   There is no dispute that Mr. Gardner, himself, says, I never gave him consent to steal or to rip off the apartment, so the facts are not much in dispute. Therefore, you must decide whether or not from all the testimony, from all the facts, and under the law which I have given to you, whether or not the Defendant, in whatever condition he was, knew that he was not licensed or privileged when he went in those premises to commit the crime of theft.

* * *

The defendant argues that under Section 401 a person cannot validly be convicted of burglary if the individual rightfully in possession has given that person permission to enter the structure.   He contends that the jury instruction was erroneous to the extent that it gave the jury the impression that if it found

---

[1] The pertinent portion of Section 401 provides:

A person is guilty of burglary if he enters or surreptitiously remains in a structure, knowing that he is not licensed or privileged to do so, with the intent to commit a crime therein.

that the defendant had intended to commit a crime within the apartment that intention would negative, for the purposes of the burglary statute, Gardner's permission to enter.

At common law, consent to enter was a complete defense to a burglary prosecution. Burglary, like arson, was conceived of as an invasion of the "right of habitation." Thus, mere entry upon the dwelling of another in the nighttime with intent to commit a felony therein was insufficient to constitute the common-law crime of burglary. The prosecution additionally had to prove a "breaking": "the actual or constructive use of some force against a part of a building in effectuating an *unconsented* entry." That the initial entry must be trespassory was established in Maine in *State v. Newbegin*, where the defendant was convicted of burglarizing a dry goods store which, at the time in question, was open for trade. The defendant lifted an unlocked latch, opened a door, stole some cloth, and escaped all without attracting the attention of the store attendants. The Court reversed the burglary conviction finding that the State had failed to establish a breaking. * * *

Since the common law required a "violation of the security designed to exclude," it was axiomatic that a person entering with the permission of the lawful possessor could not be guilty of burglary. As one authority explains, (t)he law was not ready to punish one who had been "invited" in any way to enter the dwelling. The law sought only to keep out intruders, and thus anyone given authority to come into the house could not be committing a breaking when he so entered. W. LaFave & A. Scott, CRIMINAL LAW § 96 (1972).

Although we have not had occasion to deal with a consent defense to a burglary prosecution since *Newbegin* was decided in 1846, it is nevertheless clear that consent remained a valid defense at least until such time as Maine's Criminal Code became effective in 1976. The former burglary statutes, 17 M.R.S.A. §§ 751-754, 2103, all included or incorporated by reference the familiar breaking element. Furthermore, our interpretations of that element were entirely consistent with the "security-designed- to-exclude" rationale put forth in *Newbegin*.[3]

---

[3] * * *In State v. Cookson, Me., 293 A.2d 780, 784-85 (1972), for example, Justice Weatherbee declared:

> It appears clear that the offense of burglary is one primarily against the security of the habitation. It marks the state's determination to safeguard in his dwelling the homeowner, his family and guests from the dangers that accompany felonious invasions of their sanctuaries during the particularly vulnerable periods of darkness. (footnote

Although few quarreled with the logic of including the requirement of a trespassory entry for a law designed to protect the security of the habitation, judicial interpretations of the "force" aspect of the breaking element rightly attracted the criticism of reformers. In interpreting the "force" aspect, the judges of the common law perhaps wishing to constrict the application of what was then a capital crime, created a host of fine distinctions and bewildering qualifications.[4]

With burglary no longer a capital offense, the irrationality of these interpretations became manifest. Many state legislatures have reacted by excising the breaking element from their statutes entirely. In these jurisdictions, burglary has been reduced to a three-element crime: (1) entry (2) of a structure (3) with the intent to commit a crime. Under such a statute, it is clear that consent to enter is not a defense since, no vestige of the breaking element remaining, the entry need not be trespassory to be burglarious.

In other jurisdictions, Maine among them, the word "breaking" has been eliminated and a word or phrase such as "unlawful," "unauthorized," or "without license or privilege" has been inserted in the statute to qualify "entry." Where such language has been employed in a burglary statute, the result has generally been to retain so much of the breaking element as required a trespassory entry while at the same time eliminating the illogical rules stemming from the "force" aspect of breaking. Of course, where the statute requires a trespassory entry, the lawful possessor's consent is a complete defense.

New York's burglary statute and the judicial interpretations thereof are particularly instructive since that statute makes use of the same "license or privilege" language found in our Section 401.[5] The New York courts have held that the "license or privilege" language included in Section 140.00(5) requires a trespassory entry.

---

omitted.)

[4] For example, if the defendant entered through an open door or window, no breaking occurred since no force was used: the occupant, it was said, had not sufficiently secured his dwelling and was therefore not entitled to the protection of the law. Worse still, courts were divided over the question of whether pushing open a partly open door or window was a sufficient use of force to satisfy the breaking element.

[5] Both New York and Maine appear to have adopted modified versions of the Model Penal Code's definition of burglary. Model Penal Code § 221.1(1974).

We hold that the "license or privilege" language in Maine's Section 401 requires a like construction. The portion of the statute relevant to this appeal provides that "(a) person is guilty of burglary if he enters . . . a structure, knowing that he is not licensed . . . to do so, with the intent to commit a crime therein." Breaking the statute down to its constituent parts, we discern four elements: (1) entry (2) of a structure (3) with the knowledge that the entry is not licensed and (4) with the intent to commit a crime within the structure. Obviously, the "license" referred to in the statute means the license to enter a particular structure. The "do so" clearly refers back to "enters." Accordingly, the prosecution must, as an independent proposition, prove beyond reasonable doubt that the accused knew that he was
not "licensed" to enter the structure.

The State argues that since the defendant entered the Gardners' apartment for the unlawful purpose of stealing certain valuables, any permission he may have secured from Gardner would be negated. We find no room in Section 401 for this argument. Whether or not the defendant had permission to enter is a question that must be resolved without reference to his alleged intent, another separate and distinct element of the crime. The Louisiana Supreme Court, construing that state's "unauthorized entry" statute, responded to the same argument as follows:

> As we construe the burglary statute, the entry must be unauthorized and this must be determined as a distinct element of the offense separate and apart from the intent to steal. If the legislature desired that burglary consist only of an entry with intent to steal, they would have omitted the word *unauthorized*.

State v. Dunn, supra 263 La. at 63, 267 So.2d at 195. (emphasis in original.)

Much the same can be said of Maine's Section 401. If we construed the statute to allow the existence of a criminal intent upon entry to negate the permission of the lawful possessor, the result would be, for all practical purposes, the expungement of the "license" language from the statute. If the State's argument is accepted, a burglary defendant would have to prevail on the question of his intent to commit a crime in order to prevail on the "license or privilege" issue. The State's interpretation would thus render the "license or privilege" language mere surplusage, and Section 401 would be little more than a variation on the typical three-element statute discussed earlier. We have no reason to believe that the Legislature would inject unnecessary language into any of the Code's provisions. Indeed, our familiar rule has been to construe statutes, particularly criminal ones, as being free of superfluous language.

It is true that the Comment appended to Section 401 declares that the statute eliminates "the common law requirement . . . that there be a 'breaking.'" However, the next sentence, "(t)he crime loses nothing in seriousness if the burglar enters a door inadvertently left open, rather than through a door he breaks open," indicates that the revisers intended to draft the statute in such a way as to eliminate only the "force" aspect of breaking together with the irrational judicial interpretations that accompanied it. The "license or privilege" language inserted in the statute itself indicates that the trespassory aspect of the breaking element was retained.

Turning to the instruction given by the presiding Justice, we conclude that the jury was given the mistaken impression that it could find the defendant guilty of burglary whether or not David Gardner gave him permission to enter the apartment. "There's not much of a dispute," stated the court, "that Mr. Gardner, one of the co-tenants, gave permission . . . ." That being the case, the jury's function, according to the court, was to determine whether or not the defendant "knew that he was not licensed (to enter) with the intent to commit this crime of theft . . . ." The instruction invited the jury to consider whether, in the words of the presiding Justice, a "qualified license" existed. As our analysis here indicates, Section 401 does not contemplate the kind of qualification outlined by the presiding Justice. A remand will therefore be necessary. * * *

Judgment of conviction set aside.

Case remanded for a new trial.

Note

Like burglary, extortion has aspects of a crime against the person and aspects of a crime against property. At common law, extortion was defined as a crime committed by an officer of the law who, under cover or color of his office, unlawfully and corruptly takes any money or thing of value that is not due to him, or who takes more than is due, or before it is due. No proof of threat, fear or duress was required. It was also not necessary under the common law of extortion for the public official to demand or request the thing of value; merely taking it constituted the crime. Over time, however, the crime was broadened to include actions by private individuals who had no official power to wield over their victims. Threats, fear and duress then became express elements of the crime.

In the majority of jurisdictions that incorporate the common law, extortion is understood as a crime against the person, not against property. Therefore, "honest claim of right" is not a defense. Under section 223.4 of the

Model Penal Code, however, extortion is classified as a form of theft, and governed by the Code's general claim-of-right defense. Thus, the defendant's claim that the property extorted rightfully belonged to her is a good defense. *See Woodward v. State*, 855 P.2d 423 (Alaska Ct. App. 1993) (discussing the common law and Model Penal Code approaches).

2.   Robbery

CROCKER v. STATE
Supreme Court of Mississippi
272 So.2d 664 (Miss. 1973)

INZER, Justice:

Appellant George Leon Crocker was indicted, tried and convicted in the Circuit Court of Neshoba County for the crime of robbery. He was sentenced to serve a term of ten years in the State Penitentiary. From this conviction and sentence, he appeals. We reverse and remand.

The principal contention of appellant is that the trial court was in error in refusing to grant his request for a directed verdict at the close of the state's case.

The indictment in this case in effect charged that appellant committed an assault on one Jesse S. McKenzie and did thereby put him in bodily fear of immediate injury to his person and that appellant did take $500 from the person of Jesse S. McKenzie against his will, and did then and there feloniously and violently take, steal and carry away $500.

McKenzie testified that at approximately eleven o'clock on the morning of June 26, 1971, appellant came to his home and after they had a cup of coffee, he and appellant went to the store where they drank some beer and whiskey. When they returned McKenzie changed his clothes. He had his billfold containing $500 in the bib of his coveralls which he removed. He stated that he removed the billfold and put it in his pocket. It is unclear from his testimony whether he put the billfold in the pocket of the coveralls which he removed, or whether he put it in the pocket of the clothes he put on. Apparently, he left it on the bed because he stated appellant got the billfold, removed $500 therefrom, laid the billfold down and left. Although the state attempted to get him to say that the appellant took the money from his person by force or violence, he never would say that any force or violence was used. On cross examination he stated that appellant did not in any way use force, violence, or fear to get his money. He concluded his testimony by stating that his clothes were on the bed and his wallet was in his clothes, and that appellant took his money from his wallet and left. He also stated at one point in his testimony that appellant had been gone for about an hour before he missed his money.

It is well settled that the three essential elements of robbery are as follows: (1) felonious intent, (2) force or putting in fear as a means of effectuating the intent, and (3) by that means taking and carrying away the property of another from his person or in his presence. All these elements must occur in point of time. If force is relied upon as proof of the charge it must be force by which another is deprived of and the offender gains possession of the property. If putting in fear is relied upon, it must be the fear under duress of which the owner parts with possession. It is apparent that the state failed to prove the second necessary element of the crime of robbery and therefore, the trial court was in error in refusing to grant the appellant's motion for a directed verdict, insofar as the crime of robbery is concerned.

The state, while contending the evidence is sufficient to sustain the charge of robbery, urges that although we find the evidence of the charge of robbery was insufficient to sustain the conviction, it was sufficient to sustain a conviction of the lesser included offense of larceny, and that this Court should sustain the conviction insofar as the conviction includes larceny and remand the case for proper sentencing. The state cites Section 2523, Mississippi Code 1942 Annotated (1956), which reads as follows:

> On an indictment for any offense the jury may find the defendant guilty of the offense as charged, or of any attempt to commit the same offense, or may find him guilty of an inferior offense, or other offense, the commission of which is necessarily included in the offense with which he is charged in the indictment, whether the same be a felony or misdemeanor, without any additional count in the indictment for that purpose.

Under the provisions of this section the jury could have found appellant guilty of grand larceny instead of robbery, and in that event the conviction would be upheld. The difficulty here is that the state chose to rely upon the charge of robbery, and the trial court submitted the case to the jury on that charge, instead of submitting the case to the jury on the lesser included offense of grand larceny. Under these circumstances, this Court cannot sustain a conviction of the constituent offense of grand larceny. * * *

Reversed and appellant ordered held for further action of the grand jury.

MILLER v. SUPERIOR COURT

Court of Appeal of California, 4th Appellate District, Division One
115 Cal.App.4th 216, 8 Cal.Rptr.3d 872 (Ct. App. 2004)

McIntyre, J.

Penal Code section 211 defines a robbery as "the felonious taking of personal property in the possession of another, from his person or immediate presence, and against his will, accomplished by means of force or fear." (All statutory references are to the Penal Code except as otherwise specified.) The issue presented in this case is whether the immediate presence requirement of a robbery charge is satisfied where the defendant, after stealing property belonging to the victim but not from the victim's presence, is confronted by the victim as he is attempting to carry the property to a place of temporary safety and uses forcible resistance to keep the property. We conclude that the immediate presence requirement is met under such circumstances and thus deny the defendant's petition for a writ of prohibition challenging the superior court's order denying his motion to dismiss the robbery charge.

FACTUAL AND PROCEDURAL BACKGROUND

On August 27, 2002, Jose Higareda went into the public restroom at La Jolla Cove to change into his swimming trunks. He went into one of the restroom's enclosed stalls and hung his pants, which contained his wallet (with more than $200 in cash), cellular telephone and keys, on a hook inside the stall door. As Higareda was changing, Miller walked into the restroom and entered the stall directly across from Higareda's. There was no one else in the restroom at the time.

After Higareda finished putting on his swimming trunks, he walked out of the restroom, inadvertently leaving his pants hanging inside the stall. After taking a few steps outside the restroom, Higareda realized his mistake and went back into the restroom. He checked the stall where he had left his pants and, after discovering the pants missing, began looking under the doors of the other stalls to try to locate them. Higareda heard the sound of someone opening Velcro coming from the stall directly across from the one where he had left his pants.

Because his wallet had a Velcro fastener, Higareda became suspicious, entered a stall adjacent to the one Miller was in and looked over the top into Miller's stall. Miller, who appeared to be shielding something from Higareda's view, inquired what Higareda was doing. Higareda responded that someone had taken his belongings and Miller told him to report the situation to a lifeguard.

Higareda waited outside Miller's stall for 15 to 20 minutes, expecting that Miller would come out. During that time, Miller repeatedly asked other persons who entered the restroom for toilet paper, but did not leave the stall.

Ultimately, Higareda's friend, Dennis O'Brien, entered the restroom looking for Higareda. Higareda told O'Brien that someone had taken his belongings and that he believed Miller had them. O'Brien knocked on the door of Miller's stall, demanding that Miller "give ... the stuff back." Miller told O'Brien to leave him "the 'f' alone," but Higareda continued to demand that Miller return his property. After additional exchanges, O'Brien announced that he was going to get a lifeguard, although, at Higareda's request, he did not leave the restroom.

Five to ten seconds later, Miller came out of his stall and attempted to leave the restroom, saying "[l]et me out of here." Higareda and O'Brien blocked Miller from leaving and yelled for someone to get a lifeguard. Miller charged at the men, trying to push and shove his way out of the restroom. After a great deal of scuffling, O'Brien placed Miller in a headlock and Higareda demanded to see what Miller had in his pockets. Miller gave Higareda his wallet, which Higareda held until lifeguards arrived.

Police arrested Miller at the scene and found $241 in cash in his wallet, which did not fasten with Velcro, and 2.43 grams of methamphetamine in his shorts pocket. O'Brien told the officers that he found Higareda's pants and empty wallet underneath a tremendous mound of toilet paper in the stall Miller had occupied. Officers suspected that Miller was under the influence of a controlled substance at the time of his arrest; Miller subsequently tested positive for the presence of methamphetamine.

The district attorney charged Miller with one count each of robbery and possession of a controlled substance. At an April 3, 2003 preliminary hearing on the charges against Miller, O'Brien and two police officers testified. (Although Higareda did not testify at the preliminary hearing, one of the officers testified about Higareda's statements concerning the incident. The officer's testimony was admissible pursuant to section 872, subdivision (b).) The magistrate held Miller to answer both charges.

Miller filed a section 995 motion to dismiss the robbery charge against him on the ground that the evidence did not establish that he took property from Higareda's person or immediate presence. The superior court concluded that, in accordance with *People v. Estes*, Miller's resistance to Higareda's attempt to regain the property was sufficient to establish the immediate presence requirement and that the evidence thus supported the robbery charge against Miller. Based on its findings, the court denied Miller's section 995 motion.

Miller filed the instant petition for writ of prohibition, challenging the denial order and reasserting his argument that because there is no evidence showing the property was taken from Higareda's person or immediate presence, the evidence admitted at his preliminary hearing is insufficient to support the robbery charge against him. We issued an order to show cause why the relief should not be granted and stayed further proceedings in the trial court.

DISCUSSION

* * *

2. Robbery

As noted above, a "robbery" is "the felonious taking of personal property in the possession of another, from his person or immediate presence, and against his will, accomplished by means of force or fear." (§ 211.) The crime is essentially a theft with two aggravating factors, that is, a taking (1) from victim's person or immediate presence, and (2) accomplished by the use of force or fear.

"The taking element of robbery itself has two necessary elements, gaining possession of the victim's property and asporting or carrying away the loot." "Immediate presence" is spatially, not temporally, descriptive and thus "refer[s] to the area from which the property is taken, not how far it is taken" or for what duration. "A thing is in the [immediate] presence of a person, in respect to robbery, which is so within his reach, inspection, observation or control, that he could, if not overcome by violence or prevented by fear, retain his possession of it." The "immediate presence" component focuses on whether the stolen property was located in an area in which the victim could have expected to take effective steps to retain control over his property. Traditionally, the "immediate presence" requirement has been described as relating to the "gaining possession" element of the taking rather than the "carrying away" element of a robbery charge.

To support a robbery charge, the taking must also be accomplished by force or fear. Circumstances otherwise constituting a mere theft will establish a robbery where the perpetrator peacefully acquires the victim's property, but then uses force to retain or escape with it. For example, in *People v. Anderson*, the California Supreme Court held that the defendant was properly convicted of robbery based on evidence that he examined a rifle and ammunition at a pawnshop under the guise of being interested in purchasing the items and while the pawnshop clerk was totaling the purchase price, he loaded the rifle and pointed it at the clerk to facilitate his escape.

The *Anderson* court stated "[i]n this state, it is settled that a robbery is not completed at the moment the robber obtains possession of the stolen property and that the crime of robbery includes the element of asportation, the robber's escape with the loot being considered as important in the commission of the crime as gaining possession of the property. . . . Accordingly, if one who has stolen property from the person of another uses force or fear in removing, or attempting to remove, the property from the owner's immediate presence, ... the crime of robbery has been committed."

The *Anderson* court cited with approval *People v. Phillips*, in which the defendant had a gas station attendant pump gasoline into his car and then confronted the attendant with a rifle, refusing to pay for the gas. There, the appellate court affirmed the judgment of conviction based on the taking of the gasoline, upholding the jury's implicit finding that the defendant took the gasoline from the immediate presence of the attendant by means of force or fear.

Although these cases address the peaceful acquisition of property from the immediate presence of the victim, with force or fear arising only in an effort to carry the property away, subsequent authority establishes that the victim's presence after the taking is in progress is sufficient to establish the immediate presence element of a robbery charge. In *Estes*, a department store security guard saw the defendant shoplifting items of clothing inside the store and attempted to stop the defendant, who had left the store without paying for the items. The defendant pulled out a knife, swung it at the security guard and threatened to kill the guard.

The *Estes* court rejected the defendant's contention that the merchandise was not taken from the security guard's immediate presence, stating "[t]he evidence establishe[d] that [the defendant] forcibly resisted the security guard's efforts to retake the property and used that force to remove the items from the guard's immediate presence. By preventing the guard from regaining control over the merchandise, [the] defendant is held to have taken the property as if the guard had actual possession of the goods in the first instance." The *Estes* court also observed that a "[d]efendant's guilt is not to be weighed at each step of the robbery as it unfolds. The events constituting the crime of robbery, although they may extend over large distances and take some time to complete, are linked by a single-mindedness of purpose."

Miller and the dissent suggest that because the security guard in Estes observed the thief taking clothing from the store, the immediate presence element was otherwise satisfied in accordance with the standard set forth in *People v. Hayes, supra*, (to wit, that "[a] thing is in the [immediate] presence of a person, in respect to robbery, which is so within his reach, inspection, observation or control, that he could, if not overcome by violence or prevented by fear, retain his possession of it") and that the above-quoted language in *Estes* was merely dicta. We disagree. Although the *Estes* court could have found that the immediate presence element was satisfied based on the security guard's observation of the theft, the fact remains that it did not do so. Rather the court concluded that, as the use of force or fear only in carrying the stolen property away was sufficient to support a robbery charge, the victim's immediate presence during the asportation of the property was likewise sufficient. Courts and practitioners have widely accepted this analysis, such that robberies in which the victim only comes upon the defendant after the latter has gained possession of the stolen property are commonly referred to as "*Estes* robberies."

Miller argues and the dissent agrees that to the extent *Estes* concludes the element of "immediate presence" can be satisfied by a victim's presence during a defendant's asporting or carrying away of property, the California Supreme Court subsequently overruled it on that issue in *Cooper*. However, although *Cooper* described the immediate presence element of a robbery charge as relating to the "gaining possession" element of the taking rather than the "carrying away" element the opinion did not overrule or disapprove of *Estes* in any respect, but rather cited *Estes* with approval.

Although the dissent credits us with "complet[ing] the transmogrification of the crime of robbery," in light of the widespread acceptance of the analysis of *Estes* and the fact that the California Supreme Court has not criticized or overruled *Estes* in the 20 years since that decision issued, we do not believe that our opinion expresses a change in the law, but instead reflects the current state of the law on the issue of what is sufficient to establish the immediate presence element of a robbery charge. We conclude from these authorities that, although the immediate presence and force or fear elements of robbery originally had to be satisfied at the time of the gaining possession aspect of a taking, the law has long since allowed these elements to be supplied after the defendant has initially gained possession of the victim's property.

Pursuant to the long-standing principles announced in *Estes*, Miller's use of force to retain the property after Higareda confronted him while he was attempting to get away with Higareda's money was sufficient to support the assertion of a robbery charge against him. In such circumstances, Higareda could reasonably "have expected to take effective steps to retain control over his property" and thus the immediate presence requirement is satisfied.

For the foregoing reasons, we conclude that the preliminary hearing evidence is sufficient to support the existence of a taking from Higareda's immediate presence and thus the trial court did not err in denying Miller's section 995 motion to dismiss the robbery charge against Miller.

DISPOSITION

The petition for a writ of prohibition is denied. The stay issued by this court will dissolve by its own terms when this opinion becomes final.

MCDONALD, J., dissenting.

The majority opinion completes the transmogrification of the crime of robbery from the offense defined in Penal Code section 211 as the "taking of personal property in the possession of another, from his person or immediate presence ..., accomplished by means of force or fear" to the new offense of the taking or retaining personal property under those circumstances, a change accomplished by the court without legislative assistance.

Section 211 defines "robbery" as "the felonious taking of personal property in the possession of another, from his person or immediate presence, and against his will, accomplished by means of force or fear." The taking element of robbery itself has two necessary elements, gaining possession of the victim's property and asporting or carrying away the loot. However, *Cooper* further stated:

"Although the 'immediate presence' language comes directly from section 211, this language does not pertain to the duration of robbery.... Taking from the 'person' and from the 'immediate presence' [in section 211] are alternatives. These terms are spatially, rather than temporally, descriptive. They refer to the area from which the property is taken, not how far it is taken. [Citations.] Put another way, these limitations on the scope of the robbery statute relate to the 'gaining possession' component of the taking as distinct from the 'carrying away' component."

In *People v. Hayes*, the Supreme Court adopted the following definition of "immediate presence:" "'[a] thing is in the [immediate] presence of a person, in respect to robbery, which is so within his reach, inspection, observation or control, that he could, if not overcome by violence or prevented by fear, retain his possession of it.'"

"Immediate presence" means at least an area within which the victim could reasonably be expected to exercise some physical control over his or her property. Under the Supreme Court decisions in *Cooper*, Hayes and Webster, a necessary element of a section 211 robbery is the victim's presence in a location in which he or she could reasonably expect some physical control of the personal property at the time the perpetrator gained possession of the property.

In this case, Higareda was not in that location; he was outside the public restroom at the time Miller gained possession of Higareda's trousers and the items contained in those trousers. An element of the charged robbery, as described by the Supreme Court, is absent in this case. Miller may have been guilty of burglary, assault, theft or other criminal offenses, but he was not guilty of robbery.

The majority opinion agrees that Miller did not gain possession of Higareda's personal property from either his person or from his immediate possession. It also concludes that Miller retained possession of Higareda's personal property in his immediate presence during the asportation phase of the incident, and that retention of the personal property during the asportation phase of the incident satisfied the taking "from the person or immediate presence" element of robbery.

The majority opinion's conclusion that the victim's presence during the asportation phase of the incident is sufficient to satisfy the elements of robbery is directly in conflict with language of the Supreme Court's opinion in *Cooper*. It seeks to obviate that conflict by describing the Supreme Court cases as representing the "traditional" view of robbery, which has evolved into a new and different rule creating a new and different offense known as an "*Estes* robbery." * * *

* * * The language from *Estes* quoted ante is effectively dicta because the guard was present and observed the defendant gain possession of the property; the defendant in *Estes* gained possession of the property in the guard's immediate presence under the *Hayes* test and *Estes* is factually inapposite to this case. The court in *Estes* unnecessarily stated the element of "immediate presence" was satisfied retroactively by the defendant's use of force during the asportation phase of the incident after he gained possession of the property. To the extent *Estes* stated the element of immediate presence can be satisfied by a victim's presence during a defendant's asporting or carrying away of property, it is inconsistent with *Cooper*, which concluded immediate presence applies only to the gaining possession component and not to the asporting or carrying away component. *Estes* does not establish the immediate presence element was satisfied in this case. Rather, *Estes* under its facts, established only that the force or fear element of robbery could be satisfied if present during the asportation phase of the incident. * * *

The approval by *Cooper* of *Estes* was limited to the temporal aspect of the force or fear element of robbery and confirmed the holding of *Estes*, but not its dicta, that the force or fear element of robbery may be supplied by conduct during the asportation phase of the incident even if not present at the gaining possession phase of the incident. That is an *Estes* robbery. *Cooper* gave no approval to the language of *Estes*, which was unnecessary to its decision, that the immediate presence element of robbery could be satisfied during the asportation phase of the incident although not present at the gaining possession phase.

I do not agree with the majority opinion that the crime of robbery has evolved into a retention rather than a taking crime and, because bound by my understanding of *Cooper* and *Hayes*, I conclude the preliminary hearing evidence does not support a reasonable inference that the property was on Higareda's person or in his immediate presence at the time Miller gained possession of it. The trial court therefore erred by denying Miller's section 995 motion to dismiss the robbery charge against him. I would let a peremptory writ of prohibition issue restraining the San Diego County Superior Court from taking further action on the robbery charge against petitioner, other than to dismiss it.

Note

Where is the line between theft and robbery? *Rigell v. State*, 782 So.2d 440 (Fla. Dist. Ct. App. 2001), involved the following facts:

> [T]he victim and her husband were walking through a parking lot when the victim noticed a man ahead of them. After passing the man, the victim "felt two hands go on my shoulder bag – go on my purse, wrench downwards, a sharp pain in my right shoulder. My shoulder sort of gave way, and I screamed that he has got my bag." The purse strap broke. Although she felt pain, she had no physical injuries. She attempted to chase the assailant but fell to the ground.

Rigell, 782 So.2d 440, 441.

The defendant was convicted of robbery and appealed, arguing that there was insufficient evidence of the necessary force. The appellate court, however, affirmed the conviction, with the following explanation: "[T]he key distinction in determining the level of force necessary to distinguish theft from robbery is whether more force than was necessary to remove the property from the victim was used, or force enough to overcome victim resistance." 782 So.2d at 441.

C. BEYOND THEFT

When the English common law of larceny emerged, only tangible objects were subject to theft. In the centuries since then, however, as larceny gradually expanded to become a crime against property, the concept of "property" itself expanded and altered. By the twentieth century in the United States, various kinds of intangible rights had become recognized as property, and thus protected by the law of theft. As Geraldine Moohr observes about contemporary law:

> Intangible property can be a valuable commodity or business asset. Indeed, estimates of money lost through takings of property such as copyrighted works, trade secrets, and other business information are staggering. Even as rough estimates, multi-billion-dollar losses indicate the great economic significance of intangible property. Owners of such valuable interests naturally seek the protection of criminal law.
>
> In recent years, the kinds of intangible property have multiplied. The intangible interests examined here serve as examples: Elvis Presley recordings; computer source codes, software, and games; honest services; business licenses and franchises; and business information such as the contents of a newspaper column, the paper's production schedule, and plans of one corporation to purchase another. Although these interests are diverse, they share certain characteristics and raise similar questions. Unlike tangible property, their intangible nature makes the application of traditional criminal statutes problematic. How does one take a thing whose value and essence is independent of a physical form? Conversely, how does one maintain ownership of a res that can be simultaneously possessed by others? Most tellingly for present purposes, the effort to protect intangible property interests through criminal law raises the fundamental issue of whether such interests should be afforded the full panoply of property rights, including the protection of criminal law.

Geraldine Szott Moohr, *Federal Criminal Fraud and the Development of Intangible Property Rights in Information*, 2000 U. Ill. L. Rev. 683, 684-85.

The advancements of the computer age also poses new challenges for criminal law. The final excerpt in this section offers a typology of computer crime, and suggests ways for law enforcement to prevent computer crimes from occurring.

1.   Mail Fraud and Intangible Rights

One of the most powerful tools available to contemporary federal prosecutors is the mail fraud statute and its cousin, the wire fraud statute. 18 U.S.C. § 1341, the mail fraud statute, provides as follows:

> Whoever, having devised or intending to devise any scheme or artifice to defraud, or for obtaining money or property by means of false or fraudulent pretenses, representations, or promises, . . . places in any post office or authorized depository for mail matter, any matter or thing whatever to be sent or delivered by the Postal Service, or deposits or causes to be deposited any matter or thing whatever to be sent or delivered by any private or commercial interstate carrier, . . . shall be fined not more than $1,000 or imprisoned not more than five years, or both. If the violation affects a financial institution, such person shall be fined not more than $1,000,000 or imprisoned not more than 30 years, or both.

The wire fraud statute, 18 U.S.C. § 1343, punishes the same schemes punished by mail fraud when the defendant "transmits or causes to be transmitted by means of wire, radio, or television communication in interstate or foreign commerce, any writings, signs, signals, pictures, or sounds for the purpose of executing such scheme or artifice." Telephone communications fall under the definition of wire transmissions.

In *Durland v. United States*, 161 U.S. 306 (1896), the Supreme Court held that the crime of mail fraud is broader than the common law crime of false pretenses. The crime of mail fraud also punishes not only completed frauds but also "schemes to defraud." In this sense, mail fraud is an inchoate crime, similar to conspiracy.[a] Finally, mail fraud is a powerful tool because it encompasses the taking of intangible property and services. An example of how far prosecutors have tried to push the crime of mail fraud is given in *United States v. Margiotta*, below.

---

[a] However, the Supreme Court has held that Congress did mean to transport the common law requirement of "materiality" from the common law of fraud to the mail fraud statute. *Neder v. United States*, 527 U.S. 1 (1999). Therefore, under the mail fraud, wire fraud, and bank fraud statutes, the false representations or promises must be "material," or likely to influence a decision.

UNITED STATES v. MARGIOTTA

United States Court of Appeals for the Second Circuit
688 F.2d 108 (2d Cir. 1982)

IRVING R. KAUFMAN, Circuit Judge:

The significant role played by political parties in municipal government has been an often noted characteristic of American urban life. Some critics, contributing to the prevailing mythology that machine politics have controlled the corridors of local government, have highlighted the opportunities available to those who hold the strings of political power for defrauding the citizenry and reaping personal gain, through the sale of public office and other favors. Other commentators, however, have asserted that local party leaders have often served important functions of political representation and association. In cities fragmented into diverse social and economic groups, it has been argued, party organizations have played a salutary role in organizing large numbers of people, and fulfilling their desires with patronage, jobs, services, community benefits, and opportunities for upward social mobility. In sum, the line between legitimate political patronage and fraud on the public has been difficult to draw.

Today, not unmindful of these competing visions of political history, we must consider where such lines may be drawn in the context of a criminal prosecution for mail fraud and extortion. Specifically, we are asked to determine, inter alia, when, if ever, a political party leader who holds no official government office but who participates substantially in the governance of a municipality owes a fiduciary duty to the general citizenry, and what conduct violates such a fiduciary duty. The issues before us arise out of a criminal prosecution against Joseph M. Margiotta, long-time Chairman of the Republican Committees of both Nassau County and the Town of Hempstead, New York. The Government charges Margiotta with one count of mail fraud in violation of 18 U.S.C. § 1341 (1976) and five counts of extortion in violation of 18 U.S.C. § 1951 (1976) for activities in connection with the distribution of insurance commissions on municipal properties to Margiotta's political allies. The Government presented "evidence of a scheme of fraud spun into a web of political power" at a trial before Judge Sifton, at which nearly seventy witnesses testified during a period of three weeks. After deliberating for eight days, the jury announced it was hopelessly deadlocked, and the trial judge declared a mistrial. * * *

Margiotta's retrial before Judge Sifton proved to be another closely fought contest. Following a trial lasting three weeks, the jury deliberated conscientiously for three days. It returned a verdict of guilty on all six counts, including the one count of mail fraud in violation of 18 U.S.C. § 1341 (1976) and the five counts of extortion in violation of 18 U.S.C. § 1951 (1976). Judge Sifton sentenced Margiotta to concurrent terms of imprisonment of two years on each count.

Margiotta appeals to this Court from the judgment of conviction entered by Judge Sifton. On appeal, he raises a number of claims, several of which involve novel issues. Margiotta argues that his conviction of mail fraud must be reversed and the indictment dismissed on the grounds that the federal mail fraud statute * * * does not embrace a theory of fiduciary fraud by individuals who participate in the political process but who do not occupy public office, and that Margiotta owed no fiduciary duty to the general citizenry of Nassau County and the Town of Hempstead under federal or state law. Moreover, he asserts that the evidence was insufficient to support a finding of fiduciary duty even if it were held that the trial court's instructions were not erroneous as a matter of law. In addition, Margiotta claims that the indictment and conviction violate his First Amendment rights of freedom of expression, association and petition, and that the mail fraud statute is impermissibly vague on its face and as applied to him on the facts of this case. Furthermore, he asserts that he did not fail to disclose material information in violation of the mail fraud statute. * * * For the reasons stated below, we reject Margiotta's contentions, and affirm the judgment of conviction in all respects.

I. Background

Since the conduct at issue in this case involves an intricate scheme of fraud, we must set forth the facts in detail. As noted above, Joseph M. Margiotta, was at all relevant times the Chairman of the Republican Committee of both Nassau County and the Town of Hempstead, New York. Although he held no elective office, his positions as County and Town Republican Chairman, according to the Government, afforded him sufficient power and prestige to exert substantial control over public officials in Hempstead and Nassau County who had been elected to office as candidates of the Republican Party. This control, it was charged, enabled Margiotta to exercise influence over the appointees of these elected officials as well. The spread of his political tentacles over the governments of Town and County allegedly offered Margiotta the opportunity to engage in a highly remunerative fraudulent design involving the distribution of insurance commissions on municipal properties to his political associates.

The responsibility of the Nassau County Executive and the Presiding Supervisor of the Town of Hempstead in maintaining the properties owned and operated by their respective jurisdictions was at the crux of this artifice. The holders of these public offices were responsible for obtaining insurance coverage for the properties owned by the Town and County. As a matter of practice, the authority for obtaining insurance on municipal properties was delegated to a Broker of Record designated by the entities and serving at their pleasure. The Broker of Record was the only individual who acted on behalf of these jurisdictions in placing insurance policies. The Broker received as compensation for his services commissions consisting of a portion of the monies paid by the municipalities for the insurance policies.[10]

According to the Government, this municipal insurance activity was transformed into a scheme to defraud the citizens of Hempstead and Nassau County in 1968. At that time, Margiotta allegedly contrived the appointment of Richard B. Williams & Sons, Inc., an insurance agency, (hereinafter the "Williams Agency" or "Agency"), as Broker of Record for the Town of Hempstead. Richard B. Williams determined to have the Agency designated as Broker of Record for the Town, a position then held by one Mortimer Weis. Williams allegedly met with Margiotta and Weis to strike a secret "deal": The Williams Agency would be named Broker of Record for the Town of Hempstead, and Weis would become a $10,000 a year consultant to the Town. In return for the appointment, the Williams Agency would set aside 50% of the insurance commissions and other compensation it received, to be distributed to licensed insurance brokers and others designated by Margiotta. Shortly thereafter, Ralph Caso, the Presiding Supervisor of Hempstead, appointed the Williams Agency as Hempstead's Broker of Record based on Margiotta's recommendation. In 1969, the Williams Agency began to write insurance for the Town of Hempstead, and commenced making "kickbacks" to brokers selected by political leaders of local election districts in the Town who were loyal to the appellant.

In 1970 Caso was elected County Executive of Nassau County. After his election, Richard B. Williams met with Margiotta to discuss the possibility of the Williams Agency acting as Broker of Record for Nassau County. On January 1, 1971, the day on which he took office, Ralph Caso designated the Williams Agency as Broker of Record for Nassau County based on Margiotta's recommendation. Soon thereafter, the Williams Agency commenced to distribute 50% of the commissions it earned on Nassau County properties to brokers and others politically allied with Margiotta. Between 1969 and 1978, according to the Government, the compensation paid the Broker of Record in connection with this arrangement totalled in excess of two million, two hundred thousand dollars. Among the recipients of more than five hundred thousand

---

[10] Moreover, it appears that Nassau County also occasionally compensated the Broker of Record through personal services contracts not subject to competitive bidding.

dollars in kickbacks were numerous insurance brokers who performed no legitimate work, lawyers and other friends of Margiotta who rendered no services in return for their compensation, and the appellant himself. The concealment of this fraudulent scheme, according to the Government, was fostered through the preparation of fictitious property inspection reports. As a result, it was made to appear that the recipients of the insurance commission kickbacks were legitimately earning their commissions. Moreover, the Government has charged, the insurance activities were disguised by Margiotta through false and misleading testimony during the course of an investigation by the New York State Investigation Commission.

In November, 1980, a federal grand jury indicted Margiotta on one count of mail fraud, in violation of 18 U.S.C. § 1341 (1976), and five counts of extortion, in violation of 18 U.S.C. § 1951 (1976). The mail fraud count (Count One) was based on a scheme to defraud the Town of Hempstead, Nassau County, New York State, and their citizens (1) of the right to have the affairs of the Town, County and State conducted honestly, free from corruption, fraud and dishonesty, and (2) of the right to Margiotta's honest and faithful participation in the governmental affairs of the Town, County and State. * * *

* * * Trial commenced on March 27, 1981. While the Government presented evidence to prove that Margiotta's involvement in the insurance activities was a scheme to defraud, Margiotta offered a defense of good faith. He attempted to prove that he had no secret agreement with the Williams Agency for the distribution of insurance commissions as a quid pro quo for securing the appointment of the Agency as Broker of Record. Admitting that he recommended the Agency to be Broker of Record for both the Town and the County and that he directed the distribution of insurance commissions, he argued that this behavior was merely a longstanding political patronage arrangement practiced for decades by Republicans and Democrats alike. As noted above, after deliberating carefully for more than a week, the jury announced that it could not agree on a verdict, and a mistrial was declared.

This court's second review of the Margiotta case followed Judge Sifton's declaration of the mistrial. In anticipation of another hotly contested battle at the retrial, the Government sought reconsideration of a number of legal and evidentiary rulings Judge Sifton had made at the first trial. The Government challenged Judge Sifton's instruction to the jury that for the Government to show Margiotta had defrauded the citizens of Nassau County and the Town of Hempstead of the right to have the affairs of those entities conducted honestly, free from corruption, fraud and dishonesty, in violation of the mail fraud statute as charged in Count One, the jury had to find that Margiotta owed some kind of special fiduciary duty to the citizenry. The Government also sought reconsideration of the district court's related instruction that a violation of mail fraud under Count One required an additional showing of willful concealment. * * *

At the second trial, the Government again sought to prove that Margiotta's participation in the insurance activities amounted to an elaborate scheme of fraud in violation of the federal mail fraud and extortion statutes rather than a mere political patronage system. The Government presented evidence to show that Margiotta had deeply insinuated himself into the affairs of government in the Town of Hempstead and Nassau County, to the point that he was in effect undertaking the business of government and not simply the activities of the Republican Party. This evidence was provided by testimony of Ralph Caso, who was the Presiding Supervisor of the Town of Hempstead until 1971 and Nassau County Executive until 1977. Caso stated that prior to his "break" with Margiotta in 1976, he was "controlled" by Margiotta in "the basic responsibilities that (he) was to carry out," including appointments to offices and positions such as the Broker of Record.

While Caso's successor, Francis Purcell, who still holds the office of Nassau County Executive, did not describe the same relationship of dominance over the affairs of government in Town and County, the testimony of Margiotta himself and those who carried out his directives established that the appellant exercised a vise-like grip over the basic governmental functions in Hempstead and Nassau County. * * *

Through his control over the appointment process and other aspects of municipal government, Margiotta had thus generated a "slush fund," the proceeds of which could be distributed to purchase party loyalty, to assist friends, or, for purposes he designated, in his words, "whenever the spirit moved (him)." * * *

* * * We turn now to the merits of Margiotta's claims.

II. Mail Fraud

Margiotta asserts that his conviction of mail fraud (Count One) must be reversed and the indictment dismissed on the grounds that the federal mail fraud statute does not embrace a theory of fiduciary fraud by private participants in the political process, and that Margiotta owed no fiduciary duty to the general citizenry of Nassau County or the Town of Hempstead upon which a mail fraud offense could be based. * * * Margiotta argues that an alleged deprivation of an "intangible right" to a defendant's honest and faithful services forms a predicate for a federal mail fraud violation only where the defendant shares a fiduciary relationship with the putative victim. Asserting that a fiduciary duty to the general citizenry requiring honest and faithful participation in governmental affairs has been recognized only in cases involving defendants who are public officials, Margiotta concludes that the novel application of the mail fraud statute on an "intangible rights" theory to a non-office holder such as Margiotta represents an untenable and improper extension of the mail fraud statute beyond its permissible bounds.

In construing the elements of the mail fraud statute in this case of first impression, we tread most cautiously. As we have noted in another context, § 1341 is seemingly limitless on its face. We are not unaware of the time-honored tenet of statutory construction that ambiguous laws which impose penal sanctions are to be strictly construed against the Government. Concomitantly, it is indisputable that there are situations in which the legislature has intended to define broadly the scope of criminal liability. Our task today is complicated because the broad provisions of the mail fraud statute have been applied in a context implicating two conflicting sets of values, both of which merit stringent protections. On the one hand, the prosecution under § 1341 of those who simply participate in the affairs of government in an insubstantial way, or exercise influence in the policymaking process, poses the danger of sweeping within the ambit of the mail fraud statute conduct, such as lobbying and party association, which has been deemed central to the functioning of our democratic system since at least the days of Andrew Jackson. On the other hand, an unduly restrictive reading of § 1341, leading to the formulation of a rule that precludes, as a matter of law, a finding that a person who does not hold public office owes a fiduciary duty to the citizenry, regardless of that individual's de facto control of the processes of government, eliminates a potential safeguard of the public's interest in honest and efficient government. While we conclude that there are limitations on the application of the mail fraud statute to violations of the intangible right to "good government," we believe that the statute reaches the conduct evidenced by the appellant in this case.

A. The applicability of the mail fraud statute.

Margiotta argues that the mail fraud statute cannot, as a matter of law, embrace a theory of fiduciary fraud by private participants in the political process. * * * We reject Margiotta's claim. In the private sector, it is now a commonplace that a breach of fiduciary duty in violation of the mail fraud statute may be based on artifices which do not deprive any person of money or other forms of tangible property. * * * A close reading of the statute supports this result. Section 1341 prohibits "any scheme or artifice to defraud, or for obtaining money or property by means of false or fraudulent pretenses, representations or promises." Accordingly, the prohibition against schemes or artifices to defraud is properly interpreted to be independent of the clause "for obtaining money or property." * * *

In the public sector, as the appellant correctly points out, the mail fraud statute has been employed in prosecutions of public officials who have allegedly deprived the citizenry of such intangible rights as the right to good government, or the right to the honest and loyal services of its governmental officers. A number of courts have approved the prosecution of allegedly corrupt politicians who did not deprive the citizens of anything of readily identifiable economic value. From these cases, a basic principle may be distilled: a public official may be prosecuted under 18 U.S.C. § 1341 when his alleged scheme to defraud has as its sole object the deprivation of intangible and abstract political and civil rights of the general citizenry. The definition of fraud is thus construed broadly to effectuate the statute's fundamental purpose in prohibiting the misuse of the mails to further fraudulent enterprises of all kinds.

The instant case raises the novel issue whether an individual who occupies no official public office but nonetheless participates substantially in the operation of government owes a fiduciary duty to the general citizenry not to deprive it of certain intangible political rights that may lay the basis for a mail fraud prosecution. In the private sector cases, a formal employer- employee relationship is not a prerequisite to a finding that a fiduciary duty is owed. Similarly, we do not believe that a formal employment relationship, that is, public office, should be a rigid prerequisite to a finding of fiduciary duty in the public sector.

The drawing of standards in this area is a most difficult enterprise. On the one hand, it is essential to avoid the Scylla of a rule which permits a finding of fiduciary duty on the basis of mere influence or minimum participation in the processes of government. Such a rule would threaten to criminalize a wide range of conduct, from lobbying to political party activities, as to which the public has no right to disinterested service. On the other hand, the harm to the public arising from the sale of public office and other fraudulent schemes leads us to steer a course away from the Charybdis of a rule which bars on all occasions, as a matter of law, a holding that one who does not hold public office owes a fiduciary duty to the general citizenry even if he in fact is conducting the business of government.

Although there is no precise litmus paper test, two time-tested measures of fiduciary status are helpful: (1) a reliance test, under which one may be a fiduciary when others rely upon him because of a special relationship in the government, and (2) a de facto control test, under which a person who in fact makes governmental decisions may be held to be a governmental fiduciary. These tests recognize the important distinction between party business and government affairs, permitting a party official to act in accordance with partisan preferences or even whim, up to the point at which he dominates government. Accordingly, the reliance and de facto control tests carve out a safe harbor for the party leader who merely exercises a veto power over decisions affecting his constituency.

In light of these guidelines, the prosecution of Margiotta under the mail fraud statute was permissible, notwithstanding the fact that the appellant held no official public office. It cannot be gainsaid that Margiotta had a stranglehold on the respective governments of Nassau County and the Town of Hempstead. According to Donald Woolnough, one of Margiotta's principal assistants, "everything went through his hands." The evidence established not only that he was responsible for the administration of the municipal insurance activities, but also that he acted as a virtual Department of Personnel, with substantial power over decisions concerning hiring, promotions and salary increases. Others relied upon him for the rendering of important governmental decisions, and he dominated governmental affairs as the de facto public leader. As a result, the federal mail fraud statute properly supported a prosecution for Margiotta's breach of at least a minimum duty not to sell his substantial influence and control over governmental processes.

Moreover, Judge Sifton's charge to the jury was consistent with the limitations we have delineated on the application of the mail fraud statute to participants in the political process who hold no public office. Judge Sifton did not simply instruct that the jury could find that Margiotta owed a fiduciary duty if he participated or had influence in Nassau County and the Town of Hempstead. Instead, the trial court charged that the jury should determine whether Margiotta's work "was in substantial part the business of Government, rather than being solely party business and that his performance of that work was intended by him and relied on by others in Government as part of the business of Government ...." This charge was harmonious with the guidelines we have articulated today, and ensured that the jury's consideration of the mail fraud count was properly channelled.

Margiotta's argument that the legislative history does not support the application of the mail fraud statute to private participants in the political process, regardless of the extent to which they dominate the affairs of government, is unavailing. While the mail fraud statute, originally enacted as § 301 of the Act of June 8, 1872, ch. 335, 17 Stat. 283, 323, resulted from a recommendation of a committee of postal officials for legislation "to prevent the frauds which are perpetrated by lottery swindlers through the mails," § 1341 has never been limited to this narrow purpose. Yet no legislative history exists to suggest that Congress has intended the mail fraud statute to deal only with schemes to defraud involving money or property, let alone to be subject to a hard-and-fast distinction between public officeholders and dominant non-public officeholders in cases involving intangible political rights. Accordingly, our construction of § 1341 furthers the basic purpose of the statute in proscribing the use of the mails to promote fraudulent enterprises.

Furthermore, Margiotta's prosecution does not exceed the permissible bounds of the statutory language. More than five decades ago, the Supreme Court stated that the phrase "scheme to defraud" extends to "a great variety of transactions." In his brief, appellant has conceded that a deprivation of an intangible right to a defendant's honest and faithful services properly forms the basis for a mail fraud violation where the defendant owes a fiduciary duty to the alleged victim. As a result, while the question remains whether Margiotta owed a fiduciary duty to the general citizenry of the Town of Hempstead and Nassau County, there is no merit to Margiotta's claim that the language of the federal mail fraud statute cannot embrace a theory of fiduciary fraud by one, like the appellant, who has de facto control over the processes of government and is relied upon by others in the rendering of essential governmental decisions.

B. Fiduciary Duty.

* * *

Judge Sifton, in his charge to the jury on the nature of the participation the jury had to find in deciding whether Margiotta had a special duty to disclose the corrupt agreement, adopted a standard consistent with two measures of fiduciary duty recognized under New York law. As noted above, the district court instructed the jury that it must determine whether the work done by Margiotta was "in substantial part the business of government, rather than being solely party business and that his performance of that work was intended by him and relied on by others in Government as part of the business of Government." This instruction reflects the concepts of reliance, and de facto control and dominance, which are at the heart of the fiduciary relationship. Accordingly, the jury could properly find that Margiotta owed a special duty to the electorate under New York law. * * *

D. Alleged First and Fourteenth Amendment limitations on the mail fraud conviction.

Margiotta argues that the trial court's fiduciary doctrine impairs important rights of free expression and association, as well as the right to petition government to effect political or social change. He asserts that Judge Sifton's instructions apply to all persons influencing government. As a result, Margiotta argues, the trial court's construction of § 1341 brings within the statute's ambit "the entire spectrum of political participation" in governmental affairs, and thus criminalizes a substantial amount of constitutionally protected conduct. Such overbroad regulation, Margiotta continues, carries the potential of significant chill arising from the likelihood of criminal prosecution.

Furthermore, according to the appellant, requiring a political party or its chairman to act as a "disinterested fiduciary" for the general citizenry abridges the cherished right of freedom of political association. Moreover, Margiotta alleges, the imposition of criminal liability pursuant to the district court's fiduciary doctrine eviscerates the right of petition by interfering with the efforts of political party leaders freely to lobby government officials on behalf of their supporters.

If the indictment and prosecution of Margiotta for mail fraud on the basis of his breach of a fiduciary duty to the citizenry meaningfully implicated First Amendment interests, we would be loathe to approve such an application of the mail fraud statute. One of the essential purposes of the First Amendment is to protect the unfettered discussion of governmental affairs, and the activities of lobbyists and others who seek to exercise influence in the political process are basic in our democratic system. The First Amendment concerns raised by Margiotta, however, are a chimera. Count One of the indictment and the pertinent jury instructions do not address mere participation in the political process or protected conduct such as lobbying or party association. Rather than resting on a generalized breach of duty to render disinterested services on the part of one who participates in the political process in some unspecified way, the indictment and prosecution focused on whether Margiotta's corrupt agreement breached a fiduciary duty which Margiotta owed as a result of his significant role in the governance of Hempstead and Nassau County. * * *

En passant, in response to Margiotta's contention that other political leaders are in jeopardy of prosecution, we believe his argument overlooks our narrow construction of the mail fraud statute. The necessity of meeting our restricted tests for the existence of a duty as a government fiduciary on the part of those who technically hold no public office precludes the use of § 1341 for dragnet prosecutions of party officials.

We need only briefly consider Margiotta's argument that the mail fraud statute is impermissibly vague both on its face and as applied to the facts of this case. Section 1341 has withstood repeated challenges which have raised the claim that it does not provide fair notice and warning of the conduct proscribed by the statute. The broad language of the statute, intended by Congress to be sufficiently flexible to cover the wide range of fraudulent schemes mankind is capable of devising, is not unconstitutionally vague because § 1341 contains the requirement that the defendant must have acted willfully and with a specific intent to defraud. Judge Sifton appropriately charged the jury on this element of the offense. Moreover, Margiotta knew that the conduct reached was likely to be contrary to law, since he conceded at trial that a corrupt agreement pursuant to which he recommended the Williams Agency on the condition that the Agency kick back fifty percent of its commissions could be illegal. In light of the inclusion of payments to non-brokers in the scheme, the application of the mail fraud statute to his artifice should have come as no surprise. As a result, although he may not have anticipated the precise legal theory according to which the insurance ruse was deemed fraudulent, Margiotta was given fair warning that his activities could cause him to run afoul of the federal mail fraud statute. * * *

Since all of Margiotta's claims concerning the mail fraud count are without merit, we affirm the judgment of conviction of mail fraud in violation of 18 U.S.C. § 1341. * * *

RALPH K. WINTER, Circuit Judge (concurring in part and dissenting in part):

While I do not agree in every particular with the majority's analysis of the conviction rendered under the Hobbs Act, I concur in the result. Margiotta was not the instrument of a party organization executing well understood patronage practices but instead exercised personal discretion in each case as to the recipients of kickbacks, including payments to himself. This, I believe, is sufficient to characterize the entire kickback scheme as extortionate.

I dissent, however, as to the mail fraud count. The majority's use of mail fraud as a catch-all prohibition of political disingenuousness expands that legislation beyond any colorable claim of Congressional intent and creates a real danger of prosecutorial abuse for partisan political purposes.

I

It should be emphasized at the outset that, while a kickback scheme is relevant to Margiotta's conviction for mail fraud, it is not essential. Nor is the government required to prove any loss whatsoever to taxpayers or a violation of New York law. Reduced to essentials, the majority holds that a mail fraud conviction will be upheld when a politically active person is found by a jury to have assumed a duty to disclose material facts to the general citizenry and deliberately failed to do so. Margiotta's conviction is based upon his failure as a partisan political leader with great influence to disclose to the citizens of the Town of Hempstead and Nassau County his knowledge that the Williams Agency would have been willing to act as Broker of Record for considerably smaller commissions than were actually paid. Because those citizens might have compelled the municipalities to reduce these costs had they been given this information, it is a material fact. * * *

The majority pays lip service to construing the criminal law against the government but then gives the mail fraud statute a more sweeping interpretation than any court which has addressed the statute to date. Given that this statute has occasioned a number of courts to comment apprehensively in the past about its steady expansion, that is no mean feat. * * *

* * * [N]o amount of rhetoric seeking to limit the holding to the facts of this case can conceal that there is no end to the common political practices which may now be swept within the ambit of mail fraud. Since the doctrine adopted by the majority applies to candidates as well as those holding office, a candidate who mails a brochure containing a promise which the candidate knows cannot be carried out is surely committing an even more direct mail fraud than what Margiotta did here. An elected official who for political purposes performs an act imposing unnecessary costs on taxpayers is guilty of mail fraud if disclosure is not made to the public. A partisan political leader who throws decisive support behind a candidate known to the leader to be less qualified than his or her opponent because that candidate is more cooperative with the party organization, is guilty of mail fraud unless that motive is disclosed to the public. A partisan political leader who causes elected officials to fail to modernize government to retain jobs for the party faithful is guilty of mail fraud unless that fact is disclosed. In each of these cases the undisclosed fact is as "material" as the facts which Margiotta failed to disclose, the harm to the public is at least as substantial as the harm resulting from Margiotta's scheme, and the dishonesty, partiality, bias and deceit in failing to disclose those facts is equally present. This is not to say that Margiotta's conduct as a whole is not more odious than the conduct described in these hypotheticals. That is not the issue. The point is that the actions taken by Margiotta deemed relevant to mail fraud by the majority are present in each case: a relationship calling for disclosure, a material fact known to the candidate, official or party leader, and a failure to disclose it.

The majority is quite simply wrong in brushing aside the First Amendment issues. The theory they adopt subjects politically active persons to criminal sanctions based solely upon what they say or do not say in their discussions of public affairs. The majority explicitly bottoms Margiotta's mail fraud conviction on his failure to say something. Its logic would easily extend to the content of campaign literature. Indeed, it takes no great foresight to envision an indictment framed on the theory adopted by the majority and alleging mail fraud based on public speeches.

II

My brethren are not striking out on their own in pushing the mail fraud statute to limits far exceeding any Congressional intent. To the contrary, much of what they say has substantial and direct precedent. For example, the statutory proscriptions are not limited to common law fraud or deceit but extend to dishonest schemes generally. It also seems well established that dishonest actions by an employee which violate the employee's fiduciary obligations to an employer can be a basis for a mail fraud conviction. Moreover, loss or concrete harm need not be shown beyond the fact that the employer was deprived of information which might have affected his or her judgment.

One can, with seeming logic, move from those propositions to the proposition that a person holding governmental employment is bound by the same standards. From that it seems a small leap to apply these principles to those who hold elective as well as appointed office. We then arrive at a rule that elected officials have a duty to disclose material facts concerning their conduct of public affairs. Any official who fails to disclose such facts is guilty of mail fraud without regard to whether actual loss occurred or to whether local law was violated.

Much of what the majority says thus has direct precedential support. They add only one seemingly small element to these precedents: a jury may find that a politically active person has sufficient influence and power over the acts of elective officials to be subjected to the same duty as those officials so far as those acts are concerned. The failure of such a person to disclose material information to the public can thus constitute mail fraud.

However logical this growth of the law may seem, it leads to a result which is not only greater than, but is roughly the square of, the sum of the parts. The proposition that any person active in political affairs who fails to disclose a fact material to that participation to the public is guilty of mail fraud finds not the slightest basis in Congressional intent, statutory language or common canons of statutory interpretation. This wholly impermissible result is brought about, I believe, by drawing an erroneous analogy between fiduciary relationships involving private parties based on express or implied contract and relationships between politically active persons and the general citizenry in a pluralistic, partisan, political system.

Mr. Justice Frankfurter quite appropriately underlined the fact that "to say that a man is a fiduciary only begins an analysis; it gives direction to further inquiry. To whom is he a fiduciary? What obligations does he owe as a fiduciary? In what respect has he failed to discharge these obligations? And what are the consequences of his deviation from duty?" The words fiduciary duty are no more than a legal conclusion and the legal obligations actually imposed under that label vary greatly from relationship to relationship. Nevertheless, because fiduciary relationships in the private sector have been the subject of centuries of common law development, there is a considerable body of law based on implied or express contract governing whether particular behavior is legal. Its most notable feature, however, is the degree to which fiduciary obligations vary from relationship to relationship. Partners, employees, trustees and corporate directors are all fiduciaries, yet their legal obligations may be wholly dissimilar. While an hourly employee usually may quit a job without fearing legal action even though he leaves at a time which makes it difficult for the employer to continue business, a trustee may not so easily abandon his beneficiaries. While a trustee's actions are void or voidable if tainted by a conflict of interest, the corporate officer generally can act even if he is personally interested so long as the action is fair to the corporation.

To transfer this complex, variable body of law to the political context, simply by mouthing the word fiduciary, makes the very mistake underlined by Mr. Justice Frankfurter in *Chenery*. Although the courts have, with precious little analysis, brought virtually all participants in government and politics under the rubric fiduciary, the obligations imposed are wholly the creation of recent interpretations of the mail fraud statute itself. A reading of the cases in this area, however, shows how little definition there is to these newly created obligations which carry criminal sanctions. For all one can find in the case law, no distinction is made between the fiduciary obligations of a civil servant, political appointee, elected official, candidate or partisan political leader. Juries are simply left free to apply a legal standard which amounts to little more than the rhetoric of sixth grade civics classes. One searches in vain for even the vaguest contours of the legal obligations created beyond the obligation to conduct governmental affairs "honestly" or "impartially," to ensure one's "honest and faithful participation" in government and to obey "accepted standards of moral uprightness, fundamental honesty, fair play and right dealing." The present case is no exception. While there is talk of a line between legitimate patronage and mail fraud, there is no description of its location. With all due respect to the majority, the quest for legal standards is not furthered by reference to "the right to good government" and the duty "to act in a disinterested manner."

Of course, we should all hope that public affairs are conducted honestly and on behalf of the entire citizenry. Nevertheless, we should recognize that a pluralistic political system assumes politically active persons will pursue power and self-interest. Participation in the political process is not limited to the pure of heart. Quite frankly, I shudder at the prospect of partisan political activists being indicted for failing to act "impartially" in influencing governmental acts.[5]

---

[5] Among the truths assumed by the founders was that self-interest would be a major generating force in democratic politics. The concern over "faction" motivated by "passion ... adverse ... to the interests of the community" appears again and again in The Federalist Papers. The founders suffered under no illusion that only "enlightened statesmen" would hold the reins of power. They sought safety in checks and balances and a separation of powers which would prevent the assertion of too much power in a single hand. The majority decision vests federal prosecutors with largely unchecked power to harass political opponents. It may be that we should expect only

Where a statute, particularly a criminal statute, does not regulate specific behavior, enforcement of inchoate obligations should be by political rather than criminal sanctions. Where Congress has not passed legislation specifying particular acts by the politically active as criminal, our reliance rather should be on public debate, a free press and an alert electorate. In a pluralistic system organized on partisan lines, it is dangerous to require persons exercising political influence to make the kind of disclosure required in public offerings by the securities laws.

III

* * *

My concerns in this case thus extend far beyond a disagreement over statutory interpretation. The limitless expansion of the mail fraud statute subjects virtually every active participant in the political process to potential criminal investigation and prosecution. It may be a disagreeable fact but it is nevertheless a fact that political opponents not infrequently exchange charges of "corruption," "bias," "dishonesty," or deviation from "accepted standards of ... fair play and right dealing." Every such accusation is now potentially translatable into a federal indictment. I am not predicting the imminent arrival of the totalitarian night or the wholesale indictment of candidates, public officials and party leaders. To the contrary, what profoundly troubles me is the potential for abuse through selective prosecution and the degree of raw political power the freeswinging club of mail fraud affords federal prosecutors. * * *

In arguing this case, the United States Attorney left no doubt that he prosecuted Margiotta for political corruption generally. The problem is that in stretching the mail fraud statute to fit this case, we create a crime which applies equally to persons who have not done the evil things Margiotta is said to have done, a catch-all political crime which has no use but misuse. After all, the only need served by resort to mail fraud in these cases is when a particular corruption, such as extortion, cannot be shown or Congress has not specifically regulated certain conduct. But that use creates a danger of corruption to the democratic system greater than anything Margiotta is alleged to have done. It not only creates a political crime where Congress has not acted but also lodges unbridled power in federal prosecutors to prosecute political activists. When the first corrupt prosecutor prosecutes a political enemy for mail fraud, the rhetoric of the majority about good government will ring hollow indeed.

"enlightened statesmen" to hold such office, but, with Madison, I would prefer not to take such a risk.

Note

In 1987, the Supreme Court brought the house of cards built in *Margiotta* and other cases crashing to the floor when it held in *McNally v. United States*, 483 U.S. 350, (1987), that the mail fraud statute applies only to schemes to defraud people of money or property; it does not protect, therefore, a citizenry's intangible rights to honest and impartial government. However, the following year, Congress amended the term "scheme or artifice to defraud" in the mail and wire fraud statutes to include schemes "to deprive another of the intangible right of honest services." Pub. L. No. 100-690, 102 Stat. 4508 (1994) (codified at 18 U.S.C. § 1346 (1994)).

How have prosecutors taken advantage of Congress' restoration of the honest services theory? In *United States v. Giffen*, 326 F.Supp.2d 497 (S.D.N.Y. 2004), the district attorney's office of the Southern District of New York indicted James Giffen, an American businessman, for his involvement in Kazakhstan, a former republic of the Soviet Union that became a sovereign nation in 1991. As the court described the facts:

> The indictment alleges that between 1995 and 1999, Giffen made unlawful payments totaling $78 million to senior Kazakh officials, to obtain business for his New York-headquartered company Mercator corporation ("Mercator").

> From the business obtained by Mercator, Giffen [Mercator's principal shareholder, board chairman, and Chief Executive Officer] directed millions of dollars in unreported compensation to a Mobil Oil executive, a Mercator employee and himself. The Indictment alleges a series of complex financial transactions that enabled Mercator to conceal illicit payments to the senior Kazakh officials.

> Kazakhstan, formerly a republic within the Soviet Union, became a sovereign nation in 1991. Kazakhstan has vast oil and gas reserves, which are the property of the Kazakh government. Since its independence, Kazakhstan has sold rights to its oil and gas reserves to international oil companies. The Kazakh government hired Mercator to advise it regarding these oil and gas transactions.

> The indictment alleges that on or about August 1, 1995, Giffen was named a Counselor to the President of Kazakhstan. The Counselor position was a semi-official title that enabled Giffen

> to effect numerous oil and gas transactions. In December 1994, Mercator entered into an agreement with the Kazakh Ministry of Oil and Gas Industries to assist the Ministry in developing a strategy for foreign investment in Kazakhstan's natural resources. The agreement further provided that Mercator would receive substantial success fees if the oil and gas transactions were completed. * * *

Giffen, 326 F.Supp.2d at 499–500.

The United States District Attorney's office indicted Giffen on 62 criminal counts, based on the Foreign Corrupt Practices Act (the "FCPA"), mail and wire fraud, money laundering, and federal income tax violations. Giffen did not try to challenge the mail and wire fraud counts based on the theory that he deprived the citizens of Kazakhstan of money and property. However, he did object to the counts under which he was charged with engaging in a scheme to "deprive the citizens of Kazakhstan of their intangible right to the honest services of their political leaders."

The court noted the reinstatement by statute of the honest services aspect of mail fraud. However, the question was whether any pre-McNally precedent supported prosecution of American citizens for depriving foreign nationals of the honest services of their own government officials. At the preliminary hearing, the prosecution admitted it had no precedent on which to rely. The government did allude, however, to a case called *United States v. Lazarenko*, pending in the Northern District of California. There, the defendant, a former president of the Republic of Ukraine, was charged with depriving Ukrainian citizens of the honest services of their government officials. *United States v. Lazarenko*, No. CR 00-0284(MJJ) at 1-2 (N.D.Cal. Sept. 10, 2003) (order on applicability of foreign law to Lazarenko's prosecution) ("Lazarenko I"). However, in that case the district court dismissed the honest services charge at the close of the evidence, because the government failed to prove that the defendant violated any provision of Ukrainian law analogous to Section 1346. The district attorney in *Giffen*, however, did not possess any Kazakh law on the issue. Further, the court held that the "honest services" amendment was unconstitutionally vague:

> While the pre-McNally cases applying the honest services theory to public sector corruption cases are legion, none of them apply the intangible rights theory to corruption in a foreign nation. Moreover, extension of the intangible rights theory to Giffen and the Kazakh citizenry is more ethereal. The claimed violation is the deprivation of the honest services of Kazakh government officials to the Kazakh citizenry. Deciding

that issue requires an analysis of the compact between Kazakh citizens and their government. In turn, the inquiry would require this Court to determine what constitutes honest services in the Kazakh landscape, untethered to any Kazakh statute analogous to Section 1346. Under such circumstances, this Court concludes that the application of Section 1346 to Giffen is unconstitutionally vague.

326 F. Supp. at 506-07.

In the same year that the Court decided *McNally*, the Court affirmed the application of the mail fraud statute to another kind of intangible property. As Geraldine Moohr explains:

In *United States v. Carpenter*, [484 U.S. 19 (1987)], the Court upheld the mail fraud conviction of a reporter who analyzed stock market trends in a daily Wall Street Journal column. The reporter gave unpublished material to others who profited by trading in the stocks in advance of publication. This conduct did not cause the Journal to lose money or tangible property; therefore, in light of *McNally*, the government argued that the reporter deprived the newspaper of intangible property. The Supreme Court agreed, holding that an interest in confidential information was property for purposes of mail fraud. The Court couched the loss as a property interest in the newspaper's confidential information. Consequently, the decision expanded the range of interests protected by the mail fraud statute to include intangible property such as information. At the same time, the Court reinforced its holding in *McNally* by stating that a right to honest services is "too ethereal" an interest to fall within the protection of the mail fraud statute.

The defendants argued that the crime of fraud requires that a defendant's gain come from the deceived victim. Here, even if the Journal had lost a property right, the defendants had not obtained money or property from the newspaper. The money gained by the defendants came from potential and present shareholders who had, respectively, bought stock at inflated prices or sold it for deflated prices. Thus, the Court was asked to decide whether the statute required that a defendant's gain be equivalent to, or symmetrical with, the victim's loss. In light of *McNally*'s emphasis on harm and its rejection of the loss of intangible honest services, the Court was obliged to insist on symmetry. The Court defined the victim's loss and the defendant's gain as confidential information; the Journal lost exclusive use of its information, and the defendants gained it by making use of the confidential information in their scheme. Thus, the holding in *Carpenter* requires an equivalence or symmetry between the victim's loss and the defendant's gain.

The defendants next argued that their violation of workplace rules was not a deception for purposes of pecuniary, post-*McNally*, fraud. The Court responded, however, that it was "common understanding" that "dishonest methods or schemes," or "trick, deceit, chicane or overreaching," could comprise a deception. The Court reasoned that this broad concept of fraud includes embezzlement, and that the acts of the defendants were tantamount to embezzlement. Thus, the decision also enlarges the underlying conduct that meets the deception required by fraud.

Geraldine Szott Moohr, *Mail Fraud Meets Criminal Theory*, 67 U. Cinn. L. Rev. 1, 12-13 (1998).

The dissent in *Margiotta* outlines public policy problems that could arise from the application of mail fraud to good government cases. What sorts of public policy problems might ensue from the use of mail fraud to punish takings of intangible property? Consider the excerpt that follows.

FEDERAL CRIMINAL FRAUD AND THE DEVELOPMENT OF INTANGIBLE PROPERTY RIGHTS IN INFORMATION
Geraldine Szott Moohr
2000 U. Ill. L. Rev. 683[a]

* * * [A]re copyrights property for purposes of mail and wire fraud? Two district courts that considered the issue reached, not surprisingly, contrary conclusions.

In *United States v. LaMacchia*, the district court found that copyrighted computer software was not property for purposes of wire fraud. Using the Internet, encrypted addresses, and the computer network of the Massachusetts Institute of Technology, LaMacchia devised a system that distributed free

---

[a]Copyright to the *University of Illinois Law Review* is held by The Board of Trustees of the University of Illinois.

software applications and computer games to fellow hackers. Although LaMacchia had not sought or derived any personal benefit, the scheme allegedly cost copyright holders more than one million dollars.

LaMacchia invoked *Dowling* (holding that the National Stolen Property Act did not apply to copyrights) to argue that wire fraud could not be used to enforce copyright infringement. The Government's most persuasive response was that *Carpenter* had squarely held that mail and wire fraud protected intangible property, and the software was intangible property. The court, however, found that copyright was different from the confidential business information in *Carpenter*. More specifically, Congress's enactment of a complex and responsive statutory scheme to protect copyrights was compelling evidence of the distinction.

The court also reasoned that the Supreme Court's concerns in *Dowling* applied equally to mail and wire fraud. Just as in *Dowling*, the Government's position in this case subverted Congress's carefully calibrated scheme to protect creative effort. The court also registered a concern with overcriminalization, noting that the Government's position would make criminals of home computer users who copy even a single computer software program. Even though it found "nothing edifying" about LaMacchia's conduct, the court focused on the kind of property at issue rather than on the type of interference. This choice led it to distinguish between the intangible business information protected by *Carpenter* and the intangible business property of copyrights.

In *United States v. Wang*, the court reached a contrary conclusion, holding that wire fraud applied to copyrighted material. In *Wang*, the defendants participated in a scheme to transmit a copyrighted confidential source code. The defendants argued that their conduct amounted to copyright infringement and that it could not be prosecuted as wire fraud. The court found *Dowling* to be inapposite and invoked *Carpenter* to note that valuable, confidential business information was property protected by the mail fraud statute.

In *LaMacchia*, the court followed the rationale and methodology of *Dowling* to distinguish among different kinds of intangible property. Copyright is unique; the holder "owns only a bundle of intangible rights which can be infringed, but not stolen or converted." The court in *Wang* relied on *Carpenter*, reasoning that intangible business information was protected by wire fraud, and the copyrighted source code was intangible business property; therefore, wire fraud applied. Rather than distinguishing among different kinds of business information, this reasoning accepts the broad proposition that all business information is property. * * *

The property in cases of insider trading fraud is confidential business information, which may, if made public, affect stock prices. When corporate officials or insiders, who are often privy to such information, use the information to profit personally by buying their corporation's stock, they engage in insider trading. Insider trading is a specific form of fraud. Section 10(b) of the Securities Exchange Act of 1934 prohibits the use of any "deceptive device" in connection with the purchase or sale of securities. As authorized, the Securities and Exchange Commission (SEC) adopted Rule 10b-5 to implement the statutory prohibition. Although neither provision mentions insider trading, the courts utilized the provisions to criminalize insider trading on the ground that trading based on nonpublic information was a deceptive device. * * *

* * * O'Hagan was a partner in a law firm whose client intended to make a tender offer for the common stock of Pillsbury. After learning about the intended offer from a fellow partner, O'Hagan bought call options and common stock in Pillsbury. Because O'Hagan owed no fiduciary duty to the sellers of Pillsbury stock, the Eighth Circuit held that this conduct did not comprise classic insider trading.

The Supreme Court disagreed and adopted a theory of misappropriation fraud that prohibits outsiders who possess nonpublic information from trading on that information. This theory met the statutory requirements of securities fraud: (1) a "deceptive device" or contrivance (2) used "in connection with the purchase or sale of securities." Closely following the property and fraud rationales of *Carpenter*, the Court had little difficulty in finding deception. First, confidential business information is property, which a fiduciary may not use for personal benefit. Second, deception through nondisclosure occurs when the actor does not inform the source of the information that he or she plans to use the information to trade in securities. If the actor informs the source about that intention, there is no deception and thus no violation of federal securities laws. O'Hagan violated the securities laws when he used confidential information in trading securities; he breached a duty to disclose his intention to the sources of the information, his law firm and its client. This theory premises liability on the deception of the source of the confidential information. The Court thus eliminated the requirement of classic insider trading that the actor have a fiduciary relationship with the buyers and/or sellers of stock.

The Court held that the misappropriation theory also satisfied the statutory requirement that the deception be "in connection with the purchase or sale of a security." This is a significant leap, given that the deception of the source is not connected to the ultimate trade. But the majority stated that fraud against the source was not consummated until O'Hagan used the information to purchase securities. At that point, O'Hagan deceived his law firm and its client and simultaneously harmed members of the investing public.

The majority in *O'Hagan* adhered closely to *Carpenter*. It approved *Carpenter*'s view that confidential business information, in this case a firm's plan to buy another company, was property. The opinion also endorsed the *Carpenter* view that depriving another of exclusive use of information was a violation of a property right that merited criminal sanctions. The majority again followed *Carpenter*'s lead when it condemned that kind of interference and noted that undisclosed use of employer information is akin to embezzlement. Although the Supreme Court had characterized the rule prohibiting insider trading as a catchall provision, it had insisted that "what it catches must be fraud." The Court in *O'Hagan* complied with this requirement by formulating a new theory of criminal fraud -- misappropriation fraud.

Misappropriation fraud continues the expansion of two elements of fraud--deception and harm. The theory adopts the idea that a fiduciary's failure to disclose material information is a deception. Loss of exclusive use of information, even when there has been no monetary loss, satisfies the harm element. Like honest services fraud, misappropriation fraud divorces the conduct of deception from the consequences, or harm, of that deception. In the case of insider trading, the actor's deception is a failure to disclose to one party an intent to use the information, even though the harm of trading on inside information falls on third-party victims -- the shareholders who sell their shares without complete information.

The outer limits of the theory are, at least for now, unclear. The Court emphasized that the duty to disclose runs to the source of the information. Under the facts of the case, this is not surprising; O'Hagan owed traditional fiduciary duties to both the partners of his law firm and to the client that required him to disclose his intention to trade. It was unnecessary to clarify the respective rights of the client and its agent, the law firm, because the defendant owed fiduciary duties to both entities. Yet the opinion appears to countenance a duty to disclose based on something less than the duties that arise from a confidential or fiduciary relationship. The Court suggested that a duty can arise from having been entrusted with the confidential information or that a duty emanates from the deception itself. Although courts have been generous in finding that a fiduciary duty exists in mail and wire fraud cases, finding a duty in either of the above cases represents a significant change. * * *

* * * [T]hese Supreme Court decisions and some lower court opinions recall the English common law cases that expanded the definition of larceny to protect the property of the emerging merchant class. In a strikingly similar vein, federal courts are adopting new theories of a criminal offense and broadening the concept of property in response to economic and social forces. This time, however, the offense is fraud, and the valuable interests are intangible

information. Now, as then, the result is to criminalize more conduct and to create new property rights. * * *

Decisions that rest on broad theories of fraud develop, and effectively create, new property rights. When courts find that an actor's conduct violates the mail and wire fraud statutes, they unavoidably treat the interest that was taken or interfered with as if it were property. Criminalizing the conduct sweeps whatever the victim lost into the property category. When the court focuses on the type of interference, the object of the fraud assumes the status of a protected property interest. Thus, the Court in O'Hagan effectively gave the source of information, who may in future cases be neither the creator nor the owner of the information, a property right of exclusive use of that information. Moreover, the Court conferred the property right even though one source of the information--the law firm--could not have lawfully used it. Similarly, honest services fraud gives employers a property right in the honest services of employees. It also gives the employer a property right in the information known to the employee--that a supplier would take less money, for example. In sum, the symbiotic relation between intangible property and fraud results in the creation of new forms of fraud and property. * * *

B. Information--The Newest Kind of Property

As the Supreme Court has noted, courts interpreting criminal law routinely depend upon definitions of property that were developed in civil cases. In light of this practice, the failure of courts to make similar distinctions among kinds of information is disquieting. The law does not now uniformly protect intangible rights in information and often offers only limited relief. For example, trade secret law, which is a creature of state law, confers varying levels of protection to trade secrets, and commentators are undecided about whether such information should be subject to civil misappropriation. Another example is factual compilations; the Supreme Court has characterized copyright protection of compilations as "thin" and limited to the selection and arrangement of facts. Specialists in the law of information strongly believe that a different lexicon to describe rights in information is necessary to create a balance appropriate to modern information resources. Similarly, protection of other forms of property--and the standards by which property is defined--are also developing. Finally, there is significant criticism based on the effect of expanding protection for intangible information in the civil context. In other words, whether information is property is an open and "borderline" issue.

Nevertheless, when courts determine that an interest is property in the course of interpreting a criminal statute, they reflexively assume that a full set of absolute property rights then attaches to the interest. Courts often use the term property as if the notion of property has an intrinsic meaning, a habit that masks the self-justifying circularity of the inquiry. This reflexive reaction is inconsistent with modern property law, which teaches that property rights are limited and that those limitations are determined by reference to public policy. Thus, the determination that an interest is property only begins the inquiry. The more important and sensitive task is to decide what specific rights attach to that property interest. When criminal sanctions are involved, the pertinent consideration is whether the specific interest at issue should be protected by penal sanctions. * * * [T]hat determination depends on choices between competing public policies. The following sections discuss two policies that are implicated when courts use criminal law to accord interests the status of property.

1. Efficient Use of Information

In a broad sense, intangible information is a public good, similar to Mary's carrot cake recipe. The recipe is subject to virtually costless unauthorized use, which, in turn, may discourage its original creation because Mary cannot recoup the investment of time and money required to create it. Legal rules are thus necessary to assure the creation of this form of property. The rules, however, must balance two competing goals. The first is to encourage development of knowledge and information; this is accomplished by awarding one or more exclusionary rights--property rights--to the creator. The second goal is to encourage efficient use of that knowledge, usually accomplished by limiting the right to exclude use by others in some way.

The most efficient way to use information is to allow its free use by not giving the creator any exclusionary right to block use by others. In the long run, however, this choice imperils the creation of new work; without such rights, creators have no monetary incentive to produce anything new. At the other extreme, assigning full and lasting monopoly rights to creators would permit them to charge too much for use. This option may also result in a decline in production of new work; expanded ownership rights would impede future creation by diminishing the public domain upon which new creators depend for ideas and models. Thus, providing incentives to creators may paradoxically decrease the quantity of new work. A vibrant public domain ensures and enhances cultural and scientific progress while also avoiding socially wasteful practices, such as "duplicative efforts to reinvent the wheel." Thus, efficient, optimal use rests between the two extremes.

To illustrate the problem of a reduced public domain, consider the plight of a scientist who plans a genetic research project that would investigate the treatment of disease through genetic implantation. Unfortunately for the scientist, the cell lines necessary for the research are the patented property of a university medical center, and the university charges a substantial sum for their use. The scientist cannot afford to pay and must abandon the project or delay it while she develops her own cell lines. A less dramatic, but more immediate example, is the current debate over database protection. Databases are integral to commercial and educational activities on the Internet, and their creators are pressing for a federal law to ensure that their compilations are not appropriated by others. On the other hand, scientists and librarians have expressed fears that the proposals could hamper scientific research and hurt competition in the commercial database industry.

Despite the significance of efficient use, evidence suggests that courts and legislators--in an effort to encourage production of public goods--overlook the need to encourage such use of knowledge and information. This trend tilts the balance toward creators and away from users. Criminal fraud actions, such as those surveyed here, indicate that criminal law is part of this trend to protect property rights in information. At first appraisal, the trend does not seem inappropriate; criminal laws are consistent with other legal rules that ensure the creator can recoup investment and earn profit. The interest in stimulating creative development thus argues for protecting information against unauthorized use through criminal law. Nevertheless, the profound impact of criminal sanctions on efficient use argues against the use of criminal sanctions. Criminal law is simply too blunt an instrument to achieve the required balance between creation and use * * *. Its use may shrink the public domain, both directly by extending property rights to new interests, such as those in information, and indirectly by deterring potential use.

2. Employee Mobility

A second public policy affected by expanded property interests in information, although not as global in its implications, has significant impact on employees. That policy is to foster competition and economic growth by balancing the interests of firms in protecting business information and the interests of employees in securing employment that fully rewards their skill and knowledge. An appropriate balance enables both employers and employees to pursue their separate goals, despite the natural tension that exists between their interests. Firms want to keep information regarding business practices from their competitors, while employees want freedom to change jobs or to open their own businesses. Such moves require that employees be free to utilize general skills and knowledge developed in their previous jobs. Treating all business information as if it were property limits employee mobility.

Protecting more information by according it the status of property increases the number of employees subject to an obligation to keep information confidential. Employees who unavoidably use information acquired in former employment risk a charge of fraud. The suggestion that such prosecutions are rare, although seemingly reasonable, is not an adequate response. An overbroad and vague concept of property rights in information chills employee mobility because employees and new employers may prefer not to risk criminal charges. The indiscriminate award of property rights in information thus alters the bargaining positions of employees and employers and ultimately reduces employee autonomy.

Using criminal law to protect the confidential business information of employers may even be perverse because civil courts are reluctant to enforce contracts that restrain postemployment options of employees. To subject employees to penalties when they use information learned in previous employment is inefficient in that it prevents employees from working for the firm that values them most highly. The result is incompatible with a policy that favors competition and with judicial reluctance to enforce covenants not to compete.

C. General Concerns Relating to Creating Property Through Criminal Law

Criminal law is thought to be more effective than civil law in deterring harmful conduct, and it is, therefore, tempting to use criminal law to protect valuable information. Nevertheless, criminal law is not an appropriate context in which to create property rights. First, the blunt criminal verdict may produce the unintended consequence of overdeterrence. Individuals may then be unwilling to embark upon socially beneficial activities, such as engaging in genetic research or exchanging facts from databases, because those activities risk involvement with the criminal justice system. In addition to reducing the public domain, the social costs include diminished competition when firms are afraid to collect data about their competitors or when employees are reluctant to search for optimal employment.

A second general concern stems from the intangible nature of information. In contrast to tangible property, the absence of concrete, physical boundaries creates inherent uncertainty over the boundaries of property rights in information. To prevent unwitting infringement by innocent users, property rights in information should have precise legal boundaries and articulated, specific rights. The simple determination that conduct does or does not violate a criminal statute fails to delineate such boundaries.

A criminal trial is not an appropriate or adequate forum in which to decide issues that implicate significant societal goals. Most basically, the issue of whether public policy justifies the creation of a property right is not before the court. Even if a court were inclined to consider the issue sua sponte, it has not been briefed, and there are no advocates to argue that a verdict will negatively affect social policies, such as ensuring a vibrant public domain.

Although civil trials are not immune to these problems, the narrow, well-defined issues before a criminal court leave less opportunity to consider the effects of the verdict on public policy. Moreover, despite the inadequacy of the criminal forum, determinations regarding property are likely to influence the public debate. The criminal determinations may be viewed as evidence of the need to offer increased protection to intangible interests in information.

The policy choices regarding information as property and its effect on employee mobility are abstract, and their effect on public policy is significant. The choices are ultimately political in nature, inevitably privileging one group over another. They are also not susceptible to easy resolution. These considerations argue for legislative rather than judicial action, and Congress has passed new statutes designed to address the protection of information. Thus, given the public policies at issue and the inadequacy of the criminal forum, courts should reevaluate the judicial tendency to develop property rights in information.

2.   Computer Crimes

New technologies create the possibility of new kinds of crime, and the development of the computer and the World Wide Web have enhanced criminal capacities in several different ways. Law enforcement officials have tackled computer crimes both by applying existing statutes and by creating new crimes. *State v. Schwartz* provides an illustration of both tactics. From this perspective, computer crime can be seen as the latest manifestation of the process visible in the English common law theft cases: the evolution of criminal law to meet cultural needs. However, computer crime also poses unique challenges. The excerpt by Orin Kerr provides an overview of "cyber-crime" and some suggestions about how to combat it.

STATE v. SCHWARTZ
Court of Appeals of Oregon
173 Or.App. 301, 21 P.3d 1128 (Ct. App. 2001)

DEITS, C.J.

Defendant appeals from a judgment of conviction of three counts of computer crime. We reverse the order of restitution, but otherwise we affirm.

Because a jury found defendant guilty, we set out the facts in the light most favorable to the state. Defendant worked as an independent contractor for Intel Corporation beginning in the late 1980s. Defendant's tasks included programming, system maintenance, installing new systems and software, and resolving problems for computer users. In late 1991 or early 1992, defendant began working in Intel's Supercomputer Systems Division (SSD). SSD creates large computer systems that can cost millions of dollars and are used for applications such as nuclear weapons safety. Intel considers the information stored on its SSD computers to be secret and valuable. Each person using SSD computers must use a unique password in order to gain access to electronic information stored there. Passwords are stored in computer files in an encrypted or coded fashion.

In the spring of 1992, defendant and Poelitz, an Intel systems administrator, had a disagreement about how defendant had handled a problem with SSD's e-mail system. The problem was ultimately resolved in an alternative manner suggested by Poelitz, which upset defendant and made him believe that any future decisions he made would be overridden. Accordingly, defendant decided to terminate his SSD contract with Intel. As defendant himself put it, he "hadn't left SSD on the best of terms." At that time, his personal passwords onto all but one SSD computer were disabled so that defendant would no longer have access to SSD computers. His password onto one SSD computer, Brillig, was inadvertently not disabled.

After defendant stopped working with SSD, he continued to work as an independent contractor with a different division of Intel. In March 1993, Brandewie, an Intel network programmer and systems administrator, noticed that defendant was running a "gate" program on an Intel computer called Mink, which allowed access to Mink from computers outside of Intel. "Gate" programs like the one defendant was running violate Intel security policy, because they breach the "firewall" that Intel has established to prevent access to Intel computers by anyone outside the company. Defendant was using the gate program to use his e-mail account with his publisher and to get access to his Intel e-mail when he was on the road. When Brandewie talked to defendant about his gate program, defendant acknowledged that he knew that allowing external access to Intel computers violated company policy. Even though defendant believed that precautions he had taken made his gate program secure, he agreed to alter his program.

In July 1993, Brandewie noticed that defendant was running another gate program on Mink. This program was similar to the earlier gate program and had the same effect of allowing external access to Intel computers. Defendant protested that changes he had made to the program made it secure, but Brandewie insisted that the program violated company policy. At that point, defendant decided that Mink was useless to him without a gate program, so he asked that his account on that computer be closed. Defendant then moved his gate program onto an Intel computer called Hermeis. Because that computer was too slow for him, defendant finally moved his gate program onto the SSD computer Brillig.

In the fall of 1993, defendant downloaded from the Internet a program called "Crack," which is a sophisticated password guessing program. Defendant began to run the Crack program on password files on various Intel computers. When defendant ran the Crack program on Brillig, he learned the password for "Ron B.," one of Brillig's authorized users. Although he knew he did not have the authority to do so, defendant then used Ron B.'s password to log onto Brillig. From Brillig, he copied the entire SSD password file onto another Intel computer, Wyeth. Once the SSD password file was on Wyeth, defendant ran the Crack program on that file and learned the passwords of more than 35 SSD users, including that of the general manager of SSD. Apparently, defendant believed that, if he could show that SSD's security had gone downhill since he had left, he could reestablish the respect he had lost when he left SSD. Once he had cracked the SSD passwords, however, defendant realized that, although he had obtained information that would be useful to SSD, he had done so surreptitiously and had "stepped out of my bounds." Instead of reporting what he had found to anyone at SSD, defendant did nothing and simply stored the information while he went to teach a class in California.

After he returned from California, defendant decided to run the Crack program again on the SSD password file, this time using a new, faster computer called "Snoopy." Defendant thought that, by running the Crack program on the SSD password file using Snoopy, he would have "the most interesting figures" to report to SSD security personnel. On October 28, 1993, Mark Morrissey, an Intel systems administrator, noticed that defendant was running the Crack program on Snoopy. At that point, Morrissey contacted Richard Cower, an Intel network security specialist, for advice about how to proceed. In investigating defendant's actions, Morrissey realized that defendant had been running a gate program on the SSD computer Brillig, even though defendant's access should have been canceled. On October 29, 1993, Cower, Morrissey, and others at Intel decided to contact police.

Defendant was charged with three counts of computer crime, and was convicted of all three counts by a jury. * * *

Defendant's second and third assignments of error pertain to his demurrer. Defendant demurred to count one of the indictment, arguing, among other things, that the statute under which he was charged was unconstitutionally vague and that the indictment was not definite and certain. In count one, defendant was charged with violating ORS 164.377(3), which provides: "Any person who knowingly and without authorization alters, damages or destroys any computer, computer system, computer network, or any computer software, program, documentation or data contained in such computer, computer system or computer network, commits computer crime." * * *

A criminal statute is unconstitutionally vague when it "is stated in terms from which those to whom it is addressed -- potential defendants, prosecutors, courts, and jurors -- cannot discern what conduct the lawmaker did or did not mean to include in the prohibition." The prohibition against vague criminal statutes serves the dual purposes of "provid [ing] notice, with a reasonable degree of certainty, of the conduct that is prohibited" and "prevent[ing] a judge, jury, or other law enforcer from exercising uncontrolled discretion in punishing defendants." If potential defendants and others can be reasonably certain about what conduct is prohibited, the statute at issue is not vague; absolute certainty is not required.

Defendant contends that the term "alter" in ORS 164.377(3) is unconstitutionally vague. He argues that "alter" is vague because its meaning overlaps with that of the word "access," which the legislature used in ORS 164.377(2). He also argues that, by making "alteration" of a computer a crime, the legislature has criminalized "socially tolerable" conduct as well as "socially intolerable" conduct. Defendant further argues that ORS 164.377(3) is vague because it does not require proof of harm. The state responds that ORS 164.377(3) provides reasonable certainty about what conduct is prohibited; that it was clear that defendant's conduct in particular was prohibited, necessarily defeating a facial vagueness challenge; that proof of harm is not necessary to save a law from vagueness; and that defendant's arguments confuse the concept of vagueness with the concept of overbreadth.

Defendant also contends that the phrase "without authorization" in ORS 164.377(3) is unconstitutionally vague. According to defendant, because that phrase does not identify what sort of authorization is required, or from what source it must come, it is vague. Defendant further suggests that ORS 164.377(3), as written, requires that any alteration be authorized and that such a construction is so broad as to allow ad hoc enforcement. The state responds that only substantial certainty is required. The state observes that ORS 164.377(3) criminalizes alteration of a computer only when a person knows that he or she is without authorization. The state further argues that we should read ORS 164.377(3) as a whole; as such, it is sufficiently clear that the source of the authorization must be the person in control of the computer.

We agree with the state that many of defendant's arguments confuse the concepts of vagueness and overbreadth. * * * Defendant's arguments that "access" and "alter" overlap and that the statute criminalizes any unauthorized alteration are challenges to the breadth of the statute, not its lack of definiteness, and, accordingly, are not well taken as part of a vagueness claim.

For the same reason, we reject defendant's argument that ORS 164.377(3) is unconstitutionally vague because it reaches socially tolerable conduct as well as socially intolerable conduct. We considered a similar argument in *City of Portland v. Johnson*, in which the crux of the defendant's vagueness argument was that the statute prohibited activities that no reasonable person would consider to be criminal. In *Johnson*, as in this case, the defendant relied upon *State v. Sanderson*, to support his vagueness argument. In *Sanderson*, we said that the fundamental flaw of the statute at issue was that it "g[ave] no basis to distinguish between anti-social conduct which was intended to be prohibited and socially tolerable conduct which could not reasonably have been intended to be subject to criminal sanction." In *Johnson*, although we did not expressly state that such an analysis may not be appropriate, we suggested, * * * that it might not.

We now expressly repudiate the quoted portion of *Sanderson*. First, an argument that a statute covers too much ground can never, standing alone, support a vagueness challenge. As a matter of logic, the conclusion that a law is insufficiently definite to provide guidance to its potential violators and enforcers simply does not follow from the premise that the statute criminalizes too broad a category of conduct. Secondly, such an argument cannot provide the basis for an overbreadth claim, because "[a] legislature can make a law as 'broad' and inclusive as it chooses unless it reaches into constitutionally protected ground." The sole limit on a statute's breadth is constitutionality, not our second-guessing of what the legislature could or could not have deemed "socially tolerable." * * *

In this case, a potential violator or enforcer can be reasonably certain what conduct is prohibited by the phrase "alter[ ] * * * any computer [or] computer system." To "alter" means "to cause to become different in some particular characteristic * * * without changing into something else * * *." Webster's Third New Int'l Dictionary, 63 (unabridged ed. 1993). In this case, defendant installed gate programs that allowed external access to Intel computers. That conduct clearly changed a particular characteristic of those computers, namely their imperviousness to access from outside the company. "Alter" as used in ORS 164.377(3) is not unconstitutionally vague.

Similarly, "without authorization" in ORS 164.377(3) provides sufficiently definite notice of the prohibited conduct. In this case, defendant himself acknowledged that installing gate programs was against company policy. He did not argue that, despite company policy, he had obtained permission to install a gate program. Confronted with the phrase "without authorization," a potential violator of ORS 164.377(3) would be reasonably certain that he or she would run afoul of that prohibition by doing something to a computer in violation of the policy of the company that owned the computer without having sought permission for an exception to the policy. The trial court did not err in overruling defendant's demurrer on the ground of vagueness. * * *

In his fourth assignment of error, defendant challenges the trial court's denial of his motion for judgment of acquittal on counts two and three of the indictment. In counts two and three, respectively, defendant was charged as follows:

> That the above named defendant(s) on and between August 1, 1993 and November 1, 1993, in Washington County, Oregon, did unlawfully and knowingly access and use a computer and computer network for the purpose of committing theft of the Intel SSD's password file[.] * * *

> That the above named defendant(s) on and between October 21, 1993 and October 25, 1993, in Washington County, Oregon, did unlawfully and knowingly access and use a computer and computer system for the purpose of committing theft of the Intel SSD individual user's passwords.

At the close of the state's case, defendant moved for a judgment of acquittal on counts two and three. Defendant argued that, because the state's theory was that he acted with the purpose of committing theft, the state had to prove the elements of the theft statute, ORS 164.015. According to defendant the state had failed, first, to put on evidence that he had taken property and, second, to put on evidence that he had acted with the intent or purpose to commit theft. The trial court denied defendant's motion for a judgment of acquittal. Defendant assigns error to that denial.

ORS 164.377 includes three separately defined crimes: "(2) Any person commits computer crime who knowingly accesses, attempts to access or uses, or attempts to use, any computer, computer system, computer network or any part thereof for the purpose of:

> "(a) Devising or executing any scheme or artifice to defraud;

> "(b) Obtaining money, property or services by means of false or fraudulent pretenses, representations or promises; or

> "(c) Committing theft, including, but not limited to, theft of proprietary information.

"(3) Any person who knowingly and without authorization alters, damages or destroys any computer, computer system, computer network, or any computer software, program, documentation or data contained in such computer, computer system or computer network, commits computer crime.

"(4) Any person who knowingly and without authorization uses, accesses or attempts to access any computer, computer system, computer network, or any computer software, program, documentation or data contained in such computer, computer system or computer network, commits computer crime."

Defendant argues, the state concedes, and we agree that the indictment alleged, and the state attempted to prove at trial, only that defendant violated ORS 164.377(2)(c). Accordingly, we review the evidence in the light most favorable to the state to determine whether a rational trier of fact could have found the elements of computer crime as set out in ORS 164.377(2)(c) beyond a reasonable doubt.

The parties do not dispute that the state proved that defendant "knowingly accesse[d] * * * or use[d] * * * any computer, computer system, computer network or any part thereof" as required by ORS 164.377(2)(c). The parties dispute only whether the evidence was sufficient to establish that defendant did so "for the purpose of * * * [c]ommitting theft, including, but not limited to, theft of proprietary information." ORS 164.377(2)(c). To resolve the issue, we construe that statutory wording by first examining the text and context. Context includes related statutes.

ORS 164.377 does not define "theft." However, the legislature has defined "theft" in a related statute, ORS 164.015. ORS 164.015 provides, in part:

"A person commits theft when, with intent to deprive another of property or to appropriate property to the person or to a third person, the person:

"(1) Takes, appropriates, obtains or withholds such property from an owner thereof[.]"

"Property" includes "any * * * thing of value." ORS 164.005(5). The parties do not dispute that the password file and individual passwords have value, and there is evidence in the record to support that proposition. The parties dispute, however, whether defendant "t[ook], appropriate[d], obtain[ed] or withh[e]ld" the password file and individual passwords.

Defendant argues that he could not have "taken, appropriated, obtained or withheld" the password file and individual passwords because, even though he moved them to another computer and took them in the sense that he now had them on his computer, the file and passwords remained on Intel's computers after he ran the Crack program. The individual users whose passwords defendant had obtained could still use their passwords just as they had before. Intel continued to "have" everything it did before defendant ran the Crack program and, consequently, defendant reasons, he cannot be said to have "taken" anything away from Intel.

The state responds that, by copying the passwords, defendant stripped them of their value. The state contends that, like proprietary manufacturing formulas, passwords have value only so long as no one else knows what they are. Once defendant had copied them, the passwords were useless for their only purpose, protecting access to information in the SSD computers. The loss of exclusive possession of the passwords, according to the state, is sufficient to constitute theft.

Under ORS 164.015, theft occurs, among other ways, when a person "takes" the property of another. "Take" is a broad term with an extensive dictionary entry. Webster's Third New Int'l Dictionary, 2329-31. Some of the dictionary definitions undermine defendant's argument. The first definition of "take" is "to get into one's hands or into one's possession, power, or control by force or stratagem * * *." Another definition provides "to adopt or lay hold of for oneself or as one's own * * *." Black's defines "take" to include "[t]o obtain possession or control * * *." Black's Law Dictionary, 1466 (7th ed. 1999). Those definitions indicate that the term "take" might include more than just the transfer of exclusive possession that defendant proposes. For example, "take" could include obtaining control of property, as defendant did with respect to the passwords and password file by copying them.

Turning back to the text of the statute under which defendant was charged, we note that the legislature contemplated that "theft" as used in ORS 164.377(2)(c) could be exercised upon, among other things, "proprietary information." "Proprietary information" includes "scientific, technical or commercial information * * * that is known only to limited individuals within an organization * * *." ORS 164.377(1)(i). Proprietary information, like the passwords and password files at issue here, is not susceptible to exclusive possession; it is information that, by definition, can be known by more than one person. Nevertheless, the legislature indicated that it could be subject to "theft" under ORS 164.377(2)(c).

We conclude that the state presented sufficient evidence to prove that, by copying the passwords and password file, defendant took property of another, namely Intel, and that his actions, therefore, were for the purpose of theft. The trial court did not err in denying defendant's motion for judgment of acquittal on counts two and three. * * *

Restitution order reversed and remanded for reconsideration; otherwise affirmed.

CYBERCRIME'S SCOPE: INTERPRETING "ACCESS" AND "AUTHORIZATION" IN COMPUTER MISUSE STATUTES
Orin S. Kerr
78 N.Y.U. L. Rev. 1596 (2003)

* * * The broad umbrella category of "computer crimes" can be divided into two types of substantive offenses: traditional crimes committed using computers, and crimes of computer misuse.[19]

Traditional crimes committed using computers are easy to understand. Examples include Internet fraud schemes, Internet gambling, online distribution of child pornography, and cyberstalking. These crimes involve the online commission or facilitation of traditional criminal offenses. Consider the plague of child pornography and child exploitation crimes. Two decades ago, a pedophile seeking to obtain illegal images of child pornography would seek out a book or magazine containing the images. Today, the same pedophile likely would turn to the Internet, and seek out chat rooms and underground clubs that distribute these illegal images in digital form. * * *

For the most part, traditional crimes committed using computers raise few new issues for criminal law. The basic crimes remain the same regardless of whether wrongdoers use computers or some other means to

---

[19]This is my own dichotomy; other authors have used other approaches. *See, e.g.*, Donn B. Parker, Fighting Computer Crime 17 (1983) (arguing that computer crimes can be divided into cases in which computers are used as object, subject, instrument, or symbol); Scott Charney & Kent Alexander, *Computer Crime*, 45 Emory L.J. 931, 934 (1996) (classifying computer crimes as offenses in which computer is target of offense, tool of traditional offense, or storage device for evidence). * * * I differ with Charney and Alexander primarily with regard to their third category – crimes in which a computer is used as a storage device for evidence. This is really the field of criminal procedure, as opposed to substantive criminal law, and I think it is helpful to recognize this as a distinct area.

commit them. For example, a death threat is still a death threat regardless of whether it is transmitted via e-mail or a telephone call. Reasons may exist in some circumstances to regulate such crimes differently when they occur via computers and the Internet. But in general, the basic issues raised by traditional crimes do not change when they happen to be committed using computers.

Crimes of computer misuse represent a new type of crime, however, and pose fresh challenges for criminal law. We can define computer misuse as conduct that intentionally, knowingly, recklessly, or negligently causes interference with the proper functioning of computers and computer networks. Common examples include computer hacking, distribution of computer worms and viruses, and denial-of-service attacks. Computer misuse upsets users' reliance on the rights and privileges provided by computer owners and operators. For example, a personal e-mail account ordinarily gives its owner the right to access e-mail along with the privilege of exclusive access to that e-mail. An outsider who guesses the owner's password and reads the owner's e-mails denies her the assurance that her personal e-mails have remained private, secure, and confidential. Such an act of computer misuse violates the rights and privileges that the account owner was granted when she obtained the account.[24]

At a conceptual level, computer misuse can occur in two distinct ways. First, a user can exceed her privileges on a computer, either by using a computer that she has no authority to use, or by using the computer in a way that she is not authorized to use it. For example, a person can hack into a corporate network and see secret files that the person is not supposed to view. In such a case, the hacker will have exceeded her privileges on the network; she will see more than the network was configured to allow her to view. Second, a person can cause a denial of privileges, blocking another user from being able to enjoy her full privileges on a computer. For example, a person can deliver a denial-of-service attack that incapacitates a network, blocking its use. In this case, other users will try to exercise their rights to use the

---

[24]Notably, traditional crimes and computer misuse statutes can coexist in practice. Computer misuse sometimes occurs as part of a broader scheme to commit a traditional crime. For example, imagine that a high-tech bank thief hacks into the computer network of a major banking institution, sets up a false account remotely, and instructs the bank's computer that the false account contains $10 million. The thief then steals money from the bank by withdrawing money from the account. On one hand, this is a traditional crime: bank theft. On the other hand, the bank theft was furthered by engaging in computer misuse. The computer misuse crime of hacking into the bank's computer helped further the traditional crime of bank theft.

network, but will find that they cannot. These two types of computer misuse are two sides of the same coin: In the first case, the user exceeds her privileges; in the second, the user denies privileges to others. Both interfere with the rights and privileges that computers have been configured to allow.

Computer misuse is an important new type of criminal offense because it can cause serious harms, both economic and noneconomic. For example, computer misuse that exceeds privileges often results in serious invasions of privacy. The more that individuals store their private information in electronic form, the greater the possible invasion of privacy if others obtain access to their private information without the owner's permission. Computer misuse can also trigger heavy economic losses. While comprehensive figures remain elusive, experts estimate that computer crimes cause many billions of dollars of loss every year. These economic harms vary tremendously depending on the offense, but can reach levels rarely seen in traditional criminal offenses. For example, the "I Love You" computer virus that spread around the world in May 2000 caused losses to its victims estimated to be as high as $ 10 billion.

B.   The Use of Trespass and Burglary Law to Address Computer Misuse

The enormous potential harms of computer misuse first became apparent in the early 1970s. At that time, no legislature had enacted a computer crime statute. When prosecutors considered bringing criminal charges for computer misuse, they naturally turned to existing property crime laws, such as laws prohibiting trespass, burglary, and theft. The fit proved a poor one, however. In the case of trespass and burglary, the scope of existing laws plainly did not extend to computer misuse. In the case of theft, the law could be stretched to apply, but required judicial sleight of hand and resort to an unpredictable legal fiction. Taken together, the efforts to apply existing statutes to computer misuse produced an unsatisfying, results-oriented jurisprudence that inspired the passage of dedicated computer crime statutes.
* * *

II.   Unauthorized Access Statutes as an Answer to the Problem of Computer Misuse

Congress and all fifty state legislatures responded to the difficulties of prosecuting computer misuse as a property crime by enacting new computer crime statutes. * * * While no two statutes are identical, all share the common trigger of "access without authorization" or "unauthorized access" to computers, sometimes in tandem with its close cousin, "exceeding authorized access" to computers. In most cases, the statutes prohibit accessing a computer without authorization or exceeding authorized access as a necessary but not sufficient element of criminal liability, and then create several specific offenses by combining this base with various additional statutory requirements. In other words, most statutes start with the basic building block of "unauthorized access" to computers, and then add additional elements to the offense to deal with specific types of computer misuse.

The influential federal computer crime statute codified at 18 U.S.C. 1030 provides a good example. The statute includes seven distinct crimes, listed in 1030(a)(1) through (a)(7), almost all of which are triggered by "access without authorization" to computers. For example, one crime prohibits unauthorized access to government computers, another prohibits unauthorized access to computers that results in damage, and a third prohibits unauthorized access or exceeding authorized access to computers such that the user obtains private information.

But what does the trigger of unauthorized access mean? What exactly do these statutes prohibit? * * * [W]hile legislatures often had a basic sense that the new statutes would cover the computer equivalent of traditional trespass or burglary crimes, that sense was overly simplistic - even naïve. The question of what these statutes prohibit turns out to be rich and complex, requiring courts to consider difficult questions about the meanings of access and authorization, questions that legislatures have never recognized, much less resolved. Both "access" and "without authorization" can have a wide range of meanings. Seeking certainty, legislatures ended up enacting new statutes that created almost as many questions as they answered.

The courts that have interpreted "access" and "without authorization" have offered a broad range of interpretations that run the gamut from quite narrow to extraordinarily broad. Precedents remain sparse; only a handful of cases have interpreted "access," and only a handful of cases have interpreted "without authorization." But even the few available decisions reflect a diverse range of possible approaches. Most importantly, several recent decisions point toward remarkably expansive interpretations of unauthorized access. These decisions threaten to criminalize a great deal of innocuous activity online, potentially transforming routine Internet usage into an activity that (at least based on the law on the books) risks serious criminal liability.

* * * [T]he conceptual foundation of unauthorized access statutes remains remarkably unclear. And without a clear foundation, the statutes may inadvertently end up prohibiting far more conduct than the legislatures intended or common sense would support.

D.   CRIMES OF PROPERTYLESSNESS

THE RIGHT OF PROPERTY AND THE LAW OF THEFT

Michael E. Tigar
62 Tex. L. Rev. 1443 (1984)[a]

* * * [T]he seventeenth century opened with a newly forged alliance between the common-law lawyers and the bourgeoisie. The English bourgeoisie emerged from these struggles poised for large-scale commercial capitalist ventures and entered the nineteenth century prepared for industrial capitalist expansion. In the realm of private law, these developments were mirrored in the fields of property and contract. We can also observe, in the history of capitalist development, the self-conscious use of theft law not simply to enforce the right to property as newly defined, but to suppress and eliminate vestigial systems of social relations based upon principles other than property and contract.* * *

The law of theft sometimes did more than mirror class interest. It was used as a cudgel for enforcing that interest. In 1723, Parliament passed the 'Black Act,' ostensibly a three-year temporary measure, which was not repealed until the nineteenth century. Indeed, from 1723 until about 1775, the list of capital crimes involving the nonviolent appropriation of property was steadily lengthened. The 'Blacks' were peasants, laborers, and others who were being herded out of their traditional means of livelihood in the forests of Windsor and East Hampshire. Their name -- 'Black' -- derived from a practice of blacking their faces as a disguise when engaged in poaching or in attacks upon members of the gentry.

The Black Act defined about one hundred separate felonies, all punishable by hanging. These included arson, blackmail, and forms of mob violence. For our purposes, the most interesting part of this extraordinarily savage legislation is that it made felonious the taking of rabbits from a warren, fish from a pond, or deer from a forest, as well as the cutting of any tree. To be sure, the taking or cutting had to occur in an enclosed park, garden, or forest; but the Crown and the wealthy gentry owned most of the enclosed land. The livelihood of the Hampshire peasantry depended upon access to things that abounded in the wild state: deer, fish, and rabbits to eat, and wood for burning and building. The Black Act and its extremely harsh enforcement essentially criminalized a peasant way of life.

---

[a] © Texas Law Review Association.

The Black Act was not unheralded. The peasantry had been progressively denied historic use rights for some time, and many of the Act's prohibitions are foreshadowed in earlier legislation. The Act tells us much about English politics and about an important period in English history. Concerning the Whigs, its authors and enforcers, E.P. Thompson has written:

> The Whigs, in the 1720s, were a curious junta of political speculators and speculative politicians, stock-jobbers, officers grown fat on Marlborough's wars, time-serving dependants in the law and the Church, and great landed magnates. They were the inheritors, not of the Puritan Revolution, but of the canny and controlled Settlement of 1688. The libertarian rhetoric passed down from their forefathers they wore awkwardly, like fancy-dress. They derived what political strength they had in the country from the fact that they offered themselves as the only alternative to civil war or to a Stuart and Catholic repossession of the island.[2]

The danger of public disorder from the Blacks' raids, firing of houses, and murder of game wardens was no less severe than social conflict in other times and places. Making such conduct a capital felony can hardly be considered a departure from prior law. Making hanging matters of fish stealing, or of going disguised in a wood, was a clear departure. It was a signal that the survival of older systems of social relations would not be tolerated. Parks and forests were to be fenced, marked off, and regarded as the private property of some person, even if that person put the land to no productive use. Once that was done, the deer, fish, rabbits, and trees within were also endowed with the status of private property, so that taking them subjected one to punishment.

Parliament thus legislated away the means by which many people survived, providing a substantial encouragement to leave the land and swell the ranks of the urban proletariat. How can we analyze what Parliament had done to the various legal interests at stake? The forest had been a source of food, fuel, and timber. If a yeoman had killed a deer and carted it home, and then someone had taken it, that would have been larceny. The possession conferred by expenditure of labor would have been interrupted. The Black Act recognized a law of theft based not upon possession -- for no one could possess a forest or the creatures in it -- but upon a determinate relationship of dominium, an abstract relationship between a person and a thing, betokening the right to exclude all use by all others.

---

[2]*See generally* E.P. Thompson, WHIGS AND HUNTERS: THE ORIGIN OF THE BLACK ACT 198 (1975) (recounting the background of the Black Act).

POTTINGER v. CITY OF MIAMI

United States District Court, S.D. Florida
810 F.Supp. 1551 (1992)

ATKINS, Senior District Judge.

* * *

Plaintiffs ("plaintiffs" or "class members") filed this action in December of 1988 on behalf of themselves and approximately 6,000 other homeless people living in the City of Miami. Plaintiffs' complaint alleges that the City of Miami ("defendant" or "City") has a custom, practice and policy of arresting, harassing and otherwise interfering with homeless people for engaging in basic activities of daily life – including sleeping and eating – in the public places where they are forced to live. Plaintiffs further claim that the City has arrested thousands of homeless people for such life-sustaining conduct under various City of Miami ordinances and Florida Statutes. In addition, plaintiffs assert that the City routinely seizes and destroys their property and has failed to follow its own inventory procedures regarding the seized personal property of homeless arrestees and homeless persons in general.

Plaintiffs allege, pursuant to 42 U.S.C. § 1983,[1] that the property destruction and arrests, which often result in no criminal charges, prosecutions or convictions, violate their rights under the United States and Florida Constitutions. Because the arrested plaintiffs are released without further official process, the argument continues, plaintiffs never have the opportunity to raise such valid defenses as necessity or duress. As discussed below, plaintiffs do not challenge the facial validity of the ordinances or statutes under which they are arrested. Rather, they contend that the City applies these laws

---

[1] Section 1983 provides as follows:

Every person who, under color of any statute, ordinance, regulation, custom, or usage, of any State, or Territory, or the District of Columbia, subjects, or causes to be subjected, any Citizen of the United States or any other persons within the jurisdiction thereof to the deprivation of any rights, privileges or immunities secured by the Constitution and laws, shall be liable to the person injured in an action of law, suit in equity, or other proper proceedings for redress.

42 U.S.C. § 1983.

to homeless individuals as part of a custom and practice of driving the homeless from public places. Accordingly, plaintiffs do not argue that any of the ordinances should be stricken; instead, they ask that the City be enjoined from arresting homeless individuals for inoffensive conduct, such as sleeping or bathing, that they are forced to perform in public.* * *

In essence, this litigation results from an inevitable conflict between the need of homeless individuals to perform essential, life-sustaining acts in public and the responsibility of the government to maintain orderly, aesthetically pleasing public parks and streets. The issues raised in this case reveal various aspects of this conflict which, unfortunately, has become intensified by the overwhelming increase in the number of homeless people in recent years and a corresponding decrease in federal aid to cities. Because some of these issues have arisen in prior proceedings in this case, we briefly outline the history of this litigation before turning to the merits of the present inquiries.

I. PROCEDURAL HISTORY

On December 23, 1988, plaintiffs filed this action against the City of Miami on behalf of themselves and thousands of other homeless persons living within the City. * * *

A. The Complaint

Specifically, plaintiffs allege the following in their six-count complaint:

Count I: that the ordinances under which the City arrests class members for engaging in essential, life-sustaining activities – such as sleeping, eating, standing and congregating – are used by the City to punish homeless persons based on their involuntary homeless status in violation of the protection against cruel and unusual punishment found in the Eighth Amendment to the United States Constitution;

Count II: that the City has used its legitimate arrest powers for the unlawful purpose of "pest control," that is, "sanitizing" its streets by removing unsightly homeless individuals, which amounts to malicious abuse of process * * *;

Count V: that the City's arrests of homeless individuals for essential, life-sustaining activities violate their right to due process, privacy and decisional autonomy in violation of the Fourteenth Amendment to the United States Constitution and corresponding provisions of the Florida Constitution; and

Count VI: that the right of homeless persons publicly to engage in essential activities such as sleeping, eating, bathing and congregating is "fundamental" for purposes of equal protection under the Fifth and Fourteenth Amendments to the United States Constitution; that arresting the homeless infringes upon these fundamental rights and other fundamental rights, such as the right to travel, and burdens the homeless as a suspect class; and that the City has no compelling interest in making these arrests. * * *

II. FINDINGS OF FACT

A. The Homeless Plaintiffs

The plaintiffs are homeless men, women and children who live in the streets, parks and other public areas in the area of the City of Miami bordered on the North by Interstate 395, on the South by Flagler Street, on the East by Biscayne Bay, and on the West by Interstate 95. In making the factual findings underlying this order, the court relies in large part on the testimony at trial of a number of expert witnesses familiar with the plight of these and other homeless people.

Professor James Wright, an expert in the sociology of the homeless, testified that most homeless individuals are profoundly poor, have high levels of mental or physical disability, and live in social isolation. He further testified that homeless individuals rarely, if ever, choose to be homeless. Generally, people become homeless as the result of a financial crisis or because of a mental or physical illness.

While a mental or physical illness may cause some people to become homeless, health problems are also aggravated by homelessness. Dr. Pedro J. Greer, Jr., Medical Director of the Camillus Health Concern and an expert in medical treatment of homeless individuals, testified that a higher incidence of all diseases exists among the homeless. For example, hypertension, gastro-intestinal disorders, tuberculosis and peripheral vascular disease occur at a much higher rate in homeless people. This is due to a variety of factors such as exposure to the elements, constant walking, sleeping and eating in unsanitary conditions, lack of sleep and poor nutrition. In addition, people without a home generally have no place to store medication, no clock to determine when to take a pill, and no water with which to take it. Medical treatment of the homeless is hampered by the lack of beds and other facilities in the areas where the homeless reside. Lack of transportation further enhances the difficulty of the homeless in obtaining follow-up medical care. Improper diet and the stress of living outside can also aggravate mental illness.

Substance abuse, a component of both physical and mental illness, is also a factor contributing to homelessness. Dr. Greer testified that studies have shown that people are genetically predisposed to alcoholism, but that no such genetic link has been established with regard to drug addictions. Substance abuse also may be a consequence of being homeless. Professor Wright testified that many homeless people do not begin drinking until they become homeless; they use alcohol as a self-medication to numb both psychological and physical pain.

Chronic unemployment is another problem that many homeless face. Joblessness among homeless individuals is exacerbated by certain barriers that impede them from searching for work, such as health problems, the fact that they have no place to bathe, no legal address, no transportation and no telephone.

Professor Wright also testified that the typical day in the life of a homeless individual is predominated by a quest to obtain food and shelter. Because the lines at feeding programs are often long, some homeless individuals skip meals because they will miss obtaining a space in a shelter if they wait for food.

In summary, many of the problems described by the expert witnesses are both a cause and a consequence of homelessness. Furthermore, Dr. David F. Fike, a professor of social work and an expert on homelessness in Dade County, Florida, testified that the longer a person has been on the streets, the more likely it is that he or she will remain homeless.

The City has made laudable attempts, particularly in recent years, to assist the homeless. For example, the City resolved to participate, in conjunction with Dade County, the State of Florida and all agencies providing services to the homeless, in the development of an interim plan to provide resources to the homeless. In addition, the City stopped enforcing its ordinance against sleeping in public after an Eleventh Circuit ruling called into question the validity of a similar ordinance. However, many factors have frustrated the City's efforts to alleviate the problem of homelessness. Perhaps the most significant factor is the escalating number of homeless people.

The number of homeless individuals in Miami has grown at an alarming rate. According to Dr. Greer, the number of homeless treated medically at the Camillus Health Concern increased dramatically from 1984 to 1991. A disturbing aspect of the rise in homelessness is the increase in the number of families without shelter. One of the more poignant photographs in evidence shows two small children living beneath the I-395 overpass with their pregnant mother. As Dr. Greer commented, a second generation of homeless persons is being born right under our bridges.

The lack of low-income housing or shelter space cannot be underestimated as a factor contributing to homelessness. At the time of trial, Miami had fewer than 700 beds available in shelters for the homeless. Except for a fortunate few, most homeless individuals have no alternative to living in public areas.

The evidence presented at trial regarding the magnitude of the homelessness problem was overwhelming in itself. Then, shortly after the trial, one of the worst possible scenarios for homelessness occurred when Hurricane Andrew struck South Florida. Overnight, approximately 200,000 people were left without homes. In sum, this court has no difficulty in finding that the majority of homeless individuals literally have no place to go. * * *

C. Arrests of Homeless Individuals

The City, as evidenced by the records presented at trial, has arrested thousands of homeless individuals from 1987 to 1990 for misdemeanors such as obstructing the sidewalk, loitering, and being in the park after hours. The records show that the City arrested homeless individuals for standing, sleeping or sitting on sidewalks in violation of City of Miami Code § 37-53.1 (prohibiting obstruction of sidewalks); for sleeping on benches, sidewalks or in parks in violation of Miami Code § 37-63 (prohibiting sleeping in public); for sleeping in the park in violation of Miami Code § 38-3 (prohibiting being in the park after hours); for loitering and prowling in violation of Florida Statutes § 856.021 and Miami Code §§ 37-34 and 35; and for sleeping, sitting or standing in public buildings in violation of Florida Statutes § 810.08, .09 (prohibiting trespassing).

As discussed below in greater detail, the arrest records also show that many of the arrests for being in the park after hours were made less than an hour before the park was to reopen. In addition, the narrative sections of a majority of the arrest reports indicate that the individual arrestee was not disorderly, was not involved in any drug activity, and did not pose any apparent harm to anyone. Many of the records indicate that the arrestee was doing nothing more than sleeping. Peter Carter testified that he was doing just that when he was arrested in Bicentennial Park in 1988.

Carter stated that, during the time that he was homeless, he would sleep in Bicentennial Park or near Camillus House. He preferred the park because it had a restroom and running water. While in the park, he would stay with a group of fifteen to thirty other homeless people because it was safer to do so. Carter testified that, at around midnight on the night of his arrest, police officers arrived in cars and a paddy wagon. The officers told Carter and approximately fifteen others not to move, paired them, strapped their hands, put them into the paddy wagon and took them to the station. After taking statements in a room at the station, the officers took Carter and the others to jail and detained them another hour while they checked for any outstanding warrants. The officers released Carter and the other homeless individuals at approximately 4:00 a.m. Carter then walked back to Bicentennial Park with eight to ten other people and found that all of their belongings were gone. According to Carter, he and his companions were not bothering anyone while they were in the park; at the time of the arrest, he and the others were doing nothing more than sleeping.

The testimony and the documentary evidence regarding the arrests of the homeless – in addition to the sheer volume of homeless people in the City of Miami and the dearth of shelter space – support plaintiffs' claim that there is no public place where they can perform basic, essential acts such as sleeping without the possibility of being arrested.

III. CONCLUSIONS OF LAW

* * *

C. Cruel and Unusual Punishment

Plaintiffs contend that the City's arrests of class members under various ordinances prohibit them from lying down, sleeping, standing, sitting or performing other essential, life-sustaining activities in any public place at any time. Plaintiffs argue that their status of being homeless is involuntary and beyond their immediate ability to alter and that the conduct for which they are arrested is inseparable from their involuntary homeless status. Consequently, plaintiffs argue, application of these ordinances to them is cruel and unusual in violation of the eighth amendment.

The judicial prohibition of status-based abuse of police power under the eighth amendment is not without precedent. In a leading United States Supreme Court case addressing the issue, the Court held that punishment of a person for his involuntary status of being an addict was cruel and unusual in violation of the eighth amendment. *Robinson v. California*, 370 U.S. 660 (1962). Finding the status of being an addict similar to that of being mentally or physically ill, both of which are innocent and involuntary, the Court stated the following:

> a law which made a criminal offense of such a disease would doubtless be universally thought to be an infliction of cruel and unusual punishment in violation of the Eighth and Fourteenth Amendments.

The Court distinguished the punishment of the involuntary status of being an addict and the punishment of voluntary acts such as the use, purchase, sale or possession of narcotics or the disorderly behavior resulting from their use.

Based on *Robinson*, courts have overturned vagrancy laws because they punish status or condition. * * * Again, voluntariness of the status or condition is the decisive factor.

The Supreme Court again applied the *Robinson* principle in *Powell v. Texas*, 392 U.S. 514 (1968). Justice Marshall, writing for a plurality of four Justices, found that the appellant was convicted not for his status as a chronic alcoholic, but for

> being in public while drunk on a particular occasion. The State of Texas thus has not sought to punish a mere status, as California did in *Robinson*; nor has it attempted to regulate appellant's behavior in the privacy of his own home. Rather, it has imposed upon appellant a criminal sanction for public behavior which may create substantial health and safety hazards, both for appellant and for members of the public, and which offends the moral and esthetic sensibilities of a large segment of the community. This seems a far cry from convicting one from being an addict, being a chronic alcoholic, being "mentally ill, or a leper."

Although the law is well-established that a person may not be punished for involuntary status, it is less settled whether involuntary conduct that is inextricably related to that status may be punished. An initial reading of *Powell* suggests that all conduct is outside the rule of *Robinson*. The plurality in *Powell* stated that

> [t]he entire thrust of *Robinson 's* interpretation of the Cruel and Unusual Punishment Clause is that criminal penalties may be inflicted only if the accused has committed some act, has engaged in some behavior, which society has an interest in preventing, or perhaps in historical common law terms has committed some actus reus. It thus does not deal with the question of whether certain conduct cannot constitutionally be punished because it is, in some sense, "involuntary" or occasioned by compulsion.

However, the *Powell* plurality was not confronted with a critical distinguishing factor that is unique to the plight of the homeless plaintiffs in this case: that they have no realistic choice but to live in public places. Justice White identified this distinction in his concurrence:

> The fact remains that some chronic alcoholics must drink and hence must drink somewhere. Although many chronics have homes, many others do not. For all practical purposes the public streets may become home for these unfortunates, not because their disease compels them to be there, but because, drunk or sober, they have no place else to go and no place else to be when they are drinking.... For some of these alcoholics I would think a showing could be made that resisting drunkenness is impossible and that avoiding public places when intoxicated is also impossible. As applied to them this statute is in effect a law which bans a single act for which they may not be convicted under the Eighth Amendment--the act of getting drunk.

Although Justice White joined the majority in rejecting the appellant's challenge to his conviction, he did so only because he found the record insufficient to support the appellant's claim that his alcoholic condition compelled him to appear in public while drunk.. In contrast, as discussed below, the record in the present case amply supports plaintiffs' claim that their homeless condition compels them to perform certain life-sustaining activities in public.

As a number of expert witnesses testified, people rarely choose to be homeless. Rather, homelessness is due to various economic, physical or psychological factors that are beyond the homeless individual's control.

Professor Wright testified that one common characteristic of homeless individuals is that they are socially isolated; they are part of no community and have no family or friends who can take them in. Professor Wright also testified that homelessness is both a consequence and a cause of physical or mental illness. Many people become homeless after losing their jobs, and ultimately their homes, as a result of an illness. Many have no home of their own in the first place, but end up on the street after their families or friends are unable to care for or shelter them. Dr. Greer testified that once a person is on the street, illnesses can worsen or occur more frequently due to a variety of factors such as the difficulty or impossibility of obtaining adequate health care, exposure to the elements, insect and rodent bites, and the absence of sanitary facilities for sleeping, bathing or cooking.[18] Both Professor Wright and Dr. Greer testified that, except in rare cases, people do not choose to live under these conditions.

According to Professor Wright's testimony, joblessness, like physical and mental illness, becomes more of a problem once a person becomes homeless. This is so because of the barriers homeless individuals face in searching for a job. For example, they have no legal address or telephone. Also, they must spend an inordinate amount of time waiting in line or searching for seemingly basic things like food, a space in a shelter bed or a place to bathe.

In addition to the problems of social isolation, illness and unemployment, homelessness is exacerbated by the unavailability of many forms of government assistance. Gail Lucy, an expert in the area of government benefits available to homeless people, testified that many homeless individuals are ineligible for most government assistance programs. For example, Supplemental Security Income is available only to people who are sixty-five years of age or more, who are blind or disabled and who are without other resources. Social Security Disability Insurance is available only to workers who have paid into the social security fund for five of the past ten years prior to the onset of the disability. Aid to Families with Dependent Children is available only to low-income families with physical custody of children under the age of eighteen. The only benefit that is widely available to the homeless is food stamps.

Another notable form of assistance that is unavailable to a substantial number of homeless individuals is shelter space. Lucy testified that there are approximately 700 beds available in local shelters. However, approximately 200 of these are "program beds," for which one must qualify. In addition, some of these beds are set aside for families. Given the estimated 6,000 individuals who were homeless at the time of trial and the untold number of people left homeless by Hurricane Andrew, the lack of adequate housing alternatives cannot be overstated. The plaintiffs truly have no place to go.

---

[18] The photographs admitted during Dr. Greer's testimony depicting various locations where homeless people sleep and congregate show the filth, the exposure, and the lack of adequate facilities. For example, the photographs show that many of the homeless individuals sleep in the dirt on top of pieces of cardboard. A number of the photographs showed that plastic bottles were a common possession of homeless individuals. Dr. Greer testified that, without a fresh water supply, many homeless persons store water in plastic jugs when they can get it.

In sum, class members rarely choose to be homeless. They become homeless due to a variety of factors that are beyond their control. In addition, plaintiffs do not have the choice, much less the luxury, of being in the privacy of their own homes. Because of the unavailability of low-income housing or alternative shelter, plaintiffs have no choice but to conduct involuntary, life-sustaining activities in public places. The harmless conduct for which they are arrested is inseparable from their involuntary condition of being homeless. Consequently, arresting homeless people for harmless acts they are forced to perform in public effectively punishes them for being homeless. This effect is no different from the vagrancy ordinances which courts struck because they punished "innocent victims of misfortune" and made a crime of being "unemployed, without funds, and in a public place." Therefore, just as application of the vagrancy ordinances to the displaced poor constitutes cruel and unusual punishment, arresting the homeless for harmless, involuntary, life-sustaining acts such as sleeping, sitting or eating in public is cruel and unusual.

The City suggests, apparently in reference to the aftermath of Hurricane Andrew, that even if homelessness is an involuntary condition in that most persons would not consciously choose to live on the streets, "it is not involuntary in the sense of a situation over which the individual has absolutely no control such as a natural disaster which results in the destruction of one's place of residence so as to render that person homeless." The court cannot accept this distinction. An individual who loses his home as a result of economic hard times or physical or mental illness exercises no more control over these events than he would over a natural disaster. Furthermore, as was established at trial, the City does not have enough shelter to house Miami's homeless residents. Consequently, the City cannot argue persuasively that the homeless have made a deliberate choice to live in public places or that their decision to sleep in the park as opposed to some other exposed place is a volitional act. As Professor Wright testified, the lack of reasonable alternatives should not be mistaken for choice.

For plaintiffs, resisting the need to eat, sleep or engage in other life-sustaining activities is impossible. Avoiding public places when engaging in this otherwise innocent conduct is also impossible. Moreover, plaintiffs have not argued that the City should not be able to arrest them for public drunkenness or any type of conduct that might be harmful to themselves or to others. To paraphrase Justice White, plaintiffs have no place else to go and no place else to be. This is so particularly at night when the public parks are closed. As long as the homeless plaintiffs do not have a single place where they can lawfully be, the challenged ordinances, as applied to them, effectively punish them for something for which they may not be convicted under the eighth amendment -- sleeping, eating and other innocent conduct. Accordingly, the court finds that defendant's conduct violates the eighth amendment ban against cruel and unusual punishment and therefore that the defendant is liable on this count. * * *

2. Procedural Due Process

Plaintiffs further contend that, as applied to them, the challenged ordinances violate their right to due process. To review, these ordinances prohibit sleeping in public, being in a public park after hours, obstructing the sidewalk, loitering and prowling and trespassing on public property.

The procedural due process guarantees of the Fourteenth Amendment to the United States Constitution and Article I, Section 9 of the Florida Constitution require that a criminal law be clear and precise, not overbroad. However, a law may be overbroad, even if it is clear and precise, if it reaches conduct that is constitutionally protected or conduct that is beyond the reach of the state's police power.

A number of courts have overturned vagrancy and loitering statutes on due process grounds after finding them unconstitutionally vague. Before an individual may be criminally punished, he or she must be given fair notice of what type of conduct is prohibited. Therefore, if a person of ordinary intelligence is unable to ascertain from the language of a statute what conduct will subject him to criminal penalties, the statute is unconstitutionally vague. For example, writing for a unanimous Court in a leading United States Supreme Court case, Justice Douglas stated that a Jacksonville, Florida vagrancy ordinance was void for vagueness because it failed to give fair notice of the forbidden conduct and because it encouraged arbitrary arrests and convictions. *Papachristou v. City of Jacksonville*, 405 U.S. 156, 162 (1972). In *Kolender v. Lawson*, the Supreme Court overturned a California loitering statute that punished failure by any person wandering the streets to produce credible identification when so requested by a police officer. The Court held that this statute, like the vagrancy law invalidated in Papachristou, was too vague to satisfy the requirements of due process.

Courts also have overturned vagrancy and loitering statutes on due process grounds after finding them overbroad. A statute is overbroad when it reaches constitutionally protected conduct or conduct which is beyond the police power of the state to regulate.

Like the vagrancy and loitering statutes, courts have overturned statutes against sleeping in public on overbreadth grounds. In *State v. Penley*, the court declared unconstitutional an anti-sleeping ordinance which provided as follows: "No person shall sleep upon or in any street, park, wharf or other public place

(Code 1955, ch. 25, § 47)." *State v. Penley*, 276 So.2d 180, 180 (Fla. 2d DCA1973). The court noted the similarity between the anti-sleeping ordinance and most vagrancy laws, namely, that both punish unoffending behavior. The court further reasoned that the ordinance drew no distinction between conduct that is calculated to harm and that which is essentially innocent, that the ordinance failed to provide fair notice of the forbidden conduct, and that the ordinance could result in arbitrary and erratic convictions. Similarly, another Florida court partially invalidated an ordinance prohibiting sleeping in cars parked on public streets because the ordinance criminalized conduct that "in no way impinge[d] on the rights or interests of others." *City of Pompano Beach v. Capalbo*, 455 So.2d 468, 470-71 (Fla. 4th DCA1984), *cert. denied*, 474 U.S. 82 (1985) (quoting *Lazarus v. Faircloth*, 301 F. Supp. 266, 272 (S.D.Fla.1969)). The court found that such conduct was beyond the scope of the city's police power.

The City maintains that plaintiffs' due process claim must fail because none of the challenged ordinances is facially vague. However, plaintiffs have not challenged any of the ordinances on vagueness grounds; rather, plaintiffs contend that the ordinances are overbroad, as applied to them, because they reach conduct that is beyond the reach of the City's police power. In addition, plaintiffs do not argue that the challenged ordinances should be stricken. Rather, as in their eighth amendment argument, plaintiffs ask that the City be enjoined from arresting homeless individuals for harmless, involuntary conduct. We now consider plaintiffs' due process claim based on overbreadth. * * *

The concept of overbreadth will usually only apply when a case involves constitutionally protected conduct. * * *

* * * The acts of sleeping, sitting down or eating in themselves are not constitutionally protected. However, * * * under the unique circumstances of this case, the challenged ordinances as applied to class members do implicate constitutionally protected rights under the eighth amendment and, as discussed in greater detail below, the equal protection clause of the fourteenth amendment.

While sleeping "of the general kind" may "enjoy no peculiar constitutional advantage," under the facts of this case arresting plaintiffs for performing innocent conduct in public places – in particular, for being in a park or on public streets at a time of day when there is no place where they can lawfully be – most definitely interferes with their right under the constitution to be free from cruel and unusual punishment and, as will be addressed, their right to freedom of movement. Thus, plaintiffs have shown that the challenged ordinances as applied to them are overbroad to the extent that they result in class members being arrested for harmless, inoffensive conduct that they are forced to perform in public places. Accordingly, the court finds the City liable as to this count. * * *

The City further contends that it has a compelling interest in ensuring that its parks are free of crime. The court recognizes the tremendous responsibility that the City has and agrees that the City's interest in this regard is a compelling one. However, the City has not shown that arresting the homeless for being in the park after hours when they have no place else to go is the least intrusive means of addressing the interest in crime prevention.

The City claims that the arrests are necessary, or at least justified, because unlike the arrests made under vagrancy ordinances, the arrests of homeless individuals under various ordinances are effected after citizens file complaints and police officers observe other criminal activity. However, the arrests records and the internal police memoranda refute this contention. This evidence shows that numerous arrests were made not in response to citizen complaints, but as a result of police sweeps targeting areas where the homeless were known to reside or congregate.

The City further argues that it would be disingenuous to ignore the criminal element among the homeless. However, there is a criminal element among all of society, not just among the homeless. The United States Supreme Court, in rejecting the idea that criminality can be ascribed to the unfortunate, stated that no one can seriously contend that a person without funds and without a job constitutes a "moral pestilence." The Court further stated that "[p]overty and immorality are not synonymous." In fact, the City presented no evidence that a homeless person committed any of the crimes reported in the citizen complaints. Furthermore, as the narrative sections of the arrest records show, many of the homeless individuals arrested under the park closure ordinance were doing nothing more than sleeping. * * *

[A]lthough the idea of homeless people sleeping in public parks may disturb or offend some portion of society, the answer is not in arresting individuals who have arguably only committed the offense of being without shelter. There exist other means of preventing crime that are less drastic than arresting the homeless for harmless conduct that poses no threat to society. Rather than arrest the homeless, the City could increase police patrols of the park. It could allow homeless persons who have no alternative place to sleep to remain in a limited area instead of banishing them from the park entirely. In addition, the City could issue warnings to both homeless and non-homeless people about high-crime areas. * * *

* * * For these reasons, the court finds that plaintiffs' claim for injunctive relief is warranted.* * *

Obviously, the ideal solution would be to provide housing and services to the homeless. However, assembling and allocating such resources is a matter for the government – at all levels – to address, not for the court to decide. Rather, our immediate task is to fashion relief that accommodates the two predominant interests in this litigation. First, such relief must protect the homeless from one approach that clearly is not the answer to homelessness, that is, arresting homeless people for innocent, involuntary acts. Second, any relief granted must not unduly hamper the City's ability to preserve public order. For these reasons and for the reasons set forth above in the findings of fact and conclusions of law, it is

ORDERED AND ADJUDGED that * * * plaintiffs' request for injunctive relief is granted as follows:

(3) The City, through its Police Department, is enjoined from arresting homeless individuals who are forced to live in public for performing innocent, harmless, inoffensive acts such as sleeping, eating, lying down or sitting in at least two public areas to be agreed upon by the parties;

(4) Counsel for both parties are directed to meet within fifteen (15) days from the date of this order to establish two "safe zones" where homeless people who have no alternative shelter can remain without being arrested for harmless conduct such as sleeping or eating. In establishing these arrest-free zones, counsel should consider the proximity of the areas to feeding programs, health clinics and other services. In addition, the parties are encouraged to develop a procedure for maintaining the areas. Counsel are directed to submit a joint report within thirty (30) days regarding the outcome of their meeting.

(5) Until the parties reach an agreement on two arrest-free zones, the City is enjoined from arresting homeless individuals for sleeping or eating in a portion of Bicentennial Park to be designated by the City and in the area beneath the I-395 overpass that is still occupied by the homeless;

(6) The court emphasizes that nothing in this order prevents the City from arresting any individual for any criminal activity or for any conduct that is harmful to others or to himself. In addition, nothing in this order affects the ability of police officers to make arrests on private property; * * *

Note

Although local ordinances targeting homeless people for criminal prosecution when they participate in life maintenance activities in public are common, *Pottinger* is unusual in finding such an ordinance unconstitutional. Most courts faced with constitutional challenges to such "quality of life" ordinances uphold them based on the broad "police power" of state and local government to make general rules protecting the health and welfare of their citizens. *See, e.g., Joyce v. San Francisco*, 846 F. Supp. 843 (N.D. Cal. 1994) (upholding San Francisco's "Matrix" program designed to get homeless people off the streets); *Tobe v. Santa Ana*, 40 Cal.Rptr.2d 402 (1995) (upholding anti-camping ordinance as applied against homeless people).

Chapter 10

CRIMINAL LAW DEFENSES

INTRODUCTION

Criminal law defenses are traditionally divided into two categories: case-in-chief defenses (also known as failure of proof defenses or prima facie case defenses) and affirmative defenses. A case-in-chief defense is one in which the defendant attacks the prosecution's case in chief by arguing that the prosecutor has failed its burden of proof on at least one essential element of the crime, such as the mens rea, the actus reus, causation, or concurrence. Since the government bears the burden of proving every element of the crime beyond a reasonable doubt, all the defendant has to do is raise a reasonable doubt as to the existence of one element to secure a complete acquittal. Unconsciousness and most mistakes, which we have already studied, are case-in-chief defenses.

This chapter will cover a few additional case-in-chief defenses, but our main focus will be on affirmative defenses. An affirmative defense is one in which the defense attorney admits that the government has met its burden of proof regarding the case in chief, but argues that the defendant nonetheless should be acquitted for some other reason. These "other reasons," when recognized by the law, are called affirmative defenses. The defense usually bears the burden of proof regarding affirmative defenses. The standard of proof necessary to successfully carry off an affirmative defense varies from jurisdiction to jurisdiction. Typically, however, the defendant must convince the jury by a preponderance of the evidence that the necessary elements of the affirmative defense exist.[a]

Affirmative defenses are traditionally characterized as either justification defenses or excuse defenses.[b] A justification defense is one in

---

[a]In some situations the standard of proof is even higher. For example, in *Leland v. Oregon*, 343 U.S. 790, 72 S.Ct. 1002, 96 L.Ed. 1302 (1952), the Supreme Court upheld Oregon's rule that a defendant had to prove insanity beyond a reasonable doubt.

[b]A third category of less common, crime-specific defenses also exists. For example, legal impossibility is recognized in some common law jurisdictions as a defense to the crime of attempt. Abandonment is recognized in some jurisdictions as a defense to the crime of attempt, and in some jurisdictions as a defense to the crime of

which the defendant claims he did the right thing or took the most appropriate action under the circumstances. For example, self-defense is considered a justification defense. The defendant who claims self-defense argues that under the circumstances he did what society would have wanted him to do -- kill his attacker rather than be killed himself. Justification defenses focus on the correctness or justness of the defendant's action.

Excuse defenses, in contrast, focus on the individual defendant and whether he is blameworthy or culpable. In other words, the defendant's act is presumed to have been wrongful, but the defendant asks us to excuse him for some other reason. For example, insanity is an excuse defense. The defendant who claims insanity admits that his act (e.g., killing an innocent person) was wrongful but asks for leniency on the ground that a defect in his mental condition prevented him from knowing right from wrong or being able to control his actions.

At early common law, the justification and excuse distinction was extremely important. A justification would result in a complete acquittal while an excuse defense could only help the capital defendant escape the death penalty. Today, both justification and excuse defenses can lead to complete acquittals. Nonetheless, the justification-excuse distinction is still important in certain situations having to do with accomplice liability. For example, if a defendant is justified in violating the law, then that defendant's accomplices presumably are not guilty either, for there was no wrongdoing. Excuses, however, are considered personal to the actor. Therefore, if a defendant is acquitted on the basis of an excuse, her accomplices may still be found guilty of the crime. See Joshua Dressler, UNDERSTANDING CRIMINAL LAW § 17.05 [E] (3d ed. 2001).

Justification and excuse defenses, like substantive crimes, reflect their cultural context. The justification defenses, for instance, have emerged from a social consensus, influenced by the history and practices of Anglo-American culture, that in some situations breaking the law is more desirable than obeying the law. The excuse defenses, similarly, rest on culturally-shaped moral intuitions that some people are so lacking in personal responsibility that they should not be criminally punished. As you read these materials, consider whether the cultural bases for the justification and excuse defenses are solid. Are some defenses becoming obsolete? Should certain aspects of the existing law of defenses be updated? Should the law recognize new defenses to reflect changing social norms?

---

conspiracy. We will study these crime-specific defenses in Chapters 11 (attempts) and 13 (conspiracy).

A.   JUSTIFICATION DEFENSES

1.   Self-Defense

Self-defense is usually considered a justification defense. Some scholars, however, have argued that self-defense by a mistaken actor should be considered an excuse on the theory that the killing of an innocent human being cannot be applauded.

When a defendant is successful at proving all the elements of a self-defense claim, her liability for the crime will be eliminated and she will be acquitted. In some jurisdictions, even if the defendant is not able to convince the jury that all of the elements of self-defense were present, the defendant may be convicted of a lesser-included offense. This situation is referred to as imperfect self-defense and is discussed in more detail below.

The triggering condition for a self-defense claim is the defendant's honest and reasonable belief that he or she is threatened with an imminent threat of unlawful force. Once this triggering condition has occurred, the defendant is justified in using force against the initial perpetrator as long as the defendant honestly and reasonably believes that such force is both necessary to repel the threat and proportional to the threat. Accordingly, the defense of self-defense includes a necessity requirement, an imminence requirement, and a proportionality requirement. In addition, the defendant must not have been the initial aggressor – that is, the one who started the affray.

The three requirements of necessity, imminence, and proportionality are not absolute requirements. The defendant does not have to be correct in her belief that force was necessary in order to defend against an imminent threat of unlawful force. Rather, the defendant can be acquitted as long she *reasonably* believed in the need to act in self-defense, even if her belief was mistaken. Whether the defendant honestly and reasonably believed she was threatened with imminent unlawful force and whether the force the defendant used was reasonably necessary and proportional to the threat are questions for the fact-finder to decide. Trials involving self-defense, therefore, are fact-intensive, requiring both the prosecution and defense to present detailed and competing stories about what happened.

Trials involving self-defense also raise questions of cultural bias. For example, what constitutes a *reasonable* belief with respect to the threat of imminent unlawful force? As we've seen in previous chapters, the answer may vary depending on whether certain characteristics of the defendant are factored into the reasonableness equation. The cases that follow revisit a question we encountered in our study of the doctrine of provocation: to what extent should the law employ a normative standard of reasonableness, and to what extent should it equate reasonableness with typicality?

CULVERSON v. STATE
Supreme Court of Nevada
106 Nev. 484, 797 P.2d 238 (Nev. 1990)

YOUNG, CHIEF JUSTICE:

Samuel Culverson was convicted by a jury of first degree murder and sentenced to two terms of life imprisonment without possibility of parole for killing Michael Smith. We hold that the district court erred in instructing the jury that a defendant may not use self-defense to justify a homicide unless he is in actual danger of being killed or seriously injured by his assailant; and that the district court also erred in instructing the jury that a defendant has a duty to retreat when he reasonably believes that he is about to be attacked or killed. We reverse Culverson's judgment of conviction.

FACTS

On March 27, 1988, Hollie Broadus (Broadus) and Michael Smith (Smith) agreed to pool their money to buy cocaine. Broadus went out alone to find a seller. Samuel Culverson (Culverson) drove up to Broadus and offered him a ride. Culverson had a passenger with him in the car named Joel Thomas (Thomas). Broadus, Culverson, and Thomas drove to the home of Smith. Broadus talked with Smith and then both men entered Culverson's car. At this point the testimony is conflicting.

Broadus testified that Culverson was the initial aggressor. He claimed that Culverson pulled out a gun, pointed it at Smith and said "give me all of your . . . money." Smith said "I ain't giving you . . . man" and Broadus pushed Smith out of the car and jumped out himself. As Broadus ran from the scene he saw Smith pointing a gun at Culverson and heard four shots.

Thomas testified that Smith was the initial aggressor. He claimed that when they arrived at Smith's house, Smith and Broadus asked Culverson for a ride somewhere. Culverson said he would need money before he took them anywhere. Smith took out a roll of bills and began to count them. Broadus grabbed Smith's money and stuck it in his mouth. Culverson became angry at Broadus for being "disrespectful" and stated that he was going to take the money back from him. He then told Thomas to let Smith out of the car. Smith got out of the car, pulled a gun out of his pants, and called someone a "s-o-b." Thomas ran. He heard one shot, ran further, and then heard four more shots.

Culverson testified that he shot Smith in self-defense when Smith pointed a gun at him. He further testified that he did not attempt to rob Smith.

Smith died from four bullet wounds from Culverson's gun. The police found a pellet gun next to Smith's body. Culverson was tried and found guilty of first degree murder with the use of a deadly weapon. He was sentenced to two consecutive terms of life imprisonment without possibility of parole. * * *

I. ACTUAL AND APPARENT DANGER IN RELATION TO A CLAIM OF SELF-DEFENSE.

Culverson contends that the court erred when it failed to give the jury an instruction he submitted regarding the relationship between self-defense, actual danger, and perceived danger. At his trial Culverson submitted the following jury instruction to the court:

> Actual danger is not necessary to justify self-defense. If one is confronted by the appearance of danger which arouses in his mind, as a reasonable person, an honest conviction and fear that he is about to suffer great bodily injury, and if a reasonable man in a like situation, seeing and knowing the same facts, would be justified in believing himself in like danger, and if the person so confronted acts in self-defense upon such appearances and from such fear and honest convictions, his right of self-defense is the same whether such danger is real or merely apparent.

The court refused to give this instruction.

Culverson contends that the instructions given by the court regarding self-defense were misleading. He particularly objects to a part of Instruction 17 which states:

> Homicide is also justifiable when committed either in the lawful defense of the slayer, when there is reasonable ground to apprehend a design on the part of the person slain to commit a felony or to do some great personal injury to the slayer and there is imminent danger of such design being accomplished or in the actual resistance of an attempt to commit a felony upon the slayer in his presence.

Instruction 17 appears to state that homicide is justifiable when a person reasonably believes that he is about to be seriously injured or killed and there is an actual and immediate danger that he will be killed. While homicide would be justifiable under these circumstances, it would also be justifiable if there was no actual or immediate danger to the defendant, but the defendant reasonably believed that his assailant could kill or seriously harm him.[1]

We note that Instruction 17 states that homicide is also justified under the situation mentioned in the instruction. The use of the word "also" implies that Instruction 17 is but one example of when self-defense justifies a homicide. Other instructions given to the jury do not require that the defendant be in actual danger before he uses self-defense as a justification for homicide. A careful reading of all the instructions could have led a juror to conclude that a person may use self-defense as a justification to homicide even if he is not in actual danger.

A juror should not be expected to be a legal expert. Jury instructions should be clear and unambiguous. Instruction 17 may have misled the jury into concluding that Culverson was not justified in shooting Smith because Smith carried a pellet gun which could not have seriously harmed Culverson. Accordingly, we conclude that Jury Instruction 17 was erroneous and could have prejudiced the jury.

II. THE DUTY TO RETREAT.

Culverson contends that the district court erroneously informed the jury that he had a duty to retreat before he could act in self-defense. Specifically, Culverson objects to Instruction No. 19 which states:

> In this case even if you should believe from the evidence that the deceased commenced the encounter in question and was the first to offer violence, but further believe from the evidence, beyond a reasonable doubt, that the defendant could, by making a reasonable effort, have avoided or safely withdrawn from it, and thereby avoided further trouble, and that he made no effort to do so, but voluntarily entered into and continued the

---

[1] For instance, a defendant who is approached by a person who points an unloaded shotgun at him may reasonably believe that he is in danger of being attacked if he believes the gun is loaded. Under Instruction 17, such a person might not be justified in using self-defense because he was in no actual or immediate danger of being killed or seriously injured.

encounter and shot and killed the deceased, then the killing of the deceased is not excused or justified on the ground of self-defense.

The leading Nevada case which deals with the duty to retreat is *State v. Grimmett*, 33 Nev. 531, 112 P. 273 (1910). In *Grimmett*, the victim, while standing behind a bar, took a gun from a drawer and fired one shot at the defendant who immediately fired two shots killing the victim. This court held:

> The law is well established that where a person, without voluntarily seeking, provoking, inviting, or willingly engaging in a difficulty of his own free will, is attacked by an assailant, and it is necessary for him to take the life of his assailant to protect his own, then he need not flee for safety, but has the right to stand his ground and slay his adversary.

Culverson contends that *Grimmett* stands for the proposition that Nevada does not require a person to retreat when he reasonably believes that he is about to be attacked with deadly force. We agree. First, we note that a rule requiring a non-aggressor to retreat confers a benefit on the aggressor and a detriment on the non-aggressor. Second, it is often quite difficult for a jury to determine whether a person should reasonably believe that he may retreat from a violent attack in complete safety. Thus, a rule which requires a non-aggressor to retreat may confuse the jury and lead to inconsistent verdicts. We believe that a simpler rule will lead to more just verdicts.

One reason that has been given to support the no duty to retreat rule is that the non-aggressor should be able to avoid the appearance of cowardice. We do not believe this is a valid reason to support the rule we now adopt. However, the reasons cited amply support the rule that a non-aggressor need not retreat if he reasonably believes he is about to be seriously injured or killed.

Therefore, we hold that a person, who is not the original aggressor, has no duty to retreat before using deadly force, if a reasonable person in the position of the non-aggressor would believe that his assailant is about to kill him or cause him serious bodily harm. * * *

CONCLUSION

We hold that the district court erred when it instructed the jury that self-defense cannot be used as a justification for homicide unless a person is actually in danger of being seriously injured or killed by his attacker. Self-defense may justify a homicide if a person reasonably believes that he is in danger of being seriously injured or killed by his assailant.

We further hold that a person who as a reasonable person believes that he is about to be killed or seriously injured by his assailant does not have a duty to retreat unless he is the original aggressor. The district court erred when it instructed the jury that the appellant had a duty to retreat if he could have safely withdrawn from the encounter.

Accordingly, we reverse Culverson's conviction for first degree murder and remand this matter to the district court for a new trial.

ROSE, JUSTICE, concurring, with whom SPRINGER, JUSTICE, agrees:

I agree with the majority that Instruction No. 17 may have been confusing to the jury and the instructions did not legally address the situation where a defendant is not in fact faced with actual or immediate danger, but reasonably believes that his or her assailant could kill him or her. But in considering the duty to retreat in the face of deadly force, I would require a non-aggressor to retreat if he or she could do so in complete safety. This differs somewhat from the majority's position that a non-aggressor does not have to retreat, even though he or she could do so with complete safety, if a reasonable person in his or her position would believe that death or serious bodily harm is about to be inflicted upon him or her. * * *

Other states are divided on the issue of whether a defendant has a duty to retreat. The majority of jurisdictions hold that a defendant who was not the initial aggressor is not required to retreat before using deadly force against someone whom he reasonably believes is about to kill or seriously injure him. A significant minority of states have adopted the rule that a defendant must retreat, if he can safely do so, when threatened with deadly force.

The following rationale justifies not requiring a defendant to retreat from an aggressor if he or she may do so in complete safety: (1) the State should not force a non-aggressor to act in a cowardly manner; (2) unjustified aggression should not be protected; and (3) it is too difficult for a jury to determine when it is safe for a defendant to retreat.

I disagree that it is cowardly to walk away safely from a attacker rather than to kill him or her, and the majority opinion agrees. Rather, I believe that:

> A really honorable man, a man of truly refined and elevated feeling, would perhaps always regret the apparent cowardice of a retreat, but he would regret ten times more, after the excitement of the contest was past, the thought that he had the blood of a fellow-being on his hands.

J. Beale, *Retreat From A Murderous Assault*, 16 Harv. L. Rev. 567, 581 (1903). The policy of saving one human life, even if it is that of an aggressor, outweighs the interest an individual might have in avoiding the appearance of cowardice.

The person who retreats can usually rely upon the state to punish the aggressor for his or her actions. A jury is required to make many difficult decisions and it is perfectly capable of determining whether a reasonable person should know that he or she could retreat without using deadly force.

Finally, self-defense is measured by necessity. There is no necessity to use deadly force if a defendant may retreat in complete safety.

For the preceding reasons, I believe the better rule would be that a person who has a reasonable belief that he or she is about to be killed or seriously injured has the duty to retreat, rather than use deadly force against his aggressor, if as a reasonable person he or she should know that a retreat can be made with complete safety. Whether a person should reasonably know that he or she can retreat with complete safety will be determined after examination of the totality of circumstances surrounding the attack, including but not limited to, the immediate excitement which is caused by the attack. As Justice Holmes stated, "[d]etached reflection cannot be demanded in the presence of an uplifted knife."

Note

Although the older English common law imposed a duty to retreat, the majority rule in the United States, as *Culverson* indicates, is that no retreat is necessary before using deadly force. Only a minority of jurisdictions require retreat. Even in these jurisdictions, moreover, one is not required to retreat if attacked in one's home – the so-called "castle" doctrine. Some jurisdictions have expanded the castle doctrine to include the workplace as well as the home.

The rule that no retreat is required is occasionally referred to as the "True Man" rule. *See, e.g., People v. Toler*, 9 P.3d 341, 347 (Colo. 2000). Does the no-duty-to-retreat rule reflect cultural preoccupations about masculinity? Is it peculiarly "American"?

What happens when the defendant begins a fist fight and the victim responds by pulling a gun or knife? May the defendant use deadly force herself and still successfully claim self defense? The older common law rule was that the actor had to be "free from fault" before being justified in using deadly force; thus, aggressors lost any claim to self-defense. The more modern common law rule is that an initial aggressor may regain the privilege of self-defense if she withdraws from the conflict and makes that withdrawal plain to the other person(s) involved. If the aggressor does not so withdraw, however, she loses the justification. (The aggressor, however, might have access to an "imperfect self defense" claim, as we will see.) Look closely at section 3.04(2)(b)(i) of the Model Penal Code to see how the Code drafters analyzed this kind of problem.

PEOPLE v. GOETZ
Court of Appeals of New York
68 N.Y.2d 96, 497 N.E.2d 41, 506 N.Y.S.2d 18 (1986)

WACHTLER, C.J.

A Grand Jury has indicted defendant on attempted murder, assault, and other charges for having shot and wounded four youths on a New York City subway train after one or two of the youths approached him and asked for $5. The lower courts, concluding that the prosecutor's charge to the Grand Jury on the defense of justification was erroneous, have dismissed the attempted murder, assault and weapons possession charges. We now reverse and reinstate all counts of the indictment.

I.

The precise circumstances of the incident giving rise to the charges against defendant are disputed, and ultimately it will be for a trial jury to determine what occurred. We feel it necessary, however, to provide some factual background to properly frame the legal issues before us. Accordingly, we have summarized the facts as they appear from the evidence before the Grand Jury. We stress, however, that we do not purport to reach any conclusions or holding as to exactly what transpired or whether defendant is blameworthy. The credibility of witnesses and the reasonableness of defendant's conduct are to be resolved by the trial jury.

On Saturday afternoon, December 22, 1984, Troy Canty, Darryl Cabey, James Ramseur, and Barry Allen boarded an IRT express subway train in The Bronx and headed south toward lower Manhattan. The four youths[a] rode

---

[a]Interestingly, the court omits mention of the fact that the four youths were Black and Goetz was white. This color blind attitude was replicated at Goetz's trial to the detriment of the prosecution. Law professor George Fletcher, who sat through the trial, observed that race was never explicitly by either the prosecution or the defense as if race was irrelevant. Instead, the defense covertly appealed to the Black-as-Criminal stereotype by referring to the four youths as "savages," "predators," and "vultures," terms which suggested that the teens were criminals and/or gang members

together in the rear portion of the seventh car of the train. Two of the four, Ramseur and Cabey, had screwdrivers inside their coats, which they said were to be used to break into the coin boxes of video machines.[b]

Defendant Bernhard Goetz boarded this subway train at 14th Street in Manhattan and sat down on a bench towards the rear section of the same car occupied by the four youths. Goetz was carrying an unlicensed .38 caliber pistol loaded with five rounds of ammunition in a waistband holster. The train left the 14th Street station and headed towards Chambers Street.

It appears from the evidence before the Grand Jury that Canty approached Goetz, possibly with Allen beside him, and stated "give me five dollars." Neither Canty nor any of the other youths displayed a weapon. Goetz responded by standing up, pulling out his handgun and firing four shots in rapid succession. The first shot hit Canty in the chest; the second struck Allen in the back; the third went through Ramseur's arm and into his left side; the fourth was fired at Cabey, who apparently was then standing in the corner of the car, but missed, deflecting instead off of a wall of the conductor's cab. After Goetz briefly surveyed the scene around him, he fired another shot at Cabey, who then was sitting on the end bench of the car. The bullet entered the rear of Cabey's side and severed his spinal cord.

---

preying on innocent law-abiding citizens like Goetz. Fletcher opines that "[t]he covert appeal to racial bias came out most dramatically in the recreation of the shooting, played out while Joseph Quirk was testifying. The defendant called in four props to stand in for the four victims Canty, Allen, Ramseur, and Cabey. The nominal purpose of the demonstration was to show the way in which each bullet entered the body of each victim. The defense's real purpose, however, was to recreate for the jury, as dramatically as possible, the scene that Goetz encountered when four young black passengers began to surround him. For that reason Barry Slotnick (Goetz's attorney) asked the Guardian Angels to send him the four young black men to act as the props in the demonstration. In came the four young black Guardian Angels, fit and muscular, dressed in T-shirts, to play the parts of the four victims in a courtroom minidrama." George P. Fletcher, A CRIME OF SELF-DEFENSE: BERNHARD GOETZ AND THE LAW ON TRIAL 206-207 (1988).

[b]Some newspaper accounts of the shooting erroneously reported that the youths had threatened Goetz with sharpened screwdrivers. None of the youths, however, used screwdrivers to threaten Goetz. The two youths who did not approach Goetz had screwdrivers inside their jackets which they planned to use to break into the coin boxes on some video machines. George P. Fletcher, A CRIME OF SELF-DEFENSE: BERNHARD GOETZ AND THE LAW ON TRIAL (1988).

All but two of the other passengers fled the car when, or immediately after, the shots were fired. The conductor, who had been in the next car, heard the shots and instructed the motorman to radio for emergency assistance. The conductor then went into the car where the shooting occurred and saw Goetz sitting on a bench, the injured youths lying on the floor or slumped against a seat, and two women who had apparently taken cover, also lying on the floor. Goetz told the conductor that the four youths had tried to rob him.

While the conductor was aiding the youths, Goetz headed towards the front of the car. The train had stopped just before the Chambers Street station and Goetz went between two of the cars, jumped onto the tracks and fled. Police and ambulance crews arrived at the scene shortly thereafter. Ramseur and Canty, initially listed in critical condition, have fully recovered. Cabey remains paralyzed, and has suffered some degree of brain damage.

On December 31, 1984, Goetz surrendered to police in Concord, New Hampshire, identifying himself as the gunman being sought for the subway shootings in New York nine days earlier. Later that day, after receiving *Miranda* warnings, he made two lengthy statements, both of which were tape recorded with his permission. In the statements, which are substantially similar, Goetz admitted that he had been illegally carrying a handgun in New York City for three years. He stated that he had first purchased a gun in 1981 after he had been injured in a mugging. Goetz also revealed that twice between 1981 and 1984 he had successfully warded off assailants simply by displaying the pistol.

According to Goetz's statement, the first contact he had with the four youths came when Canty, sitting or lying on the bench across from him, asked "how are you," to which he replied "fine." Shortly thereafter, Canty, followed by one of the other youths, walked over to the defendant and stood to his left, while the other two youths remained to his right, in the corner of the subway car. Canty then said "give me five dollars." Goetz stated that he knew from the smile on Canty's face that they wanted to "play with me." Although he was certain that none of the youths had a gun, he had a fear, based on prior experiences, of being "maimed."

Goetz then established "a pattern of fire," deciding specifically to fire from left to right. His stated intention at that point was to "murder [the four youths], to hurt them, to make them suffer as much as possible." When Canty again requested money, Goetz stood up, drew his weapon, and began firing, aiming for the center of the body of each of the four. Goetz recalled that the first two he shot "tried to run through the crowd [but] they had nowhere to run." Goetz then turned to his right to "go after the other two." One of these two "tried to run through the wall of the train, but * * * he had nowhere to go." The other youth (Cabey) "tried pretending that he wasn't with [the others]" by standing still, holding on to one of the subway hand straps, and not looking at Goetz. Goetz nonetheless fired his fourth shot at him. He then ran back to the first two youths to make sure they had been "taken care of." Seeing that they had both been shot, he spun back to check on the latter two. Goetz noticed that the youth who had been standing still was now sitting on a bench and seemed unhurt. As Goetz told the police, "I said '[you] seem to be all right, here's another,'" and he then fired the shot which severed Cabey's spinal cord. Goetz added that "if I was a little more under self-control * * * I would have put the barrel against his forehead and fired." He also admitted that "if I had had more [bullets], I would have shot them again, and again, and again." * * *

III.

Penal Law article 35 recognizes the defense of justification, which "permits the use of force under certain circumstances." One such set of circumstances pertains to the use of force in defense of a person, encompassing both self-defense and defense of a third person. Penal Law §35.15 (1) sets forth the general principles governing all such uses of force: "[a] person may * * * use physical force upon another person when and to the extent he *reasonably believes* such to be necessary to defend himself or a third person from what he *reasonably believes* to be the use or imminent use of unlawful physical force by such other person."

Section 35.15 (2) sets forth further limitations on these general principles with respect to the use of "deadly physical force": "A person may not use deadly physical force upon another person under circumstances specified in subdivision one unless (a) He *reasonably believes* that such other person is using or about to use deadly physical force * * * or (b) He *reasonably believes* that such other person is committing or attempting to commit a kidnapping, forcible rape, forcible sodomy or robbery."

Thus, consistent with most justification provisions, Penal Law §35.15 permits the use of deadly physical force only where requirements as to triggering conditions and the necessity of a particular response are met. As to the triggering conditions, the statute requires that the actor "reasonably believes" that another person either is using or about to use deadly physical force or is committing or attempting to commit one of certain enumerated felonies, including robbery. As to the need for the use of deadly physical force as a response, the statute requires that the actor "reasonably believes" that such force is necessary to avert the perceived threat.

Because the evidence before the second Grand Jury included statements by Goetz that he acted to protect himself from being maimed or to avert a robbery, the prosecutor correctly chose to charge the justification defense in section 35.15 to the Grand Jury. The prosecutor properly instructed the grand jurors to consider whether the use of deadly physical force was justified to prevent either serious physical injury or a robbery, and, in doing so, to separately analyze the defense with respect to each of the charges. He elaborated upon the prerequisites for the use of deadly physical force essentially by reading or paraphrasing the language in Penal Law §35.15. The defense does not contend that he committed any error in this portion of the charge.

When the prosecutor had completed his charge, one of the grand jurors asked for clarification of the term "reasonably believes." The prosecutor responded by instructing the grand jurors that they were to consider the circumstances of the incident and determine "whether the defendant's conduct was that of a reasonable man in the defendant's situation." It is this response by the prosecutor--and specifically his use of "a reasonable man" -- which is the basis for the dismissal of the charges by the lower courts. As expressed repeatedly in the Appellate Division's plurality opinion, because section 35.15 uses the term *"he* reasonably believes," the appropriate test, according to that court, is whether a defendant's beliefs and reactions were "reasonable *to him."* Under that reading of the statute, a jury which believed a defendant's testimony that he felt that his own actions were warranted and were reasonable would have to acquit him, regardless of what anyone else in defendant's situation might have concluded. Such an interpretation defies the ordinary meaning and significance of the term "reasonably" in a statute, and misconstrues the clear intent of the Legislature, in enacting section 35.15, to retain an objective element as part of any provision authorizing the use of deadly physical force.

Penal statutes in New York have long codified the right recognized at common law to use deadly physical force, under appropriate circumstances, in self-defense. These provisions have never required that an actor's belief as to the intention of another person to inflict serious injury be correct in order for the use of deadly force to be justified, but they have uniformly required that the belief comport with an objective notion of reasonableness. * * *

Had the drafters of section 35.15 wanted to adopt a subjective standard, they could have simply used the language of [Model Penal Code] section 3.04 [which omits "any requirement of reasonableness"]. "Believes" by itself requires an honest or genuine belief by a defendant as to the need to use deadly force. Interpreting the statute to require only that the defendant's belief was "reasonable to *him,"* as done by the plurality below, would hardly be different from requiring only a genuine belief; in either case, the defendant's own perceptions could completely exonerate him from any criminal liability.

We cannot lightly impute to the Legislature an intent to fundamentally alter the principles of justification to allow the perpetrator of a serious crime to go free simply because that person believed his actions were reasonable and necessary to prevent some perceived harm. To completely exonerate such an individual, no matter how aberrational or bizarre his thought patterns, would allow citizens to set their own standards for the permissible use of force. It would also allow a legally competent defendant suffering from delusions to kill or perform acts of violence with impunity, contrary to fundamental principles of justice and criminal law.

We can only conclude that the Legislature retained a reasonableness requirement to avoid giving a license for such actions. * * * Statutes or rules of law requiring a person to act "reasonably" or to have a "reasonable belief" uniformly prescribe conduct meeting an objective standard measured with reference to how "a reasonable person" could have acted. * * *

Goetz also argues that the introduction of an objective element will preclude a jury from considering factors such as the prior experiences of a given actor and thus, require it to make a determination of "reasonableness" without regard to the actual circumstances of a particular incident. This argument, however, falsely presupposes that an objective standard means that the background and other relevant characteristics of a particular actor must be ignored. To the contrary, we have frequently noted that a determination of reasonableness must be based on the "circumstances" facing a defendant or his "situation." Such terms encompass more than the physical movements of the potential assailant. As just discussed, these terms include any relevant knowledge the defendant had about that person. They also necessarily bring in the physical attributes of all persons involved, including the defendant. Furthermore, the defendant's circumstances encompass any prior experiences he had which could provide a reasonable basis for a belief that another person's intentions were to injure or rob him or that the use of deadly force was necessary under the circumstances.

Accordingly, a jury should be instructed to consider this type of evidence in weighing the defendant's actions. * * * The jury would have to determine, in light of all the "circumstances," as explicated above, if a reasonable person could have had these beliefs.

The prosecutor's instruction to the second Grand Jury that it had to determine whether, under the circumstances, Goetz's conduct was that of a reasonable man in his situation was thus essentially an accurate charge. * * *

Accordingly, the order of the Appellate Division should be reversed, and the dismissed counts of the indictment reinstated.

Note

At his subsequent trial, Goetz claimed he acted in self-defense when he shot the four youths. He was found not guilty by a predominantly white jury on all counts except for the illegal possession of a handgun charge. Nine years later, an all-minority six person civil jury found Goetz liable to Darryl Cabey, the youth who was paralyzed after Goetz shot him in the spine, and ordered Goetz to pay Cabey $43 million in damages. N.Y.L.J., Apr. 24, 1996, at 1. Joseph A. Kirby, *"Subway Vigilante" Case in Final Stage,* CHI. TRIB., Apr. 23, 1996, at 4.

STATE v. SIMON
Supreme Court of Kansas
231 Kan. 572, 646 P.2d 1119 (1982)

MCFARLAND, J.

*   *   *

The issue presented in this appeal is whether the statutory justification for the use of deadly force in defense of a person contained in K.S.A. 21-3211 is to be determined by the trier of fact using a subjective standard (from the viewpoint of the accused's state of mind) or by using an objective standard (from the viewpoint of a reasonable man in the accused's position).

The instruction given herein on self-defense was PIK Crim. 54.17 as follows:

> A person is justified in the use of force to defend himself against an aggressor's imminent use of unlawful force to the extent it *appears reasonable to him* under the circumstances then existing.

The statutory authority for any instruction relative to use of force in defense of a person is K.S.A. 21-3211 which provides:

> A person is justified in the use of force against an aggressor when and to the extent it appears to him and *he reasonably believes* that such conduct is necessary to defend himself or another against such aggressor's imminent use of unlawful force.

The Judicial Council Comments to K.S.A. 21-3211 provide in relevant part:

> The section defines the right to defend one's person against unlawful aggression. It attempts to define the phrase 'reasonably believes.' A reasonable belief implies both a belief and the existence of facts that would persuade a reasonable man to that belief.

* * *

The State contends K.S.A. 21-3211 requires the trier of fact to determine the reasonableness of the accused's actions by an objective rather than a subjective standard. The State further contends PIK Crim. 54.17 improperly instructs the jury to utilize a subjective standard in determining the reasonableness of the accused's actions. We agree with both contentions.

We note that of all the times self-defense instructions have been involved in appeals before us, this is the first time this precise issue has been raised. * * *

Defendant is an elderly homeowner in Wichita. Steffen Wong, a young man of Oriental extraction, rented half of the duplex next door. By virtue of Mr. Wong's racial heritage, defendant assumed he was an expert in the martial arts.[a] Defendant was afraid of Steffen Wong, and heated words had been exchanged between the two. Defendant was fearful because more "Orientals" were moving into the neighborhood, and one had expressed interest in purchasing defendant's home.

On May 27, 1981, Mr. Wong was fired upon as he attempted to enter his own duplex. Shortly thereafter Rickey and Brenda Douglas, the residents of the other half of the duplex, pulled into their driveway and were fired upon by the defendant. Police officers arrived a few minutes later and defendant fired a number of shots at the officers who had previously identified themselves. Defendant was charged with two counts of aggravated assault for firing at

---

[a] It appears that Mr. Simon was relying on the Asian-as-Martial Artist Stereotype which links Asians to proficiency in Karate, Kung Fu, Tae Kwando, or some other martial art form from Asia. *See* Cynthia Lee, MURDER AND THE REASONABLE MAN: PASSION AND FEAR IN THE CRIMINAL COURTROOM (NYU Press 2003); Cynthia Kwei Yung Lee, *Race and Self-Defense: Toward a Normative Conception of Reasonableness*, 81 Minn. L. Rev. 367, 438 (1996).

Steffen Wong and Rickey Douglas. At trial defendant testified as to his general fear of Mr. Wong and that Mr. Wong had walked toward him cursing just before the incident started. The defense called a clinical psychologist who testified defendant was a "psychological invalid" who was very tense and fearful. The psychologist stated defendant's mental condition permitted him to "misjudge reality" and see himself under attack. The tentative diagnosis was "anxiety neurosis."

> The jury was instructed:

> A person is justified in the use of force to defend himself against an aggressor's imminent use of unlawful force to the extent it appears reasonable to him under the circumstances then existing.

> Defense counsel argued to the jury that the evidence showed defendant believed Mr. Wong was an imminent threat to him and that the firing of the gun appeared reasonable to the defendant. The jury acquitted defendant on both counts. Under the totality of the circumstances, one must assume the acquittals were occasioned in large measure by the improper instruction on self-defense.

> We hereby disapprove the giving of PIK Crim. 54.17 as being an incorrect statement of the law of Kansas as set forth in K.S.A. 21-3211. * * * We conclude that the jury should properly have been instructed in the following language or its equivalent:

> A person is justified in the use of force against an aggressor when and to the extent it appears to him and he reasonably believes that such conduct is necessary to defend himself or another against such aggressor's imminent use of unlawful force. A reasonable belief implies both a belief and the existence of facts that would persuade a reasonable man to that belief.

> This instruction combines the language of K.S.A. 21-3211 with the necessary definition set forth in the Judicial Council Comments following the statute, and results in setting forth the requisite objective standard.

> The appeal is sustained.

MURDER AND THE REASONABLE MAN: PASSION AND FEAR IN THE CRIMINAL COURTROOM
Cynthia Lee, 2003

THE ASIAN-AS-FOREIGNER STEREOTYPE

Fear of the foreigner is sometimes a black streak that runs through America's political culture. We see instances of [this] when it involves hate crimes, not necessarily directed at black Americans, but at foreign Americans.

> - Mike McCurry, Former White House
> Press Secretary
> to President Bill Clinton

Even though it is oxymoronic to speak of "foreign" "Americans," the term "foreign Americans" conveys meaning. Asians and Latinos are usually considered foreign Americans. A person who asks an Asian American, "So, where are you from?" usually expects to hear, "I'm from Japan," or "I'm from China," or "I'm from Vietnam." If one answers, "I'm from Houston," or "I'm from New York," one is likely to be asked, "No, I mean, where are your parents from?" Even if true, it won't do to say, "My parents were also born in Houston," because the speaker is interested in finding out which foreign country the Asian person is from, even if she isn't from a foreign country.

The focus on the Asian in Asian American is deep-rooted. During World War II, when the United States was at war with Japan, hostility toward Japan extended to all persons of Japanese ancestry, even Japanese Americans born and raised in the United States for several generations. From 1942 to 1945, all persons of Japanese descent were forced to leave their homes and were incarcerated in internment camps because the American government viewed them as a potential threat.

In times of economic uncertainty, resentment and violence against Asian Americans seem to increase as individuals vent their frustrations on model-minority Asian Americans who are perceived as stealing valuable job opportunities from "real" Americans. Because many individuals can't tell Americans of Asian descent apart from Asian nationals, Asian Americans are mistaken for Asian nationals and then blamed for foreign imports that threaten domestic goods, such as America cars. In the film, *Who Killed Vincent Chin?* filmmakers Renee Tajima and Christine Choy illustrate the association between

Asians and foreign car imports by juxtaposing the image of angry White[a] American autoworkers and their friends taking turns swinging a baseball bat as hard as possible at a Japanese economy car with the actual baseball bat beating of Vincent Chin, a Chinese American man who was mistaken for a Japanese. Around the time of Chin's death, a Detroit radio station hosted "Toyota parties," encouraging people to demolish Japanese autos with a sledgehammer, and a car dealership in Detroit ran television commercials that showed a battle tank crushing a Japanese car.

The Asian-as-Foreigner stereotype continues today, although it often takes more subtle forms. During the O. J. Simpson trial, for example, much of the racial joking that arose in connection with the case was directed at two prominent Asian Americans, the presiding judge, Lance Ito, and the criminalist, Dennis Fung. Ito and Fung, both of whom speak English without a noticeable accent, were portrayed by radio station disk jockeys, publishing houses, and even a United States senator as bumbling, heavily accented Asians who could barely speak English. The 1996 campaign finance scandal involving Johnny Huang and the Democratic National Party and the December 1999 arrest of scientist Wen Ho Lee on charges of illegally downloading nuclear secrets raised the specter of the evil Asian foreigner again, prompting Neil Gotanda to opine that "The Wen Ho Lee case and the campaign finance scandals are the most serious threat to Asian Pacific Americans since the end of the Vietnam war."

Another example of the Asian-as-Foreigner stereotype at work is reflected in crimes of violence against Asians and Asian Americans. Jerry Kang has noted that Asian and Asian Americans are often targeted by muggers who assume that all Asians carry a lot of cash. The fact that some individuals from certain Asian countries do carry a lot of cash contributes to this type of targeting. A mugger who sees someone who looks Asian is not likely to know whether the person was born and raised in the United States or is from another country, and is not likely to ask. The problem is compounded by stereotypes about Asians as "physically weak and culturally adverse to defending themselves."

The Asian-as-Foreigner stereotype is complicated by the fact that approximately two-thirds of all Asians in the United States are foreigners. Frank Wu cautions us not to use this statistical information to "justify the assumption that everyone with an Asian name is a guest or a tourist," because such an assumption "leads to implications that the Asians are enjoying their sojourn and will ultimately return elsewhere."

---

[a]The author purposely capitalizes the "W" in "White" to draw attention to the fact that Whiteness is a socially constructed racial category.

Because of the constant conflation of Asian nationals and Asian Americans, symptomatic of the Asian-as-Foreigner stereotype, the tragic shooting of Yoshihiro Hattori, a Japanese foreign exchange student, has special significance for Asian Americans. Hattori died after being shot by a Louisiana homeowner who claimed he shot the unarmed Japanese teenager in self-defense.

October 17, 1992. Two sixteen-year-old high school students, Webb Haymaker and Yoshihiro Hattori, were looking for a Halloween party in the suburbs of Baton Rouge, Louisiana, when they came across the home of Rodney and Bonnie Peairs. The home was decorated for Halloween, and was just a few doors away from the correct house. Hattori was a Japanese foreign exchange student, and Haymaker was a member of his host family. Haymaker was dressed as a car accident victim. Hattori was dressed as the character played by John Travolta in the movie "Saturday Night Fever." He wore a white tuxedo jacket and carried a small black camera. The boys rang the front doorbell. No one answered the door, but the boys heard the clinking of window blinds coming from the carport area. The boys walked around the house to the carport, Haymaker leading the way. A moment later, Bonnie Peairs opened the back door leading out to the carport. She saw Haymaker, who started to say, "We're here for the party." Then Hattori came around the corner. When Bonnie Peairs saw Hattori, she emitted a scream, slammed the door, and called for her husband to "get the gun." Without asking any questions, Rodney Peairs ran to the bedroom and grabbed a laser-scoped .44 magnum Smith and Wesson, one of a number of guns he owned.

The two boys had walked away from the house and were on the sidewalk about ten yards from the house when Peairs rushed out of the house from the back door and into the carport area. The carport light and a street light in front of the house illuminated the carport and the sidewalk area. Hattori turned and approached Peairs, smiling and explaining in his broken English, "We are here for the party." Rather than telling Hattori that he had the wrong house, Peairs pointed his laser-scoped gun at Hattori and shouted, "Freeze." Hattori, who was from Japan, a country where firearms are prohibited, had never learned the English word "Freeze," so he continued to approach Peairs. Without waiting a second longer, Peairs fired one shot at Hattori's chest. Hattori collapsed and died on the spot. The entire incident – from the time Peairs opened his back door to the time he fired his gun – took place in approximately three seconds.

Peairs was charged with manslaughter. At trial, Peairs asserted that he shot Hattori in self-defense. He claimed that Hattori was skipping or walking very fast toward him and looked very scary. Peairs said Hattori, the slight teenage boy, looked like a crazy man. When Hattori did not stop after Peairs shouted at him to freeze, Peairs claimed he was terrified and thought his life was in danger. Although Hattori was carrying a camera, Peairs did not claim that he thought the camera was a gun. In fact, Peairs later admitted, during the course of the civil wrongful death action filed by Hattori's parents, that he did not see a gun, knife, stick, or club in Hattori's hand that night.

The judge instructed the jury that in order to acquit Peairs, they had to find that Peairs *reasonably* believed he was imminent danger of losing his life or receiving great bodily harm and that the killing was necessary to save Peairs from the danger. After little more than three hours of deliberation, the jury found Peairs not guilty of manslaughter. Spectators in the courtroom applauded the verdict. In contrast to the public outrage over the short deliberation process in the *O. J. Simpson* case, in which jurors reached a verdict of acquittal in less than four hours, there was little public outrage over the shortness of deliberation time leading to Peairs' acquittal. In fact, the residents of the town of Baton Rouge felt so strongly that Peairs was justified in shooting Hattori that they loudly objected to plans to erect a memorial in honor of Hattori.

The key question in the *Peairs* case was whether it was *reasonable* for Peairs to believe (1) that he was in imminent danger of death or great bodily harm, and (2) that is was necessary to shoot Hattori to protect himself from such imminent death or great bodily harm. Reasonable minds can certainly disagree on this question. On the one hand, Peairs had pointed a gun at Hattori and shouted at him to freeze. Hattori kept approaching. Arguably, the average Louisiana homeowner in Peairs' situation could have thought Hattori posed a very real threat of death or great bodily injury. If Hattori wouldn't stop after being warned to stop, there was nothing left to do but shoot. Additionally, this shooting took place in Louisiana. * * * [P]lace (i.e., geographic location) has some influence over whether the use of deadly force is seen as reasonable. Studies have shown that men in Southern states are more prone to perceive nonthreatening insults as a threat to their honor and more prone to respond violently to threats of a nondeadly nature.

On the other hand, Peairs could have completely avoided the shooting tragedy by retreating into his house and locking the door. Once inside, Peairs could have called the police. There was little reason to think Hattori would try to follow Peairs inside the house and force the door open. Recall that by the time Peairs came outside with his gun, the two boys were already on the sidewalk, leaving the premises. They were not hanging around near the back door, waiting for someone to open it so they could enter. Moreover, Peairs did not have to go outside in the first place. When his wife screamed at him to get the gun, Peairs could have asked her why she was screaming. He could have quickly locked the doors and called the police. In fact, if Hattori and Haymaker had been robbers, it would have been much safer for Peairs to lock the doors right away (to prevent entry into the home), rather than rushing to get a gun. Any of these less fatal measures would have avoided the imagined danger poised by Hattori.

How did the Asian-as-Foreigner stereotype influence the verdict in this case? The fact that Hattori was in fact a foreigner, a Japanese citizen and not an American, simply made it easier for the Baton Rouge jury to emphathize with Peairs. They could picture themselves in Peair's shoes. If an Asian teenager came onto their property and refused to freeze even with a gun pointed at his chest, that teenager was asking to be shot. Bonnie Peair's trial testimony is very revealing in this regard. When asked to describe Hattori, she responded, "I guess he appeared Oriental. He could have been Mexican or whatever." Mrs. Peairs was unable to tell whether Hattori was Asian or Mexican or neither. All she knew was that Hattori was different. He wasn't White like her.

Because of Hattori's nationality, the jurors couldn't see Hattori as one of their own sons. If Webb Haymaker, the boy from the neighborhood, had been the victim in this case, Peairs would have found it difficult to persuade the jury that he was terrified for his life and thought the boy looked like a crazy man. It would have been difficult for the defense to paint a credible picture of the victim as the bad guy. If Haymaker had been shot and killed, it is unlikely that the spectators in the courtroom would have applauded the not guilty verdict. Haymaker's parents and his siblings would have been in the courtroom, reminding the other members of that Baton Rouge community that the dead boy could have been their son. But it was a teenager from Japan who was shot and killed, and the sight of his grieving parents in the courtroom only served to remind the jurors that the victim was not one of the community's own. * * *

STATE v. STEWART
Supreme Court of Kansas
243 Kan. 639, 763 P.2d 572 (1988)

LOCKETT, J.

A direct appeal by the prosecution upon a question reserved asks whether the statutory justification for the use of deadly force in self-defense provided by K.S.A. 21-3211 excuses a homicide committed by a battered wife where there is no evidence of a deadly threat or imminent danger contemporaneous with the killing. An *amicus curiae* brief has been filed by the Kansas County and District Attorney Association.

Peggy Stewart fatally shot her husband, Mike Stewart, while he was sleeping. She was charged with murder in the first degree, K.S.A. 21-3401. Defendant pled not guilty, contending that she shot her husband in self-defense. Expert evidence showed that Peggy Stewart suffered from the battered woman syndrome. Based upon the battered woman syndrome, the trial judge instructed the jury on self-defense. The jury found Peggy Stewart not guilty.

The State stipulates that Stewart "suffered considerable abuse at the hands of her husband," but contends that the trial court erred in giving a self-defense instruction since Peggy Stewart was in no imminent danger when she shot her sleeping husband. We agree that under the facts of this case the giving of the self-defense instruction was erroneous. We further hold that the trial judge's self-defense instruction improperly allowed the jury to determine the reasonableness of defendant's belief that she was in imminent danger from her individual subjective viewpoint rather than the viewpoint of a reasonable person in her circumstances.

Following an annulment from her first husband and two subsequent divorces in which she was the petitioner, Peggy Stewart married Mike Stewart in 1974. Evidence at trial disclosed a long history of abuse by Mike against Peggy and her two daughters from one of her prior marriages. Laura, one of Peggy's daughters, testified that early in the marriage Mike hit and kicked Peggy, and that after the first year of the marriage Peggy exhibited signs of severe psychological problems. Subsequently, Peggy was hospitalized and diagnosed as having symptoms of paranoid schizophrenia; she responded to treatment and was soon released. It appeared to Laura, however, that Mike was encouraging Peggy to take more than her prescribed dosage of medication.

In 1977, two social workers informed Peggy that they had received reports that Mike was taking indecent liberties with her daughters. Because the social workers did not want Mike to be left alone with the girls, Peggy quit her job. In 1978, Mike began to taunt Peggy by stating that Carla, her 12-year-old daughter, was "more of a wife" to him than Peggy.

Later, Carla was placed in a detention center, and Mike forbade Peggy and Laura to visit her. When Mike finally allowed Carla to return home in the middle of summer, he forced her to sleep in an un-air conditioned room with the windows nailed shut, to wear a heavy flannel nightgown, and to cover herself with heavy blankets. Mike would then wake Carla at 5:30 a.m. and force her to do all the housework. Peggy and Laura were not allowed to help Carla or speak to her.

When Peggy confronted Mike and demanded that the situation cease, Mike responded by holding a shotgun to Peggy's head and threatening to kill her. Mike once kicked Peggy so violently in the chest and ribs that she required hospitalization. Finally, when Mike ordered Peggy to kill and bury Carla, she filed for divorce. Peggy's attorney in the divorce action testified in the murder trial that Peggy was afraid for both her and her children's lives.

One night, in a fit of anger, Mike threw Carla out of the house. Carla, who was not yet in her teens, was forced out of the home with no money, no coat, and no place to go. When the family heard that Carla was in Colorado, Mike refused to allow Peggy to contact or even talk about Carla.

Mike's intimidation of Peggy continued to escalate. One morning, Laura found her mother hiding on the school bus, terrified and begging the driver to take her to a neighbor's home. That Christmas, Mike threw the turkey dinner to the floor, chased Peggy outside, grabbed her by the hair, rubbed her face in the dirt, and then kicked and beat her.

After Laura moved away, Peggy's life became even more isolated. Once, when Peggy was working at a cafe, Mike came in and ran all the customers off with a gun because he wanted Peggy to go home and have sex with him right that minute. He abused both drugs and alcohol, and amused himself by terrifying Peggy, once waking her from a sound sleep by beating her with a baseball bat. He shot one of Peggy's pet cats, and then held the gun against her head and threatened to pull the trigger. Peggy told friends that Mike would hold a shotgun to her head and threaten to blow it off, and indicated that one day he would probably do it.

In May 1986, Peggy left Mike and ran away to Laura's home in Oklahoma. It was the first time Peggy had left Mike without telling him. Because Peggy was suicidal, Laura had her admitted to a hospital. There, she was diagnosed as having toxic psychosis as a result of an overdose of her medication. On May 30, 1986, Mike called to say he was coming to get her. Peggy agreed to return to Kansas. Peggy told a nurse she felt like she wanted to shoot her husband. At trial, she testified that she decided to return with Mike because she was not able to get the medical help she needed in Oklahoma.

When Mike arrived at the hospital, he told the staff that he "needed his housekeeper." The hospital released Peggy to Mike's care, and he immediately drove her back to Kansas. Mike told Peggy that all her problems were in her head and he would be the one to tell her what was good for her, not the doctors.

Peggy testified that Mike threatened to kill her if she ever ran away again. As soon as they arrived at the house, Mike forced Peggy into the house and forced her to have oral sex several times.

The next morning, Peggy discovered a loaded .357 magnum. She testified she was afraid of the gun. She hid the gun under the mattress of the bed in a spare room. Later that morning, as she cleaned house, Mike kept making remarks that she should not bother because she would not be there long, or that she should not bother with her things because she could not take them with her. She testified she was afraid Mike was going to kill her.

Mike's parents visited Mike and Peggy that afternoon. Mike's father testified that Peggy and Mike were affectionate with each other during the visit. Later, after Mike's parents had left, Mike forced Peggy to perform oral sex. After watching television, Mike and Peggy went to bed at 8:00 p.m. As Mike slept, Peggy thought about suicide and heard voices in her head repeating over and over, "kill or be killed." At this time, there were two vehicles in the driveway and Peggy had access to the car keys. About 10:00 p.m., Peggy went to the spare bedroom and removed the gun from under the mattress, walked back to the bedroom, and killed her husband while he slept. She then ran to the home of a neighbor, who called the police.

When the police questioned Peggy regarding the events leading up to the shooting, Peggy stated that things had not gone quite right that day, and that when she got the chance she hid the gun under the mattress. She stated that she shot Mike to "get this over with, this misery and this torment." When asked why she got the gun out, Peggy stated to the police:

> I'm not sure exactly what . . . led up to it . . . and my head
> started playing games with me and I got to thinking about
> things and I said I didn't want to be by myself again. . . . I got
> the gun out because there had been remarks made about me
> being out there alone. It was as if Mike was going to do
> something again like had been done before. He had gotten me
> down here from McPherson one time and he went and told them
> that I had done something and he had me put out of the house
> and was taking everything I had. And it was like he was going
> to pull the same thing over again.

Two expert witnesses testified during the trial. The expert for the defense, psychologist Marilyn Hutchinson, diagnosed Peggy as suffering from "battered woman syndrome," or post-traumatic stress syndrome. Dr. Hutchinson testified that Mike was preparing to escalate the violence in retaliation for Peggy's running away. She testified that loaded guns, veiled threats, and increased sexual demands are indicators of the escalation of the cycle.[a] Dr. Hutchinson believed Peggy had a repressed knowledge that she was in a "really grave lethal situation."

The State's expert, psychiatrist Herbert Modlin, neither subscribed to a belief in the battered woman syndrome nor to a theory of learned helplessness[b] as an explanation for why women do not leave an abusive relationship. Dr. Modlin testified that abuse such as repeated forced oral sex would not be trauma sufficient to trigger a post-traumatic stress disorder. He also believed Peggy was erroneously diagnosed as suffering from toxic psychosis. He stated that Peggy was unable to escape the abuse because she suffered from schizophrenia, rather than the battered woman syndrome.

At defense counsel's request, the trial judge gave an instruction on self-defense to the jury. The jury found Peggy not guilty. * * *

Although the State may not appeal an acquittal, it may reserve questions for appeal. We will not entertain an appeal by the prosecution merely to determine whether the trial court committed error. The appeal by the prosecution must raise a question of statewide interest, the answer to which is essential to the just administration of criminal law.

The question reserved is whether the trial judge erred in instructing on self-defense when there was no imminent threat to the defendant and no evidence of any argument or altercation between the defendant and the victim contemporaneous with the killing. We find this question and the related question of the extent to which evidence of the battered woman syndrome will be allowed to expand the statutory justification for the use of deadly force in self-defense are questions of statewide importance.

The State claims that under the facts the instruction should not have been given because there was no lethal threat to defendant contemporaneous with the killing. The State points out that Peggy's annulment and divorces from former husbands, and her filing for divorce after leaving Mike, proved that

---

[a] Dr. Hutchinson was referring to the "cycle of violence" in an abusive relationship which "begins with an initial building of tension and violence, culminates in an explosion, and end with a 'honeymoon.'" *State v. Stewart*, 243 Kan. 639 (1988) (J. Herd's dissent).

[b] According to Lenore Walker, women in abusive relationships become conditioned to believe they are helpless to stop or escape the violence. Lenore E.A. Walker, THE BATTERED WOMAN (1979)

Peggy knew there were non-lethal methods by which she could extricate herself from the abusive relationship. * * *

In *State v. Rose,* we approved an instruction on self-defense which stated in part: "[B]efore a person can take the life of another, it must reasonably appear that his own life must have been in imminent danger, or that he was in imminent danger of some great bodily injury from the hands of the person killed. No one can attack and kill another because he may fear injury at some future time." The perceived imminent danger had to occur in the present time, specifically during the time in which the defendant and the deceased were engaged in their final conflict.

These common-law principles were codified in K.S.A. 21-3211, which provides:

> A person is justified in the use of force against an aggressor when and to the extent it appears to him and he reasonably believes that such conduct is necessary to defend himself or another against such aggressor's imminent use of unlawful force.

The traditional concept of self-defense has posited one-time conflicts between persons of somewhat equal size and strength. When the defendant claiming self-defense is a victim of long-term domestic violence, such as a battered spouse, such traditional concepts may not apply. Because of the prior history of abuse, and the difference in strength and size between the abused and the abuser, the accused in such cases may choose to defend during a momentary lull in the abuse, rather than during a conflict. However, in order to warrant the giving of a self-defense instruction, the facts of the case must still show that the spouse was in imminent danger close to the time of the killing.

A person is justified in using force against an aggressor when it appears to that person and he or she reasonably believes such force to be necessary. A reasonable belief implies both an honest belief and the existence of facts which would persuade a reasonable person to that belief. A self-defense instruction must be given if there is any evidence to support a claim of self-defense, even if that evidence consists solely of the defendant's testimony.

Where self-defense is asserted, evidence of the deceased's long-term cruelty and violence towards the defendant is admissible. In cases involving battered spouses, expert evidence of the battered woman syndrome is relevant to a determination of the reasonableness of the defendant's perception of danger. Other courts which have allowed such evidence to be introduced include those in Florida, Georgia, Illinois, Maine, New Jersey, New York, Pennsylvania,

Washington, and Wisconsin. However, no jurisdictions have held that the existence of the battered woman syndrome in and of itself operates as a defense to murder.

In order to instruct a jury on self-defense, there must be some showing of an imminent threat or a confrontational circumstance involving an overt act by an aggressor. There is no exception to this requirement where the defendant has suffered long-term domestic abuse and the victim is the abuser. In such cases, the issue is not whether the defendant believes homicide is the solution to past or future problems with the batterer, but rather whether circumstances surrounding the killing were sufficient to create a reasonable belief in the defendant that the use of deadly force was necessary. * * *

Here, however, there [was] an absence of imminent danger to defendant: Peggy told a nurse at the Oklahoma hospital of her desire to kill Mike. She later voluntarily agreed to return home with Mike when he telephoned her. She stated that after leaving the hospital Mike threatened to kill her if she left him again. Peggy showed no inclination to leave. In fact, immediately after the shooting, Peggy told the police that she was upset because she thought Mike would leave her. Prior to the shooting, Peggy hid the loaded gun. The cars were in the driveway and Peggy had access to the car keys. After being abused, Peggy went to bed with Mike at 8 p.m. Peggy lay there for two hours, then retrieved the gun from where she had hidden it and shot Mike while he slept.

Under these facts, the giving of the self-defense instruction was erroneous. Under such circumstances, a battered woman cannot reasonably fear imminent life-threatening danger from her sleeping spouse. We note that other courts have held that the sole fact that the victim was asleep does not preclude a self-defense instruction. In *State v. Norman,* cited by defendant, the defendant's evidence disclosed a long history of abuse. Each time defendant attempted to escape, her husband found and beat her. On the day of the shooting, the husband beat defendant continually throughout the day, and threatened either to cut her throat, kill her, or cut off her breast. In the afternoon, defendant shot her husband while he napped. The North Carolina Court of Appeals held it was reversible error to fail to instruct on self-defense. The court found that, although decedent was napping at the time defendant shot him, defendant's unlawful act was closely related in time to an assault and threat of death by decedent against defendant and that the decedent's nap was "but a momentary hiatus in a continuous reign of terror."

There is no doubt that the North Carolina court determined that the sleeping husband was an evil man who deserved the justice he received from his battered wife. Here, similar comparable and compelling facts exist. But, as one court has stated: "To permit capital punishment to be imposed upon the subjective conclusion of the [abused] individual that prior acts and conduct of the deceased justified the killing would amount to a leap into the abyss of anarchy." Finally, our legislature has not provided for capital punishment for even the most heinous crimes.[c] We must, therefore, hold that when a battered woman kills her sleeping spouse when there is no imminent danger, the killing is not reasonably necessary and a self-defense instruction may not be given. To hold otherwise in this case would in effect allow the execution of the abuser for past or future acts and conduct. * * *

The appeal is sustained.

HERD, J., dissenting:

The sole issue before us on the question reserved is whether the trial court erred in giving a jury instruction on self-defense. We have a well-established rule that a defendant is entitled to a self-defense instruction if there is any evidence to support it, even though the evidence consists solely of the defendant's testimony. It is for the jury to determine the sincerity of the defendant's belief she needed to act in self-defense, and the reasonableness of that belief in light of all the circumstances.

It is not within the scope of appellate review to weigh the evidence. An appellate court's function is to merely examine the record and determine if there is *any* evidence to support the theory of self-defense. If the record discloses any competent evidence upon which self-defense could be based, then the instruction must be given. In judging the evidence for this purpose, all inferences should be resolved in favor of the defendant. * * *

It is evident from prior case law appellee met her burden of showing some competent evidence that she acted in self-defense, thus making her defense a jury question. She testified she acted in fear for her life, and Dr. Hutchinson corroborated this testimony. The evidence of Mike's past abuse, the escalation of violence, his threat of killing her should she attempt to leave him, and Dr. Hutchinson's testimony that appellee was indeed in a "lethal situation" more than met the minimal standard of "any evidence" to allow an instruction to be given to the jury.

Appellee introduced much uncontroverted evidence of the violent nature of the deceased and how he had brutalized her throughout their married life. It

---

[c]Two years after the decision in this case, the Kansas legislature passed a capital punishment statute, authorizing imposition of the death penalty for certain heinous crimes.

is well settled in Kansas that when self-defense is asserted, evidence of the cruel and violent nature of the deceased toward the defendant is admissible. The evidence showed Mike had a "Dr. Jekyll and Mr. Hyde" personality. He was usually very friendly and ingratiating when non-family persons were around, but was belligerent and domineering to family members. He had a violent temper and would blow up without reason. Mike was cruel to his two stepdaughters, Carla and Laura, as well as to the appellee. He took pride in hurting them or anything they held dear, such as their pets. Mike's violence toward appellee and her daughters caused appellee to have emotional problems with symptoms of paranoid schizophrenia. He would overdose appellee on her medication and then cut her off it altogether. Mike's cruelty would culminate in an outburst of violence, and then he would suddenly become very loving and considerate. This was very confusing to appellee. She lived in constant dread of the next outburst.

Appellee became progressively more passive and helpless during the marriage but finally became desperate enough to confront Mike and tell him the cruelty to her daughters had to stop. Mike responded by holding a shotgun to her head and threatening to kill her in front of the girls. The violence escalated. At one point, Mike kicked appellee so violently in the chest and ribs that she required hospitalization.

Mike threw twelve-year-old Carla out of the house without resources, and Laura left home as soon as she could. Mike would not let appellee see her daughters and ran Laura off with a shotgun when she tried to visit. Appellee's life became even more isolated. Towards the end, both the phone and utilities were disconnected from the house.

Appellee finally took the car and ran away to Laura's home in Oklahoma. It was the first time she had ever left Mike without telling him. She was suicidal and again hearing voices, and Laura had her admitted to a hospital. She was diagnosed as having toxic psychosis from a bad reaction to her medication. She soon felt better, but was not fully recovered, when Mike found out where she was and called her to say he was coming to get her. She told a nurse she felt like she wanted to shoot him, but the nurse noted her major emotion was one of hopelessness.

The hospital nevertheless released appellee to Mike's care, and he immediately drove her back to Kansas, telling her on the way she was going to have to "settle down now" and listen to him because he was the boss. *He said if she ever ran away again, he would kill her.*

When they reached the house, Mike would not let appellee bring in her suitcases and forced her to have oral sex four or five times in the next 36 hours, with such violence that the inside of her mouth was bruised. The next morning, appellee found a box of bullets in the car that had not been there before. She then discovered a loaded .357 magnum. This frightened her, because Mike had promised to keep his guns unloaded. She did not know how to unload the gun, so she hid it under the mattress of the bed in a spare room. As she cleaned house, Mike remarked she should not bother, because she would not be there long. He told her she should not bother with her things, because she could not take them with her. She took these statements to mean she would soon be dead and she grew progressively more terrified. Throughout the day Mike continued to force her to have oral sex, while telling her how he preferred sex with other women.

The sexual abuse stopped when Mike's parents came to visit. Mike's father testified everything seemed normal during their stay. After the visit, Mike again forced appellee to perform oral sex and then demanded at 8:00 p.m. she come to bed with him. The cumulative effect of Mike's past history, coupled with his current abusive conduct, justified appellee's belief that a violent explosion was imminent. As he slept, appellee was terrified and thought about suicide and heard voices in her head repeating over and over, "kill or be killed." The voices warned her there was going to be killing and to get away.

She went to the spare bedroom and removed the gun from under the mattress, walked back to the bedroom, and fatally shot Mike. After the first shot, she thought he was coming after her so she shot again and fled wildly outside, barefoot, wearing only her underwear. Ignoring the truck and car outside, although she had the keys in her purse inside, she ran over a mile to the neighbors' house and pled with them to keep Mike from killing her. She thought she had heard him chasing her. The neighbor woman took the gun from appellee's hand and gave her a robe while her husband called the sheriff. The neighbor testified appellee appeared frightened for her life and was certain Mike was alive and looking for her.

Psychologist Marilyn Hutchinson qualified as an expert on the battered woman syndrome and analyzed the uncontroverted facts for the jury. She concluded appellee was a victim of the syndrome and reasonably believed she was in imminent danger. In *State v. Hodges,* we held it appropriate to permit expert testimony on the battered woman syndrome to prove the reasonableness of the defendant's belief she was in imminent danger. Most courts which have addressed the issue are in accord.

The majority implies its decision is necessary to keep the battered woman syndrome from operating as a defense in and of itself. It has always been clear the syndrome is not a defense itself. Evidence of the syndrome is admissible only because of its relevance to the issue of self-defense. The majority of jurisdictions have held it beyond the ordinary jury's understanding why a battered woman may feel she cannot escape, and have held evidence of the battered woman syndrome proper to explain it. The expert testimony explains how people react to circumstances in which the average juror has not been involved. It assists the jury in evaluating the sincerity of the defendant's belief she was in imminent danger requiring self-defense and whether she was in fact in imminent danger.

Dr. Hutchinson explained to the jury at appellee's trial the "cycle of violence" which induces a state of "learned helplessness" and keeps a battered woman in the relationship. She testified appellee was caught in a such a cycle. The cycle begins with an initial building of tension and violence, culminates in an explosion, and ends with a "honeymoon." The woman becomes conditioned to trying to make it through one more violent explosion with its battering in order to be rewarded by the "honeymoon phase," with its expressions of remorse and eternal love and the standard promise of "never again." After all promises are broken time after time and she is beaten again and again, the battered woman falls into a state of learned helplessness where she gives up trying to extract herself from the cycle of violence. She learns fighting back only delays the honeymoon and escalates the violence. If she tries to leave the relationship, she is located and returned and the violence increases. She is a captive. She begins to believe her husband is omnipotent, and resistance will be futile at best.

It is a jury question to determine if the battered woman who kills her husband as he sleeps fears he will find and kill her if she leaves, as is usually claimed. Under such circumstances the battered woman is not under actual physical attack when she kills but such attack is imminent, and as a result she believes her life is in imminent danger. She may kill during the tension-building stage when the abuse is apparently not as severe as it sometimes has been, but nevertheless has escalated so that she is afraid the acute stage to come will be fatal to her. She only acts on such fear if she has some survival instinct remaining after the husband-induced "learned helplessness."

Dr. Hutchinson testified the typical batterer has a dichotomous personality, in which he only shows his violent side to his wife or his family. A batterer's major characteristic is the need to blame all frustration on someone else. In a typical battering relationship, she said, the husband and wife are in traditional sex roles, the wife has low self-esteem, and the husband abuses drugs or alcohol. The husband believes the wife is his property and what he does to her is no one's business. There is usually a sense of isolation, with the woman not allowed to speak with friends or children. Overlying the violence is the intimation of death, often created by threats with weapons.

It was Dr. Hutchinson's opinion Mike was planning to escalate his violence in retaliation against appellee for running away. She testified that

Mike's threats against appellee's life, his brutal sexual acts, and appellee's discovery of the loaded gun were all indicators to appellee the violence had escalated and she was in danger. Dr. Hutchinson believed appellee had a repressed knowledge she was in what was really a gravely lethal situation. She testified appellee was convinced she must "kill or be killed." * * *

The majority claims permitting a jury to consider self-defense under these facts would permit anarchy. This underestimates the jury's ability to recognize an invalid claim of self-defense. Although this is a case of first impression where an appeal by the State has been allowed, there have been several similar cases in which the defendant appealed on other grounds. In each of these cases where a battered woman killed the sleeping batterer, a self-defense instruction has been given when requested by the defendant. * * *

The majority bases its opinion on its conclusion appellee was not in imminent danger, usurping the right of the jury to make that determination of fact. The majority believes a person could not be in imminent danger from an aggressor merely because the aggressor dropped off to sleep. This is a fallacious conclusion. For instance, picture a hostage situation where the armed guard inadvertently drops off to sleep and the hostage grabs his gun and shoots him. The majority opinion would preclude the use of self-defense in such a case. * * *

In *State v. Hundley*, we joined other enlightened jurisdictions in recognizing that the jury in homicide cases where a battered woman ultimately kills her batterer is entitled to all the facts about the battering relationship in rendering its verdict. The jury also needs to know about the nature of the cumulative terror under which a battered woman exists and that a batterer's threats and brutality can make life-threatening danger imminent to the victim of that brutality even though, at the moment, the batterer is passive. Where a person believes she must kill or be killed, and there is the slightest basis in fact for this belief, it is a question for the jury as to whether the danger was imminent. I confess I am an advocate for the constitutional principle that in a criminal prosecution determination of the facts is a function of the jury, not the appellate court.

I would deny this appeal.

Note

Evidence of "battered women's syndrome" (BWS) has increasingly been admissible in court in civil and criminal cases involving domestic violence. The pioneering social science researcher in this area has been Lenore Walker, who treats BWS as a sub-category of post-traumatic stress syndrome, consisting of "a collection of thoughts, feelings, and actions that logically follow a frightening experience that one expects could be repeated." Lenore E.A. Walker, *Battered Women Syndrome and Self-Defense*, 6 Notre Dame J. L., Ethics & Pub. Pol'y 321, 327 (1992); *see also* Lenore E.A. Walker, THE BATTERED WOMAN (1979) and THE BATTERED WOMAN SYNDROME (2d ed. 1984).

Walker defines a battered woman as someone "in an intimate relationship with a man who repeatedly subjects * * * her to forceful physical and/or psychological abuse," where "repeatedly" is defined as "more than once" and "abuse" includes any of six categories of behavior, from life-threatening violence to "extreme verbal harassment and expressing comments of a derogatory nature with negative value judgments." Walker, THE BATTERED WOMAN SYNDROME 203 (2d ed. 1984). In the courts, as the *Stewart* opinion indicates, Walker's theories are often reduced to two basic psychological concepts: the "cycle of violence" and "learned helplessness."

Recently, Walker's research and the concepts of learned helplessness, the cycle of violence, and even the term "battered woman's syndrome" itself have come under fire. David L. Faigman and Amy J. Wright, for example, question the evidence for both the "cycle of violence" and "learned helplessness." Reviewing Walker's research methods, Faigman and Wright note that Walker's technique allowed subjects to guess the answer the researchers were looking for, and that her theory relies heavily on the interviewers' interpretations of their subjects' responses. Moreover, Walker's own data indicate that not all subjects, or even most subjects, actually experienced all three stages of the cycle of violence. *See* David L. Faigman & Amy J. Wright, *The Battered Woman's Syndrome in the Age of Science*, 39 Ariz. L. Rev. 67, 77-78 (1997). Faigman and Wright are also critical of Walker's use of the concept of learned helplessness, noting that it emerged from experiments with dogs and that, unlike dogs, women continue to resist their batterers in numerous ways rather than becoming completely passive and unable to respond. *Id.* at 79. Faigman and Wright conclude, "The battered woman syndrome illustrates all that is wrong with the law's use of science." *Id.* at 68.

Feminist activists and scholars, too, have been critical of the BWS concept and of Walker's theories. First, the name "battered women's syndrome" suggests that only women can be victims. Although the vast majority of intimate violence is in fact perpetrated on women by men, domestic violence exists in the gay, lesbian, bisexual, and transgender communities as well, and men may also be battered by women. Children and the elderly, as well, may suffer psychological and physical abuse from intimates. Moreover, BWS suggests that women who are abused are victims who lack agency. Elizabeth Schneider argues, in contrast, that survivors of domestic violence must be seen as exercising agency within social as well as psychological constraints. Elizabeth M. Schneider, *Particularity and Generality: Challenges of Feminist Theory and Practice in Work on Woman-Abuse*, 67 N.Y.U. L. Rev. 520, 548-550 (1992).

Second, critics fear that too-rigid application of the cycle of violence and learned helplessness theories will cause some trial judges to deny the admission of expert testimony on BWS when the defendant does not exhibit all the symptoms identified by Walker or when the defendant seems insufficiently "sick" or psychologically disturbed. The psychological focus of BWS evidence arguably reinforces longstanding stereotypes about men and women, rather than combating them. The result of these combined pressures may be that in order to get their case to the jury, lawyers for battered women may have to paint their clients as passive, frightened, and mentally disturbed, and morally pure as well -- a process that in itself may be a degrading experience for the defendant. As Michael Dowd comments:

> "Good" battered women are passive, loyal housewives, acting as loving companions to their abusers. These women must have flawless characters and continually appeal to the police and courts for help, regardless of the futility of their efforts. By contrast, the "bad" battered woman is one who fails to possess any of the virtues of the "good" woman, and who may have even obtained an education and pursued a career. This demonstration of control often operates to disqualify the "bad" battered woman from the group. Infidelity or abuse of drugs is equally discrediting.

Michael Dowd, *Dispelling the Myths About the "Battered Woman's Defense": Towards a New Understanding*, 19 Fordham Urb. L.J. 567, 581 (1992). Sharon Angella Allard adds that black women have particular difficulty being perceived by juries and judges as fitting into the "good" battered woman category. Sharon Angella Allard, *Rethinking Battered Woman Syndrome: A Black Feminist Perspective*, 1 UCLA Women's L.J. 191, 197 (1991) (arguing that black women tend to be seen as acting out of revenge and anger rather than fear).

Third, the psychological focus of BWS evidence tends to obscure its relevance to the objective elements of a self-defense claim. For example, BWS evidence could be introduced to show that the defendant was correct in believing that she was facing a threat of death because of her long experience with the batterer and her ability to read even subtle physical and verbal cues. BWS evidence could also be introduced to show that escape is much less easy than it might appear to a jury, since batterers frequently go to great lengths to hunt down their partners and since victims are most likely to be killed when they are attempting to leave the relationship.

Recent activism on battering has renamed the topic as "battering and its effects," rather than the diagnosis of a particular "syndrome" particular to women. Recent social science, as well, emphasizes physical battering as one element of a larger pattern of control. One team of researchers describes the concept of a "culture of battering":

> The culture of battering refers to the relationship context of an abusive relationship. The first of the three elements of the culture of battering is the abuse, which includes at least one of the following types: physical, emotional, sexual, familial, and property. Professionals have increasingly recognized non-physical forms of abuse as harmful to domestic violence victims. The second element is the systematic pattern of domination and control that the batterer exerts over his victim. This pattern may be initiated by the batterer's gradual imposition of a series of rules that his victim must follow or be punished for violating. * * * The third element, hiding, denying, and minimizing the abuse, refers to typical coping strategies that battered women use to reduce the psychological impact of the abuse. Each of these elements to some degree must be present in order for a culture of battering to be established. * * *

Karla Fischer, Neil Vidmar & René Ellis, *The Culture of Battering and the Role of Mediation in Domestic Violence Cases*, 46 SMU L. Rev. 2117, 2141, 2121-2122 (1993). How, if at all, does this expanded concept of "the culture of battering" fit legal concepts of self-defense?

JURIES AND EXPERT EVIDENCE: SOCIAL FRAMEWORK TESTIMONY
Neil Vidmar & Regina A. Schuller
52 Law & Contemp. Probs. 133 (1989)

During the past decade and a half, courts have been faced with an increasing number of attempts to have social science experts testify about such matters as eyewitness unreliability, post-traumatic stress disorders, or cross-cultural differences in the meaning of behavior. The purpose of the testimony, to which Walker and Monahan have given the generic label of "social framework evidence" in order to distinguish it from other forms of social science evidence, is to provide the factfinder, usually a jury, with information about the social and psychological context in which contested adjudicative facts occurred. It is presumed that knowledge about the context will help the factfinder interpret the contested adjudicative facts. * * *

A partial list of evidence that would qualify as social framework evidence would include testimony on eyewitness reliability, predictions of dangerousness, battered woman syndrome, rape trauma syndrome, behavioral and psychological symptoms of sexually abused children, battered child syndrome, "brainwashed" defendants, Vietnam veterans syndrome, discriminatory behavior, effects of cultural stress, and psycholinguistic meaning.

Despite the wide variety of substantive topics and the use of the evidence for different litigation goals, all this evidence shares the common characteristic of employing general conclusions drawn from social science research to help evaluate factual issues in a specific case. In each instance, the evidence involves general assertions about some aspect of human behavior that is intended to help the trier of fact, usually a jury, to interpret the meaning of some disputed fact or testimony at issue in the suit.

In theory, social framework testimony does not bear directly on the ultimate fact to be decided by the trier; rather, it provides a social and psychological context in which the trier can understand and evaluate claims about the ultimate fact. Thus, a psychologist called to testify about potential eyewitness unreliability does not assert that the eyewitness in the particular case is wrong, only that studies of perception and recall indicate that people in similar contexts are often wrong. To cite another example, an expert called to testify about rape trauma syndrome, in a case where the defendant disputes the complainant's testimony that she did not consent to sexual intercourse, describes studies on the characteristic reactions and behavior patterns of women who have been sexually assaulted. Although in some instances the expert may also be allowed to indicate that the complainant herself exhibits these characteristic symptoms, the testimony revolves around characteristics of a class of persons, sexual assault victims. The factfinder may then use this information to evaluate case-specific evidence.

Several matters regarding the conceptualization of social framework evidence need to be discussed at this point. First, as Walker and Monahan observe, not only is the basic thrust of social framework evidence probabilistic in nature, it may also address past, present, or future events. Where eyewitness reliability is in dispute, the issue is whether the eyewitness is mistaken about a past event. Testimony about dangerousness, of course, represents a judgment about future behavior. The expert testimony on allegations of sexual abuse of a child may relate to the validity of the child's current retraction of previous allegations. Social framework evidence, therefore, is not bounded by time constraints.

A second characteristic of social framework evidence is that the research is often, though not invariably, "off the rack." The studies relied upon by the experts are usually conducted and published well before the disputed events occurred, and involve persons having no connection to the legal proceeding. Often the research was never intended for use in a legal setting, but addressed a problem in another context. For example, the data on rape trauma syndrome were derived from studies originally intended to help devise therapeutic measures for rape victims. Many of the studies that experts cite in testimony about the unreliability of eyewitnesses were conducted in settings and contexts removed from the conditions involved in the identification offered in the specific case. In our view, however, Walker and Monahan place too much emphasis on the "off the rack" nature of social framework evidence. Research intended for social framework applications can be undertaken with the express purpose of use in a particular case. To cite one example, in cases where it is suspected that a line-up was biased, research bearing on the line-up procedure using groups of people having no connection to the case can be generated specifically for that trial. One can easily conceive of litigation-driven social framework research with respect to other issues. In short, "off the rack" research is not a necessary characteristic of social framework evidence.

Social framework evidence may be based on large sets of systematically analyzed data bases or simply on clinical experience. Walker and Monahan cite *State v. Davis* as an example of a large-scale data set. In *Davis*, a defendant who pleaded guilty to murder offered the testimony of a sociologist in the penalty trial, which was held to determine whether the defendant should be executed or receive a mandatory thirty-year minimum sentence. The sociologist's opinion was not based upon a personal evaluation of Davis. Rather, it was based upon published studies and government statistics indicating that murderers have low rates of recidivism and that persons of the age Davis would be after serving the mandatory sentence are unlikely to commit violent crimes. In contrast to these kinds of data, which are usually summarized by means of computer processing with disaggregation and probability projections according to type of offense or demographic characteristics of the offenders, consider *Barefoot v. Estelle*. In *Barefoot*, the defendant had been found guilty of murder; in the penalty trial, the prosecution called two psychiatrists to testify about the probability that someone like Barefoot would constitute a continuing danger to society. As in *Davis*, neither of these experts personally interviewed Barefoot. Unlike *Davis*, neither psychiatrist relied on aggregated statistical information. Rather, both were asked to testify about their own professional experience with convicted felons and were asked hypothetical questions about the likelihood that someone with Barefoot's characteristics would commit violence in the future. The data bases were statistical only in the sense that they involved an aggregation of the psychiatrists' own clinical experience with similar persons. Yet, in both *Davis* and *Barefoot*, the evidence referred to empirical relationships beyond the confines of the particular case.

Thus, the data bases from which social framework evidence is drawn vary along continuums of rigor and size. The type of data, the specific profession of the expert who presents the data, and other factors may affect how the jury receives and uses the evidence. Conceptually, however, social framework evidence can be defined solely by its function: to supply the triers with information about some aspect of human behavior to aid in interpreting disputed facts.

Note

The widespread acceptance of "battered women's syndrome" evidence in the courtroom is due to the activism of feminist lawyers in the 1970s and 1980s, and their sense that the law of self defense as it stood disserved women. Another feminist criticism of the law of self-defense is that it assumes that the parties involved in a physical confrontation meet on more or less equal terms. The next case, *State v. Wanrow*, illustrates one court's sensitivity to this concern.

STATE v. WANROW
Supreme Court of Washington
88 Wash. 2d 221, 559 P.2d 548 (1977)

UTTER, Associate Justice.

Yvonne Wanrow was convicted by a jury of second-degree murder and first-degree assault. She appealed her conviction to the Court of Appeals. The Court of Appeals reversed and remanded the case. * * * We granted review and affirm the Court of Appeals.

We order a reversal of the conviction on two grounds. The first is the ground stated by the Court of Appeals regarding the erroneous admission of the tape recording. The second ground is error committed by the trial court in improperly instructing the jury on the law of self-defense as it related to the defendant.

On the afternoon of August 11, 1972, defendant's (respondent's) two children were staying at the home of Ms. Hooper, a friend of defendant. Defendant's son was playing in the neighborhood and came back to Ms. Hooper's house and told her that a man tried to pull him off his bicycle and drag him into a house. Some months earlier, Ms. Hooper's 7-year-old daughter had developed a rash on her body which was diagnosed as venereal disease. Ms. Hooper had been unable to persuade her daughter to tell her who had molested her. It was not until the night of the shooting that Ms. Hooper discovered it was

William Wesler (decedent) who allegedly had violated her daughter. A few minutes after the defendant's son related his story to Ms. Hooper about the man who tried to detain him, Mr. Wesler appeared on the porch of the Hooper house and stated through the door, 'I didn't touch the kid, I didn't touch the kid.' At that moment, the Hooper girl, seeing Wesler at the door, indicated to her mother that Wesler was the man who had molested her. Joseph Fah, Ms. Hooper's landlord, saw Wesler as he was leaving and informed Shirley Hooper that Wesler had tried to molest a young boy who had earlier lived in the same house, and that Wesler had previously been committed to the Eastern State Hospital for the mentally ill. Immediately after this revelation from Mr. Fah, Ms. Hooper called the police who, upon their arrival at the Hooper residence, were informed of all the events which had transpired that day. Ms. Hooper requested that Wesler be arrested then and there, but the police stated, 'We can't, until Monday morning.' Ms. Hooper was urged by the police officer to go to the police station Monday morning and 'swear out a warrant.' Ms. Hooper's landlord, who was present during the conversation, suggested that Ms. Hooper get a baseball bat located at the corner of the house and 'conk him over the head' should Wesler try to enter the house uninvited during the weekend. To this suggestion, the policeman replied, 'Yes, but wait until he gets in the house.' (A week before this incident Shirley Hooper had noticed someone prowling around her house at night. Two days before the shooting someone had attempted to get into Ms. Hooper's bedroom and had slashed the window screen. She suspected that such person was Wesler.)

That evening, Ms. Hooper called the defendant and asked her to spend the night with her in the Hooper house. At that time she related to Ms. Wanrow the facts we have previously set forth. The defendant arrived sometime after 6 p.m. with a pistol in her handbag. The two women ultimately determined that they were too afraid to stay alone and decided to ask some friends to come over for added protection. The two women then called the defendant's sister and brother-in-law, Angie and Chuck Michel. The four adults did not go to bed that evening, but remained awake talking and watching for any possible prowlers. There were eight young children in the house with them. At around 5 a.m., Chuck Michel, without the knowledge of the women in the house, went to Wesler's house, carrying a baseball bat. Upon arriving at the Wesler residence, Mr. Michel accused Wesler of molesting little children. Mr. Wesler then suggested that they go over to the Hooper residence and get the whole thing straightened out. Another man, one David Kelly, was also present, and together the three men went over to the Hooper house. Mr. Michel and Mr. Kelly remained outside while Wesler entered the residence.

The testimony as to what next took place is considerably less precise. It appears that Wesler, a large man who was visibly intoxicated, entered the home and when told to leave declined to do so. A good deal of shouting and confusion then arose, and a young child, asleep on the couch, awoke crying. The testimony indicates that Wesler than approached this child, stating, 'My what a cute little boy,' or words to that effect, and that the child's mother, Ms. Michel, stepped between Wesler and the child. By this time Hooper was screaming for Wesler to get out. Ms. Wanrow, a 5' 4" woman who at the time had a broken leg and was using a crutch, testified that she then went to the front door to enlist the aid of Chuck Michel. She stated that she shouted for him and, upon turning around to reenter the living room, found Wesler standing directly behind her. She testified to being gravely startled by this situation and to having then shot Wesler in what amounted to a reflex action.

After Wesler was shot, Ms. Hooper called the police via a Spokane crime check emergency phone number, stating, 'There's a guy broke in, and my girlfriend shot him.' The defendant later took the phone and engaged in a conversation with the police operator. The entire conversation was tape recorded.

At trial, over defense counsel's objection, the tape was admitted into evidence. After presentation of the evidence, the jury was instructed on the law and commenced deliberations. Deliberations progressed for a time, and the jurors requested to hear the tape again. The request was granted. Not long after reviewing the tape, the jury reached its verdict of guilty as to both counts. * * *

[The court concludes that the tape recording should not have been admitted into evidence.]

Reversal of respondent's conviction is also required by a second serious error committed by the trial court. Instruction No. 10, setting forth the law of self-defense, incorrectly limited the jury's consideration of acts and circumstances pertinent to respondent's perception of the alleged threat to her person. * * *

In the opening paragraph of instruction No. 10, the jury, in evaluating the gravity of the danger to the respondent, was directed to consider only those acts and circumstances occurring 'at or immediately before the killing . . .' This is not now, and never has been, the law of self-defense in Washington. On the contrary, the justification of self-defense is to be evaluated in light of *all* the facts and circumstances known to the defendant, including those known substantially before the killing. * * *

The second paragraph of instruction No. 10 contains an equally erroneous and prejudicial statement of the law. That portion of the instruction reads:

> However, when there is no reasonable ground for the person attacked to believe that *his* person is in imminent danger of death or great bodily harm, and it appears to *him* that only an ordinary battery is all that is intended, and all that *he* has reasonable grounds to fear from *his* assailant, *he* has a right to stand *his* ground and repel such threatened assault, yet *he* has no right to repel a threatened assault with naked hands, by the use of a deadly weapon in a deadly manner, unless *he* believes, *and has reasonable grounds to believe*, that *he* is in imminent danger of death or great bodily harm.

(Italics ours.) In our society women suffer from a conspicuous lack of access to training in and the means of developing those skills necessary to effectively repel a male assailant without resorting to the use of deadly weapons. Instruction No. 12 does indicate that the 'relative size and strength of the persons involved' may be considered; however, it does not make clear that the defendant's actions are to be judged against her own subjective impressions and not those which a detached jury might determine to be objectively reasonable.
* * *

The second paragraph of instruction No. 10 not only establishes an objective standard, but through the persistent use of the masculine gender leaves the jury with the impression the objective standard to be applied is that applicable to an altercation between two men. The impression created-- that a 5' 4" woman with a cast on her leg and using a crutch must, under the law, somehow repel an assault by a 6' 2" intoxicated man without employing weapons in her defense, unless the jury finds her determination of the degree of danger to be objectively reasonable--constitutes a separate and distinct misstatement of the law and, in the context of this case, violates the respondent's right to equal protection of the law. The respondent was entitled to have the jury consider her actions in the light of her own perceptions of the situation, including those perceptions which were the product of our nation's 'long and unfortunate history of sex discrimination.' *Frontiero v. Richardson*, 411 U.S. 677, 684, 93 S.Ct. 1764, 1769, 36 L.Ed.2d 583 (1973). Until such time as the effects of that history are eradicated, care must be taken to assure that our self-defense instructions afford women the right to have their conduct judged in light of the individual physical handicaps which are the product of sex discrimination. To fail to do so is to deny the right of the individual woman involved to trial by the same rules which are applicable to male defendants. The portion of the instruction above quoted misstates our law in creating an objective standard of 'reasonableness.' It then compounds that error by utilizing language suggesting that the respondent's conduct must be measured against that of a reasonable male individual finding himself in the same circumstances.

We conclude that the instruction here in question contains an improper statement of the law on a vital issue in the case, is inconsistent, misleading and prejudicial when read in conjunction with other instructions pertaining to the same issue, and therefore is a proper basis for a finding of reversible error. * * *

In light of the errors in admission of evidence and instruction of the jury, the decision of the Court of Appeals is affirmed, the conviction reversed, and the case remanded for a new trial.

[The concurring opinion of WRIGHT, J., and the dissenting opinion of HAMILTON, J., have been omitted.]

2.   Imperfect Self-Defense

What if you honestly believe that force is necessary on the present occasion, but your belief is unreasonable? Or, what if someone attacks you with nondeadly force, and you wrongfully escalate the conflict by using deadly force? Under the traditional common law approach, if the victim dies you will be convicted of murder; you do not have a valid self-defense claim. However, in some states, your crime may be mitigated in a homicide prosecution from murder to voluntary manslaughter. This doctrine is called "imperfect self-defense." *See, e.g., In re Christian S.*, 7 Cal.4th 768, 30 Cal.Rptr.2d 33, 872 P.2d 574 (1994).

What is the rationale for this mitigation? The idea is that we need a middle ground between a complete defense and no defense. The person who honestly, even if wrongly and unreasonably, believes that force is necessary is not as culpable as someone who knows or believes that it is not. Similarly, a nondeadly aggressor who then becomes the victim of deadly violence shares some fault with the victim.

The mitigation principle incorporated in the doctrine of imperfect self-defense is incorporated, as well, in the justification defenses set out in the Model Penal Code. Section 3.09(2) provides that when the actor seeking an affirmative defense for the use of force is reckless or negligent in having a belief about the necessity of that force under the circumstances, or when the actor is reckless or negligent in acquiring or failing to acquire material knowledge concerning the justifiability of her use of force, she loses any justification defense as against prosecutions based on recklessness or negligence. The result, then, is similar to that achieved by the doctrine of imperfect self-defense. The actor who is acquitted of the charged offense on the ground of self-defense may be found guilty of a less serious crime which requires proof of recklessness or negligence as the mental state.

3. Defense of Others

A close cousin of self-defense, defense of others is a justification defense used when a person uses force against another person to defend a third person he thinks is in imminent danger of unlawful attack. Like self-defense, defense of others includes a triggering condition (a third person under imminent unlawful attack), a necessity requirement, and a proportionality requirement (deadly force may only be used to protect the third party from death or grievous bodily injury). Moreover, like self-defense, defense of others requires that the defendant honestly and *reasonably* believed the force he used was necessary to protect the third person from an imminent unlawful attack.

The older common law approach to defense of others diverged from self-defense doctrine in two ways. First, the older common law included an "Act-at-Peril" rule which permitted the use of force in defense of a third person only if the defendant was correct about the third person's ability to use force in self-defense. In other words, the defendant who came to a third person's rescue did so at his peril. If it turned out that the third person had no right to use force in self-defense, then the defendant would have no defense. Second, under the older common law approach, the defense was only available if the defendant was in a particular status relationship with the person being protected. In other words, the third person being protected had to be a close relative, or in some cases the servant or employee of the defendant.

Today, most jurisdictions have done away with both the Act-at-Peril rule and the status relationship limitation. When *People v. Young* was decided, however, the Act-at-Peril rule was the majority rule at the time. Note how the dissent makes use of the doctrine of mistake of fact in order to challenge the outcome. How would this case come out under the Model Penal Code?

PEOPLE v. YOUNG
Court of Appeals of New York
11 N.Y.2d 274, 183 N.E.2d 319 (1962)

PER CURIAM

Whether one, who in good faith aggressively intervenes in a struggle between another person and a police officer in civilian dress attempting to effect the lawful arrest of the third person, may be properly convicted of assault in the third degree[a] is a question of law of first impression here.

The opinions in the court below in the absence of precedents in this State carefully expound the opposing views found in other jurisdictions. The majority in the Appellate Division have adopted the minority rule in the other States that one who intervenes in a struggle between strangers under the mistaken but reasonable belief that he is protecting another who he assumes is being unlawfully beaten is thereby exonerated from criminal liability. The weight of authority holds with the dissenters below that one who goes to the aid of a third person does so at his own peril.

While the doctrine espoused by the majority of the court below may have support in some States, we feel that such a policy would not be conducive to an orderly society. We agree with the settled policy of law in most jurisdictions that the right of a person to defend another ordinarily should not be greater than such person's right to defend himself.[b] * * *

In this case there can be no doubt that the defendant intended to assault the police officer in civilian dress. The resulting assault was forceful. Hence motive or mistake of fact is of no significance as the defendant was not charged with a crime requiring such intent or knowledge. To be guilty of third degree assault "It is sufficient that the defendant voluntarily intended to commit the unlawful act of touching." Since in these circumstances the aggression was inexcusable the defendant was properly convicted.

Accordingly, the order of the Appellate Division should be reversed and the information reinstated.

FROESSEL, J., dissenting

---

[a] Under New York law, a person is guilty of assault in the third degree, a class A misdemeanor, when:
1. With intent to cause physical injury to another person, he causes such injury to such person or to a third person; or
2. He recklessly causes physical injury to another person; or
3. With criminal negligence, he causes physical injury to another person by means of a deadly weapon or a dangerous instrument.
N.Y. Penal Law § 120.00 (McKinney 1998).

[b] New York Penal Law § 35.27 states that "A person may not use physical force to resist an arrest, whether authorized or unauthorized, which is being effected or attempted by a police officer or peace officer when it would reasonably appear that the latter is a police officer or peace officer." N.Y. Penal Law § 35.27 (McKinney 1998).

The law is clear that one may kill in defense of another when there is reasonable, though mistaken, ground for believing that the person slain is about to commit a felony or to do some great personal injury to the apparent victim; yet the majority now hold, for the first time, that in the event of a simple assault under similar circumstances, the mistaken belief, no matter how reasonable, is no defense.

Briefly, the relevant facts are these: On a Friday afternoon at about 3:40, Detectives Driscoll and Murphy, not in uniform, observed an argument taking place between a motorist and one McGriff in the street in front of premises 64 West 54th Street, in midtown Manhattan. Driscoll attempted to chase McGriff out of the roadway in order to allow traffic to pass, but McGriff refused to move back; his actions caused a crowd to collect. After identifying himself to McGriff, Driscoll placed him under arrest. As McGriff resisted, defendant "came out of the crowd" from Driscoll's rear and struck Murphy about the head with his fist. In the ensuing struggle Driscoll's right kneecap was injured when defendant fell on top of him. At the station house, defendant said he had not known or thought Driscoll and Murphy were police officers.

Defendant testified that while he was proceeding on 54th Street he observed two white men, who appeared to be 45 or 50 years old, pulling on a "colored boy" (McGriff), who appeared to be a lad about 18, whom he did not know. The men had nearly pulled McGriff's pants off, and he was crying. Defendant admitted he knew nothing of what had transpired between the officers and McGriff, and made no inquiry of anyone; he just came there and pulled the officer away from McGriff.

Defendant was convicted of assault [in the] third degree. In reversing upon the law and dismissing the information, the Appellate Division held that one is not "criminally liable for assault in the third degree if he goes to the aid of another whom he mistakenly, but *reasonably*, believes is being unlawfully beaten, and thereby injures one of the apparent assaulters" (emphasis supplied). While in my opinion the majority below correctly stated the law, I would reverse here and remit so that the Appellate Division may pass on the question of whether or not defendant's conduct was reasonable in light of the circumstances presented at the trial.

As the majority below pointed out, assault is a crime derived from the common law. Basic to the imposition of criminal liability both at common law and under our statutory law is the existence in the one who committed the prohibited act of what has been variously termed a guilty mind, a *mens rea* or a criminal intent.

Criminal intent requires an awareness of wrongdoing. When conduct is based upon mistake of fact reasonably entertained, there can be no such awareness and, therefore, no criminal culpability. In *People ex rel. Hegeman v. Corrigan* we stated: "it is very apparent that the innocence or criminality of the intent in a particular act generally depends on the knowledge or belief of the actor at the time. An honest and *reasonable* belief in the existence of circumstances which, if true, would make the act for which the defendant is prosecuted innocent, would be a good defense." (Emphasis supplied.)

It is undisputed that defendant did not know that Driscoll and Murphy were detectives in plain clothes engaged in lawfully apprehending an alleged disorderly person. If, therefore, defendant *reasonably* believed he was lawfully assisting another, he would not have been guilty of a crime. Subdivision 3 of section 246 of the Penal Law provides that it is not unlawful to use force "When committed either by the party about to be injured or *by another person in his aid or defense, in preventing or attempting to prevent an offense against his person,* * * * if the force or violence used is not more than sufficient to prevent such offense" (emphasis supplied). The law is thus clear that if defendant entertained an "honest and reasonable belief" that the facts were as he perceived them to be, he would be exonerated from criminal liability.

By ignoring one of the most basic principles of criminal law -- that crimes *mala in se* require proof of at least general criminal intent -- the majority now hold that the defense of mistake of fact is "of no significance." We are not here dealing with one of "a narrow class of exceptions" where the Legislature has created crimes which do not depend on *criminal* intent but which are complete on the mere intentional doing of an act *malum prohibitum.*

There is no need, in my opinion, to consider the law of other States, for New York policy clearly supports the view that one may act on appearances reasonably ascertained. * * * Our Penal Law, to which I have already alluded, is a statement of that policy. The same policy was expressed by this court in *People v. Maine.* There, the defendant observed his brother fighting in the street with two other men; he stepped in and stabbed to death one of the latter. The defense was justifiable homicide under the predecessor of section 1055. The court held it reversible error to admit into evidence the declarations of the defendant's brother, made before defendant happened upon the scene, which tended to show that the brother was the aggressor. We said: "Of course the acts and conduct of the defendant must be judged solely with reference to the situation as it was when he first and afterwards saw it." Mistake of relevant fact, reasonably entertained, is thus a defense to homicide under section 1055, and one who kills in defense of another and proffers this defense of justification is to be judged according to the circumstances as they appeared to him.

The mistaken belief, however, must be one which is reasonably entertained, and the question of reasonableness is for the trier of the facts. "The question is not merely what did the accused believe, but also, what did he have the right to believe?" Without passing on the facts of the instant case, the Appellate Division had no right to assume that defendant's conduct was reasonable, and to dismiss the information as a matter of law. Nor do we have the right to reinstate the verdict without giving the Appellate Division the opportunity to pass upon the facts.

Although the majority of our court are now purporting to fashion a policy "conducive to an orderly society," by their decision they have defeated their avowed purpose. What public interest is promoted by a principle which would deter one from coming to the aid of a fellow citizen who he has reasonable ground to apprehend is in imminent danger of personal injury at the hands of assailants? Is it reasonable to denominate, as justifiable homicide, a slaying committed under a mistaken but reasonably held belief, and deny this same defense of justification to one using less force? Logic, as well as historical background and related precedent, dictates that the rule and policy expressed by our Legislature in the case of homicide, which is an assault resulting in death, should likewise be applicable to a much less serious assault not resulting in death.

I would reverse the order appealed from and remit the case to the Appellate Division pursuant to section 543-b of the Code of Criminal Procedure "for determination upon the questions of fact raised in that court."

4.   Defense of Habitation

In contrast to the long acceptance in Anglo-American law of the right to use deadly force to defend oneself or, in some cases, another person from a deadly attack, it is well-settled that deadly force is not permissible simply in defense of property. Between these two clear rules lies a gray area: the so-called "defense of habitation." Under what circumstances should the law permit the occupant of a dwelling to use deadly force against an intruder?

The original common law rule permitted an occupant of the dwelling to use any force necessary, including deadly force, if he reasonably believed the force was necessary to prevent an imminent unlawful entry. In some jurisdictions that follow the common law, the original rule has been modified to restrict the use of deadly force to cases in which the occupant reasonably believes such force is necessary to prevent imminent unlawful entry *and* the intruder intends to commit a felony or cause injury to the occupant or another occupant of the dwelling. In other jurisdictions that incorporate the common law, the requirements are even more stringent. In these states, the occupant of a dwelling may use deadly force against an intruder only if he reasonably believes that such force is necessary to prevent imminent unlawful entry *and* that the intruder intends to commit a forcible felony or kill or cause grievous bodily injury to the occupant or another occupant of the dwelling. Note that in these jurisdictions, the defense of habitation can be described as a kind of "accelerated" self-defense or defense of others.

People v. Brown examines the question whether entry onto an unenclosed front porch constitutes an entry into the residence under California's defense of habitation.

PEOPLE v. BROWN
Court of Appeal of California, Third District
6 Cal. App. 4th 1489, 8 Cal.Rptr.2d 513 (Ct. App. 1992)

Davis, J.

A jury convicted defendant of assault with a deadly weapon and found he personally used a firearm, but did not personally inflict great bodily injury on the victim. There was evidence showing the victim entered defendant's front porch and advanced toward defendant with a hammer raised back at shoulder-height after the two had argued about a contract under which the victim was to perform landscaping work at defendant's house. At this point, defendant, standing in the doorway of his home, shot the victim in the leg. According to defendant he did so in fear for his life.

In the published portion of this opinion, we hold that defendant was not entitled to a requested instruction based on section 198.5, the "Home Protection Bill of Rights."[a] Although there was evidence that the victim's entry onto defendant's front porch was unlawful and forcible, an entry onto a front porch like defendant's does not constitute entry into a residence as required under section 198.5. The porch in this case is an unenclosed front porch, without any

---

[a] Section 198.5 [of the California Penal Code] provides: "Any person using force intended or likely to cause death or great bodily injury within his or her residence shall be presumed to have held a reasonable fear of imminent peril of death or great bodily injury to self, family, or a member of the household when that force is used against another person, not a member of the family or household, who unlawfully and forcibly enters or has unlawfully and forcibly entered the residence and the person using the force knew or had reason to believe that an unlawful and forcible entry occurred. As used in this section, great bodily injury means a significant or substantial physical injury."

signs, gates or other indications that would tend to show the residential occupant did not expect intrusion into that area. The porch is connected to a walkway, which is connected to a driveway, which in turn is connected to a public sidewalk. There is a doorbell adjacent to the front door to signal the arrival of persons on the porch. * * * Using principles developed by this court in *People v. Nible,* we conclude that, under these circumstances, a residential occupant does not have a reasonable expectation of protection from unauthorized intrusion onto the porch and thus an entry there does not entitle a defendant occupant to an instruction based on section 198.5. In this situation, the occupant is left with the standard instructions on self-defense. * * *

Background

What began as a minor contract dispute between a homeowner and a bricklayer ended with the homeowner shooting the bricklayer in the leg. About a month before the incident in question, defendant, the homeowner, and Jason Neal, the bricklayer, entered into a contract. Neal was to lay a brick flower bed at defendant's home, and defendant was to pay for labor and certain materials. The contract was to be completed over a two-week period in April because defendant had guests arriving at the end of that time. Prior to April 14, defendant and Neal had some minor disagreement regarding Neal's performance, but Neal was to finish the job.

On April 14, Neal arrived at defendant's house around 11:30 a.m. to continue his work. This time he brought an acquaintance, Butler, to help him. Neal, Butler and defendant gave varying accounts of what happened next.

Neal's Testimony

As soon as Neal arrived at defendant's house on April 14, defendant came out of the garage and told Neal he thought Neal was going to be there earlier that morning. Defendant told Neal he should get his tools and leave without finishing the job. Defendant then said Neal could go ahead and finish, because he (defendant) had company arriving the next day. Defendant then changed his mind again and told Neal to get his tools from the porch; defendant also said he was keeping the tools Neal had stored in defendant's backyard because he had paid for them.

At this point, Neal acknowledges that defendant and he had a "disagreement." However, Neal maintained it never escalated to anything more than a "man-to-man discussion." After that, defendant shut the garage door and went into his house. Neal then took his tools from the porch, put them beside his car, and walked back toward the house with a hammer in his hand. When he reached the flower bed, he began knocking off the top layer of bricks because he was angry at being fired. Neal testified he was turned oblong with his back towards the front door of defendant's house, approximately seven feet from the door.

After defendant walked into the house, Neal did not see defendant again until after he heard the gun go off. He did not hear defendant say anything other than his name before he heard the gunshot. Neal denied threatening or attacking defendant.

Butler's Testimony

When Butler and Neal arrived at defendant's house on April 14, defendant told Neal to pack up his tools and go home, "he was through." Neal and defendant then had a "heated discussion." Neal got some tools from the porch and set them by his car, then walked back toward the porch with empty hands. After defendant went into the garage, Neal picked up the rest of his tools and starting hitting the bricks he had laid, saying, "he [defendant] wasn't going to pay him for it, so he [Neal] was going to take it out."

Neal was facing the front door while he was hitting the bricks. Defendant came to the screen door and told Neal "you better," then shot Neal in the leg. Neal never attempted to throw the hammer, attack defendant, or strike anything but the bricks in the flower bed. Neal never tried to enter the house. Butler testified he could not remember how high Neal swung the hammer, but Neal was intent on hammering the bricks.

Defendant's Testimony

On April 14, defendant reminded Neal their agreement was that the work would be finished within two weeks, which meant Neal had only until the next day to complete the job. Yet, Neal had just delivered the balance of the bricks the previous day. Defendant did not think Neal could finish in that short time, so he told Neal to get his tools and go, that he would find someone else to finish the job.

At this point Neal picked up a "brick carry," walked over to defendant and started waving it around. Defendant backed further into the garage and warned Neal he was going to close the garage door. When Neal left the garage and passed a stack of bricks, he angrily kicked the pile down. Once inside the house, defendant heard a "hammering noise." Defendant hurried to the front door and saw Neal hammering away at the flower bed; defendant then started out the screen door and said something like, "Cut it out! Stop! Stop! Stop!"

Once defendant opened the screen door and started out, Neal looked up and saw defendant. He raised up and swung back with the hammer, then came off the flower bed with the hammer in his right hand, raised to his shoulder. He whirled around and began moving towards defendant, "not fast, but deliberate." Defendant testified Neal was like a "raging" animal and was in a "very antagonistic mood."

When defendant realized that only the screen door stood between himself and Neal, he jumped back inside and tried closing the screen door. He was very afraid, and concerned only with how to stop Neal and protect himself. Because of some problem with the hydraulic on the screen door, defendant believed he had to hold onto it or else it would fly open. Defendant testified he could not reach around the wooden door, which was open and to his left, in time to shut it, without letting go of the screen door. So, while holding onto the screen door handle, defendant picked up a handgun, which was lying under a cloth on a room divider next to the door. By this time, Neal had stepped over the flower bed and had come up to the first level of the porch, approximately five feet from defendant. Defendant fired the gun through the screen door, hitting Neal in the leg.

Defendant was afraid and "knew [Neal] was going to attack [him] with that hammer ...." Defendant testified he intended to shoot down at the ground and sidewalk. He wasn't trying to hit Neal, but rather to stop him. Neal's right leg was on the porch when defendant shot him.

Discussion

1. Defendant's Requested Jury Instruction on Section 198.5

Section 198.5, enacted in 1984 and entitled the "Home Protection Bill of Rights," creates a rebuttable presumption that a residential occupant has a reasonable fear of death or great bodily injury when he or she uses deadly force against an unlawful and forcible intruder into the residence. For section 198.5 to apply, four elements must be met. There must be an unlawful and forcible entry into a residence; the entry must be by someone who is not a member of the family or the household; the residential occupant must have used "deadly" force against the victim within the residence; and finally, the residential occupant must have had knowledge of the unlawful and forcible entry.

These four elements would comprise the heart of any instruction based on section 198.5. The trial court refused defendant's request to instruct under section 198.5 because the court found no evidence of "entry" into the "residence."

It is undisputed there was evidence showing that Neal's entry onto the porch was unlawful and forcible; that Neal was not a member of defendant's family or household; that defendant's firing of the gun constituted use of deadly force under section 198.5; and that defendant knew of Neal's unlawful and forcible entry, since he testified he ordered Neal off the property and then saw Neal approach menacingly with a hammer and told him to stop. The issue narrows to whether Neal's entry onto defendant's front porch constituted an entry into defendant's residence. In other words, is an entry onto an unenclosed front porch (a porch that has no access barriers from a public sidewalk) an entry into a residence, so that a residential occupant who uses deadly force against an unlawful and forcible intruder becomes entitled, upon request, to a jury instruction based on section 198.5? We conclude there was no residential entry here.

This issue requires us to examine the scope of the term "residence" in section 198.5 as it relates to a front porch. The plain language of section 198.5 shows the statute was intended to give residential occupants additional protection in situations where they are confronted in their own homes by unlawful intruders such as burglars. It is appropriate, therefore, to look at relevant burglary cases to determine whether there was an entry into a residence in this case.

Preliminarily, we note that California's statutory definition of burglary is broader than the common law definition. Under California law, a breaking is no longer required. Furthermore, California case law has expanded the definition of a burglarious entry into a building or residence, to encompass situations where burglary would be inapplicable under the common law.

The California Courts of Appeal have formed various tests for determining the scope of the terms "residence" or "building" for burglarious entry. We conclude the reasonable expectation test this court formulated in *Nible* is the appropriate one to employ here. Since one of the purposes of the burglary statute is to protect against unauthorized entry and the attendant danger that the occupant will react violently to the intrusion, the reasonable expectation test focuses on the protection the inhabitants of a structure reasonably expect. In situations implicating this particular purpose, the proper question is whether the nature of a structure's composition is such that a reasonable person would expect some protection from unauthorized intrusions. In *Nible*, this court held that a reasonable person would believe a window screen provides some protection against unauthorized intrusions, noting that even an open door or window affords some expectation of such protection because reasonable persons understand the social convention that portals may not be crossed without permission from the structure's owner.

This safety-based reasonable expectation test is appropriate for the issue presented here involving section 198.5. This is because section 198.5 gives a defendant a rebuttable presumption that he was in reasonable fear of imminent danger when he used deadly force within his residence against an intruder (most likely a burglar) who unlawfully and forcibly entered the residence. As noted in *Owen*, section 198.5 establishes a presumption "'that the very act of forcible entry entails a threat to the life and limb of the homeowner.'"

Applying this reasonable expectation test to the ordinary, unenclosed front porch at issue here, we conclude that Neal's entry onto the porch cannot constitute entry into defendant's residence for purposes of section 198.5. A reasonable person would not expect protection from unauthorized intrusion onto this kind of porch. Quite the contrary. Social convention dictates that anyone wishing to summon the occupant's presence or gain entry into the home must first enter the porch. The porch is not a portal. Absent "no soliciting" signs or a gate or some other barrier, Girl Scouts selling cookies, the person delivering the newspaper, the door-to-door salesperson or any stranger will likely come onto a front porch of this nature, without permission. The reasonable residential occupant would not react violently to this entry. We find that a residential occupant does not have a reasonable expectation of protection from unauthorized intrusion onto a front porch like the one involved in this case.

Defendant argues that a reasonable person would have an expectation of protection because of the threat of immediate access to the home. It is true that once on the porch, particularly if the front door is open (as it was in this case), an intruder would have ready access to the home. It is nonetheless a qualitatively lesser expectation of protection than that recognized in section 198.5, and a situation which is adequately covered by the self-defense doctrine. If a residential occupant reasonably believes that bodily injury is about to be inflicted upon him or her by the intruder's presence on the porch, then the occupant can use reasonable force to repel the intruder, and the occupant, if tried, would be entitled to self-defense instructions.

Defendant relies on *In re Christopher J.* That reliance is misplaced. There, the Fourth District held that entry into a carport with intent to commit theft constituted a burglary because the carport was "an integral part of the dwelling house." The carport was roofed and attached to the dwelling house on one side; also, it was enclosed in the rear with a half-wall and open on two sides. * * *

We hold that a residential occupant does not have a reasonable expectation of protection from unauthorized intrusion onto the kind of front porch involved in this case, and therefore entry onto such a porch does not constitute entry into a residence for section 198.5 purposes. The trial court correctly denied defendant's request for a jury instruction based on section 198.5, which would have given defendant a rebuttable presumption that he was in reasonable fear of imminent danger when he used deadly force against Jason Neal. * * *

We remand for resentencing in accord with the views expressed in this opinion. In all other respects, the judgment is affirmed.

5.   Defense of Property

As a general matter, one is not allowed to use deadly force in defense of property. As we have seen, however, the existence of a "defense of habitation" or a privilege to use deadly force against home intruders, blurs the line between defense of property and defense of self and others. In *People v. Ceballos* and the article that follows, note the overlap, in fact, in law, and in culture, between defending one's self and defending one's property. *Ceballos* also addresses the problems raised by the use of automatic protection devices.

PEOPLE v. CEBALLOS
Supreme Court of California
12 Cal.3d 470, 526 P.2d 241, 116 Cal.Rptr. 233 (1974)

BURKE, J.

Don Ceballos was found guilty by a jury of assault with a deadly weapon. Imposition of sentence was suspended and he was placed on probation. He appeals from the judgment, contending primarily that his conduct was not unlawful because the alleged victim was attempting to commit burglary when hit by a trap gun mounted in the garage of defendant's dwelling and that the court erred in instructing the jury. We have concluded that the former argument lacks merit, that the court did not commit prejudicial error in instructing the jury, and that the judgment should be affirmed.

Defendant lived alone in a home in San Anselmo. The regular living quarters were above the garage, but defendant sometimes slept in the garage and had about $2,500 worth of property there. In March 1970 some tools were stolen from defendant's home. On May 12, 1970, he noticed the lock on his garage doors was bent and pry marks were on one of the doors. The next day he mounted a loaded .22 caliber pistol in the garage. The pistol was aimed at the center of the garage doors and was connected by a wire to one of the doors so that the pistol would discharge if the door was opened several inches.

The damage to defendant's lock had been done by a 16-year-old boy named Stephen and a 15-year-old boy named Robert. On the afternoon of May 15, 1970, the boys returned to defendant's house while he was away. Neither boy was armed with a gun or knife. After looking in the windows and seeing no one, Stephen succeeded in removing the lock on the garage doors with a crowbar, and, as he pulled the door outward, he was hit in the face with a bullet from the pistol. Stephen testified: He intended to go into the garage "[for] musical equipment" because he had a debt to pay to a friend. His "way of paying that debt would be to take [defendant's] property and sell it" and use the proceeds to pay the debt. He "wasn't going to do it [i.e., steal] for sure, necessarily." He was there "to look around," and "getting in, I don't know if I would have actually stolen."

Defendant, testifying in his own behalf, admitted having set up the trap gun. He stated that after noticing the pry marks on his garage door on May 12, he felt he should "set up some kind of a trap, something to keep the burglar out of my home." When asked why he was trying to keep the burglar out, he replied, ". . . Because somebody was trying to steal my property . . . and I don't want to come home some night and have the thief in there . . . usually a thief is pretty desperate . . . and . . . they just pick up a weapon . . . if they don't have one . . . and do the best they can." When asked by the police shortly after the shooting why he assembled the trap gun, defendant stated that "he didn't have much and he wanted to protect what he did have."

As heretofore appears, the jury found defendant guilty of assault with a deadly weapon. An assault is "an unlawful attempt, coupled with a present ability, to commit a violent injury on the person of another."

Defendant contends that had he been present he would have been justified in shooting Stephen since Stephen was attempting to commit burglary, that * * * defendant had a right to do indirectly what he could have done directly, and that therefore any attempt by him to commit a violent injury upon Stephen was not "unlawful" and hence not an assault. The People argue that * * * as a matter of law a trap gun constitutes excessive force, and that in any event the circumstances were not in fact such as to warrant the use of deadly force.

The issue of criminal liability under statutes such as Penal Code section 245 where the instrument employed is a trap gun or other deadly mechanical device appears to be one of first impression in this state, but in other jurisdictions courts have considered the question of criminal and civil liability for death or injuries inflicted by such a device.

At common law in England it was held that a trespasser, having knowledge that there are spring guns in a wood, cannot maintain an action for an injury received in consequence of his accidentally stepping on the wire of such gun. That [rule] aroused such a protest in England that it was abrogated seven years later by a statute, which made it a misdemeanor to set spring guns with intent to inflict grievous bodily injury but excluded from its operation a spring gun set between sunset and sunrise in a dwelling house for the protection thereof.

In the United States, courts have concluded that a person may be held criminally liable under statutes proscribing homicides and shooting with intent to injure, or civilly liable, if he sets upon his premises a deadly mechanical device and that device kills or injures another. However, an exception to the rule that there may be criminal and civil liability for death or injuries caused by such a device has been recognized where the intrusion is, in fact, such that the person, were he present, would be justified in taking the life or inflicting the bodily harm with his own hands. The phrase "were he present" does not hypothesize the actual presence of the person, but is used in setting forth in an indirect manner the principle that a person may do indirectly that which he is privileged to do directly.

Allowing persons, at their own risk, to employ deadly mechanical devices imperils the lives of children, firemen and policemen acting within the scope of their employment, and others. Where the actor is present, there is always the possibility he will realize that deadly force is not necessary, but deadly mechanical devices are without mercy or discretion. Such devices "are silent instrumentalities of death. They deal death and destruction to the innocent as well as the criminal intruder without the slightest warning. The taking of human life [or infliction of great bodily injury] by such means is brutally savage and inhuman."

It seems clear that the use of such devices should not be encouraged. Moreover, whatever may be thought in torts, the foregoing rule setting forth an exception to liability for death or injuries inflicted by such devices "is inappropriate in penal law for it is obvious that it does not prescribe a workable standard of conduct; liability depends upon fortuitous results." We therefore decline to adopt that rule in criminal cases. * * *

Furthermore, even if that rule were applied here, * * * defendant was not justified in shooting Stephen. Penal Code section 197 provides: "Homicide is . . . justifiable . . . 1. When resisting any attempt to murder any person, or to commit a felony, or to do some great bodily injury upon any person; or, 2. When committed in defense of habitation, property, or person, against one who manifestly intends or endeavors, by violence or surprise, to commit a felony. .

. . ." Since a homicide is justifiable under the circumstances specified in section 197, *a fortiori* an attempt to commit a violent injury upon another under those circumstances is justifiable.

By its terms subdivision 1 of Penal Code section 197 appears to permit killing to prevent any "felony," but in view of the large number of felonies today and the inclusion of many that do not involve a danger of serious bodily harm, a literal reading of the section is undesirable. *People v. Jones* read into section 197, subdivision 1, the limitation that the felony be "some atrocious crime attempted to be committed by force." * * *

* * * [W]hatever may have been the very early common law, the rule developed at common law that killing or use of deadly force to prevent a felony was justified only if the offense was a forcible and atrocious crime. * * *

Examples of forcible and atrocious crimes are murder, mayhem, rape and robbery. In such crimes "from their atrocity and violent human life [or safety] either is, or is presumed to be, in peril."

Burglary has been included in the list of such crimes. However, in view of the wide scope of burglary under Penal Code section 459, as compared with the common law definition of that offense, in our opinion it cannot be said that under all circumstances burglary under section 459 constitutes a forcible and atrocious crime.[2]

Where the character and manner of the burglary do not reasonably create a fear of great bodily harm, there is no cause for exaction of human life, or for the use of deadly force. The character and manner of the burglary could not reasonably create such a fear unless the burglary threatened, or was reasonably believed to threaten, death or serious bodily harm.

In the instant case the asserted burglary did not threaten death or serious bodily harm, since no one but Stephen and Robert was then on the premises. A defendant is not protected from liability merely by the fact that the intruder's conduct is such as would justify the defendant, were he present, in believing that

---

[2] At common law burglary was the breaking and entering of a mansion house in the night with the intent to commit a felony. Burglary under Penal Code section 459 differs from common law burglary in that the entry may be in the daytime and of numerous places other than a mansion house, and breaking is not required. For example, under section 459 a person who enters a store with the intent of committing theft is guilty of burglary. It would seem absurd to hold that a store detective could kill that person if necessary to prevent him from committing that offense.

the intrusion threatened death or serious bodily injury. There is ordinarily the possibility that the defendant, were he present, would realize the true state of affairs and recognize the intruder as one whom he would not be justified in killing or wounding.

We thus conclude that defendant was not justified under Penal Code section 197, subdivisions 1 or 2, in shooting Stephen to prevent him from committing burglary. * * *

We recognize that our position regarding justification for killing under Penal Code section 197, subdivisions 1 and 2, differs from the position of section 143, subdivision (2), of the Restatement Second of Torts, regarding the use of deadly force to prevent a "felony . . . of a type . . . involving the breaking and entry of a dwelling place" but in view of the supreme value of human life we do not believe bodily force can be justified to prevent all felonies of the foregoing type, including ones in which no person is, or is reasonably believed to be, on the premises except the would-be burglar. * * *

Defendant also argues that had he been present he would have been justified in shooting Stephen under subdivision 4 of Penal Code section 197, which provides, "Homicide is . . . justifiable . . . 4. When necessarily committed in *attempting*, by lawful ways and means, *to apprehend* any person for any felony committed. . . ." (Italics added.) The argument cannot be upheld. The words "attempting. . . to apprehend" contain the idea of acting for the purpose of apprehending. * * * Here no showing was made that defendant's intent in shooting was to apprehend a felon. Rather it appears from his testimony and extrajudicial statement heretofore recited that his intent was to prevent a burglary, to protect his property, and to avoid the possibility that a thief might get into defendant's house and injure him upon his return. * * *

Defendant also does not, and could not properly, contend that the intrusion was in fact such that, were he present, he would be justified under Civil Code section 50 in using deadly force. That section provides, "Any necessary force may be used to protect from wrongful injury the person or property of oneself. . . ." This section also should be read in the light of the common law, and at common law in general deadly force could not be used solely for the protection of property. "'The preservation of human life and limb from grievous harm is of more importance to society than the protection of property.'" * * *

At common law an exception to the foregoing principle that deadly force could not be used solely for the protection of property was recognized where the property was a dwelling house in some circumstances. * * * Also at common law if another attempted to burn a dwelling the owner was privileged to use deadly force if this seemed necessary to defend his "castle" against the threatened harm. Further, deadly force was privileged if it was, or reasonably seemed, necessary to protect the dwelling against a burglar.

Here we are not concerned with dispossession or burning of a dwelling, and, as heretofore concluded, the asserted burglary in this case was not of such a character as to warrant the use of deadly force. * * *

We conclude that as a matter of law the exception to the rule of liability for injuries inflicted by a deadly mechanical device does not apply under the circumstances here appearing. * * *

The judgment is affirmed.

KILLER OF THIEF WINS WIDE SUPPORT
Jeffrey Bair
The San Diego Union Tribune, Dec. 27, 1994, at A-8[1]

ERIE, Pa. – Barkeeper Thomas Radu shot an unarmed thief in the back of the head. That much is clear. The question is whether he had good reason.

The 70-year-old tavern owner is accused of killing James Blum after catching Blum with his hand in the till Nov. 4 in the latest in a series of robberies at what a neighbor called a workingman's bar. As Blum's partner watched, Radu grabbed his gun and fired, police said. Blum – who had been a suspect in some of the 10 robberies at the bar during the previous three months – fell near the door of the nearly empty tavern with a bullet in his brain and a wad of bills in his possession.

A prosecutor has been considering for nearly two months whether to drop a homicide charge against Radu, who has considerable support from friends and strangers. "He's no hero, but I think that he should be relieved of the whole thing," grocer Mike Dowd said. "Look at what he was facing. The only people in there were two baddy-bads, so to speak. And they had no intention of leaving. They had the intention of beating the hell out of him." Radu is free pending a hearing Jan. 6 and has been back at Radu's Tavern, which he has operated for 35 years. His lawyer, David Ridge, said Radu was defending himself. District

---

[1] Reprinted with permission of The Associated Press.

Attorney Rusty Cunningham must determine whether Radu himself was threatened, as required by law for a finding of justifiable homicide.

History could be on Radu's side. In 1991, a jury in Erie needed only two hours to clear garage owner Daniel Strong of wounding two stereo thieves with a shotgun. "I hope the man gets off," Strong said about Radu. "If somebody is willing to take the risk of robbing somebody, of maybe doing harm, of being lazy and breaking the law to take what someone else like me has worked hard for, then he is taking the chance of losing his life, too."

When WLKK talk show host Barry Dain Steinhagen suggested Radu should be prosecuted because he was not in danger, callers overwhelmingly favored dropping the charge. "Some of them are saying, 'Enough is enough.'" Steinhagen said. "Sure, people are frustrated. But what I was saying was that Radu had no right to take matters into his own hands."

Radu's neighbors say he was frustrated with frequent robberies at the brick tavern where he was known to have a low tolerance for sloppy drunks and other troublemakers. He cherished the metal shop and paper mill workers who unwound at Radu's Tavern after their shifts – hard-working men like him. Radu has said he does not want to discuss the shooting.

Note

As indicated in *People v. Ceballos*, another situation in which force, including deadly force, may sometimes be justified is when a person is attempting to prevent the commission of a felony, or attempting to apprehend a fleeing felon. The older common law approach permitted any force, including deadly force, in both the prevention and the detention of felons, although in some jurisdictions the privilege to use deadly force to stop a fleeing felon was limited by a kind of "Act-at-Peril" rule under which the privilege was lost if the person killed or injured turned out to be an innocent bystander. *See, e.g., People v. Piorkowski*, 41 Cal.App.3d 324 (Cal. Ct. App. 1974) (the use of deadly force by a private citizen in arresting a fleeing felon is only privileged if a felony was in fact committed and the defendant had reasonable cause for believing the person arrested to have committed it).

As *Ceballos* also suggests, whether and in what circumstances deadly force should be used to defend oneself against burglary remains a contested issue. Consider the case that follows.

PEOPLE v. QUESADA

113 Cal.App.3d 533, 169 Cal.Rptr. 881 (Cal.App.1980)

GRODIN, J.

Defendant's house was burglarized during the night while no one was at home. Two days later, under circumstances we shall describe, defendant shot and killed the burglar. In response to charges of murder with use of a firearm, defendant claimed justification under Penal Code section 197, subdivision 4, which provides that "[h]omicide is ... justifiable ... When necessarily committed in attempting, by lawful ways and means, to apprehend any person for any felony committed, ..." By case law, that justification exists "only where the felony committed is one which threatens death or great bodily harm." The trial court instructed the jury that it was its duty to determine whether the burglary met that description, taking into account the surrounding facts. The jury, apparently rejecting the asserted justification defense, found defendant guilty of involuntary manslaughter and found also that he used a firearm in the commission of that offense. The trial court suspended imposition of sentence, and defendant was admitted to probation conditioned on confinement in the county jail for one year.

On appeal, appellant contends that burglary at night is *necessarily* a felony which threatens death or bodily injury for purposes of determining the justifiability of deadly force used by a citizen to apprehend the burglar, and that the trial court erred in not so instructing the jury. Alternatively, he contends that the firearm use finding should be stricken because such use was an element of the involuntary manslaughter offense which he was found to have committed. We are not persuaded by either contention for the reasons which follow, and therefore affirm.

The Factual Setting. The following synopsis is based primarily on appellant's testimony at trial. In the evening of January 24, 1979, appellant left his apartment to go bowling. When he returned at 2 a.m. the following morning he found that it had been ransacked and that a number of valuable items, including his stereo, had been stolen. No one was in the apartment when the burglary occurred.

Later that day appellant told a neighbor, Art Sanchez, about the theft. The following day, January 26, Sanchez informed appellant that a person named Edie had asked Sanchez if he knew anyone who wanted to buy a stereo. Sanchez related to appellant Edie's description of the stereo and appellant concluded from the description that the stereo might be his.

Sanchez asked appellant not to contact the police, since Edie was married to a cousin of Sanchez and they were not positive that the stereo belonged to appellant. Accordingly, appellant devised a plan for recovering his property: Sanchez would have Edie bring the stereo to Sanchez' house for sale, appellant and some friends would grab Edie, and then they would notify the police. Sanchez warned appellant that Edie was dangerous and unpredictable: he was a narcotics addict usually "high" on drugs; he had just been released from prison, where he had been a member of a prison gang; he stole for a living; and he sometimes carried a gun.

That night, as planned, Sanchez and a companion, Cabrera, visited Edie, saw the stereo, agreed to purchase it for $400 (which appellant supplied), and returned to Sanchez' house to complete the transaction. There, Cabrera gave the $400 to Edie, who then helped to carry the stereo speakers into the house from his car, and left.

Meanwhile, appellant and friends were waiting in the bedroom. When Cabrera announced that Edie was leaving, appellant went to the kitchen, identified the stereo as his, and went outside, where he saw Edie in his car. Appellant tried to open the driver's door, but it was locked. Appellant told Edie to "freeze" and get out of the car. Cabrera opened the passenger door and tried to grab Edie, telling him to stop and get out. Edie then reached under his seat, causing both appellant and Cabrera to believe that he was reaching for a gun. They both stepped back and Edie accelerated, hitting two trees with his open passenger door. Appellant, who was armed with a loaded 9-mm. automatic pistol, then fired into the driver's door of the car. He feared, he testified, that Edie would run over him or Cabrera and get away. Edie then shifted forward and accelerated down the street, and appellant gave chase. Appellant testified that he saw the brake lights go on, and thought Edie was going to stop and shoot, so appellant fired at the car, emptying the gun. Edie died of a bullet wound in his chest.

I.

As regards appellant's conviction for involuntary manslaughter, the sole issue is whether the trial court erred in refusing to give an instruction, which appellant's counsel requested, to the effect that homicide is justifiable "when necessarily committed in attempting, by lawful ways and means, to apprehend any person who has committed burglary of the first degree." * * *

In [*People v. Ceballos*] the defendant was convicted of assault with a deadly weapon after a trap gun, which he had mounted in the garage of his dwelling, fired and hit a person who entered the garage in an attempt to commit burglary. * * *

In considering whether the burglary in that case involved an "atrocious crime" within the meaning of the common-law (and therefore statutory) rule, the court in *Ceballos* stated: "Where the character and manner of the burglary do not reasonably create a fear of great bodily harm, there is no cause for exaction of human life, or for the use of deadly force. The character and manner of the burglary could not reasonably create such a fear unless the burglary threatened, or was reasonably believed to threaten, death or serious bodily harm. In the instant case the asserted burglary did not threaten death or serious bodily harm, since no one but [the burglars] was then on the premises."

Appellant characterizes this last quoted sentence from *Ceballos* as dictum, but clearly it is more than that. It is a necessary element of the court's analysis, supporting the conclusion that the use of deadly force to prevent the burglary of an unoccupied premises is not justified under Penal Code section 197. And since a burglary committed when no one is on the premises is not a crime which threatens death or serious bodily harm so as to justify the use of deadly force in preventing its occurrence, it would seem to follow that it is not, or at least not per se, the sort of crime which justifies the use of deadly force by a citizen in apprehending the criminal. In the latter case, as well as the former, the modern common law rule limits the use of deadly force to "dangerous" felonies: "The law does not permit the use of deadly force for the mere purpose of preventing a nondangerous felony, and a private person cannot defeat this restriction merely by saying his purpose is arrest rather than prevention."[3] Indeed, the court in *Piorkowski* expressly determined that "[t]he reasoning of the court in *Jones* [limiting subdivision 1 of section 197 to dangerous felonies on the basis of common law] applies with like force and effect in construing subdivision 4 of section 197." We conclude that the trial court did not err by refusing to give the instruction requested. * * *

The order granting probation is affirmed.

---

[3]Whether the common law has developed similar limitations upon the use of deadly force by police officers is more debatable. It is interesting to note that "[t]he privilege of using deadly force had its common-law development primarily in the areas of law enforcement and crime prevention, and the extent of the development is not surprising since all felonies were punishable by death in those early days. As the felon had forfeited his life by the perpetration of his crime, it was quite logical to authorize the use of deadly force if this reasonably seemed necessary to bring him to justice." Since escape from arrest is not a crime punishable by death, the justification for licensing a private citizen to impose capital punishment upon persons fleeing from crimes outside that category is not readily apparent. We do not, of course, reach that policy question.

Note

The traditional common law permitted citizens to use reasonable, non-deadly force to resist unlawful arrests, such as arrests based on less than probable cause, and to resist arrests in which the law enforcement officer uses excessive force. Although most states have altered this rule in order to create a legal duty to submit to even unlawful arrests, some have left in place the privilege to use force against excessively forceful arrests. *See, e.g., People v. Curtis*, 70 Cal.2d 347, 74 Cal.Rptr. 713, 450 P.2d 33 (1969) (upholding the right of a citizen to defend herself against excessive force used by law enforcement, even though that citizen has a statutory duty to submit to unlawful arrest).

What constitutes excessive force by a police officer? In *Tennessee v. Garner*, 471 U.S. 1, 105 S.Ct. 1694, 85 L.Ed.2d 1 (1985), the Supreme Court considered a case brought against (among other defendants) the City of Memphis, Tennessee, the Memphis Police Department, and the State of Tennessee by the father of a 15-year-old African American boy named Edward Garner. In October of 1974, Memphis, Tennessee police officers investigating a prowler call around 10:45 p.m. saw someone running away in a residential backyard. Officer Elton Hymon saw the suspect stop at a chain link fence at the edge of the yard. He could not see any sign of a weapon and was "reasonably sure" that the suspect was unarmed. Hymon shouted "Police, halt" and began to advance. The suspect, however, began to climb over the fence and in order to keep him from escaping, Officer Hymon shot and killed him. Officer Hymon later testified that he had believed the suspect to be 17 or 18 years old and about 5' 5" or 5' 7" tall; Garner, an eighth-grader, was in fact 5' 4" tall and around 100 or 110 pounds.

The killing of Garner was in accordance with Memphis police department policy and a Tennessee statute permitting officers to use "all the necessary means" to arrest a suspect if, after notice of the intention to arrest, the suspect either tried to flee or to forcibly resist arrest. Garner's father, however, argued that the law violated the Fourth, Fifth, Sixth, Eighth, and Fourteenth Amendments of the United States Constitution. The Supreme Court agreed that the law violated the Fourth Amendment guaranteeing protection against unreasonable searches and seizures. Balancing the suspect's right to life against the public interest in effective law enforcement, the Court observed that "the use of deadly force is a self-defeating way of apprehending a suspect and so setting the criminal justice mechanism in motion," noted that most police departments in the country had already forbidden the use of deadly force against nonviolent suspects, and concluded that the facts in this case did not justify the use of deadly force.

The Court articulated a new rule required in its view by the Fourth Amendment:

> Where the officer has probable cause to believe that the suspect poses a threat of serious physical harm, either to the officer or to others, it is not constitutionally unreasonable to prevent escape by using deadly force. Thus, if the suspect threatens the officer with a weapon or there is probable cause to believe that he has committed a crime involving the infliction or threatened infliction of serious physical harm, deadly force may be used if necessary to prevent escape, and if, where feasible, some warning has been given.

471 U.S. at 11-12.

Although the United States Constitution applies to all government actors, the limitations of the Fourth Amendment do not apply to private parties. The possibility remains, therefore, that in some circumstances private citizens, in jurisdictions that have not modified their reliance on the old common law rules, will have a greater privilege to use force against suspected felons than law enforcement. Consider, also, the scope of the privilege exercisable by private security guards and officials in private prisons.

6.   Necessity

In a sense, the justification defenses we have just studied – self-defense, defense of others, defense of habitation, defense of property, crime prevention and crime apprehension – are special applications of a more general defense of "necessity." The idea behind necessity as a general defense (also sometimes called "choice of evils") is that sometimes the greater good is served by breaking the law than by obeying it. In such circumstances, the defendant should not be criminally punished. Necessity therefore provides an affirmative defense to the actor in situations in which, from an objective perspective, the harm caused by breaking the law is less than the harm avoided by the action.

While the specific elements of the necessity defense vary from jurisdiction to jurisdiction, as a general matter, a defendant claiming necessity as a defense in jurisdictions incorporating the common law may be acquitted if:

1.   The harm the defendant was seeking to avoid was greater than the harm the defendant would likely cause by breaking the law (the balance of harms inquiry);

2.   The legislature has not determined the matter in a way that goes against the defendant;

3.   There is a causal connection between the defendant's illegal act and the harm the defendant was seeking to avoid. In other words, it was reasonable for the defendant to believe his illegal conduct would abate the threatened harm;

4.   No effective legal alternative was available to the defendant;

5.   The defendant was seeking to avoid a clear and imminent danger; and

6.   The defendant was not at fault for creating the dangerous situation.

The Model Penal Code's version of the necessity defense is found in section 3.02, which provides that "conduct that the actor believes to be necessary to avoid a harm or evil to himself or others is justifiable provided that: (a) the harm or evil sought to be avoided by such conduct is greater than that sought to be prevented by the law defining the offense charged; and (b) neither the Code nor other law defining the offense provides exceptions or defenses dealing with the specific situation involved; and (c) a legislative purpose to exclude the justification claimed does not otherwise plainly appear." Model Penal Code § 3.02.

Like the common law version of the necessity defense, the Model Penal Code focuses on a balancing of the relative harms. However, there are also some key differences. First, under the Model Penal Code, there is no "imminence" requirement. As long as the jury finds the harm avoided greater than the harm caused and the defendant believes the action was necessary, the harm need not be imminent. Second, the common law tradition provides that necessity is not a defense to homicide on the theory that it can never constitute the greater good to kill an innocent person. (Recall the *Dudley & Stevens* case in Chapter 1.) Under the Model Penal Code, however, there is no such explicit limitation; it is possible, therefore, that under certain circumstances killing an innocent person could be successfully defended as necessary.

Most common law judges, and the drafters of the Model Penal Code, seem to have imagined the necessity defense being used in cases without broader social or political implications: for example, the person lost in a blizzard who breaks into a mountain cabin to stay alive, or the person who deliberately burns another's property in order to create a firebreak during a dangerous wildfire. As it happens, however, the necessity defense is frequently invoked in cases involving political protest. In such cases, judges are often reluctant to instruct juries on the defense and to admit evidence that might support the defense. Consider the case that follows.

UNITED STATES v. SCHOON
United States Court of Appeals for the Ninth Circuit
939 F.2d 826 (9th Cir. 1991)

BOOCHEVER, C.J.

Gregory Schoon, Raymond Kennon, Jr., and Patricia Manning appeal their convictions for obstructing activities of the Internal Revenue Service Office in Tucson, Arizona, and failing to comply with an order of a federal police officer. Both charges stem from their activities in protest of United States involvement in El Salvador. They claim the district court improperly denied them a necessity defense. Because we hold the necessity defense inapplicable in cases like this, we affirm.

I.

On December 4, 1989, thirty people, including appellants, gained admittance to the IRS office in Tucson, where they chanted "keep America's tax dollars out of El Salvador," splashed simulated blood on the counters, walls, and carpeting, and generally obstructed the office's operation. After a federal police officer ordered the group, on several occasions, to disperse or face arrest, appellants were arrested.

At a bench trial, appellants proffered testimony about conditions in El Salvador as the motivation for their conduct. They attempted to assert a necessity defense, essentially contending that their acts in protest of American involvement in El Salvador were necessary to avoid further bloodshed in that country. While finding appellants motivated solely by humanitarian concerns, the court nonetheless precluded the defense as a matter of law, relying on Ninth Circuit precedent. The sole issue on appeal is the propriety of the court's exclusion of a necessity defense as a matter of law.

II.

A district court may preclude a necessity defense where "the evidence, as described in the defendant's offer of proof, is insufficient as a matter of law to support the proffered defense." To invoke the necessity defense, therefore, the defendants colorably must have shown that: (1) they were faced with a choice of evils and chose the lesser evil; (2) they acted to prevent imminent harm; (3) they reasonably anticipated a direct causal relationship between their conduct and the harm to be averted; and (4) they had no legal alternatives to violating the law. We review *de novo* the district court's decision to bar a necessity defense.

The district court denied the necessity defense on the grounds that (1) the requisite immediacy was lacking; (2) the actions taken would not abate the evil; and (3) other legal alternatives existed. Because the threshold test for admissibility of a necessity defense is a conjunctive one, a court may preclude invocation of the defense if "proof is deficient with regard to any of the four elements. . . ."

While we could affirm substantially on those grounds relied upon by the district court, we find a deeper, systemic reason for the complete absence of federal case law recognizing a necessity defense in an indirect civil disobedience case. Indirect civil disobedience involves violating a law which is not, itself, the object of protest, whereas direct civil disobedience involves protesting the existence of a particular law by breaking that law. This case involves indirect civil disobedience because these protestors were not challenging the laws under which they were charged. In contrast, the civil rights lunch counter sit-ins, for example, constituted direct civil disobedience because the protestors were challenging the rule that prevented them from sitting at lunch counters.

While our prior cases consistently have found the elements of the necessity defense lacking in cases involving indirect civil disobedience, we have never addressed specifically whether the defense is available in cases of indirect civil disobedience. * * * Today, we conclude, for the reasons stated below, that the necessity defense is inapplicable to cases involving indirect civil disobedience.

III.

Necessity is, essentially, a utilitarian defense. It therefore justifies criminal acts taken to avert a greater harm, maximizing social welfare by allowing a crime to be committed where the social benefits of the crime outweigh the social costs of failing to commit the crime. Pursuant to the defense, prisoners could escape a burning prison; a person lost in the woods could steal food from a cabin to survive; an embargo could be violated because adverse weather conditions necessitated sale of the cargo at a foreign port; a crew could mutiny where their ship was thought to be unseaworthy; and property could be destroyed to prevent the spread of fire.

What all the traditional necessity cases have in common is that the commission of the "crime" averted the occurrence of an even greater "harm."

In some sense, the necessity defense allows us to act as individual legislatures, amending a particular criminal provision or crafting a one-time exception to it, subject to court review, when a real legislature would formally do the same under those circumstances. For example, by allowing prisoners who escape a burning jail to claim the justification of necessity, we assume the lawmaker, confronting this problem, would have allowed for an exception to the law proscribing prison escapes.

Because the necessity doctrine is utilitarian, however, strict requirements contain its exercise so as to prevent nonbeneficial criminal conduct. For example, "'if the criminal act cannot abate the threatened harm, society receives no benefit from the criminal conduct.'" Similarly, to forgive a crime taken to avert a lesser harm would fail to maximize social utility. The cost of the crime would outweigh the harm averted by its commission. Likewise, criminal acts cannot be condoned to thwart threats, yet to be imminent, or those for which there are legal alternatives to abate the harm.

Analysis of three of the necessity defense's four elements leads us to the conclusion that necessity can never be proved in a case of indirect civil disobedience. We do not rely upon the imminent harm prong of the defense because we believe there can be indirect civil disobedience cases in which the protested harm is imminent.

A.

1. Balance of Harms

It is axiomatic that, if the thing to be averted is not a harm at all, the balance of harms necessarily would disfavor any criminal action. Thus, if an insane person bombed a welfare office for "helping those who won't help themselves," that person should be prevented from claiming necessity because the operation of a welfare system is simply not a cognizable harm. Welfare cannot constitute a harm where society has expressed its preference for such a system. * * *

Just as welfare was not a cognizable harm in our hypothetical, the El Salvador policy has been chosen by society and, therefore, cannot be deemed a cognizable harm here. The El Salvador policy does not violate the Constitution. Appellants have never suggested as much. There is no evidence that the procedure by which the policy was adopted was in any way improper; nor is there any evidence that appellants were prevented systematically from participating in the democratic processes through which the policy was chosen.

Under these circumstances, as a matter of law, whenever Congress has decided a matter exclusively within its constitutionally-delineated realm of authority, its decision, be it in the form of policy or law, cannot constitute a cognizable harm. If there is no cognizable harm to prevent, the harm resulting from any criminal action taken to prevent it necessarily outweighs any benefit.

2. Causal Relationship Between Criminal Conduct and Harm to be Averted

This inquiry requires a court to judge the likelihood that an alleged harm will be abated by the taking of illegal action. In the sense that the likelihood of abatement is required in the traditional necessity cases, there will never be such likelihood in cases of indirect political protest. In the traditional cases, a prisoner flees a burning cell and averts death, or someone demolishes a home to create a firebreak and prevents the conflagration of an entire community. The nexus between the act undertaken and the result sought is a close one. Ordinarily it is the volitional illegal act alone which, once taken, abates the evil.

In political necessity cases involving indirect civil disobedience against congressional acts, however, the act alone is unlikely to abate the evil precisely because the action is indirect.[1] Here, the IRS obstruction, or the refusal to comply with a federal officer's order, are unlikely to abate the killings in El Salvador, or immediately change Congress's policy; instead, it takes another *volitional* actor not controlled by the protestor to take a further step; Congress must change its mind.

3. Legal Alternatives

A final reason the necessity defense does not apply to these indirect civil disobedience cases is that legal alternatives will never be deemed exhausted when the harm can be mitigated by congressional action. In *Dorrell*, which involved a protestor's trespass on Vandenburg Air Force Base to protest the MX missile program, we answered Dorrell's claims that legal alternatives, like lobbying Congress, were futile by noting that "he differed little from many whose passionate beliefs are rejected by the will of the majority legitimately expressed." The necessity defense as applied in the traditional context requires that one have no legal *alternative* to the illegal conduct contemplated *that would*

---

[1] Obviously, the same may not be true of instances of direct civil disobedience. For example, if the evil to be abated was a particular shipment of weapons to El Salvador and the protestors hijacked the truck or destroyed those weapons, the precise evil would have been abated. Because our case does not involve direct civil disobedience, we do not address the applicability of the necessity defense to such incidents.

abate the evil. For the existence of a legal alternative to preclude the taking of illegal action, it would necessarily have to be one which *would abate the evil.* Thus, a person fleeing a burning jail would not be asked either to perish or wait in his cell because someone might conceivably save him (both legal alternatives) because neither are well-suited to the purpose of avoiding death. In other words, a reasonableness requirement is implied into judging whether legal alternatives exist.

The legal alternatives requirement has been treated differently in the political context, however. *Dorrell* did not inquire into the "likelihood" that petitioning Congress would succeed. It merely assumed that the "possibility" of Congress changing its mind was sufficient. Yet, certainly an inquiry into the efficacy of legal alternatives available to a fleeing prisoner would have been undertaken. Without expressly saying so, *Dorrell* decided that petitioning Congress to change a policy is *always* a legal alternative, regardless of the likelihood of the plea's success.

Reading between the lines in *Dorrell*, it appears we took the reasonable position that, once Dorrell had a chance to convince Congress, the necessity defense became unavailable because otherwise he would be granted license to violate the law without the concomitant, and outweighing, benefit that the necessity doctrine envisions. That this is so in every indirect political protest does not change the fact that we failed to measure the reasonableness of the legal alternative of petitioning Congress. The cases involving protest of congressional policy have implicitly decided that, because Congress can change its mind at any time in response to citizen protest, petitioning Congress is always an adequate legal alternative. Thus there is never an absence of legal alternatives in cases where congressional action is the protest's aim.

B.

As have courts before us, we could assume, as a threshold matter, that the necessity defense is conceivably available in these cases, but find the elements never satisfied. Such a decision, however, does not come without significant costs. First, the failure of the federal courts to hold explicitly that the necessity defense is unavailable in these cases results in district courts expending unnecessary time and energy trying to square defendants' claims with the strict requirements of the doctrine. Second, such an inquiry oftentimes requires the courts to tread into areas constitutionally committed to other branches of government. For example, in *May*, which involved trespass on a naval base to protest American nuclear weapons policy, we noted that, "to consider defendants' argument [that trespassing was justified by the nefariousness of the Trident missile] would put us in the position of usurping the functions that the Constitution has given to the Congress and to the President."

Third, holding out the possibility of the defense's applicability sets a trap for the unwary civil disobedient, rather than permitting the individual to undertake a more realistic cost-benefit analysis before deciding whether to break the law in political protest. Fourth, assuming the applicability of the defense in this context may risk its distortion in traditional cases. Finally, some commentators have suggested that the courts have sabotaged the usually low threshold for getting a defense theory before the jury as a means of keeping the necessity defense from the jury.

The real problem here is that litigants are trying to distort to their purposes an age-old common law doctrine meant for a very different set of circumstances. What these cases are really about is gaining notoriety for a cause – the defense allows protestors to get their political grievances discussed in a courtroom. It is precisely this political motive that has left some courts, like the district court in this case, uneasy. Because these attempts to invoke the necessity defense "force the courts to choose among causes they should make legitimate by extending the defense of necessity," and because the criminal acts, themselves, do not maximize social good, they should be subject to a *per se* rule of exclusion.

Thus, we see the failure of any federal court to recognize a defense of necessity in a case like ours not as coincidental, but rather as the natural consequence of the historic limitation of the doctrine. Indirect protests of congressional policies can never meet all the requirements of the necessity doctrine. Therefore, we hold that the necessity defense is not available in such cases.

CONCLUSION

Because the necessity defense was not intended as justification for illegal acts taken in indirect political protest, we affirm the district court's refusal to admit evidence of necessity.

AFFIRMED.

COMMONWEALTH v. HUTCHINS

Supreme Judicial Court of Massachusetts, Essex
410 Mass. 726, 575 N.E.2d 741(1991)

O'CONNOR, J.

The defendant was convicted of drug offenses at a bench trial in the District Court. He requested a jury trial de novo. Thus, any errors that may have occurred during the bench trial are without consequence. In a jury session of the District Court, the charges were first amended to charges of cultivation of THC (a chemical found in marihuana) and of marihuana, and of possession of both substances with intent to distribute. Subsequently, the charges were reduced to simple possession or cultivation of THC and marihuana, and the defendant waived trial by jury.

Before trial, the defendant filed a motion to dismiss the complaints "on the ground that any possession of controlled substances by the [d]efendant is within the [d]efense of [m]edical [n]ecessity." The motion states that counsel "wishes to present a clear record for the reviewing court," and therefore requests the court to "state that it is denying the [d]efendant the right to assert a defense of medical necessity as a matter of law." * * * After a hearing, a judge complied, and endorsed the motion. "10/24/85. Motion denied. Def[endant] will not be allowed to introduce [evidence] re defense of medical necessity." Following a bench trial, the defendant was convicted of both reduced charges, and appealed. * * * We now affirm the convictions.

In support of his motion, as an offer of proof, the defendant submitted affidavits, excerpts from his medical records, literature on a disease known as progressive systemic sclerosis (scleroderma) and on the medicinal uses of marihuana and other materials. Through these materials, the defendant offered to prove the following facts: The defendant is a forty-seven year old man who has been diagnosed as having scleroderma accompanied by Raynaud's phenomenon, related to his service in the Navy. Scleroderma is a chronic disease that results in the buildup of scar tissue throughout the body. The cause of scleroderma is not known and no effective treatment or cure has been discovered. In the most severe cases, scleroderma may result in death. The defendant's medical history includes episodes of fatigue, hypertension, loss of appetite, weight loss of up to twenty-five pounds, diarrhea, nausea, vomiting, reflux of food and stomach acid into the mouth, reduced motility and constriction of the esophagus, extreme difficulty and pain in swallowing, and swollen, painful joints and extreme sensitivity to the cold in his hands and feet. He also suffers from severe depression, related at least in part to his disease, and was briefly hospitalized after attempting suicide. As a result of his illness, the defendant has been unable to work since 1978.

According to the offer of proof, the defendant's medical condition has been unsuccessfully treated with numerous medications and therapies by physicians of the Veterans Administration. The constriction of his esophagus has been treated by dilation and in 1974 was so severe that his treating physician advised him to have his esophagus surgically removed and replaced with a piece of his own intestine. The defendant has informed his treating physicians that since 1975, with some success, he has used marihuana, in lieu of antidepressants and surgery, to alleviate certain symptoms of his illness including nausea, loss of appetite, difficulty in eating, drinking or swallowing, loss of motility of the esophagus, spasticity, hypertension, and anxiety. Two of his treating physicians state that, although they are unable to "confirm [the defendant's] claim that his use of mari[h]uana has caused his remarkable remission, . . . it does appear that his use of mari[h]uana does alleviate the previously mentioned symptoms." These two physicians also state that "there appears to be a sufficient basis to conduct a scientific and medical investigation into the possible use of mari[h]uana to treat the disease of scleroderma." A research study of its therapeutic potential and medical uses indicates that the use of marihuana, indeed, may be effective to treat loss of appetite, nausea, vomiting, and weight loss and may relieve severe anxiety and depression. One of the defendant's other treating physicians, however, does not find that marihuana "had any effect in [the defendant's] case" and that he is "unaware of any published or unpublished evidence of [a] beneficial effect of mari[h]uana in this condition." Through correspondence with his physicians, the Veterans Administration, and members of the Massachusetts Legislature and the United States Congress, the defendant has made numerous, albeit unsuccessful, attempts lawfully to obtain either a prescription for marihuana or permission to participate in a research study on the use of marihuana to treat scleroderma. The Massachusetts Legislature has considered a bill providing for the use of marihuana in therapeutic research on more than one occasion, but no such statute has been enacted in the Commonwealth. The Veterans Administration has determined that presently there is no research study on the use of marihuana to treat scleroderma and therefore will not dispense marihuana for the defendant's treatment.

In *Commonwealth v. Hood,* we said, "It is, perhaps, 'more prudent for the judge to follow the traditional, and constitutionally sounder, course of waiting until all the evidence has been introduced at trial before ruling on its sufficiency to raise a proffered defense. If, at that time, the defendant has failed to produce some evidence on each element of the defense, the judge should decline to instruct on it. . . . In that event, the judge, may if appropriate, give curative instructions to caution the jury against considering evidence not properly before them.'" However, the defendant cannot fairly complain about the procedure adopted by the judge in this case if, as the Commonwealth contends and the judge appears to have concluded, the proof offered would not support a necessity defense. Our question, then, is whether, if the defendant were able to prove by admissible evidence at trial the facts contained in the offer of proof, a properly instructed fact finder could determine that the defendant had established the defense which he asserts.

"Under the common law defense of justification by necessity, a crime committed under the pressure of imminent danger may be excused if the harm

sought to be avoided far exceeds the harm resulting from the crime committed."
"In essence, the 'competing harms' defense exonerates one who commits a
crime under the 'pressure of circumstances' if the harm that would have resulted
from compliance with the law significantly exceeds the harm actually resulting
from the defendant's violation of the law." At its root is an appreciation that
there may be circumstances where the value protected by the law is, as a matter
of public policy, eclipsed by a superseding value which makes it inappropriate
and unjust to apply the usual criminal rule.

"We have ruled that 'the application of the defense is limited to the
following circumstances: (1) the defendant is faced with a clear and imminent
danger, not one which is debatable or speculative; (2) the defendant can
reasonably expect that his [or her] action will be effective as the direct cause of
abating the danger; (3) there is [no] legal alternative which will be effective in
abating the danger; and (4) the Legislature has not acted to preclude the defense
by a clear and deliberate choice regarding the values at issue.'" It must be
understood, however, that that oft-repeated principle, that the necessity defense
is limited to certain specified circumstances, does not mean that, whenever those
circumstances obtain, the defense automatically applies. Rather, the first
question always is whether the harm that would have resulted from compliance
with the law significantly outweighs the harm that reasonably could result from
the court's acceptance of necessity as an excuse in the circumstances presented
by the particular case. Only when a comparison of the "competing harms" in
specific circumstances clearly favors excusing what would otherwise be
punishable conduct, is it appropriate then to inquire whether the standards
enumerated in the cases cited above, standards which themselves do not call for
a comparison of competing harms, have been met.

We mention two illustrative cases. In *Commonwealth v. Thurber* the
defendant was convicted of escape from the Massachusetts Correctional
Institution at Concord. At the trial, the defendant presented evidence that he had
escaped because his life was in imminent danger at the prison. In discussing the
necessity defense we quoted with approval a statement in a California case of
the circumstances in which an escape from prison might be excused, one of the
circumstances being that the escape be accomplished without violence, and
another being that "[t]he prisoner immediately reports to the proper authorities
when he has attained a position of safety from the immediate threat." In *Thurber*
we "[a]ssum[ed] that we would apply the doctrine [of necessity] as a
justification for escape in a proper case." The extent of public harm likely to
attend a peaceful escape from prison, followed by the prisoner's prompt
submission to the authorities, would be minimal compared to the likely harm to
the prisoner, as demonstrated by the defendant's evidence in *Thurber*, if he were
to comply with the law. Common sense tells us that, in the absence of a clear

and specific contrary statutory expression, the court would not frustrate legislative intent in a *Thurber*-type situation by recognizing a necessity defense.

Commonwealth v. Iglesia provides another illustration. There, the defendant was charged with unlawfully carrying a firearm. He testified that he was attacked by a man with a gun, that he wrested the gun from the man, and that he immediately went to the police station with it. Again, as we did in *Commonwealth v. Thurber,* we "assume[d] . . . that, when 'a defendant seizes a firearm from one who had expressed an immediate intention to use it, and flees to a place of safe-keeping,' such possession might be lawful." In *Iglesia*, as in *Thurber*, the likely harm to society that would be likely to result from recognition of a necessity defense, carefully limited as to circumstances, would be significantly outweighed by the potential harm to the defendant, if his evidence were to be believed, if he were to comply with the law. It is fair to assume, in the absence of a specifically expressed contrary legislative intent, that judicial recognition of a necessity defense in the circumstances of the *Iglesia* case would not contradict any legislative policy determination.

Accepting the defendant's offer of proof, and assuming, as we do without decision, that the circumstances referred to above as enumerated * * * obtain, nevertheless we rule that the defendant's proffered evidence does not raise the defense of necessity. In our view, the alleviation of the defendant's medical symptoms, the importance to the defendant of which we do not underestimate, would not clearly and significantly outweigh the potential harm to the public were we to declare that the defendant's cultivation of marihuana and its use for his medicinal purposes may not be punishable. We cannot dismiss the reasonably possible negative impact of such a judicial declaration on the enforcement of our drug laws, including but not limited to those dealing with marihuana, nor can we ignore the government's overriding interest in the regulation of such substances. Excusing the escaped prisoner in the circumstances presented by *Thurber,* or the carrier of a gun in the circumstances of *Iglesia,* is quite different from excusing one who cultivates and uses marihuana in the circumstances of this case.

Judgment affirmed.

LIACOS, C.J. (dissenting, with whom NOLAN, J., joins).

I believe that a jury, not a judge, ordinarily should be allowed to determine whether medical necessity is a defense to a charge of possession or cultivation of marihuana. "The defendant[ ] presented sufficient evidence to raise such a defense. Neither the judge below nor this court should substitute its judgment for the sound deliberations of the jury."

The court today engages in speculative judicial fact finding by concluding that "the alleviation of the defendant's medical symptoms, the importance to the defendant of which we do not underestimate, would not clearly and significantly outweigh the potential harm to the public were we to declare that the defendant's cultivation of marihuana and its use for his medicinal purposes may not be punishable. We cannot dismiss the reasonably possible negative impact of such a judicial declaration on the enforcement of our drug laws, including but not limited to those dealing with marihuana, nor can we ignore the government's overriding interest in the regulation of such substances." While I recognize that the public has a strong interest in the enforcement of drug laws and in the strict regulation of narcotics, I do not believe that the interest would be significantly harmed by permitting a jury to consider whether the defendant cultivated and used marihuana in order to alleviate agonizing and painful symptoms caused by an illness. The court seems to suggest that we should not condone the use of marihuana, regardless of a particular individual's reasons for using the drug. Although the court appears to recognize the defense by taking this position, it fails to give sufficient consideration to the rationale behind the common law defense of necessity. That rationale is based on the recognition that, under very limited circumstances, "the value protected by the law is, as a matter of public policy, eclipsed by a superseding value which makes it inappropriate and unjust to apply the usual criminal rule."

The superseding value in a case such as the present one is the humanitarian and compassionate value in allowing an individual to seek relief from agonizing symptoms caused by a progressive and incurable illness in circumstances which risk no harm to any other individual. In my view, the harm to an individual in having to endure such symptoms may well outweigh society's generalized interest in prohibiting him or her from using the marihuana in such circumstances. On a proper offer of proof I would recognize the availability of a necessity defense when marihuana is used for medical purposes.

To recognize a medical necessity defense based on the use of marihuana for medical purposes would not allow *every* defendant charged with possessing or cultivating marihuana to present such a defense to the jury. Instead, "the application of the defense [would be] limited to the following circumstances: (1) the defendant is faced with a clear and imminent danger, not one which is debatable or speculative; (2) the defendant can reasonably expect that his [or her] action will be effective as the direct cause of abating the danger; (3) there is [no] legal alternative which will be effective in abating the danger; and (4) the Legislature has not acted to preclude the defense by a clear and deliberate choice regarding the values at issue." The defendant's offer of proof satisfied all the elements of a necessity defense. The judge erred in not allowing the defendant to present evidence of medical necessity to a jury of his peers.

The defendant's offer of proof contained sufficient allegations that he faced a "clear and imminent danger." The defendant presented affidavits from two physicians who stated that the defendant's esophagus was dangerously constricted as a result of his illness, and that, without treatment, his esophagus would constrict to the point where the defendant would be unable to eat or drink without great difficulty and pain. The physicians also stated in the affidavits "that it does appear that [the defendant's] use of mari[h]uana does alleviate [his nausea, loss of appetite, difficulty in swallowing, spasticity, hypertension, and anxiety]." Thus, the defendant offered to prove the second element of a necessity defense by showing that he had a "reasonable expectation" that smoking marihuana would be effective in abating the danger. The third element was satisfied when the defendant offered to prove that he had unsuccessfully attempted to acquire marihuana legally by seeking authorization from the Federal government to use marihuana for medical research. Finally, the fourth element was satisfied in this case since the Legislature has not precluded the medical necessity defense by clearly and deliberately choosing among the values at stake.

Since the defendant's offer of proof satisfied the four elements of a necessity defense, the judge's refusal to allow the defendant to present evidence of medical necessity to the jury improperly prevented the jury from exercising their vital functions of "[1] temper[ing] the application of strict rules of law by bringing the common sense judgment of a group of laymen to the case [and] . . . [2] stand[ing] as a check on arbitrary enforcement of the law. 'Fear of unchecked power, so typical of our State and Federal Governments in other respects, found expression in the criminal law in this insistence upon community participation in the determination of guilt or innocence.' The court today once again unnecessarily interferes with the proper functions of the jury. I dissent.

UNITED STATES v. OAKLAND CANNABIS BUYERS' COOPERATIVE

Supreme Court of the United States
532 U.S. 483, 121 S.Ct. 1711, 149 L.Ed.2d 722 (2001)

JUSTICE THOMAS delivered the opinion of the Court.

Controlled Substances Act, 84 Stat. 1242, 21 U.S.C. § 801 *et seq.*, prohibits the manufacture and distribution of various drugs, including marijuana. In this case, we must decide whether there is a medical necessity exception to these prohibitions. We hold that there is not.

I

In November 1996, California voters enacted an initiative measure entitled the Compassionate Use Act of 1996. Attempting "to ensure that seriously ill Californians have the right to obtain and use marijuana for medical purposes," the statute creates an exception to California laws prohibiting the possession and cultivation of marijuana. These prohibitions no longer apply to a patient or his primary caregiver who possesses or cultivates marijuana for the patient's medical purposes upon the recommendation or approval of a physician. In the wake of this voter initiative, several groups organized "medical cannabis dispensaries" to meet the needs of qualified patients. Respondent Oakland Cannabis Buyers' Cooperative is one of these groups.

The Cooperative is a not-for-profit organization that operates in downtown Oakland. A physician serves as medical director, and registered nurses staff the Cooperative during business hours. To become a member, a patient must provide a written statement from a treating physician assenting to marijuana therapy and must submit to a screening interview. If accepted as a member, the patient receives an identification card entitling him to obtain marijuana from the Cooperative.

In January 1998, the United States sued the Cooperative and its executive director, respondent Jeffrey Jones (together, the Cooperative), in the United States District Court for the Northern District of California. Seeking to enjoin the Cooperative from distributing and manufacturing marijuana, the United States argued that, whether or not the Cooperative's activities are legal under California law, they violate federal law. Specifically, the Government argued that the Cooperative violated the Controlled Substances Act's prohibitions on distributing, manufacturing, and possessing with the intent to distribute or manufacture a controlled substance. Concluding that the Government had established a probability of success on the merits, the District Court granted a preliminary injunction.

The Cooperative did not appeal the injunction but instead openly violated it by distributing marijuana to numerous persons. To terminate these violations, the Government initiated contempt proceedings. In defense, the Cooperative contended that any distributions were medically necessary. Marijuana is the only drug, according to the Cooperative, that can alleviate the severe pain and other debilitating symptoms of the Cooperative's patients. The District Court rejected this defense, however, after determining there was insufficient evidence that each recipient of marijuana was in actual danger of imminent harm without the drug. The District Court found the Cooperative in contempt and, at the Government's request, modified the preliminary injunction to empower the United States Marshal to seize the Cooperative's premises.

Although recognizing that "human suffering" could result, the District Court reasoned that a court's "equitable powers [do] not permit it to ignore federal law." Three days later, the District Court summarily rejected a motion by the Cooperative to modify the injunction to permit distributions that are medically necessary. * * *

The denial of the Cooperative's motion to modify the injunction, however, presented a live controversy that was appealable under 28 U.S.C. § 1292(a)(1). Reaching the merits of this issue, the Court of Appeals reversed and remanded. According to the Court of Appeals, the medical necessity defense was a "legally cognizable defense" that likely would apply in the circumstances. * * *

Remanding the case, the Court of Appeals instructed the District Court to consider "the criteria for a medical necessity exemption, and, should it modify the injunction, to set forth those criteria in the modification order." Following these instructions, the District Court granted the Cooperative's motion to modify the injunction to incorporate a medical necessity defense.[2]

The United States petitioned for certiorari to review the Court of Appeals' decision that medical necessity is a legally cognizable defense to violations of the Controlled Substances Act. Because the decision raises significant questions as to the ability of the United States to enforce the Nation's drug laws, we granted certiorari.

II

The Controlled Substances Act provides that, "except as authorized by this subchapter, it shall be unlawful for any person knowingly or intentionally . . . to manufacture, distribute, or dispense, or possess with intent to manufacture, distribute, or dispense, a controlled substance." The subchapter, in turn, establishes exceptions. For marijuana (and other drugs that have been classified as "schedule I" controlled substances), there is but one express exception, and it is available only for Government-approved research projects, § 823(f). Not conducting such a project, the Cooperative cannot, and indeed does not, claim this statutory exemption.

---

[2] The amended preliminary injunction reaffirmed that the Cooperative is generally enjoined from manufacturing, distributing, and possessing with the intent to manufacture or distribute marijuana, but it carved out an exception for cases of medical necessity. * * *

The Cooperative contends, however, that notwithstanding the apparently absolute language of § 841(a), the statute is subject to additional, implied exceptions, one of which is medical necessity. According to the Cooperative, because necessity was a defense at common law, medical necessity should be read into the Controlled Substances Act. We disagree.

As an initial matter, we note that it is an open question whether federal courts ever have authority to recognize a necessity defense not provided by statute. A necessity defense "traditionally covered the situation where physical forces beyond the actor's control rendered illegal conduct the lesser of two evils." Even at common law, the defense of necessity was somewhat controversial. And under our constitutional system, in which federal crimes are defined by statute rather than by common law, it is especially so. As we have stated: "Whether, as a policy matter, an exemption should be created is a question for legislative judgment, not judicial inference." Nonetheless, we recognize that this Court has discussed the possibility of a necessity defense without altogether rejecting it.

We need not decide, however, whether necessity can ever be a defense when the federal statute does not expressly provide for it. In this case, to resolve the question presented, we need only recognize that a medical necessity exception for marijuana is at odds with the terms of the Controlled Substances Act. The statute, to be sure, does not explicitly abrogate the defense. But its provisions leave no doubt that the defense is unavailable.

Under any conception of legal necessity, one principle is clear: The defense cannot succeed when the legislature itself has made a "determination of values." In the case of the Controlled Substances Act, the statute reflects a determination that marijuana has no medical benefits worthy of an exception (outside the confines of a Government-approved research project). Whereas some other drugs can be dispensed and prescribed for medical use, the same is not true for marijuana. Indeed, for purposes of the Controlled Substances Act, marijuana has "no currently accepted medical use" at all.

The structure of the Act supports this conclusion. The statute divides drugs into five schedules, depending in part on whether the particular drug has a currently accepted medical use. The Act then imposes restrictions on the manufacture and distribution of the substance according to the schedule in which it has been placed. Schedule I is the most restrictive schedule.[5] The Attorney

---

[5] As noted, *supra*, at 5, the only express exception for schedule I drugs is the Government-approved research project, see 21 U.S.C. § 823(f). Unlike drugs in other schedules, see § 829, schedule I drugs cannot be dispensed under a prescription.

General can include a drug in schedule I only if the drug "has no currently accepted medical use in treatment in the United States," "has a high potential for abuse," and has "a lack of accepted safety for use . . . under medical supervision." Under the statute, the Attorney General could not put marijuana into schedule I if marijuana had any accepted medical use. * * *

The Cooperative further argues that use of schedule I drugs generally -- whether placed in schedule I by Congress or the Attorney General -- can be medically necessary, notwithstanding that they have "no currently accepted medical use." According to the Cooperative, a drug may not yet have achieved general acceptance as a medical treatment but may nonetheless have medical benefits to a particular patient or class of patients. We decline to parse the statute in this manner. It is clear from the text of the Act that Congress has made a determination that marijuana has no medical benefits worthy of an exception. The statute expressly contemplates that many drugs "have a useful and legitimate medical purpose and are necessary to maintain the health and general welfare of the American people," but it includes no exception at all for any medical use of marijuana. Unwilling to view this omission as an accident, and unable in any event to override a legislative determination manifest in a statute, we reject the Cooperative's argument. * * *

For these reasons, we hold that medical necessity is not a defense to manufacturing and distributing marijuana.[7] The Court of Appeals erred when it held that medical necessity is a "legally cognizable defense." It further erred when it instructed the District Court on remand to consider "the criteria for a medical necessity exemption, and, should it modify the injunction, to set forth those criteria in the modification order." * * *

---

[7] Lest there be any confusion, we clarify that nothing in our analysis, or the statute, suggests that a distinction should be drawn between the prohibitions on manufacturing and distributing and the other prohibitions in the Controlled Substances Act. Furthermore, the very point of our holding is that there is no medical necessity exception to the prohibitions at issue, even when the patient is "seriously ill" and lacks alternative avenues for relief. Indeed, it is the Cooperative's argument that its patients are "seriously ill," and lacking "alternatives." We reject the argument that these factors warrant a medical necessity exception. If we did not, we would be affirming instead of reversing the Court of Appeals.

Finally, we share JUSTICE STEVENS' concern for "showing respect for the sovereign States that comprise our Federal Union." However, we are "construing an Act of Congress, not drafting it." Because federal courts interpret, rather than author, the federal criminal code, we are not at liberty to rewrite it. Nor are we passing today on a constitutional question, such as whether the Controlled Substances Act exceeds Congress' power under the Commerce Clause.

In this case, the Court of Appeals erred by considering relevant the evidence that some people have "serious medical conditions for whom the use of cannabis is necessary in order to treat or alleviate those conditions or their symptoms," that these people "will suffer serious harm if they are denied cannabis," and that "there is no legal alternative to cannabis for the effective treatment of their medical conditions." As explained above, in the Controlled Substances Act, the balance already has been struck against a medical necessity exception. Because the statutory prohibitions cover even those who have what could be termed a medical necessity, the Act precludes consideration of this evidence. It was thus error for the Court of Appeals to instruct the District Court on remand to consider "the criteria for a medical necessity exemption, and, should it modify the injunction, to set forth those criteria in the modification order."

* * * The judgment of the Court of Appeals is reversed, and the case is remanded for further proceedings consistent with this opinion.

It is so ordered.

[A concurring opinion by JUSTICE STEVENS, joined by JUSTICES SOUTER and GINSBURG, is omitted. JUSTICE BREYER took no part in the consideration or decision of this case.]

In re EICHORN

Court of Appeal of California, Fourth Appellate District, Division Three
69 Cal. App. 4th 382, 81 Cal.Rptr. 2d 535 (Ct. App. 1998)

CROSBY, J.

James Warner Eichorn was convicted of a misdemeanor violation of a City of Santa Ana ordinance banning sleeping in designated public areas. The appellate department affirmed his conviction and denied his request to transfer the cause. Eichorn thereafter petitioned for writ of habeas corpus in this court. We conclude his conviction must be set aside.

I

James Eichorn was cited for violation of the city's anticamping ordinance (Santa Ana Mun. Code, ch. 10, art. VIII, §10-402) on the evening of

January 25, 1993.[1] Following a detour to the Supreme Court that established the ordinance was facially constitutional, Eichorn's case eventually went to trial.

In a significant pretrial ruling, the court (Judge James M. Brooks) determined Eichorn could not present a necessity defense to a jury. Eichorn had offered to prove that on the night of the violation every shelter bed within the city that was available to a homeless single man with no children was occupied, and that he was involuntarily homeless, i.e., he had done everything he could to alleviate his condition. Due to circumstances beyond his control, defendant, a 14-year resident of Santa Ana, had been unable to find work as a manual laborer that paid enough to allow him to find an alternative place to sleep.

The court determined defendant had not made a sufficient showing to allow a jury to consider his necessity defense: "It appears that the defense of necessity is not supported by the offer of proof. The first element wasn't satisfied, in the court's view, no significant, imminent evil for this defendant or any other person."[2] Defendant objected that the court's ruling "not only goes against what we understand to have been the statements and admissions by the People and by [Judge Margines, who had previously handled the case] but undermines the whole reason why we were going forward at trial . . . it's clearly eviscerated our entire defense."

In light of Judge Brooks's ruling on the necessity defense, and noting there was no dispute Eichorn was in a sleeping bag in the civic center on the night in question, Eichorn's lawyer agreed to go forward without a jury on the constitutional issue whether the ordinance was unconstitutional as applied to him based on his alleged involuntary homelessness.

Trial commenced without a jury in May 1996. Officer Carol Craig testified defendant was in a sleeping bag on the ground about 10:30 p.m. outside a county office building in the civic center. He was using his clothes as a pillow. Craig asked (as she always did) why Eichorn wasn't at the National Guard Armory (a homeless shelter several miles away). A bus from the civic center to

---

[1] Section 10-402 reads as follows: "Unlawful Camping. [P] It shall be unlawful for any person to camp, occupy camp facilities or use camp paraphernalia in the following areas, except as otherwise provided: (a) Any street; (b) Any public parking lot or public area, improved or unimproved." Camp paraphernalia included a sleeping bag.

[2] The court's questions and comments suggested it was not impressed with defendant's claim lack of sleep was a significant evil ("what do you mean 'bodily harm?' Like tired eyelids or blood?"; "[I]f he didn't sleep here, he'd lose sleep and this would be a horrible physical thing to impose on him?").

the armory usually picked up people between 5:00 and 6:00 p.m. According to Craig's police report, defendant replied he had tried "a while back." It was full, so he never returned. The court judicially noticed that the walk between the civic center and the armory was "through very dangerous areas of town." Police photographed and cited Eichorn, then asked him to move on. He complied.

James Meeker, a professor at the University of California, Irvine in the department of criminology, law and society, testified he had conducted a study on homelessness in January and February 1993. There were more than 3,000 homeless individuals in Orange County during this period. Most homeless were longtime residents of Orange County (average 14 years) who had lost jobs and could not afford housing. The county had relatively little affordable housing, and it had been decreasing. Single men had a particularly difficult time because they were less likely to receive the support from family, friends, or governmental agencies. Most were sleeping outdoors because they had no other choice. Homeless individuals were 10 times as likely to be victimized by crime than the average population. Many homeless stayed in urban areas because of proximity to assistance providers (food, clothing and shelter), day jobs (just 8 percent were unemployed and not looking for jobs), public facilities (restrooms, etc.) and the lack of transportation.

Timothy Shaw was the executive director of the Orange County Homeless Issues Task Force. He pegged the number of homeless in Santa Ana at about 1,500 persons in 1993. There were about 118 shelter beds available for single men like Eichorn, most available on a first-come, first-served basis. In addition, the armory could accomodate 125 persons during the winter (although it frequently exceeded its capacity). As was routine, these shelters were full on the night Eichorn was cited.

Maria Mendoza was the county's homeless coordinator and oversaw use of the armory as a shelter. The armory was available only on cold winter nights. She explained how the bus to the armory would leave from the civic center in the late afternoon. Those on the bus had priority at the armory. Eichorn had spent some 20 nights there in December and January. On January 25, the armory was 13 persons over capacity, which was not uncommon. That the armory would accept excess capacity was not a given. Usually, only those "at risk" (e.g., women and children) would be admitted after the maximum was reached, and generally only when it was raining.

Eichorn, 49 years old, testified he had moved to Costa Mesa in 1972, a few years after his discharge from the Marine Corps. The Vietnam veteran lost his job in a machine shop in 1980, and subsequently ended up without a place to live. He moved to Santa Ana because a friend told him about a job driving an ice cream truck. He sold ice cream for about a year and was able to afford a motel room. When he lost that job, he frequented the casual labor office in Santa Ana until it closed. When he worked and could save enough, he would live in a motel. He also relied on general relief and food stamps. However, general relief was no longer enough to secure affordable housing because most of the less expensive motels had been torn down. If he could not get into a shelter, Eichorn would sleep in the civic center, where he was close to services (including restrooms) and where there was "safety in numbers" (i.e., where it was less likely someone would steal or attack him while he slept). He loved to work and did so every chance he got. He did not like living outside. He had been turned away from the armory in the past and had a "nervous walk" back to the civic center. On January 25, he did not recall whether he had tried to find a spot at a shelter or whether he heard that the shelters were full. He recalled eating around 7:00 p.m. He was in his sleeping bag listening to his radio when Craig arrived around 10:30 p.m. Eichorn's mother and stepfather lived in Long Beach, but staying with them was not an option because he was "an adult responsible for" himself. Defendant denied a problem with alcohol or drugs.

June Marcott, program manager for food stamps and general relief of the County of Orange, testified Eichorn received food stamps on a regular basis from 1989 through 1993, except when he was employed in parts of 1991 and 1992. He was eligible for $307 monthly in general relief if he participated in a work program (working nine days a month) and looked for work (four job applications per day). He last received general relief in November 1990 and was terminated because he did not submit a job search report. He applied for relief in March and June 1992, but was denied.

The court found Eichorn had violated the camping ordinance and was not involuntarily homeless on the night in question, finding he chose not to go to the armory. He also suggested defendant should have sought out familial assistance and should have applied for general relief. The court ordered him to perform 40 hours of community service. By a two-to-one margin, the appellate department of the superior court affirmed the conviction without opinion and declined to certify the case to this court for direct review. Eichorn filed this petition for habeas corpus and seeks to set aside his conviction.

II

Eichorn makes a multipronged attack on his conviction. One of his contentions is that he was induced to waive his right to a jury trial by the court's pretrial ruling that he could not present a necessity defense. As noted above, the court ruled the defense's offer of proof was inadequate, i.e., defendant had not presented enough evidence to get to a jury on the issue of whether he violated the law to prevent a significant evil. This ruling was error, and we vacate the judgment accordingly.

California appellate courts have recognized the necessity defense "despite the absence of any statutory articulation of this defense and rulings from the California Supreme Court that the common law is not a part of the criminal law in California."

In *Tobe v. City of Santa Ana,* the Supreme Court, while holding the camping ordinance was facially valid, declined to decide whether and how it might be unconstitutionally applied. The court refused to assume that the ordinance would be enforced "against persons who have no alternative to 'camping' or placing 'camp paraphernalia' on public property." Indeed, the *Tobe* court was given assurances by the People "that a necessity defense might be available to 'truly homeless' persons and that prosecutorial discretion would be exercised." * * *

An instruction on the defense of necessity is required where there is evidence "sufficient to establish that defendant violated the law (1) to prevent a significant evil, (2) with no adequate alternative, (3) without creating a greater danger than the one avoided, (4) with a good faith belief in the necessity, (5) with such belief being objectively reasonable, and (6) under circumstances in which he did not substantially contribute to the emergency." * * *

Whether necessity exists is generally a question of fact.

At a minimum, reasonable minds could differ whether defendant acted to prevent a "significant evil." Sleep is a physiological need, not an option for humans. It is common knowledge that loss of sleep produces a host of physical and mental problems (mood irritability, energy drain and low motivation, slow reaction time, inability to concentrate and process information). Certainly, no one would suggest that a groggy truck driver who stops his rig on the side of a road rather than risk falling asleep at the wheel does not act to prevent a significant evil, i.e., harm to himself and others. Indeed, Judge Margines had denied Eichorn's request for funds to hire an expert to testify about the harmful effects of sleep loss: "I mean it doesn't take an expert to tell us that, to convince a person, that there are ill effects that arise from sleep [deprivation]."

The court must instruct if the evidence could result in a finding defendant's criminal act was justified by necessity. Eichorn's offer of proof was sufficient. There was substantial if not uncontradicted evidence that defendant slept in the civic center because his alternatives were inadequate and economic forces were primarily to blame for his predicament. Thus, whether denominated a denial of his right to jury trial or of his due process right to present a defense the court's error was clear, fundamental, and struck at the heart of the trial process. * * *

The writ is granted and the cause remanded to the former municipal court with directions to set aside the judgment of conviction and to proceed in conformity with this opinion.

Note

According to Mr. Eichorn's appellate counsel, the District Attorney did not refile charges against Mr. Eichorn after the case was remanded.

In *United States v. Arellano-Rivera*, 244 F.3d 1119 (9th Cir. 2001), *cert. denied*, 535 U.S. 976 (2002), the defendant was convicted of unlawfully reentering the United States after being deported in violation of a federal statute, 8 U.S.C. § 1326, and argued that he was wrongfully precluded from submitting evidence to support a necessity defense. Arellano-Rivera was detained, along with four other individuals, by a U.S. Border Patrol agent in the hills near Andrade, California, about two miles from the United States-Mexico border, and he admitted that he was a citizen of Mexico and had no legal right to be in the United States. At trial, Arellano-Rivera offered to prove that he suffered from an advanced case of Acquired Immune Deficiency Syndrome (AIDS), along with related illnesses, and that he was entering the United States to receive treatment he was unable to obtain in Mexico. The Ninth Circuit, citing *Schoon*, held that the district court properly refused to allow Arellano-Rivera to submit his evidence, because there was a legal alternative: Arellano-Rivera could have petitioned the United States Attorney General for temporary admission into the United States on the basis of his dire medical condition, but he did not. The court held that this failure barred a necessity claim, even though it was extremely unlikely that the United States Attorney General would have granted such a claim. Indeed, even if Arellano-Rivera had petitioned the Attorney General and the petition was denied, the Ninth Circuit held that necessity would not have been a cognizable defense. According to the court, "an alien cannot lawfully overrule the Attorney General and parole himself as a matter of 'necessity.'" 244 F.3d 1119, at 1126.

B.   EXCUSE DEFENSES

In contrast with the justification defenses, which share a common logical structure, the excuses developed under the common law and the Model Penal Code have various structures. What they share is the intuition that under some circumstances, even though the defendant broke the law and was not morally justified in doing so, the defendant should nevertheless not be punished because she lacks moral responsibility for her actions. Sometimes this lack of responsibility is situational: the defendant who acts under duress, for example, is conceived of as an ordinary, reasonable person caught in unreasonable circumstances. In other situations the defendant's lack of responsibility is rooted in her very personality: the criminal defendant who is insane, whose capacity is diminished, or who is a minor is conceived of as lacking full moral agency across the board.

1. Duress

Duress, also known as coercion, is an affirmative defense in which the defendant claims she was threatened by another person with physical force (either to herself or a third person) unless she committed a specific crime. While the elements of duress vary from jurisdiction to jurisdiction, the basic elements of the duress defense in jurisdictions that have incorporated the common law include the following:

1. The defendant acted in response to an imminent threat of death or serious bodily injury;

2. The defendant had a well-grounded (or reasonable) fear that the threat would be carried out unless she committed a specified crime;

3. The defendant had no reasonable opportunity to escape the threatened harm.

See Alafair S. Burke, *Rational Actors, Self-Defense, and Duress: Making Sense, Not Syndromes, Out of the Battered Woman,* 81 N.C. L. Rev. 211, 253 (2002).

There is often confusion in the courts about the difference between necessity and duress, and in some jurisdictions the judges use terms like "lesser evil," "choice of evils," "justification," "compulsion," "coercion," "duress," and "necessity" more or less interchangeably. The key difference between necessity and duress is that conduct under duress is a response to a threat from a specific individual to commit the acts that constitute the crime. Conduct under necessity, in contrast, involves a response to a dire situation.

At early common law, the duress defense was limited to cases in which the defendant or members of her family were threatened. Today, most jurisdictions that follow the common law allow a threat to kill or seriously injure the defendant or any other person to satisfy element one.

The imminence requirement in element one has been strictly construed in some cases. For example, in one case, a man agreed to cooperate with the government and testify against a defendant in a criminal trial. Right before trial, the man was threatened by armed assailants who nearly ran him over. The man gave false testimony at trial. At his subsequent trial for perjury, the man asserted duress as a defense. The court rejected his duress defense because it felt the threat of death or serious bodily harm was not imminent or impending when he testified falsely at trial. *See State v. Rosillo*, 282 N.W.2d 872 (Minn. 1979).

Section 2.09 of the Model Penal Code, which sets out the defense of duress, excuses criminal conduct that was coerced by the use of, or threat to use, unlawful force against the actor's person or the person of another that a "person of reasonable firmness in his situation would have been unable to resist." Thus, unlike the common law formulation, the duress defense is not limited to situations involving threats of death or great bodily harm. Nor is there any explicit imminence requirement, although the question of the imminence of the threat is relevant to the issue of whether a person of reasonable firmness would have been able to resist it. Finally, within the common law tradition the principle seems to have been accepted that duress can never be a defense to murder, at least where the defendant was the principal actor. Under the Model Penal Code, a duress defense to homicide is possible, even if the victim is an innocent.

UNITED STATES v. CONTENTO-PACHON
United States Court of Appeals for the Ninth Circuit
723 F.2d 691 (9th Cir. 1984)

BOOCHEVER, C.J.

This case presents an appeal from a conviction for unlawful possession with intent to distribute a narcotic controlled substance in violation of 21 U.S.C. § 841(a)(1). At trial, the defendant attempted to offer evidence of duress and necessity defenses. The district court excluded this evidence on the ground that it was insufficient to support the defenses. We reverse because there was sufficient evidence of duress to present a triable issue of fact.

I. FACTS

The defendant-appellant, Juan Manuel Contento-Pachon, is a native of Bogota, Colombia and was employed there as a taxicab driver. He asserts that one of his passengers, Jorge, offered him a job as the driver of a privately-owned car. Contento-Pachon expressed an interest in the job and agreed to meet Jorge and the owner of the car the next day.

Instead of a driving job, Jorge proposed that Contento-Pachon swallow cocaine-filled balloons and transport them to the United States. Contento-Pachon agreed to consider the proposition. He was told not to mention the proposition to anyone, otherwise he would "get into serious trouble." Contento-Pachon testified that he did not contact the police because he believes that the Bogota police are corrupt and that they are paid off by drug traffickers.

Approximately one week later, Contento-Pachon told Jorge that he would not carry the cocaine. In response, Jorge mentioned facts about Contento-Pachon's personal life, including private details which Contento-Pachon had never mentioned to Jorge. Jorge told Contento-Pachon that his failure to cooperate would result in the death of his wife and three year-old child.

The following day the pair met again. Contento-Pachon's life and the lives of his family were again threatened. At this point, Contento-Pachon agreed to take the cocaine into the United States.

The pair met two more times. At the last meeting, Contento-Pachon swallowed 129 balloons of cocaine. He was informed that he would be watched at all times during the trip, and that if he failed to follow Jorge's instruction he and his family would be killed.

After leaving Bogota, Contento-Pachon's plane landed in Panama. Contento-Pachon asserts that he did not notify the authorities there because he felt that the Panamanian police were as corrupt as those in Bogota. Also, he felt that any such action on his part would place his family in jeopardy.

When he arrived at the customs inspection point in Los Angeles, Contento-Pachon consented to have his stomach x-rayed. The x-rays revealed a foreign substance which was later determined to be cocaine.

At Contento-Pachon's trial, the government moved to exclude the defenses of duress and necessity. The motion was granted. We reverse.

A. DURESS

There are three elements of the duress defense: (1) an immediate threat of death or serious bodily injury, (2) a well-grounded fear that the threat will be carried out, and (3) no reasonable opportunity to escape the threatened harm. Sometimes a fourth element is required: the defendant must submit to proper authorities after attaining a position of safety.

Factfinding is usually a function of the jury, and the trial court rarely rules on a defense as a matter of law. If the evidence is insufficient as a matter of law to support a duress defense, however, the trial court should exclude that evidence.

The trial court found Contento-Pachon's offer of proof insufficient to support a duress defense because he failed to offer proof of two elements: immediacy and inescapability.[1] We examine the elements of duress.

Immediacy: The element of immediacy requires that there be some evidence that the threat of injury was present, immediate, or impending. "[A] veiled threat of future unspecified harm" will not satisfy this requirement. The district court found that the initial threats were not immediate because "they were conditioned on defendant's failure to cooperate in the future and did not place defendant and his family in immediate danger."

Evidence presented on this issue indicated that the defendant was dealing with a man who was deeply involved in the exportation of illegal substances. Large sums of money were at stake and, consequently, Contento-Pachon had reason to believe that Jorge would carry out his threats. Jorge had gone to the trouble to discover that Contento-Pachon was married, that he had a child, the names of his wife and child, and the location of his residence. These were not vague threats of possible future harm. According to the defendant, if he had refused to cooperate, the consequences would have been immediate and harsh.

Contento-Pachon contends that he was being watched by one of Jorge's accomplices at all times during the airplane trip. As a consequence, the force of the threats continued to restrain him. Contento-Pachon's contention that he was operating under the threat of immediate harm was supported by sufficient evidence to present a triable issue of fact.

Escapability: The defendant must show that he had no reasonable opportunity to escape. The district court found that because Contento-Pachon was not physically restrained prior to the time he swallowed the balloons, he could have sought help from the police or fled. Contento-Pachon explained that he did not report the threats because he feared that the police were corrupt. The trier of fact should decide whether one in Contento-Pachon's position might believe that some of the Bogota police were paid informants for drug traffickers and that reporting the matter to the police did not represent a reasonable opportunity of escape.

If he chose not to go to the police, Contento-Pachon's alternative was to flee. We reiterate that the opportunity to escape must be reasonable. To flee,

---

[1] We believe that a triable issue was presented as to the [second] element, that the fear be well-grounded, based on the same facts that lead us to the conclusion as to the immediacy of the threats.

Contento-Pachon, along with his wife and three year-old child, would have been forced to pack his possessions, leave his job, and travel to a place beyond the reaches of the drug traffickers. A juror might find that this was not a reasonable avenue of escape. Thus, Contento-Pachon presented a triable issue on the element of escapability.

Surrender to Authorities: As noted above, the duress defense is composed of at least three elements. The government argues that the defense also requires that a defendant offer evidence that he intended to turn himself in to the authorities upon reaching a position of safety. Although it has not been expressly limited, this fourth element seems to be required only in prison escape cases. Under other circumstances, the defense has been defined to include only three elements.

The Supreme Court in *United States v. Bailey,* noted that "escape from federal custody . . . . is a continuing offense and . . . . an escapee can be held liable for failure to return to custody as well as for his initial departure." This factor would not be present in most crimes other than escape.

In cases not involving escape from prison there seems little difference between the third basic requirement that there be no reasonable opportunity to escape the threatened harm and the obligation to turn oneself in to authorities on reaching a point of safety. Once a defendant has reached a position where he can safely turn himself in to the authorities he will likewise have a reasonable opportunity to escape the threatened harm.

That is true in this case. Contento-Pachon claims that he was being watched at all times. According to him, at the first opportunity to cooperate with authorities without alerting the observer, he consented to the x-ray. We hold that a defendant who has acted under a well-grounded fear of immediate harm with no opportunity to escape may assert the duress defense, if there is a triable issue of fact whether he took the opportunity to escape the threatened harm by submitting to authorities at the first reasonable opportunity.

B. NECESSITY

The defense of necessity is available when a person is faced with a choice of two evils and must then decide whether to commit a crime or an alternative act that constitutes a greater evil. Contento-Pachon has attempted to justify his violation of 21 U.S.C. § 841(a)(1) by showing that the alternative, the death of his family, was a greater evil.

Traditionally, in order for the necessity defense to apply, the coercion must have had its source in the physical forces of nature. The duress defense was applicable when the defendant's acts were coerced by a human force. This distinction served to separate the two similar defenses. But modern courts have tended to blur the distinction between duress and necessity. * * *

The defense of necessity is usually invoked when the defendant acted in the interest of the general welfare. For example, defendants have asserted the defense as a justification for (1) bringing laetrile into the United States for the treatment of cancer patients; (2) unlawfully entering a naval base to protest the Trident missile system; (3) burning Selective Service System records to protest United States military action.

Contento-Pachon's acts were allegedly coerced by human, not physical forces. In addition, he did not act to promote the general welfare. Therefore, the necessity defense was not available to him. Contento-Pachon mischaracterized evidence of duress as evidence of necessity. The district court correctly disallowed his use of the necessity defense.

II. CONCLUSION

Contento-Pachon presented credible evidence that he acted under an immediate and well-grounded threat of serious bodily injury, with no opportunity to escape. Because the trier of fact should have been allowed to consider the credibility of the proffered evidence, we reverse. The district court correctly excluded Contento-Pachon's necessity defense.

REVERSED and REMANDED.

COYLE, DISTRICT JUDGE (dissenting in part and concurring in part):

In order to establish a defense of duress, the trial court in this case required Contento-Pachon to show (1) that he or his family was under an immediate threat of death or serious bodily injury; (2) that he had a well grounded fear that the threat would be carried out; and (3) that he had no reasonable opportunity to escape the threat. Applying this three-part test, the trial court found that the defendant's offer of proof was insufficient to support a defense of duress. The government argues that this holding should be affirmed and I agree. * * *

In granting the government's motion in limine excluding the defense of duress, the trial court specifically found Contento-Pachon had failed to present sufficient evidence to establish the necessary elements of immediacy and inescapability. In its Order the district court stated:

The first threat made to defendant and his family about three weeks before the flight was not immediate; the threat was conditioned upon defendant's failure to cooperate in the future and did not place the defendant and his family in immediate danger or harm. Moreover, after the initial threat and until he went to the house where he ingested the balloons containing cocaine, defendant and his family were not physically restrained and could have sought help from the police or fled. No such efforts were attempted by defendant. Thus, defendant's own offer of proof negates two necessary elements of the defense of duress.

In cases where the defendant's duress has been raised, the courts have indicated that the element of immediacy is of crucial importance. The trial court found that the threats made against the defendant and his family lacked the requisite element of immediacy. This finding is adequately supported by the record. The defendant was outside the presence of the drug dealers on numerous occasions for varying lengths of time. There is no evidence that his family was ever directly threatened or even had knowledge of the threats allegedly directed against the defendant.

Moreover, the trial court found that the defendant and his family enjoyed an adequate and reasonable opportunity to avoid or escape the threats of the drug dealers in the weeks before his flight. Until he went to the house where he ingested the balloons containing cocaine, defendant and his family were not physically restrained or prevented from seeking help. The record supports the trial court's findings that the defendant and his family could have sought assistance from the authorities or have fled. Cases considering the defense of duress have established that where there was a reasonable legal alternative to violating the law, a chance to refuse to do the criminal act and also to avoid the threatened danger, the defense will fail. Duress is permitted as a defense only when a criminal act was committed because there was no other opportunity to avoid the threatened danger.

The district court is vested with broad discretion whether to admit or exclude proffered evidence and its rulings will not be overturned on review without a clear showing of abuse of discretion. Because the district court's decision granting the government's motion *in limine* is fully and adequately supported by the record, I cannot agree that the district court abused its discretion and I therefore respectfully dissent.

I agree with the majority, however, that the district court properly excluded Contento-Pachon's necessity defense.

STATE v. HUNTER

Supreme Court of Kansas
241 Kan. 629, 740 P.2d 559 (1987)

LOCKETT, J.

Defendant James C. Hunter appeals his convictions of two counts of felony murder, two counts of aggravated kidnapping, one count of aggravated robbery, one count of aggravated battery on a law enforcement officer, and one count of aggravated battery. Hunter raises numerous issues, among them that the trial judge committed reversible error by refusing Hunter's requested instruction on his defense of compulsion. We reverse and remand for a new trial.

In February 1985 James C. Hunter, a resident of Amoret, Missouri, was hitchhiking from Texas back to the Kansas City area. He arrived in Wichita on February 12, 1985. On February 13, Hunter hitched a ride with Mark Walters, Lisa Dunn, and Daniel Remeta. On the way north on I-135, Remeta displayed two weapons, a .357 Magnum and an inoperative .22 pistol. Hunter repaired the .22 and Remeta fired the .22 out of the car window several times. When they reached the intersection of I-135 and I-70, Hunter asked to be let off. At that point Remeta began talking about another hitchhiker he wished he had killed and also described prior crimes he had committed, including several murders.

At the Levant exchange on I-70, Dunn, Walters, Remeta, and the defendant were pulled over by a police car. The driver of the police car was Thomas County Undersheriff Benjamin F. Albright, who had been asked to investigate a vehicle matching the description of the car. Albright instructed the occupants to remain in the car and put their hands on the ceiling. One of the passengers exited the car and fired two shots through Albright's windshield. Albright identified the person who fired these shots as having shoulder-length brown hair and a full beard. This description matched that of the defendant. Immediately thereafter, Albright was shot by the same person in the arm and chest. At trial, Albright identified James Hunter as his assailant. Hunter, Dunn, and Remeta all testified that it was Remeta who shot Albright. Hunter testified that, after Albright was shot, he attempted to shoot Remeta with the .22 handgun but accidentally wounded Dunn. Dunn and Remeta corroborated this testimony.

Shortly after the Albright shooting, the Remeta vehicle reached the Bartlett Elevator in Levant, Kansas. There were eight individuals at the elevator: Maurice Christie, the elevator manager; Fred Sager, the assistant manager; and Dennis Tubbs, Raymond Haremza, Rick Schroeder, Glenn Moore, and two others. The testimony concerning Hunter's activities at the Levant elevator conflicted greatly. Christie testified that he observed "a bearded man," later identified as Hunter, holding a gun in the face of Rick Schroeder and forcing him into a pickup truck. Sager testified that he saw a bearded man with a gun in his hand and that Rick Schroeder got into the pickup by himself. Dennis Tubbs testified that Hunter held Schroeder's arm and told him to get into the pickup; he further testified he saw only one person with a gun. After Rick Schroeder and Glenn Moore were taken as hostages and loaded into Moore's pickup truck, Christie, while attempting to call the sheriff from the scale house, was shot by Remeta.

Following the shooting at the elevator, the hostages were driven to a point north of U.S. Highway 24 near Colby, Kansas. Remeta testified that he killed both Schroeder and Moore and left them at the side of the road. Police caught up with the pickup truck and forced it off the road at a farm. During an exchange of gunfire, Walters was killed. Subsequently, Remeta, Dunn, and Hunter were arrested.

Remeta, Dunn, and Hunter were formally charged on February 15, 1985. A preliminary hearing was held, after which all three defendants were bound over. At the arraignment, all defendants refused to enter a plea and the trial court entered pleas of not guilty on behalf of all three. Prior to trial, Remeta entered a plea of guilty to all charges. Dunn and Hunter were tried by a jury, found guilty of all counts, and sentenced to consecutive terms. Hunter now appeals his conviction of two counts of felony murder (Schroeder and Moore), two counts of aggravated kidnapping (Schroeder and Moore), one count of aggravated battery on a law enforcement officer (Albright), one count of aggravated battery (Christie), and one count of aggravated robbery. * * *

COMPULSION

* * * Hunter contends that the trial court committed reversible error by refusing to instruct the jury on his defense of compulsion. We agree. K.S.A. 21-3209 provides for the defense of compulsion to crimes other than murder or manslaughter, stating:

> (1) A person is not guilty of a crime other than murder or voluntary manslaughter by reason of conduct which he performs under the compulsion or threat of the imminent infliction of death or great bodily harm, if he reasonably believes that death or great bodily harm will be inflicted upon him or upon his spouse, parent, child, brother or sister if he does not perform such conduct.

(2) The defense provided by this section is not available to one who willfully or wantonly places himself in a situation in which it is probable that he will be subjected to compulsion or threat.

Defendant's requested instruction, taken from PIK Crim. 2d 54.13, stated:

It is a defense to the charges of Aggravated Battery Against a Law Enforcement Officer, Aggravated Robbery and Aggravated Kidnapping, if the defendant acted under compulsion or threat of immediate infliction of death or great bodily harm, and if said defendant reasonably believed that death or great bodily harm would have been inflicted upon said defendant had he or she not acted as he or she did.

The trial court refused to give the compulsion instruction because the defendant was charged with premeditated and felony murder. * * *

Whether the defense of compulsion is available to a criminal defendant charged with felony murder under K.S.A. 21-3401 is an issue of first impression. * * * [E]arly cases refused to recognize any compulsion as sufficient to excuse intentional killing.[a] The rationale is that, when confronted by a choice between two evils of equal magnitude, the individual ought to sacrifice his own life rather than escape by the murder of an innocent.

A number of jurisdictions, including Kansas, have incorporated by statute the common-law denial of the compulsion defense in crimes of murder. While not all jurisdictions have considered the applicability of these statutes to crimes of felony murder, we note that both Arizona and Missouri have held that defendants are barred from claiming the compulsion defense in felony-murder cases. They reason that the person charged need only have the required intent to commit or participate in the underlying felony and no other mental state on his part need be demonstrated because of the strict liability imposed by the felony-murder rule.

---

[a] The Model Penal Code, in contrast to the common law, allows a defendant charged with any offense, including murder, to argue duress. *See* Model Penal Code § 2.09(1) providing that "it is an affirmative defense that the actor engaged in the conduct charged ... because he was coerced to do so by the use of, or a threat to use, unlawful force against his person ... that a person of reasonable firmness in his situation would have been unable to resist." Model Penal Code § 2.09(1).

We are not, however, persuaded by the reasoning of these decisions. The better view, consistently adhered to by commentators, is that any limitation to the defense of duress be confined to crimes of intentional killing and not to killings done by another during the commission of some lesser felony. As LaFave and Scott have explained:

> [I]f *A* compels *B* at gunpoint to drive him to the bank which *A* intends to rob, and during the ensuing robbery *A* kills a bank customer *C, B* is not guilty of the robbery (for he was justified by duress) and so is not guilty of felony murder of *C* in the commission of robbery. The law properly recognizes that one is justified in aiding a robbery if he is forced by threats to do so to save his life; he should not lose the defense because his threateners unexpectedly kill someone in the course of the robbery and thus convert a mere robbery into a murder.

*   *   *

There were three versions of the events at the grain elevator in Levant. First, State's witnesses Christie, Sager, and Tubbs all testified that Hunter had played an active role in the kidnapping of Schroeder and Moore and the theft of the pickup truck. Christie and Sager testified that Hunter had a weapon. Second, Hunter testified that he had no weapon at the elevator and that he was ordered by Remeta to go to the other end of the building to watch to see if anyone tried to exit through the back door. According to Hunter, he then walked around to the back of the building and stopped there to wait to see what happened, and Remeta then ordered him back around to the other side and into the pickup. Hunter testified that he never felt he had a chance to escape. Third, Remeta testified that he had both guns at all times. He further stated that he asked Hunter to watch Schroeder and Moore at the pickup truck and that he would have shot Hunter if he had not followed orders.

In order to constitute the defense of compulsion, the coercion or duress must be present, imminent, and impending, and of such a nature as to induce a well-grounded apprehension of death or serious bodily injury if the act is not done. The doctrine of coercion or duress cannot be invoked as an excuse by one who had a reasonable opportunity to avoid doing the act without undue exposure to death or serious bodily harm. In addition, the compulsion must be continuous and there must be no reasonable opportunity to escape the compulsion without committing the crime.

The only opportunity Hunter would have had for escape would have been when he was out of sight of Remeta at the point when he went around the north side of the building at the Levant elevator. Hunter testified that Remeta came around the building and ordered him to return to the pickup. There was testimony that the total time which elapsed at the grain elevator was approximately five minutes. From the record, it is impossible to tell how long Hunter remained out of sight of Remeta. Viewed in the light most favorable to Hunter, however, and particularly in light of the fact that it was undisputed that Remeta had possession of the .357 Magnum at all times, it cannot be said that Hunter had a reasonable opportunity to escape.

Although some of the evidence supporting Hunter's defense of compulsion came from Hunter's own testimony, this court has held that a defendant is entitled to an instruction on his or her theory of the case even though the evidence is slight and supported only by defendant's own testimony. In this case, evidence came not only from Hunter, but also from Remeta and the State's witnesses Christie, Sager, and Tubbs. There was ample evidence presented from which the jury could have concluded that Hunter's acts were justified by compulsion.

Here, the record is replete with testimony that Daniel Remeta was a person to be feared. It was the function of the jury as the exclusive trier of fact to determine if it was believable that Hunter was afraid for his life, if such fear was reasonable, and if such fear justified any criminal acts which Hunter may have performed. When the trial judge refused the requested compulsion instruction, he effectively prevented the jury from considering the evidence presented in Hunter's defense. This denial of the jury's right to determine the facts constitutes reversible error. We reverse and remand this case for a new trial in accordance with this opinion. Because the resolution of this issue is dispositive of this appeal, we do not reach the other issues raised.

Note

Professor Phillip Johnson reports that "On retrial Hunter obtained a change of venue and was acquitted of all charges by the jury after almost 3 years in prison. According to [a] UPI news story dated January 21, 1988, Hunter made these comments after the acquittal:

> Asked if he was bitter, Hunter replied, 'Yeah I'm bitter. Basically at Ben Albright. I know what happened that day. He (Albright) just freaked out and lost it. He never looked up from that car. I thought that idiot was going to save my life. He's a police officer and he can't admit he turned tail.'

> * * * [Hunter] said he has often wished he had taken the advice he has heard throughout life – never hitchhike. 'I wouldn't do

it (now) unless I got to. If a car breaks down, I can understand,' he said. 'I had been told for years you shouldn't hitchhike, you shouldn't hitchhike. I just wish them folks there had never stopped and picked me up.'

Hunter died a week later of a heart attack at the age of 35." Phillip E. Johnson, CRIMINAL LAW: CASES, MATERIALS AND TEXT (6th ed. 2000).

Increasingly, courts have been asked to consider whether evidence of battered woman's syndrome should be admitted in cases in which an abused woman defendant claims she committed the charged offense under duress from her abuser. A few courts have decided that such evidence is relevant and should be admitted. *See, e.g., People v. Romero*, 26 Cal. App. 4th 315, 13 Cal.Rptr.2d 332 (Ct. App. 1992). Most courts, however, have deemed battered woman syndrome evidence irrelevant to claims of duress on the ground that the defense of duress requires an objectively reasonable fear of imminent death or grievous bodily injury and evidence of battered woman syndrome supports only a subjective fear. Alafair S. Burke, *Rational Actors, Self-Defense, and Duress: Making Sense, Not Syndromes, Out of the Battered Woman*, 81 N.C. L. Rev. 211, 265 (2002) (noting "although battered women who claim duress have had some success in relying upon the battered woman syndrome theory, they have enjoyed less success than battered women who claim self-defense."). If courts are willing to admit battered woman syndrome evidence as relevant to the reasonableness of the battered woman's belief in the need to use deadly force against her abuser in self-defense, should they also admit battered woman syndrome evidence in cases involving claims of duress?

2. Insanity

The defendant's mental competency is a possible issue at three stages of the criminal proceeding. Before trial, the defense may argue that the defendant is incompetent to stand trial. The test for determining competency to stand trial is whether the defendant is capable of understanding the proceedings and assisting his counsel in presenting a defense. If the court decides that the defendant is incapable of understanding the proceedings or cannot assist in his defense, criminal proceedings are generally suspended until the defendant is deemed competent to stand trial.[a]

---

[a]The United States Supreme Court recently addressed the issue whether the government can forcibly medicate an incompetent defendant to make him competent to stand trial and held that the government may forcibly administer anti-psychotic drugs to render a mentally ill defendant competent to stand trial if the treatment is (1) medically appropriate, (2) substantially unlikely to have side effects that may

Second, the defendant may put his or her mental competency into issue by claiming that he or she should be found not guilty by reason of insanity. Over the years, many different common law tests for determining whether a defendant is legally insane have been adopted. All of these tests examine the defendant's mental capacity at the time he or she committed the criminal act. The first case in this section, *United States v. Freeman*, discusses these various tests in detail and provides a cogent critique of the *M'Naghten* test, once the leading test for insanity.

Section 4.01 of the Model Penal Code provides an alternative definition of insanity. Section 4.01 provides a defense when, as a result of mental disease or defect, the actor "lacked substantial capacity to appreciate the criminality or wrongfulness of his conduct." As Christopher Slobogin notes:

> This formulation works two changes in the M'Naghten Test. One is that, on its face, the ALI test does not require the black-or-white analysis that M'Naghten does. It speaks in terms of *substantial* lack of experience and capacity, as opposed to an *inability* to know the wrongfulness of the act. Second, the ALI test uses the word "appreciate" as opposed to the word "know." The latter modification was meant to provide an excuse to those who might "know" that the criminal act was wrong, but who are unable to internalize the wrongfulness of the act.

Christopher Slobogin, *The Integrationist Alternative to the Insanity Defense: Reflections of the Exculpatory Scope of Mental Illness in the Wake of the Andrea Yates Trial*, 30 Am. J. Crim. L. 315, 318 (2003).

Well over half the states initially moved from the *M'Naghten* test to the Model Penal Code test. However, the 1982 acquittal of John Hinckley, who had tried to assassinate President Ronald Reagan, on insanity grounds caused a public outcry. In response, many jurisdictions, including the federal government, re-adopted some version of the stricter *M'Naghten* test. (The federal statute, however, kept the word "appreciate" rather than "know," defining insanity as an inability "to appreciate the nature and quality or the wrongfulness of [the defendant's] acts." 18 U.S.C. § 20 (1984).) As of 1995, approximately twenty-five states were using some version of the M'Naghten Test, approximately twenty states were using the ALI Model Penal Code test, and a few states had

---

undermine the trial's fairness, and (3) necessary to significantly further important governmental interests. *Sell v. United States,* 539 U.S. 166 (2003).

abolished the insanity defense. Deborah W. Denno, *Who is Andrea Yates? A Short Story About Insanity*, 10 Duke J. Gender L. & Pol'y 1, 13 (2003).

One question that has split the courts is whether to construe the term "wrong" or "wrongfulness," which appears in both of the leading tests, as "legal wrongfulness" (i.e., the defendant knew that he was acting illegally) or "moral wrongfulness" (i.e. the defendant knew that he was acting contrary to morality). The majority in *State v. Crenshaw* discusses the distinction between legal and moral wrongfulness, and concludes that this is a distinction without a difference because a defendant who knows that he is acting illegally will often also realize that he is acting in contradistinction to society's moral values. The dissent in *Crenshaw* argues that this is not always the case, and that the trial court's instruction to the jury that "right and wrong" refers to the knowledge of a person that he is acting contrary to law usurped the power of the jury to decide whether the defendant knew the difference between right and wrong.

Third, the mental capacity of a convicted defendant on death row may be an issue prior to execution. In *Ford v. Wainwright*, 477 U.S. 399 (1986), the United States Supreme Court ruled that the execution of an insane person constitutes cruel and unusual punishment in violation of the Eighth Amendment. Whether the state can forcibly medicate a defendant to make him sane for execution is an issue that has not yet been addressed by the high court.

UNITED STATES v. FREEMAN
United States Court of Appeals for the Second Circuit
357 F.2d 606 (2d Cir. 1966)

KAUFMAN, CIRCUIT JUDGE

*   *   *

After a trial before Judge Tenney without a jury, Charles Freeman was found guilty on two counts of selling narcotics in violation of 21 U.S.C. §§ 173, 174, and sentenced to concurrent terms of five years on each count. Although Freeman denied commission of the substantive offense, his principal allegation at trial was that, at the time of the alleged sale of narcotics, he did not possess sufficient capacity and will to be held responsible for the criminality of his acts. In rejecting this contention, the District Court understandably relied upon the familiar *M'Naghten* Rules which, in their traditional formulation, permit acquittal only when it is proved that, "at the time of the committing of the act, the party accused was laboring under such a defect of reason, from disease of the mind as not to know the nature and quality of the act he was doing, or, if he did know it, that he did not know he was doing what was wrong." Since he could not find that Freeman's condition satisfied the rigid requirements of this test, Judge Tenney had no alternative but to hold the defendant guilty as charged. * * *

THE EVIDENCE OF SALE

If the issue of criminal responsibility is put to one side for the moment, the facts of Freeman's case do not rise above the routine. The government's evidence established that on the evening of June 24, 1963, narcotics agents Coursey and Fluhr met one James Lockhart, an informant (or, in the more polite lexicon of the government, a "special employee"), in uptown Manhattan. After making the usual search of the informant in order to be sure he did not possess narcotics prior to contact with the suspect, Lockhart and Coursey walked to the corner of 110th Street and Broadway while Fluhr remained behind. Lockhart introduced Freeman to Coursey and, after some preliminary discussion, Freeman stated, "I hear you want to buy some heroin." When Coursey indicated that he did and inquired about the price, Freeman replied that it would be $230 a "piece." At Freeman's suggestion, the three men then proceeded to the close-by Gold Rail bar, where Freeman gave Coursey a sealed brown paper bag in return for which Coursey mistakenly paid the defendant $130 instead of the stipulated $230. Coursey then left the bar and met Agent Fluhr and Agent Casale. Together they performed a field test on the contents of the brown paper bag which revealed the presence of heroin. A chemical analysis subsequently confirmed this result.

Shortly thereafter, Coursey was notified by car radio that Lockhart had called him. Coursey returned to 110th Street and Broadway and entered a taxi in which Freeman and Lockhart had been riding. When Freeman asked if Coursey was trying to "beat" him out of $100, Coursey explained that the failure to make full payment in the bar had been a mistake and he turned over an additional $100.

On August 1, 1963, a second transaction took place; in many respects it was a sequel to the first. This time, Coursey and a different informant, Alfred Roach, entered Marvin's Bar on Broadway near 111th Street. Freeman, standing at the bar, said that he had been sick, but, nevertheless, had heard that Coursey had been buying large amounts of heroin and indicated that he would like to make another sale. A price of $235 per ounce was agreed upon and Freeman and Coursey adjourned to the men's room where Freeman handed Coursey another brown paper bag.[6] Coursey made payment, this time in the correct amount, and departed. A field test on the contents of the bag showed that it contained heroin and a chemical analysis confirmed the accuracy of this result.

While Freeman admitted taking part in the transactions of June 24 and August 1, he presented a different version of his participation. He testified that rather than being the culprit, he was merely a conduit being used by the informant to pass the brown paper packages to Agent Coursey. The money which the agent paid, Freeman said, was not his to keep, but was turned over to the informant who had furnished him in each instance with the brown paper bag. Judge Tenney chose to discredit Freeman's version of these transactions and we see no reason to disagree with his resolution of the credibility issue.

THE DEFENSE OF LACK OF RESPONSIBILITY

As is not uncommon in cases in which the defense is raised, the bulk of the evidence directly relating to the issue of criminal responsibility took the form of expert psychiatric testimony of witnesses called by both the government and the defense. Freeman's expert witness at trial was Dr. Herman Denber, Associate Professor of Clinical Psychiatry at New York Medical College and Director of Psychiatric Research at Manhattan State Hospital. Dr. Denber, who had examined the defendant on the previous afternoon, testified that Freeman was not only a narcotics addict, but also a confirmed alcoholic. The Doctor noted that Freeman's body had become accustomed to the consumption of large amounts of heroin over a fourteen-year period, and that the defendant was in the habit of drinking one or two bottles of wine daily to increase the potency of the narcotics. In addition, he observed, Freeman regularly imbibed six to nine "shots" of whiskey each day.

Describing his examination in some detail, Dr. Denber testified that Freeman displayed no depth or variation in his emotional reactions, spoke in a flat monotone and paused for excessively long periods before responding to questions. Dr. Denber also noted that as a result of taking impure narcotics for

---

[6]Freeman apparently was uneasy in Marvin's Bar because he and the informant were the only Negroes present. Thus, Freeman hurrying to complete the transaction told Coursey, "Hurry up, man, because I got the stuff in my pocket and we look suspicious here because there is a whole lot of white people in here, we look suspicious in here."

so long a time, Freeman suffered from frequent episodes of toxic psychosis[7] leading to a clouding of the sensorium (inability to know what one is doing or where one is) as well as delusions, hallucinations, epileptic convulsions and, at times, amnesia.[8] The witness testified, moreover, that Freeman had suffered "knock-outs" on three occasions while engaging in prize fighting, and that these had led to a general vagueness about details. Finally, Dr. Denber observed that Freeman had experienced "innumerable brain traumata" which produced such organic and structural changes as destroyed brain tissue.

Restricted to stating a conclusory opinion within the confines of *M'Naghten*, Dr. Denber initially averred that Freeman was incapable of knowing right from wrong, even under a strict interpretation of that limited test. However, upon amplifying this conclusion, the defense expert acknowledged that Freeman had an awareness of what he was doing on the nights of June 24 and August 1 in the sense that he possessed cognition that he was selling heroin. The Doctor also added that Freeman was not in "such a state of toxicity that he did not remember the dates. He told me the story [of the narcotics transactions] clearly, but it is my feeling about him, in particular, that as far as the social implications or the nature or meaning of what this meant to him at that moment he was not aware of it."

To respond to Dr. Denber's testimony, the government called on Dr. Robert S. Carson, a former staff physician at Payne-Whitney Clinic of The New

---

[7] Dr. Denber defined a "psychosis" as "a disorder of the brain in which the individual's reality appreciation is altered and in which symptoms of thinking and feeling become abnormal." The term "toxic psychosis" refers to a "state of impaired mental functioning with clouding of the senses, non-awareness of time and place produced by some compound, usually medicinal, taken in excess over and above the usual requirements that are prescribed, and usually have been taken for a period of time by the individual."

[8] Dr. Denber testified that because of Freeman's extensive and prolonged use of narcotics such as heroin, cocaine, morphine, and benzedrine, amphetamines and sleeping pills, he did not derive satisfaction from the standard "fix" and was not, in any respect, just an ordinary drug addict. This massive infusion of drugs produced a condition which made Freeman at times, as he put it, so "messed up with the stuff" that he would fall "knocked cold in the street," with resultant head and other injuries. In addition, Freeman suffered from vomiting and chills and approximately twelve times a year for the last eight years, experienced auditory and visual hallucinations as well as paranoid delusions. For example, Freeman saw people in miniature and heard them call his name from under his bed. Indeed, Freeman told the Doctor, "At times I would think something was wrong with my head. I think the drugs I was using was eating up my brain."

York Hospital and Clinical Instructor in Psychiatry at Cornell University. Dr. Carson testified that Freeman was able to distinguish between right and wrong within the meaning of the *M'Naghten* test despite his heavy use of narcotics and alcohol. He noted that Freeman possessed the capacity to enter into purposeful activity such as the sale of narcotics, and he expressed the opinion that the defendant had been aware of the wrongfulness of his acts. In support of this view, Dr. Carson pointed to the fact that on the evening of August 1, 1963, Freeman had been sufficiently fearful of being apprehended that he had suggested that the transfer of narcotics take place in the privacy of the men's room of Marvin's Bar. In summary, Dr. Carson significantly acknowledged that Freeman had "some limitations" on his ability to distinguish right from wrong, but not to the degree required by the *M'Naghten* test. * * *

We are now concerned with whether the Court at trial should have applied a test less rigid than that provided by *M'Naghten*, so that the essential examination and psychiatric testimony could have been directed towards Freeman's capacity to exercise will or appreciate the wrongfulness of his conduct, rather than being confined to the relatively narrow inquiry required by *M'Naghten*. * * *

II.

We are here seeking a proper test of criminal responsibility. That we are not instead deciding the initial question -- whether lack of such responsibility, however defined, should be a defense in criminal prosecutions -- itself seems significant and worthy of at least some brief comment.

The criminal law, it has been said, is an expression of the moral sense of the community. The fact that the law has, for centuries, regarded certain wrong-doers as improper subjects for punishment is a testament to the extent to which that moral sense has developed. Thus, society has recognized over the years that none of the three asserted purposes of the criminal law -- rehabilitation, deterrence and retribution -- is satisfied when the truly irresponsible, those who lack substantial capacity to control their actions, are punished.

What rehabilitative function is served when one who is mentally incompetent and found guilty is ordered to serve a sentence in prison? Is not any curative or restorative function better achieved in such a case in an institution designed and equipped to treat just such individuals? And how is deterrence achieved by punishing the incompetent? Those who are substantially unable to restrain their conduct are, by definition, undeterrable and their "punishment" is no example for others; those who are unaware of or do not appreciate the nature and quality of their actions can hardly be expected rationally to weigh the consequences of their conduct. Finally, what segment of society can feel its desire for retribution satisfied when it wreaks vengeance upon the incompetent? Although an understandable emotion, a need for retribution can never be permitted in a civilized society to degenerate into a sadistic form of revenge.

A recognition that traditional notions of crime and punishment were inapplicable to the truly "irresponsible" hence came early to Anglo-American criminal law. We turn now to a consideration of those early stirrings.

III.

M'Naghten and its antecedents can, in many respects, be seen as examples of the law's conscientious efforts to place in a separate category, people who cannot be justly held "responsible" for their acts. As far back as 1582, William Lambard of Lincolns' Inn set forth what can be viewed as the forerunner of the *M'Naghten* test as we know it: "If a man or a natural fool, or a lunatic in the time of his lunacy, or a child who apparently has no knowledge of good or evil do kill a man, this is no felonious act * * * for they cannot be said to have any understanding will." By 1724, the language had shifted from "good or evil" to the more familiar emphasis on the word "know." Thus, in *Rex v. Arnold,* the "Wild Beast" test was enunciated. It provided for exculpation if the defendant "doth not *know* what he is doing, no more than * * * a wild beast."

* * * Daniel M'Naghten suffered from what now would be described as delusions of persecution. Apparently, he considered his major persecutor to be Robert Peel, then Prime Minister of England, for M'Naghten came to London with the intention of assassinating the chief of the Queen's government. His plan would have succeeded but for the fact that Peel chose to ride in Queen Victoria's carriage because of her absence from the city, while Drummond, his secretary, rode in the vehicle which normally would have been occupied by Peel. M'Naghten, believing that the Prime Minister was riding in his own carriage, shot and killed Drummond in error.

After a lengthy trial in 1843, M'Naghten was found "not guilty by reason of insanity." M'Naghten's exculpation from criminal responsibility was most significant for several reasons. His defense counsel had relied in part upon Dr. Isaac Ray's historic work, MEDICAL JURISPRUDENCE OF INSANITY which had been published in 1838. This book, which was used and referred to extensively at the trial, contained many enlightened views on the subject of criminal responsibility in general and on the weaknesses of the right and wrong test in particular. Thus, for example, the jury was told that the human mind is not compartmentalized and that a defect in one aspect of the personality could spill over and affect other areas. As Chief Judge Biggs tells us in his Isaac Ray lectures compiled in THE GUILTY MIND, the court was so impressed with this and other medical evidence of M'Naghten's incompetency that Lord Chief Justice Tindal practically directed a verdict for the accused.

For these reasons, M'Naghten's case could have been the turning point for a new approach to more modern methods of determining criminal responsibility. But the Queen's ire was raised by the acquittal and she was prompted to intervene. Mid-19th Century England was in a state of social upheaval and there had been three attempts on the life of the Queen and one on the Prince Consort. Indeed, Queen Victoria was so concerned about M'Naghten's acquittal that she summoned the House of Lords to "take the opinion of the Judges on the law governing such cases." Consequently, the fifteen judges of the common law courts were called in a somewhat extraordinary session under a not too subtle atmosphere of pressure to answer five prolix and obtuse questions on the status of criminal responsibility in England. Significantly, it was Lord Chief Justice Tindal who responded for fourteen of the fifteen judges, and thus articulated what has come to be known as the *M'Naghten* Rules or *M'Naghten* test. Rather than relying on Dr. Ray's monumental work which had apparently impressed him at M'Naghten's trial, Tindal, with the Queen's breath upon him, reaffirmed the old restricted right-wrong test despite its 16th Century roots and the fact that it, in effect, echoed such uninformed concepts as phrenology and monomania. In this manner, Dr. Ray's insights were to be lost to the common law for over one hundred years except in the small state of New Hampshire.

The foregoing necessarily abbreviated historical account makes manifest some of the critical infirmities of the *M'Naghten* test, not the least of which are the manner in which it was formulated and the charged atmosphere in which it was spawned. Even contemporaries questioned the validity of a rule that was not the product of the case-by-case method traditional with common law judges. Thus, Mr. Justice Maule, the fifteenth member of the panel summoned by the House of Lords, concurred in the use of the right-wrong test but expressed deep reservations about answering questions put to the judges abstractly without the benefit of a concrete case and argument. * * *

But the principal objection to *M'Naghten* is not that it was arrived at by this extraordinary process. Rather, the rule is faulted because it has several serious deficiencies which stem in the main from its narrow scope. Because *M'Naghten* focuses only on the cognitive aspect of the personality, i.e., the ability to know right from wrong, we are told by eminent medical scholars that it does not permit the jury to identify those who can distinguish between good and evil but who cannot control their behavior. The result is that instead of being treated at appropriate mental institutions for a sufficiently long period to bring about a cure or sufficient improvement so that the accused may return with relative safety to himself and the community, he is ordinarily sentenced to a prison term as if criminally responsible and then released as a potential recidivist with society at his mercy. To the extent that these individuals continue to be released from prison because of the narrow scope of *M'Naghten*, that test poses a serious danger to society's welfare.

Similarly, *M'Naghten*'s single track emphasis on the cognitive aspect of the personality recognizes no degrees of incapacity. Either the defendant knows right from wrong or he does not and that is the only choice the jury is given. But such a test is grossly unrealistic; our mental institutions, as any qualified psychiatrist will attest, are filled with people who to some extent can differentiate between right and wrong, but lack the capacity to control their acts to a substantial degree. As the commentary to the American Law Institute's Model Penal Code observes, "The law must recognize that when there is no black and white it must content itself with different shades of gray."

A further fatal defect of the *M'Naghten* Rules stems from the unrealistically tight shackles which they place upon expert psychiatric testimony. When the law limits a testifying psychiatrist to stating his opinion whether the accused is capable of knowing right from wrong, the expert is thereby compelled to test guilt or innocence by a concept which bears little relationship to reality. He is required thus to consider one aspect of the mind as a "logic-tight compartment in which the delusion holds sway leaving the balance of the mind intact. * * *"

Prominent psychiatrists have expressed their frustration when confronted with such requirements. Echoing such complaints, Edward de Grazia has asked, "How [does one] translate 'psychosis' or 'psychopathy' or 'dementia praecox' or even 'sociopathy' or 'mental disorder' or 'neurotic character disorder' or 'mental illness' into a psychiatric judgment of whether the accused knew 'right' from 'wrong.'" In stronger and more vivid terms, Dr. Lawrence Kolb, Director of the New York Psychiatric Institute, Professor and Chairman of the Department of Psychiatry at Columbia University and Director of the Psychiatric Service at Presbyterian Hospital, expressed a similar viewpoint when he declared that "answers supplied by a psychiatrist in regard to questions of rightness or wrongness of an act or 'knowing' its nature constitute a professional perjury."

* * * The tremendous growth of psychiatric knowledge since the Victorian origins of *M'Naghten* and even the near-universal disdain in which it is held by present-day psychiatrists are not by themselves sufficient reasons for abandoning the test. At bottom, the determination whether a man is or is not held responsible for his conduct is not a medical but a legal, social or moral judgment. Ideally, psychiatrists -- much like experts in other fields -- should provide grist for the legal mill, should furnish the raw data upon which the legal

judgment is based. It is the psychiatrist who informs as to the mental state of the accused -- his characteristics, his potentialities, his capabilities. But once this information is disclosed, it is society as a whole, represented by judge or jury, which decides whether a man with the characteristics described should or should not be held accountable for his acts. In so deciding, it cannot be presumed that juries will check their common sense at the courtroom door. As Professor Wechsler has rightly commented, "It's not to be expected that juries will lightly accept the proposition that one who seemingly knew in a true sense did not know. One would expect jury skepticism and the system is the healthier for that jury skepticism."

The true vice of *M'Naghten* is not, therefore, that psychiatrists will feel constricted in artificially structuring their testimony but rather that the ultimate deciders -- the judge or the jury -- will be deprived of information vital to their final judgment. For whatever the social climate of Victorian England, today's complex and sophisticated society will not be satisfied with simplistic decisions, based solely upon a man's ability to "know" right from wrong. * * *

IV.

Efforts to supplement or replace the *M'Naghten* Rules with a more meaningful and workable test have persisted for generations, with varying degrees of success. Perhaps the first to receive judicial approval, however, was more an added fillip to *M'Naghten* than a true substitute: the doctrine which permits acquittal on grounds of lack of responsibility when a defendant is found to have been driven by an "irresistible impulse" to commit his offense. In one form or another, the "irresistible impulse" test has become encrusted on the law of several jurisdictions, including the District Courts of this Circuit, and is now a familiar part of the vocabulary of millions since it was successfully invoked by the defendant of Robert Travers' celebrated novel and motion picture, "Anatomy of a Murder."

As it has commonly been employed, however, we find the "irresistible impulse" test to be inherently inadequate and unsatisfactory. Psychiatrists have long questioned whether "irresistible impulses" actually exist; the more basic legal objection to the term "irresistible impulse" is that it is too narrow and carries the misleading implication that a crime impulsively committed must have been perpetrated in a sudden and explosive fit. Thus, the "irresistible impulse" test is unduly restrictive because it excludes the far more numerous instances of crimes committed after excessive brooding and melancholy by one who is unable to resist sustained psychic compulsion or to make any real attempt to control his conduct. In seeking one isolated and indefinite cause for every act, moreover, the test is unhappily evocative of the notions which underlay

M'Naghten -- unfortunate assumptions that the problem can be viewed in black and white absolutes and in crystal-clear causative terms.

In so many instances the criminal act may be the reverse of impulsive; it may be coolly and carefully prepared yet nevertheless the result of a diseased mind. The "irresistible impulse" test is therefore little more than a gloss on *M'Naghten*, rather than a fundamentally new approach to the problem of criminal responsibility. It is, as one professor explained, "a relatively unobnoxious attempt to improve upon *M'Naghten*."

With the exception of New Hampshire, American courts waited until 1954 and Judge Bazelon's opinion for the District of Columbia Circuit in *Durham v. United States*, for legal recognition that disease or defect of the mind may impair the whole mind and not a subdivided portion of it. The *Durham* court swept away the intellectual debris of a century and articulated a test which was as simple in its formulation as its sources were complex. A defendant is not criminally responsible, wrote Judge Bazelon, "if his unlawful act was the product of mental disease or mental defect."

The advantages of *Durham* were apparent and its arrival was widely hailed. The new test entirely eliminated the "right-wrong" dichotomy, and hence interred the overriding emphasis on the cognitive element of the personality which had for so long plagued *M'Naghten*. The fetters upon expert testimony were removed and psychiatrists were permitted and indeed encouraged to provide all relevant medical information for the common sense application of judge or jury.

Finally, *Durham* ended to a large degree the "professional perjury" decried by psychiatrists -- the "juggling" of legal standards made inevitable by *M'Naghten* and rightly deplored by Justice Frankfurter. Too often, the unrealistic dogma of *M'Naghten* had compelled expert witnesses to "stretch" its requirements to "hard cases;" sympathetic to the plight of a defendant who was not, in fairness, responsible for his conduct, psychiatrists had found it necessary to testify that the accused did not know his act was "wrong" even when the defendant's words belied this conclusion. In its frank and express recognition that criminality resulting from mental disease or defect should not bring forth penal sanctions, *Durham* brought an end to this all too-frequent practice of "winking" at legal requirements, a practice which had contributed little to the self-respect and integrity of either medicine or the law.

In the aftermath of *Durham*, however, many students of the law recognized that the new rule, despite its many advantages, also possessed serious deficiencies. It has been suggested, for example, that *Durham's* insistence that an offense be the "product" of a mental disease or defect raised near-impossible problems of causation, closely resembling those encountered by the *M'Naghten* and irresistible impulse tests.

The most significant criticism of *Durham*, however, is that it fails to give the fact-finder any standard by which to measure the competency of the accused. As a result, psychiatrists when testifying that a defendant suffered from a "mental disease or defect" in effect usurped the jury's function. This problem was strikingly illustrated in 1957, when a staff conference at Washington's St. Elizabeth's Hospital reversed its previous determination and reclassified "psychopathic personality" as a "mental disease." Because this single hospital provides most of the psychiatric witnesses in the District of Columbia courts, juries were abruptly informed that certain defendants who had previously been considered responsible were now to be acquitted. It seems clear that a test which permits all to stand or fall upon the labels or classifications employed by testifying psychiatrists hardly affords the court the opportunity to perform its function of rendering an independent legal and social judgment.

V.

In 1953, a year before *Durham*, the American Law Institute commenced an exhaustive study of criminal conduct including the problem of criminal responsibility. In the ensuing months and years, under the scholarly direction of Professors Herbert Wechsler of Columbia University, its Chief Reporter, and Louis B. Schwartz of the University of Pennsylvania, Co-Reporter, the leading legal and medical minds of the country applied themselves to the task. Gradually and painstakingly a new definition of criminal responsibility began taking shape as Section 4.01 of the Model Penal Code was evolved. * * *

Section 4.01 provides that "A person is not responsible for criminal conduct if at the time of such conduct as a result of mental disease or defect he lacks substantial capacity either to appreciate the wrongfulness of his conduct or to conform his conduct to the requirements of law." For reasons which will be more fully set forth, we believe this test to be the soundest yet formulated and we accordingly adopt it as the standard of criminal responsibility in the Courts of this Circuit.

* * * The Model Penal Code formulation views the mind as a unified entity and recognizes that mental disease or defect may impair its functioning in numerous ways. The rule, moreover, reflects awareness that from the perspective of psychiatry absolutes are ephemeral and gradations are inevitable. By employing the telling word "substantial" to modify "incapacity," the rule emphasizes that "any" incapacity is not sufficient to justify avoidance of criminal responsibility but that "total" incapacity is also unnecessary. The choice of the word "appreciate," rather than "know" in the first branch of the test

also is significant; mere intellectual awareness that conduct is wrongful, when divorced from appreciation or understanding of the moral or legal import of behavior, can have little significance.

While permitting the utilization of meaningful psychiatric testimony, the American Law Institute formulation, we believe, is free of many of the defects which accompanied *Durham*. Although it eschews rigid classification, the Section is couched in sufficiently precise terms to provide the jury with a workable standard when the judge charges in terms comprehensible to laymen. Expert testimony, in short, will be admissible whenever relevant but always *as* expert testimony -- and not as moral or legal pronouncement. Relieved of their burden of divining precise causal relationships, the judge or jury can concentrate upon the ultimate decisions which are properly theirs, fully informed as to the facts.

Under the American Law Institute formulation, an inquiry based on meaningful psychological concepts can be pursued. The most modern psychiatric insights will be available, but, even more importantly, the legal focus will be sharper and clearer. The twin branches of the test, significantly phrased in the alternative, will remove from the pale of criminal sanctions precisely those who are in no meaningful sense responsible for their actions.

We do not delude ourselves in the belief that the American Law Institute test is perfect. Perfection is unattainable when we are dealing with a fluid and evolving science. * * *

We believe, in sum, that the American Law Institute test -- which makes no pretension at being the ultimate in faultless definition -- is an infinite improvement over the *M'Naghten* Rules, even when, as had been the practice in the courts of this Circuit, those Rules are supplemented by the "irresistible impulse" doctrine. All legal definitions involve elements of abstraction and approximation which are difficult to apply in marginal cases. The impossibility of guaranteeing that a new rule will always be infallible cannot justify continued adherence to an outmoded standard, sorely at variance with enlightened medical and legal scholarship. No one would suggest that a physician-expert called to state an opinion with respect to a litigant's orthopedic or neurological condition should be restricted in his reply to a single isolated cause to the exclusion of other relevant and important findings and conclusions -- much less to concepts developed at the outset of Victoria's reign. In a criminal trial, when life and liberty hang in the balance, such arbitrary limitations on expert and jury are all the less defensible.

The genius of the common law has been its responsiveness to changing times, its ability to reflect developing moral and social values. Drawing upon the past, the law must serve -- and traditionally has served -- the needs of the present. In the past century, psychiatry has evolved from tentative, hesitant groupings in the dark of human ignorance to a recognized and important branch of modern medicine. The outrage of a frightened Queen has for too long caused us to forego the expert guidance that modern psychiatry is able to provide.

VI.

Since Freeman's responsibility was determined under the rigid standards of the *M'Naghten* Rules, we are compelled to reverse his conviction and remand the case for a new trial in which the criteria employed will be those provided by Section 4.01 of the Model Penal Code.

And lest our opinion be misunderstood or distorted, some additional discussion is in order. First, we wish to make it absolutely clear that mere recidivism or narcotics addiction will not *of themselves* justify acquittal under the American Law Institute standards which we adopt today. Indeed, the second clause of Section 4.01 explicitly states that "the terms 'mental disease or defect' do not include an abnormality manifested only by repeated criminal or otherwise anti-social conduct." We approve and adopt this important caveat.

There may be instances where recidivists will not be criminally responsible, but this will be for determination in each individual case depending upon other evidence of mental disease augmenting mere recidivism with the ultimate determination dependent upon the proper application of the standards we have adopted. But, we stress, repeated criminality cannot be the *sole* ground for a finding of mental disorder; a contrary holding would reduce to absurdity a test designed to encourage full analysis of all psychiatric data and would exculpate those who knowingly and deliberately seek a life of crime.

Nor may narcotics addiction without more be the sole evidence of abnormality under the American Law Institute test. We have observed that the defense of lack of responsibility is essentially an acknowledgment on the part of society that because of mental disease or defect certain classes of wrongdoers are not properly the subjects of criminal punishment. In light of the severe penalties imposed by Congress for the possession and sale of narcotics, it would be unwise at this stage of medical knowledge, for a court to conclude that those addicted to narcotics should be, for that reason alone, immune from criminal sanctions.

Secondly, in order to avoid any misapprehension as to the thrust of our opinion some mention should be made of the treatment to be afforded individuals found to lack criminal responsibility under the test we adopt. There is no question but that the security of the community must be the paramount interest. Society withholds criminal sanctions in cases of incompetence out of a sense of compassion and understanding. It would be obviously intolerable if those suffering from a mental disease or defect of such a nature as to relieve them from criminal responsibility were to be set free to continue to pose a threat to life and property.

A verdict of "not guilty by reason of incompetency" has, in the past, been equivalent in the federal judicial system to a simple "not guilty" verdict because of the existing void in provisions for commitment and treatment. As a result of the comparatively recent adoption by various federal courts of more enlightened tests of responsibility, we trust that Congress will explore its power to authorize commitment of those acquitted on these grounds. Such was the result of *Durham* in the District of Columbia; shortly after that decision, Congress provided for mandatory post-trial commitment in all cases in the District resulting in acquittals on grounds of lack of responsibility. Pending Congressional action, however, we are confident that the several states will continue to step into the breach as they have in the past. Accordingly, we suggest that those adjudged criminally irresponsible promptly be turned over to state officials for commitment pursuant to state procedures.

Effective procedures for institutionalization and treatment of the criminally irresponsible are vital as an implementation to today's decision. Throughout our opinion, we have not viewed the choice as one between imprisonment and immediate release. Rather, we believe the true choice to be between different forms of institutionalization -- between the prison and the mental hospital. Underlying today's decision is our belief that treatment of the truly incompetent in mental institutions would better serve the interests of society as well as the defendant's.

      * * * Reversed and remanded.

STATE v. CRENSHAW
Supreme Court of Washington
98 Wash. 2d 789, 659 P.2d 488 (1983)

BRACHTENBACH

Rodney Crenshaw was convicted by a jury of first degree murder. Finding that the trial court committed no reversible error, we affirm the conviction.

Petitioner Rodney Crenshaw pleaded not guilty and not guilty by reason of insanity to the charge of first degree murder of his wife, Karen Crenshaw. A

jury found him guilty. Petitioner appealed his conviction, assigning error to a number of the trial court's rulings. After the Court of Appeals affirmed the trial court in all respects, petitioner raised the same issues before this court. * * *

Before turning to the legal issues, the facts of the case must be recounted. While [petitioner] and his wife were on their honeymoon in Canada, petitioner was deported as a result of his participation in a brawl. He secured a motel room in Blaine, Washington, and waited for his wife to join him. When she arrived 2 days later, he immediately thought she had been unfaithful -- he sensed "it wasn't the same Karen . . . she'd been with someone else."

Petitioner did not mention his suspicions to his wife; instead he took her to the motel room and beat her unconscious. He then went to a nearby store, stole a knife, and returned to stab his wife 24 times, inflicting a fatal wound. He left again, drove to a nearby farm where he had been employed and borrowed an ax. Upon returning to the motel room, he decapitated his wife with such force that the ax marks cut into the concrete floor under the carpet and splattered blood throughout the room.

Petitioner then proceeded to conceal his actions. He placed the body in a blanket, the head in a pillowcase, and put both in his wife's car. Next, he went to a service station, borrowed a bucket and sponge, and cleaned the room of blood and fingerprints. Before leaving, petitioner also spoke with the motel manager about a phone bill, then chatted with him for awhile over a beer.

When Crenshaw left the motel he drove to a remote area 25 miles away where he hid the two parts of the body in thick brush. He then fled, driving to the Hoquiam area, about 200 miles from the scene of the crime. There he picked up two hitchhikers, told them of his crime, and enlisted their aid in disposing of his wife's car in a river. The hitchhikers contacted the police and Crenshaw was apprehended shortly thereafter. He voluntarily confessed to the crime.

The defense of not guilty by reason of insanity was a major issue at trial. Crenshaw testified that he followed the Moscovite religious faith, and that it would be improper for a Moscovite not to kill his wife if she committed adultery. Crenshaw also has a history of mental problems, for which he has been hospitalized in the past. The jury, however, rejected petitioner's insanity defense, and found him guilty of murder in the first degree. * * *

Insanity is an affirmative defense the defendant must establish by a preponderance of the evidence.[a] Sanity is presumed, even with a history of prior institutional commitments from which the individual was released upon sufficient recovery.

The insanity defense is not available to all who are mentally deficient or deranged; legal insanity has a different meaning and a different purpose than the concept of medical insanity. A verdict of not guilty by reason of insanity completely absolves a defendant of any criminal responsibility. Therefore, "the defense is available only to those persons who have lost contact with reality so completely that they are beyond any of the influences of the criminal law."

Petitioner assigned error to insanity defense instruction 10 which reads:

In addition to the plea of not guilty, the defendant has entered a plea of insanity existing at the time of the act charged.

Insanity existing at the time of the commission of the act charged is a defense.

For a defendant to be found not guilty by reason of insanity you must find that, as a result of mental disease or defect, the defendant's mind was affected to such an extent that the defendant was unable to perceive the nature and quality of the acts with which the defendant is charged or was unable to tell right from wrong with reference to the particular acts with which defendant is charged.

What is meant by the terms "right and wrong" refers to knowledge of a person at the time of committing an act that he was acting contrary to the law.

But for the last paragraph, this instruction tracks the language of WPIC 20.01, which is the *M'Naghten* test. * * * Petitioner contends, however, that the trial court erred in defining "right and wrong" as legal right and wrong rather than in the moral sense.

We find this instruction was not reversible error on three alternative grounds: (1) The *M'Naghten* opinion amply supports the "legal" wrong

---

[a]Insanity is indeed an affirmative defense. States, however, may choose to place the burden of proving sanity on the government or they may place the burden of proving insanity on the defendant.

definition as used in this case, (2) under these facts, "moral" wrong and "legal" wrong are synonymous, therefore the "legal" wrong definition did not alter the meaning of the test, and (3) because Crenshaw failed to prove other elements of the insanity defense, any error in the definition of wrong was harmless.

I

The definition of the term "wrong" in the *M'Naghten* test has been considered and disputed by many legal scholars. Courts from other jurisdictions are divided on the issue. In Washington, we have not addressed this issue previously. [The court concludes that the *M'Naghten* opinion supports the definition of "right and wrong" in Instruction 10, which referred to the defendant's knowledge of whether he was acting contrary to law.]

II

Alternatively, the statement in instruction 10 may be approved because, in this case, legal wrong is synonymous with moral wrong. This conclusion is premised on two grounds.

First, in discussing the term "moral" wrong, it is important to note that it is society's morals, and not the individual's morals, that are the standard for judging moral wrong under *M'Naghten*. If wrong meant moral wrong judged by the individual's own conscience, this would seriously undermine the criminal law, for it would allow one who violated the law to be excused from criminal responsibility solely because, in his own conscience, his act was not morally wrong. This principle was emphasized by Justice Cardozo:

> The anarchist is not at liberty to break the law because he reasons that all government is wrong. The devotee of a religious cult that enjoins polygamy or human sacrifice as a duty is not thereby relieved from responsibility before the law
> . . .

More recently the Arizona Supreme Court stated:

> We find no authority upholding the defendant's position that one suffering from a mental disease could be declared legally insane if he knew that the act was morally and legally wrong but he personally believed that act right. We believe that this would not be a sound rule, because it approaches the position of exonerating a defendant for his personal beliefs and does not take account of society's determination of defendant's capacity to conform his conduct to the law.

There is evidence on the record that Crenshaw knew his actions were wrong according to society's standards, as well as legally wrong. Dr. Belden testified:

I think Mr. Crenshaw is quite aware on one level that he is in conflict with the law *and with people*. However, this is not something that he personally invests his emotions in.

We conclude that Crenshaw knew his acts were morally wrong from society's viewpoint and also knew his acts were illegal. His personal belief that it was his duty to kill his wife for her alleged infidelity cannot serve to exculpate him from legal responsibility for his acts.

A narrow exception to the societal standard of moral wrong has been drawn for instances wherein a party performs a criminal act, knowing it is morally and legally wrong, but believing, because of a mental defect, that the act is ordained by God: such would be the situation with a mother who kills her infant child to whom she is devotedly attached, believing that God has spoken to her and decreed the act. Although the woman knows that the law and society condemn the act, it would be unrealistic to hold her responsible for the crime, since her free will has been subsumed by her belief in the deific decree.

This exception is not available to Crenshaw, however. Crenshaw argued only that he followed the Moscovite faith and that Moscovites believe it is their duty to kill an unfaithful wife. This is not the same as acting under a deific command. Instead, it is akin to "[t]he devotee of a religious cult that enjoins . . . human sacrifice as a duty [and] is *not* thereby relieved from responsibility before the law." Crenshaw's personal "Moscovite" beliefs are not equivalent to a deific decree and do not relieve him from responsibility for his acts.

Once moral wrong is equated with society's morals, the next step, equating moral and legal wrong, follows logically. The law is, for the most part, an expression of collective morality. Most cases involving the insanity defense involve serious crimes for which society's moral judgment is identical with the legal standard. Therefore, a number of scholars have concluded that, as a practical matter, the way in which a court interprets the word "wrong" will have little effect on the eventual outcome of a case.

As one scholar explained:

[S]ince by far the vast majority of cases in which insanity is pleaded as a defense to criminal prosecutions involves acts which are universally regarded as morally wicked as well as illegal, the hair-splitting distinction between legal and moral wrong need not be given much attention.

Society's morals and legal wrong are interchangeable concepts in the context of this case. Petitioner's crime, killing his wife by stabbing her 24 times then hacking off her head, is clearly contrary to society's morals as well as the law. Therefore by defining wrong in terms of legal wrong, the trial court did not alter the meaning of the *M'Naghten* test.

III

We also find that, under any definition of wrong, Crenshaw did not qualify for the insanity defense under *M'Naghten*; therefore, any alleged error in that definition must be viewed as harmless. * * *

Here, any error is harmless for two alternate reasons. First, Crenshaw failed to prove an essential element of the defense because he did not prove his alleged delusions stemmed from a mental defect; second, he did not prove by a preponderance of the evidence that he was legally insane at the time of the crime.

In addition to an incapacity to know right from wrong, *M'Naghten* requires that such incapacity stem from a mental disease or defect. Assuming, arguendo, that Crenshaw did not know right from wrong, he failed to prove that a mental defect was the cause of this inability.

Petitioner's insanity argument is premised on the following facts: (1) he is a Moscovite and Moscovites believe it is their duty to assassinate an unfaithful spouse; (2) he "knew," without asking, that his wife had been unfaithful when he met her in Blaine and this was equivalent to an insane delusion; and (3) at other times in his life, he had been diagnosed as a paranoid personality and had been committed to mental institutions. A conscientious application of the *M'Naghten* rule demonstrates, however, that these factors do not afford petitioner the sanctuary of the insanity defense.

To begin, petitioner's Moscovite beliefs are irrelevant to the insanity defense, because they are not insane delusions. Some notion of morality, unrelated to a mental illness, which disagrees with the law and mores of our society is not an insane delusion.

Nor was petitioner's belief that his wife was unfaithful an insane delusion. Dr. Trowbridge, a psychiatrist, explained:

A man suspects his wife of being unfaithful. Certainly such suspicions are not necessarily delusional, even if they're ill based. Just because he suspected his wife of being unfaithful doesn't mean that he was crazy.

*   *   *

Certainly when a man kills his wife he doesn't do it in a rational way. No one ever does that rationally. But that is not to suggest that every time a man kills his wife he was [sic] insane.

Finally, evidence of prior commitments to mental institutions is not proof that one was *legally* insane at the time the criminal act was committed. As we stated in State v. McDonald:

> Those who are commonly regarded as "odd" or "unsound" or even "deranged" would not normally qualify [for the insanity defense]. Many, if not most, mentally ill persons presently being treated in the mental institutions of this state who are there under the test of "likelihood of serious harm to the person detained or to others," . . . would not meet the *M'Naghten* test, if charged with a crime.

Thus, petitioner does not establish the necessary connection between his criminal acts and his psychological problems to qualify for the insanity defense.

In addition, the preponderance of the evidence weighs against finding Crenshaw legally insane. All of the psychological experts, save one, testified that defendant was not insane at the time of the murder. The only doctor who concluded defendant (petitioner) was legally insane, Dr. Hunter, was a psychologist who had not examined petitioner for a year and a half.

Given the various qualifications of the experts, the time they spent with the petitioner, and the proximity in time of their examinations to the murder, the testimony does not establish by a preponderance of the evidence that petitioner was legally insane at the time of the murder.

Furthermore, in addition to the expert testimony, there was lay testimony that petitioner appeared rational at the time of the killing. After cleaning the motel room, Crenshaw resolved a phone bill dispute with the manager, then shared a beer with him without arousing any suspicion in the manager's mind. Also, the woman who gave him the ax testified as to his behavior the day before the murder:

Well, he seemed very normal or I certainly wouldn't have handed him an ax or a hoe. He was polite, he done his work. He didn't, I wasn't afraid of him or anything. I mean we were just out there working and I certainly wouldn't have handed him an ax or anything like that if I would have thought that there was anything even remotely peculiar about him.

And, with specific reference to the time when petitioner borrowed the ax to decapitate his wife:

Q. . . . did he seem rational to you?
A. Oh, yes, he was very nice.
Q. Did he seem coherent when he spoke to you?
A. Oh, yes. . . .
. . .
Q. Did he appear to be sane to you then? . . .
A. Yes. . . .

Thus, at the same time that he was embroiled in the act of murdering his wife, he was rational, coherent, and sane in his dealings with others.

Finally, evidence of petitioner's calculated execution of the crime and his sophisticated attempts to avert discovery support a finding of sanity. Crenshaw performed the murder methodically, leaving the motel room twice to acquire the knife and ax necessary to perform the deed. Then, after the killing he scrubbed the motel room to clean up the blood and remove his fingerprints. Next, he drove 25 miles to hide the body in thick brush in a remote area. Finally, he drove several hundred miles and ditched the car in a river.

Such attempts to hide evidence of a crime manifest an awareness that the act was legally wrong. Moreover, petitioner testified that he did these things because he "didn't want to get caught."

To summarize thus far, we find no error in instruction 10 for the following reasons: (1) As we interpret the *M'Naghten* case, it was not improper for the trial court to instruct with reference to the law of the land, under the facts of this case; (2) because the concept of moral wrong refers to the mores of society and not to the individual's morals, "moral" wrong is synonymous with "legal" wrong with a serious crime such as this one, therefore, instructing in terms of legal wrong did not alter the meaning of the *M'Naghten* rule; (3) any error was harmless because (a) Crenshaw did not show that at the time of the crime his mind was affected as a result of a mental disease or defect and without this essential element the insanity defense was not available to him, and (b) an overwhelming preponderance of the evidence supports the finding that

Crenshaw was not legally insane when he killed his wife. We thus conclude that the additional statement in instruction 10 was not improper, or, at the very least, that it was harmless error.

Nevertheless, we do not believe that, in the future, such a comment should be necessary. As the Legislature has chosen to codify the *M'Naghten* test in statutory form, it would be preferable to have this test presented to the jury without any elaboration. This would permit both parties to argue their theories of the case. * * * Thus, we hold prospectively that as a general rule no definition of wrong should accompany an insanity defense instruction. * * *

As stated above, we find that the Court of Appeals thoughtfully and correctly resolved the other assignments of error raised by petitioner, and we see no need to repeat their reasoning here. Finding no reversible error was committed by the trial court, we affirm the judgment.

DORE, J., dissenting

The major issue of the subject appeal is whether the jury was properly instructed on insanity and, if not, whether this constituted prejudicial error.

The majority, in affirming the trial court and the Court of Appeals, upholds the validity of instruction 10, instructing the jurors the defendant would be "insane" only if he couldn't distinguish between *legal* right and wrong. The majority eliminated the *moral* right and wrong test by concluding that "moral" wrong and "legal" wrong are synonymous.

I disagree, for I believe that although at times moral and legal are "synonymous," sometimes they are distinguishable. This is a factual issue to be determined by the trier of the fact, and not by the courts as a matter of law. The submission of instruction 10 constituted prejudicial error. I would reverse for a new trial based on the instruction's erroneous statement of the law on insanity. * * *

Washington's test for insanity, a codification of *M'Naghten*'s rule, reads:

To establish the defense of insanity, it must be shown that:

(1) At the time of the commission of the offense, as a result of mental disease or defect, the mind of the actor was affected to such an extent that:

(a) He was unable to perceive the nature and quality of the act with which he is charged; or

(b) He was unable to tell right from wrong with reference to the particular act charged.

(2) The defense of insanity must be established by a preponderance of the evidence.

The issue before us is whether the terms "right" and "wrong" as used in RCW 9A.12.010(1)(b) should be qualified for the jury. At trial, the jury was instructed the defendant would not be legally insane if he knew "legal right" from "legal wrong." Crenshaw contends the trial court erred in defining "right and wrong" as "legal right" and "legal wrong." The majority of the Court of Appeals held that

> If the accused knew his act was wrong -- either legally or morally -- then he cannot be excused for his crime by the insanity defense.

The Court of Appeals concluded that the trial court did not err in its instruction on insanity because, if the defendant knew his conduct was contrary to law, he could not be found legally insane even if he could not distinguish moral right from moral wrong. The majority avoids the problem by holding that legal right and moral right are "synonymous."

The defendant urges this court to define the terms solely as "moral right and wrong" or, alternatively, to leave the terms undefined for the jury, as does the pattern instruction. The Court of Appeals argued that if the moral sense of the terms becomes the standard, the defense would be broadened significantly. Anyone would be able to argue that his actions were justifiable by reference to his personal morality. * * *

The majority and the Court of Appeals miss the point. Of course, as they contend, the standard of right and wrong must be an objective one. That is not to say, however, that only the criminal code can provide that standard. I agree with the dissenting judge, Ringold, J., of the Court of Appeals, that if a defendant knows his acts are contrary to law, an inference may be drawn, *by a jury*, that defendant knew his acts were morally wrong. * * *

I do not believe that a jury's function in this regard should be usurped. As used in RCW 9A.12.010(1)(b), the terms "right" and "wrong" refer to their moral sense, and not to a defendant's knowledge that he has acted contrary to the law.

It is not the mere assertion by a defendant that he "thought" he committed no moral wrong which would excuse his otherwise criminal act. The statute requires that such belief be the result of mental disease or defect and that such defect existed at the time of the commission of the offense. As Justice Cardozo stated in *People v. Schmidt*:

> It is not enough, to relieve from criminal liability, that the prisoner is morally depraved. It is not enough that he has views of right and wrong at variance with those that find expression in the law. The variance must have its origin in some disease of the mind. The anarchist is not at liberty to break the law because he reasons that all government is wrong. The devotee of a religious cult that enjoins polygamy or human sacrifice as a duty is not thereby relieved from responsibility before the law. In such cases the belief, however false according to our own standards, is not the product of disease. Cases will doubtless arise where criminals will take shelter behind a professed belief that their crime was ordained by God . . . We can safely leave such fabrications to the common sense of juries.

I also agree with Judge Ringold, who pointed out that

> if we are to be consistent in our application of the maxim that ignorance of the law excuses no man, then a person's knowledge of the law must be immaterial to culpability.

This court has previously indicated that the *M'Naghten* test involved the moral definition of right and wrong. Prior to codification of the *M'Naghten* rule into our statutory scheme, we held that a jury was correctly instructed when it was told that the insanity defense would lie if defendant "was unable to perceive the *moral qualities*" of his act. The sole question is whether we want to hold a defendant answerable to our criminal law, notwithstanding the barbaric or cruel nature of the defendant's acts. A mind which cannot distinguish moral right from wrong cannot be held accountable for acts performed as a result of that illness and while suffering under that influence.

The majority, at page 798, surprisingly seems to concede that at times there is a difference between legal right and wrong and moral right and wrong, stating:

> A narrow exception to the societal standard of moral wrong has been drawn for instances wherein a party performs a criminal act, knowing it is morally and legally wrong, but believing,

because of a mental defect, that the act is ordained by God: such would be the situation with a mother who kills her infant child to whom she is devotedly attached, believing that God has spoken to her and decreed the act. Although the woman knows that the law and society condemn the act, it would be unrealistic to hold her responsible for the crime, since her free will has been subsumed by her belief in the deific decree.

This is exactly the point I wish to make in the subject case. Crenshaw knew if he killed his wife he was violating the law, but he believed he had a duty to do it under the teaching of his Moscovite "religious" beliefs. To determine his insanity under *M'Naghten*, as codified in RCW 9A.12.010, a determination must be made as to what was morally right and wrong. The jury had this duty and responsibility, but to do so it had to be properly instructed. Instruction 10 wrongly limited the jury to the *legal* right and wrong test and prevented it from determining whether Crenshaw knew the difference between *moral* right and wrong at the time he killed his wife. This constituted prejudicial error.

The majority concludes at page 805, "Thus, we hold *prospectively* that as a general rule no definition of wrong should accompany an insanity defense instruction" (italics mine), impliedly admitting and agreeing that instruction 10 is defective and that the jury should be instructed under *both moral* and *legal* wrong in order to correctly determine insanity. Without saying so, the majority adopts WPIC 20.01 as a correct instruction on insanity. Crenshaw argued use of WPIC 20.01 would have permitted his lawyers to argue moral right and wrong as the true test of insanity in his case, and that his jury should have been so instructed. The majority holds that future defendants shall have the benefit of WPIC 20.01, but not defendant Crenshaw.

I would reverse and remand to the trial court for a new trial on the basis that instruction 10 was defective and constituted prejudicial error.

3.   Diminished Capacity

Sometimes a defendant who cannot prove he was insane at the time of the crime will nevertheless seek to introduce evidence about her mental illness as a way of mitigating or eliminating her responsibility for the crime. The use of evidence of mental illness in this way is generally described as a "diminished capacity" defense.

In jurisdictions that follow the common law, diminished capacity defenses have been articulated in several different ways. One variant of the diminished capacity defense is called the "mens rea variant" of the defense. Under this variant, a defendant who can show that he was suffering from a mental disease or defect not amounting to insanity at the time he committed his crime and therefore lacked the mental state required for commission of the charged offense will be found not guilty of the charged offense. Diminished capacity of the mens rea variant is a case-in-chief defense because it attacks an element of the crime, the mens rea, and accordingly results in a complete acquittal. *Compare* Model Penal Code § 4.02 (permitting evidence of mental disease or defect to be admitted whenever relevant to prove that the defendant did or did not have a state of mind which is an element of the offense).

Another variant of the diminished capacity defense is the "partial responsibility variant." Under this variant, the defendant argues that because of some mental disease or defect not amounting to insanity, he (or she) is less blameworthy than others charged with the same offense. If the jury agrees, they can acquit him of the charged offense and find him guilty of a lesser offense. Before 1981, the California courts were receptive to several different versions of this kind of claim. For example, in *People v. Wolff*, 61 Cal.2d 795, 40 Cal.Rptr. 271, 349 P.2d 959 (1964), and ten years later in *People v. Poddar*, 10 Cal.3d 750 (1974), mentally disturbed defendants successfully argued that evidence that they were incapable of the "mature and meaningful reflection" necessary for a first-degree murder conviction (in Wolff's case) or the awareness of a necessity to act within the law necessary for a second-degree murder conviction (in Poddar's case) should have been admissible to reduce their responsibility. In these and other cases, diminished capacity acted as a partial defense.

California's openness to such claims ended after the infamous Dan White case, in which a former police officer and City Supervisor named Dan White shot and killed former San Francisco Mayor George Moscone and then Supervisor Harvey Milk (the first openly gay person to hold this office) in their offices in City Hall. White, who had resigned as City Supervisor, was upset because Mayor Moscone refused to reappoint White to his position as City Supervisor. At his 1979 trial, White successfully argued that he should be acquitted of murder and found guilty of voluntary manslaughter because he was suffering from diminished capacity. A prominent psychiatrist testified for the defense that one cause of White's outburst was high blood sugar caused by eating too much junk food, and the media dubbed the defense's argument the "Twinkie defense." The verdict in the case (seen as anti-gay by Milk's constituents) sparked rioting in the streets of San Francisco, and ultimately led the California legislature to abolish the defense of diminished capacity.[a]

4.   Infancy

In re DEVON T.
Court of Special Appeals of Maryland
85 Md. App. 674, 584 A.2d 1287 (Ct. Spec. App. 1991)

MOYLAN, J.

The Present Case

The juvenile appellant, Devon T., was charged with committing an act which, if committed by an adult, would have constituted the crime of possession of heroin with intent to distribute. In the Circuit Court for Baltimore City, Judge Roger W. Brown found that Devon was delinquent. The heart of the case against Devon was that when on May 25, 1989, Devon was directed to empty his pockets by the security guard at the Booker T. Washington Middle School, under the watchful eye of the Assistant Principal, the search produced a brown bag containing twenty zip-lock pink plastic bags which, in turn, contained heroin. Upon this appeal, Devon raises the following contentions:

1. That the State did not offer legally sufficient evidence to rebut his presumptive incapacity because of infancy;

2. That the security guard's direction that he empty his pockets violated his Fourth Amendment right against unreasonable search and seizure. * * *

The Infancy Defense Generally

At the time of the offense, Devon was 13 years, 10 months, and 2 weeks of age. He timely raised the infancy defense. * * *

The case law and the academic literature alike conceptualize the infancy defense as but an instance of the broader phenomenon of a defense based upon

---

[a] See Cal.Pen. Code § 25a ("The defense of diminished capacity is hereby abolished."). Evidence of mental illness may still be used, however, to prove that the defendant lacked the mens rea required for the commission of the crime. *See* Miguel A. Mendez, *Diminished Capacity in California: Premature Reports of Its Demise*, 3 Stan. L. & Pol'y Rev. 216 (1991).

lack of moral responsibility or capacity. The criminal law generally will only impose its retributive or deterrent sanctions upon those who are morally blameworthy -- those who know they are doing wrong but nonetheless persist in their wrongdoing.

After several centuries of pondering the criminal capacity of children and experimenting with various cut-off ages, the Common Law settled upon its current resolution of the problem by late Tudor and early Stuart times. As explained by LaFave & Scott, *Criminal Law*, (2d ed. 1986), at 398, the resolution was fairly simple:

> At common law, children under the age of seven are conclusively presumed to be without criminal capacity, those who have reached the age of fourteen are treated as fully responsible, while as to those between the ages of seven and fourteen there is a rebuttable presumption of criminal incapacity.

The authors make clear that infancy was an instance of criminal capacity generally:

> The early common law infancy defense was based upon an unwillingness to punish those thought to be incapable of forming criminal intent and not of an age where the threat of punishment could serve as a deterrent.

*　　*　　*

Clark & Marshall, *A Treatise on the Law of Crimes*, emphasizes that the mental quality that is the *sine qua non* of criminal responsibility is the capacity to distinguish right from wrong:

> *Children Under the Age of Seven Years.*
> – Children under the age of seven years are, by an arbitrary rule of the common law, conclusively presumed to be *doli incapax*, or incapable of entertaining a criminal intent, and no evidence can be received to show capacity in fact.

> *Children Between the Ages of 7 and 14.*
> – Children between the ages of 7 and 14 are presumed to be incapable of entertaining a criminal intent, but the presumption is not conclusive, as in the case of children under the age of 7. It may be rebutted by showing in the particular case that the accused was of sufficient intelligence to distinguish between

right and wrong, and to understand the nature and illegality of the particular act, or, as it is sometimes said, that he was possessed of 'a mischievous discretion.' (footnotes omitted).

The reasoning behind the rule is made very clear, at 391:

A child is not criminally responsible unless he is old enough, and intelligent enough, to be capable of entertaining a criminal intent; and to be capable of entertaining a criminal intent he must be capable of distinguishing between right and wrong as to the particular act.

Walkover, *The Infancy Defense in the New Juvenile Court*, distills the rationale to a single sentence:

The infancy defense was an essential component of the common law limitation of punishment to the blameworthy.

*   *   *

What is Criminal Capacity in an Infant?

Before the juvenile master, the appellant timely raised the infancy defense. One party or the other (it matters not which) introduced the undisputed fact (it would not have mattered if the fact had been disputed) that at the time of the allegedly delinquent act, Devon was 13 years, 10 months, and 2 weeks of age. Thus, the issue of mental incapacity due to infancy was properly generated and before the court.

On that issue, Devon initially had the benefit of presumptive incapacity. The presumption having been generated, the State had the burdens (of both production and persuasion) of rebutting that presumption. * * * To overcome the presumption of incapacity, then, what precisely was that quality of Devon's mind as to which the State was required to produce legally sufficient evidence? It was required to produce evidence permitting the reasonable inference that Devon -- the Ghost of *M'Naghten* speaks: -- "at the time of doing the act knew the difference between right and wrong." * * *

In short, when Devon walked around the Booker T. Washington Middle School with twenty zip-lock bags of heroin, apparently for sale or other distribution, could Devon pass the *M'Naghten* test? Was there legally sufficient data before him to permit Judge Brown to infer that Devon knew the difference between right and wrong and knew, moreover, that what he was doing was wrong?

The Legal Sufficiency of the Evidence to Prove Devon's Knowledge of Right and Wrong

As we turn to the legal sufficiency of the evidence, it is important to know that the only mental quality we are probing is the cognitive capacity to distinguish right from wrong. Other aspects of Devon's mental and psychological make-up, such as his scholastic attainments, his I.Q., his social maturity, his societal adjustment, his basic personality, etc., might well require evidentiary input from psychologists, from parents, from teachers or other school authorities, etc. On knowledge of the difference between right and wrong, however, the general case law, as well as the inherent logic of the situation, has established that that particular psychic phenomenon may sometimes permissibly be inferred from the very circumstances of the criminal or delinquent act itself. * * *

Before looking at the circumstances of the delinquent act in this case, as well as at other data pointing toward Devon's awareness that he was doing wrong, a word is in order about the quantity of proof required. *In re William A,* quotes with approval from *Adams v. State,* in pointing out:

> It is generally held that the presumption of *doli incapax* is 'extremely strong at the age of seven and diminishes gradually until it disappears entirely at the age of fourteen . . . .' Since the strength of the presumption of incapacity decreases with the increase in the years of the accused, the quantum of proof necessary to overcome the presumption would diminish in substantially the same ratio.

That kind of a sliding standard of proof or inverse proportion is relatively rare in law. * * * Some analysis may be helpful as to how a presumption "diminishes gradually until it disappears entirely," as to how "incapacity decreases" as age increases, and as to how "the quantum of proof . . . diminish[es] in substantially the same ratio." * * *

The applicable common law on *doli incapax* with relation to the infancy defense establishes that on the day before their seventh birthday, no persons possess cognitive capacity. (0 per cent). It also establishes that on the day of their fourteenth birthday, all persons (at least as far as age is concerned) possess cognitive capacity. (100 per cent). On the time scale between the day of the seventh birthday and the day before the fourteenth birthday, the percentage of persons possessing such capacity steadily increases. The statistical probability is that on the day of the seventh birthday, at most a tiny fraction of one per cent will possess cognitive capacity. Conversely, on the day before the fourteenth birthday, only a tiny fraction of one per cent will lack such cognitive capacity.

Assuming a steady rate of climb, the mid-point where fifty per cent of persons will lack cognitive capacity and fifty per cent will possess it would be at 10 years and 6 months of age. That is the scale on which we must place Devon.

We stress that the burden in that regard, notwithstanding the probabilities, was nonetheless on the State. The impact of the allocation of the burden of proof to the State is that the infant will enjoy the benefit of the doubt. The fact that the quantum of proof necessary to overcome presumptive incapacity diminishes in substantially the same ratio as the infant's age increases only serves to lessen the State's burden, not to eliminate it. The State's burden is still an affirmative one. It may not, therefore, passively rely upon the mere absence of evidence to the contrary.

We hold that the State successfully carried that burden. A minor factor, albeit of some weight, was that Devon was essentially at or near grade level in school. The report of the master, received and reviewed by Judge Brown, established that at the time of the offense, Devon was in middle school, embracing grades 6, 7, and 8. The report of the master, indeed, revealed that Devon had flunked the sixth grade twice, with truancy and lack of motivation as apparent causes. That fact nonetheless revealed that Devon had initially reached the sixth grade while still eleven years of age. That would tend to support his probable inclusion in the large majority of his age group rather than in a small and subnormal minority of it.

We note that the transcript of the hearing before the juvenile master shows that the master was in a position to observe first-hand Devon's receiving of legal advice from his lawyer, his acknowledgment [sic] of his understanding of it, and his acting upon it. His lawyer explained that he had a right to remain silent and that the master would not infer guilt from his exercise of that right. He acknowledged understanding that right. His lawyer also advised him of his right to testify but informed him that both the assistant state's attorney and the judge might question him about the delinquent act. Devon indicated that he wished to remain silent and say nothing. Although reduced to relatively simple language, the exchange with respect to the risk of self-incrimination and the privilege against self-incrimination forms a predicate from which an observer might infer some knowledge on Devon's part of the significance of incrimination.

The exchange, moreover, might have significance in two distinct evidentiary regards. It suggests that Devon's lawyer, who presumably had significant opportunity to talk to him before the hearing, concluded that Devon understood the significance of criminality and incrimination. * * *

The significance of the colloquy in this case, moreover, is far more direct. Here, the master was in a position to observe Devon closely throughout the exchange. It does, to be sure, require us to extrapolate that Devon's mental capacity on the day of the hearing, July 20, reflected his mental capacity two months earlier on May 25. * * *

We turn, most significantly, to the circumstances of the criminal act itself. As we do so, we note the relevance of such circumstances to the issue at hand. R. Perkins & R. Boyce, CRIMINAL LAW, (3d ed. 1982), point out, at 938:

> The prosecution, in brief, cannot obtain the conviction of such a person without showing that he had such maturity in fact as to have a guilty knowledge that he was doing wrong. Conduct of the defendant such as concealing himself or the evidence of his misdeed may be such under all the circumstances as to authorize a finding of such maturity.

W. LaFave & A. Scott, CRIMINAL LAW, (2d ed. 1986), speak to the same effect, at 399-400:

> Conduct of the defendant relating to the acts charged may be most relevant in overcoming the presumption. Thus hiding the body, inquiry as to the detection of poison, bribery of a witness, or false accusation of others have all been relied upon in finding capacity.

* * * Just such a use of a secluded location or concealment was present in this case. The case broke when a grandmother, concerned enough to have had her own live-in grandson institutionalized, complained to the authorities at Booker T. Washington Middle School that several of her grandson's classmates were being truant on a regular basis and were using her home, while she was out working, as the "hide out" from which to sell drugs. Although the initial suspicion was directed toward Edward, it ultimately appeared that Edward and Devon were in the enterprise together. Children who are unaware that what they are doing is wrong have no need to hide out or to conceal their activities.

The most significant circumstance was the very nature of the criminal activity in which Devon engaged. It was not mere possession of heroin. It was possession of twenty packets of heroin with the intent to distribute. This was the finding of the court and it was supported by the evidence. There were no needle marks or other indications of personal use on Devon's body. Nothing in the information developed by the Juvenile Services Agency on Devon and his family gave any indication that this sixth grader, directly or indirectly, had the affluence to purchase drugs for himself in that amount. Indeed, a statement he gave to the interviewer from the Juvenile Services Agency acknowledged that he had been selling drugs for two days when the current offense occurred. His motivation was "that he just wanted something to do."

The evidence in this case affirmatively indicated that Devon and Edward and several other students had been regularly using the absent grandmother's home as a base from which to sell drugs. The circumstances clearly indicated that Devon and his companions were not innocent children unaware of the difference between games and crimes but "street wise" young delinquents knowingly involved in illicit activities. Realistically, one cannot engage in the business of selling drugs without some knowledge as to sources of supply, some pattern for receiving and passing on the money, some network of potential customers, and some *modus operandi* to avoid the eye of the police and of school authorities. It is almost inconceivable that such a crime could be engaged in without the drug pusher's being aware that it was against the law. That is, by definition, criminal capacity.

We hold that the surrounding circumstances here were legally sufficient to overcome the slight residual weight of the presumption of incapacity due to infancy.

JUDGMENT AFFIRMED; COSTS TO BE PAID BY APPELLANT.

5. Intoxication

The defense of intoxication is traditionally understood as comprising two distinct defenses: voluntary intoxication and involuntary intoxication. As we have seen in Chapter 4 (Mens Rea), in jurisdictions that follow the common law, the traditional rule has been that whether a defendant can argue voluntary intoxication as a defense turns on whether the crime with which she is charged is considered a specific intent crime or a general intent crime. If the charged offense is a general intent crime, then the defendant will not be permitted to introduce evidence of her intoxication. If the offense is a specific intent crime, the defendant will be allowed to present evidence of her voluntary intoxication. In order to secure an acquittal, however, the defendant must show that because of his intoxicated condition, he did not have the specific intent required for commission of the crime.

In recent years, common law courts have become increasingly hostile toward the defense of voluntary intoxication. In *People v. Register*, for example, the Court of Appeals of New York refuses to allow a defendant charged with depraved heart murder to present evidence of voluntary intoxication, rejecting his claim that because of his intoxicated condition he was not *aware* of and did not *consciously* disregard a substantial and unjustifiable risk. How would this case be decided under the Model Penal Code? *See* § 2.08.

Some states have decided to abolish the defense of voluntary intoxication, disallowing evidence of voluntary intoxication in all cases regardless of whether the charged offense is a specific intent or general intent crime. In 1996, the U.S. Supreme Court was asked to decide whether a legislature's decision to abolish the defense of voluntary intoxication is consistent with a criminal defendant's constitutional right to present evidence in his or her behalf. The Court answers this question in *Montana v. Egelhoff.*

Involuntary intoxication has been treated very differently by courts that follow the common law. In some jurisdictions, evidence of involuntary intoxication is admissible to negate either specific or general intent (although since general intent is often treated as "intent to do the physical actions that constitute the crime," it is unlikely that one would ever be so intoxicated as to not have such intent unless comatose). In most jurisdictions, involuntary intoxication can be the basis for a temporary insanity claim. In this way, involuntary intoxication can be used as an affirmative defense. Some jurisdictions acknowledge only this second use of involuntary intoxication evidence, holding that involuntary intoxication is only a defense if it caused the defendant to become temporarily insane.

What constitutes involuntary intoxication? The court in *Commonwealth v. Smith* reviews the common law precedents, and ultimately concludes that Pennsylvania law has incorporated the Model Penal Code on this point.

PEOPLE v. REGISTER

Court of Appeals of New York
60 N.Y.2d 270, 457 N.E.2d 704, 469 N.Y.S.2d 599 (1983)

SIMONS, J.

Defendant appeals from an order of the Appellate Division which affirmed a judgment entered after a jury trial convicting him of murder in the second degree (Penal Law, §125.25, subd 2 [depraved mind murder]) and two counts of assault in the first degree (Penal Law, §120.10, subd 1). The charges arose from a barroom incident in which defendant shot and killed one man and seriously injured two others. He alleges that the evidence was insufficient to support the murder conviction and that the trial court erred in refusing to instruct the jury that it could consider intoxication evidence to negate an element of the crime of depraved mind murder. * * * There should be an affirmance. The evidence supports the conviction and the court's instructions were correct. * * *

The shootings occurred about 12:30 a.m. on January 15, 1977 in a crowded barroom in downtown Rochester. The evidence established that defendant and a friend, Duval, had been drinking heavily that day celebrating the fact that Duval, through an administrative mixup, would not have to spend the weekend in jail. Sometime between 7:00 p.m. and 8:00 p.m., the two men left home for the bar. Defendant took a loaded pistol with him and shortly after they arrived at the bar, he produced it when he got into an argument with another patron over money owed him. Apparently the dispute ended without incident and defendant continued his drinking. After midnight another argument developed, this time between Duval and Willie Mitchell. Defendant took out the gun again, shot at Mitchell but mistakenly injured Lawrence Evans who was trying to stop the fight. He then stepped forward and shot Mitchell in the stomach from close range. At that, the 40 or 50 patrons in the bar started for the doors. Some of the bystanders tried to remove Mitchell to a hospital and while they were doing so, the decedent, Marvin Lindsey, walked by defendant. Lindsey was apparently a friend or acquaintance of defendant although that was the first time he had seen him that night. For no explained reason, defendant turned and fired his gun killing Lindsey.

Defendant did not contest the shootings. In defense, his counsel elicited evidence during the prosecution's case of defendant's considerable drinking that evening and he called as his only witness a forensic psychiatrist who testified on the debilitating effects of consuming alcoholic beverages. The jury acquitted defendant of intentional murder but convicted him of depraved mind murder and the two assault counts.

The murder conviction must be supported by evidence that defendant "[under] circumstances evincing a depraved indifference to human life * * * recklessly [engaged] in conduct which [created] a grave risk of death to another person, and thereby [caused] the death of another person." A person acts recklessly when he is aware of and consciously disregards a substantial and unjustifiable risk, but to bring defendant's conduct within the murder statute, the People were required to establish also that defendant's act was imminently dangerous and presented a very high risk of death to others and that it was committed under circumstances which evidenced a wanton indifference to human life or a depravity of mind. The crime differs from intentional murder in that it results not from a specific, conscious intent to cause death, but from an indifference to or disregard of the risks attending defendant's conduct.

Whether the risk of defendant's conduct was of the type condemned by the Penal Law was to be decided by the trier of the facts aided by appropriate instructions. The jury's proper role, as the Appellate Division found, was to make a qualitative judgment whether defendant's act was of such gravity that it placed the crime upon the same level as the taking of life by premeditated design. It had to determine from the evidence if defendant's conduct, though reckless, was equal in blameworthiness to intentional murder.

The evidence in the record supports the verdict. Defendant's awareness of and indifference to the attendant risks was established by evidence that he entered a crowded bar with a loaded gun, he said that he was "going to kill somebody tonight," or similar words, several times, and he had brought the gun out in the bar once before during the evening only to be told to put it away. Ultimately, he fired the gun three times in the "packed" barroom, conduct which presented a grave risk of death and did in fact result in the death of Marvin Lindsey. His conduct was well within that defined by the statute.

At the conclusion of the evidence and after the charge, defendant requested the court to instruct the jury on the effect of intoxication. The court complied with the request when discussing the intentional murder and assault counts, but it refused to charge the jury that it could consider defendant's intoxication in determining whether he acted "[under] circumstances evincing a depraved indifference to human life" in causing the death of Marvin Lindsey. The court held that the *mens rea* required for depraved mind murder is recklessness and that subdivision 3 of section 15.05 of the Penal Law precludes evidence of intoxication in defense of reckless crimes because it provides that "[a] person who creates such a risk but is unaware thereof solely by reason of voluntary intoxication also acts recklessly." That ruling is assigned as error by defendant. He contends that depraved mind murder contains a different or additional element of mental culpability, namely "circumstances evincing a depraved indifference to human life," which elevates defendant's conduct from manslaughter to murder and that this additional element may be negatived by evidence of intoxication.

The Penal Law does not expressly define the term "element." However, it does set forth what the "elements" of an offense are and identifies them, as does the common law, as a culpable mental state (*mens rea*) and a voluntary act (*actus reus*). Both are required in all but the strict liability offenses. Consistent with that provision, the statutory definition of depraved mind murder includes both a mental element ("recklessly") and a voluntary act ("engaging in conduct which creates a grave risk of death to another person"). Recklessness refers to defendant's conscious disregard of a substantial risk and the act proscribed, the risk creating conduct, is defined by the degree of danger presented. Depraved mind murder resembles manslaughter in the second degree (a reckless killing which includes the requirement that defendant disregard a substantial risk), but the depraved mind murder statute requires in addition not only that the conduct which results in death present a grave risk of death but that it also occur "[under] circumstances evincing a depraved indifference to human life." This additional requirement refers to neither the *mens rea* nor the *actus reus*. If it states an element of the crime at all, it is not an element in the traditional sense but rather a definition of the factual setting in which the risk creating conduct must occur -- objective circumstances which are not subject to being negatived by evidence of defendant's intoxication.

The view is supported by an analysis of the statutory development of the crime. Because of an inability to quantify homicidal risks in precise terms, the Legislature structured the degree of risk which must be present in nonintentional killings by providing that in a depraved mind murder the actor's conduct must present a grave risk of death whereas in manslaughter it presents the lesser substantial risk of death. The phrase "[under] circumstances evincing a depraved indifference to human life" refers to the wantonness of defendant's conduct and converts the substantial risk present in manslaughter into a *very* substantial risk present in murder. The predecessor statute referred to "a depraved mind, regardless of human life" and the older cases, in attempting to explicate this factor, speak of a "depraved heart devoid of social duty and fatally bent on mischief." Such phrases, suggesting malice aforethought, have provoked statements that malice or intent is inferred in depraved mind murder. However, the focus of the offense is not upon the subjective intent of the defendant, as it is with intentional murder, but rather upon an objective assessment of the degree of risk presented by defendant's reckless conduct. * * *

In sum, the statutory requirement that the homicide result from conduct evincing a depraved indifference to human life is a legislative attempt to qualitatively measure egregiously reckless conduct and to differentiate it from manslaughter. It does not create a new and different *mens rea*, undefined in the Penal Law, or a voluntary act which can be negatived by evidence of intoxication. If the objective circumstances under which the crime is committed constitute an element of it, they do so only in the sense that carrying a gun or acting in concert with another are elements of the crime of robbery or that the theft of more than $250 is an element of grand larceny. It is an element which elevates the severity of the offense but it is not an element subject to being negatived by evidence of intoxication as may intent or the physical capacity to act.

In conclusion, it is worth noting that at common law intoxication was not a defense or excuse to criminal charges, but was viewed instead as an aggravating circumstance which heightened moral culpability. The common-law courts viewed the decision to drink to excess, with its attendant risks to self and others, as an independent culpable act. Despite widespread acceptance of this rule, legal authorities began to recognize that the debilitating impact of voluntarily consuming excessive amounts of alcohol warranted the admission of evidence of intoxication in some cases, particularly to negative proof that defendant possessed the physical capacity to commit the crime, by striking a blow, for example. In New York the Legislature further modified the common-law rule by permitting the defendant to introduce evidence of intoxication to aid the jury in determining his motive or intent in committing an act.

Notwithstanding this relaxation of the prohibition against use of intoxication evidence, the present statute when enacted in 1967 continued to foreclose the use of intoxication evidence in cases involving recklessness. The rationale is readily apparent: the element of recklessness itself -- defined as conscious disregard of a substantial risk -- encompasses the risks created by defendant's conduct in getting drunk.

Ultimately, the only intended purpose in permitting the jury to consider intoxication in a reckless crime is to negate defendant's awareness and disregard of the risk. It is precisely that point -- the inconsistency of permitting reckless and otherwise aggravating conduct to negate an aspect of the offense -- that persuades us that intoxication evidence should be excluded whenever recklessness is an element of the offense. In utilitarian terms, the risk of excessive drinking should be added to and not subtracted from the risks created by the conduct of the drunken defendant for there is no social or penological purpose to be served by a rule that permits one who voluntarily drinks to be exonerated from failing to foresee the results of his conduct if he is successful at getting drunk.

Accordingly, the order of the Appellate Division should be affirmed.

JASEN, J., dissenting

The majority holds that the element of "circumstances evincing a depraved indifference to human life" set forth in subdivision 2 of section 125.25 of the Penal Law is not part of the *mens rea* of murder in the second degree and that evidence of intoxication is, therefore, inadmissible to negate that element. Since I believe the Legislature intended that a defendant's alleged intoxication could be used to negate that element of the crime, I respectfully dissent.

Subdivision 2 of section 125.25 of the Penal Law provides that a person is guilty of murder in the second degree when "[under] circumstances evincing a depraved indifference to human life, he recklessly engages in conduct which creates a grave risk of death to another person, and thereby causes the death of another person." This statute evolved without substantial change from the Revised Statutes of 1829 which, *inter alia*, characterized a homicide as murder "[w]hen perpetrated by any act imminently dangerous to others, and evincing a depraved mind, regardless of human life, although without any premeditated design to effect the death of any particular individual." While this statutory language was changed slightly in 1967, the new statute was intended to be "substantially a restatement" of the former provision. The majority's unexplained refusal to recognize this crucial piece of legislative history represents the fundamental flaw in its reasoning. As the majority concedes, the predecessor statutes to subdivision 2 of section 125.25 of the Penal Law defined the requisite *mens rea* "as a depraved mind." Thus, unless a significant change was intended by the Legislature in enacting subdivision 2 of section 125.25, this statute must be similarly construed as characterizing "depraved indifference" as a *mens rea*. That no such change was intended was made abundantly clear by the State commission in declaring that the new statute was intended to be "substantially a restatement" of the former. Nevertheless, the majority disregards entirely the legislative intent behind the statute and states, without any authority in support thereof, that "[the] concept of depraved indifference was retained in the news statute not to function as a *mens rea* element, but to objectively define the circumstances which must exist to elevate a homicide from manslaughter to murder." Inasmuch as the cases construing this statute have consistently held that "depraved mind" and "depraved indifference" connote a culpable mental state, I see no reason why the majority should reach a different result now.

In *Darry v People,* our court held that the statute was designed "to provide for that class of cases, and no others, where the acts resulting in death are calculated to put the lives of [many] persons in jeopardy, without being aimed at any one in particular, *and are perpetrated with a full consciousness of the probable consequences.*" Thus, in construing the 1854 version of the statute, a version which included the element "depraved mind" but not "recklessly," as requiring proof that the accused was aware of and consciously disregarded the probable consequences of his act, the court viewed the "depraved mind" element as a culpable mental state. Indeed, the plain wording of the statute compelled that conclusion. Similarly, in *People v. Jernatowski*, this court held that where a person is "aware that there are human beings in a house [and] fires several shots into it, *knowing* that some one may be killed and with reckless indifference whether he is or not, he ought not to be relieved from the natural consequences of his act." Recognizing that the depraved mind murder statute required proof of consciousness of the risks of defendant's conduct and a disregard of same, the court placed great emphasis on the fact that defendant was fully aware of the consequences of his act. It seems clear, therefore, that the defendant in the case before us should be treated similarly and be allowed to show that as a result of his intoxication he was not aware of what he was doing and the risks involved and was not, therefore, competent to consciously disregard those risks. If such proof were offered and believed, defendant could be convicted only of manslaughter.

This conclusion finds strong support in a recent decision of this court where it was reasoned that, under the present version of the statute, "circumstances evincing a depraved indifference to human life" plus "recklessness," constitutes conduct of "graver culpability" which involves something more serious than mere recklessness. Although the majority chooses to ignore this plain language, by speaking in terms such as "graver culpability" this court made it abundantly clear that "depraved indifference" was to be construed as a *mens rea* involving a state of mind more vicious than recklessness but less so than intent. Inasmuch as proof of intoxication is admissible "whenever it is relevant to negative an element of the crime charged," it should have been admitted here to show that defendant did not possess a state of mind sufficiently culpable to warrant a conviction for murder rather than manslaughter.

While the majority correctly states that "[the] crime differs from intentional murder in that it results not from a specific, conscious intent to cause death, but from an indifference to or disregard of the risks attending defendant's conduct," can there be any doubt that to disregard the risks attending his conduct defendant must have at least been aware of those risks? As stated by Arnold D. Hechtman, Counsel to the Commission on Revision of the Penal Law and Criminal Code, the fatal conduct must be performed with "a depraved kind of wantonness." Wantonness, a term used by the majority in defining what a defendant's conduct must amount to before a conviction for depraved mind murder can be sustained is commonly defined as requiring a conscious doing of some act with knowledge of existing conditions and an awareness of the risks involved. Thus, it should be clear beyond cavil that "depraved indifference" was intended by the Legislature to constitute a culpable state of mind which could be negated by proof that the actor was so intoxicated he was not aware of existing conditions or the risks inherent in his conduct.

The construction which I would give the depraved mind murder statute is not only consistent with the Legislature's intent, the history of the statute and precedent of this court, but is also in line with the basic underpinnings of our system of criminal justice. The rule announced by the majority today effectively eviscerates the distinction between manslaughter in the second degree and murder in the second degree with respect to the accused's state of mind. The majority holds that mere recklessness is a sufficient *mens rea* under the depraved mind murder statute if the objective circumstances surrounding the killing "presented a grave risk of death and did in fact result in the death" of another.

Historically, our criminal law is based upon a theory of "punishing the vicious will." It is a deep-rooted part of our jurisprudence that, in the ordinary case, only those offenders who consciously choose to do evil rather than good will be punished. Under the majority's rule, however, a person who possessed only a reckless state of mind when he caused the death of another could be convicted of depraved mind murder and sentenced to a term of 15 years to life imprisonment simply because objective circumstances surrounding the killing presented a "grave risk" of death even though the actor, due to intoxication, was unaware of those circumstances and could not appreciate the risks. The majority would also hold that another person who is fully aware of a "substantial and unjustifiable risk" and consciously disregards that risk can only be found guilty of manslaughter in the second degree and sentenced to as little as one and one-half years in jail. While there may be a technical distinction between a "grave" risk and a "substantial" one, the only real difference is about 15 years in prison. To accept this distinction as justification for the disparate penalties which the respective crimes carry defies basic principles of fairness and logic. I simply cannot agree that the Legislature intended that convictions for murder as opposed to manslaughter would turn upon the nature of the objective surrounding circumstances regardless of whether or not the accused was aware of those circumstances or could appreciate the consequences of his conduct.[2]

In my view, the Legislature purposely distinguished between reckless manslaughter and depraved mind murder, intending that depraved indifference plus recklessness would connote a *mens rea* more culpable than recklessness alone and nearly as culpable as intent. The differences between the mental states set forth in the reckless manslaughter, depraved mind murder and intentional murder statutes are easily delineated, although somewhat difficult to apply. A person acts recklessly in causing the death of another when he is aware of and consciously disregards a substantial and unjustifiable risk. A person intentionally kills another when his "conscious objective" is to cause the death of the victim. A person acts with depraved indifference, however, when he engages in conduct whereby he does not intend to kill but is so indifferent to the consequences, which he knows with substantial certainty will result in the death of another, as to be willing to kill. It is at this point that reckless homicide becomes knowing homicide and the killing differs so little from an intentional killing that parity of punishment is required. This is so not because the surrounding circumstances happened to create a "grave" as opposed to a

---

[2]While I would agree with the majority that the Legislature could constitutionally exclude intoxication as a factor which negates the element of "depraved indifference" just as it has with respect to the element of "recklessness" (see Penal Law, § 15.05, subd 3), the simple fact is that the Legislature has not done so; indeed section 15.25 of the Penal Law has done just the opposite.

"substantial" risk, but because the accused has acted with greater culpability and a wickedness akin to that of one whose conscious objective is to kill. * * *

Finally, with respect to the majority's statement that "the risk of excessive drinking should be added to and not subtracted from the risks created by the conduct of the drunken defendant for there is no social or penological purpose to be served by a rule that permits one who voluntarily drinks to be exonerated from failing to foresee the results of his conduct if he is successful at getting drunk," I would only note that although this may be an accurate representation of what the majority believes the law should be, the Legislature has decided otherwise and it is this court's responsibility to construe the statute accordingly.

Inasmuch as the legislative history of subdivision 2 of section 125.25 of the Penal Law, prior precedent of this court and basic notions of justice make clear that the element of "depraved indifference" should be construed as a mental state more culpable than recklessness, evidence of defendant's intoxication should have been admitted, pursuant to section 15.25 of the Penal Law, to negate that element of the offense.

Accordingly, I would reverse the conviction and order a new trial.

MONTANA v. EGELHOFF
Supreme Court of the United States
518 U.S. 37, 116 S.Ct. 2013, 135 L.Ed.2d 361 (1996)

JUSTICE SCALIA announced the judgment of the Court and delivered an opinion, in which THE CHIEF JUSTICE, JUSTICE KENNEDY, and JUSTICE THOMAS join.

We consider in this case whether the Due Process Clause is violated by Montana Code Annotated §45-2-203, which provides, in relevant part, that voluntary intoxication "may not be taken into consideration in determining the existence of a mental state which is an element of a criminal offense."

I

In July 1992, while camping out in the Yaak region of northwestern Montana to pick mushrooms, respondent made friends with Roberta Pavola and John Christenson, who were doing the same. On Sunday, July 12, the three sold the mushrooms they had collected and spent the rest of the day and evening drinking, in bars and at a private party in Troy, Montana. Some time after 9 p.m., they left the party in Christenson's 1974 Ford Galaxy station wagon. The drinking binge apparently continued, as respondent was seen buying beer at 9:20 p.m. and recalled "sitting on a hill or a bank passing a bottle of Black Velvet back and forth" with Christenson.

At about midnight that night, officers of the Lincoln County, Montana, sheriff's department, responding to reports of a possible drunk driver, discovered Christenson's station wagon stuck in a ditch along U.S. Highway 2. In the front seat were Pavola and Christenson, each dead from a single gunshot to the head. In the rear of the car lay respondent, alive and yelling obscenities. His blood-alcohol content measured .36 percent over one hour later. On the floor of the car, near the brake pedal, lay respondent's .38 caliber handgun, with four loaded rounds and two empty casings; respondent had gunshot residue on his hands.

Respondent was charged with two counts of deliberate homicide, a crime defined by Montana law as "purposely" or "knowingly" causing the death of another human being. A portion of the jury charge, uncontested here, instructed that "a person acts purposely when it is his conscious object to engage in conduct of that nature or to cause such a result," and that "a person acts knowingly when he is aware of his conduct or when he is aware under the circumstances his conduct constitutes a crime; or, when he is aware there exists the high probability that his conduct will cause a specific result." Respondent's defense at trial was that an unidentified fourth person must have committed the murders; his own extreme intoxication, he claimed, had rendered him physically incapable of committing the murders, and accounted for his inability to recall the events of the night of July 12. Although respondent was allowed to make this use of the evidence that he was intoxicated, the jury was instructed, pursuant to Mont. Code Ann. §45-2-203 (1995), that it could not consider respondent's "intoxicated condition . . . in determining the existence of a mental state which is an element of the offense." The jury found respondent guilty on both counts, and the court sentenced him to 84 years' imprisonment.

The Supreme Court of Montana reversed. It reasoned (1) that respondent "had a due process right to present and have considered by the jury all relevant evidence to rebut the State's evidence on all elements of the offense charged," and (2) that evidence of respondent's voluntary intoxication was "clearly . . . relevant to the issue of whether respondent acted knowingly and purposely." Because §45-2-203 prevented the jury from considering that evidence with regard to that issue, the court concluded that the State had been "relieved of part of its burden to prove beyond a reasonable doubt every fact necessary to constitute the crime charged," and that respondent had therefore been denied due process. We granted certiorari.

II

The cornerstone of the Montana Supreme Court's judgment was the proposition that the Due Process Clause guarantees a defendant the right to present and have considered by the jury "*all relevant evidence* to rebut the State's evidence on all elements of the offense charged." Respondent does not [challenge] this categorical rule; he acknowledges that the right to present relevant evidence "has not been viewed as absolute." That is a wise concession, since the proposition that the Due Process Clause guarantees the right to introduce all relevant evidence is simply indefensible. As we have said: "The accused does not have an unfettered right to offer [evidence] that is incompetent, privileged, or otherwise inadmissible under standard rules of evidence." Relevant evidence may, for example, be excluded on account of a defendant's failure to comply with procedural requirements. And any number of familiar and unquestionably constitutional evidentiary rules also authorize the exclusion of relevant evidence. For example, Federal (and Montana) Rule of Evidence 403 provides: "*Although relevant*, evidence may be excluded if its probative value is substantially outweighed by the danger of unfair prejudice, confusion of the issues, or misleading the jury, or by considerations of undue delay, waste of time, or needless presentation of cumulative evidence." Hearsay rules, *see* Fed. Rule Evid. 802, similarly prohibit the introduction of testimony which, though unquestionably relevant, is deemed insufficiently reliable. Of course, to say that the right to introduce relevant evidence is not absolute is not to say that the Due Process Clause places *no* limits upon restriction of that right. But it is to say that the defendant asserting such a limit must sustain the usual heavy burden that a due process claim entails:

> Preventing and dealing with crime is much more the business of the States than it is of the Federal Government, and . . . we should not lightly construe the Constitution so as to intrude upon the administration of justice by the individual States. Among other things, it is normally "within the power of the State to regulate procedures under which its laws are carried out," . . . and its decision in this regard is not subject to proscription under the Due Process Clause unless "it offends some principle of justice so rooted in the traditions and conscience of our people as to be ranked as fundamental."

Respondent's task, then, is to establish that a defendant's right to have a jury consider evidence of his voluntary intoxication in determining whether he possesses the requisite mental state is a "fundamental principle of justice."

Our primary guide in determining whether the principle in question is fundamental is, of course, historical practice. Here that gives respondent little support. By the laws of England, wrote Hale, the intoxicated defendant "shall have no privilege by this voluntary contracted madness, but shall have the same judgment as if he were in his right senses." According to Blackstone and Coke, the law's condemnation of those suffering from *dementia affectata* was harsher still: Blackstone, citing Coke, explained that the law viewed intoxication "as an aggravation of the offence, rather than as an excuse for any criminal misbehaviour." This stern rejection of inebriation as a defense became a fixture of early American law as well. The American editors of the 1847 edition of Hale wrote:

> Drunkenness, it was said in an early case, can never be received as a ground to excuse or palliate an offence: this is not merely the opinion of a speculative philosopher, the argument of counsel, or the *obiter dictum* of a single judge, but it is a sound and long established maxim of judicial policy, from which perhaps a single dissenting voice cannot be found. But if no other authority could be adduced, the uniform decisions of our own Courts from the first establishment of the government, would constitute it now a part of the common law of the land.

In an opinion citing the foregoing passages from Blackstone and Hale, Justice Story rejected an objection to the exclusion of evidence of intoxication as follows:

> This is the first time, that I ever remember it to have been contended, that the commission of one crime was an excuse for another. Drunkenness is a gross vice, and in the contemplation of some of our laws is a crime; and I learned in my earlier studies, that so far from its being in law an excuse for murder, it is rather an aggravation of its malignity.

The historical record does not leave room for the view that the common law's rejection of intoxication as an "excuse" or "justification" for crime would nonetheless permit the defendant to show that intoxication prevented the requisite *mens rea*. Hale, Coke, and Blackstone were familiar, to say the least, with the concept of *mens rea*, and acknowledged that drunkenness "deprive[s] men of the use of reason." It is inconceivable that they did not realize that an offender's drunkenness might impair his ability to form the requisite intent; and inconceivable that their failure to note this massive exception from the general rule of disregard of intoxication was an oversight. Hale's statement that a drunken offender shall have the same judgment "as if he were in his right senses" must be understood as precluding a defendant from arguing that, because of his intoxication, he could not have possessed the *mens rea* required to commit the crime. * * *

Against this extensive evidence of a lengthy common-law tradition decidedly against him, the best argument available to respondent is the one made by his *amicus* and conceded by the State: Over the course of the 19th century, courts carved out an exception to the common law's traditional across-the-board condemnation of the drunken offender, allowing a jury to consider a defendant's intoxication when assessing whether he possessed the mental state needed to commit the crime charged, where the crime was one requiring a "specific intent." The emergence of this new rule is often traced to an 1819 English case, in which Justice Holroyd is reported to have held that "though voluntary drunkenness cannot excuse from the commission of crime, yet where, as on a charge of murder, the material question is, whether an act was premeditated or done only with sudden heat and impulse, the fact of the party being intoxicated [is] a circumstance proper to be taken into consideration." * * *

[B]y the end of the 19th century, in most American jurisdictions, intoxication could be considered in determining whether a defendant was capable of forming the specific intent necessary to commit the crime charged.

On the basis of this historical record, respondent's *amicus* argues that "the old common-law rule . . . was no longer deeply rooted at the time the Fourteenth Amendment was ratified." That conclusion is questionable, but we need not pursue the point, since the argument of *amicus* mistakes the nature of our inquiry. It is not the State which bears the burden of demonstrating that its rule is "deeply rooted," but rather respondent who must show that the principle of procedure *violated* by the rule (and allegedly required by due process) is "'so rooted in the traditions and conscience of our people as to be ranked as fundamental.'" Thus, even assuming that when the Fourteenth Amendment was adopted the rule Montana now defends was no longer generally applied, this only cuts off what might be called an *a fortiori* argument in favor of the State. The burden remains upon respondent to show that the "new common-law" rule -- that intoxication may be considered on the question of intent -- was so deeply rooted at the time of the Fourteenth Amendment (or perhaps has become so deeply rooted since) as to be a fundamental principle which that Amendment enshrined.

That showing has not been made. Instead of the uniform and continuing acceptance we would expect for a rule that enjoys "fundamental principle" status, we find that fully one-fifth of the States either never adopted the "new common-law" rule at issue here or have recently abandoned it. * * *

It is not surprising that many States have held fast to or resurrected the common-law rule prohibiting consideration of voluntary intoxication in the determination of *mens rea*, because that rule has considerable justification -- which alone casts doubt upon the proposition that the opposite rule is a "fundamental principle." A large number of crimes, especially violent crimes, are committed by intoxicated offenders; modern studies put the numbers as high as half of all homicides, for example. Disallowing consideration of voluntary intoxication has the effect of increasing the punishment for all unlawful acts committed in that state, and thereby deters drunkenness or irresponsible behavior while drunk. The rule also serves as a specific deterrent, ensuring that those who prove incapable of controlling violent impulses while voluntarily intoxicated go to prison. And finally, the rule comports with and implements society's moral perception that one who has voluntarily impaired his own faculties should be responsible for the consequences.

There is, in modern times, even more justification for laws such as §45-2-203 than there used to be. Some recent studies suggest that the connection between drunkenness and crime is as much cultural as pharmacological -- that is, that drunks are violent not simply because alcohol makes them that way, but because they are behaving in accord with their learned belief that drunks are violent. This not only adds additional support to the traditional view that an intoxicated criminal is not deserving of exoneration, but it suggests that juries -- who possess the same learned belief as the intoxicated offender -- will be too quick to accept the claim that the defendant was biologically incapable of forming the requisite *mens rea*. Treating the matter as one of excluding misleading evidence therefore makes some sense.

In sum, not every widespread experiment with a procedural rule favorable to criminal defendants establishes a fundamental principle of justice. Although the rule allowing a jury to consider evidence of a defendant's voluntary intoxication where relevant to *mens rea* has gained considerable acceptance, it is of too recent vintage, and has not received sufficiently uniform and permanent allegiance, to qualify as fundamental, especially since it displaces a lengthy common law tradition which remains supported by valid justifications today.

III

* * * *In re Winship* announced the proposition that the Due Process Clause requires proof beyond a reasonable doubt of every fact necessary to constitute the charged crime, and *Sandstrom v. Montana,* established a corollary, that a jury instruction which shifts to the defendant the burden of proof on a requisite element of mental state violates due process. These decisions simply are not implicated here because, as the Montana court itself recognized, "the

burden is not shifted" under §45-2-203. The trial judge instructed the jury that "the State of Montana has the burden of proving the guilt of the Defendant beyond a reasonable doubt," and that "[a] person commits the offense of deliberate homicide if he purposely or knowingly causes the death of another human being." Thus, failure by the State to produce evidence of respondent's mental state would have resulted in an acquittal. That acquittal did not occur was presumably attributable to the fact, noted by the Supreme Court of Montana, that the State introduced considerable evidence from which the jury might have concluded that respondent acted "purposely" or "knowingly." For example, respondent himself testified that, several hours before the murders, he had given his handgun to Pavola and asked her to put it in the glove compartment of Christenson's car. That he had to retrieve the gun from the glove compartment before he used it was strong evidence that it was his "conscious object" to commit the charged crimes; as was the execution-style manner in which a single shot was fired into the head of each victim. * * *

"The doctrines of *actus reus, mens rea*, insanity, mistake, justification, and duress have historically provided the tools for a constantly shifting adjustment of the tension between the evolving aims of the criminal law and changing religious, moral, philosophical, and medical views of the nature of man. This process of adjustment has always been thought to be the province of the States." The people of Montana have decided to resurrect the rule of an earlier era, disallowing consideration of voluntary intoxication when a defendant's state of mind is at issue. Nothing in the Due Process Clause prevents them from doing so, and the judgment of the Supreme Court of Montana to the contrary must be reversed.

It is so ordered.

JUSTICE O'CONNOR, with whom JUSTICE STEVENS, JUSTICE SOUTER, and JUSTICE BREYER join, dissenting.

The Montana Supreme Court unanimously held that Mont. Code Ann. §45-2-203 (1995) violates due process. I agree. Our cases establish that due process sets an outer limit on the restrictions that may be placed on a defendant's ability to raise an effective defense to the State's accusations. Here, to impede the defendant's ability to throw doubt on the State's case, Montana has removed from the jury's consideration a category of evidence relevant to determination of mental state where that mental state is an essential element of the offense that must be proved beyond a reasonable doubt. Because this disallowance eliminates evidence with which the defense might negate an essential element, the State's burden to prove its case is made correspondingly easier. The justification for this disallowance is the State's desire to increase the likelihood of conviction of a certain class of defendants who might otherwise be able to prove that they did not satisfy a requisite element of the offense. In my view, the statute's effect on the criminal proceeding violates due process.

I

This Court's cases establish that limitations placed on the accused's ability to present a fair and complete defense can, in some circumstances, be severe enough to violate due process. "The right of an accused in a criminal trial to due process is, in essence, the right to a fair opportunity to defend against the State's accusations." Applying our precedent, the Montana Supreme Court held that keeping intoxication evidence away from the jury, where such evidence was relevant to establishment of the requisite mental state, violated the due process right to present a defense and that the instruction pursuant to §45-2-203 was not harmless error. In rejecting the Montana Supreme Court's conclusion, the Court emphasizes that "any number of familiar and unquestionably constitutional evidentiary rules" permit exclusion of relevant evidence. It is true that a defendant does not enjoy an absolute right to present evidence relevant to his defense. But none of the "familiar" evidentiary rules operates as Montana's does. The Montana statute places a blanket exclusion on a category of evidence that would allow the accused to negate the offense's mental-state element. In so doing, it frees the prosecution, in the face of such evidence, from having to prove beyond a reasonable doubt that the defendant nevertheless possessed the required mental state. In my view, this combination of effects violates due process. * * *

Meaningful adversarial testing of the State's case requires that the defendant not be prevented from raising an effective defense, which must include the right to present relevant, probative evidence. To be sure, the right to present evidence is not limitless; for example, it does not permit the defendant to introduce any and all evidence he believes might work in his favor, nor does it generally invalidate the operation of testimonial privileges. Nevertheless, "an essential component of procedural fairness is an opportunity to be heard. That opportunity would be an empty one if the State were permitted to exclude competent, reliable evidence" that is essential to the accused's defense. Section 45-2-203 forestalls the defendant's ability to raise an effective defense by placing a blanket exclusion on the presentation of a type of evidence that directly negates an element of the crime, and by doing so, it lightens the prosecution's burden to prove that mental-state element beyond a reasonable doubt.

This latter effect is as important to the due process analysis as the former. A state legislature certainly has the authority to identify the elements of the offenses it wishes to punish, but once its laws are written, a defendant has the right to insist that the State prove beyond a reasonable doubt every element of an offense charged. "The Due Process Clause protects the accused against conviction except upon proof beyond a reasonable doubt of every fact necessary to constitute the crime with which he is charged." Because the Montana Legislature has specified that a person commits "deliberate homicide" only if he "purposely or knowingly causes the death of another human being," the prosecution must prove the existence of such mental state in order to convict. That is, unless the defendant is shown to have acted purposely or knowingly, *he is not guilty of the offense of deliberate homicide.* The Montana Supreme Court found that it was inconsistent with the legislature's requirement of the mental state of "purposely" or "knowingly" to prevent the jury from considering evidence of voluntary intoxication, where that category of evidence was relevant to establishment of that mental-state element.

Where the defendant may introduce evidence to negate a subjective mental-state element, the prosecution must work to overcome whatever doubts the defense has raised about the existence of the required mental state. On the other hand, if the defendant may *not* introduce evidence that might create doubt in the factfinder's mind as to whether that element was met, the prosecution will find its job so much the easier. A subjective mental state is generally proved only circumstantially. If a jury may not consider the defendant's evidence of his mental state, the jury may impute to the defendant the culpability of a mental state he did not possess. * * *

A State's placement of a significant limitation on the right to defend against the State's accusations "requires that the competing interest be closely examined." Montana has specified that to prove guilt, the State must establish that the defendant acted purposely or knowingly, but has prohibited a category of defendants from effectively disputing guilt through presentation of evidence relevant to that essential element. And the evidence is indisputably relevant: The Montana Supreme Court held that evidence of intoxication is relevant to proof of mental state and furthermore, §45-2-203's exception for involuntary intoxication shows that the legislature does consider intoxication relevant to mental state. Montana has barred the defendant's use of a category of relevant, exculpatory evidence for the express purpose of improving the State's likelihood of winning a conviction against a certain type of defendant. * * *

The plurality brushes aside this Court's precedents as variously fact bound, irrelevant, and dicta. I would afford more weight to principles enunciated in our case law than is accorded in the plurality's opinion today. It seems to me that a State may not first determine the elements of the crime it wishes to punish, and then thwart the accused's defense by categorically disallowing the very evidence that would prove him innocent.

II

The plurality does, however, raise an important argument for the statute's validity: the disallowance, at common law, of consideration of voluntary intoxication where a defendant's state of mind is at issue. Because this disallowance was permitted at common law, the plurality argues, its disallowance by Montana cannot amount to a violation of a "fundamental principle of justice."

From 1551 until its shift in the 19th century, the common-law rule prevailed that a defendant could not use intoxication as an excuse or justification for an offense, or, it must be assumed, to rebut establishment of a requisite mental state. "Early law was indifferent to the defence of drunkenness because the theory of criminal liability was then too crude and too undeveloped to admit of exceptions. . . . But with the refinement in the theory of criminal liability . . . . a modification of the rigid old rule on the defence of drunkenness was to be expected." As the plurality concedes, that significant modification took place in the 19th century. Courts acknowledged the fundamental incompatibility of a particular mental-state requirement on the one hand, and the disallowance of consideration of evidence that might defeat establishment of that mental state on the other. In the slow progress typical of the common law, courts began to recognize that evidence of intoxication was properly admissible for the purpose of ascertaining whether a defendant had met the required mental-state element of the offense charged.

This recognition, courts believed, was consistent with the common-law rule that voluntary intoxication did not excuse commission of a crime; rather, an element of the crime, the requisite mental state, was not satisfied and therefore the crime had not been committed. As one influential mid-19th century case explained: "Drunkenness is no excuse for crime; yet, in that class of crimes and offences which depend upon guilty knowledge, or the coolness and deliberation with which they shall have been perpetrated, to constitute their commission . . . . [drunkenness] should be submitted to the consideration of the Jury"; for, where the crime required a particular mental state, "it is proper to show any state or condition of the person that is adverse to the proper exercise of the mind" in order "to rebut" the mental state or "to enable the Jury to judge rightly of the matter."

Courts across the country agreed that where a subjective mental state was an element of the crime to be proved, the defense must be permitted to show, by reference to intoxication, the absence of that element. One court commented that it seemed "incontrovertible and to be universally applicable" that "where the nature and essence of the crime are made by law to depend upon the peculiar state and condition of the criminal's mind at the time with reference to the act done, drunkenness may be a proper subject for the consideration of the jury, not to excuse or mitigate the offence but to show that it was not committed."

With similar reasoning, the Montana Supreme Court recognized the incompatibility of a jury instruction pursuant to §45-2-203 in conjunction with the legislature's decision to require a mental state of "purposely" or "knowingly" for deliberate homicide. It held that intoxication is relevant to formation of the requisite mental state. Unless a defendant is proved beyond a reasonable doubt to have possessed the requisite mental state, he did not commit the offense. Elimination of a critical category of defense evidence precludes a defendant from effectively rebutting the mental-state element, while simultaneously shielding the State from the effort of proving the requisite mental state in the face of negating evidence. It was this effect on the adversarial process that persuaded the Montana Supreme Court that the disallowance was unconstitutional.

The Due Process Clause protects those "'principle[s] of justice so rooted in the traditions and conscience of our people as to be ranked as fundamental.'" At the time the Fourteenth Amendment was ratified, the common-law rule on consideration of intoxication evidence was in flux. The plurality argues that rejection of the historical rule in the 19th century simply does not establish that the "'new common-law'" rule is a principle of procedure so "deeply rooted" as to be ranked "fundamental." But to determine whether a fundamental principle of justice has been violated here, we cannot consider only the historical disallowance of intoxication evidence, but must also consider the "fundamental principle" that a defendant has a right to a fair opportunity to put forward his defense, in adversarial testing where the State must prove the elements of the offense beyond a reasonable doubt. * * *

III

Because the management of criminal justice is within the province of the States, this Court is properly reluctant to interfere in the States' authority in these matters. Nevertheless, the Court must invalidate those rules that violate the requirements of due process. The plurality acknowledges that a reduction of the State's burden through disallowance of exculpatory evidence is unconstitutional if it violates a principle of fairness. I believe that such a violation is present here. Montana's disallowance of consideration of voluntary-intoxication evidence removes too critical a category of relevant, exculpatory evidence from the adversarial process by prohibiting the defendant from making an essential argument and permitting the prosecution to benefit from its suppression. Montana's purpose is to increase the likelihood of conviction of a certain class of defendants, who might otherwise be able to prove that they did not satisfy a requisite element of the offense. The historical fact that this disallowance once existed at common law is not sufficient to save the statute today. I would affirm the judgment of the Montana Supreme Court.

COMMONWEALTH v. SMITH
Superior Court of Pennsylvania
831 A.2d 636 (Pa. Super. 2003)

ORIE MELVIN, J.

Appellant, Karen Smith, appeals from the judgment of sentence of 48 hours to 18 months' incarceration imposed following her conviction of driving under the influence (DUI) and related summary offense. Appellant claims she established the affirmative defense of "involuntary intoxication" thereby negating the state of mind necessary to support a conviction of DUI. After review, we affirm.

The facts and procedural history of this matter may be summarized as follows. On March 29, 2002, Officer James E. Ott, of the Greenfield Township Police Department, observed Appellant driving a Ford truck on State Route 101 in Greenfield Township, Blair County, Pennsylvania. Officer Ott observed Appellant's vehicle drift completely into the oncoming lane and proceed to travel in the lane for oncoming traffic for one tenth of a mile until he activated his emergency lights. Appellant then pulled her vehicle to the side of the road, leaving a large portion of the vehicle protruding into the roadway, even though there was sufficient space to park the vehicle totally off of the roadway. Upon making contact with the Appellant, Officer Ott observed that her eyes were glassy and bloodshot and she emanated a strong odor of alcohol. When asked to exit her vehicle, Appellant stumbled and staggered numerous times. Appellant admitted to consuming beer earlier in the evening.

Officer Ott administered three field sobriety tests, all of which Appellant failed. Appellant was placed under arrest for DUI and transported to the hospital for a blood alcohol test, which she refused. On September 24, 2002, a bench trial was held. On direct examination, Appellant testified that she consumed alcohol while wearing a prescribed "duragesic" patch for pain. She testified that she did not realize that the patch would heighten the effects of alcohol. Appellant admitted that she did not read the directions or warnings for the patch. Moreover, Appellant offered no expert testimony whatsoever to support her allegation that the patch heightened the effects of the alcohol she consumed. The Honorable Thomas J. Peoples, Jr. found Appellant guilty and imposed sentence on October 17, 2002. Appellant filed a post sentence motion that was denied. This timely appeal followed.

Appellant's sole question on appeal reads as follows: I. IS THE DEFENSE OF INVOLUNTARY INTOXICATION OR INVOLUNTARY DRUGGED CONDITION A DEFENSE COGNIZABLE IN PENNSYLVANIA?

Initially, we note that Appellant was convicted of driving while under the influence of alcohol to a degree that rendered her incapable of safe driving. In order to prove a violation of this section, the Commonwealth must show: (1) that the defendant was the operator of a motor vehicle and (2) that while operating the vehicle, the defendant was under the influence of alcohol to such a degree as to render him or her incapable of safe driving. To establish the second element, it must be shown that alcohol has substantially impaired the normal mental and physical faculties required to safely operate the vehicle. Substantial impairment, in this context, means a diminution or enfeeblement in the ability to exercise judgment, to deliberate or to react prudently to changing circumstances and conditions. Evidence that the driver was not in control of himself, such as failing to pass a field sobriety test, may establish that the driver was under the influence of alcohol to a degree which rendered him incapable of safe driving, notwithstanding the absence of evidence of erratic or unsafe driving.

Appellant asserts that involuntary intoxication is a cognizable affirmative defense in a DUI prosecution. Specifically, she claims that "[i]n the pharmaceutical age, the labeling of drugs places on the physician in Pennsylvania, the duty to warn the patient of the side effects of drugs. When labeling is not on bold print but on minute instructions in tiny print inside of a box, it is not the consumer who is expected to be aware of the consequences, but the physician. Where testimony is offered, unrebutted, nor challenged, that the user was unaware of the polypharmacology of the drug a cognizable defense should be recognized in Pennsylvania." Appellant's brief, at 9. In effect, Appellant urges this Court to find that she was not criminally culpable for her conduct because she was unaware that the newly increased strength of the prescribed duragesic patch she was wearing would heighten the effects of the alcohol she voluntarily ingested. We are not persuaded.

Pennsylvania like many other jurisdictions, either by statute or caselaw, specifically limits the availability of a voluntary intoxication defense but does not specify whether an involuntary intoxication defense is available. In *Commonwealth v. Collins*, we recently noted that "the issue of whether involuntary intoxication is a defense to a DUI charge is unclear in Pennsylvania." Moreover, in the context of a DUI prosecution, assuming the defense applies, we have held that the defendant has the burden of proving the affirmative defense of involuntary intoxication by a preponderance of the evidence.

Generally speaking, many of the other jurisdictions that permit an accused to be completely relieved of criminal responsibility based on involuntary intoxication do so premised upon the notion that he or she was temporarily rendered legally insane at the time he or she committed the offense. The defense of involuntary intoxication has been recognized in other jurisdictions in four types of situations: (1) where the intoxication was caused by the fault of another (i.e., through force, duress, fraud, or contrivance); (2) where the intoxication was caused by an innocent mistake on the part of the defendant (i.e., defendant took hallucinogenic pill in reasonable belief it was aspirin or lawful tranquilizer); (3) where a defendant unknowingly suffers from a physiological or psychological condition that renders him abnormally susceptible to a legal intoxicant (sometimes referred to as pathological intoxication); and (4) where unexpected intoxication results from a medically prescribed drug.[2] These widely varying circumstances make it difficult to formulate a comprehensive definition of the defense; nonetheless, it would appear that a key component is lack of culpability on the part of the defendant in causing the intoxication.

Instantly, Appellant's argument is most similar to the situation described above in type number four. This type is premised upon the notion that "because a patient is entitled to assume that an intoxicating dose would not be prescribed or administered by a physician, where intoxication results from medicine which has been prescribed (and taken as prescribed) or administered by a physician, such intoxication is generally considered involuntary." Significantly, Appellant's argument differs from a pure type four involuntary intoxication defense in that she does not claim that the patch alone caused an unknowing and unexpected intoxicating effect. Rather, she claims that a higher dose of the patch combined with her voluntary ingestion of an allegedly moderate amount of alcohol caused an unexpected intoxication. It would seem, however, that her intoxication was "self-induced" as defined by the Model Penal Code. Clearly, she "knowingly introduce[d]" a substance--alcohol--"the tendency of which to cause intoxication" she "ought to [have known]." Model Penal Code § 2.08(5)(b). In fact, this Court and our Supreme Court have previously rejected similar arguments in *Commonwealth v. Todaro* and *Commonwealth v. Hicks*.

In *Todaro*, the defendant was charged with involuntary manslaughter, recklessly endangering another person, and driving under the influence. This Court held that an instruction on involuntary intoxication was not required

---

[2] Like the insanity defense, the defendant is excused from criminality because intoxication affects the ability to distinguish between right and wrong. W. Lafave & A. Scott, Handbook on Crim. Law, § 45 at 342 (1972). Thus, the mental state of an involuntarily intoxicated defendant is measured by the test of legal insanity.

where the defendant inadvertently mixed alcoholic beverages with prescribed medication because there was no evidence to support a finding that defendant's intoxication was not voluntary. In *Hicks*, prior to the victim's murder the defendant had consumed a large quantity of alcohol and an amphetamine based diet pill. Defendant asserted that the record did not establish that he was sane so as to be criminally responsible for his conduct. He argued that his mental state was involuntarily induced from a mixture of the prescribed medication and alcohol because he was not warned of the possible effect of such combination. On appeal our Supreme Court held that the trial court properly weighed the evidence and found that defendant's behavior resulted from the voluntary ingestion of alcohol and not mental disease. The Court further noted that "[e]ven accepting the remote possibility of the existence of a pathological disorder, it was at best a passive condition triggered by the ingestion of alcohol. In either event [defendant] was not entitled to escape the responsibility for his conduct under the M'Naghten Rule."

Thus, it would appear that Pennsylvania law is consonant with the Model Penal Code's definition and would not characterize intoxication produced by the voluntary consumption of a prescription drug and alcohol as "involuntary" even if that consumption was without knowledge of a synergistic effect. Here, as in *Todaro* the evidence merely established that Appellant drank alcohol without regard to the effects of its combination with medication she was taking. Thus, even assuming the proffered defense is viable, these facts alone cannot establish involuntary intoxication.

Moreover, upon our careful review of the facts of this case even if we were to assume that such a defense is cognizable under Appellant's theory, she still cannot show that the trial court erred in rejecting this defense because she has failed to establish the necessary factual foundation to support her claimed defense. To absolve Appellant of criminal behavior by the complete defense of involuntary intoxication, she had the burden to show such intoxication by a preponderance of the evidence. If this defense is to be relied upon, Appellant must show that the combination is capable of causing the extreme intoxication which is alleged. The trial court cannot take judicial notice of this fact. Thus, at a minimum it will be necessary to present expert witnesses to establish this effect. Here, the only evidence of record is Appellant's self-serving statements that she had not read any of the labeling and was not told by her doctor of any possible side effects and thus was unaware of the alleged heightened effect of the patch when combined with alcohol consumption. Appellant did not present her physician or any other medical expert to establish that an increased inebriating effect was even possible. It follows that Appellant has not come close to putting the integrity of the conviction into question. Because Appellant was unable to establish the factual foundation for her proffered defense, it does not bear upon the sufficiency of the evidence in the case, and the trial court properly denied Appellant's motion in arrest of judgment.

Judgment of sentence affirmed.

C.   OTHER DEFENSE THEORIES

In this last section, we consider defenses (or, more accurately, defense theories) which have not been widely accepted by the courts, such as "black rage," the "cultural defense," "brainwashing," and "rotten social background."

1.   Black Rage

BLACK RAGE CONFRONTS THE LAW
Paul Harris, 1997

What is the black rage defense? It is a legal strategy that centers on the racial oppression experienced by the defendant. It is an attempt to explain to the judge and jury how the defendant's environment contributed to his or her crime. It shows how concrete instances of racial discrimination impacted on the mental state of the defendant.

It is essential to understand that the black rage defense is not an independent, freestanding defense. That is, one cannot argue that a defendant should be acquitted of murdering his boss because the boss fired him out of racial prejudice. The innovation inherent in the black rage defense is that it merges racial oppression with more conventional criminal defenses.

The law has always recognized state-of-mind defenses. For example, if a person is insane at the time of the criminal act, he can raise his mental condition as a defense. So if, in the above example, the white boss's racist behavior caused the black worker to lose the ability to control himself, a defense of diminished capacity would be allowed. Such a defense would reduce first-degree murder to second-degree murder or manslaughter. Another example is a young African American surrounded by three skinheads wearing Nazi symbols and calling him "nigger." If he pulls a gun and shoots one of them, he can raise a self-defense claim. As part of the defense he would be allowed to argue that given his experience with racists it was "reasonable" for him to assume that he was in danger of serious bodily injury, and therefore it was legally justifiable to shoot before he was actually attacked.

State-of-mind defenses allow us to bring the racial reality of America into the court by presenting "social context" or "social framework" evidence.

I have also described it to judges as 'social reality" or "racial reality" evidence. The phrase "black rage defense" describes a lawyer's gestalt, a theory of the case, an all-encompassing strategy that uses racial reality evidence to establish self-defense, diminished capacity, insanity, mistake of fact, duress, or other state-of-mind defenses allowed by the criminal law.

In a larger sense, the black rage defense educates the judge and jury about society's role in contributing to the criminal act. It is part of a growing body of recognized criminal defenses that have forced the courts to consider the effects of environmental hardship. The Vietnam Vet Syndrome and post-traumatic stress disorder used to defend veterans scarred by the war in Vietnam and African American teenagers scarred by the war in urban America illustrates state-of-mind defenses rooted in social reality. The battered woman defense parallels the black rage defense, in introducing evidence of gender oppression in defense of women charged with crimes of violence against their abusive husbands and boyfriends. The cultural defense, another rapidly growing legal strategy, uses evidence of a defendant's culture (e.g., Laotian and Vietnamese refugees, Chinese immigrants, or Native Americans) to explain his or her state-of-mind in defense or mitigation of criminal charges. * * *

* * * In a riot situation where a defendant injures someone and is charged with attempted murder, a traditional defense is to argue that the defendant did not have the "specific intent to kill." In these situations attorneys have presented evidence of racial tension leading up to the riot in order to show that their clients were caught up in the violence, and that although they attacked people they did not intend to kill anyone. Therefore, they argue, the defendants may be guilty of assault but not attempted murder. The epitome of this type of case took place during the 1992 riot that rocked Los Angeles after the Rodney King verdicts. It involved the prosecution of a young African American man named Damian Williams for smashing a brick into the head of a white truck driver Reginald Denny, an incident videotaped by a local news helicopter and shown on television in every city in America. The South-Central Los Angeles riots were black rage in action. Williams was consumed by that anger and his defense team took on the task of making that rage understandable to a jury.

The fires of 1992 find their kindling in the economic hopelessness and political resignation that is daily reality for residents in South-Central. They were fueled by institutional racism and continual acts of police misconduct. In 1990 alone, the City of Los Angeles paid victims of police abuse over a million dollars. Those who did not believe the police were capable of systematic unconstitutional behavior were shocked on March 3, 1991, to see a videotape of policemen repeatedly clubbing and kicking Rodney King. Two weeks later, a fifteen-year-old African American girl, Latasha Harlins, was shot to death by a middle-aged Korean American woman grocer, Soon Ja Du, after a dispute in a

South Los Angeles grocery store. In November 1991 Soon Ja Du, convicted of manslaughter, was given probation, community service, and a five thousand dollar fine. California State Senator Diane Watson responded to the extremely lenient sentence by saying, "This might be the time bomb that explodes." Two weeks later, Los Angeles police officers fatally shot a twenty-eight-year-old black man, Henry Peco, causing a standoff with more than a hundred residents of the Imperial Court housing project in Watts. Two months later, the trial of the four policemen charged with assaulting King began, after the case was moved from Los Angeles to the primarily white, conservative venue of Simi Valley.

On April 29, 1992, a jury devoid of African Americans returned a verdict of not guilty on all charges except one count of excessive force against officer Lawrence Powell. The verdict was announced on live television. More than two thousand people gathered for a peaceful rally at the First African Methodist Episcopal Church in South-Central. But other residents took to the streets. There was a small confrontation between police and angry people at the intersection of Florence and Normandie in South-Central. The police left and a mob furious at the not guilty verdicts poured into the area. Reginald Denny was driving his large truck through the intersection. Bricks were thrown into his windows. As he came to a stop he was pulled from the truck and beaten. A television helicopter videotaped the scene. Twenty-nine-year-old Henry Watson was seen with his foot on Denny's neck as he lay on the ground. Nineteen-year-old Damian Williams was videotaped as he smashed a brick against Denny's head and strutted away in celebration. Denny managed to crawl back into his truck, where sympathetic blacks climbed into the cab of the vehicle to help him. One person held him in her arms while another man drove the truck to a hospital, saving Denny's life.

The riots swept through Los Angeles and nearby areas. Fifty-eight people were reported killed. There were more than two thousand injuries, more than seven thousand fires, $3 billion worth of damage, and 12,111 arrests. Though at least as many Latinos as blacks were arrested, the events were perceived nationally as a black riot. Many, if not most, of the participants were burning and looting out of economic envy and class rage, but there is no question that the injustice of the not guilty verdicts was the catalyst.

Williams and Watson were charged with the beatings of Denny and seven other motorists. Included in the charges were attempted murder and aggravated mayhem, both of which carry life imprisonment. A defense committee called "Free the LA Four" was formed for them and two other defendants. Williams was fortunate to obtain the services of an outstanding lawyer, Edi M.O. Faal. Faal was born in Gambia, West Africa, and trained at Middle Temple Inn of Court in London, where he became a barrister. A dignified-looking man in his late thirties, he was highly regarded among his peers for both his legal ability and his political acumen. His primary strategy was to show that any criminal acts Williams committed were a result of the unthinking emotion generated by the riot.

In early 1993 the four police officers who beat King were tried in federal court for violating his civil rights. Two were acquitted, but Officer Powell and Sergeant Stacy Koon were convicted. Facing a maximum of ten years and a $250,000 fine, they each received a thirty-month sentence. Two weeks later, Williams and Watson went to trial in front of a racially mixed jury consisting of four blacks, four Latinos, three whites, and one Asian.

Faal, with the aid of Wilma Shanks and David Lynn, attempted a two-pronged strategy that can be described as "he didn't do it, but if he did, he didn't do what the prosecutor is charging him with." Once in a while, a jury will accept this defense when they recognize that the defendant has committed a crime, but that the district attorney is guilty of overcharging. In Williams's case, Faal argued that Williams was mistakenly identified as the perpetrator. However, even if the jury believed that his client was the perpetrator, he argued that they should still find him not guilty of the two most serious crimes because he did not specifically intend to kill or permanently disfigure Denny.

Faal delivered a six-hour closing argument over two days. He had to go over all the evidence regarding each of the people Williams had been charged with assaulting. The *Los Angeles Times* described his closing as one that combined "sarcasm, eloquence, indignation and wit." After putting forth the weak defense of mistaken identification, Faal began a persuasive discussion of the riot and how the collective frenzy of the group was responsible for his client's acts. His legal point was quite clear: in order to convict Williams of attempted murder and aggravated mayhem, the jury had to find premeditation and specific intent. Faal had presented as an expert witness a local sociologist named Armando Morales. Morales testified to the phenomenon of mob psychology, in which individuals are caught up in the "mass hysteria and mass convulsions" of the crowd. People act without reflection, without rationally considering what they are doing; they act impulsively, unpredictably. Faal tied Morales's testimony to the riot and put it all in the social context of a community's frustrated and indignant reaction to the not guilty verdicts of the four police officers.

> We know that on April 29, 1992, many people in many communities; Black, White, Hispanic, experienced tremendous disappointment from the verdicts that came down from Simi Valley. I'm talking about the acquittal of the police officers that were accused of beating Rodney King.

People near Florence and Normandie congregated to grieve together or to express their disappointments together. The police came, there was a slight confrontation, the police left. A mob developed. The mob, true to its name which is a mob, got into a frenzy. People started acting in manners that they would not act otherwise and that whole situation became the 1992 riots, the L.A. Riots.

People caught up in that frenzy were acting out their frustration, their anger, their disappointment. They were so consumed with emotions that they could not have rationally been entertaining the type of reflective thought which gives rise to specific intent to kill or to disfigure.

The defense was in the favorable situation of being able to contrast the injustice of the Simi Valley verdicts on assault charges against the police with the more serious charges of attempted murder and mayhem against their clients. Earl Broady, counsel for codefendant Watson, specifically told the jury that the defendants were in court because four L.A. policemen had been found not guilty of beating Rodney King. This was strongly contested by prosecutor Janet Moore:

I say Mr. Faal and Mr. Broady are dead wrong. We are in court because of what these two men chose to do on April 29, 1992. They have no one else to blame but themselves.

They are here because they acted in a violent and unconscionable way. They are not here because we are holding them responsible for the entire Los Angeles riot.

Faal was sophisticated in his concluding words. Instead of referring specifically to the Simi Valley verdict he talked about "justice," and he urged the racially mixed jury to rely on their personal experiences in coming to a fair result. His underlying theme was that the riot was caused by an injustice, and that by their verdict they could balance the scales of justice.

Ladies and gentlemen, before I conclude the closing argument that I am giving on behalf [of] Mr. Damian Monroe Williams I have to remind you of a few things: number one, that justice does not exist in a vacuum. It's not a concept that you say justice and just put it in isolation.

Justice exists in the real world. The court has given you the law to evaluate and the law to apply, and you are to evaluate the facts of this case. And in evaluating the facts and coming to your determination as to what facts have been proven and what facts have not been proven, you are not relying on the law alone, you are relying on your common sense. You are relying on your personal experiences and you are relying on your sense of fairness and justice in evaluating the facts of this case.

At the end of Faal's closing argument, supporters in the courtroom stood and applauded, some even wept. As Faal left the courtroom, he was embraced. People appreciated that throughout the long trial he had consciously articulated the frustration and rage of the African American community.

The jury deliberated for more than two weeks. They acquitted Williams of attempted murder and aggravated mayhem, the two charges that carried life imprisonment. They also acquitted him of all the other felonies except one – simple mayhem. He was also convicted of four misdemeanor assaults. Williams was sentenced to eight years in prison. As of 1995, he was in Pelican Bay – California's notorious high-tech, maximum security prison where conditions are so bad that a federal judge held that it had violated the cruel and unusual punishment prohibitions of the Constituion.

Reginald Denny seemed to understand the social context of the crimes against him. He said, "Things could have been a lot worse. I mean the next step for me would have been death. But I've been given a chance, and so I'm gonna extend that courtesy towards some guys who obviously were a little bit confused."

One woman, Cynthia Henry, who lived near the now infamous intersection, spoke for many people when she said, "I'm happy with the verdicts. I know that what they did was wrong, but it was in the heat of passion. I was watching what happened [in the King trial] on TV, and it hurt me to see that. But I could understand because I was angry too."

Note

Arguing black rage may lead to favorable results for individual black defendants, but do such arguments harm the greater black community by perpetrating negative stereotypes about blacks as deviant criminals? Anthony Alfieri argues that criminal defense attorneys should forego racialized narratives like the group contagion theory used by Edi Faal, lead counsel for Damian Williams, because such narratives harm the greater black community by reinforcing negative stereotypes. Anthony V. Alfieri, *Defending Racial Violence*, 95 Colum. L. Rev. 1301 (1995). Alfieri grounds his argument in legal ethics, arguing that "criminal defense lawyers representing black males in cases of racially-motivated violence bear a race-conscious responsibility to forego narratives or stories that construct racial identity in terms of individual, group, or community deviance." *Id*. at 1306. Abbe Smith disagrees, arguing that the rules of professional responsibility required criminal defense attorneys to zealously represent their clients. Abbe Smith, *Burdening the Least of Us: "Race-Conscious" Ethics in Criminal Defense*, 77 Tex. L. Rev. 1585 (1999). Smith explains that a criminal defense attorney who puts the interests of the black community over the interests of his or her client violates this duty. *Id*. at 1601.

Paul Harris explains that the black rage "defense" is not really a new defense but is a strategy that uses "social framework" evidence to support traditional criminal defenses such as self-defense, diminished capacity, insanity, mistake, and duress. Social framework evidence is used in many other contexts as explained in the next excerpt by Neil Vidmar and Regina Schuller.

2.   The "Cultural Defense"

PEOPLE v. APHAYLATH
Court of Appeals of New York
68 N.Y.2d 945, 502 N.E.2d 998, 510 N.Y.S.2d 83 (1986)

Defendant, a Laotian refugee living in this country for approximately two years, was indicted and tried for the intentional murder of his Laotian wife of one month. At trial, defendant attempted to establish the affirmative defense of extreme emotional disturbance to mitigate the homicide on the theory that the stresses resulting from his status of a refugee caused a significant mental trauma, affecting his mind for a substantial period of time, simmering in the unknowing subconscious and then inexplicably coming to the fore. Although the immediate cause for the defendant's loss of control was his jealousy over his wife's apparent preference for an ex-boyfriend, the defense argued that under Laotian culture the conduct of the victim wife in displaying affection for another man and receiving phone calls from an unattached man brought shame on defendant and his family sufficient to trigger defendant's loss of control.

The defense was able to present some evidence of the Laotian culture through the cross-examination of two prosecution witnesses and through the testimony of defendant himself, although he was hampered by his illiteracy in both his native tongue and English. Defendant's ability to adequately establish his defense was impermissibly curtailed by the trial court's exclusion of the proffered testimony of two expert witnesses concerning the stress and disorientation encountered by Laotian refugees in attempting to assimilate into the American culture. It appears from the record before us that the sole basis on which the court excluded the expert testimony was because "neither one * * * was going to be able to testify as to anything specifically relating to this defendant." It is unclear from this ruling whether the Trial Judge determined that she had no discretion to allow the testimony because the experts had no knowledge of this particular defendant or that she declined to exercise her discretion because of the experts' lack of knowledge of the defendant or his individual background and characteristics. Under either interpretation, however, the exclusion of this expert testimony as a matter of law was erroneous because the admissibility of expert testimony that is probative of a fact in issue does not depend on whether the witness has personal knowledge of a defendant or a defendant's particular characteristics. Whether or not such testimony is sufficiently relevant to have probative value is a determination to be made by the Trial Judge in the exercise of her sound discretion.

Accordingly, because the court's ruling was not predicated on the appropriate standard and the defendant may have been deprived of an opportunity to put before the jury information relevant to his defense, a new trial must be ordered.

CULTURAL EVIDENCE AND MALE VIOLENCE: ARE FEMINIST AND MULTICULTURALIST REFORMERS ON A COLLISION COURSE IN CRIMINAL COURTS?
Holly Maguigan
70 N.Y.U. L. Rev. 36 (1995)

Introduction

The American criminal justice system faces an important question: Can the courts permit defendants to introduce evidence of cultural background without condoning violence by men against women and children? In those trials in which cultural evidence is received, is the information entitled to such unquestioning deference that its receipt signals the recognition of a "cultural defense" to male violence? Two cases illustrate the problem.

At his 1988 murder trial in Brooklyn, Chinese immigrant Dong Lu Chen did not deny that he had killed his wife, also an immigrant from China, by bludgeoning her with a claw hammer. Instead, he offered evidence that he had killed her after learning of her infidelity. The trial court admitted defense testimony from an anthropologist that Chen's rage and violent impulses were normal in his culture of origin. The cultural expert testified that in Chen's village in China others would have intervened before the event resulted in a killing, and that in his new country Chen was removed from the moderating influences that would have prevented the homicide. Largely on the basis of the cultural evidence, the defendant was convicted of manslaughter, rather than murder, and sentenced to probation.

Similarly, at his 1981 rape trial in Los Angeles, African American Jacinto Rhines did not deny that he had had intercourse with the complainant, who was also African American and who testified that the defendant raped her by using physical force and an intimidating tone of voice. Instead, the defense contended that Rhines made a reasonable mistake about the complainant's consent. The defendant proffered testimony from a psychologist that there are cultural differences among races and that Black people speak to each other very loudly. In this case, however, the trial court excluded the proffered cultural information. The defendant was convicted of rape and the exclusion of the cultural evidence was upheld on appeal.

Chen and Rhines frame this Article's inquiry: whether the work of some reformers -- toward increasing judicial responsiveness to claims of pluralism raised by defendants who are not part of the dominant culture -- conflicts with the goals of other reformers, who focus their efforts on increasing the court's vigor in prosecuting crimes of family and anti-woman violence. Some observers see multiculturalist and feminist values on a collision course in the criminal courts. The perceived risk is that two overlapping groups of outsider voices -- those of people not from the dominant culture (including women) and those of women (including women not from the dominant culture) -- cannot be heard simultaneously in this country's criminal courts. * * *

I   The Misplaced Focus on a Separate Cultural Defense as the Cause of Tension Between Feminist and Multiculturalist Reform Goals

Advocates of a new, separately defined defense argue that its recognition is necessary to overcome the injustice of holding defendants from different cultures to the monolithic standards of the dominant one. Some opponents of the creation of a separate defense argue that recognition of pluralism, at the expense of the presumption that all know the law's requirements, would lead to relativism and chaos. Others, including some feminists scholars, argue that such a defense has already been recognized, but should be rejected because it condones violence against women.

Discussion of these issues is not, in fact, joined in any other than a purely theoretical fashion. There is not and will not be a separate cultural defense because as a practical matter such a defense can be neither defined nor implemented. In short, debate over a new cultural defense is misguided because the use of cultural information is not new, a workable legal definition of culture is impossible to develop, and the information is not being offered in court to create a separate defense. The current separate-defense debate obscures the real, practical problems of accomplishing reform goals that appear to be in competition with each other.

The multiculturalist reform goal is a system that takes a more pluralistic approach to the assessment of blame and the imposition of punishment. The operation of the current criminal justice system results in higher conviction rates and longer sentences for outsider defendants than for defendants who are part of the dominant culture. Scholars have suggested that at least part of the explanation for those disparities is that the present system does not reflect the shared values of a multicultural society but instead reinforces the white, traditionally male-identified values of the dominant culture. * * *

In apparent tension with a multiculturalist reform agenda is the feminist goal of vigilant protection of a value only recently and tentatively recognized by this criminal justice system: the right of women to be free from physical violence at the hands of men. Some observers believe that courts' receipt of cultural information, when offered to excuse or mitigate responsibility for violence against women, leads to dispositions that condone that violence. Simply admitting the evidence is seen as tantamount to excusing the criminal conduct. Some authors suggest that a cultural defense, if it were used to excuse or mitigate punishment for male violence against women and children, would violate international human rights norms. In this theoretical debate, a cultural defense is seen both as a quick-fix solution to the problem of pluralistic ignorance and as anathema to feminist reform goals. * * *

Many observers, both advocates and opponents of a formal "cultural defense," share the belief that increasing numbers of people accused of crime in this country are asserting such a defense. They view the phenomenon as a by-product of a recent "influx" of immigrants, mainly Asians, to this country. Some observers incorrectly posit a situation in which defendants use "cultural defenses" primarily in family violence cases. In fact, the use of cultural information is not a new phenomenon. It is not limited to immigrants. It does not occur primarily in cases involving violence against women or children. Finally, most culturally different defendants who try to introduce background evidence do not assert a freestanding cultural defense. * * *

For many years, cultural background evidence has been proffered to challenge the sufficiency of prosecution evidence regarding a defendant's state of mind. In guilty pleas, the information has been used to convince prosecutors and courts that, because they lacked the mens rea necessary for a conviction on the top count charged, defendants should be permitted to plead to lesser offenses or should receive lighter sentences than would seem warranted in the absence of cultural information. In trials, the information -- often in the form of both lay and expert testimony -- has been offered for a similar purpose: to demonstrate that the defendant's mens rea differed from that required for conviction. The information has been proffered in connection with both excuse and justification defenses.

The necessity of introducing evidence of a defendant's background results from the reality that individuals with decisionmaking roles in the American criminal courts are often culturally different from those accused of crime. A study of courtroom dynamics in the 1960s yielded the following conclusion:

> Examination of the courtroom culture ... indicates that several factors work to the disadvantage of the culturally different in the trial process. These factors are: the value system of the legal profession, the procedures by which juries are selected, the value system of the jurors, the lack of articulation in communication between the culturally different and the professionals and nonprofessionals composing the court, and the negative stereotypes of cultural minorities held by the professionals.

In order to overcome "the lack of ... communication between the culturally different and the professionals and nonprofessionals composing the court," defendants offer information about their backgrounds. This information, sometimes called "social framework evidence," is meant to maximize the information available to those charged with adjudication:

> The purpose of "social framework evidence" ... is to provide the fact-finder, usually a jury, with information about the social and psychological context in which contested adjudicative facts occurred. It is presumed that knowledge about the context will help the fact-finder interpret the contested adjudicative facts.

Defendants use cultural evidence to give dominant-culture courts an information framework within which to assess questions of individual culpability under existing criminal law definitions. * * *

It is when "social framework" evidence, in the form of cultural information, is offered by men accused of family or anti-woman violence that there appears to be competition between feminist and multiculturalist values. The theoretical debate about recognition of a formal cultural defense misses that point. A separate cultural defense is not the cause of a conflict between multiculturalism and women's rights in criminal trials. Nor is it the answer to the current problems defendants face when trying to use cultural information. The real issue facing the courts is the adequacy of the current mechanisms to receive cultural information and to do so without endorsing family violence.

(MIS)IDENTIFYING CULTURE: ASIAN WOMEN AND THE "CULTURAL DEFENSE"
Leti Volpp
17 Harv. Women's L.J. 57 (1994)[a]

I. INTRODUCTION

The "cultural defense" is a legal strategy that defendants use in attempts to excuse criminal behavior or to mitigate culpability based on a lack of requisite mens rea. Defendants may also use "cultural defenses" to present evidence relating to state of mind when arguing self defense or mistake of fact. The theory underlying the defense is that the defendant, usually a recent immigrant to the United States, acted according to the dictates of his or her "culture," and therefore deserves leniency. There is, however, no formal "cultural defense"; individual defense attorneys and judges use their discretion to present or consider cultural factors affecting the mental state or culpability of a defendant. In my discussion of this strategy, I focus on the significance of its use for Asian women.

When examining the "cultural defense" and its effect on Asian women, I write from the subject position of an Asian American woman. I also write with the benefit of collective insight of Asian American women working with the Asian Women's Shelter in San Francisco, who created the "Cultural Defense" Study Group. The Study Group arose from concern about the use of the "cultural defense" and from the pressing need for Asian American women to articulate a position on its use.

The "cultural defense" presents several complex problems inherent in essentializing a culture and its effect on a particular person's behavior. I analyze the use of the defense in two cases in order to illustrate problems with the defense and situations in which allowing cultural information into the courtroom might be appropriate. I argue that any testimony about a defendant's cultural background must embody an accurate and personal portrayal of cultural factors

---

[a] Copyright © (1993) by the President and Fellows of Harvard College and the Harvard Women's Law Journal.

used to explain an individual's state of mind and should not be used to fit an individual's behavior into perceptions about group behavior. * * *

II. INVISIBLE WOMAN: THE PEOPLE V. DONG LU CHEN

In 1989, Brooklyn Supreme Court Justice Edward Pincus sentenced Chinese immigrant Dong Lu Chen to five years probation for using a claw hammer to smash the skull of his wife, Jian Wan Chen. The defense sought to demonstrate that the requisite state of mind was lacking by introducing evidence about Chen's cultural background. After listening to a white anthropologist "expert," Burton Pasternak, provide a "cultural defense" for Dong Lu Chen, Pincus concluded that traditional Chinese values about adultery and loss of manhood drove Chen to kill his wife.

The defense introduced most of the information about Dong Lu Chen's cultural backgrond through Pasternak's expert testimony. Defense Attorney Stewart Orden presented Pasternak with a lengthy hypothetical designed to evoke a response about the "difference" between how an "American" and a "Mainland Chinese individual" might respond to a particular set of events. This hypothetical was in fact a history of Dong Lu Chen and provided the defense's explanation for why he killed Jian Wan Chen. * * *

In September, 1986, the Chen family immigrated to the United States. While Dong Lu Chen worked as a dish washer in Maryland, Jian Wan Chen and the three children stayed in New York. During a visit when Jian Wan Chen refused to have sex with him and "became abusive," Dong Lu Chen became suspicious she was having an affair. He returned to Maryland, burdened with the stress of his wife's assumed infidelity.

In June, 1987, Dong Lu Chen moved to New York. On August 24 he rushed into his wife's bedroom and grabbed her breasts and vaginal area. They felt more developed to him and he took that as a sign she was having affairs. When he confronted her the next day, she said she was seeing another man. On September 7, when he again confronted her and said he wanted to have sex, "she said I won't let you hold me because I have other guys who will do this." His head felt dizzy, and he "pressed her down and asked her for how long had this been going on. She responded, for three months." Confused and dizzy, he picked something up and hit her a couple of times on the head. He passed out.

After presenting the above "facts" as part of his hypothetical, Orden asked Pasternak if this history was consistent with reactions "under normal conditions for people from Mainland China." Pasternak responded:

Yes. Well, of course, I can't comment on the mental state of this particular person. I am not a psychiatrist. I don't know this particular person. But the events that you have described, the reactions that you have described would not be unusual at all for Chinese in that situation, for a normal Chinese in that situation. Whether this person is normal or not I have no idea . . . . If it was a normal person, it's not the United States, they would react very violently. They might very well have confusion. It would be very likely to be a chaotic situation. I've witnessed such situations myself.

Orden also asked Pasternak to verify that a "normal Chinese person from Mainland China" would react in a more extreme and much quicker way than an "American" to the history as given in the hypothetical. Pasternak answered:

In general terms, I think that one could expect a Chinese to react in a much more volatile, violent way to those circumstances than someone from our own society. I think there's no doubt about it.

This initial testimony highlights some important issues. First, the distinction Orden and Pasternak draw between "American," "someone from our own society," and "Chinese" implies that "Chinese" and "American" are two utterly distinct categories: "American" does not encompass immigrant Chinese. This dichotomy rests on the lingering perception of Asians in America as somehow "foreign," as existing in "America" while not being "American." Importantly, the perspective that Chinese living in the United States are not "American" is the very basis for the assertion of the "cultural defense," on the grounds that someone from a distinctly "non-American" culture should not be judged by "American" standards. * * *

After dichotomizing "American" and "Chinese," Orden and Pasternak's second step in creating a "cultural defense" was to assert that a man considered "normal" in the category "Chinese" would react very differently from someone in the category "American" to the belief that his wife was having an affair. Their third step collapsed the history of a particular person with specific mental problems into the category "normal person from Mainland China." * * *

Continuing his description of Chinese familial life and values, Pasternak asserted that "casual sex, adultery, which is an even more extreme violation, and divorce" are perceived as deviations from these social mores. "In the Chinese context," adultery by a woman was considered a kind of "stain" upon the man, indicating that he had lost "the most minimal standard of control" over her. Pasternak contrasted the condemnation of adultery in China with the United

States, "where we take this thing normally in the course of an event." He claimed that the Chinese woman was likely to be "thrown out" and that both parties would have difficulty remarrying. * * *

Pasternak's bizarre portrayal of divorce and adultery in China in fact had little basis in reality. When Assistant District Attorney Arthur Rigby pressed Pasternak for his sources during cross-examination, Pasternak mentioned fieldwork he did between the 1960s and 1988 (he could not remember the title of his own article), incidents he saw, such as a man chasing a woman with a cleaver, and stories he heard. He admitted he could not recall a single instance in which a man in China killed his wife or having ever heard about such an event, yet he suggested that this was accepted in China. Pasternak's description of "Chinese society" thus was neither substantiated by fact nor supported by his own testimony. The description was in fact his own American fantasy.

During his cross-examination of Pasternak, Rigby attempted to undermine Chen's "cultural defense" by deconstructing Pasternak's identification of "American," his description of Chinese as insulated from Western influence and his depiction of Chinese Americans as completely non-assimilated. Rigby began his questioning by asking, "What would you consider your average American?" Pasternak responded, "I think you are looking at your average American."

With this statement Pasternak situated his own subjective position as the definition of the "average American." In other words, Pasternak defined the "average American" to be a white, professional male. By situating himself as the "average American," Pasternak exposed his subjective identification as the "average American" against whom the "foreigner," Dong Lu Chen, was to be compared.

* * * Justice Pincus was swayed by the "persuasiveness" of Pasternak's testimony about the "cultural" roots of Dong Lu Chen's actions. He held:

> Were this crime committed by the defendant as someone who was born and raised in America, or born elsewhere but primarily raised in America, even in the Chinese American community, the Court [*sic*] would have been constrained to find the defendant guilty of manslaughter in the first degree. But, this Court [*sic*] cannot ignore . . . the very cogent forceful testimony of Doctor Pasternak, who is, perhaps, the greatest expert in America on China and interfamilial relationships.

Pincus specifically found significant Pasternak's testimony that Chen lacked a Chinese community to act as a "safety valve" to keep Chen from killing his wife. Yet the alleged motivation for Chen's actions was his "shame" and humiliation before this very same community. The inconsistency in this reasoning is self-evident. * * *

In his decision to grant probation rather than impose a jail sentence, Pincus also took other unrelated "cultural" considerations into account. Pincus believed that the possible effect of Chen's incarceration on his daughters' marriage prospects should be a factor in determining Chen's sentence. Pincus told a reporter, "Now there's a stigma of shame on the whole family. They have young, unmarried daughters. To make them marriageable prospects, they must make sure he succeeds so they succeed." In the sentencing colloquy Pincus indicated that he also learned that Dong Lu Chen was a "victim":

> Based on the cultural background of this individual he has also succeeded in partially destroying his family and his family's reputation . . . . There are victims in this case: The deceased is a victim, her suffering is over. The defendant is a victim, a victim that fell through the cracks because society didn't know where or how to respond in time.

Thus Pincus was able to justify his probationary sentencing: Dong Lu Chen did not serve time for killing his wife because in balancing this action and the surrounding circumstances he was just as much a "victim" as she was.

But where was Jian Wan Chen in this story? The defense strategy rendered her invisible. She was most notably present in the testimony as a dead body and as a reputed "adulteress," bringing a "stain" upon her husband. Jian Wan Chen did not exist as a multi-faceted person but was instead flattened into the description "adulteress." Any discussion of her at trial was premised upon her characterization as a woman who provoked her husband into jealousy. How should this flattening be interpreted? This invisibility and erasure of the woman, Jian Wan Chen?

Jian Wan Chen's invisibility involved more than the disappearance of a victim in a trial focused on the guilt or innocence of a defendant. The defense presented a narrative that relied on her invisibility as an Asian woman for its logical coherence. This invisibility was manifest through the absence of Jian Wan Chen as a subject, a void that was filled only by stereotypes of the sexual relationships of "Chinese women" and an image of her silent physicality. She appeared as an object, whose silence devalued her humanity to the extent that the taking of her life did not merit a prison sentence.

Jian Wan Chen's invisibility is a legacy of an intersection of race and gender that erases the existence of women of color from the popular consciousness. Because white male citizens personify what is considered "normal" in the United States, a status as "other" that is more than one deviation away from the "norm" rarely exists in popular consciousness. The exclusion of Jian Wan Chen exemplifies the difficulty that women of color have when attempting to express themselves as holistic subjects, as Asian women whose identity lies at the intersection of multiple forms of subordination.

Applying an intersectional analysis, it is clear that what Pasternak presented as "Chinese culture" privileged race over any consideration of gender oppression. Pasternak's perspective was "male," obviating the possibility that a woman, and specifically a Chinese immigrant woman, might describe divorce, adultery and male violence within "Chinese culture" very differently. The perspective, was, of course, also "white." The "whiteness" of Pasternak's perspective allowed him to situate Dong Lu Chen in a category labelled "Chinese" diametrically opposite to Pasternak's own "average," white, male citizen position. Yet this placement ignored that Jian Wan Chen was, in fact, the person categorically opposite to Pasternak: she was Chinese, immigrant and female. Thus, the "cultural defense" served in this case to legitimize male violence against women by glossing over the gendered aspects of Pasternak's testimony about "culture."

The Chen trial suffered from a complete absence of any female perspective: Dong Lu Chen, Pasternak, Orden, Rigby and Pincus were all male. Jian Wan Chen was dead, symbolizing how ideologies that subordinate groups of people literally transpire over the body of an "other." Thus, Jian Wan Chen's invisibility is not only the product of the racist notion that "Asian life is cheap," it also is a remnant of the indifference with which many in the United States treat the epidemic of violence against women. Furthermore, the complete disregard for her life also reflected the way racism and sexism intersect to render insignificant violence against women of color, and here specifically, Asian immigrant women.

The impact of the trial and probationary sentencing resonated beyond the courtroom, sending a message to the wider community. Jian Wan Chen's life was not valued; her life was worth less than other lives; her murderer did not deserve punishment in jail. Other Chinese immigrant women living with abuse at the hand of their partners and husbands identified with Jian Wan Chen and clearly understood that violence against them by their partners and husbands had the implicit approval of the state.

The Chen decision sent a message to battered immigrant Asian women that they had no recourse against domestic violence. One battered Chinese woman told a worker at the New York Asian Women's Center, "Even thinking about that case makes me afraid. My husband told me: 'If this is the kind of sentence you get for killing your wife, I could do anything to you. I have the money for a good attorney.'" In other words, her husband could afford to hire someone to testify as an expert to bolster a "cultural defense" that legitimized his violence. * * *

INDIVIDUALIZING JUSTICE THROUGH MULTICULTURALISM: THE LIBERALS' DILEMMA[a]

Doriane Lambelet Coleman
96 Colum. L. Rev. 1093 (1996)

Introduction

In California, a Japanese-American mother drowns her two young children in the ocean at Santa Monica and then attempts to kill herself; rescuers save her before she drowns. The children's recovered bodies bear deep bruises where they struggled as their mother held them under the water. The mother later explains that in Japan, where she is from, her actions would be understood as the time-honored, customary practice of parent-child suicide. She spends only one year in jail - the year she is on trial.

In New York, a Chinese-American woman is bludgeoned to death by her husband. Charged with murder, her husband explains that his conduct comports with a Chinese custom that allows husbands to dispel their shame in this way when their wives have been unfaithful. He is acquitted of murder charges.

Back in California, a young Laotian-American woman is abducted from her place of work at Fresno State University and forced to have sexual intercourse against her will. Her Hmong immigrant assailant explains that, among his tribe, such behavior not only is accepted, but expected -- it is the customary way to choose a bride. He is sentenced to 120 days in jail, and his victim receives $ 900 in reparations.

A Somali immigrant living in Georgia allegedly cuts off her two-year old niece's clitoris, partially botching the job. The child was cut in accordance with the time-honored tradition of female circumcision; this custom attempts to ensure that girls and women remain chaste for their husbands. The State charges the woman with child abuse, but is unable to convict her.

---

[a] This article originally appeared at 96 Colum. L. Rev. 1093 (1996). Reprinted by permission.

In these cases, the defense presented, and the prosecutor or court accepted, cultural evidence as an excuse for the otherwise criminal conduct of immigrant defendants. These official decisions appear to reflect the notion that the moral culpability of an immigrant defendant should be judged according to his or her own cultural standards, rather than those of the relevant jurisdiction. Although no state has formally recognized the use of exonerating cultural evidence, some commentators and judges have labelled this strategy the "cultural defense."

The cultural defense (and the issues it raises about the rights of immigrants to retain aspects of their cultures when they come to the United States) is an important part of the larger debate about multiculturalism which currently is prominent in academic, social, and political circles. In particular, this larger debate concerns whether there is and should be a unifying American culture that guides our institutions, including the justice system, or whether the United States is and should be a culturally pluralistic nation in all respects, including in the law.

The introductory illustrations exemplify this debate in the legal arena with an unusual clarity, because they pit foreign customs and cultural practices directly against essential elements of contemporary American legal culture, including the antidiscrimination principle that is central to equal protection doctrine and related principles of universal rights that are at the foundation of feminist legal doctrine.

Allowing sensitivity to a defendant's culture to inform the application of laws to that individual is good multiculturalism. It also is good progressive criminal defense philosophy, which has as a central tenet the idea that the defendant should get as much individualized (subjective) justice as possible. The illustrations that introduce this Article may be interpreted as reflecting this sort of sensitivity on the part of some prosecutors and judges.

For legal scholars and practitioners who believe in a progressive civil and human rights agenda, these illustrations also raise an important question: What happens to the victims - almost always minority women and children - when multiculturalism and individualized justice are advanced by dispositive cultural evidence? The answer, both in theory and in practice, is stark: They are denied the protection of the criminal laws because their assailants generally go free, either immediately or within a relatively brief period of time. More importantly, victims and potential victims in such circumstances have no hope of relief in the future, either individually or as a group, because when cultural evidence is permitted to excuse otherwise criminal conduct, the system effectively is choosing to adopt a different, discriminatory standard of criminality for immigrant defendants, and hence, a different and discriminatory level of protection for victims who are members of the culture in question. This different standard may defeat the deterrent effect of the law, and it may become precedent, both for future cases with similar facts, and for the broader position that race- or national origin-based applications of the criminal law are appropriate. Thus, the use of cultural defenses is anathema to another fundamental goal of the progressive agenda, namely the expansion of legal protections for some of the least powerful members of American society: women and children.

Margaret Fung, Executive Director of the Asian-American Defense and Education Fund, provided what is perhaps the best evidence of the tension that is created for progressives by these cases. When Ms. Fung first publicly addressed the decision in *People v. Chen*, the New York spousal killing case described above, she is reported to have expressed her concern that the result was bad for Asian women and for the image of Asian-Americans: "You don't want to import [immigrant] cultural values into our judicial system ... We don't want women victimized by backward customs ... We don't want so-called cultural experts perpetuating certain stereotypes that may not be accurate, ... and putting that out to the American public." Later, however, Ms. Fung was reported to have reformulated her position on the use of cultural evidence by criminal defendants: To bar the cultural defense "would promote the idea that when people come to America, they have to give up their way of doing things. That is an idea we cannot support."

In addition to highlighting the dilemma posed by these cases, Margaret Fung's reactions highlight the two-fold discriminatory effect of the cultural defense. First, to the extent that cultural evidence is used to determine the outcome of criminal cases and to excuse some perpetrators of crimes, it results in disparate treatment of immigrants and other members of American society. Second, the particular cultural norms at issue in these cases are also inherently discriminatory in that they incorporate values about the lesser status of women and children; these values are contrary to those the contemporary international progressive agenda embraces. When the American legal system chooses to recognize such traditions in the context of pursuing individualized justice for the defendant, it condones the chauvinism that is at the core of these traditions.

The question of how to resolve the competing interests that Margaret Fung's turnaround so clearly sets out -- a question that I call the "Liberals' Dilemma" -- is the focus of this Article. Unlike existing scholarship in the area, most of which does not appear to recognize this dilemma, it is my premise that the answer for legal (rather than moral) purposes should not be made in an ad hoc fashion, based on political and professional affiliations. Rather, I believe the law must reflect a broader, more considered resolution of this question, and that this resolution can be accomplished only by engaging in a balancing of the two substantial and conflicting interests. Thus, the defendant's interest in using cultural evidence that incorporates discriminatory norms and behaviors must be weighed against the victims' and potential victims' interests in obtaining protection and relief through a non-discriminatory application of the criminal law. Contemporary jurisprudence favors just this sort of balancing, which considers the interests of the two parties in a given case, as well as those of society generally, in determining the outcome. Using this approach, I conclude that victims' interests in this area are more compelling than those of defendants. In the process, I acknowledge that my position is contrary to that pure vein of multiculturalism that decries ethnocentrism in any form; and I agree that it also is contrary to those aspects of the liberal agenda that traditionally have sought to embrace (at least in theory) simultaneously both cultural pluralism and individual rights, including the rights of defendants and of the women and children who are often their victims. In this context, I believe that there are several reasons for choosing rights over culture.

First, the criminal justice system already affords defendants substantial opportunities to raise established, nondiscriminatory arguments in support of their innocence or of a reduced sentence.

Second, permitting the use of culture-conscious, discriminatory evidence as part of the defendant's case-in-chief distorts the substantive criminal law and affords little or no protection to victims, whose assailants are left, as a result of this distortion, relatively free from broader societal strictures. There presently is no acceptable alternative to cure this deficiency.

Third, the use of cultural evidence risks a dangerous balkanization of the criminal law, where non-immigrant Americans are subject to one set of laws and immigrant Americans to another. This is a prospect that is inconsistent not only with one of the law's most fundamental objectives, the protection of society and all of its members from harm, but also with the important human and civil rights doctrines embodied in the Equal Protection Clause. Thus, society as a whole is best served by a balance that avoids the use of discriminatory cultural evidence.

Fourth, despite the benevolent interpretation I earlier afforded the modern acceptance of immigrant cultural evidence by some prosecutors and judges, there also is the substantial concern that culture consciousness -- at least of the sort that leads to discriminatory results -- may not be a good thing for a judicial system that is already plagued by a racist and sexist history. As Justice Brennan commented in his dissenting opinion in *McCleskey v. Kemp*, "formal dual criminal laws may no longer be in effect, and intentional discrimination may no longer be prominent. Nonetheless ... subtle, less consciously held racial attitudes' continue to be of concern." It is at best ironic that progressive forces would purposefully give back to the system a new and lawful opportunity to treat immigrant women, children, and other minority victims of crimes as less valuable. At worst, this trend may foreshadow a return to overtly racist decisionmaking by some prosecutors and judges. * * *

3.   Brainwashing

ASCRIPTION OF CRIMINAL STATES OF MIND: TOWARD A DEFENSE THEORY FOR THE COERCIVELY PERSUADED ("BRAINWASHED") DEFENDANT
Richard Delgado
63 Minn. L. Rev. 1 (1978)

I. INTRODUCTION

Coercive persuasion, or thought reform, has been extensively described by psychologists and psychiatrists in field studies of prisoners of war, victims of Chinese "revolutionary universities," captives of outlaw or extremist groups, and members of religious cults. In more controlled settings, behavioral scientists have explored the contributions that isolation, physiological depletion, assertions of authority, guilt manipulation, peer pressure, and cognitive dissonance" can have in bringing about behavioral compliance and attitudinal change. * * *

Many authorities, including the drafters of a Department of Defense report prepared in response to evidence of widespread collaboration by American prisoners of war (POW) during the Korean conflict, have concluded that a determined captor, possessing total control over the life and environment of a captive, can produce behavioral and attitudinal change in even the most strongly resistant individual.

Apart from Korean POW cases, allegations of the use of thought reform techniques have arisen in two areas of recent controversy. The first concerns a number of new-age religious cults that, according to their critics, utilize high-pressure thought reform methods to induce college-age youths to join them as devotees, fund raisers, and street-corner proselytizers. The second involves individuals such as Patricia Hearst who are tried for criminal acts asserted to have been induced by coercive persuasion.

Both of these situations involve the use of similar methods and the goal of controlling the minds of others for given purposes. Because the legal contexts in which these cases arise are distinct, however, each area of controversy involves unique issues. For example, the primary question in connection with the use of such methods by religious cults is the extent to which their peculiar conversion practices merit the protection of the [F]irst [A]mendment. In prosecutions of criminal defendants, by contrast, the fundamental issue is the extent to which coercive treatment interferes with the victim's capacity to formulate voluntarily the criminal intent required to uphold a criminal charge. These two areas of controversy can overlap: a religious convert might be induced by his leaders to commit acts - such as soliciting donations for nonexisting social programs - that violate the criminal law. At trial he might attempt to interpose his forcible conversion as a defense.

* * * [T]he present Article addresses the question of how the legal system should treat the coercively persuaded criminal defendant. Although not dictated by the number of victims of wartime or religious coercive persuasion, the present inquiry is of interest for several reasons. The frequency with which such cases arise is likely to accelerate as social conditions conducive to terrorism and other forms of psychologically totalistic behavior continue, and as the potential utility of thought reform methods becomes more widely known among extremist groups. Moreover, commentators who have considered the problem of the coercively persuaded defendant have concluded, largely on an analysis of the Patricia Hearst case, that no legal defense is available to such an individual. If they are correct, their conclusion is a troubling one, for it means denying a defense to a class of defendants who are, by ordinary moral intuitions, often more victims than perpetrators.

Consider a hypothetical individual captured by an outlaw gang and subjected to lengthy thought reform techniques, beginning with threats and terror, and continuing with isolation, starvation, sleep deprivation, and guilt manipulation carried out by seemingly all-powerful captors. At various intervals in the process, that individual's captors demand that he perform criminal acts for their benefit. Under traditional criminal defense theories, exculpation would be available for those crimes the victim commits during the initial stages of captivity, when classic duress and coercion exist, but not during the latter stages, when such overt coercion no longer is necessary for the captors to maintain control. Such a result is surely wrong. The breakdown of the victim's identity and will in the latter stages of the coercive persuasion process destroys the very mechanisms by which he might have offered resistance. Thus, acquiescence is rendered more certain than in the early stages when simple duress is applied. A person under direct threats of death will rarely cling to even deeply held beliefs. Rarer still is the individual who can resist protracted, unremitting, coercive thought reform techniques.

Consideration of theories traditionally believed to justify punishment also suggests that coercive persuasion should be taken into account in assessing a defendant's criminal guilt. Prison law decisions hold that punishment, to be constitutional, must advance one or more of the accepted rationales of the criminal justice system - societal safety, rehabilitation, deterrence, or retribution. Punitive treatment of coercively persuaded defendants is difficult to reconcile with this requirement. Past experience demonstrates that most such victims, once removed from the coercive environment, soon lose their inculcated responses and return to their former modes of thinking and acting. This return often is accompanied by expressions of anger, in which the former captive accuses his captors of the "rape" of his mind and personality. Punishment of such individuals does little to promote the rationales of the criminal justice system.

If punishment of the coercively persuaded defendant conflicts with both basic intuitions and the justifications advanced for invocation of criminal punishment, yet cannot be avoided under any existing defense theory, it becomes necessary to fashion a new theory of defense. Occam's razor dictates that any such new defense should constitute, insofar as is possible, a logical extension of existing concepts of act, intent, and blame. The actus reus of defendants who have undergone coercive persuasion is undisputed, they apparently are neither insane, coerced, nor acting under diminished capacity, and yet they seem less than fully responsible for their acts. This is so because the coercively persuaded defendant's choice to act criminally was not freely made and, indeed, appears to be not his choice at all. Traditional mens rea analysis has inquired only whether a defendant who committed an allegedly criminal act possessed the requisite state of criminal mind at the time of the act. In the case of the coercively persuaded defendant, it is appropriate to ask also whether the intent the actor possessed can properly be said to be his own.

The victim of thought reform typically commits criminal acts fully aware of their wrongfulness. He acts consciously, even enthusiastically, and without overt coercion. Yet, in an important sense, the guilty mind with which he acts is not his own. Rather, his mental state is more appropriately ascribed to the captors who instilled it in him for their own purposes. Explication of the concept of transferred or superimposed mens rea - criminal intent that is not the actor's own - is thus the principal task of this Article. Initially, an example is presented in which characterization of a person's actions as stemming from an intent other than his own seems intuitively plausible. Then, various existing legal doctrines are reviewed in order to ascertain the extent to which analogous concepts of transferred or superimposed mental states have been applied to relieve the actor of liability in other contexts. Concluding that the notion of implanted mens rea offers, both intuitively and doctrinally, a tenable basis for a new criminal defense, a third section offers criteria for determining when such a transfer has occurred. A final section considers possible objections to the new defense, including the criticisms that the defense would have no clearly defined boundaries and that it would destroy the concept of free will that underlies the criminal justice system. * * *

III. ANALOGOUS CONCEPTS INVOLVING INDUCED MENTAL STATES

In a number of contexts, courts have expressed a willingness to relieve individuals from responsibility for criminal acts based on transferred intent or design.

One illustration of the concept of transferred mens rea is found in cases of posthypnotic suggestion. California recognizes a defense of hypnosis, and the Model Penal Code incorporates a hypnosis defense under its treatment of actus reus, justifying it by the marked dependency and helplessness of the subject. It would seem that the hypnosis defense might more appropriately be analyzed according to the transferred mens rea concept. Regardless of its theoretical moorings, however, the doctrine assigns criminal responsibility to the hypnotist who procures the illegal behavior, not to the subject who physically carries it out. This approach recognizes that the hypnotized subject is more a victim of the crime than its perpetrator, and that a search beyond the primary actor will reveal another to whom the criminal action may more appropriately be ascribed.

The Model Penal Code also refuses to inculpate when an otherwise criminal act results from reflex, convulsion, unconsciousness, or an active state of automatism, because of the involuntary nature of the act committed. The victim of brainwashing, by contrast, acts voluntarily and is usually aware of the wrongfulness of his acts. Thus, such cases do not fit squarely into the Code's treatment of hypnosis transferred actus reus. Yet the recognition that there can be transferred actus reus is an important step toward recognizing a new defense for the coercively persuaded defendant. If a showing that the actus reus originates outside the defendant results in exoneration, the same consequence should follow when it is the element of mens rea that is externally induced.

Presumably, this extension has not previously occurred because until recently it was considered impossible to interfere with the mental states of others to the same extent as with their physical acts. The development of potent techniques of organic and psychological behavior control, however, suggests that such an extension is now appropriate. Like the addition of newly discovered elements to the periodic table, recognition of a defense based on transferred mens rea simply fills in an existing asymmetry in the theory of criminal excuses.

Another existing legal doctrine that employs the concept of transferred mens rea is entrapment. The prevailing test for entrapment examines the extent to which criminal intent originates not with the defendant but with the police authorities. In the leading case of *Sorrells v. United States*, a government agent, whose sole purpose was to entrap the defendant, posed as a tourist and convinced the defendant to sell him liquor for a friend. The Court found that the defendant had no previous disposition to commit the crime and was lured into doing so only by the agent's persistent solicitation and appeals to wartime reminiscences. Observing that the government may provide the opportunity or the facilities for the commission of an act so as "to reveal the [preexisting] criminal design," the Court held that a different case was presented when "the criminal design originates with . . . the Government [agents], and they implant in the mind of an innocent person the disposition to commit the alleged offense. In such a case, the criminal act is not properly ascribable to the defendant, but is "the creature of" the agent who procured it. * * *

PROFESSOR DELGADO'S "BRAINWASHING" DEFENSE: COURTING A DETERMINIST LEGAL SYSTEM

Joshua Dressler
63 Minn. L. Rev. 335 (1979)

I. INTRODUCTION

In 1951, journalist Edward Hunter wrote a book describing "brainwashing," a process of abrupt attitudinal change that was used in the People's Republic of China. At that time, the United States was involved in a "hot" war with the Communist government of North Korea and a "cold" war with the ideology of Marxism. This situation caused both the unfamiliar term and the concept underlying it hat people can have their life-long values involuntarily and suddenly changed to become the subjects of widespread general interest and copious scientific literature. Except for some interest engendered by military court-martial proceedings against American prisoners of war, however, brainwashing was largely ignored in legal circles until recently, when kidnapping victim Patricia Hearst was prosecuted for joining her captors in a bank robbery.

The absence of debate within the legal community is unfortunate, because the subject of coercive persuasion raises more than esoteric scientific questions. Its consideration leads to fundamental philosophical quandaries concerning the continued viability of the concept of free will, one of the basic premises of our substantive criminal justice system.

Nor can it any longer be said that the issue of coercive persuasion, and the related debate regarding free will, are of mere academic interest. The likelihood that a defense based on coercive persuasion will be raised in the future is great. Prosecution following "terrorist" kidnaping is but one situation raising the issue. Another is in connection with certain religious cults that allegedly not only coercively indoctrinate new members to their religious views but also indoctrinate them to commit fraudulent acts. In response to the conversion techniques adopted by the cults, parents and professional deprogrammers have imprisoned cultists in order to reverse this influence. * * *

It is critical, then, for both practical and jurisprudential reasons, that legal scholarship in this field flourish. Three recent articles addressing the question of coercive persuasion as a criminal defense have initiated this process, but more is needed. Unfortunately, two of the articles rejected in relatively perfunctory fashion the idea that the law should permit this new defense. An article written by Professor Richard Delgado, however, presents for the first time in legal literature a lucid rationalization for such a new claim.

Because Professor Delgado is the first to call for such a defense, and because he states a convincing case for it, it is to his analysis that this Article directly responds. It is the thesis of this author that Delgado erroneously applies certain criminal law doctrines. * * *

II. DELGADO'S THESIS

Professor Delgado sets for himself the goal of justifying a new criminal defense theory for the coercively persuaded defendant which is a "logical extension of existing concepts of act, intent, and blame" and which does not "fatally [erode] the [criminal law's] assumption of freedom of the will."

Delgado premises his theory on a new criminal law doctrine he variously describes as "transferred," "superimposed," or "implanted" mens rea. He readily concedes that the typical coercively persuaded defendant is neither insane, coerced, nor the victim of diminished capacity when the criminal acts are performed. In addition, he grants that such a person acts consciously, even enthusiastically, fully aware of the wrongfulness of his actions. By all traditional indices, the requisite mens rea is therefore present. Delgado nevertheless suggests that because such intent is coercively indoctrinated into the actor, "the guilty mind with which he acts is not his own," and should instead be ascribed solely to the captor. In light of the criminal law's "insistence that any requisite mental state be found to be that of the defendant himself," Delgado asserts, the defendant should be exculpated and the captor prosecuted. * * *

III. CRITICISM OF DELGADO'S THESIS

*   *   *

Implicit in the concept of mens rea is the idea of choice, for an actor cannot be said to have "intended" to commit an act if he had no choice but to commit it. The existence of general human free will, however, is conclusively presumed. Although the philosophical and scientific arguments for determinism may seem persuasive to some, the criminal justice system rejects, as a matter of policy, any doctrine that conflicts with a free will theory. * * *

As noted earlier, Delgado's doctrinal argument is predicated on the unique theory of a superimposed mens rea. Because the mental state of the coercively persuaded victim is inculcated by another person, Delgado would create a new legal fiction by treating the actor's mens rea as legally noncognizable. Legal blame would attach solely to the indoctrinator.

Such a proposal is doctrinally untenable. All ideas and intents originate outside the individual, in the sense that they are shaped by experiences and environments. As we have seen, however, the law nevertheless considers intent to be personal - to be a product of each individual's free will. This is true whether the intent to commit the crime is initiated by an inanimate object ("I saw the painting and it made me think of killing"), an innocent third party ("X told me the victim had a lot of money so I killed the victim"), or a guilty third party. If this were not the case, one could plausibly argue that all mental states for example, criminal intentions, or political or religious views are inauthentic, thus unacceptably blurring concepts of moral and legal responsibility.

Coercive persuasion obviously falls within the category of intentions originating with a guilty third person. To say that no legally cognizable mens rea is present in the perpetrator in such cases conflicts with current, and sensible, law. Consider this hypothetical situation: A solicits B to steal X's car. B agrees and steals the car. The idea of theft originated wholly in A's mind. It was "implanted" into B's mind verbally, with the help, possibly, of an offer of money. A, of course, is guilty of theft, as a solicitor, but B is also guilty because, regardless of where the intent originated, it became his when he accepted it as his. His reason for stealing the car, whether for profit, fun, or jealousy, or because he is suggestible, does not, in itself, negate the existence of mens rea. The criminal law has no aversion to convicting more than one person for a single crime, although one may be considered the originator of the design and another the follower. * * *

It can be argued, however, that this hypothetical situation does a disservice to Delgado, because he is concerned only with cases in which intention is transplanted forcefully. But the particular means through which intent is transferred is irrelevant; so long as the actor remains free to choose his course of action, he is responsible for his blameworthy acts. Of course, if it can be said that B has little choice but to steal the car - where, for example, A holds a gun to B's head and orders the theft - B would be exulpated on grounds of duress. Duress as a defense, however, is not predicated on the theory of the negation or nonrecognition of a personal mens rea, but rather on the basis that despite mens rea, the defendant is morally blameless because he committed a relatively minor crime under circumstances involving severely limited and unacceptable choices.

The error in Delgado's mens rea analysis becomes clearer if one carefully analyzes a hypothetical situation posited in his article. Delgado notes the existence of "stimoceivers," devices that may be used to apply electrical currents to a person's brain, causing him to feel particular emotions. Delgado hypothesizes a case in which an evil third person triggers such a device by remote control, causing the actor to feel "inexplicably and overwhelmingly angry." The actor "might discharge the aggressive impulse by attacking a hapless bystander." Delgado then states that in a prosecution of the actor for assault, acquittal is proper because "[i]f the defendant possessed mens rea at all, it seems more natural to attribute it, not to the [defendant], but to the [impulse] sender. . ."

The difficulty with Delgado's mens rea analysis is that the actor does possess the requisite mental state: intent to batter the hapless victim. Although his anger is inauthentic, like fear in duress, in that it originates from external forces, the decision on how to release the anger is personal, as is the decision on how to alleviate fear. The defendant could have vented his anger in many noncriminal ways: by throwing an object at the wall of his house, screaming, or running around the block. Instead, he exercised an independent and personal choice when he elected to hit the hapless bystander. The mens rea necessary to prove the prima facie case for battery is thus present, even in Delgado's bizarre example.

Mens rea is not absent in cases of coercive persuasion. Although theories of the etiology of coercive persuasion abound, all are premised on the view that the captive comes to share the captor's view, and later commits supportive crimes, because he wants - that is, intends - to commit the acts. The intent itself may derive from any one of various psychological sources but the mens rea is clearly present. One cannot do as Delgado suggests: pretend it is not there. If the law creates such a fiction in some cases by ignoring the intent of the actor because of dismay over the way he came to have it, there is no logical reason to limit such inquiry. Delgado's mens rea thesis, therefore, violates his own goal of logically but minimally extending the law. His concept would constitute an abrupt, unprecedented, and potentially unlimitable change in legal doctrine. * * *

4.   Rotten Social Background

"ROTTEN SOCIAL BACKGROUND": SHOULD THE CRIMINAL LAW RECOGNIZE A DEFENSE OF SEVERE ENVIRONMENTAL DEPRIVATION?
Richard Delgado
3 Law & Inequality J. 9 (1985)

Introduction

No jurisdiction in the United States or elsewhere recognizes a criminal defense based on socioeconomic deprivation *simpliciter*. Is this refusal principled and justified, or only a timid response to the prospect of changing to accommodate that which appears alien? That environment plays a significant role in shaping an individual's values and behavior is beyond dispute. For over two decades preferential treatment and affirmative action have been incorporated within our liberal-democratic heritage as means of compensating for unequal opportunity resulting from discrimination, inadequate education and material deprivation.

There is also a strong relationship between environmental adversity and criminal behavior. Of course, not all poor persons violate the law and not all those from privileged backgrounds are law-abiding; it remains, however, that of more than one million offenders entangled in the correctional system, the vast majority are members of the poorest class. Unless we are prepared to argue that offenders are poor because they are criminal, we should be open to the possibility that many turn to crime because of their poverty – that poverty is, for many, a determinant of criminal behavior.

Assuming that socioeconomic deprivation causes criminal behavior rather than the converse, should that mitigate criminal responsibility? * * *

Judge Bazelon first raised the possibility that extreme poverty might give rise to an RSB defense in *United States v. Alexander*, a 1973 opinion by the D.C. Circuit Court of Appeals. In *Alexander*, one of the defendants shot and killed a marine in a tavern after the marine called him a "black bastard." The defense attempted to show that the youth's action stemmed from an irresistible impulse to shoot, which they, in turn, traced to an emotionally and economically deprived childhood in Watts, California. The defendant reported that when he was young, his father deserted the family and the boy grew up with little money or attention. He was subjected to racist treatment and learned to fear and hate white persons.

A psychiatrist testified that the defendant suffered from impaired behavior controls rooted in his "rotten social background." The psychiatrist refused to label the defendant insane, however. The trial judge instructed the jury to disregard the testimony about the defendant's deprived background and to consider only whether or not his mental condition met the legal standard of insanity. The jury found him sane and the defendant was sentenced to twenty years to life.

The court of appeals affirmed. In a lengthy, troubled opinion that concurred in part and dissented in part, Judge Bazelon laid out his early thoughts on the RSB defense. For Bazelon, the trial judge erred in instructing the jury to disregard the testimony about defendant's social and economic background. That testimony might well have persuaded the jury that the defendant's behavioral controls were so impaired as to require acquittal, even though that impairment might not render him clinically insane. Apart from this, exposure to the testimony would benefit society. As a result of learning about the wretched conditions in which some of its members live, society would presumably decide to do something about them.

Nevertheless, Bazelon was not prepared to abandon all the trappings of the "disease" model. Among other things, that model provides a rationale for detaining dangerous persons following acquittal. Bazelon reviewed other possible dispositions for the RSB defendant – outright release, preventive detention, and psychological reprogramming – finding each unacceptable. According to Bazelon, the ultimate solution to the problem of violent crime in our society is some form of income redistribution coupled with other social reform measures. The current narrow insanity test conceals the need for such reform and thus should be broadened, although disposition of offenders not "sick" in any classic sense remained a problem for Bazelon.

Judge Bazelon further developed his views on an RSB defense in his Hoover lecture and in a reply article. In his Hoover address, Bazelon declared that "law's aims must be achieved by a moral process cognizant of the realities of social injustice." Persons must obey the law not out of fear, but because they personally believe its commands to be just. Punishment is justified only when inflicted upon persons whose actions are morally condemnable. This, in turn, requires that society's conduct in relation to the defendant entitle it to sit in condemnation, and that the defendant's mental, emotional, and behavioral controls were intact at the time of the crime. Citing the example of the defendant in *United States v. Alexander*, Bazelon urged that when these two conditions are not met, society is not entitled to inflict punishment.

In a response to Judge Bazelon and a short rejoinder, Professor Stephen Morse argued against Judge Bazelon's position. For Morse, all environments affect choice, making some choices easy and others hard. Rarely, however, will environmental adversity completely eliminate a person's power of choice. Poor persons are free to choose or not choose to commit crimes, and the criminal law may justifiably punish them when they give in to temptation and break the law. Although he conceded a statistical correlation between poverty and crime, Morse denied that poverty causes crime. He pointed out that some poor persons are law-abiding, while some wealthy persons break the law, and that economic improvements often result in more, not less, crime. Moreover, Bazelon's social-welfare suggestions would be impractical because there is not enough money to eradicate all poverty; giving money to the poor would entail higher taxation, thus endangering such goals as free accumulation and disposition of wealth; and though eradicating poverty may eliminate some crime, it is a wasteful way to do it. Consequently, Bazelon's broadened inquiry into culpability could exonerate dangerous criminals without generating socially useful knowledge or experience. Indeed, Bazelon's defense skirts paternalism. When an individual has freely broken the law, respect for that individual's personhood *demands* punishment; any other treatment demeans the defendant, and treats him or her as something less than an autonomous individual.

The Bazelon-Morse debate thus raises, but does not answer, a number of key questions concerning a "rotten social background" defense. Does economic and cultural disadvantage impair controls or otherwise cause crime, and if so, how? If severe impairment can be shown in a particular case, what effect should this have on criminal responsibility? What should be done with the successful RSB defendant? The remainder of this article explores these and related questions. * * *

IV.   A New Defense

An environment of extreme poverty and deprivation creates in individuals a propensity to commit crimes. In some cases, a defendant's impoverished background so greatly determines his or her criminal behavior that we feel it unfair to punish the individual. This sense of unfairness arises from the morality of the criminal law itself, in that "our collective conscience does not allow punishment where it cannot impose blame." And blame is inappropriate when a defendant's criminal behavior is caused by extrinsic factors beyond his or her control.

Still, the criminal law does not recognize a rotten social background, as such, as relevant to the issue of guilt. Commentators have noted this seeming inconsistency. For example, Professor Packer observes:

If a person engages in criminal conduct while in an epileptic fit, we say that he was incapable of performing a voluntary act and we acquit. . . . At the other extreme, we recognize that cultural deprivation of a kind associated with urban poverty may in a very real sense restrict the individual's capacity to choose and make him more susceptible to engaging in antisocial conduct than the "average" member of society. However, we regard those constraints as too remote to justify an excuse on the ground that the person could not have helped acting as he did.

Professor Norval Norris, in commenting on the insanity defense, argues:

Why not permit the defense of dwelling in a Negro ghetto? Such a defense would not be morally indefensible. Adverse social and subcultural background is statistically *more* criminogenic than is psychosis; like insanity, it also severely circumscribes the freedom of choice. . . . You argue that insanity destroys, undermines, diminishes a man's capacity to reject what is wrong and adhere to what is right. So does the ghetto – more so.

Indeed, why *not* permit a defense of dwelling in a ghetto? I have two purposes in this part of the article: (1) to analyze the legal and moral arguments for a new defense of rotten social background; and (2) to suggest possible models for such a defense. * * *

B.   *Possible Models.*

Evidence of a rotten social background could be introduced in criminal trials in various ways. It could be relevant to a defense of excuse or justification, to a public policy defense relating to a society's responsibility for the rotten social background, or to considerations in the sentencing stage. In any of these ways, information about extreme poverty and deprivation can have the beneficial effect hoped for by Judge Bazelon in "compell[ing] us to explore these problems, and thereby offer[ing] some slight hope that we will learn, in the course of deciding individual cases, something about the causes of crime."

1.   Excuses.

The previous discussion suggested a number of possible excuse defenses; the particular circumstances of each case would determine the appropriateness of each approach.

a.   *Involuntary rage.*

Under this model, the RSB defendant would argue that a precipitating event evoked rage so powerful as to block his or her consciousness, rendering subsequent actions involuntary. Studies of repressed anger reviewed in part II indicate that long-term exposure to environmental insult can make an individual a virtual "time bomb." Such a person may react to a seemingly minor provocation with a violent response of which he or she is scarcely aware. Professor Hart summarizes the conventional theory of cases of automatic behavior as follows:

> What is missing in these cases appears to most people as a vital link between mind and body; and both the ordinary man and the lawyer might well insist on this by saying that in these cases there is not "really" a human action at all and certainly nothing for which anyone should be made criminally responsible. . . .

What extreme environmental deprivation causes the type of physical disorder required by the conventional defense, then the RSB person should be exculpated. The defense, however, should not be limited to cases of physical disorder, like epilepsy or brain tumor. The kind of pent-up rage and despair that can result from living in a crowded, violent neighborhood can cause an explosion of violence just as disordered brain circuitry can. When this occurs, a defense should be available. The defense would require proving: (i) that the defendant was acting automatically; and (ii) that the automatic state was caused by the extreme deprivation of a rotten social background.

b.   *Isolation from dominant culture.*

The theory underlying this model of the defense is that some urban ghettos are social and cultural islands unto themselves, with their own rules, norms and values. A person who has lived since birth in such an environment may be so strongly socialized by it that he or she has little sense of the values of the larger society or opportunity to acquire the norms necessary to function responsibly in that society. This defense would be particularly appropriate for a younger defendant who has had little or no exposure to life outside the ghetto, and for whom acquiescence to ghetto norms was required to survive. It would require a psychological and sociological analysis of the defendant's development, and proof that the defendant did not adequately internalize the values of the larger society, while in fact living by ghetto norms endorsing violence and other criminal behavior.

c.   *Inability to control conduct.*

This model assumes that a rotten social background can cause inability to control conduct, as insanity does. This defense would require a broad definition of disability, for instance, that proposed by Judge Bazelon in *Alexander*: that at the time of the defendant's unlawful conduct his or her mental or emotional processes or behavioral controls were impaired to such an extent that he or she cannot justly be held responsible for his or her act. This test is an advancement over the current medical-model tests for responsibility in that it allows for broad, socioeconomic explanations for loss of control. To a greater extent, it also preserves the dignity of an RSB defendant by not forcing him or her to opt, for strategic purposes, for a plea of insanity when he or she is not insane. * * *

4. Mitigation of sentence.

Evidence of rotten social background should be admissible during sentencing as a special circumstance which made conforming to the law especially difficult. When this is shown, the sentence should be reduced accordingly.

Sentence mitigation is probably appropriate for any RSB defendant:

The special features of mitigation are that a good reason for administering a less severe penalty is made out if the situation or mental state of the convicted criminal is such that he was exposed to an unusual or specially great temptation, or his ability to control his actions is thought to have been impaired or weakened otherwise than by his own action, so that conformity to the law which he has broken was a matter of special difficulty for him as compared with normal persons normally placed.

When a defendant could not be acquitted on the basis of rotten social background, consideration of his or her background is still relevant to sentencing.

C.   *Summary.*

From both individual and societal perspectives, a strong case can be made for new defenses for the criminal defendant whose crime stems from poverty, mistreatment, or a legitimate and frustrated desire for self-respect. Destitution and neglect affect individual behavior and choice; they are thus highly relevant to issues of criminal responsibility. Broader considerations favor a new defense, as well. If the criminal law reflects and reinforces a system of morality, then a criminal trial is an obvious and appropriate place to apply, test, and develop that morality. As Judge Bazelon observed: "We cannot rationally decry crime and brutality and racial animosity without at the same time struggling to enhance the fairness and integrity of the criminal justice system. That system has first-line responsibility for probing and coping with these complex problems." The simplest meaning of fairness in criminal trials is that no one should be punished without first having the opportunity to argue the issue of his or her culpability. The best reason for a defense acknowledging a rotten social background is that it is unfair to ignore it. * * *

Chapter 11

ATTEMPTS

INTRODUCTION

At common law, an attempt was defined as "an act, done with intent to commit a crime, and tending but failing to effect its commission." *People v. Rizzo*, 246 N.Y. 334 (1927). Most attempts were classified as misdemeanors regardless of the seriousness of the target offense. Today, most jurisdictions classify an attempt to commit a felony as a felony and an attempt to commit a misdemeanor as a misdemeanor. Generally speaking, the attempt in either case is treated as a less serious crime than the target offense.[a]

The first three cases in this chapter, *People v. Rizzo*, *People v. Staples*, and *State v. LaTraverse*, discuss the actus reus of an attempt. As will become evident from the cases, there is no single common law test for determining whether and when a defendant's acts go beyond mere preparation and become sufficient for an attempt. Instead, there are many tests, most of which focus on how much (or how little) remains to be done in order to complete the target offense. The Model Penal Code's provision on attempt, in contrast, requires a "substantial step" towards the culmination of the commission of the targeted offense. The Model Penal Code focuses on what the defendant has done, rather than on what remains to be done, and whether the defendant's acts or omissions are strongly corroborative of his criminal purpose.

The mens rea of an attempt is the specific intent to commit the targeted offense. *People v. Harris* explains how the mental state required for commission of an attempt can be narrower than the mental state or mental states required for commission of the target offense. *State v. Hinkhouse* provides an interesting fact pattern to test your understanding of the mens rea required for an attempt.

---

[a]Some states treat the attempt and the target offense as mutually exclusive crimes. D, the defendant, either attempts to commit crime X (and fails) or he commits crime X (i.e., he succeeds). Other states treat the attempt as a lesser included offense of the target offense. In these states, if D commits crime X, s/he also commits attempted crime X. D, however, cannot be punished for both crime X and attempted crime X because this would constitute punishment for the same offense in violation of double jeopardy principles.

The law of attempts recognizes two defenses specific to attempts: the defense of impossibility and the defense of abandonment. *State v. LaTraverse* (the third case in this section) discusses the elements of the defense of abandonment. The last case in this chapter, *United States v. Thomas*, discusses the defense of impossibility.

A.   THE ACTUS REUS REQUIREMENT

PEOPLE v. RIZZO
Court of Appeals of New York
246 N.Y. 334, 158 N.E. 888 (1927)

CRANE, J.

The police of the city of New York did excellent work in this case by preventing the commission of a serious crime. It is a great satisfaction to realize that we have such wide-awake guardians of our peace. Whether or not the steps which the defendant had taken up to the time of his arrest amounted to the commission of a crime, as defined by our law, is, however, another matter. He has been convicted of an attempt to commit the crime of robbery in the first degree and sentenced to State's prison. There is no doubt that he had the intention to commit robbery if he got the chance. An examination, however, of the facts is necessary to determine whether his acts were in preparation to commit the crime if the opportunity offered, or constituted a crime in itself, known to our law as an attempt to commit robbery in the first degree. Charles Rizzo, the defendant, appellant, with three others, Anthony J. Dorio, Thomas Milo and John Thomasello, on January 14th planned to rob one Charles Rao of a payroll valued at about $1,200 which he was to carry from the bank for the United Lathing Company. These defendants, two of whom had firearms, started out in an automobile, looking for Rao or the man who had the payroll on that day. Rizzo claimed to be able to identify the man and was to point him out to the others who were to do the actual holding up. The four rode about in their car looking for Rao. They went to the bank from which he was supposed to get the money and to various buildings being constructed by the United Lathing Company. At last they came to One Hundred and Eightieth street and Morris Park avenue. By this time they were watched and followed by two police officers. As Rizzo jumped out of the car and ran into the building all four were arrested. The defendant was taken out from the building in which he was hiding. Neither Rao nor a man named Previti, who was also supposed to carry a payroll, were at the place at the time of the arrest. The defendants had not found or seen the man they intended to rob; no person with a payroll was at any of the places where they had stopped and no one had been pointed out or identified by Rizzo.

The four men intended to rob the payroll man, whoever he was; they were looking for him, but they had not seen or discovered him up to the time they were arrested.

Does this constitute the crime of an attempt to commit robbery in the first degree? The Penal Law, section 2, prescribes, "An act, done with intent to commit a crime, and tending but failing to effect its commission, is 'an attempt to commit that crime.'" The word "*tending*" is very indefinite. It is perfectly evident that there will arise differences of opinion as to whether an act in a given case is one *tending* to commit a crime. "Tending" means to exert activity in a particular direction. Any act in preparation to commit a crime may be said to have a tendency towards its accomplishment. The procuring of the automobile, searching the streets looking for the desired victim, were in reality acts tending toward the commission of the proposed crime. The law, however, has recognized that many acts in the way of preparation are too remote to constitute the crime of attempt. The line has been drawn between those acts which are remote and those which are proximate and near to the consummation. The law must be practical, and, therefore, considers those acts only as tending to the commission of the crime which are so near to its accomplishment that in all reasonable probability the crime itself would have been committed but for timely interference. The cases which have been before the courts express this idea in different language, but the idea remains the same. The act or acts must come or advance very near to the accomplishment of the intended crime. In *People v. Mills* it was said: "Felonious intent alone is not enough, but there must be an overt act shown in order to establish even an attempt. An overt act is one done to carry out the intention, and it must be such as would naturally effect that result, unless prevented by some extraneous cause." In *Hyde v. U. S.* it was stated that the act amounts to an attempt when it is so near to the result that the danger of success is very great. "There must be dangerous proximity to success." Halsbury in his "Laws of England" says: "An act, in order to be a criminal attempt, must be immediately, and not remotely, connected with and directly tending to the commission of an offence." *Commonwealth v. Peaslee* refers to the acts constituting an attempt as coming *very near* to the accomplishment of the crime.

The method of committing or attempting crime varies in each case so that the difficulty, if any, is not with this rule of law regarding an attempt, which is well understood, but with its application to the facts. As I have said before, minds differ over proximity and the nearness of the approach.

How shall we apply this rule of immediate nearness to this case? The defendants were looking for the payroll man to rob him of his money. This is the charge in the indictment. Robbery is defined in section 2120 of the Penal Law as "the unlawful taking of personal property, from the person or in the presence of another, against his will, by means of force, or violence, or fear of injury, immediate or future, to his person;" and it is made robbery in the first degree by section 2124 when committed by a person aided by accomplices actually present. To constitute the crime of robbery the money must have been taken from Rao by means of force or violence, or through fear. The crime of attempt to commit robbery was committed if these defendants did an act tending to the commission of this robbery. Did the acts above describe[d] come dangerously near to the taking of Rao's property? Did the acts come so near the commission of robbery that there was reasonable likelihood of its accomplishment but for the interference? Rao was not found; the defendants were still looking for him; no attempt to rob him could be made, at least until he came in sight; he was not in the building at One Hundred and Eightieth street and Morris Park avenue. There was no man there with the payroll for the United Lathing Company whom these defendants could rob. Apparently no money had been drawn from the bank for the payroll by anybody at the time of the arrest. In a word, these defendants had planned to commit a crime and were looking around the city for an opportunity to commit it, but the opportunity fortunately never came. Men would not be guilty of an attempt at burglary if they had planned to break into a building and were arrested while they were hunting about the streets for the building not knowing where it was. Neither would a man be guilty of an attempt to commit murder if he armed himself and started out to find the person whom he had planned to kill but could not find him. So here these defendants were not guilty of an attempt to commit robbery in the first degree when they had not found or reached the presence of the person they intended to rob.

For these reasons, the judgment of conviction of this defendant, appellant, must be reversed and a new trial granted. * * *

PEOPLE v. STAPLES

Court of Appeal of California, Second District, Division 5
6 Cal. App. 3d 61, 85 Cal.Rptr. 589 (1970)

REPPY, J.

Defendant was charged in an information with attempted burglary. Trial by jury was waived, and the matter submitted on the testimony contained in the transcript of the preliminary hearing together with exhibits. Defendant was found guilty. * * *

I. The Facts

In October 1967, while his wife was away on a trip, defendant, a mathematician, under an assumed name, rented an office on the second floor of a building in Hollywood which was over the mezzanine of a bank. Directly below the mezzanine was the vault of the bank. Defendant was aware of the layout of the building, specifically of the relation of the office he rented to the bank vault. Defendant paid rent for the period from October 23 to November 23. The landlord had 10 days before commencement of the rental period within which to finish some interior repairs and painting. During this prerental period defendant brought into the office certain equipment. This included drilling tools, two acetylene gas tanks, a blow torch, a blanket, and a linoleum rug. The landlord observed these items when he came in from time to time to see how the repair work was progressing. Defendant learned from a custodian that no one was in the building on Saturdays. On Saturday, October 14, defendant drilled two groups of holes into the floor of the office above the mezzanine room. He stopped drilling before the holes went through the floor. He came back to the office several times thinking he might slowly drill down, covering the holes with the linoleum rug. At some point in time he installed a hasp lock on a closet, and planned to, or did, place his tools in it. However, he left the closet keys on the premises. Around the end of November, apparently after November 23, the landlord notified the police and turned the tools and equipment over to them. Defendant did not pay any more rent. It is not clear when he last entered the office, but it could have been after November 23, and even after the landlord had removed the equipment. On February 22, 1968, the police arrested defendant. After receiving advice as to his constitutional rights, defendant voluntarily made an oral statement which he reduced to writing.

Among other things which defendant wrote down were these:

Saturday, the 14th ... I drilled some small holes in the floor of the room. Because of tiredness, fear, and the implications of what I was doing, I stopped and went to sleep.

At this point I think my motives began to change. The actual [*sic*] commencement of my plan made me begin to realize that even if I were to succeed a fugitive life of living off of stolen money would not give the enjoyment of the life of a mathematician however humble a job I might have.

I still had not given up my plan however. I felt I had made a certain investment of time, money, effort and a certain psychological commitment to the concept.

I came back several times thinking I might store the tools in the closet and slowly drill down (covering the hole with a rug of linoleum square. As time went on (after two weeks or so). My wife came back and my life as bank robber seemed more and more absurd.

II. Discussion of Defendant's Contentions

Defendant's position in this appeal is that, as a matter of law, there was insufficient evidence upon which to convict him of a criminal attempt under Penal Code section 664. Defendant claims that his actions were all preparatory in nature and never reached a stage of advancement in relation to the substantive crime which he concededly intended to commit (burglary of the bank vault) so that criminal responsibility might attach.

In order for the prosecution to prove that defendant committed an attempt to burglarize as proscribed by Penal Code section 664, it was required to establish that he had the specific intent to commit a burglary of the bank and that his acts toward that goal went beyond mere preparation.

The required specific intent was clearly established in the instant case. Defendant admitted in his written confession that he rented the office fully intending to burglarize the bank, that he brought in tools and equipment to accomplish this purpose, and that he began drilling into the floor with the intent of making an entry into the bank.

The question of whether defendant's conduct went beyond "mere preparation" raises some provocative problems. The briefs and the oral argument of counsel in this case point up a degree of ambiguity and uncertainty that permeates the law of attempts in this state. Each side has cited us to a different so-called "test" to determine whether this defendant's conduct went beyond the preparatory stage. Predictably each respective test in the eyes of its proponents yielded an opposite result. * * *

We suggest that the confusion in this area is a result of the broad statutory language of section 664, which reads in part: "Any person who attempts to commit any crime, but fails, or is prevented or intercepted in the perpetration thereof, is punishable . . . ." This is a very general proscription against all attempts not specifically made a crime. The statute does not differentiate between the various types of attempts which may be considered culpable. Reference must be made to case law in order to determine precisely what conduct constitutes an attempt. However, the statute does point out by the words "fails," "prevented," and "intercepted," those *conditions* which separate an attempt from the substantive crime. * * *

Our courts have come up with a variety of "tests" which try to distinguish acts of preparation from completed attempts. "The preparation consists in devising or arranging the means or measures necessary for the commission of the offense; the attempt is the direct movement toward the commission after the preparations are made." "'[The] act must reach far enough towards the accomplishment of the desired result to amount to the commencement of the consummation.'" "[Where] the intent to commit the substantive offense is . . . clearly established . . . [,] acts done toward the commission of the crime may constitute an attempt, where the same acts would be held insufficient to constitute an attempt if the intent with which they were done is equivocal and not clearly proved."

None of the above statements of the law applicable to this category of attempts provide a litmus-like test, and perhaps no such test is achievable. Such precision is not required in this case, however. There was definitely substantial evidence entitling the trial judge to find that defendant's acts had gone beyond the preparation stage. Without specifically deciding where defendant's preparations left off and where his activities became a completed criminal attempt, we can say that his "drilling" activity clearly was an unequivocal and direct step toward the completion of the burglary. It was a fragment of the substantive crime contemplated, i.e., the beginning of the "breaking" element. Further, defendant himself characterized his activity as the *actual commencement of his plan.* The drilling by defendant was obviously one of a series of acts which logic and ordinary experience indicate would result in the proscribed act of burglary. * * *

The order is affirmed.

STATE v. LATRAVERSE
Supreme Court of Rhode Island
443 A.2d 890 (1982)

KELLEHER, J.

The defendant, Paul A. Latraverse (Latraverse), was found guilty by a Superior Court justice, after a jury-waived trial, of attempting knowingly and maliciously to dissuade a Woonsocket police officer from giving testimony before a grand jury, a violation of * * * the Anti-intimidation of Witnesses and Crime Victims statute.

Salvatore Lombardi (Lombardi) is a member of the Woonsocket police department. As a member of the detective division, he has done undercover work numerous times using the name Frank Torro. As Frank Torro, he had purchased four stolen cars from Latraverse, who owns and operates a Woonsocket used-car dealership. Following the sale, Latraverse was arrested and arraigned in the District Court on several charges of receiving stolen goods. At the time of the incident we are about to describe, Latraverse was free on bail while awaiting the grand jury's consideration of his dealings with "Torro."

On June 26, 1980, Lombardi arrived at his Morton Avenue home sometime between 11 p.m. and midnight after completing a tour of duty. At approximately 1:40 a.m. on June 27, he and his wife were watching a television program when a car with a faulty muffler passed by. The resulting noise caused Lombardi to look out the front window. There on the street he observed a late-model Ford Thunderbird bearing a license plate assigned to Latraverse's automobile agency. Lombardi was aware that the "T-bird" belonged to Latraverse. Once the vehicle had passed by, Lombardi took his walkie-talkie, went outside his home, and secreted himself in the darkness. Lombardi told the trial justice that he kept a vigilant eye on the early-morning traffic passing by his house because he had received threats as a result of his undercover work. He also testified that on one occasion while working under cover he was asked by Latraverse if his real name was "Salvatore Lombardi."

Lombardi watched the T-bird as it proceeded along Morton Avenue and then took a left onto Bellevue Street, and within a matter of twenty to thirty seconds, he observed the T-bird coming "down" Harrison Avenue. When the vehicle came to a halt, it was parked in front of 203 Harrison Avenue. Its lights were then extinguished. Harrison Avenue runs perpendicular to Morton Avenue and is almost directly across the street from the Lombardi residence. After a wait of a minute or so, Lombardi radioed headquarters for a "backup" because, in his words, he "wasn't going to take any chances" and he "felt" that Latraverse wanted to see him injured. As the backup vehicle came onto Morton Avenue from Hamlet Avenue, its lights were on, and the vehicle was proceeding at forty miles per hour toward the Harrison Avenue-Morton Avenue intersection. As the backup headed toward the intersection, the T-bird backed up on Harrison, made a U-turn, and headed away from the Morton Avenue area toward Park Place. The backup caught up with the darkened T-bird in front of 138 Harrison Avenue.

When the police looked at the interior of the car, they saw the following items: a can of gasoline; a rag; matches; an aluminum baseball bat; a wire coat hanger that had been stretched out so that it could be used to open a car door; and a note that read, "Hi, Sal, know [sic][2] it's my turn asshole."

---

[2]In order to appreciate the full flavor of the note, the word "know" must be read as "now" because the intended reading was, "Hi, Sal, now it's my turn asshole."

After the defense had rested without presenting any evidence, Latraverse moved for a judgment of acquittal. Thereafter, the trial justice gave a bench decision in which, after first noting that this court had yet to express itself on the subject of criminal liability for attempting to commit a crime, he referred to several cases in which various courts in Connecticut, the District of Columbia, Maine, and Maryland had had their say in regard to whether an accused's conduct fell within the parameters of each jurisdiction's definition of what constituted criminal attempt.

Since the issues presented by Latraverse are those of first impression for this court, we shall briefly detail the evolution of the law of criminal attempt, noting as we proceed the differing views expressed through the years about what are the essential elements of the crime.

Although the criminal law is of ancient origin, the concept that there could be criminal liability for an attempt, even if ultimately unsuccessful, is of comparatively recent origin, beginning with *Rex v. Scofield*, Cald 397 (1784). In *Scofield*, Lord Mansfield observed:

> The *intent* may make an act, innocent in itself, criminal; nor is the *completion* of an act, criminal in itself, necessary to constitute criminality. Is it no offence to set fire to a train of gunpowder with intent to burn a house, because by accident, or the interposition of another, the mischief is prevented?

The classic elements of a common-law attempt are an intent to commit a crime, the execution of an overt act in furtherance of the intention, and a failure to consummate the crime. However, this common-law view fails to indicate how far the accused's conduct must proceed toward the actual consummation of the crime in order to be considered an attempt to commit that crime. It is generally agreed that neither the intent to commit a crime nor mere preparation in and of itself constitutes an attempt. The difficulty is to establish a standard that excludes preparation prior to the actual attempt to commit the crime while including as punishable those acts which have reached the point where intervention by the police is justified.

In looking to the tests formulated by the various courts that have sought to distinguish preparation from perpetration, we first look to our northern New England neighbor, Vermont, where "attempt" is defined as an act which "must reach far enough towards the accomplishment of the desired result to amount to the commencement of the consummation." Again, shortly before the turn of the century in Massachusetts, Mr. Justice Oliver Wendell Holmes, in considering an appeal involving an attempted poisoning, observed that "the act done must come pretty near to accomplishing that result before the law will notice it." A few years later, when the question was attempted arson, he said:

> Preparation is not an attempt. But some preparations may amount to an attempt. It is a question of degree. If the preparation comes very near to the accomplishment of the act, the intent to complete it renders the crime so probable that the act will be a misdemeanor * * *.

The learned jurist also stressed that the arson attempt was complete even though an accused had an opportunity to experience a change of mind. Twenty-four years later Mr. Justice Cardozo in *People v. Werblow,* expressed the belief that acts performed in furtherance of a criminal project do not reach the stage of attempt unless "they carry the project forward within dangerous proximity to the criminal end to be attained * * *."

Later, in *United States v. Coplon,* Judge Learned Hand, in considering whether the defendant's claim that her conduct "remained in the zone of 'preparation' and that the evidence did not prove an 'attempt,'" rejected a suggested doctrine whereby the crime of attempt would be proved by a showing that the accused had done all that was in his power to do but had been prevented from proceeding further by outside intervention. Judge Hand noted that there were many decisions in the United States in which the accused had passed beyond preparation even though he had been interrupted before taking the last of his intended steps. This noted jurist found the notion that the instant of consummation could serve as the dividing line between the areas of preparation and attempt to be most unpersuasive.

It should be obvious by now that much has been written trying to establish the exact placement of the dividing line where preparation ends and attempt begins, and we have no intention of contributing one whit to what has been described as the preparation-attempt "quagmire." Instead, we adopt the sensible approach to the question now before us embodied in § 5.01 of the American Law Institute's Model Penal Code, which reads in part as follows:

Criminal Attempt.

1) *Definition of Attempt.* A person is guilty of an attempt to commit a crime if, acting with the kind of culpability otherwise required for commission of the crime, he:

(a) purposely engages in conduct which would constitute the crime if the attendant circumstances were as he believes them to be; or

(b) when causing a particular result is an element of the crime, does or omits to do anything with the purpose of causing or with the belief that it will cause such result without further conduct on his part; or

(c) purposely does or omits to do anything which, under the circumstances as he believes them to be, is an act or omission constituting a substantial step in a course of conduct planned to culminate in his commission of the crime.

(2) *Conduct Which May Be Held Substantial Step Under Subsection (1)(c).* Conduct shall not be held to constitute a substantial step under Subsection (1)(c) of this Section unless it is strongly corroborative of the actor's criminal purpose. Without negativing the sufficiency of other conduct, the following, if strongly corroborative of the actor's criminal purpose, shall not be held insufficient as a matter of law:

(a) lying in wait, searching for or following the contemplated victim of the crime;

(b) enticing or seeking to entice the contemplated victim of the crime to go to the place contemplated for its commission;

(c) reconnoitering the place contemplated for the commission of the crime;

(d) unlawful entry of a structure, vehicle or enclosure in which it is contemplated that the crime will be committed;

(e) possession of materials to be employed in the commission of the crime, which are specially designed for such unlawful use or which can serve no lawful purpose of the actor under the circumstances;

(f) possession, collection or fabrication of materials to be employed in the commission of the crime, at or near the place contemplated for its commission, where such possession, collection or fabrication serves no lawful purpose of the actor under the circumstances;

(g) soliciting an innocent agent to engage in conduct constituting an element of the crime. * * *

(4) *Renunciation of Criminal Purpose.* When the actor's conduct would otherwise constitute an attempt under Subsection (1)(b) or (1)(c) of this Section, it is an affirmative defense that he abandoned his effort to commit the crime or otherwise prevented its commission, under circumstances manifesting a complete and voluntary renunciation of his criminal purpose. The establishment of such defense does not, however, affect the liability of an accomplice who did not join in such abandonment or prevention.

Within the meaning of this Article, renunciation of criminal purpose is not voluntary if it is motivated, in whole or in part, by circumstances, not present or apparent at the inception of the actor's course of conduct, which increase the probability of detection or apprehension or which make more difficult the accomplishment of the criminal purpose. Renunciation is not complete if it is motivated by a decision to postpone the criminal conduct until a more advantageous time or to transfer the criminal effort to another but similar objective or victim."

In taking this approach, we follow the path previously taken by our appellate colleagues in the Second and Fifth Federal Circuit Courts of Appeals as well as the Supreme Courts of the States of Ohio and Washington.

It is obvious from a reading of the code that the intent of the drafters was to extend criminal responsibility for attempted criminal behavior by * * * drawing the line between attempt and noncriminal preparation further away from the final act so as to make the crime essentially one of criminal purpose implemented by an overt act strongly corroborative of such purpose. * * *

More to the point, however, is the substantial-step clause. Under §5.01(1)(c) of the code, an attempt occurs when one "purposely does or omits to do anything which * * * is an act or omission constituting a substantial step in a course of conduct planned to culminate in his commission of the crime." To constitute a substantial step, the conduct must be "strongly corroborative of the actor's criminal purpose." The application of this standard will, of course, depend upon the nature of the intended crime and the facts of the particular case. A substantial step in the commission of robbery may be quite different from that in arson, rape, or some other crime, but this standard properly directs attention to overt acts of the defendant which convincingly demonstrate a firm purpose to commit a crime. In subscribing to the substantial-step doctrine, we endorse the sentiments expressed by Chief Judge Kaufman in *United States v. Stallworth*, in which the court, in rejecting the defendants' contention that they could not be convicted of an attempted bank robbery because they neither entered the bank nor brandished weapons, said:

> We reject this wooden logic. Attempt is a subtle concept that requires a rational and logically sound definition, one that enables society to punish malefactors who have unequivocally set out upon a criminal course without requiring law enforcement officers to delay until innocent bystanders are imperiled.

The code's requirement of a substantial step shifts the emphasis from what remains to be done to what already has been done. Thus, liability for a relatively remote preparatory act is precluded, but at the same time dangerous individuals may be lawfully apprehended at an earlier stage of their nefarious enterprises than would be possible under the [common law]. * * *

Having made our choice concerning the pertinent legal principles, we now turn to the merits of Latraverse's appeal. His argument is simple and straightforward. He argues that in taking the evidence adduced by the state in its best light, his actions in the early-morning hours of June 27, 1980, add up to nothing more than pure preparations that, in turn, must be considered abandoned by his decision to turn around on Harrison Avenue and leave the area.

With all due deference to Latraverse's claim of preparation and/or abandonment, the code's requirement of proof (1) that Latraverse must have been acting with the kind of culpability otherwise required for the commission of the crime he is charged with attempting and (2) that he must have been engaged in conduct which constituted a substantial step toward the commission of the crime emphasizes the importance of the necessity of encouraging early police intervention when a suspect is clearly bent on the commission of crime. There is no necessity that the police had to wait until Latraverse poured the gasoline or struck the match.

The evidence presented before the trial justice indicates that Latraverse had indeed taken substantial steps to effectuate his effort to intimidate Lombardi. There is no question that at 1:40 a.m. on the morning in question he was reconnoitering Lombardi's neighborhood and in the process continued his observation while parked in a darkened automobile 100 feet from the Lombardi household. No one disputes the fact that Latraverse carried with him a homemade tool for unlocking a motor vehicle as well as material that could cause an incendiary episode, and, the most persuasive evidence of Latraverse's intentions to enter Lombardi's property in the early-morning hours of June 27, 1980, his "billet-doux" to Lombardi in which he reminded "Sal" that it was now Latraverse's turn. We have no hesitancy whatsoever in holding that Latraverse's conduct constituted a substantial step in his endeavor to give Lombardi something to think about as the officer awaited his summons to appear before the grand jury.

The trial justice, rejecting Latraverse's abandonment defense, relied on *Wiley v. State,* in which the Maryland Court of Appeals observed that a voluntary abandonment of a criminal attempt that had proceeded beyond mere preparation into an overt act or acts in furtherance of the commission of the attempt does not serve as a defense because the crime has already been committed. We cannot fault the trial justice for his reliance on the legal principles expressed in the *Wiley* case. There is a divergence of opinion about whether or not a defendant can rely upon the doctrine of abandonment after he or she has gone so far as to commit a criminal attempt. The *Wiley* case represents one side. The code expresses a different point of view in that it recognizes as a defense to an attempted crime the abandonment of efforts to commit the crime when circumstances manifest a complete and voluntary renunciation of criminal purpose.

The code stresses that abandonment or renunciation is not complete and voluntary if it is motivated because either (*a*) the defendant has failed to complete the attempt because of unanticipated difficulties, unexpected resistance, or circumstances that increase the probability of detection or apprehension or (*b*) the defendant fails to consummate the attempted offense after deciding to postpone his endeavors until another time or to substitute another victim or another but similar objective. * * *

Since abandonment is an affirmative defense, Latraverse, if he wishes, has the opportunity and the burden of establishing by a preponderance of the evidence that he in fact voluntarily and completely abandoned his nefarious efforts on the evening in question when he turned around on Harrison Avenue and drove away from Lombardi's home toward Park Place. In placing the burden of abandonment upon the defendant, we perceive no constitutional limitations. Voluntary abandonment, as we view the doctrine, does not negate any element of the offense. Our adoption of the code's approach to abandonment is motivated solely by our belief that our actions are consonant with the purpose of the substantial-step rationale, which recognizes the desirability of early preventive action by the police before a defendant comes dangerously close to committing the intended crime. In like manner, the sole motivation for our recognition of an abandonment defense is the hope that individuals will desist from pursuing their criminal designs, thereby reducing the risk that the intended substantive crime will be accomplished.

Having recognized the abandonment defense, we now afford Latraverse the opportunity to establish by the fair preponderance of the evidence that his departure from Lombardi's neighborhood constituted a voluntary and complete abandonment of his criminal purposes on the evening in question. If this evidentiary hearing is not commenced within ten days of the filing date of this opinion, an order will be entered affirming the judgment of conviction entered in the Superior Court. If he accepts this mandate, the record in this case will be remanded to the Superior Court for a hearing so that the evidence may be presented forthwith to the trial justice for his evaluation. Jurisdiction will be retained by us for further appellate review if such is required.

B.   THE MENS REA REQUIREMENT

PEOPLE v. HARRIS
Supreme Court of Illinois
72 Ill. 2d 16, 377 N.E.2d 28 (1978)

WARD, C.J.

*   *   *

[T]he defendant was convicted on a charge, made by information, of the attempted murder of Joyce Baker on the night of November 18, 1975, in a country area east of Champaign. In a separate count the defendant was charged with aggravated kidnapping.

The alleged murder attempt took place while Miss Baker was sitting inside her car and the defendant was standing behind the car with a pistol in his hand. The defendant and Miss Baker had been keeping company. For much of the evening they had been engaged in an argument in which the defendant accused the victim of infidelity. As the argument became more heated, the defendant, who was driving, reached down and picked up a revolver from the floor of the car and placed it in his lap with the barrel pointed toward Miss Baker. He made several remarks which Miss Baker interpreted as threats to kill her.

Alarmed, she opened the door on her side of the car, got out and began to run away, but ran into a barbed wire fence, injuring her leg. The defendant also got out of the car. He did not pursue her, but remained standing by the car. After her collision with the fence, Miss Baker returned to the car, and made an unsuccessful attempt to capture the gun, which the defendant was holding in his hand and pointing in her general direction. Miss Baker then got into the car on the driver's side, and drove off toward a nearby farmhouse. She testified that as she drove off she looked in the rear vision mirror and saw the defendant standing behind the car. He was holding the gun with both hands, and pointing it at her.

Then she heard something strike the rear window, and the broken pane of glass in the rear window fell out of its frame. There were no other witnesses, but following this episode the police were summoned, and they found the defendant walking down the road near the scene of the episode just described. When the car was located, the police officers testified, the rear glass was broken, and a bullet fragment was found on the left side of the rear seat.

The jury returned a verdict of guilty on the charge of attempted murder and a verdict of not guilty on the aggravated kidnapping charge. The defendant was sentenced to serve a term of not less than 4 years and not more than 12 years. * * *

The following instructions to the jury were tendered by the State and were given, over the objection of the defendant:

> A person commits the crime of attempt who, with intent to commit the crime of murder, does any act which constitutes a substantial step toward the commission of the crime of murder. The crime attempted need not have been committed.

> To sustain the charge of attempt, the State must prove the following propositions:

> *First*: That the defendant performed an act which constituted a substantial step toward the commission of the crime of murder; and

> *Second*: That the defendant did so with intent to commit the crime of murder.

> A person commits the crime of murder who kills an individual if, in performing the acts which cause the death, he *intends to kill or do great bodily harm to that individual.* (emphasis added).

The defendant objected to the last of the instructions on the ground that it told the jury it could find him guilty of attempted murder if the jury found that he had acted only with the intent to do great bodily harm and did not have the intent to cause death. * * *

The central difficulty * * * arises out of the difference between the elements of the offense of attempt and those of the specific offense attempted, murder. The definition of attempt, contained in section 8 -- 4(a) of the Criminal Code of 1961, is:

A person commits an attempt when, *with intent to commit a specific offense*, he does any act which constitutes a substantial step toward the commission of that offense. (emphasis added).

The statutory definition of murder is found in section 9 -- 1(a) of the Code, and reads:

A person who kills an individual without lawful justification commits murder if, in performing the acts which cause the death:

(1) He either intends to kill or do great bodily harm to that individual or another, or knows that such acts will cause death to that individual or another; or

(2) He knows that such acts create a strong probability of death or great bodily harm to that individual or another; or

(3) He is attempting or committing a forcible felony other than voluntary manslaughter.

The crime of murder is thus committed not only when a person intends to kill another individual, but also when he intends to do great bodily harm, or when he knows that his acts create a strong probability of death or great bodily harm, or when he is attempting or committing a forcible felony. * * *

[In this case] the third instruction states that a person is guilty of the crime of murder "if, in performing the acts which cause the death, he intends to kill or do great bodily harm to that individual." * * * [T]his instruction * * * permits the jury to return a verdict of guilty upon evidence that the defendant intended only to cause great bodily harm short of death. An instruction must make it clear that to convict for attempted murder nothing less than a criminal intent to kill must be shown. * * *

Observations of LaFave and Scott are representative of authority that it is not sufficient to prove attempted murder to show that the accused intended to cause serious bodily harm:

Some crimes, such as murder, are defined in terms of acts causing a particular result plus some mental state which need not be an intent to bring about that result. Thus, if A, B, and C have each taken the life of another, A acting with intent to kill, B with an intent to do serious bodily injury, and C with a reckless disregard of human life, all three are guilty of murder because the crime of murder is defined in such a way that any one of these mental states will suffice. However, if the victims do not die from their injuries, then only A is guilty of attempted murder; on a charge of attempted murder it is not sufficient to show that the defendant intended to do serious bodily harm or that he acted in reckless disregard for human life. Again, this is because intent is needed for the crime of attempt, so that attempted murder requires an intent to bring about that result described by the crime of murder (*i.e.*, the death of another). * * *

Reversed and remanded.

STATE v. HINKHOUSE
Court of Appeals of Oregon
139 Or. App. 446, 912 P.2d 921 (1996)

LANDAU, J.

Defendant is infected with the human immunodeficiency virus (HIV). He was convicted of ten counts of attempted murder and ten counts of attempted assault I, based on his conduct of engaging in unprotected sexual intercourse with a number of victims without disclosing his medical condition. On appeal, he argues that the convictions must be set aside, because the evidence is insufficient to establish that he intended to cause the death of or serious physical injury to any of his several victims. The state argues that the evidence is sufficient to support the convictions. We agree with the state and affirm.

We state the facts in the light most favorable to the state. Defendant learned that he had tested positive for HIV in 1989. That year, he began a sexual relationship with P.B., who was 15 years old at the time. At the end of the summer, defendant moved to California, but he returned six months later and renewed his sexual relationship with P.B. During that relationship, defendant refused to use condoms, saying that he did not like them. He and P.B. did not discuss HIV. In July 1990, defendant again left. P.B. asked defendant why he was leaving. In the course of his explanation, defendant told P.B. that she might want to get tested for HIV. P.B. was tested and, in August 1990, she learned that she was HIV-positive. A few months later, defendant called P.B. and said that he wanted to meet with her. When they met, defendant asked whether she had been tested. P.B. responded, "Well, you should know my status because you gave it to me." Defendant did not deny the accusation, but just "brushed it off."

On November 3, 1990, defendant told his probation officer, Bill Carroll, that defendant was HIV-positive. Carroll immediately advised defendant of the implications of his HIV status, explaining the seriousness of the disease and the manner in which it is transmitted. Carroll explained that using a condom limits the risks of transmitting the virus, but he also explained that it would not eliminate the risk entirely. He told defendant that if he passed the virus to another person, "he would be killing someone." Over the next several months, Carroll and defendant continued to have conversations about HIV and the need to take precautions to avoid transmitting the virus. In a telephone conversation in 1991, Carroll again cautioned defendant: "If you infect anyone, that is murder." Defendant said that he understood and agreed that he would take appropriate precautions.

In 1992, defendant was taken into custody on a probation violation. He and Carroll continued their conversations about the danger defendant posed by continuing to engage in sexual relationships. According to Carroll, defendant said that he understood the situation and that "he would cease and desist from any kind of [sexual] activity." Nevertheless, defendant continued to engage in sexual relations with a number of women. When he was taken into custody again for another probation violation later that year, he was heard bragging about his sexual prowess with women, expressing neither concern nor remorse for the people whom he might have exposed to HIV. As a condition of his release, however, he signed a probation agreement that included a commitment not to engage in any unsupervised contact with women without express permission from his parole officer.

In 1993, defendant began several sexual relationships without notifying Carroll. In each case, he refused to use a condom during sex and failed to disclose his HIV status. In May of that year, he began a sexual relationship with P.D. He never used a condom and said nothing about HIV.

In June of 1993, defendant began having sex with L.K. She demanded that defendant use a condom, and he did so for three or four weeks. On one occasion, he promised to use a condom, but then he penetrated her without one, in spite of L.K.'s protests. L.K. and defendant then had a long talk about safe sex, in which defendant told her that he had just ended a long-term relationship, that he had not engaged in any risky behavior since then, and that he had recently tested negative for HIV. Defendant and L.K. resumed their sexual relationship. Defendant, however, persisted in failing to use a condom. When L.K. expressed concern about his behavior, defendant replied that there was no need to wear condoms, because, if either of them had HIV, the other already had been exposed. Defendant agreed to be tested for HIV, but never followed through.

After a brief hiatus, defendant and L.K. continued their sexual relationship. Defendant's sexual behavior became very rough. He would engage in intercourse so vigorously that L.K. would bleed. When L.K. complained, defendant's attitude was "very casual," even proud. Defendant also insisted on engaging in anal intercourse, and, although L.K. said that she was "dead set" against it, defendant attempted anal sex several times. She complained that, although at times he could be gentle, he was becoming "very rough and very rude," and that he would be "mean and spiteful and try[] to be hurtful." L.K. ended her relationship with defendant in August of 1993.

The following month, defendant began a sexual relationship with R.L. She suggested that defendant buy condoms, but he told her, "I don't believe in them." R.L. suggested that defendant might have HIV, but he denied that, saying, "I don't have it, and whoever is telling you is lying."

Throughout 1993, defendant continued to meet with his probation officer on a weekly basis. During that time they would discuss defendant's HIV status. At no time did defendant mention P.D., L.K. or R.L.

Around the same time that defendant began seeing R.L., he also began a romantic relationship with M.S. Defendant hopes that he and M.S. will marry someday. M.S. was aware of his HIV status, and defendant always wore condoms when he had sexual intercourse with her.

At trial, Dr. Beers explained that HIV is transmitted through bodily fluids, including semen. He said that even nontraumatic sexual intercourse is an effective method of transmitting the disease and that more violent sex or anal sex increases the risk of transmission, because of the increased likelihood that tears in tissue break down the body's barriers to the virus. He explained that a person may be infected after a single sexual exposure.

Defendant's psychologist, Dr. Norman, testified that defendant had a long history of acting out sexually and that he suffered from attention deficit disorder. He opined that defendant understood how HIV is transmitted and that it is a fatal disease. Norman also testified that, although defendant had reportedly threatened in 1991 to "go out and spread" HIV, he did not lend much credence to such threats. According to Norman, defendant simply did not think about the consequences of his behavior.

The state's expert, Dr. Johnson, agreed that defendant suffers from attention deficit disorder. Johnson testified that defendant also suffers from a borderline personality disorder and is antisocial. He recounted that defendant had acknowledged that his parole officer had warned him not to infect other people, and that defendant had responded that "he was going to do whatever he wanted, whenever he wanted." Johnson also thought that it was significant that defendant agreed to use, and in fact used, condoms when having intercourse with a woman for whom he expressed affection, but he did not use condoms with the other women with whom he had sex. Johnson also reported a conversation with another of defendant's former sexual partners, who said that, although defendant had denied that he was HIV-positive, he said that if he were positive, he would spread the virus to other people. In Johnson's opinion, such statements, coupled with defendant's behavior, showed intentional, deliberate conduct. Particularly in the light of the pattern of systematically recruiting and exploiting multiple partners over a long period of time, Johnson said, he found no evidence to suggest that defendant was acting impulsively or without the intent to harm.

Defendant moved for a judgment of acquittal, which the trial court denied. On appeal, defendant argues that the trial court erred in denying his motion, because the evidence is insufficient to support convictions for either attempted murder or attempted assault. He argues that there is no evidence that he intended to cause death or serious bodily injury, only evidence that--at most-- he acted in reckless disregard of the consequences of his conduct. The state contends that the evidence is sufficient to support the convictions on both sets of charges, based on the undisputed evidence that defendant concealed or lied about his HIV status, refused to wear condoms, and intentionally had unprotected sex with a number of women, while fully aware of the fact that he was exposing them to the virus.

We review a denial of a motion for judgment of acquittal to determine whether, viewing the evidence in the light most favorable to the state, a rational trier of fact could have found the essential elements of the crime beyond a reasonable doubt. We must give the state the benefit of all reasonable inferences that properly may be drawn. A person is guilty of attempting to commit a crime "when the person intentionally engages in conduct which constitutes a substantial step toward commission of the crime." A person commits assault in the first degree when "the person intentionally causes serious physical injury to another by means of a deadly or dangerous weapon."

A person commits attempted murder when he or she attempts, without justification or excuse, intentionally to cause the death of another human being. To act "intentionally" is to "act[] with a conscious objective to cause the result or to engage in the conduct so described."

Viewing the evidence in the light most favorable to the state, we conclude that there is sufficient evidence for a rational trier of fact to find that defendant intended to cause both physical injury and death. He knew that he was HIV positive and that his condition was terminal. He knew that if he transmitted the virus to another person, that person eventually would die as well. He understood that having unprotected sex would expose his sexual partners to the virus and that a single sexual encounter could transmit the virus. He had been told, and he acknowledged, that having unprotected sex and transmitting the disease was "murder." He even signed an agreement that he would refrain from any unsupervised contact with women without the approval of his probation officer.

In spite of that awareness, defendant engaged in a persistent pattern of recruiting sexual partners over a period of many months. He consistently concealed or lied about his HIV status. He refused to wear condoms, or pretended to wear them, penetrating women without protection and against their protestations. He engaged in unprotected sex, including rough and violent intercourse, which increased the chances of passing the virus to his partners. He bragged about his sexual prowess, even after acknowledging his HIV status, and told at least one person that he intended to spread the disease to others by such conduct.

Defendant insists that he meant only to satisfy himself sexually, and that that is insufficient to prove intent to harm or to cause death. His conduct, however, demonstrates that his objective was more than mere sexual gratification. When he engaged in sexual intercourse with the woman he hoped to marry, he consistently wore condoms and made no attempt to conceal his HIV status. When he had sex with others, in contrast, he concealed or lied about his condition and refused any protection. Particularly in the light of the pattern of exploitation over a long period of time, a rational fact finder could conclude beyond a reasonable doubt that defendant did not act impulsively merely to satisfy his sexual desires, but instead acted deliberately to cause his victims serious bodily injury and death. The trial court did not err in denying defendant's motion for a judgment of acquittal.

Affirmed.

C. THE DEFENSE OF IMPOSSIBILITY

UNITED STATES v. THOMAS
United States Court of Military Appeals
32 C.M.R. 278, 13 U.S.C.M.A. 278 (1962)

KILDAY, Judge:

The accused herein, Thomas and McClellan, were tried in common by general court-martial. Separate charges against the pair alleged the offenses of conspiracy to commit rape, rape, and lewd and lascivious conduct, in violation of Articles 81, 120, and 134, Uniform Code of Military Justice, 10 USC §§ 881, 920, and 934, respectively. Upon arraignment, both men entered pleas of not guilty. Each was acquitted of rape, but the court-martial found them guilty of attempted rape, contrary to Article 80 of the Uniform Code, 10 USC § 880, and likewise convicted them of the other two charges upon which they were brought to trial. Both received identical sentences to dishonorable discharge, confinement at hard labor for three years, forfeiture of all pay and allowances for a like period, and reduction to the grade of airman recruit.

Thereafter, the findings and sentences adjudged by the trial court were approved by the officer exercising general court-martial jurisdiction. The board of review, however, set aside the findings of guilty of attempted rape and conspiracy as to both accused. It approved a modified finding of lewd and lascivious conduct as to each and reassessed the punishment, reducing the sentences of the pair to bad-conduct discharge, confinement at hard labor for five months, total forfeitures, and reduction. The case is before this Court on the following questions certified to us by the Acting Judge Advocate General of the Navy in accordance with Article 67(b)(2), Uniform Code of Military Justice, 10 USC § 867:

> I. Was the Board of Review correct in setting aside, with respect to both accused, the findings of guilty of Charge I, attempted rape?

> II. Was the Board of Review correct in setting aside, with respect to both accused, the findings of guilty of the Additional Charge, conspiracy to commit rape?

The evidence adduced at the trial presents a sordid and revolting picture which need not be discussed in detail other than as necessary to decide the certified issues. In brief, both these young accused -- Thomas being twenty years of age, and McClellan only nineteen, at the time of the instant offenses -- started their fateful evening on a "bar hopping" spree. They were accompanied by an eighteen-year-old companion, Abruzzese, who, like both accused, held the grade of airman in the Navy. The latter was a co-actor in these offenses, but was granted immunity from prosecution for his criminality in the incidents, and testified as a witness for the Government.

After several stops the trio entered a tavern known as "Taylor's Place" where McClellan began dancing with a girl. Almost at once she collapsed in McClellan's arms. Thereafter, he, with his two companions, volunteered to take her home. They placed the apparently unconscious female in McClellan's car and left. Abruzzese was seated beside McClellan, who drove; Thomas was in the left rear seat next to the girl. Before they had proceeded very far McClellan, in frank, expressive language, suggested that this was a good chance for sexual intercourse as apparently this woman was just drunk and would never know the difference. Each of the three subsequently did or attempted to consummate this act and then started their return to town. The three became concerned as the woman had not regained consciousness.

In the meantime they dropped Abruzzese off at the USO. The accused, unable to find the female's home and becoming more concerned about her condition, stopped at a service station seeking help. The attendant called the police who, upon arriving at the service station, examined the girl and determined she was dead. An ambulance was called and she was taken to a hospital for further examination. An autopsy, later performed, revealed that she apparently died of "acute interstitial myocarditis." In general terms this is a weakening of the heart muscles with edema and inflammation which occurs more in young people without its presence being suspected. It was the general undisputed opinion that her death probably occurred at the time she collapsed on the dance floor at Taylor's Place or very shortly thereafter. Apparently, in deaths of this type, rigor mortis does not usually begin for some time and as a result the accused were unaware of the fact she was dead.

The chief witness for the prosecution was the co-actor Abruzzese who, as we have noted, had been granted immunity. He implicated himself and both accused in his testimony. A written statement by McClellan concerning the alleged offenses was introduced through an agent of the Office of Naval Intelligence, a witness for the prosecution. The accused Thomas discussed the alleged incident with this same Office of Naval Intelligence agent, but no statement by Thomas was introduced into evidence. Numerous other witnesses testified, including medical experts, and the record of trial and exhibits in this case are voluminous. However, as the board of review stated, no factual dispute exists as to the death of the female involved and the cause thereof. It is clear, as that appellate body concluded, the victim was dead at the time she was removed from the tavern or relatively shortly thereafter, and the prosecution adduced no convincing evidence that she was alive at the time the offenses were committed. Indeed, on the merits trial counsel argued there could be no question but that the accused were guilty of attempted rape, "because the evidence shows that they would be guilty of rape if it wasn't for the fact that the government failed in its proof, perhaps, that she was alive at the time of the intercourse." Neither -- at least as we need be concerned, since we deal here only with convictions for conspiracy and attempt, and not with the substantive offense of rape itself -- can there be any real controversy regarding the acts done by Abruzzese and the two accused.

Despite the fact that defense counsel at trial vigorously urged to the law officer that the offenses of attempt and conspiracy could not be found validly if the victim's death occurred prior to the commission of the alleged acts, the law officer ruled otherwise. He instructed the court that to find the accused guilty of rape, or of assault, assault and battery, assault with intent to commit rape, or indecent assault as lesser included offenses thereto, it must be shown beyond a reasonable doubt that the victim was alive at the time of the alleged acts. Otherwise, he admonished the court members, the accused must be acquitted of those offenses. The law officer then continued, and instructed the court on the elements of attempt as an included lesser crime to rape. However, unlike the instructions given as to rape and the other lesser offenses previously mentioned, the law officer did not instruct that being alive was essential to a finding of attempt. That clearly drawn distinction is illuminated by the following colloquy which subsequently ensued between a member of the court and the law officer:

> Cdr. Carpenter: I don't remember you pointing this out in your instructions -- you said the woman must be alive if raped but you didn't say whether she had to be alive for attempted rape, although I think you implied it.

> LO: Yes, sir. There is no requirement under the instructions which I have given you that there be a finding she be alive before the accused may be convicted of attempted rape. However, before you can make a finding of guilty of rape or the other lesser included offenses, not including attempted rape, you must so find as a matter of fact that she was alive at that time.

Likewise, the court-martial was not required to find that the alleged victim was alive in order to find the accused guilty of conspiracy.

Before the board of review, appellate defense counsel contended that the law officer erred in his instructions to the court on the attempt and conspiracy offenses. In support of that position, the defense argued that where circumstances beyond the accused's control make it legally impossible to commit a crime, as distinguished from factual impossibility to do so, there can be no attempt nor can there be a conspiracy to commit the substantive offense.

In substance, then, the question thus presented to the board of review was, whether the law officer was correct in his instructions to the court-martial that a finding the victim was alive was not essential to a conviction for attempt as a lesser included offense of rape. As noted above, the law officer had replied to the question of a court member that there was no requirement under the instructions given that there be a finding that she be alive before the accused could be convicted of attempted rape.

The board faced up squarely to the issue, stating:

> Factually, the evidence adduced clearly indicates an attempt made by the accused to effect sexual relations with the victim without her consent. Whether the act was ever consummated is a matter of conjecture. However, the question the board must resolve goes to the legal possibility of such offense as attempt to rape being committed upon a woman, whom the evidence strongly and clearly indicates, was not alive at the time of the attempt.

The board of review held that an attempt to commit a crime must be directed to an object on which it is possible to commit the crime. Reasoning that a corpse is not a person, the board of review determined that the law officer erred in his instruction that there was no requirement that the victim be alive before the accused could be convicted of attempted rape. Thus, the board stated, "If the consummation was not an offense, the attempt herein was not an offense," and concluded, "Legally under the facts and law before us the offense of rape and the lesser included offenses including attempts were impossible of commission." Similarly, it was found that the accused could not be found guilty of conspiring to do that which if effected or consummated would not be an offense. Accordingly, the board of review set aside both accused's convictions for attempt to commit rape and for conspiracy to commit rape.

It is this action of the board which gives rise to the certified questions.

The rules of law applying to attempts and those applying to conspiracies are very closely related. Our principal discussion shall be confined to attempts. However, we shall, in essence, treat of the two certified issues together. * * *

In all candor we must confess that we claim no particular expertise as to the question of attempts as they have troubled our brothers on the bench of tribunals in the civilian community. We profess no mastery of the subject and do not purport to be more competent than other judges to resolve the conflicts in the civilian authorities which trouble them. However, as shall later be developed, we do not consider it necessary to evaluate the civilian decisions ourselves, nor to take a stand with or opposed to any one or group thereof. Nevertheless, as a backdrop against which to consider the problem, we deem it appropriate to explore the intricacies of the civilian holdings in the area.

As might be anticipated, a subject so intriguing has frequently received the attention of legal scholars as reflected by numerous articles and papers appearing in law school publications. Among others we have read the following with interest and profit: [citations omitted].

Text writers have covered the subject extensively, and we refer the interested reader to the following: [citations omitted].

In practically all of the foregoing articles and texts, the specific question involved in this case -- impossibility of completion of the substantive crime -- is discussed at very considerable length. The two reasons for "impossibility" are treated in this connection: (1) If the intended act is not criminal, there can be no criminal liability for an attempt to commit the act. This is sometimes described as a "legal impossibility." (2) If the intended substantive crime is impossible of accomplishment because of some physical impossibility unknown to the accused, the elements of a criminal attempt are present. This is sometimes described as "impossibility in fact."

The authorities seem to be in fair accord that (1), above, is not punishable as an attempt. There is some considerable conflict of authority as to whether (2), above, is punishable as an attempt, but the preponderance seems to be that such instances do constitute attempts. What is abundantly clear, however, is that it is most difficult to classify any particular state of facts as positively coming within one of these categories to the exclusion of the other.

Practically all writers on this subject, whether in law journal articles, texts, or judicial opinions, cite and discuss the same relatively limited number of decisions. These decisions are generally placed in the two following categories:

> 1. "Legal impossibility" in which attempt convictions have been set aside on the ground that it was legally impossible for the accused to have committed the crime contemplated. These are as follows:

> (a) A person accepting goods which he believed to have been stolen, but which were not then "stolen" goods, was not guilty of an attempt to receive stolen goods.

> (b) An accused who offered a bribe to a person believed to be a juror, but who was not a juror, could not be said to have attempted to bribe a juror.

(c) An official who contracted a debt which was unauthorized and a nullity, but which he believed to be valid, could not be convicted of an attempt to illegally contract a valid debt.

(d) A hunter who shot a stuffed deer believing it to be alive had not attempted to take a deer out of season.

(e) It is not an attempt to commit subornation of perjury where the false testimony solicited, if given, would have been immaterial to the case at hand and hence not perjurious.

2. Instances in which a claim of impossibility has been rejected and convictions sustained, are included below. Apparently these can all be classified as "impossibility in fact." These decisions are:

(a) It is now uniformly held that one is guilty if he attempts to steal from an empty pocket. The same is true as to an empty receptacle, and an empty house. The rule is applied whether the attempt is to commit burglary, robbery, extortion, or obtaining by false pretenses.

(b) One can attempt to possess narcotics, even though accused obtained possession of talcum believing it to be narcotics. And, one can be convicted of attempted use of a narcotic drug even though there is a reasonable doubt as to whether the substance was a narcotic.

(c) An accused may be guilty of attempted murder who, suspecting that a policeman on the roof was spying upon him through a hole, but ignorant that the policeman was then upon another part of the roof, fired at the hole with intent to kill. It is attempted murder to shoot into the intended victim's bed believing he is there asleep when in fact he is some place else. An accused is not absolved from the charge of attempted murder when he points an unloaded gun at his wife's head and pulls the trigger, if he actually thought at the time that it was loaded.

(d) In attempted abortion cases an accused may be guilty in the absence of proof that the woman was pregnant. Where the statute refers to "any woman," it is immaterial whether she was pregnant or not if the defendant believed she was.

*   *   *

The lack of logic between some of the holdings, the inherent difficulty in assigning a given set of facts to a proper classification; the criticism of existing positions in this area; and, most importantly, the denial of true and substantial justice by these artificial holdings have led, quite naturally, to proposals for reform in the civilian legal concepts of criminal attempts.

In addition to a progressive and modern view now evident in some judicial decisions and writings, The American Law Institute in its proposal of a "Model Penal Code" defines Criminal Attempts, in Article 5.01, as follows:

> (1) Definition of attempt. A person is guilty of an attempt to commit a crime if, acting with the kind of culpability otherwise required for commission of the crime, he:
>
> (a) purposely engages in conduct which would constitute the crime if the attendant circumstances were as he believes them to be; or
>
> (b) when causing a particular result is an element of the crime, does or omits to do anything with the purpose of causing or with the belief that it will cause such result, without further conduct on his part; or
>
> (c) purposely does or omits to do anything which, under the circumstances as he believes them to be, is a substantial step in a course of conduct planned to culminate in his commission of the crime."

The import of that suggested statute is made clear in Tentative Draft No. 10 of the Model Penal Code of The American Law Institute, supra, at page 25, where it is stated:

> ... It should suffice, therefore, to indicate at this stage what we deem to be the major results of the draft. They are:
>
> (a) to extend the criminality of attempts by sweeping aside the defense of impossibility (including the distinction between so-called factual and legal impossibility) and by drawing the line between attempt and non-criminal preparation further away from the final act; the crime becomes essentially one of criminal purpose implemented by an overt act strongly corroborative of such purpose; ...

After having given this entire question a great deal more than casual attention and study, we are forced to the conclusion that the law of attempts in military jurisprudence has tended toward the advanced and modern position, which position will be achieved for civilian jurisprudence if The American Law Institute is completely successful in its advocacy of this portion of the Model Penal Code.

Because of the legal acumen of the law officer of this general court-martial, the trial was conducted in accordance with this approach. We conclude that his instructions to the court-martial with reference to the offense of rape, the lesser included offenses thereto, including attempt to rape, and conspiracy, furnished correct advice on impossibility insofar as the same is affected by the death of the victim. * * *

We hold, therefore, in accordance with the foregoing authorities, that in this instance the fact that the female, upon whom these detestable acts were performed, was already dead at the time of their commission, is no bar to conviction for attempted rape. * * *

For the above stated reasons, we hold that the law officer did not err in the instructions given to the court-martial in connection with attempted rape and conspiracy to commit rape.

It is clear from this record, by the findings of the court-martial and the facts as sustained by the board of review, that each of these appellants was guilty of each element necessary to the crime of attempted rape. That is, each of the appellants did:

1. A certain overt act.

2. The act was done with the specific intent to commit the offense of rape; that is, each intended to have sexual intercouse with a female not his wife by force and without her consent.

3. The act amounted to more than mere preparation.

4. It apparently tended to effect the commission of the intended offense, even though

5. The intended offense failed of completion because, unknown to either appellant and as a matter beyond their control, their victim was already dead.

Likewise, all of the necessary elements of conspiracy to commit the offense of rape are present. That is:

1. Each of these accused and their co-actor Abruzzese mutually entered into an agreement to commit rape on the female alleged.

2. Thereafter, while the agreement continued in existence and while each of appellants remained a party thereto, each performed an overt act to effect the object of the agreement.

All the elements of both attempted rape and conspiracy to commit rape are present and were returned by the members of the court-martial under correct standards set out in the law officer's instructions. The board of review, therefore, erred in holding to the contrary.

The certified issues are answered in the negative, and the decision of the board of review is reversed. This case is returned to The Judge Advocate General of the Navy for action not inconsistent with this opinion.

[The opinion of FERGUSON, Judge, concurring in part and dissenting in part, has been omitted.]

Chapter 12

ACCOMPLICE LIABILITY (COMPLICITY)

INTRODUCTION

One who intentionally assists another in the commission of a crime can be convicted of that offense as an accomplice. At common law, the different parties involved were divided into principals and accessories. These distinctions were extremely important at common law. For example, at common law, the charging document had to state correctly whether the defendant was a principal or an accessory. If the indictment said the defendant was a principal and it turned out that the defendant was only an accessory, the indictment would be dismissed. These distinctions were also important in terms of timing. An accessory could not be tried before the principal in the first degree, and an accessory could not be convicted unless the principal in the first degree was convicted first. Additionally, while principals would be prosecuted in the jurisdiction in which the crime was perpetrated, an accessory could only be prosecuted in the jurisdiction in which his acts of assistance occurred. Although these common law rules have largely been abandoned, many courts still use the terminology of principal in the first degree, principal in the second degree, accessory before the fact, and accessory after the fact.

The "principal in the first degree" was the person who actually committed the acts constituting the offense or used an "innocent instrumentality" to commit the crime. The innocent instrumentality could be either a non-culpable person, such as a mentally incompetent person, or a non-human agent, such as a trained animal.

The "principal in the second degree" was the person who intentionally assisted the commission of the crime *in the presence of* the principal in the first degree. The "in the presence of" requirement could be satisfied by actual or constructive presence. For example, an accomplice just outside a bank watching for police officers is constructively present at the scene of a bank robbery even though he is not inside the bank (not actually present) during the robbery.

An "accessory before the fact" was a person who intentionally assisted in the commission of the crime, but who was not present when the crime was being committed. For example, the person who buys the guns used to rob the bank but who does not accompany the others to the bank is an accessory before the fact.

An "accessory after the fact" was a person who helped the principal in the first degree and his or her accomplices avoid arrest, trial or conviction.

An accomplice must intentionally assist the principal in the first degree in committing a crime. Some kind of assistance is required. Mere presence generally is not sufficient for accomplice liability. In *Pace v. State* and *State v. Parker*, however, we see the courts trying to decide whether and when presence can be sufficient to constitute the assistance required for accomplice liability. In *Wilson v. People*, the court deals with the question whether a "feigning accomplice" who intentionally assists another in the commission of a crime can be held liable as an accomplice to that crime. In *Brewer v. State*, the court decides whether a man who allows an intoxicated friend to drive may be held responsible for the criminal acts of his friend.

PACE v. STATE
Supreme Court of Indiana
248 Ind. 146, 224 N.E.2d 312 (1967)

HUNTER, Judge

This is an appeal from a jury finding and judgment of conviction of the defendant for the crime of accessory before the fact of robbery by placing in fear.

The defendant was charged by an affidavit filed in the St. Joseph Superior Court No. 2, May 26, 1964, with the crime of Accessory Before the Fact to Robbery by Putting in Fear, to-wit:

Arthur Madaras, being first duly sworn upon his oath, deposes and says:

That on or about the 23rd day of May, 1964, at and in the County of St. Joseph, State of Indiana, one William Eugene Rootes did then and there unlawfully, feloniously and forcibly and by putting Richard Leon Reppert in fear, rob, take and steal from the said Richard Leon Reppert Two ($ 2.00) Dollars in good and lawful currency of the United States of America, belonging to the said Richard Leon Reppert, and one Benrus wrist watch with gold band valued in the sum of Fifty ($ 50.00)

Dollars belonging to the said Richard Leon Reppert, and the said Carl Lemual Pace, Jr., at and in the County and State aforesaid, did then and there unlawfully and feloniously aid and abet, counsel and encourage the said William Eugene Rootes to do and commit the said felony in the manner and form aforesaid, contrary to the form of Statutes in such cases made and provided and against the peace and dignity of the State of Indiana.

The appellant waived arraignment and entered a plea of not guilty and was represented by court appointed public defender. Trial was to a jury. At the close of State's evidence, defendant filed [a] written motion for directed verdict which was overruled. The jury rendered its verdict against the defendant and found him guilty as charged.

Thereafter on April 6, 1964 the court sentenced the defendant to the Indiana Reformatory for a period of not less than ten (10) or more than twenty-five (25) years. On April 23, 1965 a motion for new trial was filed which was overruled by the trial court. In the assignment of errors, the principal point urged is that the verdict of the jury is not sustained by sufficient evidence and the verdict of the jury is contrary to law. We are of the opinion that the principal ground for reversal presented by the assignment of errors which questions the sufficiency of the evidence to sustain the jury's finding of guilty is determinative of this case.

Viewing the evidence most favorable to the State, the record shows the following: appellant, his wife and two infant children were in a car driving from South Bend to LaPorte. Eugene Rootes was riding with them. The appellant was driving with his wife and one child in the front seat. Rootes and appellant's other child were in the back seat. While in South Bend, appellant after asking his wife for permission stopped to pick up a hitchhiker, Mr. Reppert, who sat next to Rootes in the back seat with one of appellant's infant children. Later Rootes pulled a knife and took Reppert's wallet. After driving further, Reppert got out of the car, Rootes then took his watch. The appellant said nothing during the entire period and they continued driving to LaPorte. This is all of the evidence presented by the record which would have any bearing on the crime charged, i.e., accessory before the fact of robbery by placing in fear.

The main question presented in the facts at bar is what evidence beyond the mere presence of a person at the scene of a crime is sufficient to sustain a connection as an accessory before the fact? This court has previously stated that negative acquiescence is not enough to constitute a person guilty of aiding and abetting the commission of a crime. Consequently, this court has always looked for affirmative conduct either in the form of acts or words from which reasonable inferences of a common design or purpose to effect the commission of a crime might be drawn. However, it has been further stated by this court in *Mobley v. State*:

> . . . in the absence of anything in his conduct showing a design to encourage, incite, aid, abet or assist in the crime, the trier of the facts may consider failure of such person to oppose the commission of the crime in connection with other circumstances and conclude therefrom that he assented to the commission of the crime, lent his countenance and approval thereto and thereby aided and abetted it . . .

It should be noted that the court in *Mobley*, in stating that a failure to oppose the commission of a crime may be considered as aiding and abetting, impliedly qualified this statement wherein the Court stated at p. 343:

> This, it seems to us, is particularly true when the person who fails to interfere owes a duty to protect as a parent owes to a child.

In other cases relying on *Mobley*, there has normally been some course of conduct of an affirmative nature to connect the defendant with the crime.

In the facts at bar we have found no evidence or reasonable inferences therefrom which might demonstrate that the appellant aided and abetted in the alleged crime. While he was driving the car, nothing was said nor did he act in any manner to indicate his approval or countenance of the robbery. While there is evidence from which a jury might reasonably infer that he knew the crime was being committed, his situation was not one which would demonstrate a duty to oppose it. We do not intend to draw any hard and fast rules in this area of the law. Each case must be reviewed on its own facts; in so doing we hold that the verdict is not sustained by substantial evidence of probative value and is therefore contrary to law.

We hold that the appellant's (defendant's) motion for a directed verdict should have been sustained by the trial court. Now, therefore, the judgment of the trial court should be reversed.

Judgment reversed.

STATE v. PARKER

Supreme Court of Minnesota

282 Minn. 343, 164 N.W.2d 633 (1969)

NELSON, Justice

Defendant, John William Parker, appeals to this court from a judgment of conviction of aggravated robbery. On January 10, 1967, he was sentenced to the Youth Conservation Commission for an indeterminate term or until thence discharged by due course of law or by competent authority.

The victim, Larry Leventhal, was a 25-year-old senior at the University of Minnesota Law School who spent the summer of 1966 working on a research project at the University and did further research at the Legal Aid Center in downtown Minneapolis. He testified that [the defendant, John William Parker, Calvin Earl Sam, and Paul Peter Roy beat him up and robbed him of his wallet which contained $30 to $35, his watch, and his car.] * * *

Detective Michael Hlady of the Minneapolis Police Department interviewed defendant on August 8, 1966. After a full Miranda warning, defendant stated he understood his rights and consented to discuss the case. Detective Hlady informed defendant that they were investigating an assault and robbery that had occurred August 6, 1966, and that defendant was suspected of being involved with two other men. Defendant said that he had been picked up by Larry and Sam, "then they drove around some more, and they spotted another party, and they picked him up," and the four of them drove up to the Franklin Avenue area. Defendant stated that the four of them stopped at the scene of a homicide and "looked about."

[According to Detective Hlady], "* * * And then they got back in the car. And then they drove on a little further. And the driver at that time was Larry Leventhal. And they stopped. And when they made this last stop he [defendant] told me that Calvin Sam took and dragged Larry Leventhal in the back of the car and handed him the keys. And [defendant] John Parker said he drove the car for several blocks, and Calvin Sam said he wanted to drive. So Calvin Sam took over the wheel, and [defendant] John Parker rode on the passenger side of the car in the front. And they drove out to Columbia Heights. And he said while they were driving out there this third party in the back seat with the victim was administering a beating to him [victim Larry Leventhal]. He said it sounded awful. And when they got out to Columbia Heights he said Larry was just a bloody mess. And during this assault on the victim he was told -- John [the defendant] told me that the victim never lost consciousness. And when he stopped in Columbia Heights, that Larry leaped through the window and fled. And they returned to the Franklin area in Minneapolis, and shortly thereafter they were picked up by the police."

Defendant, however, denied that he took any part in the assault or that he had taken any of Larry's property.

Defendant took the stand in his own behalf. His testimony is, in the main, in conflict with the testimony produced by the state as to how he happened to meet the victim and as to how defendant and his two cohorts, one of whom he claimed to have seen only once before, got together. He testified that he was talking to his cousin, Jean Lagard, in front of the Sparkle Cafe on Franklin Avenue when Larry and Sam came there. Sam introduced Larry to defendant and Jean. Larry and Sam asked them if they wanted to go to a party. Jean declined, but defendant reluctantly agreed to go. He got into the back seat of Larry's car and they went to Seven Corners, where Sam got some beer and liquor. They returned to the Sparkle Cafe and near there met "another Indian guy." Defendant said the stranger asked to go along, Larry agreed, and defendant and "the other guy, we got in the back seat. Sam and Leventhal [Larry] was in the front. Leventhal was driving." The foursome "started riding around just looking for, you know, girls, Jean Lagard or somebody, and a party." The "unknown Indian" claimed he, too, wanted to pick up some beer and "we went to his house and got them [two six-packs], too." A little later, defendant stated, Larry and the "unknown Indian" started fighting in the back seat; "[t]he other guy was hitting Leventhal"; "[i]t just kept going on, and he kept beating him." * * *

Defendant said that they kept on driving and reached Columbia Heights, where Larry then told them to stop the car. Defendant claimed that they drove to the end of a dead-end street and Sam turned the car around and stopped; that Sam, defendant, and the other Indian got out of the car; and that thereupon Larry crawled out of the door and started running while the three Indians "all just stood there and looked." Then the three of them got back into the car. He said Sam drove back to the Franklin Avenue area and they let the "unknown Indian" off on their way; that they went to the Band Box and found Roy there; and that they were about to give him a ride home when the squad car appeared and the officers pursued and arrested them.

Defendant conceded in his testimony that Larry, when he left the car, was full of blood and that he was "beat up." Defendant, however, denied that he assisted in the beating and said that he had told Sam to "knock it off." He said that he "knew the guy [Larry] had run to the cops -- run to the police and say he had been beaten anyway. I didn't think he would say he had been robbed."

After the trial the jury returned for instructions, asking clarification on the point of "aiding and abetting." The foreman explained:

> * * * There is a little confusion as to how far -- how much a person has to do to say that he is aiding, even at the point of can a person aid by inaction, by not leaving, if it's quite apparent to him that there is trouble * * *. Can he aid by his, say, just by his inaction at that point * * *.

The court then said:

> The Court can do nothing but read you the law on aiding and abetting. Is that the only point that is troubling you? * * *

> * * * The Court then, with the permission of counsel, will reread to the jury that portion of the instructions covering aiding and abetting. And after the Court has done so, that is as far as the Court can go in assisting you with your deliberations.

> * * * 609.05 of the Statutes reads as follows: "A person is criminally liable for a crime committed by another if he intentionally aids, advises, hires, counsels, or conspires with or otherwise procures the other to commit the crime. The guilt of a defendant may be established without proof that the accused personally did every act constituting the offense charged. Whoever commits an offense or wilfully aids, abets, counsels, commands, induces or procures its commission is punishable as a principal. Whoever wilfully causes an act to be done which if directly performed by him or another would be an offense is punishable as a principal. Every person who thus wilfully participates in the commission of a crime may be found to be guilty of that offense. Participation is wilful if done voluntarily and purposely and with specific intent to do some act the law forbids or with specific intent to fail to do some act the law requires to be done. That is to say, with evil motive or bad purpose either to disobey or disregard the law.

> You may now resume your deliberations, ladies and gentlemen.

Mr. Nicklaus, counsel for defendant, then stated: "* * * Your Honor, in the light of what has happened here, could I see you with Mr. Winick [counsel for the state] in chambers? * * *"

In the court's chambers Mr. Nicklaus stated:

* * * May the record show that following the instructions, counsel and the Court adjourned to chambers and at this time I am asking the Court for an additional instruction to the effect and somewhat in these words, that on the other hand that if they find that the defendant did not aid, abet, counsel -- and here the words of the Statute can be used -- then there is no moral obligation on the part of the defendant to come to the aid of any party who has been the victim of a crime after the crime has been committed, and the accused did not participate in that crime directly, as instructed by the Court, or by participating in the manner of aiding, abetting, procuring, counseling, et cetera.

Mr. Winick: "State would oppose the motion and feels that the instruction speaks in the negative as well as the positive since it says you have to find this. * * *"

The Court: "Motion will be denied."

Defendant now contends that the foreman's question shows that the jury rejected Larry's testimony that defendant directly participated in the assault and robbery. He contends that the trial court in effect instructed the jury that defendant might in fact have owed a legal obligation to render aid to the victim. Defendant contends that he did not have such an obligation and that the failure to discharge a moral obligation to aid Larry is not enough to convict defendant of the crime charged.

1. We think it clear that the foreman's remarks fail to prove rejection by the jury of the victim's testimony about defendant's participation in the assault and robbery. The verdict indicates that the jurors resolved whatever questions they initially had. However, the question whether a person can aid by inaction may well be answered in the affirmative since inaction is often the distinguishing characteristic of the aider and abettor and is encompassed within the statute. In this regard the "lookout" is a classic example. The presence of one at the commission of a felony by another is evidence to be considered in determining whether or not he was guilty of aiding or abetting, and it has been held that presence, companionship, and conduct before and after the offense are circumstances from which one's participation in the criminal intent may be inferred.

In the instant case defendant was present during the criminal activity. He did nothing to prevent the offenses committed or the brutal beating which the victim endured. He must have known of the robbery and made no effort to stop it, and we think, under the circumstances, his presence and acts helped to make all the crimes possible. Therefore, his lack of objection under the circumstances supports his conviction.

2. It has been established that a person may aid or abet without actively participating in the overt act. If the proof shows that a person is present at the commission of a crime without disapproving or opposing it, it is competent for the jury to consider this conduct in connection with other circumstances and thereby reach the conclusion that he assented to the commission of the crime, lent to it his approval, and was thereby aiding and abetting its commission. Certainly mere presence on the part of each would be enough if it is intended to and does aid the primary actors. * * *

3. Evidence of subsequent acts is competent to prove participation in the criminal acts charged. The testimony of defendant and other witnesses appearing in his behalf was definitely weakened by the circumstances of the flight of the defendant and his accomplices which took place when police authority appeared.

We conclude that defendant's close association with the other men who appeared in the stolen car in front of the Band Box on the early morning of August 6, 1966, both before and after the crimes charged were committed, and the fact that the three of them were apprehended fleeing from the convertible stolen from the victim, all tend reasonably to justify the conclusion that defendant joined with the other two cohorts in the common purpose of assaulting the victim, robbing him, and stealing his automobile.

Affirmed.

WILSON v. PEOPLE
Supreme Court of Colorado, en banc.
103 Colo. 441, 87 P.2d 5 (1939)

MR. JUSTICE BOCK delivered the opinion of the court.

PLAINTIFF in error was charged and convicted under two counts of having unlawfully and feloniously aided, abetted and assisted one Dwight J. Pierce in the commission of a burglary and larceny. One of his defenses was the absence of felonious intent on his part to commit the crimes in question, because he acted solely as a decoy to detect the commission of the crime and to report it to the proper officers, so that Pierce might be apprehended. Plaintiff in error will hereinafter be referred to as Wilson.

The facts, substantially, are as follows: On the night of February 19, 1938, Wilson, son of the deputy district attorney of the thirteenth judicial district, and employed by him for several months prior thereto, was in Johnson's Cafe in Sterling, Colorado. Some time after 10 o'clock p.m. Pierce entered. Pierce had been drinking and was looking for a place where he could purchase more liquor. Without previous arrangement, Pierce approached Wilson and prevailed upon him to make an effort to find such a place. The two left the cafe and went to the Commercial Hotel, where Pierce borrowed some money. Wilson left and came back to report to Pierce that no whiskey could be had, but he could get a pint of sloe gin. This was satisfactory to Pierce, and Wilson procured a bottle of the gin which he delivered to Pierce, and both returned to the Johnson Cafe, where they drank some of the liquor. During that time a wrist watch which Wilson had been wearing disappeared while he was in the company of Pierce. When Wilson missed his watch he immediately accused Pierce of taking it. He continued to make the accusation through the evening, and at one time threatened to fight Pierce because of the alleged theft. Pierce denied the theft. The argument about the wrist watch became so noisy that the participants were asked to leave the cafe. They then went to another cafe and Wilson bought Pierce a cup of coffee, and the argument concerning the watch was resumed until Pierce, as he testified, thought they would be thrown out there.

While drinking the liquor at the Johnson Cafe, Pierce first commenced to talk about jobs that he had done and specifically mentioned his burglary of the Wheat Growers Cafe. This talk came up in connection with the disappearance of Wilson's wrist watch. Finally they reached the Commercial Hotel, where Pierce was a janitor, and in the furnace room the conversation about burglaries continued between them. There also was some talk concerning tools, and Pierce procured a piece of paper and wrote down a list of tools that would be needed, not that night, but at some future time, and Wilson said that he could get them for him. The subject of the watch again came up in the furnace room, and Pierce again denied taking it. Wilson suggested that they go to his father's office, to which he had the keys, to start on the jobs, and they there conceived the idea of breaking into Hecker Brothers' Drugstore. Wilson did not first propose the burglarizing, the idea originating with Pierce, and after the latter had told Wilson that he had burglarized the Wheat Growers Cafe several days before. There is some conflict in the evidence as to who first suggested breaking into Hecker Brothers' Drugstore, but they proceeded to the building in which it was located, tried several doors, finally going outside, and effecting an entry through the front transom. After Wilson had boosted Pierce up so that he could break the glass in the transom, and after looking around to see if anyone had heard them, Wilson again lifted Pierce and the latter handed the broken glass to Wilson, who dropped it on the cement. Thereupon Wilson again lifted Pierce up so that he could crawl through the transom. Pierce then proceeded to the cash register. Immediately after Pierce was inside the store Wilson ran to his father's office and telephoned the police to come to Hecker Brothers' Drugstore. He then returned to where the entry had been effected, and a few moments before the police arrived, Pierce handed to Wilson, through the transom, two or three bottles of liquor which he placed on the cement. Pierce noticed after he entered the store that Wilson had disappeared. Immediately after arrival of the police Wilson told them that Pierce was inside, designating him as "that guy from the Commercial Hotel." The police officer asked him how he knew, and he replied, "I boosted him in." Pierce escaped through the back door and Wilson immediately volunteered to track him down, and did so by going to Pierce's room at the Commercial Hotel, where he identified Pierce as the burglar in the presence of the police authorities. Wilson told the police, shortly after the apprehension of Pierce, that his connection with the burglary was for the purpose of getting even with Pierce for taking his watch, and that that was the only way he hoped to recover it. He also stated later that evening that he wanted to apprehend Pierce and turn him over to the authorities -- he wanted to catch him in the act.

The record indicates that Wilson was sincere in his belief that Pierce had taken his watch. Moreover, there is evidence in the people's case that tends to support his defense that he acted only as a decoy to apprehend Pierce in the act of committing the crime. Wilson's testimony at the trial substantially supported his defense that he had no criminal intent to feloniously burglarize or steal.

Plaintiff in error classifies his assignments of error under two headings: 1. That the court erred in giving to the jury Instruction No. 10. 2. That the court erred in not sustaining the defendant's motion for a nonsuit at the conclusion of the people's testimony, and that it again erred in not directing a verdict of not guilty at the conclusion of all of the evidence.

Taking up first the second ground of error, we are of the opinion that the evidence was sufficient to warrant the trial court's submission of the case to the jury. The motions for nonsuit, and for a directed verdict of not guilty, were properly denied.

Instruction No. 10, to the giving of which defendant assigns error, reads as follows: "One may not participate in the commission of a felony and then obtain immunity from punishment on the ground that he was a mere detective or spy. One who attempts to detect the commission of crime in others must himself stop short of lending assistance, or participation in the commission of the crime."

Defendant contends that this instruction is erroneous because it left no question of fact for the determination of the jury on his defense of decoy and detection. Wilson did assist Pierce in entering the drugstore. This he never denied and immediately revealed to the police his part in the transaction when they arrived in response to his call. The instruction inferentially placed guilt upon Wilson, because he did not "stop short of lending assistance," but actually gave assistance.

We find the following language in 16 Corpus Juris at page 128, section 115: "For one to be guilty as principal in the second degree, it is essential that he share in the criminal intent of the principal in the first degree; the same criminal intent must exist in the minds of both." And on page 129: "One who participates in a felony as a feigned accomplice, in order to entrap the other, is not criminally liable, and he need not take an officer of the law into his confidence to avoid an imputation of criminal intent."

In *Price v. People* the Supreme Court of the state of Illinois had before it an issue similar to the one here presented. There Price, with two others, was convicted of the crime of burglary. It appears the defendant in that case accompanying two others went to Milroy's house for the purpose of robbing him. He, with the others, entered the house where the holdup was committed, carried a gun, which he displayed, but which was not loaded, and did assist to a far greater extent than did Wilson in the instant case. Because of an interruption, the crime of robbery was not carried to a successful conclusion. Price testified that on the previous day he had talked to a constable about the matter and to an ex-sheriff. The evidence whether or not he did so was conflicting. Price insisted that his object in accompanying the other two was to expose the contemplated crime and to bring the real perpetrators to justice. We quote from the language of the court: "Waiving all controverted questions, the undisputed facts, as appears from the foregoing, are, that the accused, on the day of the attempted robbery, went deliberately to a constable of the town in which he lived and told him all about the contemplated crime, giving the true names of the parties, and telling him when and where it was to take place, and the name of the intended victim; that the attempt was made at the very time and place, and by the parties, stated by him, and that on the following morning he, in like manner, went to a justice of the peace and told him all about what had been done, and furnished him with the true names of the parties implicated, by means of which, on the same day, they were brought to trial, and were subsequently convicted of the crime. That a sane person, really guilty of committing so grave a crime as the one imputed to the accused, would thus act, is so inconsistent with all human experience as not to warrant the conviction of any one under the circumstances shown." The judgment of conviction was reversed.

In the case of *State v. Bigley,* the defendant, who with others was charged with committing a burglary, made substantially the same defense as did Wilson in the instant case. The assistance rendered by Bigley was to a greater degree than by Wilson here. In reversing the conviction the Supreme Court of

Idaho uses the following language at page 640: "The defect in this reasoning is that Bigley can only be held responsible for his intent at the time the crime was committed, that is, the entering into the bank and taking of the money, and the only evidence in the record of his intent at that time was that while he desired the crime to be fully consummated by Coppinger and Lawley, his intention was not that he should be a participant therein with the intent of permanently depriving the bank of the money to be taken." * * *

Counsel for the people contend that the principle involved here has been set at rest by the opinion in *Connor v. People.* In that case we sustained the defense of entrapment and reversed the judgment of conviction. In the instant case we have the defense of detection and not entrapment, and any language relating to the defense of Connor is not applicable here.

In this connection we cite also Wharton's Criminal Law (12th ed.), volume 1, section 271, which reads in part as follows: "A detective entering apparently into a criminal conspiracy already formed for the purpose of exploding it is not an accessory before the fact. For it should be remembered that while detectives, when acting as decoys, may apparently provoke the crime, the essential element of *dolus,* or malicious determination to violate the law, is wanting in their case. And it is only the formal, and not the substantive, part of the crime that they provoke. They provoke, for instance, in larceny, the asportation of the goods, but not the ultimate loss by the owner. They may be actuated by the most unworthy of motives, but the *animus furandi* in larcency is not imputable to them; and it is in larcenous cases or cheats that they are chiefly employed."

It may be that the jury in the instant case placed more stress on the motives that actuated Wilson in his participation in the transaction than they did on the necessity of determining his felonious intent under the circumstances.

Reverting to Instruction No. 10, by judicial fiat this instruction makes any assistance in the perpetration of an offense criminal, whether felonious or not. The determination of whether the assistance by Wilson under the evidence in this case was given with felonious intent was solely the province of the jury, and this instruction erroneously invaded that province. There may be offenses and circumstances when any assistance rendered may make a participant guilty of a criminal offense; but here we are concerned only with the facts, circumstances and defenses in this case. Forfeiture of individual liberty through criminal procedure, by courts, must on our part meet all the demands of impartial justice. The giving of Instruction No. 10 constituted prejudicial error.

The judgment is reversed and the cause remanded for new trial.

MR. JUSTICE BAKKE and MR. JUSTICE BURKE not participating.

BREWER v. STATE
Court of Criminal Appeals of Texas
140 Tex. Crim. 9, 143 S.W.2d 599 (1940)

BEAUCHAMP, Judge.

The appellant was convicted of murder in the District Court of DeWitt County and his punishment assessed at five years in the penitentiary. The victim was a five months' old baby.

The indictment contains two counts, the first being a charge of murder with malice by causing an automobile to collide with another car on the public highway, resulting in the death of the baby. The second count alleges murder by operating an automobile upon the public highway while intoxicated and through accident and mistake, while so driving the car, killing a child. The charge of the court submitted both counts to the jury and the verdict returned is a general one.

A large number of witnesses testified in the case, detailing observations of transactions with and conduct by the appellant and his companion throughout a large portion of the day, during which time both parties were shown to have been intoxicated. The car which they were driving belonged to the appellant. He had placed the same in the hands of Leo Spears, his companion, who drove the car at all times while the appellant sat by his side on the front seat. Both were credited with conversations and participation in incidents of the day. They visited many way-side drinking and eating places, both in Yoakum and in Cuero. The only business which they transacted was that of leaving a check with one party for the payment of a debt owing to another. From all indications, the two men were engaging themselves voluntarily in association with each other for the purpose of "staging a drunk" in the appellant's 1937 Ford V-8 on the highways and at such places as they may choose to go, which were many. At several stations they were so drunk upon their arrival, or before leaving, that the proprietors refused to sell them further drinks. They were admonished to keep off the highways and to retire to some place so that they could sober up. This they refused to do and boasted that they could stay on the highway drunk and not be disturbed. This boast they made good until in the afternoon when the tragic event culminated in the death of an innocent baby and the injury to others, wrecking two automobiles and sending himself and his companion to the hospital, still too drunk to realize fully what had taken place.

Further details of the facts may not be essential to a proper disposition of the case except as they are hereinafter stated in connection with the issues discussed.

Both parties were indicted and the appellant was separately tried. * * * The appellant did not testify on the trial of the case in his own behalf but produced a long list of witnesses, prominent citizens of the county in which he lives, who testified to his good reputation up to that time. Further than that the defense is technical, reliance being had on the contention that appellant was not driving the car, that he was too intoxicated to have authorized his companion to drive it; and that without knowledge of the presence of the deceased on the highway, and under the other admitted facts there could be no malice; and that the court, therefore, committed an error of law in his charge to the jury on murder with malice. * * *

First, we will consider whether or not the appellant, under the circumstances of the case, may be held to be responsible for the acts of his companion in whose hands he had placed the automobile. The case of *Schorr v. State*, is relied upon. That case is an important one, but we do not believe it helpful to the appellant. Under Article 69 of the Penal Code, it is provided that a person who advises or agrees to the commission of an offense and who is present when the same is committed is a principal whether he aid or not in the illegal act. In the *Schorr* case, it was held that the appellant had not advised or agreed to the commission of the offense and that his presence when the offense was committed was not, under the facts of that case, sufficient to constitute him a principal offender. If the appellant has advised and agreed to all the acts and conduct of a companion whom he has placed in charge of his car and acts with him for hours, as in the instant case, in recklessly driving upon the streets and public highways in an intoxicated condition, where it may be known that the driver of the car is incapable of judicious control and the owner who places it in his hands continues with him and permits him to use it while in that condition, watches him make one reckless drive after another, as the record discloses in this case, crashing into other automobiles, a cattle-guard, into and across ditches, and repeatedly acts without judgment or discretion and without regard for the rights of others, it would seem that there would be no difficulty in concluding that he is responsible as a principal for whatever might result therefrom, provided it could have been reasonably anticipated as a result. This conclusion is not contrary to the *Schorr* case, supra, but is clearly indicated by the citation in that opinion of the case of *Story v. United States*, in which it is said: "If the owner of a dangerous instrumentality like an automobile knowingly puts that instrumentality in the immediate control of a careless and reckless driver, sits by his side, and permits him without protest so recklessly and negligently to operate the car as to cause the death of another, he is as much responsible as the man at the wheel."

We have held that an automobile is not a dangerous weapon per se, but when placed under the control of "alcohol at the wheel and gasoline in the tank" and driven upon the highway, the results are so uncertain that the owner agreeing thereto may be held responsible for the resulting death as though he himself had, with his own hands, guided the wheel. We think that the facts of the Story case justify us in applying the law as there laid down to the facts of the case at bar. The trial court properly held that the appellant was responsible as a matter of law under the facts before him.

The next question for our consideration is that raised by the objections to the court's charge on murder with malice. In *Cockrell v. State,* the drunken driver of a car recklessly and negligently ran into two small boys and killed them. He was given forty-five years. The question of malice was considered in an opinion by Judge Graves of this court, the opinion on motion for rehearing being by Judge Hawkins. It was there held that the facts of that case were sufficient to give the jury "some substantial ground upon which to base their belief that he was possessed of a heart regardless of social duty and fatally bent on mischief." The opinion further applies the law of malice to the facts of that case in a very logical and forceful discussion of the authorities, and the reasoning there may well be adopted for this case. For a further consideration of the subject, see authorities discussed in the *Cockrell* case.

By Bills of Exception Nos. 3 to 12, inclusive, appellant complains of the admission in evidence of testimony showing his conduct and drunken condition at several places during the day preceding the collision resulting in the death for which he is charged. There is no denial in the record of his drunken condition, and we think that this testimony is pertinent and proper to show malice. By this is not meant a mature intent to take a human life but it shows a continuous conduct, dangerous to others, so recklessly and wantonly as to manifest a depravity of mind and disregard for human life, supplying the constituent elements embraced in an accepted definition of malice. * * *

We find no error in the ruling of the court or in his charge.

The judgment of the trial court is affirmed.

Chapter 13

CONSPIRACY

INTRODUCTION

In Chapter 12 we examined the law of complicity, which provides rules for holding more than one person responsible for a given crime. This chapter considers a different but related question: criminal behavior that is the product of collective action.

One response to such criminal behavior is the law of conspiracy. The common law tradition understands collective criminality to pose special dangers, and conspiracy thus makes an agreement to commit a crime itself criminal. The idea of conspiracy liability, however, raises a number of new questions. What distinguishes a conspiracy from simple complicity? Who counts as a member of a conspiracy, and who is responsible for substantive crimes committed pursuant to a larger conspiracy? When does a conspiracy begin and end? Can a person withdraw from a conspiracy? What is the relationship between punishment for the conspiracy and punishment for the criminal conduct that is the object of the conspiracy?

The traditional common law definition of conspiracy is an agreement by two or more persons to commit either one or more criminal acts, or one or more acts that are non-criminal but are "corrupt, dishonest, fraudulent, immoral, and in that sense illegal." *See State v. Burnham*, 15 N.H. 396 (1844). Like attempt, conspiracy is an "inchoate" crime: the defendant is not charged with conspiracy in the abstract, but conspiracy to do something. In contrast to the law of attempt, however, in conspiracy law there is no need to prove that the defendants ever came close to actually committing the target act: the agreement itself is a crime. Moreover, in jurisdictions that incorporate the common law, conspiracy does not "merge" into the target crime as attempt does. Rather, a defendant can be convicted both of the target crime and the conspiracy to commit that crime.

In jurisdictions that continue to follow the older common law, proof of an agreement completes the crime, and the jury may infer the existence of the agreement from circumstantial evidence. In other jurisdictions, however, proof of some "overt act" in furtherance of the conspiracy is required in order to demonstrate the existence of the conspiracy. This overt act need not be illegal or even central to accomplishing the ultimate goal of the conspiracy. A telephone call or meeting will satisfy the overt act requirement so long as done for the purpose of furthering the conspiracy.

Under English common law, conspiracy was a misdemeanor. In contemporary United States jurisdictions that have incorporated the common law, however, the rules vary. Some states continue to punish conspiracy as a misdemeanor. Other states calibrate the severity of a conspiracy conviction to the severity of the target crime. For example, a conspiracy to commit a felony is itself a felony in these jurisdictions, but conspiracy to commit a misdemeanor is only a misdemeanor. In yet other states, however, a conspiracy to commit certain misdemeanors constitutes a felony. *See, e.g., People v. Tatman*, 24 Cal.Rptr.2d 480 (Cal. Ct. App. 1993) (upholding felony conviction for conspiracy to unlawfully possess red abalone, a misdemeanor).

Conspiracy is a crime that is frequently charged by prosecutors, particularly under federal law. Indeed, Judge Learned Hand famously called conspiracy "the darling of the modern prosecutor's nursery." *Harrison v. United States*, 7 F.2d 259 (2d Cir. 1925). It is also the subject of continuing controversy. First, under the common law definition of a conspiracy, the scope of conduct that can be punished is potentially very broad. Many commentators have attacked, for example, the notion that a person could be convicted of conspiracy to commit a legal act merely because the act is immoral or dishonest. Contemporary conspiracy convictions typically involve illegal goals.

Second, there are significant procedural consequences of charging defendants with conspiracy that tend to benefit the prosecution. For example, the trial of a conspiracy case may be held in any locale where any overt act by any of the conspirators took place. *See* Wayne R. LaFave and Austin Scott, Jr., CRIMINAL LAW 528 (2d ed. 1986). Accused co-conspirators may be tried together, increasing the possibility that the jury will transfer suspicions of guilt from one defendant to another. *Id.* at 529. The law of evidence contains special accommodations for conspiracy cases, including exceptions to the rule against hearsay evidence. *Id.* at 528. Finally, given the subjective nature of an "agreement," judges are often liberal in permitting the admission of circumstantial evidence to prove guilt. *Id.* at 592.

Because of the broad scope of conspiracy law and the favorable procedural consequences for the government, many scholars have commented on -- and objected to -- the potential abuses of conspiracy law. Others, however, defend conspiracy law, pointing to the inherent difficulty of proving something as ephemeral as an "agreement," as well as the difficulty of investigating and proving very complex criminal behavior involving many actors. Most significantly, commentators who defend the law of conspiracy point to the special dangers of collective action. Is it the case that collective criminality poses special dangers? The essay by Neal Katyal, below, supports the traditional defense of conspiracy with contemporary social science evidence.

The Model Penal Code diverges from the common law approach to conspiracy in some important ways. Conceptually, the drafters of the Model Penal Code saw conspiracy as worthy of punishment for a different reason than the common law judges. To the Code drafters, conspiracy should be punished because a person who has entered into a conspiracy has demonstrated a firm commitment to criminal activity, and therefore poses a greater threat of actual social harm than a person who has not so agreed. As a consequence of this perspective, under the Model Penal Code the crime of conspiracy "merges" with the completed crime. The actor cannot be punished for both a conspiracy and the target crime. *See* Model Penal Code 1.07(1)(b). It also follows from this perspective on conspiracy that punishment for conspiracy under the Code is linked to the punishment for the target crime. *See* Model Penal Code 5.05(1).

The Model Penal Code departs from the common law approach to conspiracy in a few other ways, as well. Under section 5.03(1), a conspiracy must have a crime as its object, and in this way the Code is narrower than the common law approach. The Model Penal Code also expands criminal liability beyond the common law in some ways. For example, the Model Penal Code imposes criminal responsibility not only when the actor intends to promote or facilitate the commission of the target crime herself, but also when she intends only to aid others in its promotion or facilitation.

A.   THE AGREEMENT

STATE v. PACHECO
Supreme Court of Washington
882 P.2d 183 (1994)

JOHNSON, J.

The Defendant, Herbert Pacheco, appeals his convictions for conspiracy to commit first degree murder and conspiracy to deliver a controlled substance. He contends he did not commit conspiracy within the meaning of RCW 9A.28.040 because no genuine agreement existed between him and his sole coconspirator, an undercover police agent. We hold RCW 9A.28.040 and RCW 69.50.407 require an actual agreement between two coconspirators, and, therefore, reverse his convictions for conspiracy to commit murder in the first degree and conspiracy to deliver a controlled substance.

FACTS

Herbert Pacheco met Thomas Dillon in 1985, when Pacheco worked about 2 months for Dillon's private investigation firm. Pacheco bragged to Dillon about his involvement in illegal activities, including enforcement, collecting debts, procuring weapons, providing protection, and performing "hits."

In 1989, Dillon learned that Pacheco was a Clark County deputy sheriff. Dillon contacted the FBI and volunteered to inform on Pacheco. The FBI began an investigation of Pacheco. The Clark County Sheriff's office joined, and later directed the investigation.

The investigation involved the recording of conversations, face-to-face and over the telephone, between Dillon and Pacheco. During these conversations Dillon asked Pacheco to perform various jobs, including collections and information checks on individuals.

On March 26, 1990, according to a plan designed by the sheriff's office and the FBI, Dillon called Pacheco and told him he would like to meet to discuss a possible deal. Dillon and Pacheco met at a restaurant. Dillon said he had ties to the "Mafia" and offered Pacheco $500 in exchange for protection during a cocaine deal. Dillon told Pacheco that a buyer (an undercover FBI agent) would arrive shortly, and Pacheco was to protect Dillon during the transaction. Pacheco agreed. The undercover agent arrived and the purported drug transaction took place. Afterward, Dillon paid Pacheco $500.

The same scenario was replayed at a second purported drug transaction on April 2, 1990. Dillon again paid Pacheco $500. Later that night Dillon called Pacheco and pretended he had been shortchanged $40,000 in that afternoon's drug transaction. Dillon said he had been given $10,000 by his superiors to take care of the situation. Dillon agreed to meet Pacheco at a convenience store. At the store, Pacheco offered to kill the drug buyer for $10,000. Pacheco indicated if he had to kill anyone else, it would cost more. Pacheco proposed he go get his gun while Dillon located the drug buyer at his motel.

Dillon and Pacheco met at a lounge near the motel. They decided Pacheco would go to the lobby of the motel, call the buyer and convince him to come down to the lobby where Pacheco would then shoot him. Pacheco went to the lobby with a loaded gun, but he did not call the buyer's room. As Pacheco left the lobby, sheriff's deputies arrested him. Pacheco contended he was collecting evidence to build a case against Dillon and he thought he was following police procedures.

Pacheco was charged with conspiracy to commit first degree murder, attempted first degree murder, two counts of unlawful delivery of a controlled substance, two counts of conspiracy to deliver a controlled substance, and offidal misconduct. The offidal misconduct charge was dismissed. The jury found Pacheco not guilty of attempted first degree murder, but convicted him on all other counts.

The Court of Appeals affirmed the convictions. We accepted review of the conspiracy convictions, limited to the issue of whether a conspiracy exists when the sole coconspirator is an undercover agent.

ANALYSIS

The Defendant contends he did not commit conspiracy within the meaning of RCW 9A.28.040 because his sole coconspirator was an undercover police agent who never "agreed" to commit the crime of murder in the first degree.

The Defendant argues the statute retains the common law, bilateral approach to conspiracy, which requires an actual agreement to commit a crime between the defendant and at least one other. Therefore, a government agent feigning agreement with the defendant does not constitute a conspiracy under the common law approach because no genuine agreement is reached. The Defendant asserts Washington is among those states whose statutes are patterned after the Model Penal Code but have been interpreted as adopting only a limited form of the code's unilateral approach, and retaining the requirement of a bilateral underlying agreement.

The State contends RCW 9A.28.040 follows the code's purely unilateral approach. Under the code, actual agreement is not required as long as the defendant believes another is agreeing to commit the criminal act. Therefore, a purported agreement between a government agent and a defendant would satisfy the code's unilateral conspiratorial agreement approach.

Adopted in 1975, as a part of the overhaul of the criminal code, RCW 9A.28.040 provides in part:

> (1) A person is guilty of criminal conspiracy when, with intent that conduct constituting a crime be performed, he agrees with one or more persons to engage in or cause the performance of such conduct, and any one of them takes a substantial step in pursuance of such agreement.
>
> (2) It shall not be a defense to criminal conspiracy that the person or persons with whom the accused is alleged to have conspired:
>
> (a) Has not been prosecuted or convicted; or
>
> (b)Has been convicted of a different offense; or
>
> (c) Is not amenable to justice; or

(d) Has been acquitted; or

(e) Lacked the capacity to commit an offense.

In construing a statute, our primary objective is to carry out the intent of the Legislature. When a term is not defined in a statute, the court may look to common law or a dictionary for the definition. As a general rule, we presume the Legislature intended undefined words to mean what they did at common law.

Subsection (1) of RCW 9A.28.040 expressly requires an *agreement,* but does not define the term. Black's Law Dictionary defines *agreement as,* "[a] meeting of two or more minds; a coming together in opinion or determination; the coming together in accord of two minds on a given proposition." Similarly, *agreement* is defined in *Webster's* as "1a: the act of agreeing or coming to a mutual agreement . . . b: oneness of opinion . . . ." The dictionary definitions thus support the Defendant's argument.

Likewise, the common law definition of the agreement required for a conspiracy is defined not in unilateral terms but rather as a confederation or combination of minds. A conspiratorial agreement necessarily requires more than one to agree because it is impossible to conspire with oneself. We conclude that by requiring an agreement, the Legislature intended to retain the requirement of a genuine or bilateral agreement.

Subsection (2) provides the conspiratorial agreement may still be found even though the coconspirator cannot be convicted. In this sense, the statute incorporates a limited form of the code's unilateral conspiracy in that it is no longer necessary that agreement be proved against both conspirators. Thus, under subsection (2)'s unilateral approach, the failure to convict an accused's sole coconspirator will not prevent proof of the conspiratorial agreement against the accused. However, this does not indicate the Legislature intended to abandon the traditional requirement of two criminal participants reaching an underlying agreement.

Our case law supports this interpretation of RCW 9A.28.040. In *State v. Valladares,* two codefendants were charged with conspiracy to deliver cocaine. In a joint trial, one defendant was acquitted and the other, Valladares, was found guilty.

On appeal, the court held acquittal of Valladares' only alleged coconspirator mandated reversal of Valladares' conviction because the two outcomes were logically inconsistent. The inconsistent verdicts to the charge of conspiracy in the same trial nullified the possibility that the two coconspirators reached an agreement, a necessary element of the conspiracy. We said:

RCW 9A.28.040(2)(d) provides that it shall not be a defense to a charge of criminal conspiracy that the person with whom the accuse is alleged to have conspired has been acquitted. In this regard, the Washington Legislature appears to have adopted a unilateral approach to conspiracy by focusing on the culpability of the individual actor. At the same time, however, RCW 9A.28.040(1) makes *an agreement* with one or more persons a necessary element of the crime of conspiracy.

Valladares thus makes clear the Legislature adopted the unilateral approach to the limited extent set out in RCW 9A.28.040(2). However, the element of the "requisite corrupt agreement," or the bilateral agreement, is still necessary as set out in RCW 9A.28.040(1). Indeed, the essence of a conspiracy is the agreement to commit a crime. We will not presume the Legislature intended to overturn this long-established legal principle unless that intention is made very dear.

Additionally, the unilateral approach fails to carry out the primary purpose of the statute. The primary reason for making conspiracy a separate offense from the substantive crime is the increased danger to society posed by group criminal activity. However, the increased danger is nonexistent when a person "conspires" with a government agent who pretends agreement. In the feigned conspiracy there is no increased chance the criminal enterprise will succeed, no continuing criminal enterprise, no educating in criminal practices, and no greater difficulty of detection.

Indeed, it is questionable whether the unilateral conspiracy punishes criminal activity or merely criminal intentions. The "agreement" in a unilateral conspiracy is a legal fiction, a technical way of transforming nonconspiratorial conduct into a prohibited conspiracy. When one party merely pretends to agree, the other party, whatever he or she may believe about the pretender, is in fact not conspiring with anyone. Although the deluded party has the requisite criminal intent, there has been no criminal act.

The federal courts agree. In *Sears v. United States,* the Court of Appeals established the rule that "as it takes two to conspire, there can be no indictable conspiracy with a government informer who secretly intends to frustrate the conspiracy." Every federal court which has since considered the issue has adopted this approach.

Another concern with the unilateral approach is its potential for abuse. In a unilateral conspiracy, the State not only plays an active role in creating the offense, but also becomes the chief witness in proving the crime at trial. We agree with the Ninth Circuit this has the potential to put the State in the improper position of manufacturing crime. At the same time, such reaching is unnecessary because the punishable conduct in a unilateral conspiracy will almost always satisfy the elements of either solicitation or attempt. The State will still be able to thwart the activity and punish the defendant who attempts agreement with an undercover police officer.

* * * [T]he State has not persuaded us the Legislature intended to abandon the traditional requirement of an actual agreement. We hold RCW 9A.28.040 and RCW 69.50.407 require the defendant to reach a genuine agreement with at least one other coconspirator. The Defendant's convictions for conspiracy to commit murder in the first degree and conspiracy to deliver a controlled substance are reversed.

DURHAM, J. [dissenting]

The jury found that Herbert Pacheco, an aspiring hit man, planned a murder for money. Moreover, he took a substantial step toward that objective. Yet the majority overturns his conviction for conspiracy to commit murder solely because he conspired with a government agent rather than with another hit man. The Washington conspiracy statute does not require a co-conspirator to be a nongovernment actor. In fact, the statute explicitly envisages so-called unilateral conspiracies, as the majority admits. Because neither our case law, the statute, nor the rationale of conspiracy crimes compel the result arrived at by the majority, I dissent.

We accepted review solely to determine whether Washington's conspiracy statute countenances unilateral conspiracies. Yet the majority fails to provide even a cursory analysis of the essential differences between the bilateral and unilateral approaches to conspiracy. The bilateral approach asks whether there is an agreement between two or more persons to commit a criminal act. Its focus is on the content of the agreement and whether there is a shared understanding between the conspirators. The unilateral approach is not concerned with the content of the agreement or whether there is a meeting of minds. Its sole concern is whether the agreement, shared or not, objectively manifests the criminal intent of at least one of the conspirators. The majority does not even mention this crucial difference, and instead merely assumes that all conspiracies must be bilateral. In other words, the majority assumes precisely what it is supposed to prove; it begs the question.

The result is a tangle of inaccuracies. First, the majority repeatedly contends that our decision in *State v. Valladares,* either adopted or supports the bilateral theory of conspiracies. That is not true. In fact, *Valladares* explicitly reserved the question. * * *

Next, the majority portrays the unilateral approach to conspiracy as an outdated relic from a bygone era. The Model Penal Code endorses unilateral conspiracies, the majority admits, but "every federal court, which has since considered the issue" has adopted the bilateral approach. The majority neglects to mention that all the federal courts adopting bilateral conspiracy are construing a different statute, one whose language requires bilateral conspiracies. In contrast, the Model Penal Code defines conspiracy "in terms of one person's agreeing with another, rather than in terms of an agreement among or between two or more people."

The code embodies a significant change in emphasis. In its view, the major basis of conspiratorial liability is not the group nature of the activity but the firm purpose of an individual to commit a crime which is objectively manifested in conspiring. The Washington conspiracy statute tracks the Model Penal Code's language rather than the "two or more persons" language of the general federal conspiracy statute. In any event, far from being antiquated or obsolete, the "movement toward a unilateral theory of the crime is the modern trend in conspiracy law."

A comparison of the revised Washington conspiracy statute with its predecessor is far more revealing of legislative intent than the majority's simplistic and premature resort to dictionary definitions. The predecessor statute used the phrase "whenever two or more persons shall conspire", which parallels the federal conspiracy statute and clearly requires bilateral conspiracy. The revised statute, in contrast, tracks the definitional language of the Model Penal Code, which adopts unilateral conspiracy.

Under a unilateral formulation, the crime of conspiracy is committed when a person agrees to proceed in a prohibited manner; under a bilateral formulation, the crime of conspiracy is committed when two or more persons agree to proceed in such manner. * * * The contrast between the prior and the present statute is clear, precise, and determinative.

Next, the majority constructs a straw man by claiming that the primary purpose of conspiracy is "the increased danger to society posed by group criminal activity." Preventing group criminal activity is the rationale behind bilateral conspiracy, but that rationale was decisively rejected by the Model Penal Code. At best, controlling group criminal activity is only one rationale for conspiracy statutes.

> A bilateral theory of conspiracy and the rigid standard of mutuality that it demands . . . are inconsistent with the recognition of an independent rationale for conspiracy law based on a conspirator's firm expectation of committing a crime.

Broderick, 94 Yale L.J. at 906 n.64.

The majority compounds its own confusion by contending that unilateral conspiracies are factually impossible and therefore presumptively invalid. Majority at 9 ("When one party merely pretends to agree, the other party, whatever he or she may believe about the pretender, is in fact not conspiring with anyone."). This argument amounts to the truism that it is factually impossible to have a "meeting of minds" on the commission of a future crime if one of the minds is a government agent who does not intend to commit the criminal act. However, a "meeting of minds" is not a prerequisite of unilateral conspiracy. In any event, factual impossibility is not a recognized defense. The majority does nothing more than restate the discredited assumption that all conspiracies must be bilateral because conspiracy statutes attempt to target only group criminal activity.

Finally, I share the majority's concern about the potential for abuse of unilateral conspiracy. However, the majority fails to take into consideration the effect of the entrapment defense. The potential for abuse is further restricted by the statute itself, which requires not only an agreement to engage in criminal conduct but also "a substantial step in pursuance of such agreement." In the end, the majority succeeds only in providing a superfluous protection to criminal defendants at the price of hamstringing government attempt nip criminal acts in the bud.

B.   THE PINKERTON RULE

When two or more people agree with another to commit a crime, what is their responsibility for ancillary crimes committed that promote their agreement? Applying agency law to the offense of conspiracy, in 1946 the Supreme Court announced what has come to be known as the "Pinkerton rule" of vicarious liability. *Pinkerton v. United States*, 328 U.S. 640 (1946), involved two brothers, Daniel and Walter Pinkerton, who were indicted for bootlegging on ten substantive counts and one conspiracy count of Internal Revenue Code violations. Although there was no evidence to show that Daniel had participated directly in the commission of all the substantive offenses (since he was in prison during some of them), the Supreme Court upheld his conviction for those offenses anyway. The Court commented: "A different case would arise if the substantive offense committed by one of the conspirators was not in fact done in furtherance of the conspiracy, did not fall within the scope of the unlawful project, or was merely a part of the ramifications of the plan which could not be reasonably foreseen as a necessary or natural consequence of the unlawful agreement. But as we read this record, that is not this case." In dissent, Justice Rutledge objected that principles of vicarious liability taken from commercial law and tort law were inappropriate in the context of criminal responsibility.

The case that follows illustrate the outer limits of the *Pinkerton* rule as interpreted by one federal circuit.

UNITED STATES v. MOTHERSILL
U.S. Court of Appeals for the Eleventh Circuit
87 F.3d 1214 (1996)

JOHN H. MOORE, II, Senior District Judge:

On February 1, 1992, on a highway located in Jefferson County, Florida, Florida Highway Patrol Trooper James Fulford observed a car exceeding the speed limit and made a routine traffic stop. After making the usual inquiries, he discovered the car was a rental, and the driver was without a license; he arrested the driver of the vehicle for operating a vehicle without a license. After the driver consented, and while waiting for the car to be impounded, Trooper Fulford opened a gift-wrapped package found in the truck of the vehicle, purportedly containing a microwave oven. Unfortunately, there was a homemade pipe bomb inside the microwave oven, which was triggered to explode when the microwave was opened. Trooper Fulford died from the extensive injuries he received from the blast.

After law enforcement conducted a thorough investigation, the government indicted several individuals, ultimately filing a third superseding indictment on October 16, 1992, which included charges ranging from drug and RICO conspiracies to felony murder and the murder of a law enforcement officer. On March 9, 1993, after an eight-week criminal jury trial, Appellants were convicted of several counts.

Appellants Patrick and Paul Howell, Michael Morgan, Patricia Clarke, Norris Mothersill, Egnatius Johnson, and Errol Morrison were all found guilty of either Counts I or III, which alleged a conspiracy to commit racketeering pursuant to 18 U.S.C. § 1962(d) and conspiracy to traffic in controlled substances pursuant to 21 U.S.C. § 846, respectively. For purposes of the discussion below, it is noteworthy that Appellants Patrick and Paul Howell, Morgan, Clarke, Mothersill, and Johnson were all found guilty of Count XXVIII of the Third Superseding Indictment.[2] Count XXVIII dealt with Trooper

---

[2] Count XXVIII, in pertinent part, alleged Appellants:

did maliciously damage and destroy by means of fire and explosive materials property which was used in interstate or foreign commerce and in activities affecting interstate or foreign commerce, that is: a Sharpe microwave ... and a 1991 Mitsubishi Galant ... and as a direct and proximate result did cause the death of Florida Highway Patrol Trooper James Fulford, a public safety officer in the performance of his duties, in violation of Title 18, United States Code, Sections 844(I) and 2.

Fulford's death, and Appellants Morgan, Clarke, Johnson and Mothersill were found guilty under the co-conspirator liability theory outlined in *Pinkerton v. United States*, 328 U.S. 640 (1946). Defendant Paul Howell was convicted pursuant to the *Pinkerton* liability theory for his role in the creation of the bomb that led to Trooper Fulford's death. Patrick Howell was convicted under *Pinkerton* liability and for aiding and abetting the crime.[3]

After the district court sentenced Appellants to life or "life-plus" terms of imprisonment, Appellants appealed their convictions to this Court. * * * Appellants raise several issues, only one of which merits discussion, namely, the imposition of *Pinkerton* co-conspirator liability. The remaining issues are meritless and we affirm them without discussion. We affirm.

I. STANDARD OF REVIEW

The scope of our review is limited since the application of the *Pinkerton* doctrine to the facts of a case lies within the jury's domain. In determining whether the trial court was correct in submitting the *Pinkerton* issue to the jury, we must ascertain "whether the evidence was sufficient for a reasonable jury to have concluded, beyond a reasonable doubt, that the murder was a reasonably foreseeable consequence of the drug conspiracy alleged in the indictment." In making our determination, we view the evidence in the light most favorable to the government and accept all the jury's reasonable inferences and credibility choices which support the verdict.

II. DISCUSSION

a. Background Facts

Patrick Howell, Michael Morgan and Egnatius Johnson, among others, were the principal leaders of an elaborate drug operation, dating back to 1988, that supplied, distributed and sold crack cocaine throughout Florida, Alabama, Mississippi, Georgia, and North and South Carolina. Most of the leaders were Jamaican citizens residing in the Ft. Lauderdale, Florida area. Patrick's brother, Paul Howell, Johnson's former girlfriend and Morgan's sister, Patricia Clarke, Norris Mothersill and Errol Morrison were also major players in the sophisticated and expansive operation. For purposes of our discussion, the precise scope and history of the conspiracy need not be recited; however, certain

---

[3] "A defendant charged with conspiracy and the substantive offense 'normally will be responsible for the substantive crime under the *Pinkerton* theory and also may be responsible for the substantive crime under an aiding and abetting theory.'" *United States v. Meester*, 762 F.2d 867, 878 (11th Cir.1985) (quoting *United States v. Monaco*, 702 F.2d 860, 881 (11th Cir.1983)).

events and individuals, pertinent to the issue examined below, warrant mentioning.

Egnatius Johnson distributed and supplied a great deal of crack cocaine from a source located in the Bahamas, employing individuals to import the cocaine on cruise ships sailing to and from Florida. Appellant Clarke, along with her brother, had been trafficking drugs from South Florida to Marianna, Florida, Georgia and Alabama; they joined Johnson in his endeavors sometime in early 1992. Patrick Howell, introduced to the area by Michael Morgan, sold cocaine in the Marianna Garden Apartments in Marianna, Florida throughout the 1980s, and later expanded his business to Georgia and South Carolina. Mothersill, assisted by Morrison, started dealing drugs in Marianna during the late 1980s.

In August of 1991, Patrick Howell and Michael Morgan were plotting to rob a Ft. Lauderdale drug dealer named Alfonso Tillman. With Clarke and Johnson present, Howell and Morgan obtained a car rented by Paul Howell, and Morgan secured a weapon. Morgan, while Patrick Howell drove, shot and killed Tillman. After the shooting, the inside of the car needed extensive cleaning, and Clarke and Patrick and Paul Howell commenced the clean-up efforts. Tammie Bailey and Yolanda McCalister were the girlfriends of Michael Morgan and Patrick Howell respectively. Patrick Howell had informed McCalister of the murder, and warned her if she told anybody, he would kill her and her family. McCalister and Bailey ultimately rode in the rental car, noticing blood and bullet holes in the interior, and blood on Patrick Howell's shorts.

In October of 1991, after returning from a trip to Jamaica, Patrick Howell was detained by immigration officials and ultimately arrested. While Patrick was incarcerated, Paul took over the supervisory role in their drug operation. During this time, law enforcement officials were progressing in the investigation of the Tillman murder. In the wake of the Tillman murder, appellant Paul Howell, concerned about the possibility of Ms. Bailey "straying" and turning to the authorities, constructed a pipe bomb with the intention of killing her in an apparent attempt to ensure she would not talk. To that end, he ordered the delivery of a gift-wrapped package containing a microwave oven to Ms. Bailey; inside the oven was the homemade pipe bomb that took Trooper Fulford's life.

b. *Pinkerton/Alvarez* co-conspirator liability

Basic to criminal law principles is the concept that the "commission of a substantive offense and a conspiracy to commit it are separate and distinct offenses." Each party to a continuing conspiracy may be vicariously liable for substantive criminal offenses committed by a co-conspirator during the course and in the furtherance of the conspiracy, notwithstanding the party's non-participation in the offenses or lack of knowledge thereof. Liability will not lie, however, if the substantive crime "did not fall within the scope of the unlawful project, or was merely a part of the ramifications of the plan which could not be reasonably foreseen as a necessary or natural consequence of the unlawful agreement." *Pinkerton*, 328 U.S. at 647-48. Hence, a court need not assess the individual culpability of a particular conspirator provided the "substantive crime was a reasonably foreseeable consequence of the conspiracy."

Generally, *Pinkerton* co-conspirator liability applies in two situations. First, where the substantive crime is also a goal of the conspiracy, e.g., where there is a narcotics conspiracy and a corresponding substantive crime of possession or distribution of cocaine. The second scenario is where the substantive offense differs from the precise nature of the ongoing conspiracy, but facilitates the implementation of its goals. For example, a particular co-conspirator, found guilty of conspiring to distribute drugs, may also be held liable for the substantive crime of possession of a firearm.

In *Alvarez*, this circuit expanded the breadth of *Pinkerton* liability to include reasonably foreseeable but originally unintended substantive crimes, in other words, embracing substantive crimes occurring "as a result of an unintended turn of events." Despite the fact that murder was not within the originally intended scope of the conspiracy in that case, the *Alvarez* Court found individual culpability of the defendants sufficient to support their murder convictions pursuant to the *Pinkerton* co-conspirator doctrine.

The extension of co-conspirator liability to "reasonably foreseeable but originally unintended substantive crimes" must be limited by due process as *Alvarez* realized. Thus, *Alvarez*'s holding is limited to conspirators "who played more than a 'minor' role in the conspiracy, or who had actual knowledge of at least some of the circumstances and events culminating in the reasonably but unintended substantive crime."

It seems clear the primary goal of Appellants' conspiracy in the instant case was not specifically to cause the death of a state trooper on a highway by means of a pipe bomb; their principal objective was to engage in the sale and distribution of illegal drugs. As applied to this case, therefore, *Alvarez*'s holding means that liability properly attaches to Appellants if the substantive crime of causing the death of Trooper Fulford was a reasonably foreseeable but originally unintended outcome, provided Appellants were more than "minor" players in the conspiracy or had some actual knowledge of some of the circumstances and events leading to the death of Trooper Fulford.

The Court in Alvarez focused on two factors in finding that there was sufficient evidence to support the jury's conclusion that murder was a reasonably foreseeable consequence of the conspiracy. The first was the substantial amount of drugs and money involved in the drug conspiracy; as that court states, it was not a "nickel-and-dime" operation. The second involved the jury's ability to infer -- given the amount of drugs and money involved in the operation -- that the conspirators must have been aware of the likelihood that another member of their coterie would be using or carrying weapons and that, if necessary, deadly force would be used to protect the conspirators' interests. We find both factors are present in this case.

Appellants argue that the bombing was an attenuated, unintended act, and that it does not compare, for example, to the use of firearms for stealing or protecting drugs and monies derived from a conspiracy to distribute drugs. Appellants also maintain that Trooper Fulford's death was the result of an irrational act by Paul Howell which could not have been reasonably foreseen as a natural and probable consequence of the alleged conspiracy. The government, conversely, argues that deadly force and violence were more than peripheral possibilities; rather, they were routine practices and central to the goals and implementation of the conspiracy. A review of the record supports the government's position.

When viewed in light of the *Alvarez* theory of co-conspirator liability, it is clear that the trial court did not err by submitting the *Pinkerton* issue to the jury. There was sufficient evidence for a reasonable jury to have concluded beyond a reasonable doubt that the murder was a reasonably foreseeable consequence of the drug conspiracy. We further find that the court's jury instructions are sound and without error. We therefore find that *Pinkerton* liability was properly imposed on Appellants. * * *

An exhaustive examination of the record reveals abundant evidence supporting the jury's conclusion that the killing of individuals was a reasonably foreseeable consequence of the ongoing conspiracy, especially given the frequency with which weapons and violence, actual or threatened, were used in order to further the interests of the conspiracy. One need not look further than the Tillman murder to support its conclusion. Moreover, the record is replete with references to the conspirators being continuously armed and using such weapons either to protect or advance their interest, most notably by armed robberies.

Cognizant of the due process considerations promoted by *Alvarez*, and bound by its narrow holding, we find the individual culpability of Appellants sufficient to support their convictions pursuant to *Pinkerton*. Further, we conclude the relationship between Appellants and Trooper Fulford's death was not so attenuated as to transgress the due process limitations on *Pinkerton* co-conspirator liability and preclude its application.

Patrick Howell, Michael Morgan and Egnatius Johnson were the principal leaders of the drug operation, and their role was more than "minor" in the conspiracy. Appellants Paul Howell, Clarke, and Mothersill also played important roles in the implementation of the conspiracy's unlawful goals and deserve the label "more than minor participants." Therefore, we hold that the imposition of *Pinkerton* liability on Appellants Morgan, Clarke, Johnson, Mothersill and Patrick Howell for the death of Trooper Fulford was proper, and hence, reject Appellants' attempts to reverse their convictions on this ground.

AFFIRMED.

C. THE MENS REA OF CONSPIRACY

In jurisdictions that have incorporated the common law, conspiracy is usually considered a specific intent crime. This required specific intent involves two elements: (1) the intent to enter into an agreement; and (2) the intent to commit, or aid in the commission of, the act or acts constituting the target crime. *People v. Swain* examines these two requirements in the context of a conspiracy to commit second degree murder.

Despite the designation of conspiracy as a specific intent crime, on occasion convictions for conspiracy have been permitted based not on evidence of what under the Model Penal Code would be called "purpose," but rather on some form of what the Model Penal Code calls "knowledge." *People v. Lauria* and *United States v. Lanza* explores the limits of conspiracy responsibility based on knowledge.

Under section 5.03 of the Model Penal Code, to be convicted of conspiracy the actor must have the purpose to promote or facilitate the target offense, or to aid others in committing, attempting, or soliciting the action that constitutes the crime.

PEOPLE v. SWAIN
Supreme Court of California
909 P.2d 994, 49 Cal.Rptr.2d 390 (1996)

BAXTER, ASSOCIATE JUSTICE.

Defendants Jamal K. Swain and David Chatman were each convicted of conspiracy to commit murder and other crimes, stemming from the drive-by shooting death of a 15-year-old boy. As we shall explain, we hold that intent to kill is a required element of the crime of conspiracy to commit murder. In light of the jury instructions given, and general verdicts returned, we cannot determine beyond a reasonable doubt whether the jury found that the defendants conspired with an intent to kill. That conclusion requires us to reverse defendants' conspiracy convictions.

FACTS AND PROCEDURAL BACKGROUND

The question before us is one of law; the facts found by the Court of Appeal, summarized below, are not disputed.

Prosecution evidence established that a brown van passed through the Hunter's Point neighborhood of San Francisco about 2:00 a.m. on January 13, 1991. It slowed down near the spot where the young victim, who was of Samoan descent, and his friends were listening to music on the street.

A young Black male who appeared to have no hair was driving the van. Suddenly several shots were fired from the front of the van. Defendant Chatman and another young man also fired guns from the rear of the van. One of the intended victims had yelled out "drive-by" as a warning of the impending shooting, so most of the people on the street ducked down. The 15-year-old victim, Hagbom Saileele, who was holding the radio from which music was playing, was shot twice from behind. He later died in surgery.

Afterward, defendant Swain was in jail and boasted to jailmates about what good aim he had with a gun: "He was talking about what a good shot he was. He was saying he had shot that Samoan kid when they were in the van going about 30 miles an hour up a hill." The area where the shooting occurred is hilly; the van would have had to have been traveling uphill as it passed by the scene of the shooting. * * *

The abandoned brown van was recovered by police; in the van and nearby were found surgical gloves, expended cartridges, a hooded ski mask, and two handguns: a .380-caliber semi-automatic and a .25-caliber automatic. Defendant Swain's fingerprint was on the inside of the driver's side window. The forensic evidence established that whoever had used the .380-caliber semi-automatic handgun, from which the fatal shots were fired, had been sitting in the driver's side front seat of the van.

The .380-caliber gun was traced, through a series of owners and transactions involving narcotics, to defendant Chatman. Chatman was interrogated by police; he denied any knowledge of the van and claimed he had not purchased the gun. When this story proved false, Chatman admitted he had bought the gun, but claimed it had been stolen from him. Still later, he claimed he had sold it to someone else.

A warrant was obtained for Chatman's arrest. After waiving his rights, Chatman told police he and two other people, not including Swain, had driven the van to the crime scene in order to get revenge for a car theft by a rival gang.

Chatman insisted, to the police and at trial, that Swain had not been in the van. He could not, however, explain Swain's fingerprint inside the van.

The owner of the van testified Swain had never been inside his van prior to the incident, but that Swain had intimidated him into telling police he (Swain) had previously been inside the vehicle, since otherwise "he was going to have something done to him."

At trial, Chatman admitted he had been in the van, which was driven to Hunter's Point to retaliate for a car theft attributed to a neighborhood youth who was not the victim of the shooting. The original plan was allegedly to steal the car of the thief. Chatman admitted he had fired shots, but claimed he fired wildly and only in self-defense. In support of this self-defense theory, he testified he heard an initial shot and thought it was fired by someone outside the van shooting at him, so he returned the fire. As noted, Chatman claimed Swain was not in the van.

Swain testified he was not in the van during the shooting and did not do any shooting. He claimed he had entered the van earlier in the evening, but had left because "the smell of marijuana bothered him." He claimed he took BART (Bay Area Rapid Transit) to Berkeley, where he spent the evening at a relative's home. He denied boasting about shooting the victim and denied having threatened any witnesses.

The jury first returned a verdict finding defendant Chatman guilty of second degree murder and conspiracy. As instructed, the jury also made a finding that the target offense of the conspiracy was murder in the second degree. Several days later, the jury returned verdicts against defendant Swain, finding him not guilty of murder or its lesser included offenses, but guilty of conspiracy and of attempting to dissuade a witness from testifying by threats. Once again, the jury made a finding under the conspiracy count that the target offense of the conspiracy was murder in the second degree. * * *

Both defendants appealed on several grounds, including the question of whether intent to kill is a required element of the crime of conspiracy to commit murder. More particularly, where, as here, the target offense is determined to be murder in the second degree, does conviction of conspiracy to commit murder necessarily require proof of express malice -- the functional equivalent of intent to kill -- or can one conspire to commit implied malice murder? * * *

DISCUSSION
I

Defendants contend the jury should have been instructed that proof of intent to kill is required to support a conviction of conspiracy to commit murder, whether the target offense of the conspiracy -- murder -- is determined to be in the first or second degree. More particularly, defendants assert it was error to instruct the jury on the principles of implied malice second degree murder in connection with the determination of whether they could be found guilty of conspiracy to commit murder, since implied malice does not require a finding of intent to kill. As we shall explain, we agree.

We commence our analysis with a brief review of the elements of the crime of conspiracy, and of murder, the target offense of the conspiracy here in issue.

Conspiracy is an inchoate crime. It does not require the commission of the substantive offense that is the object of the conspiracy. "As an inchoate crime, conspiracy fixes the point of legal intervention at [the time of] agreement to commit a crime," and "thus reaches further back into preparatory conduct than attempt...." (Model Pen. Code & Commentaries (1985) com. 1 to § 5.03, pp. 387-388.)

The crime of conspiracy is defined in the Penal Code as "two or more persons conspir[ing]" "[t]o commit any crime," together with proof of the commission of an overt act "by one or more of the parties to such agreement" in furtherance thereof. "Conspiracy is a 'specific intent' crime.... The specific intent required divides logically into two elements: (a) the intent to agree, or conspire, and (b) the intent to commit the offense which is the object of the conspiracy.... To sustain a conviction for conspiracy to commit a particular offense, the prosecution must show not only that the conspirators intended to agree but also that they intended to commit the elements of that offense." In some instances, the object of the conspiracy "is defined in terms of proscribed conduct." (Model Pen.Code & Commentaries, supra, com. 2(c) to § 5.03, p. 402.) In other instances, it "is defined in terms of ... a proscribed result under specified attendant circumstances."

Penal Code, section 182, the current version of which was enacted in 1955, prescribes the punishment for the crime of conspiracy. "If the felony is one for which different punishments are prescribed for different degrees, the jury or court which finds the defendant guilty thereof shall determine the degree of the felony defendant conspired to commit. If the degree is not so determined, the punishment for conspiracy to commit such felony shall be that prescribed for the lesser degree, except in the case of conspiracy to commit murder, in which case the punishment shall be that prescribed for murder in the first degree."

Turning next to the elements of the target offense of the conspiracy here in issue, Penal Code section 187 defines the crime of murder as the "unlawful killing of a human being ... with malice aforethought." Malice aforethought "may be express or implied." "It is express when there is manifested a deliberate intention unlawfully to take away the life of a fellow creature. It is implied, when no considerable provocation appears, or when the circumstances attending the killing show an abandoned and malignant heart."

This court has observed that proof of unlawful "intent to kill" is the functional equivalent of express malice.

Penal Code section 189 distinguishes between murders in the first degree and murders in the second degree. "All murder which is perpetrated by means of a destructive device or explosive ..., poison, lying in wait, torture, or by any other kind of willful, deliberate, and premeditated killing, or which is committed in the perpetration of, or attempt to perpetrate, [certain enumerated felonies], or any murder which is perpetrated by means of discharging a firearm from a motor vehicle, intentionally at another person outside of the vehicle with the intent to inflict death, is murder of the first degree. All other kinds of murders are of the second degree." * * *

As noted, the jury in this case was instructed on the elements of murder, including principles of implied malice second degree murder. Under the instructions given, the jury could have based its verdicts finding defendants guilty of conspiracy to commit murder in the second degree on a theory of implied malice murder. * * *

We have noted that conspiracy is a specific intent crime requiring an intent to agree or conspire, and a further intent to commit the target crime, here murder, the object of the conspiracy. Since murder committed with intent to kill is the functional equivalent of express malice murder, conceptually speaking, no conflict arises between the specific intent element of conspiracy and the specific intent requirement for such category of murders. Simply put, where the conspirators agree or conspire with specific intent to kill and commit an overt act in furtherance of such agreement, they are guilty of conspiracy to commit express malice murder. The conceptual difficulty arises when the target offense of murder is founded on a theory of implied malice, which requires no intent to kill.

Implied malice murder, in contrast to express malice, requires instead an intent to do some act, the natural consequences of which are dangerous to human life. * * * In such circumstances, ". . . it is not necessary to establish that the defendant intended that his act would result in the death of a human being." Hence, under an implied malice theory of second degree murder, the requisite mental state for murder -- malice aforethought -- is by definition "implied," as a matter of law, from the specific intent to do some act dangerous to human life together with the circumstance that a killing has resulted from the doing of such act. * * *

The element of malice aforethought in implied malice murder cases is therefore derived or "implied," in part through hindsight so to speak, from (i) proof of the specific intent to do some act dangerous to human life and (ii) the circumstance that a killing has resulted therefrom. It is precisely due to this nature of implied malice murder that it would be illogical to conclude one can be found guilty of conspiring to commit murder where the requisite element of malice is implied. Such a construction would be at odds with the very nature of the crime of conspiracy -- an "inchoate" crime that "fixes the point of legal intervention at [the time of] agreement to commit a crime," and indeed "reaches further back into preparatory conduct than [the crime of] attempt" (Model Pen. Code & Commentaries, supra, com. 1 to § 5.03, pp. 387-388) -- precisely because commission of the crime could never be established, or deemed complete, unless and until a killing actually occurred.

By analogy, we have reached similar conclusions respecting the nature of proof of the element of malice required to establish the inchoate crimes of assault with intent to commit murder and attempted murder. * * *

We conclude that a conviction of conspiracy to commit murder requires a finding of intent to kill, and cannot be based on a theory of implied malice. * * *

That portion of the Court of Appeal's judgment affirming defendants' convictions of conspiracy to commit murder must therefore be reversed.

PEOPLE v. LAURIA

Court of Appeal, Second District, Division 2, California
251 Cal. App. 2d 471 (1967)

FLEMING, J.

In an investigation of call-girl activity the police focused their attention on three prostitutes actively plying their trade on call, each of whom was using Lauria's telephone answering service, presumably for business purposes.

On January 8, 1965, Stella Weeks, a policewoman, signed up for telephone service with Lauria's answering service. Mrs. Weeks, in the course of her conversation with Lauria's office manager, hinted broadly that she was a prostitute concerned with the secrecy of her activities and their concealment from the police. She was assured that the operation of the service was discreet and "about as safe as you can get." It was arranged that Mrs. Weeks need not leave her address with the answering service, but could pick up her calls and pay her bills in person.

On February 11, Mrs. Weeks talked to Lauria on the telephone and told him her business was modelling and she had been referred to the answering service by Terry, one of the three prostitutes under investigation. She complained that because of the operation of the service she had lost two valuable customers, referred to as tricks. Lauria defended his service and said that her friends had probably lied to her about having left calls for her. But he did not respond to Mrs. Weeks' hints that she needed customers in order to make money, other than to invite her to his house for a personal visit in order to get better acquainted. In the course of his talk he said "his business was taking messages."

On February 15, Mrs. Weeks talked on the telephone to Lauria's office manager and again complained of two lost calls, which she described as a $50 and a $100 trick. On investigation the office manager could find nothing wrong, but she said she would alert the switchboard operators about slip-ups on calls.

On April 1 Lauria and the three prostitutes were arrested. Lauria complained to the police that this attention was undeserved, stating that Hollywood Call Board had 60 to 70 prostitutes on its board while his own service had only 9 or 10, that he kept separate records for known or suspected prostitutes for the convenience of himself and the police. When asked if his records were available to police who might come to the office to investigate call girls, Lauria replied that they were whenever the police had a specific name. However, his service didn't "arbitrarily tell the police about prostitutes on our board. As long as they pay their bills we tolerate them." In a subsequent voluntary appearance before the grand jury Lauria testified he had always cooperated with the police. But he admitted he knew some of his customers were prostitutes, and he knew Terry was a prostitute because he had personally used her services, and he knew she was paying for 500 calls a month.

Lauria and the three prostitutes were indicted for conspiracy to commit prostitution, and nine overt acts were specified. Subsequently the trial court set aside the indictment as having been brought without reasonable or probable cause. The People have appealed, claiming that a sufficient showing of an unlawful agreement to further prostitution was made.

To establish agreement, the People need show no more than a tacit, mutual understanding between coconspirators to accomplish an unlawful act. Here the People attempted to establish a conspiracy by showing that Lauria, well aware that his codefendants were prostitutes who received business calls from customers through his telephone answering service, continued to furnish them with such service. This approach attempts to equate knowledge of another's criminal activity with conspiracy to further such criminal activity, and poses the question of the criminal responsibility of a furnisher of goods or services who knows his product is being used to assist the operation of an illegal business. Under what circumstances does a supplier become a part of a conspiracy to further an illegal enterprise by furnishing goods or services which he knows are to be used by the buyer for criminal purposes?

The two leading cases on this point face in opposite directions. In *United States v. Falcone,* the sellers of large quantities of sugar, yeast, and cans were absolved from participation in a moonshining conspiracy among distillers who bought from them, while in *Direct Sales Co. v. United States,* a wholesaler of drugs was convicted of conspiracy to violate the federal narcotic laws by selling drugs in quantity to a codefendant physician who was supplying them to addicts. The distinction between these two cases appears primarily based on the proposition that distributors of such dangerous products as drugs are required to exercise greater discrimination in the conduct of their business than are distributors of innocuous substances like sugar and yeast.

In the earlier case, *Falcone*, the sellers' knowledge of the illegal use of the goods was insufficient by itself to make the sellers participants in a conspiracy with the distillers who bought from them. Such knowledge fell short of proof of a conspiracy, and evidence on the volume of sales was too vague to support a jury finding that respondents knew of the conspiracy from the size of the sales alone.

In the later case of *Direct Sales*, the conviction of a drug wholesaler for conspiracy to violate federal narcotic laws was affirmed on a showing that it had actively promoted the sale of morphine sulphate in quantity and had sold codefendant physician, who practiced in a small town in South Carolina, more than 300 times his normal requirements of the drug, even though it had been repeatedly warned of the dangers of unrestricted sales of the drug. The court contrasted the restricted goods involved in *Direct Sales* with the articles of free commerce involved in *Falcone*: "All articles of commerce may be put to illegal ends," said the court. "But all do not have inherently the same susceptibility to harmful and illegal use. . . . This difference is important for two purposes. One is for making certain that the seller knows the buyer's intended illegal use. The other is to show that by the sale he intends to further, promote, and cooperate in it. This intent, when given effect by overt act, is the gist of conspiracy. While it is not identical with mere knowledge that another purposes unlawful action it is not unrelated to such knowledge. . . . The step from knowledge to intent and agreement may be taken. There is more than suspicion, more than knowledge, acquiescence, carelessness, indifference, lack of concern. There is informed and interested cooperation, stimulation, instigation. And there is also a 'stake in the venture' which, even if it may not be essential, is not irrelevant to the question of conspiracy."

While *Falcone* and *Direct Sales* may not be entirely consistent with each other in their full implications, they do provide us with a framework for the criminal liability of a supplier of lawful goods or services put to unlawful use.

Both the element of *knowledge* of the illegal use of the goods or services and the element of *intent* to further that use must be present in order to make the supplier a participant in a criminal conspiracy.

Proof of *knowledge* is ordinarily a question of fact and requires no extended discussion in the present case. The knowledge of the supplier was sufficiently established when Lauria admitted he knew some of his customers were prostitutes and admitted he knew that Terry, an active subscriber to his service, was a prostitute. In the face of these admissions he could scarcely claim to have relied on the normal assumption an operator of a business or service is entitled to make, that his customers are behaving themselves in the eyes of the law. Because Lauria knew in fact that some of his customers were prostitutes, it is a legitimate inference he knew they were subscribing to his answering service for illegal business purposes and were using his service to make assignations for prostitution. On this record we think the prosecution is entitled to claim positive knowledge by Lauria of the use of his service to facilitate the business of prostitution.

The more perplexing issue in the case is the sufficiency of proof of *intent* to further the criminal enterprise. The element of intent may be proved either by direct evidence, or by evidence of circumstances from which an intent to further a criminal enterprise by supplying lawful goods or services may be inferred. Direct evidence of participation, such as advice from the supplier of legal goods or services to the user of those goods or services on their use for illegal purposes, such evidence as appeared in a companion case we decide today, *People* v. *Roy, ante*, provides the simplest case. When the intent to further and promote the criminal enterprise comes from the lips of the supplier himself, ambiguities of inference from circumstance need not trouble us. But in cases where direct proof of complicity is lacking, intent to further the conspiracy must be derived from the sale itself and its surrounding circumstances in order to establish the supplier's express or tacit agreement to join the conspiracy.

In the case at bench the prosecution argues that since Lauria knew his customers were using his service for illegal purposes but nevertheless continued to furnish it to them, he must have intended to assist them in carrying out their illegal activities. Thus through a union of knowledge and intent he became a participant in a criminal conspiracy. Essentially, the People argue that knowledge alone of the continuing use of his telephone facilities for criminal purposes provided a sufficient basis from which his intent to participate in those criminal activities could be inferred.

In examining precedents in this field we find that sometimes, but not always, the criminal intent of the supplier may be inferred from his knowledge of the unlawful use made of the product he supplies. Some consideration of characteristic patterns may be helpful.

1. Intent may be inferred from knowledge, when the purveyor of legal goods for illegal use has acquired a stake in the venture. For example, in *Regina v. Thomas,* a prosecution for living off the earnings of prostitution, the evidence showed that the accused, knowing the woman to be a convicted prostitute, agreed to let her have the use of his room between the hours of 9 p.m. and 2 a.m. for a charge of £3 a night. The Court of Criminal Appeal refused an appeal from the conviction, holding that when the accused rented a room at a grossly inflated rent to a prostitute for the purpose of carrying on her trade, a jury could find he was living on the earnings of prostitution.

In the present case, no proof was offered of inflated charges for the telephone answering services furnished the codefendants.

2. Intent may be inferred from knowledge, when no legitimate use for the goods or services exists. The leading California case is *People v. McLaughlin,* in which the court upheld a conviction of the suppliers of horse-racing information by wire for conspiracy to promote bookmaking, when it had been established that wire-service information had no other use than to supply information needed by bookmakers to conduct illegal gambling operations.

In *Rex v. Delaval,* the charge was unlawful conspiracy to remove a girl from the control of Bates, a musician to whom she was bound as an apprentice, and place her in the hands of Sir Francis Delaval for the purpose of prostitution. Lord Mansfield not only upheld the charges against Bates and Sir Francis, but also against Fraine, the attorney who drew up the indentures of apprenticeship transferring custody of the girl from Bates to Sir Francis. Fraine, said Lord Mansfield, must have known that Sir Francis had no facilities for teaching music to apprentices so that it was impossible for him to have been ignorant of the real intent of the transaction.

In *Shaw* v. *Director of Public Prosecutions*, the defendant was convicted of conspiracy to corrupt public morals and of living on the earnings of prostitution, when he published a directory consisting almost entirely of advertisements of the names, addresses, and specialized talents of prostitutes. Publication of such a directory, said the court, could have no legitimate use and serve no other purpose than to advertise the professional services of the prostitutes whose advertisements appeared in the directory. The publisher could be deemed a participant in the profits from the business activities of his principal advertisers.

Other services of a comparable nature come to mind: the manufacturer of crooked dice and marked cards who sells his product to gambling casinos; the tipster who furnishes information on the movement of law enforcement officers to known lawbreakers. In such cases the supplier must necessarily have an intent to further the illegal enterprise since there is no known honest use for his goods.

However, there is nothing in the furnishing of telephone answering service which would necessarily imply assistance in the performance of illegal activities. Nor is any inference to be derived from the use of an answering service by women, either in any particular volume of calls, or outside normal working hours. Night-club entertainers, registered nurses, faith healers, public stenographers, photographic models, and free lance substitute employees, provide examples of women in legitimate occupations whose employment might cause them to receive a volume of telephone calls at irregular hours.

3. Intent may be inferred from knowledge, when the volume of business with the buyer is grossly disproportionate to any legitimate demand, or when sales for illegal use amount to a high proportion of the seller's total business. In such cases an intent to participate in the illegal enterprise may be inferred from the quantity of the business done. For example, in *Direct Sales,* the sale of narcotics to a rural physician in quantities 300 times greater than he would have normal use for provided potent evidence of an intent to further the illegal activity. In the same case the court also found significant the fact that the wholesaler had attracted as customers a disproportionately large group of physicians who had been convicted of violating the Harrison Act. In *Shaw* v. *Director of Public Prosecutions*, almost the entire business of the directory came from prostitutes.

No evidence of any unusual volume of business with prostitutes was presented by the prosecution against Lauria.

Inflated charges, the sale of goods with no legitimate use, sales in inflated amounts, each may provide a fact of sufficient moment from which the intent of the seller to participate in the criminal enterprise may be inferred. In such instances participation by the supplier of legal goods to the illegal enterprise may be inferred because in one way or another the supplier has acquired a special interest in the operation of the illegal enterprise. His intent to participate in the crime of which he has knowledge may be inferred from the existence of his special interest.

Yet there are cases in which it cannot reasonably be said that the supplier has a stake in the venture or has acquired a special interest in the enterprise, but in which he has been held liable as a participant on the basis of knowledge alone. Some suggestion of this appears in *Direct Sales,* where both the knowledge of the illegal use of the drugs and the intent of the supplier to aid that use were inferred. In *Regina* v. *Bainbridge*, a supplier of oxygen-cutting equipment to one known to intend to use it to break into a bank was convicted as an accessory to the crime. In *Sykes* v. *Director of Public Prosecutions*, one having knowledge of the theft of 100 pistols, 4 submachine guns, and 1,960 rounds of ammunition was convicted of misprision of felony for failure to disclose the theft to the public authorities. It seems apparent from these cases that a supplier who furnishes equipment which he *knows* will be used to commit a serious crime may be deemed from that knowledge alone to have intended to produce the result. Such proof may justify an inference that the furnisher intended to aid the execution of the crime and that he thereby became a participant. For instance, we think the operator of a telephone answering service with positive knowledge that his service was being used to facilitate the extortion of ransom, the distribution of heroin, or the passing of counterfeit money who continued to furnish the service with knowledge of its use, might be chargeable on knowledge alone with participation in a scheme to extort money, to distribute narcotics, or to pass counterfeit money. The same result would follow the seller of gasoline who knew the buyer was using his product to make Molotov cocktails for terroristic use.

Logically, the same reasoning could be extended to crimes of every description. Yet we do not believe an inference of intent drawn from knowledge of criminal use properly applies to the less serious crimes classified as misdemeanors. The duty to take positive action to dissociate oneself from activities helpful to violations of the criminal law is far stronger and more compelling for felonies than it is for misdemeanors or petty offenses. In this respect, as in others, the distinction between felonies and misdemeanors, between more serious and less serious crime, retains continuing vitality. In historically the most serious felony, treason, an individual with knowledge of the treason can be prosecuted for concealing and failing to disclose it. In other felonies, both at common law and under the criminal laws of the United States, an individual knowing of the commission of a felony is criminally liable for concealing it and failing to make it known to proper authority. But this crime, known as misprision of felony, has always been limited to knowledge and concealment of felony and has never extended to misdemeanor. A similar limitation is found in the criminal liability of an accessory, which is restricted to aid in the escape of a principal who has committed or been charged with a *felony*. We believe the distinction between the obligations arising from knowledge of a felony and those arising from knowledge of a misdemeanor continues to reflect basic human feelings about the duties owed by individuals to society. Heinous crime must be stamped out, and its suppression is the responsibility of all. Venial crime and crime not evil in itself present less of a danger to society, and perhaps the benefits of their suppression through the modern equivalent of the posse, the hue and cry, the informant, and the citizen's arrest, are outweighed by the disruption to everyday life brought about by amateur law enforcement and private officiousness in relatively inconsequential delicts which do not threaten our basic security. * * *

With respect to misdemeanors, we conclude that positive knowledge of the supplier that his products or services are being used for criminal purposes does not, without more, establish an intent of the supplier to participate in the misdemeanors. With respect to felonies, we do not decide the converse, viz., that in all cases of felony knowledge of criminal use alone may justify an inference of the supplier's intent to participate in the crime. The implications of *Falcone* make the matter uncertain with respect to those felonies which are merely prohibited wrongs. But decision on this point is not compelled, and we leave the matter open.

From this analysis of precedent we deduce the following rule: the intent of a supplier who knows of the criminal use to which his supplies are put to participate in the criminal activity connected with the use of his supplies may be established by (1) direct evidence that he intends to participate, or (2) through an inference that he intends to participate based on, (a) his special interest in the activity, or (b) the aggravated nature of the crime itself.

When we review Lauria's activities in the light of this analysis, we find no proof that Lauria took any direct action to further, encourage, or direct the call-girl activities of his codefendants and we find an absence of circumstance from which his special interest in their activities could be inferred. Neither excessive charges for standardized services, nor the furnishing of services without a legitimate use, nor an unusual quantity of business with call girls, are present. The offense which he is charged with furthering is a misdemeanor, a category of crime which has never been made a required subject of positive disclosure to public authority. Under these circumstances, although proof of Lauria's knowledge of the criminal activities of his patrons was sufficient to charge him with that fact, there was insufficient evidence that he intended to further their criminal activities, and hence insufficient proof of his participation in a criminal conspiracy with his codefendants to further prostitution. Since the conspiracy centered around the activities of Lauria's telephone answering service, the charges against his codefendants likewise fail for want of proof.

In absolving Lauria of complicity in a criminal conspiracy we do not wish to imply that the public authorities are without remedies to combat modern manifestations of the world's oldest profession. Licensing of telephone answering services under the police power, together with the revocation of licenses for the toleration of prostitution, is a possible civil remedy. The furnishing of telephone answering service in aid of prostitution could be made a crime. (*Cf.* Pen. Code, § 316, which makes it a misdemeanor to let an apartment with knowledge of its use for prostitution.) Other solutions will doubtless occur to vigilant public authorities if the problem of call-girl activity needs further suppression.

The order is affirmed.

UNITED STATES v. LANZA
United States Court of Appeals, Second Circuit
790 F.2d 1015 (1986)

PIERCE, CIRCUIT JUDGE:

These appeals are from judgments of conviction in the United States District Court for the Southern District of New York, Inzer B. Wyatt, Judge, after a jury trial for conspiracy to commit wire fraud, in violation of 18 U.S.C. § 371. Appellants Anthony Lanza and Vyscheslav Lyubarsky were sentenced to four years' imprisonment, and appellant Roman Zonenashvili to three years' imprisonment. * * *

Lyubarsky and Zonenashvili * * * challenge the court's instructions to the jury concerning conscious avoidance with regard to knowledge and specific intent.

We affirm.

BACKGROUND

* * *

Zubok testified that he immigrated to the United States in 1976; in 1980, he found employment in New York City with Lemiro International (Lemiro), a jewelry store owned by Gregory Lekach. Zubok worked intermittently at Lemiro between 1980 and August 1983, during which time he met Lyubarsky. In 1983, Zubok left Lemiro and opened his own jewelry business in Chicago, Illinois, which he named Keyiasso. He later learned that there had been a burglary at Lemiro and suspected that it was a fraudulent burglary to obtain insurance proceeds. He testified that thereafter Lyubarsky suggested to him that they do at Keyiasso "exactly what Lekach did" at Lemiro.

In April, 1984, Zubok went to New York where he met with agents from the FBI. He told the agents of his conversation with Lyubarsky, and thus began his cooperation with the FBI. On April 26, 1984, Zubok met Lyubarsky in Forest Hills, Queens, and Lyubarsky asked him about the safe and alarm system at Keyiasso and told him that he would "talk with people, and . . . decide what he will do in my office." The next day Zubok met Lyubarsky in Manhattan and was driven to Bay Ridge, Brooklyn. En route, he told Zubok that he would introduce him to his "boss". Upon arrival, Zubok was introduced to a man later identified by Zubok as Anthony Lanza. At the meeting, Lanza also questioned Zubok about the safe and alarm system at Keyiasso.

On April 30, 1984, Lyubarsky introduced Zubok to Nuzio and Zonenashvili at a restaurant in Brooklyn, at which time Zubok was checked with a metal detector. During the meeting, Nuzio told Zubok that the operation would have to "go the right way" or "we will crush your head". Nuzio inquired about insurance coverage and whether Zubok would need any help in order to raise his inventory to the appropriate level. Zubok told them that Keyiasso had $750,000 of insurance coverage and declined further assistance. Zubok also testified that it was "agreed that the [burglary] would take place at the time when [Keyiasso] had somewhere between 500 and 800 thousand dollars worth of merchandise".

On May 2, 1984, Lyubarsky and Zonenashvili met with Zubok at Keyiasso in Chicago, and informed him that he would be visited by individuals who would survey his safe and alarm system. According to the testimony of Zubok's son, Eugene, and Nuzio, on May 7, 1984, Lyubarsky, Zonenashvili and Nuzio inspected the Keyiasso premises.

Three days later, Lyubarsky and Nuzio met Zubok at Kennedy Airport in New York. Zubok was told by Lyubarsky that the operation was proceeding smoothly and that "the most important task now [was] to acquire merchandise." It was the government's theory, as explained in opening argument, that Zubok's role in the phony burglary scheme was to obtain jewelry on credit and store it in his vault at Keyiasso. After the jewelry was stolen by burglars hired by Lanza, the jewelry was to be divided and held by each of the conspirators until the insurance proceeds were received. During this trip to New York, Zubok met with Lanza, Nuzio and Lyubarsky at a Brooklyn restaurant. During the meeting, Lanza discussed the manner in which the merchandise would be divided between them, and Nuzio again threatened Zubok's life unless he carried out his part of the scheme.

In late May, sometime after an unsuccessful attempt by Lyubarsky, Zonenashvili and Zubok to obtain jewelry on credit, Zubok came to New York and was unexpectedly met at the airport by Lyubarsky, Zonenashvili and Nuzio. They took him to a private social club in Brooklyn, where Lanza joined them. Lanza informed Zubok that the burglars had already been paid $150,000 for their part in the scheme and told him that if he failed to obtain the required merchandise he would be killed.

In addition to testimony by Zubok and Zubok's adult son, Eugene, the government played taped telephone conversations between Nuzio and Zubok. In these tapes, Nuzio is heard to threaten to kill Zubok if he failed to obtain certain merchandise on credit. Nuzio also makes references to "my boss" and to "Tony" during discussions of the scheme.

Only Lanza presented a defense case. He called Nuzio as a witness and Nuzio testified that Lanza was not present at any of the meetings with Zubok, but his testimony otherwise corroborated much of Zubok's testimony. Nuzio testified that the objective of the scheme was to "con" Zubok into obtaining merchandise and giving it, as well as the $150,000 compensation for the supposed burglars, to the three of them, but that there was never any agreement to actually go through with the burglary or to defraud the insurance company. Nuzio testified that Lanza was not his boss and that the references to "my boss" and to "Tony" on the tape recordings were intended to scare Zubok into thinking that Nuzio had powerful "Italians" working with him.

The sole theory of defense for Lyubarsky and Zonenashvili was that while all these events did occur the purpose behind them was not the conspiracy charged in the indictment, i.e., "a scheme to stage a sham burglary at a Chicago, Illinois, jewelry store and thereby to defraud the store's insurance carrier", but was a scheme to ultimately extort money directly from Zubok. Lanza's defense was based upon his denial of any participation whatsoever in the unlawful activities charged in the indictment.

DISCUSSION

* * *

C. Issues Regarding The Jury Charge

Lyubarsky and Zonenashvili assert that the district judge did not charge the jury with sufficient particularity as to the specific intent required for a conspiracy conviction. They challenge the use of a "conscious avoidance" charge as unwarranted given their denial of participation in the offense charged and their defense that they intended to commit a different crime. Appellants also argue that such a charge was improper since it allowed the jury to convict without finding beyond a reasonable doubt that appellants had knowledge of the specific conspiracy charged.

As for the first of these contentions, we note that Judge Wyatt began his instruction by reading the indictment to the jury and that the indictment was sent into the jury room during deliberations. Thereafter, the jury was charged at least twice that they must find the existence of a conspiracy "as charged in the indictment". On two other occasions the judge specifically stressed that the object of the conspiracy must have been to defraud the insurer of Zubok's Chicago jewelry store. Then, during deliberation, in response to a note from the jury and in order to satisfy objections raised by Lyubarsky's counsel, the trial judge emphasized in supplemental instructions that the appellants' "guilty knowledge" must have related to "a scheme as charged in this indictment here on trial". Thus, it is clear that the jury was adequately instructed on the finding of intent required to warrant conviction. * * *

The conscious avoidance of knowledge language is to be found in the Model Penal Code's definition of "knowledge."

> When knowledge of the existence of a particular fact is an element of an offense, such knowledge is established if a person is aware of a high probability of its existence unless he actually believes that it does not exist.

Model Penal Code § 2.02(7) (Proposed Official Draft 1962). * * *

The conscious avoidance charge commonly has been used where a defendant has claimed lack of some specific aspect of knowledge necessary to conviction but where the evidence may be construed as deliberate ignorance. * * * These cases also instruct that conscious avoidance charges have been upheld on appeals: a) from convictions for substantive offenses that require "knowledge" or "knowing" activity, b) from convictions for conspiracy to commit such offenses, and c) from convictions for both. Accordingly, we reject appellants' argument that the conscious avoidance charge was inappropriate in this conspiracy case simply because the underlying substantive offense was not charged.

There are at least two aspects of knowledge involved in a conspiracy: 1) knowing participation or membership in the scheme charged and 2) some knowledge of the unlawful aims and objectives of the scheme. * * * Here there is no question regarding appellants' participation in an unlawful scheme, the appellants' defense admits as much. The only question is whether appellants had knowledge of the unlawful aims and objectives of the scheme charged in the indictment. *United States v. Reed*, 790 F.2d 208 (2d Cir. 1986) (Where, as here, the defendant has become a member of a joint undertaking, he cannot avoid responsibility for acts by closing his eyes to what is readily apparent.) While it is not necessary to a conviction for conspiracy for the government to prove that the accused knew all of the unlawful aims and objectives of the scheme charged, the government must demonstrate that the accused had some knowledge of its unlawful aims. Here, a conscious avoidance charge was appropriate vis-a-vis knowledge of the objectives of the scheme charged since the appellants assert what amounts to ignorance of the specific objectives alleged in the indictment.

Whether appellants participated in a scheme aware of the objective of defrauding Zubok's insurance carrier or participated in a scheme to "con" Zubok was an issue for the jury to decide from all the evidence presented. This evidence included, inter alia, Zubok's testimony that Nuzio inquired of him, in the presence of Lyubarsky and Zonenashvili, on April 30, 1984, at Nino's Restaurant in Brooklyn, about Zubok's insurance coverage, and whether he needed any help to raise his level of inventory. During direct examination Zubok testified as follows:

> Q. And was there a conversation at Nino's?
>
> A. Yes. . . . The conversation started whereby Tony Nuzio told me how they were serious people, and if something does not go the right way, then be advised that we will break your head. We will crush your head.
>
> Q. Please continue.
>
> A. Then he asked me in what amount is my insurance. I told him it was $750,000. Later on he asked me if I needed some help in order to raise my inventory so he would also help me.
>
> Q. What was the purpose of building the inventory?
>
> A. We agreed that the robbery would take place at the time when I had somewhere between 500 to 800,000 worth of merchandise.

Since we conclude that a conscious avoidance charge was appropriate in this case, we now turn to appellants' final arguments regarding the specific language used by Judge Wyatt to explain the conscious avoidance principle. * * * Judge Wyatt charged as follows:

> In determining whether a particular defendant acted knowingly, or in other words, had guilty knowledge, you may consider whether the defendant deliberately closed his eyes to what otherwise would have been obvious to him. By this I mean that a finding of guilty knowledge cannot be avoided by a showing that the defendant deliberately closed his eyes to the essential nature of the conspiracy and its unlawful purpose.
>
> It is not necessary that the government prove to a certainty that a particular defendant knew a scheme existed to defraud the insurer of Zubok's Chicago jewelry store by staging a sham burglary. Rather, it is enough if the government proves beyond a reasonable doubt that the defendant was aware of a high probability that such a scheme was in existence, unless you find that the defendant actually believed that he and his associates were acting in a lawful manner.

I must emphasize at this point that guilty knowledge cannot be established by showing mere negligence or even foolishness on the part of a defendant.

Appellants argue that the use of the high probability language served to effectively reduce the government's burden of proof and allowed conviction where the proof of knowledge of the specific conspiracy charged in the indictment was less than beyond a reasonable doubt. We conclude that appellants have failed to establish plain error in this regard.

While the "high probability" language derives directly from the same source as the charge itself, the Model Penal Code, courts have warned that reliance upon the language of a legal definition, from the Model Penal Code or elsewhere, may confuse and ultimately mislead the jury. Though there are other formulations of this particular instruction, the question presented here is whether Judge Wyatt's charge, when read in context, required something less than proof beyond a reasonable doubt. It did not. The use of the high probability language occurs right in the midst of language which instructs that proof beyond a reasonable doubt was required to establish the requisite specific intent. Also, within the very paragraph containing this language, reference is made to the specific conspiracy charged in the indictment regarding a scheme to defraud the insurer of Zubok's Chicago Jewelry store. In *United States v. Aulet*, 618 F.2d 182 (2d Cir.1980), after review of the relevant cases, we stated:

> The principle to be gleaned from these cases is that a conscious avoidance charge must include references to a purposeful avoidance of the truth, ... an awareness of high probability, ... and the absence of defendant's actual belief in the nonexistence of the crucial fact,.... All of these elements were present in [the] charge, and, therefore, there is no error.

Id. at 191. Judge Wyatt was equally careful to include all of these necessary elements in his charge to the jury. Therefore, we find no error as to these challenged portions of the district judge's conscious avoidance charge. * * *

We affirm the judgments of conviction.

Note

What mens rea is required as to the attendant circumstances of a crime? In *United States v. Feola*, 420 U.S. 671 (1975), two drug dealers agreed to attack a third person, who turned out to be a federal officer working undercover. Were they guilty of conspiracy to commit simple assault, or the more serious crime of conspiracy to commit assault on a federal officer in the performance of his official duties? The Supreme Court held that the defendants could be convicted of the more serious crime, even though they did not know at the time that the victim was a federal officer. The Court relied in part on the legal wrong doctrine discussed in Chapter 5:

> This interpretation poses no risk of unfairness to defendants. It is no snare for the unsuspecting. Although the perpetrator of a narcotics [offense], such as the one involved here, may be surprised to find that his intended victim is a federal officer in civilian apparel, he nonetheless knows from the very outset that his planned course of conduct is wrongful.

United States v. Feola, 420 U.S. 671, 685.

Feola represents the Court's interpretation of a particular statute, and thus does not make precedent on the broader point of the mens rea for attendant circumstances of a crime. Other courts have disagreed with *Feola*'s reasoning. Consider the criticism of one judge in the Southern District of New York:

> The trouble with *Feola* as a guiding precedent is that it purported to treat the statute as both "an aggravated assault statute," and as one involving a federal provision that was "jurisdictional only." But the Court did not acknowledge that some mens rea requirement is necessary with respect to the officers' status in order to effectuate Congress' intent to punish assaults upon federal officers more severely. At a minimum, the defendant must know that the assault victim is some kind of official, whether federal or state, or such a provision has no additional deterrent effect beyond the existing general laws prohibiting assaults. The contention that the defendants knew their conduct was criminal is no answer where the legislature is interested in punishing a particular form of assault more severely. One can easily imagine the undercover agents in *Feola* providing their criminal counterparts during their negotiations with assurances that they were real drug dealers and not law enforcement officers. *Feola* is typical of the failure, exhibited in many of the decisions of the lower federal courts discussed below, to apply the integral connections between the mens rea principle and the general purposes of the criminal law.

United States v. Cordoba-Hincapie, 825 F.Supp. 485, 511 (E.D.N.Y. 1993).

D.   THE SHAPE AND BOUNDARIES OF CONSPIRACIES

KOTTEAKOS v. UNITED STATES
Supreme Court of the United States
328 U.S. 750 (1946)

MR. JUSTICE RUTLEDGE delivered the opinion of the Court.

The only question is whether petitioners have suffered substantial prejudice from being convicted of a single general conspiracy by evidence which the Government admits proved not one conspiracy but some eight or more different ones of the same sort executed through a common key figure, Simon Brown. Petitioners were convicted under the general conspiracy section of the Criminal Code, 18 U. S. C. § 88, of conspiring to violate the provisions of the National Housing Act, 12 U. S. C. §§ 1702, 1703, 1715, 1731. The judgments were affirmed by the Circuit Court of Appeals. We granted certiorari because of the importance of the question for the administration of criminal justice in the federal courts.

The indictment named thirty-two defendants, including the petitioners. The gist of the conspiracy, as alleged, was that the defendants had sought to induce various financial institutions to grant credit, with the intent that the loans or advances would then be offered to the Federal Housing Administration for insurance upon applications containing false and fraudulent information.

Of the thirty-two persons named in the indictment nineteen were brought to trial and the names of thirteen were submitted to the jury. Two were acquitted; the jury disagreed as to four; and the remaining seven, including petitioners, were found guilty.

The Government's evidence may be summarized briefly, for the petitioners have not contended that it was insufficient, if considered apart from the alleged errors relating to the proof and the instructions at the trial.

Simon Brown, who pleaded guilty, was the common and key figure in all of the transactions proven. He was president of the Brownie Lumber Company. Having had experience in obtaining loans under the National Housing Act, he undertook to act as broker in placing for others loans for modernization and renovation, charging a five per cent commission for his services. Brown knew, when he obtained the loans, that the proceeds were not to be used for the purposes stated in the applications.

In May, 1939, petitioner Lekacos told Brown that he wished to secure a loan in order to finance opening a law office, to say the least a hardly auspicious professional launching. Brown made out the application, as directed by Lekacos, to state that the purpose of the loan was to modernize a house belonging to the estate of Lekacos' father. Lekacos obtained the money. Later in the same year Lekacos secured another loan through Brown, the application being in the names of his brother and sister-in-law. Lekacos also received part of the proceeds of a loan for which one Gerakeris, a defendant who pleaded guilty, had applied.

In June, 1939, Lekacos sent Brown an application for a loan signed by petitioner Kotteakos. It contained false statements.[5] Brown placed the loan, and Kotteakos thereafter sent Brown applications on behalf of other persons. Two were made out in the names of fictitious persons. The proceeds were received by Kotteakos and petitioner Regenbogen, his partner in the cigarette and pinball machine business. Regenbogen, together with Kotteakos, had indorsed one of the applications. Kotteakos also sent to Brown an application for a loan in Regenbogen's name. This was for modernization of property not owned by Regenbogen. The latter, however, repaid the money in about three months after he received it.

The evidence against the other defendants whose cases were submitted to the jury was similar in character. They too had transacted business with Brown relating to National Housing Act loans. But no connection was shown between them and petitioners, other than that Brown had been the instrument in each instance for obtaining the loans. In many cases the other defendants did not have any relationship with one another, other than Brown's connection with each transaction. As the Circuit Court of Appeals said, there were "at least eight, and perhaps more, separate and independent groups, none of which had any connection with any other, though all dealt independently with Brown as their agent." As the Government puts it, the pattern was "that of separate spokes meeting in a common center," though, we may add, without the rim of the wheel to enclose the spokes.

The proof therefore admittedly made out a case, not of a single conspiracy, but of several, notwithstanding only one was charged in the indictment. The Court of Appeals aptly drew analogy in the comment, "Thieves who dispose of their loot to a single receiver -- a single 'fence' -- do not by that

---

[5]The application stated that the house on which the loan was sought was bought in 1936 rather than in 1938, that the purchase price was $ 8500 rather than $ 7200, and that the assessed valuation was $ 9500 rather than $ 6500. The application further stated that among the repairs contemplated was a repainting of the house, whereas in fact only the basement hallway and garage were repainted.

fact alone become confederates: they may, but it takes more than knowledge that he is a 'fence' to make them such." It stated that the trial judge "was plainly wrong in supposing that upon the evidence there could be a single conspiracy; and in the view which he took of the law, he should have dismissed the indictment." Nevertheless the appellate court held the error not prejudicial, saying among other things that "especially since guilt was so manifest, it was 'proper' to join the conspiracies," and "to reverse the conviction would be a miscarriage of justice." This is indeed the Government's entire position. It does not now contend that there was no variance in proof from the single conspiracy charged in the indictment. Admitting that separate and distinct conspiracies were shown, it urges that the variance was not prejudicial to the petitioners.

In *Berger v. United States,* this Court held that in the circumstances presented the variance was not fatal where one conspiracy was charged and two were proved, relating to contemporaneous transactions involving counterfeit money. One of the conspiracies had two participants; the other had three; and one defendant, Katz, was common to each. "The true inquiry," said the Court, "is not whether there has been a variance in proof, but whether there has been such a variance as to 'affect the substantial rights' of the accused."

The Court held the variance not fatal, resting its ruling on what has become known as "the harmless error statute," § 269 of the Judicial Code, as amended (28 U. S. C. § 391), which is controlling in this case and provides:

> On the hearing of any appeal, certiorari, writ of error, or motion for a new trial, in any case, civil or criminal, the court shall give judgment after an examination of the entire record before the court, without regard to technical errors, defects, or exceptions which do not affect the substantial rights of the parties.

* * * The question we have to determine is whether the same ruling may be extended to a situation in which one conspiracy only is charged and at least eight having separate, though similar objects, are made out by the evidence, if believed; and in which the more numerous participants in the different schemes were, on the whole, except for one, different persons who did not know or have anything to do with one another.

The salutary policy embodied in § 269 was adopted by the Congress in 1919 (Act of February 26, 1919, c. 48, 40 Stat. 1181) after long agitation under distinguished professional sponsorship, and after thorough consideration of various proposals designed to enact the policy in successive Congresses from the Sixtieth to the Sixty-fifth. It is not necessary to review in detail the history of the abuses which led to the agitation or of the progress of the legislation through the various sessions to final enactment without debate. But anyone familiar with it knows that § 269 and similar state legislation grew out of widespread and deep conviction over the general course of appellate review in American criminal causes. This was shortly, as one trial judge put it after § 269 had become law, that courts of review "tower above the trials of criminal cases as impregnable citadels of technicality." So great was the threat of reversal, in many jurisdictions, that criminal trial became a game for sowing reversible error in the record, only to have repeated the same matching of wits when a new trial had been thus obtained.

In the broad attack on this system great legal names were mobilized, among them Taft, Wigmore, Pound and Hadley, to mention only four. The general object was simple: To substitute judgment for automatic application of rules; to preserve review as a check upon arbitrary action and essential unfairness in trials, but at the same time to make the process perform that function without giving men fairly convicted the multiplicity of loopholes which any highly rigid and minutely detailed scheme of errors, especially in relation to procedure, will engender and reflect in a printed record.

The task was too big, too various in detail, for particularized treatment. The effort at revision therefore took the form of the essentially simple command of § 269. It comes down on its face to a very plain admonition: "Do not be technical, where technicality does not really hurt the party whose rights in the trial and in its outcome the technicality affects." It is also important to note that the purpose of the bill in its final form was stated authoritatively to be "to cast upon the party seeking a new trial the burden of showing that any technical errors that he may complain of have affected his substantial rights, otherwise they are to be disregarded." But that this burden does not extend to all errors appears from the statement which follows immediately. "The proposed legislation affects only technical errors. If the error is of such a character that its natural effect is to prejudice a litigant's substantial rights, the burden of sustaining a verdict will, notwithstanding this legislation rest upon the one who claims under it." * * *

If, when all is said and done, the conviction is sure that the error did not influence the jury, or had but very slight effect, the verdict and the judgment should stand, except perhaps where the departure is from a constitutional norm or a specific command of Congress. But if one cannot say, with fair assurance, after pondering all that happened without stripping the erroneous action from the whole, that the judgment was not substantially swayed by the error, it is impossible to conclude that substantial rights were not affected. The inquiry cannot be merely whether there was enough to support the result, apart from the phase affected by the error. It is rather, even so, whether the error itself had substantial influence. If so, or if one is left in grave doubt, the conviction cannot stand. * * *

The Government's theory seems to be, in ultimate logical reach, that the error presented by the variance is insubstantial and harmless, if the evidence offered specifically and properly to convict each defendant would be sufficient to sustain his conviction, if submitted in a separate trial. For reasons we have stated and in view of the authorities cited, this is not and cannot be the test under § 269. But in apparent support of its view the Government argues that there was no prejudice here because the results show that the jury exercised discrimination as among the defendants whose cases were submitted to it. As it points out, the jury acquitted some, disagreed as to others, and found still others guilty. From this it concludes that the jury was not confused and, apparently, reached the same result as would have been reached or would be likely, if the convicted defendants had been or now should be tried separately.

One difficulty with this is that the trial court itself was confused in the charge which it gave to guide the jury in deliberation. The court instructed:

> The indictment charges but one conspiracy, and to convict each of the defendants of a conspiracy the Government would have to prove, and you would have to find, that each of the defendants was a member of that conspiracy. You cannot divide it up. It is one conspiracy, and the question is whether or not each of the defendants, or which of the defendants, are members of that conspiracy.

On its face, as the Court of Appeals said, this portion of the charge was plainly wrong in application to the proof made; and the error pervaded the entire charge, not merely the portion quoted. The jury could not possibly have found, upon the evidence, that there was only one conspiracy. The trial court was of the view that one conspiracy was made out by showing that each defendant was linked to Brown in one or more transactions, and that it was possible on the evidence for the jury to conclude that all were in a common adventure because of this fact and the similarity of purpose presented in the various applications for loans.

This view, specifically embodied throughout the instructions, obviously confuses the common purpose of a single enterprise with the several, though similar, purposes of numerous separate adventures of like character. It may be that, notwithstanding the misdirection, the jury actually understood correctly the purport of the evidence, as the Government now concedes it to have been; and came to the conclusion that the petitioners were guilty only of the separate conspiracies in which the proof shows they respectively participated. But, in the face of the misdirection and in the circumstances of this case, we cannot assume that the lay triers of fact were so well informed upon the law or that they disregarded the permission expressly given to ignore that vital difference.

As we have said, the error permeated the entire charge, indeed the entire trial. Not only did it permit the jury to find each defendant guilty of conspiring with thirty-five other potential co-conspirators, or any less number as the proof might turn out for acquittal of some, when none of the evidence would support such a conviction, as the proof did turn out in fact. It had other effects. One was to prevent the court from giving a precautionary instruction such as would be appropriate, perhaps required, in cases where related but separate conspiracies are tried together under § 557 of the Code, namely, that the jury should take care to consider the evidence relating to each conspiracy separately from that relating to each other conspiracy charged. The court here was careful to caution the jury to consider each defendant's case separately, in determining his participation in "the scheme" charged. But this obviously does not, and could not, go to keeping distinct conspiracies distinct, in view of the court's conception of the case.

Moreover, the effect of the court's misconception extended also to the proof of overt acts. Carrying forward his premise that the jury could find one conspiracy on the evidence, the trial judge further charged that, if the jury found a conspiracy, "then the acts or the statements of any of those whom you so find to be conspirators between the two dates that I have mentioned, may be considered by you in evidence as against all of the defendants whom you so find to be members of the conspiracy." The instructions in this phase also declared:

> It is not necessary, as a matter of law, that an overt act be charged against each defendant. It is sufficient if the conspiracy be established and the defendant be found to be a member of the conspiracy -- it is sufficient to allege overt acts on the part of any others who may have been members of the conspiracy, if those acts were done in furtherance of, and for the purpose of accomplishing the conspiracy.

On those instructions it was competent not only for the jury to find that all of the defendants were parties to a single common plan, design and scheme, where none was shown by the proof, but also for them to impute to each defendant the acts and statements of the others without reference to whether they related to one of the schemes proven or another, and to find an overt act affecting all in conduct which admittedly could only have affected some.

* * * Guilt with us remains individual and personal, even as respects conspiracies. It is not a matter of mass application. There are times when of necessity, because of the nature and scope of the particular federation, large numbers of persons taking part must be tried together or perhaps not at all, at any rate as respects some. When many conspire, they invite mass trial by their conduct. Even so, the proceedings are exceptional to our tradition and call for use of every safeguard to individualize each defendant in his relation to the mass. Wholly different is it with those who join together with only a few, though many

others may be doing the same and though some of them may line up with more than one group.

Criminal they may be, but it is not the criminality of mass conspiracy. They do not invite mass trial by their conduct. Nor does our system tolerate it. That way lies the drift toward totalitarian institutions. True, this may be inconvenient for prosecution. But our Government is not one of mere convenience or efficiency. It too has a stake, with every citizen, in his being afforded our historic individual protections, including those surrounding criminal trials. About them we dare not become careless or complacent when that fashion has become rampant over the earth.

Here toleration went too far. We do not think that either Congress, when it enacted § 269, or this Court, when deciding the *Berger* case, intended to authorize the Government to string together, for common trial, eight or more separate and distinct crimes, conspiracies related in kind though they might be, when the only nexus among them lies in the fact that one man participated in all. * * *

Reversed.

UNITED STATES v. BRUNO
Circuit Court of Appeals, Second Circuit
105 F.2d 921 (1939)

Before L. HAND, AUGUSTUS N. HAND, and CLARK, CIRCUIT JUDGES.

PER CURIAM.

Bruno and Iacono were indicted along with 86 others for a conspiracy to import, sell and possess narcotics; some were acquitted; others, besides these two, were convicted, but they alone appealed. They complain [inter alia] that if the evidence proved anything, it proved a series of separate conspiracies, and not a single one, as alleged in the indictment. * * *

The first point was made at the conclusion of the prosecution's case: the defendants then moved to dismiss the indictment on the ground that several conspiracies had been proved, and not the one alleged. The evidence allowed the jury to find that there had existed over a substantial period of time a conspiracy embracing a great number of persons, whose object was to smuggle narcotics into the Port of New York and distribute them to addicts both in this city and in Texas and Louisiana. This required the cooperation of four groups of persons; the smugglers who imported the drugs; the middlemen who paid the smugglers and distributed to retailers; and two groups of retailers - one in New York and one in Texas and Louisiana - who supplied the addicts. The defendants assert that there were, therefore, at least three separate conspiracies; one between the smugglers and the middlemen, and one between the middlemen and each group of retailers. The evidence did not disclose any cooperation or communication between the smugglers and either group of retailers, or between the two groups of retailers themselves; however, the smugglers knew that the middlemen must sell to retailers, and the retailers knew that the middlemen must buy of importers of one sort or another. Thus the conspirators at one end of the chain knew that the unlawful business would not, and could not, stop with their buyers; and those at the other end knew that it had not begun with their sellers. That being true, a jury might have found that all the accused were embarked upon a venture, in all parts of which each was a participant, and an abettor in the sense that the success of that part with which he was immediately concerned, was dependent upon the success of the whole. That distinguishes the situation from that in *United States v. Peoni,* where Peoni, the accused, did not know that Regno, his buyer, was to sell the counterfeit bills to Dorsey, and had no interest in whether he did, since Regno might equally well have passed them to innocent persons himself. It might still be argued that there were two conspiracies; one including the smugglers, the middlemen and the New York group, and the other, the smugglers, the middlemen and the Texas & Louisiana group, for there was apparently no privity between the two groups of retailers. That too would be fallacious. Clearly, quoad the smugglers, there was but one conspiracy, for it was of no moment to them whether the middlemen sold to one or more groups of retailers, provided they had a market somewhere. So too of any retailer; he knew that he was a necessary link in a scheme of distribution, and the others, whom he knew to be convenient to its execution, were as much parts of a single undertaking or enterprise as two salesmen in the same shop. We think therefore that there was only one conspiracy. * * *

E.   SPECIAL DEFENSES TO CONSPIRACY: WITHDRAWAL AND IMPOSSIBILITY

UNITED STATES v. READ
United States Court of Appeals, Seventh Circuit
658 F.2d 1225 (1981)

BAUER, CIRCUIT JUDGE.

Defendants-appellants Ralph Read, Ronald E. Spiegel, and Howard Swiger appeal their convictions for conspiracy, mail fraud, and securities fraud. We affirm the judgments of conviction entered for Ralph Read and Howard Swiger in Nos. 80-1017 and 80-1019. We reverse Ronald Spiegel's conviction for conspiracy in No. 80-1018 and remand for a new trial. We affirm Spiegel's conviction on the substantive counts.

I

The indictment charged a scheme to artificially inflate the year-end inventory of Cenco Medical Health Supply Corporation ("CMH") and thus increase its reported profits. The defendants-appellants were officers of CMH and Cenco, CMH's parent corporation. Ralph Read was president of Cenco and a member of its board of directors; Ronald Spiegel was a vice-president of Cenco, and president of CMH; Howard Swiger was also a vice-president of Cenco and comptroller of CMH. Other defendants Russell Rabjohns, Bernard Magdovitz, and Jack Carlson pled guilty to two counts and testified for the government. Another defendant, Robert Smith, was acquitted.

We need only briefly outline the evidence at trial showing defendants' massive manipulation of CMH's finances from 1970 to 1975. The greatest amount of the fraud was accomplished by overstating CMH's inventory. During annual inventory, each CMH branch recorded the amount of every item in stock on computer cards. When the cards were returned to the central Chicago office for processing, some of the defendants, at Spiegel's direction, increased the numbers on the cards. Thousands of cards were altered in this fashion; defendants made additional changes in the computer listings of the inventory that CMH submitted to its auditors. In 1970, defendants increased the reported inventory of CMH by 3.5 million dollars. In each succeeding year, defendants increased the inventory by several millions more and carried the previous years' inflation forward. The overstatement of inventory decreased CMH's cost of sales, which in turn produced greater reported profits, dollar-for-dollar. This practice continued until 1975. Estimates of the total fraud ranged from 20 to 25 million dollars.

Other methods included inflating profits by accruing sales in one year and deferring expenses for those sales until the next fiscal year. The defendants also increased reported sales by listing the sales from August 1972 on computer printouts for March 1973 sales. They also created fake documents showing hundreds of thousands of dollars of non-existent inventory to be in transit between warehouses so that it could not be physically counted.

In 1974, Curtiss-Wright Corporation, a large conglomerate, purchased five percent of Cenco's shares. Curtiss-Wright's accountants, while examining Cenco's finances for a possible loan, found discrepancies in Cenco's inventory records. Alarmed, the defendants sought to create the appearance of $10 million of non-existent inventory should Curtiss-Wright's auditors physically check the inventory. In order to do so, they ordered the repacking of obsolete inventory in boxes of expensive products. Finally, in 1975, the defendants implemented an inventory destruction program to cover up the fraud. The defendants persuaded Cenco's board of directors to approve the destruction of $16 million of obsolete inventory as part of a supposed tax savings program. Almost all of the "destroyed" inventory existed only on paper.

The ultimate result of the fraud was to overstate the profitability of Cenco, thereby defrauding its board, its stockholders, and the SEC. The prosecution also showed that Read's compensation was linked to the company's profits.

The indictment charged the defendants with conspiracy, mail fraud, and securities fraud. On September 6, 1979, the case proceeded to trial against Read, Spiegel, Swiger, and Smith. On October 29, 1979, following almost eight weeks of testimony, the jury returned guilty verdicts on all counts as to Read, Spiegel, and Swiger. Smith was acquitted. Read, Spiegel, and Swiger appeal their convictions. * * *

III

Ronald Spiegel's main defense at trial was that he withdrew from the conspiracy more than five years before the indictment was filed. He argued that his prosecution therefore was barred by the statute of limitations. 18 U.S.C. § 3282. Spiegel argues on appeal that the trial court gave erroneous instructions on the issue of withdrawal.

The trial court instructed the jury:

> Now, we talked about withdrawal. How does a person withdraw from a conspiracy? A person can withdraw from a conspiracy, and in such a case he is not liable for the acts of his former co-conspirators after his withdrawal. A defendant may withdraw by notifying co-conspirators that he will no longer participate in the undertaking. A defendant may also withdraw from a conspiracy by engaging in acts inconsistent with the objects of the conspiracy. These acts or statements need not be known or communicated to all other co-conspirators as long as they are communicated in a manner reasonably calculated to reach some of them. To withdraw from a conspiracy there is no requirement that a conspirator try to convince the other co-conspirators to abandon their undertaking or that he go to public authorities or others to expose the conspiracy or to prevent the carrying out of an act involved in the conspiracy. But a withdrawal defense requires that a defendant completely abandon the conspiracy and that he do so in good faith. If you find that a defendant completely withdrew from the conspiracy before the 24th of April, 1974, you should acquit him. If you find that he was a member on April 24, 1974, and that an overt

act was committed while he was still a member, his later withdrawal, if any, standing alone, is not a defense.

Why do we pick the date "April 24th, 1974"? We do that because the indictment in this case, as you will see, bears a stamp, the Clerk's stamp that it was filed on April 24th, 1979. There is a five year statute of limitations for criminal conspiracy and the charge and the five year statute of limitations runs from the date of the last overt act in the indictment to the date of the filing of the indictment. Accordingly, if you find that an overt act was committed within five years before April 24, 1979 another way of saying that is that if you find that an overt act was committed between April 24th, 1974 and August of 1975, the conspiracy count in its entirety may be considered by you, going all the way back to 1970 or earlier.

Spiegel objected to the above instructions. He claimed before the trial court, and here, that the instructions put the burden of proving withdrawal on Spiegel and failed to put the burden of disproving withdrawal beyond a reasonable doubt on the government. He also attacks the propriety of instructing the jury that the withdrawal must be in good faith. He further asserts that the instruction erroneously allowed the jury to find that he participated in the conspiracy after the limitations date by proof of overt acts not alleged in the indictment.

Spiegel also claims he withdrew before commission of the securities and mail fraud crimes. He complains that the jury was not instructed that his withdrawal was effective if it occurred before the dates of the sales or mailings charged in the indictment.

We agree that the instructions concerning withdrawal were erroneous and require a remand for a new trial on the conspiracy charge. We disagree, however, that withdrawal is a defense to the substantive crimes, and affirm Spiegel's conviction on those counts.

A

Due process requires that the prosecution prove beyond a reasonable doubt every fact necessary to constitute the crime charged. *In re Winship*, 397 U.S. 358, 364 (1970); *Mullaney v. Wilbur*, 421 U.S. 684, 685 (1975); *Patterson v. New York*, 432 U.S. 197 (1977). The prosecution's burden often includes disproving defenses because they bring into question facts necessary for conviction. This rule has been well-settled with regard to some defenses.

Patterson requires us to inquire whether the particular defense negates an essential element of the offense as defined by the legislature. As held in *Holloway v. McElroy*, 632 F.2d 605, 625 (5th Cir. 1980), the government "may not place the burden of persuasion on (an) issue upon the defendant if the truth of the 'defense' would necessarily negate an essential element of the crime charged."

18 U.S.C. § 371 provides:

> If two or more persons conspire either to commit any offense against the United States, or to defraud the United States, or any agency thereof in any manner or for any purpose, and one or more of such persons do any act to effect the object of the conspiracy, each shall be fined not more than $10,000 or imprisoned not more than five years, or both.

The statute, as long construed, requires the prosecution to prove (1) that the alleged conspiracy existed; (2) that an overt act was committed in furtherance of the conspiracy; and (3) that the defendant knowingly and intentionally became a member of the conspiracy.

Prosecution for conspiracy is also subject to a five-year statute of limitations, which runs from the date of the last overt act. In practice, to convict a defendant the prosecution must prove that the conspiracy existed and that each defendant was a member of the conspiracy at some point in the five years preceding the date of the indictment.

Withdrawal marks a conspirator's disavowal or abandonment of the conspiratorial agreement. By definition, after a defendant withdraws, he is no longer a member of the conspiracy and the later acts of the conspirators do not bind him. The defendant is still liable, however, for his previous agreement and for the previous acts of his co-conspirators in pursuit of the conspiracy. Withdrawal is not, therefore, a complete defense to the crime of conspiracy. Withdrawal becomes a complete defense only when coupled with the defense of the statute of limitations. A defendant's withdrawal from the conspiracy starts the running of the statute of limitations as to him. If the indictment is filed more than five years after a defendant withdraws, the statute of limitations bars prosecution for his actual participation in the conspiracy. He cannot be held liable for acts or declarations committed in the five years preceding the indictment by other conspirators because his withdrawal ended his membership in the conspiracy. It is thus only the interaction of the two defenses of withdrawal and the statute of limitations which shields the defendant from liability.[4]

Withdrawal, then, directly negates the element of membership in the conspiracy during the period of the statute of limitations. Under *Patterson, Mullaney,* and *Winship,* the government should disprove the defense of withdrawal beyond a reasonable doubt.

The government, however, insists that *Hyde v. United States,* 225 U.S. 347 (1912), a long-established Supreme Court case, placed the burden of proving withdrawal on the defendant. Indeed, *Hyde* has often been cited for that proposition in the courts of appeals. Almost every case we researched holds that the burden is on the defendant to "prove" or "establish" withdrawal. Within this Circuit, we recently held that it "is well-settled (that) this burden of establishing withdrawal lies on the defendant."

We have, however, reexamined *Hyde.* Our research convinces us that the cases, including our own, have misinterpreted *Hyde.* According to our interpretation, *Hyde* placed only the burden of going forward on the defendant. To understand what *Hyde* did hold, however, it is important to understand the law of conspiracy as it existed pre-*Hyde.*

Turn-of-the-century law held that the crime of conspiracy was complete with the agreement. Under old law, the statute of limitations ran from the first overt act. To prove that a conspiracy was still "live," the government had to prove each defendant's membership in the conspiracy with evidence from within the statute of limitations. Put another way, the government had to prove that each defendant had not withdrawn prior to the running of the statute of limitations.

In *Hyde v. United States,* the Supreme Court reacted to the problems of proving membership in a conspiracy that did not end with one agreement, but rather was a continuous series of agreements, such as gambling or liquor and drug smuggling. The old rule envisioned a static conspiracy, with the relation of the conspirators fixed at one moment in time. The *Hyde* Court rejected that image. It held that if a conspiracy may continue, "it would seem necessarily to

---

[4] Dropping out during the limitations period does not absolve a defendant. He is still liable for the agreement and acts committed before he withdraws. Since a continuing conspiracy is alleged as one crime, he is also liable in effect for the crimes of his co-conspirators even after his withdrawal. Severance is not ordinarily justified because the circumstances usually provide sufficient basis for joinder under the rules of criminal procedure.

follow (that) the relation of the conspirators to it must continue, being to (the conspiracy) during its life as it was to it the moment it was brought into life." Since liability for conspiracy is predicated on the responsibility of the participants for each other's acts, "(i)f each conspirator was the agent of the others" at one time, "he remains an agent during all (other) time(s)." Thus, the Court held, the government need only prove a defendant's membership in the conspiracy at one point in time.

The Court next responded to debate that its new theory of group responsibility would make conspirators perpetually liable. The Court stated that its new theory would not "take from a conspirator the power to withdraw from the execution of the offense or to avert a continuing criminality." The Court stated the defense of the statute of limitations was viable in a continuing conspiracy, but that its "application" was "different." Withdrawal from a conspiracy, the Court held, "requires affirmative action, but certainly that is no hardship. Having joined in an unlawful scheme ... to be continuous until full fruition be secured, until he does some act to disavow or defeat the purpose he is in no situation to claim the delay of the law." The Court justified its new requirement of affirmative proof of withdrawal by saying:

> As the offense has not been terminated or accomplished he is still offending. And we think, consciously offending, offending as certainly ... as at the first moment of his confederation, and consciously through every moment of its existence .... As he has started evil forces he must withdraw his support from them or incur the guilt of their continuance.

Hyde made one definite change in the law the prosecution no longer had to show each defendant's participation in the conspiracy during the statute of limitations. Instead, the prosecution could prove a defendant's membership at any time during the life of the conspiracy. It was then up to the defendant to show that he did "some act to disavow or defeat the purpose" of the conspiracy to mark his withdrawal. If his withdrawal predated the statute of limitations, he could then "claim the delay of the law."

Hyde said nothing explicit about the amount of evidence the defendant must offer to show "some act to disavow or defeat the purpose" of the conspiracy. As one commentator noted, the *Hyde* language "might have been interpreted as merely shifting the production burden on the issue of withdrawal to the defendant, and leaving the persuasion burden with the state." *Developments in the Law-Criminal Conspiracy*, 72 Harv. L. Rev. 920, 958 (1959). Two early cases interpreted *Hyde* in this manner. * * *

Other cases, however, reached strikingly different conclusions. * * *

At the same time, courts grappled with the issue of what acts constituted withdrawal. * * *

A subtle, but important, change was occurring. Within decades, the *Hyde* rule that a defendant show some "affirmative action" to trigger the withdrawal defense was transformed into a rule that the defendant must meet "rigorous requirements" to show his withdrawal. * * *

The withdrawal rule is based on a misinterpretation of *Hyde*'s requirement that the defendant do "some act to disavow or defeat the purpose" of the conspiracy to withdraw. We have traced back the citation of authority in our own cases; they lead back to only the same language in *Hyde*.

As withdrawal negates the essential element of membership, it must be disproved beyond a reasonable doubt by the government. We therefore overrule those cases imposing the burden of proving withdrawal on the defendant. We hold today that the burden of going forward with evidence of withdrawal and with evidence that he withdrew prior to the statute of limitations remains on the defendant. However, once he advances sufficient evidence, the burden of persuasion is on the prosecution to disprove the defense of withdrawal beyond a reasonable doubt. As in the cases of other defenses, once the jury has been instructed on the withdrawal defense, the jury should be instructed that the government bears the burden of disproving withdrawal beyond a reasonable doubt. * * *

[The court goes on to point out that withdrawal is not a defense to securities fraud or mail fraud.]

Since we hold that withdrawal is not an available defense to the substantive counts, Spiegel was not entitled to an instruction regarding withdrawal. Although the court erred, Spiegel could not have been prejudiced by the giving of an instruction favorable to him. His conviction on the securities and mail fraud counts was therefore proper. * * *

We affirm the judgment of convictions of Read and Swiger entered in numbers 80-1017 and 80-1019. We reverse Spiegel's conviction on Count I in 80-1018 and remand for a new trial; we affirm his conviction on the remaining counts.

UNITED STATES v. RECIO
Supreme Court of the United States
537 U.S. 270, 123 S.Ct. 819, 154 L.Ed.2d 744 (2003)

JUSTICE BREYER delivered the opinion of the Court.

We here consider the validity of a Ninth Circuit rule that a conspiracy ends automatically when the object of the conspiracy becomes impossible to achieve -- when, for example, the Government frustrates a drug conspiracy's objective by seizing the drugs that its members have agreed to distribute. In our view, conspiracy law does not contain any such "automatic termination" rule.

I

In *United States v. Cruz*, 127 F.3d 791, 795 (9th Cir.1997), the Ninth Circuit, following the language of an earlier case, *United States v. Castro*, 972 F.2d 1107, 1112 (9th Cir. 1992), wrote that a conspiracy terminates when "'there is affirmative evidence of abandonment, withdrawal, disavowal *or defeat of the object of the conspiracy.*'" (Emphasis added.) It considered the conviction of an individual who, the Government had charged, joined a conspiracy (to distribute drugs) after the Government had seized the drugs in question. The Circuit found that the Government's seizure of the drugs guaranteed the "defeat" of the conspiracy's objective, namely, drug distribution. The Circuit held that the conspiracy had terminated with that "defeat," i.e., when the Government seized the drugs. Hence the individual, who had joined the conspiracy after that point, could not be convicted as a conspiracy member.

In this case the lower courts applied the *Cruz* rule to similar facts: On November 18, 1997, police stopped a truck in Nevada. They found, and seized, a large stash of illegal drugs. With the help of the truck's two drivers, they set up a sting. The Government took the truck to the drivers' destination, a mall in Idaho. The drivers paged a contact and described the truck's location. The contact said that he would call someone to get the truck. And three hours later, the two defendants, Francisco Jimenez Recio and Adrian Lopez-Meza, appeared in a car. Jimenez Recio drove away in the truck; Lopez-Meza drove the car away in a similar direction. Police stopped both vehicles and arrested both men.

A federal grand jury indicted Jimenez Recio, Lopez-Meza, and the two original truck drivers, charging them with having conspired, together and with others, to possess and to distribute unlawful drugs. A jury convicted all four. But the trial judge then decided that the jury instructions had been erroneous in respect to Jimenez Recio and Lopez-Meza. The judge noted that the Ninth Circuit, in *Cruz*, had held that the Government could not prosecute drug conspiracy defendants unless they had joined the conspiracy before the Government seized the drugs. That holding, as applied here, meant that the jury could not convict Jimenez Recio and Lopez-Meza unless the jury believed they had joined the conspiracy before the Nevada police stopped the truck and seized the drugs. The judge ordered a new trial where the jury would be instructed to that effect. The new jury convicted the two men once again.

Jimenez Recio and Lopez-Meza appealed. They pointed out that, given *Cruz*, the jury had to find that they had joined the conspiracy before the Nevada stop, and they claimed that the evidence was insufficient at both trials to warrant any such jury finding. The Ninth Circuit panel, by a vote of 2 to 1, agreed. All three panel members accepted *Cruz* as binding law. Two members concluded that the evidence presented at the second trial was not sufficient to show that the defendants had joined the conspiracy before the Nevada drug seizure. One of the two wrote that the evidence at the first trial was not sufficient either, a circumstance she believed independently warranted reversal. The third member, dissenting, believed that the evidence at both trials adequately demonstrated preseizure membership. He added that he, like the other panel members, was bound by *Cruz*, but he wrote that in his view *Cruz* was "totally inconsistent with long established and appropriate principles of the law of conspiracy," and he urged the Circuit to overrule it en banc "at the earliest opportunity."

The Government sought certiorari. It noted that the Ninth Circuit's holding in this case was premised upon the legal rule enunciated in *Cruz*. And it asked us to decide the rule's validity, i.e., to decide whether "a conspiracy ends as a matter of law when the government frustrates its objective." We agreed to consider that question.

II

In *Cruz*, the Ninth Circuit held that a conspiracy continues "'until there is affirmative evidence of abandonment, withdrawal, disavowal or defeat of the object of the conspiracy.'" The critical portion of this statement is the last segment, that a conspiracy ends once there has been "'defeat of [its] object.'" The Circuit's holdings make clear that the phrase means that the conspiracy ends through "defeat" when the Government intervenes, making the conspiracy's goals impossible to achieve, even if the conspirators do not know that the Government has intervened and are totally unaware that the conspiracy is bound to fail. In our view, this statement of the law is incorrect. A conspiracy does not automatically terminate simply because the Government, unbeknownst to some of the conspirators, has "defeat[ed]" the conspiracy's "object."

Two basic considerations convince us that this is the proper view of the law. First, the Ninth Circuit's rule is inconsistent with our own understanding of basic conspiracy law. The Court has repeatedly said that the essence of a conspiracy is "an agreement to commit an unlawful act." That agreement is "a distinct evil," which "may exist and be punished whether or not the substantive crime ensues." The conspiracy poses a "threat to the public" over and above the threat of the commission of the relevant substantive crime -- both because the "[c]ombination in crime makes more likely the commission of [other] crimes" and because it "decreases the probability that the individuals involved will depart from their path of criminality." Where police have frustrated a conspiracy's specific objective but conspirators (unaware of that fact) have neither abandoned the conspiracy nor withdrawn, these special conspiracy-related dangers remain. *Cf.* 2 W. LaFave & A. Scott, SUBSTANTIVE CRIMINAL LAW §6.5, p. 85 (1986) ("[i]mpossibility" does not terminate conspiracy because "criminal combinations are dangerous apart from the danger of attaining the particular objective"). So too remains the essence of the conspiracy -- the agreement to commit the crime. That being so, the Government's defeat of the conspiracy's objective will not necessarily and automatically terminate the conspiracy.

Second, the view we endorse today is the view of almost all courts and commentators but for the Ninth Circuit. No other Federal Court of Appeals has adopted the Ninth Circuit's rule. Three have explicitly rejected it. * * * One treatise, after surveying lower court conspiracy decisions, has concluded that "[i]mpossibility of success is not a defense." 2 LaFave & Scott, SUBSTANTIVE CRIMINAL LAW §6.5, at 85; see also *id.*, §6.5(b), at 90-93. And the American Law Institute's Model Penal Code §5.03, p. 384 (1985), would find that a conspiracy "terminates when the crime or crimes that are its object are committed" or when the relevant "agreement . . . is abandoned." It would not find "impossibility" a basis for termination.

The *Cruz* majority argued that the more traditional termination rule threatened "endless" potential liability. To illustrate the point, the majority posited a sting in which police instructed an arrested conspirator to go through the "telephone directory . . . [and] call all of his acquaintances" to come and help him, with the Government obtaining convictions of those who did so. The problem with this example, however, is that, even though it is not necessarily an example of entrapment itself, it draws its persuasive force from the fact that it bears certain resemblances to entrapment. The law independently forbids convictions that rest upon entrapment. And the example fails to explain why a different branch of the law, conspiracy law, should be modified to forbid entrapment-like behavior that falls outside the bounds of current entrapment law. At the same time, the *Cruz* rule would reach well beyond arguable police misbehavior, potentially threatening the use of properly run law enforcement sting operations. *See Lewis v. United States*, 385 U.S. 206, 208-09 (1966) (Government may "use decoys" and conceal agents' identity); *see also* M. Lyman, CRIMINAL INVESTIGATION 484-485 (2d ed. 1999) (explaining the importance of undercover operations in enforcing drug laws). * * *

III

We conclude that the Ninth Circuit's conspiracy-termination law holding set forth in *Cruz* is erroneous in the manner discussed. We reverse the present judgment insofar as it relies upon that holding. Because Jimenez Recio and Lopez-Meza have raised other arguments not here considered, we remand the case, specifying that the Court of Appeals may consider those arguments, if they were properly raised.

The judgment of the Ninth Circuit is reversed, and the case is remanded for further proceedings consistent with this opinion.

It is so ordered.

[JUSTICE STEVENS' opinion concurring in part and dissenting in part is omitted.]

F.   CONSPIRACY AND THE DANGERS OF COLLECTIVE ACTION

Courts and commentators typically assume that a conspiracy poses distinct dangers quite apart from those of the substantive offense.

> [C]ollective criminal agreement -- partnership in crime -- presents a greater potential threat to the public than individual delicts. Concerted action both increases the likelihood that the criminal object will be successfully attained and decreases the probability that the individuals involved will depart from their path of criminality. Group association for criminal purposes often, if not normally, makes possible the attainment of ends more complex than those which one criminal could accomplish. Nor is the danger of a conspiratorial group limited to the particular end toward which it has embarked. Combination in crime makes more likely the commission of crimes unrelated to the original purpose for which the group was formed. In sum, the danger which a conspiracy generates is not confined to the substantive offense which is the immediate aim of the enterprise.

Ianelli v. United States, 420 U.S. 770, 778 (1975) (quoting *Callanan v. United States*, 364 U.S. 587, 593-594 (1961)).

Is the long-held idea that concerted action is uniquely dangerous supported by contemporary social science evidence? Consider the argument that follows.

CONSPIRACY THEORY
Neal Katyal
112 Yale L.J. 1307 (2003)

* * * Why should conspiracy liability begin at the moment of "agreement," before any crime is committed? Why can a conspirator be charged with both the inchoate offense of conspiracy and the robbery? Why should the law punish conspirators even if it's impossible for them to commit the crime they planned? Why is withdrawal from a conspiracy so difficult? And what about that oddball *Pinkerton* doctrine?

For more than 50 years, these questions have prompted a series of critiques of conspiracy law. The major scholarly articles have alleged the doctrine "unnecessary" and stated that the "assumed dangers from conspiracy . . . have never been verified empirically." And such views have successfully permeated the criminal law. The Model Penal Code, a blueprint for state law first written by a commission of experts in the early 1950s, rejected many of the traditional features of conspiracy law. Over the past fifteen years, the Federal Sentencing Commission similarly eliminated many of the traditional features of conspiracy doctrine, so that, for example, it is not generally possible to punish someone for conspiring to commit a crime and for committing it.

These cutbacks are likely to be a mistake. * * * Psychologists have made many advances in understanding the ways in which people in groups act differently than they do as individuals. So, too, economists have developed sophisticated explanations for why firms promote efficiency, leading to new theories in corporate law. These insights can be "reverse-engineered" to make conspiracies operate less efficiently. In reverse engineering corporate law principles and introducing lessons from psychology, a rich account of how government should approach conspiracy begins to unfold.

This is a central issue in criminal law, since more than one-quarter of all federal criminal prosecutions and a large number of state cases involve prosecutions for conspiracy. Virtually every state recognizes the crime. Yet criticisms of the doctrine are pervasive, and generally take two forms. First, the rationale for the offense of conspiracy is questioned. Why should group behavior receive additional punishment, and why should any punishment at all attach at the moment of agreement? In the second critique, conspiracy law is excoriated for giving prosecutors too much power. This Article concerns itself with answering the first of these criticisms by offering a functional justification for punishing conspiracy. * * *

[There are] two reasons why conspiracies are harmful: the specialization of labor/economies of scale and the development of a pernicious group identity.

The former is easily understood by thinking about how difficult it is for an individual to rob a bank alone. Several individuals are needed to carry weapons and provide firepower (economies of scale), someone needs to be the "brains behind the operation" (a form of specialization of labor), and another should serve as a lookout (specialization again). Conspiracy creates obvious efficiencies, efficiencies predicted by Ronald Coase in his path-breaking article about why firms develop.

What are somewhat less obvious, but at least as important, are psychological accounts of the dangers of group activity. Advances in psychology over the past thirty years have demonstrated that groups cultivate a special social identity. This identity often encourages risky behavior, leads individuals to behave against their self-interest, solidifies loyalty, and facilitates harm against nonmembers. The psychological and economic accounts explain why law treats conspiracy in a distinctive way. The law focuses on "agreement" because that decision has drastic consequences. The law seeks to attach a broad and potentially uncognizable set of penalties at this early stage to deter many from becoming conspirators. * * *

1. Psychological Analysis of Social Identity

A wide body of psychological research over the last century reveals that people tend to act differently in groups than they do as individuals. Some of the work is tentative, thereby precluding robust results. Nevertheless, it is generally accepted that groups are more likely to polarize toward extremes, to take courses of action that advance the interests of the group even in the face of personal doubts, and to act with greater loyalty to each other. Much of the most influential research focuses on how group membership changes an individual's personal identity to produce a new social identity. In this process, a person's self-esteem becomes linked to the group's successes and failures. Group members thus tend to refer more to each other than they do to outsiders, listen more to each other, and reward each other more often.

The work on social identity began with studies of group conformity. Muzafer Sherif's 1936 experiments showed that people estimating how far a pinpoint of light moved in a dark room tended to conform to what others in the room said. Even a wildly off-base group member influenced the results. Follow-up studies confirmed that individuals internalized the views of others and adhered to them even a year later. Furthermore, when individuals left a group and were replaced by others, the group views remained constant over "generations" of subjects -- so much so that an entirely new group of subjects at the end of an experiment had the same views as the initial group of subjects.

Finding somewhat similar results, early studies by Solomon Asch asked individuals in groups which of three "comparison" lines placed at a distance matched a "standard" line. Each group was staffed largely with Asch's confederates; when they voiced clearly wrong answers, the naive subjects would conform over one-third of the time to these obviously incorrect answers (compared to a one percent error rate when confederates voiced correct answers). When even one confederate broke ranks with the off-base match, however, the subject was very unlikely to support the wrong answer -- even when seven other people voiced support for it. The lesson here is not that individuals blindly follow groups; rather, it is that groups suppress dissent and induce conformity when they are visibly unanimous. Rules that provide incentives to break ranks, such as conspiracy's withdrawal doctrine, may therefore unravel conformist dynamics.

More generally, the psychological research will underscore why conspiracy law cannot be understood as a device that merely deters individuals. Rather, the doctrine functions on a group level, for in groups a variety of psychological processes come into play, such as the relationship between leaders and followers, the emergence of a social identity, and polarization. By thinking about the individual, as the dominant mode of legal scholarship has sought to do, these processes are slighted -- yet they explain why conspiracy should be treated in a distinctive way. * * *

a. Polarization and Risk-Taking

Groups are more likely to have extreme attitudes and behavior. This research began with findings showing "risky shifts" -- predictability in the conformity result in that people take greater risks in groups. Subsequent work found that the phenomenon was not limited to shifts in risk, and that groups polarize in the direction their members were already tending. For example, French students who already liked de Gaulle liked him even more after discussing him in a group, and those who did not like Americans liked them even less after discussing Americans in a group. Once the problem is conceptualized as polarization, it becomes possible to understand why some groups behave with extreme caution.

From one perspective, criminal risk-taking might be good because lawbreakers may commit acts with a high probability of detection. While more empirical research is necessary, there are reasons to doubt that polarization will occur along this dimension. Polarization arises because individuals exaggerate their conformity to perceived traits of a group's social identity. It is therefore possible to have a group of criminals acting more cautiously with respect to what targets to attack, and more riskily with respect to the number of crimes that they commit. A study of active burglars provides some support for this dual shift, for it found that burglars working in groups committed more burglaries and that they were more cautious about which targets to burgle. The study also found that burglars in groups are more likely to be aroused, raising the possibility that group crimes lead to unplanned violence.

b. Acting Against Self-Interest

Groups encourage individuals to submerge their self-interest to that of the group. Some of the most interesting work on this point is being done by two economists, Nobel laureate George Akerlof and his colleague Rachel Kranton. Their model puts forth a theory for why individuals act against their own interests in order to preserve or augment their group identity. Flouting the perceived ideals of the group generates personal anxiety over self-image. Standard economic theory, Akerlof and Kranton underscore, does not take these considerations into account, and therefore has a difficult time explaining activities that are against individual self-interest, such as self-mutilation through tattoos or piercing.

Akerlof and Kranton's work follows from a number of psychological studies about behavior in groups. In a series of famous experiments, Sherif studied group dynamics in a boys' summer camp. Upon arrival, the boys were free to form spontaneous friendships, but after a few days they were split into two groups. Under isolation, the groups "developed a cohesive structure and they came to strongly prefer the members of their own group." When the groups were brought together for a tournament, "overt group hostility . . . [and] minor acts of discrimination and aggression" were found, and "in-group loyalty, solidarity and cooperation" were at their height.

A second series of experiments, dubbed the "minimal group" ones, found that even arbitrary formation of groups with no previous history between the members produces similar results. Henri Tajfel's initial studies divided schoolchildren into two groups by showing them some abstract paintings and asking which ones they liked best. The students were told that they were assigned to their groups on the basis of their answers (in actuality they were randomly assigned, and in later experiments, they were not even shown paintings, but assigned by a coin toss or by being told they were in a red or blue group). The subjects were not told who else was in the group and were placed in individual cubicles. They were then asked to award money between the two groups, and Tajfel found that there was significant discrimination in favor of one's own group. Indeed, individuals favored their group even when it was against their absolute self-interest: They gave their group the largest relative gains instead of giving their group and the other group greater absolute gains. This research suggests that the initial decision to agree to conspire is an important pivot point. Once an individual has made such an agreement, group identity can take hold and lead her to submerge self-interest to the group's interest.

c. Dissuasion

Contracts scholars have spoken of a moral obligation to fulfill contracts -- an obligation that increases the probability of performance. When A agrees to engage in a crime with B, the agreement thus makes the crime more likely. What is now understood about groups is that, apart from this obligation, groups are far more difficult to dissuade than are individuals because they develop self-serving inferences. Such inferences permit members of groups to justify their conduct as furthering either social or group goals.

One common inference is for group members to believe that other members are more likely to be correct and that nonmembers are more likely to be wrong. Another inference is that group members are fairer than nonmembers. As a result of these and other group biases, members of a group will listen to one another far more than they will listen to other people. Consequently, people in groups are more likely to escalate their commitments to failing courses of action and more likely to continue with these failing courses of action. Chip Heath, in a related finding, discovered that people are far more likely to experience doubts about their performance and disillusionment when they act as individuals compared to when they act in groups.

Dissuasion and disillusionment are critical ways for the government to fight conspiracy. When criminal groups develop self-serving inferences, it reinforces their tendencies toward crime. Members may feel more justified in pursuing criminal activity to help other members and may develop rationalizations (some drug dealers, for example, believe they perform the positive work of pharmacists and steer customers away from violent dealers). Such rationalizations can also thwart cooperation with law enforcement. Consider the recent startling results of two psychologists who found that prisoners' dilemma players induced to feel empathy for the other party cooperate almost fifty percent of the time even when they know that the other party has already defected. Game theory predicts constant defection, and yet cooperation is manifested repeatedly. Such research explains why many do not defect from conspiracies. The group encourages a feeling of solidarity and cultivates the view that each member needs the cooperation of the others. It is harder to get people to defect -- to flip -- when they share an identity.

d. Success in Tasks

Studies of group performance appear to be in some tension with each other. On the one hand, some studies show that people perform less well in groups than they do as individuals. For example, German experiments in the nineteenth century found that when the size of a group asked to pull a rope was increased, the total pull exerted would increase, but the amount each participant pulled would drop. Dyads pulled at 93%, trios at 85%, and groups of eight at only 49% of their individual performance levels. Taylorism, a management theory dominant in the early part of the twentieth century, was based on such notions of group inefficiency. More recent work has argued that groups suppress dissent and stifle creativity, an idea captured by Irving Janis's term "groupthink."

On the other hand, a number of studies find that groups enhance performance. Early work showed that when word puzzles were provided to individuals and groups, groups performed better. Other research has found that groups tend to have more solutions to problems, to generate them faster, and to find more creative solutions than do individuals. Indeed, a psychological literature review found a "general consensus . . . that, on average, groups outperform individuals" on tasks ranging from intellectual problems to decisionmaking ones.

The findings from these studies are reconcilable in two ways. First, the rope-pulling and other such experiments were beset with what we will later call "team-production" problems -- circumstances in which an individual's input to the team product was not visible and shirking therefore more likely. So, for example, individuals asked to cheer will not do so as loudly in a group as they will on their own, but will cheer as loudly in a group setting if they are told that a computer can discern their individual level of cheering. * * * Second, the group-inefficiency studies often slighted social identity. With a shared identity, performance increases markedly. One literature review found that "loyalty, rule-following and extra-role behaviour increase when employees define themselves in terms of a relevant team or organizational identity" so that when groups are given tasks that "encourage participants to define themselves in terms of a shared sense of self, group productivity can match that of isolated individuals and may also exceed it." Conspiracies, which often cultivate such an identity, therefore can be more productive (and impose greater harm) than isolated individuals.

2. Economic Analysis of Specialization of Labor and Economies of Scale

Businesses take advantage of their size in two ways: They permit their employees to specialize (and thereby increase production and/or quality), and they use their purchasing power to obtain larger advantages in the marketplace. Much early twentieth-century work in economics was preoccupied with understanding these phenomena. Coase argued that the benefit from merger arises because the manager of one firm will have control over the other and will not need to price incentives for additional output. A preexisting firm will economize on the search costs involved in finding labor for each new activity, and on the costs incurred in setting a wage structure from scratch. The firm develops because it is cheaper to avoid marketplace contracts.

A conspiracy, too, can exploit these benefits -- the criminal firm creates a framework of trust to reduce the transaction costs involved in forming new contracts with each other. A criminal enterprise can hire specialists and use its size to obtain benefits that uncoordinated individuals cannot. Conspiracies also create efficiencies for criminal enterprises because they minimize competition among members. Competing against each other imposes costs (such as the resources spent fighting) and reduces profits (due to a greater number of suppliers).

Economies of scale also have another set of advantages: They can reduce the probability of detection. Although larger entities may be more visible, they are also better bribers. The laws against bribery, which punish a small bribe with a large penalty, create marginal deterrence problems in that police and prosecutors only take large bribes since small ones are not worth the risk; individuals can rarely afford to pay these bribes. Conspiracies can also reduce the probability of detection in two other ways: by committing numerous crimes within a short time period in a jurisdiction and overpowering limited resources for investigation, and by assigning people as "lookouts" to avoid committing crimes in the presence of witnesses or law enforcement.

Specialization also permits crimes of diffusion, where the responsibility for a single crime is spread over many persons. These strategies help members evade punishment because of the difficulty involved in proving a person's actus reus and mens rea. The former is obscured by the number of other actors who committed parts of the crime; the latter because the individual might only have intended to carry out a minor role and because proof of a more culpable mental state is difficult to prove for those performing discrete tasks. In general, those insulated will be leaders, who orchestrate actions to maintain plausible deniability. (I first became painfully aware of this phenomenon while investigating war-crimes cases; imputing wrongdoing is exceptionally difficult because leaders hide their actions behind layers of middlepersons.) Conspiracy liability partially compensates for diffusion by punishing those who hide behind the veneer of the group.

Diffusion can also remove internal restraints to crime. Like the prison warden who flips a switch to carry out a death sentence, a person who drives a person from Point A to Point B may not feel that he is doing something gravely immoral, even when he is driving away from the scene of a crime. A person who "bags" cocaine for individual consumption may not consider herself responsible for the cocaine dependence of buyers. The forces of morality and social norms are thus subverted through strategies that disaggregate human behavior, playing on the idea that little bad acts are excusable. This makes crime easier and cheaper to carry out. * * *

B. The Benefits to Society from Group Behavior

    1. Information Extraction

    The chief benefit conspirators provide is information. In the Oklahoma City bombing prosecution, for example, Michael Fortier's testimony was indispensable because it "connected the government's 'bricks of evidence' by providing the only direct evidence of the plan, motivation, and preparation" of Timothy McVeigh and Terry Nichols. Because many conspiracies operate in a shadowy netherworld without complaining "victims," conspirators are valuable sources, and many prosecutions would not be possible without them.

    The primary way that a conspirator can be induced to provide information is by threatening penalties against that individual. A 1998 study found that flipping helped the government obtain guilty pleas of co-defendants, prosecution of new defendants, additional convictions and arrests, recovery of assets, cooperation of known and new co-defendants, and deportations. Indeed, flipping is so common that when the Tenth Circuit briefly decided to shut down the practice, the Justice Department complained that its ruling made "a criminal out of nearly every federal prosecutor" and that the government "relies on witnesses who testify in return for leniency in literally thousands of cases each year, including major cases."

    The classic co-conspirator exception to hearsay at trial, which permits a prosecutor to introduce all sorts of evidence about the parties without the actual speakers themselves in the courtroom, facilitates information extraction. The conspirator must "bear the risk of what his agents say as well as the risk of what they do." As such, it is a powerful tool to harvest information from a cooperator because it increases the range of statements to which she can testify. The permissiveness of joinder in conspiracy cases similarly furthers information extraction. Joinder induces each defendant to testify and lay responsibility for the crimes at the feet of the other defendants. * * *

    * * * [T]he basic point [is] that a conspiracy can sometimes aid law enforcement. The criminal who robs a house by himself may be less likely to get caught than the duo who robs two houses. Working in a group can expose a criminal to additional law enforcement risks because his partners can implicate him. Prosecutors can also obtain information about entirely unrelated crimes of which a conspirator learns from dealings with other members of a criminal syndicate. * * *

2. Physical Evidence and Perpetration Cost

Working in a group often results in physical evidence that increases the probability of being caught and sentenced. Because conspirators need to communicate with each other, their messages can be intercepted. E-mails can be captured, phone conversations tapped, mail read, and discussions in public places overheard. The lone criminal does not face these risks. * * *

In addition, conspiracy may be financially costly. A leader who runs a conspiracy has to devote time to management: making sure that employees are happy, the books are working, the suppliers are paid, and so on. Profits need to be split among many different actors. At some point, a conspiracy gets large enough that it does not generate enough profits for each participant. This is particularly the case when changes to architecture, such as better locks and more powerful lighting, require criminals to work in larger groups or to expend money on better equipment. These costs, by reducing gains to the criminal, can diminish incentives to commit crime.

Note

A doctrinal corollary of the theory behind conspiracy liability that the collective decision to commit a crime merits punishment distinct from punishment for the crime itself is represented by the common law doctrine called "Wharton's Rule." Under Wharton's Rule, certain crimes – among them adultery, incest, bigamy, and dueling – cannot be the subject of a conspiracy conviction, because they are inherently crimes requiring more than one person. Thus, it would constitute double punishment to convict someone both of the target crime and the conspiracy. Wharton's Rule does have certain exceptions:

> An exception to the Rule generally is thought to apply in the case in which the conspiracy involves more persons than are required for commission of the substantive offense. For example, while the two persons who commit adultery cannot normally be prosecuted both for that offense and for conspiracy to commit it, the third-party exception would permit the conspiracy charge where a "matchmaker" -- the third party -- had conspired with the principals to encourage commission of the substantive offense. The rationale supporting this exception appears to be that the addition of a third party enhances the dangers presented by the crime. Thus, it is thought that the legislature would not have intended to preclude punishment for a combination of greater dimension than that required to commit the substantive offense.

Iannelli v. United States, 420 U.S. 770, 782 n. 15 (1975).

G.   CONSPIRACY AND CONSTITUTIONAL VALUES

DENNIS v. UNITED STATES
Supreme Court of the United States
341 U.S. 494, 71 S.Ct. 857, 95 L.Ed. 1137 (1951)

MR. CHIEF JUSTICE VINSON announced the judgment of the Court and an opinion in which MR. JUSTICE REED, MR. JUSTICE BURTON and MR. JUSTICE MINTON join.

Petitioners were indicted in July, 1948, for violation of the conspiracy provisions of the Smith Act, 54 Stat. 671, 18 U.S.C. (1946 ed.) § 11, during the period of April, 1945, to July, 1948. * * * A verdict of guilty as to all the petitioners was returned by the jury on October 14, 1949. The Court of Appeals affirmed the convictions. We granted certiorari, limited to the following two questions: (1) Whether either § 2 or § 3 of the Smith Act, inherently or as construed and applied in the instant case, violates the First Amendment and other [provisions] of the Bill of Rights; (2) whether either § 2 or § 3 of the Act, inherently or as construed and applied in the instant case, violates the First and Fifth Amendments because of indefiniteness.

Sections 2 and 3 of the Smith Act, 54 Stat. 671, 18 U.S.C. (1946 ed.) §§ 10, 11 (*see* present 18 U.S.C. § 2385), provide as follows:

'Sec. 2.

(a) It shall be unlawful for any person–

(1) to knowingly or willfully advocate, abet, advise, or teach the duty, necessity, desirability, or propriety of overthrowing or destroying any government in the United States by force or violence, or by the assassination of any officer of any such government;

(2) with intent to cause the overthrow or destruction of any government in the United States, to print, publish, edit, issue, circulate, sell, distribute, or publicly display any written or printed matter advocating, advising, or teaching the duty, necessity, desirability, or propriety of overthrowing or destroying any government in the United States by force or violence;

(3) to organize or help to organize any society, group, or assembly of persons who teach, advocate, or encourage the overthrow or destruction of any government in the United States by force or violence; or to be or become a member of, or affiliate with, any such society, group, or assembly of persons, knowing the purposes thereof.

(b) For the purposes of this section, the term 'government in the United States' means the Government of the United States, the government of any State, Territory, or possession of the United States, the government of the District of Columbia, or the government of any political subdivision of any of them.

Sec. 3. It shall be unlawful for any person to attempt to commit, or to conspire to commit, any of the acts prohibited by the provisions of * * * this title.'

The indictment charged the petitioners with wilfully and knowingly conspiring (1) to organize as the Communist Party of the United States of America a society, group and assembly of persons who teach and advocate the overthrow and destruction of the Government of the United States by force and violence, and (2) knowingly and wilfully to advocate and teach the duty and necessity of overthrowing and destroying the Government of the United States by force and violence. The indictment further alleged that § 2 of the Smith Act proscribes these acts and that any conspiracy to take such action is a violation of § 3 of the Act.

The trial of the case extended over nine months, six of which were devoted to the taking of evidence, resulting in a record of 16,000 pages. Our limited grant of the writ of certiorari has removed from our consideration any question as to the sufficiency of the evidence to support the jury's determination that petitioners are guilty of the offense charged. Whether on this record petitioners did in fact advocate the overthrow of the Government by force and violence is not before us, and we must base any discussion of this point upon the conclusions stated in the opinion of the Court of Appeals, which treated the issue in great detail. That court held that the record in this case amply supports the necessary finding of the jury that petitioners, the leaders of the Communist Party in this country, were unwilling to work within our framework of democracy, but intended to initiate a violent revolution whenever the propitious occasion appeared. Petitioners dispute the meaning to be drawn from the evidence, contending that the Marxist -Leninist doctrine they advocated taught that force and violence to achieve a Communist form of government in an existing democratic state would be necessary only because the ruling classes of that state would never permit the transformation to be accomplished peacefully, but would use force and violence to defeat any peaceful political and economic gain the

Communists could achieve. But the Court of Appeals held that the record supports the following broad conclusions: By virtue of their control over the political apparatus of the Communist Political Association, petitioners were able to transform that organization into the Communist Party; that the policies of the Association were changed from peaceful cooperation with the United States and its economic and political structure to a policy which had existed before the United States and the Soviet Union were fighting a common enemy, namely, a policy which worked for the overthrow of the Government by force and violence; that the Communist Party is a highly disciplined organization, adept at infiltration into strategic positions, use of aliases, and double-meaning language; that the Party is rigidly controlled; that Communists, unlike other political parties, tolerate no dissension from the policy laid down by the guiding forces, but that the approved program is slavishly followed by the members of the Party; that the literature of the Party and the statements and activities of its leaders, petitioners here, advocate, and the general goal of the Party, was, during the period in question, to achieve a successful overthrow of the existing order by force and violence.

I.

It will be helpful in clarifying the issues to treat next the contention that the trial judge improperly interpreted the statute by charging that the statute required an unlawful intent before the jury could convict. More specifically, he charged that the jury could not find the petitioners guilty under the indictment unless they found that petitioners had the intent 'to overthrow * * * the Government of the United States by force and violence as speedily as circumstances would permit.'

Section 2(a)(1) makes it unlawful 'to knowingly or willfully advocate, * * * or teach the duty, necessity, desirability, or propriety of overthrowing or destroying any government in the United States by force or violence * * *.'; Section 2(a)(3), 'to organize or help to organize any society, group, or assembly of persons who teach, advocate or encourage the overthrow * * *.' Because of the fact that § 2(a)(2) expressly requires a specific intent to overthrow the Government, and because of the absence of precise language in the foregoing subsections, it is claimed that Congress deliberately omitted any such requirement. We do not agree. * * * The structure and purpose of the statute demand the inclusion of intent as an element of the crime. Congress was concerned with those who advocate and organize for the overthrow of the Government. Certainly those who recruit and combine for the purpose of advocating overthrow intend to bring about that overthrow. We hold that the statute requires as an essential element of the crime proof of the intent of those who are charged with its violation to overthrow the Government by force and violence.

Nor does the fact that there must be an investigation of a state of mind under this interpretation afford any basis for rejection of that meaning. A survey of Title 18 of the U.S. Code indicates that the vast majority of the crimes designated by that Title require, by express language, proof of the existence of a certain mental state, in words such as 'knowingly,' 'maliciously,' 'wilfully,' 'with the purpose of,' 'with intent to,' or combinations or permutations of these and synonymous terms. The existence of a mens rea is the rule of, rather than the exception to, the principles of Anglo-American criminal jurisprudence. * * *

The obvious purpose of the statute is to protect existing Government, not from change by peaceable, lawful and constitutional means, but from change by violence, revolution and terrorism. That it is within the power of the Congress to protect the Government of the United States from armed rebellion is a proposition which requires little discussion. Whatever theoretical merit there may be to the argument that there is a 'right' to rebellion against dictatorial governments is without force where the existing structure of the government provides for peaceful and orderly change. We reject any principle of governmental helplessness in the face of preparation for revolution, which principle, carried to its logical conclusion, must lead to anarchy. No one could conceive that it is not within the power of Congress to prohibit acts intended to overthrow the Government by force and violence. The question with which we are concerned here is not whether Congress has such power, but whether the means which it has employed conflict with the First and Fifth Amendments to the Constitution.

One of the bases for the contention that the means which Congress has employed are invalid takes the form of an attack on the face of the statute on the grounds that by its terms it prohibits academic discussion of the merits of Marxism-Leninism, that it stifles ideas and is contrary to all concepts of a free speech and a free press. * * *

The very language of the Smith Act negates the interpretation which petitioners would have us impose on that Act. It is directed at advocacy, not discussion. Thus, the trial judge properly charged the jury that they could not convict if they found that petitioners did 'no more than pursue peaceful studies and discussions or teaching and advocacy in the realm of ideas.' He further charged that it was not unlawful 'to conduct in an American college and university a course explaining the philosophical theories set forth in the books which have been placed in evidence.' Such a charge is in strict accord with the statutory language, and illustrates the meaning to be placed on those words. Congress did not intend to eradicate the free discussion of political theories, to destroy the traditional rights of Americans to discuss and evaluate ideas without fear of governmental sanction. Rather Congress was concerned with the very kind of activity in which the evidence showed these petitioners engaged.

III.

But although the statute is not directed at the hypothetical cases which petitioners have conjured, its application in this case has resulted in convictions for the teaching and advocacy of the overthrow of the Government by force and violence, which, even though coupled with the intent to accomplish that overthrow, contains an element of speech. For this reason, we must pay special heed to the demands of the First Amendment marking out the boundaries of speech.

We pointed out in [an earlier case] that the basis of the First Amendment is the hypothesis that speech can rebut speech, propaganda will answer propaganda, free debate of ideas will result in the wisest governmental policies. It is for this reason that this Court has recognized the inherent value of free discourse. An analysis of the leading cases in this Court which have involved direct limitations on speech, however, will demonstrate that both the majority of the Court and the dissenters in particular cases have recognized that this is not an unlimited, unqualified right, but that the societal value of speech must, on occasion, be subordinated to other values and considerations.

No important case involving free speech was decided by this Court prior to *Schenck v. United States*. * * * That case involved a conviction under the Criminal Espionage Act, 40 Stat. 217. The question the Court faced was whether the evidence was sufficient to sustain the conviction. Writing for a unanimous Court, Justice Holmes stated that the 'question in every case is whether the words used are used in such circumstances and are of such a nature as to create a clear and present danger that they will bring about the substantive evils that Congress has a right to prevent.' * * * The charge was causing and attempting to cause insubordination in the military forces and obstruct recruiting. The objectionable document denounced conscription and its most inciting sentence was, 'You must do your share to maintain, support and uphold the rights of the people of this country.' Fifteen thousand copies were printed and some circulated. This insubstantial gesture toward insubordination in 1917 during war was held to be a clear and present danger of bringing about the evil of military insubordination.

In several later cases involving convictions under the Criminal Espionage Act, the nub of the evidence the Court held sufficient to meet the 'clear and present danger' test enunciated in *Schenck* was as follows: *Frohwerk v. United States* – publication of twelve newspaper articles attacking the war; *Debs v. United States* – one speech attacking United States' participation in the war; *Abrams v. United States* – circulation of copies of two different socialist circulars attacking the war; *Schaefer v. United States* – publication of a German language newspaper with allegedly false articles, critical of capitalism and the war; *Pierce v. United States* – circulation of copies of a four-page pamphlet written by a clergyman, attacking the purposes of the war and United States' participation therein. Justice Holmes wrote the opinions for a unanimous Court in *Schenck*, *Frohwerk* and *Debs*. He and Justice Brandeis dissented in *Abrams*, *Schaefer* and *Pierce*. The basis of these dissents was that, because of the protection which the First Amendment gives to speech, the evidence in each case was insufficient to show that the defendants had created the requisite danger under *Schenck*. But these dissents did not mark a change of principle. The dissenters doubted only the probable effectiveness of the puny efforts toward subversion. In *Abrams*, they wrote, 'I do not doubt for a moment that by the same reasoning that would justify punishing persuasion to murder, the United States constitutionally may punish speech that produces or is intended to produce a clear and imminent danger that it will bring about forthwith certain substantive evils that the United States constitutionally may seek to prevent.' * * *

The rule we deduce from these cases is that where an offense is specified by a statute in nonspeech or nonpress terms, a conviction relying upon speech or press as evidence of violation may be sustained only when the speech or publication created a 'clear and present danger' of attempting or accomplishing the prohibited crime, e.g., interference with enlistment. * * *

In this case we are squarely presented with the application of the 'clear and present danger' test, and must decide what that phrase imports. We first note that many of the cases in which this Court has reversed convictions by use of this or similar tests have been based on the fact that the interest which the State was attempting to protect was itself too insubstantial to warrant restriction of speech. * * * Overthrow of the Government by force and violence is certainly a substantial enough interest for the Government to limit speech. Indeed, this is the ultimate value of any society, for if a society cannot protect its very structure from armed internal attack, it must follow that no subordinate value can be protected. If, then, this interest may be protected, the literal problem which is presented is what has been meant by the use of the phrase 'clear and present danger' of the utterances bringing about the evil within the power of Congress to punish.

Obviously, the words cannot mean that before the Government may act, it must wait until the putsch is about to be executed, the plans have been laid and the signal is awaited. If Government is aware that a group aiming at its overthrow is attempting to indoctrinate its members and to commit them to a course whereby they will strike when the leaders feel the circumstances permit, action by the Government is required. The argument that there is no need for Government to concern itself, for Government is strong, it possesses ample powers to put down a rebellion, it may defeat the revolution with ease needs no answer. For that is not the question. Certainly an attempt to overthrow the Government by force, even though doomed from the outset because of inadequate numbers or power of the revolutionists, is a sufficient evil for

Congress to prevent. The damage which such attempts create both physically and politically to a nation makes it impossible to measure the validity in terms of the probability of success, or the immediacy of a successful attempt. In the instant case the trial judge charged the jury that they could not convict unless they found that petitioners intended to overthrow the Government ' as speedily as circumstances would permit.' This does not mean, and could not properly mean, that they would not strike until there was certainty of success. What was meant was that the revolutionists would strike when they thought the time was ripe. We must therefore reject the contention that success or probability of success is the criterion. * * *

Chief Judge Learned Hand, writing for the majority below, interpreted the phrase as follows: 'In each case (courts) must ask whether the gravity of the 'evil,' discounted by its improbability, justifies such invasion of free speech as is necessary to avoid the danger.' We adopt this statement of the rule. As articulated by Chief Judge Hand, it is as succinct and inclusive as any other we might devise at this time. It takes into consideration those factors which we deem relevant, and relates their significances. More we cannot expect from words.

Likewise, we are in accord with the court below, which affirmed the trial court's finding that the requisite danger existed. The mere fact that from the period 1945 to 1948 petitioners' activities did not result in an attempt to overthrow the Government by force and violence is of course no answer to the fact that there was a group that was ready to make the attempt. The formation by petitioners of such a highly organized conspiracy, with rigidly disciplined members subject to call when the leaders, these petitioners, felt that the time had come for action, coupled with the inflammable nature of world conditions, similar uprisings in other countries, and the touch-and-go nature of our relations with countries with whom petitioners were in the very least ideologically attuned, convince us that their convictions were justified on this score. And this analysis disposes of the contention that a conspiracy to advocate, as distinguished from the advocacy itself, cannot be constitutionally restrained, because it comprises only the preparation. It is the existence of the conspiracy which creates the danger. If the ingredients of the reaction are present, we cannot bind the Government to wait until the catalyst is added. * * *

V.

There remains to be discussed the question of vagueness -- whether the statute as we have interpreted it is too vague, not sufficiently advising those who would speak of the limitations upon their activity. It is urged that such vagueness contravenes the First and Fifth Amendments. This argument is particularly nonpersuasive when presented by petitioners, who, the jury found, intended to overthrow the Government as speedily as circumstances would permit. A claim of guilelessness ill becomes those with evil intent.

We agree that the standard as defined is not a neat, mathematical formulary. Like all verbalizations it is subject to criticism on the score of indefiniteness. But petitioners themselves contend that the verbalization, 'clear and present danger' is the proper standard. We see no difference, from the standpoint of vagueness, whether the standard of 'clear and present danger' is one contained in haec verba within the statute, or whether it is the judicial measure of constitutional applicability. We have shown the indeterminate standard the phrase necessarily connotes. We do not think we have rendered that standard any more indefinite by our attempt to sum up the factors which are included within its scope. We think it well serves to indicate to those who would advocate constitutionally prohibited conduct that there is a line beyond which they may not go -- a line which they, in full knowledge of what they intend and the circumstances in which their activity takes place, will well appreciate and understand. Where there is doubt as to the intent of the defendants, the nature of their activities, or their power to bring about the evil, this Court will review the convictions with the scrupulous care demanded by our Constitution. But we are not convinced that because there may be borderline cases at some time in the future, these convictions should be reversed because of the argument that these petitioners could not know that their activities were constitutionally proscribed by the statute.

We hold that §§ 2(a)(1), 2(a)(3) and 3 of the Smith Act, do not inherently, or as construed or applied in the instant case, violate the First Amendment and other provisions of the Bill of Rights, or the First and Fifth Amendments because of indefiniteness. Petitioners intended to overthrow the Government of the United States as speedily as the circumstances would permit. Their conspiracy to organize the Communist Party and to teach and advocate the overthrow of the Government of the United States by force and violence created a 'clear and present danger' of an attempt to overthrow the Government by force and violence. They were properly and constitutionally convicted for violation of the Smith Act. The judgments of conviction are affirmed.

Affirmed.

MR. JUSTICE JACKSON, concurring. * * *

What really is under review here is a conviction of conspiracy, after a trial for conspiracy, on an indictment charging conspiracy, brought under a statute outlawing conspiracy. With due respect to my colleagues, they seem to me to discuss anything under the sun except the law of conspiracy. One of the dissenting opinions even appears to chide me for 'invoking the law of conspiracy.' As that is the case before us, it may be more amazing that its reversal can be proposed without even considering the law of conspiracy. * * *

The basic rationale of the law of conspiracy is that a conspiracy may be an evil in itself, independently of any other evil it seeks to accomplish. Thus, we recently held in *Pinkerton v. United States*, 'It has been long and consistently recognized by the Court that the commission of the substantive offense and a conspiracy to commit it are separate and distinct offenses. The power of Congress to separate the two and to affix to each a different penalty is well established. * * * And the plea of double jeopardy is no defense to a conviction for both offenses. * * *'

So far does this doctrine reach that it is well settled that Congress may make it a crime to conspire with others to do what an individual may lawfully do on his own. This principle is illustrated in conspiracies that violate the antitrust laws as sustained and applied by this Court. Although one may raise the prices of his own products, and many, acting without concert, may do so, the moment they conspire to that end they are punishable. The same principle is applied to organized labor. Any workman may quit his work for any reason, but concerted actions to the same end are in some circumstances forbidden.

The reasons underlying the doctrine that conspiracy may be a substantive evil in itself, apart from any evil it may threaten, attempt or accomplish, are peculiarly appropriate to conspiratorial Communism.

> The reason for finding criminal liability in case of a combination to effect an unlawful end or to use unlawful means, where none would exist, even though the act contemplated were actually committed by an individual, is that a combination of persons to commit a wrong, either as an end or as a means to an end, is so much more dangerous, because of its increased power to do wrong, because it is more difficult to guard against and prevent the evil designs of a group of persons than of a single person, and because of the terror which fear of such a combination tends to create in the minds of people.

There is lamentation in the dissents about the injustice of conviction in the absence of some overt act. Of course, there has been no general uprising against the Government, but the record is replete with acts to carry out the conspiracy alleged, acts such as always are held sufficient to consummate the crime where the statute requires an overt act.

But the shorter answer is that no overt act is or need be required. The Court, in antitrust cases, early upheld the power of Congress to adopt the ancient common law that makes conspiracy itself a crime. * * * It is not to be supposed that the power of Congress to protect the Nation's existence is more limited than its power to protect interstate commerce.

Also, it is urged that since the conviction is for conspiracy to teach and advocate, and to organize the Communist Party to teach and advocate, the First Amendment is violated, because freedoms of speech and press protect teaching and advocacy regardless of what is taught or advocated. I have never thought that to be the law.

I do not suggest that Congress could punish conspiracy to advocate something, the doing of which it may not punish. Advocacy or exposition of the doctrine of communal property ownership, or any political philosophy unassociated with advocacy of its imposition by force or seizure of government by unlawful means could not be reached through conspiracy prosecution. But it is not forbidden to put down force or violence, it is not forbidden to punish its teaching or advocacy, and the end being punishable, there is no doubt of the power to punish conspiracy for the purpose.

The defense of freedom of speech or press has often been raised in conspiracy cases, because, whether committed by Communists, by businessmen, or by common criminals, it usually consists of words written or spoken, evidenced by letters, conversations, speeches or documents. Communication is the essence of every conspiracy, for only by it can common purpose and concert of action be brought about or be proved. However, when labor unions raised the defense of free speech against a conspiracy charge, we unanimously said:

> It rarely has been suggested that the constitutional freedom for speech and press extends its immunity to speech or writing used as an integral part of conduct in violation of a valid criminal statute. We reject the contention now. * * *

> * * * It is true that the agreements and course of conduct here were as in most instances brought about through speaking or writing. But it has never been deemed an abridgment of freedom of speech or press to make a course of conduct illegal merely because the conduct was in part initiated, evidenced, or carried out by means of language, either spoken, written, or printed. * * * Such an expansive interpretation of the constitutional guaranties of speech and press would make it practically impossible ever to enforce laws against agreements in restraint of trade as well as many other agreements and conspiracies deemed injurious to society.

In conspiracy cases the Court not only has dispensed with proof of clear and present danger but even of power to create a danger: It long has been settled, however, that a 'conspiracy to commit a crime is a different offense from the crime that is the object of the conspiracy.' * * * Petitioners, for example, might have been convicted here of a conspiracy to monopolize without ever having acquired the power to carry out the object of the conspiracy * * *.

Having held that a conspiracy alone is a crime and its consummation is another, it would be weird legal reasoning to hold that Congress could punish the one only if there was 'clear and present danger' of the second. This would compel the Government to prove two crimes in order to convict for one.

When our constitutional provisions were written, the chief forces recognized as antagonists in the struggle between authority and liberty were the Government on the one hand and the individual citizen on the other. It was thought that if the state could be kept in its place the individual could take care of himself.

In more recent times these problems have been complicated by the intervention between the state and the citizen of permanently organized, well-financed, semisecret and highly disciplined political organizations. Totalitarian groups here and abroad perfected the technique of creating private paramilitary organizations to coerce both the public government and its citizens. These organizations assert as against our Government all of the constitutional rights and immunities of individuals and at the same time exercise over their followers much of the authority which they deny to the Government. The Communist Party realistically is a state within a state, an authoritarian dictatorship within a republic. It demands these freedoms, not for its members, but for the organized party. It denies to its own members at the same time the freedom to dissent, to debate, to deviate from the party line, and enforces its authoritarian rule by crude purges, if nothing more violent.

The law of conspiracy has been the chief means at the Government's disposal to deal with the growing problems created by such organizations. I happen to think it is an awkward and inept remedy, but I find no constitutional authority for taking this weapon from the Government. There is no constitutional right to 'gang up' on the Government.

While I think there was power in Congress to enact this statute and that, as applied in this case, it cannot be held unconstitutional, I add that I have little faith in the long-range effectiveness of this conviction to stop the rise of the Communist movement. Communism will not go to jail with these Communists. No decision by this Court can forestall revolution whenever the existing government fails to command the respect and loyalty of the people and sufficient distress and discontent is allowed to grow up among the masses. Many failures by fallen governments attest that no government can long prevent revolution by outlawry. Corruption, ineptitude, inflation, oppressive taxation, militarization, injustice, and loss of leadership capable of intellectual initiative in domestic or foreign affairs are allies on which the Communists count to bring opportunity knocking to their door. Sometimes I think they may be mistaken. But the Communists are not building just for today -- the rest of us might profit by their example.

UNITED STATES v. RAHMAN

United States District Court, Southern District of New York
854 F.Supp. 254 (1994)

MUKASEY, DISTRICT JUDGE.

Defendant El Sayyid Nosair has moved to strike from Count One of the indictment references to the murder of Meir Kahane, and to sever Counts Five, Six, Seven, Eight and Ten. Further, defendant Mohammed Abouhalima has moved to strike from Count One references to a plan to assassinate Egyptian president Hosni Mubarak, and to bar all reference at trial to either of these incidents as unduly prejudicial under Fed. R. Evid. 403. In addition, Nosair, Omar Ahmad Ali Abdel Rahman, Mohammed Abouhalima, Fares Khallafalla, Mohammed Saleh and Matarawy Mohammed Said Saleh have moved to sever all counts against them and for separate trials. All defendants have been permitted to join in one another's motions to the extent those motions relate to them, with the exception of Ibrahim El-Gabrowny, who disclaimed any motions other than those he made, a waiver apparently in aid of his unsuccessful motion for a severance and an early trial.

The government has responded with an unusually detailed and lengthy brief meant to serve as a partial evidentiary proffer in opposition to the motions.

For the reasons set forth below, the motion to strike the references in Count One to the Kahane murder is granted. The other motions are denied.

I.

Count One of the indictment charges a seditious conspiracy to levy a war of urban terrorism against the United States through a series of violent acts principally in New York, both accomplished and proposed. These violent acts, set forth in that section of Count One listing the means allegedly used by the defendants to further the objects of the conspiracy include the bombing of the World Trade Center in February 1993, the planned bombing of buildings and vehicular tunnels in June 1993, and the assassination of various public figures. They include also the commission of unspecified "acts of terrorism designed to undermine the foreign relations of the United States."

The overt acts allegedly taken in furtherance of this scheme include both the murder in November 1990 at a New York hotel of Meir Kahane -- a rabbi and leader of a small radical group opposed, among other things, to any Arab presence within the biblically defined borders of Israel --and the proposed assassination of Egyptian president Hosni Mubarak during his 1993 visit to the United Nations.

II.

Defendants argue as to the assassination of Kahane and the planned assassination of Mubarak that, whatever those acts might accomplish or assist, they are simply unrelated to any goal reasonably defined as sedition, and therefore they cannot be included within a count that charges conspiracy to commit sedition. Defendants note that Kahane was not a federal official (indeed, he was an Israeli citizen), that the shooting of the postal officer after the Kahane slaying was entirely unrelated to that officer's governmental function, and that Mubarak is an Egyptian; they argue that killing foreign citizens and incidentally related acts cannot be sedition against the United States.

The government's response is that the conspirators themselves saw both acts as furthering a seditious goal: Thus, for example, they regarded Kahane as a proponent of Jewish emigration to Israel and the United States as a supporter of Zionists and pro-Israeli groups, and Kahane presumably as one who fit in one or both categories. Therefore, a blow against Kahane, the government argues, was a blow that was "part of a greater struggle" against the " 'infidel' West, of which the United States was deemed the leader," a struggle that included the bombing of the World Trade Center. Further, the conspirators allegedly regarded Mubarak as a puppet of the United States, and thus a blow against him presumably was a blow against the United States. The crux of the government's argument, however, is not the actual connection between either Kahane or Mubarak and official acts and policies of the United States. The government argues that because both acts were on the agenda of the conspirators and were perceived by them as furthering a goal that included sedition, they should be provable as acts in furtherance of a conspiracy to accomplish sedition:

> Aside from the fact that there need have been no furthering [of the goal of sedition] at all for [statutory] liability to be established, ... the material issue in this case is not what the government (or, for that matter, defense counsel or the Court) believes, however objectively, might advance a war against the United States. The question for the jury is what the defendants intended -- and the appropriate inquiry is whether the evidence the government seeks to introduce, considered in the context of all the proof to be offered, would form an adequate basis for a

rational juror to conclude that the defendants intended to levy war on the United States or oppose its authority by force.

An evaluation of the parties' arguments requires a comparison of the charges in the indictment with the statute that defines and proscribes seditious conspiracy, 18 U.S.C. § 2384:

> If two or more persons in any State ... conspire to overthrow, put down, or to destroy by force the Government of the United States, or to levy war against them, or to oppose by force the authority thereof, or by force to prevent, hinder or delay the execution of any law of the United States ... they shall each be fined not more than $20,000 or imprisoned not more than 20 years, or both.

The theory of the indictment is that the defendants conspired "to levy a war of urban terrorism against the United States, to oppose by force the authority of the United States, and by force to prevent, hinder and delay the execution of laws of the United States." The indictment charges that the defendants planned to commit five separate kinds of acts in furtherance of the conspiracy's objectives: bombings of government and landmark buildings and of vehicular tunnels and bridges; kidnaping of particular government, law enforcement and judicial officers; obstruction of justice designed to secure the release of imprisoned members of the organization; concealment of their unlawful activities; and opposition to the federal government through unspecified "acts of terrorism designed to undermine the foreign relations of the United States."

To be sure, the kind of "war" punishable under § 2384 does not require the presence of a foreign power, or an actual war in the sense of forcible conquest of territory and supplanting of the government. "Congress enacted Section 2384 to help the government cope with and fend off urban terrorism." The interests to be protected by enforcing the statute include the government's interest "in safeguarding public security." That is perhaps the most basic function of government, and is what those who established our government had in mind when they drafted a Constitution whose purpose, among others, was "to insure domestic Tranquility." U.S. Const. pmbl.

However, although this statute protects basic societal interests and must be read to cover a wide spectrum of activities, for the reasons summarized below I cannot agree with the government when it argues, as it seems to in the above quoted portion of its memorandum, that the law has no objective limits whatever. Oddly, the government seems to have arrived at this mistaken view through a series of correct arguments strung together to reach an incorrect result. Thus, the government is correct when it insists that the statute requires "no furthering at all" of the goal of sedition for liability to attach because the crime is the agreement to promote the ends the law forbids. Indeed, the statute contains no requirement of an overt act. The government is correct also when it points out that "[t]he question for the jury is what the defendants intended," in the sense that because the gist of the crime is agreement, the defendants' intent determines whether or not they committed it.

The government is correct as well when it states that "the appropriate inquiry is whether the evidence the government seeks to introduce, considered in the context of all the proof to be offered, would form an adequate basis for a rational juror to conclude that the defendants intended to levy war on the United States or oppose its authority by force." But it is here that the government's argument goes astray, conflating the issue of what conduct furthers a seditious end within the meaning of the statute with the entirely separate issue of what evidence may be admissible to help prove an agreement to achieve that end. Not all conduct admissible to prove the existence of a charged conspiracy is necessarily conduct in furtherance of that conspiracy. If it were, there would be no such thing as other crimes evidence in a conspiracy case. *See* Fed. R. Evid. 404(b).

The Kahane murder, if it were proved to have been the act of more than one of these defendants, would be admissible for a variety of reasons at a joint trial, even if had not been charged in a separate substantive count or mentioned in the conspiracy count. Those reasons include to show that defendants associated with one another, to demonstrate a common scheme of which the conspiracy charged in Count One was a part, to prove that defendants intended to do more than talk about acts of violence, to explain why other defendants were intent on freeing Nosair after he was convicted on weapons charges relating to the murder, and perhaps for other reasons as well. In that sense, proof of the murder would help prove the seditious conspiracy -- but in that sense only. The murder of Kahane could not be in itself an overt act tending to accomplish the goals of a seditious conspiracy unless, objectively, that murder could further an end that the statute prohibits agreeing to further, wholly apart from what the defendants thought or believed. Were the rule otherwise, the seditious conspiracy statute would expand infinitely to embrace the entire agenda of anyone who violated it, whether or not that agenda also included an objectively non-seditious plan.

The flaw in the government's argument may be illustrated by an example having nothing to do with this case. Consider a defendant charged with conspiracy to distribute narcotics. If that defendant distributes a package that contains only flour, in the belief that the substance in fact is heroin, he can be convicted of conspiracy because he intends to distribute heroin and has agreed to do so, although he cannot be convicted of the substantive offense. In such a case, a conspiracy count properly could allege the overt act of distributing flour, because the defendant thought the flour was heroin. But if it is alleged that he knew the package contained flour, and that he agreed to distribute it in the belief that flour is a narcotic drug, then such an act could not be alleged as one in furtherance of the conspiracy.

Moreover, he could not be convicted of conspiring to distribute narcotics if the distribution of flour is the only proof of his agreement to distribute narcotics. Even if there is other proof of the hypothetical defendant's agreement to distribute narcotics, the knowing distribution of flour cannot be transformed into an overt act in furtherance of that agreement simply because the defendant has been shown by other proof to have agreed also to distribute narcotics.

The subject of proof is significant because the indictment has charged that the Kahane murder was an overt act in furtherance of the seditious conspiracy, and a jury presumably would be asked to consider it as such, and not merely as evidence tending to establish the conspiracy in the more remote ways suggested above. However, the government's extensive memorandum does not suggest any way in which the Kahane murder could have furthered the goals of a seditious conspiracy beyond the statement that the defendants thought it did. That is not enough.

Nor does the equation change simply because the statute in question does not require the commission of an overt act. The government chose to put before the grand jury an indictment that included an allegation that certain overt acts were taken in furtherance of the conspiracy. Presumably, the government intends the jury to consider such acts, if proved, as evidence that the defendants agreed not simply to engage in miscellaneous criminal conduct, but agreed specifically to oppose the United States government in the ways the statute forbids. Once the acts have been alleged in the indictment, the government is not relieved from the rigors of logic simply because the statute did not require that the acts be included in the first place.

The alleged plan to assassinate Mubarak presents a different issue, even though the government has argued for its inclusion as an overt act on the same basis as it argues for inclusion of the Kahane murder: that the defendants thought of Mubarak in essence as a representative of the United States, and therefore thought of his murder as a blow against the United States. The indictment charges that one of the means employed by the conspirators to further the objects of the conspiracy was to "oppose by force the government of the United States by planning and committing acts of terrorism designed to undermine the foreign relations of the United States." It is at least objectively plausible that the plot to murder a foreign head of state while he was on United States soil would have a direct impact on this country's ability to conduct its foreign relations, and thus would constitute an agreement "to oppose by force the authority" of the United States to conduct its foreign relations. Therefore, the alleged plan to assassinate Mubarak, accompanied by proof of animus against the United States, may be proved as a step in furtherance of the seditious conspiracy charged in the indictment. Proof of such animus is crucial, however, because without it the defendants would be shown merely to have engaged in conduct that conflicted incidentally with some policy of the United States. If that were enough to constitute sedition, then our hypothetical defendant charged with narcotics conspiracy, if he were armed, could be charged with sedition as well, because in agreeing to traffic in narcotics with the aid of force he would be agreeing, albeit incidentally, to oppose by force a policy of the United States.

Accordingly, the motion to strike from Count One reference to the Kahane murder is granted, but the motion to strike the reference to the Mubarak assassination plan is denied.

Note

In *Brandenburg v. Ohio*, 395 U.S. 444 (1969), the Supreme Court revisited the conflict between criminal syndicalism and sedition statutes and the First Amendment, and announced the current test for the constitutionality of such prosecutions: "the constitutional guarantees of free speech and free press do not permit a State to forbid or proscribe advocacy of the use of force or of law violation except where such advocacy is directed to inciting or producing imminent lawless action and is likely to incite or produce such action." Sedition trials tend to emerge when the United States is at war. As John Cohan notes:

> Society's preoccupation with criminal anarchy during World War I provides the most notable examples of prosecutions for seditious speech during the Twentieth Century. There were thousands of prosecutions for violation of sedition under the Espionage Acts of 1917 and 1918. A resurgence of sedition cases occurred immediately following World War II, with the specter of international Communism corrupting American society from within. Underlying these cases was the attitude that any advocacy of communist ideas and opinions was inherently an extremely dangerous incitement to overthrow the existing social order. During the Vietnam War and the black liberation movement of the 1960s and 1970s there were further efforts to prosecute people for sedition in one form or another.

John Allen Cohan, *Seditious Conspiracy, the Smith Act, and Prosecution for Religious Speech Advocating the Violent Overthrow of Government*, 17 St. John's J. Legal Comment 199, 202-03 (2003). In addition, prosecutions for sedition and syndicalism tend to proliferate in times of domestic political unrest. Abolitionists, labor organizers, civil rights organizers, and anti-war protesters, along with suspected Communists and anarchists, have been the target of such prosecutions. *See generally* David B. Filvaroff, *Conspiracy and the First*

Amendment, 121 U. Pa. L. Rev. 189 (1972). Cohan observes that in contemporary times, "Prosecutions of seditious conspiracy are more likely to occur in a climate of society's heightened apprehension about terrorist plots against the nation." Cohan, *supra* at 203.

The modern seditious conspiracy statute reads in full:

If two or more persons in any State or Territory, or in any place subject to the jurisdiction of the United States, conspire to overthrow, put down, or to destroy by force the Government of the United States, or to levy war against them [sic.], or to oppose by force the authority thereof, or by force to prevent, hinder, or delay the execution of any law of the United States, or by force to seize, take, or possess any property of the United States contrary to the authority thereof, they shall each be fined not more than $20,000 or imprisoned not more than twenty years, or both.

18 U.S.C. §2384 (1994).

Cohan notes, "Much of the case against Sheik Rahman * * * was based on evidence of * * * sermons and religious guidance given by the cleric to members of his flock. * * * His blindness and frailty prevented him from carrying out specific terrorist plans with the others. In fact, the evidence showed that Rahman did not even participate in any actual plotting against the government or in the preparatory activities undertaken by his co-defendants." Cohan, *supra* at 202, 205.

Should the government's focus on sermons and other religious speech raise special constitutional problems? Recently the executive branch has shown increased interest in such speech. One commentator reports:

Federal agents are now permitted to infiltrate religious groups without any particularized suspicion of criminal activity -- perhaps simply based on a hunch that people in a certain religious group warrant closer scrutiny.

The authority for such investigations lies in a new set of investigative guidelines that Attorney General John Ashcroft issued in May 2002. He ended a twenty-six-year-old policy that had prohibited F.B.I. agents from infiltrating a religious organization without some suspicion of specific criminal activity by the organization or its members. Prior to May 2002, criminal investigations generally "ended at the door" of a religious institution unless law enforcement agents could articulate some reason for suspecting that a person inside the building might be involved in a crime. Ashcroft argued that the F.B.I. needed to expand its infiltration of religious organizations in order to investigate terrorist cells. * * *

Predictably, mosques have occupied most of the F.B.I.'s attention since Ashcroft eased the restrictions on investigations of religious organizations. In January 2003, F.B.I. Director Robert Mueller ordered all fifty-six of the F.B.I.'s branch offices to count the number of mosques within their jurisdictional boundaries. An F.B.I. spokesman initially told Congress that this inventory of mosques was useful as a starting point for proactive investigations of potential terrorists. After civil libertarians raised concerns about the burdens on religious freedom, the F.B.I. offered an entirely different rationale, claiming in public statements that mosque-counting was necessary to protect Muslims from hate crimes. * * *

Published reports indicate that the F.B.I. has used a variety of investigative techniques to monitor worshippers at mosques. The F.B.I. has utilized confidential informants, undercover agents, surveillance cameras, flyovers, and subpoenas for phone records, among other investigative techniques. Federal law enforcement agencies have not only infiltrated mosques in the United States, but also in foreign countries.

Tom Lininger, *Sects, Lies, and Videotape: The Surveillance and Infiltration of Religious Groups*, 89 Iowa L. Rev. 1201 (2004).

In the wake of the destruction of the twin towers of New York City's World Trade Center on September 11, 2001 and President George W. Bush's announcement of a "War on Terror," Congress, by a Senate vote of 98-1, passed the Uniting and Strengthening America by Providing Appropriate Tools Required to Intercept and Obstruct Terrorism (USA PATRIOT) Act of 2001, Pub. L. No. 107-56, 115 Stat. 272. The USA PATRIOT Act is complex and contains a number of procedural provisions giving the executive branch new powers of surveillance, investigation, detention, and the deportation of foreign nationals. *See* Kim Lane Scheppele, *Law in a Time of Emergency: States of Exception and the Temptations of 9/11*, 6 U. Pa. J. Const. L. 1001, 1034-1040 (2004). The USA PATRIOT Act joins a number of other statutes and executive orders directed at permitting the federal government to cut off the financial support of terrorist organizations:

Current criminal statutes allow the prosecution of individuals who "knowingly provide material support or resources to a foreign terrorist organization, or attempt[] or conspire to do so." And Executive Order 13224 allows the seizure of assets from persons determined by the secretary of the Treasury to assist designated foreign persons who pose a risk of terrorism, or to be "otherwise associated" with such persons. These are the statutes that the Justice Department has invoked in its prosecution of so-called "sleeper cells," based not on any violent conduct but on conspiracies to give money or other "material support" to individuals or organizations that may engage in such conduct. The statutes extend to organizations that engage in both violent and nonviolent activities (like the Irish Republican Army ("IRA") or the African National Congress ("ANC")), as well as foundations that may be "associated with" such organizations. * * *

Faced with such statutes, there is a strong incentive to steer clear of controversial associations. The administration of the University of California San Diego recently decided to forbid a student website from linking to the website of the Revolutionary Armed Forces of Colombia for fear that this might be construed as "providing material support," but backed off in the face of protests. That incident is, perhaps, amusing but especially combined with the "material witness" power claimed by the Justice Department, matters may get deadly serious in short order. * * *

For non-citizen residents of the United States, the threat of retaliation is even more foreboding. In the backwash of September 11, the administration rounded up over one thousand men of near eastern origin, held them for an extended time period, and deported most of them, notwithstanding the absence in many cases of any substantial connection with terrorist threats. The USA PATRIOT Act makes even unknowing association with terrorists a deportable offense, and allows the attorney general to order detention of aliens without any prior showing or court ruling that the person is dangerous where he "has reasonable grounds to believe that the alien is engaged in any other activity that endangers the national security of the United States." And the administration claims the right to choose political bases to deport non-citizens for immigration violations, no matter how trivial, at its sole discretion.

Seth Kreimer, *Watching the Watchers: Surveillance, Transparency, and Political Freedom in the War on Terror*, 7 U. Pa. J. Const. L. 133 (2004). Nina J. Crimm observes further:

Not only did the USA Patriot Act fortify the previously existing criminal and civil laws that can be used to combat terrorists and terrorism, but it also added new ones to the arsenal. Moreover, the Bush administration dedicated resources to existing and newly created governmental structures that would be responsible for enforcing these laws and for waging the financial war on terrorism.

The enhanced legal and structural arsenal produced by these swift reactions contains multiple means by which the U.S. government, as well as citizens injured by activities of foreign terrorists, can pursue economic or criminal sanctions against terrorists and their private sponsors, including individuals, foreign nongovernmental organizations, and domestic charitable organizations and their governing bodies. For example, the available arsenal enables the U.S. government to freeze assets in order to "starve" terrorists of their financial "life-blood." The government can bring a criminal action against persons who knowingly provide "material support or resources" to a terrorist or a foreign terrorist organization, or who intentionally or knowingly collect or provide funds for use in carrying out terrorist activities. Moreover, the government has authority in connection with an individual's violation of either of these criminal offenses to impose a civil penalty on a domestic entity, including a § 501(c)(3) organization, if the perpetrator was responsible for the management or control of that entity and committed the offense in that capacity. The government also can bring charges pursuant to the Racketeer Influenced and Corrupt Organizations Act (RICO) based on predicate crimes that include the offenses of providing material support or resources to a foreign terrorist organization, or intentionally or knowingly collecting or providing funds for use in carrying out terrorist activities, as well as money laundering. Congress recently proposed legislation to permit the Internal Revenue Service (IRS) to suspend the tax-exempt status under Internal Revenue Code (I.R.C.) § 501(a) of an organization that is identified or designated as a terrorist organization.

Nina J. Crimm, *High Alert: The Government's War on the Financing of Terrorism and Its Implications for Donors, Domestic Charitable Organizations, and Global Philanthropy*, 45 Wm. & Mary L. Rev. 1341 (2004).

Chapter 14

CORPORATE CRIMINAL LIABILITY

INTRODUCTION

The law of conspiracy is one mechanism used to address collective criminal behavior. A second response to the problem of collective criminal behavior is corporate criminal liability. The corporate form was originally created in order to promote the beneficial, rather than malign, aspects of collective action. But what happens when corporations commit crimes? In some ways a corporation that is committing crimes can be thought of as a kind of institutionalized conspiracy, posing the same dangers of more efficient action and greater commitment to the ultimate goal.

Like conspiracy, corporate criminal liability raises difficult questions for substantive criminal law. How should the criminal responsibility of the corporation itself be distinguished from the responsibility of the natural persons who make and implement corporate decisions? Although for many civil purposes, corporations have the rights of natural persons, does it make sense to treat corporations as persons under criminal law, given criminal law's highly moralized focus on culpability?

Another difficult issue with respect to corporate criminal responsibility is punishment. A corporation, as opposed to a natural person, cannot be imprisoned; and if fines are levied upon it, those costs may be passed on to consumers, employers, and shareholders. As some observers have concluded, a corporation has "no soul to damn, and no body to kick." Nevertheless, the corporate form is a powerful tool for wrongdoing, and both the common law tradition and the Model Penal Code offer methods of holding corporations criminally responsible.

A. CONCEPTUAL ISSUES IN CORPORATE CRIMINAL RESPONSIBILITY

STATE v. CHAPMAN DODGE CENTER, INC.
Supreme Court of Louisiana.
428 So.2d 413 (1983)

FRED C. SEXTON, JR., JUSTICE AD HOC.

1045

Defendants, Chapman Dodge Center, Inc., and John Swindle were charged by bill of information with 20 counts of theft, in violation of LSA-R.S. 14:67. On July 13-16, 1981, defendants were tried before a six person jury which found them guilty of the lesser included offense of unauthorized use of a movable in violation of LSA-R.S. 14:68. Thereafter, the trial court sentenced Chapman Dodge Center, Inc., to pay $100 on each of the 20 counts and actual court costs pursuant to LSA-C.Cr.P. Art. 887; in addition to the $100 fines and court costs, defendant John Swindle was sentenced to serve six months in parish prison on each of the 20 counts, the sentences to run consecutively. The sentences were suspended, however, and Swindle was placed on two years supervised probation, with the special conditions that he:

> (a) Make restitution to each of the victims listed in the bill of information for their loss and inconvenience pursuant to LSA-C.Cr.P. Art. 895.1, (total sum of $8,460.35); and

> (b) Serve five days in jail on each count, or in lieu thereof serve five days on the City-Parish litter detail on each count.

The defendants have appealed citing 14 assignments of error. We reverse as to both defendants on the assignment of insufficient evidence and pretermit discussion of the other assignments of error.

FACTS

Chapman Dodge Center, Inc., a Baton Rouge Dodge dealership, closed its doors because of financial difficulty on September 12, 1980. Shortly thereafter the district attorney's office began receiving complaints from Dodge customers that they had not received their permanent license plates for their cars because the dealership had neither registered the cars purchased, nor paid the sales tax due. The usual practice was for the customer to pay the amount due for sales tax to the car dealer who, in turn, would register the car with the state and tender the tax. After a car is registered and the tax paid, the state issues a permanent license plate. In the meantime, the dealership is authorized to give the customer a temporary plate that is valid for 35 days. Dodge customers were being stopped for expired temporary license plates since they had not received their permanent tags.

Chapman Dodge had been in financial trouble for about a year prior to its closing. Aside from the general economic situation, Chapman's difficulties were due in great part to Chapman's financial relationship to the financially troubled Chrysler Corporation. According to the trial record, at the time Chapman closed, Chrysler Corporation owed between $250,000 and $400,000 to Chapman Dodge. In addition, Chrysler Credit Corporation, a subsidiary of Chrysler Motors, had $140,000 of Chapman's money "on reserve" for potential losses on loans Chrysler Credit made to Chapman customers.

After Chapman Dodge closed its doors, Chrysler Credit Corporation took possession of Chapman Dodge. On the premises, employees of Chrysler Credit Corporation found between 180 and 190 registration forms for purchased cars which had not been filed with the state and for which no sales tax had been paid. Since Chrysler Credit Corporation owned the mortgages on 159 of these cars, it paid the sales taxes due on them (approximately $68,000) in order to register the cars and the chattel mortgages with the state.

The defendant, John Swindle, personally paid the sales taxes (about $11,000) on the remaining cars which had not been financed by Chrysler Credit Corporation. The defendant did so after he was notified by the district attorney's office that the taxes were due. The defendant's attorney in Mississippi, however, testified that he advised the defendant that Chrysler Credit Corporation should be responsible for all taxes due since it had possession of all of Chapman Dodge's assets, and was therefore responsible for discharging Chapman's tax liability.

The original bill of information charged 159 counts of theft, but was later amended to 20 counts with a reservation to prosecute the remaining 139 at a later time.

Defendant John Swindle testified that he was the sole owner of Barony Corporation, a holding company for several food service corporations. Barony Corporation owned a subsidiary called Center Management which was formed to hold automobile dealerships when Swindle expanded his operations to include that business. Chapman Dodge was one of four dealerships owned by Center Management. Center Management, after acquiring the necessary funding, then purchased Chapman Dodge. Subsequently Chapman Dodge endorsed the notes Center Management had signed in obtaining financing. Each month a check was sent by Chapman Dodge to Center Management to cover the payment due by Center Management on the notes.

The evidence showed that the defendant, a resident of Jackson, Mississippi, was seldom at the dealership more than twice a month. It was Donald Barrett that was in charge of the daily operations of Chapman Dodge as general manager. All department managers were responsible to Barrett, who in turn answered to Swindle. According to the testimony of James Duvall, Chapman Dodge's accountant, he and Barrett made the decisions as to which bills were to be paid.

Swindle testified that when the dealership was showing continued financial trouble, he discussed this matter with James Duvall. Since the dealership was behind in paying withholding taxes, as well as sales taxes, he ordered Duvall to pay all of the taxes owed, particularly the federal withholdings. When the dealership was closed, Swindle asked Barrett if all the taxes had been paid. The record shows that in the presence of Johnilyn Smith, an administrative assistant to Swindle, and Frank Peel, a business associate of Swindle, Barrett stated that all taxes had been paid. Barrett testified that he did not say all the taxes had been paid, only that the federal taxes had been paid. On cross-examination however Barrett stated that he "may" have said that all the taxes were paid.

The defendant received no indication that the sales taxes were not paid until a week or ten days after closing the dealership when the district attorney contacted Chapman Dodge's lawyer. Duvall testified that he was instructed by Donald Barrett to retain the sales tax money. Donald Barrett however testified that he had told James Duvall in June of 1980 to pay only those obligations necessary to keep the dealership open; but that he never told Duvall to retain the contracts and sales taxes on the purchased vehicles.

Donald Barrett was originally indicted on the theft charges along with John Swindle and Chapman Dodge. Both he and James Duvall were granted "use" immunity in order to compel their testimony against Chapman Dodge and John Swindle. Duvall was granted immunity at the preliminary examination. Barrett was granted immunity when his counsel invoked his privilege against compulsory self-incrimination when he was called to testify at the trial. Barrett stated on cross-examination that the district attorney's office had told him three weeks earlier that he would not be prosecuted if he testified for the state.

OPINION ON SWINDLE

John Swindle was charged with the crime of theft. The jury, however, apparently found that the elements of theft had not been proven by the state and returned a verdict of the lesser included offense of unauthorized use of a movable. Unauthorized use of a movable is defined in LSA-R.S. 14:68 as follows:

> Unauthorized use of a movable is the intentional taking or use of a movable which belongs to another, either without the other's consent, or by means of fraudulent conduct, practices, or representations, but without any intention to deprive the other of the movable permanently. The fact that the movable so taken or used may be classified as an immovable, according to the law pertaining to civil matters, is immaterial.

We find that the evidence produced at trial was insufficient to show that Swindle had the necessary criminal intent to commit the crime of unauthorized use of a movable.

Unauthorized use of a movable requires an "intentional taking or use of a movable." LSA-R.S. 14:68. In the recent case of *State v. Bias*, involving the non-payment of rental on a television set, this court, in setting aside the conviction, stated that: "A person commits the crime of unauthorized use of a movable when he either takes or uses another's property without the owner's consent or by means of fraudulent practices. R.S. 14:68, although not requiring that a person act with an intent to deprive the owner permanently of his property, must reasonably be construed to require the existence of fraudulent intent."

In the instant case, the state has failed to prove any intent on the part of Swindle, fraudulent or otherwise. The facts show that Swindle was the owner of a corporation (Barony) which owned another corporation (Central Management) which in turn owned Chapman Dodge, Inc. Swindle, although the actual owner of Chapman Dodge, had very little control over its day to day operations. The testimony of Duvall indicated that he and Donald Barrett were responsible for the daily operation of the business.

Swindle had little contact with the dealership. The testimony reveals that Swindle was seldom at the dealership more than twice a month, since he resided in Jackson, Mississippi.

Aside from the lack of contact with the dealership, the most convincing evidence as to Swindle's lack of intent, was the testimony of James Duvall. Duvall stated that Swindle had instructed him to pay the taxes. This, in our mind, certainly negates any fraudulent intent on the part of Swindle and shifts the blame elsewhere. Also important, is the testimony of several witnesses for the defense, who stated that Donald Barrett, upon being asked by Swindle, had informed him that "all the taxes had been paid."

Thus the record is devoid of any evidence indicating that Swindle issued direct orders, or even implied, that the taxes in question were not to be paid. Certainly it is less than clear from the record who made the decision, but we feel that the evidence shows that it was not Swindle. In summary, there is insufficient evidence that Swindle had sufficient fraudulent intent to commit the offense of unauthorized use of a movable. There may be various civil wrongs for which the defendant Swindle is responsible, but the requisite mens rea or criminal intent necessary to hold this defendant responsible for a criminal offense is lacking. * * *

OPINION ON CHAPMAN DODGE

The question of the criminal liability of the corporate defendant in this cause is a more difficult proposition involving fundamental issues of the nature of criminal responsibility. These issues have not been generally considered with respect to corporations in this jurisdiction. Certainly our law contemplates corporate criminal defendants. Louisiana law delineates a number of acts the commission or omission of which creates corporate criminal responsibility.[3]

The problem of what criminal liability a corporation should bear for the unauthorized acts of its officers and managers is indeed a grave and troubling one. Recent allegations of corporate responsibility for large train derailments and massive pollution of water sources underscore the importance of this troubling topic. Certainly there is civil responsibility under such circumstances. The question is whether a corporation should be criminally responsible in the absence of a specific statute which defines and describes the corporate act, prohibits that act, and establishes a specific punishment therefor.

Criminal liability in our system of justice has always been founded upon the simultaneous existence of two distinct elements namely: (1) actus reus, and (2) mens rea. The existence of only one of these elements does not make one criminally liable. Both must be present to invoke the sanctions society has placed on what is termed "criminal conduct." Certainly one cannot be held criminally liable for simply thinking of a criminal act without the act occurring. A somewhat more difficult, but logically consistent idea, is that an act, committed without the required criminal intent or mens rea, is not criminally punishable. We do not criminally punish those that do not know what they are doing -- such as the insane. Neither do we punish those who, while aware of what they are doing, have no control over their actions -- the victims of threats or coercion. We do not impose criminal liability on those who act without criminal intent for the simple reason that such an imposition would not achieve the main goal of our criminal law: deterrence.

Given these basic ruminations on the topic of criminal intent, we should now consider the nature of a corporation. Our Civil Code in Article 427 defines a corporation as:

---

[3] LSA-R.S. 12:172 (Failure to Keep Records); LSA-R.S. 37:850 (Violation of Embalming Laws); LSA-R.S. 14:106 (Obscenity); LSA-R.S.47:1953 (Tax Assessment of Corporations); LSA-R.S. 51:125, 126 (Transactions Lessening Competition); LSA-R.S. 30:217 (Unauthorized Prospecting); LSA-R.S. 30:1096 (Pollution).

... an intellectual body, created by law, composed of individuals united under a common name, the members of which succeed each other, so that the body continues always the same, notwithstanding the change of the individuals which compose it, and which, for certain purposes, is considered as a natural person.

The corporation as a fictitious person is capable of entering into contracts, owning property and making and receiving donations. In short, it is capable of doing virtually anything that a natural person is capable of doing.

A corporation by the very nature of its operation is dependent upon people to carry out its business. Some of these people may rightfully be regarded as the "mind" of the corporation. This group, known as the board of directors, is responsible for the direction that the corporation takes in its business activity. Plans for the corporation, developed by the board of directors, are transmitted to the officers of the corporation and through them to the employees. This latter group may be regarded as the "hands" of the corporation. But here our analogy to the human form must end. For unlike ordinary human hands, corporate "hands" have minds of their own and are capable of self direction.

When a corporation is accused of committing a crime which requires intent, it must be determined who within the corporate structure had the intent to commit the crime. If the crime was the product of a board of directors' resolution authorizing its employees to commit specific criminal acts, then intent on the part of the corporation is manifest. However, a more difficult question arises if the crime is actually committed by an employee of the corporation not authorized to perform such an act. Holding a corporation criminally responsible for the acts of an employee may be inconsistent with basic notions of criminal intent, since such a posture would render a corporate entity responsible for actions which it theoretically had no intent to commit.

Common law jurisdictions hold corporations criminally liable for the acts of low-ranking employees. In such jurisdictions, corporate criminal liability is based on an extension of the tort doctrine of vicarious liability. The theme of vicarious criminal liability, however, is varied. Some jurisdictions impose criminal liability where there has been an act or an authorization to act by a managerial officer, some where there has been an act committed within the scope of the actor's employment, and still others where there has been an act done which benefits the corporation. These varied applications notwithstanding, common law jurisdictions have found corporations liable for forms of homicide, theft, extortion -- in short, virtually every crime other than rape and carnal knowledge.

Although this merger of tort and criminal law doctrine has found wide acceptance, it has also generated significant theoretical problems. Admittedly, tort law and criminal law are cousins, causing concern as to whether their relationship is within the prohibited degree such that a union of the two might produce unwanted offspring. It should be remembered that the main function of the law of torts is compensation and to a much lesser degree, deterrence.

Tort law attempts to distribute the loss of a harmful occurrence. Causation is the important ingredient therein. Holding a corporation vicariously liable for the torts of its employees dovetails with the idea of compensating the victim. The corporation is in a more likely position to compensate.

On the other hand, as mentioned earlier, the primary function of criminal law is to deter future criminal liability. To impose such liability on another party who had no part in the act and, as in the case of most corporate crimes, no intent to commit such an act, seems at first glance to be contrary to the purpose of our criminal legal system.

It is important to point out that while corporate criminal liability is recognized and applied in common law jurisdictions, the maxim that *societas delinguere non potest* (a corporation cannot do wrong) is still firmly recognized in the civil law. Only the natural person acting for the corporation can incur criminal guilt. Courts cannot, as often occurs in common law jurisdictions, convict the corporation alone so that the individual defendant may escape punishment.

In France, the jurisdiction recognized most often as our principal civilian ancestor, the courts reason that corporate criminal liability is irreconcilable with the principle of guilt. Corporate criminal liability is considered ineffective as a deterrent because it is deterrence addressed to no mind at all. The same line of thinking with no material difference is followed by virtually every other civil law country.

One of the most interesting aspects of the concept that a corporation may be guilty of an offense without specific statutory authority is the question of how one punishes a corporation. It cannot be imprisoned. Obviously it may not be sentenced to death in the sense that an individual may be. Of course, the charter may be revoked but obviously in that circumstance there would have to be a statute which authorizes this sanction.

The only method of punishing a corporation that is guilty of an offense not proscribed to corporations statutorily is by the imposition of a fine. Certainly it may be argued that a fine in such instances punishes those not guilty of the offense, for funds lost from the corporate treasury can be recouped either by withholding dividends from shareholders or increasing the price of the product to the consumer. On the other hand, serious fines levied against corporations can modify the behavior of corporate officers who want to keep their jobs, and the behavior of voting shareholders who will vote to elect officers that will avoid such costly fines. But obviously there are certain theoretical inconsistencies between a fine to a corporation for an offense not delineated statutorily and the concept that the purpose of criminal statutes is to punish and deter.

But the most interesting theoretical problem arising from the idea that a corporation may be fined where it commits an offense such as theft or unauthorized use is presented by contemplation of the converse. What punishment should be exacted where the authorized penalty is only a jail term? This dilemma would arise if one of the managers or upper level employees of a company authorized the burglary of the home of a senior officer of a competitor in order to obtain vital information. It would then not be possible to effectively punish the corporation as the burglary of an inhabited dwelling requires a minimum jail sentence which cannot be suspended.

These are interesting theoretical problems some of which are actually presented by the circumstances of this cause and others which arise more indirectly as extensions of those actually presented.

The instant defendant is a closely held holding corporation which is accused of a basic "Ten Commandment Crime" -- theft -- and convicted of a lesser included offense. Thus the finder of fact in effect determined that the defendant corporation kept the money in question with fraudulent intent, but with the intent to eventually return the funds. The evidence further indicates that "retention" of the funds was not specifically authorized by the board of directors or by the president or any other officer of the corporation. The record does not indicate, moreover, that any of these entities had any real knowledge of that action. Of course the corporation, its board of directors, its parent corporations and its president are for all practical purposes the same entity -- the individual defendant Swindle. Furthermore, as discussed earlier, the evidence preponderates that it was a party other than Swindle who determined to "retain the funds."

Thus, the facts of this case can be narrowed to a fine point. In so doing, however, broad questions of a complex nature are visited upon us. While recognizing the potential disservice to the jurisprudence we are nevertheless unable, within the confines of this appeal, to resolve these extremely complex issues. We simply determine that under the circumstances of this case, criminal intent has not been adequately established. * * * We hold that since this record reveals no evidence of complicity by the officers or the board of directors, explicit or tacit, that the actions of these managers and/or employees were insufficient to cause this corporate entity to be guilty of the offense of an unauthorized use of a movable.

We thus reverse as to both defendants and order their discharge.

REVERSED AND DISCHARGED AS TO BOTH DEFENDANTS.

LEMMON, JUSTICE, dissenting in part.

The evidence supports a conclusion that a high managerial agent, in whom the corporation had vested the authority to manage its day-to-day business operations, knowingly committed a criminal offense on behalf of the corporation and for its benefit while acting in the scope of his employment. The corporation should therefore be held criminally liable. See Model Penal Code § 2.07(1)(c).

CORPORATE ETHOS:
A STANDARD FOR IMPOSING CORPORATE
CRIMINAL LIABILITY
Pamela H. Bucy
75 Minn. L. Rev. 1095 (1991)

Responsible social policy mandates that we deter those who victimize society through egregious and dangerous acts. Historically, the criminal law has been the vehicle for such deterrence. Corporations are increasingly significant actors in our economy and, to the extent their actions can victimize society, they too should be deterred. For this reason, criminal prosecution of corporations has routinely occurred in American courts for almost a century. Commentators, however, have consistently questioned this use of the criminal law. Moreover, the debate over corporate criminal liability will likely intensify as the government increasingly prosecutes prominent corporate defendants. Two major issues have dominated this debate. One is the failure to identify or prove corporate intent. Traditionally, the criminal law has been reserved for intentional violations of the law. Yet, our prosecutions of corporations have been marked by floundering efforts to identify the intent of intangible, fictional entities. A second issue in the debate concerns sanctions. In addition to proof of intent, a major distinguishing characteristic of the criminal law has been the threat of imprisonment. Critics of corporate criminal liability suggest that because a corporation cannot be imprisoned, the criminal law is not an appropriate vehicle for controlling corporate behavior. Much of the recent scholarship on corporate crime has addressed the sanctioning issue. This Article, however, addresses corporate intent and suggests that a better resolution of this issue would eliminate much of the controversy concerning corporate criminal liability, including the controversy over sanctions. * * *

This Article proposes a standard of corporate criminal liability that uses a new conceptual paradigm for identifying and proving corporate intent. This standard assumes that each corporate entity has a distinct and identifiable personality or "ethos." The government can convict a corporation under this standard only if it proves that the corporate ethos encouraged agents of the corporation to commit the criminal act. Central to this approach is the assumption that organizations possess an identity that is independent of specific individuals who control or work for the organization. This corporate identity, or "ethos," results from the dynamic of many individuals working together toward corporate goals. The living cell provides an apt analogy: Just as a living cell has an identity separate from the activities of its constituent molecules, a corporation has an identity separate from its individual agents.

In a sense, this corporate ethos standard takes its cue from notions of intent developed in the context of individual liability. When considering whether an individual should be held criminally liable we ask, did this person commit this act accidentally or purposely. If the individual committed the act purposely, we consider it to be a crime, while if the individual committed the act accidentally, we do not. Similarly, the standard proposed herein imposes criminal liability on a corporation only if the corporation encouraged the criminal conduct at issue. If it did, the criminal conduct is not an accident or the unpredictable act of a maverick employee. Instead, the criminal conduct is predictable and consistent with corporate goals, policies, and ethos. In the context of a fictional entity, this translates into intention.

This proposed standard offers the following four advantages over the current standards of liability. To the extent that historical and current standards of corporate criminal liability allow criminal convictions without proof of the corporation's intent, they encourage the blurring of criminal and civil liability. This blurring dilutes the impact of a criminal conviction, and, ultimately, erodes the power of the criminal law. The theoretical and practical framework of the corporate ethos standard provides a method for identifying and proving the intent of corporate actors. This is its first and major advantage.

The second advantage of the corporate ethos standard is that it distinguishes among diverse corporations. The current standards of corporate criminal liability often treat all corporations alike by imposing criminal liability on corporations for the acts of their individual agents, regardless of the circumstances within a particular corporation. From Bentham on, scholars and practitioners have recognized that a fundamental requirement for any criminal justice system is that the system treat like actors alike and different actors differently. Anyone, from the average person on the street to the most respected scholar in organizational behavior, recognizes that no two corporations are alike. Our criminal justice system should not treat them as if they were.

The third advantage of the corporate ethos standard is that it rewards those corporations that make efforts to educate and motivate their employees to follow the letter and spirit of the law. This encourages responsible corporate behavior. This advantage is in sharp contrast to the Model Penal Code's standard of liability that discourages higher echelon employees from properly supervising lower echelon employees. This advantage also contrasts with the minimal deterrence achieved by imposing criminal liability on individuals within the corporation. Convicting individual agents and employees of a corporation does not stop other corporate employees from committing future criminal acts if sufficient internal corporate pressure to violate the law continues to exist. In such an environment, the agents are cogs in a wheel. Those convicted are simply replaced by others whose original propensity to obey the law is similarly overcome by a corporate ethos that encourages illegal acts. Unless inside or outside forces change the lawless ethos, it will corrupt each generation of corporate agents. The proposed standard of liability addresses this problem by punishing any corporation that establishes a lawless ethos which overcomes its employees' propensity to obey the law.

The last advantage of the corporate ethos standard is that it is practical, workable, and provable, from concrete information already available in grand jury investigations of corporate crime. To ascertain the ethos of a corporation, and to determine if this ethos encouraged the criminal conduct at issue, the factfinder should examine: the corporate hierarchy, the corporate goals and policies, the corporation's historical treatment of prior offenses, the corporation's efforts to educate and monitor employees' compliance with the law, and the corporation's compensation scheme, especially its policy on indemnification of corporate employees. These facts are typically, or easily, examined in any criminal investigation of corporate misdeeds and are subject to proof in a courtroom. * * *

I. BACKGROUND

A. THE CURRENT STANDARDS OF CORPORATE CRIMINAL LIABILITY

American jurisprudence has employed two major standards to determine when a corporation should be criminally liable. Both impose vicarious liability by imputing the criminal acts and intent of corporate agents to the corporation. The traditional or respondeat superior approach is a common law rule developed primarily in the federal courts and adopted by some state courts. Derived from agency principles in tort law, it provides that a corporation "may be held criminally liable for the acts of any of its agents [who] (1) commit a crime (2) within the scope of employment (3) with the intent to benefit the corporation." As construed by most courts, the latter two requirements are almost meaningless. Courts deem criminal conduct to be "within the scope of employment" even if the conduct was specifically forbidden by a corporate policy and the corporation made good faith efforts to prevent the crime. Similarly, courts deem criminal conduct by an agent to be "with the intent to benefit the corporation" even when the corporation received no actual benefit from the offense and no one within the corporation knew of the criminal conduct at the time it occurred. With these latter two requirements thus weakened, a corporation may be criminally liable whenever one of its agents (even an independent contractor in some circumstances) commits a crime related in almost any way to the agent's employment.

The American Law Institute's Model Penal Code (MPC) provides the major alternative standard for corporate criminal liability currently found in American jurisprudence. In the 1950s, the American Law Institute addressed the issue of corporate criminal liability, ultimately agreeing on three standards for such liability. The type of criminal offense charged determines which standard applies. The option that applies to the majority of criminal offenses provides that a court may hold a corporation criminally liable if the criminal conduct was "authorized, requested, commanded, performed or recklessly tolerated by the board of directors or by a high managerial agent acting in behalf of the corporation within the scope of his office or employment." This standard still uses a respondeat superior model, but in a limited fashion: the corporation will be liable for conduct of only some agents (its directors, officers, or other higher echelon employees).

The critical weakness in both the traditional respondeat superior and MPC standards of liability is that they fail to sufficiently analyze corporate intent. Cases where a corporate employee acted contrary to express corporate policy and yet the court still held the corporation liable best exemplify this weakness. *United States v. Hilton Hotels Corp.* [467 F.2d 1000 (9th Cir. 1972), cert. denied, 409 U.S. 1125 (1973)] provides an apt example. The purchasing agent at a Hilton Hotel in Portland, Oregon, threatened a supplier of goods with the loss of the hotel's business if the supplier did not contribute to an association that was formed to attract conventions to Portland. The corporate president testified that such action was contrary to corporate policy. Both the manager and assistant manager of the Portland Hilton Hotel also testified that they specifically told the purchasing agent not to threaten suppliers. Nevertheless, the court convicted the Hilton Hotel Corporation of antitrust violations under the respondeat superior standard of liability.

Because the respondeat superior standard focuses solely on an individual corporate agent's intent and automatically imputes that intent to the corporation, a corporation's efforts to prevent such conduct are irrelevant. Under this approach all corporations, honest or dishonest, good or bad, are convicted if the government can prove that even one maverick employee committed criminal conduct.

The MPC's requirement that a higher echelon employee commit, or recklessly supervise, the criminal conduct is an improvement over the traditional respondeat superior approach. Recognizing the unfairness of holding a corporation liable for the acts of all its agents, the MPC views the corporation as the embodiment of the acts and intent of only its "high managerial agent[s]." High managerial agents are those individuals "having duties of such responsibility that [their] conduct may fairly be assumed to represent the policy of the corporation or association."

The MPC's refinement of traditional respondeat superior suffers from three serious problems, however. The first problem, the maverick employee, still arises because the MPC uses the same conceptual paradigm as does respondeat superior -- that is, the MPC automatically imputes the intent of individual corporate agents (albeit only the higher echelon agents) to the corporation. According to the MPC standard, a corporation whose higher echelon official performed or supervised illegal conduct is criminally liable even if the higher echelon official was a maverick acting contrary to express corporate policy. For example, in Hilton Hotels, if the factfinder found that the purchasing agent had "duties of such responsibility that his conduct may fairly be assumed to represent the policy of the corporation or association," the agent would be a "high managerial agent," and the Hilton Hotels Corporation would be criminally liable. By automatically imputing the intent of an individual within the corporation to the corporation, the MPC standard, like the traditional respondeat superior standard, provides for inappropriately broad liability.

The second problem with the MPC standard is that even if a clear corporate policy caused a lower echelon employee to commit an offense, the corporation is liable only if there is evidence that a specific higher echelon official recklessly tolerated this conduct. Injustice also results from this problem but here the liability is too narrow: a corporation is not held criminally liable when it should be.

The third problem with the MPC standard is commonly, and deservedly, identified. The MPC standard encourages higher echelon officials to insulate themselves from knowledge of corporate employee activity. Under this standard, if higher echelon officials can maintain unawareness of illegal conduct by corporate employees, it is difficult to prove that they tolerated such conduct, and therefore nearly impossible to hold the corporation criminally liable. By encouraging such unawareness, the MPC discourages corporations from policing themselves. Thus, although the MPC is somewhat successful in refining the traditional respondeat superior standard, it still provides an inadequate approach to assessing corporate intent. * * *

II. THE CORPORATE ETHOS STANDARD OF CORPORATE CRIMINAL LIABILITY

The standard of corporate criminal liability proposed herein focuses on the "ethos" of a corporation and provides as follows: A corporation should be held criminally liable only when its ethos encourages criminal conduct by agents of the corporation. Under this standard, the government must prove, beyond a reasonable doubt, four elements: (1) a corporate ethos (2) that encourages (3) criminal conduct (4) by agents of the corporation. * * *

Scholars and practitioners of organizational theory have long recognized that organizations differ from each other: "It is not true that all big companies are the same -- they aren't. . . . Companies develop their own distinctive personality and ethos which is so ingrained, so much a part of them, that the corporate identity expresses itself in their every action."

Much of the voluminous business literature on corporate culture is premised on the notion that organizations have distinctive cultures. For example, one commentator has described the distinct personalities of the world's dominant oil companies as follows: Texaco "with its selfishness and greed cultivates a reputation for meanness and secrecy"; Mobil "is in many ways the most sophisticated of American [oil companies] . . . much concerned with communications and image"; Exxon maintains a "tranquil style." Its headquarters are "silent" and "elegant," its atmosphere "rarefied," Exxon is "full of rhetorics of global responsibilities [and] likes to stress that it serves not only its American shareholders but all the nations where it operates." Shell, "lordly and sedate," demonstrates an "obsessive introversion" and "self containment" -- "Shellmen . . . cultivate . . . diplomacy [and]. . . prefer not to talk about anything as squalid as profits."

In their popular work, CORPORATE CULTURES, Deal and Kennedy identify five elements of a company's culture: business environment, values, heroes, rites and rituals, and cultural network. By analyzing these elements, these authors develop four types of corporate cultures: the "Tough-guy, Macho" culture, where stakes are high and feedback is quick (construction and entertainment companies); the "Work hard/Play hard" culture, where the employees live in a world of small risks -- no one sale will make or break a player (real estate and door-to-door sales); the "Bet-Your-Company" culture, where high risk but slow feedback prevails because players often must invest millions in a project that takes years to develop (capital goods and oil companies); and the "process" culture where the low risk and slow feedback forces employees to focus on how they do something, not what they do (utilities and insurance companies). * * *

For criminal justice purposes, some of the most interesting work on organizational character has been conducted by sociologists who have examined the commission of corporate crime to determine the characteristics of lawful and unlawful organizations. These scholars suggest that certain social structures and processes internal to an organization encourage unlawful behavior.

Marshall Clinard interviewed sixty-four retired middle management employees of fifty-one Fortune 500 corporations engaged in industrial manufacturing. Clinard focused his study on unethical as well as unlawful behavior. Through his interviews, Clinard found that most of the executives believed that "unethical corporate behavior can usually be traced to internal rather than external forces." The interviewees identified two internal factors as primarily determinative of whether the corporation promoted lawful or unlawful behavior. The first was top management. The interviewees portrayed top management as generally knowledgeable about the unethical or unlawful activity before or after it occurred. Not surprisingly, they therefore deemed top management to be "largely responsible for the unethical or illegal behavior within a corporation." The interviewees also associated the following management characteristics with the law-abiding corporation: an appreciation of applicable government regulations, explicit instructions and enforcement of these regulations, open lines of communication between top and middle management about compliance problems, and stable and respected leadership that came from within the corporate ranks. The second factor identified by the interviewees as influencing a corporation's propensity to comply with the law was the internal pressure on middle management to show a profit and maintain satisfactory employee relations.

Interestingly, the executives thought that these two internal factors contributed more to whether a corporation complied with the law than did the external factors such as a poor financial situation, unfair practices of competitors, or the type of industry. This focus on internal rather than external factors supports the view that an ethos developed within a corporation can encourage, or discourage, criminal conduct by corporate employees. * * *

2. The Existence of a Corporate Ethos

To apply this standard of liability, it is not necessary to ascertain the overall and complete ethos of an organization. The corporate ethos standard is concerned only with the ethos relevant to the criminal conduct in question. Thus, a corporation's ethos or "characteristic spirit" toward employees' rights, competitors, research and development, marketing, and the like is relevant only to the extent it sheds light on whether there exists a corporate ethos that encouraged the particular criminal conduct at issue.

Identifying the corporate ethos relevant to the criminal behavior in question will require a resort to circumstantial evidence, as does proof of intent in every criminal case. Although the actual evidence available will always turn on the particular facts of each case, there are certain guides for every factfinder. When the defendant is an individual, the factfinder looks to the statements and actions of the defendant before, during, and after the crime as well as corroboration for and explanations of such statements and actions. From this information, the factfinder assesses the defendant's mens rea for the criminal conduct charged. By comparison, in applying the corporate ethos standard of liability, the factfinder should look to the following types of facts to determine whether a corporate ethos existed which encouraged corporate employees to commit the criminal conduct. If so, the government has proven the corporate mens rea. These facts concern the internal, formal and informal, structure of the corporation.

Two practical points should be borne in mind when applying the following factors. First, as noted, sometimes it may not be possible to determine which individual within an organization actually performed the illegal conduct, much less encouraged it. The corporate ethos test does not require that the government prove which individual is at fault. It does, however, require the government to prove that the criminal conduct was committed by a corporate agent and that a corporate ethos existed that encouraged the criminal conduct. Thus, if the government shows that the criminal conduct occurred in the accounting department, proof of a corporate ethos that encourages criminal conduct in the research and development division is not sufficient; only evidence of such an ethos in the accounting department will suffice. Second, like Aristotle's speakers who were taught to identify and then to control and alter their own character to suit their audience, a corporation can manipulate and control its corporate ethos from within. Accordingly, the factfinder using a corporate ethos standard of liability, like an audience listening to a politician, must determine whether they are observing fact or fiction.

a. The Hierarchy

The inquiry into corporate hierarchy should begin with the board of directors' role. Does the board operate as a figurehead or does it, or any member of it, monitor the corporation's efforts to comply with the law? If the board or any member allegedly performs this function, does the board or the member have the access and resources to do so effectively?

Lockheed provides an example of how a defective board can contribute to corporate crime. Investigations initiated in the 1970s revealed that Lockheed regularly bribed foreign officials. Between 1970 and 1975, corporate agents made $30 million to $38 million in questionable payments to win foreign aircraft sales. Investigators' inquiries revealed that one of the factors contributing to this bribery was a deficiency in Lockheed's board of directors. Although the board had an audit committee, this committee "failed to function as it should because it was shielded from critical information."

Lockheed's subsequent reforms demonstrate the powerful and productive role that a board can play in establishing a law abiding ethos. In response to the scandal, the Lockheed board appointed additional directors, including an auditing director, who came from outside the corporate structure; substantially increased the staff assigned to the board's auditing committee; made the audit group's budget independent of the groups that it audited; and, opened the lines of communication so that auditors no longer reported to the heads of their local divisions, but to the Director of Auditing who reported directly to the Chairman. These reforms led to intangible changes as well: "[N]ow [Lockheed] directors ask probing questions and demand more detailed information in audit committee reports that they previously passed without challenge."

In addition to examining the role played by the board of directors, the factfinder should also examine management's organizational structure. As Braithwaite stated: "The key to understanding so much organizational crime . . . is the way that organizational complexity can be used to protect people from . . . exposure to criminal liability." The factfinder should focus its inquiries on whether management left unattended or inaccessible positions within the corporation where illegal behavior could have easily occurred. If positions were left unattended, the factfinder should scrutinize the reason for this: was there an honest and good faith oversight, or a callous recognition that if corporate employees commit illegal activity, it is best done outside the usual channels of supervision? Braithwaite's study of the pharmaceutical industry provides a graphic example of the latter. He found that many companies have systemic policies to protect the chief executive from the taint of knowledge of illegalities. They do so by having "vice-presidents responsible for going to jail." The corporate directors tell the vice presidents: "'I don't want to know how you do it . . . just get the job done.'" * * *

b. Corporate Goals

When considering the corporate goals, the factfinder should examine whether the goals set by the corporation for the relevant division, subsidiary, or employee promote lawful behavior or are so unrealistic that they encourage illegal behavior. As the American Law Institute noted in devising the Model Penal Code's standard of corporate criminal liability, "the economic pressures within the corporate body [may be] sufficiently potent to tempt individuals to hazard personal liability for the sake of company gain."

An apt example of this was Ford's ambitious production and earnings goals for 1973: It was imperative that Ford obtain EPA certification of its emission testing standards if it was to meet these goals. The Company was unable to obtain certification legitimately, so Ford employees tampered with its 1973 engines to obtain the needed certification. By comparison Exxon, following its bribery scandal, demonstrates goals a corporation can establish to promote compliance with the law. In a memorandum sent to all employees, Exxon stated:

> An overly-ambitious employee might have the mistaken idea that we do not care how results are obtained, as long as he gets results. He might think it best not to tell higher management all that he is doing, not to record all transactions accurately in his books and records, and to deceive the Corporation's internal and external auditors. He would be wrong on all counts.

> We do care how we get results. We expect compliance with our standard of integrity throughout the organization. We will not tolerate an employee who achieves results at the cost of violation of laws or unscrupulous dealing. By the same token, we will support, and we expect you to support, an employee who passes up an opportunity or advantage which can only be secured at the sacrifice of principle. . . .

Rarely will cases be as extreme as the Ford and Exxon examples. The point, however, is that institutional goals can encourage, or discourage, illegal activity by corporate employees. When illegal activity is encouraged, such goals weigh in favor of imposing criminal liability on a corporation. When the goals discourage illegal activity, they mitigate against a finding of criminal liability, even though corporate employees committed illegal acts. * * *

Most of the factfinders' work in applying the corporate ethos standard of liability will occur in the analysis of whether there existed a corporate ethos that encouraged the criminal conduct. The factfinders should examine the corporation's internal structure to make this finding. Beginning with the corporate hierarchy, the factfinders should determine whether the directors' supervision of officers, or management's supervision of employees was dilatory. Next, factfinders should examine the corporate goals, as communicated to the employees, to determine whether these goals could be achieved only by disregarding the law. The third and fourth factors focus on the corporation's affirmative steps to educate and monitor employees and are more relevant in some fields than others. In highly technical fields where corporate employees daily decide issues involving legal compliance or violation, the factfinders should view the corporation's failure to educate its employees as encouraging criminal acts. In other fields where few corporate employees deal in issues affected by law and regulations, the corporation has a minimal duty to educate its employees and its failure to do so is less relevant. In examining the fifth factor, the commission of the present offense, the factfinders should examine the facts considered under the traditional respondeat superior and MPC standards. Unlike these current standards that look to these facts as the sine qua non in imposing liability, however, the corporate ethos standard considers these facts to be relevant, but not conclusive indicia, of corporate liability. The factfinders should assess the sixth factor, how the corporation has reacted to past violations, to further evaluate whether the corporation encourages or discourages illegal behavior. Consideration of the last factor, compensation by the corporation, is extremely important because often a corporation's compensation policies most directly influence its employees' behavior. Assessing the message inherent in compensation is complicated because most corporations use at least one form of compensation, indemnification, in a way that encourages corporate crime, thus making most corporations criminally liable under the corporate ethos standard. This Article suggests a different approach toward indemnification and insurance coverage of convicted executives: If corporations follow this approach, the factfinder can more fairly weigh this component of a corporation's compensation package. * * *

In conclusion, the corporate ethos standard explicitly retains only the first portion of the traditional requirement that a court can hold a corporation criminally liable only for the conduct of an agent acting within the scope of employment and with the intent to benefit the corporation, namely, that an agent of the corporation perform the criminal act. A corporation should not be liable for every person in the world who might stumble in and use corporate resources to commit a crime. The corporate ethos test does not explicitly include the requirement "within the scope of employment" because simply applying the corporate ethos standard will include this proof. Nor does the corporate ethos standard explicitly require proof that the agent at issue was acting "for the benefit of the corporation." Historically, this requirement has been read into nonexistence with one caveat: Corporate liability cannot result when the corporation itself is the victim of the illegality. This seems to be such an obvious caveat for corporate liability that it needs no emphasizing and certainly does not warrant the currently broad overstatement. Moreover, it is not clear how courts could reasonably apply a "benefit" element. For all of these reasons, the third element of the corporate ethos standard is simply that an agent of the corporation perform the criminal act.

B.   PRACTICAL ISSUES IN CORPORATE CRIMINAL RESPONSIBILITY

TO LET THE PUNISHMENT FIT THE ORGANIZATION: SANCTIONING CORPORATE OFFENDERS THROUGH CORPORATE PROBATION
Richard Gruner
16 Am. J. Crim. L. 1 (1988)

Corporate probation is an important new sentencing option for corporations violating federal laws. More than a means of mitigating corporate punishment, corporate probation is a flexible vehicle for imposing a wide range of sanctions having the common feature of continued judicial control over aspects of corporate conduct. Through the proper tailoring of these conduct restrictions, corporate probation can be used to punish, deter, incapacitate, or rehabilitate corporate offenders.

Because of its flexibility, corporate probation can be used to fill current gaps in sentencing strategies for corporate offenders. Unlike fines and other entity sanctions that pound like bludgeons at the periphery of large corporations with somewhat unpredictable results, corporate probation terms can better focus the impact of corporate sanctions to strike like an epee at narrow targets within large firms. If properly matched to the features and criminal activities of defendant firms, corporate probation terms can further criminal sentencing goals more effectively and more efficiently than traditional corporate sanctions like fines. Furthermore, since it is available as a sentence for most federal crimes, corporate probation can reform corporate practices in areas beyond the range of civil regulatory enforcement.

Under provisions of the Sentencing Reform Act of 1984, effective November 1, 1987, corporate probation is the primary alternative to a fine as a sanction for corporate offenders. Given the unavailability of incarceration for corporations and the frequent inadequacy of corporate fines, corporate probation may be the most potent sanction available for corporate offenders.

Although fines have been by far the most common criminal sanction for corporate offenders, numerous courts and commentators have recognized the limitations of such sanctions. Past corporate fines have frequently been so small that they have had little impact on large firms. Although larger corporate fines are now authorized under the Sentencing Reform Act, larger fines risk inflicting unfair hardship on innocent corporate employees, shareholders, or customers because firms are driven out of business, stock prices are driven down, or product prices are driven up. Furthermore, regardless of their size, threatened corporate fines will often fail to deter individuals in large corporate bureaucracies from illegal behavior. The interests of these individuals may depart from those of their firms so that criminal actions may be advantageous to the individuals, even though costly to their firms. In light of these weaknesses, there is a clear need for the sort of sanctions that can now be imposed through corporate probation.

Probation offers several advantages over fines as a corporate sanction. First, unlike fines which may simply be paid with no change in corporate operations, probation conditions can force top executives to adopt specific measures to avoid criminal conduct in the future. Second, probation can help insure that firms carry out corrective internal measures by providing for the external monitoring of corporate activities by probation officers, expert consultants, or the sentencing court. Third, if used for punishment or deterrence, corporate probation can impose punitive burdens on firms and executives that will be more difficult to transfer than the economic impact of fines. Fourth, probation conditions can require actions that lower the reputation of firms and their executives, thereby imposing greater punishment and deterrence than mere economic sanctions. Finally, judicial control of a few misbehaving corporations under probation conditions may forestall the need for more elaborate and inefficient regulatory schemes of general applicability.

Although corporate probation was occasionally imposed under prior federal law through the suspension of another sentence, the Sentencing Reform Act has broadened the legitimate goals of corporate probation, the circumstances under which it may be imposed, and the types of conditions that may be attached. Corporate probation may be imposed as either a substitute for economic sanctions, such as fines and restitution orders, or in addition to such sanctions. Probation is an authorized sentence for essentially all federal crimes that corporations are likely to commit. Conditions of probation need not be limited to rehabilitative ends nor to mitigating punishment, but may be imposed for purposes of increasing punishment, specific deterrence, or general deterrence. Sentencing courts have broad discretion to develop probation conditions matched to corporate defendants and their crimes. * * *

In July, 1988, the Commission circulated two substantially different guideline proposals authorizing varying degrees of organizational probation. Neither of these proposals has been adopted by the Commission; rather, they have been distributed to encourage public discussion about the proper scope of organizational probation and other organizational penalties as federal sanctions. The Commission has scheduled further public hearings on organizational sanctions in New York on October 11, 1988, and in Los Angeles on December 2, 1988.

One proposal circulated by the Commission focuses primarily on the role of corporate probation as a valuable supplement to monetary sanctions for convicted firms. This proposal was drafted by the author, John C. Coffee, Jr. of the Columbia Law School, and Christopher Stone of the USC Law Center. It authorizes corporate probation in connection with serious crimes for the following purposes:

(1) To improve management policies or practices, including inadequate internal controls, found by sentencing courts to have substantially contributed to illegal behavior or delayed its detection;

(2) To require factual reports on a defendant corporation's criminal behavior (prepared by outside counsel or such other parties as the sentencing court shall appoint) where a sentencing court finds that the circumstances surrounding the defendant's offense have not been adequately clarified to insure accountability of corporate personnel to shareholders;

(3) To force convicted organizations to provide restitution to victims in all circumstances where promulgation of a restitution order is reasonable in light of both the need of victims for restitution and the likely complication or prolongation of the sentencing process if restitution is ordered;

(4) To obligate organizational defendants to provide essential community service or interim relief for the benefit of the victims of its crime where an order of restitution is either infeasible or an inadequate substitute; and

(5) To require an organization also sentenced to pay a fine, make restitution, comply with an order for notice to its victims, or perform community service to take steps necessary to ensure its deferred performance where these obligations will not be fully performed within 30 days of sentencing.

The proposal authorizes the appointment of outside counsel and other experts as special probation officers to oversee corporate compliance with probation terms. Recommended sanctions for probation violations include resentencing of the probationer and prosecution of corporate officials or employees willfully impeding compliance with probation terms or the reporting of probation violations. Overall, this proposal is consistent with the role advocated in this article for organizational probation.

The second proposal being circulated by the Commission was developed by members of its staff to address all types of organizational sanctions. The primary penalties authorized for organizations would be monetary sanctions determined in accordance with the following formula:

Sanctions = [(Offense Losses) x (Offense Multiplier)] + Enforcement Costs

where

Offense Losses = the total harm (or risk of harm in some instances) caused by the offense

Offense Multiplier = a factor intended to reflect the difficulty of detecting and punishing the defendant's offense

Enforcement Costs = the costs of detecting and prosecuting the particular offender

The proposal strongly emphasizes the importance of monetary sanctions as an economic incentive for proper corporate behavior; consequently, the proposal minimizes the significance of non-monetary sanctions, including organizational probation. It does, however, authorize such probation to require actions necessary to ensure deferred payment of monetary sanctions or, in very limited circumstances, to require reforms of management practices or policies following an extended pattern of corporate recidivism.

Note

In the wake of a number of scandals involving corporate misconduct, Congress passed the Sarbanes-Oxley Act of 2002, Pub. L. No. 107-204, 116 Stat. 745 (2002). The Act holds corporate officials personally liable, rather than the corporation itself, for material misstatements or omissions that result in false or misleading information for investors. If misstatements or omissions are identified, officials may be subject to extensive criminal penalties. The Act also increases penalties for individual fraudulent acts, and extends criminal liability to consultants, such as accountants, who provide the basis for misleading and fraudulent representations.

Chapter 15

CULTURE AND CRIME

INTRODUCTION

In Chapter 1, we suggested that criminal law can be viewed as a system of cultural meaning. In this final chapter, now that we have had an overview of doctrinal and policy issues in the criminal law, we explore the concept of the interaction of law and culture in more detail.

First, what do we mean by "culture"? We follow the common practice of using the word to mean several different things. We use the term "culture" to generally describe the social world outside the law, which gives legal rules and practices meaning. Scholars from the humanities, such as philosophy and literature, have long spoken of criminal punishment as a "language." More recently, scholars from the social sciences, steeped in the language of economics and sociology, have begun to write about criminal law and criminal punishment as a site where legal rules interact with "social norms." The first two readings in this chapter introduce you to these ways of understanding "law" and "culture" as a single integrated system.

Another, popular use of the word "culture" refers to the practices particular to a subgroup within a society. In the commission of crimes and in the practices of punishment, people may act in ways patterned by their awareness of gender, nationality, sexuality and race; these ways can be also described as "cultural," or as pertaining to a "subculture." The law itself can be said to have a culture: legal culture includes the patterns of thought and behavior common to people who work within the legal system, especially lawyers and judges.

Finally, another meaning of the word "culture" points outside the boundaries of a particular society. In the context of the "cultural defense," immigrants to the United States (especially immigrants from Asian countries) are often treated as coming from a particular national "culture" that may have relevance to their criminal culpability.

In this chapter, we explore the meaning of the term "culture" for criminal law in four different contexts. Section A considers crime as a cultural practice. What does the commission of a crime mean to the lawbreaker? Is criminal behavior wholly idiosyncratic and personal to the offender, or are there broader social determinants of the commission of, and the meanings of, crime?

Section B addresses punishment as a cultural practice. The criminal justice system is usually said to serve the traditional reasons for punishment: deterrence, rehabilitation, incapacitation, and retribution. Does criminal punishment serve other functions as well? What does punishment mean to citizens? What does punishment mean to offenders? How do the practices associated with criminal punishment – criminalization, policing, incarceration – interact with other influences on lawbreakers' behavior, such as social norms and cognitive structures? What effect does criminal punishment have on communities and on neighborhoods?

Section C addresses the effects of criminal justice administration on legal culture. In Chapter 2, we examined police and prosecutorial discretion as a constitutional problem. In this chapter, taking the "war on drugs" as a case study, we consider the effects of that war on the criminal justice system, on civil rights and liberties, and on substantive criminal law.

Section D examines the role of culture in the courtroom. In Chapter 10, we saw one example of a case in which the defendant sought to rely on a "cultural defense" to crime. What is the role, if any, of a specific cultural defense in American criminal law? What might be the drawbacks of such a defense? Do "cultural defenses" already exist?

Finally, Section E considers the alternatives to the existing criminal justice system, with its emphasis on punitive punishment. The theory of restorative justice attempts to transcend punishment as the ultimate goal of the criminal justice system, seeking instead to reintegrate the offender into society. Other alternative sanctions, such as "shaming" punishments and procedural innovations such as drug courts, similarly seek to change our legal culture's dependency on incarceration as the primary tool of criminal justice.

A. CRIME AS A CULTURAL PRACTICE

CRIMINAL LAW, CRIMINOLOGY, AND THE SMALL WORLD OF LEGAL SCHOLARS
Robert Weisberg
63 U. Colo. L. Rev. 521 (1992)[a]

* * * In our positive law, an intentional killing is presumptively a murder; only an express exception to the rule can justify, excuse, or mitigate it. Jack Katz [in his book *Seductions of Crime*] argues, however, that if we are to understand the moral and psychological dynamics of crime, we must look at things in an opposite manner: That is, we must view the typical homicide as presumptively feeling in the mind of the killer as if it is a legitimately justified act of law enforcement.

In spousal killings, the killer, usually male, may act to assert his sexual rights, to punish an insult to his honor, or to preserve a certain orderly image of the relationship. Many spousal killings also occur, however, over disputes concerning the proper handling of domestic business, such as a dispute over the proper priority (by legal or moral standards) among a couple's financial obligations--that is, over the principle of how one affirms to the world that one is a debtor of integrity. Many killings occur over slight insults, disputes over parking places or the proper level of respect or civility required in a bar or concerning a pool table. It is important, Katz argues, to see that such trivial matters are viewed by the killers not only as assertions of legitimate property rights, but as affirmations of civil order. Ironically, though killings of this sort are greater among the poorer classes, the issue underlying the killings might be seen as a defense of bourgeois values -- marital order, property rights, responsible debt.

In describing the psychological stages of these killings, Katz notes that, although intentional, they are not premeditated in the sense of including a plan for escape. The killer engages in a mixture of resignation and justification. In one sense, he stays at the scene because he views his act as one of legitimate law enforcement, merely to be reported when the police arrive. On the other hand, to the extent that the killer recognizes that his claim of justification will not be legally recognized, he simply awaits his fate, because, given the demands of the moral norms to which he was responding, he views himself as having had no choice -- he was commanded by the situation to affirm the good and the orderly. (In this sense, the sane killer is like the psychotic killer; each believes his act is

---

[a]Reprinted with permission of the *University of Colorado Law Review*.

justified because it was obligatory.) This sort of killer may feel innocent of any willful violence because his own law was "transparent"; he was merely the medium for the natural, automatic retribution that certain evil acts merit.

Now one might argue that this notion of the modal killer is irrelevant to the other large category of killings -- the category which most people (wrongly) fear they are most likely to fall victim: the so-called senseless killings of total strangers. But Katz's theory of righteous slaughter extends to these killings as well. Many "senseless" killers think they are engaged in righteous slaughter -- they kill "Nietzscheanly." They punish people under a private norm of strict liability, to replicate the "unjust" world in which they have personally suffered. * * *

* * * [Mercer Sullivan] shows how individual volition can connect with economic forces to produce crime. Indeed, he defines what might be called the criminal's culture of money. For Sullivan, * * * labor intersects with crime in complex ways. In a boy's life, crime precedes even the possibility of work, and occasional crime overlaps with early employment. Ironically, opportunities for manual shop work may help cause crime by teaching necessary skills. Criminals are fairly good entrepreneurs who sometimes test, alternately or simultaneously, the legitimate and criminal job markets. Among the groups Sullivan studied, one specializing in drug sales and con games simultaneously got real job training in people-skill clerical and service jobs. On the whole, work opportunities somewhat moderate crime * * * and, if one looks at neighborhoods with some particularity, there is some crime-unemployment correlate in richer neighborhoods where there were more jobs. But the influence of employment is long-term and character building, not immediate, and from a broader perspective, the key is not the employment of the individual, but the density of consistent unemployment in the neighborhood.

But the economic causes and effects of crime are complex. Some are far away -- the macroeconomic forces that create the unstable secondary labor market in which most youths live. Others are closer to home -- the ambivalent attitude about crime in poor neighborhoods where some residents denounce crime as much as rich people do -- for the obvious reason that they are the most frequent victims and hold mainstream moral values. Other residents tolerate crime out of cynicism or exhaustion, and still others appreciate crime because, as Sullivan finds, though these young criminals are no Robin Hoods, there is a fair amount of wealth redistribution in the acts of young capitalist criminals. Crime gives the neighborhood a positive balance of trade and is not the least efficient form of welfare.

Sullivan finds a fair amount of rational planning and mutually rational group activity among young criminals. Though crime begins as theft-play, not work, it soon takes on entrepreneurial calculations. Ethnographers like Sullivan look to bounded spheres where coherent culture can operate, but these are very small cultures. Sullivan sees crime as a matter of the social and economic ecology of particular neighborhoods. He steers away from rigid free market assumptions of equal opportunity as well as reductive Marxist explanations that prove too much. As powerful as economic forces may be, there are, in Sullivan's ethnography, individual creative responses to the social situation. Ironically, Sullivan is reluctant to use the term "culture" only because it sounds too reductionist and determinist to describe the nexus of forces at play. Indeed, he is wary of the old culture-of-poverty theories of the 1960s. For him, culture is a mixture of the anthropologist's shared symbols and beliefs and the economist's patterning of market interactions. The ghettoes he studies are ruled by many non-market relations of reciprocity and redistribution and exchanges of goods and services among kin who are cut off from normal markets.

Thus, Sullivan manages to construct an economic model that assumes neither the extreme individualist model of the neoconservative nor the sentimental strain theory of some liberals. Criminals do often live and work in groups. To some extent, these groups are cliques that share thrills, drugs, and trendy consumer goods. To some extent they are entrepreneurial teams, as where local car-theft/chop-shop schemes are cottage industries. Crime represents a locus of cultural symbols related to age, labor, household organization, and ethnicity, a male "limbo" between work, school, and home. And to some extent the young criminals blend with the larger non-criminal "community" which is ambivalent about crime, but accepts its local benefits. But crime--or membership among criminals--is still individually chosen. It is a short term "occupation" of leisure, a construction of a self the criminal has somehow become locked into. It is not a free market choice, nor is it deranged and isolated. It is a logical adaptation to a situation.

Sullivan's work exemplifies what is called for in David Garland's refreshingly sensible argument for how sociological analysis and ethnography can enhance the study of criminal justice. Garland portrays the power of sociology to provide perspectives -- not reductionist or essentialist theories -- to illuminate the role crime and the criminal justice system play in the wider culture. Moreover, while praising Durkheim's insights into the role of criminal justice as an expression of social norms, Garland warns against viewing the rules and ceremonies of belief and punishment which constitute the criminal justice system as being coterminous with society or as necessarily promoting social harmony. The history of punishment is in part the history of sensibility; societies punish in ways they find culturally permissible as a matter of social taste, and in a manner consistent with their perception of themselves as having made moral progress toward higher levels of civilization.

"THE BLACK COMMUNITY," ITS LAWBREAKERS, AND A POLITICS OF IDENTIFICATION

Regina Austin[a]

65 S. Cal. L. Rev. 1769 (1992)

* * * In the black vernacular, a "bad" person may be a potent and respected force for good rather than a despised source of evil. In the culture of "the community," there has historically been a subtle admiration of criminals who are bold and brazen in their defiance of the legal regime of the external enemy. * * * A further reflection of this phenomenon is the respect shown to drug dealers by their neighbors and the beneficiaries of their philanthropic largess. Blacks, of course, are hardly unique in idolizing the criminal element of their ethnic group or race as social critics and resisters of oppression. It is possible to mount a substantial and quite coherent case for the appreciation of the black male lawbreaker.

Those who identify with black male lawbreakers accept the validity of the justification the lawbreakers offer to rationalize their behavior. For some blacks who commit crimes, it makes economic sense to engage in such conduct. It is the best job available. The rewards to be gained by young urban males from the drug trade-for example, money ("paper"), fancy cars ("Benzo's," "Beemers," and "'vettes"), and fine females-seem worth the risk, given the alternatives of unemployment or a dead-end job. As one Detroit gang member put it:

> I didn't do shit in school, my people ain't got no paper. I tried to join the Marines, I couldn't pass their written test. Ain't got no transportation to get a job. So what's a fella to do? You talk all that righteous shit, but you got a job. Got one for me? So I'm going to get with somebody rolling.... That's the only job for fellas like me.

The willingness to risk incarceration and physical harm, together with the high demand for drugs, can make drug dealing quite remunerative. Jail may be delayed or avoided even if one is caught because the criminal justice system is overburdened, and should one wind up serving time, the harshness of prison life may be cushioned by access to liquor, drugs, friends, and some of the comforts of home. Furthermore, death and injury from violence are constants in some urban areas whatever one does. Where one's physical survival is always in jeopardy, the line between offensive and defensive toughness and aggression wears thin.

The relativity of what is legal and what is illegal is not lost on the lawbreakers:

> It's like this, if we don't sell the shit, somebody else will. Niggahs getting paid in full, slinging dope hard every day. So why should we take some bullshit ass minimum wage McDonalds' job? Fuck, everything is illegal [laughing]. Pork is deadly, bacon can kill niggahs, whiskey, cigarettes, cars, guns, but ain't nobody stopping them companies from selling them!

The refusal to surrender to the stranglehold of material deprivation and social constraints has a heroic quality, as is suggested by John Edgar Wideman's brother Robert in *Brothers and Keepers*:

> See. Ain't all of us out there in the street crazy. We know what's going down. We look round and what do we see? Homewood look like five miles of bad road. Ain't nothing happening.... We see what's going down. We supposed to die. Take our little welfare checks and be quiet and die. That ain't news to nobody.... Them little checks and drugs. What else is out there? The streets out there. The hard-ass curb. That's why the highest thing you can say about a cat is he made his from the curb.... What else he be but bad if he made all his shit from that hard rock.

The resistance he and others see in black lawbreaking produced in Robert Wideman such feelings of admiration that he was inspired to pursue the street life himself. (He is presently serving a life term for felony murder.):

> [W]e can't help but feel some satisfaction seeing a brother, a black man, get over on these people, on these people, on their system without playing by their rules. No matter how much we have incorporated these rules as our own, we know that they were forced on us by people who did not have our best interests at heart. So this hip guy, this gangster or player or whatever label you give these brothers that we like to shun because of the poison they spread, we, black people, still look at them with some sense of pride and admiration, our children openly, us adults somewhere deep inside. We know they represent rebellion -- what little is left in us.

Similar sentiments are shared by many blacks who, unlike Robert Wideman, do not act on them. For example, Martin Sanchez Jankowski reports that "a significant number of adults from low-income areas identify with the 'resistance component' of gangs." He continues:

> These people empathize with the desires, frustrations, and resentments that the youth of low-income neighborhoods experience because they have experienced them too. Thus they identify with the gang because they are sympathetic to the members' attempts to resist their poor socioeconomic position. Take the comments of Wayne, a fifty-seven- year-old African-American machinist who was the father of two girls:
>
>> I know people think gangs are terrible and that the kids are just disgusting individuals, but that just ain't what's going down with these kids. Hell, they ain't bad kids, sure you gots some, but most ain't bad, they just not willing to quietly sit back and let the society take everything and give them nothing.... Sometimes I think some of the gangs go too far, but I understand where they're coming from, and I say, they ain't bad, they just made a bad decision that time, that's all.

Some blacks follow the exploits of deviants with interest and sympathy because their criminal behavior generates tangible and intangible benefits. Through the antisocial acts of others, the law-abiding experience a vicarious release of the hostility and anger they cannot express themselves without jeopardizing their own respectability. Moreover, criminals whose illegal behavior brings additional resources into economically marginal neighborhoods achieve a greater degree of acceptance than criminals whose conduct simply recycles the wealth that is already there. Additionally, local gang members and lawbreakers have been known to provide a community with such services as protection from more dangerous malefactors and unscrupulous entrepreneurs. Finally, the lawbreakers' presence justifies the existence of anti-crime or anti-gang social programs that employ community residents and otherwise benefit the law-abiding population.

All in all, then, identification with lawbreakers seems justified to some. It is based on a recognition of the need for critical assessments of the dominant society's laws and for some kind of resistance against material and cultural subjugation.

But so much for the romance. Ordinary lawbreaking is a lame manifestation of revolt. Most lawbreakers are not social bandits. Even the majority of their admirers are ambivalent about their activities and have good reasons for refusing to join their campaign of the streets. A praxis based on a literal association of lawbreakers with race-war guerrillas could be justified only by a gross magnification of the damage black criminals actually inflict on white supremacy and a gross minimization of the injuries the criminals cause themselves and other blacks. * * *

These young people's lawless resistance also misfires because more often than not their targets are similarly situated minority folks. Either for lack of access to or identification of more suitable marks, the anger and alienation poor blacks feel are displaced upon those close at hand: family, peers, and neighbors. Though those who resort to violent lawlessness may cite self-preservation as their justification, an element of self-destruction is operating as well. The killings of young blacks by other young blacks are mass suicide disguised as murder. In his seminal work *The Wretched of the Earth*, Frantz Fanon maintains that "a community of victims, unaware of its history and unable to control its destiny, tends to victimize itself viciously." So-called black-on-black crime "constitutes expressions of misdirected rebellion and collective autodestruction" that "cannot be explained apart from the prevailing structural and institutional violence in society." Unfortunately, Fanon's insights are rarely invoked in analyses of contemporary black urban violence.

Black lawbreaking is in addition a form of collective economic suicide. Gauging the winners and losers of the underground economy is a complicated matter. To be sure, blacks are included among the realtors, clothiers (including purveyors of athletic shoes), car dealers (including the sellers of fancy foreign cars and popular cheap jeeps), and other business and professional persons (including lawyers) who are profiting from criminal enterprises in minority neighborhoods. Sales to white, middle-class suburban customers who frequent inner-city drug markets probably do contribute to the economies of the surrounding neighborhoods. But black drug dealers have few qualms about who their customers are. Women and older persons, segments of the population never before involved in drug usage, smoke crack; this means that profits are now being extracted from a broader base than ever before. Crack dealing to other poor folks depletes the resources of the community; the money travels out of the neighborhood, out of the state, and out of the country. Ansley Hamid's assessment of the overall negative redistributive effect of the political economy of crack seems justified:

> Crack may be thought of as a super-efficient "vacuum cleaner" that is going over the physical and social rubble of [the decaying Caribbean-American neighborhoods that were Hamid's chosen] study sites to detect and draw in overlooked wealth. In my study sites, crack dollars are not reinvested at the

local level. These dollars have not contributed a single vegetarian cookshop, nor is there evidence of other local-level secondary economic activity that it [sic] has stimulated. Instead, as youthful crack distributors spend on "gold cables" and luxury motorcars, there is evidence of more apartments being abandoned and more buildings being rendered derelict (and of others being gentrified). Crack dollars for the most part travel abroad to the supplier countries, leaving significant deposits only in the hands of corporate institutions that launder drug money or perform other roles in distribution.

* * * In sum, then, the young lawbreakers wind up with little control over their images and less control than they imagine over their lives and their own world views. Far from being self-conscious political insurrection, most ordinary black male criminal behavior may not even be progressive. The lawbreakers' rebellion is limited because it is not based on a thoroughgoing critique that attacks the systemic sources of their material deprivation. Nor is it likely to generate or exploit the sort of material and ideological dislocations that lead to economic and political reform.

GENDER VIOLENCE, RACE, AND CRIMINAL JUSTICE
Angela P. Harris
52 Stan. L. Rev. 777 (2000)

* * *

Manliness is one of those ideas that is often made real with violence. Violent acts often carry idiosyncratic moral or emotional meanings to the perpetrator. But violent acts are also, sometimes, the result of the character of masculinity itself as a cultural ideal. In these cases, men use violence or the threat of violence as an affirmative way of proving individual or collective masculinity, or in desperation when they perceive their masculine self-identity to be under attack.

For some years now, feminist criminologists have insistently called attention to a fact that previously seems to have escaped criminology's notice: Criminals are overwhelmingly male. As criminologist James Messerschmidt observes,

[a]rrest, self-report, and victimization data all reflect that men and boys both perpetrate more conventional crimes and the more serious of these crimes than do women and girls. Men

also have a virtual monopoly on the commission of syndicated, corporate, and political crime . . . . Indeed, gender has consistently been advanced by criminologists as the strongest predictor of criminal involvement.

Men predominate not only in crime but also in criminal justice. Policing, for example, has traditionally been a male occupation. Messerschmidt observes that "until the 1970s, women officers engaged in such 'feminine' functions as working primarily with juveniles, women offenders, women victims, vice-squad assignments, and community relations . . . . Although by the 1970s women were increasingly assigned to routine patrol duty, today [1989] less than 10 percent of all police officers are women." Nearly ten years later, the numbers had not improved significantly. The National Center for Women and Policing (NCWP) found that "[a]mong the largest law enforcement agencies in the country in 1998, women comprise[d] only 13.8% of all sworn law enforcement positions." A similar history and continuing gender asymmetry holds for jobs in corrections.

Some researchers suspect the cause for this startling sex difference is biological in origin. Sociologists, true to their discipline, are instead interested in the systems of social meaning that link crime with masculinity. The literature on "masculinities" suggests that men are disproportionately violent, at least in part, because being violent is one socially recognized way of being a man. * * *

Some men routinely use violence or the threat of violence as a way of presenting themselves as masculine. Other men, ordinarily nonviolent, may on occasion transform intolerable feelings of shame and humiliation into rage and commit violent acts to protect their sense of masculine identity. Men in groups sometimes use violence to raise or protect their esteem in the eyes of other men or their comrades. Some of these violent acts violate the law. Some of these violent acts are committed in the name of the law.

The link between doing crime and doing gender has received a fair amount of attention from sociologists. For example, Jack Katz argues that the violent crimes of some men are part and parcel of a masculine persona to which these men aspire, the desired image being that of the impervious coldness of the "hardman" or the crazy, unpredictable "badass." But gender-based criminal violence is not limited to such men. Ordinarily law-abiding and peaceful men may find themselves committing violent criminal acts when (in public settings) their manhood is threatened by conflict with other men or when (in private settings) women threaten to reveal them as sexually inadequate, fail to submit to their patriarchal authority, or threaten to leave them. In these situations, the potential loss of masculinity brings shame and humiliation, and the man who finds these emotions intolerable may turn them into rage and act violently in expression of that rage.

The need to be seen as a man by other men may require violence. Sociologists Dov Cohen and Joe Vandello describe "cultures of honor" as sharing "a common conception of the insult as something that drastically reduces one's social standing and a belief that violence can be used to restore that standing once it has been jeopardized." In this kind of culture, they argue,

> people react not just to physical threats but to verbal affronts
> and insults as well because these are the probes by which one
> man tests another to see what he is made of. Letting infractions
> to honor go unanswered amounts to announcing that one is soft
> or can be walked over with impunity.

As the slide from "people" to "man" in the quote suggests, Cohen and Vandello's "cultures of honor" involve relations among men. Criminal law casebooks are full of homicides that emerge from seemingly trivial encounters between men who are strangers to one another, interactions that would seem inexplicable unless it is understood that manhood is at stake.

Another distinctively masculine form of humiliation that may quickly lead to rage and then criminal violence occurs not in public among other men, but in "private" in connection with women. For example, both actual humiliation by women and the fear of being humiliated play a large role in men's accounts of why they rape women. Rapists tend to experience themselves as the humiliated victims of female sexual power. As one man succinctly noted, "Just the fact that they can come up to me and just melt me and make me feel like a dummy makes me want revenge." Similarly, researchers of domestic violence interpret the actions of some men who batter women as efforts to establish and maintain male dominance. In other instances, men beat or kill their wives or girlfriends when the women attempt to leave the relationship. In these cases, criminal violence emerges not simply out of the desire to control, but out of an extreme emotional dependence, coupled with an unwillingness or inability to see the woman as a separate and independent person. In this form of love, masculine style, a woman's attempt to end the relationship is experienced as an intolerable threat to the self: "If I can't have her, no one can" is the response.

In the situations I have described, individual men resort to violence when other men or women threaten their masculinity. Another dynamic that produces criminal gender violence emerges from the behavior of men in groups. The violence of street gangs provides an example. Katz argues that these gangs, which are usually made up of very young men, use violence as a way of heightening the drama of their moral and sensual lives and as a way of demanding that others take them seriously as adults rather than children:

> In the hands of adolescent street elites, violence has a constructive power sufficient (1) to transform the significance of their principles of association from demeaning indications of childhood to the social requirements for glorious combat, (2) to establish a metaphor of sovereignty respected by peers, observed by the police, and duly reported by the mass media, and (3) most essentially, to sustain the claim of elite status in an aura of dread.

Each of these goals is accomplished by using violence in the service of masculine gender performance. The lords, kings, and princes whose names have traditionally been taken by gangs exemplify glorious and hegemonic manhood. Membership in a gang serves many different purposes, but one of them is the desire to establish unquestioned masculinity.

Wealthier, more privileged young men have their own brotherhoods from which violence may emerge. Criminologists Patricia Yancey Martin and Robert A. Hummer argue, for example, that campus "fraternities create a sociocultural context in which the use of coercion in sexual relations with women is normative and in which the mechanisms to keep this pattern of behavior in check are minimal at best and absent at worst." Because fraternities promote masculine brotherhood as the center of campus social life and treat the casual use of women as an important element of the brotherhood, date rapes and even occasional gang rapes can be expected to occur with depressing regularity.

Finally, men in groups may engage in "hate crimes" and other spontaneous violent attacks as a way of performing their gender. In one survey of gay men and lesbians who were the victims of bias crimes, it was noted that the perpetrators commonly boasted about their own alleged hyper-heterosexuality while attacking men, and derided feminism and women in general while attacking women. This violence was, then, as much about the perpetrators' purportedly secure and superior masculinity as it was about bigotry. Indeed, criminologist Jana L. Bufkin argues that these displays of hypermasculinity are connected with nationalist pride. As Bufkin comments, "These individuals obviously wish to separate themselves from all that is feminine and non-heterosexual and feel as though they are American heroes when the task is completed."

In a wide variety of situations, then, male criminal violence is gender violence. The term "gender violence" should not be used to ignore the currents of race, ethnicity, religion, and sexuality that shape who becomes a victim and who a perpetrator. But I want to suggest that, when studying racial violence and other kinds of bias crimes, we should not forget about the codes of gender that make this violence explicable; similarly, when studying violence against women, we should place it in the context of gender violence as a whole.

B.   PUNISHMENT AS A CULTURAL PRACTICE

1.   Crime, Punishment, and Culture: A Humanities Perspective

MAKING SENSE OF WHAT WE DO:
THE CRIMINAL LAW AS A SYSTEM OF MEANING
James Boyd White
HERACLES' BOW: ESSAYS ON THE RHETORIC AND POETICS OF THE LAW
(1985)

When a person comes to law school, he (or she) leaves behind a world he knows and understands and turns to another world, that of the law, which at the beginning he cannot comprehend. The body of literature in which he is immersed is at once assertive and confusing, and it is not at all clear what he should do with it. He attends a series of classes in which his teacher seems to make the unsettling assumption that he already knows what he came to learn. One question he will naturally ask himself about all this – his experience of the law – is whether it makes any sense. And for a long time, if he is honest with himself, he will find that it does not. * * *

When I say that the criminal law does not "make sense" when talked about in a certain way, I do not mean that it is impossible for a lawyer to learn to make appropriate arguments for and against a particular defendant, for that can be done and done well. The question is not whether one can learn the arguments but what, if anything, they all add up to, and how they fit together. * * *

Most contemporary writing about the nature of criminal law and whether, and how far, each of [the traditional justifications for punishment] serves as a justification either of the practice of punishment in general or of its infliction in a particular case or class of cases. The idea is that once the purposes have been agreed upon, they can form a basis upon which the institution of the criminal law can be shaped and action within it guided and controlled. * * * This is the mechanical and instrumental language of systems design and cost-benefit analysis. Of this way of talking it is sometimes said that it, and it alone, is "rational."

I want to put aside for the moment the question whether this kind of talk about institutional and collective life can ever be rational. For present purposes let us accept its premises and accept the further claim that each of the purposes stated is, standing alone, a valid one. My question then is this: What can it mean to say that the law serves all of these purposes at once? * * *

When it is conceived of in the traditional way, the criminal law forces a choice among its competing purposes but affords no method by which that choice can be made and explained. * * *

* * * Each of the four purposes of the criminal law implies its own conception of the character both of the individual and of the judge. If you act with a genuine solicitude for the offender's welfare, and seek – however misguidedly in practice – to rehabilitate him (or her), you can properly be said to respect his humanity. You treat him as a person in a different sense when you act to restrain him – for you do no more than he should be required to recognize it is necessary to do, to him and to others, who threaten the security of the community. * * * But when you impose a punishment not required by any of the particular characteristics of the defendant's personality or the circumstances of his life or the nature of his conduct, merely to make him serve as an example to others, what you have done is to convert him from a person into a resource or object to be employed in the public interest. You have, as it were, drafted him into a population control program. * * *

Is there another way to conceive of the practice of punishment that would render it intelligible and coherent? Is there some way, that is, in which we can make sense of this activity after all?

I think that the first step is to abandon the "purpose-structure" or "ends-means" language of bureaucratic analysis. The assumption of such a way of talking is that we can produce in schematic language, like a blueprint, both a description of the mechanism of a social institution and a statement of the goals by which it is to be directed. * * * In my view, to talk this way about the criminal law misrepresents the nature of human action and experience and misconceives the nature of language. * * *

I want to begin by thinking of communal punishment as a practice of a special kind, the function of which is to claim a certain kind of meaning for events. In this it is like law more generally, which * * * is in my view best regarded not as a machine for social control, but as what I call a system of constitutive rhetoric: a set of resources for claiming, resisting, and declaring significance. It is a way of asking and responding to questions; of defining roles and positions from which, and voices with which, to speak; of creating and maintaining relations; of justifying and explaining action and inaction. It is one of the forms in which a culture lives and changes, drawing connections in special ways between past and present, near and far. The law, of which legal punishment is a part, is a system of meaning; it is language and should be evaluated as such. * * *

The old common law formulation, that there can be no criminal guilt without a "mens rea" (guilty mind) reflects a conception of the criminal law as a species of blaming. The Model Penal Code, which codifies enlightened modern opinion, states as its central principle the allocation of criminal responsibility according to blameworthiness. Within the criminal law as well as outside it, punishment has traditionally been regarded as a special form of the social and intellectual practice we call "blaming." If we can make sense of that practice, we may be able to make sense of the criminal law as well, and indeed discover a ground, very different from a statement of purposes, upon which that activity may be shaped and guided.* * *

* * * Blaming can * * * be seen as a way of limiting one's imaginative or sympathetic identification with the actor, but this is done in the interest of maintaining one's capacities to remember what one knows and feels about others as well. It is a way of saying to the offender and to his victim that in the eyes of the community both have claims to recognition and sympathy. For one's identification with the victim is also qualified by the practice of blaming. The victim is not entitled, that is, to demand public condemnation on a showing of some injury alone; he or she must speak a language of fault and blame. * * *

* * * The community insists to each of the characters that it will recognize the existence of the other, and it forces each to speak a language that does this too. In doing this, the community claims and performs a meaning for its action or inaction; it defines and maintains a character of its own. This last, indeed, is the critical achievement of the practice of blaming, for there is no guarantee that the communal insistence I describe will much affect the subjective view either of a particular defendant or of his or her victim. The one may simply want to get off; the other may simply want revenge. It is in its own interest above all that the community acts when it insists upon recognizing the claims of both, for this insistence gives the community an important part of its character. * * *

The community so created is not an abstraction but is a living world defined by the actions of individual people responsible for particular judgments. For the judgment of blame is made by one jury or one judge about one person; the sentence a person must suffer is passed upon him or her by another who is responsible for the judgment. The law happens, as it should be studied, one case at a time. * * * The defendant speaks to the person who is responsible for his case, the proper disposition of which requires an individualized judgment about him. This is an important way in which the criminal law defines the citizen and his relation to the community.

Even when he (or she) is sent to a special place of punishment, the defendant remains a member of his community, entitled to all protections and recognitions not taken away as punishment. * * *

2.   **Crime, Punishment, and Culture: A Social Science Perspective**

UPDATING THE STUDY OF PUNISHMENT
Tracey L. Meares, Neal Katyal, & Dan M. Kahan
56 Stan. L. Rev. 1171 (2004)

* * * Recent years have witnessed a tremendous outpouring of research in economics, psychology, sociology, and other disciplines concerning how institutions, incentives, and rules actually affect behavior. This research has had a significant impact on criminal law scholarship. But it has had almost none on popular criminal law textbooks and thus (we suspect) next to none on the education of criminal lawyers. * * *

I. Punishment and Social Science: What Works, What Doesn't, and Why

To the detriment of students, legal casebooks largely limit their focus to classic deterrence insights. The standard trope in criminal law, both in scholarship as well as contemporary public understanding, is that enacting high penalties on a particular crime will deter offenders from committing it. The traditional analysis simply turns on whether the penalty is set at an appropriate level to optimize deterrence -- balancing the cost of the activity against the cost of enforcement. We do not dispute the central insights of economic theory that people generally act to maximize their preferences and that crime is an area ripe for application of these concepts. However, modern deterrence analysis must incorporate several refinements to the deterrence function, particularly: substitution effects, decision framing, educational impact of laws, social control, and perceived legitimacy. We will discuss each in turn.

A. Substitution Effects

The most pervasive economic conception of criminal law, made famous in modern times by economist Gary Becker, views the legal sanction for a given act as its "price" and asks whether that price will exceed the benefit of the criminal act to the criminal. Within the economic tradition itself, some (most preeminently George Stigler) have explained that this calculation misses a crucial variable for optimality: marginal deterrence. The idea is essentially the problem of cliffs -- exacting equal penalties for crimes of lesser and greater magnitude leads to crimes of greater magnitude: "If the thief has his hand cut off for taking five dollars, he had just as well take $5,000." The marginal deterrence argument, therefore, is one about creating incentives for individuals to refrain from committing the same crime on a greater scale. While the traditional question asks whether a penalty for X deters X, the marginal deterrence one asks whether a penalty for X may prompt commission of the marginally more severe crime X + 1 because that crime receives the same magnitude of punishment as X. Unfortunately, contemporary casebooks, when they mention deterrence, generally omit this key point. Instead, the analysis is framed as whether a higher penalty on X will produce greater "deterrence," without asking what activity precisely is being deterred and what behavior is being encouraged through the law.

Once economics is taken seriously, the problems with contemporary criminal law analysis become even more acute. Marginal deterrence is only the tip of the iceberg, for it functions as an illustration of a broader concept at work: substitution effects. Put simply, two products are substitutes when they compete with each other and are complements when they "go together." Consumers will tend to use more of a good -- to substitute in favor of the good -- when its relative price falls, and to use less of it -- to substitute away from the good -- when its relative price increases. If the price of tea increases, for example, substitution theory predicts that the demand for coffee would increase. But the demand for other products that go with tea, such as lemons, may drop because tea and lemons are complementary products. * * *

* * * The whole point of deterrence is to make the price of a crime high enough so that a criminal will "substitute" forgoing the crime. Just as a high price on train rides means that some people will not take them and ride bicycles instead, a high price on a crime, it is thought, means people will not commit that criminal act. When it comes to crime, however, most of us don't take the economics seriously enough to examine whether an analogue to the bicycles exists: We assume that deterrence works and -- poof! -- a would-be lawbreaker is now magically converted into a law-abider.

Consider, for example, the way our government treats crack cocaine. Congress passed dramatic penalties against crack cocaine only a few days after learning of the drug's existence. The mandatory-minimum scheme Congress enacted provides that a minor crack dealer caught with five grams of crack will be in jail for at least sixty months, even on a first offense. Yet legislators never gave serious consideration to what the impact of high crack penalties would be on consumption of other drugs. Much attention has been given to the racial implications of the disparity between powder cocaine and crack cocaine. But none on substitution effects.

This lack of attention to substitution issues is troubling given the significant disparity between punishments for possessing crack and punishments for possessing other drugs. Simply by weight, the ratio of crack to heroin penalties can be as high as 20:1. Indeed, a dealer can carry 375 grams of heroin and be punished at the same level -- 5 to 6 years -- as the 5-gram crack dealer. When drug dosage is factored into the equation, the crack to heroin punishment ratio can be 80:1 or even higher. As such, drug dealers, who are motivated at least in part by money and a desire to avoid incarceration, would be much better off carrying heroin instead of crack. And while it is difficult to test the substitution effect here without better data, crack consumption has decreased since 1988 while heroin consumption has increased. * * *

* * * [E]ven crimes of passion may be examined in terms of substitution. * * *

Take what seems like the quintessential example in which substitution would not occur: rape. Insofar as these categories are separable -- and the argument does not depend on their separation -- is rape a crime of sex, violence, or domination? If rapists seek sex, it might follow that legalizing prostitution will reduce the frequency of rape. If they seek to dominate and humiliate, legalized prostitution may provide a substitute as well. To the extent that rapists seek violence, lowering the penalties for other violence, say assaults, may reduce the commission of rapes. Conversely, a high penalty for rape may mean that there are more instances of spousal abuse and other violence. These ideas are not policy suggestions, only possible illustrations of substitution at work. There may be many reasons why legalized prostitution is problematic -- including its potential complementarity to rape. But the complementarity between prostitution and rape itself suggests that interrelationships between behavior cannot be ignored.

Even when the penalties for a crime are so high that it appears that all the crime that can be deterred will be deterred, substitution presents other possible problems. After all, one result of a higher penalty may be an increase in criminal activity -- both of the particular crime and of other crimes. As explained above, at high prices, many crimes may substitute for one crime. The rapist who is determined to rape a particular woman and is not deterred by a high penalty for rape may go out and commit other crimes. He may first commit the rape, then kill the victim, and finally assault unrelated others, because the cost of future criminal activity is negligible. If, on the other hand, the penalty for rape is not high, the marginal cost of additional criminal activity may be much higher.

To take another example, imagine the potential consequences of the "three strikes you're out" rule that has recently been implemented in several jurisdictions. If offenders know that on their third offense they will be jailed for life, they may be less likely to commit that third offense; but if they do, the offenders may make the third crime a drastic one. Indeed, they may even decide to kill the witnesses to their crimes, because -- at least in states without a death penalty -- there is nothing more that the government can do to them.

Viewed in these terms, the death penalty could provide an incentive for additional crime. * * *

The inattention to substitution in contemporary criminal law is even more striking when it is juxtaposed against the everyday attention received by its economic opposite, complementarity. Prosecutors, for example, often will justify their aggressive prosecutions of narcotics traffickers on the ground that drug traffickers are likely to engage in violence. In other words, drug dealing has a complementary relationship to violence, and even if drug dealing is not a terrible evil, punishing that dealing can avert greater harm to society. Policymakers, for their part, criminalize certain drugs like marijuana on the ground that they are "gateway" drugs that lead to consumption of harder, more dangerous, drugs. And yet the casebooks never point out that the policymakers get the question backwards: Shouldn't it be asked whether, by branding the common act of smoking marijuana a crime, criminalization creates the gateway effect in the first place? After all, those who smoke marijuana are now introduced to a variety of dealers who carry other illegal drugs, and the cost of undertaking a second criminal act is much lower than it is the first time around (particularly when the first time might produce beliefs in the illegitimacy of the criminal law in, for example, teenagers who question why marijuana is punished in a way that alcohol is not).

Relationships of substitution and complementarity underscore a fundamental point about criminal law -- that it will often influence tastes or preferences rather than constrain opportunity. Criminal law may be said to set itself apart from many other areas of the law because it concentrates more on altering people's preferences, particularly with its focus on criminal intent, which can be understood as a proxy for taste. Taste shaping explains why potential substitutes for a particular crime may radiate well beyond crimes with similar characteristics to the original one. * * *

Substitution theory expands on this insight by demonstrating that the law may shape tastes in perverse ways. If the penalty for consumption of one drug induces people to use other drugs, for example, these penalties are altering those people's desires. Punishment, therefore, can breed crime by increasing the taste for it and by reducing the "price" of future criminal activity.

B. Decision Framing

Consider an additional wrinkle in the deterrence story: Traditional understandings of deterrence ignore a wealth of research from psychology about the way in which people frame choices. * * * Here is a clear example: Simonson and Tversky offered subjects a choice between $6 and "an elegant Cross pen." 36% chose the pen and 64% took the cash. A second group was given the choice between $6, the Cross pen, and a second, less attractive, pen. This time, 46% took the Cross and 52% chose the cash. * * * [T]he cheap pen option should not influence the choice between the Cross pen and the cash. Yet it does. Closely related to this is the finding of extremeness aversion, which shows that within an offered set, options with extreme values are relatively less attractive than those with intermediate values.

* * *The substitution perspective predicts that individuals do not view the costs and benefits of a particular crime in a vacuum. Rather, they examine them in light of the costs and benefits of other crimes. The psychological addendum to substitution suggests that people evaluate the relative harms and benefits of a particular crime by using reference points. Consequently, when the law proclaims, through a harsh penalty, that the cost of a particular activity is very high, it might make other crimes appear more attractive than they were before the penalty. * * *

C. Educational Impact of Criminal Law

Implicit in the discussion up to this point has been the assumption that people know what the penalties actually are. The skeptic is rightfully concerned: How can policymakers expect would-be lawbreakers to know such details? And if people do not know the law and do not understand the penalties, then how can deterrence ever function? * * *

* * * The educational impact of the criminal law is not a brittle Skinnerian stimulus and response, but rather one that works through a complex process of social interaction. A small group of people may look at the sentencing structure and be influenced by its relative treatment of crimes. As time passes, the information this group possesses will trickle down but now in a way no longer tied to sentencing. Instead, it may simply be said that activity X is worse than activity Y. People who have never eaten caviar, for example, do not need to know its cost for their preferences to be affected by the price -- particularly when the high price places a stigma on caviar-eaters as being greedy and selfish. In such circumstances, even if the monetary price of the good is unknown, the social price (which is in part a function of the monetary one) will deter consumption.

In this way, contemporary understanding of deterrence must take into account the educational impact of the criminal law. As Andenaes argued, penalties send out "messages" to members of society, and these messages exert a moral influence that inculcates social norms. This theory of messages thus gives meaning to English jurist James Fitzjames Stephen's statement on why most men abstain from murder:

> Some men, probably, abstain from murder because they fear that, if they committed murder, they would be hung. Hundreds of thousands abstain from it because they regard it with horror. One great reason why they regard it with horror is, that murderers are hung with the hearty approbation of all reasonable men.

Stephen realized that a penalty can have an unconscious deterrent effect through a subtle changing of social norms. Stephen's words, therefore, mark him for more than the general deterrence theory for which he is cited today. Stephen believed that a penalty can affect the behavior of more than the individual punished -- the general deterrence point. But he also argued that the criminal law has an educational effect and that this effect may dwarf general deterrence. * * *

But the claim about creating social prices, through punishment's inculcation of social "norms," itself misses a fundamental problem -- punishment's effect on the criminal. By segregating such actors from mainstream America, the criminal law may reinforce a tendency towards criminal action. In economic terms, when an individual cannot get hired for lawful work because she was once an outlaw, the relative cost of illegal activity decreases. Moreover, from a psychological perspective, those branded outlaws may begin to internalize such labels and fulfill the expectation that they believe the criminal system and society have for them. Instead of reducing crime, stigmatization strategies may increase the criminal activity of particular actors. * * *

* * * First, criminal punishment imposes a stigma on individuals that may lead criminals to avoid contact with law-abiding people. For the criminal, outside contact becomes problematic because of the risk that normal people will disapprove or define a criminal only in terms of his stigma. Outsiders, for their part, will avoid a criminal because of the possibility that being seen with one will contaminate them both socially and legally. Criminals may use the stigma as a way to justify their career choices, much the way those with scars and harelips may justify their decisions. Thus, those who have already committed crime may feel that other options are closed to them and continue their criminal activity.

Second, stigmatization from the law-abiding world will prompt criminals to band together with others like them. The stigma imposed from outsiders is celebrated within this group, and their norms differ from the world of the nonstigmatized. They develop subnorms that may be antithetical to those of the law-abiding world. This may become both an inducement to further crime, as lawbreaking is seen as a socially positive act within the group, and a disincentive to noncriminal alternatives. * * *

In this fashion, social norms strategies can force additional crimes. The youth who is caught selling one vial of crack emerges from confinement as a social pariah. He internalizes that belief and avoids contact with the law-abiding world. His isolation from the lawful world leads him to keep company with other pariahs. The subnorms of this group reward the criminal activity that the law-abiding world punishes, and devalues the lawful alternatives that the law-abiding world celebrates. The punishment, then, produces the crime it was intended to prevent. What is more, it may even produce other types of crime, substitutions of sorts, both because stigmatized individuals avoid the law-abiding world and because they may learn new ways of earning money from members of the stigmatized group.

D. Inverse Sentencing Effect

Incorporating social norms into criminal law analysis also illustrates other defects in the opportunity-shaping view of behavior. The traditional approach ignores the way in which people react to high penalties. Such penalties create what may be termed an inverse sentencing effect. High penalties, instead of increasing conviction rates, may decrease them. As penalties increase, people may not be as willing to enforce them because of the disproportionate impact on those caught.

Several different mechanisms are responsible for the inverse sentencing effect. When the penalties are high, for example, the public may not be willing to turn lawbreakers in, police and prosecutors may not want to prosecute, and jurors may not vote to convict. Legal scholar Frederick Beutel observed this phenomenon in his study of bad check laws. He found that in Colorado fewer bad checks were written because the punishment was weaker but enforcement was more consistent. In Nebraska, by contrast, he discovered that Nebraska's severe punishment for bad checks hampered enforcement and conviction. Similarly, in the eighteenth and nineteenth centuries, even though the number and severity of English penal laws had increased, English jurors regarded the penalties as excessive and were lenient in applying them. Of course, the law is only one variable that affects social norms, but when increasing the penalty on a particular law is out of step with norms in a community, it may reduce deterrence instead of promoting it. This real world effect is, again, contrary to most treatments of deterrence, which treat the probability of enforcement as a variable fungible with the extent of the sanction.

E. Impact of Social Control

* * *

A final factor that should be assessed when discussing the purposes of punishment is the offender's community context and social role within that community. Understanding this broader context of social control is essential to understanding deterrence. * * *

Examination of connections to work (or a lack of them) provides a specific example of the impact on deterrence of the interaction between legal punishment and social controls. Research shows individuals with regularized paying jobs have commitments that enhance the deterrent effect of formal legal sanctions. However, as economist Richard Freeman and criminologist Jeff Fagan have noted, a sustained decline in wages for unskilled workers has weakened both attachments to work and incentives to participate. The returns from illegal work often exceed legal wages for workers with limited human capital or access to higher wage jobs and neutralize incentives to avoid crime and possible punishment. This is especially true in communities where large numbers of the jobless are concentrated. The attractions of illegal work are reflected in variables often unmeasured in quantitative studies on crime and work, especially "tastes and preferences" that inflate the nonmonetary dimensions of illegal work.

A fuller understanding of the purposes of punishment can be gained through an assessment of punishment at the community level rather than simply that of the individual -- a macro rather than a micro level if you will. Sociological studies of communities provide just such a lens. * * *

* * * One such study that looks at the costs of incarceration was implemented by anthropologist (and soon-to-be lawyer) Donald Braman. He conducted more than two hundred interviews over a three-year period with fifty families living in the Washington, DC area. Each of these families was located in a poor, mostly minority neighborhood where the male incarceration rate exceeded two percent. These interviews contain valuable insights concerning the effects of incarceration on family life. Through a recounting of the experiences of several families, Braman explains that the most costly expense that families of the incarcerated must regularly bear is collect calls from the inmate. It turns out that correctional facilities contract out for phone services, and facilities select carriers based on which carrier will provide the facility with the highest fee -- not which company will provide cheapest service for the inmate.

According to the families Braman interviewed, ten dollar fees for ten-minute conversations were not uncommon. In addition to phone calls, families bear the expenses of visits, which can include car rental or some other form of transportation, hotels, childcare, and, of course, food. If costs associated with maintaining legal battles on appeal and with stress-related medical expenses that some left-behind family members experience when a loved one is incarcerated are added to the list, it is easy to see how these direct costs of incarceration add up quickly -- especially given that such expenses must be borne by families in the worst position to deal with them.

Braman also shows how family members left behind withdraw from their own families. Increased economic costs sometimes force female partners of the incarcerated (or their mothers or sisters) to turn to extended family for financial assistance, childcare, and other resources. But the assistance extended family members can offer is limited by their own constrained finances. Eventually, extended family members begin to resent the burden of caring for family members whose partners are incarcerated. One woman Braman interviewed shares, "My mother can't even hear me talk about him. She'll be like, 'What? Are you crazy?'" This woman stopped talking to her own extended family about her husband and ended up turning only to his sisters for help. This kind of isolation from family networks is clearly inconsistent with promotion of social norms in favor of positive neighborhood outcomes. * * *

E. Punishment Practice and Legitimacy

One area where there is increasing interest among criminal law scholars is the work of social psychologists and the theories that they have offered to explain compliance with the law. The issue is a critical one in criminal law as the basic theories of deterrence taught in criminal law courses posit promotion of compliance with the law as an important reason for punishing people. Theories of deterrence assume that compliance is instrumental. That is, people comply with the law because they fear the consequences of failing to do so. But social psychologists offer another view of compliance with the law -- a view that is notably absent from widely used criminal law casebooks.

The social psychologists point to normative bases for compliance rather than instrumental ones, and they have connected voluntary compliance with the law to the fact that individuals believe the law is "just" or because they believe that the authority enforcing the law has the right to do so. These factors are considered normative because individuals respond to them differently from the way they respond to rewards and punishments. In contrast to the individual who complies with the law because she is responding to externally imposed punishments, the individual who complies for normative reasons does so because she feels an internal obligation. * * *

When one is thinking about punishment, this idea is a central one. Reliance on carrots and sticks to produce compliance can be a costly strategy. Programs featuring rewards and punishments can be costly because instrumental means of producing compliance are rarely self-sustaining; rather, authorities must be willing to maintain mechanisms of instrumental compliance. For example, if deterrence is to be produced by maintaining a certain probability of detection of rule-breakers, then authorities must be willing to devote resources to maintenance (or increase) of the desired level of police to ensure that the requisite probability of detection is met. Therefore, instrumental means of producing compliance always depend on resource limits. Legitimacy as a means of producing compliance, in contrast, does not always depend on resource limits because legitimacy can be acquired simply by changing procedures and practices of current officials in ways that require almost no additional resources. For example, some research indicates that police who regularly treat arrestees with courtesy are more likely than those who do not to be viewed as legitimate. While police officers may not like to be told to be more polite to arrestees, this research suggests that law enforcement gains could be achieved more cheaply than through more instrumental means simply by telling officers to "be nice." Once established, perceived legitimacy can support acceptance of decisions. We should, therefore, expect greater compliance in communities where police treat arrestees with greater respect than communities where police do not, even if the former community does not hire any more police officers. The lesson of this work for criminal law is that the practice and procedures of punishment can matter just as much (if not more) than the amount of punishment itself to achieving the goal of compliance. * * *

This novel area of scholarship is just one of a series of sweeping changes in method and focus that have convulsed the study of criminal law in the last decade. The classical economic conception of how the law regulates criminal behavior has been enriched (if not displaced) by a variety of insights drawn from social psychology, sociology, and behavioral economics. * * * The scholastic debate between "retributivists" and "utilitarians" has been displaced by a new, sociologically informed interest in the social meanings that law expresses.

Note

What kinds of criminal justice policies are suggested by the new literature on the social implications of criminal punishment? One type of policy is a focus not on individual lawbreakers but rather on communities as a whole. In the excerpts that follow, Bernard Harcourt critically examines a new style of policing – "order-maintenance policing" – that attempts to prevent serious crime in urban neighborhoods. Randall Kennedy and Tracey Meares consider the impact of the "war on drugs" on African American communities.

REFLECTING ON THE SUBJECT:
A CRITIQUE OF THE SOCIAL INFLUENCE
CONCEPTION OF DETERRENCE,
THE BROKEN WINDOWS THEORY, AND
ORDER-MAINTENANCE POLICING NEW YORK
STYLE

Bernard E. Harcourt
97 Mich. L. Rev. 291 (1998)[a]

* * * Order-maintenance policing is a law-enforcement strategy that seeks to create public order by aggressively enforcing laws against public drunkenness, loitering, vandalism, littering, public urination, panhandling, prostitution, and other minor misdemeanors. It is one variation of community policing, a variation that emphasizes police presence and arrests. Order-maintenance policing traces its origins to the broken windows theory, first articulated in James Q. Wilson and George L. Kelling's article, Broken Windows, which appeared in the Atlantic Monthly in 1982. The hypothesis of the broken windows theory is that minor disorder in a neighborhood, if left unchecked, will result in increased serious crime, and, therefore, that eliminating minor disorder will have a deterrent effect on major crime. * * *

The Broken Windows essay is premised on the idea that "disorder and crime are usually inextricably linked, in a kind of developmental sequence." According to Wilson and Kelling, minor disorders (like littering, loitering, public drinking, panhandling, and prostitution) if tolerated, produce an environment that is likely to attract crime. They signal to potential criminals that delinquent behavior will not be reported or controlled -- that no one is in charge. One broken window, left unrepaired, invites other broken windows. These progressively break down community standards, leaving the community vulnerable to crime.

In the essay, disorder breeds crime in a highly scripted manner:

---

[a] Reprinted from MICHIGAN LAW REVIEW, November 1988, Vol. 97, No. 2. Copyright 1988 by the Michigan Law Review Association. Revised and updated in Bernard E. Harcourt, ILLUSION OF ORDER: THE FALSE PROMISE OF BROKEN WINDOW POLICING (Harvard University Press 2001).

A stable neighborhood of families who care for their homes, mind each other's children, and confidently frown on unwanted intruders can change, in a few years or even a few months, to an inhospitable and frightening jungle. A piece of property is abandoned, weeds grow up, a window is smashed. Adults stop scolding rowdy children; the children, emboldened, become more rowdy. Families move out, unattached adults move in. Teenagers gather in front of the corner store. The merchant asks them to move; they refuse. Fights occur. Litter accumulates. People start drinking in front of the grocery; in time, an inebriate slumps to the sidewalk and is allowed to sleep it off. Pedestrians are approached by panhandlers.

At this point it is not inevitable that serious crime will flourish or violent attacks on strangers will occur. But many residents will think that crime, especially violent crime, is on the rise, and they will modify their behavior accordingly. They will use the streets less often, and when on the streets will stay apart from their fellows, moving with averted eyes, silent lips, and hurried steps. . . .

Such an area is vulnerable to criminal invasion. Though it is not inevitable, it is more likely that here . . . drugs will change hands, prostitutes will solicit, and cars will be stripped. * * *

In 1993, New York City began implementing the quality-of-life initiative, an order-maintenance policing strategy targeting minor misdemeanor offenses like turnstile jumping, aggressive panhandling, and public drinking. The policing initiative is premised on the broken windows theory of deterrence, namely the hypothesis that minor physical and social disorder, if left unattended in a neighborhood, causes serious crime. New York City's new policing strategy has met with overwhelming support in the press and among public officials, policymakers, sociologists, criminologists and political scientists. The media describe the "famous" Broken Windows essay as "the bible of policing" and "the blueprint for community policing." Order-maintenance policing has been called the "Holy Grail of the '90s." "There is little dispute that the theory works," says the ABA Journal. It has sparked "a revolution in American policing," according to the Christian Science Monitor, in an article captioned "One Man's Theory Is Cutting Crime in Urban Streets." Even the recent U.S. News & World Report cover story on crime -- a cover story that debunks nearly every hypothesis for the national decline in crime -- makes a passing curtsy to the quality-of-life initiative: "Clearly, smarter policing was spectacularly decisive in some cities like New York." Former Police Commissioner William Bratton, the principal architect of the quality-of-life initiative, credits the broken windows theory with falling crime rates in New York City. "These successes didn't just happen," Bratton contends. "They were achieved by embracing the concept of community policing." Wesley Skogan, a political scientist at Northwestern University, has conducted an empirical study of the broken windows theory and concludes that "'[b]roken windows' do need to be repaired quickly." George Kelling, co-author of Broken Windows and of a recent book entitled Fixing Broken Windows, contends that Skogan "established the causal links between disorder and serious crime -- empirically verifying the 'Broken Windows' hypotheses." In this euphoria of support, it is today practically impossible to find a single scholarly article that takes issue with the quality-of-life initiative. It stands, in essence, uncontested -- even in the legal academy. * * *

     * * * [O]rder-maintenance policing is one of the leading recommendations along what Kahan calls "the new path of deterrence." The new path is a loosely grouped set of initiatives in the area of crime and punishment, ranging from order-maintenance policing to curfews, gang-loitering laws, informal public-space zoning, reverse stings, and shaming penalties. The new path seeks to revitalize the argument for deterrence by infusing it with cutting-edge social science. Social norm proponents locate the new path of deterrence between economics and sociology. The new path represents, according to Kahan, "a third way, one that combines the virtues of both economics and sociology without succumbing to the vices of either." From economics, the new path appropriates the idea that individuals are rational actors maximizing their utility. From sociology, the new path appropriates the idea that individuals are influenced, and their conduct is shaped, by social phenomena. The new path of deterrence is presented as an application of social norm theory to criminal law.

     In this Article, I critically examine the empirical evidence and the social influence explanation supporting New York City's experiment with order-maintenance policing. At the empirical level, I replicate the principal social scientific study that has attempted to establish the disorder-crime nexus, namely Wesley Skogan's Disorder and Decline: Crime and the Spiral of Decay in American Neighborhoods. I conclude that Skogan's data do not support the claim that reducing disorder deters more serious crime. As a preliminary matter, the data are missing a large number of values (thirty to forty percent, on average, of the relevant dependent and independent variables) for such a small sample of neighborhoods (at most, forty neighborhood observations). But even setting aside that problem, my replication of Skogan's study establishes that (a) certain types of crime like rape, purse snatching, and pocket-picking are not significantly related to disorder; (b) other types of crime like physical assault and burglary are not significantly related to disorder when neighborhood poverty, stability, and race are held constant; and (c) although robbery remains significantly related to disorder, a cluster of five Newark neighborhoods exert excessive influence on the statistical findings. When those five Newark neighborhoods are set aside, the relationship between robbery victimization and disorder disappears. Accordingly, the data do not support the broken windows hypothesis.

Social norm proponents advance a second empirical argument in support of order-maintenance policing, namely the precipitous decline in crime rates in New York City. The conventional explanations for the drop in crime, they argue, do not account for the magnitude of the drop in relation to other large cities. As we speak, however, there is a hotly contested debate raging among criminologists, legal scholars, policy-makers, journalists, and other experts over the causes of the decline in crime in New York City and nationally. I review the various leading explanations and argue that it is far too simplistic to suggest that the quality-of-life initiative explains the extent of the decline of the crime rate in New York City. * * *

Running through the social influence explanation and the broken windows theory is a recurrent and pervasive dichotomy between, what we could call in vulgar terms, honest people and the disorderly; between "committed law-abiders" and "individuals who are otherwise inclined to engage in crime"; between "families who care for their homes, mind each other's children, and confidently frown on unwanted intruders" and "disreputable or obstreperous or unpredictable people: panhandlers, drunks, addicts, rowdy teenagers, prostitutes, loiterers, the mentally disturbed." Hand-in-hand with this set of categories is another ubiquitous dichotomy between order and disorder; between "norms of orderliness" and "[p]ublic drunkenness, prostitution, aggressive panhandling and similar behavior"; between a "stable neighborhood" and "an inhospitable and frightening jungle."

The social influence conception of deterrence is grounded on these categories. The mechanisms of social influence assume these fixed identities because disorder operates on honest people and on the disorderly in different ways. Neighborhood disorder influences honest people to move out of the neighborhood or to lock themselves in their homes, but it influences the disorderly and especially criminals to move into the neighborhood and commit crimes.

These categories, however, do not have a pre-existent fixed reality, independent of the techniques of punishment implemented by the quality-of-life initiative. In other words, they do not pre-date the policing strategy. To the contrary, the category of the disorderly is itself a reality produced by the method of policing. It is a reality shaped by the policy of aggressive misdemeanor arrests. It is the product of a technique of punishment that combines several different historical modalities, including classical strategies of excessive force and modern disciplinary mechanisms like surveillance and spatial control. Michel Foucault's study, Discipline and Punish, details these techniques of punishment, and it is there, Isuggest, that we should turn to overcome the problems with the Durkheimian approach -- first, by rehearsing Foucault's analysis, but second, and more importantly, by refining his analysis.

The techniques of punishment that comprise the quality-of-life initiative create the disorderly person as an object of suspicion, surveillance, control, relocation, micromanagement, and arrest. According to the unwritten rules of a Newark police officer enforcing order, "[d]runks and addicts could sit on the stoops, but could not lie down. People could drink on side streets, but not at the main intersection. Bottles had to be in paper bags. Talking to, bothering, or begging from people waiting at the bus stop was strictly forbidden." The fine art of policing creates the disorderly as a person with a full biography of habits, inclinations and desires. It simultaneously creates the disorderly as an object of surveillance and control. The disorderly is closely analogous to the delinquent, in Foucault's work, the end product of the penitentiary system. But the disorderly also differs in important ways from the delinquent. He is not coddled, he is not reformed, he is not part of the psychotherapeutic project of rehabilitation. The disorderly is, instead, watched, controlled, relocated, and, ideally, excluded from the neighborhood. The disciplinary techniques captured by the quality-of-life initiative operate on an axis of order and disorder, rather than on the axis of psychotherapeutic rehabilitation.

Order-maintenance policing helps create the category of the disorderly and this, in turn, facilitates the very policy of aggressive arrests for minor disorderly conduct. Once the category is in place, there is little else to do but crack down on the disorderly. Who in their right mind, after all, would side with people who urinate in the street, break windows, aggressively accost passers-by, or vandalize other people's property? The category triggers an aggressive response, even absent evidence supporting the broken windows theory.

At the same time, the category overshadows the numerous costs associated with the new policing strategy. Order maintenance in New York City has been achieved, in large part, by means of a fifty percent increase in misdemeanor arrests -- up from 133,446 in 1993 to 205,277 in 1996. Those arrests can be quite an ordeal: being arrested, handcuffed, transported, booked, often strip-searched, and spending the night in jail is an experience that many of us, readers of this Article, have had the good fortune to avoid. The quality-of-life initiative has been accompanied by a significant increase in the number of complaints of police brutality. The Civilian Complaint Review Board in New York City received 5,550 and 4,816 complaints of police brutality for 1996 and 1997, respectively, up from 3,580 complaints in 1993. Moreover, a law enforcement strategy that emphasizes misdemeanor arrests has a disproportionate effect on minorities -- not necessarily in relation to the racial composition of misdemeanor offenders but simply in relation to the racial composition of the community. The brute fact is that the decision to arrest for misdemeanors results in the arrest of many minorities. In cities in the United States, for example, 46.4% of persons arrested for vagrancy and 58.7% of persons arrested for suspicion in 1995 were black although the population inside metropolitan areas was approximately 13% African-American. Order-maintenance policing may also delegate the power to define order and disorder to police officers and designated community members in a manner inconsistent with our conception of democratic theory or constitutional principles. And the costs of arrest and prosecution of minor misdemeanor offenses may add up to a considerable investment. These are some aspects of order-maintenance policing that are not being heard in today's euphoria, in large part because of the category of the disorderly underlying the social influence conception of deterrence. They suggest that a much stronger empirical showing is needed before we proceed down the new path of deterrence.

I should emphasize * * * that I am extremely sympathetic with the motivation behind the new path of deterrence. Its primary motive, Kahan explains, is political, not conceptual. "By focusing on how law can be used to regulate norms, the new deterrence scholarship can be used to identify morally acceptable and politically feasible alternatives to the severe punishments that dominate contemporary criminal law." I share Kahan's motivation. New York City's quality-of-life initiative, however, does not fulfill that aspiration.

THE STATE, CRIMINAL LAW, AND RACIAL DISCRIMINATION: A COMMENT
Randall Kennedy
107 Harv. L. Rev. 1255 (1994)[a]

Crime is widely perceived as a major blight that decreases happiness, productivity, and security in the United States. Defining crimes and protecting people from criminality are central tasks that we assign to the state. Like many social ills, crime afflicts African-Americans with a special vengeance. African-Americans are considerably more likely than whites to be raped, robbed, assaulted, and murdered. Many of those who seek to champion the interests of African-Americans, however, wrongly retard efforts to control criminality. They charge that the state, at least in its role as administrator of criminal justice, is now (as it has been historically) an instrument of racist oppression. In all too many instances, these allegations are overblown and counterproductive; they exaggerate the extent of racial prejudice in the criminal justice system and detract attention from other problems of law enforcement that warrant more consideration. What such critiques ignore or minimize is that the main problem confronting black communities in the United States is not excessive policing and invidious punishment but rather a failure of the state to provide black communities with the equal protection of the laws. Although this failure often stems from a pervasive and racist devaluation of black victims of crime, ironically, a substantial contributing cause is a misguided antagonism toward efforts to preserve public safety. * * *

[Kennedy discusses the case of *State v. Russell*, excerpted in Chapter 2.]

The court's hostility to the Minnesota sentencing statute stemmed from its perception that, in Justice Wahl's words, the law "appears to impose a substantially disproportionate burden" on blacks, "the very class of persons whose history [of oppression] inspired the principles of equal protection." There are two related difficulties with this statement: one has to do with what constitutes a "burden," and the second has to do with what makes a law or policy racially discriminatory.

First, Justice Wahl's portrayal of Minnesota's sentencing statute as a "burden" to blacks as a class is simplistic. Assuming that one believes in criminalizing the distribution of crack cocaine, punishing this conduct is a public good. It is a "burden" on those who are convicted of engaging in this conduct. But it is presumably a benefit for the great mass of law-abiding people. Professor Kate Stith articulates this point with clarity. Commenting on *Russell*, she keenly observes:

> While it appears true that the enhanced penalties for crack cocaine more often fall upon black defendants, the legislature's action might also have been viewed as a laudatory attempt to provide enhanced protection to those communities -- largely black, according to the court's own statistics -- who are ravaged by abuse of this potent drug.... [I]f dealers in crack cocaine have their liberty significantly restricted, this will afford greater liberties to the majority of citizens who are the potential victims of drug dealing and associated violent behaviors. This is the logic of the criminal law, and it is distressing that a majority of the Minnesota Supreme Court recognized only half of this logic -- the denial of liberty to lawbreakers.

When discussing racial issues and the administration of criminal justice, some commentators think immediately and, all too often, solely about invidious criminal prosecution of people of color. There is reason for that. Throughout American history, officials have wielded the criminal law as a weapon with which to intimidate blacks and other people of color. But the flip side of racially invidious over-enforcement of the criminal law is often minimized. Racially invidious under-enforcement purposefully denies African-American victims of violence the things that all persons legitimately expect from the state: civil order and, in the event that crimes are committed, best efforts to apprehend and punish offenders. For most of the nation's history, blacks were denied this public good. The history of anti-black lynching and the failure of the states and the federal government to combat it effectively offers only the most notorious example. In many contexts, in comparison to the treatment accorded to whites, blacks have been denied quite literally the equal protection of the law.

Many have observed that, all too frequently, politicians, newspaper editors, and police officials express concern about crime only if they perceive that it inflicts injury upon whites. The more crime affects whites, the more likely officials are to respond. The less whites are harmed, the less likely officials are to respond. This critique suggests a very different approach to the crack cocaine-powdered cocaine distinction from that taken by the Minnesota Supreme Court. It suggests that we ought to commend rather than condemn the legislature's distinction between crack and powdered cocaine.

If it is true that blacks as a class are disproportionately victimized by the conduct punished by the statute at issue, then it follows that blacks as a class may be helped by measures reasonably thought to discourage such conduct.

To get at the second difficulty with the *Russell* court's perception of the punishment at issue -- its conception of the sentencing statute as an instance of "racial" discrimination -- one must focus on the punishment's relationship to those on whom it does place a burden, namely, persons convicted of possessing a certain amount of crack cocaine. The Minnesota Supreme Court condemned the statute as imposing an unjustifiable racially discriminatory burden. But what is "racial" about the punishment? Justice Wahl writes as though the punishment falls upon blacks as a class. But to the extent that the heavier punishment for possession of crack falls upon blacks, it falls not upon blacks as a class but rather upon a subset of the black population -- those in violation of the law who are apprehended.

It is possible for a facially race neutral law that affects only a subset of the black population to be intentionally aimed at blacks as a class, and thus to injure the group as a whole. For example, one of the methods used by Alabama to minimize the electoral power of blacks as a class was a state constitutional provision, silent on its face with respect to race, that permanently disenfranchised those convicted of committing certain crimes. In that instance, the delegates to the state constitutional convention openly admitted that the provision was purposefully being used as a weapon to disenfranchise blacks, and that they included as disenfranchising offenses only those crimes that blacks were thought likely to commit. In *Russell*, by contrast, the court made no finding that the purpose of the legislature's harsher punishment for possession of crack cocaine was to oppress blacks as a class. * * *

* * * [T]o return to the point of departure -- the intersection of state crime control policy and racial politics -- it is worth noting that, to an increasing extent, across the political spectrum and within black communities, priority of sympathetic identification is flowing to victims as opposed to perpetrators of crime. Sometimes people with these sentiments become inhibited when they confront the paradox that increasing the extent and severity of state crime control policy to protect law-abiding blacks will result in higher rates of incarceration and heavier punishments for black perpetrators, as most of those who commit crimes against blacks are themselves black. Perhaps, however, they will come to accept that disparities like those in *Russell* may be the mark, not of a white-dominated state apparatus "discriminating" against blacks, but instead, of a state apparatus responding sensibly to the desires of law-abiding people -- including the great mass of black communities -- for protection against criminals preying upon them. * * *

DRUGS: IT'S A QUESTION OF CONNECTIONS
Tracey L. Meares
31 Val. U. L. Rev. 579 (1997)

* * * In his book *Streetwise*, Elijah Anderson compellingly recounts how the weakened structural fabric of an urban community attended the transmission of diffuse norms in the community of "Northton." Anderson describes in great detail the clash between "decent" values (norms associated with hard work, family life, the church and law-abiding behavior) held by some families in Northton and "streetwise" values (norms associated with drug culture, unemployment, little family responsibility, and crime) held by others. A central part of Anderson's story is the gradual breakdown of a community tradition involving the transmission of decent values by neighborhood "old heads" to neighborhood youngsters that accompanied the constriction of employment opportunities for youngsters, increased neighborhood transience, and increased crime. Anderson's ethnography of Northton reflects the predictions of social organization theory. As the social networks in Northton weakened and contracted due to residential instability, unemployment, and increased drug use, a rival set of values-streetwise values-flourished. The streetwise norms that Anderson describes are at once a product of affirmative reinforcement of lifestyles that focus on drug use and crime, and the vacuum

created by the breakdown of social networks. For example, when work is not available for significant numbers of a community's residents, a value system among nonworkers that affirms the pursuit of economic opportunities in the informal economy or even the illegal drug economy may arise. And these values are less likely to be countered by values that emphasize the importance of seeking work in the formal labor market when social networks are weak.

Anderson's finding that streetwise values did not completely overtake decent values in Northton is critical to thinking about cultural disorganization in a community. While many in Northton continued to adhere to decent values, the streetwise code of conduct presented a significant and rival set of values that Northton residents were forced to negotiate in their daily lives. It should be obvious that it is more difficult for a community in which there are competing value systems to achieve and reinforce a common set of values. Such a community can be considered culturally disorganized. In Northton, the link between streetwise value and crime, and decent values and promotion of law-abidingness, has much relevance to a general discussion of crime prevention. The good news for Northton residents is that the proponents of decent values provide a counterweight to proponents of streetwise values, creating a barrier to community consensus on streetwise values as the common set of goals for community pursuit. The bad news is transparent.* * *

* * * Randall Kennedy has argued that the disparity in sentencing benefits law-abiding African Americans in neighborhoods in which crack dealing is prevalent.

Residents of these neighborhoods might welcome a sentencing regime that removes offenders for long periods of time -- especially if such residents are unable to leave the neighborhoods for a less crime-prone area. If the people I have in mind are convinced that "get tough" strategies reduce crime, they might also hope to achieve long-term crime reduction benefits if the organization of their community also improves as crime is reduced. * * * Less crime could and should promote better social organization, which in turn should lead to long-term crime reduction.

Note, however, that the power of this argument depends absolutely on the potential for "get tough" strategies to reduce crime. If crime is not appreciably reduced, there is no reason to be confident that already weakened structures of community social organization will be strengthened. Does our current "get tough" approach to drug offending reduce such offending? There are many reasons to be skeptical of the potential of our "get tough" approach to drug offending, which relies on incapacitation and deterrence through long sentences, to reduce such crimes in communities where social organization is low -- very poor communities in central cities that are disproportionately African American.

Joblessness is the hallmark of many very poor inner city communities. The significance of this point for a theory of community social organization directed at solving problems related to crime cannot be understated. Some proportion of those without jobs will, unsurprisingly, resort to drug-selling. The interaction between "get tough" policies and jobless ghettoes should be obvious. When one drug-seller is caught, convicted, and incarcerated for a long period, another eager seller will take the first dealer's place. In the absence of a deterrent effect of drug-law enforcement, huge numbers of drug offenders must be incarcerated before any meaningful impact on the population of offenders will be detected. Shaw and McKay predicted as much over fifty years ago. They wrote, "individualized methods of treatment probably will not be successful in a sufficiently large number of cases to result in any substantial diminution of the volume of delinquency and crime." In other words, individualistic strategies are unlikely to effectively fight delinquency in communities where the level of social organization is low.

What about deterrence? The little empirical work on the topic suggests that tough sanctions do little to deter those who already have offended from offending again. One reason that tough sanctions may be associated with low levels of specific deterrence is that despite a high lifetime likelihood of arrest, the probability that an individual will be caught committing a particular offense is incredibly low. Inciardi and Pottieger's work provides an especially striking example of this phenomenon. In their sample of 254 crack dealers from Miami, approximately 87% had been arrested at some point within the year of the survey. However, out of over 220,000 offenses the likelihood of arrest for each particular incident was less than 1%!

Inciardi and Pottieger's work refers to specific deterrence, but the theory of community social organization places emphasis on how law-abiders remain so. Assessment of the potential for long sentences to effect general deterrence is a difficult problem. It is possible that the law-abiding African American community in general and the subset of poor African Americans in particular who reside in impoverished neighborhoods in central cities interpret the disproportionate impact of long sentences on the drug offenders among them as a way to prevent individuals on the margin from slipping across the line of the law. If this is true we might expect greater general deterrence to flow from the current drug-law enforcement regime among African Americans. However, I think it is likely that the asymmetry in drug incarceration undermines, rather than enhances, the deterrent potential of long sentences for at least three categories of reasons: (1) group distrust of law enforcement for historical reasons kept alive by current scandals suggests that African Americans are not going to jump on the harshest law enforcement remedy possible to solve their problems; (2) African American belief in linked fate both in terms of empathy with family and friends and in terms of group identity is likely to make African Americans less likely to desire to treat harshly members of the group who may victimize them; and (3) when presumably law-abiding victims of crime in one instance are law-breaking offenders in the next instance, and when there is mutual support between so-called law-abiders and lawbreakers, it may be difficult to draw lines between them by penalizing lawbreakers very harshly for nonviolent offenses.

Recall that the theory advanced above hypothesizes that structures of community social organization will improve when crime decreases. We now have several reasons to be skeptical of arguments in support of significant crime reduction in poor minority communities. An additional problem for "get tough" law enforcement policy that depends on accelerated and disproportionate involvement of the minority poor in the criminal justice system is that such a policy is bound to exacerbate the precursors to social disorganization. While the number of African Americans incarcerated in state correctional facilities has long been disproportionate to the percentage of African Americans in the population, African Americans now comprise about half the state prison population. And as the numbers of those incarcerated for drug offenses has increased over time the racial gap in the demographics of prisoners has widened. My analysis of Bureau of Justice Statistics data is illustrative. These data indicate that incarceration for drug offending of African Americans with less than a high school education has increased from 60 in 100,000 in 1979 to 800 in 100,000 in 1991. The same rates for whites with a high school education increased from 6 in 100,000 in 1979 to 20 in 100,000 in 1991. The bottom line? High levels of drug-law enforcement, as currently implemented anyway, are likely to generate negative consequences for community social organization -- family disruption, unemployment, and low socioeconomic status. Less obviously, high levels of incarceration of poor, minority individuals for drug offending is likely to lead to lower levels of civic participation. Twenty-First Century Vote excepted, convicted felons are unlikely to be active politically, and in many states convicted felons are disenfranchised. People who do not vote are less likely to be politically active than those who do. Formal organization participation is an important component of community social organization.

Moreover, the asymmetry of drug-law enforcement affects African American communities in a unique way because such asymmetry reinforces negative stereotypes that compromise African American crime prevention efforts in at least two important ways. First, the stereotyping of African Americans as criminals affects how law enforcement agents relate to African Americans and how African Americans in turn relate to them. This is especially true when law enforcement agents are white. Some white law enforcement agents may view

African Americans, law-abiding or not, through the negative lens of criminality. Though the change in African American representation on city police forces has been positive and dramatic, poor African Americans continue to face a high probability of being policed by non-African American officers. Additionally, high levels of criminal offending in poor communities relative to offending in other areas can exacerbate the negative perceptions police officers have of those they are sworn to protect. The mutual distrust between African Americans and law enforcement officers makes it less likely that African Americans will report crimes to the police, assist the police in criminal investigations, and participate in community policing programs that lead to greater social control of neighborhoods. Second, by crystallizing the connection between African American men and criminality, a high-incarceration strategy promotes distrust within African American communities. Reverend Jesse Jackson is not unique among African Americans in fearing victimization by young African American men. Neighborly distrust leads to greater atomization of African Americans in poor communities, which leads, in turn, to a breakdown in social cohesion in the places where the need for social cohesion is the greatest. Individuals who keep to themselves reduce opportunities for enforcement of law-abiding norms in the community.

When evaluated through the lens of social organization theory, it appears that the current strategy fails on two levels. First, the strategy appears very unlikely to effectively reduce crime in the communities that are the most plagued by crime. Second, the strategy itself is criminogenic in that it exacerbates the precursors to social disorganization in a community. If harsh sentences for drug offenders are unlikely to remedy problems associated with teen drug use and violence, what will help?

An effective policy should have as its main goal increasing the social organization of inner city communities. Greater social organization promotes community guardianship and makes crime less likely. Greater social cohesion also creates more fertile ground for the transmission of law-abiding social norms. Thus, a drug-law enforcement policy that pays greater attention to the responses of the community as opposed to the incentives of an individual is likely to have beneficial long-term effects. Perhaps counterintuitively, the key point for policymakers and lawmakers is that law enforcement can and should help to strengthen social organization by strengthening social networks.

Probably the most important goal for law enforcement policy directed toward social organization improvement is redistribution of the social networks among both young people and adults in communities where social organization is weak. For example, supervision of teen peer groups is likely to be more effective when the level of social capital among adults exceeds that among teens in the community. If parents cannot count on each other to supervise each other's children, then individual parents may be forced to counteract the norms developed by groups of teens-norms that may promote lawbreaking behavior.

Unfortunately, when the social capital among teens is high, which often is true in the communities containing street gangs, individual parents face a dilemma. Each parent has little power to counteract the power of the teen group; moreover, the power of the teen group may cause the individual parent to attempt to exert even less supervisory control than she otherwise would. This is, of course, a very general description of some of the mechanisms that underlay the withdrawal of Northton's "old heads" from community life. Such consequences to structural and cultural community organization should be prevented. * * *

By making it difficult for teens to congregate on street corners and in other public areas, law enforcement strategies such as curfews and loitering ordinances have the potential to redistribute the proportion of social capital away from a community's teens to a community's adults. These law enforcement strategies impede the accumulation of social capital among teens in a neighborhood and allow promotion of social organization structure and transmission of law-abiding norms that disfavor drug-selling. Additionally, disorder-reducing strategies such as reverse drug stings can have a similar social organization improvement effect. Reverse drug stings focus on buyers who come into poor inner city neighborhoods, often from crime-free suburbs, to purchase drugs. The reverse sting procedure reduces disorder by making it more difficult for suburban drug users to locate inner city dealers. Street drug prices fall, and the open-air market constricts. When disorder in a crime-prone neighborhood is reduced then, fear, a prominent barrier to local friendship network formation, also is reduced. Finally, each of these law enforcement strategies is less likely than the current "get tough" approach to brand teens with the scarlet letter that reduces employment opportunities and levels of civic participation.

C. LEGAL CULTURE AND THE ADMINISTRATION ON CRIMINAL JUSTICE

Another way to think about the interplay of criminal law and culture is to consider the legal and political effects of fighting crime on the state and on political and legal culture itself. The first two excerpts in this section criticize the "war on drugs" for its seeming ineffectiveness and its deleterious effects on American legal culture. John T. Schuler & Arthur McBride argue that criminalization of the drug trade has unintended deleterious consequences, including an increase in certain kinds of violence. Amanda Park outlines a "harm reduction" approach to substance abuse that might ameliorate these unintended consequences.

The second two excerpts in this section consider the tension between the desire to prevent and punish crime and the protection of civil liberties and civil rights. Markus Dirk Dubber argues that the "war on drugs" has eroded protection of civil liberties by affecting the law of possession. Erik Luna addresses the dilemma of discretion in law enforcement generally, and suggests a tool – "transparent policing" – for making that discretion visible and hence subject to greater democratic control.

NOTES FROM THE FRONT: A DISSIDENT LAW-ENFORCEMENT PERSPECTIVE ON DRUG PROHIBITION
John T. Schuler & Arthur McBride
18 Hofstra L. Rev. 893 (1990)[a]

* * *

III. VIOLENCE: A CONSEQUENCE OF PROHIBITION

The violence related to illegal drug trafficking is an inescapable consequence of prohibition. Decriminalization will not eliminate all the violence in inner-city neighborhoods where brutality has been a central element for generations, manifesting itself in child abuse, domestic violence, and other brutal forms. What decriminalization can do is stop financing and feeding trafficking-related violence. It will prevent drug traffickers from being the primary successful role models in neighborhoods where poverty and unemployment make affluent and unafraid drug traffickers people to emulate.

"Drug-related"' violence can be separated into three broad categories: intramural violence between drug traffickers, violence intended to hinder law-enforcement efforts, and violence ascribed to the consumption of illegal drugs. This Article will address only the first two categories.

Violence intended to hinder law-enforcement efforts takes a number of forms, in categories which overlap: (1) assassinations, force, or threats intended to intimidate or eliminate public officials, (2) avoiding apprehension during an arrest; (3) intimidating or eliminating prospective, past or potential witnesses and (4) intimidating citizens, often neighborhood activists or public figures, who

---

[a]Reprinted with the permission of the Hofstra Law Review Association.

speak out against drug dealers. Intramural violence has variations. Such violence is also intended to hinder law enforcement efforts: one trafficker kills or threatens an associate or former associate because of the victim's perceived cooperation with the authorities. This can either be anticipatory, or retaliatory in order to set an example and deter others from cooperating.

Other drug-related violence among criminals involves wars over markets, usually over a geographical area, often as small as one block on a city street. A portion of intramural violence involves the avoidance of paying debts. Some violence involves one individual, group, or trafficker, robbing or kidnapping drug traffickers or their families. These last two actions are often interrelated: one group kills the members of another group, and at the same time steals money and drugs. This serves several goals at once: it eliminates a competitor, serves as a warning to other potential competitors, and also provides the spoils of conquest. Some violence is merely retaliation for past injury, such as selling "beat'" drugs,[54] larceny, past attacks, or is meant to serve as a show of force.

There are also "non-combatants;" unintentional victims, often children, who are mistakenly killed or maimed either by stray bullets, or because they are standing near a target. It is characteristic of much drug violence that bystanders do not matter. It is also an inevitable, if horrific, fact of criminal law enforcement that police officers and investigators will sometimes accidently harm innocent persons or each other. Finally, there are killings of private attorneys, which are hard to categorize.

Drug-related violence imposes an enormous burden not only on the criminal-justice system, but on health-care delivery systems as well.

These levels of violence should not be unexpected. James Bakalar and Lester Grinspoon have observed:

> It is certainly hypocritical to pretend to indignation and alarm about the murderousness of drug trafficking itself, since we have in effect deliberately tried to shape it in a way that makes it attractive to the most reckless and callous people and as nerve-racking as possible for everyone involved.

---

[54] "Beat" drugs are substances which purport to be drugs but which in fact are some relatively worthless substance, such as talcum powder for amphetamine, baking soda, milk sugar or flour for cocaine, or oregano for marijuana.

One of the primary purposes of criminalizing an activity is to forbid people from participating in that activity. Not only is the goal to subject them to the risk of state force, but also to place them outside the protection of the law, in a world which by definition is very dangerous. Drug traffickers cannot complain to the authorities if they are robbed, assaulted, defrauded or the victims of theft.

Violence is not only the clear result of prohibition, but also the consequence of prohibition; it is the natural and probable result of the use of criminal sanctions.

Criminal sanctions alone do not make violence a sine qua non. Increased sanctions together with serious enforcement attempts create the necessary conditions for violence to flourish -- both intramural violence and violence against others. When the risk of apprehension (or the expected punishment when apprehended) increases, the most risk-averse and relatively law-abiding amateurs leave the business, and the more aggressive and anti-social "'professionals'" remain in or enter the business. Similarly, individuals unwilling to engage in violence may enter the field of drug trafficking, but will not remain unless they acquire a capacity for intramural violence engaged in by the professionals, or at least acquire the ability to give the appearance of that capacity, or ally themselves with others who will provide them with protection. * * *

IV. CORRUPTION

When narcotics enforcement is tightened and the stakes are made higher through increased punishment, or the odds made less advantageous for traffickers through increased enforcement, the incentive to avoid detection and prosecution is increased. There are four sets of responses available to traffickers: leave the business, respond with increased violence, respond with increased innovation, or attempt to subvert the process itself by corrupting those who enforce the law and can aid traffickers in avoiding detection and punishment. Corruption is a concomitance of narcotics enforcement.

An inevitable cost of criminal law is that violators will attempt to evade those laws. However, murderers, car thieves, shoplifters, and drunken drivers are generally in no position to offer compensation which is worth the risk of capture to persons in a position to be corrupted. Drug traffickers, because of the large amounts of money available in the market, are more likely to be able to absorb the costs of corrupting law enforcement officials.

Corruption has all the characteristics of other "victimless'" crimes which make those offenses hard to detect and prosecute. None of the parties to the transaction has reason to complain (unless to later offer the information as part of a plea bargain), and the crime leaves little if any physical evidence which triggers an investigation or supports a prosecution. And where the corrupted person is a law-enforcement professional, one or more of the parties is an expert in avoiding detection and prosecution. Consequently, as in narcotics investigations, those detected and prosecuted will tend to be the least intelligent and resourceful, the neophyte, and the unlucky. Clever and unscrupulous public officials are more likely to remain undetected and prosper. * * *

V. CRIMINAL JUSTICE SYSTEM: CAPACITY

If prohibition continues, the headlines will probably not change: there will still be reports of large seizures, flashy arrests and trials, occasional reports of public officials arrested or indicted for drug related corruption, and reports of the deaths of people who get in the way of drug traffickers, such as neighborhood activists, police officers, other drug dealers, and people caught in the cross-fire.

The sale and purchase of illegal drugs will continue, and if we build more prisons, they will be filled as soon as they are completed. In some jurisdictions, there have been pleas for more police officers, which, even if acted upon, are not always followed by commensurate plans to expand the rest of the criminal system, such as the prosecutors, judges, public defenders, court-appointed counsel, or the support staff necessary to stop the system from grinding towards a halt. Although some jurisdiction have massively expanded their prison capacities, there is no sign that capacity is moving ahead of the supply of cases awaiting disposition and convicted defendants awaiting incarceration.

The natural response to the "drug problem"' -- especially for elected officials -- is to hire more police officers. This facile response can produce a result which is the opposite of that intended: "logjams"' at each stage of the disposition process subsequent to arrest. Such a response is eloquent testimony to the symbolic role police officers play in our society, and to the great demands we place on the police to resolve social conflict. The conflict of those demands and the realities of the criminal justice system can exact a toll on police officers.

VI. CRIMINAL JUSTICE SYSTEM; COURT OVERCROWDING

Narcotics enforcement is driven more and more by the public's demand for results, and by the need of elected officials to appear to be providing those results. Law enforcement agencies, like all bureaucracies, will respond with what bureaucrats in every society respond with: numbers. This invites police and investigative agencies to focus on the numbers of arrests, and the amounts of drugs and assets seized.* * * Our public officials emphasize the need to increase caseloads for our criminal justice system, but, unfortunately, less often discuss the importance of the rest of the system's role in handling that expanding caseload.

Concern with the arrest numbers on the part of police managers tends to encourage a lot of low-level street cases, and provides no incentive for even those cases to be properly investigated and prepared. This in turn leads to the litany of complaints which have been made for decades about the state of the criminal justice system: overcrowded court dockets, and overburdened prosecutors and public defenders. Whether or not this is truer now than in the past is for the most part irrelevant. The conditions in the criminal justice system in most, if not all of our major cities are deplorable, and those conditions relate in large part to the volume of cases.

VII. DISRESPECT FOR THE LAW

This Article does not suggest that our drug problem will be solved if capacity in the criminal justice system is increased so that all cases can be thoroughly and rapidly prosecuted, even with adequate prison space for all drug arrests. The problem with court congestion is that it diminishes respect for the legal system, and particularly diminishes respect for the system's deterrent capacity.

The large volume means that cases are handled as fungible. The need to dispose of cases may outweigh the goal of just dispositions of cases. Careful examination of each case in order to avoid convicting the innocent is sacrificed. These practices can only promote disrespect for the legal system, not only by the rare outside observer, but also by police officers, practitioners, judges, and defendants as well. This is ironic; for it is among criminal defendants that we most hope to instill respect for the legal system. As Charles Silberman has noted:

> In a large and complex society such as ours, respect for law -- the willingness to obey the law because it is the law -- is a more effective instrument of social control than is fear of punishment.

In the short run, shabby courtrooms and shoddy legal practices may be the only way to deal with a crisis caused by a surfeit of cases. In the long run, those conditions foster the circumstances which underlie and have lead to the crisis in the first place. "'Crisis'" has become a permanent state of affairs -- it has become normalcy.

Despite the hyperbolic rhetoric, there is little to indicate that the United States has the political will to increase all of the criminal justice resources devoted to enforcing narcotics laws. Even if we had the political will to radically expand the criminal system, we would probably be in the same place five years from now with respect to the availability of drugs. There will always be new dealers, either U.S. citizens and residents, or new immigrants from other countries. The bottom line is that as long as demand exists, someone will try to satisfy it. The criminal sanction can only achieve a "holding action'" against traffickers. It is also of limited utility in any efforts to end demand. * * *

X. CONSEQUENCES OF DEMAND STRATEGY

Recently there has been a renaissance of narcotics enforcement via prosecution of illegal drug consumers. Although there are some justifications for strenuously enforcing narcotics laws against buyers, the adverse consequences of such a policy outweigh the benefits.

Because possession of certain substances is illegal, it can be argued that enforcing the law is good in and of itself. The fact that the law may be ill-conceived or unenforceable does not relieve citizens from their obligation to obey it. For this reason, it may be the obligation of drug consumers to speak out against laws that they find unjust or unuseful and petition for changes in the law.

The prosecutions of buyers are relatively inexpensive and are, from the point of view of the prosecutor, easier to prove than a case against a seller. One problem with minor possession cases is that juries may be more inclined to show compassion through acquittal or hung jury for persons accused of being buyers than for those accused of being sellers. These cases do have the virtue of being generally safer for police officers: the suspects are less likely to be armed. Users have less to lose by being arrested than traffickers because the charges are less serious. Therefore, they have less incentive to resort to violence to avoid arrest.

Although emphasizing buyer arrests may deter some people from drug purchases, the general effect will be towards indoor purchases. Once the trade is driven inside, it's more dangerous for officers. Indoors, people and weapons may be more easily concealed; officers entering a building will also be separated from other officers who can come to their aid. Therefore, one of the unintended consequences of prohibition is that circumstances become more dangerous for all law-enforcement personnel in the long-run.

A buyer-focused strategy can be a useful enforcement tool if the aim is to drive a major retail trafficking organization out of business by reducing the customers and potential profits. In the short run, these tactics appear promising if accompanied by substantial media attention. The publicity surrounding these drives doesn't take away the demand, it merely warns buyers of a particular mode or place of purchasing drugs. The cycle of innovation and response will ensure that other modes or places of transacting business will take the place of the publicized enforcement efforts. * * *

Enforcement of a buyer-focused strategy fails in direct proportion to the size of the market. The use of such a general enforcement strategy is doomed in regard to drugs with widespread popularity. If the number of prosecuted traffickers threatens to overwhelm the criminal justice system, the crisis that would result from enhanced enforcement of buyers would be far greater. * * *

XII. THE BENEFITS OF PROHIBITION: CUI BONO?

There is no question that prohibition is not without its benefits. It is equally clear that only some of those benefits have anything to do with drugs, drug misuse, or public health. The benefits which do have a connection with drugs and public health are few, mixed and shallow. The other benefits are political, parochial and symbolic.

Prohibition presumably keeps some people away from drugs. And it's not unreasonable to assume that some of the population, had they used illegal drugs, might have suffered some harm from them. Some or all of that group may be misusing licit drugs now. On the other side of this equation, many of the people who have been harmed by illegal drugs might well have been saved from that injury through labeling, honest public health information campaigns, and regulation of dosage and purity. But the law is now, and will always be, ineffective in deterring anyone who really wants to use or misuse legal or illegal drugs: those who are unaffected by the social opprobrium associated with illegal drug use and feel no internal compunctions about violating the law. The people least likely to violate the law may also be the least problematic drug users. The most reckless drug users -- the polysubstance misuser, for instance, are going to be dysfunctional regardless of the licit or illicit status of her or his drugs of choice.

Ironically, the greatest beneficiaries of our commitment to the "war on drugs"' are our sworn enemies -- drug traffickers. Drug dealers are the last people in the world who want decriminalization and competition from legitimate sources. It is prohibition which creates an illicit market and the profit opportunities that flow from illicit markets. Drug traffickers sell not only a product, but the service of illegal delivery. In a non-criminalized commercial context, they will not have the skills to compete successfully. Traffickers are selling their skills as outlaws. In a legal market, those skills are virtually useless.

Most of the price of illegal drugs is overhead for the illegal delivery of drugs -- not cultivation and production. Under decriminalization, this overhead cost would no longer be an ingredient in the price structure.

The "drug war'" is clearly good for the "armies'" which fight it, including police, prosecutors, drug-treatment centers, prison administrations, antidrug agencies, and for politicians. There is little or no political constituency which wants to be seen as "for'" illegal drugs. This may be, in part, because decriminalization, unlike the "war on drugs'" cannot be easily explained in thirty seconds or less. All of the constituencies listed above profit -- even if overburdened. Their budgets cannot be cut, and the popularity of fighting drugs will help them in any bureaucratic struggle.

Political leaders also have an interest in the drug issue. A better issue could not have been invented. As Lewis Lapham noted:

> To politicians in search of sound opinions and sustained applause, the war on drugs presents itself as a gift from heaven .... The war against drugs provides them with something to say that offends nobody, requires them to do nothing difficult, and allows them to postpone, perhaps indefinitely, the more urgent and specific questions about the state of the nation's schools, housing, employment opportunities for young black men -- i.e., the conditions to which drug addiction speaks as a tragic symptom, not a cause.... The war on drugs becomes the perfect war for people who would rather not fight a war, a war in which the politicians who stand so fearlessly on the side of the good, the true, and the beautiful need to nothing else but strike noble poses as protectors of the people and defenders of the public trust.

Maintaining drug prohibition saves face and prevents us, as a nation, from admitting that we may have made a mistake. The mere discussion of decriminalization may be very painful for the families of police officers slain during narcotics enforcement, and for the survivors of others killed during America's drug wars. America's overdue reconciliation with those who performed military service in Vietnam may provide use with a guide: our admiration and respect for those who fought in their nation's service stands apart from our judgment of the wisdom of that war. If we are to decriminalize, there should be no need for a reconciliation, no failure to recognize the sacrifices made -- the lives lost -- in a fight against profiteering. Decriminalization can be the final, winning salvo in the battle against illegal drug trafficking.

XIII. WHAT DO WE REALLY WANT?

In the authors' view, the best aspirations we can have regarding drug policy are a maximization of personal liberty, a minimization of violence for law enforcement personnel and civilians, and better education as to the general and specific nature of drugs. The more we truly know about drugs, the more safely drugs can be used and wiser decisions can be made by individuals about which ones to use and when, the more they can be respected. When drugs are reified as objects of fear and loathing, we are led as individuals and as a society to make less rational, rather than more rational, choices about their use.

Our goal should also be to keep children and drugs apart from each other. While this is not the place to determine what an appropriate age of majority is, both small children and adolescents are, in our view, not equipped to make decisions regarding drug use, and often make bad choices. Prohibition and propaganda, however, don't help children make better choices.

Wanting people not to misuse drugs and to stop hurting themselves and their families with their drug use is a good thing. However, it has little to do with criminal law enforcement. Where people who use or misuse drugs also assault family members or others, they should be prosecuted criminally, and the defense or mitigating argument that the defendant has "a drug problem" should be dismissed for the cant it is.

XIV. DRUG, SET AND SETTING

One of the greatest risks of decriminalization is that people who have not previously used illegal drugs will carelessly experiment with them. One of the greatest dangers of drug use -- legal and illegal -- is not use per se, but unknowing, careless and uneducated use. Because initial use is so easily accompanied by a lack of accurate knowledge of the drug's pharmacology, it carries a special danger. The other critical factors which increase or reduce risk are strength and purity of the drug, use of more than one drug at once, pre-existing medical conditions in the user, and the context of the use. Decriminalization, although we assume it will expose more people to experimentation, still impacts favorably upon most of these variables.

Strength and purity can be regulated in a non-criminal context, such as requiring warning labels on all drugs, including information about hazardous drug combinations and the risks associated with the use by persons with specified medical conditions. Moreover, all of these factors, and especially the context of use, can be affected through honest and accurate public education programs.

Critical to analyzing these problems is understanding the way in which individual drugs, human beings, and society interact -- and what makes some combinations of those three factors dangerous. The late Dr. Norman Zinberg and Dr. Andrew Weil have provided the best explanations of these factors, referred to respectively as "drug," "set," and "setting." Set is a person's expectations of what a drug will do to him, considered in the context of his whole personality. Setting is the environment, both physical and social, in which a drug is taken.

Thus, the drug itself is only one variable in a complex equation. As Weil notes, "all drugs are dangerous."' Some drugs are more dangerous than others. It is our hope that we can encourage people, to the extent that they use drugs, to use them in the least dangerous manner possible, and, all other things being equal, to use the least dangerous drugs. In any case, criminal sanctions are not the most useful tools in encouraging this sort of behavioral and cultural change.

The fact that all drugs are dangerous does not mean that all drugs are equally dangerous, or that there are no differences in the form of drugs, or in the mode of ingestion. There are good public health reasons for encouraging the use of certain drugs as against others simply because some drugs and some forms of drugs are more dangerous than others. The ideal should be to encourage the wisest combinations of drugs, set and setting.

Realistic drug education, and not scare tactics, is an essential component of any drug decriminalization program.

XV. PROPOSALS

The most radical decriminalization option would be to immediately repeal all federal and state criminal laws regarding all illegal drugs without replacing prohibition with a regulatory scheme. This would create a chaotic situation which is neither desirable nor necessary. It would forfeit an ideal opportunity to regulate purity, impose excise taxes, and attempt to encourage and discourage various patterns of use.

The most prudent course of action is to start with the least dangerous and most popular drugs, and encourage a licit market in those drugs that will in the short term, displace some portion of the illicit market. Starting with the least dangerous drugs, in their least dangerous forms, will cut into the eventual licit market in other, more dangerous drugs. Probably, the first drug decriminalized would be marijuana. At the same time, enforcement of weapons possession, assault and other trafficking-related violence would be enhanced. The apprehension and prosecution of intoxicated drivers, and of those selling to minors would continue. Given the current political context, it may be all that can be managed in the short term to decriminalize marijuana. The degree of progress that would provide depends in large measure on what the substitution curve of marijuana and other drugs looks like. Marijuana prices have risen over the last decade, as cocaine prices have dropped. A lower legal price for marijuana would draw an unknown number of consumers away from still-forbidden drugs. It is unknown how many current illegal drug consumers are concerned about the illegality of their drug use, and whether that concern would lead them to make a choice of, for example, legal marijuana as against illicit cocaine.

If we are going to do anything less than full decriminalization, newly freed resources must be thoughtfully reallocated. There should be a focus on the drugs which are the most dangerous: PCP, crack cocaine, amphetamines. Direct enforcement and prosecution resources should not be directed towards "soft targets"' which make for easy publicity, but on the most violent traffickers -- those who corrupt or attempt to corrupt public officials. Where there is a choice between enforcing against street traffic in a commercial or a residential area, resources should be allocated towards residential areas and schools. A path of least resistance for retail dealers should be made to move into areas where they will have the least impact on people's lives.

If we were to decriminalize drugs, we must immediately regulate labelling, including health warnings and notices of content and strength. Regardless of whether we decriminalize for "recreational"' use, at a minimum marijuana, methaqualone, heroin and LSD should be rescheduled for medical use.

A criminal requirement should be imposed that narcotics traffickers label the substances they sell for active ingredients, adulterants, and relative strength. Those people violating labelling laws must be prosecuted harshly, to give a real incentive to all retail traffickers to avoid endangering drug consumers.

An excise tax structure should be imposed, both on the state and federal level, on substances as they are decriminalized. The taxation structure should be such that the least harmful drug, in the least harmful and weakest form, should bear the lowest tax; the more harmful the drug, the stronger the form, the higher the tax.

Distributors of whatever is decriminalized should be licensed, either by the federal government, state governments, or both. This is a question best left to those who already possess expertise in regulating the distribution of drugs, and who will have to do the regulation, such as the Food and Drug

Administration, the Treasury Department, and the parallel state agencies. Because the price of illegal drugs represents payment for illegal services, prices would be lower in a decriminalized system. It is, however, unclear which is the most desirable form for such a market to take: an entirely government controlled market; or a relatively free market, like the one for alcohol, that sets its own prices but is subject to government regulation and taxation; or some combination of these two markets.

Also unanswered are questions of who should produce or be allowed to produce these drugs. Like alcohol, there is the option of micro-managing price through the use of excise taxes. These questions, including the pricing of decriminalized drugs, are questions to be answered after debate and experimentation, and are beyond the scope of this Article.

XVI. CONCLUSION

If we are committed to thinking about drug prohibition via the metaphor of the "war on drugs," we should bear in mind that it is a civil war. It is one group of citizens, probably a numerical minority, defying the dominant group's command not to purchase or use certain substances. Drug traffickers exploit that defiance to make a profit.

Decriminalization is no panacea -- but further prohibition will only lead us to another generation of violence, corruption and a diversion of resources from other problems. Every law-enforcement dollar spent on narcotics enforcement is a dollar not spent on investigating or prosecuting sexual assault, domestic violence, or child abuse. Similarly, every dollar spent on law-enforcement, including imprisonment, is a dollar not spent on national defense, social programs, education, or, a dollar not remaining in the pocket of a taxpayer.

The hallmark of the underground narcotics economy, the intense and seemingly random violence, the constant need for participants to prove their "toughness"' are not a pharmacological consequence of using illegal drugs no matter how much or how many public officials wish to accept such a theory. They are consequences of the contraband economy itself. If it is not crack, it will be whatever other illegal substance becomes popular. Prohibition, combined with pervasive poverty, fuels the fire of inner-city violence and social destruction.

But the role of the criminal justice system is of limited utility in controlling the use and distribution of a socially destructive commodity that is in high demand. Increased enforcement merely raises the stakes for the participants: they either get tougher or they get out. Those who remain and the new entrants increasingly appear to belong to two groups: those without other meaningful options; and the avaricious with a capacity or appetite for ruthlessness and violence. Most of those who had a meaningful place to go, or with no stomach for the high stakes of drug trafficking are already gone.

It doesn't seem to be too strong a statement to say that our preoccupation with "winning the war on drugs'" has led us to a point where selling crack in a liquor store or tobacconist could hardly make our city neighborhoods any worse. This may horrify some. Given the choice between a violent, Hobbesian world ruled by drug dealers, and the likely alternative of a world with many drug users but no lucrative role for violent outlaws, the latter seems a better choice. At least then the life and death stakes of living in our urban areas would be lowered and, given the proper political will, we could begin to address our social problems.

It would be a disservice to the memories of those who have sacrificed their lives enforcing our laws to embrace tyranny in the pursuit of an unobtainable "'drug-free'" society. Benjamin Franklin wisely noted that the sacrifice of liberty in pursuit of an illusory safety entitles us to neither liberty nor safety. The best way to honor the memories of those who have already died is to create a world in which it will not be necessary for more people to die enforcing an unenforceable policy.

THE AGONY OF ECSTASY: RECONSIDERING THE PUNITIVE APPROACH TO UNITED STATES DRUG POLICY
Amanda Kay
29 Fordham Urb. L.J. 2133 (2002)

Introduction

People think they can stop the drug traffic by putting people in jail and by having terribly long sentences. But, of course, it doesn't do any good.

-- Judge Whitman Knapp

In the past few years, legislators and judges have become more vocal in their opposition to the "war on drugs"[1] in the United States. However,

---

[1] * * * The "war on drugs" describes the United States' drug policy of the past three decades. Frontline Teachers' Guide - Drug Wars at
http://www.pbs.org/wgbh/pages/frontline/teach/american/drugs (last visited Apr. 25,

challenging punitive drug laws is politically difficult; the challenger risks being perceived by the public as someone "weak on crime" who "condones drug use." Tom Campbell, a congressman from California, commented on this phenomenon: "The most common reaction I get from my colleagues is 'You're absolutely right, but, boy, I'm not going to take that risk.'" While the public is decreasingly supportive of punitive laws, many still cling to the belief that such laws will reduce drug use because of fear -- fear that drug use among children will increase and that less stringent drug laws will lead to moral decline and empower minority groups.[7]

United States drug laws implicate complex matters such as race, gender, class, the national budget, prison overcrowding, civil liberties, and the spread of diseases such as HIV/AIDS and hepatitis. In fact, efforts to reduce drug use may cause more harm than the drugs themselves. For example, increased funding for enforcement of criminal drug laws couple[d] with escalating criminal sentences has led to a rise in drug related convictions and a significant need for prison beds; the war on drugs has created and supported a prison-industrial complex that costs taxpayers over $24 billion per year. Enforcement is often directed at racial minorities and lower class communities; civil liberties are sacrificed in cases of racial profiling, illegal searches, and excessive wiretapping. The direct financial cost of the war on drugs is in the billions, with most of the national budget allocated for enforcement. The additional indirect costs are unknown. Yet needle exchange programs aimed at reducing harm by slowing the spread of HIV/AIDS go without funding and often without legal authority to operate. These are merely a few examples of the collateral consequences of the drug war.

An objective cost/benefit analysis of the current drug policy is difficult to ascertain. In 1999, Americans spent an estimated $63.2 billion on illicit drugs. Most of that spending was by hard-core addicts, a group that makes up less than one-quarter of the drug users in this country, but consumes over

---

2002). It began with Former President Nixon's declaration that illegal drug consumption is public enemy number one, and that an all out war on drugs was necessary. *Id.* After his declaration, the federal government applied a new zeal to the four components of this war: (1) treatment; (2) law enforcement; (3) eradication; and (4) interdiction. President Nixon also established the Drug Enforcement Agency. *Id.*

[7] * * * David Musto, THE AMERICAN DISEASE 294-95 (Oxford University Press, 1999) (1973) (stating that the strongest support for drug prohibition has been associated with fear of a given drug's effect on a minority group as demonstrated by the prohibition of cocaine for fear that it would enable blacks to withstand bullets, the prohibition of opium for fear that it would stimulate sexual contact between Chinese and white Americans, and the prohibition of alcohol for fear that it would encourage immigrants to crowd into large cities) * * * .

two-thirds of the illegal drugs. Given that drugs are less expensive and more widely available than ever before, and that punitive drug laws have increasingly negative social consequences, finding advantages of the current approach is a challenge. One commentator believes the important question about any drug control program is whether it "contribute[s] materially to the reduction of drug use and drug-related harms." Whether there is a "material" difference depends on whether "the effect is sizeable and, in particular, whether it is sizeable compared to the costs."

Examining the effects of United States drug policy under this rubric may prove frustrating. For example, more drug convictions could mean a reduction in the number of drug dealers and addicts, but could also mean that more people are using and selling drugs. Fewer drug-related emergency room visits could mean that fewer people are getting sick from using drugs. It could also indicate that fewer people are seeking treatment for drug-related illnesses. Less marijuana use among teenagers than in the past could mean that they are using fewer drugs in general, or it could simply mean they are using more of other drugs. Even if the number of drug users were known, that knowledge might not prove an effective measure of the success of drug policy. The effects of the drug war remain open to interpretation, providing fuel for the politics of the debate. Yet, as the drug war enters its thirtieth year, public sentiment is migrating toward frustration and disapproval of the present system; many people claim that the war on drugs has simply failed.

Solutions are proffered by proponents of two traditionally opposed ideologies. On one side of the debate are prohibitionists, those advocating a punitive approach through the criminal justice system, believing that tougher laws will deter new drug dealers and users while removing current ones from society. Their opponents are those advocating harm reduction, who believe that education, prevention, and treatment reduce the harm caused by drug use -- harm, that is, to some extent, inevitable. * * *

B. Harm Reduction

Harm reduction rests on two premises: first, that psychoactive drug use has been a part of every culture since the beginning of civilization, rendering eradication unrealistic and probably impossible, and second, that drug use is primarily a social and public health issue as opposed to a penal issue. In practice, harm reduction encompasses programs that attempt to make drug use as safe as possible for both the users and the community. Examples of specific programs include syringe exchanges for intravenous drug users; treatment programs; "safer-use" educational campaigns that offer objective, factual information to drug users; and treatment as an alternative to incarceration for convicted drug offenders. Harm reduction advocates recognize that drug use can never be completely safe, and some acknowledge the need for law enforcement in certain circumstances.

Harm reduction is often confused with legalization. Legalization involves removing criminal penalties for possession of some or all illicit drugs and usually involves implementing a system of regulated distribution similar to that which is in place for alcohol and cigarettes, with state-run sales, quality and price control, and a ban on advertising. Legalization advocates often point to crime caused by prohibitive drug laws themselves as support for legalization. Although many harm reduction advocates support legalization to some extent, legalization is a broader approach to drug policy that is not necessarily informed by the social and medical concerns underlying harm reduction. In fact, most legalization arguments are economic.

Decriminalization may be a component of harm reduction, but it is a distinct approach advocating that selected laws not be enforced and that penalties for possession be substantially reduced. In practice, decriminalization directs law enforcement efforts away from minor possession of less harmful drugs and toward larger distribution networks involving more dangerous drugs. By altering the manner in which criminal drug laws are enforced, decriminalization aims to reduce harms to drug users arising from the criminal justice system itself, while more efficiently utilizing government resources. Examining the development of harm reduction in the Netherlands and its subsequent migration to the United Kingdom and North America enables a complete understanding of this approach and its various applications.

1. The Netherlands

The Dutch established a drug policy guided by harm reduction ideology with the development of three innovative concepts. The first concept is that different drugs carry different risks, some acceptable and some not. This concept was developed as a response to the increase in drug use in the 1960s. This increase led to broad public concern about the operation of the criminal justice system. Specific concerns about the effect of drug laws on personal choice, the consequences of criminalization, and the risks to the user, led the Dutch government to create an official commission (the "Commission") to study the increased use of narcotics and issue a report proposing possible solutions. The Commission's thorough report proposed that the bases for all future drug policy be "risk-criteria," principles for legislation and policy-making that would take into account the relative risks of illegal drugs. In 1972, the emergence and rapid spread of heroin put pressure on the government to seriously discuss the Commission's report and consider legal reforms. Applying risk criteria, legislators decided that the law should distinguish between "drugs presenting unacceptable risks," such as heroin, cocaine, LSD, and amphetamines, and drugs presenting acceptable risks, such as hashish and marijuana. This concept, that "hard" and "soft" drugs should be separated both legally and in the public's perception, is one of the most significant and effective elements of Dutch harm reduction. In 1976, the Dutch codified this policy by creating two classes of drugs, schedule I and schedule II, which reflect the respective risks of the drugs.

Prevention, treatment, and risk minimization comprise the second aspect of Dutch harm reduction. By preventing nonusers from trying "hard" drugs and helping current users abstain, the Dutch believed they could reduce risks both to drug users and society. Professionals in the field soon realized that abstinence-only methods were inadequate; relying solely on treatment and prevention left the majority of drug users, who were not seeking abstinence, without a range of necessary services. These professionals began providing medical and social assistance to injection drug users who were not seeking abstinence, allowing them to monitor and influence the health, social, and legal status of the users while reducing damage to society.

The third and most widely known element of Dutch drug policy is decriminalization. Decriminalization is based on the "normalization" or "cultural integration" that the state reaches when the public believes the eradication of drugs is unattainable. The Dutch enacted a policy of pragmatic nonenforcement for violations involving the sale or possession of up to approximately one-fifth of an ounce of marijuana. Marijuana's decriminalization keeps transactions public to prevent a health issue from becoming a crime problem. * * *

Prevention education has long been considered an integral part of a comprehensive drug policy, but how to use it most effectively is a subject of great debate. The national prevention program, Drug Abuse Resistance Education ("DARE"), advocates abstinence and is taught in eighty percent of the nation's school districts. However, extensive research during the past two decades has identified a number of other prevention strategies that measurably reduce drug use. These strategies share a common goal: strengthening "protective factors" (i.e., well-developed social skills, strong family bonds, attachment to school, and active involvement in the community and religious organizations), while reducing "risk factors" that increase vulnerability to drug abuse (i.e., substance abuse by a parent, lack of parental guidance, disruptive, abusive family relationships, school failure, early experimentation with drugs, and living in a community where substance abuse and dealing are pervasive). Harm reduction education efforts usually encompass "safer-use" campaigns meant to inform current users of accurate risks. * * *

POLICING POSSESSION: THE WAR ON CRIME AND THE END OF CRIMINAL LAW

Markus Dirk Dubber

91 J. Crim. L. & Criminology 829 (2001)[a]

* * *

Possession has replaced vagrancy as the most convenient gateway into the criminal justice system. Possession shares the central advantages of vagrancy as a policing tool: flexibility and convenience. Yet, as we shall see, it is in the end a far more formidable weapon in the war on crime: it expands the scope of policing into the home, it results in far harsher penalties and therefore has a far greater incapacitative potential, and it is far less vulnerable to legal challenges.

Millions of people commit one of its variants every day, from possessing firearms and all sorts of other weapons, dangerous weapons, instruments, appliances, or substances, including toy guns, air pistols and rifles, tear gas, ammunition, body vests, and anti-security items, to burglary tools or stolen property, and of course drugs, and everything associated with them, including drug paraphernalia, drug precursors, not to mention instruments of crime, graffiti instruments, computer related material, counterfeit trademarks, unauthorized recordings of a performance, public benefit cards, forged instruments, forgery devices, embossing machines (to forge credit cards), slugs, vehicle identification numbers, vehicle titles without complete assignment, gambling devices, gambling records, usurious loan records, prison contraband, obscene material, obscene sexual performances by a child, "premises which [one] knows are being used for prostitution purposes," eavesdropping devices, fireworks, noxious materials, and taximeter accelerating devices (in New York), spearfishing equipment (in Florida), or undersized catfish (in Louisiana), and the list could go on and on.

And that's the first prerequisite for a sweeping offense. Lots of people must be guilty of it. Thanks to the erosion of constitutional constraints on police behavior in the state declared emergency of the war on crime, possession is easy to detect. Every physical or merely visual search, every frisk, every patdown, is also always a search for possession. Like vagrancy (and pornography), then,

---

[a] Reprinted by special permission of Northwestern University School of Law, *Journal of Criminal Law and Criminology.*

police officers know possession when they see it. Unlike vagrancy, they also know it when they feel it.

Police officers have become experts at detecting "bulges" in various articles of clothing, each of which signal an item that may be illegally possessed. Similarly, police officers and the judges who occasionally review their actions have long been particularly imaginative in their interpretation of the particular nature of these bulges, when the time has come to confirm one's visual suspicion with a physical frisk. Here the search for one illegally possessed item -- say a concealed weapon -- may actually bear fruit in the form of the discovery of another illegally possessed item -- say a bag of cocaine. Possession offenses in this way manage to bootstrap themselves, each giving the other a helping hand. * * *

In 1998, possession offenses accounted for 106,565, or 17.9%, of all arrests made in New York State. Of these cases, 295 (or 0.27%) resulted in a verdict (by a judge or a jury), a whopping 129 (0.12%) in an acquittal. Of those originally arrested for possession, 33,219 (31.2%) went to prison or jail. New York boasts no fewer than 115 felony possession offenses, all of which require a minimum of one year in prison; eleven of them provide for a maximum sentence of life imprisonment.

Possession has become the paradigmatic offense in the current campaign to stamp out crime by incapacitating as many criminals as we can get our hands on. Every minute of every day, police pull over cars and sweep neighborhoods looking for, or just happening upon, "possessors" of one thing or another. Prosecutors throw in a possession count for good measure or, if nothing else sticks, make do with possession itself. Why, as one Michigan prosecutor remarked before the U.S. Supreme Court, why bother charging more involved offenses if you can get life imprisonment without parole for a possession conviction?

In many cases, possession statutes also save prosecutors the trouble of proving that other major ingredient of criminal liability in American criminal law, mens rea, or a guilty mind. This means that many possession statutes, particularly in the drug area--where some of the harshest campaigns in the war on crime have been prosecuted--are so-called strict liability crimes. In other words, you can be convicted of them if you don't know that you are "possessing" a drug of any kind, what drug you are "possessing," how much of it you've got, or--in some states--even that you are possessing anything at all, drug or no drug.

* * * Possession * * * also does away with the traditional requirement that criminal liability must be predicated on an actus reus, an affirmative act or

at least a failure to act (rather than a status, like being in possession of something). So even if some sort of intent (or at least negligence) is required for conviction, there is no need to worry about the actus reus.

Plus, it turns out that other defenses also don't apply to possession offenses. We've already seen that * * * culpability and responsibility defenses have no place in a possession case. But what about other defenses, such as self-defense or necessity?

Say you're riding in the back seat of your friend's car as a couple of men try to jack the car, guns drawn. You notice a gun under the driver seat, bend down and grab it, and then shoot one of the men in the leg. You're cleared of the assault on grounds of self-defense. Still, since you weren't licensed to carry the gun, you're liable for possessing it illegally. This is so because the defense of self-defense applies only to the use, but not to the possession of the gun. * * *

By now, you may not be surprised to learn that you didn't even have to pick up the gun to be guilty of possessing it illegally. Again in New York -- but in many other jurisdictions as well -- you may well have "constructively" possessed the weapon simply by having been in the car at the same time. So to possess something in the eye of the criminal law doesn't mean you owned it, nor does it mean you physically possessed it. It's generally enough that you could have brought it within your physical possession or at least kept others from bringing it within theirs. (Technically, you constructively possessed the gun if you "exercise[d] dominion or control over" it.)

And, as though proving possession isn't easy enough, the law of possession also teems with evidentiary presumptions. Not only can you constructively possess something you don't have in your hands or on your person, you can also be presumed to constructively possess it. In our example, this means that it will be up to you to prove to the jury -- should you be among the minuscule percentage of possession defendants who make it to a jury trial -- that you did not in fact possess the gun, constructively, which is a tough row to hoe, given what we just learned about how little it takes to establish possession.

The most popular choice among legislatures anxious to further reduce prosecutorial inconvenience associated with the enforcement of possession offenses is to establish the rule that mere presence constitutes presumptive possession. The more eager the state is to get certain possessors off the street, and the more dangerous these possessors have revealed themselves to be through their possession, the more dangerous the item possessed, the greater the temptation will be to do away with evidentiary requirements, and thereby to accelerate the incapacitation process. Small wonder that these presumptions from presence to possession pop up in gun and drug possession cases.

In the New York Penal Law, for example, merely being around drugs not only amounts to presumptively possessing them. It further simplifies the prosecutor's incapacitative task by also establishing a presumption of "knowing" possession. So, from evidence of being in the same car or room with a controlled substance, the prosecutor gets, without additional evidence, to jump to the conclusion that you possessed the drugs, and knew that you did. And, as we just saw, this conclusion will stand, unless you convince the fact finder otherwise. And that fact finder is, in virtually every possession case, none other than the prosecutor himself, who offers you a reduced sentence in exchange for a guilty plea.

The use of mere presence as a foundation of criminal liability has an additional benefit. Presence not only simplifies the prosecutorial task of connecting a given object with a particular possessor. Presence can with one fell swoop ensnare not just one, but several, persons in the web of possession liability emanating from a piece of contraband at its center. * * *

PRINCIPLED ENFORCEMENT OF PENAL CODES
Erik Luna
4 Buff. Crim. L.Rev. 515 (2000)

* * *

A. THE RULE OF LAW AS FULL ENFORCEMENT

One historic definition of the rule of law argues that discretionary power has no place in legitimate government. This interpretation, referred to by Kenneth Culp Davis as "the extravagant version of the rule of law," would seek the elimination of all executive discretion in the enforcement of the penal code. If the legislature enacts a criminal law, the executive branch has no discretion but to fully enforce the provisions in each and every possible circumstance. The police must investigate all known crimes and arrest all known criminals; prosecutors, in turn, must charge and try such criminals to the limits of the penal code. Under this interpretation, the rule of law is synonymous with full enforcement of criminal statutes.

But the full enforcement conception of the rule of law is untenable in the real world, with scholars describing the ideal as a "myth," "chimera," and "false pretense." Little more than a third of all crime is reported to law enforcement; of those offenses known to police, less than a quarter are eventually cleared by an arrest. Vaguely worded statutes coupled with the intrinsic limits of language also preclude full enforcement, requiring government agents to guess as to whether some conduct is criminal or not. Understandably, conscientious police officers and prosecutors often err on the side of not arresting or not charging.

Inflexible application of the penal code, in fact, would likely prove unbearable in a free society. Every day millions of otherwise law-abiding Americans engage in criminal activity such as petty gambling, drug possession, and consensual (but illegal) sexual activity. Even if the public wanted full enforcement, the executive branch has insufficient resources to comply; there are simply not enough police officers, prosecutors, courts, and prisons to accommodate full enforcement in a system that is already bursting at the seams. The full enforcement conception also assumes that the purpose of the executive is merely ministerial, that its function is to mechanically enforce the penal code without introducing policy considerations. This robo-branch interpretation is dubious, even on a theoretical level, as the executive is a coordinate branch with policymaking powers independent of the legislature and the judiciary.

At best, the full enforcement conception of the rule of law serves as an aspirational norm, like the Ten Commandments, to be aspired to regardless of real-world practice. Yet even this moderate claim is difficult to sustain; behavioral control, whether by aspiration or force, is only one potential function of law. In addition, it can distribute power among individuals and entities or can serve a procedural function, announcing the steps that must be taken for a particular event to occur. Law can also serve a symbolic or educational function separate from direct behavioral modification. By disaggregating its objectives, law becomes a much more complex creature than depicted in the full enforcement conception of the rule of law.

Penal proscriptions obviously seek to influence conduct in a utilitarian sense or punish bad behavior consistent with retributive thought. An original purpose of criminal law enforced by government was to curb a particular type of behavior -- private revenge and the blood feud. But less provocative forms of behavioral control have become necessary components of the modern regulatory state. Take, for example, the traffic code. It prevents utter chaos on the roads; one can imagine how (much more) dangerous driving would be if there were no rules, no signs or signals, no enforcement of any kind. Traffic laws are a pure attempt at manipulating conduct for the good of the individual driver and society at large.

For better or worse, law also serves a symbolic function. This, of course, is not a new idea, but the implications are still important. Law expresses the values and expectations of society; it makes a statement about what is good or bad, right or wrong. By damning particular behavior or extolling a course of conduct, legal commands in secular government have thereby replaced the overt moralizing of the theocratic state. These symbolic pronouncements often eschew behavioral modification or retribution and instead seek some type of social catharsis, publicly announcing a community's outrage and disgust by condemning certain anti-social acts. Even without transgressions or enforcement, the penal code thereby offers a symbolic gesture that arouses reflection rather than action.

Law, particularly criminal law, also serves an educational function -- to express boundaries between the acceptable (but possibly distasteful) and the forbidden -- illuminating the border and suggesting that the public steer clear. Under this theory, criminal law acts as a tutor to both the deviant and the general public, and what it teaches is the dominant social morality. Yet the penal code does more than delineate good from bad behavior; it also discriminates between individuals worthy of praise and those deserving reproach. In this way, criminal statutes can create, alter, or buttress status hierarchies within a society, distinguishing the ins from the outs, the haves from the have-nots, and serving as an expression of power and prestige.

Once the primary functions are disaggregated, law emerges as a diverse and dangerous tool of government. There is no single goal of law; instead, there are numerous potential ends served by legal pronouncements, particularly in the criminal justice system. The full enforcement conception of the rule of law is not the inescapable theory of the executive branch, for instance, as it is neither practical in the real world nor preordained by a single function of law. Rather, criminal bans sometimes further an expressive function without coercive enforcement by the executive. The legislature enacts a criminal law for its symbolic message and the judiciary acquiesces to the statutory provisions -- but the executive branch selectively enforces the law due to resource limitations, other incompatible interests, paternalism or bigotry. * * *

When the legislature declares certain behavior criminal and the courts validate both the crime and related enforcement procedures, police and prosecutors exercise virtually limitless discretion to administer the relevant code section. Within the confines of this discretionary authority, law enforcement has the leeway to investigate, arrest, and prosecute as it sees fit.

With that said, two basic points about executive discretion in criminal justice should be acknowledged. First, such discretion is inevitable. For better or worse, various legal and political limitations impede the narrowing of executive discretion by the legislative and judicial branches. The boundaries of language and foresight, for example, prevent the legislature from formulating appropriate behavior in every law enforcement scenario, while the process of judicial interpretation and case-based analogy suffer from similar restrictions.

Second, executive discretion is not an inherent evil within the criminal justice system. Instead, discretion is a tool much like a hammer; it may be used for positive goals (mending your neighbor's fence) or malevolent ends (striking your neighbor in anger). The key question, therefore, is not whether executive discretion should or should not exist. The issues are how much discretion, under what standards, and in what circumstances -- more or less, whether discretionary enforcement comports with the procedural justice conception of the rule of law.

Let me reiterate, as to be clear on what is being said and, more importantly, what is not being said. Some laws, like traffic regulations, are both necessary in modern society and facially innocuous. This does not mean that such laws will be used only for benevolent ends; the deplorable phenomenon of "driving while black" clearly demonstrates as much. Moreover, the fact that law can serve a symbolic function apart from behavioral modification and has the power to delineate between socially acceptable conduct and repulsive nonconformity does not mean that it should be used in such a manner.

Instead, I am suggesting that: (1) discretion is inevitable; (2) expressive lawmaking also seems inevitable in modern day America; (3) discretion can be abused; and (4) society needs to accept the first and second propositions while doing everything in its power to preclude the third. An appropriate normative goal, I believe, is limiting executive discretion that produces procedural injustice, rather than eliminating discretion altogether.* * *

* * * [T]he exercise of executive discretion often follows predictable patterns, with drug offenses, prostitution, and other vice crimes being particularly illustrative. William Stuntz has recently argued that throughout American history police have focused vice enforcement efforts on the lower socio-economic classes of society. This approach seems logical enough: Vice offenses harm poor communities more than their affluent counterparts, with lower-class vice frequently resulting in violence unknown to successful neighborhoods. Vice is also intimately connected to ghetto-producing pathologies and weak social organization.

Most importantly, lower-class markets are fundamentally different from those in high-income, low-unemployment communities. While the financially secure consumer can purchase his vice in private transactions with little chance of police involvement, poor customers and suppliers tend to deal on the streets. Because street transactions are both highly visible and relatively inexpensive to monitor, lower-class citizens face a much greater possibility of being nabbed by vice enforcers. And given that police and prosecutors have limited resources to catch a nearly unlimited supply of offenders, enforcement efforts generally focus on vice-ridden inner cities.

This might not be so troublesome except for one fact -- poor urban citizens are almost exclusively African-American or Hispanic. To be clear, the likely goal of modern vice policy is not racist -- intentional discrimination based on skin color -- but instead pragmatic, putting anti-vice resources to their most efficient and effective use. "But in a society where racial division is all too real," Stuntz notes, "decisions that have no racial cause may still have a very powerful racial meaning."

Ninety percent of all prostitution arrests and eighty-five percent of those incarcerated are minority women. Drug enforcement statistics are equally disturbing. Blacks suffer more than one-third of all drug arrests, receive fifty-three percent of state drug convictions, incur seventy-four percent of all prison sentences for drug possession, and constitute nearly half of all inmates in the United States -- despite the fact that they represent thirteen percent of the American population.

So vice enforcement statistics carry the appearance of racism and, in the war on vice, appearances do matter. About two-thirds of African-Americans believe that the police are racially biased, and one-third rate the honesty and ethical standards of law enforcement as low or very low. In fact, one in four black citizens has no confidence in the police and is dissatisfied with police service, while more than forty percent of blacks are afraid that police will stop and arrest them despite their innocence. The major source of this discontent is the disproportionate effect of vice prohibition on minority citizens, with disparate enforcement undermining not only the credibility of vice statutes but also the authority of all law.

Paul Robinson and John Darley contend that a particular statute can draw upon law's general pool of moral authority. Under this theory, a law that prohibits seemingly harmless (and maybe enjoyable) activity may nonetheless be self-enforcing. If the criminal law "has developed a reputation as a reliable statement of existing norms, people will be willing to defer to its moral authority in cases where there exists some ambiguity as to the wrongfulness of the contemplated conduct." In this way, law co-opts private norms as a means of altering behavior. It drafts behind the powerful influence of social customs and conventions, shaping conduct without the costs of active law enforcement. But the converse is also true: "When a criminal law offends the moral intuitions of the governed community, the power of the entire criminal code to gain compliance is risked." In this way, social disrespect for an important set of criminal statutes has the potential to generalize to all legal commands.

The same phenomenon occurs, I believe, when the administration of the penal code appears to deviate from the procedural justice conception of the rule of law. Whether intended or not, the racial disproportionality in vice enforcement has the possibility, if not the reality, of undercutting the moral credibility of legal pronouncements. Although there may be altruistic motives behind the concentration of vice enforcement in urban neighborhoods, the current exercise of executive discretion carries the perception of invidious racial discrimination. The process of selectively enforcing vice law appears unprincipled, based on the color of one's skin and the subjective beliefs of the beat cop, not pursuant to understandable and fair procedures that allow affected individuals to order their affairs. And when police and prosecutors are perceived as racist in the administration of vice crime, it is only natural that this image carries over to all executive decisions in the criminal justice system.

* * * Vice law and its enforcement in poor, urban, largely minority communities offer a disturbing illustration of this dilemma. Whether stemming from religiously motivated moralism, self-righteous paternalism, or self-serving protectionism, the electorate has demanded stiffer vice enforcement and the executive branch has obliged. And because law enforcement is generally not called upon to provide a legitimate, substantiated rationale for its administration of vice law, many minority communities have filled in the theoretical vacuum with the logic of cause-and-effect: Racially disproportionate enforcement statistics reflect the intentional use of executive discretion against minorities.

But the racial tensions between law enforcement and residents of poor minority neighborhoods are not inevitable. What is missing, I believe, is a level of procedural justice in the administration of vice law. "While law enforcement discretion must be preserved," one civil rights organization argues, "the type of unchecked, unreviewable discretion that police and prosecutors currently wield breeds racial disparity and resentment." If community members were persuaded that there was rhyme or reason to the exercise of executive discretion, that it was founded on a legitimate theory, they might come to accept the resulting pattern of enforcement -- or at least they would have the opportunity to challenge the underlying rationale. All told, discretionary vice enforcement needs to be infused with concepts of procedural justice; distrusting residents should be informed of how and why police discretion will be exercised, as well as being allowed to participate in most decisionmaking, to help achieve optimal principles for law enforcement while legitimating the process for affected individuals.

The question is how to control and limit discretion so it squares with the procedural justice conception of the rule of law and (re)establishes the moral authority of legal commands in distrusting communities. One possible solution is what I call "transparent policing" and, in particular, a sub-constitutional, sub-statutory administrative-type rulemaking process in an open, dialogic forum. By incorporating procedural justice into law enforcement discretion, the process of executive decisionmaking pursuant to announced, legitimate principles has the potential to strengthen or even regain institutional credibility. The balance of this article will provide an overview of what I have in mind.

A. THE STRATEGY OF TRANSPARENT POLICING

Consistent with notions of procedural justice, sustaining, augmenting, or regaining the moral authority of law enforcement requires a certain level of transparency in policing. Transparency simply means the ability of the citizenry to observe and scrutinize the substantive and procedural policy choices of government, as well as their underlying rationales, and to have a direct say in the formation and reformulation of these decisions.

Transparent policing contains three procedural justice-enhancing values: (1) visibility, (2) voice, and (3) justification. The first value requires that most policy decisions be perceived or perceptible to those affected by their implementation, while the second value ensures that these same individuals are allowed to participate in the decisionmaking process. Comprehensive policies-- those typically made by police chiefs, district attorneys, and their immediate lieutenants--generally should be formulated in public arenas, not closed door sessions, so that both lay citizens and experts are allowed to contribute to the debate. Likewise, authoritative resolutions should be readily available to individual citizens, the media, and the academy.

The third value requires that policy decisions further -- or at least not be inconsistent with -- an announced theory of the citizen and the state. In other words, transparent policing requires not only visibility of policy choices but an articulated justification for these decisions. It can therefore be viewed as an invitation to expressly incorporate political, economic, sociological, or psychological theory into the decisionmaking process. Transparent policing is like an empty glass; it demands that policy be made and reviewed in a publicly accessible forum, and that those policies be informed by an overarching theory of the relationship between individuals and law enforcement. Although it necessitates that a policy be justified in a philosophical sense, it does not require allegiance to any particular political theory, such as modern individualism or communitarianism. Instead, it establishes a visible process -- a transparent glass, if you will -- to fill with policies and their justifications. * * *

So let me now be specific: How might transparent policing work? Transparent policing techniques would include open community review boards and mandatory videotaping of police-citizen confrontations on the streets or confessions derived by custodial interrogation. A more sweeping example -- and the one that will occupy the balance of this article -- involves the open adoption of sub-statutory, sub-constitutional principles to limit and guide executive discretion. * * *

A floor of procedural justice, both theoretical and practical, would seem to have at least three elements consistent with the values of transparency. First, the public must be provided sufficient notice of impending rulemaking. Second, affected and interested citizens must have an opportunity to participate in the rulemaking process. And third, the relevant agency must announce both the final principle and its justification. These criteria are imprecise by necessity; effective notice, for example, is highly dependent on the means of law enforcement and community members. A publicly accessible web-site could provide adequate notice for an affluent neighborhood--with its well-funded police force and on-line citizenry -- but might be insufficient in a poor, urban community lacking in both law enforcement resources and private computer ownership. * * *

Against this background, the formulation of principles (in the broader sense) for executive discretion might proceed along the following lines: The police chief and his lieutenants would sit down with the district attorney and her main deputies to pinpoint troublesome areas of selective enforcement; other important officials, such as the city counsel and mayor, might also be in attendance. After defining the compass of problematic selective enforcement, these officials would forge principles for the administration of relevant criminal laws -- principles that they would be willing to apply in all like cases, in every part of town, and against all potential offenders. The proposed principles would then be publicized and feedback would be solicited from community members in an open forum or town meeting. Based on community input and political debate, law enforcement would formally and publicly adopt those principles that withstood scrutiny and would instruct front-line officers on the import and application of the principles. To reiterate, a modest rulemaking process would call for (1) preparation of enforcement principles, (2) publication and invitation for comments, (3) public deliberation in an open forum, (4) revision based on the comments, (5) publication of the final principles, and (6) inculcation of the principles among rank-and-file officers.

Some might claim that the adoption of sub-constitutional, sub-statutory principles will handcuff police and prosecutors by giving rise to new causes of action. An official's failure to follow some principle of executive discretion, for instance, might be used by the criminal defendant to avoid well-deserved punishment. This concern is largely unfounded, however, as the Supreme Court has held that the failure of law enforcement agents to follow self-imposed regulations does not create a cognizable right in a criminal defendant. Transparency through administrative-type rulemaking is not a judicial remedy but a political strategy to enhance the legitimacy and accountability of law enforcement.

Inertia provides the greatest barrier to the adoption of enforcement principles. Many communities might be pleased with the current state of law enforcement, giving officials little incentive to take the time and effort to delineate their discretion; in these regions, the adoption of principles pursuant to administrative-type rulemaking is, at best, wishful thinking. Nonetheless, there are many neighborhoods that are thoroughly dissatisfied with the discretionary judgments of police and prosecutors, with the enforcement of vice law in poor minority communities serving as the archetype of public disillusionment. It is in these neighborhoods where principled enforcement might receive popular support while helping to restore the moral credibility of law. * * *

Some communities undoubtedly espouse a "sausage theory" of criminal justice: They don't want to know how law enforcement is using its discretion, they just want safe streets and low crime. In these areas, the penal code will continue to be administered in an obscured (if not ad hoc) manner with transparent policing and its manifestations having next to no chance of adoption. The criminal law will continue to ban vice of all kinds and, for the most part, successful communities will be content with this state of affairs. Affluent but thrill-seeking individuals in these communities will continue to snort, smoke, and otherwise ingest all types of banned substances -- in private. Businessmen (and maybe businesswomen?) will continue to partake in illicit assignations with professionals -- once again, in private. Most importantly, these communities and their members will continue to prosper despite silent and unseen rebellions against the code.

The same cannot be said in poor, urban, and largely minority neighborhoods. These communities are confronted with a seemingly intractable dilemma: They are debilitated by open vice activity and the resulting street violence; yet the communities are often mistrusting of the police and prosecutors empowered to snuff out this social disease, whether due to racially disproportionate enforcement statistics, a perception of the police as occupying force, or the general lack of moral authority in law. But whatever the reason, there is a need, in Remington's words, "to clarify police authority to deal with a variety of community problems not adequately dealt with in the Code [and] to give further recognition to the propriety of administrative discretion and to develop means for more effective control of its exercise."

Transparent policing and administrative-type rulemaking offer possible alternatives for reestablishing the moral credibility of law in distrusting communities. There may be other amenable solutions, of course, but thoughtless enforcement of the current codes is not among them. The framers of the MPC and their contemporaries took the first step toward procedural justice in criminal law, bringing a heightened level of inner morality to the penal codes. Yet they also recognized that principled codification did not guarantee principled administration of the criminal law. The next step for comprehensive procedural justice in the penal system requires that society think outside of the box, beyond today's codes, to meaningfully address the problems of discretionary law enforcement.

D.   CULTURE IN THE COURTROOM

A JUSTIFICATION OF THE CULTURAL DEFENSE AS PARTIAL EXCUSE

Alison Dundes Renteln[a]
2 S. Cal. Rev. L. & Women's Stud. 437 (1993)

In pluralistic societies, culture conflict is inevitable. When some of these conflicts reach the legal system, the question arises whether the cultural background of the defendant should be admissible as evidence in a court of law. The issue is not simply whether cultural evidence can be introduced, but whether such evidence can function to exonerate a defendant.

Necessarily, cultural data is admitted into courtrooms whenever a culture conflict case occurs--it would be impossible to exclude it entirely. But in the absence of any official policy guidelines, the cultural evidence is treated differently from one case to the next, and from one court to the next. This can lead to gross injustices, in which one defendant who commits murder goes free, while another defendant who commits a less serious offense receives too harsh a punishment.

The purpose of this essay is to offer arguments in favor of the establishment of an official "cultural defense." A cultural defense is a defense asserted by immigrants, refugees, and indigenous people based on their customs or customary law. A successful cultural defense would permit the reduction (and possible elimination) of a charge, with a concomitant reduction in punishment. The rationale behind such a claim is that an individual's behavior is influenced to such a large extent by his or her culture that either (i) the individual simply did not believe that his or her actions contravened any laws (cognitive case), or (ii) the individual was compelled to act the way he or she did (volitional case). In both cases the individual's culpability is lessened.

---

[a] Reprinted by permission of the author. For further analysis, see Alison Dundes Renteln, THE CULTURAL DEFENSE (Oxford University Press 2004).

The reason for admitting a cultural defense lies not so much in a desire to be culturally sensitive, although that is surely a large part of it, but rather in a desire to ensure equal application of the law to all citizens. By equality I mean, not merely the desire to treat all culture conflict cases in a more uniform manner, but also the desire to treat all individuals in society as equals. As I shall argue, individual justice demands that the legal system focus on the actor as well as the act, on motive as well as intent. This, in turn, necessitates the introduction of cultural information into the courtroom. Oftentimes cultural information is brought into the courtroom by defense attorneys in the context of a pre-existing defense, such as provocation or insanity. For many reasons, however, this strategy is unsatisfactory for the generic culture conflict case. The most salient drawback is that the standards against which a defendant's actions are judged are those of "the reasonable person." But it is precisely this idea of reasonableness that lies at the heart of the conflict. As I shall argue, the actions of defendants should be judged against behavioral standards that are reasonable for a person of that culture in the context of this culture. This would balance the requirements of individual justice and cultural accommodation with the competing demands of social order and the rule of law.

It must be emphasized from the outset that the consideration of cultural evidence in no way requires that it be dispositive. A common fear is that the establishment of a cultural defense may force us to condone practices which contravene the rights of historically disenfranchised groups, including women and children. The argument seems to be that, although human rights are respected in the United States, the rest of the world is still barbaric. Ignoring the culturally patronizing overtones of such an argument, I should like to point out that sometimes it is women (and children) who benefit from the existence of cultural defenses.

More importantly, as I shall explain in more detail below, the sort of cultural defense I advocate is one which functions as a partial excuse. The advantage of such a formulation is that a demonstration of cultural influence is not sufficient to acquit. Juries must decide whether cultural factors were determinative in a defendant's behavior, and, if so, whether that is sufficient to warrant either a lesser charge or complete acquittal. By employing the cultural defense as a partial excuse, courts would be better able to fit the punishment to the crime, which is surely one of the goals of the criminal justice system. * * *

There have been some cases in which the defense counsel has advanced a defense combining the mental illness and cultural considerations all in one. Under some circumstances this approach may be necessary, because the defendant suffers from some sort of mental trauma related to his or her culture. The case of *People v. Kimura* is one such example. It provides an illustration of a case in which the cognitive insanity defense was successfully employed. The other case I shall consider, *People v. Metallides*, is an illustration of the use of the volitional insanity defense.

3. *People v. Kimura*

When Fumiko Kimura, a Japanese American living in Santa Monica, California, learned of the infidelity of her husband, she attempted oyako- shinju, parent-child suicide, by wading into the Pacific Ocean with her two children. The two children died, but she survived and was charged with first-degree murder with special circumstances which could have brought the death penalty. Oyako-shinju, while illegal in Japan, is not unheard of as a means by which a family can avoid an otherwise unacceptable social predicament. The Japanese-American community gathered a petition with over 25,000 signatures appealing to the Los Angeles County district attorney not to prosecute her, arguing that her actions were based on a different worldview. According to this worldview, it is more cruel to leave the children behind with no one to look after them than it is for the mother to take them with her to the afterlife.

Six psychiatrists testified that Kimura was suffering from temporary insanity. Some based their conclusion on her failure to distinguish between her own life and the lives of her children. Through a plea bargain her homicide charge was reduced to voluntary manslaughter and she was sentenced to one year in county jail (which she had already served), five years probation, and psychiatric counseling. She was subsequently reunited with her husband(!).

Though her attorney, Mr. Klausner, claimed that his argument relied on psychiatric testimony, commentators believe that cultural factors played a role in the process. It is worth pointing out that Kimura appears to have benefitted from a cultural defense though she had resided in the United States for several years. As she had remained culturally isolated, she had not become assimilated. This suggests that assimilation often does not occur as rapidly as many believe.

Another important point is that the children's rights dimension of this case has hardly been discussed in the literature. While the court may have been correct in considering the cultural aspects of the case, it is arguable that probation was an unjustifiably light sentence to impose.

4. *People v. Metallides*

In the Miami, Florida case of *People v. Metallides* a Greek immigrant, Kostas Metallides, killed his best friend when he found out that he had raped Kostas' daughter. Metallides' attorney, a public defender, used a temporary insanity argument based on culture. Though not recognized as a defense in

Florida, the attorney relied on the "irresistible impulse" test. Metallides' attorney constructed an argument around the cultural idea that the "law of the old country" is that "you do not wait for the police if your daughter has been raped." Though the jury was given temporary insanity as the official issue to decide, apparently it recognized that honor was a cultural concept. Metallides was acquitted because the jury technically found him not guilty by reason of temporary insanity, but those involved say it was because of arguments based on Greek culture. The defense attorney said that the judge may have allowed the cultural evidence because the judge's wife was Greek.

It seems unfair that it was possible to introduce the cultural defense only surreptitiously. Had the judge been unwilling to consider the irresistible impulse test, due to the absence of statutory authorization, or to interpret the cultural evidence as relevant, Metallides would not have had the benefit of a cultural defense. Moreover, the accuracy of the claims made concerning Greek culture could have been questioned, considering that no expert witness was consulted on this point.

While it was appropriate to allow the cultural argument to be heard, it appears that the jury gave excessive weight to it. Although one can only speculate about the jury's reasoning, it may have been that the jury felt that a vote to convict would lead to an excessive punishment under the circumstances, and so the preferred option was acquittal. One of the reasons for instituting the cultural defense as a separate defense is to avoid such artificial dichotomies.

Under the current system, a defendant's fate would appear to hinge upon the attitude of the judge to the relevancy of the cultural evidence and on the availability of particular insanity tests. Although Metallides was able to escape punishment by relying on the irresistible impulse test, other defendants may not have such good fortune. Another reason for adopting a cultural defense is to achieve a greater degree of uniformity in the handling of such cases. * * *

The major obstacle to the use of the provocation defense by defendants in cultural defense cases is judicial adherence to the "objective" reasonable person standard. Critics contend that it is absurd to judge whether an "objective" reasonable person would have been provoked, when the reality is that this "objective" being is simply the persona of the dominant culture. Their position is that the court should modify the standard, so that the application of the test evaluates whether the reasonable person from the defendant's culture would have been provoked. Whether or not the cultural defense can be effectively raised through the provocation defense depends entirely upon the judge's interpretation of the reasonable person standard: if the test is "objective," almost invariably no provocation will be found; if the test is "subjective," then ordinarily provocation will be found. This controversy is well illustrated in the cases of *People v. Aphaylath*, *Regina v. Ly*, and *People v. Chen*.

1. *People v. Aphaylath*

In 1982, May Aphaylath, a Laotian refugee residing in Rochester, New York stabbed his wife to death in a jealous rage when she received a phone call from a former boyfriend. The public defender tried to argue that Aphaylath's loss of self control was culturally based: "under Laotian culture the conduct of the victim wife in displaying affection for another man and receiving phone calls from an unattached man brought shame on defendant and his family sufficient to trigger defendant's loss of control." Defense counsel sought to introduce expert witnesses to establish that: (1) Aphaylath was suffering from culture shock or extreme disorientation and (2) the infidelity of one's wife brings great shame on the family. The public defender attempted to construct an argument that in Laotian culture the combination of the disgrace of his wife's conduct and the stress of resettlement could have triggered his disproportionate rage.

The judge disallowed the testimony of experts on the cultural issues because they had not evaluated the defendant and could, therefore, only testify about Laotian culture and refugee problems generally. The court took the view that jealousy was not a subject beyond the comprehension of the jury for which expert evidence was needed.

Aphaylath was convicted of murder in the second degree. The Supreme Court, Appellate division, denied the appeal based on the exclusion of expert evidence because it found the trial court's judgment appropriate with respect to excluding cultural evidence. The dissenting judge would have granted a new trial because the excluded testimony would have been "highly probative of whether there was a reasonable explanation for defendant's conduct from the perspective of his internal point of view." In his view, the evidence might have established extreme emotional disturbance that could serve as a mitigating factor.

The Court of Appeals of New York held that it was reversible error to exclude the testimony of expert witnesses concerning culture shock suffered by Laotian refugees. As a result the Court of Appeals ordered that the lower court decision be reversed and the case remanded for a new trial. This was not necessary because the prosecutor negotiated a plea bargain whereby an admission of guilt would lead to a conviction of manslaughter. Since the reduction in sentence from 15 years to life to 8 1/3 years to 25 years in prison was precisely what the public defender sought, the plea bargain was accepted.

Although this might have been a major coup for advocates of the relevance of culture for judicial decision-making, the opinion left much to be desired. Only four paragraphs long, the memorandum of the court gives little guidance as to when culture is relevant and how the ascertainment of culture should proceed. The public defender had hoped for a landmark decision and was bitterly disappointed.

2. *Regina v. Ly*

The relevance of culture for a defense of provocation was the central issue in the Canadian case of *Regina v. Ly.* The facts resemble those in *Aphaylath*. A Vietnamese refugee became suspicious that his common-law wife was no longer faithful to him. When he confronted her about this initially, explaining that he felt he had lost face in the eyes of the community, he spoke of committing suicide which his wife supposedly encouraged him to do. He took some pills but was treated in a hospital and survived. On one particular night he expected his wife home early and when she returned at two o'clock in the morning, he questioned her again. After she told him that where she had been was none of his business, he strangled her and tried again to kill himself.

At the trial he tried to emphasize the cultural significance of his wife's conduct, testifying that: "his wife's infidelity had caused him to lose 'face' and 'honour' and this had special importance to him because of his Vietnamese upbringing." The chairman of a Vietnamese refugee association corroborated the cultural argument. But the trial judge's instruction to the jury on provocation diminished the power of the cultural argument.

According to the Criminal Code of Canada, reducing a murder charge to manslaughter requires passing a two-pronged test. First, there must be a determination that the wrongful act or insult was of such a nature that it would deprive an ordinary person of self control. Second, the accused must have reacted to provocation, promptly before there was time for his passion to cool. One rationale for combining an "objective" reasonable person test and a "subjective" test of actual provocation is that an ordinary person might be provoked by something even though the accused was not.

The crux of the appeal was based on the trial judge's instruction that the jury not consider culture in assessing the first part of the test, namely whether the "ordinary person" would have been sufficiently provoked. As far as the judge was concerned, culture only goes to the question of whether the accused was actually provoked. But the defendant contended that the insult "could only be properly measured against the cultural background of the appellant." As the jury did not evaluate the reaction of an average Vietnamese male, Ly was convicted of second degree murder. The three judges of the British Columbia Court of Appeal affirmed the decision of the lower court.

Until the Canadian judiciary clarifies the nature of the test for provocation, the relevance of culture arguments will be ambiguous. In *Regina v. Ly* the judges followed precedent and took an unduly narrow view of provocation, one based almost exclusively on racial slurs. It is hard to fathom their reasoning. It is also curious that American and Canadian appellate courts came to diametrically opposed conclusions in similar cases within a year of each other.

3. *People v. Chen*

Dong Lu Chen, a Chinese born man living in New York, bludgeoned his wife to death after she confessed to adultery. A professor of anthropology at Hunter College, Burton Pasternak, testified that in China women are sometimes severely punished for adultery. He said that it is viewed as an "enormous stain" that reflects not only on the husband but "is a reflection on his ancestors and his progeny." Pasternak also observed that adultery rarely ends in a wife's murder in China. In China when irate husbands confront wives suspected of infidelity, the community normally intervenes to prevent any acts of violence. In fact, Pasternak could not cite any cases where Chinese men had killed adulterous wives, though he did know of beatings. Nor did he present evidence to show that a jealousy killing would go unpunished under either customary or modern Chinese law. It seems that no effort was made to discover what punishment would be imposed in the case of a husband who murders an adulterous wife, either under traditional or modern Chinese law. Some commentators have pointed out that at least under modern law such a husband would be punished.

Nevertheless, after a non-jury trial New York State Supreme Court Judge Edward Pincus relied heavily on Pasternak's testimony when he found Chen guilty of second degree manslaughter and decided to sentence him to only five years probation. This "sentence" of five years probation essentially represented a complete defense rather than mitigation.

Women's organizations, Asian-American groups, and Elizabeth Holtzman condemned the decision. They even went so far as to file a complaint with the State of New York Commission on Judicial Conduct asking for an investigation into the judge's decision.

4. What is Reasonable About Provocation?

The notion of an "objective" test of what an ordinary person believes is fraught with perils. The concept masks the subjective biases of the culture of the dominant group. In many cases throughout the world the application of the ordinary or reasonable person test has meant the forceful imposition of one set of values upon individuals whose own value system differs. * * *

* * * [R]etention of the "objective" reasonable person standard is grossly unfair because it means that the provocation defense, which is supposed to be available to all, is a defense only for those who belong to the dominant culture. There are two reasonable responses. Either the provocation defense should be abandoned altogether or the standard should be that of the culture to which the defendant belongs. After all, different things provoke different people. The purpose of the provocation defense is to hold less culpable those individuals who cannot control their actions. If the reasonable defendant from another culture cannot control his or her actions in the face of a certain provocation, what is the basis for holding that individual guilty of first-degree (premeditated) murder? * * *

A[]* * * practical query is what groups would be entitled to raise cultural defenses. There is realistically no way to limit their use, nor would it be fair to do so. However, to ensure that the defense not be subject to abuse, statutory authorization of cultural arguments should require that the defendant prove the authenticity of the tradition in question. The defendant would have the burden of proving that: (1) the group to which the defendant belongs remains committed to the cultural practice, and (2) the defendant was, in fact, motivated by the tradition.

One of the most vexing questions is how to limit the use of the cultural defense to bona fide ethnic minority groups and to prevent its use by sub-cultures. The reason why subcultures should not be entitled to use a cultural defense is that their worldview is not radically different from the rest of society. For example, gang members do not believe in witchcraft, coining, or other customs integral to a markedly different conceptual system. It may well be that the social and economic background of sub-cultural defendants should be raised in some cases. The suitable defense for this purpose is not the cultural defense but what has been called the "rotten social background" defense.

The sub-cultural defense has more to do with class differences than cultural differences. If individuals who come from lower socio-economic backgrounds were to rely on the cultural defense, then there would be nothing to prevent aristocrats from raising a "Great Gatsby" defense when they drive while intoxicated. Use of the rotten social background defense ensures that only those who have experienced life in the ghetto, or something akin to it, are entitled to a criminal defense. In reality it may not be possible to thwart the use of the cultural defense by sub-cultures. However, just because a cultural argument is advanced does not obligate a judge or jury to accept the argument.

Courts may be reluctant to allow cultural defenses because they fear that it will be difficult to ascertain the validity of the practice in question. Invoking a cultural defense might be unjustifiable because the practice may never have existed, may be considerably different from that described by a defendant * * * or may have ceased to exist * * *. One real danger of allowing cultural defenses might be the unwarranted assumption on the part of lawyers and judges that traditions do not change. Of course, cultures evolve, and so courts must guard against basing decisions on information that is anachronistic.

Some may object to a formal cultural defense on the grounds that putting the culture on trial may have adverse consequences for members of the group. There is concern that decisions based on group characteristics may lead to the reinforcement of social stereotypes. But it is important to recognize that members of groups do share common characteristics, and the desire to obliterate prejudice and hatred should not lead to the unfair treatment of individuals. That is, individualized justice based on group traits may be necessary to safeguard the rights of individual defendants and thus be more important than the promotion of a progressive social policy. Furthermore, since the cultural defense will only serve as a partial, rather than complete, excuse, this will ensure that the rights of children and other vulnerable groups are not violated in deference to culture.

The law must make many difficult determinations, e.g., questions of insanity and causation. There is no reason to suppose than cultural evidence is any more difficult to interpret than any other data. If it turns out to be the case that the process of verifying the cultural claim demonstrates its falsity, then it should obviously be rejected.

ON CULTURE, DIFFERENCE, AND DOMESTIC VIOLENCE
Leti Volpp
11 Am. U.J. Gender, Soc. Pol'y & Law 393 (2003)[a]

How should we consider cultural difference when we think about domestic violence? Elizabeth Schneider's path-breaking representation of Yvonne Wanrow, described in her book, Battered Women and Feminist Lawmaking, gives us an important example of how one can contemplate this question in the context of legal representation. In arguing that Yvonne Wanrow's perspective as a Native American woman had been excluded from her claim of self defense, Elizabeth Schneider and other attorneys at the Center for Constitutional Rights successfully asserted that the way one's specific identity

---

[a]Reprinted with permission.

shapes experiences must be factored into the consideration of a defendant's state of mind. What was missing, they argued, was evidence that would have explained why Yvonne Wanrow would react as she did when an uninvited white man, who she believed had tried to molest one of her children, entered her babysitter's home. This evidence included information as to the general lack of police protection in such situations, the pervasiveness of violence against women and children, Wanrow's belief that the man was a child molester, Wanrow's lack of trust in the police, and her belief that she could successfully defend herself only with a weapon.

But I fear that this representation was exceptional in its careful attention to particularized detail. I am concerned that when attempts to represent a woman's difference are less careful, what can accompany or underlie culturally based advocacy can be quite problematic. Very often, discussions of cultural alterity rely upon invocations of culture that are little more than crass, group based stereotypes that may, in fact, be quite remote from the individual experiences at issue. Moreover, unlike in Wanrow's case where the failures of the police were pivotal to the argument, invocations of culture often suggest that culture somehow exists apart from the state.

This reflects outmoded, although popular, perceptions of culture. Culture is still fused with ethnicity, and not understood as a descriptor explaining all kinds of social interactions. Moreover, culture is generally thought of as a noun, a fixed and static thing, rather than conceived as an adjective modifying particular practices. Discussions of the way culture can shape domestic violence occur in a broader context of already existing stereotypes about culture, that reflect problematic notions as to how culture is believed to link to race.

Despite the valiant attempts of organizations such as the Family Violence Prevention Fund to inform the American public that domestic violence in the United States is a universal phenomenon occurring at epidemic rates, behavior that we condemn, such as domestic violence, is more often conceptualized as cultural for nonwhite communities. In fact, some have argued that it appears that many feminists and battered women's advocates suspect that "other" cultures actually support domestic violence -- without turning to ask whether this may also be the case in their own communities. This tendency to describe domestic violence as "cultural" when occurring in communities of color, and not through the language of power and control used to describe domestic violence in "mainstream" communities, is linked to the uninterrogated assumption that devalued and less powerful groups are somehow more culturally determined. This description suggests that members of communities of color behave in certain ways, because they follow cultural dictates, as if they are encoded with culture.

We can see this in the reaction to the case of Andrea Yates. Her killing of her five children was primarily explained as a result of mental illness, with a diagnosis of postpartum psychosis. While there was some discussion suggesting Andrea Yates inhabited a particular cultural location due to her family's Christian beliefs, that engendered their living in a school bus left by a traveling preacher, or that led her to keep having children without using birth control because the children came from God, the primary lens through which her behavior was understood was psychological. We thus heard about her experience with the mental health system, medications she had stopped taking, and suicide attempts.

Psychology is used to explain why people positioned as Western subjects act irrationally. In contrast, culture is used to explain why those considered non-Western subjects act irrationally. We could thus compare the coverage of Andrea Yates with other cases involving mothers who killed their children. One such case involved Khoua Her, a Hmong immigrant, who in Minnesota in 1998 strangled her six children and then hanged herself in a failed suicide attempt. Police had been called to the family's home at least sixteen times in the previous two years, and there was a long history of domestic violence. In searching for explanations, the media invoked a "cultural clash," and "the American pull to be an individual versus the Hmong orientation of putting the group first." Described as the worst mass murder in Minnesota memory, the Her case was invoked -- along with tales of animal cruelty, religious sacrifice of small dogs, the statistic that nearly half of the Hmong community was on state welfare, a string of gang rapes, and a thirteen year old who smothered her newborn -- by a popular radio talk show host who said, "Those people should either assimilate or hit the road."

We see here the process of selective blaming of culture. The same act is understood as the product of Hmong culture in one case, but not white American culture in the other. Rather, Andrea Yates, whether she is condemned or pitied, is primarily depicted as a mother under enormous pressure, her life uninflected [sic] by a racialized culture. Khoua Her, in contrast, is described as if her life is completely circumscribed by a racialized culture.

A particular academic description of culture that reflects some of these problems is an article which appeared in a symposium issue of the Stanford Law Review, authored by Nilda Rimonte, who was once the director of a battered women's shelter in Los Angeles that serves Asian women and children. In the article, Rimonte points to a number of reasons for domestic violence in Asian immigrant communities: the Pacific-Asian family's traditionally patriarchal system and the attendant belief in the supremacy of the male; the socialization goals and processes which favor the family and community over the individual; the cultural emphasis on silent suffering versus open communication of needs and feelings; and the enormous adjustment pressures which test the limits of immigrants' and refugees' survival skills. Rimonte also suggests that few Asian countries have woman's rights movements whose energy and goals might significantly influence the women in their society, asserts that Asians have a different sense of time, claims that the idea of choices and rights may not be appropriate for Asians, and states that, unlike the Western ideal of the healthy family, the Asian family is structured around male privilege, authority, and superiority. The article presents a frozen, monolithic description of culture for an enormous region of the world that elides any difference or heterogeneity. Rimonte's sweeping and inaccurate generalizations have allowed other writers to make blanket statements about gender subordination in "Asian cultures" and to assert that there is something more misogynistic about Asian immigrant communities than "our own."

In the face of this selective stereotyping, the appeal of universalist descriptions of domestic violence, to suggest that specific cultural formations have no impact, is understandable. Two examples that surfaced in discussions I recently had with Asian American and Pacific Islander domestic violence advocates come to mind. The first was the response of one advocate to the query of a "mainstream" women's shelter (meaning one not serving diverse populations), that inquired for advice about the "cultural shame" of an Indian immigrant who had been sexually assaulted; this cultural shame, said the shelter staff, prohibited the woman from using the shelter's public shower. The response of the advocate was to tell the shelter that any woman who had been sexually assaulted would have issues around privacy and bodily integrity. The second was the response of another advocate to the question as to what, specifically, were the issues for battered lesbians. The advocate's response was that a battered lesbian's experience of domestic violence will reflect her class position, whether she is disabled, whether she is an immigrant, or whether she lives in a rural area, like any other woman in those situations. She then reflected that perhaps the fear of being outed by the abusive partner, if the battered woman was not already out, was specific to lesbians -- but then reflected that any battered woman fears being outed, as battered. This kind of approach, to shift attention away from a focus on particular assumptions about how cultural identities shape domestic violence, to examining how experiences are similar, seems necessary.

Yet I would agree with Sherene Razack, who, in examining narratives of sexual violence against South Asian women, cautions against a simple turn to universalist narratives. She argues that there are three problems with reacting against culturalist stereotypes through using universal arguments. Razack asserts that deculturalized narratives rarely have enough traction to displace orientalist fantasies that are believed in mainstream communities, are too abstract to use in conversations within communities that are the subject of description, and lastly, fail to grapple with the fact that violent acts are committed in culturally specific ways.

But then how do we describe the specifics of culture? One important shift would be to understand that cultural practices are imbricated with material and political forces. Usually when cultural explanations are given, a static and insular culture is blamed, detracting attention away from one's limited access to services, or from the policies of the state. Thus, part of what I am arguing for here is an understanding of culture that does not strip away the economic and the political from its content. Take, for example, the idea that Asian immigrants have difficulty gaining access to the Violence Against Women Act ("VAWA") self-petitioning process. When this is blamed on "cultural limitations" of Asian communities -- such as passivity, or shame -- it removes the onus from agencies or the government to try to make services more accessible. Thus, invocations of culture can erase the racism of agencies and entities that fail to provide appropriate services to battered women by hiring diverse staff who speak relevant languages or translate materials. Further, invocations of culture can detract attention away from the policies of the state: VAWA self-petitioning was only required as a remedy to fix U.S. immigration laws that gave batterers tools with which they could abuse partners, after Congress enacted the Marriage Fraud Act. For an example that foregrounds the importance of economic concerns, we could return to the case of Khoua Her. Recently, an article in the Hmong Times suggested that Her strangled her six children because she saw death as the only means of saving them from poverty, after she lost the low-paying job that had provided food and benefits for her family. Understanding Her's acts as solely the product of "Hmong culture" completely subsumes the role material forces may have played in shaping her perceptions.

Another important shift was evident in the second advocate's response, described above, when she insisted on invoking class, disability, immigrant status, and geographical location as relevant to any particular battered lesbian's experience. Identities and experiences do shape perspectives, but we must be attentive to the way in which this transpires through a complex process that reflects an individual's specific position. Essentializing narratives about particular cultures can often serve to mask reality. For example, a battered woman who is an immigrant may have failed to call the police, not because her culture condones passivity on the part of women, but because her partner was a police officer in her country of origin, because she has witnessed a failure of police protection and practices of police brutality, and because the police in her present location do not speak her language. Granting explanatory power to essentialized depictions of "culture," as purportedly made up of unchanging rituals that cement the subordinate location of women in a fixed system of social practices, will inevitably fail to accurately describe the relationship of culture, difference, and domestic violence.

E. CHANGING THE CULTURE OF CRIMINAL PUNISHMENT

A FUTURE WHERE PUNISHMENT IS MARGINALIZED: REALISTIC OR UTOPIAN?
John Braithwaite
46 UCLA L. Rev. 1727 (1999)

Restorative justice is a process of bringing together the individuals who have been affected by an offense and having them agree on how to repair the harm caused by the crime. The purpose is to restore victims, restore offenders, and restore communities in a way that all stakeholders can agree is just. One value of restorative justice is that we should be reluctant to resort to punishment. Punishment adds to the amount of hurt in the world, but justice has more meaning if it is about healing rather than hurting. "Crime hurts; justice heals": This captures the essence of the paradigm shift. It involves rejection of a justice that balances the hurt of the crime with proportionately hurtful punishment.

The term "restorative justice" was first used in the late 1970s to describe victim-offender mediation programs of various kinds in North America and Europe. These mostly involved a meeting of a single offender with a single victim in the presence of a professional mediator. Initially, they had a pragmatic emphasis, especially in England, on material reparation for victims, which was thought of as a kind of sentencing alternative. While a lot of these programs sprung up, they tended to be tiny, marginalized, and did not inspire a transformative agenda for the criminal justice system during the 1980s.

Restorative justice became a global social movement in the 1990s as a result of learning from indigenous practices of restorative justice: the ways in which individualistic Western victim-offender mediation was impoverished. The most influential wisdom was from the oral justice traditions of the New Zealand Maori and North American native peoples. These restorative justice traditions were more radically communitarian. Instead of two individuals mediating a dispute across a table, members of two communities (one supporting a victim, another an offender, with other individuals supporting both) would come together as one community in a circle. This gave rise to the names "sentencing circle" or "healing circle" for the 1990s North American variants of restorative justice. The southern hemisphere variants were called "conferences." In both the Maori and North American traditions, the supporters in the circle were not limited to parents and siblings. Grandparents, aunts, uncles, cousins, close friends, teachers, sporting coaches, and many other kinds of concerned community members would often attend. Sometimes there would be more than thirty people in the circle, but more typically fewer than ten. Westerners like those in my own research team who observed a lot of conferences and circles almost universally concluded that it was rarely a problem to have too many people in the circle. This surprised us because we assumed that large numbers, especially of children, would lead to chaos.

The second big lesson we learned from indigenous practice was that material reparation was much less important than emotional or symbolic reparation. Victims often wanted an apology more than compensation. Forgiveness from their families was often more important to the restoration of offenders than anything else. The surprise was that talk about justice could sit so comfortably alongside talk about love.

There were many other lessons from peoples who had not let older restorative traditions die, but these were the key shifts we made from that learning: from dyad to circle, from dialogue about material reparation to symbolic plus material reparation, from justice to justice intertwined with love and caring.

In a typical conference or circle, the consequences of the crime will first be discussed. Who has suffered as a result of the crime: the victim, the family of the offender? How have they suffered? Then the conference considers a plan of action to heal that suffering. Often the plan will include ways of making amends to the victim or the community that many will conceive as punishment. But it may also include apology, forgiveness, ways of helping victims to feel safer and preventing a recurrence of the crime.

There is an overwhelming amount of evidence now that participant (victim, offender, community, police) satisfaction with such restorative justice processes is extremely high, typically 90%-95%, and in some studies even higher. Participant perceptions of the fairness of conferences is at comparably high levels. Most, though far from all, victims feel safer after a conference than they did before and experience healing. Moreover, for cases randomly assigned to conference rather than court, perceptions of fairness and overall satisfaction are higher in conference than in court cases for all types of participants. * * *

Restorative justice can also be used to improve crime prevention. Elsewhere I have argued that there are some good theoretical reasons for predicting that restorative justice programs will outperform punitive justice in terms of crime prevention, but that restorative justice processes in themselves are unlikely to have a major impact on the crime rate. The reason for the latter is that it is implausible that what happens during a one- or two-hour encounter will often turn around all the other variables operating during all the other hours of a person's life. One hope about restorative justice is that it might be a superior vehicle for implementation of the other crime-prevention strategies that evidence-based criminology shows to work. * * *

It seems to me we know five things that are important to making crime prevention work:

1. You need to motivate crime prevention to get it to work. The emotion of the circle's rituals of remorse-apology-forgiveness, the tears of disappointed and relieved mums and dads, create an environment where motivation to do difficult things becomes possible.

2. You need community ownership to get crime prevention to work. It is easier to get citizens to attend a conference to support a victim or an offender they love than it is to get them to a neighborhood watch meeting or a police-community liaison committee.

3. You need to bring out the perspectives of a plurality of stakeholders for it to work. With an incident of violence at a pub, there may be a girlfriend who can commit to sorting out a relationship problem that was engendering jealousy. There may be drinking mates who can commit to changing drinking practices. There may be a bar manager who can commit to the kind of self-regulatory program Homel found to reduce pub violence in Australia. Getting all these actors to turn up and speak up is difficult, but conferences have had remarkable success at accomplishing this.

4. You need citizens to freely choose to change their behavior rather than being coerced into change by the state. This is especially true of rehabilitation programs. Offenders must choose them, own them. It follows that state monopolies of therapeutic provision -- the state's professionals deciding what is best for the offender or the victim -- are inferior to citizens choosing a rehabilitation program from a diversity of options funded in civil society. Such citizen choice can be discussed and decided in a restorative justice circle.

5. You need crime prevention to be transacted within bonds of social support. Rehabilitation programs that an individual commits to alone are less likely to succeed than rehabilitation programs that the offender commits to with the active support of a boyfriend, a mother, a respected schoolteacher or employer. Citizens are invited to conferences or circles precisely because of their desire to support a victim or an offender. This means that restorative justice allows crime prevention to advance within networks of social support.

In sum, restorative justice processes might have greater potential for orchestrating the conditions to make crime prevention work than any other node for organization in the criminal justice system. Certainly they have more potential than criminal trials controlled by lawyers. To date this potential has not been developed very well in existing restorative justice programs. * * *

Note

Related to James Boyd White's argument that the criminal law is better understood as a system of meaning than as a tool for achieving certain goals is the argument that one of the most important functions of the criminal law is its *expressive* function. Thus, Dan M. Kahan argues that "we can give a satisfactory account of crime and punishment only if we pay close attention to their social meaning." Dan M. Kahan, *What Do Alternative Sanctions Mean?* 63 U. Chi. L. Rev. 591, 597 (1996). Kahan argues that the expressive theory of criminal law explains why certain kinds of punishment that might achieve the pragmatic goals of deterrence, incapacitation, and/or retribution – such as corporal punishment – are nevertheless politically unpopular: in a nation with a history of slavery, argues Kahan, "corporal punishment is an unacceptable reminder of America's history of slavery and racial inequality." *Id.* at 615.

Taking the expressive function of criminal law further, Kahan argues that "shaming" punishments – punishments that seek to humiliate the offender – might be a useful, less harsh alternative to incarceration. Kahan divides these shaming punishments into four types: stigmatizing publicity, literal stigmatization, self-debasement, and contrition. As Kahan describes these types:

> Stigmatizing publicity is the most straightforward. Penalties in this class attempt to magnify the humiliation inherent in conviction by communicating the offender's status to a wider audience. Some municipalities, for example, publish offenders' names in newspapers or even on billboards, a disposition that is especially common for men convicted of soliciting prostitutes. Other jurisdictions broadcast the names of various types of offenders on community-access television channels.

> Literal stigmatization is just that – the stamping of an offender with a mark or symbol that invites ridicule. Some judges order petty thieves to wear t-shirts announcing their crimes. Others achieve the same effect with brightly colored bracelets that read "DUI Convict," "I Write Bad Checks," and the like. One judge ordered a woman to wear a sign declaring "I am a convicted child molester."

Less dramatic but even more common are penalties that attach stigmatizing marks to property. Some jurisdictions now require persons guilty of drunk driving to display special license plates or bumper stickers. Courts have also ordered those convicted of sexual assaults and other crimes to post signs at their residences warning others to steer clear.

Self-debasement penalties involve ceremonies or rituals that publicly disgrace the offender. In a contemporary version of the stocks, for example, some communities require offenders simply to stand in public spaces, such as the local courthouse, with signs describing their offenses. More imaginative forms of self-debasement attempt to match the penalty to the character of the offense. A judge in Tennessee orders convicted burglars to permit their victims to enter their homes and remove items of their choosing. In New York, a slumlord was sentenced to house arrest in one of his rat-infested tenements (where tenants greet ed him with the banner, "Welcome, You Reptile!"). Hoboken, New Jersey, requires Wall Street brokers and others who urinate in public to clean the city's streets. This is only a small sample; self-debasement sanctions are as diverse and particular as the crimes that they are used to punish.

Contrition penalties come in two forms. The first requires offenders to publicize their own convictions, describing their crimes in first-person terms and apologizing for them. These penalties combine stigmatizing publicity with an element of self-debasement; the sincerity of the offenders' remorse seems largely irrelevant.

Another form of contrition is the apology ritual. In Maryland, for example, juvenile offenders must apologize on their hands and knees and are released from confinement only if they persuade their victims that their remorse is sincere. Other jurisdictions use community-based sanctions that include public apologies and appropriate reparations.

Id. at 631-34.

Are shaming sanctions likely to be effective? What objections might be made to them? Are they consistent with the theory of restorative justice?

BOOK REVIEW ESSAY: JUDGING IN A THERAPEUTIC KEY: THERAPEUTIC JURISPRUDENCE AND THE COURTS

Charity Scott

25 J. Legal Med. 377 (2004)

"Therapeutic jurisprudence" represents a shift in perspective on the role of law and courts in our society. *Judging in a Therapeutic Key*[2] is a collection of thought-provoking essays that illustrates this shift, often through the various authors' descriptions of the roles of judges and litigants in our legal system. These authors – many of whom are judges – do not promote the traditional view of the judge as just a neutral arbiter of cases who is uninvolved in the conflict before her, or as only an adjudicator of historical facts who chooses between two conflicting positions to determine a winner and a loser, or as simply the final decision-maker who renders judgment in one case and moves on to the next case without looking back. Instead, they depict the judge as a "coach," a "member of the treatment team," a "case manager" or a "risk manager," and a "leading actor in the therapeutic drama" of the courtroom. Judges are described as "listeners, translators, educators, and if possible, facilitators," and above all, as versatile "problem-solvers" who craft solutions to the underlying social and behavioral problems that gave rise to the cases before her.

New kinds of specialized problem-solving courts that reflect the principles of therapeutic jurisprudence have been springing up all over the country during the past 15 years. In these courtrooms, the judge may assume "the role of confessor, task master, cheerleader, and mentor" to the criminal offender. The offender is often referred to as a "client," and the judge-offender relationship is described as a "rich therapeutic opportunity" to reduce recidivism and "make a positive difference in people's lives before it's too late." Offenders are encouraged to confront their "cognitive distortions," and victims might be the beneficiaries of "symbolic reparation." These are courtrooms where judges practice an "ethic of care," where treating defendants with respect and dignity is as important as knowing the law, and where "behavioral contracts" and "graduation ceremonies" may be more the order of the day than sentencing and incarceration. Judges in these new courts are encouraged to place less emphasis on efficiency in case processing and more emphasis on "repentance, education, reform, catharsis, and healing."

---

[2] Bruce J. Winick & David B. Wexler, JUDGING IN A THERAPEUTIC KEY: THERAPEUTIC JURISPRUDENCE AND THE COURTS 6 (2003).

What's going on here? A transformation of the judicial role has been steadily taking place across the country in trial-level courts that specialize in certain kinds of cases or problems, such as adult and juvenile drug treatment courts, mental health courts, and domestic violence courts. Key characteristics common to these and other such "problem-solving courts" are "active judicial involvement and the explicit use of judicial authority to motivate individuals to accept needed services and to monitor their compliance and progress." Despite their unconventional vocabulary, these well-respected judicial and academic writers are not pushing political correctness or touchy-feely reforms. Rather, they are advocating a concerted national effort to combine common sense with the lessons of the behavioral sciences to transform our courts into opportunities to ensure public safety, to aid victims in reconciling with their abusers and coping with their injuries, to re-cast criminal offenders as actively contributing members of society, and to increase public trust of and respect for our judicial system.

THERAPEUTIC JURISPRUDENCE EXPLAINED

What, then, is therapeutic jurisprudence? Therapeutic jurisprudence (TJ) is the interdisciplinary study of law as a social force that has considerable impact on people's emotional lives and psychological well-being. Its fundamental premise is that a person's involvement with the legal system can have both positive (therapeutic) and negative (anti-therapeutic) consequences for him or her, even independent of the win/lose outcome of the case. In other words, like medications, legal rules and legal procedures can have unintended adverse side effects.

TJ scholars analyze these therapeutic and anti-therapeutic consequences and ask to what extent the law, lawyers, and judges should attempt to maximize the potential for therapeutic outcomes. TJ suggests that people's encounters with the legal system, like their encounters with the health care system, ideally should leave them better off, not worse off, than they were before the encounter. In other words, like medicine, law should strive first to "do no harm."

Therapeutic jurisprudence was founded in the late 1980s and early 1990s through the work of the author-editors of this book, law professors Bruce Winick and David Wexler, who were doing interdisciplinary research in mental health law. Examining such issues as competency to consent to treatment, the commitment process, and the insanity defense, these scholars looked at the therapeutic implications of mental health laws. In particular, they focused on how legal rules, legal procedures, and legal actors could contribute to the psychological dysfunction of patients and defendants. For example, laws restricting confidentiality could negatively impact a mentally ill person's willingness to fully disclose important information to a therapist, or the doctrine of incompetence to stand trial could either prolong a criminal defendant's mental illness or encourage unnecessary treatment.

Over the past decade, therapeutic jurisprudence has attracted the attention of a widely diverse group of scholars and practitioners who have extended its principles into such fields as criminal law, family law, juvenile law, tort law, contract law, disability law, and health law. To get a quick glimpse of the enormous impact that TJ has had on legal scholarship and practice, the reader may visit the TJ website for a lengthy, cumulative bibliography of videos, books, book chapters, monographs, and articles on the application of TJ in many different contexts. Rarely does the academic work of law scholars have such a clear-cut impact in shaping the research agendas of a broad range of legal academics. Rarer still are the times when such legal scholarship positively impacts the working lives of judges and practicing lawyers. As these essays make abundantly clear, therapeutic jurisprudence has come of age as a legal discipline in its own right, ready to be further tested carefully and strategically within our judicial system.

HOW THE NEW PROBLEM-SOLVING COURTS WORK

Judging in a Therapeutic Key describes how these new problem-solving courts work and also sets out the underlying rationale for creating them. * * * Part I, titled "The New Judicial Approaches," consists largely of short newspaper stories that provide a highly readable and engaging introduction to the workings of these new courts. These journalistic accounts develop a basic theme of problem-solving courts, which is to end the "revolving-door" effect that returns ex-offenders back to criminal courts. The new courts partly grew out of frustration that judges were "processing cases like a vegetable factory. Instead of cans of peas, you've got cases. You just move 'em, move 'em, move 'em . . . . I feel like I work for McJustice: we sure aren't good for you, but we are fast." With rising criminal caseloads, judges were frustrated that their courtrooms were turning into "plea bargain mills"; attorneys were frustrated by the sense they were working on an "assembly line"; and the public's confidence in the criminal justice system was declining as rates of criminal activity were rising.

The first news story succinctly sets the stage by introducing the concept of revolving-door justice through Nando, a young man from the Bronx who, within a few hours of his release from an eight-month prison term for selling crack, had been offered drugs on the street and an opportunity to return to his old job dealing drugs. In releasing Nando back to the community with little more than subway fare, the traditional judicial system had not addressed the underlying social or psychological problems that might have fostered his drug-related activities in the first place and that might again prove too strong an influence for him to withstand in the future.

Subsequent news accounts describe the new approaches that various courts across the country are taking to break the cycle of re-involvement by individuals like Nando with the criminal justice system. These courts attempt to intervene in the life of criminal offenders by addressing their underlying problems, such as mental illness, poverty, substance abuse, or the lack of a home, job, or education. For example, various drug treatment courts in Florida (where they first got their start in Miami in 1989 through the efforts of Janet Reno, then Dade County's district attorney), Pennsylvania, California, and elsewhere employ a variety of strategies to break the cycle of addiction and recidivism by developing drug treatment plans for offenders. These treatment plans are tailored to the needs of the individual offender, and could include, among other things, writing an essay on what recovery means to the offender, participating in group therapy, job training, completing a GED program, or referral to a residential treatment center.

Similarly, juvenile drug treatment courts in North Dakota make young offenders "earn their freedom" by taking random drug screens, attending drug counseling sessions, participating in community service, and reporting regularly on their progress to the judge. If they stay clean and offense-free for two years, they may have their juvenile records expunged. In Texas, over 80 so-called Teen Courts provide an alternative forum to the regular juvenile courts. Young offenders can plead guilty and opt for a sentencing "trial" by other teens who play the roles of prosecutor, defense counsel, and the jurors who determine the sentence, which can include apologies, community service, the writing of research papers, and service as jurors in future Teen Court sessions.

Other news stories recount the successes of specialized domestic violence courts in Utah and Idaho in breaking the cycle of abuse by violent partners or parents and in aiding the recovery of their victims. The first specialized mental health court was established in 1997 in Florida to stop the revolving door for mentally ill persons who are often repeatedly arrested and sent to jail (which may worsen their health) instead of being offered treatment to address their underlying mental health problems. Since then, about 20 other such courts have been established and a dozen others have been proposed in various cities nationwide to divert mentally ill offenders into treatment programs.

APPLYING THERAPEUTIC JURISPRUDENCE PRINCIPLES IN THE NEW COURTS

* * *

Part II * * * provides tools and techniques, drawn from empirical research in psychology and the behavioral sciences, that judges can employ to achieve therapeutic outcomes in their courts. For example, one essay describes how "relationship factors" – that is, whether there is empathy, acceptance, and warmth in a client-counselor relationship – are among the most important contributors to any therapy's effecting a successful change in behavior. Another essay hypothesizes how aspects within the judge-defendant interaction – such as demeanor, speech, body language, and listening skill -- might create a "shared respect process" that could contribute to positive offender behavior.

In this book, the court is often portrayed as the critical first step in the process of therapy and behavioral change; hence, the authors advocate for judicial education in psychology, the science of human behavior. Two essays on the civil commitment process, for example, discuss how the commitment hearing itself can have therapeutic implications for both the patient and his or her caregivers and can increase the likelihood that any subsequent hospitalization and treatment will be successful.

Another pair of essays explores how permitting a nolo contendere plea, in which the offender is allowed to claim innocence while accepting punishment, might have anti-therapeutic consequences for both the offender and the victim. Sex offenders in particular may suffer from cognitive distortions, "denial and minimization" that they have done anything wrong. Therapeutically speaking, however, "[a]dmitting one's wrong is the first step toward moving past it . . . . Admissions are so central to therapy that most sex-offender programs refuse to admit offenders who deny any sexual conduct." A judge who accepts a nolo contendere plea may thereby allow the offender to remain in denial and to resist treatment while one who, instead, accepts a guilty plea and requires admission of guilt under oath could enable the offender to begin the process of "cognitive resturcturing" which can lead to successful recovery.

Several essays examine how judges can facilitate an offender's motivation to change by, among other things, taking advantage of the offender's "crisis" at the outset of court proceedings as a "teachable moment or therapeutic opportunity": instilling self-confidence that change is possible, respecting autonomy and avoiding paternalism and coercion, and engaging in reflective listening that helps offenders both to acknowledge their problems and to buy into solutions that they had an active part in shaping. Wexler also shows how techniques used by health care professionals to increase patient compliance with medical treatment might be applied in the judicial context to ensure compliance by insanity acquittees with court-ordered conditions for their release (such as medical or psychiatric treatment regimens). Winick separately elaborates on how a behavioral psychology technique called "behavioral contracting" can increase an individual's motivation to comply with a treatment or rehabilitative program when the individual has been involved in advance in setting the goals, rewards for success, and punishments for non-compliance.

Are judges being encouraged to go beyond the realistic limits of their expertise by applying research in psychology, therapy, and other behavioral sciences in their courtrooms? While this concern is surely legitimate, one essay is particularly noteworthy in attempting to dispel it. The author, Michael Clark, a Michigan social worker and consultant to drug treatment courts, discusses studies that suggest that experience and training make little difference in achieving effective therapeutic outcomes. In one study, for example, experienced therapists were no more helpful than untrained college professors, and in another study, novice graduate students were more effective than trained professionals at couples therapy. Evidently, effective therapy depends less on a particular therapeutic approach and more on a therapist's ability to promote certain factors common to all effective therapy, such as: employing the client as the fundamental "engine" of change, taking into account each client's personality, skills, and circumstances, establishing a trusting relationship with the client, and instilling hope and positive expectation in the client that therapy will work. Clark concludes that "the 'good news' of this common factors research is that therapeutic work is not just the domain of treatment professionals" and that judges, lawyers, and other court-related staff can use these techniques to induce positive behavior change.

DO THESE NEW APPROACHES WORK?

In these problem-solving courts, judges are viewed as active "therapeutic agents" who attempt to foster therapeutic outcomes for the offenders who come before them – whether by ending the drug addict's addiction, checking the violent propensities of a child or spouse abuser, or forestalling the "public acts of bizarreness" that formerly had resulted in repetitive criminal arrests of the mentally ill. These are high aspirations, but do these courts actually achieve their goal of "healing"?

To date, success has been gauged largely in anecdotal reports. Throughout this book, the need for more empirical research is freely and repeatedly acknowledged. There is some empirical evidence that these new approaches have reduced recidivism. Further, judges and participants have reported increased satisfaction with these new approaches. Some studies, however, indicate that in practice these courts may not consistently implement the therapeutic principles espoused in these essays but, instead, continue traditional approaches that provide negative sanctions more often than positive feedback.

Nevertheless, without waiting for all the empirical evidence to come in, some legislatures, courts, and other legal authorities have recently begun to "codify" TJ principles in their statutes, court procedures, and recommendations for legal system reform. For example, the Florida statute on drug treatment courts provides that such programs "shall include therapeutic jurisprudence principles." Commentary on Maryland's Family Divisions Performance Standard 5.1 acknowledges the "therapeutic potential of court intervention" in the lives of families and children. Expressly referencing therapeutic jurisprudence, judges have set forth key principles and components of effective domestic violence and mental health courts. One state court has declared in a "vision statement" that it would be guided by the principles of therapeutic jurisprudence. Impressively, in 2000, the Conference of Chief Justices and the Conference of State Court Administrators adopted a joint resolution in support of problem-solving courts and therapeutic jurisprudence principles.

CRITICS OF THERAPEUTIC JURISPRUDENCE AND THE NEW COURTS

So, what's not to love? Despite this enthusiastic reception in many legal circles, these problem-solving courts and TJ's role in them are not without critics. As acknowledged in these essays, questions are often raised about the preservation of individual rights in these new courts. Is the defendant's choice to opt out of the traditional courts and to participate in these new judicial programs after a guilty plea truly voluntary and not coerced? Do the lawyers who represent these defendants remain their zealous advocates? Do the judges sacrifice impartiality as they become more closely involved in the defendants' progress in therapy and in life generally? Do problem-solving courts cross the line into the executive branch of government when they so actively manage the defendants' behavior?

The authors do not duck such questions. Rather, they confront them squarely and make suggestions for addressing these potential problems. Winick and Wexler note the procedural due process concerns in the very first pages of the book and urge judges in problem-solving courts to heed the Supreme Court's decision in In re Gault, which "recognized the importance of not dropping the due process guard simply because of governmental 'good intentions,' such as a goal of rehabilitation rather than punishment." In several essays, the therapeutic benefits of procedural due process are offered alongside of the historic justifications of fairness to encourage judges to take care to ensure procedural justice. Showing respect for the offenders, allowing them a real voice in the proceedings, and evidencing genuine concern for their well-being increases litigants' sense of fair treatment. Furthermore, these judicial behaviors can encourage compliance with treatment regimens and adherence to other conduct requirements of continued participation.

Thus, for both philosophical and utilitarian reasons, the authors caution against cutting procedural corners in these new courts. Winick, for example, acknowledges the potential for a judge in a specialized domestic court to become cynical over time about those accused of violence and to over-identify with the victims of violence. He suggests that requesting a transfer to a court of general jurisdiction may become appropriate at that point.

TJ proponents do not claim that therapeutic jurisprudence should displace other perspectives on the law or that therapeutic effects should trump other values or considerations in our legal system, such as individual autonomy, constitutional rights, community safety, or economic efficiency. Their intentions are more modest: to encourage more empirical research to identify the therapeutic consequences of legal rules and legal procedures and more scholarly reflection on whether such rules and procedures should be changed, taking into account those consequences as well as other important social values.

THE ANALOGY TO HEALTH CARE

As the name implies, therapeutic jurisprudence borrows heavily from the experiences in health-related fields, and health care analogies appear throughout the book. At one point, courts are described as functioning as "trauma centers," serving families in crisis. Several essays promote the concept of "risk management" in the context of releasing potentially dangerous offenders back to the community. TJ's emphasis on interdisciplinary teamwork among court staff, social workers, and lawyers and on taking a holistic, coordinated approach to criminal offenders finds parallels in current interdisciplinary approaches to patient care and to public health in general. Indeed, the authors even suggest that TJ and the new problem-solving courts represent a public health approach to the problems of juvenile delinquency, drug addiction, domestic violence, and mental illness.

There is a striking similarity as well between many of TJ's core principles and the lessons coming out of the patient safety movement in health care. Both perspectives urge taking a systemic approach to problems in their respective arenas, be they medical errors or criminal behavior. Just as health care providers do a root cause analysis after a medical mishap has occurred in order to prevent similar accidents from occurring in the future, so do judges in problem-solving courts applying TJ principles seek to understand the root causes of an offender's behavior, to resolve the underlying psychological conditions or social circumstances that led to that behavior, and thereby to prevent future criminal behavior.

CONCLUSION

Are judges being encouraged to stray too far from their traditional roles in these new problem-solving courts? Some may think so. An alternative view is that this new book and the movement it promotes challenge judges to act like decent human beings who genuinely care about the citizens who appear before them, about their victims, about their families, and about their communities. Judges wield enormous power – both overtly and in subtle psychological ways – and TJ encourages them to use the power and prestige of their office responsibly and in the best interests of the parties as well as the public. The authors assembled in this worthy volume believe strongly in the law's potential to serve as a "healing agent" and seek to cast judges and lawyers in the roles of peacemakers and creative problem-solvers. Their vision deserves our serious consideration.

Note

At the 2003 Annual Meeting of the American Bar Association, U.S. Supreme Court Justice Anthony Kennedy gave a surprising speech.

> [S]peaking without notes in the grand setting of the San Francisco Opera House, Justice Kennedy delivered his now-famous verdict on the American criminal justice system: "Our resources are misspent, our punishments too severe, our sentences too long." In his characteristically low-key style, he challenged every lawyer there, and implicitly the entire legal profession, to take responsibility for a regime of punishments that he plainly believed had become morally indefensible.
>
> Noting the legal profession's "obsessive focus" on the process for determining guilt or innocence, Justice Kennedy asked us to consider what happens "when the door is locked against the prisoner":
>
>> We have a greater responsibility. As a profession, and as a people, we should know what happens after the prisoner is taken away. To be sure the prisoner has violated the social contract; to be sure he must be punished to vindicate the law; to acknowledge the suffering of the victim, and to deter future crimes. Still, the prisoner is a person; still, he or she is part of the family of humankind.

Justice Kennedy remarked on the sheer number of people incarcerated in this country, the disproportionate impact of incarceration on minority communities, and the dehumanizing impact of the prison experience. He asked the ABA "to help start a new public discussion about the prison system." He asked us to remember that the "two million inmates in the United States are human beings whose minds and spirits we must try to reach."

This was the same Justice Kennedy who, in the Term just completed, had provided the crucial fifth vote in the Court's rejection of a constitutional attack on California's three strikes law, *Lockyer v. Andrade*, 123 S.Ct. 1166 (2003); *Ewing v. California*, 123 S.Ct. 1179 (2003), and had written the opinion upholding the constitutionality of Michigan's restrictions on noncontact prison visits. (*Overton v. Bazetta*, 539 U.S. 126 (2003).) He seemed to be saying that American sentencing and corrections policies and practices have a moral dimension that cannot be reached through legal process, and he called upon "the energies and diverse talents of the entire Bar to address this matter."

Margaret Colgate Love, *The American Way of Punishment: ABA Justice Kennedy Commission Recommends Sweeping Changes,* 19 Criminal Justice 32, 32-33 (Winter 2005).

The ABA responded by appointing a commission, dubbed the "Kennedy Commission," to investigate the current state of criminal justice law, sentencing, and policy. One year after Justice Kennedy's speech, the Kennedy Commission issued a report recommending a list of policy reforms. Margaret Love, one of two reporters for the Commission, asserts that these reforms "call into question the most fundamental tenet of the war on crime: that locking people up is the linchpin of an effective crime control strategy." *Id.* at 34. Love further contends:

The reports document a growing official skepticism about the efficacy of imprisonment as a crime control strategy in light of mushrooming prison populations and skyrocketing prison budgets, and a developing consensus among state lawmakers and corrections officials that mandatory minimum sentences are not necessary to provide appropriately stiff prison sentences for serious and violent offenders. Increasingly in the states, considerations of efficiency and humanity combine to support less reliance on prison and more reliance on alternative rehabilitative strategies such as drug courts, intensive

> probation, and prison education and job training programs. Only the federal government, unconstrained by budgetary pressures, seems unwilling to question the old orthodoxy.

Id. at 35. Love concludes on a note of optimism:

> Surely, in time, the spirit of reform that is evidently abroad in the land will reach the federal government. For now, it seems hopeful that so many states have reached beyond the "tough on crime" vocabulary that framed the conversation during the 1980s and 1990s, and are experimenting with innovative approaches to crime control that recognize both the complexity of the causes of crime, and the limited usefulness of incarceration in discouraging it. Like Justice Kennedy, many states have evidently come to understand that the goal of the criminal justice system must be to reunite offenders with the community that has been injured, not to create a class of social outcasts whose reduced legal status forever sets them apart from the family of humankind.

Id.

Is "therapeutic jurisprudence" adequate to addressing the problems Justice Kennedy and the ABA have identified? Is it consistent with the American adversarial system? For some critical commentary on therapeutic jurisprudence, *see, e.g.*, James L. Nolan, Jr., *Redefining Criminal Courts: Problem-Solving and the Meaning of Justice*, 40 Am. Crim. L. Rev.1541 (2003); *see also* Timothy Casey, *When Good Intentions Are Not Enough: Problem-Solving Courts and the Impending Crisis of Legitimacy,* 57 SMU L. Rev.1459 (2004).

Appendix

Model Penal Code

PART I. GENERAL PROVISIONS
ARTICLE 1. PRELIMINARY
...
Section 1.02. Purposes; Principles of Construction.

(1) The general purposes of the provisions governing the definition of offenses are:

(a) to forbid and prevent conduct that unjustifiably and inexcusably inflicts or threatens substantial harm to individual or public interests;
(b) to subject to public control persons whose conduct indicates that they are disposed to commit crimes;
(c) to safeguard conduct that is without fault from condemnation as criminal;
(d) to give fair warning of the nature of the conduct declared to constitute an offense;
(e) to differentiate on reasonable grounds between serious and minor offenses.

(2) The general purposes of the provisions governing the sentencing and treatment of offenders are:

(a) to prevent the commission of offenses;
(b) to promote the correction and rehabilitation of offenders;
(c) to safeguard offenders against excessive, disproportionate or arbitrary punishment;
(d) to give fair warning of the nature of the sentences that may be imposed on conviction of an offense;
(e) to differentiate among offenders with a view to a just individualization in their treatment;
(f) to define, coordinate and harmonize the powers, duties and functions of the courts and of administrative officers and agencies responsible for dealing with

offenders;

(g) to advance the use of generally accepted scientific methods and knowledge in the sentencing and treatment of offenders;

(h) to integrate responsibility for the administration of the correctional system in a State Department of Correction [or other single department or agency].

(3) The provisions of the Code shall be construed according to the fair import of their terms but when the language is susceptible of differing constructions it shall be interpreted to further the general purposes stated in this Section and the special purposes of the particular provision involved. The discretionary powers conferred by the Code shall be exercised in accordance with the criteria stated in the Code and, insofar as such criteria are not decisive, to further the general purposes stated in this Section. * * *

Section 1.04. Classes of Crimes; Violations.

(1) An offense defined by this Code or by any other statute of this State, for which a sentence of [death or of] imprisonment is authorized, constitutes a crime. Crimes are classified as felonies, misdemeanors or petty misdemeanors.

(2) A crime is a felony if it is so designated in this Code or if persons convicted thereof may be sentenced [to death or] to imprisonment for a term that, apart from an extended term, is in excess of one year.

(3) A crime is a misdemeanor if it is so designated in this Code or in a statute other than this Code enacted subsequent thereto.

(4) A crime is a petty misdemeanor if it is so designated in this Code or in a statute other than this Code enacted subsequent thereto or if it is defined by a statute other than this Code that now provides that persons convicted thereof may be sentenced to imprisonment for a term of which the maximum is less than one year.

(5) An offense defined by this Code or by any other statute of this State constitutes a violation if it is so designated in this Code or in the law defining the offense or if no other sentence than a fine, or fine and forfeiture or other civil penalty is authorized upon conviction or if it is defined by a statute other than this Code that now provides that the offense shall not constitute a crime. A violation does not constitute a crime and conviction of a violation shall not give rise to any disability or legal disadvantage based on conviction of a criminal offense.

(6) Any offense declared by law to constitute a crime, without specification of the grade thereof or of the sentence authorized upon conviction, is a

misdemeanor.

(7) An offense defined by any statute of this State other than this Code shall be classified as provided in this Section and the sentence that may be imposed upon conviction thereof shall hereafter be governed by this Code. * * *

Section 1.13. General Definitions.

In this Code, unless a different meaning plainly is required:

(1) "statute" includes the Constitution and a local law or ordinance of a political subdivision of the State;

(2) "act" or "action" means a bodily movement whether voluntary or involuntary;

(3) "voluntary" has the meaning specified in Section 2.01;

(4) "omission" means a failure to act;

(5) "conduct" means an action or omission and its accompanying state of mind, or, where relevant, a series of acts and omissions;

(6) "actor" includes, where relevant, a person guilty of an omission;

(7) "acted" includes, where relevant, "omitted to act";

(8) "person," "he" and "actor" include any natural person and, where relevant, a corporation or an unincorporated association;

(9) "element of an offense" means (i) such conduct or (ii) such attendant circumstances or (iii) such a result of conduct as

(a) is included in the description of the forbidden conduct in the definition of the offense; or
(b) establishes the required kind of culpability; or
(c) negatives an excuse or justification for such conduct; or
(d) negatives a defense under the statute of limitations; or
(e) establishes jurisdiction or venue;

(10) "material element of an offense" means an element that does not relate exclusively to the statute of limitations, jurisdiction, venue, or to any other matter similarly unconnected with (i) the harm or evil, incident to conduct, sought to be prevented by the law defining the offense, or (ii) the existence of

a justification or excuse for such conduct;

(11) "purposely" has the meaning specified in Section 2.02 and equivalent terms such as "with purpose," "designed" or "with design" have the same meaning;

(12) "intentionally" or "with intent" means purposely;

(13) "knowingly" has the meaning specified in Section 2.02 and equivalent terms such as "knowing" or "with knowledge" have the same meaning;

(14) "recklessly" has the meaning specified in Section 2.02 and equivalent terms such as "recklessness" or "with recklessness" have the same meaning;

(15) "negligently" has the meaning specified in Section 2.02 and equivalent terms such as "negligence" or "with negligence" have the same meaning;

(16) "reasonably believes" or "reasonable belief" designates a belief that the actor is not reckless or negligent in holding.

ARTICLE 2. GENERAL PRINCIPLES OF LIABILITY

Section 2.01 Requirement of Voluntary Act; Omission as Basis of Liability; Possession as an Act.

(1) A person is not guilty of an offense unless his liability is based on conduct that includes a voluntary act or the omission to perform an act of which he is physically capable.

(2) The following are not voluntary acts within the meaning of this Section:

(a) a reflex or convulsion;
(b) a bodily movement during unconsciousness or sleep;
(c) conduct during hypnosis or resulting from hypnotic suggestion;
(d) a bodily movement that otherwise is not a product of the effort or determination of the actor, either conscious or habitual.

(3) Liability for the commission of an offense may not be based on an omission unaccompanied by action unless:

(a) the omission is expressly made sufficient by the law defining the offense; or
(b) a duty to perform the omitted act is otherwise imposed by law.

(4) Possession is an act, within the meaning of this Section, if the possessor knowingly procured or received the thing possessed or was aware of his control

thereof for a sufficient period to have been able to terminate his possession.

Section 2.02. General Requirements of Culpability.

(1) *Minimum Requirements of Culpability*. Except as provided in Section 2.05, a person is not guilty of an offense unless he acted purposely, knowingly, recklessly or negligently, as the law may require, with respect to each material element of the offense.

(2) *Kinds of Culpability Defined.*

(a) *Purposely.*

A person acts purposely with respect to a material element of an offense when:

(i) if the element involves the nature of his conduct or a result thereof, it is his conscious object to engage in conduct of that nature or to cause such a result; and
(ii) if the element involves the attendant circumstances, he is aware of the existence of such circumstances or he believes or hopes that they exist.

(b) *Knowingly.*

A person acts knowingly with respect to a material element of an offense when:

(i) if the element involves the nature of his conduct or the attendant circumstances, he is aware that his conduct is of that nature or that such circumstances exist; and
(ii) if the element involves a result of his conduct, he is aware that it is practically certain that his conduct will cause such a result.

(c) *Recklessly.*

A person acts recklessly with respect to a material element of an offense when he consciously disregards a substantial and unjustifiable risk that the material element exists or will result from his conduct. The risk must be of such a nature and degree that, considering the nature and purpose of the actor's conduct and the circumstances known to him, its disregard involves a gross deviation from the standard of conduct that a law-abiding person would observe in the actor's situation.

(d) *Negligently.*

A person acts negligently with respect to a material element of an offense when he should be aware of a substantial and unjustifiable risk that the material element exists or will result from his conduct. The risk must be of such a nature and degree that the actor's failure to perceive it, considering the nature and purpose of his conduct and the circumstances known to him, involves a gross deviation from the standard of care that a reasonable person would observe in the actor's situation.

(3) *Culpability Required Unless Otherwise Provided.* When the culpability sufficient to establish a material element of an offense is not prescribed by law, such element is established if a person acts purposely, knowingly or recklessly with respect thereto.

(4) *Prescribed Culpability Requirement Applies to All Material Elements.* When the law defining an offense prescribes the kind of culpability that is sufficient for the commission of an offense, without distinguishing among the material elements thereof, such provision shall apply to all the material elements of the offense, unless a contrary purpose plainly appears.

(5) *Substitutes for Negligence, Recklessness and Knowledge.* When the law provides that negligence suffices to establish an element of an offense, such element also is established if a person acts purposely, knowingly or recklessly. When recklessness suffices to establish an element, such element also is established if a person acts purposely or knowingly. When acting knowingly suffices to establish an element, such element also is established if a person acts purposely.

(6) *Requirement of Purpose Satisfied if Purpose Is Conditional.* When a particular purpose is an element of an offense, the element is established although such purpose is conditional, unless the condition negatives the harm or evil sought to be prevented by the law defining the offense.

(7) *Requirement of Knowledge Satisfied by Knowledge of High Probability.* When knowledge of the existence of a particular fact is an element of an offense, such knowledge is established if a person is aware of a high probability of its existence, unless he actually believes that it does not exist.

(8) *Requirement of Wilfulness Satisfied by Acting Knowingly.* A requirement that an offense be committed wilfully is satisfied if a person acts knowingly with respect to the material elements of the offense, unless a purpose to impose further requirements appears.

(9) *Culpability as to Illegality of Conduct.* Neither knowledge nor recklessness or negligence as to whether conduct constitutes an offense or as to the existence, meaning or application of the law determining the elements of an offense is an

element of such offense, unless the definition of the offense or the Code so provides.

(10) *Culpability as Determinant of Grade of Offense.* When the grade or degree of an offense depends on whether the offense is committed purposely, knowingly, recklessly or negligently, its grade or degree shall be the lowest for which the determinative kind of culpability is established with respect to any material element of the offense.

Section 2.03. Causal Relationship Between Conduct and Result; Divergence Between Result Designed or Contemplated and Actual Result or Between Probable and Actual Result.

(1) Conduct is the cause of a result when:

(a) it is an antecedent but for which the result in question would not have occurred; and
(b) the relationship between the conduct and result satisfies any additional causal requirements imposed by the Code or by the law defining the offense.

(2) When purposely or knowingly causing a particular result is an element of an offense, the element is not established if the actual result is not within the purpose or the contemplation of the actor unless:

(a) the actual result differs from that designed or contemplated, as the case may be, only in the respect that a different person or different property is injured or affected or that the injury or harm designed or contemplated would have been more serious or more extensive than that caused; or
(b) the actual result involves the same kind of injury or harm as that designed or contemplated and is not too remote or accidental in its occurrence to have a [just] bearing on the actor's liability or on the gravity of his offense.

(3) When recklessly or negligently causing a particular result is an element of an offense, the element is not established if the actual result is not within the risk of which the actor is aware or, in the case of negligence, of which he should be aware unless:

(a) the actual result differs from the probable result only in the respect that a different person or different property is injured or affected or that the probable injury or harm would have been more serious or more extensive than that caused; or
(b) the actual result involves the same kind of injury or harm as the probable result and is not too remote or accidental in its occurrence to have a [just] bearing on the actor's liability or on the gravity of his offense.

(4) When causing a particular result is a material element of an offense for which absolute liability is imposed by law, the element is not established unless the actual result is a probable consequence of the actor's conduct.

Section 2.04. Ignorance or Mistake.

(1) Ignorance or mistake as to a matter of fact or law is a defense if:

(a) the ignorance or mistake negatives the purpose, knowledge, belief, recklessness or negligence required to establish a material element of the offense; or
(b) the law provides that the state of mind established by such ignorance or mistake constitutes a defense.

(2) Although ignorance or mistake would otherwise afford a defense to the offense charged, the defense is not available if the defendant would be guilty of another offense had the situation been as he supposed. In such case, however, the ignorance or mistake of the defendant shall reduce the grade and degree of the offense of which he may be convicted to those of the offense of which he would be guilty had the situation been as he supposed.

(3) A belief that conduct does not legally constitute an offense is a defense to a prosecution for that offense based upon such conduct when:

(a) the statute or other enactment defining the offense is not known to the actor and has not been published or otherwise reasonably made available prior to the conduct alleged; or
(b) he acts in reasonable reliance upon an official statement of the law, afterward determined to be invalid or erroneous, contained in (i) a statute or other enactment; (ii) a judicial decision, opinion or judgment; (iii) an administrative order or grant of permission; or (iv) an official interpretation of the public officer or body charged by law with responsibility for the interpretation, administration or enforcement of the law defining the offense.

(4) The defendant must prove a defense arising under Subsection (3) of this Section by a preponderance of evidence.

Section 2.05. When Culpability Requirements Are Inapplicable to Violations and to Offenses Defined by Other Statutes; Effect of Absolute Liability in Reducing Grade of Offense to Violation.

(1) The requirements of culpability prescribed by Sections 2.01 and 2.02 do not apply to:

(a) offenses that constitute violations, unless the requirement involved is included in the definition of the offense or the Court determines that its application is consistent with effective enforcement of the law defining the offense; or

(b) offenses defined by statutes other than the Code, insofar as a legislative purpose to impose absolute liability for such offenses or with respect to any material element thereof plainly appears.

(2) Notwithstanding any other provision of existing law and unless a subsequent statute otherwise provides:

(a) when absolute liability is imposed with respect to any material element of an offense defined by a statute other than the Code and a conviction is based upon such liability, the offense constitutes a violation; and

(b) although absolute liability is imposed by law with respect to one or more of the material elements of an offense defined by a statute other than the Code, the culpable commission of the offense may be charged and proved, in which event negligence with respect to such elements constitutes sufficient culpability and the classification of the offense and the sentence that may be imposed therefor upon conviction are determined by Section 1.04 and Article 6 of the Code.

Section 2.06. Liability for Conduct of Another; Complicity.

(1) A person is guilty of an offense if it is committed by his own conduct or by the conduct of another person for which he is legally accountable, or both.

(2) A person is legally accountable for the conduct of another person when:

(a) acting with the kind of culpability that is sufficient for the commission of the offense, he causes an innocent or irresponsible person to engage in such conduct; or

(b) he is made accountable for the conduct of such other person by the Code or by the law defining the offense; or

(c) he is an accomplice of such other person in the commission of the offense.

(3) A person is an accomplice of another person in the commission of an offense if:

(a) with the purpose of promoting or facilitating the commission of the offense, he

(i) solicits such other person to commit it, or

(ii) aids or agrees or attempts to aid such other person in planning or committing it, or

(iii) having a legal duty to prevent the commission of the offense, fails to make proper effort so to do; or

(b) his conduct is expressly declared by law to establish his complicity.

(4) When causing a particular result is an element of an offense, an accomplice in the conduct causing such result is an accomplice in the commission of that offense if he acts with the kind of culpability, if any, with respect to that result that is sufficient for the commission of the offense.

(5) A person who is legally incapable of committing a particular offense himself may be guilty thereof if it is committed by the conduct of another person for which he is legally accountable, unless such liability is inconsistent with the purpose of the provision establishing his incapacity.

(6) Unless otherwise provided by the Code or by the law defining the offense, a person is not an accomplice in an offense committed by another person if:

(a) he is a victim of that offense; or

(b) the offense is so defined that his conduct is inevitably incident to its commission; or

(c) he terminates his complicity prior to the commission of the offense and

(i) wholly deprives it of effectiveness in the commission of the offense; or

(ii) gives timely warning to the law enforcement authorities or otherwise makes proper effort to prevent the commission of the offense.

(7) An accomplice may be convicted on proof of the commission of the offense and of his complicity therein, though the person claimed to have committed the offense has not been prosecuted or convicted or has been convicted of a different offense or degree of offense or has an immunity to prosecution or conviction or has been acquitted.

Section 2.07. Liability of Corporations, Unincorporated Associations and Persons Acting, or Under a Duty to Act, in Their Behalf.

(1) A corporation may be convicted of the commission of an offense if:

(a) the offense is a violation or the offense is defined by a statute other than the Code in which a legislative purpose to impose liability on corporations plainly appears and the conduct is performed by an agent of the corporation acting in behalf of the corporation within the scope of his office or employment, except that if the law defining the offense designates the agents for whose conduct the corporation is accountable or the circumstances under which it is accountable, such provisions shall apply; or

(b) the offense consists of an omission to discharge a specific duty of affirmative performance imposed on corporations by law; or

(c) the commission of the offense was authorized, requested, commanded, performed or recklessly tolerated by the board of directors or by a high managerial agent acting in behalf of the corporation within the scope of his office or employment.

(2) When absolute liability is imposed for the commission of an offense, a legislative purpose to impose liability on a corporation shall be assumed, unless the contrary plainly appears.

(3) An unincorporated association may be convicted of the commission of an offense if:

(a) the offense is defined by a statute other than the Code that expressly provides for the liability of such an association and the conduct is performed by an agent of the association acting in behalf of the association within the scope of his office or employment, except that if the law defining the offense designates the agents for whose conduct the association is accountable or the circumstances under which it is accountable, such provisions shall apply; or
(b) the offense consists of an omission to discharge a specific duty of affirmative performance imposed on associations by law.

(4) As used in this Section:

(a) "corporation" does not include an entity organized as or by a governmental agency for the execution of a governmental program;
(b) "agent" means any director, officer, servant, employee or other person authorized to act in behalf of the corporation or association and, in the case of an unincorporated association, a member of such association;
(c) "high managerial agent" means an officer of a corporation or an unincorporated association, or, in the case of a partnership, a partner, or any other agent of a corporation or association having duties of such responsibility that his conduct may fairly be assumed to represent the policy of the corporation or association.

(5) In any prosecution of a corporation or an unincorporated association for the commission of an offense included within the terms of Subsection (1)(a) or Subsection (3)(a) of this Section, other than an offense for which absolute liability has been imposed, it shall be a defense if the defendant proves by a preponderance of evidence that the high managerial agent having supervisory responsibility over the subject matter of the offense employed due diligence to prevent its commission. This paragraph shall not apply if it is plainly inconsistent with the legislative purpose in defining the particular offense.

(6)(a) A person is legally accountable for any conduct he performs or causes to be performed in the name of the corporation or an unincorporated association or in its behalf to the same extent as if it were performed in his own name or behalf.

(b) Whenever a duty to act is imposed by law upon a corporation or an unincorporated association, any agent of the corporation or association having primary responsibility for the discharge of the duty is legally accountable for a reckless omission to perform the required act to the same extent as if the duty were imposed by law directly upon himself.

(c) When a person is convicted of an offense by reason of his legal accountability for the conduct of a corporation or an unincorporated association, he is subject to the sentence authorized by law when a natural person is convicted of an offense of the grade and the degree involved.

Section 2.08. Intoxication.

(1) Except as provided in Subsection (4) of this Section, intoxication of the actor is not a defense unless it negatives an element of the offense.

(2) When recklessness establishes an element of the offense, if the actor, due to self-induced intoxication, is unaware of a risk of which he would have been aware had he been sober, such unawareness is immaterial.

(3) Intoxication does not, in itself, constitute mental disease within the meaning of Section 4.01.

(4) Intoxication that (a) is not self-induced or (b) is pathological is an affirmative defense if by reason of such intoxication the actor at the time of his conduct lacks substantial capacity either to appreciate its criminality [wrongfulness] or to conform his conduct to the requirements of law.

(5) *Definitions.* In this Section unless a different meaning plainly is required:

(a) "intoxication" means a disturbance of mental or physical capacities resulting from the introduction of substances into the body;

(b) "self-induced intoxication" means intoxication caused by substances that the actor knowingly introduces into his body, the tendency of which to cause intoxication he knows or ought to know, unless he introduces them pursuant to medical advice or under such circumstances as would afford a defense to a charge of crime;

(c) "pathological intoxication" means intoxication grossly excessive in degree, given the amount of the intoxicant, to which the actor does not know he is susceptible.

Section 2.09. Duress.

(1) It is an affirmative defense that the actor engaged in the conduct charged to constitute an offense because he was coerced to do so by the use of, or a threat to use, unlawful force against his person or the person of another, that a person of reasonable firmness in his situation would have been unable to resist.

(2) The defense provided by this Section is unavailable if the actor recklessly placed himself in a situation in which it was probable that he would be subjected to duress. The defense is also unavailable if he was negligent in placing himself in such a situation, whenever negligence suffices to establish culpability for the offense charged.

(3) It is not a defense that a woman acted on the command of her husband, unless she acted under such coercion as would establish a defense under this Section. [The presumption that a woman acting in the presence of her husband is coerced is abolished.]

(4) When the conduct of the actor would otherwise be justifiable under Section 3.02, this Section does not preclude such defense.

Section 2.10. Military Orders.

It is an affirmative defense that the actor, in engaging in the conduct charged to constitute an offense, does no more than execute an order of his superior in the armed services that he does not know to be unlawful.

Section 2.11. Consent.

(1) *In General.* The consent of the victim to conduct charged to constitute an offense or to the result thereof is a defense if such consent negatives an element of the offense or precludes the infliction of the harm or evil sought to be prevented by the law defining the offense.

(2) *Consent to Bodily Injury.* When conduct is charged to constitute an offense because it causes or threatens bodily injury, consent to such conduct or to the infliction of such injury is a defense if:

(a) the bodily injury consented to or threatened by the conduct consented to is not serious; or
(b) the conduct and the injury are reasonably foreseeable hazards of joint participation in a lawful athletic contest or competitive sport or other concerted activity not forbidden by law; or
(c) the consent establishes a justification for the conduct under Article 3 of the

Code.

(3) *Ineffective Consent.* Unless otherwise provided by the Code or by the law defining the offense, assent does not constitute consent if:

(a) it is given by a person who is legally incompetent to authorize the conduct charged to constitute the offense; or
(b) it is given by a person who by reason of youth, mental disease or defect or intoxication is manifestly unable or known by the actor to be unable to make a reasonable judgment as to the nature or harmfulness of the conduct charged to constitute the offense; or
(c) it is given by a person whose improvident consent is sought to be prevented by the law defining the offense; or
(d) it is induced by force, duress or deception of a kind sought to be prevented by the law defining the offense.

Section 2.12. De Minimis Infractions.

The Court shall dismiss a prosecution if, having regard to the nature of the conduct charged to constitute an offense and the nature of the attendant circumstances, it finds that the defendant's conduct:

(1) was within a customary license or tolerance, neither expressly negatived by the person whose interest was infringed nor inconsistent with the purpose of the law defining the offense; or
(2) did not actually cause or threaten the harm or evil sought to be prevented by the law defining the offense or did so only to an extent too trivial to warrant the condemnation of conviction; or
(3) presents such other extenuations that it cannot reasonably be regarded as envisaged by the legislature in forbidding the offense.

The Court shall not dismiss a prosecution under Subsection (3) of this Section without filing a written statement of its reasons.

Section 2.13. Entrapment.

(1) A public law enforcement official or a person acting in cooperation with such an official perpetrates an entrapment if for the purpose of obtaining evidence of the commission of an offense, he induces or encourages another person to engage in conduct constituting such offense by either:

(a) making knowingly false representations designed to induce the belief that such conduct is not prohibited; or
(b) employing methods of persuasion or inducement that create a substantial risk

that such an offense will be committed by persons other than those who are ready to commit it.

(2) Except as provided in Subsection (3) of this Section, a person prosecuted for an offense shall be acquitted if he proves by a preponderance of evidence that his conduct occurred in response to an entrapment. The issue of entrapment shall be tried by the Court in the absence of the jury.

(3) The defense afforded by this Section is unavailable when causing or threatening bodily injury is an element of the offense charged and the prosecution is based on conduct causing or threatening such injury to a person other than the person perpetrating the entrapment.

ARTICLE 3. GENERAL PRINCIPLES OF JUSTIFICATION

Section 3.01. Justification an Affirmative Defense; Civil Remedies Unaffected.

(1) In any prosecution based on conduct that is justifiable under this Article, justification is an affirmative defense.

(2) The fact that conduct is justifiable under this Article does not abolish or impair any remedy for such conduct that is available in any civil action.

Section 3.02. Justification Generally: Choice of Evils.

(1) Conduct that the actor believes to be necessary to avoid a harm or evil to himself or to another is justifiable, provided that:

(a) the harm or evil sought to be avoided by such conduct is greater than that sought to be prevented by the law defining the offense charged; and
(b) neither the Code nor other law defining the offense provides exceptions or defenses dealing with the specific situation involved; and
(c) a legislative purpose to exclude the justification claimed does not otherwise plainly appear.

(2) When the actor was reckless or negligent in bringing about the situation requiring a choice of harms or evils or in appraising the necessity for his conduct, the justification afforded by this Section is unavailable in a prosecution for any offense for which recklessness or negligence, as the case may be, suffices to establish culpability.

Section 3.03. Execution of Public Duty.

(1) Except as provided in Subsection (2) of this Section, conduct is justifiable when it is required or authorized by:

(a) the law defining the duties or functions of a public officer or the assistance to be rendered to such officer in the performance of his duties; or
(b) the law governing the execution of legal process; or
(c) the judgment or order of a competent court or tribunal; or
(d) the law governing the armed services or the lawful conduct of war; or
(e) any other provision of law imposing a public duty.

(2) The other sections of this Article apply to:

(a) the use of force upon or toward the person of another for any of the purposes dealt with in such sections; and
(b) the use of deadly force for any purpose, unless the use of such force is otherwise expressly authorized by law or occurs in the lawful conduct of war.

(3) The justification afforded by Subsection (1) of this Section applies:

(a) when the actor believes his conduct to be required or authorized by the judgment or direction of a competent court or tribunal or in the lawful execution of legal process, notwithstanding lack of jurisdiction of the court or defect in the legal process; and
(b) when the actor believes his conduct to be required or authorized to assist a public officer in the performance of his duties, notwithstanding that the officer exceeded his legal authority.

Section 3.04. Use of Force in Self-Protection.

(1) *Use of Force Justifiable for Protection of the Person.* Subject to the provisions of this Section and of Section 3.09, the use of force upon or toward another person is justifiable when the actor believes that such force is immediately necessary for the purpose of protecting himself against the use of unlawful force by such other person on the present occasion.

(2) *Limitations on Justifying Necessity for Use of Force.*

(a) The use of force is not justifiable under this Section:
(i) to resist an arrest that the actor knows is being made by a peace officer, although the arrest is unlawful; or
(ii) to resist force used by the occupier or possessor of property or by another person on his behalf, where the actor knows that the person using the force is

doing so under a claim of right to protect the property, except that this limitation shall not apply if:

(A) the actor is a public officer acting in the performance of his duties or a person lawfully assisting him therein or a person making or assisting in a lawful arrest; or

(B) the actor has been unlawfully dispossessed of the property and is making a re-entry or recaption justified by Section 3.06; or

(C) the actor believes that such force is necessary to protect himself against death or serious bodily injury.

(b) The use of deadly force is not justifiable under this Section unless the actor believes that such force is necessary to protect himself against death, serious bodily injury, kidnapping or sexual intercourse compelled by force or threat; nor is it justifiable if:

(i) the actor, with the purpose of causing death or serious bodily injury, provoked the use of force against himself in the same encounter; or

(ii) the actor knows that he can avoid the necessity of using such force with complete safety by retreating or by surrendering possession of a thing to a person asserting a claim of right thereto or by complying with a demand that he abstain from any action that he has no duty to take, except that:

(A) the actor is not obliged to retreat from his dwelling or place of work, unless he was the initial aggressor or is assailed in his place of work by another person whose place of work the actor knows it to be; and

(B) a public officer justified in using force in the performance of his duties or a person justified in using force in his assistance or a person justified in using force in making an arrest or preventing an escape is not obliged to desist from efforts to perform such duty, effect such arrest or prevent such escape because of resistance or threatened resistance by or on behalf of the person against whom such action is directed.

(c) Except as required by paragraphs (a) and (b) of this Subsection, a person employing protective force may estimate the necessity thereof under the circumstances as he believes them to be when the force is used, without retreating, surrendering possession, doing any other act that he has no legal duty to do or abstaining from any lawful action.

(3) *Use of Confinement as Protective Force.* The justification afforded by this Section extends to the use of confinement as protective force only if the actor takes all reasonable measures to terminate the confinement as soon as he knows that he safely can, unless the person confined has been arrested on a charge of crime.

Section 3.05. Use of Force for the Protection of Other Persons.

(1) Subject to the provisions of this Section and of Section 3.09, the use of force upon or toward the person of another is justifiable to protect a third person

when:

(a) the actor would be justified under Section 3.04 in using such force to protect himself against the injury he believes to be threatened to the person whom he seeks to protect; and

(b) under the circumstances as the actor believes them to be, the person whom he seeks to protect would be justified in using such protective force; and

(c) the actor believes that his intervention is necessary for the protection of such other person.

(2) Notwithstanding Subsection (1) of this Section:

(a) when the actor would be obliged under Section 3.04 to retreat, to surrender the possession of a thing or to comply with a demand before using force in self-protection, he is not obliged to do so before using force for the protection of another person, unless he knows that he can thereby secure the complete safety of such other person; and

(b) when the person whom the actor seeks to protect would be obliged under Section 3.04 to retreat, to surrender the possession of a thing or to comply with a demand if he knew that he could obtain complete safety by so doing, the actor is obliged to try to cause him to do so before using force in his protection if the actor knows that he can obtain complete safety in that way; and

(c) neither the actor nor the person whom he seeks to protect is obliged to retreat when in the other's dwelling or place of work to any greater extent than in his own.

Section 3.06. Use of Force for Protection of Property.

(1) *Use of Force Justifiable for Protection of Property.* Subject to the provisions of this Section and of Section 3.09, the use of force upon or toward the person of another is justifiable when the actor believes that such force is immediately necessary:

(a) to prevent or terminate an unlawful entry or other trespass upon land or a trespass against or the unlawful carrying away of tangible, movable property, provided that such land or movable property is, or is believed by the actor to be, in his possession or in the possession of another person for whose protection he acts; or

(b) to effect an entry or re-entry upon land or to retake tangible movable property, provided that the actor believes that he or the person by whose authority he acts or a person from whom he or such other person derives title was unlawfully dispossessed of such land or movable property and is entitled to possession, and provided, further, that:

(i) the force is used immediately or on fresh pursuit after such dispossession; or

(ii) the actor believes that the person against whom he uses force has no claim of right to the possession of the property and, in the case of land, the circumstances, as the actor believes them to be, are of such urgency that it would be an exceptional hardship to postpone the entry or re-entry until a court order is obtained.

(2) *Meaning of Possession.* For the purposes of Subsection (1) of this Section:

(a) a person who has parted with the custody of property to another who refuses to restore it to him is no longer in possession, unless the property is movable and was and still is located on land in his possession;

(b) a person who has been dispossessed of land does not regain possession thereof merely by setting foot thereon;

(c) a person who has a license to use or occupy real property is deemed to be in possession thereof except against the licensor acting under claim of right.

(3) *Limitations on Justifiable Use of Force.*

(a) *Request to Desist.* The use of force is justifiable under this Section only if the actor first requests the person against whom such force is used to desist from his interference with the property, unless the actor believes that:

(i) such request would be useless; or

(ii) it would be dangerous to himself or another person to make the request; or

(iii) substantial harm will be done to the physical condition of the property that is sought to be protected before the request can effectively be made.

(b) *Exclusion of Trespasser.* The use of force to prevent or terminate a trespass is not justifiable under this Section if the actor knows that the exclusion of the trespasser will expose him to substantial danger of serious bodily injury.

(c) *Resistance of Lawful Re-entry or Recaption.* The use of force to prevent an entry or re-entry upon land or the recaption of movable property is not justifiable under this Section, although the actor believes that such re-entry or recaption is unlawful, if:

(i) the re-entry or recaption is made by or on behalf of a person who was actually dispossessed of the property; and

(ii) it is otherwise justifiable under Subsection (1)(b) of this Section.

(d) *Use of Deadly Force.* The use of deadly force is not justifiable under this Section unless the actor believes that:

(i) the person against whom the force is used is attempting to dispossess him of his dwelling otherwise than under a claim of right to its possession; or

(ii) the person against whom the force is used is attempting to commit or consummate arson, burglary, robbery or other felonious theft or property destruction and either:

(A) has employed or threatened deadly force against or in the presence of the actor; or

(B) the use of force other than deadly force to prevent the commission or the consummation of the crime would expose the actor or another in his presence to substantial danger of serious bodily injury.

(4) *Use of Confinement as Protective Force.* The justification afforded by this Section extends to the use of confinement as protective force only if the actor takes all reasonable measures to terminate the confinement as soon as he knows that he can do so with safety to the property, unless the person confined has been arrested on a charge of crime.

(5) *Use of Device to Protect Property.* The justification afforded by this Section extends to the use of a device for the purpose of protecting property only if:

(a) the device is not designed to cause or known to create a substantial risk of causing death or serious bodily injury; and
(b) the use of the particular device to protect the property from entry or trespass is reasonable under the circumstances, as the actor believes them to be; and
(c) the device is one customarily used for such a purpose or reasonable care is taken to make known to probable intruders the fact that it is used.

(6) *Use of Force to Pass Wrongful Obstructor.* The use of force to pass a person whom the actor believes to be purposely or knowingly and unjustifiably obstructing the actor from going to a place to which he may lawfully go is justifiable, provided that:

(a) the actor believes that the person against whom he uses force has no claim of right to obstruct the actor; and
(b) the actor is not being obstructed from entry or movement on land that he knows to be in the possession or custody of the person obstructing him, or in the possession or custody of another person by whose authority the obstructor acts, unless the circumstances, as the actor believes them to be, are of such urgency that it would not be reasonable to postpone the entry or movement on such land until a court order is obtained; and
(c) the force used is not greater than would be justifiable if the person obstructing the actor were using force against him to prevent his passage.

Section 3.07. Use of Force in Law Enforcement.

(1) *Use of Force Justifiable to Effect an Arrest.* Subject to the provisions of this Section and of Section 3.09, the use of force upon or toward the person of another is justifiable when the actor is making or assisting in making an arrest and the actor believes that such force is immediately necessary to effect a lawful arrest.

(2) *Limitations on the Use of Force.*

(a) The use of force is not justifiable under this Section unless:

(i) the actor makes known the purpose of the arrest or believes that it is otherwise known by or cannot reasonably be made known to the person to be arrested; and

(ii) when the arrest is made under a warrant, the warrant is valid or believed by the actor to be valid.

(b) The use of deadly force is not justifiable under this Section unless:

(i) the arrest is for a felony; and

(ii) the person effecting the arrest is authorized to act as a peace officer or is assisting a person whom he believes to be authorized to act as a peace officer; and

(iii) the actor believes that the force employed creates no substantial risk of injury to innocent persons; and

(iv) the actor believes that:

(A) the crime for which the arrest is made involved conduct including the use or threatened use of deadly force; or

(B) there is a substantial risk that the person to be arrested will cause death or serious bodily injury if his apprehension is delayed.

(3) *Use of Force to Prevent Escape from Custody.* The use of force to prevent the escape of an arrested person from custody is justifiable when the force could justifiably have been employed to effect the arrest under which the person is in custody, except that a guard or other person authorized to act as a peace officer is justified in using any force, including deadly force, that he believes to be immediately necessary to prevent the escape of a person from a jail, prison, or other institution for the detention of persons charged with or convicted of a crime.

(4) *Use of Force by Private Person Assisting an Unlawful Arrest.*

(a) A private person who is summoned by a peace officer to assist in effecting an unlawful arrest, is justified in using any force that he would be justified in using if the arrest were lawful, provided that he does not believe the arrest is unlawful.

(b) A private person who assists another private person in effecting an unlawful arrest, or who, not being summoned, assists a peace officer in effecting an unlawful arrest, is justified in using any force that he would be justified in using if the arrest were lawful, provided that (i) he believes the arrest is lawful, and (ii) the arrest would be lawful if the facts were as he believes them to be.

(5) *Use of Force to Prevent Suicide or the Commission of a Crime.*

(a) The use of force upon or toward the person of another is justifiable when the actor believes that such force is immediately necessary to prevent such other person from committing suicide, inflicting serious bodily injury upon himself, committing or consummating the commission of a crime involving or threatening bodily injury, damage to or loss of property or a breach of the peace, except that:

(i) any limitations imposed by the other provisions of this Article on the justifiable use of force in self-protection, for the protection of others, the protection of property, the effectuation of an arrest or the prevention of an escape from custody shall apply notwithstanding the criminality of the conduct against which such force is used; and

(ii) the use of deadly force is not in any event justifiable under this Subsection unless:

(A) the actor believes that there is a substantial risk that the person whom he seeks to prevent from committing a crime will cause death or serious bodily injury to another unless the commission or the consummation of the crime is prevented and that the use of such force presents no substantial risk of injury to innocent persons; or

(B) the actor believes that the use of such force is necessary to suppress a riot or mutiny after the rioters or mutineers have been ordered to disperse and warned, in any particular manner that the law may require, that such force will be used if they do not obey.

(b) The justification afforded by this Subsection extends to the use of confinement as preventive force only if the actor takes all reasonable measures to terminate the confinement as soon as he knows that he safely can, unless the person confined has been arrested on a charge of crime.

Section 3.08. Use of Force by Persons with Special Responsibility for Care, Discipline or Safety of Others.

The use of force upon or toward the person of another is justifiable if:

(1) the actor is the parent or guardian or other person similarly responsible for the general care and supervision of a minor or a person acting at the request of such parent, guardian or other responsible person and:

(a) the force is used for the purpose of safeguarding or promoting the welfare of the minor, including the prevention or punishment of his misconduct; and

(b) the force used is not designed to cause or known to create a substantial risk of causing death, serious bodily injury, disfigurement, extreme pain or mental distress or gross degradation; or

(2) the actor is a teacher or a person otherwise entrusted with the care or supervision for a special purpose of a minor and:

(a) the actor believes that the force used is necessary to further such special purpose, including the maintenance of reasonable discipline in a school, class or other group, and that the use of such force is consistent with the welfare of the minor; and

(b) the degree of force, if it had been used by the parent or guardian of the minor, would not be unjustifiable under Subsection (1)(b) of this Section; or

(3) the actor is the guardian or other person similarly responsible for the general care and supervision of an incompetent person and:

(a) the force is used for the purpose of safeguarding or promoting the welfare of the incompetent person, including the prevention of his misconduct, or, when such incompetent person is in a hospital or other institution for his care and custody, for the maintenance of reasonable discipline in such institution; and

(b) the force used is not designed to cause or known to create a substantial risk of causing death, serious bodily injury, disfigurement, extreme or unnecessary pain, mental distress, or humiliation; or

(4) the actor is a doctor or other therapist or a person assisting him at his direction and:

(a) the force is used for the purpose of administering a recognized form of treatment that the actor believes to be adapted to promoting the physical or mental health of the patient; and

(b) the treatment is administered with the consent of the patient or, if the patient is a minor or an incompetent person, with the consent of his parent or guardian or other person legally competent to consent in his behalf, or the treatment is administered in an emergency when the actor believes that no one competent to consent can be consulted and that a reasonable person, wishing to safeguard the welfare of the patient, would consent; or

(5) the actor is a warden or other authorized official of a correctional institution and:

(a) he believes that the force used is necessary for the purpose of enforcing the lawful rules or procedures of the institution, unless his belief in the lawfulness of the rule or procedure sought to be enforced is erroneous and his error is due to ignorance or mistake as to the provisions of the Code, any other provision of the criminal law or the law governing the administration of the institution; and

(b) the nature or degree of force used is not forbidden by Article 303 or 304 of the Code; and

(c) if deadly force is used, its use is otherwise justifiable under this Article; or

(6) the actor is a person responsible for the safety of a vessel or an aircraft or a person acting at his direction and:

(a) he believes that the force used is necessary to prevent interference with the operation of the vessel or aircraft or obstruction of the execution of a lawful order, unless his belief in the lawfulness of the order is erroneous and his error is due to ignorance or mistake as to the law defining his authority; and

(b) if deadly force is used, its use is otherwise justifiable under this Article; or

(7) the actor is a person who is authorized or required by law to maintain order or decorum in a vehicle, train or other carrier or in a place where others are assembled, and:

(a) he believes that the force used is necessary for such purpose; and

(b) the force used is not designed to cause or known to create a substantial risk of causing death, bodily injury, or extreme mental distress.

Section 3.09. Mistake of Law as to Unlawfulness of Force or Legality of Arrest; Reckless or Negligent Use of Otherwise Justifiable Force; Reckless or Negligent Injury or Risk of Injury to Innocent Persons.

(1) The justification afforded by Sections 3.04 to 3.07, inclusive, is unavailable when:

(a) the actor's belief in the unlawfulness of the force or conduct against which he employs protective force or his belief in the lawfulness of an arrest that he endeavors to effect by force is erroneous; and

(b) his error is due to ignorance or mistake as to the provisions of the Code, any other provision of the criminal law or the law governing the legality of an arrest or search.

(2) When the actor believes that the use of force upon or toward the person of another is necessary for any of the purposes for which such belief would establish a justification under Sections 3.03 to 3.08 but the actor is reckless or negligent in having such belief or in acquiring or failing to acquire any knowledge or belief that is material to the justifiability of his use of force, the justification afforded by those Sections is unavailable in a prosecution for an offense for which recklessness or negligence, as the case may be, suffices to establish culpability.

(3) When the actor is justified under Sections 3.03 to 3.08 in using force upon or toward the person of another but he recklessly or negligently injures or creates a risk of injury to innocent persons, the justification afforded by those Sections is unavailable in a prosecution for such recklessness or negligence towards innocent persons.

Section 3.10. Justification in Property Crimes.

Conduct involving the appropriation, seizure or destruction of, damage to, intrusion on or interference with property is justifiable under circumstances that would establish a defense of privilege in a civil action based thereon, unless:

(1) the Code or the law defining the offense deals with the specific situation involved; or

(2) a legislative purpose to exclude the justification claimed otherwise plainly appears.

Section 3.11 Definitions.

In this Article, unless a different meaning plainly is required:

(1) "unlawful force" means force, including confinement, that is employed without the consent of the person against whom it is directed and the employment of which constitutes an offense or actionable tort or would constitute such offense or tort except for a defense (such as the absence of intent, negligence, or mental capacity; duress; youth; or diplomatic status) not amounting to a privilege to use the force. Assent constitutes consent, within the meaning of this Section, whether or not it otherwise is legally effective, except assent to the infliction of death or serious bodily injury.

(2) "deadly force" means force that the actor uses with the purpose of causing or that he knows to create a substantial risk of causing death or serious bodily injury. Purposely firing a firearm in the direction of another person or at a vehicle in which another person is believed to be constitutes deadly force. A threat to cause death or serious bodily injury, by the production of a weapon or otherwise, so long as the actor's purpose is limited to creating an apprehension that he will use deadly force if necessary, does not constitute deadly force.

(3) "dwelling" means any building or structure, though movable or temporary, or a portion thereof, that is for the time being the actor's home or place of lodging.

ARTICLE 4. RESPONSIBILITY

Section 4.01. Mental Disease or Defect Excluding Responsibility.

(1) A person is not responsible for criminal conduct if at the time of such conduct as a result of mental disease or defect he lacks substantial capacity either to appreciate the criminality [wrongfulness] of his conduct or to conform his conduct to the requirements of law.

(2) As used in this Article, the terms "mental disease or defect" do not include an abnormality manifested only by repeated criminal or otherwise antisocial conduct.

Section 4.02. Evidence of Mental Disease or Defect Admissible When Relevant to Element of the Offense [; Mental Disease or Defect Impairing Capacity as Ground for Mitigation of Punishment in Capital Cases].

(1) Evidence that the defendant suffered from a mental disease or defect is admissible whenever it is relevant to prove that the defendant did or did not have a state of mind that is an element of the offense.

[(2) Whenever the jury or the Court is authorized to determine or to recommend whether or not the defendant shall be sentenced to death or imprisonment upon conviction, evidence that the capacity of the defendant to appreciate the criminality [wrongfulness] of his conduct or to conform his conduct to the requirements of law was impaired as a result of mental disease or defect is admissible in favor of sentence of imprisonment.]

Section 4.03. Mental Disease or Defect Excluding Responsibility Is Affirmative Defense; Requirement of Notice; Form of Verdict and Judgment When Finding of Irresponsibility Is Made.

(1) Mental disease or defect excluding responsibility is an affirmative defense.

(2) Evidence of mental disease or defect excluding responsibility is not admissible unless the defendant, at the time of entering his plea of not guilty or within ten days thereafter or at such later time as the Court may for good cause permit, files a written notice of his purpose to rely on such defense.

(3) When the defendant is acquitted on the ground of mental disease or defect excluding responsibility, the verdict and the judgment shall so state.

Section 4.04. Mental Disease or Defect Excluding Fitness to Proceed.

No person who as a result of mental disease or defect lacks capacity to understand the proceedings against him or to assist in his own defense shall be tried, convicted or sentenced for the commission of an offense so long as such incapacity endures. * * *

Section 4.10. Immaturity Excluding Criminal Conviction; Transfer of Proceedings to Juvenile Court.

(1) A person shall not be tried for or convicted of an offense if:

(a) at the time of the conduct charged to constitute the offense he was less than sixteen years of age [, in which case the Juvenile Court shall have exclusive jurisdiction*]; or

(b) at the time of the conduct charged to constitute the offense he was sixteen or seventeen years of age, unless:

(i) the Juvenile Court has no jurisdiction over him, or

(ii) the Juvenile Court has entered an order waiving jurisdiction and consenting to the institution of criminal proceedings against him.

(2) No court shall have jurisdiction to try or convict a person of an offense if criminal proceedings against him are barred by Subsection (1) of this Section. When it appears that a person charged with the commission of an offense may be of such an age that criminal proceedings may be barred under Subsection (1) of this Section, the Court shall hold a hearing thereon, and the burden shall be on the prosecution to establish to the satisfaction of the Court that the criminal proceeding is not barred upon such grounds. If the Court determines that the proceeding is barred, custody of the person charged shall be surrendered to the Juvenile Court, and the case, including all papers and processes relating thereto, shall be transferred.

ARTICLE 5. INCHOATE CRIMES

Section 5.01. Criminal Attempt.

(1) *Definition of Attempt*. A person is guilty of an attempt to commit a crime if, acting with the kind of culpability otherwise required for commission of the crime, he:

(a) purposely engages in conduct that would constitute the crime if the attendant circumstances were as he believes them to be; or

(b) when causing a particular result is an element of the crime, does or omits to do anything with the purpose of causing or with the belief that it will cause such result without further conduct on his part; or

(c) purposely does or omits to do anything that, under the circumstances as he believes them to be, is an act or omission constituting a substantial step in a course of conduct planned to culminate in his commission of the crime.

(2) *Conduct That May Be Held Substantial Step Under Subsection (1)(c)*. Conduct shall not be held to constitute a substantial step under Subsection (1)(c) of this Section unless it is strongly corroborative of the actor's criminal purpose. Without negativing the sufficiency of other conduct, the following, if strongly

---

*The bracketed words are unnecessary if the Juvenile Court Act so provides or is amended accordingly.

corroborative of the actor's criminal purpose, shall not be held insufficient as a matter of law:

(a) lying in wait, searching for or following the contemplated victim of the crime;

(b) enticing or seeking to entice the contemplated victim of the crime to go to the place contemplated for its commission;

(c) reconnoitering the place contemplated for the commission of the crime;

(d) unlawful entry of a structure, vehicle or enclosure in which it is contemplated that the crime will be committed;

(e) possession of materials to be employed in the commission of the crime, that are specially designed for such unlawful use or that can serve no lawful purpose of the actor under the circumstances;

(f) possession, collection or fabrication of materials to be employed in the commission of the crime, at or near the place contemplated for its commission, if such possession, collection or fabrication serves no lawful purpose of the actor under the circumstances;

(g) soliciting an innocent agent to engage in conduct constituting an element of the crime.

(3) *Conduct Designed to Aid Another in Commission of a Crime.* A person who engages in conduct designed to aid another to commit a crime that would establish his complicity under Section 2.06 if the crime were committed by such other person, is guilty of an attempt to commit the crime, although the crime is not committed or attempted by such other person.

(4) *Renunciation of Criminal Purpose.* When the actor's conduct would otherwise constitute an attempt under Subsection (1)(b) or (1)(c) of this Section, it is an affirmative defense that he abandoned his effort to commit the crime or otherwise prevented its commission, under circumstances manifesting a complete and voluntary renunciation of his criminal purpose. The establishment of such defense does not, however, affect the liability of an accomplice who did not join in such abandonment or prevention.

Within the meaning of this Article, renunciation of criminal purpose is not voluntary if it is motivated, in whole or in part, by circumstances, not present or apparent at the inception of the actor's course of conduct, that increase the probability of detection or apprehension or that make more difficult the accomplishment of the criminal purpose. Renunciation is not complete if it is motivated by a decision to postpone the criminal conduct until a more advantageous time or to transfer the criminal effort to another but similar objective or victim.

Section 5.02. Criminal Solicitation.

(1) *Definition of Solicitation*. A person is guilty of solicitation to commit a crime if with the purpose of promoting or facilitating its commission he commands, encourages or requests another person to engage in specific conduct that would constitute such crime or an attempt to commit such crime or would establish his complicity in its commission or attempted commission.

(2) *Uncommunicated Solicitation*. It is immaterial under Subsection (1) of this Section that the actor fails to communicate with the person he solicits to commit a crime if his conduct was designed to effect such communication.

(3) *Renunciation of Criminal Purpose*. It is an affirmative defense that the actor, after soliciting another person to commit a crime, persuaded him not to do so or otherwise prevented the commission of the crime, under circumstances manifesting a complete and voluntary renunciation of his criminal purpose.

Section 5.03. Criminal Conspiracy.

(1) *Definition of Conspiracy*. A person is guilty of conspiracy with another person or persons to commit a crime if with the purpose of promoting or facilitating its commission he:

(a) agrees with such other person or persons that they or one or more of them will engage in conduct that constitutes such crime or an attempt or solicitation to commit such crime; or
(b) agrees to aid such other person or persons in the planning or commission of such crime or of an attempt or solicitation to commit such crime.

(2) *Scope of Conspiratorial Relationship*. If a person guilty of conspiracy, as defined by Subsection (1) of this Section, knows that a person with whom he conspires to commit a crime has conspired with another person or persons to commit the same crime, he is guilty of conspiring with such other person or persons, whether or not he knows their identity, to commit such crime.

(3) *Conspiracy with Multiple Criminal Objectives*. If a person conspires to commit a number of crimes, he is guilty of only one conspiracy so long as such multiple crimes are the object of the same agreement or continuous conspiratorial relationship.

(4) *Joinder and Venue in Conspiracy Prosecutions*.

(a) Subject to the provisions of paragraph (b) of this Subsection, two or more persons charged with criminal conspiracy may be prosecuted jointly if:

(i) they are charged with conspiring with one another; or

(ii) the conspiracies alleged, whether they have the same or different parties, are so related that they constitute different aspects of a scheme of organized criminal conduct.

(b) In any joint prosecution under paragraph (a) of this Subsection:

(i) no defendant shall be charged with a conspiracy in any county [parish or district] other than one in which he entered into such conspiracy or in which an overt act pursuant to such conspiracy was done by him or by a person with whom he conspired; and

(ii) neither the liability of any defendant nor the admissibility against him of evidence of acts or declarations of another shall be enlarged by such joinder; and

(iii) the Court shall order a severance or take a special verdict as to any defendant who so requests, if it deems it necessary or appropriate to promote the fair determination of his guilt or innocence, and shall take any other proper measures to protect the fairness of the trial.

(5) *Overt Act.* No person may be convicted of conspiracy to commit a crime, other than a felony of the first or second degree, unless an overt act in pursuance of such conspiracy is alleged and proved to have been done by him or by a person with whom he conspired.

(6) *Renunciation of Criminal Purpose.* It is an affirmative defense that the actor, after conspiring to commit a crime, thwarted the success of the conspiracy, under circumstances manifesting a complete and voluntary renunciation of his criminal purpose.

(7) *Duration of Conspiracy.* For purposes of Section 1.06(4):

(a) conspiracy is a continuing course of conduct that terminates when the crime or crimes that are its object are committed or the agreement that they be committed is abandoned by the defendant and by those with whom he conspired; and

(b) such abandonment is presumed if neither the defendant nor anyone with whom he conspired does any overt act in pursuance of the conspiracy during the applicable period of limitation; and

(c) if an individual abandons the agreement, the conspiracy is terminated as to him only if and when he advises those with whom he conspired of his abandonment or he informs the law enforcement authorities of the existence of the conspiracy and of his participation therein.

Section 5.04. Incapacity, Irresponsibility or Immunity of Party to Solicitation or Conspiracy.

(1) Except as provided in Subsection (2) of this Section, it is immaterial to the

liability of a person who solicits or conspires with another to commit a crime that:

(a) he or the person whom he solicits or with whom he conspires does not occupy a particular position or have a particular characteristic that is an element of such crime, if he believes that one of them does; or

(b) the person whom he solicits or with whom he conspires is irresponsible or has an immunity to prosecution or conviction for the commission of the crime.

(2) It is a defense to a charge of solicitation or conspiracy to commit a crime that if the criminal object were achieved, the actor would not be guilty of a crime under the law defining the offense or as an accomplice under Section 2.06(5) or 2.06(6)(a) or (6)(b).

Section 5.05. Grading of Criminal Attempt, Solicitation and Conspiracy; Mitigation in Cases of Lesser Danger; Multiple Convictions Barred.

(1) Grading. Except as otherwise provided in this Section, attempt, solicitation and conspiracy are crimes of the same grade and degree as the most serious offense that is attempted or solicited or is an object of the conspiracy. An attempt, solicitation or conspiracy to commit a [capital crime or a] felony of the first degree is a felony of the second degree.

(2) Mitigation. If the particular conduct charged to constitute a criminal attempt, solicitation or conspiracy is so inherently unlikely to result or culminate in the commission of a crime that neither such conduct nor the actor presents a public danger warranting the grading of such offense under this Section, the Court shall exercise its power under Section 6.12 to enter judgment and impose sentence for a crime of lower grade or degree or, in extreme cases, may dismiss the prosecution.

(3) Multiple Convictions. A person may not be convicted of more than one offense defined by this Article for conduct designed to commit or to culminate in the commission of the same crime.

Section 5.06. Possessing Instruments of Crime; Weapons.

(1) Criminal Instruments Generally. A person commits a misdemeanor if he possesses any instrument of crime with purpose to employ it criminally. "Instrument of crime" means:

(a) anything specially made or specially adapted for criminal use; or

(b) anything commonly used for criminal purposes and possessed by the actor under circumstances that do not negative unlawful purpose.

(2) Presumption of Criminal Purpose from Possession of Weapon. If a person possesses a firearm or other weapon on or about his person, in a vehicle occupied by him, or otherwise readily available for use, it is presumed that he had the purpose to employ it criminally, unless:

(a) the weapon is possessed in the actor's home or place of business;
(b) the actor is licensed or otherwise authorized by law to possess such weapon; or
(c) the weapon is of a type commonly used in lawful sport.

"Weapon" means anything readily capable of lethal use and possessed under circumstances not manifestly appropriate for lawful uses that it may have; the term includes a firearm that is not loaded or lacks a clip or other component to render it immediately operable, and components that can readily be assembled into a weapon.

(3) Presumptions as to Possession of Criminal Instruments in Automobiles. If a weapon or other instrument of crime is found in an automobile, it is presumed to be in the possession of the occupant if there is but one. If there is more than one occupant, it is presumed to be in the possession of all, except under the following circumstances:

(a) it is found upon the person of one of the occupants;
(b) the automobile is not a stolen one and the weapon or instrument is found out of view in a glove compartment, car trunk, or other enclosed customary depository, in which case it is presumed to be in the possession of the occupant or occupants who own or have authority to operate the automobile;
(c) in the case of a taxicab, a weapon or instrument found in the passengers' portion of the vehicle is presumed to be in the possession of all the passengers, if there are any, and, if not, in the possession of the driver. * * *

ARTICLE 6. AUTHORIZED DISPOSITION OF OFFENDERS.

Section 6.01. Degrees of Felonies.

(1) Felonies defined by this Code are classified, for the purpose of sentence, into three degrees, as follows:

(a) felonies of the first degree;
(b) felonies of the second degree;
(c) felonies of the third degree.

A felony is of the first or second degree when it is so designated by the Code. A crime declared to be a felony, without specification of degree, is of the third degree.

(2) Notwithstanding any other provision of law, a felony defined by any statute of this State other than this Code shall constitute, for the purpose of sentence, a felony of the third degree. * * *

Section 6.04.　Penalties Against Corporations and Unincorporated Associations; Forfeiture of Corporate Charter or Revocation of Certificate Authorizing Foreign Corporation to Do Business in the State.

(1) The Court may suspend the sentence of a corporation or an unincorporated association that has been convicted of an offense or may sentence it to pay a fine authorized by Section 6.03.

(2)(a) The [prosecuting attorney] is authorized to institute civil proceedings in the appropriate court of general jurisdiction to forfeit the charter of a corporation organized under the laws of this State or to revoke the certificate authorizing a foreign corporation to conduct business in this State. The Court may order the charter forfeited or the certificate revoked upon finding

(i) that the board of directors or a high managerial agent acting in behalf of the corporation has, in conducting the corporation's affairs, purposely engaged in a persistent course of criminal conduct and
(ii) that for the prevention of future criminal conduct of the same character, the public interest requires the charter of the corporation to be forfeited and the corporation to be dissolved or the certificate to be revoked.
(b) When a corporation is convicted of a crime or a high managerial agent of a corporation, as defined in Section 2.07, is convicted of a crime committed in the conduct of the affairs of the corporation, the Court, in sentencing the corporation or the agent, may direct the [prosecuting attorney] to institute proceedings authorized by paragraph (a) of this Subsection.
(c) The proceedings authorized by paragraph (a) of this Subsection shall be conducted in accordance with the procedures authorized by law for the involuntary dissolution of a corporation or the revocation of the certificate authorizing a foreign corporation to conduct business in this State. Such proceedings shall be deemed additional to any other proceedings authorized by law for the purpose of forfeiting the charter of a corporation or revoking the certificate of a foreign corporation. * * *

Section 6.06.　Sentence of Imprisonment for Felony; Ordinary Terms.

A person who has been convicted of a felony may be sentenced to imprisonment, as follows:

(1) in the case of a felony of the first degree, for a term the minimum of which shall be fixed by the Court at not less than one year nor more than ten years, and the maximum of which shall be life imprisonment;

(2) in the case of a felony of the second degree, for a term the minimum of which shall be fixed by the Court at not less than one year nor more than three years, and the maximum of which shall be ten years;

(3) in the case of a felony of the third degree, for a term the minimum of which shall be fixed by the Court at not less than one year nor more than two years, and the maximum of which shall be five years. * * *

Section 6.08. Sentence of Imprisonment for Misdemeanors and Petty Misdemeanors; Ordinary Terms.

A person who has been convicted of a misdemeanor or a petty misdemeanor may be sentenced to imprisonment for a definite term which shall be fixed by the Court and shall not exceed one year in the case of a misdemeanor or thirty days in the case of a petty misdemeanor. * * *

Section 6.12. Reduction of Conviction by Court to Lesser Degree of Felony or to Misdemeanor.

If, when a person has been convicted of a felony, the Court, having regard to the nature and circumstances of the crime and to the history and character of the defendant, is of the view that it would be unduly harsh to sentence the offender in accordance with the Code, the Court may enter judgment of conviction for a lesser degree of felony or for a misdemeanor and impose sentence accordingly. * * *

PART II. DEFINITION OF SPECIFIC CRIMES

OFFENSES INVOLVING DANGER TO THE PERSON

ARTICLE 210. CRIMINAL HOMICIDE

Section 210.0. Definitions.

In Articles 210-213, unless a different meaning plainly is required:

(1) "human being" means a person who has been born and is alive;

(2) "bodily injury" means physical pain, illness or any impairment of physical condition;

(3) "serious bodily injury" means bodily injury which creates a substantial risk

of death or which causes serious, permanent disfigurement, or protracted loss or impairment of the function of any bodily member or organ;

(4) "deadly weapon" means any firearm or other weapon, device, instrument, material or substance, whether animate or inanimate, which in the manner it is used or is intended to be used is known to be capable of producing death or serious bodily injury.

Section 210.1. Criminal Homicide.

(1) A person is guilty of criminal homicide if he purposely, knowingly, recklessly or negligently causes the death of another human being.

(2) Criminal homicide is murder, manslaughter or negligent homicide.

Section 210.2. Murder.

(1) Except as provided in Section 210.3(1)(b), criminal homicide constitutes murder when:

(a) it is committed purposely or knowingly; or
(b) it is committed recklessly under circumstances manifesting extreme indifference to the value of human life. Such recklessness and indifference are presumed if the actor is engaged or is an accomplice in the commission of, or an attempt to commit, or flight after committing or attempting to commit robbery, rape or deviate sexual intercourse by force or threat of force, arson, burglary, kidnapping or felonious escape.

(2) Murder is a felony of the first degree [but a person convicted of murder may be sentenced to death, as provided in Section 210.6].

Section 210.3. Manslaughter.

(1) Criminal homicide constitutes manslaughter when:

(a) it is committed recklessly; or
(b) a homicide which would otherwise be murder is committed under the influence of extreme mental or emotional disturbance for which there is reasonable explanation or excuse. The reasonableness of such explanation or excuse shall be determined from the viewpoint of a person in the actor's situation under the circumstances as he believes them to be.

(2) Manslaughter is a felony of the second degree.

Section 210.4. Negligent Homicide.

(1) Criminal homicide constitutes negligent homicide when it is committed negligently.

(2) Negligent homicide is a felony of the third degree.

Section 210.5. Causing or Aiding Suicide.

(1) *Causing Suicide as Criminal Homicide.* A person may be convicted of criminal homicide for causing another to commit suicide only if he purposely causes such suicide by force, duress or deception.

(2) *Aiding or Soliciting Suicide as an Independent Offense.* A person who purposely aids or solicits another to commit suicide is guilty of a felony of the second degree if his conduct causes such suicide or an attempted suicide, and otherwise of a misdemeanor.

Section 210.6. Sentence of Death for Murder; Further Proceedings to Determine Sentence.

(1) *Death Sentence Excluded.* When a defendant is found guilty of murder, the Court shall impose sentence for a felony of the first degree if it is satisfied that:

(a) none of the aggravating circumstances enumerated in Subsection (3) of this Section was established by the evidence at the trial or will be established if further proceedings are initiated under Subsection (2) of this Section; or
(b) substantial mitigating circumstances, established by the evidence at the trial, call for leniency; or
(c) the defendant, with the consent of the prosecuting attorney and the approval of the Court, pleaded guilty to murder as a felony of the first degree; or
(d) the defendant was under 18 years of age at the time of the commission of the crime; or
(e) the defendant's physical or mental condition calls for leniency; or
(f) although the evidence suffices to sustain the verdict, it does not foreclose all doubt respecting the defendant's guilt.

(2) *Determination by Court or by Court and Jury.* Unless the Court imposes sentence under Subsection (1) of this Section, it shall conduct a separate proceeding to determine whether the defendant should be sentenced for a felony of the first degree or sentenced to death. The proceeding shall be conducted before the Court alone if the defendant was convicted by a Court sitting without a jury or upon his plea of guilty or if the prosecuting attorney and the defendant waive a jury with respect to sentence. In other cases it shall be conducted before

the Court sitting with the jury which determined the defendant's guilt or, if the Court for good cause shown discharges that jury, with a new jury empanelled for the purpose.

In the proceeding, evidence may be presented as to any matter that the Court deems relevant to sentence, including but not limited to the nature and circumstances of the crime, the defendant's character, background, history, mental and physical condition and any of the aggravating or mitigating circumstances enumerated in Subsections (3) and (4) of this Section. Any such evidence, not legally privileged, which the Court deems to have probative force, may be received, regardless of its admissibility under the exclusionary rules of evidence, provided that the defendant's counsel is accorded a fair opportunity to rebut such evidence. The prosecuting attorney and the defendant or his counsel shall be permitted to present argument for or against sentence of death.

The determination whether sentence of death shall be imposed shall be in the discretion of the Court, except that when the proceeding is conducted before the Court sitting with a jury, the Court shall not impose sentence of death unless it submits to the jury the issue whether the defendant should be sentenced to death or to imprisonment and the jury returns a verdict that the sentence should be death. If the jury is unable to reach a unanimous verdict, the Court shall dismiss the jury and impose sentence for a felony of the first degree.

The Court, in exercising its discretion as to sentence, and the jury, in determining upon its verdict, shall take into account the aggravating and mitigating circumstances enumerated in Subsections (3) and (4) and any other facts that it deems relevant, but it shall not impose or recommend sentence of death unless it finds one of the aggravating circumstances enumerated in Subsection (3) and further finds that there are no mitigating circumstances sufficiently substantial to call for leniency. When the issue is submitted to the jury, the Court shall so instruct and also shall inform the jury of the nature of the sentence of imprisonment that may be imposed, including its implication with respect to possible release upon parole, if the jury verdict is against sentence of death.

Alternative formulation of Subsection (2):

(2) *Determination by Court.* Unless the Court imposes sentence under Subsection (1) of this Section, it shall conduct a separate proceeding to determine whether the defendant should be sentenced for a felony of the first degree or sentenced to death. In the proceeding, the Court, in accordance with Section 7.07, shall consider the report of the pre-sentence investigation and, if a psychiatric examination has been ordered, the report of such examination. In addition, evidence may be presented as to any matter that the Court deems

relevant to sentence, including but not limited to the nature and circumstances of the crime, the defendant's character, background, history, mental and physical condition and any of the aggravating or mitigating circumstances enumerated in Subsections (3) and (4) of this Section. Any such evidence, not legally privileged, which the Court deems to have probative force, may be received, regardless of its admissibility under the exclusionary rules of evidence, provided that the defendant's counsel is accorded a fair opportunity to rebut such evidence. The prosecuting attorney and the defendant or his counsel shall be permitted to present argument for or against sentence of death.

The determination whether sentence of death shall be imposed shall be in the discretion of the Court. In exercising such discretion, the Court shall take into account the aggravating and mitigating circumstances enumerated in Subsections (3) and (4) and any other facts that it deems relevant but shall not impose sentence of death unless it finds one of the aggravating circumstances enumerated in Subsection (3) and further finds that there are no mitigating circumstances sufficiently substantial to call for leniency.

(3) *Aggravating Circumstances.*

(a) The murder was committed by a convict under sentence of imprisonment.

(b) The defendant was previously convicted of another murder or of a felony involving the use or threat of violence to the person.

(c) At the time the murder was committed the defendant also committed another murder.

(d) The defendant knowingly created a great risk of death to many persons.

(e) The murder was committed while the defendant was engaged or was an accomplice in the commission of, or an attempt to commit, or flight after committing or attempting to commit robbery, rape or deviate sexual intercourse by force or threat of force, arson, burglary or kidnapping.

(f) The murder was committed for the purpose of avoiding or preventing a lawful arrest or effecting an escape from lawful custody.

(g) The murder was committed for pecuniary gain.

(h) The murder was especially heinous, atrocious or cruel, manifesting exceptional depravity.

(4) *Mitigating Circumstances.*

(a) The defendant has no significant history of prior criminal activity.

(b) The murder was committed while the defendant was under the influence of extreme mental or emotional disturbance.

(c) The victim was a participant in the defendant's homicidal conduct or consented to the homicidal act.

(d) The murder was committed under circumstances which the defendant believed to provide a moral justification or extenuation for his conduct.

(e) The defendant was an accomplice in a murder committed by another person and his participation in the homicidal act was relatively minor.

(f) The defendant acted under duress or under the domination of another person. .

(g) At the time of the murder, the capacity of the defendant to appreciate the criminality [wrongfulness] of his conduct or to conform his conduct to the requirements of law was impaired as a result of mental disease or defect or intoxication.

(h) The youth of the defendant at the time of the crime.]

ARTICLE 211. ASSAULT; RECKLESS ENDANGERING; THREATS

Section 211.0. Definitions.

In this Article, the definitions given in Section 210.0 apply unless a different meaning plainly is required.

Section 211.1. Assault.

(1) *Simple Assault.* A person is guilty of assault if he:

(a) attempts to cause or purposely, knowingly or recklessly causes bodily injury to another; or

(b) negligently causes bodily injury to another with a deadly weapon; or

(c) attempts by physical menace to put another in fear of imminent serious bodily injury.

Simple assault is a misdemeanor unless committed in a fight or scuffle entered into by mutual consent, in which case it is a petty misdemeanor.

(2) *Aggravated Assault.* A person is guilty of aggravated assault if he:

(a) attempts to cause serious bodily injury to another, or causes such injury purposely, knowingly or recklessly under circumstances manifesting extreme indifference to the value of human life; or

(b) attempts to cause or purposely or knowingly causes bodily injury to another with a deadly weapon.

Aggravated assault under paragraph (a) is a felony of the second degree; aggravated assault under paragraph (b) is a felony of the third degree.

Section 211.2. Recklessly Endangering Another Person.

A person commits a misdemeanor if he recklessly engages in conduct which places or may place another person in danger of death or serious bodily injury. Recklessness and danger shall be presumed where a person knowingly points a firearm at or in the direction of another, whether or not the actor believed the firearm to be loaded.

Section 211.3. Terroristic Threats.

A person is guilty of a felony of the third degree if he threatens to commit any crime of violence with purpose to terrorize another or to cause evacuation of a building, place of assembly, or facility of public transportation, or otherwise to cause serious public inconvenience, or in reckless disregard of the risk of causing such terror or inconvenience.

ARTICLE 212. KIDNAPPING AND RELATED OFFENSES; COERCION

Section 212.0. Definitions.

In this Article, the definitions given in Section 210.0 apply unless a different meaning plainly is required.

Section 212.1 Kidnapping.

A person is guilty of kidnapping if he unlawfully removes another from his place of residence or business, or a substantial distance from the vicinity where he is found, or if he unlawfully confines another for a substantial period in a place of isolation, with any of the following purposes:

(a) to hold for ransom or reward, or as a shield or hostage; or
(b) to facilitate commission of any felony or flight thereafter; or
(c) to inflict bodily injury on or to terrorize the victim or another; or
(d) to interfere with the performance of any governmental or political function.

Kidnapping is a felony of the first degree unless the actor voluntarily releases the victim alive and in a safe place prior to trial, in which case it is a felony of the second degree. A removal or confinement is unlawful within the meaning of this Section if it is accomplished by force, threat or deception, or, in the case of a person who is under the age of 14 or incompetent, if it is accomplished without the consent of a parent, guardian or other person responsible for general supervision of his welfare.

Section 212.2. Felonious Restraint.

A person commits a felony of the third degree if he knowingly:

(a) restrains another unlawfully in circumstances exposing him to risk of serious bodily injury; or

(b) holds another in a condition of involuntary servitude.

Section 212.3. False Imprisonment.

A person commits a misdemeanor if he knowingly restrains another unlawfully so as to interfere substantially with his liberty.

Section 212.4. Interference with Custody.

(1) *Custody of Children.* A person commits an offense if he knowingly or recklessly takes or entices any child under the age of 18 from the custody of its parent, guardian or other lawful custodian, when he has no privilege to do so. It is an affirmative defense that:

(a) the actor believed that his action was necessary to preserve the child from danger to its welfare; or

(b) the child, being at the time not less than 14 years old, was taken away at its own instigation without enticement and without purpose to commit a criminal offense with or against the child.

Proof that the child was below the critical age gives rise to a presumption that the actor knew the child's age or acted in reckless disregard thereof. The offense is a misdemeanor unless the actor, not being a parent or person in equivalent relation to the child, acted with knowledge that his conduct would cause serious alarm for the child's safety, or in reckless disregard of a likelihood of causing such alarm, in which case the offense is a felony of the third degree.

(2) *Custody of Committed Persons.* A person is guilty of a misdemeanor if he knowingly or recklessly takes or entices any committed person away from lawful custody when he is not privileged to do so. "Committed person" means, in addition to anyone committed under judicial warrant, any orphan, neglected or delinquent child, mentally defective or insane person, or other dependent or incompetent person entrusted to another's custody by or through a recognized social agency or otherwise by authority of law.

Section 212.5. Criminal Coercion.

(1) *Offense Defined.* A person is guilty of criminal coercion if, with purpose unlawfully to restrict another's freedom of action to his detriment, he threatens to:

(a) commit any criminal offense; or

(b) accuse anyone of a criminal offense; or

(c) expose any secret tending to subject any person to hatred, contempt or ridicule, or to impair his credit or business repute; or

(d) take or withhold action as an official, or cause an official to take or withhold action.

It is an affirmative defense to prosecution based on paragraphs (b), (c) or (d) that the actor believed the accusation or secret to be true or the proposed official action justified and that his purpose was limited to compelling the other to behave in a way reasonably related to the circumstances which were the subject of the accusation, exposure or proposed official action, as by desisting from further misbehavior, making good a wrong done, refraining from taking any action or responsibility for which the actor believes the other disqualified.

(2) *Grading.* Criminal coercion is a misdemeanor unless the threat is to commit a felony or the actor's purpose is felonious, in which cases the offense is a felony of the third degree.

ARTICLE 213. SEXUAL OFFENSES

Section 213.0. Definitions.

In this Article, unless a different meaning plainly is required:

(1) the definitions given in Section 210.0 apply;

(2) "Sexual intercourse" includes intercourse per os or per anum, with some penetration however slight; emission is not required;

(3) "Deviate sexual intercourse" means sexual intercourse per os or per anum between human beings who are not husband and wife, and any form of sexual intercourse with an animal.

Section 213.1. Rape and Related Offenses.

(1) *Rape.* A male who has sexual intercourse with a female not his wife is guilty of rape if:

(a) he compels her to submit by force or by threat of imminent death, serious bodily injury, extreme pain or kidnapping, to be inflicted on anyone; or

(b) he has substantially impaired her power to appraise or control her conduct by administering or employing without her knowledge drugs, intoxicants or other means for the purpose of preventing resistance; or

(c) the female is unconscious; or

(d) the female is less than 10 years old.

Rape is a felony of the second degree unless (i) in the course thereof the actor inflicts serious bodily injury upon anyone, or (ii) the victim was not a voluntary social companion of the actor upon the occasion of the crime and had not previously permitted him sexual liberties, in which cases the offense is a felony of the first degree.

(2) *Gross Sexual Imposition.* A male who has sexual intercourse with a female not his wife commits a felony of the third degree if:

(a) he compels her to submit by any threat that would prevent resistance by a woman of ordinary resolution; or
(b) he knows that she suffers from a mental disease or defect which renders her incapable of appraising the nature of her conduct; or
(c) he knows that she is unaware that a sexual act is being committed upon her or that she submits because she mistakenly supposes that he is her husband.

Section 213.2. Deviate Sexual Intercourse by Force or Imposition.

(1) *By Force or Its Equivalent.* A person who engages in deviate sexual intercourse with another person, or who causes another to engage in deviate sexual intercourse, commits a felony of the second degree if:

(a) he compels the other person to participate by force or by threat of imminent death, serious bodily injury, extreme pain or kidnapping, to be inflicted on anyone; or
(b) he has substantially impaired the other person's power to appraise or control his conduct, by administering or employing without the knowledge of the other person drugs, intoxicants or other means for the purpose of preventing resistance; or
(c) the other person is unconscious; or
(d) the other person is less than 10 years old.

(2) *By Other Imposition.* A person who engages in deviate sexual intercourse with another person, or who causes another to engage in deviate sexual intercourse, commits a felony of the third degree if:

(a) he compels the other person to participate by any threat that would prevent resistance by a person of ordinary resolution; or
(b) he knows that the other person suffers from a mental disease or defect which renders him incapable of appraising the nature of his conduct; or
(c) he knows that the other person submits because he is unaware that a sexual act is being committed upon him.

Section 213.3. Corruption of Minors and Seduction.

(1) *Offense Defined*. A male who has sexual intercourse with a female not his wife, or any person who engages in deviate sexual intercourse or causes another to engage in deviate sexual intercourse, is guilty of an offense if:

(a) the other person is less than [16] years old and the actor is at least [four] years older than the other person; or
(b) the other person is less than 21 years old and the actor is his guardian or otherwise responsible for general supervision of his welfare; or
(c) the other person is in custody of law or detained in a hospital or other institution and the actor has supervisory or disciplinary authority over him; or
(d) the other person is a female who is induced to participate by a promise of marriage which the actor does not mean to perform.

(2) *Grading*. An offense under paragraph (a) of Subsection (1) is a felony of the third degree. Otherwise an offense under this section is a misdemeanor.

Section 213.4. Sexual Assault.

A person who has sexual contact with another not his spouse, or causes such other to have sexual contact with him, is guilty of sexual assault, a misdemeanor, if:

(1) he knows that the contact is offensive to the other person; or

(2) he knows that the other person suffers from a mental disease or defect which renders him or her incapable of appraising the nature of his or her conduct; or

(3) he knows that the other person is unaware that a sexual act is being committed; or

(4) the other person is less than 10 years old; or

(5) he has substantially impaired the other person's power to appraise or control his or her conduct, by administering or employing without the other's knowledge drugs, intoxicants or other means for the purpose of preventing resistance; or

(6) the other person is less than [16] years old and the actor is at least [four] years older than the other person; or

(7) the other person is less than 21 years old and the actor is his guardian or otherwise responsible for general supervision of his welfare; or

(8) the other person is in custody of law or detained in a hospital or other institution and the actor has supervisory or disciplinary authority over him.

Sexual contact is any touching of the sexual or other intimate parts of the person for the purpose of arousing or gratifying sexual desire.

Section 213.5. Indecent Exposure.

A person commits a misdemeanor if, for the purpose of arousing or gratifying sexual desire of himself or of any person other than his spouse, he exposes his genitals under circumstances in which he knows his conduct is likely to cause affront or alarm.

Section 213.6. Provisions Generally Applicable to Article 213.

(1) *Mistake as to Age.* Whenever in this Article the criminality of conduct depends on a child's being below the age of 10, it is no defense that the actor did not know the child's age, or reasonably believed the child to be older than 10. When criminality depends on the child's being below a critical age other than 10, it is a defense for the actor to prove by a preponderance of the evidence that he reasonably believed the child to be above the critical age.

(2) *Spouse Relationships.* Whenever in this Article the definition of an offense excludes conduct with a spouse, the exclusion shall be deemed to extend to persons living as man and wife, regardless of the legal status of their relationship. The exclusion shall be inoperative as respects spouses living apart under a decree of judicial separation. Where the definition of an offense excludes conduct with a spouse or conduct by a woman, this shall not preclude conviction of a spouse or woman as accomplice in a sexual act which he or she causes another person, not within the exclusion, to perform.

(3) *Sexually Promiscuous Complainants.* It is a defense to prosecution under Section 213.3 and paragraphs (6), (7) and (8) of Section 213.4 for the actor to prove by a preponderance of the evidence that the alleged victim had, prior to the time of the offense charged, engaged promiscuously in sexual relations with others.

(4) *Prompt Complaint.* No prosecution may be instituted or maintained under this Article unless the alleged offense was brought to the notice of public authority within [3] months of its occurrence or, where the alleged victim was less than [16] years old or otherwise incompetent to make complaint, within [3] months after a parent, guardian or other competent person specially interested in the victim learns of the offense.

(5) *Testimony of Complainants.* No person shall be convicted of any felony under this Article upon the uncorroborated testimony of the alleged victim. Corroboration may be circumstantial. In any prosecution before a jury for an offense under this Article, the jury shall be instructed to evaluate the testimony of a victim or complaining witness with special care in view of the emotional involvement of the witness and the difficulty of determining the truth with respect to alleged sexual activities carried out in private.

OFFENSES AGAINST PROPERTY

ARTICLE 220. ARSON, CRIMINAL MISCHIEF, AND OTHER PROPERTY DESTRUCTION

Section 220.1. Arson and Related Offenses.

(1) *Arson.* A person is guilty of arson, a felony of the second degree, if he starts a fire or causes an explosion with the purpose of:

(a) destroying a building or occupied structure of another; or
(b) destroying or damaging any property, whether his own or another's, to collect insurance for such loss. It shall be an affirmative defense to prosecution under this paragraph that the actor's conduct did not recklessly endanger any building or occupied structure of another or place any other person in danger of death or bodily injury.

(2) *Reckless Burning or Exploding.* A person commits a felony of the third degree if he purposely starts a fire or causes an explosion, whether on his own property or another's, and thereby recklessly:

(a) places another person in danger of death or bodily injury; or
(b) places a building or occupied structure of another in danger of damage or destruction.

(3) *Failure to Control or Report Dangerous Fire.* A person who knows that a fire is endangering life or a substantial amount of property of another and fails to take reasonable measures to put out or control the fire, when he can do so without substantial risk to himself, or to give a prompt fire alarm, commits a misdemeanor if:

(a) he knows that he is under an official, contractual, or other legal duty to prevent or combat the fire; or
(b) the fire was started, albeit lawfully, by him or with his assent, or on property in his custody or control.

(4) *Definitions.* "Occupied structure" means any structure, vehicle or place adapted for overnight accommodation of persons, or for carrying on business therein, whether or not a person is actually present. Property is that of another, for the purposes of this section, if anyone other than the actor has a possessory or proprietary interest therein. If a building or structure is divided into separately occupied units, any unit not occupied by the actor is an occupied structure of another.

220.2. Causing or Risking Catastrophe.

(1) *Causing Catastrophe.* A person who causes a catastrophe by explosion, fire, flood, avalanche, collapse of building, release of poison gas, radioactive material or other harmful or destructive force or substance, or by any other means of causing potentially widespread injury or damage, commits a felony of the second degree if he does so purposely or knowingly, or a felony of the third degree if he does so recklessly.

(2) *Risking Catastrophe.* A person is guilty of a misdemeanor if he recklessly creates a risk of catastrophe in the employment of fire, explosives or other dangerous means listed in Subsection (1).

(3) *Failure to Prevent Catastrophe.* A person who knowingly or recklessly fails to take reasonable measures to prevent or mitigate a catastrophe commits a misdemeanor if:

(a) he knows that he is under an official, contractual or other legal duty to take such measures; or
(b) he did or assented to the act causing or threatening the catastrophe.

Section 220.3. Criminal Mischief.

(1) *Offense Defined.* A person is guilty of criminal mischief if he:

(a) damages tangible property of another purposely, recklessly, or by negligence in the employment of fire, explosives, or other dangerous means listed in Section 220.2(1); or
(b) purposely or recklessly tampers with tangible property of another so as to endanger person or property; or
(c) purposely or recklessly causes another to suffer pecuniary loss by deception or threat.

(2) *Grading.* Criminal mischief is a felony of the third degree if the actor purposely causes pecuniary loss in excess of $5,000, or a substantial interruption or impairment of public communication, transportation, supply of water, gas or

power, or other public service. It is a misdemeanor if the actor purposely causes pecuniary loss in excess of $100, or a petty misdemeanor if he purposely or recklessly causes pecuniary loss in excess of $25. Otherwise criminal mischief is a violation.

ARTICLE 221. BURGLARY AND OTHER CRIMINAL INTRUSION

Section 221.0. Definitions.

In this Article, unless a different meaning plainly is required:

(1) "occupied structure" means any structure, vehicle or place adapted for overnight accommodation of persons, or for carrying on business therein, whether or not a person is actually present.

(2) "night" means the period between thirty minutes past sunset and thirty minutes before sunrise.

Section 221.1. Burglary.

(1) *Burglary Defined.* A person is guilty of burglary if he enters a building or occupied structure, or separately secured or occupied portion thereof, with purpose to commit a crime therein, unless the premises are at the time open to the public or the actor is licensed or privileged to enter. It is an affirmative defense to prosecution for burglary that the building or structure was abandoned.

(2) *Grading.* Burglary is a felony of the second degree if it is perpetrated in the dwelling of another at night, or if, in the course of committing the offense, the actor:

(a) purposely, knowingly or recklessly inflicts or attempts to inflict bodily injury on anyone; or
(b) is armed with explosives or a deadly weapon.

Otherwise, burglary is a felony of the third degree. An act shall be deemed "in the course of committing" an offense if it occurs in an attempt to commit the offense or in flight after the attempt or commission.

(3) Multiple Convictions. A person may not be convicted both for burglary and for the offense which it was his purpose to commit after the burglarious entry or for an attempt to commit that offense, unless the additional offense constitutes a felony of the first or second degree.

Section 221.2. Criminal Trespass.

(1) Buildings and Occupied Structures. A person commits an offense if, knowing that he is not licensed or privileged to do so, he enters or surreptitiously remains in any building or occupied structure, or separately secured or occupied portion thereof. An offense under this Subsection is a misdemeanor if it is committed in a dwelling at night. Otherwise it is a petty misdemeanor.

(2) *Defiant Trespasser*. A person commits an offense if, knowing that he is not licensed or privileged to do so, he enters or remains in any place as to which notice against trespass is given by:

(a) actual communication to the actor; or
(b) posting in a manner prescribed by law or reasonably likely to come to the attention of intruders; or
(c) fencing or other enclosure manifestly designed to exclude intruders.

An offense under this Subsection constitutes a petty misdemeanor if the offender defies an order to leave personally communicated to him by the owner of the premises or other authorized person. Otherwise it is a violation.

(3) *Defenses.* It is an affirmative defense to prosecution under this Section that:

(a) a building or occupied structure involved in an offense under Subsection (1) was abandoned; or
(b) the premises were at the time open to members of the public and the actor complied with all lawful conditions imposed on access to or remaining in the premises; or
(c) the actor reasonably believed that the owner of the premises, or other person empowered to license access thereto, would have licensed him to enter or remain.

ARTICLE 222. ROBBERY

Section 222.1. Robbery.

(1) *Robbery Defined.* A person is guilty of robbery if, in the course of committing a theft, he:

(a) inflicts serious bodily injury upon another; or
(b) threatens another with or purposely puts him in fear of immediate serious bodily injury; or
(c) commits or threatens immediately to commit any felony of the first or second degree.

An act shall be deemed "in the course of committing a theft" if it occurs in an attempt to commit theft or in flight after the attempt or commission.

(2) *Grading*. Robbery is a felony of the second degree, except that it is a felony of the first degree if in the course of committing the theft the actor attempts to kill anyone, or purposely inflicts or attempts to inflict serious bodily injury.

ARTICLE 223. THEFT AND RELATED OFFENSES

Section 223.0. Definitions.

In this Article, unless a different meaning plainly is required:

(1) "deprive" means: (a) to withhold property of another permanently or for so extended a period as to appropriate a major portion of its economic value, or with intent to restore only upon payment of reward or other compensation; or (b) to dispose of the property so as to make it unlikely that the owner will recover it.

(2) "financial institution" means a bank, insurance company, credit union, building and loan association, investment trust or other organization held out to the public as a place of deposit of funds or medium of savings or collective investment.

(3) "government" means the United States, any State, county, municipality, or other political unit, or any department, agency or subdivision of any of the foregoing, or any corporation or other association carrying out the functions of government.

(4) "movable property" means property the location of which can be changed, including things growing on, affixed to, or found in land, and documents although the rights represented thereby have no physical location; "immovable property" is all other property.

(5) "obtain" means: (a) in relation to property, to bring about a transfer or purported transfer of a legal interest in the property, whether to the obtainer or another; or (b) in relation to labor or service, to secure performance thereof.

(6) "property" means anything of value, including real estate, tangible and intangible personal property, contract rights, choses-in-action and other interests in or claims to wealth, admission or transportation tickets, captured or domestic animals, food and drink, electric or other power.

(7) "property of another" includes property in which any person other than the actor has an interest which the actor is not privileged to infringe, regardless of the fact that the actor also has an interest in the property and regardless of the fact that the other person might be precluded from civil recovery because the property was used in an unlawful transaction or was subject to forfeiture as contraband. Property in possession of the actor shall not be deemed property of another who has only a security interest therein, even if legal title is in the creditor pursuant to a conditional sales contract or other security agreement.

Section 223.1. Consolidation of Theft Offenses; Grading; Provisions Applicable to Theft Generally.

(1) *Consolidation of Theft Offenses.* Conduct denominated theft in this Article constitutes a single offense. An accusation of theft may be supported by evidence that it was committed in any manner that would be theft under this Article, notwithstanding the specification of a different manner in the indictment or information, subject only to the power of the Court to ensure fair trial by granting a continuance or other appropriate relief where the conduct of the defense would be prejudiced by lack of fair notice or by surprise.

(2) *Grading of Theft Offenses.*

(a) Theft constitutes a felony of the third degree if the amount involved exceeds $500, or if the property stolen is a firearm, automobile, airplane, motorcycle, motor boat, or other motor-propelled vehicle, or in the case of theft by receiving stolen property, if the receiver is in the business of buying or selling stolen property.

(b) Theft not within the preceding paragraph constitutes a misdemeanor, except that if the property was not taken from the person or by threat, or in breach of a fiduciary obligation, and the actor proves by a preponderance of the evidence that the amount involved was less than $50, the offense constitutes a petty misdemeanor.

(c) The amount involved in a theft shall be deemed to be the highest value, by any reasonable standard, of the property or services which the actor stole or attempted to steal. Amounts involved in thefts committed pursuant to one scheme or course of conduct, whether from the same person or several persons, may be aggregated in determining the grade of the offense.

(3) *Claim of Right.* It is an affirmative defense to prosecution for theft that the actor:

(a) was unaware that the property or service was that of another; or
(b) acted under an honest claim of right to the property or service involved or that he had a right to acquire or dispose of it as he did; or

(c) took property exposed for sale, intending to purchase and pay for it promptly, or reasonably believing that the owner, if present, would have consented.

(4) *Theft from Spouse.* It is no defense that theft was from the actor's spouse, except that misappropriation of household and personal effects, or other property normally accessible to both spouses, is theft only if it occurs after the parties have ceased living together.

Section 223.2. Theft by Unlawful Taking or Disposition.

(1) *Movable Property.* A person is guilty of theft if he unlawfully takes, or exercises unlawful control over, movable property of another with purpose to deprive him thereof.

(2) *Immovable Property.* A person is guilty of theft if he unlawfully transfers immovable property of another or any interest therein with purpose to benefit himself or another not entitled thereto.

Section 223.3. Theft by Deception.

A person is guilty of theft if he purposely obtains property of another by deception. A person deceives if he purposely:

(1) creates or reinforces a false impression, including false impressions as to law, value, intention or other state of mind; but deception as to a person's intention to perform a promise shall not be inferred from the fact alone that he did not subsequently perform the promise; or

(2) prevents another from acquiring information which would affect his judgment of a transaction; or

(3) fails to correct a false impression which the deceiver previously created or reinforced, or which the deceiver knows to be influencing another to whom he stands in a fiduciary or confidential relationship; or

(4) fails to disclose a known lien, adverse claim or other legal impediment to the enjoyment of property which he transfers or encumbers in consideration for the property obtained, whether such impediment is or is not valid, or is or is not a matter of official record.

The term "deceive" does not, however, include falsity as to matters having no pecuniary significance, or puffing by statements unlikely to deceive ordinary persons in the group addressed.

Section 223.4. Theft by Extortion.

A person is guilty of theft if he purposely obtains property of another by threatening to:

(1) inflict bodily injury on anyone or commit any other criminal offense; or

(2) accuse anyone of a criminal offense; or

(3) expose any secret tending to subject any person to hatred, contempt or ridicule, or to impair his credit or business repute; or

(4) take or withhold action as an official, or cause an official to take or withhold action; or

(5) bring about or continue a strike, boycott or other collective unofficial action, if the property is not demanded or received for the benefit of the group in whose interest the actor purports to act; or

(6) testify or provide information or withhold testimony or information with respect to another's legal claim or defense; or

(7) inflict any other harm which would not benefit the actor.

It is an affirmative defense to prosecution based on paragraphs (2), (3) or (4) that the property obtained by threat of accusation, exposure, lawsuit or other invocation of official action was honestly claimed as restitution or indemnification for harm done in the circumstances to which such accusation, exposure, lawsuit or other official action relates, or as compensation for property or lawful services.

Section 223.5. Theft of Property Lost, Mislaid, or Delivered by Mistake.

A person who comes into control of property of another that he knows to have been lost, mislaid, or delivered under a mistake as to the nature or amount of the property or the identity of the recipient is guilty of theft if, with purpose to deprive the owner thereof, he fails to take reasonable measures to restore the property to a person entitled to have it.

Section 223.6. Receiving Stolen Property.

(1) *Receiving.* A person is guilty of theft if he purposely receives, retains, or disposes of movable property of another knowing that it has been stolen, or believing that it has probably been stolen, unless the property is received,

retained, or disposed with purpose to restore it to the owner. "Receiving" means acquiring possession, control or title, or lending on the security of the property.

(2) *Presumption of Knowledge.* The requisite knowledge or belief is presumed in the case of a dealer who:

(a) is found in possession or control of property stolen from two or more persons on separate occasions; or
(b) has received stolen property in another transaction within the year preceding the transaction charged; or
(c) being a dealer in property of the sort received, acquires it for a consideration which he knows is far below its reasonable value.

"Dealer" means a person in the business of buying or selling goods including a pawnbroker.

Section 223.7. Theft of Services.

(1) A person is guilty of theft is he purposely obtains services which he knows are available only for compensation, by deception or threat, or by false token or other means to avoid payment for the service. "Services" includes labor, professional service, transportation, telephone or other public service, accommodation in hotels, restaurants or elsewhere, admission to exhibitions, use of vehicles or other movable property. Where compensation for service is ordinarily paid immediately upon the rendering of such service, as in the case of hotels and restaurants, refusal to pay or absconding without payment or offer to pay gives rise to a presumption that the service was obtained by deception as to intention to pay.

(2) A person commits theft if, having control over the disposition of services of others, to which he is not entitled, he knowingly diverts such services to his own benefit or to the benefit of another not entitled thereto.

Section 223.8. Theft by Failure to Make Required Disposition of Funds Received.

A person who purposely obtains property upon agreement, or subject to a known legal obligation, to make specified payment or other disposition, whether from such property or its proceeds or from his own property to be reserved in equivalent amount, is guilty of theft if he deals with the property obtained as his own and fails to make the required payment or disposition. The foregoing applies notwithstanding that it may be impossible to identify particular property as belonging to the victim at the time of the actor's failure to make the required payment or disposition. An officer or employee of the government or of a financial institution is presumed: (i) to know any legal obligation relevant to his criminal liability under this Section, and (ii) to have dealt with the property as his own if he fails to pay or account upon lawful demand, or if an audit reveals a shortage or falsification of accounts.

Section 223.9. Unauthorized Use of Automobiles and Other Vehicles.

A person commits a misdemeanor if he operates another's automobile, airplane, motorcycle, motorboat, or other motor-propelled vehicle without consent of the owner. It is an affirmative defense to prosecution under this Section that the actor reasonably believed that the owner would have consented to the operation had he known of it.

ARTICLE 224. FORGERY AND FRAUDULENT PRACTICES

Section 224.0. Definitions

In this Article, the definitions given in Section 223.0 apply unless a different meaning plainly is required.

Section 224.1. Forgery.

(1) *Definition.* A person is guilty of forgery if, with purpose to defraud or injure anyone, or with knowledge that he is facilitating a fraud or injury to be perpetrated by anyone, the actor:

(a) alters any writing of another without his authority; or
(b) makes, completes, executes, authenticates, issues or transfers any writing so that it purports to be the act of another who did not authorize that act, or to have been executed at a time or place or in a numbered sequence other than was in fact the case, or to be a copy of an original when no such original existed; or
(c) utters any writing which he knows to be forged in a manner specified in paragraphs (a) or (b).

"Writing" includes printing or any other method of recording information, money, coins, tokens, stamps, seals, credit cards, badges, trade-marks, and other symbols of value, right, privilege, or identification.

(2) *Grading.* Forgery is a felony of the second degree if the writing is or purports to be part of an issue of money, securities, postage or revenue stamps, or other instruments issued by the government, or part of an issue of stock, bonds or other instruments representing interests in or claims against any property or enterprise. Forgery is a felony of the third degree if the writing is or purports to be a will, deed, contract, release, commercial instrument, or other document

evidencing, creating, transferring, altering, terminating, or otherwise affecting legal relations. Otherwise forgery is a misdemeanor. * * *

Section 224.5. Bad Checks.

A person who issues or passes a check or similar sight order for the payment of money, knowing that it will not be honored by the drawee, commits a misdemeanor. For the purpose of this Section as well as in any prosecution for theft committed by means of a bad check, an issuer is presumed to know that the check or order (other than a post-dated check or order) would not be paid, if:

(1) the issuer had no account with the drawee at the time the check or order was issued; or

(2) payment was refused by the drawee for lack of funds, upon presentation within 30 days after issue, and the issuer failed to make good within 10 days after receiving notice of that refusal.

Section 224.6. Credit Cards.

A person commits an offense if he uses a credit card for the purpose of obtaining property or services with knowledge that:

(1) the card is stolen or forged; or

(2) the card has been revoked or cancelled; or

(3) for any other reason his use of the card is unauthorized by the issuer.

It is an affirmative defense to prosecution under paragraph (3) if the actor proves by a preponderance of the evidence that he had the purpose and ability to meet all obligations to the issuer arising out of his use of the card. "Credit card" means a writing or other evidence of an undertaking to pay for property or services delivered or rendered to or upon the order of a designated person or bearer. An offense under this Section is a felony of the third degree if the value of the property or services secured or sought to be secured by means of the credit card exceeds $500; otherwise it is a misdemeanor.

Section 224.7. Deceptive Business Practices.

A person commits a misdemeanor if in the course of business he:

(1) uses or possesses for use a false weight or measure, or any other device for falsely determining or recording any quality or quantity; or

(2) sells, offers or exposes for sale, or delivers less than the represented quantity of any commodity or service; or

(3) takes or attempts to take more than the represented quantity of any commodity or service when as buyer he furnishes the weight or measure; or

(4) sells, offers or exposes for sale adulterated or mislabeled commodities. "Adulterated" means varying from the standard of composition or quality prescribed by or pursuant to any statute providing criminal penalties for such variance, or set by established commercial usage. "Mislabeled" means varying from the standard of truth or disclosure in labeling prescribed by or pursuant to any statute providing criminal penalties for such variance, or set by established commercial usage; or

(5) makes a false or misleading statement in any advertisement addressed to the public or to a substantial segment thereof for the purpose of promoting the purchase or sale of property or services; or

(6) makes a false or misleading written statement for the purpose of obtaining property or credit; or

(7) makes a false or misleading written statement for the purpose of promoting the sale of securities, or omits information required by law to be disclosed in written documents relating to securities.

It is an affirmative defense to prosecution under this Section if the defendant proves by a preponderance of the evidence that his conduct was not knowingly or recklessly deceptive. * * *

OFFENSES AGAINST THE FAMILY

ARTICLE 230. OFFENSES AGAINST THE FAMILY

Section 230.1. Bigamy and Polygamy.

(1) Bigamy. A married person is guilty of bigamy, a misdemeanor, if he contracts or purports to contract another marriage, unless at the time of the subsequent marriage:

(a) the actor believes that the prior spouse is dead; or
(b) the actor and the prior spouse have been living apart for five consecutive years throughout which the prior spouse was not known by the actor to be alive; or
(c) a Court has entered a judgment purporting to terminate or annul any prior disqualifying marriage, and the actor does not know that judgment to be invalid; or
(d) the actor reasonably believes that he is legally eligible to remarry.

(2) *Polygamy.* A person is guilty of polygamy, a felony of the third degree, if he marries or cohabits with more than one spouse at a time in purported exercise of the right of plural marriage. The offense is a continuing one until all cohabitation and claim of marriage with more than one spouse terminates. This section does not apply to parties to a polygamous marriage, lawful in the country of which they are residents or nationals, while they are in transit through or temporarily visiting this State.

(3) *Other Party to Bigamous or Polygamous Marriage.* A person is guilty of bigamy or polygamy, as the case may be, if he contracts or purports to contract marriage with another knowing that the other is thereby committing bigamy or polygamy.

Section 230.2. Incest.

A person is guilty of incest, a felony of the third degree, if he knowingly marries or cohabits or has sexual intercourse with an ancestor or descendant, a brother or sister of the whole or half blood [or an uncle, aunt, nephew or niece of the whole blood]. "Cohabit" means to live together under the representation or appearance of being married. The relationships referred to herein include blood relationships without regard to legitimacy, and relationship of parent and child by adoption. * * *

Section 230.4. Endangering Welfare of Children.

A parent, guardian, or other person supervising the welfare of a child under 18 commits a misdemeanor if he knowingly endangers the child's welfare by violating a duty of care, protection or support.

Section 230.5. Persistent Nonsupport.

A person commits a misdemeanor if he persistently fails to provide support which he can provide and which he knows he is legally obliged to provide to a spouse, child or other dependent. * * *

OFFENSES AGAINST PUBLIC ORDER AND DECENCY

ARTICLE 250. RIOT, DISORDERLY CONDUCT, AND RELATED OFFENSES

Section 250.1. Riot; Failure to Disperse.

(1) *Riot.* A person is guilty of riot, a felony of the third degree, if he participates

with [two] or more others in a course of disorderly conduct:

(a) with purpose to commit or facilitate the commission of a felony or misdemeanor;

(b) with purpose to prevent or coerce official action; or

(c) when the actor or any other participant to the knowledge of the actor uses or plans to use a firearm or other deadly weapon.

(2) *Failure of Disorderly Persons to Disperse upon Official Order.* Where [three] or more persons are participating in a course of disorderly conduct likely to cause substantial harm or serious inconvenience, annoyance or alarm, a peace officer or other public servant engaged in executing or enforcing the law may order the participants and others in the immediate vicinity to disperse. A person who refuses or knowingly fails to obey such an order commits a misdemeanor.

Section 250.2. Disorderly Conduct.

(1) *Offense Defined.* A person is guilty of disorderly conduct if, with purpose to cause public inconvenience, annoyance or alarm, or recklessly creating a risk thereof, he:

(a) engages in fighting or threatening, or in violent or tumultuous behavior; or

(b) makes unreasonable noise or offensively coarse utterance, gesture or display, or addresses abusive language to any person present; or

(c) creates a hazardous or physically offensive condition by any act which serves no legitimate purpose of the actor.

"Public" means affecting or likely to affect persons in a place to which the public or a substantial group has access; among the places included are highways, transport facilities, schools, prisons, apartment houses, places of business or amusement, or any neighborhood.

(2) *Grading.* An offense under this section is a petty misdemeanor if the actor's purpose is to cause substantial harm or serious inconvenience, or if he persists in disorderly conduct after reasonable warning or request to desist. Otherwise disorderly conduct is a violation. * * *

Section 250.4. Harassment.

A person commits a petty misdemeanor if, with purpose to harass another, he:

(1) makes a telephone call without purpose of legitimate communication; or

(2) insults, taunts or challenges another in a manner likely to provoke violent or

disorderly response; or

(3) makes repeated communications anonymously or at extremely inconvenient hours, or in offensively coarse language; or

(4) subjects another to an offensive touching; or

(5) engages in any other course of alarming conduct serving no legitimate purpose of the actor.

Section 250.5. Public Drunkenness; Drug Incapacitation.

A person is guilty of an offense if he appears in any public place manifestly under the influence of alcohol, narcotics or other drug, not therapeutically administered, to the degree that he may endanger himself or other persons or property, or annoy persons in his vicinity. An offense under this Section constitutes a petty misdemeanor if the actor has been convicted hereunder twice before within a period of one year. Otherwise the offense constitutes a violation.

Section 250.6. Loitering or Prowling.

A person commits a violation if he loiters or prowls in a place, at a time, or in a manner not usual for law-abiding individuals under circumstances that warrant alarm for the safety of persons or property in the vicinity. Among the circumstances which may be considered in determining whether such alarm is warranted is the fact that the actor takes flight upon appearance of a peace officer, refuses to identify himself, or manifestly endeavors to conceal himself or any object. Unless flight by the actor or other circumstance makes it impracticable, a peace officer shall prior to any arrest for an offense under this section afford the actor an opportunity to dispel any alarm which would otherwise be warranted, by requesting him to identify himself and explain his presence and conduct. No person shall be convicted of an offense under this Section if the peace officer did not comply with the preceding sentence, or if it appears at trial that the explanation given by the actor was true and, if believed by the peace officer at the time, would have dispelled the alarm. * * *

ARTICLE 251. PUBLIC INDECENCY

Section 251.1. Open Lewdness.

A person commits a petty misdemeanor if he does any lewd act which he knows is likely to be observed by others who would be affronted or alarmed.

Section 251.2. Prostitution and Related Offenses.

(1) *Prostitution*. A person is guilty of prostitution, a petty misdemeanor, if he or she:

(a) is an inmate of a house of prostitution or otherwise engages in sexual activity as a business; or

(b) loiters in or within view of any public place for the purpose of being hired to engage in sexual activity.

"Sexual activity" includes homosexual and other deviate sexual relations. A "house of prostitution" is any place where prostitution or promotion of prostitution is regularly carried on by one person under the control, management or supervision of another. An "inmate" is a person who engages in prostitution in or through the agency of a house of prostitution. "Public place" means any place to which the public or any substantial group thereof has access.

(2) *Promoting Prostitution*. A person who knowingly promotes prostitution of another commits a misdemeanor or felony as provided in Subsection (3). The following acts shall, without limitation of the foregoing, constitute promoting prostitution:

(a) owning, controlling, managing, supervising or otherwise keeping, alone or in association with others, a house of prostitution or a prostitution business; or

(b) procuring an inmate for a house of prostitution or a place in a house of prostitution for one who would be an inmate; or

(c) encouraging, inducing, or otherwise purposely causing another to become or remain a prostitute; or

(d) soliciting a person to patronize a prostitute; or

(e) procuring a prostitute for a patron; or

(f) transporting a person into or within this state with purpose to promote that person's engaging in prostitution, or procuring or paying for transportation with that purpose; or

(g) leasing or otherwise permitting a place controlled by the actor, alone or in association with others, to be regularly used for prostitution or the promotion of prostitution, or failure to make reasonable effort to abate such use by ejecting the tenant, notifying law enforcement authorities, or other legally available means; or

(h) soliciting, receiving, or agreeing to receive any benefit for doing or agreeing to do anything forbidden by this Subsection.

(3) *Grading of Offenses Under Subsection* (2). An offense under Subsection (2) constitutes a felony of the third degree if:

(a) the offense falls within paragraph (a), (b) or (c) of Subsection (2); or

(b) the actor compels another to engage in or promote prostitution; or

(c) the actor promotes prostitution of a child under 16, whether or not he is aware of the child's age; or

(d) the actor promotes prostitution of his wife, child, ward or any person for whose care, protection or support he is responsible.

Otherwise the offense is a misdemeanor.

(4) *Presumption from Living off Prostitutes.* A person, other than the prostitute or the prostitute's minor child or other legal dependent incapable of self-support, who is supported in whole or substantial part by the proceeds of prostitution is presumed to be knowingly promoting prostitution in violation of Subsection (2).

(5) *Patronizing Prostitutes.* A person commits a violation if he hires a prostitute to engage in sexual activity with him, or if he enters or remains in a house of prostitution for the purpose of engaging in sexual activity.

(6) *Evidence.* On the issue whether a place is a house of prostitution the following shall be admissible evidence: its general repute; the repute of the persons who reside in or frequent the place; the frequency, timing and duration of visits by non-residents. Testimony of a person against his spouse shall be admissible to prove offenses under this Section.

Section 251.3. Loitering to Solicit Deviate Sexual Relations.

A person is guilty of a petty misdemeanor if he loiters in or near any public place for the purpose of soliciting or being solicited to engage in deviate sexual relations.

Index

1230